The Routledge Companion to Organizational Change

Organizations change. They grow, they adapt, they evolve. The effects of organizational change are important, varied and complex, so analysing and understanding them is vital for students, academics and researchers in all business schools.

The Routledge Companion to Organizational Change offers a comprehensive and authoritative overview of the field. The volume brings together the very best contributors not only from the field of organizational change, but also from adjacent fields, such as strategy and leadership. These contributors offer fresh and challenging insights to the mainstream themes of this discipline.

Surveying the state of the discipline and introducing new, cutting-edge themes, this book is a valuable reference source for students and academics in this area.

David M. Boje is Bill Daniels Ethics Fellow, and Professor in the Management Department at New Mexico State University, USA.

Bernard Burnes is Professor of Organisational Change at the University of Manchester, UK.

John Hassard is Professor of Organisational Analysis at Manchester Business School, UK and Fellow in Management Learning at the Judge Business School, Cambridge, UK.

The Routledge Companion to Organizational Change

Edited by David M. Boje,
Bernard Burnes and John Hassard

Routledge
Taylor & Francis Group

LONDON AND NEW YORK

First published 2012
by Routledge
2 Park Square, Milton Park, Abingdon, Oxon OX14 4RN

Simultaneously published in the USA and Canada
by Routledge
270 Madison Ave, New York, NY 10016

Routledge is an imprint of the Taylor & Francis Group, an informa business

British Library Cataloguing in Publication Data
A catalogue record for this book is available from the British Library

Library of Congress Cataloging-in-Publication Data
The Routledge companion to organizational change / edited by David M. Boje, Bernard
Burnes and John Hassard.
p. cm.
Includes bibliographical references and index.
1. Organizational change. I. Boje, David M. II. Burnes, Bernard, 1953-III. Hassard, John, 1953-
HD58.8.R693 2011
658.4'06 – dc22
2010053479

ISBN: 978-0-415-55645-3 (hbk)
ISBN: 978-0-203-81027-9 (ebk)

Typeset in Bembo
by Integra Software Services Pvt. Ltd, Pondicherry, India

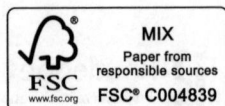

MIX
Paper from
responsible sources
FSC
www.fsc.org   FSC® C004839

Printed and bound in Great Britain by
CPI Antony Rowe, Chippenham, Wiltshire

Contents

List of figures

List of tables

List of contributors

Stephen Ackroyd (Professor Emeritus, Management School, Lancaster University, Lancaster, UK)

Elena Antonacopoulou (Professor of Organizational Behaviour, Management School, University of Liverpool, Liverpool, UK)

Richard Badham (Associate Dean (Research) and Professor of Management, Macquarie Graduate School of Management, Macquarie University, Sydney, NSW, Australia)

David Bargal (Professor, Paul Baerwald School of Social Work and Social Welfare, Hebrew University, Jerusalem, Israel)

Nic Beech (Professor and Head of the School of Management, University of St Andrews, St Andrews, UK)

Emma Bell (Senior Lecturer in Organisation Studies, Department of Management, Business School, University of Exeter, Exeter, UK)

Suzanne Benn (Professor of Sustainable Enterprise, UTS Faculty of Business, Sydney, NSW, Australia)

David M. Boje (Professor and Bill Daniels Ethics Fellow, Management Department College of Business, New Mexico State University, Las Cruces, NM, USA)

Melanie Bryant (Senior Lecturer in Management, School of Business, Charles Sturt University, Wagga Wagga, NSW, Australia)

Bernard Burnes (Professor of Organisational Change, Manchester Business School, University of Manchester, Mancester, UK)

Gervase R. Bushe (Professor of Leadership and Organization Development, Segal Graduate School of Business, Simon Fraser University, Vancouver, BC, Canada)

Rune Todnem By (Academic Group Leader (Organisational Behaviour, Leadership and Change), Business School, Staffordshire University, Stoke-on-Trent, UK)

George Cairns (Professor and Head, School of Management, RMIT University, Melbourne, VIC, Australia)

Ted Chambers (Doctoral candidate, Institute for Advanced Studies, Colorado Technical University-IAS, Colorado Springs, CO, USA)

Richard Claydon (Research Fellow, Macquarie Graduate School of Management, Macquarie University, Sydney, NSW, Australia)

Stewart Clegg (Professor of Organization Studies, UTS Business School, University of Technology, Sydney, NSW, Australia)

David Coghlan (Associate Professor of Organisation Development, School of Business, Trinity College Dublin, Dublin, Ireland)

David Collins (Reader in Management, Essex Business School, University of Essex, Colchester, UK)

Bill Cooke (Professor of Management and Society, Lancaster University Management School, Lancaster University, Lancaster, UK)

Krisha Coppedge (Doctoral candidate, Institute for Advanced Studies, Colorado Springs, CO, USA)

Patrick Dawson (Professor in School of Management and Marketing, Faculty of Commerce, University of Wollongong, NSW, Australia and University of Aberdeen Business School, University of Aberdeen, Business School, UK)

Simon Down (Senior Lecturer, Business School, Newcastle University, Newcastle upon Tyne, UK)

Helga Drummond (Professor of Decision Sciences, The Management School, University of Liverpool, Liverpool, UK)

Ivy DuRant (Doctoral candidate, Institute for Advanced Studies, Colorado Technical University, Colorado Springs, CO, USA)

David Grant (Professor of Organisational Studies, Business School, University of Sydney, NSW, Australia)

John Gray (Associate Professor of Management, UTS Business School, University of Technology, Sydney, NSW, Australia)

Richard Hall (Professor of Work and Organisational Studies, Business School, University of Sydney, Sydney, NSW, Australia)

Philip Hancock (Professor, Essex Business School, University of Essex, Colchester, UK)

John Hassard (Professor of Organisational Analysis Manchester Business School, University of Manchester, Mancester, UK and Fellow in Management Learning at the Judge Business School, Cambridge, UK)

Mary Ann Hazen (Professor, College of Business Administration, University of Detroit Mercy, Detroit, MI, USA)

Paula Hyde (Senior Lecturer, Manchester Business School, University of Manchester, Manchester, UK)

Kate Kearins (Professor, Faculty of Business and Law, Auckland University of Technology, Auckland, New Zealand)

Ann Langley (Professor, Service de l'enseignement du management, HEC Montréal, QC, Canada)

Hugo Letiche (Professor at University for Humanistics, Utrecht ,The Netherlands)

Charlotta Levay (Associate Professor, Department of Business Administration, Lund University, Sweden)

Michael R. Lissack (Executive Director, Institute for the Study of Coherence and Emergence, Naples, Italy)

Robert MacIntosh (Professor, Business School, University of Glasgow, Glasgow, UK)

Sławomir Magala (Professor and Head, Department of Organization and HRM, Rotterdam School of Management, Erasmus University, The Netherlands)

Marilu Marcillo-Gomez (Adjunct Faculty, Berkeley College, NJ and Associate Professor at Colorado Technical University Online, USA)

Robert J. Marshak (Professor and Senior Scholar in Residence in Department of Public Administration and Policy, School of Public Affairs, American University, Washington, DC, USA)

Amanda Mead (PhD student, Graduate School of Management, Macquarie University, Sydney, NSW, Australia)

Albert J. Mills (Professor and Director, PhD Business Administration (Management), Sobey School of Business, Saint Mary's University, Halifax, NS, Canada)

Jean Helms Mills (Professor of Management, Sobey School of Business, Saint Mary's University, Halifax, NS, Canada)

Ali Mir (Professor, Cotsakos College of Business, William Paterson University, Wayne, NJ, USA)

Raza Mir (Seymour Hyman Professor of Management, Cotsakos College of Business, William Paterson University, Wayne, NJ, USA)

Cliff Oswick (Chair in Organization Theory and Deputy Dean, Cass Business School, City University, University of London, UK)

Stephen Procter (Alcan Chair of Management, Business School, Newcastle University, Newcastle upon Tyne, UK)

Julian Randall (Senior Lecturer, Business School, University of Aberdeen, Aberdeen, UK)

Christopher J. Rees (Senior Lecturer in Human Resources and Organisational Change, Institute for Development Policy and Management, University of Manchester, Manchester, UK)

Carl Rhodes (Professor, School of Business and Economics, Swansea University, Swansea, UK)

Kathy Sanderson (Sessional Lecturer, Lakehead University, Thunder Bay, ON, Canada)

Pamela Sloan (Adjunct Professor, Service de l'enseignement du management, HEC Montréal, Montréal, QC, Canada)

André Spicer (Professor of Organizational Behaviour, Warwick Business School, Warwick University, Coventry, UK)

John Storey (Professor of Human Resource Management, Business School, The Open University, Milton Keynes, UK)

Theodore Taptiklis (Founder and joint CEO, The Storymaker Partnership, Princes Risborough, UK)

Scott Taylor (Senior Lecturer in Leadership Studies, Centre for Leadership Studies, Business School, University of Exeter, Exeter,UK)

Jo A. Tyler (Assistant Professor, Penn State Harrisburg, Middletown, PA, USA)

Maxim Voronov (Associate Professor of Strategic Management, Department of Marketing, International Business and Strategy Faculty of Business Brock University, St. Catharines, ON, Canada)

Tonya Wakefield (Colorado Technical University, Colorado Springs, CO, USA)

Julie Wolfram Cox (Professor of Management, Department of Management, Monash University Caulfield East, VIC, Australia)

Warner P. Woodworth (Professor, Department of Organizational Leadership & Strategy, Brigham Young University, Provo, UT, USA)

Introduction
The emergence of organizational change

David M. Boje, Bernard Burnes and John Hassard

'Change? Change? Why do we need change? Things are quite bad enough as they are.'
(Lord Salisbury, nineteenth-century British Prime Minister,
to Queen Victoria, quoted in Wilson, 1999)

To maintain their competitiveness and viability, firms need to continuously adjust by
initiating and implementing changes.

(Sackmann et al., 2009: 521)

The above two quotations, though separated by over 100 years, neatly sum up most people's
attitude to organizational change: 'we don't like it, but it's inevitable'. We live in an era where change
is seen as essential if organizations and, indeed, the human race are to survive, but we are doubtful that
change will be for the better (Dunphy et al., 2007; Kanter, 2008). Nevertheless, such is the
importance now given to change that it is seen as the prime responsibility of those who lead
organizations, as the rise of the transformational leader shows (Bass, 1995; Burns, 1978; Yukl, 2010).
   Yet, despite its posited importance and inevitability, most organizations find change very difficult
to implement, and there is much debate in the field as to how change should be accomplished (Beer
and Nohria, 2000; Boje, 2010; Burnes, 2009a; Smith, 2002, 2003). In particular, there is a growing
concern that change management has become too managerialist, that most stakeholders' voices
have been marginalizad and that ethical considerations have been sidelined (Boje and Hillon, 2008;
Burnes, 2009b; Wood and Gray, 1991). There is also a growing awareness that many of the changes
organizations initiate have an adverse effect on the global climate and environmental sustainability;
hence the calls for the natural world to be considered as a legitimate and equal stakeholder in the
change process. These developments are influenced by the work of writers from outside the change
field, such as Bakhtin (1990), Freire (1970) and Marcuse (1964), which provides support for a
dialogical approach to change and transformation that would embrace all stakeholders, including
Nature. In addressing these issues, and in taking a comprehensive view of the field, *The Routledge
Companion to Organizational Change* is distinguished from previous such books.
   Bennis et al.'s (1961) *The Planning of Change* was one of the earliest and most influential readers
on organizational change. Indeed, its managerialist approach could be said to have defined the

field for the next four decades. The overall approach of the book treated Kurt Lewin as the seminal founding figure of change management, but did not delve below the surface of Lewin's work. For example, in the 1969 edition, Berne and Burnbaum state that ' ... the planning of change has become part of the responsibility of management in all contemporary institutions' (Bennis et al., 1969: 328). However, Lewin's approach saw the planning of change as the responsibility of all the parties involved, not just managers. Bennis et al. embraced a managerialist orientation by viewing Lewin's 'planned change' as the golden mean between what they saw as two unpalatable alternatives: Adam Smith's laissez-faire economics and Marx's class-struggle perspective. By so doing, they dismiss Marxist critical theory which sees radical intervention in the workplace as a means of bringing about democratic governance in organizations.

In turning planned change into a managerialist golden mean, they also left out any concern with material conditions and the consequences of their managerialism. Change management became just a 'method of social technology' used to redress the inability of Taylor's scientific management to deal with instrumental ethics (Bennis et al., 1969: 4). Bennis et al. legitimized their change practices by basing them on the science of social psychology in the same way that Taylor had tried to use the science of engineering. In their final move, Bennis et al. redefine Kurt Lewin's field theory by scripting management's role as the driver of change, and the worker's role as a restraining obstacle to change.

By presenting a narrow and managerialist portrayal of Lewin, the true value of his work was lost to many scholars who learnt their trade from the 1970s onwards. This accounted for the decline of interest in and the misunderstanding of his work. Lewin's views were anything but managerialist. Whilst Lewin argued that all those affected by the change process had to be involved in planning and implementing change, the managerialist approach takes the view that the greater good of all stakeholders can best be achieved by limiting involvement to just a few managers who are capable of discerning the needs and views of all stakeholders (Calton and Kurland, 1996). In this 'stakeholders of the mind' approach, as Mitroff (1983) termed it, the assumption is that managers and their change agents can speak for owners, for workers and for Nature herself instead. The result is that the managerialist mind substitutes for actual dialogical engagement. Not only does this monophonic managerialist approach to change exclude the legitimate voices of other stakeholders, but it does not even bring economic benefits to organizations (Boje and Wolfe, 1987; Lewicki and Bunker, 1995; Wood and Gray, 1991). As Calton and Kurland (1996: 160) observe: 'without [real] stakeholder participation in a trust-building process, the prospect of lower transaction or contracting costs remains problematic'.

In contrast, writers in this *Companion* advocate a multi-voice, polyphonic approach to stakeholder involvement (e.g. Hazen, Chapter 32) which sits easily with Lewin's approach. In support of the polyphonic approach, Carlton and Kurland (1996) cite the case of emerging postmodern network organizational forms where issues of participation, democratic discourse and trust-building dialogue are critical to the change process. Real stakeholder participation in change management allows stakeholders their own voice instead of a few managers and change agents attempting to understand and balance conflicting stakeholder voices, logics and prefer-ences. Examples of where this has been made to work successfully are participative work design (Emery and Emery, 1974), transorganizational network change (Boje and Hillon, 2008) and intervention research (Boje, 2011; Savall et al., 2011).

In developing a polyphonic approach to stakeholder involvement, Nature needs to be included as a stakeholder in the change process (Dunphy et al., 2007). This is a point which arises forcibly from the work of Marcuse (1964). He argues that the outcome of a one-dimensional positivistic ethic and 'technological rationality' is the destruction of Nature in the name of scientific progress (Marcuse, 1964: 234). Marcuse maintains that the repression of critical thinking by positivistic social science blinds its practitioners to their own complicity in the negation of Nature. Marcuse's argument is that the pursuit of materialism requires greater and greater consumption of natural resources, which in turn leads inexorably to the ill-treatment of Nature, including animals and humans. Business seeks to overcome its destruction of the natural environment through recourse to the creation of a 'technological transformation of the world' and the creation of a totalitarian 'administered society' (Marcuse, 1964: 239). *The Routledge Companion to Organizational Change* seeks to promote an alternative transformation, one that challenges the technocratic-scientific management conquest of Nature. The wholesale destruction and exhaustion of the planet's natural resources, through developments such as forest clearing and subsequent soil erosion, is brought about by one-dimensional positivistic thinking not being ethically answerable for its own complicity in such actions. In its place we need to promote an ethical approach to change which includes, and is accountable to, all stakeholders.

In compiling this *Companion,* we take an inclusive view of change, viewing it not just as a social phenomenon affecting people in organizations, but one which also impacts on the natural environment and sees Nature as a key stakeholder. It follows that this *Companion* needs to engage critically with the broad spectrum of views on and approaches to change – whether they be established and respected or new and heretical. This was our aim in producing this *Companion* – to create an essential reference work which spans the field of organizational change, covering its origins and development, and examining the main theories, challenges and controversies.

In contrast to other such books, the *The Routledge Companion to Organizational Change*:

1   presents a more sophisticated reading of the work of Kurt Lewin, including the implications of field theory for understanding how change is influenced by and affects material conditions;
2   provides a broader picture of resistance to change, and sees it as arising from managerialist actions and not from any predisposition to resistance by workers;
3   adopts a participative and ethical rather than a managerialist approach to change;
4   argues that change takes place in the material world and in real communities – as such, change arises out of shifts in material conditions, and change also affects material conditions, including who is involved in shaping that change;
5   brings together established perspectives on change with those drawn from critical theory, postcolonialism, environmentalism and feminist studies, in order to examine current and past change management practices and to develop a new, inclusive, liberatory pedagogy which embraces stakeholders from the social and natural worlds;
6   approaches change management from an 'ethics of practic' stance which requires the voices of all stakeholders to be heard. In so doing, it rejects the 'stakeholders of the mind' perspective which only gives consideration a few voices.

This *Companion* comprises 40 chapters by the very best established and developing contributors to the field of organizational change and to fields related to organizational change. It is organized into six parts.

Part 1, 'Planned change and organization development', focuses on the work of Kurt Lewin. The seven chapters are by Bernard Burnes; David Bargal; David Coghlan; Bill Cooke; Christopher J. Rees; Gervase R. Bushe; and Cliff Oswick and Robert J. Marshak. Their contributions show how Lewin's work transformed organizational change from a collection of idiosyncratic and confusing nostrums into the coherent, theory-based and practice-orientated discipline of Organization Development (OD). It shows that even today, despite the criticisms and challenges it has faced, OD in its various forms still remains the most widely used approach to organizational change, and one which has spread from its origins in the US to be adopted across the world.

Part 2, 'Newer approaches to change', comprises five chapters by Patrick Dawson; Bernard Burnes; Hugo Letiche; Michael R. Lissack; and David Boje and Tonya Wakefield. These writers explore the main theories which have arisen as challengers to OD. It shows that attempts to replace OD as the dominant approach to change have come from three main quarters: processual change, emergent change and the complexity-based approach to change. Despite support for all three approaches, as Part II shows, only the complexity approach still appears to be gaining adherents.

Part 3, 'Perspectives on change', contains seven chapters by Richard Badham, Amanda Mead and Elena Antonacopoulou; George Cairns; Paula Hyde; Stephen Ackroyd; Stewart Clegg and John Gray; Ann Langley and Pamela Sloan; and André Spicer and Charlotta Levay. The chapters challenge the managerialist perspective on change and explore various theoretical and metho-dological perspectives relating to organizational change and development. These include dra-maturgy, psychodynamics, realism, institutional theory, dialectics and critical theory. By moving away from traditional ways of viewing change, these chapters open up new ways of changing organizations and the prospect of achieving outcomes which benefit a wider range of stakeholders.

Part 4, 'Change in practice', features eight chapters by Rune Todnem By and Bernard Burnes; David Collins; Helga Drummond; David Grant and Richard Hall; Slawomir Magala; Stephen Procter and Julian Randall; Melanie Bryant and Julie Wolfram Cox; and John Storey. These writers are largely concerned with how change policies, programmes and practices are developed and prosecuted. Issues dealt with in this part include the ethics of change, fads and fashions, power and discourse, cultural change, the use of narrative and the role of governance.

Part 5, 'Key issues', comprises eight chapters by Richard Badham, Richard Claydon and Simon Down; Raza Mir and Ali Mir; Maxim Voronov and Warner P. Woodworth; Nic Beech and Rob McIntosh; Mary Ann Hazen; Jo A. Tyler; Albert Mills, Kathy Sanderson and Jean Mills; and Carl Rhodes. These chapters are devoted to understanding resistance to change and, in particular, challenging the managerialist construction of resistance. Drawing on perspectives from imperialism, power, domination and gender, the chapters share the view that resistance should be seen in a positive light rather than as a futile attempt to hold back the tide of change.

Part 6, 'The future', features five chapters by Phil Hancock; Suzanne Benn and Kate Kearins; Theodore Taptiklis; Scott Taylor and Emma Bell; and David M. Boje, Ivy DuRant, Krisha Coppedge, Ted Chambers and Marilu Marcillo-Gomez. These contributors address the future of organizational change. Each in their own way calls for a radical rethink of how we view and manage change. The chapters focus on topics such as aesthetics, trust, posthumanism, sustain-ability and spirituality. One of the interesting facets of these chapters is that they are not necessarily calling for a break with the past, but for a need to revisit and reclaim non-managerialist perspectives on change with a view to using them to develop approaches to change appropriate for the twenty-first century. This is particularly the case with the final chapter, which seeks to reclaim Lewin's work and ally it with newer perspectives on change. It may come as a surprise to many that this *Companion* begins and ends with a favourable take on Lewin's work, but, as any student of the topic should know, change and surprise go hand in hand.

This *Companion* concludes with a brief 'Postscript: change in a changing world – where now?' Each of the editors gives their view of how the field will or should develop and what the important issues will be. For Boje, the key issue is to move away from an over-reliance on social constructionism and get 'real' about the materiality of power, politics and world ecology. For him, looking forward requires us to look back; in order to create a new theory and practice of organizational change, we need to return to the work of Weber and Lewin. For Burnes, current change practices are too dominated by senior managers, focus on the wrong issues – riches for the few and not the sustainability of the planet – and are often based on unethical practices. For him, the main reasons for this are a breakdown of the link between theory and practice and between scholars and practitioners. Burnes argues that we need to learn from and build on the past, and in particular understand the continuing importance of Lewin's work. For Hassard, an understanding of materiality, ideology and politics is essential for organizational change. He draws attention to renewed interest in the work of Marx and structuralist, formalist and modernist organizational research. He argues that it is time for a return to more formal and material explanations of what organizations are and how they are changing, explanations which account for the tangible political, economic and ideological environments in which organizations operate.

The pre-history of organizational change

Before moving on to Part 1, it is important to recognize that our current preoccupation with change is relatively new, as is the study of change itself. It was only with the advent of the Industrial Revolution that organizations began to focus on change rather than stability. Only in the last 70 years has organizational change emerged as a subject for systematic academic study and, indeed, it is really only since the 1980s that it has become a mainstream subject on undergraduate and postgraduate courses in management and business.

To understand why this is so, we have to recognize that whilst organizational change is as old as organizations, it has not always been the case that those who lead organizations have welcomed change or seen it as the norm. For most of recorded human history, leaders appear to have favoured stability and tradition rather than change and newness. In a review of managerial practices in the 2500 years before the Christian era, Rindova and Starbuck (1997) showed how Chinese leaders fostered stable social structures and established a bureaucratic state apparatus geared to the purpose of maintaining the status quo rather than challenging it. Though Weber (1948) saw bureaucracy as a modern approach to achieving order, predictability and control, the Chinese example shows that this is not the case. Nor is it an isolated example. We can see this preference for stability across the ancient world. In Egypt, Greece and Rome, the structure, laws and practice of the state, and social norms such as ancestor worship and respect for age, promoted tradition and stability over newness and change (Antonaccio, 1994; Beyer, 1959; Jones, 1984). As Robbins (1987) noted, this preference for bureaucratic-type organization can be found in the Bible. When Moses, having led his people out of Egypt, began to find the strain of leadership too much, his father-in-law offered the following advice:

> … thou shalt provide out of all the people able men … and place such over them, to be rulers of thousands, and rulers of hundreds, rulers of fifties, and rulers of tens: and let them judge the people at all seasons: and it shall be, that every great matter they shall bring unto thee, but every small matter they shall judge: so shall it be easier for thyself, and they shall bear the burden with thee.
>
> (Exodus 18, 21–23, the Bible, 1962)

Of course, it could be argued that these examples are not typical organizations, but nation states, or in the case of Moses and the Israelites, a proto-state. This, though, would miss the point that until the emergence of craft guilds in Europe around the fourteenth century the only organizations of any significance were feudal states/principalities and, from the fourth century onwards, the 'one, holy catholic church' whose structure tended to mirror that of the states in which it operated (Gonzalez, 1999; Keen, 1991).

In the Christian world, man was subject to two sets of laws: Divine Law, protected and promoted by the Catholic Church; and Human Law, enforced by civil government (Foster, 1977). However, the belief was that rulers were appointed by God and only subject to God's laws (which later grew into the Divine Right of Kings). Therefore, Human Law was seen as subservient to Church Law. This was enshrined in the doctrine of Natural Law, which states that there are certain enduring rules of behaviour to which humans are subject, primarily obedience to the laws of God as prescribed by the church. Anything or anyone who challenged these laws and the pre-eminence of the church, or the Divine Right of Kings, was deemed to be heretical and had to be suppressed, often, as the Inquisition demonstrated, in an extremely violent manner (Green, 2008). It follows that the preference for stability in the church, the state and their institutions was regarded not merely as an attitude of mind, but as the natural order of things as laid down by God.

Even when the duopoly of church and state started to be challenged by the advent of powerful and rich craft guilds, this did not noticeably challenge the preference for stability over change. A guild was a monopoly which regulated entry into a trade or craft in a city and sought to control price and supply, quality and methods of production (Gadd and Wallis, 2006). Technological or organizational innovations were seen as threats by guilds as these could undermine their control over their craft. Consequently, for guilds, the pursuit of stability was an economic necessity rather than a religious imperative, but no less powerful for that. This of course did not mean that changes did not take place in church, state or guild; they clearly did and were often momentous in nature (Davis, 1997; Epstein and Prak, 2010). However, the point is that stability rather than change was seen as the norm. The leaders of organizations, whether they be popes, kings or guild masters, saw it as their duty to maintain the status quo, whether that be in terms of religious doctrine, existing social relations or methods of production.

It was only with the commencement of the British Industrial Revolution in the eighteenth century, buttressed by the rise of sectarian Protestantism and the new thinking of the Enlightenment, that change began to be seen as preferential to stability (Hampson, 1990; Hobsbawm, 1979). The emergence of the factory system led to the creation of a new entrepreneurial-industrial class who saw stability and tradition as obstacles to their pursuit of wealth and power. They saw organizational, technological and scientific progress as the key to increased wealth. However, for their workers, the reverse appeared to be the case. They saw change as a threat to their skills and livelihood, and tradition and stability as things to be valued and protected (Burnes, 2009a). Therefore, even at the beginning of what Morgan (1986) refers to as the 'organizational society', the fault lines between employers and employees were evident. Change posed a challenge for both. For employers the challenge was how to accomplish it; for employees the challenge was how to prevent it.

As Burnes (2009a: 14) observed:

British employers based their attitude towards employees on two basic propositions:

1 Labour is unreliable, lazy and will only work when tightly controlled and closely supervised.
2 The main controllable business cost is labour; therefore the key to increased profits is to make it cheaper, and/or increase its productivity, by getting employees to work harder, or for longer hours, for the same, or less, money.

The Industrial Revolution was built on both technological and organizational innovation, and employers used both to increase the productivity and reduce the cost of labour. In terms of the latter, the division of labour, as epitomized by Adam Smith's pin factory, was perhaps the most significant development (Smith, 1776). Josiah Wedgwood pioneered its application to factory production at his Etruria pottery works, where he developed a production system which reduced the skill involved in each operation to a minimum in order, in Wedgwood's words, 'to make machines of men as cannot err' (quoted in Tillett, 1970: 37). The following quotes from a contemporary source illustrate how technology was viewed:

> In the spirit of the Egyptian task-masters the operative printers dictate to the manufacturers the number and quality of apprentices to be admitted to the trade, the hours of their own labour, and the wages to be paid to them. At length capitalists sought deliverance from this intolerable bondage in the resources of science, and were speedily re-instated in their legitimate rule, that of the head over the inferior members ... This ... confirms the great doctrine ... that when capital enlists science in her service, the refractory hand of labour will always be taught docility.
>
> Ure (1835: 368–69)

> By developing machines ... which require only unskilled instead of skilled labour, the cost of labour can be reduced [and] the bargaining position of the worker reduced.
>
> Ure (1836: viii–ix)

Despite the increasing diffusion of organizational and technological innovations throughout the nineteenth century, it was not the case that 'the refractory hand of labour' was 'taught docility'. Workers responded by developing their own organizational innovations – trade unions (Pelling, 1976). Management–labour disputes increased rather than decreased, especially in the USA, where explosive growth fuelled bitter industrial tensions which challenged the legitimacy of managerial power (Pelling, 1960; Zinn, 1980).

Managers were desperate for an effective method of overcoming resistance to change. At the beginning of the twentieth century, Frederick Taylor declared that he had developed such a method – Scientific Management. His aim in developing Scientific Management was to overcome workers' resistance to change by providing managers and workers with an approach to change which he argued was fair, neutral and based on scientific objectivity (Taylor, 1911). Taylor argues that his system did not seek to promote the interests of employers over employees, but instead sought to offer workers a fair day's pay for a fair day's work (Rose, 1988; Scott, 1987; Sheldrake, 1996). As Taylor (1911: 1) put it: 'The principal object of management should be to secure the maximum prosperity for the employer, coupled with the maximum prosperity for each employee.' Taylor maintained that it is possible and desirable to establish, through methodical study and the application of scientific principles, the one best way of carrying out any job. Once established, the way must be implemented totally and made to operate consistently.

There have rightly been many criticisms of Taylor's approach to the organization of work, particularly that it was neither scientific nor effective (Littler, 1978; Locke, 1982; Sheldrake, 1996). However, in terms of his approach to managing change, there are three points that are particularly worth noting. First, Taylor's approach was a pragmatic response to the issue of how to overcome workers' resistance to change. Second, his understanding of human nature and motivation was badly flawed; he portrayed organizations as machines and people as 'greedy robots' (Rose, 1988). Lastly, Taylor saw only a passive role for workers. Their job was to carry out the instructions of managers and to perform any new tasks they were given in the manner laid down and not to deviate by one iota. Scientific Management was neither the systematic nor neutral approach to change which Taylor claimed (Rose, 1988). Indeed, despite its later popularity, it appeared to meet with as much opposition as the adhocracy it sought to replace (Rose, 1988; Schachter, 2010; Sheldrake, 1996).

In the 1930s, a very different perspective on people and organizations began to emerge from two of the early pioneers of the Human Relations movement – Elton Mayo (1933) and Chester Barnard (1938). Unlike Scientific Management, the Human Relations approach appeared to reject the notion of organizations as split along a management–labour axis, and it challenged Taylor's notion that change was primarily concerned with overcoming the resistance of labour. Instead, Mayo and Barnard portrayed organizations as cooperative, social systems rather than mechanical ones, and they emphasized that people's emotional and social needs can have more influence on their behaviour at work than financial incentives (Burnes, 2009a).

There have been many critiques of the early Human Relations work (Gillespie, 1991; Landsberger, 1958; Rose, 1988). However, focusing solely on its implications for organizational change, there are three points to note. First, unlike Scientific Management, Human Relations portrays people as having an active and to an extent voluntary role to play in the life of the organization. Second, it is an approach which is long on philosophy, i.e. it promotes a positive view of human nature and the benefits of participatory management, but it is short on practicalities, i.e. there is no blueprint, set of guidelines or tools for bringing about change. Lastly, the work of Mayo and Barnard is more about managing organizations in a steady state rather than how to change organizations.

Neither Scientific Management nor the early Human Relations movement could justifiably claim to offer the world an effective approach to change. Taylor offered the manager a box of tools to analyse and plan work, but failed to understand the nature of organizational and human behaviour. Mayo and Barnard offered a better understanding of both, but failed to provide the tools necessary to bring about change. In order for the study and management of organizational change to come of age, it was necessary to develop an empirical-based theory and a theory-based practice. Such an approach to change began to emerge at the end of the 1930s in the work of Kurt Lewin. His development of planned change and the ethical values which accompanied it created the philosophical, ethical and practical basis for what was later to become OD (Burnes, 2004, 2007).

It is really with Lewin that theory and practice come together to create the modern discipline of organizational change. Therefore, it is right that Part 1 of this *Companion* is devoted to Lewin and OD.

References

Antonaccio, C.M. (1994) Contesting the Past: Hero Cult, Tomb Cult and Epic in Early Greece. *American Journal of Archaeology*, 98 (3), 398–410.

Bakhtin, M.M. (1990) *Art and Answerability*. Michael Holquist and Vadim Liapunov (eds). Translation and notes by Vadim Liapunov; supplement translated by Kenneth Brostrom. University of Texas Press: Austin, TX.

Barnard, C. (1938) *The Functions of the Executive*. Harvard University Press: Cambridge, MA.

Bass, B.M. (1995) Transformational Leadership Redux. *Leadership Quarterly*, 6, 463–78.

Beer, M. and Nohria, N. (eds) (2000) *Breaking the Code of Change*. Harvard Business School Press: Boston, MA.

Bennis, W.G., Benne, K.D. and Chin, R. (eds) (1961) *The Planning of Change* (1st edition). Holt, Rinehart and Winston: New York.

Bennis, W.G., Benne, K.D. and Chin, R. (eds) (1969) *The Planning of Change* (2nd edition). Holt, Rinehart and Winston: New York.

Beyer, W.C. (1959) The Civil Service in the Ancient World. *Public Administration Review*, 19 (4), 243–49.

Bible, The – Authorized Version (1962) The British & Foreign Bible Society: London.

Boje, D.M. (2010) Sideshadowing Appreciative Inquiry: One Storyteller's Commentary. *Journal of Management Inquiry*, 19 (3), 242–44.

Boje, D.M. (2011) Postscript: An Antenarrative Theory of Socioeconomic in Intervention Research (pp. 363–72). In David M. Boje (ed.) *Shaping the Future of Storytelling and Organizations: An Antenarrative Handbook*. Routledge: London.

Boje, D.M. and Hillon, M. (2008) Transorganizational Development (Chapter 34, pp. 651–664). In Tom Cummings (ed.) *Handbook of Organizational Development*. Sage: Thousand Oaks, CA.

Boje, D.M. and Wolfe, T. (1987) Transorganizational Development: Contributions to Theory and Practice (pp. 733–54). In Harold J. Leavitt, Louis R. Pondy and David M. Boje (eds) *Readings in Managerial Psychology*. University of Chicago Press: Chicago, IL.

Burnes, B. (2004) Kurt Lewin and the Planned Approach to Change: A Re-appraisal. *Journal of Management Studies*, 41(6), 977–1002.

Burnes, B. (2007) Kurt Lewin and the Harwood Studies: The Foundations of OD. *Journal of Applied Behavioral Science*, 43 (2), 213–31.

Burnes, B. (2009a) *Managing Change*. (5th edition). FT/Prentice Hall: Harlow.

Burnes, B. (2009b) Reflections: Ethics and Organizational Change – Time for a Return to Lewinian Values. *Journal of Change Management*, 9 (4), 359–81.

Burns, J.M. (1978) *Leadership*. Harper & Row: New York.

Calton, J. and Kurland, N. (1996) A Theory of Stakeholder Enabling: Giving Voice to an Emerging Postmodern Praxis of Organizational Discourse (pp. 154–80). In D. Boje, R.P. Gephart and T.J. Thatchenkery (eds) *Postmodern Management and Organization Theory*. Sage: London.

Davis, N. (1997) *Europe: A History*. Pimlico: London.

Dunphy, D., Griffiths, A. and Benn, S. (2007) *Organizational Change for Corporate Sustainability* (2nd edition). Routledge: London.

Emery, F. and Emery, M. (1974) Participative Design: Work and Community Life (pp. 100–122). Reprinted in M. Emery (ed.) (1993) *Participative Design for Participative Democracy*. Centre for Continuing Education, Australian National University, Canberra, Australia.

Epstein, S.R. and Prak, M. (2010) *Guilds, Innovation and the European Economy, 1400–1800*. Cambridge University Press: Cambridge.

Foster, M.B. (1977) *Masters of Political Thought (Vol 1)*. Harrap: London.

Freire, P. (1970) *Pedagogy of the Oppressed*. Translated by Myra Bergman Ramos. The Seabury Press (A Continuum Book): New York.

Gadd, I.A. and Wallis, P. (2006) 'Guilds and Associations in Europe, 900–1900' Centre for Metropolitan History, University of London: London.

Gillespie, R. (1991) *Manufacturing Knowledge: A History of the Hawthorne Experiments*. Cambridge University Press: Cambridge.

Gonzalez, J.L. (1999) *The Story of Christianity: The Early Church to the Present Day*. Prince Press: Peabody, MA.

Green, T. (2008) *Inquisition: The Reign of Fear*. Pan: London.

Hampson, N. (1990) *The Enlightenment*. Penguin: Harmondsworth.

Hobsbawm, E.J. (1979) *The Age of Revolution*. Abacus: London.

Jone, A.H.M. (1984) *The Greek City from Alexander to Justinian*. Oxford University Press: Oxford.

Kanter, R.M. (2008) Transforming Giants. *Harvard Business Review*, 86, January, 43–52.

Keen, M. (1991) *The Penguin History of Medieval Europe*. Penguin: Harmondsworth.

Landsberger, H.A. (1958) *Hawthorne Revisited: 'Management and the Worker'. Its Critics and Developments in Human Relations in Industry*. Cornell University Press: Ithaca, NY.

Lewicki, R.J. and Bunker, B.B. (1995) Trust in Relationships: A Model of Development and Decline. In B.B. Bunker and J.Z. Rubin (eds) *Conflict, Cooperation and Justice: Essays Inspired by the Work of Moreton Deutsch*. Jossey-Bass: San Francisco, CA.

Littler, C.R. (1978) Understanding Taylorism. *British Journal of Sociology*, 29 (2), 185–202.

Locke, E.W. (1982) The Ideas of Frederick W. Taylor. *Academy of Management Review*, 7 (1), 14–24.

Marcuse, H. (1964) *One-Dimensional Man*. Boston: Beacon Press.

Mayo, E. (1933) *The Human Problems of Industrial Civilization*. Macmillan: New York.

Mitroff, I. (1983) *Stakeholders of the organizational mind*. Jossey-Bass: San Francisco, CA.

Morgan, G. (1986) *Images of Organizations*. Sage: Beverly Hills, CA.

Pelling, H. (1960) *American Labor*. Chicago University Press: Chicago.

Pelling, H. (1976) *A History of British Trade Unionism*. Pelican: Harmondsworth.

Rindova, V.P. and Starbuck, W.H. (1997) Ancient Chinese Theories of Control. *Journal of Management Inquiry*, 6 (2), 144–59.

Robbins, S.P. (1987), *Organization Theory: Structure, Design, and Applications*, Prentice-Hall, Englewood Cliffs, NJ.

Rose, M. (1988) *Industrial Behaviour*. Penguin: Harmondsworth.

Sackmann, S.A., Eggenhofer-Rehart, P.M. and Friesl, M. (2009) Sustainable Change: Long-Term Efforts Toward Developing a Learning Organization. *Journal of Applied Behavioral Science*, 45 (4), 521–49.

Savall, H. Zardet, V. and Péron, M. (2011) 'The "Evolutive" and Interactive Actor Polygon in the Theater of Organizations' (pp. 346–62). In D. M. Boje (ed.) *Shaping the Future of Storytelling and Organizations: An Antenarrative Handbook*. Routledge: London.

Schachter, H.L. (2010) The Role Played by Frederick Taylor in the Rise of the Academic Management Fields. *Journal of Management History*, 16 (4), 437–48.

Scott, W.R. (1987) *Organizations: Rational, Natural and Open Systems*. Prentice Hall: Englewood Cliffs, NJ.

Sheldrake, J. (1996) *Management Theory: From Taylorism to Japanization*. International Thompson Business Press: London.

Smith, A. (1776) *The Wealth of Nations*, Volume 1. Methuen (1950 edition): London.

Smith, M.E. (2002) Success Rates for Different Types of Organizational Change. *Performance Improvement*, 41 (1), 26–33.

Smith, M.E. (2003) Changing an Organization's Culture: Correlates of Success and Failure. *Leadership & Organization Development Journal*, 24 (5), 249–61.

Taylor, F.W. (1911) *The Principles of Scientific Management*. Dover (1998 edition): New York.

Tillett, A. (1970) Industry and Management. In A. Tillett, T. Kempner and G. Willis (eds) *Management Thinkers*. Pelican: Harmondsworth.

Ure, A. (1835) *The Philosophy of Manufactures*. Frank Cass (1967 edition): London.

Ure, A. (1836) *The Cotton Manufacture of Great Britain*, Vol. 1. Johnson (1970 edition): London.

Weber, M. (1948) *From Max Weber: Essays in Sociology*. Translated, edited and with an introduction by H.H. Gerth and C. Wright Mills. Routledge & Kegan Paul: London.

Wilson, R. (1999) Permanent Revolution? Yes, Minister, from the inaugural Vice Chancellor's lecture at City University given by the head of the Home Civil Service. *Independent*, 11 May. Available at www.independent.co.uk.

Wood, D.J. and Gray, B. (1991) Toward a Comprehensive Theory of Collaboration. *Journal of Applied Behavioral Science*, 27 (2), 139–62.

Yukl, G. (2010) *Leadership in Organizations* (7th edition). Pearson: Upper Saddle River, NJ.

Zinn, H. (1980) *A People's History of the United States*. Longman: London.

Part 1

Planned change and organization development

Introduction

Bernard Burnes

Though the practice of organizational change is as old as organizations themselves, its emergence as an academic discipline seeking to develop and utilize theory to understand and better implement change is relatively new. Kurt Lewin (1890–1947) is usually considered as the founding father of the discipline. It was Lewin's creation of 'planned change' which transformed organizational change from a collection of idiosyncratic and confusing nostrums into the coherent, theory-based and practice-orientated discipline of Organization Development (OD). Coalescing around planned change, OD emerged in the 1950s and 1960s and went on to dominate the theory and practice of organizational change until the early 1980s. Social, economic and technical changes in the late 1970s and early 1980s led to a challenging of previous views of the nature of organizations and how change occurs (Burnes, 2009). This gave rise to a number of alternative perspectives on change, most notably the processual, emergent and complexity approaches, which are reviewed and discussed in Part II. In particular, these criticized Lewin's planned approach to change as at best being unsuitable for modern organizations, and at worst fundamentally flawed (Burnes, 2004). It also led to a general questioning of the appropriateness and future of OD by both its detractors and supporters (Greiner and Cummings, 2004). However, nearly 30 years after these challenges began, OD still remains the most widely used approach to organizational change, and one which has spread from its origins in the US to be adopted across the world.

As the seven chapters in this part will show, OD has not stood still. From its inception to the present day, it has continued to grow, adapt and diversify. These adaptations and diversifications have led even its proponents to question whether OD has lost its way and abandoned its original purpose and values. Others, though, see them as appropriate responses to changing times, multiple challenges and different national cultures, which have allowed OD to remain true to its origins whilst maintaining its practical relevance. Central to this debate is the legacy of Kurt Lewin. Is Lewin's work as relevant now as it was 70 years ago and is it still central to OD?

In Chapter 1, Burnes describes Lewin's background and examines the development and substance of his planned approach to change. In so doing, he shows how planned change became the core of OD. He also argues that Lewin provided OD with an ethical rationale which focused on the human side of the organization and the promotion of democratic-humanist values. In addition, Burnes maintains that far from being outdated, the organizational challenges addressed by Lewin, and the methods and values he espoused, are still vital for today's organizations.

Lewin passionately believed that theory and practice go hand in hand. Indeed, it was he who coined the phrase 'There is nothing so practical as a good theory' (Lewin, 1943–4: 169). Bargal explores Lewin's pioneering work in uniting theory and practice in Chapter 2. He focuses on the importance of Lewin's action research paradigm and its significance for organizational and social change. Bargal argues that in developing action research, Lewin removed the barriers between theory, research and action/action practice. He argues that Lewin led the move from an epistemological approach, which gave priority to formal knowledge (theory and research), to a dialogical (interdependent) approach, which perceived production and utilization of knowledge as a mutual enterprise shared by all parties involved. In addition, Bargal's exploration of Lewin's psychological-phenomenological approach to reality shows that Lewin's work had more than a touch of the postmodern about it.

In Chapter 3, Coghlan extends the discussion of action research by showing that it has important roots and strands that exist outside of OD, e.g. action learning, action science, Appreciative Inquiry, cooperative inquiry and developmental action inquiry. Similarly, he shows that the forms and challenges of OD have developed over time. Despite these separate developments, Coghlan maintains that in today's postmodern world, the collaboration of OD and action research is, if anything, more relevant than ever before.

It has to be recognized, of course, that the birth and development of OD did not take place in a politically neutral or value-free climate. In Chapter 4, Cooke draws attention to the seemingly paradoxical situation whereby OD, which its proponents saw as a vehicle for progressive social change, came to maturity in the US in the Cold War era. This was a time when many left-leaning, New Deal liberals were hounded by Senator McCarthy and his sympathisers. This made life very difficult for those seeking to promote OD, with its participative-democratic ethos. Cooke shows how the work of leading figures in the creation of OD, Kurt Lewin, Ronald Lippitt, John Collier and Goodwin Watson, was affected by the political climate of their times.

Though the 1950s and 1960s saw OD make major strides in establishing itself as the main approach to organizational change in the US, it has not stood still in the intervening years. In Chapter 5, Rees addresses two key questions which have arisen in OD's journey from the 1950s to the twenty-first century. First, as it has been applied to a wider range of change situations, to what extent has OD lost its identity and has merely become an amorphous collection of tools and techniques which no longer constitute a distinct, coherent and value-based approach to change? Second, as OD has become a truly international movement, how have practitioners operating in different countries under different national cultures adapted OD to their specific situations without undermining its distinct ethos and values?

In Chapter 6, Bushe discusses Appreciative Inquiry (AI), which he describes as one of the first post-Lewinian forms of OD. He sees AI as having catalysed the subsequent proliferation of Dialogic OD methods that operate outside the Lewinian paradigm. Bushe argues that one of the fundamental underpinnings of AI is that it sees organizations as socially constructed realities which are constrained only by human imagination and the shared beliefs of organizational members. Thus AI seeks to accommodate OD to the rise of postmodern, social constructionist perspectives on organizations. For Bushe, AI offers the possibility of OD practitioners working with organizations to transcend the limitations imposed by their 'objective' reality in order to create a new, more favourable reality.

Oswick and Marsham, in Chapter 7, examine the role played by metaphor in shaping traditional and newer forms of OD. Traditional OD, they argue, is based on the twin metaphors of change as a journey and organizations as sick/ill and in need of treatment. However, they see newer forms of OD as being based on the twin metaphors of change as a conversation and organizations as mystery. Oswick and Marsham do not see traditional OD as being superseded by newer forms of OD. Instead, just as Bushe sees social constructionism as helping to renew and maintain the relevance of OD, Oswick and Marsham see traditional and newer forms of OD as mutually supportive. Rather than the two sets of metaphors leading to conflicting outcomes, they maintain that they are complementary.

In summary, the key challenge for OD since its inception has been how to maintain its relevance in a changing world without losing its core values. As such, it has had to expand out from its original concern with the human side of the organization, especially its focus on the effectiveness of small groups, to address the full range of organization-wide and inter-organizational issues that modern organizations face. OD has also had to address the changing landscape of the academic debate on the nature of organizations and organizational change, whether this be the processualists with their focus on power and politics, the postmodernists and their multiple realities, or the complexity theorists with their recourse to the mind-boggling mathematics which govern change in the natural world.

Returning to the question posed earlier: Is Lewin's work as relevant now as it was 70 years ago and is it still central to OD? In the 1980s, the expectation was that planned change and OD would collapse under the weight of the challenges they faced; however, this has clearly not happened. OD has shown a remarkable capacity to address new challenges and incorporate new perspectives. As Bushe shows in Chapter 6, in some cases, this has led to the development of post-Lewinian forms of OD. However, as Oswick and Marsham argue in Chapter 7, these appear to sit side by side with rather than overthrow Lewinian OD. Perhaps the most remarkable aspect of the last 30 years has been that Lewin's work, rather than being sidelined, seems to have developed a new relevance. The attacks on his work have led to its being reinvestigated and re-evaluated. This has not only shown that Lewin's work is still central to OD but also that instead of being replaced by newer perspectives on organizational change, such as postmodernism and complexity, Lewin's work appears to have remarkable synergies with them (Boje and Rosile, 2010; Burnes, 2005).

The fact that planned change and OD have survived the controversies and challenges that they have faced does not mean that these have been resolved – far from it. However, it does indicate that the battle has not been the walkover it once appeared. This first part of *The Routledge Companion to Organizational Change* seeks to illustrate and discuss the development, challenges and controversies faced by planned change and OD over the last 70 years. In so doing, the seven chapters in this part portray OD not as a fixed and cohesive whole, but as a developing and contested terrain whose proponents can be as critical of it as its opponents. The key measure of its continuing relevance must be Lewin's (1943–4: 169) assertion that 'There is nothing so practical as a good theory'. For Lewin, any approach to change had to be based on robust theory and produce practical results. This continues to be the yardstick by which OD, in whatever form, must be evaluated. It is also the yardstick against which newer approaches to organizational change must be measured if they are to be considered potential successors to OD.

References

Boje, D. and Rosile, G.A. (2010) Lewin's Action Research Meets Aristotle on the STORYTELLING FIELD: Maybe it's a Distinctive Niche for CTU. Colorado Technical University, Colorado Springs, CO, 11 July.

Burnes, B. (2004) Kurt Lewin and the Planned Approach to Ahange: A Re-appraisal. *Journal of Management Studies*, 41 (6), 977–1002.

Burnes, B. (2005) Complexity Theories and Organisational Change, *International Journal of Management Reviews*, 7 (2), 73–90.

Burnes, B. (2009) *Managing Change* (5th edition). FT/Prentice Hall: Harlow.

Greiner, L.E. and Cummings, T.G. (2004) Wanted: OD More Alive Than Dead! *Journal of Applied Behavioral Science*, 40 (4), 374–91.

Lewin, K. (1943–4) Problems of Research in Social Psychology. In D. Cartwright (ed.) (1952): *Field Theory in Social Science*. Social Science Paperbacks: London.

1

Kurt Lewin and the origins of OD

Bernard Burnes

Introduction

> Freud the clinician and Lewin the experimentalist – these are the two men whose names will stand out before all others in the history of our psychological era.
>
> (Edward C. Tolman's memorial address for Kurt Lewin delivered at the
> 1947 Convention of the American Psychological Association,
> quoted in Marrow, 1969: ix)

> There is little question that the intellectual father of contemporary theories of applied behavioural science, action research and 'planned change' is Kurt Lewin. His seminal work on leadership style and the experiments on planned change which took place in World War II in an effort to change consumer behavior launched a whole generation of research in group dynamics and the implementation of change programs.
>
> (Schein, 1988: 239)

Few social scientists can have received the level of praise and admiration that has been heaped upon Kurt Lewin (Ash, 1992; Bargal et al., 1992; Dent and Goldberg, 1999; Dickens and Watkins, 1999; Tobach, 1994). Though his work has also attracted much criticism (Dawson, 1994; Hatch, 1997; Kanter et al., 1992; Marshak, 1993; Weick, 2000), this chapter will show that the praise Lewin has received is well deserved (Burnes, 2004b; Burnes, 2007).

It needs to be recognized that Lewin's primary focus was on human behaviour in general and not organizational behaviour in particular. His main preoccupation was the resolution of social conflict and, in particular, the problems of minority or disadvantaged groups. Underpinning this preoccupation was a strong belief that only the permeation of democratic values into all facets of society, including organizations, could prevent the worst extremes of social conflict (Cartwright, 1952; G. W. Lewin and Allport, 1948).

To a large extent, his interests and beliefs stemmed from his background as a German Jew. Lewin was born in 1890 and, for a Jew growing up in Germany at this time, officially approved anti-Semitism was a fact of life. Few Jews could expect to achieve a responsible post in the civil service or universities. Despite this, Lewin was awarded a doctorate at the University of Berlin in 1916 and went on to teach there. Though he was never awarded tenured status, Lewin achieved a growing international reputation in the 1920s as a leader in his field (M. Lewin, 1992). However, with the rise of the Nazi Party, Lewin recognized that the position of Jews in Germany was increasingly threatened. The election of Hitler as Chancellor in 1933 was the final straw for him; he resigned from the University and moved to America (Marrow, 1969). In America, Lewin found a job first as a 'refugee scholar' at Cornell University and then, from 1935 to 1945, at the University of Iowa. Here he was to embark on an ambitious programme of research which covered topics such as child–parent relations, conflict in marriage, styles of leadership, worker motivation and performance, conflict in industry, group problem-solving, communication and attitude change, racism, anti-Semitism, discrimination and prejudice, integration-segregation, peace, war and poverty (Bargal et al., 1992; Cartwright, 1952; G. W. Lewin and Allport, 1948). As Cooke (1999) notes, given the prevalence of racism and anti-Semitism in America at the time, much of this work, especially his increasingly public advocacy in support of disadvantaged groups, put Lewin on the political left.

During the years of the Second World War, Lewin did much work for the American war effort. This included studies of the morale of front-line troops and psychological warfare, and his famous study aimed at persuading American housewives to buy cheaper cuts of meat (K. Lewin, 1943a; Marrow, 1969). He was also much in demand as a speaker on minority and inter-group relations (Smith, 2001). With the end of the war, Lewin established the Research Center for Group Dynamics at the Massachusetts Institute of Technology. The aim of the Center was to investigate all aspects of group behaviour, especially how it could be changed. At the same time, he was also chief architect of the Commission on Community Interrelations (CCI). Founded and funded by the American Jewish Congress, its aim was the eradication of discrimination against all minority groups.

In addition, in 1946, the Connecticut State Inter-Racial Commission asked Lewin to help train leaders and conduct research on the most effective means of combating racial and religious prejudice in communities. This led to the development of sensitivity training and the creation, in 1947, of the now famous National Training Laboratories (NTL). However, his huge workload took its toll on his health, and on 11 February 1947 he died of a heart attack (M. Lewin, 1992).

The remainder of this chapter will examine Lewin's contribution to the field of organizational change, especially his development of planned change, his contribution to the creation of the Organization Development (OD) movement and the continuing relevance of his work. It will begin by a brief examination of approaches to organization change before Lewin.

Change management before Lewin

The origins of the academic study of organizational change as we know it today can be said to have begun with Lewin (Burnes, 2004b, 2009a, 2009b; Greiner and Cummings, 2004; Schein, 1988). He was also in the advance guard of those psychologists who sought to move the study of human behaviour out of the laboratory and into the real world (Burnes, 2007). At a practical level, of course, organizational change had been a preoccupation of employers since the advent of the Industrial Revolution. However, in the eighteenth and nineteenth centuries, this was very much in terms of introducing technology and work practices which allowed employers to exert greater control over the workforce in order to extract the maximum effort from labour for the minimum pay (Burnes, 1989; Pollard, 1965). Indeed, one of the leading advocates of the factory system, Ure (1835: 368–69), neatly summed up the employers' view of the purpose and process of technological change:

> In the spirit of the Egyptian task-masters the operative printers dictate to the manufacturers the number and quality of apprentices to be admitted to the trade, the hours of their own labour, and the wages to be paid to them. At length capitalists sought deliverance from this intolerable bondage in the resources of science, and were speedily re-instated in their legitimate rule, that of the head over the inferior members ... This ... confirms the great doctrine ... that when capital enlists science in her service, the refractory hand of labour will always be taught docility.

However, it was not until the beginning of the twentieth century that employers were offered a systematic approach to managing change in the form of Frederick Taylor's Scientific Management. One of Taylor's key objectives was to overcome workers' resistance to change by, for the first time, developing an approach to change based on scientific objectivity, which offered workers a fair day's pay for a fair day's work, and applied equally to employers and employees (Rose, 1988; Sheldrake, 1996). As Taylor put it:

> The principal object of management should be to secure the maximum prosperity for the employer, coupled with the maximum prosperity for each employee.
>
> (Taylor, 1911a: 1)

> The man at the head of the business under scientific management is governed by rules and laws ... just as the workman is, and the standards which have been developed are equitable.
>
> (Taylor, 1911b: 189)

There have rightly been many criticisms of Taylor's approach to the organization of work, particularly that it was neither scientific nor effective (Littler, 1978; Locke, 1982; Rose, 1988). However, in terms of his approach to managing change, there are two points that are particularly worth noting. First, Taylor's approach was a pragmatic response to the issue of how to overcome workers' resistance to change. He found that arbitrary imposition was counterproductive and, therefore, sought to overcome resistance by an approach he portrayed as fair, neutral and scientific. Second, Taylor saw only a passive role for workers. Their job was to carry out the instructions of managers and to perform any new tasks they were given in the manner laid down and not deviate by one iota. In effect, Taylor believed, as the pioneers of the Industrial Revolution believed, that workers should do as they were told by managers. They had no other role to play in the management of change.

In the 1930s, a very different approach to managing organizations began to emerge from the work of two of the early pioneers of the Human Relations movement – Elton Mayo (1933) and Chester Barnard (1938). Unlike Scientific Management, the Human Relations approach, as it became known, sought to highlight the importance of human beings and human emotions. In particular, as Burnes (2009a) notes, it argued that:

- People are emotional rather than economic-rational beings. Human needs are far more diverse and complex than the one-dimensional image painted by Taylor and his supporters. People's emotional and social needs can have more influence on their behaviour at work than financial incentives.

- Organizations are cooperative, social systems rather than mechanical ones. People seek to meet their emotional needs through the formation of informal but influential workplace social groups.
- Organizations are composed of informal structures, rules and norms as well as formal practices and procedures. These informal rules, patterns of behaviour and communication, norms and friendships are created by people to meet their own emotional needs and are as important to the effective running of an organization as the formal systems laid down by management.

Mayo (1933) drew his arguments partly from the findings of the Hawthorne studies and to a large extent from his own views on how to achieve industrial harmony (Rose, 1988; Sheldrake, 1996). He believed that industrial unrest did not arise from any basic conflict between managers and workers, but from workers' underlying psychological flaws, which could be resolved by addressing their emotional rather than economic needs (Gillespie, 1991). Therefore, Mayo, like Taylor, was concerned with resolving industrial conflict and overcoming resistance to change.

Barnard (1938) drew his arguments from his experience as President of the New Jersey Bell Telephone Company and also from his extensive contacts with academics, especially Mayo and his colleagues at the Harvard Business School. One of the key arguments in his book *The Functions of the Executive* (1938) is the idea of organizations as cooperative systems: managers cannot run their businesses effectively and efficiently without the cooperation – the partnership – of workers. Whilst Taylor attempted to appeal to the rational side of workers and managers, Barnard (1938: 279) recognized the need to win their hearts as well as their minds by stressing moral and ethical leadership:

> The distinguishing mark of the executive responsibility is that it requires not merely conformance to a complex code of morals but also the creation of moral codes for others. The most generally recognized aspect of this function is called securing, creating, inspiring of 'morale' in an organization. This is the process of inculcating points of view, fundamental attitudes, loyalties, to the organization or cooperative system, and to the system of objective authority, that will result in subordinating individual interests and the minor dictates of personal codes to the good of the cooperative whole. This includes (also important) the establishment of the morality standards of workmanship.

There have been many critiques of the early Human Relations work (Gillespie, 1991; Rose, 1988; Sheldrake, 1996). However, focusing solely on organizational change, there are two points of note. First, unlike Scientific Management, Human Relations portrays people as having an active and to an extent voluntary role to play in the life of the organization. Nevertheless, the work of Mayo and Barnard is more about managing organizations in a steady state rather than how to change organizations. In essence it is theory of stability and not change. Second, it is an approach which is long on philosophy, i.e. it promotes a positive view of human nature and the benefits of participatory management, but it is short on practicalities, i.e. there is no blueprint, set of guidelines or tools for bringing about change.

The early Human Relations approach can be seen to have started to create a climate of readiness for the ideas of Lewin and his collaborators. It is perhaps, then, no coincidence that towards the end of the 1930s, Lewin began to move his work out of the laboratory and into the real world, and move his focus from children to adults. In so doing, he created the philosophical, ethical and practical basis for what was later to become OD through the development of his planned approach to managing change and his participative approach to managing organizations (Burnes, 2004b, 2007).

Lewin's contribution to OD

According to Greiner and Cummings (2004: 376):

> The intellectual foundation for OD began in the 1940s with the research and writing of Kurt Lewin and his protégés. Their application of participative methods to small groups was found to lead to attitude change, higher performance, and greater commitment to individual action.

Perhaps Lewin's major contribution to OD was his emphasis on developing the human side of the organization through his planned approach to change. As French and Bell (1995: 1–2) note:

> Organization development is about people *and* organizations and people *in* organizations and how they function. OD is also about planned change, that is getting individuals, teams and organizations to function better. Planned change involves common sense, hard work applied diligently over time, a systematic, goal-oriented approach, and valid knowledge about organizational dynamics and how to change them. Valid knowledge derives from the behavioral sciences such as psychology, social psychology, sociology, anthropology, systems theory, and the practice of management.

The main events in Lewin's creation of planned change can be seen in Table 1.1 (Burnes, 2007). The table shows that his work covered many subjects and fields but, as Gold (1999: 295) states, 'It is quite clear that Lewin thought of his professional activities as a piece, seamless and integrated.' Lewin's humanitarian philosophy was the glue that held his work together and gave it focus. He believed that only by resolving social conflict, whether it be religious, racial, marital or industrial, could the human condition be improved. For Lewin, the key to resolving social conflict was to facilitate learning and so enable individuals, through their own volition, to understand and restructure their perceptions of the world around them. In this he was much influenced by the Gestalt psychologists he had worked with in Berlin (Smith, 2001). The central focus of his approach to behavioural change was the notion that ' … the group to which an individual belongs is the ground for his perceptions, his feelings and his actions' (Allport, 1948: vii). Therefore, the three core beliefs which underpin Lewin's planned approach to behavioural change are:

Change must be voluntary and participative.
Change is a learning process.
Change must focus on the group rather than the individual or the organization.

Two events in 1939 laid the basis of planned change: the publication of Lewin's work on the impact of different leadership styles on children's behaviour; and the beginning of his involvement with the Harwood Manufacturing Corporation (Burnes, 2009a).

The first of these, Lewin's leadership research, was based on classic laboratory experiments. Three groups of children were exposed to three different styles of leadership: autocratic; laissez faire and democratic. The results showed that the two groups which operated under autocratic and laissez-faire leadership behaved in a dysfunctional manner. However, the group which operated under democratic leadership behaved in a co-operative and effective manner (K. Lewin et al., 1939). This confirmed Lewin's belief that democratic leadership – participative

Table 1.1 Lewin – key projects and events 1939–1947

Date	Study/Event	Location	Focus	Concepts	Citation
1938/9	Autocracy–Democracy	Iowa	The effects of different leadership styles on children's behaviour	Participation and group decision-making	K. Lewin et al. (1939)
1939	Employee Turnover	Harwood	Employee retention	Changing supervisory behaviour	Marrow (1969)
1940/1	Group Decision-making	Harwood	Democratic participation and productivity	Participation and group decision-making	Marrow (1969)
1941	Training in Democratic Leadership	Iowa	Improving leadership behaviours and techniques	Sensitivity Training	Bavelas and K. Lewin (1942)
1942	Food Habits	Iowa	Changing the food-buying habits of housewives	Participation and group decision-making	K. Lewin (1943a)
1942?	Self-management	Harwood	Increasing workers' control over the pace of work	Group decision-making	Marrow (1969)
1944/5	Leadership Training	Harwood	Improving the interpersonal skills and effectiveness of supervisors	Role Play	French (1945)
1944/5	Commission on Community Interrelations (CCI)	New York	The problems and conflicts of group and community life	Action Research	Marrow (1969)
1945	Research Center for Group Dynamics	MIT	Understanding and changing group behaviour	Action Research	Marrow (1969)
1946	Changing Stereotypes	Harwood	Changing attitudes to older workers	Information gathering, discussion and reflection	Marrow (1957 & 1972)
1946	Connecticut State Inter-Racial Commission	New Britain, Connecticut	Leadership Training	Sensitivity Training/Role Play	Marrow (1969)
1947	National Training Laboratory	Bethel, Maine	Leadership Training	T-groups (sensitivity training/role play)	Marrow (1967 & 1969)
1947	Overcoming Resistance to Change	Harwood	The impact of different approaches to change on productivity	Participative change/force field analysis	Coch and French (1948)

Source: Burnes (2007)

management – was the most effective way of managing groups and changing group behaviour (K. Lewin, 1943b, 1934c). Indeed, as Zimmerman (1978) pointed out, modern concepts of participative management began with Lewin's work.

The second event, the beginning of Lewin's work with the Harwood Manufacturing Corporation, allowed Lewin to move from the laboratory to the workplace and to show that participative management could be applied and succeed in the real world (Burnes, 2007). The importance of the Harwood studies was noted by Dent (2002: 272):

> ... although this comprehensive effort is much less well-known than the Hawthorne studies, the research which came out of it has perhaps had a greater impact on group decision-making processes, self-management, leadership development, meeting management, stereotyping and resistance to change, among others.

Burnes (2007) also shows that the Harwood studies constitute a milestone in the practice of organizational change. Harwood became the arena where Lewin developed, tested and proved planned change, and as such laid the foundations of OD.

Planned change

Though many writers see Lewin's Three-Step model as the totality of his work on organizational change (see Dawson, 1994; Hatch, 1997; Kanter et al., 1992), this is just one element of his planned approach. In fact, planned change has four elements – Field Theory, Group Dynamics, Action Research and the Three-Step model. Though they are often treated as separate aspects of his work, Lewin saw them as a unified whole with each element supporting and reinforcing the others, and all of them necessary to understand and bring about planned change.

Field Theory

Lewin maintained that for group behaviour to change, it was necessary to 'unfreeze' the forces restraining change, such as personal defences or group norms (Weick and Quinn, 1999). Field Theory is an approach to understanding group behaviour by identifying and mapping the totality and complexity of the field in which the behaviour takes place (Back, 1992). Lewin believed that to understand any situation it was necessary that 'One should view the present situation – the status quo – as being maintained by certain conditions or forces' (K. Lewin, 1943b: 172). The status quo is maintained because forces driving change are in balance with the forces restraining change. Lewin (K. Lewin, 1947b) postulated that individual behaviour is a function of the group environment or 'field', as he termed it. Consequently, any changes in behaviour stem from changes, be they small or large, in the forces within the field, i.e. either an increase in the driving forces or a decrease in the restraining forces (K. Lewin, 1947a). Lewin believed that a field was in a continuous state of adaptation and that 'Change and constancy are relative concepts; group life is never without change, merely differences in the amount and type of change exist' (K. Lewin, 1947a: 199). This is why Lewin used the term 'quasi-stationary equilibrium' to indicate that, whilst there might be a rhythm and pattern to the behaviour and processes of a group, these tended to fluctuate constantly owing to changes in the forces or circumstances that impinge on the group.

Lewin argued that if one could identify, plot and establish the potency of these forces, then it would be possible not only to understand why individuals, groups and organizations behave as they do, but also what forces would need to be diminished or strengthened in order to bring about change. With Lewin's death, the interest in Field Theory waned (Back, 1992; Gold, 1992; Hendry, 1996). However, in the past two decades, it has once again begun to attract interest, especially in terms of understanding and overcoming resistance to change (Argyris, 1990; Hirschhorn, 1988). According to Hendry (1996), even critics of Lewin's work have drawn on Field Theory to develop their own models of change (e.g. Pettigrew et al., 1989; Pettigrew et al., 1992). Indeed, parallels have even been drawn between Lewin's work on Field Theory and the work of complexity theorists (Back, 1992; Kippenberger, 1998).

Group Dynamics

Lewin was the first psychologist to write about 'group dynamics' and the importance of the group in shaping the behaviour of its members (Allport, 1948; Bargal et al., 1992). Drawing on Lewin's work, Cartwright (1951: 382) offers the following definition:

> What is "group dynamic"? Perhaps it will be most useful to start by looking at the derivation of the word "dynamics". It comes from a Greek word meaning force. In careful usage of the phrase, "group dynamics" refers to the forces operating in groups. The investigation of group dynamics, then, consists of a study of these forces: what gives rise to them, what conditions modify them, what consequences they have, etc.

Lewin's (K. Lewin, 1939: 165) definition of a 'group' is still generally accepted: ' … it is not the similarity or dissimilarity of individuals that constitutes a group, but interdependence of fate'. As Kippenberger (1998) notes, Lewin was addressing two questions:

- What is it about the nature and characteristics of a particular group that causes it to respond (behave) as it does to the forces which impinge on it?
- How can these forces be changed in order to elicit a more desirable form of behaviour?

It was to address these questions that Lewin began to develop the concept of Group Dynamics. Group Dynamics stresses that group behaviour, rather than that of individuals, should be the main focus of change (Bernstein, 1968; Dent and Goldberg, 1999). Lewin (K Lewin, 1947b) maintained that it is fruitless to concentrate on changing the behaviour of individuals because the individual in isolation is constrained by group pressures to conform. Consequently, the focus of change must be at the group level and should concentrate on factors such as group norms, roles, interactions and socialization processes to create 'disequilibrium' and change (Schein, 1988).

Lewin's pioneering work on Group Dynamics not only laid the foundations for our understanding of groups (Dent and Goldberg, 1999; Cooke, 1999; French and Bell, 1984; Marrow, 1969; Schein, 1988) but, as with Field Theory, it has also been linked to complexity theories by researchers examining self-organizing theory and non-linear systems (Tschacher and Brunner, 1995).

Lewin was perhaps the first to recognize the need to study and understand the internal dynamics of a group – the different roles people play and how groups need to change over time. However, for him, this understanding was not sufficient by itself to bring about change. Lewin also recognized the need to provide a process whereby group members could be engaged in and committed to changing their behaviour. This led Lewin to develop Action Research and the Three-Step model of change.

Action Research

This term was coined by Lewin (K. Lewin, 1946) in an article entitled 'Action Research and Minority Problems'. Lewin stated in the article: 'In the last year and a half I have had occasion to have contact with a great variety of organizations, institutions, and individuals who came for help in the field of group relations' (K. Lewin, 1946: 201). However, though these people exhibited

> ... a great amount of good-will, of readiness to face the problem squarely and really do something about it. ... These eager people feel themselves to be in a fog. They feel in a fog on three counts: 1. What is the present situation? 2. What are the dangers? 3. And most importantly of all, what shall we do?
>
> (K. Lewin, 1946: 201)

Lewin conceived of Action Research as a two-pronged process which would allow groups to address these three questions:

- Firstly, it emphasizes that change requires action, and is directed at achieving this.
- Secondly, it recognizes that successful action is based on analysing the situation correctly, identifying all the possible alternative solutions and choosing the one most appropriate to the situation at hand.

> (Bennett, 1983)

To be successful, though, there has also to be a 'felt-need'. Felt-need is an individual's inner realization that change is necessary. If felt-need is low in the group or organization, introducing change becomes problematic. The theoretical foundations of Action Research lie in Gestalt psychology, which stresses that change can only successfully be achieved by helping individuals to reflect on and gain new insights into the totality of their situation. Lewin (K. Lewin, 1946: 206) stated that Action Research ' ... proceeds in a spiral of steps each of which is composed of a circle of planning, action, and fact-finding about the results of the action'. As Figure 1.1 shows, it is an iterative process whereby research leads to action, and action leads to evaluation and further

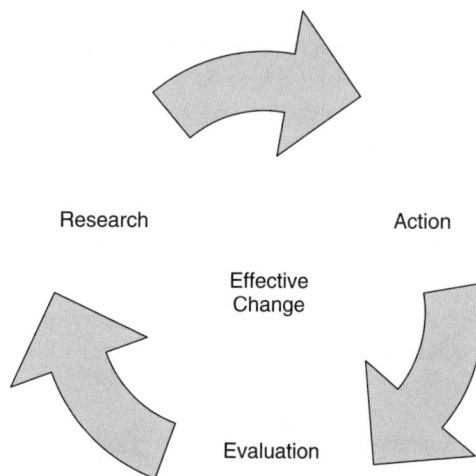

Research   Action

Effective
Change

Evaluation

Figure 1.1 Action research

research. As Schein (1996: 35) comments, it was Lewin's view that ' ... one cannot understand an organization without trying to change it ... '. Indeed, Lewin's view was very much that the understanding and learning that this process produces for the individuals and groups concerned, which then feeds into changed behaviour, is more important than any resulting change as such (K. Lewin, 1946).

To this end, Action Research draws on Lewin's work on Field Theory to identify the forces that focus on the group to which the individual belongs. It also draws on Group Dynamics to understand why group members behave in the way they do when subjected to these forces. Lewin stressed that the routines and patterns of behaviour in a group are more than just the outcome of opposing forces in a force field. They have a value in themselves and have a positive role to play in enforcing group norms (K. Lewin, 1947a). Action Research stresses that for change to be effective, it must take place at the group level, and must be a participative and collaborative process which involves all of those concerned (Allport, 1948; Bargal et al., 1992; Darwin et al., 2002; Dickens and Watkins, 1999; French and Bell, 1984; K. Lewin, 1947b; McNiff, 2000).

Lewin's first Action Research project was to investigate and reduce violence between Catholic and Jewish teenage gangs. This was quickly followed by a project to integrate black and white sales staff in New York department stores (Marrow, 1969). However, Action Research was also adopted by the Tavistock Institute in Britain, and used to improve managerial competence and efficiency in the newly nationalized coal industry. Since then it has acquired strong adherents throughout the world (Dickens and Watkins, 1999; Eden and Huxham, 1996; Elden and Chisholm, 1993). However, Lewin (K. Lewin, 1947a: 228) was concerned that

> A change towards a higher level of group performance is frequently short lived; after a 'shot in the arm', group life soon returns to the previous level. This indicates that it does not suffice to define the objective of a planned change in group performance as the reaching of a different level. Permanency at the new level, or permanency for a desired period, should be included in the objective.

It was for this reason that he developed his Three-Step model of change.

Three-Step model

This is often cited as Lewin's key contribution to organizational change. It needs to be recognized, however, that when he developed his Three-Step model Lewin was not thinking solely of organizational change. Nor did he intend it to be used separately from the other three elements which comprise his planned approach to change (i.e. Field Theory, Group Dynamics and Action Research). Rather Lewin saw the four concepts as forming an integrated approach to analysing, understanding and bringing about change whether it be in organizations or in society at large.

A successful change project, Lewin (K. Lewin, 1947a) argued, involved three steps (see Figure 1.2).

STEP 1: UNFREEZING
Lewin believed that the stability of human behaviour was based on a quasi-stationary equilibrium supported by a complex field of driving and restraining forces. Others refer to this as inertia – the

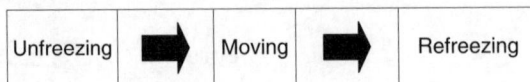

Figure 1.2 Lewin's Three-Step model of change

inability of organizations or groups to change as fast as the environment in which they operate (Pfeffer, 1997). Miller (1993, 1994) argues that the more successful a group has been, the greater the inertia. This is because success tends to make groups focus on those factors which are seen as having brought success and to discard those which are seen as peripheral. Successful groups also tend to ignore signals which might indicate the need for change. The result is that they sacrifice adaptability and increase inertia. This is why Lewin argued that the equilibrium (the forces of inertia) needs to be destabilized (unfrozen) before old behaviour can be discarded (unlearnt) and new behaviour successfully adopted. Given the type of issues that Lewin was addressing, as one would expect, he did not believe that change would be easy or that the same approach could be applied in all situations:

> The 'unfreezing' of the present level may involve quite different problems in different cases. Allport ... has described the 'catharsis' which seems necessary before prejudice can be removed. To break open the shell of complacency and self-righteousness it is sometimes necessary to bring about an emotional stir up.
>
> (K. Lewin, 1947a: 229)

STEP 2: MOVING

As Schein (1996: 32) notes, unfreezing is not an end in itself; it ' ... creates motivation to learn but does not necessarily control or predict the direction of learning'. This echoes Lewin's view that any attempt to predict or identify a specific outcome from planned change is very difficult because of the complexity of the forces concerned. Instead, one should seek to take into account all the forces at work and identify and evaluate, on a trial and error basis, all the available options (K Lewin, 1947a). This is, of course, the learning approach promoted by Action Research. It is this iterative approach of research, action and more research that enables groups and individuals to move from a less acceptable to a more acceptable set of behaviours. However, as noted above, Lewin (K. Lewin, 1947a) recognized that, without reinforcement, change could be short-lived.

STEP 3: REFREEZING

This is the final step in the Three-Step model. Refreezing seeks to stabilize the group at a new quasi-stationary equilibrium in order to ensure that the new behaviours are relatively safe from regression. The main point about refreezing is that new behaviour must be, to some degree, congruent with the rest of the behaviour, personality and environment of the learner or it will simply lead to a new round of disconfirmation (Schein, 1996). This is why Lewin saw successful change as a group activity, because unless group norms and routines are also transformed, changes to individual behaviour will not be sustained. In organizational terms, refreezing often requires changes to organizational culture, norms, policies and practices (Cummings and Huse, 1989).

With the advent of newer approaches to change, Lewin's Three-Step model has attracted much criticism (Dawson, 1994; Hatch, 1997; Kanter et al., 1992). Nevertheless, such is its continuing influence that, as Hendry (1996: 624) commented:

> Scratch any account of creating and managing change and the idea that change is a three-stage process which necessarily begins with a process of unfreezing will not be far below the surface. Indeed, it has been said that the whole theory of change is reducible to this one idea of Kurt Lewin's ...

Hendry's view is supported by the work of Elrod and Tippett (2002), who reviewed a wide range of change models. They found that most approaches to organizational change were strikingly similar to Lewin's Three-Step model. When they extended their research to other forms of human and organizational change, Elrod and Tippett (2002: 288) also found that:

> Models of the change process were identified in diverse and seemingly unrelated disciplines [such as bereavement theory, personal transition theory, creative processes, cultural revolutions and scientific revolutions]. Examination of most of these models revealed … most followed Lewin's [K. Lewin,1947b] three-phase model of change.

Others also support this view (see Burnes, 2004b, 2007; Zell, 2003).

Lewin's legacy

As Cummings and Worley (2005) observe, OD evolved from five major developments:

The growth of the National Training Laboratory (NTL)
Action Research/Survey Feedback
Participative Management
Quality of Working Life
Strategic Change

The first three developments derived from work by Lewin on planned change in the 1940s, whilst the latter two did not emerge until the 1960s/1970s (Burnes, 2007; Marrow, 1969; Zimmerman, 1978). However, Lewin did not just provide OD with a range of theories, tools, techniques and approaches; he also imbued it with a set of democratic–humanist values which provided the ethical basis of OD (Conner, 1977; French and Bell, 1999; Gellerman et al., 1990; Hurley et al., 1992; Warwick and Thompson, 1980). Therefore, as can be seen, Lewin provided OD with its theoretical, practical and philosophical foundations.

With the emergence of newer approaches to change in the 1980s, Lewin's work has attracted much criticism, especially that it is simplistic and outmoded (Dawson, 1994; Hatch, 1997; Kanter et al., 1992). However, it is difficult to see how an approach based on building understanding, generating learning, gaining new insights, and identifying and testing (and retesting) solutions is either simplistic or outmoded (Bargal and Bar, 1992; Darwin et al., 2002). Nor have the organizational concerns which Lewin sought to address, such as of group effectiveness, behaviour and change, etc., diminished in importance in the years since his death, though they may often now be labelled differently. This can be seen from the enormous emphasis that continues to be placed on the importance of group behaviour, involvement and empowerment (Argyris, 1992; Handy, 1994; Hannagan, 2002; Huczynski and Buchanan, 2001; Kanter, 1989; Mullins, 2002; Peters, 1993; Schein, 1988; Senge, 1990; Wilson, 1992). Indeed, the advent of the complexity perspective appears to be leading to a renewed interest in Lewin's work (Back, 1992; Burnes, 2004a; Kippenberger, 1998; MacIntosh and MacLean, 2001; Tschacher and Brunner, 1995). In addition, Lewin's work has had enormous implications for the way that organizations are now managed. In particular, the Harwood studies marked the point at which the era of autocratic management started to give way to the more participative approaches that began to characterize academic thought and managerial practice in the 1950s and 1960s (Burnes, 2007; Lowin, 1968).

Despite the criticisms, or perhaps because of them, the last two decades have seen a renewed interest in understanding and applying Lewin's approach to change (Bargal and Bar, 1992; Boje and Rosile, 2010; Elrod and Tippett, 2002; Hendry, 1996; Kippenberger, 1998; MacIntosh and

MacLean, 2001; Wooten and White, 1999). In many respects, this should not come as a surprise given the tributes and acknowledgments paid to him by major figures such as Chris Argyris (et al., 1985) and Edgar Schein (1988). Above all, though, it is a recognition of the rigour of Lewin's work, based as it was on a virtuous circle of theory, experimentation and practice, which is best expressed by his famous dictum that ' ... there is nothing so practical as a good theory' (K. Lewin, 1943–44: 169).

In examining work which was conducted more than 60 years ago, there is a tendency to see it as having little relevance for today's world. However, the issues Lewin addressed have a very contemporary ring to them. What Lewin and his colleagues referred to as group decision-making and self-management, we would now call empowerment. Their work on changing stereotypes/combating age discrimination we would now refer to as managing diversity. In other cases, the terminology has remained the same, namely, resistance to change and leadership training. These issues are all still seen as central challenges faced by organizations today, and many of the methods used by OD practitioners to tackle them are still based on the pioneering work of Lewin and his colleagues (Bradford and Burke, 2004; Cummings and Worley, 2005; Jones et al., 2000; French and Bell, 1999; Yukl, 2002). Indeed, at a time when the OD movement appears to have lost its sense of direction (Greiner and Cummings, 2004), it is timely to remember where it all started and what it was trying to achieve.

References

Allport, G.W. (1948) Foreword. In G.W. Lewin, and G.W. Allport (eds) *Resolving Social Conflict*. Harper & Row: London.

Argyris, C. (1990) *Overcoming Organizational Defenses: Facilitating Organizational Learning*. Allyn & Bacon: Boston, MA.

Argyris, C. (1992) *On Organizational Learning*. Blackwell: Oxford.

Argyris, C., Putnam, R. and McLain-Smith, D. (1985) *Action Science: Concepts, Methods and Skills for Research and Intervention*. Jossey Bass: San Francisco, CA.

Ash, M.G. (1992) Cultural contexts and scientific change in psychology – Lewin, Kurt in Iowa. *American Psychologist*, 47(2), 198–207.

Back, K.W. (1992) This business of topology. *Journal of Social Issues*, 48(2), 51–66.

Bargal, D. and Bar, H. (1992) A Lewinian approach to intergroup workshops for Arab-Palestinian and Jewish youth. *Journal of Social Issues*, 48(2), 139–54.

Bargal, D., Gold, M. and Lewin, M. (1992) The heritage of Kurt Lewin – introduction. *Journal of Social Issues*, 48(2), 3–13.

Barnard, C. (1938) *The Functions of the Executive*. Harvard University Press: Cambridge, MA.

Bavelas, A. and Lewin, K. (1942) Training in democratic leadership. *Journal of Abnormal Psychology*, 37, 115–19.

Bennett, R. (1983) *Management Research: Guide for Institutions and Professionals*. Management Development Series No. 20. Geneva: International Labour Office.

Bernstein, L. (1968) *Management Development*. Business Books: London.

Boje, D. and Rosile, G.A. (2010) *Lewin's Action Research meets Aristotle on the STORYTELLING FIELD: Maybe it's A Distinctive Niche for CTU*. Colorado Technical University, Colorado Springs, CO, July 11.

Bradford, D.L. and Burke, W.W. (2004) Introduction: Is OD in Crisis? *Journal of Applied Behavioral Science*, 40(4), 369–373.

Burnes, B. (1989) *New Technology in Context*. Gower: Aldershot.

Burnes, B. (2004a) Kurt Lewin and complexity theories: back to the future? *Journal of Change Management*, 4(4), 309–25.

Burnes, B. (2004b) Kurt Lewin and the planned approach to change: a re-appraisal. *Journal of Management Studies*, 41(6), 977–1002.

Burnes, B. (2007) Kurt Lewin and the Harwood studies: the foundations of OD. *Journal of Applied Behavioral Science*, 43(2), 213–31.

Burnes, B. (2009a) *Managing Change* (5th edition). FT/Prentice Hall: Harlow.

Burnes, B. (2009b) Organisational change in the public sector: the case for planned change. In R.T. By, and C. Macleod (eds) *Managing Organisational Change in Public Services: International Issues, Challenges and Cases*. Routledge: London.

Cartwright, D. (1951) Achieving change in people: some applications of group dynamics theory. *Human Relations*, 6(4), 381–92.

Cartwright, D. (ed.) (1952) *Field Theory in Social Science*. Social Science Paperbacks: London.

Coch, L. and French, J.R.P., Jr (1948) Overcoming resistance to change. *Human Relations*, 1, 512–32.

Conner, P.E. (1977) A critical enquiry into some assumptions and values characterizing OD. *Academy of Management Review*, 2(1), 635–44.

Cooke, B. (1999) Writing the left out of management theory: the historiography of the management of change. *Organization*, 6(1), 81–105.

Cummings, T.G. and Huse, E.F. (1989) *Organization Development and Change* (4th edition). West: St Paul, MN.

Cummings, T.G. and Worley, C.G. (2005) *Organization Development and Change* (8th edition). South-Western College Publishing: Mason, OH.

Darwin, J., Johnson, P. and McAuley, J. (2002) *Developing Strategies for Change*. FT/Prentice Hall: Harlow.

Dawson, P. (1994) *Organizational Change: A Processual Approach*. Paul Chapman Publishing: London.

Dent, E.B. (2002) The messy history of OB&D: How three strands came to be seen as one rope. *Management Decision*, 40, 266–80.

Dent, E.B. and Goldberg, S.G. (1999) Challenging resistance to change. *Journal of Applied Behavioral Science*, 35(1), 25–41.

Dickens, L. and Watkins, K. (1999) Action research: rethinking Lewin. *Management Learning*, 30(2), 127–40.

Eden, C. and Huxham, C. (1996) Action research for the study of organizations. In S.R. Clegg, C. Hardy and W.R. Nord (eds) *Handbook of Organization Studies*. London: Sage.

Elden, M. and Chisholm, R.F. (1993) Emerging varieties of action research: Introduction to the Special Issue. *Human Relations*, 46(2), 121–42.

Elrod II, P.D. and Tippett, D.D. (2002) The 'death valley' of change. *Journal of Organizational Change Management*, 15(3), 273–91.

French, J.R.P., Jr (1945) Role playing as a method of training foremen. *Sociometry*, 8, 410–25.

French, W.L. and Bell, C.H. (1984) *Organization Development* (4th edition). Prentice Hall: Englewood Cliffs, NJ.

French, W.L. and Bell, C.H. (1995) *Organization Development* (5th edition). Prentice Hall: Englewood Cliffs, NJ.

French, W.L. and Bell, C.H. (1999) *Organization Development* (6th edition). Prentice Hall: Upper Saddle River, NJ.

Gellerman, W., Frankel, M.S. and Ladenson, R.F. (1990) *Values and Ethics in Organizational and Human Systems Development: Responding to Dilemmas in Professional Life*. Jossey-Bass: San Francisco, CA, USA.

Gillespie, R. (1991) *Manufacturing Knowledge: A History of the Hawthorne Experiments*. Cambridge University Press: Cambridge.

Gold, M. (1992) Metatheory and field theory in social psychology: relevance or elegance? *Journal of Social Issues*, 48(2), 67–78.

Gold, M. (ed.) (1999) *The Complete Social Scientist: A Kurt Lewin Reader*. American Psychological Association: Washington, DC.

Greiner, L.E. and Cummings, T.G. (2004) Wanted: OD more alive than dead! *Journal of Applied Behavioral Science*, 40(4), 374–91.

Handy, C. (1994) *The Empty Raincoat*. Hutchinson: London.

Hannagan, T. (2002) *Management: Concepts and Practices* (3rd edition). FT/Pearson: Harlow.

Hatch, M.J. (1997) *Organization Theory: Modern, Symbolic and Postmodern Perspectives*. Oxford University Press: Oxford.

Hendry, C. (1996) Understanding and creating whole organizational change through learning theory. *Human Relations*, 49(5), 621–41.

Hirschhorn, L. (1988) *The Workplace Within*. MIT Press: Cambridge, MA.

Huczynski, A. and Buchanan, D. (2001) *Organizational Behaviour* (4th edition). FT/Prentice Hall: Harlow.

Hurley, R.F., Church, A.H., Burke, W.W. and Van Eynde, D.F. (1992) Tension, change and values in OD. *OD Practitioner*, 29, 1–5.

Jones, G.R., George, J.M. and Hill, C.W.L. (2000) *Contemporary Management* (2nd edition). McGraw-Hill: Boston, MA.

Kanter, R.M. (1989) *When Giants Learn to Dance: Mastering the Challenges of Strategy, Management, and Careers in the 1990s*. Unwin: London.

Kanter, R.M., Stein, B.A. and Jick, T.D. (1992) *The Challenge of Organizational Change*. Free Press: New York, USA.

Kippenberger, T. (1998) Planned change: Kurt Lewin's legacy. *The Antidote*, 3(4), 10–12.

Lewin, G.W. and Allport, G.W. (eds) (1948). *Resolving Social Conflict*. London: Harper & Row.

Lewin, K. (1939) When facing danger. In G.W. Lewin and G.W. Allport (eds) (1948) *Resolving Social Conflict*. Harper & Row: London.

Lewin, K. (1943a) Forces behind food habits and methods of change. *Bulletin of the National Research Council*, 108, 35–65.

Lewin, K. (1943b) Psychological ecology. In D. Cartwright (ed.) *Field Theory in Social Science*. London: Social Science Paperbacks.

Lewin, K. (1943c) The special case of Germany. In G.W. Lewin and G.W. Allport (eds) (1948) *Resolving Social Conflict*. London: Harper & Row.

Lewin, K. (1943/4) Problems of research in social psychology. In D. Cartwright (ed.) (1952) *Field Theory in Social Science*. Social Science Paperbacks: London.

Lewin, K. (1946) Action research and minority problems. In G.W. Lewin and G.W. Allport (eds) (1948) *Resolving Social Conflict*. Harper & Row: London.

Lewin, K. (1947a) Frontiers in group dynamics. In D. Cartwright (ed.) (1952) *Field Theory in Social Science*. Social Science Paperbacks: London.

Lewin, K. (1947b) Group decisions and social change. In T.M. Newcomb and E.L. Hartley (eds) (1959) *Readings in Social Psychology*. Henry Holt: New York.

Lewin, K., Lippitt, R. and White, R. (1939) Patterns of aggressive behavior in experimentally created "social climates." *Journal of Social Psychology*, 10, 271–99.

Lewin, M. (1992) The impact of Kurt Lewin's life on the place of social issues in his work. *Journal of Social Issues*, 48(2), 15–29.

Littler, C.R. (1978) Understanding Taylorism. *British Journal of Sociology*, 29(2), 185–202.

Locke, E.W. (1982) The ideas of Frederick W Taylor. *Academy of Management Review*, 7(1), 14–24.

Lowin, A. (1968) Participative decision making: a model, literature critique, and prescriptions for research. *Organizational Behavior and Human Performance*, 3, 68–106.

MacIntosh, R. and MacLean, D. (2001) Conditioned emergence: researching change and changing research. *International Journal of Operations and Production Management*, 21(10), 1343–57.

Marrow, A.J. (1957) *Making Management Human*. New York: McGraw-Hill.

Marrow, A.J. (1967). Events leading to the establishment of the National Training Laboratories. *The Journal of Applied Behavioral Science*, 3, 144–50.

Marrow, A.J. (1969) *The Practical Theorist: The Life and Work of Kurt Lewin*. New York: Basic Books.

Marrow, A.J. (1972) The effects of participation on performance. In A.J. Marrow (ed.) *The Failure of Success* (pp. 90–102). New York: Amacom.

Marshak, R.J. (1993) Lewin meets Confucius: a re-view of the OD model of change. *The Journal of Applied Behavioral Science*, 29(4), 393–415.

Mayo, E. (1933) *The Human Problems of Industrial Civilization*. Macmillan: New York.

McNiff, J. (ed.) (2000) *Action Research in Organisations*. Routledge: London.

Miller, D. (1993) The architecture of simplicity. *Academy of Management Review*, 18(1), 116–38.

Miller, D. (1994) What happens after success: the perils of excellence. *Journal of Management Studies*, 31(3), 325–58.

Mullins, L. (2002) *Management and Organisational Behaviour* (6th edition). FT/Pearson: Harlow.

Peters, T. (1993) *Liberation Management*. Pan: London.

Pettigrew, A.M., Ferlie, E. and McKee, L. (1992) *Shaping Strategic Change*. Sage: London.

Pettigrew, A.M., Hendry, C. and Sparrow, P. (1989) *Training in Britain: Employers' Perspectives on Human Resources*. HMSO: London.

Pfeffer, J. (1997) *New Directions for Organization Theory*. Oxford University Press: Oxford.

Pollard, S. (1965) *The Genesis of Modern Management*. Pelican: Harmondsworth.

Rose, M. (1988) *Industrial Behaviour*. Penguin: Harmondsworth.

Schein, E.H. (1988) *Organizational Psychology* (3rd edition). Prentice Hall: Englewood Cliffs, NJ, USA.

Schein, E.H. (1996) Kurt Lewin's change theory in the field and in the classroom: notes towards a model of management learning. *Systems Practice*, 9(1), 27–47.

Senge, P.M. (1990) *The Fifth Discipline: The Art and Practice of the Learning Organization*. Century Business: London.

Sheldrake, J. (1996) *Management Theory: From Taylorism to Japanization*. International Thompson Business Press: London.

Smith, M.K. (2001) Kurt Lewin: groups, experiential learning and action research. *The Encyclopedia of Informal Education*, 1–15, available at www.infed.org/thinkers/et-lewin.htm.

Taylor, F.W. (1911a) *The Principles of Scientific Management*. Dover (1998 edition): New York.

Taylor, F.W. (1911b) *Shop Management*. Harper (1947 edition): New York.

Tobach, E. (1994) Personal is political is personal is political. *Journal of Social Issues*, 50(1), 221–44.

Tschacher, W. and Brunner, E.J. (1995) Empirical-studies of group-dynamics from the point-of-view of self-organization theory. *Zeitschrift fur Sozialpsychologie*, 26(2), 78–91.

Ure, A. (1835) *The Philosophy of Manufactures*. Frank Cass (1967 edition): London.

Warwick, D.P., and Thompson, J.T. (1980) Still crazy after all these years. *Training and Development Journal*, 34(2), 16–22.

Weick, K.E. (2000) Emergent change as a universal in organisations. In M. Beer and N. Nohria (eds) *Breaking the Code of Change*. Harvard Business School Press: Boston, MA.

Weick, K.E. and Quinn, R.E. (1999) Organizational Change and Development. *Annual Review of Psychology*, 50, 361–86.

Wilson, D.C. (1992) *A Strategy of Change*. Routledge: London.

Wooten, K.C. and White, L.P. (1999) Linking OD's philosophy with justice theory: postmodern implications. *Journal of Organizational Change Management*, 12(1), 7–20.

Yukl, G. (2002) *Leadership in Organizations* (5th edition). Prentice Hall: Upper Saddle River, NJ.

Zell, D. (2003) Organizational change as a process of death, dying, and rebirth. *Journal of Applied Behavioral Science*, 39 (1), 73–96.

Zimmerman, K.D. (1978) Participative management: A reexamination of the classics. *Academy of Management Review*, 3, 896–901.

2

Kurt Lewin's vision of organizational and social change

The interdependence of theory, research and action/practice

David Bargal

Introduction

This chapter will present systematic arguments and documentation that highlight Lewin's involvement in theory formulation and research in the domains of social and organizational change. As a result of Lewin's involvement, planned organizational and social change became an important issue in social and behavioral sciences. The evidence presented here is an intriguing example of a dialectical thought process, which resulted in the construction of action research as a research paradigm, a methodology, and a means of interventions aimed at improvement of social systems.

Lippitt's eulogy following Lewin's premature death opened with the following observation:

> Although his life line could be analyzed in terms of many themes, I believe the most persistent and central was his continuous scientific study of the mysteries of interdependence in the successful functioning of individual personality, of group life and of science as an ongoing operation made of many subparts.
>
> (1947, p. 87)

In the following chapter, it will be argued that by introducing the action research paradigm, Lewin was one of the first intellectuals to pave the way for a shift from an epistemological approach, which gave priority to formal knowledge (theory and research), to a dialogical (interdependent) approach, which perceived production and utilization of knowledge as a mutual enterprise shared by all parties involved. Furthermore, it will be argued that the action research paradigm, which Lewin never established formally due to his untimely death, developed gradually over a period of eight years through a dialogical process of epistemological refinement. Lewin integrated three interdependent components into that paradigm: theory, research, and action/practice.

In so doing, he foresaw the issue that has become a major concern in all professions – that is, the relationship between theory and practice (Anderson et al., 2001; Rynes et al., 2001; Van De Ven and Johnson, 2006). By proposing the action research paradigm for systematic intervention in problems relating to organizational and social change, he addressed many issues that leading scholars today have dealt with in a similar way. Two such paradigms will be discussed later in more detail: participatory action research (Reason and Bradbury, 2001, 2008), and engaged scholarship (Van De Ven, 2007).

The interdependent relationships among the three components of the action research paradigm will be highlighted. All three components are embedded in the Gestalt school of psychology, which reflected Lewin's philosophical orientation.

First, some highlights in Lewin's personal and intellectual background will be presented, in an attempt to shed light on his concepts and theories. Afterwards, the four clusters that shaped his approach towards social and organizational change will be presented (Figure 2.1):

Cluster one: theory. This cluster consists of three themes—the metatheoretical principles underlying gestalt psychology and the field theory approach; Lewin's commitment to democratic values and ideology; and Lewin's principles of social change.
Cluster two: research. This cluster consists of two fields of study—small groups and leadership.
Cluster three. This cluster consists of Lewin's real-life interventions and actions in the field of organizational and social change, as reflected in the Harwood studies (Burnes, 2004; Marrow, 1969), and in the field of intergroup relations (Lewin, 1946/1948; Lippitt, 1949).
Cluster four. This cluster consists of the action research paradigm and its principles.

The action research paradigm was developed gradually, and became the main methodology for organizational change and development. The paradigm will be presented and elaborated on the basis of Lewin's last two papers (Lewin 1947a, 1997b). The chapter will conclude with a discussion of the implications of Lewin's thinking for understanding interventions aimed at

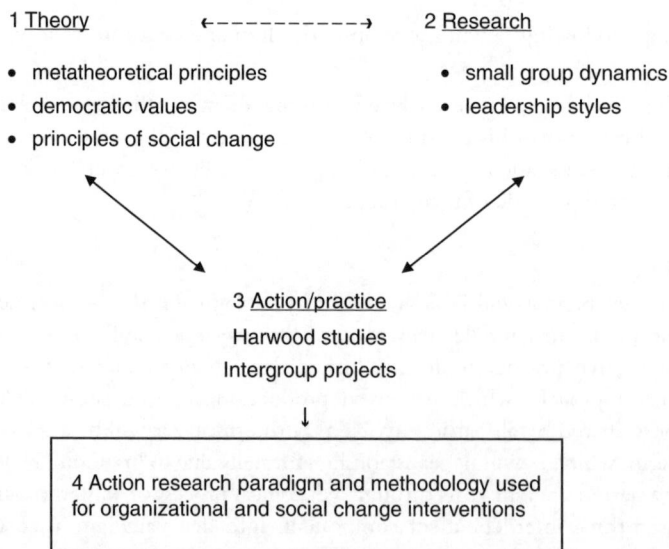

Figure 2.1 The interdependence of theory, research, and action/practice and their effect on organizational and social change issues

organizational and social change, and the relevance of his approach to the debate on the gap between theory and practice, as reflected in contemporary literature on organizational studies.

Kurt Lewin's personal and intellectual background (1890–1947)

Kurt Lewin was born in 1890 in Mogilno, a small town near the former Prussian province of Posen, Germany (now in Poland). He was the second of four children in a middle-class family that made a living from a farm and a small store. When Lewin was 14, his family moved to Berlin, and he spent most of his adolescence in an atmosphere of open discrimination against Jews, including direct manifestations of anti-Semitism (Lewin, 1992).

Initially, Lewin aspired to become a physician and began medical school in Freiburg, where he specialized in medicine and philosophy. In 1910, he abandoned the study of medicine and moved to Berlin, where he studied philosophy and psychology. In World War I, Lewin served in the German army. He rose to the rank of lieutenant, and earned a military award of excellence after being wounded in the war. In 1916, he was granted a Ph.D. degree for his doctoral research on "The Psychic Activity on Interrupting the Process of the Will and the Fundamental Laws of Association." Although he devoted his career to the social sciences, he was strongly influenced by philosophers such as Cassirer and Brentano, who provided the epistemological basis for Lewin's future theoretical and experimental work.

At the University of Berlin, Lewin developed an interest in Gestalt psychology under the leadership of Carl Stumpf, and was also influenced by colleagues such as Wertheimer, Kofka, and Köhler. Whereas his colleagues mainly developed theories on perception and its organization, Lewin started to apply theories on memory, will, and intention. Later he applied those theories to the field of group dynamics and intergroup relations. From 1921 to 1926, Lewin served as an assistant professor at the Psychology Institute of the University of Berlin. However, this promotion was obstructed because of his Jewish identity. From 1926 to 1932, he served as a professor of psychology and philosophy at the Institute, and his work focused on performing several experiments on will, tension, needs, motivation, and learning. The experiments stand out even today as exemplary works in the literature of psychology (De Rivera, 1976).

Following a lecture series in Europe, the United States, and Russia, Lewin served as a visiting professor at Stanford University in California. When he heard that Hitler rose to power in 1933, Lewin returned to Germany, wrapped up all of his affairs, and moved to the United States with his family. His sorrow and ingratitude about having to leave his intellectual and cultural roots behind are reflected in a detailed letter to his former professor Wolfgang Köhler, which he never sent (Lewin, 1933/1987). In that letter, two themes stand out. First, Lewin described the suffering, injustice, and discriminatory acts that he personally experienced in Germany, even though his behavior had been patriotic. Second, he emphasized his deep sorrow about being forced to abandon his personal and cultural assets and face an uncertain future in the United States.

As a visiting professor at Cornell University, he negotiated a position at the Hebrew University, and prepared a plan for the establishment of an institute of psychology there. According to the plan, Lewin proposed that the institute conduct research on problems of acculturation among immigrants (Bargal, 1998). Even though he was not appointed to the chair of psychology, probably owing to lack of resources, Lewin decided to pursue his career in the United States.

From 1935 to 1944, Lewin served on the faculty of the University of Iowa, where he headed a research institute on child welfare. In that capacity, he conducted experiments on leadership styles, and examined the impact of leadership styles on performance of tasks as well as on the

33

social-emotional atmosphere and productivity in groups, and on the personal adaptation of group members (Lewin et al., 1939). The list of scholars who studied and worked with Lewin and later became leaders in the field of social psychology in America includes: Lippitt, White, Kelley, Deutsch, Horowitz, French, Raven, Cartwright, Zander, and Festinger, among many others (Ash, 1992; Patnoe, 1988).

Lewin was involved in projects aimed at organizational change. The term "action research" was first used in reference to a project conducted at the Harwood Manufacturing Corporation in a rural community in Virginia (Burnes, 2004; Marrow, 1969). For eight years thereafter, the term continued to be used, as will be described in further detail in subsequent sections of this chapter. Lewin's vision of interdependence between theory, research, and practice led him to establish the Research Center for Group Dynamics, where he sought to realize his vision.

Toward the end of World War II, Lewin moved from Iowa to the Massachusetts Institute of Technology, where he established The Research Center for Group Dynamics (Lewin, 1945). The Institute was involved not only in research and theoretical work, but also in efforts to solve social problems. Through contacts with the American Jewish Committee, Lewin invested considerable time and energy in dealing with problems of discrimination and with minority and majority relations. The fact that Lewin himself was a minority group member as a Jew, and still carried the experience of anti-Semitic humiliation in Germany, made him especially sensitive to these problems. His intense involvement in these issues led to the development of a new research methodology, as part of an attempt to find solutions to social issues and contribute to the development of an intervention theory. This was the basis for Lewin's conceptualization of action research (1946/1948), which he formulated during the last two years of his life (1945–47). The Research Center for Group Dynamics at MIT conducted numerous action research studies. In light of Lewin's personal experiences, it is understandable that he chose intergroup relations as the central issue for his action research interventions.

During one of the action research projects, which was constructed to prepare community leaders to work towards promoting the improving intergroup relations (Lippitt, 1949), the T-Group technology was discovered. The T-Group became a principal means of promoting change through interventions aimed at organizational development. Those efforts led to the establishment of the National Training Laboratories, which served for many years as a haven for the formulation and refinement of group interventions as well as for the application of group dynamics in organizational development activities (French and Bell, 1995).

Theory: the metatheoretical principles of field theory

Interdependence was a key term in Lewin's metatheoretical perspective. It represented his holistic conception of phenomena in the psychological universe, and emphasized the major role that relationships and interactions played in his metatheoretical assumptions. In that context, Lewin (1935) applied Cassirer's distinction between "thing concepts" and "relation or function concepts." In line with the principles of Gestalt psychology, he conceived every behavior of individuals, groups, or organizations to be the result of the total situation in which it occurs. For Lewin, the total situation was the life space, or the field where interdependent forces existed. Life space was defined as "the totality of facts which determine the behavior (B) of an individual (or group/organization) at a certain moment. The life space (L) represents the totality of possible events. The life space includes the person (P) and the environment (E). $B = f(L) = f(P.E)$" (Lewin, 1936, p. 216).

Lewin formulated six metatheoretical principles that characterize the field theory approach (Lewin, 1942/1951), and stressed that theory building in psychology must always rest on those principles. This section will briefly elaborate on five relevant principles: (1) an emphasis on the total situation; (2) the psychological approach; (3) the constructive versus the classificatory approach; (4) systemic versus historical causation; and (5) the dynamic approach.

1   *An emphasis on the total situation*: According to Lewin, all psychological events (e.g., hoping, dreaming, thinking, and planning) are conceived of as a consequence of the interaction between the person and the environment. In Lewin's words, the psychological processes of the individual must "always be derived from the relation of the concrete individual to the concrete situation and, so far as internal forces are concerned, from the mutual relations of the various functional systems that make up the individual" (Lewin, 1935, p. 41). This principle leads the researcher to focus on understanding the immediate situation in which behavior takes place. Field theory emphasizes the interdependence among variables that characterize a phenomenon. The method of field theory "proceeds step by step from the general to the particular, and thereby avoids the danger of 'wrong simplification' by abstraction" (1936, p. 17).

2   *The psychological approach*: According to Lewin, all psychological phenomena must be explained in psychological terms. Consistent with the constructivist tradition, Lewin asserts that psychological phenomena are real, and that there is no need to search for neurological correspondence to emotions such as hope, aspiration and skill. In Lewin's own terms: "The field which influences an individual should be described not in 'objective physicalistic' terms, but in the way which it exists for that person at that time" (1942/1951, p. 62).

3   *The constructive versus the classificatory approach*: Lewin derived this meta-principle from the philosophy of Cassirer, who suggested two different theoretical approaches for concep-tualizing situations. The classificatory approach focuses on generalization from particular objects to an ideal object, which is an abstraction from the particular object. The con-structive approach, by contrast, stresses relation concepts, as Lewin described them: "The essence of the constructive method is the representation of an individual case with the help of a few elements" (1942/1951, p. 61). According to the constructive approach, no contradiction should exist between general laws and the individual case if appropriate scientific concepts have been provided. Thus, Lewin favored the method that preserves the uniqueness of the phenomenon but remains applicable to other similar instances.

4   *Systematic versus historical concepts of causation*. Lewin described this metaprinciple as "behavior as a function of the field at the time it occurs." That is, past events count in the chain of causation only if they exert influence in the present time. According to Lewin, derivation of behavior from the past is not valid, because "the past psychological field is one of the 'origins' of the present field and this, in turn, affects behavior" (1942/1951, p. 64). This criticism is directed towards associationism as well as toward psychoanalysis. Lewin did not mean to underestimate past events and their effect on behavior, as he stressed that "to link behavior with a past field … supposes that one knows sufficiently how the past event has changed the field at that time, and whether or not in the meantime other events have modified the field again" (1942/1951, p. 64).

5   *The dynamic approach*. According to this metaprinciple, behavior is conceived of as emanating from a constant equilibrium, which is achieved as a consequence of the forces that impinge on people and on situations. Thus, individual or group behavior is analyzed in the context of the forces which enhance efforts to achieve goals, while there are inhibiting conditions which prevent it. In that context, reality is characterized as an ongoing process of achieving equilibrium in the social unit, while it is disrupted by the ever changing field of forces.

Hand in hand with Lewin's almost formal, well-established metatheoretical principles, he also advocated an open, flexible approach to choosing the appropriate theoretical conceptualization for social-science research and interventions. According to Lewin, the choice should be based on the same procedure used in systematic exploration of the resources of a new land: small paths are pushed out through the unknown; measurements are made with simple and primitive instruments; and much is left to assumption and lucky intuition. "Slowly, certain paths are widened; guess and luck are gradually replaced by experience and systematic exploration with more elaborate instruments … " (1940/1951, p. 3).

Theory: the democratic principles guiding Lewin's worldview

Lewin placed democracy at the center of his writing when he related to the system of values that guide the work of the researcher-facilitator. Allport (1948, p. xi) wrote that

> there is a striking kinship between the work of Kurt Lewin and the work of John Dewey. Both agree that democracy must be learned anew in each generation and that it is a far more difficult form of social structure to attain and maintain than is autocracy.

Lewin did not relate to democracy in a systematic way, and therefore did not devote an entire paper or article to the topic. However, many of his writings are imbued with his deep conviction and high respect for democracy, and they highlight its merits and advantages – especially as compared to the "laissez faire" regimes, or to the autocratic regime that Lewin was exposed to and fled from in Germany. He was aware that "nations need generations to learn the democratic way of living" (1941/1999, p. 321); he referred to British history in this regard, while criticizing the "mistakes which the German democrats made after 1918 when they tried to build up a democratic government with a people who were without democratic tradition and without adequately trained leadership" (p. 321).

The components of action research rely on democratic principles of cooperation among researchers, practitioners, and clients. Those principles are based on rational, transparent decision-making procedures and high regard for humanistic values. In the context of school leadership, the following conception of democratic leadership proposed by Lewin is particularly relevant (Lewin, 1941/1999):

Democracy is opposed to both autocracy and laissez-faire. It includes long-range planning by the group on the basis of self responsibility; it recognizes the importance of leadership, but this leadership remains responsible to the group as a whole and does not interfere with the basic equality of rights of every member. The safeguard of this equality of status is the emphasis on reason and fairness rather than personal willfulness. The right to influence group policy must have as its counterpart the willingness to accept majority decisions (1941/1999, p. 325).

As emphasized in this definition and in many other writings by Lewin, the democratic leader is the most important gatekeeper of the group, organization, or culture. Beginning with his famous pioneering experiment on leadership styles in experimentally created "social climates" in 1939, Lewin perceived leadership as playing a central role in democratic life. He even believed that "Germany can culturally be reconstructed after the war with a group of democratically trained new leaders." In 1945, Lewin formulated a working definition of democracy as follows:

It is the larger pattern of group life and group atmosphere … it includes … form of leadership, type of interdependence of subgroups, the way in which the policy of the

36

group depends on the will of its various sections or members ... This holds for a small group ... for the life of a whole community or state, or for the organization of the world.

(1945b, p. 302–3)

Lewin perceived the democratic society as a pluralistic entity, and emphasized the need to grant freedom of expression and respect for diversity of groups in the population. He formulated the definition in 1943, before "cultural diversity" became a central coin of language in American society: "The parallel to democratic freedom for the individual is cultural pluralism for groups" (1943/1948, p. 36). However, he was also realistic enough to express his views about restricting freedom of expression for extreme groups in society, an issue which continues to be debated to this very day. In this connection, he argued that democratic society has a right to defend itself against destructive, intolerant cultures: "Intolerance against intolerant cultures is therefore a prerequisite to any organization of permanent peace" (1943/1948, p. 36).

Theory: Lewin's principles of social change

Lewin's conception of social change has focused on two interdependent dimensions: the individual and the social system (more concretely, the small group). He first dealt theoretically with the individual, and with the processes of change that the individual experiences in regard to acquisition of new information and values (Lewin, 1945/1948). At a later date, very close to his death, he formulated the theory of planned change (Lewin, 1947/1951), which has been expressed in terms of a change of force fields. I will refer first to processes of change in individuals.

Lewin used the term "reeducation" to describe a process of change that involves more than merely acquiring new information, habits, and social skills. According to Lewin, reeducation is a process of effecting change in self-perceptions and enabling individuals to overcome inner resistance. Because behavior patterns are anchored in norms and interpersonal relations originating in the groups to which one belongs or aspires to belong, successful reeducation must include changes in one's own culture.

Changes in values, in the self, and in one's social perceptions can only be effected if the individual is part of a small group. Lewin characterized the optimal conditions for change in terms of group norms. Then he described the social climate that must prevail, and the central role of the facilitator. The group is the major leverage for changing the individual's attitude and behavior because

> only by anchoring his conduct in something as large, substantial and super-individual as the culture of the group, can the individual stabilize his new beliefs sufficiently to keep them immune from the day-by-day fluctuations of moods and influences to which he, as an individual, is subject.
>
> (Lewin, 1945/1948, p. 59)

In order for reeducation to succeed, the group facilitator must create a strong "we feeling." As Lewin formulated it, "the establishment of this feeling that everybody is in the same boat, has gone through the same difficulties, and speaks the same language is stressed as one of the main conditions facilitating the reeducation" (1945/1948, p. 67).

According to Lewin, provision of information is insufficient to change the individual's values and opinions about the other group. "We know that lectures or other similarly abstract methods of transmitting knowledge are of little avail in changing his subsequent outlook and conduct" (1945/1948, p. 60). Moreover, Lewin felt that even the experience of meeting representatives of different attitudes and values is not enough. In his view, only revision of self perceptions and social perceptions will enable the individual to perceive people and social events in a way that reaches beyond common stereotypes or false notions.

Lewin likened false stereotypes and prejudices to erroneous concepts and theories. In his view, the first step to changing those concepts and theories is to reexamine them. Reexamination should be carried out through an alternative perception of the self and one's social relations. This process cannot be left to accident, and group experiences should be planned as a forum for it. Lewin suggested that through the group one can acquire new norms and means for learning new perceptions and behaviors. In that process, individuals develop commitment to self-examination; they learn to actively confront their own perceptions and the perceptions held by the other group members; they become actively involved in problem solving; and they develop willingness to expose themselves to empirical examination of ideas and conceptions.

Lewin's approach to the topic of social change is elaborated in his last paper "Frontiers in Group Dynamics" (1947/1951). Under the subheading: "The Creation of Permanent Changes" (p. 224), Lewin described social change as a change of force fields. As he put it:

> In discussing the means of bringing about a desired state of affairs, one should not think in terms of "the goal to be reached" but rather in terms of change "from the present level to the desired one " ... A planned change consists of supplanting the force field corresponding to an equilibrium at the beginning level L^1 by a force field having its equilibrium at the desired level L^2. It should be emphasized that the total force field has to be changed at least in the area between L^1 and L^2 .

Lewin applied the principle of behavior to his theory of social change as "a function of the total situation" as follows: "For changing a social equilibrium, one has to consider the total social field" (p. 224). In the same vein, Lewin claimed that changing people's attitudes or behavior "means trying to break a well-established 'custom' or 'social habit.' Social habits usually are conceived of as obstacles to change" (p. 224). He later termed those habits as "inner resistance" to change. "To overcome this inner resistance an additional force seems to be required, a force sufficient to break the 'habit,' to 'unfreeze' the custom" (p. 225). Lewin's more general, sociological explanation for the inhibiting or resisting forces is that "social life proceeding on a certain level leads frequently to the establishment of organizational institutions. They become equivalent to 'vested interests' in a certain social level. A second possible source of social habits is related to the value system, the ethos of a group" (p. 225).

Lewin applied the force-field approach to individuals and groups alike. On the individual level, he referred to the pressure that group members exert on individuals who deviate excessively from group standards. In that connection, group standards become a "central force field which keeps the individual in line with the standards of the group" (p. 226). In this connection, Lewin used the following principle to summarize his view regarding the issue of social habit and resistance to change: "The greater the social value of a group standard, the greater is the resistance of the individual group member to move away from this level" (p. 227).

Lewin believed that the best and most effective means for bringing about change in individuals is through group encounters. In Lewin's own words: "Experience in leadership training, in changing of food habits, work production, criminality, alcoholism, prejudice – all seem to indicate that it is usually easier to change individuals formed into a group than to change any one of them separately" (p. 228).

Toward the end of the paper "Frontiers in Group Dynamics," Lewin characterized the change process as follows: "A successful change includes, therefore, three aspects: unfreezing (if necessary) the present level L^1, moving to the new level L^2, and freezing group life on the new level" (p. 228). When elaborating on each of the steps, he claimed that at the unfreezing stage, the individuals who participate in the process of change need to be emotionally stirred up many times. Allport (1954) referred to this process as catharsis, which he defined as the situation that is necessary before prejudices can be removed. In Lewin's words, unfreezing is important in order "to break open the shell of complacency and self righteousness."

The "moving" stage, or the change process, is best demonstrated through the principles of change, or reeducation. Lewin formulated these principles in his paper "Conduct, Knowledge and Acceptance of New Values" (1945/1948; see above).

The third stage in the change process proposed by Lewin (1947/1951) is termed "refreezing," namely, following the group's advancement from level L^1 to level L^2, group life will be determined on a new level. Lewin summarized this stage as follows: "Since any level is determined by a force field, permanency implies that the new force field is made relatively secure against change" (p. 229).

Lewin's theory of social change derived in part from the findings of his research on group dynamics and leadership styles. It also derived from his experience with real-life social and organizational interventions.

Research on group dynamics and leadership styles

As mentioned, Lewin began his academic career as an experimental psychologist. All of Lewin's research activity prior to his immigration to the United Sates in 1933 focused on the individual and on cognitive and emotional dynamics (Lewin, 1935), as well as on topics related to the philosophy of science. From the moment he entered the United States, he gradually shifted his research interest to the topic of social processes and issues. In that domain, he focused on small-group dynamics, and social and organizational change (Marrow, 1969).

Lewin conducted two types of research in the field of group dynamics and leadership styles: laboratory and quasi-laboratory experiments, and field experiments. He conducted the first type of studies together with his students (Lewin et al., 1939). Those studies focused on the group climate or atmosphere, as well as on leadership styles (autocratic, democratic, and *laissez faire*), and on patterns of aggressive behavior that developed in those settings. His later research dealt with decision making in small groups (Lewin, 1947/1951), and with change processes (Lewin, 1947/1951). The knowledge and insights gained through these studies contributed to Lewin's premise regarding the central role of small groups in society and social institutions (Burnes, 2007). This premise became the cornerstone of Lewin's theory of change, and was an important component of his action research paradigm.

Action and practice interventions in organizational and social-change issues

Kurt Lewin placed heavy emphasis on theory, but by no means was he an armchair social scientist. He was deeply concerned with social issues in the real world from a relatively early stage in his career. In 1939, he began an action research project at the Harwood Manufacturing Company (Burnes, 2007; Marrow, 1969), and he continued his involvement there until his sudden death in 1947. Intervention in the real world, as was the case at Harwood, gave Lewin an opportunity to establish an *in vivo* laboratory, where he attempted to apply his theories while modifying and adapting them to specific organizational conditions.

[Because] lawfulness in social as in physical science means an "if so" relation, a linkage between hypothetical conditions and hypothetical effects. These laws do not tell what conditions exist locally at any given time. In other words, the laws do not do the job of diagnosis which has to be done locally.

(Lewin, 1943/1948, p. 203)

These words clearly echo the technology of Organization Development (OD), which developed later directly from Lewin's work (French and Bell, 1995; Schein, 1996).

An additional domain of real-life interventions was intergroup relations, a domain that was promoted by the Commission on Community Interrelations (CCI) (Marrow, 1969). With administrative and financial support from that source, Lewin initiated and conducted several action research projects. Those projects focused on topics such as discrimination against Blacks and Jews, stereotype development and change, and management of social and community conflicts. Of those projects, one of the most famous was the Connecticut Workshop for Training in Community Relations. According to Lippitt (1949), that workshop brought community leaders and social scientists together "for a 'change experiment' where it would be possible to diagnose some of the problems of change and evaluate the effects of certain training techniques" (p. 10). Lippitt's book summarized the process of planning the workshop, the training techniques, and evaluation of change achieved in the community leaders, and it became a blueprint and inspiration for the development of the T-Group technique (Bradford et al., 1964). The book was dedicated to Kurt Lewin, who "stimulated the integration of research, training and action ... within one dynamic personality." It is the most detailed account of an entire project that operationalized Lewin's paradigm of action research.

The action research paradigm: the interdependence among theory, research, and practice/action

One of Lewin's colleagues and closest disciples, Dorwin Cartwright, later became Lewin's successor as head of the Center for Group Dynamics. Cartwright mentioned that Lewin believed he was on the brink of proposing a new paradigm for understanding and changing social and organizational entities. Based on my reading of the last three papers published by Lewin (1946, 1947a, 1947b), it is my view that, had Lewin lived, he would have argued that action research is the preferred paradigm to effect change, because it focuses on the interdependence among theory, research, and practice.

In the present chapter, an attempt is made to show that the action research paradigm integrates the aforementioned components of Lewin's theory (field theory) with his research in group dynamics with his emphasis on small groups, leadership styles, and changing attitudes via participation in groups. The paradigm also reflects Lewin's experience with the "real world," as evidenced in the Harwood factory projects (Burnes, 2004, 2007) and through his involvement in the field of intergroup relations (Lippitt, 1949). These three components of theory, research, and practice are deeply embedded in two additional metatheoretical origins—the Gestalt school, and the values of democracy—as described and discussed in detail above.

The following are the components of the action research paradigm, which emanated from Lewin's worldview (Lewin, 1946/1948, 1947a, 1947b; italics added):

a) Action research is a *problem solving, rational process*, which extends over a period of time and aims *to study and solve/change organizational and social issues.*

b) It is an interpersonal process, in which the relationships between researchers and the parties involved in action research (AR) activities are *democratic, egalitarian, and cooperative. Open communication and feedback regarding the results of intervention* exist among the parties. The parties' *objectives, values, and power needs are taken into account.*

c) It is a process in which the *small group* is the principal vehicle of *decision making* as well as the means to *achieve social change. Decision making is mutual,* and is carried out in a *public way.*

d) It is a process that relies on *scientific, proven* (evidence-based) *knowledge,* which is derived and formulated in the *social and behavioral science* literature but carefully adapted to the organizational unit where intervention takes place. It also creates and formulates relevant *principles of intervention,* develops instruments for selection and training, and *codifies them as actionable relevant practice wisdom.*

a) Action research as a problem-solving process

Lewin conceived of action research as a problem-solving process, which occurs in a constantly changing environment. It includes a spiral process of data collection aimed at determining goals, followed by action aimed at implementing goals and assessment of the results of the intervention. In principle, the intervention is continuous, because problems that need to be addressed arise all the time. In contrast to the normal scientific model, where the researcher's main task is to study a problem or to test a hypothesis, the action researcher is expected to provide intervention solutions to organizational and social issues. Notably, the Harwood studies are an example of an organizational intervention (Burnes, 2004, 2007; Marrow, 1969), and Lippitt (1949) is an example of an intergroup intervention project.

The first component of action research reflects several of Lewin's theoretical and metatheoretical principles. The action research paradigm deals with the interdependence between the systematic study of a social problem and efforts to solve the problem. This is an example of the Gestalt school perspective, which emphasizes the total context and the need for researchers to take into account the concrete organizational situation. The spiral process of data collection aimed at determining goals followed by implementation and assessment of goals reflects an additional metaprinciple of field theory: the dynamic nature of the forces in the field where the research intervention (AR) takes place. The action research paradigm also embodies the metatheoretical principle of the constructive approach, namely, the need to construct a concrete unit for intervention (the idiographic, Galilean approach; Lewin, 1931) rather than rely on a mechanical act of classifying the situation as a type of behavior in accordance with a certain nomenclature.

b) Action research as a democratic process

Lewin's profound belief in and commitment to the principles of democracy are reflected in the AR paradigm. In this regard, he wrote: "To believe in reason means to believe in democracy, because it grants to the reasoning partners a status of equality" (Lewin, 1943/1999, p. 325). According to the conventional scientific research model, the researcher directs the operation, and is sometimes the only one familiar with the objectives or hypotheses of the study. In action research, by contrast, all of the parties involved in the process are equal partners. They are all responsible for decisions that affect their lives, and they are urged to understand the rationale underlying the intervention. Equal partnership in the research project and knowledge of the context and rationale for the decisions that are made enables the parties involved to maintain high motivation and commitment.

This component of action research also reflects Lewin's pluralistic perspective, which grants equal weight to the opinions and ideology of all parties involved in the AR project. Because each party has its own set of priorities and values, the only way for the AR project to succeed is to deal openly with conflicts that arise. An ongoing process of managing and solving these power and value conflicts guarantees that the research will proceed as planned. This is in contrast to the conventional research design, where the principal investigator usually has the sole power to make decisions and solves conflicts unilaterally.

c) The small group as a principal vehicle for achieving social change

Lewin perceived the small group as the most important vehicle for making democratic decisions and achieving change in people (Lewin, 1945/1948). The same conclusion was reached by other theoretical scholars in the field (Coch and French, 1948; Forsyth, 1990; Lieberman, 1980). According to Lewin, society is made up of numerous and diverse groups. To quote Lewin's dictum: "The parallel to democratic freedom for the individual is cultural pluralism for groups" (1943/1948, p. 36). This speaks for the need to create harmonious intergroup relations in a heterogeneous, democratic society. However, the small group is also the cornerstone for reaching decisions in politics, in the family, in the community, and in organizations. The dynamics created within the group make it possible for the individual to grow, to be socialized, to reach effective decisions, and to plan the activities of the group. In this regard, we are reminded that the group leader's central role in this process is "not to interfere with the basic equality of rights of every member. The safeguard of this equality of status is the emphasis on reason and fairness rather than personal willfulness" (Lewin, 1943/1999, p. 325). Every group member is expected to exert his or her influence on its activities. Here, the prerequisite is that the group member is willing to accept majority decisions.

d) Action research utilizes scientific knowledge as well as accumulates and codifies actionable relevant practice wisdom, like principles of intervention and instruments for selection and training

Because the main objective of action research is to bring about change in human organizations and communities, it is essential to invest in the change agents for effecting change in those systems. "We should consider action, research and training as a triangle that should be kept together for the sake of any corner" (Lewin, 1946/1948, p. 211). Bargal and Bar (1992, 1994) and Bargal (2004) present a detailed description of conflict management workshops that were conducted in an action research project designed for Arab and Jewish youth in Israel. Recently, the conflict-management workshop idea has also been adapted to North American culture. For several years, high schools in Michigan have been running intergroup education programs for adolescents (Garvin and Bargal, 2008). Those programs are conducted as action research projects, which interweave "action, research, and training". In that connection, Aguinis (1993) and Cassell and Johnson (2006) have argued that action research methodology can be used while also preserving appropriate scientific standards.

Discussion

By introducing the action research paradigm (Lewin, 1946/1948, 1947a), Lewin essentially erased the boundaries between theory, research, and action/practice, and focused on the continuous interdependence among those three components.

The energy that Lewin devoted to action research projects from 1939 until the end of his life in 1947 point to the centrality of the paradigm in his mind and in his professional worldview. His professional activities at the Center for Group Dynamics at MIT attest to his real passion for action research. In her recollections of her father, Miriam Lewin (1992) wrote: "I believe doing social action research was in part his response to his mother's death" (Lewin's mother and aunt were killed by the Nazis). His memory of the rampant anti-Semitism and discrimination in Germany, which he expressed candidly in his letter to Köhler (1933/1987), evidently provided the impetus for his efforts to alleviate discrimination and tensions among minorities in the United States.

The idea of action research evolved gradually in Lewin's mind. In his article "Problems of Research in Social Psychology" (1943–44/1951), he spoke about the relationships between theory and practice, and emphasized the primacy of theory ("there is nothing as practical as a good theory", p. 169). However, in one of his last papers, "Action Research and Minority Problems" (1946/1948), he stated that two sources of knowledge are needed for practice or for action research: "Social research concerns itself with two different types of questions: the study of general laws of group life and the diagnosis of a specific situation ... For any field of action, both types of scientific research are needed" (p. 204). The "general laws" he referred to are the product of academic research and theoretical speculation (theory, research). "The diagnosis of a specific situation" represents action and practice. Had Lewin survived, he probably would have changed the famous statement quoted above to: "There is nothing as effective as the interdependence between theory, research, and practice."

When discussing the relevance of Lewin's theories and constructs (Burnes, 2007), one should realize that in a way Lewin foresaw the issue of the gap between theory and practice, which the action research paradigm aimed to solve. The organizational behavior literature is heavily engaged with the issue of how to solve practical problems by bridging the gap between theory and practice (Anderson et al., 2001; Baldridge et al., 2004; Beer, 2001; Mohrman et al., 2001; Rynes et al., 2001).

Lewin's notion about the difference between knowledge created through academic research and knowledge created for practical implementation led to the development of two epistemological constructs—"reflection 'in action' and 'on action'" (Schon, 1983), and "actionable knowledge" (Argyris, 1993)—which are direct offshoots of Lewin's action research paradigm. Two leading contemporary scholars in the field of organizational research suggested several variants of that research paradigm. Reason and Bradbury (2001, 2008) introduced PAR (Participatory Action Research), "which seeks to bring together action and reflection, theory and practice in participation with others ..." (2001, p. 1); and Van De Ven and Johnson proposed "engaged scholarship" as a means of bridging the gap between theory and practice: "Engaged scholarship is a collaborative form of inquiry in which academics and practitioners leverage their different perspectives and competencies to coproduce knowledge about a complex problem or phenomenon that exists under conditions of uncertainty found in the world" (2006, p. 803). The following are several operational principles of engaged scholarship that echo Lewin's components of action research: "designing a collaborative learning community"; "designing the study for an extended duration"; and "employing multiple models and methods to study the problem".

In a paper dedicated to his former teacher Ernst Cassirer, Lewin stated the following:

To proceed beyond the limitations of a given level of knowledge, the researcher, as a rule, has to break down methodological taboos which condemn as "unscientific" or "illogical" the very methods or concepts which later on prove to be basic for the next major progress.

(Lewin, 1949, p. 275)

43

Kurt Lewin coined the paradigm of action research through his vision of the interdependence among theory, research, and practice as a means of pursuing the goals of organizational and social change. In order to legitimize the paradigm as a tool for research and intervention, he had to "break down methodological taboos". Sixty years later, the paradigm is much appreciated and frequently used in numerous projects and studies of activities aimed at organizational and social change.

References

Aguinis, H. (1993). Action research and scientific method: Presumed discrepancies and actual similarities. *Journal of Applied Behavioral Science*, 29, 416–31.

Allport, G. (1948). Foreword. In G. Lewin (ed.), *Resolving social conflicts* (pp. i–x). New York: Harper & Row.

Allport, G. (1954). *The nature of prejudice*. Reading, MA: Addison Wesley.

Anderson, N., Herriot, P. and Hodgkinson, G. (2001). The practitioner – researcher divide in industrial work and organizational (IWO) psychology: Where are we now and where do we go from here? *Journal of Occupational and Organizational Psychology*, 74, 391–411.

Argyris, C. (1993). *Knowledge for action*. San Francisco, CA: Jossey Bass.

Argyris, C. (1997). Kurt Lewin award lecture: Field theory as a basis for scholarly consulting. *Journal of Social Issues*, 53, 811–27.

Ash, M. (1992). Cultural contexts and change in psychology. *American Psychologist*, 47, 198–207.

Baldridge, D., Floyd, S. and Markoczy, L. (2004). Are managers from Mars and academicians from Venus? Toward an understanding of the relationship between academic quality and practical relevance. *Strategic Management Journal*, 25, 1063–74.

Bargal, D. (1998). Kurt Lewin and the first attempts to establish a department of psychology at the Hebrew University. *Minerva*, 36, 49–68.

Bargal, D. (2004). Structure and process in reconciliation transformation encounters between Jewish and Palestinian youth. *Small Group Research*, 35, 596–616.

Bargal, D. and Bar, H. (1992). A Lewinian approach to intergroup workshops for Arab-Palestinian and Jewish youth. *Journal of Social Issues*, 48, 139–54.

Bargal, D. and Bar, H. (1994). The encounter of social selves approach in conducting intergroup workshops for Arab and Jewish youth in Israel. *Social Work with Groups*, 17(3), 39–59.

Beer, M. (2001). Why management research findings are unimplementable: An action science perspective. *Reflections*, 2(3), 58–65.

Bradford, L., Gibb, J. and Benne, K. (1964). *Group theory and laboratory method: Innovation in re-education*. New York: John Wiley & Sons.

Burnes, B. (2004). Kurt Lewin and the planned change approach to change: A reappraisal. *Journal of Management Studies*, 41, 977–1002.

Burnes, B. (2007). Kurt Lewin and the Harwood studies: The foundations of OD. *The Journal of Applied Behavioral Science*, 43, 213–31.

Cassell, C. and Johnson, P. (2006). Action research: Explaining the diversity. *Human Relations*, 59, 783–814.

Coch, L. and French, J. (1948). Overcoming resistance to change. *Human Relations*, 1, 51–53.

De Rivera, J. (1976). *Field theory as human science: Contributions of Lewin's Berlin group*. New York: Gardner Press.

Forsyth, D. (1990). *Group dynamics*. Pacific Grove, CA: Brooks/Cole.

French, W. and Bell, C. (1995). *Organizational development* (5th ed.). Englewood Cliffs, NJ: Prentice-Hall.

Garvin, C. and Bargal, D. (eds.) (2008). Enabling high school students to cope with intergroup conflict: An action research study. *Small Group Research*, 39, 3–16.

Lewin, K. (1931). The conflict between Aristotelian and Galilean modes of thought in contemporary psychology. *Journal of General Psychology*, 5, 141–77.

Lewin, K. (1933/1987). Everything within me rebels: A letter to Wolfgang Köhler. *Journal of Social Issues*, 42(4), 39–47.

Lewin, K. (1935). *A dynamic theory of personality*. New York: McGraw-Hill.

Lewin, K. (1936). *Principles of topological psychology*. New York: McGraw Hill.

Lewin, K. (1940/1951). Formalization and progress in psychology. In D. Cartwright (ed.), *Field theory in social science: Selected theoretical papers by Kurt Lewin* (pp. 1–29). New York: Harper & Row.

Lewin, K. (1941/1999). Democracy and the school. In M. Gold (ed.), *The complete social scientist: A Kurt Lewin reader* (pp. 321–26). Washington, DC: American Psychological Association.

Lewin, K. (1942/1951). Field theory and learning. In D. Cartwright (ed.), *Field theory in social science: Selected theoretical papers by Kurt Lewin* (pp. 60–86). New York: Harper & Row.

Lewin, K. (1943/1948). Cultural reconstruction. In G. Lewin (ed.), *Resolving social conflicts: Selected papers on group dynamics* (pp. 34–42). New York: Harper & Row.

Lewin, K. (1943–4/1951). Problems of research in social psychology. In D. Cartwright (ed.), *Field theory in social science: Selected theoretical papers by Kurt Lewin* (pp. 155–69). New York: Harper & Row.

Lewin, K. (1943/1999). Psychology and the process of group living. In M. Gold (ed.), *The complete social scientist: A Kurt Lewin reader* (pp. 333–45). Washington, DC: American Psychological Association.

Lewin, K. (1945a). The research center for group dynamics at the Massachusetts Institute of Technology. *Sociometry*, 8, 126–36.

Lewin, K. (1945b). The practicality of democracy. In G. Murphy (ed.), *Human nature and enduring peace: Third yearbook of the society for the psychological study of social issues* (pp. 295–323). Boston MA: Houghton Mufflin.

Lewin, K. (1945/1948). Conduct, knowledge and acceptance of new values. In G. Lewin (ed.), *Resolving social conflicts: Selected papers on group dynamics* (pp. 56–70). New York: Harper & Row.

Lewin, K. (1946/1948). Action research and minority problems. In G. Lewin (ed.), *Resolving social conflicts: Selected papers on group dynamics* (pp. 201–16). New York: Harper & Row.

Lewin, K. (1947a) Frontiers in group dynamics I. *Human Relations*, 1, 2–38.

Lewin, K. (1947b). Frontiers in group dynamics II. *Human Relations*, 1, 143–53.

Lewin, K. (1947/1951). Frontiers in group dynamics. In D. Cartwright (ed.), *Field theory in social science: Selected theoretical papers by Kurt Lewin* (pp. 188–237). New York: Harper & Row.

Lewin, K. (1949) Cassirer's philosophy of science and the social sciences. In A. Schelipp (ed.), *The philosophy of Ernst Cassirer* (pp. 269–88). Evanston IL: Library of Living Philosophers.

Lewin, K., Lippitt, R. and White, R. (1939). Patterns of aggressive behavior in experimentally created social climates. *Journal of Social Psychology*, 10, 277–99.

Lewin, M. (1992). The impact of Kurt Lewin's life on the place of social issues in his work. *Journal of Social Issues*, 48(2), 15–30.

Lieberman, M. (1980). Group methods. In F. Kanfer and A. Goldstein (eds.), *Helping people to change* (pp. 470–536). New York: Pergamon.

Lippitt, R. (1947). Kurt Lewin 1890–1947: Adventures in the exploration of interdependence. *Sociometry*, 10, 87–97.

Lippitt, R. (1949). *Training in community relations*. New York: Harper & Row.

Marrow, A. (1969). *The practical theorist*. New York: Basic Books.

Mohrman, S., Gibson, C. and Mohrman, A. (2001). Doing research that is useful to practice: A model and empirical exploration. *Academy of Management Journal*, 44, 357–75.

Patnoe, S. (1988). *A narrative history of experimental social psychology: The Lewin tradition*. New York: Springer.

Reason, P. and Bradbury, H. (eds.) (2001). *Handbook of action research: Participative inquiry and practice*. Thousand Oaks, CA: Sage.

Reason, P. and Bradbury, H. (eds.) (2008). *The Sage handbook of action research: Participative inquiry and practice* (2nd ed.). Thousand Oaks, CA: Sage.

Rynes, S., Bartunek, J. and Daft, R. (2001). Across the great divide: knowledge creation and transfer between practitioners and academics. *Academy of Management Journal*, 44, 340–55.

Schein, E. (1996). Kurt Lewin's change theory in the field and in the classroom: Notes towards a model of management learning. *Systems Practice*, 9, 27–47.

Schon, D. (1983). *The reflective practitioner: How professionals think in action*. New York: Basic Books.

Van De Ven, A. (2007). *Engaged scholarship: A guide for organizational and social research*. New York: Oxford University Press.

Van De Ven, A. and Johnson, P. (2006). Knowledge for theory and practice. *Academy of Management Review*, 31, 801–21.

3

Organization development and action research
Then and now

David Coghlan

Introduction

While organization development (OD) and action research (AR) are closely related, they exist independently of one another and there are important roots and strands of action research existing outside of OD (McArdle and Reason, 2008). In parallel with Burnes' and Bargal's contributions (Chapters 1 and 2) in this volume, this chapter reflects on the joint origins of organization development and action research in the work of Kurt Lewin and explores how organization development through action research was understood and practised in the latter half of the last century and how it is understood and practised now.

The roots of action research

Action research is one of the distinctive features of OD and one of its core origins (French and Bell, 1999). Schein (1989) argues that the tap root of OD was Lewin's seminal work. Lewin was able to combine the methodology of experimentation with sold theory and a concern for action around important social concerns. For Lewin, it was not enough to try to explain things; one also had to try to change them. It was clear to Lewin and others that working at changing human systems often involved variables that could not be controlled by traditional research methods, developed in the physical sciences. These insights led to the development of action research and the powerful notion that human systems could only be understood and changed if one involved the members of the system in the inquiry process itself. So the tradition of involving the members of an organization in the change process which is the hallmark of OD originated in a scientific premise that this is the way (a) to get better data and (b) to effect change. Action research is not only a methodology and a set of tools but is also a theory of social science (Peters and Robinson, 1984). The roots of OD are in science and Lewin built a cadre of colleagues and students whose work in group dynamics and organizational research became the foundation for what emerged later as OD. As Bargal's chapter in this volume demonstrates, Lewin framed the interdependence of theory, research and practice. In Schein's view OD was a 'quiet revolution'.

Argyris et al. (1985) summarize Lewin's concept of action research:

1   It involves change experiments on real issues in social systems. It focuses on a particular issue and seeks to provide assistance to the client system.
2   It, like social management more generally, involves iterative cycles of identifying a problem, planning, acting and evaluating.
3   The intended change in an action research project typically involves re-education, a term that refers to changing patterns of thinking and action that are presently well established in individuals and groups. Effective re-education depends on participation by clients in diagnosis, fact-finding and free choice to engage in new kinds of action.
4   It challenges the status quo from a participative perspective, which is congruent with the requirements of effective re-education.
5   It is intended to contribute simultaneously to basic knowledge in social science and to social action in everyday life. High standards for developing theory and empirically testing propositions organized by theory are not be to be sacrificed nor the relation to practice lost.

Approaching the relationship between OD and action research from the other perspective, OD is one of the roots and expressions of action research. Action research has several roots (Greenwood and Levin, 2007; Reason and Bradbury, 2008). While the work of Lewin and the OD tradition which grew out of the T group and NTL Institute, the socio-technical work of the Tavistock Institute in the UK and the workplace democracy work in Scandinavia are the major roots in the northern hemisphere (Pasmore, 2001; Bradbury et al., 2008), there are important roots and strands of action research existing outside of OD. The consciousness raising work of Freire and the Marxist-based liberation movements in the southern hemisphere (frequently referred to as emancipatory or participatory action research), feminist approaches to research, the return to epistemological notions of praxis and the hermeneutic school of philosophy associated with the work of Habermas are important strands and expressions of action research which did not grow out of the OD tradition (Reason and Bradbury, 2008).

The two fundamental differences between the action research tradition within OD and the emancipatory action research tradition lie in the purpose and location of the research. The OD tradition of action research occurs within organizations and aims to help organizations change and at the same time to generate knowledge. The emancipatory action research tradition tends to be located in rural and urban communities and aims to empower the participants to take control of some aspect of their own environment, which frequently pits the less economically powerful against the more powerful. Indeed OD action research may be criticized by the emancipatory tradition as supporting the capitalist status quo and not being radical enough. So while OD and action research are closely interlinked, each has an existence independent of the other.

Organization development and action research then

The action research model that developed in OD in the 1960s, 1970s, 1980s and 1990s was a consistent one and was captured in a number of important publications (Shepard and Katzell, 1960; Clarke, 1972; Foster, 1972; Frohman et al., 1976; Shani and Pasmore, 1985; Cunningham, 1993; French and Bell, 1999) and found application in published cases (Coch and French, 1948; Shepard and Katzell, 1960; Pasmore and Friedlander, 1982; Burnes, 2007). This model is captured by the following definition that expresses both traditions.

47

Action research may be defined as an emergent inquiry process in which applied behavioural science knowledge is integrated with existing organizational knowledge and applied to solve real organizational problems. It is simultaneously concerned with bringing about change in organizations, in developing self-help competencies in organizational members and in adding to scientific knowledge. Finally it is an evolving process that is undertaken in a spirit of collaboration and co-inquiry.

(Shani and Pasmore, 1985: 439)

One of the most clear and practical accounts of the relationship between OD and action research is found in Frohman et al. (1976). This article may be judged to be a seminal and typical piece in how it captures the essence of how OD and action research complemented each other and differed from each other at this time. The authors describe how action research used with OD is based on collaboration between the behavioural-scientist-researcher and the client where they collaborate on exploring problems and generating valid data on the problem (the research activity), and jointly in examining the data to understand the problem. They then develop action plans to address the problems and implement them. They evaluate the outcomes of the actions, both intended and unintended. This evaluation may then lead to further cycles of diagnosis, action planning and action. Cyclical-sequential phases may be identified that capture the movements of collaboration from initial scouting to evaluation. Frohman et al. (1976) note that these activities may serve also to generate new behavioural science knowledge, which is fed into the depository of information for other behavioural scientists as general laws, types of problems or the process of consultant – client collaboration, thus addressing issues beyond the specific case.

What was distinctive about OD and action research at this time was that both followed a cyclical process of consciously and deliberately (a) diagnosing the situation, (b) planning action, (c) taking action, (d) evaluating the action, leading to further diagnosing, planning and so on. The second dimension is that both approaches were collaborative, in that, with the help of a consultant/facilitator, the members of the system participated actively in the cyclical process. This action research approach to organization development was powerful. It engaged people as participants in seeking ideas, planning, taking actions, reviewing outcomes and learning what worked and didn't work, and why. This approach was in stark contrast with programmed approaches that mandated following pre-designed steps and which tended not to be open to alteration. These latter approaches were based on the assumption that the system should adopt the entire package as designed. Action research and OD, on the other hand, were based on assumptions that each system is unique and that a change process has to be designed with that uniqueness in mind and adapted in the light of ongoing experience and emergent learning.

Process consultation and clinical inquiry/research

A significant counter-position within the OD field that challenged the underlying framework of phased activities whereby organization development/action researchers enter a system, gather data, make a diagnosis and plan and implement interventions has been Schein's notion of process consultation (1969, 1988, 1999). Here, Schein focuses on the efforts of the OD consultant to be helpful to the client and so he argues strongly that, through collaborative engagement, diagnosis and intervention are concurrent as the process consultant works to help the client make sense of his/her own organizational experience. From reflection on his experience as a process consultant, Schein (1987, 1995, 2008) developed an expression of the form action research takes within OD as what he calls 'clinical inquiry'. This notion is built on the assumption that the OD practitioner is invited into an organization to help (and be paid for it) and that diagnostic and intervention activity is aimed towards enabling the system to function more healthily. In Schein's view (1995, 2008) there is a fundamental difference between clinical inquiry and action research. In action research the researcher may be present in the organization at the researcher's instigation and, to meet the researcher's needs, clinical inquiry takes place at the organization's instigation to meet the organization's need for help. As Schein argues, when the researcher is present in the organization at the organization's instigation and is being paid for it in order to be helpful, then the data which are made available are likely to be of a higher quality because as the members of the organization want help they are more likely to reveal what is really going on.

In summary, the OD tradition of action research as expressed in clinical inquiry is built on four working principles (Schein, 1997):

The issues that one works on are important.

One accepts the assumption that unless one attempts to change a system one cannot really understand it.

The primary source of organizational data is not what is 'out there' but is in the effects of and responses to interventions.

The OD process whereby the external OD practitioner is contacted and then enters and begins to learn how to be helpful is central.

For Schein, this approach constitutes authentic OD. As Coghlan (2009) demonstrates, it has a rich underpinning philosophy, whereby the method of intervention needs to cater for the need of the client system and the need of rigorous social science that advances useful and valid practical knowledge.

OD/action research in universities

It has to be noted that OD and action research also developed an ambivalent relationship, particularly in the universities. While the central role that action research held in the definition and heritage of OD was acknowledged, it tended to be relegated to the practice of OD and excluded from the forum of scholarly research. This was due to the dominance of the positivist approach to research in the academy and the denigration of forms of research that incorporate action as smacking of subjectivism and consequently which excluded action research from the universities, especially in the Anglo-Saxon academy, led by the United States (Greenwood, 2002; Levin, 2003). Despite action research's solid grounding in Dewey's pragmatic philosophy (Pasmore, 2001; Greenwood and Levin, 2007) and Aristotelian praxis (Eikeland, 2006), action research was not understood to be 'scientific'. This perspective perpetuated although, as it is well argued, its methods are far more scientific in the sense of knowledge tested in action and in mobilizing relevant knowledge from people in a position to know their conditions better than conventional researcher can (Greenwood, 2002). OD research, therefore, was typically expressed through traditional research modes (Bowers and Franklin, 1972; Culbert, 1972). Recent reviews of the state of the field of OD (e.g. Bradford and Burke, 2004 and Bradford and Burke, 2005) made no reference to action research.

The transition from then to now

At the same time, there was a growing unease that positivist science was not being useful to the world of practice. Susman and Evered (1978) argued that the conditions from which people try to learn in everyday life are better explored through a range of philosophical viewpoints: Aristotelian praxis, hermeneutics, existentialism, pragmatism, process philosophies and phenomenology. They proposed that action research provides a corrective to the deficiencies of positivist science by being future-oriented, collaborative, implying system development, generating theory grounded in action, agnostic and situational. Schon (1995) contrasted how researchers can view practice from the high ground, where they can study issues from a distance, for example because they are not organizational members or because their data are based on pre-constructed surveys or interviews. Or they can be immersed in 'swampy lowlands' where problems are messy and confusing and incapable of a technical solution, because they are either organizational members, whose actions influence the reality they see, or are outsiders who are contracted to influence what they see. He concluded that unimportant issues may be studied from the high ground according to predetermined standards and rigor, while the critically important ones, such as how to generate whatever changes in practice we wish to see, can only be confronted by being immersed in the swampy lowlands. In his view work in the swampy lowlands involves a new scholarship which requires a new epistemology.

The changing view of research

Understanding of the nature of research is changing also. As Gibbons et al. (1994) have argued it is time for a mode of research (which they call Mode 2 research) that is transdisciplinary, heterogeneous, socially accountable, reflexive and is produced in the context of application. 'The new production of knowledge' as articulated by Gibbons and his colleagues is a network activity and research, therefore, needs to follow and move away from a model whereby it is embedded currently in the expertise of isolated individuals operating from a top-down expert model (Gustavsen, 2003). MacLean et al. (2002) make the point that action-oriented research, such as action research, has the potential to meet the criteria of Mode 2 research. Levin and Greenwood (2008) note wryly that action research has been engaging in Mode 2 research since the first action research experiments in the 1940s and 1950s. Shani et al. (2008) argue for the notion of collaborative management research and focus on the dynamics of collaboration between practitioners and academic researchers and between insiders and outsiders as central to the formation of communities of inquiry emphasize the generation of actionable knowledge that meets the requirements of both practitioner and academic communities.

Action research has also undergone a transition. In what was a radical, if not revolutionary exploration of 'new paradigm' research, Reason and Rowan (1981) identified a range of approaches to human inquiry that provided alternatives to orthodox ways of doing research in human sciences. That landmark publication opened the way to viewing action research in broader terms than the OD approaches described above.

Organization development and action research now

Both OD and action research have continued to develop. Rees' chapter in this volume discusses the challenges that have confronted OD as it has developed from its early expressions and practice. The premise underpinning action research began to clarify that the purpose of research is to forge a more direct link between intellectual knowledge/theory and action so that each inquiry contributes directly to the flourishing of human persons and their communities (Reason and Bradbury, 2008). Action research rejects the separation between thought and action that underlies the pure – applied distinction that has traditionally characterized management and social research. Action research incorporates a collaborative enactment of cycles of action and reflection whereby the intended research outcome is the construction of actionable knowledge.

OD now

Bushe and Marshak (2008) explore the emergence of new forms of OD in the postmodern world. They contrast classical and postmodern OD. Classical OD is grounded classical science and modernist philosophy and thought and views organizations as living systems. Postmodern OD is influenced by the new sciences and postmodern thought and philosophy and views organizations as meaning-making systems. Accordingly, postmodern OD views reality as socially constructed with multiple realities which are socially negotiated rather than a single objective reality that is diagnosed. Data collection is less about applying objective problem-solving methods and more about raising collective awareness and generating new possibilities which lead to change. In sum, postmodern OD emphasizes changing the conversation in organizations by surfacing, legitimating and learning from multiple perspectives and generating new images and narratives on which people can act. In a subsequent piece, Bushe and Marshak (2009) describe classical OD as 'diagnostic OD' where reality is an objective fact and diagnosis infers collecting and applying data and using objective problem-solving methods to achieve change to an articulated desired future. As an alternative, they propose what they call 'dialogic OD', where organizations are viewed as meaning-making systems, containing multiple realities, which are socially constructed. Accordingly, the focus of OD is to create the space for changing the conversation. See Oswick and Marshak's chapter in this volume for a specification discussion of the role metaphors play as a form of 'dialogic' OD.

A feature of the newer forms of OD is the large-group intervention (Bunker and Alban, 1997). While these large-group interventions have different names – search conferences, future search, open space among several terms (Holman et al., 2007; Purser and Griffin, 2008) – what they have in common is the notion of bringing the whole system in the room and engaging in conversation about present realities and how to create future realities. While large-group interventions have had their origins and expressions in traditional OD (Beckhard, 1967) they have flourished as 'dialogic OD' in how they provide the setting for multiple perspectives to be shared and how they aim to develop new shared agreement. Such large-group processes have integral links to action research (Martin, 2001).

Action research now

Now it is understood that, as Reason and Bradbury (2008: 1) put it, action research is 'a family of practices of living inquiry … it is not so much a methodology as an orientation to inquiry'. As Greenwood (2007: 131) expresses it:

> Action research is neither a method or a technique; it is an approach to living in the world that include the creation of areas for collaborative learning and the design, enactment and evaluation of liberating actions … it combines action and research, reflection and action in an ongoing cycle of cogenerative knowledge.

Accordingly, what is noticeable is that there is a wide diversity, not only in practice, but in the discourse on action research practice. Raelin (2009) reflects on the multiplicity of what he refers to as 'action modalities' and identifies a number of similarities. These modalities focus on contextualized and useful theory rather than testing decontextualized and impartial theory. They invite learners to be active participants, leading to change in both self and the system in

51

question. They emphasize reflection-in-action, rather than reflection-on-action, the development of double-loop rather than single loop learning, and meta-competence over competence. Reflection needs to be facilitated rather than taught. They are comfortable with tentativeness rather than certainty. They follow a dialectic, rather than a didactic classroom approach. The normal learning outcomes are often more practice-based than theory-based.

Within action research we can now identify multiple 'action modalities': action learning, action science, appreciative inquiry, cooperative inquiry and developmental action inquiry, to name a selection (Raelin, 1999; Coghlan and Brannick, 2010; Coghlan, 2010).

Action learning: For Revans (1998), the founder of action learning, action learning involves engagement with real problems rather than with fabrications, is both scientifically rigorous in confronting the problem and critically subjective through managers learning in action. While its practice is demonstrated through many different approaches, two core elements are consistently in evidence: participants work on real organizational problems that do not appear to have clear solutions; and participants meet on equal terms to report to one another and to discuss their problem and progress (O'Neil and Marsick, 2007). Action learning has traditionally been directed towards enabling professionals to learn and develop through engaging in reflecting on their experience as they seek to solve real-life problems in their own organizational settings. As such it is a powerful OD approach (Rigg, 2006). As a form of research that seeks to generate knowledge beyond the direct experience of its participants it has not received a great deal of attention. In recent years, there have been explorations of action learning's philosophical grounds (Pedler and Burgoyne, 2008; Coghlan and Coughlan, 2010), and, from a research perspective, on research accessible through empirical engagement in practice and in collaboration with those who seek to resolve problems.

Action science: Action science is a term used by Argyris (1983), who considered that action research had lost its scientific edge and so he wanted to bring the word 'science' back into the study of practice and intervention. Argyris (1993, 2004) places an emphasis on the cognitive processes of individuals' 'theories-in-use', which he describes in terms of Model I (strategies of control, self-protection, defensiveness and covering–up embarrassment) and Model II (strategies eliciting valid information, free choice and commitment). In Argyris' (1987) view, practice-oriented OD scholars became so client-centred that they failed to question how clients themselves defined their problems and ignored the building and testing of propositions embedded in their own practice. On the theoretical side, OD scholars conducted research that met the criteria of rigour of normal science but was disconnected from everyday life. As Friedman and Rogers (2008) demonstrate action science is more of a grounding of action research than a discrete method of practice.

Appreciative inquiry: Appreciative inquiry aims at large system change through an appreciative focus on what already works in a system, rather than what is deficient (Ludema and Fry, 2008). It utilizes a cycle of appreciative inquiry, that is sometimes expressed as the 4 Ds (Discovery, Dream, Design, Delivery/Destiny) or alternatively the 4 Is (Initiate, Inquire, Imagine, Innovate) (Watkins and Mohr, 2001; Reed, 2007). Appreciative inquiry is often misunderstood and perceived to be a simple process of focusing on the positive. As Bushe argues in his chapter in this volume, appreciative inquiry did not begin its life as an intervention technique. Rather, it began as a research method for making grounded theory building more generative. Accordingly, as Bushe (2010) argues, it is a deeper and richer process than a change technique and has an underlying capacity to leverage the generative capacity of metaphors and conversation in order to facilitate transformational action. Appreciative inquiry has become a prolific way of engaging in OD (e.g. Yaeger et al., 2005).

Cooperative inquiry: Heron and Reason (2008: 366) define cooperative inquiry 'in which the participants work together in an inquiry group as co-researchers and co-subjects'. The participants research a topic through their own experience of it in order to understand their world, make sense of their life, develop new and creative ways of looking at things, and learn how to act to change things they might want to change and find out how to do things better.

Developmental action inquiry: Developmental action inquiry is an expression of action science in that Torbert adds the developmental dynamic of learning to inquire-in-action, emphasising that as leaders progress through adulthood they may intentionally develop new 'action-logics' by progressing through stages of development (Torbert and Associates, 2004). Developmental theory offers an understanding of leaders' transformation through a series of stages so that they gain insight into their own action-logics as they work to transform their organizations (Fisher et al., 2000).

These five 'action modalities' provide examples of contemporary OD that may be considered to be 'dialogic OD' in Bushe and Marshak's (2009) terms. In each of them the emphasis is on exploring subjective experience and how the participants construct the meaning of the situations in which they find themselves, which they seek to change and how they frame and implement action strategies. Selecting a modality as appropriate to a given situation requires an insight into both a given modality and to what might be required in a given situation (Coghlan, 2010).

OD and action research now: towards a synthesis

A synthesis between then and now for OD through action research is possible through exploring different forms of change programmes and different approaches through the lenses of diagnostic and dialogic OD.

Mitki et al. (2000) cluster change programmes as, limited, focused and holistic:

Limited change programmes are aimed at addressing a specific problem, such as team building, communication improvement, management development operational improvement and so on.

Focused change programmes are ones that identify a few key aspects, such as time, quality, customer value, and then use these, by-design, as levers for changing the organization system-wide.

Holistic change programmes are aimed by-design to simultaneously address all (or most) aspects of the organization.

While OD has always espoused working with the whole system, this has not always been realized. Many OD projects have and continue to be have limited and focused programmes. In such settings, 'diagnostic' OD continues to be operative though there is also potential for 'dialogic' OD in these programmes.

Buono and Kerber (2008) make an important distinction between three approaches to change: directed change, planned change and guided changing:

Directed change is where there are tightly defined goals and leadership directs and commands.

Planned change is where there is a clear goal and vision of the future and leadership devises a roadmap to reach it and influences how it is reached.

Guided changing is where the direction is loosely defined and leadership points the way and keeps watch over the process.

Table 3.1 Approaches to OD through action research in different change programmes and approaches

Change Programmes	Change Approaches	Organization Development/Action Research
Limited	■ Directed approach ■ Planned approach	Focus is likely to be diagnostic, drawing on traditional action research. May also be dialogic and draw on any of the action modalities
Focused	■ Directed approach ■ Planned approach	Focus is likely to be diagnostic, drawing on traditional action research. May also be dialogic and draw on any of the action modalities
Holistic	■ Guided changing	Focus is dialogic and builds on conversation about change and changing

Mitki et al.'s and Buono and Kerber's frameworks provide a way of framing how both old and new OD/action research may sit side by side (Table 3.1). In limited and focused change programmes where management adopts 'directed' or 'planned' approaches as diagnostic OD, the action research approach is likely to be one that accords with what was discussed above under Frohman et al.'s (1976) description. In limited and focused change programmes where management adopts 'directed' or 'planned' approaches as dialogic OD, the action research approach is likely to be one that works with some of the action modalities outlined above. In a holistic change programme 'guided changing' for fits with much of what is understood as dialogic OD and accordingly builds on dialogue and conversation about change.

Insight into the type of change programme under consideration and the type of approach adopted by leadership opens up insights into how OD can be of help to an organization. At the same time, attention to the act of insight itself provides critique of core assumptions as to how programmes and approaches are framed and what role OD may play (Coghlan, 2008, 2010).

Conclusions

This chapter has explored the relationship between organization development and action research. It has examined the nature of this relationship and how it evolved over the past sixty years. It is critical to note that not only has the theory and practice of each entity developed respectively but also that their relationship has also developed and continues to do so. With regard to organization development, Coghlan and Shani (2010) noted seven themes, which, in their view, continue to capture the essence and challenges of OD. These themes apply equally to action research and to OD enacted through action research.

- OD through action research is continuously evolving and timely as it has the ability to adapt and respond to the variety of emerging challenges experienced by individuals, groups, organizations, communities and societies.
- OD through action research is reflexive and continues to be self-aware, reflexive and to be open to its own learning and development, in the light of emerging economic, social and business trends and learning how to be relevant in each generation.
- OD is collaborative research in that it has always espoused research *with* people rather than *on* or *for* them. At the core of most OD work there is commitment to the generation of

scientific knowledge that can guide practice. Action research provides a clear approach to achieving these conditions.

- OD work is embedded in relationships, between OD practitioners and clients, between OD scholars and clients, between members of the system that are involved in an OD project, between OD practitioners that work together and, between OD scholars and OD practitioners, the quality of which have a direct impact on both process and outcomes of any OD project. Action research provides a clear approach to achieving these conditions.

- OD continues to focus on the sustainable development of human, social, economic and ecological resources. Action research provides a clear approach to achieving these conditions.

- OD through action research is relevant in any context. While any context has its own particular characteristics and challenges, the core values and processes of OD and action research have remained relevant.

- Educating for OD and action research remains a constant challenge.

The nature of action research in OD as a collaborative, interventionist form of research makes demands on the OD scholars to attend explicitly to their own learning in action, to the dynamics and quality of their engagement of OD with a client system and to the generation of actionable knowledge (Reason, 2001; Coghlan and Rashford, 2006; Shani et al., 2008; Coghlan, 2009; Coghlan and Brannick, 2010). While the academic world has struggled traditionally to accept such forms of inquiry and action as 'scientific', in the postmodern world this is increasingly less so. In today's context there are increasing demands for organizational research to be rigorous, reflective and relevant (Pasmore et al., 2008). OD through action research continues to provide such rich possibilities.

References

Argyris, C. (1983). Action science and intervention. *Journal of Applied Behavioral Science*, 19 (2), 115–35.

Argyris, C. (1987). Reasoning, action strategies and defensive routines: The case of OD practitioners. In R.W. Woodman and W.A. Pasmore (eds) *Research in organizational change and development* (Vol. 1, pp. 89–128). Greenwich, CT: JAI.

Argyris, C. (1993). *Knowledge for action*. San Francisco: Jossey

Argyris, C. (2004). *Reasons and rationalizations*. New York: Oxford University Press.

Argyris, C., Putnam, R. and Smith, D. (1985). *Action science*. San Francisco: Jossey-Bass.

Beckhard, R. (1967). The confrontation meeting. *Harvard Business Review*, 45 (2), 149–55.

Bowers, D. and Franklin, J. (1972). Survey-guided development: Using human resources measurement in organizational change. *Journal of Contemporary Business*, 1 (3), 43–55.

Bradbury, K., Mirvis, P., Neilsen, E. and Pasmore, W.A. (2008). Action research at work: Creating the future following the path from Lewin. In P. Reason and H. Bradbury (eds) *Handbook of action research*. 2nd edn (pp. 77–92). London: Sage.

Bradford, D. and Burke, W.W. (guest eds) (2004) Is organization development in crisis? Special issue *Journal of Applied Behavioral Science*, 40 (4).

Bradford, D. and Burke, W.W. (2005). *Reinventing organization development*. San Francisco: Pfeiffer.

Bunker, B. and Alban, B. (1997). *Large group interventions*. San Francisco: Jossey-Bass.

Buono, A. and Kerber, K. (2008). The challenge of organizational change: Enhancing organizational change capacity. *Revue Science de Gestion*, 65, 99–118.

Burnes, B. (2007). Kurt Lewin and the Harwood Studies: The foundations of OD. *Journal of Applied Behavioral Science*. 43 (2), 213–31.

Bushe, G.R. (2010). Generativity and the transformational potential of appreciative inquiry. In D. Zandee, D.L. Cooperrider and M. Avital (eds) *Organizational generativity: Advances in appreciative inquiry*, Vol. 3. Bingley, UK: Emerald.

Bushe, G. and Marshak, R. (2008). The postmodern turn in OD. *OD Practitioner*, 40 (4), 9–11.

Bushe, G. and Marshak, R. (2009). Revisioning organization development: Diagnostic and dialogic premises and patterns of practice. *Journal of Applied Behavioral Science*, 45 (3), 248–368.

Clarke, P.A. (1972). *Action research and organizational change*. London: Harper & Row.

Coch, L. and French, J. (1948). Overcoming resistance to change, *Human Relations*, 1, 512–32.

Coghlan, D. (2008). Exploring insight: The role of insight in a general empirical method in action research for organization change and development. *Revue Science de Gestion*, 65, 343–55.

Coghlan, D. (2009). Toward a philosophy of clinical inquiry/research. *Journal of Applied Behavioral Science*, 45 (1), 106–21.

Coghlan, D. (2010). Seeking common ground in the diversity and diffusion of action research and collaborative management research action modalities: Toward a general empirical method. In W.A. Pasmore, A.B. (Rami) Shani and R. Woodman (eds) *Research in organization change and development* (Vol. 18, pp. 149–81). Brinkley, UK: Emerald.

Coghlan, D. and Brannick, T. (2010). *Doing action research in your own organization*. 3rd edn. London: Sage.

Coghlan, D. and Coughlan, P. (2010). Notes toward a philosophy of action learning research. *Action Learning: Research and Practice*, 7 (2), 195–205.

Coghlan, D. and Rashford, N.S. (2006). *Organization change and strategy: An interlevel dynamics approach*. Abingdon: Routledge.

Coghlan D. and Shani, A.B. (Rami) (2010). Editors' Introduction: Organization development: Toward a mapping of the terrain. In D. Coghlan and, A.B. (Rami) Shani (eds) *Fundamentals of organization development*, (Vol 1. pp. xxiii–xxviii). London: Sage.

Culbert, S.A. (1972). Using research to guide an organization development project. *Journal of Applied Behavioral Science*, 8 (20), 2013–236.

Cunningham, B.C. (1993). *Organizational development and action research*. New York: Praeger.

Eikeland, O. (2006). Phronesis, Aristotle and action research. *International Journal of Action Research*, 2 (1), 5–53.

Fisher, D., Rooke, D. and Torbert, W.R. (2000). *Personal and organizational transformations through action inquiry*. Boston: Edge/work Press.

Foster, M. (1972). An introduction to the theory and practice of action research in work organizations. *Human Relations*, 25, 529–56.

French, W. and Bell, C. (1999). *Organization development*. 6th edn. Upper Saddle River, NJ: Prentice-Hall.

Friedman, V.J. and Rogers, T. (2008). Action science: Linking causal theory and meaning making in action research. In P. Reason, and H. Bradbury (eds) *Handbook of action research*. 2nd edn (pp. 252–65). London: Sage.

Frohman, M.A., Sashkin, M. and Kavanagh, M.J. (1976). Action-research as applied to organization development. *Organization and Administrative Science*, 7, 129–61.

Gibbons, M., Limoges, C., Nowotny, H., Schwartzman, S., Scott, P. and Trow, M. (1994). *The new production of knowledge*. London: Sage.

Greenwood, D. (2002). Action research: Unfulfilled promises and unmet challenges. *Concepts and Transformation*, 7 (2), 117–40.

Greenwood, D. (2007). Pragmatic action research. *International Journal of Action Research*, 3 (1 and 2), 131–48.

Greenwood, D. and Levin, M. (2007). *Introduction to action research*. 2nd edn. Thousand Oaks, CA: Sage.

Gustavsen, B. (2003). New forms of knowledge production and the role of action research. *Action Research*, 1 (2), 153–64.

Heron, J. and Reason, P. (2008). Extending epistemology with a co-operative inquiry. In P. Reason and H. Bradbury (eds) *Handbook of action research*. 2nd edn (pp. 367–380). London: Sage.

Holman, P., Devane, T. and Cady, S. (2007). *The change handbook*. 2nd edn. San Francisco: Berrett-Koehler.

Levin, M. (2003). Ph.D. programs in action research: Can they be housed in universities? *Concepts and Transformation*, 8 (3), 219–38.

Levin, M. and Greenwood, D. (2008). The future of universities: Action research and the transformation of higher education. In P. Reason and H. Bradbury (eds) *Handbook of action research*. 2nd edn (pp. 211–26). London: Sage.

Ludema, J. and Fry, R. (2008). The practice of appreciative inquiry. In P. Reason and H. Bradbury (eds) *Handbook of action research*. 2nd edn (pp. 280–96). London: Sage.

MacLean, D., MacIntosh, R. and Grant, S. (2002) Mode 2 management research. *British Journal of Management*, 13, 189–207.

Martin, A.W. (2001). Large group processes as action research. In P. Reason and H. Bradbury (eds) *Handbook of action research* (pp. 200–208). London: Sage.

McArdle, K. and Reason, P. (2008). Action research and organization development. In T. Cummings (ed.) *Handbook of organization development* (pp. 123–36). Thousand Oaks, CA: Sage.

Mitki, Y. Shani, A.B. (Rami), and Stjernberg, T. (2000). A typology of change programs and their differences from a solid perspective. In R.T. Golembiewski (ed.) *Handbook of organizational consultation*, 2nd edn (pp. 777–85). New York: Marcel Dekker Inc.

O'Neil, J. and Marsick, V. (2007). *Understanding action learning*. New York: American Management Association.

Pasmore, W.A. (2001). Action research in the workplace: The socio-technical perspective. In P. Reason, and H. Bradbury (eds) *Handbook of action research* (pp. 38–47). London: Sage.

Pasmore, W.A. and Friedlander, F. (1982). An action research program for increasing employee involvement in problem solving. *Administrative Science Quarterly*, 27, 343–62.

Pasmore, W.A., Woodman, R. and Simmons, A.L. (2008). Toward a more rigorous, reflective, and relevant science of collaborative management research. In A.B. (Rami) Shani, S.A. Mohrman, W.A. Pasmore, B. Stymne, and N. Adler (2008). *Handbook of collaborative management research* (pp. 567–82). Thousand Oaks, CA: Sage.

Pedler, M. and Burgoyne, J. (2008). Action learning. In P. Reason and H. Bradbury (eds) *Handbook of action research*. 2nd edn (pp. 319–32). London: Sage.

Peters, M. and Robinson, V. (1984). The origins and status of action research. *Journal of Applied Behavioral Science*, 20 (2), 113–24.

Purser, R. and Griffin, T. (2008). Large group interventions: Whole system approaches to organizational change. In T. Cummings (ed.) *Handbook of organization development* (pp. 261–76). Thousand Oaks, CA: Sage.

Raelin, J. (1999). Preface. *Management Learning*, 30 (1), 115–25.

Raelin, J. (2009). Seeking conceptual clarity in the action modalities. *Action Learning: Research and Practice*, 6 (1), 17–24.

Reason, P. (2001). Learning and change through action research. In J. Henry, (ed.) *Creative management*. 2nd edn (pp. 182–94). London: Sage.

Reason, P. and Bradbury, H. (2008). *Handbook of action research*. 2nd edn. London: Sage.

Reason, P. and Rowan, J. (1981). *Human inquiry: a sourcebook for new paradigm research*. London: Sage.

Reed, J. (2007). *Appreciative inquiry: Research for change*. Thousand Oaks, CA: Sage.

Revans, R. (1998). *ABC of action learning*. London: Lemos and Crane.

Rigg, C. (2006). *Action learning: Leadership and organizational development in public services*: Abingdon: Routledge.

Schein, E.H. (1969). *Process consultation: Its role in organization development*. Reading, MA: Addison-Wesley.

Schein, E.H. (1987). *The clinical perspective in fieldwork*. Thousand Oaks, CA: Sage.

Schein, E.H. (1988). *Process consultation, volume I: Its role in organization development*. Reading, MA: Addison-Wesley.

Schein, E.H. (1989). Organization development: Science, technology or philosophy? *MIT Sloan School of Management Working Paper*, 3065–89-BPS. (Reproduced in D. Coghlan and A.B. (Rami) Shani (eds) *Fundamentals of organization development*, Vol 1. (pp. 91–100). London: Sage, 2010.)

Schein, E.H. (1995). Process consultation, action research and clinical inquiry: Are they the same? *Journal of Managerial Psychology*, 10 (6), 14–19.

Schein, E.H. (1997). Organizational learning: What is new? In M.A. Rahim, R.T. Golembiewski and L.E. Pate (eds) *Current topics in management* (Vol. 2. pp. 11–26). Greenwich, CT: JAI Press.

57

Schein, E.H. (1999). *Process consultation revisited: Building the helping relationship*. Reading, MA: Addison-Wesley.

Schein, E.H. (2008). Clinical inquiry/research. In P. Reason and H. Bradbury, *Handbook of action research*. 2nd edn (pp. 226–79). London: Sage.

Schon, D.A. (1995). Knowing-in-action: The new scholarship requires a new epistemology. *Change*, November/December, 27–34.

Shani, A.B. (Rami) and Pasmore W.A. (1985). Organization inquiry: Towards a new model of the action research process. In D.D. Warrick (ed.) *Contemporary organization development: Current thinking and applications* (pp. 438–48). Scott Foresman and Company: Glenview, ILL.

Shani, A.B. (Rami), Mohrman, S.A., Pasmore, W., Stymne, B. and Adler, N. (2008). *Handbook of collaborative management research*. Thousand Oaks, CA: Sage.

Shepard, H. and Katzell, R.A. (1960). *An action research program for organization improvement*. Foundation for Research on Human Behavior. (Reproduced in B. Cooke and J. Woolfram-Cox (eds.) *Fundamentals of action research* (Vol II, pp. 317–34). London: Sage.)

Susman, G.I. and Evered, R.D. (1978). An assessment of the scientific merits of action research. *Administrative Science Quarterly*, 23, 582–601.

Torbert, W. and Associates (2004). *Action inquiry*. San Francisco: Berrett-Koehler.

Watkins, K.M. and Mohr, B. (2001). *Appreciative inquiry: Change at the speed of imagination*. San Francisco: Jossey-Bass.

Yaeger, T., Sorensen, P. and Bengtsson, U. (2005). Assessment of the state of appreciative inquiry: Past, present and future. In R. Woodman and W.A. Pasmore (eds) *Research in organization change and development*, Vol 15 (pp. 197–319). Oxford: Elsevier.

4

The early Cold War politics of action research and group dynamics

Bill Cooke

Introduction

> But, my friends, the period of social pioneering is only at its beginning. And make
> no mistake about it – the same qualities of heroism and faith and vision that were required
> to bring the forces of nature into subjection will be required – in even greater measure – to
> bring under proper control the forces of modern society.
>
> Franklin Delano Roosevelt, cited in Lewin (1945: 126)

With this quote, Kurt Lewin introduced the newly founded Research Center for Group
Dynamics (RCGD) at MIT. The article was published in May 1945, days after Roosevelt's
sudden death in office. But when the same piece was published in 1947 in a monograph, soon
after Lewin's own even more sudden death aged 56, "with comments and bibliography by
Ronald Lippitt", the FDR quote had been removed (Lewin 1947). If there were politics to the
removal of this quote, it was not that the pioneers of action research and group dynamics'
commitment to the use of science for social change had diminished. Indeed, significant for my
conclusion is that this commitment to science was a permanent, if debated, feature from the
1930s to the 1960s. The more likely political concern was the reference to Roosevelt himself, and
by implication, the endorsement of the progressive values of his New Deal administration.

Ybarra (2004) describes what happened within the post-Roosevelt Cold War US as partly
connected to the conflict in the wider world with Communism; but also as:

> ... essentially a conservative reaction to the New Deal, a long-simmering series of resent-
> ments and antipathies that boiled over into an awful, scalding mess during the late 1940s.
> The sources of bitterness that fueled this reaction were many: rural rancor toward urban
> elites, nativist dread of encroaching minorities, fundamentalist anxiety over the spread of
> secular values, Jeffersonian scorn for a growing and activist government.
>
> (2004: 5)

Antipathy towards the New Deal from conservatives, who saw it as a leftist interregnum,
predated the post-1945 McCarthy era,[1] as did their confrontational deployment of red-baiting

modes of interrogation, as I will show. Early enthusiasts for action research and group dynamics – and here I focus, in addition to Kurt Lewin and Ronald Lippitt, on John Collier and Goodwin Watson – were indeed members of urban elites, advocates of activist government, associated with the New Deal and government activism members of, and/or sympathetic to minorities, and, as proselytizing social scientists, advocates of secular values. As such, they were in constant danger of becoming embroiled in all of these sources of bitterness.

One pertinent illustration is the case of the eminent psychologist Edward Tolman. In 1947 he addressed the American Psychological Association (APA) on the occasion of Kurt Lewin's death, referring to his friend and colleague as one of the two greatest psychologists of all time (Marrow 1969: ix). Two years later, he was fired by the University of California for leading opposition to its loyalty oath, his dismissal only eventually overturned by the California Supreme Court (Cooke et al. 2005). Another case is Goodwin Watson, about whom more follows. This, then, was the formative context of group dynamics and action research; and in what follows, I demonstrate how this context impinged on the everyday lives of the early pioneers. Their response, though, was not passive retreat in the face of an increasingly dominant right-wing, anti-progressive politics. Rather, the evidence is that these founders believed in scientifically based action research and group dynamics as rational socio-political progressive responses to this politics. In the case of group dynamics I argue that the emergence of the group-dynamics-based T-group can be understood as a knowing, social-psychological challenge to the politics of the US at the time. It was also clear that adherence to the scientific persona was thought to protect T-group proponents from political attack. For action research, too, the model of scientific "indifference" arguably helped it through politically difficult times, whereas the evidence is that activist forms of scientific action research experienced a political downfall. I have addressed both action research and group dynamics individually elsewhere, drawing on the same empirical material as I do here, but each in more detail Cooke (2006, 2007); see also (Cooke 1999);[2] and this chapter is synthesized from these two articles. However, this is the first time that action research and group dynamics, between which there are strong historical overlaps, have been juxtaposed in this way.

Chapter outline

In the next section, "From New Britain 1946 to Twenty-first-century change management", I provide a more detailed historical explanation of the emergence of group dynamics. I describe the key individuals involved in my historiographical analysis (John Collier, Kurt Lewin, Ronald Lippitt and Goodwin Watson), and the events, institutions and publications through which they, with others, developed the idea of action research and group dynamics, and the broader contribution both have made to contemporary change management. Following on, I dedicate a section – "Group – and Cold War interpersonal – dynamics" – to revealing the extent to which politics impinged on the interpersonal at the time in which the notion of group dynamics, and then the T-group emerged. Here, in particular, I use Kurt Lewin's and Goodwin Watson's FBI files (see also Cooke 2006, 2007) for the data they contain, for what they symbolize in terms of the state of interpersonal relations at that time. The files also stand as comparators to other accounts of Lewin, Watson and group dynamics. That section concludes with, first, Watson's 1963 case that the scientific persona is politically useful; and second, with a 1966 excerpt from Watson's FBI file charging that the first ever book about action research, *Action for Unity* (1947), which Watson wrote, promoted a Communist Party line.

This moves me into my second empirical section, "Action Research: Activist or Neutral Science?" My data here are from a correspondence between John Collier and Ronald Lippitt, the former arguing for an activist, overtly engaged version of action research, the latter for a purer form of science-based intervention free of "content goals". Alongside this correspondence I contrast the fortunes of Collier and Lippitt, and of the respective institutions that they were associated with – the Institute for Ethnic Affairs for Collier, National Training Laboratories for Lippitt. Collier's activist action research in practice appears to have had dire political consequences for the survival of his institute; whereas Lippitt's (ostensibly?) more objective casting of science was accompanied by institutional success.

In my conclusion I both use and challenge Fuller (2003) on the relation between science, social science and the Cold War, to suggest an adherence to science may be seen as having oppositional value, as well as signifying evasion of or compliance with a dominant right-wing polity.

From New Britain 1946 to twenty-first-century change management

In this section I describe the key actors in my account. I then set out a history of the early development in the field of action research and group dynamics, and then their contemporary relevance.

Dramatis personae: Collier, Lewin, Lippitt and Watson

This difference is particularly evident in an exchange between two of Lewin's associates, Ronald Lippit and John Collier. Collier was closely associated with FDR's New Deal. As FDR's Commissioner of the Bureau of [US] Indian Affairs, John Collier was responsible for the Indian Reorganization Act also called The New Deal for Indians (Cooke 1999, 2006), and inter alia saw himself as a colonial administrator in the British imperial tradition. Three other dramatis personae feature in this chapter; again, their stories are told elsewhere, so I will keep biography brief. First is Kurt Lewin (1890–1947). Lewin was inventor of force field analysis, and the unfreeze change refreeze model. Also attributed to him is the invention of group dynamics (although Highhouse 2002a suggests the Tavistock Institute may have got there first) and action research (in the same vein see below on Collier). According to Schein (1980: 238), "there is little question that the intellectual father of contemporary theories of applied behavioral science, action research and planned change is Kurt Lewin"; and in a widely cited article Burnes (2004) has demonstrated his contemporary relevance.

Second is Ronald Lippitt. With Lewin and White, Lippitt conducted the famous research on democratic versus laissez-faire and authoritarian leadership styles in Iowa (Lewin et al. 1939). He remained close to Lewin until 1947, working for him at Research Center for Group Dynamics (RCGD) at MIT. He was active from the 1930s onwards in the Society for the Psychological Study of Social Issues (SPSSI), was first editor of its journal (*Social Issues*) and later co-authored the change-management classics *The Dynamics of Planned Change* (Lippitt et al. 1958) and *The Consulting Process in Action* (Lippitt and Lippitt 1978). Third is Goodwin Watson, author of the first ever book about action research, *Action for Unity* (1948), also active in the SPSSI, founding editor of the *Journal of Applied Behavioral Sciences* and in the 1960s leader of the National Training Laboratories' T-group movement which sought to apply group dynamics in the workplace (Kleiner 1996, Highhouse 2002b).

In 1946 a training workshop on inter-ethnic relations in New Britain, Connecticut, was organized by the Commission for Community Inter-Relations (CCI) of the American Jewish Congress (Lippitt 1949; Cooke 2006), in conjunction with the Research Centre for Group Dynamics at MIT (RGCD). Kurt Lewin was founder of both organizations, and among the organizers of the workshop was Ronald Lippitt. Received history has it that this was a break-through. There it was realized that reflection and feedback on the interactions of group members (from a range of difference ethnic backgrounds) per se, and what it revealed to them their own and others attitudes, cognitive processes and feelings, brought about apparently transformational learning and change (Kleiner 1996; Cooke 1999; French and Bell 1999).[3]

This workshop is thus represented as a foundation event in the invention of group dynamics. From this emerged the concept of the content-less and structure-less training group. Group-member interaction as it happened – in *the here and now* – became the data on which participants individually and collectively focused, and undertook to act upon, in the group and subsequently. Trainer input was on what was happening in the group, that is on interpersonal interactions. When Lewin died soon after New Britain, the CCI baton was taken up by the National Training Laboratories (NTL), which became the foremost amongst the institutions promoting and running structure-less/content-less group training through its Bethel, Maine workshops. These started off being known a basic skills training (BST) groups, and then just training, or T-groups (Benne 1964; Kleiner 1996).

Group dynamics' contribution to change management

T-groups formed an important foundation of Organization Development (OD), bringing to it a focus on the small group as unit of analysis and vehicle for organizational change (French and Bell 1999; Cummings and Worley 2004). This focus remains (albeit not exclusively so) in OD, and in contemporary team-building practices. T-groups per se have been unfashionable for a while (Pettigrew 1985), although there are still consultancies doing T-group work. The T-group/group dynamics heritage, however, is evident in, for example, the ongoing use of distinctions between group task and process, and attention to the latter, and the focus on the relationship between the intra- and the inter-personal. There has, however, been a permanent managerial interest in the uses of teamwork and team-building as a component of culture change programmes, and as means for improving organizational effectiveness in their own right (see McCardle et al. 1995 and Grint 1994 in relation to TQM and Business Process Reengineering (BPR) respectively); and as Kleiner (1996) and Hanson and Lubin (1995) have argued managerial team-building processes are built on theories of group dynamics.

The achievement of empowerment through T-groups, and consequently team-building, was also originally connected to T-group participants' experience of their changed self-awareness as profoundly empowering and liberating personal transformation (French and Bell 1999). The case for the humanistic value of this personal transformation was particularly made by Abraham Maslow (1964, 1965), for whom T-groups were forums for engendering the quasi-religious yet secular "peak experience" in which he argued self-actualization should culminate. Kleiner's (1996) popular, but nonetheless rigorously researched, history of change management demonstrates how much (apparently) liberating personal transformation was part of the T-group story, not least because those so transformed often became ardent proselytizers of the process. Yet, interestingly this deep personal change is otherwise nowadays barely mentioned by the successors to the T-group tradition. For example, in the present day, NTL's world-wide-web history makes no mention of this aspect (NTL 2010). More generally, the mainstream empowerment discourse the T-group movement endowed nowadays typically addresses empowerment at a much more shallow level, of control over elements of the labour process, and at best the consequences thereof for personal motivation (e.g. archetypally Fisher 1999).

Action research's contribution to change management

While the story of New Britain and group dynamics is oft-repeated, its status as a very early action research intervention is often overlooked, as indeed comparatively is the early history of action research per se. Ronald Lippitt (1949) describes the workshop as action research, and did likewise while it was being planned (see below). Lewin famously wrote little about action research, notwithstanding the attribution of its invention to him; however, one of the three articles he did write, "Action Research and Minority Problems" (1946), was an account of the New Britain workshop. A year later, the first book about action research, by Goodwin Watson, entitled *Action for Unity* (1947) had been published, detailing a range of CCI interventions during WWII. But by this time, it was being claimed that action research had been being conducted from the mid- to late 1930s (the specific dates are not clear) by US government agents working with Native Americans under the leadership of John Collier. Writing about this work, Collier claimed that his main principle:

> ... I would call the first and the last; that research and then more research is essential to the program, that in the ethnic field research can be made a tool of action essential to all the other tools, indeed that it ought to be the master tool ... since the finding of the research must be carried into effect by the administrator and the layman, and must be criticized by them through their experience, the administrator and the layman must participate creatively in the research, impelled as it is from their own area of need.
>
> (1945: 275)

This is close to the basic premise of action research. Standard texts make action research's status as the foundational OD method explicit (e.g. French and Bell call it "a cornerstone" (1999: 130); see also Frohman et al. 1976; Senior 2001; Cummings and Worley 2004).

Action research has four defining features which it passes on to OD, and subsequently to other change-management approaches, not least other contemporary approaches to participatory change like appreciative inquiry (AI) (Cooperrider and Srivastva 1987; Golembiewksi 1998; French and Bell 1999). First, as the terms first set out by Collier in 1945 make clear, action research is the source of the general idea of, and of specific techniques for, collaboration between researcher and the researched, often translated managerially to *consultant* and *client*. This is supposed to result in more effective change management; there is "ownership" of the problem-solving process and the subsequent solution on the part of the client system, which is able to contribute its own situational expertise (French and Bell 1999; Cummings and Worley 2004).

Second, following on from this, action research pays particular attention to particular demands – interpersonal, organizational, political – of the researcher in the action research process. In change management/organizational terms this developed into the notion of the change agent, notably in Lippit et al. (1958), although there is evidence that the terms was used at least as early as 1948. Notably this plays out in the work of Schein on Process Consultation (1969, 1987, 1998), and his advocacy of an empowering mode of intervention-style, process consultation.

Third, action research offers participatory change management a stepped action sequence or recipe. This runs from building an agreement between consultant and client, through data collection, data analysis, action planning, action, evaluation, and so on. This sequence, besides being applied in its own right, is used in OD, informs models of the consultancy process (Lippitt

63

and Lippitt 1978; Kubr 2003), and planned change (Lippitt et al. 1958; French and Bell 1999; Cummings and Worley 2004). It can arguably be seen, via Lippitt et al., in contemporary versions of change management, like Kotter's eight-step change process (1996); and even, to stretch a point, in some Total Quality Management processes (Cooke 1992) and Hammer and Champy's (1993) five-stage Business Process Reengineering recipe (which claims to be sequences and data based, and to work on "ownership", although clearly absent are notions of serious collaboration and open ended inquiry).

Fourth, there is a claim to some version of science, or at least rigour, that action research brings participatory change management. The research in "action research" is seriously meant (see, for example, Burfield 2009; Cooke 2009), and requires a process of data collection and data analysis. In the early times of action research when particularly positivist views of social science prevailed, the full panoply of hypothesis testing was often marshalled in definitions of action research, albeit harder to identify in accounts of action research in practice (Cooke and Wolfram Cox 2005) This claim to science is central to this chapter.

Group – and Cold War interpersonal – dynamics

In this section I use empirical data explored in greater detail in Cooke (2007) to demonstrate, first, the ongoing political surveillance, and worse, of Goodwin Watson and Kurt Lewin, and how this was likely to create a culture in which interpersonal relationships were dominated by questions of authenticity and trust in the face of inquisition from authority. After Lewin died, and after further difficulties in the 1950s, it appears that advocates of the T-group, and thus group dynamics, in the person of Goodwin Watson at least, moved to a more overtly scientist value-neutral position. However, it is too simplistic to suggest that this was a political caving-in. As the citation from FDR evidences, there had always been some commitment to science. The move was therefore one of degree and knowing, rightly or wrongly underpinned by a faith in the emancipatory potential of the T-group.

Watson, Lewin, and a World War II "red scare"

In November 1941, Watson was appointed as director of the Foreign Broadcast Monitoring Service (FBMS) of the Federal Communications Commission (FCC) (Brinson 2001), and relocated to Washington, DC from New York. On 18 November 1941, Representative Martin Dies, Chairman of the Special Committee to Investigate Un-American Activities (i.e. HUAC, or then "the Dies Committee") denounced Watson as a "propagandist for communism and the Soviet Union" (in Brinson 2001: 65). This was the start of a tortuous sequence of events which led to Watson having to defend his unpaid position as head of FBMS, and subsequently, in need of income, returning to New York. There, inter alia he worked for Lewin's CCI (Cooke 1999). Given the timing, *Action for Unity* is likely an output of that work. Lewin's 1942 SPSSI Presidential address stated:

> [t]he study of social groups and of their culture will, of necessity, bring us in close contact with all the social forces which are ruling the life of these groups. We might be able to handle these problems more or less cautiously and more or less wisely. But we will have to be prepared for occasional attacks by local or national politicians. Goodwin Watson, the editor of the yearbook of the SPSSI ... has been honoured by such an attack.
> (In Nicholson 1997: 480)

The Dies accusation saw the FBI at the behest of J. Edgar Hoover launch their own investigation into Watson. Watson's FBI file is substantial. It runs from 1942 to 1967, and comprises 275 pages, including, particularly during the Dies inquiry, data from many interviews with Watson's work colleagues. Pertinent, and an exemplar in terms of my subsequent argument about the T-group as the result of a particular historical moment, is one episode where an FBI special agent recalls interviewing an informant about a year previously on another matter:

> ... she remembered definitely ... Dr. GOODWIN WATSON ... She stated that this party, a few years ago, was openly advocating the overthrow of the United States government in his classes ... that the same man served on the same joint Committees and that they were all actually shocked by his denunciation of the government of the United States and his advocacy of Communism. She stated that she had nearly come to blows with some of the members of the committee over the expression of his ideas. She did not know that he had ever been a member of the Communist Party, but she stated that there is no doubt of his Communist philosophy, and she could think of no worse place for him than on the Committee.

However, on re-interview, "... this informant was much less definite in her statements, and could only remember that in her associations on various committees with WATSON he had made some statements taken and positions which she considered Communistic" (FBI: Watson File: report made at New York City 1/28/42 p. 5). Nearly 70 years on, one can still project into this particular interview record (of which there are many more on file) the emotions and uncertainties which might have led to this apparent change of view, a realization of the consequences – for Watson, or perhaps for the informant – of what is reported.

Almost simultaneously with Watson's HUAC episode, Lewin himself was being investigated by the FBI. This, though was as a background check – following Lewin's application to go and work for Watson at the FBMS – an opportunity, not surprisingly, which was never pursued. FBI agents visited places where Lewin had worked, and interviewed colleagues and neighbours – in Boston, Palo Alto and in Iowa. Notable apart from anything else is the extent to which people in Iowa in particular presented a particularly coherent account of Lewin as pro-American, in the sense that was to emerge in Marrow's biography, *The Practical Theorist* (1969) Hence:

> ... everyone feels that LEWIN is a thoroughly loyal American. He stated that LEWIN had been very much taken with the aims and ideals of democracy. [Name deleted] said that some of LEWIN'S Jewish friends feel that LEWIN has become non-critical of our institutions, he is such a thorough believer in democracy. He stated LEWIN was willing to do whatever he could to be of service to the United States in this emergency but that it was not with any idea of bitterness toward Germany [Name deleted] said LEWIN was completely American an is motivated to be of service to his country, America ...
>
> (FBI: Lewin File: Report made at Des Moines, 3-6-42, p. 2)

And the next interviewee says:

> ... LEWIN was one of the five or six greatest living psychologist [sic] in the world today and predicted that in the next ten years he would be the number one psychologist in the world. He said LEWIN was never in any sort of political activity in Germany or this country. [Name deleted] added that LEWIN has never had any student of his have any

radical political attitude. ... LEWIN has shown, he advised, that the American way of life in the long run is more effective.

(FBI: Lewin File: Report made at Des Moines, 3-6-42, p. 2)

Such is the unanimity between the five Iowa interviewees one cannot but speculate whether they agreed a "line" beforehand, a line that was to pass into historical certainty via Marrow. Or, alternatively, perhaps they were being more-or-less accurate, and Lewin was sincerely pro-American. But Lewin *was* politically active on the left in Germany and in the US, and indeed had had students from the Soviet Union (Cooke 1999). A Palo Alto neighbour was aware of this. While claiming he and Lewin "did not have a great deal in common", "it had been indicated to him [name deleted] that the applicant had "radical, left wing tendencies. ..." that as to the Socialist Party. ... and the Communist Party in the United States, strictly speaking, the applicant would not fit into either but would be in between the two parties, as far as his sympathies would be concerned. Perhaps most damning for the mythologized *Practical Theorist* is not these politics but the continuation that "[name deleted] further advised that the applicant is an intellectual and a theorist; that he does not have the ability to handle practical problems and that because of these reasons would be inclined to instil his doctrines by literary means and lectures."

Radical social change and/or corporation friendly science?

Interviewed in 1963 for an oral history project, Watson said he hoped, but couldn't be certain, that, notwithstanding Dies and a second 1953 "red scare" in Westchester, New York, when the American Legion agitated to have him removed from the management committee of a child-guidance centre, the political controversy had died down (Watson 1963). He then recounts being approached about becoming dean of the state college of education in Santa Barbara, California, there being encouraging progress, but then being dropped. This could, he says, have been for legitimate reasons, but also because of his political history. That it is Watson's own analysis that his corporate T-group work enabled him to escape these circumstances is clear, however. He continues that in the last two weeks.

> I have been working for the fourth time in what's called the Key executive training programme of the [NTL], where we have men who are pretty high up in business representing many of our major corporations ... nobody has asked a question indication any knowledge of this aspect of my background.

(1963: 86)

By that time Watson had shifted towards an ideal of the psychologist as disinterested and value neutral. He had also become an advocate and leader of corporate T-groups, and more engaged with problems of business management. According to Nicholson this reflects a loss of radicalism on Watson's part. However, Watson's 1963 oral history also records a detailed acknowledgement of that radicalism, and Nicholson argues there is an important continuity throughout Watson's life in the (also Lewinian) desire for progress to a scientifically managed, more socially and economically democratic society. In his oral history, in response to a direct question on whether he has "veered to the right", Watson says the goal remains the same, but that he sees more opportunities for progress to this end through the transformation, via T-groups of corporate bureaucracies (Watson 1963: 62). In pursuing this aim, a value neutral psychologist had greater social legitimacy, as a scientist, and was less vulnerable to political attack (Nicholson 1997, 1998).

While empirical data has only been skimmed over, what I hope to have shown through the excerpts from Watson's and Lewin's FBI files is that there developed during World War II, and became strongly established in the McCarthy era, an interpersonally destabilized culture. Within this, workmates and neighbours were interrogated by the US state, and had to guess the consequences for the person in question, and for themselves, of their responses, not least in the light of what others might have said – prisoner's dilemma style. This helped create a domestic culture centred on questions of interpersonal (in)authenticity – questions of what does a person really think, and second, what are the real motivations behind their behaviour. These precisely were the T-group addressed. Appositely, but unwitting to the political context Kleiner describes the breakthrough at New Britain as a solution to the eternal experimental problem of "trying to guess a subject's thoughts" (1996: 35). What the T-group delivered alongside this was the apparently emancipatory, empowering effect that, Kleiner aside, few now acknowledge.

Moreover, the very here-and-now-ness, the absence of structure and agenda, make the T-group an attractive form of political intervention in its particular historical moment. This immunized the T-group from McCarthy style attacks on the basis of overt ideology or political agenda. Should the inquisition come and knock on the door of the T-group there is nothing there to attack, literally no agenda, just people in a room restricting their discussion to what is happening within it. People were enabled to come to terms with the dark personal and interpersonal consequences of (proto) Cold War culture.[4] But simultaneously in so doing an interpersonal solidarity – in the foundation event in New Britain, a class solidarity across ethnic distinctions – appeared to be achievable. None of this precludes, with hindsight, psychologistic naïvety and/or collusion in group dynamics' managerialist cooptation on the part of the T-group's inventors. Watson's claims for the T-group as a vehicle of social as well as personal change may be seen to exemplify this naïvety, when set alongside the extent of state surveillance of him, of which he had suspicions, but the extent of which he was unaware. A pertinent example in point is that towards the end of Watson's FBI file, in 1966 the following occurs:

> In 1953 a confidential source,[5] who has furnished reliable information in the past, advised that he considered Goodwin Watson … to be a concealed Communist, though he could offer no positive proof of this fact … This source advised that Watson has written a book "Action For Unity" which advocates the line followed by various Communist Party front groups.
>
> (FBI: Goodwin Watson File: Confidential Memorandum,
> FBI New York, 2 March 1966)

Action research: activist or neutral science?

Action for Unity is, of course, nothing more than an account of the CCI's action research work in the 1940s. Of course, its focus on inter-ethnic solidarity is consistent with US Communist Party (CPUSA) policy at the time, but really the direction of travel is that the CPUSA was trying to align itself (publically at least) with general progressive/New Deal politics. *Action for Unity* certainly embodies many of the bundle of elements that Ybarra saw provoking the political right during the Cold War – secularism, a concern for minorities, and so on. But it is a very long stretch to read any form of Marxism-Leninism into it.

What this does reveal, though, is the extent to which methodological ideals like action research were part of, and susceptible to, Cold War politics. Here our focus shifts to Lippitt and Collier. What remains the same are issues around science and action research as progressive intervention for social change. To a large extent, it can be argued that the historic outcome was, for US action researchers at the time, similar to that for group dynamics and the T-group, in which a value-free, scientifically neutral identity became more prominent. This is not to argue that all action research ended up in this way, recognizing the politically radical goals of those in the action research tradition like Orlando Fals-Borda – see Cooke and Wolfram Cox (2005). And what is also clear is that this pro-science thread was always present in action research. This time, though, our point of reference is not just Lewin's citation of Roosevelt. What is different here in comparison to my account of group dynamics/the T-group is that this negotiation around science and politics did not take place tacitly, or at least in processes lost to the historical record. Rather, it played out, first, in a correspondence between Ronald Lippitt and John Collier which is still in the archive[6] (Collier 1980 is the source of citations from correspondence that follow), and, second, in the founding and then collapse of Collier's Institute for Ethnic Affairs, arguably the first named action research institution, while, in parallel, the NTL thrived.

Collier, Lippitt and the ghost of Kurt Lewin

John Collier knew both Lewin and Lippitt. His autobiography contains a photographic portrait of Lewin, claiming he had become "… one of my own intimate friends …" (1963: 233). Speaking particularly of group dynamics, Collier continues, however, that Lewin's "… human insights and principles faltered at the hands of somewhat lesser men." It is hard to read this as other than a slighting of Lippitt, given what follows here. The irony is that Collier's status as separate but simultaneous co-inventor of action research invariably tracks back to one source, French and Bell (1999) who in turn cite personal correspondence from Lippitt crediting Collier. Lewin and Lippitt had been on the board of Collier's Institute of Ethnic Affairs, founded when Collier left the Federal Administration. Indeed, Lippitt sent apologies for not attending the 29 May 1946 launch dinner because he would be at New Britain. Lippit states "It is organized as a genuine action research project and is giving us an opportunity to test out a number of hypotheses in a way which I think is rather exciting" (Lippitt to Collier, 14 May 1946).

Lippitt's use of "genuine" may have been pointed, given that he had already expressed doubts about whether what the IEA proposed constituted authentic action research: "… the process of action-research as we have meant it and developed it in usage denotes quite a new thing. It is not research-to-be-followed-by-action, or research-on-action, but research-as-action …"; and subsequently, that "[m]any of the projects mentioned in the prospectus are of course not action-research …" (letter to Collier, 12 August 1945).

The IEA prospectus starts by defining action research as a familiar, stepped, process:

> The Institute's approach to these problems will stress the importance of "action-research"… [which] combines these essential elements: (a) assembling data, published or unpublished, experimentally proven or subjectively experienced in the lives of people (b) sharing the task of research with the very people whose hazards and whose needs are under scrutiny – indeed inviting and encouraging the leaders of people to assume a prime responsibility in working out the task.

> (IEA 1945: 2)

In fact, the term "subjectively experienced" puts Colliers definition, recognizing cultural dimensions, ahead of its time compared with the psychological postitivism that dominated the Lippitt – Lewin discourse. What follows turns away from the now accepted more managerial definition, and indeed from Collier (1945) calling for broader political and institutional engagement:

(c) calling to assistance all the agencies of government, of private and public finance, of public opinion, and of conscience, in programs of action which arise out of the needs of people and move toward a better ordered world.

Point (c) was the nub of a disagreement between Lippitt and Collier, and the basis of a substantial correspondence between them (in Cooke 2006).

We get closest to the essence of Lippitt's case in a letter of 5 January 1949 wherein he accuses the IEA of having of "content goals" which, while supported in principle by Lippitt, are inconsistent with "… the clearer and clearer differentiation which I have been forced to make between citizen activities toward political goals and social scientist's activities toward social science values. The only political role permitted a social scientist is to lobby for the use of social science, "in the solution of the problems of human affairs and human relations".

Lippitt continues that the social scientist should seek to be the "methodological-middle man", because

> If I identify with the content goals of the United Auto Workers with whom we are now working, then I tend to lose the possibility of furthering this goal of scientific skills and outlook with the American Telegraph and Telephone Company or the Ford Motor Company, and vice versa. But to the extent that I can clearly define my role as that of the methodological collaborator or consultant, oriented to the job of helping them find out the consequences about their own goals and their own ways of locomoting toward these goals then I find I can work effectively with these and many other groups which are even more incompatible in their "content goals".

As in previous correspondence, Lippitt stresses how well his version of action research is doing. If Collier is interested in training an IEA action research team at NTL "please let us know as soon as possible because the program of the past two summers seems to have resulted in quite a flood of applications for next summer".

Collier's position is best summarized later in the exchange, on 27 April 1949. First, Collier acknowledges, the scope of social research and social science "includes inter-personal relations and intra- and inter-group dynamics", but more beside – "economics … ; population problems; organization of industry, of government …". He continues:

> As soon as the breadth of scope of social science is held in mind … it seems to become plain that the social scientist must be possessed of value and purpose, whether or not he chooses a socially visible or a socially less visible role. I mean, not just as a man but as a scientist; for otherwise there will be no assurance that he will choose problems of critical importance to work on or that he *will not* wind up by becoming simply a technician for power groups, ideological groups, etc.

And, with some justification, he concludes not just the letter, but apparently (because one can never be sure of the completeness of archives) the correspondence:

> A generalized quote from Kurt Lewin … From *Action Research and Minority Problems*, Nov 1946. "Unfortunately there is nothing in social laws or social research which will force the practitioner toward the good. Science gives more freedom and power to both the doctor and the murderer, to democracy and fascism. The social scientist should recognize his responsibility also in respect to this."

The moral and rhetorical force of this citation of the founding father – from an article in a journal edited by Lippitt – is the stronger given that in *Action Research and Minority Problems* Lewin concludes with a detailed and strong endorsement of Collier's content goals.

The Cold War consequences of content-driven action research

However, what seems to be clear, according to Collier's own account, is that this adherence to overt content goals caused the Institute of Ethnic Affairs to collapse. Throughout their correspondence, Collier alludes to the financial difficulties of the IEA, which he believes stem from the withholding of it tax exemption (used elsewhere as a Cold War tactic against the Institute for Pacific Relations – Cooke 2007). Collier is clear that to him this was a form of state victimization (Collier 1963). Exemption was initially denied on the basis of an IEA telegram to President Truman calling for Guam to be returned to civilian rule, which according to the Internal Revenue made the IEA a political organization disqualified from tax exempt status. On the IEA appealing the decision, the Revenue shifted. The IEA was "oriented to action-research. Research which involved action was by definition (Internal Revenue's definition) political, and the tax privilege must be denied it" (Collier 1963: 333). While this was no doubt an opportunistic response by the Internal Revenue, the bitter irony – not acknowledged by Collier – is that its definition and logic on action research was in fact closer to Collier's than Lippitt's.

Collier then attempted to establish a pure non-action research foundation. The eventual verdict of the Internal Revenue came closer still to Collier's analysis in his correspondence with Lippitt. It was: "[s]ocial research, if experimental at all, involved action. Such had been the Institute's own definition. Action by the Internal Revenue's definition was *ipso facto* political. And by the institute's definition, social action involved research. Hence the tax privilege was to be denied" (Collier 1963: 333). No research without action, no action without research had a political price. Meanwhile, NTL thrived.

Conclusion

Fuller (2003) argues that if intellectual accountability is required of those intellectuals who engaged with Nazism (e.g. Heidegger) and Stalinism (e.g. Lukacs, Sartre) then it too is required of those who engaged with history's winners, not least in Cold War terms, the US military-industrial complex. But, says Fuller, compared to intellectuals who were "explicitly solicitous of a dominant regime", "more challenging and morally problematic are the cases in which entire bodies of thought appear to be crafted so as to avoid having to acknowledge the regimes that sustain both the legitimacy of what the authors describe and the authors' own legitimacy" (2003: 23). Fuller accuses Kuhn, in an echo of the Collier–Lippitt correspondence, of basing his paradigmatic model on a view of science as puzzle-solving, suggesting an image of scientists "as self determining and self-organizing" rather than as potentially or even inevitably politically compromised. Behind this kind of circumspection is a normative principle "central to the politics of intellectual compliance: *You can often accomplish your scientific and political goals with minimum difficulty by not resisting the larger forces in your environment*" (2003: 24–25; Fuller's italics).

It is therefore tempting to see in Collier's fate evidence of what happens when such forces are resisted; and in Lippitt's a scientist-ist advocacy of a path of least resistance. Yet the identification of Collier as hero, and Lippitt as villain from the progressive viewpoint is problematic. Collier's heroism is compromised by his espoused colonialism (see Cooke 2003a, 2003b), and enlistment of action research to that cause. Lippitt's villainy would require a downplaying of his ongoing engagement with the SPSSI, and that even in the correspondence considered above, for all his claims for technocratic neutrality, Lippitt does make clear, he chooses to work for labour, for the United Auto Workers. Lippitt's commitment to a particular version of science, inasmuch as it may be seen to be there at the start of his correspondence with Collier, also predates McCarthyist inquisition, if not wholly, as we have seen in the wartime case of Watson, a longer-established red-baiting.

In this chapter we are now also able to consider Watson alongside Lippitt. As we have seen, Watson was explicit that the adoption of the neutral-scientist identity was tactic to shield himself, and his ongoing activism from a punitive Cold War culture. This use of science was not, according to Watson, and later to Nicholson, merely about self-preservation. Watson and his NTL colleagues (likely to therefore to have included Lippitt) did believe that the T-group, group dynamics and social/behavioural science per se were truly a vehicle for progressive social change, as well as personal transformation (Watson 1963; Nicholson 1997, 1998). Moreover, Lippitt's and Watson's tactical "compliance", if that is what it is, compared to Collier's "resistance", did at least ensure the survival of action research and group dynamics notwithstanding their New Deal, progressive associations. Despite everything, I would argue, this was for the better rather than for the worse.

Notes

1 McCarthyism was bigger than McCarthy – as Ybarra points out, it was more of a general social movement than the consequence of a single demagogue. Ybarra's book, for example, focuses on Senator Pat McCarran.
2 In addition, space means it has not been possible to address the post-development, post-colonial account of these events in Cooke (2003a, 2003b).
3 As Highhouse 2002b points out, while the T-group contribution to team development was important, there are other often unacknowledged contributors to the emergence of team development, not least London's Tavistock Clinic (part of which become the Tavistock Institute of Human Relations) which was using the term "here and now" in the early 1940s.
4 And in Lewin's case, lest we forget, of the Nazism of which he had direct personal experience, and which helped kill his mother and his sisters.
5 Circumstantially, the contents of the file for 1953 suggest this informant was the infamous Louis Budenz.
6 Excerpts from John Collier's correspondence are reproduced with the kind permission of Mrs Grace Collier. Excerpts from Ronald Lippitt's correspondence are reproduced with the kind permission of Dr Larry Lippitt.

References

Benne, K.D. History of the T group in the laboratory setting. In L.P. Bradford, J.R. Gibb and K.D. Benne (eds) *T-Group theory and laboratory method*: 80–135. New York: Wiley, 1964.

Brinson, S.L. War on the homefront in World War II: The FCC and the House Committee on Un-American Activities. *Historical Journal of Film, Radio and Television*, 2001, 21, 1, 63–75.

Burnes, B. Kurt Lewin and the planned approach to change: A re-appraisal. *Journal of Management Studies*, 2004, 41, 6, 977–1002.

Burfield, D. Tavistock Publications: A partial history. *Management & Organizational History*, 2009, 4, 2, 207–22.

Collier, J. *Microfilm archive of the John Collier papers 1922–68*. Ann Arbor, MI: Microfilm Corporation of America, 1980.

Collier, J. United States Indian Administration as a laboratory of ethnic relations. *Social Research*, 1945, 12, May, 265–303.

Collier, J. *From every zenith*. Denver: Sage, 1963.

Cooke, B. Culture, quality and local government, in I. Saunders (ed.) *Managing quality in local government*. Longman, 1992, 142–63.

Cooke, B. Writing the left out of management theory: The historiography of the management of organizational change. *Organization*, 1999, 6, 1, 81–105.

Cooke, B. A new continuity with colonial administration: Participation in development management. *Third World Quarterly*, 2003a, 24, 1, 47–61.

Cooke, B. "Managing organizational culture and imperialism". In A. Prasad (ed.) *Postcolonial theory and organizational analysis*. London: St Martin's Press, 2003b.

Cooke, B. The Cold War origin of action research as managerialist cooptation. *Human Relations*, 2006, 59, 5, 665–93.

Cooke, B. The Kurt Lewin/Goodwin Watson FBI files: A 60th anniversary "there and then" of the "here and now". *Human Relations*, 2007, 60, 3, 435–62.

Cooke, B. On the multiple significances of DB, scholar publisher. *Management and Organizational History*, 2009, 4, 2, 203–6.

Cooke, B., Mills, A. and Kelley, E. Situating Maslow in Cold War America. *Group and Organization Management*, 2005, 30, 2, 129–52.

Cooke, B. and Wolfram Cox, J. Introduction. In B. Cooke and J. Wolfram Cox (eds) *The fundamentals of action research, vol. 1*. London: Sage, 2005.

Cooperrider, D. and Srivastva, S. Appreciative inquiry in organizational life. In R.W. Woodman and W. Pasmore (eds) *Research in organizational change and development*, volume 1. Greenwich CT: JAI Press, 1987.

Cummings, T. and Worley, C.G. *Organization development and change*, 8th edn. Mason OH: South Western, 2004.

Federal Bureau of Investigation. *File on Goodwin Watson*. Washington, DC: FBI, 1942–167.

Federal Bureau of Investigation. *File on Kurt Lewin*. Washington, DC: FBI, 1942–56.

Fisher, K. *Leading self directed work teams*. New York: McGraw Hill, 1999.

French, W.L. and Bell, C.H. *Organization development – behavioral science interventions for organizational improvement*, 6th edn. Englewood Cliffs, NJ: Prentice Hall, 1999.

Frohman, M.A., Sashkin, M. and Kavanagh, M.J. Action research as applied to organization development. *Organization and Administrative Science*, 1976, 7, 1 and 2, 129–61.

Fuller, S. The critique of intellectuals in a time of pragamatist captivity. *History of the Human Sciences*, 2003, 16, 4 19–38.

Golembiewski, R. Appreciating appreciative inquiry: Diagnosis and perspectives on how to do it better. In R.W. Woodman and W. Pasmore (eds) *Research in Organizational Change and Development*, vol. 11. Greenwich CT: JAI Press, 1998.

Grint, K. Reengineering history: social resonances and business process reengineering. *Organization*, 1994, 1, 179–201.

Hammer, M. and Champy, J. *Rengineering the corporation*. New York: HarperBusiness. 1993.

Highhouse, S. A history of the T-group and its early applications in management. Development. *Group Dynamics: Theory Research and Practice*, 2002a, 6, 4, 277–90.

Highhouse. S. Assessing the candidate as a whole. A historical and critical analysis of individual psychological assessment for personnel decision making. *Personnel Psychology*, 2002b, 55, 363–96.

IEA. *The Institute of Ethnic Affairs Inc*. Washington, DC: The Institute of Ethnic Affairs, 1945.

Jahoda, M. and Cook, S. Ideological compliance as a social psychological process. In C.J. Friederich (ed.) *Totalitarianism*. Cambridge, MA: Harvard, 1954.

Kleiner, A. *The age of heretics*. London: Nicholas Brealey, 1996.

Kotter, J. *Leading change*. Boston, MA: Harvard Business School Press, 1996.

Kubr, M. *Management consulting*. Geneva: ILO, 2003.

Lewin, K. Action research and minority problems. *Journal of Social Issues*, 1946, 2, 4, 34–46.

Lewin, K. The research centre for group dynamics at Massachusetts Institute of Technology. *Sociometry*, 1945, May, 8, 2, 126–36.

Lewin, K. The research centre for group dynamics, with comments and bibliography by Ronald Lippitt. *Sociometry Monographs*, no. 17. New York: Beacon House Inc, 1947.

Lewin, K., Lippitt, R. and White, R.K. Patterns of aggressive behavior in experimentally created social climates. *Journal of Social Psychology*, 1939, 10, 271–99.

Lippitt, R. *Training in community relations*. New York: Harper, 1949.

Lippitt, R. and Lippitt, G. *The consulting process in action*. La Jolla, CA: University Associates, 1978.

Lippitt, R., Watson, J. and Westley, B. *The dynamics of planned change*. New York: Harcourt Brace, 1958.

Marrow, A.J. *The practical theorist*. New York: Basic Books, 1969.

Maslow, A. *Religions, values and peak experiences*. Cleveland: Ohio State University Press, 1964.

Maslow, A. *Eupsychian management*. Homewood, IL: Richard D. Irwin, Inc, 1965.

McCardle, L., Rowlinson, M., Procter, S., Hassard, J. and Forrester, P. (1995) TQM and participation. In A. Wilkinson and H. Willmott (eds) *Making quality critical*. London: Routledge.

National Training Laboratories (2010) *60 Years of Success*, www.ntl.org/inner.asp?id=178&category=2 (accessed 24 May).

Nicholson, I. The politics of scientific social reform: Goodwin Watson and the Society for the Psychological Study of Social Issues. *Journal of the History of the Behavioral Sciences*, 1997, 33, 39–60.

Nicholson, I. The approved bureaucratic torpor: Goodwin Watson, critical psychology, and the dilemmas of expertise. *Journal of Social Issues*, 1998, 54, 29–52.

Pettigrew, A. *The awakening giant*. Oxford: Blackwell, 1985.

Schein, E.H. *Organizational psychology*. Englewood Cliffs, NJ: Prentice Hall, 1980.

Schein, E.H. *Process consultation volume 1: its role in organization development*. Boston: Addison Wesley. 1969.

Schein, E.H. *Process consultation volume 2: lessons for managers and consultants*. Boston: Addison Wesley. 1987.

Schein, E.H. *Process consultation revisted: building the helping relationship*. Prentice Hall 1998.

Schein, E.H. *The clinical perspective in fieldwork*. Beverly Hills: Sage Publications, 1987.

Schrecker, E. *No ivory tower: McCarthyism & the universities*. New York: Oxford University Press, 1986.

Senior, B. *Organizational change*. London: FT, 2001.

Watson, G. *Action for unity*. New York: Harper, 1947.

Watson, G. *Oral history interview microform, columbia oral history project*. New York: Columbia University Press: 1963.

Ybarra, M.J. *Washington gone crazy*. Hanover, NH: Steerforth Press, 2004.

5

Organization development and international contexts
Values, controversies and challenges

Christopher J. Rees

Introduction

The multi-disciplinary nature of organizational change literature and research provides opportunities and challenges for both academics and practitioners working in this area (Marshak and Grant, 2008; Pettigrew et al., 2001; Schwarz and Huber, 2008). In terms of opportunities, knowledge from associated disciplines such as psychology, sociology, anthropology, and economics can be mined and then applied in imaginative ways to understand and inform organizational change designs and interventions (Rees, 2008a). In terms of challenges, however, the absence of universally acknowledged defining criteria makes it extremely difficult to trace trends and developments relating to the theory and practice of organizational change. As a result, key issues surrounding the aims, values, leadership, practice, and evaluation of organizational change interventions are often shrouded in ambiguity and controversy. For example, the perceived purpose of an organizational change intervention is likely to be multi-dimensional, perhaps unstated, and, in some cases, unconsciously strategized and resisted by various stakeholders involved in the process. In view of these tensions and uncertainties, it is often difficult to discuss in an overt manner the objectives and hence evaluation of an organizational change intervention; what may be viewed as an organizational change intervention failure by one group of stakeholders may be seen as a successful change intervention by another group of stakeholders.

Despite the challenges presented by the fluid nature of the subject, the main aim of this chapter is to identify and consider a number of specific developments and controversies associated with the subject of organizational change. In order to address this aim in a focused way, it is necessary to restrict this analysis to particular aspects of organizational change theory and practice. Specifically, the chapter will examine a number of developments and challenges in relation to the values of a specific approach to organizational change, namely Organization Development (OD). Given its origins, history and defining values, the study of OD provides an opportunity to identify some of the influences and challenges that are faced by those working in the field of organizational change more generally. The chapter is structured as follows. First, a brief overview is provided of the nature of the OD movement. The discussion proceeds to explore the search for a clearer business orientation within OD theory and practice, the changing values of OD, and the use of OD in international settings where prevailing values may conflict or complement the values held by OD professionals working in these settings.

The OD movement

At a general level, OD is all about developing organizations and individuals through the use of carefully planned change-management interventions. The origins of OD can be traced back to the 1940s when Kurt Lewin and his colleagues worked to develop change management technologies in the National Training Laboratories. Lewin was committed to promoting social empowerment and democracy partly as a result of his own adverse experiences of the authoritarian and racist culture of Nazi Germany (Burnes, 2004). Key texts which chart the history of OD acknowledge that, in its early stages at least, OD was a field of social action with goals that extended beyond the maximization of performance outputs (Cummings and Worley, 2009). Over the years, the field of OD has been associated to various degrees with technologies and applications including force-field analysis, T-group training, attitude surveys, action research and grid OD (Rees, 2008b). More recently, OD practitioners have sought to apply all-embracing organizational change processes such as Total Quality Management (TQM) and Business Process Re-engineering (BPR) which are most obviously associated with corporate strategy and strategic management (Cummings and Worley, 2009). There is evidence that OD practitioners are also adopting more specific processes such as scenario planning in order to formulate corporate strategy on the basis of identifying possible futures (McLean and Egan, 2008). Thus, it is highlighted that a performance focus has recently emerged within the field of OD. For example, the author of one recent textbook on OD cites the American Society for Training and Development's definition of OD that now proposes that the practice of OD must be in alignment with organization and business objectives (McLean, 2007: 12).

The difficulties associated with formally defining OD are well documented (Egan, 2002; Schifo, 2004). For example, there are disparities in the use of the term OD by various parties including OD theorists, OD practitioners, and general change-management consultants. While it would be an oversimplification to suggest that OD theorists may be defining OD in a completely different way to OD practitioners, there is some evidence to suggest that operational definitions of OD which emanate from within organizations may not correspond to definitions presented in theoretically driven OD literature (Quijano-Ramos and Rees, 2008). One of the emerging themes surrounding OD is the extent to which activities placed under the banner of OD have, in recent years, converged with the activities of business-focused HRM and HRD functions (McLean, 2007; Rees, 2008b; Ruona and Gibson, 2004). Ellis (2007: 32) has highlighted that the boundaries between HR activities and OD activities within organizations are becoming " ... increasingly blurred", a trend which does provide a further indication that organizationally based OD practitioners are adopting practices that are closely aligned to the strategic aims of business organizations.

In the past, classical definitions emphasized that OD could be defined with reference to a planned approach to change, the behavioural sciences, organizational culture, organizational effectiveness and health, and the holistic nature of OD (Beckhard, 1969), with the caveat that OD practice was underpinned by humanistic values (Rees, 2008b). Yet given the manner in which OD theorists and practitioners have tended to discard some of the traditional OD technologies such as T-group training and the managerial grid and replace them with approaches designed around, for example, TQM, BPR, and scenario planning, it is debatable whether the nature of the OD that was practised in the 1950s and 1960s is fundamentally different to the OD that is practised in the twenty-first century. Worren et al. (1999: 284) state that: 'OD practitioners, who have thought about people all along, now concede they forgot about markets, strategies, and computers'. This emerging performance-orientated focus in OD, which has been characterized as the 'joint optimization of the work and human systems' (Hornstein, 2001: 225), raises questions about the current meaning of the term OD. These questions tend to be answered with reference to the values which are associated with the field of OD.

Values and OD

The inextricable link between change management and values is well illustrated by considering the nature of values. One oft-cited definition of values is offered by Rokeach (1973). He states that values are: 'Enduring beliefs that a specific mode of conduct or end state of existence is personally or socially preferable to an opposite or converse mode of conduct or end state of existence.' This definition emphasizes various features of values. First, values are acquired over a period of time and, as a result, are likely to be deep-rooted. In relation to change management, this raises questions over the extent to which a change management intervention can, or even should be, designed to change the basic values of, for example, employees. Second, the definition introduces the notion that values are used in decision-making processes. For example, values form one element of the perceptual process which individuals use to determine whether an action or a state of affairs is 'right' or 'wrong'. Third, by implication, the definition proposes that values are closely linked to behaviour. That is, individuals evaluate the conduct of others using our own system of values. In this way, values are applied not only to assess the behaviour of others but also to act as an instrumental influence on our own behaviour. Thus, they are used in order to determine whether an action is 'right' or 'wrong' and also to select an action from a repertoire of possible behaviours. Fourth, in relation to social preference, values are considered as a key element of organizational culture (Meglino and Revlin, 1998).

As noted above, OD has traditionally been associated with humanistic values. These values are based on assumptions surrounding the innate worth and goodness of the person; organizational change based on these values will seek to create an environment (or culture) in which employees can develop and achieve psychological growth in order to help fulfil innate potential (Rees and Sharifi, 2002). Margulies and Raia (1990: 38) state their position clearly:

> Professional managers are neither barbarians nor automatons. They are, in fact, decent with honourable intentions. OD technology provides them with an automatic, built in conscience. The techniques in and of themselves are both "right" and "good" ... the more (managers) are involved with OD, the more humane they and their organizations become.

OD strategies that are centred on these humanistic assumptions place a heavy emphasis on designing organizations that motivate employees through participation, empowerment, and honesty in the workplace (Deaner, 1994).

Before considering the extent to which OD has encountered difficulties in relation to its practice in business organizations, it is apposite to highlight one of the main value–related tensions associated with traditional OD philosophy and practice. That is, OD is an approach to organizational change which is intended to provide employees with increased levels of autonomy and freedom by means of a pre-determined plan. While authors use different terminology to describe various steps contained in this pre-determined OD plan, the plan usually consists of an ordered sequence involving (a) a preliminary clarification and contracting stage, (b) a stage involving diagnostic activities, (c) a feedback stage, and (d) an evaluation and process re-entry stage

(Rees, 2008b). One can see a certain irony in situations where OD strategies, informed by a non-directive philosophy of Rogerian nature (Rogers, 1945) are implemented by means of these types of pre-determined step-by-step plans. McKendall (1993: 96) makes a similar point; citing Warwick (1978) she recognizes that some of the most serious concerns surrounding OD '... lie in the area of human freedom; planned change by its very nature subsumes human freedom'. Arguably, classical OD interventions represent the imposition of planned organizational change practices which are underpinned by a set of corresponding values; further, these values are not necessarily shared by some or all of the employees participating in the change intervention.

While some theorists, particularly those writing from a critical-management perspective, have commented on the way in which OD interventions have been used (or misused) by dominant groups to consolidate power structures within organizations (Marshak and Grant, 2008), the potential tension between the humanistic values underpinning a classical OD change intervention and the values of employees involved with the intervention is rarely explored in OD literature as representing a challenge to the assumptions underpinning humanistic values. The resistance to change that may result from this tension is rarely attributed to an informed reluctance on the part of individuals to adopt humanistic values as manifested by specific elements an OD intervention, even though reference to sources which explore a wide range of issues from Freud's portrayal of the self-centred pre-socialized id to religious concepts of 'original sin' quickly indicate that humanistic values are based on a disputed and controversial set of assumptions about human nature. Rather, the resistance to change that may result from this tension is often explained by deficiencies in the manner in which the OD plan has been implemented. In OD literature, resistance to change is usually attributed to a variety of systems-related and psychologically related factors (Lipton, 1996). As a result, OD literature '...presents a solid consensus that change and resistance can and should be "managed" by developing a strategy for and using the OD tool kit of interventions...' (Agócs, 1997: 46). Brown and Harvey (2005: 166) summarize this line of thinking clearly when they state: 'Resistance to change is a signal that something is not working in the implementation of the (OD) program.' In this sense, the existence of resistance to change would indicate that either the OD interventionist has not adhered to OD values or that further OD work is needed to identify the environmental or cultural factors that are creating the resistance to change.

The potential conflict that may exist between classical OD values and the values held by individuals and groups within organizations is particularly disconcerting when one returns to the fundamental issue of " ... who the client is in organization development interventions" (Hubbell, 2004: 339). For example, the client may be defined as the person who is working with the OD practitioner to implement change interventions based on a set of prescribed values. Alternatively, the client may be defined as the person whose values the OD practitioner is seeking to change. Given the changes that have occurred in the field of OD in recent years, as discussed above, there is even an argument to suggest that the client can be defined as the person whose values the OD practitioner adopts. In their analysis of 'What OD practitioners believe', Van Eynde et al. (1992: 44) conclude by stating that the challenge to OD in the future may be to satisfy many diverse values including 'enhancing performance and advocating social and environmental reforms'. Yet, as Hubbell (2004: 409) also concludes, it can be highly problematic for the OD practitioner to work for the entire organization ' ... especially in America where organizational members typically cherish individualistic and hierarchical values over communitarian and egalitarian values. Sometimes the OD practitioner must take a side in a situation of great import to the organization'. Issues connected to Hubbell's statement which links the values associated with organizational change and geographical contexts are pursued further in the next section of the chapter which considers OD from an international perspective.

OD from an international perspective

Recent reviews of OD theory and practice provide evidence that OD is being explored and practised from international perspectives. For example, in terms of theory, the longitudinal review of journal papers conducted by Piotrowski and Armstrong (2005) identified 'international/cultural' as one of the major topical research areas in the field of OD from 1992 to 2004. In terms of practice, the survey of OD practitioners conducted by Mozenter (2002) identified diversity (countries, languages and cultures) as a key emerging macro-force that is likely to exert an increasing influence on the work of OD practitioners. Similarly, from the results of their survey of 907 OD practitioners, Wirtenberg et al. (2004: 475) identified 'globalization, multi-cultural and whole system perspective' as a key integrated theme which presents numerous possibilities for OD professionals to contribute and add knowledge; for example: 'OD can help businesses align strategies and execute them in a way that meets the firms' financial goals and core values.'

This international theme that has emerged in OD theory and practice is highly relevant to the discussion of the challenges and controversies facing those working in the field of OD. While OD emanated from the work of writers in Western countries such as the USA and the UK, it is apparent that there is a growing use of OD in international settings. As Neumann et al. (2009: 171) state, international OD and change can be understood as 'an emerging field of applied behavioural and social science and of practice-based research'. For example, there are recent publications which have explored the theory and/or application of OD in settings such as Afghanistan (Zaldivar, 2008), Africa (James, 2004; Ukpata and Olukotun, 2008), Bhutan (O'Flynn and Blackman, 2009), China (Head et al., 2006; Nyberg and Jensen, 2009) Israel and South Korea (Raz, 2009), India (Rao and Vijayalakshmi, 2000), and Japan (Kyjar, 2007). Arguably, this level of international interest in organizational change reflects the scale of the socio-economic change which is evident in both developed and less developed countries across the world (Rees and Miazhevich, 2009). This socio-economic change, often described using adjectives such as 'tumultuous' (Darling and Heller, 2009), 'unprecedented' (Newman, 1998), and 'radical' (Alas and Rees, 2006), inevitably impacts upon organizations and raises serious questions about how change should be led and managed at the organizational level.

While globalization may have resulted in opportunities for those working in the field of OD to engage and practice in an array of different environments, this expansion of the geographical field of practice calls into question the nature of OD that is being practised in these various settings. For example, at a basic level, in diverse cultural settings, what are OD practitioners attempting to achieve? There is evidence that OD practice does vary according to the context in which it is taking place (Fagenson-Eland et al., 2004; Head and Sorensen, 1993). Writing about the implications of globalization for Human Resource Management (HRM) roles generally (as opposed to OD roles specifically), Friedman (2007: 162) proposes that there is a global challenge for HRM change agents in facilitating 'change that comprehends cultural differences and local customs'. For example, he states that 'equalitarian-based interventions such as empowerment and participatory decision-making may meet leadership resistance where power distance is high'. Yet, this variation in practice strikes at the heart of the nature of OD, for if OD practices vary according to geographical contexts, do the values underpinning international OD interventions also vary from one national context to context? If so, this raises many challenges and dilemmas for those seeking to explain the nature of OD as well for those seeking to practice OD in international contexts.

OD values and international OD

When designing OD interventions, assessments have to be made as to whether, in terms of ethics, the intervention is fundamentally morally right or morally wrong. For example, the design of an OD intervention may raise issues such as: Is it right to employ children on a full-time basis? Is the payment of bribes sometimes acceptable? Should women be segregated from men in the workplace? Should women receive the same pay as men for doing the same work? Should workers be paid a minimum wage? Do workers have a right to rest breaks? Should work processes be made as interesting as possible for the workers possibly at the expense of productivity? Different people, using their own values systems, are likely to provide different answers to these types of ethical questions when issues arise in OD work. McDevitt et al. (2007) propose that ethical decision-making of this nature involves the interaction of *individual variables* (for example, age, gender, religious beliefs, locus of control), *organizational variables* (for example, peer influence, organizational goals, rewards and punishments, leadership, availability of resources), and the *external environment* (for example, competitors, societal norms, legal system, personal and family obligations). In a specific OD intervention, specific individual, organizational, and external environmental variables are likely to exert relatively strong or relatively weak influence in decision-making processes surrounding the intervention. For example, in some cases, societal norms and the legal system will, to all intents and purposes, dictate how these types of questions are answered at the organizational level.

It should be noted that there is an informative and established body of work that has examined from a value-based perspective the role in different national settings of what has been termed here classical OD. Aspects of this literature directly explore the fit between OD values and national cultures (Lau et al., 1996; White and Rhodeback, 1992). However, although there is open recognition that OD designs are not homogeneous in nature (Golembiewski, 1991: 40), the discussion of fit between OD values and national cultures has tended to assume, albeit on occasions with some reservations (Johnson and Golembiewski, 1992), that OD practitioners possess and promote the humanistic values that have been traditionally associated with classical OD (Head and Sorensen, 1993; Jaeger, 1986) As a result, discussion of the use of OD in international contexts has often wrestled with the issue of the extent to which OD technologies should be adapted to suit cultural contexts (Fagenson-Eland et al., 2004) rather than with changing OD values to fit various international contexts. For example, Golembiewski and Luo (1994: 296) suggest that OD practitioners involved with cross-cultural applications of OD see themselves as working towards their values 'rather than insisting on them ab initio ... For most practical purposes then, the issues for ODers relate to the scope and speed of the progress beyond the original condition and toward closer approximations to OD values'.

What is apparent from the above discussion about recent developments in the general field of OD is that there is now real debate surrounding the very nature of OD (Weidner II, 2004). Hence, discussions surrounding its use in international contexts cannot be based on the assumption that change interventions labelled as OD are based upon the humanistic values that classical OD theorists promulgated. In his discussion of making OD global, Shevat (2003: 92) argues that there are now many, what he terms, OD dialects; he suggests that the two most prominent dialects are the 'dialect of the more traditional value driven OD person and the dialect of the management consultant'. This is a useful distinction in that it highlights that the values of OD practitioners vary and this variation in the OD practitioners' values (rather than solely differences in national cultures and norms) will lead to differences in OD practices in international settings. That is, in situations where the values prevalent in a particular international context tend to vary dramatically from the values espoused by the OD practitioner, there are a number of approaches that the OD practitioner may adopt (see Table 5.1).

Table 5.1 Value-based OD approaches in international settings

OD Approaches and International Settings	Summary Explanation	Summary Justification	Summary Criticism
Isolationist	The OD practitioner rejects work in certain international contexts because the prevalent contextual values conflict with the values held by the OD practitioner. Further, the OD practitioner is likely to cause unnecessary tension and conflict within these contexts.	The values held by the practitioner are non-negotiable. The OD practitioner working in a value-challenged context may, by association, be seen to be condoning unethical working practices	Isolationism is unlikely to bring about incremental changes to the values prevalent in certain international contexts. Exposure to alternative values may result in incremental value-related changes which improve the lives of those working in disadvantageous contexts.
Missionary	The OD practitioner attempts to change the values of those present in the context to match the values held by the OD practitioner. Values which the OD practitioner finds unacceptable in the local context are identified and challenged and, if possible, changed through change interventions.	Certain values relate to absolute standards which are cross-culturally transferable. Some of the values prevalent in certain international contexts need to be changed. The OD practitioner is in an ideal position to challenge unacceptable work practices and the values that underpin them.	This approach is underpinned by the view that the OD practitioner's values are superior to the values held by locals in certain international contexts. Further, the OD practitioner works for the client not vice versa.
Complaisant	The OD practitioner, while retaining certain non-negotiable core values, actively seeks to adapt the values underpinning change interventions to suit local values held in international contexts.	OD practitioners should be accommodating in their approach and accept that, within certain parameters, it is for clients to decide the values that they wish to promote in the workplace.	The boundaries between the OD practitioner's negotiable and non-negotiable values are likely to become blurred and result in tension between clients and OD practitioners.
Chameleonic	The OD practitioner adopts, wholesale, the values held by those working in the international context, particularly the values held by the commissioning client.	It is not for OD practitioners to seek to change values which, for example, underpin longstanding local traditions and customs. OD practitioners are not revolutionists.	The approach is a mercenary form of change management practice. In the absence of value-based boundaries maintained by the OD practitioner, anything becomes permissible under the guise of OD.

Thus, in an international context in which bribery is commonplace, some OD practitioners may decide to act as *isolationists* and refuse to work in this setting. Alternatively, other OD practitioners may view a particular OD assignment as an opportunity to change the values of local workers who consider bribery to be an acceptable form of business practice; in such situations some OD practitioners may approach the assignment with a *missionary* zeal. Another more *complaisant* approach that some OD practitioners could adopt is to encourage the local workforce in this setting to explore the effects of bribery without necessarily taking a standpoint as to whether bribery is, for example, to be condemned in all settings. In real-life settings, there is a further possibility that some OD practitioners could change in a *chameleonic* manner in order to fit in with the prevalent values in a given international context; in an extreme case, this may even involve adopting the values prevalent in the international context in order to obtain the OD assignment in the first place.

The literature discussed above indicates that people who call themselves OD practitioners are adopting a range of value-based approaches in international settings. This has implications for the manner in which OD is practised at the different stages of the OD process described above. For example, as noted above, the initial stage of OD is typically used to clarify boundaries and to initiate working relationships between OD practitioners and their clients (Rees, 2008b). The current uncertainty surrounding the value base of OD does, however, reveal the emergent need for both OD practitioners and clients to engage in a two-way clarification of the values that they wish to promote through an OD intervention. Arguably, when engaging in this clarification of values, the OD practitioner becomes a participant in the OD process rather than a traditional facilitator who is there to help clients to reach an understanding of the values that they wish to integrate into the OD intervention. In some international settings, there is a case for arguing that OD practitioners should play an active role in discussions surrounding issues such as bribery and empowerment in order for both the clients and individual OD practitioners to understand their respective value frameworks. Given the range of people who now call themselves OD practitioners, these discussions, perhaps involving the use of real-life examples of ethical dilemmas (see Scenarios 1 and 2 below), are necessary to reveal similarities and differences between the values of an OD practitioner and the values prevalent in an international setting.

Scenario 1: bribery

This is a real-life example of a scenario which, through discussion with potential clients, may reveal the extent of an OD practitioner's willingness to work in an international setting where bribery is endemic throughout an organization and national culture.

You recently commenced work as a senior police officer in a former Soviet state. One day, one of your traffic officers comes to see you. He explains that he is experiencing some financial difficulties after paying for his daughter to have urgent medical treatment. He asks you to move him from patrolling a 60km per hour zone to patrolling a 40km per hour zone. He openly acknowledges to you that he wants to move his patrol area as this will enable him to obtain more bribes from the motorists he stops for speeding. As his commanding officer, how would you deal with his request?

Scenario 2: openness and empowerment

This is a real-life example which challenges OD practitioners to assess the extent to which values traditionally associated with OD theory and practice such as openness and empowerment, are negotiable in complex international settings.

You work as a senior logistics manager for a humanitarian relief agency. Following an environmental catastrophe in a strictly Muslim country in Asia, your agency arranges to distribute food among those who have been made homeless. The food is urgently needed. Just before the food distribution begins, you receive a telephone call from the food supplier. She tells you that there has been a mistake in the food–manufacturing process. Apparently, while the food is perfectly safe, it contains alcohol. This alcohol was included as a preservative albeit in relatively small amounts. The food labels do not indicate the existence of the alcohol. The supplier offers to replace the food. After seeking further information, you estimate that there will be a delay of approximately four weeks regardless of whether the food is replaced by the original supplier or alternatively sourced. You realize that though, from a faith perspective, the circumstances probably permit the food to be consumed, some of the people may nevertheless refuse the food if they know it contains alcohol. Further, if it becomes common knowledge that the food contains alcohol, local distributors and tribal leaders (rather than the homeless people) may refuse to handle it; hence the homeless people themselves may not be given the opportunity to decide whether to eat the food or not as it may never reach them. In your role as senior logistics manager, how will you handle this situation?

It is highlighted that the subject of value-related dilemmas in international OD has been explored in OD literature. For example, White and Rhodeback (1992: 669), using a scenario-based research approach, concluded that there was a need for '...OD practitioner training directed at enhancing an understanding of cross-cultural differences in ethical values'. However, the developments which are discussed above indicate that a major challenge facing OD is whether to accommodate the wide range of different cultural values that are apparent in international settings and, as importantly, whether to accept the wide range of different values that are now evident among those who call themselves OD practitioners.

Conclusion

The chapter has considered the manner in which classical OD has developed from a distinct approach to organizational change and development based on humanistic values to a more amorphous field of change–management theory and practice. It has been argued that this development is, in part, evident in the reported convergence between OD practice and performance-based management functions and practices such as HRM and TQM. One of the contributions of the chapter is to highlight that the diversity of value frameworks which are used by OD practitioners will inevitably result in the use of different approaches to OD in international settings where the prevailing values may or may not complement the individualistic values of the OD practitioner. These differences in approaches extend beyond differences in the use of OD technologies. Whereas classical OD may once have presented a fairly uniform set of humanistic values against which to assess value-based OD dilemmas in international settings, the situation has become all the more complex owing to the diverse values and practices that have emerged within the field of OD itself. As a result, it has been proposed in this chapter that OD practitioners, particularly those working in complex international settings, will be required, on an increasingly frequent basis, to move from an OD facilitation role to the role of an OD participant in order to understand their own values and the compatibility of these values with those that are present or desired in the clients' national cultures and organizations.

The inextricable link between change management and values has been emphasized in this chapter. The specific case of OD serves to highlight the complexities surrounding value-based change-management interventions that are being implemented on an increasingly frequent basis in a plethora of different international contexts. Over past years, professional organizations in the field of OD have, commendably, sought to articulate the values that have traditionally been associated with their discipline (for example, see OD Institute, 1991; OD Network, 2008). Yet, the value-based challenges that OD professionals now face in relation to the practice of OD in international settings indicate that there is an emerging need for developments in the general field of organizational change to be informed by concepts and themes associated with fields such as business ethics and international development. Thus, while concerns relating to, for example, child labour, religion, equal pay, punishment, and bribery may, to an extent, be viewed as fairly peripheral concerns in change-management literature emanating from Western countries, wider literature indicates that these types of concerns are relevant to organizational change practices in some contexts (Bartram et al., 2009; Debrah, 2007; Lévy, 2007; Renwick, 2009). One of the conclusions drawn from this discussion is that, as the international nature of change-management theory and practice becomes more apparent, so too will questions surrounding the aims and values which underpin change management interventions in international contexts.

References

Agócs, C. (1997) Institutionalized Resistance to Organizational Change: Denial, Inaction and Repression. *Journal of Business Ethics*, 16(9): 917–31.

Alas, R. and Rees, C.J. (2006) Work-related Attitudes, Values and Radical Change in Post-Socialist Contexts: A Comparative Study. *Journal of Business Ethics*, 68(2): 181–89.

Bartram, T., Stanton, P., and Thomas, K. (2009) Good Morning Vietnam: New Challenges for HRM. *Management Research News*, 32(10): 891–904.

Beckhard, R. (1969) *Organization Development: Strategies and Models*. Reading, MA: Addison Wesley Publishing.

Brown, D. and Harvey B. (2005) *An Experiential Approach to Organization Development* (7th edn). Englewood Cliffs, NJ: Prentice-Hall.

Burnes, B. (2004) Kurt Lewin and the Planned Approach to Change: A Reappraisal. *Journal of Management Studies*, 41(6): 977–1002.

Cummings, T.G. and Worley, C.G (2009) *Organization Development and Change* (9th edn). Mason, OH: South-Western Cengage Learning.

Darling, J.R. and Heller, V.L. (2009) Organization Development in an Era of Socioeconomic Change: A Focus on The Key to Successful Management Leadership. *Organization Development Journal*, 27(2): 9– 26.

Deaner, C.M.D. (1994) A Model of Organization Development Ethics. *Public Administration Quarterly*, 17(4): 435–46.

Debrah, Y. (2007) Promoting the Informal Sector as a Source of Gainful Employment in Developing Countries: Insights from Ghana. *International Journal of Human Resource Management*, 18(6): 1063–84.

Egan, T.M. (2002) Organization Development: An Examination of Definitions and Dependent Variables. *Organization Development Journal*, 20(2): 59–69.

Ellis, F. (2007) The Benefits of Partnership for OD and HR. *Strategic HR Review*, 6(4): 32–35.

Fagenson-Eland, E., Ensher, E.A. and Burke, W.W. (2004) Organization Development and Change Interventions: A Seven-Nation Comparison. *Journal of Applied Behavioral Science*, 40(4): 432–64.

Friedman, B.A. (2007) Globalization Implications for Human Resource Management Roles. *Employee Responsibilities and Rights Journal*, 19(3): 157–71.

Golembiewski, R.T. (1991) Organizational Development in the Third World: Values, Closeness of Fit and Culture-Boundness. *International Journal of Human Resource Management*, 2(1): 39–53.

Golembiewski, R.T. and Luo, H. (1994) OD Applications in Developmental Settings: An Addendum About Success Rates. *International Journal of Organizational Analysis*, 2(3): 295–308.

Head, T.C., Gong, C., Ma, C., Sorensen, P.F. and Yaeger, T. (2006) Chinese Executives' Assessment of Organization Development Interventions. *Organization Development Journal*, 24(1): 28–40.

Head, T.C. and Sorensen, P.F. (1993) Cultural Values and Organizational Development: A Seven-Country Study. *Leadership and Organization Development Journal*, 14(2): 3–7.

Hornstein, H. (2001) Organizational Development and Change Management: Don't Throw the Baby Out with the Bath Water. *The Journal of Applied Behavioral Science*, 37(2): 223–26.

Hubbell, L. (2004) Struggling with the Issue of Who the Client is in Organization Development Interventions. *Leadership and Organization Development Journal*, 25(5): 399–410.

Jaeger, A.M. (1986) Organization Development and National Culture: Where's the Fit? *Academy of Management Review*, 11(1): 178–90.

James, R. (2004) Exploring OD in Africa: a Response to David Lewis. *Nonprofit Management and Leadership*, 14(3): 313–24.

Johnson, K.R. and Golembiewski, R.T. (1992) National Culture in Organization Development: A Conceptual and Empirical Analysis. *International Journal of Human Resource Management*, 3(1): 71–84.

Kyjar, R.C. (2007) A Time of Transition: Lessons in Global OD from a Successful Japanese Firm. *Organization Development Journal*, 25(3): 11–16.

Lau, C., McMahan, G.C., and Woodman, R.W. (1996) An International Comparison of Organization Development Practices: The USA and Hong Kong. *Journal of Organizational Change Management*, 9(2): 4–19.

Lévy, B. (2007) The Interface Between Globalization, Trade and Development: Theoretical Issues for International Business Studies. *International Business Review*, 16(5): 594–612.

Lipton, M. (1996) When Clients Resist Change. *Consulting to Management*, 9(2): 16–21.

Margulies, N. and Raia, A. (1990) 'The Significance of Core Values on the Theory and Practice of Organizational Development'. In F. Massarick (ed.), *Advances in Organization Development* (Vol. 1). Norwood: Ablex Publishing, pp. 27–41.

Marshak, R.J. and Grant, D. (2008) Organizational Discourse and New Organization Development Practices. *British Journal of Management*, 19: S7–S19.

McDevitt, R., Giapponi, C. and Tromley, C. (2007) A Model of Ethical Decision Making: The Integration of Process and Content. *Journal of Business Ethics*, 73: 219–29.

McKendall, M. (1993) The Tyranny of Change: Organizational Development Revisited. *Journal of Business Ethics*, 12(2): 93–104.

McLean, G.N. (2007) *Organization Development: Principles, Processes, Performance*. San Francisco: Berrett-Koehler.

McLean, G. and Egan, T.M. (2008) Applying Organization Development Tools in Scenario Planning. *Advances in Developing Human Resources*, 10(2): 240–57.

Meglino, B.M. and Revlin, E.C. (1998) Individual Values in Organizations: Concepts, Controversies and Research. *Journal of Management*, 24(3): 351–89.

Mozenter, J. (2002) Recent Research Links: Macro forces, Emerging Trends and OD's Expanding Role. *Organization Development Journal*, 20(2): 48–57.

Newman, K.L. (1998) Leading Radical Change in Transition Economies. *Leadership and Organization Development Journal*, 19(6): 309–24.

Neumann, J.E., Lau, C.M. and Worley, C.G. (2009) Ready for Consideration: International Organizational Development and Change as an Emerging Field of Practice. *Journal of Applied Behavioral Science*, 45(2): 171–85.

Nyberg, R.S. and Jensen, T.C. (2009) Honoring the Kun Lun Way: Cross-Cultural Organization Development Consulting to a Hospitality Company in Datong, China. *Journal of Applied Behavioral Science*, 45(2): 305–37.

OD Institute (1991) *The International Organization Development Code Of Ethics* (December, 1991, 22nd Revision). Available on-line from: www.odinstitute.org/ethics.htm (accessed 25 May 2010).

OD Network (2008) *Principles of OD Practice*. Available online from: www.odnetwork.org/aboutod/principles.php (accessed 25th May 2010).

O'Flynn, J. and Blackman, D. (2009) Experimenting with Organisational Development in Bhutan: A Tool for Reform and the Achievement of Multi-level Goals? *Public Administration and Development*, 29(2): 133–44.

Pettigrew, A.M., Woodman, R.W., and Cameron, K.S. (2001) Studying Organizational Change and Development: Challenges for Future Research. *Academy of Management Journal*, 44(4): 697–713.

Piotrowski, C. and Armstrong. T.R. (2005) Major Research Areas in Organization Development. *Organization Development Journal*, 23(4): 86–91.

Quijano-Ramos, C.V. and Rees C.J. (2008) The Current State of Organization Development: Organizational Perspectives from Western Europe. *Organization Development Journal*, 26(4): 67–80.

Rao, T.V. and Vijayalakshmi, M. (2000) Organization Development in India. *Organization Development Journal*, 18(1): 51–63.

Raz, A.E. (2009) Transplanting Management: Participative Change, Organizational Development, and the Glocalization of Corporate Culture. *Journal of Applied Behavioral Science*, 45(2): 280–304.

Rees, C.J. (2008a) Editorial: Organisational Change and Development: Perspectives on Theory and Practice. *Journal of Business Economics and Management*, 9(2): 87–89.

Rees, C.J. (2008b) Organization Development in the 21st Century. In C. Wankel (ed.) *Handbook of 21st Century Management*. New York: Sage Publications, pp. 433–41.

Rees, C.J. and Miazhevich, G. (2009) Socio-Cultural Change and Business Ethics in Post-Soviet Countries: The Cases of Belarus and Estonia. *Journal of Business Ethics*, 86(1): 51–63.

Rees, C.J. and Sharifi, S. (2002) Organisation Development: From Beliefs to Practice. *Zagreb International Review of Economics and Business*, 5: 109–22.

Renwick, D. (2009) The Origins of Employee Wellbeing in Brazil: An Exploratory Analysis. *Employee Relations*, 31(3): 312–21.

Rokeach, M. (1973) *The Nature of Human Values*. New York: Free Press.

Rogers, C.R. (1945) The Nondirective Method as a Technique for Social Research. *American Journal of Sociology*, 50(4): 279–83.

Ruona, W.E. and Gibson, S.K. (2004) The Making of Twenty-first Century HR: An Analysis of the Convergence of HRM, HRD and OD. *Human Resource Management*, 43(1): 49–66.

Schifo, R. (2004) OD in Ten Words or Less: Adding Lightness to the Definitions of Organizational Development. *Organization Development Journal*, 22(3): 74–85.

Schwarz, G.M. and Huber, G.P. (2008) Challenging Organizational Change Research. *British Journal of Management*, 19: S1–S6.

Shevat, A. (2003) Making OD Global. *Organization Development Journal*, 21(2): 87–92.

Ukpata, I.S. and Olukotun, G.A. (2008) The Effect of Organizational Development on the Nigerian Economy. *African Journal of Business Management*, 2(5): 85–92.

Van Eynde, D.F., Church, A., Hurley, R.F. and Burke, W.W. (1992) What OD Practitioners Believe. *Training and Development*, 46(4): 41–44.

Warwick, D. (1978) 'Moral Dilemmas in Organizational Development'. In G. Bermant, H. Kelman, and D. Warwick (eds), *The Ethics of Social Intervention*. Washington, DC: Hemisphere Publishing.

Weidner II, C.K. (2004) A Brand in Dire Straits: Organization Development at Sixty. *Organization Development Journal*, 22(2): 37–47.

White, L.P. and Rhodeback, M.J. (1992) Ethical Dilemmas in Organization Development: A Cross-Cultural Analysis. *Journal of Business Ethics*, 11: 663–70.

Wirtenberg, J., Abrams, L. and Ott, C. (2004) Assessing the Field of Organization Development. *Journal of Applied Behavioral Science*, 40(4): 465–79.

Wooten, K.C. (2008) Ethical Issues Facing OD in the New Paradigm Organizations: Back to the Future. *Organization Development Journal*, 26(4): 11–23.

Worren, N.A.M., Ruddle, K. and Moore, K. (1999) From Organizational Development to Change Management: The Emergence of a New Profession. *Journal of Applied Behavioral Science*, 35(3): 273–85.

Zaldivar, S.M. (2008) International Development Through OD: My Experience in Afghanistan. *OD Practitioner*, 40(1): 4–9.

6

Appreciative Inquiry
Theory and critique

Gervase R. Bushe

Appreciative Inquiry (AI) was one of the first post-Lewinian organization development (OD) methods and probably catalysed the subsequent proliferation of dialogic OD methods (Bushe and Marshak, 2009) that operate outside the Lewinian paradigm. Firmly grounded in social constructionist theory (Gergen, 1978; 2009), AI emerged out of the Department of Organizational Behavior (OB) at Case Western Reserve University in Cleveland, Ohio and many academic writers on AI received their doctorates there (e.g. Barrett, Bright, Bushe, Carter, Cooperrider, Johnson, Ludema, Powley, Sekerka, Stavros, Thatchenkery). Eschewing "diagnosis" as a necessary or even useful step in organizational change, and incorporating post-modern perspectives on narrative and discourse (Barrett, Thomas and Hocevar, 1995), the original, seminal article on AI (Cooperrider and Srivastva, 1987) was a revolutionary statement and a precursor to later developments in "positive organizational studies" (Cameron et al., 2003) and the "strengths based" movement (Buckingham and Clifton, 2001; Cameron and Lavine, 2006) in American management.

This review begins with a brief description of the AI method followed by the underlying theories of change that support AI practice and the rather scanty evidence that exists supporting them. This review will also consider moderators of AI practice and important critiques of AI, and conclude with some of the more pressing research questions that require addressing for a deeper understanding of how and when AI transforms organizations.

The method of Appreciative Inquiry

David Cooperrider, the creator of AI, resisted writing a book on how to do AI until the turn of the millennium because he wanted people to focus on the philosophy behind this approach and not see it as a technique. As a result, many different ways of doing AI have proliferated and it is inaccurate to say AI is done in any one way. For the first 15 years or so AI practitioners based their methods on the initial set of four principles (Cooperrider and Srivastva, 1987) which stated that inquiry into the social potential of a social system should begin with appreciation, should be collaborative, should be provocative and should be applicable. The original method called for a collective discovery process using (1) grounded observation to identify the best of what is,

(2) vision and logic to identify ideals of what might be, (3) collaborative dialogue and choice to achieve consent about what should be, and (4) collective experimentation to discover what can be. It was not until 1997 that the 4D model of AI, now almost universally described as *the* AI method, was created. Diana Whitney, Cooperrider's collaborator on some of the first AI projects in the 1990s, had a major impact on the evolution of the practice of AI and the most authoritative sources on AI practice are Cooperrider et al. (2008), Ludema et al. (2003), and Whitney and Trosten-Bloom (2003). The general outline of the 4D method is as follows:

1   *Discovery*. During this stage participants reflect on and discuss the best of *what is* concerning the object of inquiry. Sometimes it is an inquiry into the "life giving properties" of the organization (Cooperrider and Srivastva, 1987). Sometimes it is the "positive core" (Cooperrider and Whitney, 2001), where an attempt is made to catalogue the signature strengths of the organization (Ludema et al., 2003). Other times it is a specific capacity or process. For example, if the inquiry is about improving customer service, participants might inquire into their best experiences as a customer, or the best experiences of their customers, or study the best customer-service organizations they can find. The extent to which the fruits of this inquiry are then analysed or summarized varies widely by application. Most often (and this appears to be a key innovation of the AI method) participants are interviewed about their own "best of" experience. Another important innovation has been to have organizational stakeholders act as both interviewers and interviewees, that is, to fully engage all members in the act of inquiry itself (Carter and Johnson, 1999).

2   *Dream*. During this stage participants are asked to imagine their group, organization or community at its best and an attempt is made to identify the common aspirations of system members and to symbolize this in some way. The amount of preparation and the degree to which clarity about that common dream are sought vary widely by application. The dream phase often results in something more symbolic, like a graphical representation, than a mission statement.

3   *Design*. With a common dream in place, participants are asked to develop concrete proposals for the new organizational state. Initially Cooperrider called these "provocative propositions" – a phrase linked to generative theory (discussed below) that still appears in some models. More commonly, social architecture processes are employed where a model of design elements is used to identify categories for participants to organize around and create change proposals, often called possibility statements or design statements. (Mohr et al., 2003; Watkins and Mohr, 2001). Often, participants self-select into small groups to develop specific proposals within a specific category The design company IDEO (Brown, 2009) has been both a source of ideas and a participant in the evolution of the design phase of AI, and use of rapid prototyping processes is increasingly common.

4   *Delivery/Destiny*. In the initial 4D model the fourth stage was called Delivery but this was subsequently changed by Cooperrider to Destiny as he found that Delivery evoked images of traditional change-management implementation. Exactly what ought to happen in this phase has provoked the most confusion and the least consensus amongst AI advocates who recognize that using the outcomes of Design to create new targets, gaps to fill and objectives to achieve is counter to the very philosophy of AI. At the same time, one of the most common complaints about AI from users is that while energy for change is high after the Design phase, implementation can be very spotty.

Building on Barrett's (1998) work on improvisational processes in organizations, I have described Bushe (2007, 2010b; Bushe and Kassam, 2005) an improvisational as opposed to implementation approach to Destiny consistent with a vaguely developing consensus on the topic. In this approach, widespread agreement for the design statements is sought, an event is orchestrated where participants make self-chosen, personal commitments to take action consistent with any design element and leadership makes clear that there will be no action plans or committees – instead everyone is authorized to take those actions they believe will help bring the design to fruition. Leadership's role then becomes "tracking and fanning" (Bushe, 2009), finding and amplifying those innovations they want to nurture, and creating events and processes to energize self-organizing momentum.

A number of practitioner critiques pointed out that the 4D model omitted an important first step in the AI process of identifying the focus of the inquiry itself. The Clergy Leadership Institute in the US suggested "Define" as the first step and some AI models refer to a 5D model. Cooperrider's dissertation called this the "affirmative topic" and many models have retained that label. How, exactly, that topic is defined has not been well articulated but is generally regarded as essential to the overall success of the effort. Engaging the right people, especially powerful sponsors, in identifying a focus that is both of high interest to those leading the organization and will be compelling to stakeholders, is commonly held to be critical to overall success (Barrett and Fry, 2005).

Whitney and Trosten-Bloom (2003) identified eight "forms of engagement" used by AI practitioners. These ranged from interventions where a sole consultant or a small representative group of people do the AI on behalf of a larger group of people to those where most or all of the whole system is engaged in the entire 4D process. The majority of case studies of transformational change have been of the latter variety (Barrett and Fry, 2005; Barros and Cooperrider, 2000; Bushe and Kassam, 2005; Fry et al., 2002; Ludema et al., 2003; Ludema and Hinrichs, 2003; Powley et al., 2004) leading to an increasing emphasis in the AI literature on widespread engagement as central to successful AI change efforts (Bushe, 2011 in press; Cooperrider and Sekerka, 2006; Mee-Yan and Powley, 2006). The Appreciative Inquiry Summit (Ludema et al., 2003; Whitney and Cooperrider, 2000), which has probably become the most often advocated form of engagement, melds elements of Future Search (Emery and Purser, 1996; Weisbord, 1993) with AI.

Theoretical bases of Appreciative Inquiry

In their seminal article (Cooperrider and Srivastva, 1987) argued three main points in support of AI. First, they critiqued the problem-solving approach that, at that time, dominated action research, arguing that problem-solving, as a tool for social innovation, did not do a very good job and might, in fact be counterproductive. Second, they argued that organizations were best viewed as socially constructed realities, and that forms of organization were constrained only by human imagination and the shared beliefs of organizational members. As socially constructed realities, forms of inquiry were potent in constructing the systems they inquired into, and that problem-solving approaches were just as likely to create more of the very problems they were intended to solve. Third, they argued that the most important force for change were new ideas. They decried the lack of new ideas generated by conventional action research, and proposed AI as a method that was more likely to create new ideas, images, and theories that would lead to social innovations.

As the method of AI has evolved, so have the theoretical justifications and explanations for AI as a change process. The most influential statement has been Cooperrider and Whitney's (2001) five principles of AI. While some have proposed additional principles (Barrett and Fry, 2005; Whitney and Trosten-Bloom, 2003), these five have been the most widely accepted, showing up in reviews of AI (Bushe and Kassam, 2005) and non-organizational applications of AI (e.g. Stavros and Torres, 2005; Kelm, 2005). As scholars study the successes and failures of AI, a variety of underlying change mechanism have surfaced and are identifiable. In the remainder of this section ten of the theoretical levers for change underlying AI practice are reviewed.

Inquiry as intervention

Appreciative Inquiry did not begin life as an organizational change technique – it began as a research method for making grounded theory building more generative (Cooperrider, 1986; Cooperrider and Sekerka, 2006). A key underlying theory of change in AI comes from a constructive reimagining of postmodern theory. Acknowledging that all social research is inherently biased by the positioning of the researcher, Cooperrider argued this was not a reason to throw up our hands and give up the pursuit of knowledge. On the contrary, it frees us to take the idea that organizations are made and imagined to its logical conclusion: that organizational inquiry is simultaneously the production of self-and-world. What researchers choose to study and how they study it creates as much as it discovers the world, and therefore a wide field of creative, positive, possibility beckons to us (Cooperrider et al., 1995).

This is the first and most important contribution that AI made to a post-Lewinian theory of organizational change. In the modernist mind-set of the Lewinian action-research model, and most change-management models, the purpose of questions is to uncover data – to discover what is there. In the post-modern social constructionism of AI, questions are seen as actually creating what is there. Questions about conflict create more conflict. Questions about the life-giving properties of the organization create more vitality. AI theorists have stressed the importance of the questions that guide the inquiry process (Barrett and Fry, 2005; Ludema, Cooperrider and Barrett, 2000; Whitney and Cooperrider, 2001). I argue (2011) that a lack of attention to the generative potential of questions used in AI processes may explain why some interventions succeed and some fail.

Generativity

Kenneth Gergen's (1978; 1982) concept of generative theory is central to understanding AI's theory of practice. Gergen proposed that we should aim to create a social science focused on its "generative capacity" defined as the "... capacity to challenge the guiding assumptions of the culture, to raise fundamental questions regarding contemporary social life, to foster reconsideration of that which is 'taken for granted' and thereby furnish new alternatives for social actions" (1978, p.1346). AI was developed as a methodology that would meet Gergen's criteria.

The first AI change project focused on the idea of "generative metaphor" as an engine for change (Barrett and Cooperrider, 1990). My studies (Bushe, 1998) of AI in teams found that AI can surface generative metaphors capable of resolving the kind of paradoxical dilemmas (Smith and Berg, 1987) that get groups stuck. My research (Bushe, 2010b, 2011, Bushe and Kassam, 2005) has found that the generativity of AI is a key variable associated with transformational change outcomes.

> AI can be generative in a number of ways. It is the quest for new ideas, images, theories and models that liberate our collective aspirations, alter the social construction of reality and, in the process, make available decisions and actions that were not available or did not occur to us before. When successful, AI generates spontaneous, unsupervised, individual, group and organizational action toward a better future.
>
> (Bushe, 2007: 30)

90

The importance of generativity is encased in Cooperrider and Whitney's (2001) constructionist principle, which has been boiled down to a saying popular in AI circles that "words create worlds". This also highlights the important connections between generativity and discourse.

Discourse and narrative

Appreciative Inquiry is heavily influenced by theories of discourse and narrative especially as applied to organizational change (Barrett et al., 1995; Boje, 1991; Marshak and Grant, 2008; Oswick, Grant, Michaelson and Wailes, 2005). In their poetic principle, Cooperrider and Whitney (2001) propose that organizations are more like a book than a living organism, that organizational life is expressed in the stories people tell each other every day, and the story of the organization is constantly being co-authored. The initial storytelling that participants engage in, when they describe their "best of" stories, is a key innovation of the AI method and widely regarded as essential for setting the tone of an AI intervention (Ludema, 2002; Khalsa, 2002). Barrett and Fry (2005) stress the impact that telling and hearing stories has on participants as a catalyst for change. They propose that stories heard and told during the Discovery phase have a positive impact on relationships, reveal deeply held values and provide coherence and meaning. I describe (2001) how AI can elicit new stories that change the taken for granted assumptions in a group and as a result, change the behaviours of group members quite profoundly. Ludema (2002) argues that the collection, telling, and re-telling of people's best of stories results in a wave of countervailing micro-narratives that combine, over time, to change the prevailing macro-narrative of the organization.

Discursive theories stress that it is through relationships that words come to have meaning and through discourse that relationships are created, maintained and changed. AI theorists stress the importance of word choice from the moment of contact between AI practitioner and client system (Cooperrider and Whitney, 2001). Calling for the "unconditional positive question" (Ludema, Cooperrider and Barrett, 2000) they argue that the language of inquiry shapes the relationships that get formed and the entire process of inquiry (Barrett and Fry, 2005). AI advocates note that organizations consist of multiple stories and perspectives and seek to ensure that no particular history or story is considered more significant than another (Whitney, 1996). They note that in every culture or organization there are marginalized voices and that these voices are often the ones where important innovations reside (Whitney, 1996; Whitney and Trosten-Bloom, 2003). They describe AI as a process where such marginalized voices are more likely to be heard and received.

Anticipatory reality

In one of his first theoretical statements, Cooperrider (1990) proposed a "heliocentric hypothesis" to support the AI practice of inquiring into the most positive images members hold of their organizations. This hypothesis proposed that in every social system members hold an implicit or explicit image of the system at its very best, what Cooperrider called the affirmative image, and, just as plants grow towards the light, social systems naturally evolve towards the prevailing affirmative image. Therefore, conscious evolution of the system's affirmative image is a viable path for organization development.

In his later writing, Cooperrider dropped the heliotropic hypothesis and offered a more Heideggarian formulation with his "anticipatory principle" (McAdam and Mirza, 2009):

> Much like a movie projector on a screen, human systems are forever projecting ahead of themselves a horizon of expectation (in their talk in the hallways, in the metaphors and

language they use) that brings the future powerfully into the present as a mobilizing agent. To inquire in ways that serves to refashion anticipatory reality – especially the artful creation of positive imagery on a collective basis – may be the most prolific thing any inquiry can do.

(Cooperrider and Whitney, 2001: 21)

The idea of anticipatory reality as a change lever can be found in a variety of change processes that endorse a "possibility centric versus a problem centric" approach to organizational change (Boyd and Bright, 2007). Boyd and Bright argue that problem-centric change processes assume that something is broken and needs fixing, thus making organizational members more wary of consultants and change agents. This, they argue, makes it more likely that organizational members will be more defensive and resistant to the change processes and more focused on self-interests than the common good. The conservative press of fear and negative emotions make it less likely that current norms will be transformed. Focusing inquiry on positive possibilities, they argue, builds relationships and trust and identifies possibilities for shifting normative expectations.

Recently, Bright and Cameron (2009) have revisited the heliotropic hypothesis, arguing that research on positive organizational climates, positive energy networks and high-quality relationships substantiate the proposition that heliotropism exists in social organizations. They also point out that since "bad is stronger than good" (Baumeister et al., 2001) an emphasis on the positive must be sufficiently pervasive and strong enough to overcome the natural tendency of people and organizations to be more effected by negative events, situations and interactions than positive ones.

Positive affect

While the anticipatory principle focuses on the utility of positive images for supporting change, Cooperrider and Whitney's (2001) "positive principle" highlights the utility of positive affect for building rapport among people to support and sustain change processes. Cooperrider and Sekerka (2006) assert that inquiry into what people appreciate strengthens their relationships and increases positive emotions. They argue that elevation of positive emotions is a first and vital step in the change process. They point to studies that show positive feelings lead people to be more flexible, creative, integrative, open to information and efficient in their thinking (Isen, 2000). People experiencing positive affect are more resilient and able to cope with occasional adversity, have an increased preference for variety and accept a broader array of behavioural options (Fredrickson, 2001, 2006). Closely aligned is Ludema's articulation of the nature and importance of hope for organizational change (Ludema et al., 1997) and the way in which AI can provide hope (Ludema, 2000).

I contend (2007, 2011) that it may be the ability of AI to quickly create good feelings amongst people and towards a change process that has made it so popular among managers and consultants, but I caution that positive affect by itself may be too fleeting for it to sustain organization change. I propose that the transformational potential of AI is more likely when positive imagery and affect are used in the service of generativity. Bright et al. (2011) echo this view, and provide a perspective on how to inquire into negative emotional states in appreciative, generative ways. There are, however, cases where the positive affect elicited by AI appears to have been central to the change process (e.g. Khalsa, 2002), leading to profound reductions of inter-group conflict and the emergence of shared identities. We will look at this in more detail below in the section on moderators of AI.

Building on strength

Citing research in sports psychology, education and the Pygmalion effect, Cooperrider (1990) argued that we tend to get more of whatever we pay attention to. I have emphasized (Bushe and

Pitman, 1991; 2008, Bushe, 2001, 2011) this aspect of "the positive" – not so much positive anticipations or positive affect but focusing the attention of leaders and followers on the positive traits and processes they want more of, that already exist, as a key engine of change. In his later theoretical formulations, Cooperrider provides a model for understanding the transformational potential of AI as a three-phase process where "elevating inquiry" (an inquiry into what we value that increases relatedness and positive emotions) leads to a "fusion of strengths" (awareness of group resources and increased motivation to cooperate) which leads to "activation of energy" (heightened creativity and the courage to take innovative actions) (Cooperrider and Sekerka, 2006).

Commonalities between this notion of focusing on the positive to guide change and those offered in other change models like Asset Based Community Development (Kretzmann and McKnight, 1993), Positive Deviance (Spreitzer and Sonenshein, 2004; Sternin and Choo, 2000) and Solution-Focused Therapy (de Shazer, 1985; Molnar and de Shazer, 1987) are noteworthy. However, much of the strengths-based movement in organizations focuses on the elucidation and engagement of individual competencies (Buckingham and Clifton, 2001), ignoring relational realities and for the most part doing little to transform the nature of organization itself. Appreciative Inquiry not only focuses on the best of what is, but engages all stakeholders in a processes of re-imagining what could be and taking ownership for what will be. This "fusion of strengths" and "activation of energy" is generally considered essential to the generative momentum of the change process.

Stakeholder engagement

A number of AI advocates describe the engagement of large numbers of stakeholders as a critical change lever (Cooperrider and Sekerka, 2006; Powley et al. 2004; Whitney and Trosten-Bloom 2003). The idea of widespread participation in change is in no way unique to AI, having been a cornerstone of change practice since Roethlisberger and Dickson's (1939) and Coch and French's (1948) seminal research on participation in change. What is different is the degree to which widespread participation as *inquirers* is encouraged (Gergen and Thatchenkery, 1996; Thatchenkery, 1994). Conventional organization development generally involves a small group of inquirers who talk to a large number of stakeholders to get their ideas and views. That small group then analyzes and feeds back what it has gathered. New ideas that have been validated by social science enter the system through consultants and other experts. AI, in contrast, seeks to uncover and stimulate new ideas from stakeholders in the system; ideas that will, at least be new in their status within the system. Ideally, all stakeholders participate in gathering and making sense of the ideas and views of other stakeholders and participate as theorists, dreamers and designers. AI practitioners have incorporated a number of other large group engagement processes, notably Future Search (Emery and Purser, 1996; Weisbord, 1993), World Café (Brown and Issacs, 2005) during the discovery phase, and Open Space (Owen, 1992, 2008) during the design phase.

While getting very large groups engaged in events that lead to change is not unique to AI (Bunker and Alban, 2006), AI advocates make the point that a focus on the positive in AI supports more widespread, voluntary, multi-stakeholder engagement in change activities (Boyd and Bright, 2007; Powley et al., 2004). People who might not otherwise be willing to participate in a change process are more likely to join in when the inquiry is appreciative. Additionally, the credibility and reach of AI have encouraged organizational leaders to experiment with extreme scale of the whole change processes. For example, World Vision is a federation of approximately 200 fairly independent organizations spread across the globe. It recently used AI for a strategic planning event that included 6,000 members using a combination of face-to-face and internet-based participation.

Working with self-organizing processes

A more recent trend in AI theorizing is to incorporate perspectives on the self-organizing properties of social systems (Jantsch, 1979; Owen, 2008; Wheatley, 1994) into AI practice, particularly in the Design and Destiny phases (Barrett and Fry, 2005; Cooperider and Sekerka, 2006; Bushe, 2011). From this perspective, one might argue that the Discovery and Dream phases create the conditions for self-organizing processes to coalesce in positive directions. Attempts to create new cultures by having leaders prescribe and then try to implement a new culture have a propensity to generate negative, unintended outcomes (Kotter and Heskett, 1992; Ogbonna and Wilkinson, 2003). I (Bushe 2007) argue that leaders can't create new cultures so much as they can unleash cultural change. How the culture then changes is very difficult to prescribe or direct, but having a large number of members engaged in an inquiry into the best of whatever stakeholders want more of greatly increases the chances that the new culture will be better than the old one. Having a more or less shared vision of where members in the system want to go (Dream), the use of self-organizing design processes appear to increase the speed, engagement and buy-in to the plans and proposals that emerge. With that level of engagement and commitment, use of self-organizing implementation processes, what Bushe and Kassam (2005) label an improvisational as opposed to implementation form of the "action phase" in an OD process, appears to result in more change, more quickly.

Life-giving properties of social systems

Perhaps the most under-explored theory of change behind AI is the one that started it all – the idea that every social system contains a set of properties, processes and/or characteristics that "give it life", and that attention to these and intentional actions toward strengthening them increase an organization's vitality and capacity (Cooperrider and Srivastva, 1987; Cooperrider and Avital, 2004). Though it remains central to Cooperrider's personal view of what AI should focus on (personal correspondence), it hardly shows up in his or other people's writing, instead having been replaced with the idea of a "positive change core" (Cooperrider and Whitney, 2001; Cooperrider and Sekerka, 2006). Perhaps this is because what gives life to anything is spirit, and from this point of view, AI might be considered a spiritual practice (Barge and Oliver, 2003; Drogin, 1997; Reason, 2000) or an inquiry into the organization's soul (Johnson, 2011). As the language of spirituality is not well received in either the worlds of business or academia, it may explain why this perspective on AI has gained little attention. Even a paper on AI entitled "The spiritual heart of human science inquiry" skirts the issue (Cooperrider and Barrett, 2002). Yet, as an explanation for the remarkable interest in and spread of AI as a change process, and the many spin-offs that have come from it, the spiritual aspect of AI may be worth more examination by scholars and practitioners. Powley (2004), for example, brings the sacred in through the back door in his examination of AI summits as rites of passage. Though his language and focus are secular, the power of ritual for transformative change has ever been connected with spiritual concerns (e.g. Driver, 1991; Eliade, 1958).

Certainly, a focus on AI as an inquiry into what gives life, rather than an inquiry into "the positive", would overcome concerns expressed when more simplistic visions of AI as a study of the best of what is, to get more of it, are raised. "Could AI have been used to help Hitler gas people better?" is the kind of question the focuses on such concerns. An application of AI that was like benchmarking the most efficient gas chambers might indeed have helped Hitler. But properly understood, AI would force gas-chamber operators to explore what gave life to their daily existence, to be in authentic relationship with each other, to consider their highest human aspirations. Could a death cult survive such an inquiry?

Moderators of AI practice

As experience with AI increases and greater numbers of scholars and practitioners study successes and failures, there is an emerging literature on conditions which moderate AI practice and AI outcomes. Two, in particular, are worth noting.

My studies of AI in small groups, combined with my research on group development and team effectiveness (Bushe and Coetzer, 2007), led me to propose that AI works differently in pre-identity and post-identity social systems (Bushe, 2002). A pre-identity system is defined as one in which the majority of members do not identify with the system and a post-identity system as one in which a majority of members do identify with the system. The former would include Appreciative Inquiries that bring together members of different groups, which are used to launch new organizations or networks, as well as those used in existing systems where there is very little sense of psychological membership. I argued that in pre-identity systems, members don't really care that much about the system's needs and instead, see the group or organization as one more thing in their environment that must be dealt with in the pursuit of personal interests. In post-identity systems, by contrast, members take the needs and interests of the system into account and, in some cases, might even be willing to sacrifice personal interests for the betterment of the group.

I argue (Bushe, 2002) that the nature of the inquiry and resulting "vision" must be different in these two types of groups. Mirroring my findings on group state guides (Bushe and Coetzer, 2007; Coetzer and Bushe, 2003), I argue that pre-identity groups are best served by an inquiry into the ideal (group, organization, society) but that post-identity groups are best served by an inquiry into the "ought" (what we ought to do given this group or organization's responsibilities, goals and environment). Inquiry into the ideal, when successful, helps a group achieve a post-identity state and research by Head (2000) found evidence to support this assertion. I argue a post-identity group will be impatient with inquiry into the ideal, and experience it as navel gazing. Instead, members want to increase the group or organization's efficacy and will be engaged by inquiries that are more focused around increasing the system's competence and capacity. As described in Bushe (2011) this model explains findings in two published cases of AI; one in the US Navy (Powley et al., 2004) and one with an executive team (Newman and Fitzgerald, 2001).

Another moderating influence on AI may be the extent to which appreciation, discussion of ideals and a focus on strengths exists prior to an AI. Fitzgerald et al. (2010) suggest that in organizations where discussion of such things are absent, AI can be viewed as an inquiry into the organization's "shadow". Defining the shadow as censored feeling and cognition, they suggest the transformative effect of AI may sometimes be a result of energy and creativity that is unleashed when shadow material is re-integrated into the system. Bright (2009; Bright and Cameron, 2009) offers a different way to think about similar issues in his model of normative momentum. He argues that systems tend towards a normal, functional state of operations, with occasional swings toward either more dysfunctional forms of operation or more extraordinary forms of operation. All else being equal, he argues that organizations will experience "normative momentum" toward an "ordinary state" of being, a state of equilibrium in which maintaining operating procedures, efficiency and effectiveness are the pre-eminent concern and are normally accomplished through reinforcing conformity and standards. The current position of the organization along the continuum from negative deviance to positive deviance will affect both how people experience a change process and how the change process works. Bright argues (2009) that the discovery phase of AI in an organization that is in a dysfunctional, negatively deviant period will have a more dramatic, positive impact than it will in one that is already at the extraordinary, positively deviant end of the continuum. He also suggests (Bright and Cameron, 2009) that the normative press toward the ordinary means that in a dysfunctional state, any change process works with the natural flow as it moves the system back into functionality, but that moving a system towards an extraordinary state must work against that same equilibrating force.

Both these perspectives bring into question my assertion (Bushe, 2007, 2011) that a simple focus on the positive is not enough for transformational change and offers an explanation for why and when a focus on the positive may, by itself, be transformational (with pre-identity systems, and with negatively deviant systems). It also suggests that the transformational power of AI may diminish as discussion of strengths and aspirations becomes common place in a system. This fits with reports of people expressing discomfort with continuing to use AI in organizations that have had years of success using it (Fitzgerald, et al., 2010).

Critiques of Appreciative Inquiry

Critiques of AI have become more sophisticated in recent years, overcoming earlier critiques which came from people not very conversant with the underlying theory. More recent critiques have come from scholar practitioners who use AI and are aware of its limitations. A common concern is with the possibility that a focus on positive stories and experiences during the discovery phase will invalidate the negative organizational experiences of participants and repress potentially important and meaningful conversations that need to take place (Egan and Lancaster, 2005; Miller et al., 2005; Pratt, 2002; Reason, 2000). Christine Oliver (Barge and Oliver, 2003; Fitzgerald et al., 2010; Oliver, 2005a, 2005b) has provided a series of cogent arguments for thinking of AI as more than just studying "the best of" and bringing greater reflexivity to AI practice. Oliver's (2005a) critique of AI's habit of decontextualized polarization, with positive and negative treated as having intrinsic meaning, instead of acknowledging that what is positive for some may be negative for others, goes to the heart of the matter. Social constructionists argue that such meanings can't be pre-assigned by a third party; they only emerge in relationship and even then such meanings are multiple, partial and dynamic. It's hard to argue that such polarization doesn't show up with regularity in descriptions of AI, but is that really what is going on in successful AI practice? Is it even possible to inquire into images of a positive future without evoking the negative past or present? Just as AI theorists argue that behind every negative image lies the positive (Bright et al., 2011), social constructionists would argue that behind every positive image lies a negative one (Fineman, 2006). Fitzgerald et al. (2010) provide numerous examples to show that AI can surface repressed or censored thoughts and feelings.

Johnson (2011) explores the many ways casting an appreciative eye can generate "negative" experiences and how, in turn, exploring those experiences appreciatively can result in "positive", generative, outcomes. She acknowledges the dilemma at the heart of the AI project: "AI could only be differentiated *by using the language of deficit discourse to define the problem that AI would solve*" (Johnson, 2011). By polarizing AI and problem-solving, an either/or dynamic was set that continues to manifest in descriptions of AI. AI is described as a method of change that doesn't focus on problems, but research suggests transformational change will not occur from AI unless it addresses problems of real concern to organizational members (Bushe, 2010b). Rather than staying stuck in a dualistic, either/or discourse of positive or negative, Johnson argues that the generative potential of AI is most likely to come from embracing the polarities of human existence and that it is the tensions of those very forces that most give life and vitality to organizations.

While Cooperrider would not disagree with Johnson's nuanced and sensitive exploration of light and shadow, he is suspicious of the nagging desire to bring deficit based theories of change back into play:

> I think we are still on this quest for a full blown non-deficit theory of change. I'm not saying that the other isn't a way of change but I am saying that we are still in our infancy in understanding non-deficit, strength-based or life-centric approaches to change. William James called for it back in 1902, in *Varieties of Religious Experience*, when he said we know a lot about the kind of change that happens when people feel threatened, feel fear and violence is coming at them, but we don't know much about the kind of change that happens when, in his words, "everything is hot and alive within us and everything reconfigures itself around that". Whether someone would call the initiating experience "positive" or "negative", the transformational moment is a pro-fusion moment when something so deeply good and loving is touched in us that everything is changed – that's the kind of change I'm talking about … I don't think we really understand the possibilities in that kind of change yet and we aren't going to understand them until we take this to the extremes.
>
> (Personal correspondence, 30 March 2010)

The future of Appreciative Inquiry

After 20 years it is abundantly clear that AI, when skilfully done with proper sponsorship and resources, is a potent planned, transformational change process (Bushe and Kassam, 2005; Fry et al., 2002). There are now many published accounts of extraordinary results from its use in a variety of countries. One example is Brazil-based Nutrimental Foods which engaged all 750 employees in two AI summits and within one year absenteeism decreased by 300 per cent, sales increased by 27 per cent, productivity increased by over 23 per cent and profits increased by 200 per cent (Barros and Cooperrider, 2000; Powley et al., 2002). A very different example is Roadway, a unionized trucking firm in the United States that has had many dozens of AI summits at its various locations since the turn of millennium which have transformed union–management relations and dramatically improved performance (Ludema et al., 2003). An internal audit completed in 2004 found sites that had gone through AI summits had achieved cost savings almost seven times higher than sites which had not (Barrett and Fry, 2005).

While the potential for transformation has been established, there may be increasing disenchantment with AI amongst managers and consultants arising from a predictable fad phenomenon that seems to plague all organizational-change methods. The buzz created by new, successful change processes create increasing requests from organizations that consultants want to meet. Ever more poorly trained consultants provide ever more poorly designed applications leading to a situation where managers think "we tried that [fill in the change process] but it didn't work here". After a while what seemed like a silver bullet becomes yesterday's story and everyone moves on.

Anecdotal evidence is that a majority of OD consultants and many other kinds of consultants and change agents now use aspects of AI in their practice. This review has only considered AI from the organizational point of view but there have been applications at the level of individuals (Kelm, 2005), relationships (Stavros and Torres, 2005), groups (Bushe, 1998, 2002; Bushe and Coetzer, 1995), communities (Browne and Jain, 2002; Finehold et al., 2002) and, in the case of Nepal, even nations (Cooperrider et al., 2008, p. vii). As well, AI has been adapted for use in strategic planning (Stavros and Saint, 2009), programme evaluation (Preskill and Catsambas, 2006) and even quality audits (Morris, 2008). One of the downsides of this is that a lot of different things end up getting called Appreciative Inquiry, which further dilutes general understanding of the really important innovations in this theory of practice.

What we most need are studies that explore successes and failures of AI to explain the moderators and contingencies that influence AI outcomes (Head, 2005). We are long past the need for articles breathlessly describing this "new" change process or providing short anecdotes of AI success, but unfortunately that continues to be mainly what is published. Instead, we need longitudinal case studies that are detailed and nuanced, like that by Bryan (2009), Messerschmidt (2008) and Miller et al. (2005). We also need comparative studies that track contingencies, mediators and moderators when AI is used repetitively in the same or similar organizations (e.g. Bushe, 2010b; Richer et al., 2009). Due to the proliferation of methods called AI, and the variety of theoretical levers behind AI practice, these need to be carefully detailed in published reports. We also need to build a body of common models and terms so that studies can be compared. Besides the "4D model" and the "5 principles" few if any of the other useful models and lens reviewed in this chapter are being used consistently in studying and reporting on AI.

When is AI the most appropriate change process? What contingencies are important to consider when planning an AI? What organizational factors most influence the success or failure of AI? At present we have little evidence-based answers to those questions. We also don't have any good theoretical way of thinking about scale-of-the-whole change processes. It seems a common-sense proposition that if everyone in the system can agree on what needs doing, execution will be much easier, but is that all that is happening when very large numbers of people come together in an AI summit? Are there other, as yet undescribed, network effects from large scales that support organizational change? Can AI processes be scaled up infinitely? How many members in a system need to be engaged for scale-of-the-whole effects to kick in?

There are many more questions that could be asked, as so few have been empirically studied and answered but I will conclude with one final one – the competencies required of the AI facilitator/consultant. Very little has been written about this. Can any clever person with a "positive attitude" learn to facilitate AI summits well? Does it require a "healthy and spiritually grounded" individual (Murrell, 2005: 111)? Is lack of facilitator characteristics or skills related to AI failure? Maybe – we just don't know.

References

Barge, J.K. and Oliver, C. (2003) Working with appreciation in managerial practice. *Academy of Management Review*, 28: 1, 124–42.

Barrett, F.J. (1998) Creativity and improvisation in jazz and organizations: Implications for organizational learning. *Organization Science*, 9, 605–23.

Barrett, F.J. and Cooperrider, D.L. (1990) Generative metaphor intervention: A new approach for working with systems divided by conflict and caught in defensive perception. *Journal of Applied Behavioral Science*, 26, 219–39.

Barrett, F.J. and Fry, R.E. (2005) *Appreciative Inquiry: A Positive Approach to Building Cooperative Capacity*. Chagrin Falls, OH: Taos Institute.

Barrett, F.J., Thomas, G.F. and Hocevar, S.P. (1995) The central role of discourse in large-scale change: A social construction perspective. *Journal of Applied Behavioral Science*, 31: 3, 352–72.

Barros, I.O. and Cooperrider, D.L. (2000) A story of Nutrimental in Brazil: How wholeness, appreciation, and inquiry bring out the best in human organization. *Organization Development Journal*, 18: 2, 22–27.

Baumeister, R., Bratslavsky, E., Finkenauer, C. and Vohns, K.K. (2001) Bad is stronger than good. *Review of General Psychology*, 5: 4, 323–70.

Boje, D.M. (1991) Consulting and change in the storytelling organization, *Journal of Organizational Change Management*, 4: 3, 7–17.

Boyd, N.M. and Bright, D.S. (2007) Appreciative Inquiry as a mode of action research for community psychology. *Journal of Community Psychology*, 35: 8, 1019–36.

Bright, D.S. (2009) Appreciative Inquiry and positive organizational scholarship: A philosophy of practice for turbulent times. *OD Practitioner*, 41: 3, 2–7.

Bright, D.S. and Cameron, K. (2009) Positive organizational change: What the field of POS offers to OD practitioners. In Rothwell, W.J., Stavros, J.M., Sullivan, R.L. and Sullivan, A. (eds) *Practicing Organization Development: A Guide for Managing and Leading Change*, 3rd edn (pp. 397–410). San Francisco, CA: Pfeiffer-Wiley.

Bright, D.S., Powley, E.H., Fry, R.E. and Barrett, F.J. (2011) The generative potential of cynical conversations. In Avital, M., Cooperrider, D.L. and Zandee, D. (eds) *Generative Organization: Advances in Appreciative Inquiry*, Vol. 4. Bingley, UK: Emerald Publishing.

Brown, J. and Issacs, D. (2005) *World Café: Shaping Our Futures Through Conversations That Matter*. San Francisco, CA: Berrett-Koehler.

Brown, T. (2009) *Change by Design: How Design Thinking Transforms Organizations and Inspires Innovation*. New York: HarperBusiness.

Browne, B.W. and Jain, S. (2002). *Imagine Chicago: Ten Years of Imagination in Action*. Chicago: Imagine Chicago.

Bryan, J.A. (2009) New symbiosis for forest care: A trial of forest action research in the Atlantic forest of Brazil. *Journal of Sustainable Forestry*, 28: 1, 243–68.

Buckingham, M. and Clifton, D.O. (2001) *Now Discover Your Strengths*. New York: Free Press.

Bunker, B.B. and Alban, B.T. (2006) *Handbook of Large Group Methods*. San Francisco, CA: Jossey-Bass.

Bushe, G.R. (1998) Appreciative Inquiry with teams. *Organization Development Journal*, 16: 3, 41–50.

Bushe, G.R. (2001) Five theories of change embedded in appreciative Inquiry. In Cooperrider, D.L., Sorenson, P., Whitney, D. and Yeager, T. (eds) *Appreciative Inquiry: An Emerging Direction for Organization Development (117–127)*. Champaign, IL: Stipes.

Bushe, G.R. (2002) Meaning making in teams: Appreciative Inquiry with preidentity and postidentity groups. In Fry, R., Barrett, F., Seiling, J. and Whitney, D. (eds) *Appreciative Inquiry and Organizational Transformation: Reports from the Field* (pp. 39–63). Westport, CT: Quorum.

Bushe, G.R. (2007) Appreciative Inquiry is not (just) about the positive. *Organization Development Practitioner*, 39: 4, 30–35.

Bushe, G.R. (2009) *Clear Leadership*, rev. edn. Boston: Davies-Black.

Bushe, G.R. (2010a) Commentary on Appreciative Inquiry as shadow process. *Journal of Management Inquiry*, 19: 3, 234–237.

Bushe, G.R. (2010b) A comparative case study of Appreciative Inquiries in one organization: Implications for practice. *Revista de Cercetare si Interventie Sociala/Review of Research and Social Intervention* (Special Issue on Appreciative Inquiry), 29: 7–24.

Bushe, G.R. (2011) Generativity and the transformational potential of Appreciative Inquiry. In Avital, M., Cooperrider, D.L. and Zandee, D. (eds) *Organizational Generativity: Advances in Appreciative Inquiry*, Vol. 4. Bingley, UK: Emerald Press.

Bushe, G.R. and Coetzer, G. (1995) Appreciative inquiry as a team development intervention: A controlled experiment. *Journal of Applied Behavioral Science*, 31: 1, 13–30.

Bushe, G.R. and Coetzer, G.H. (2007) Group development and team effectiveness: Using shared cognitions to measure the impact of group development on task performance and group viability. *Journal of Applied Behavioral Science*. 43: 2, 184–212.

Bushe, G.R. and Kassam, A. (2005) When is Appreciative Inquiry transformational? A meta-case analysis. *Journal of Applied Behavioral Science*, 41: 2, 161–81.

Bushe, G.R. and Marshak, R.J. (2009) Revisioning OD: Diagnostic and dialogic premises and patterns of practice. *Journal of Applied Behavioral Science*, 45: 3, 348–68.

Bushe, G.R. and Pitman, T. (1991) Appreciative process: A method for transformational change. *Organization Development Practitioner*, 23: 3, 1–4.

Bushe, G.R. and Pitman, T. (2008) Performance amplification: Building the strength based organization. *Appreciative Inquiry Practitioner*, 10: 4, 23–26.

Cameron, K.S., Dutton, J.E. and Quinn, R.E. (eds) (2003) *Positive Organizational Scholarship*. San Francisco, CA: Berrett-Koehler.

Carter, J.D. and Johnson, P.D. (1999) The roundtable project. In Elliott, C. (ed.) *Locating the Energy for Change: An Introduction to Appreciative Inquiry* (pp. 255–279). Winnipeg, MB: International Institute for Sustainable Development.

Cameron, K.S. and Lavine, M. (2006) *Making the Impossible Possible: Leading Extraordinary Performance*. San Francisco, CA: Berret-Koehler.

Cheung-Judge, M. and Powley, E.H. (2006) Innovation at the BBC: Engaging an entire organizational system. In Bunker, B.B. and Albion, B.T. (eds) *The Handbook of Large Group Methods* (pp. 45–61). San Francisco, CA: Jossey-Bass.

Coch, L. and French, J.R.P. (1948) Overcoming resistance to change. *Human Relations*, 1: 4, 512–32.

Coetzer, G.H. and Bushe, G.R. (2003) Using discrepancy theory to examine the relationship between shared cognition and group outcomes. *Best Paper Proceedings of the 63rd Academy of Management*, Managerial and Organizational Cognition Division, pp. MOC: B1–B6.

Cooperrider, D.L. (1990) Positive image, positive action: The affirmative basis of organizing. In S. Srivastva and D.L. Cooperrider (eds), *Appreciative Management and Leadership* (pp. 91–125). San Francisco, CA: Jossey-Bass.

Cooperrider, D.L. (1986) *Appreciative Inquiry: Toward a Methodology for Understanding and Enhancing Organizational Innovation*. Unpublished doctoral dissertation. Department of Organizational Behavior, Case Western Reserve University, Cleveland, OH.

Cooperrider, D.L. and Avital, M. (2004) Introduction. In Cooperrider, D.L. and Avital, M. (eds) *Constructive Discourse And Human Organization: Advances In Appreciative Inquiry*, Vol. 1. Oxford: Elsevier Science.

Cooperrider, D.L. and Barrett, F. (2002) An exploration of the spiritual heart of human science inquiry. *Reflections*, 3: 3, 56–62.

Coopperrider, D.L. and Sekerka, L.E. (2006) Toward a theory of positive organizational change. In Gallos, J.V. (ed.) *Organization Development: A Jossey-Bass Reader* (pp. 223–238). San Francisco, CA: Jossey-Bass.

Cooperrider, D.L. and Srivastva, S. (1987) Appreciative Inquiry in organizational life. In Woodman, R.W. and Pasmore, W.A. (eds) *Research In Organizational Change And Development, Vol. 1 (pp. 129–169)*. Stamford, CT: JAI Press.

Cooperrider, D.L. and Whitney, D. (2001) A positive revolution in change. In Cooperrider, D.L., Sorenson, P., Whitney, D. and Yeager, T. (eds) *Appreciative Inquiry: An Emerging Direction for Organization Development* (pp. 9–29). Champaign, IL: Stipes.

Cooperrider, D.L., Barrett, F. and Srivastva, S. (1995) Social construction and Appreciative Inquiry: A journey in organizational theory. In Hosking, D., Dachler, P. and Gergen, K. (eds) *Management and Organization: Relational Alternatives to Individualism* (pp. 157–200). Aldershot, UK: Avebury.

Cooperrider, D.L., Whitney, D. and Stavros, J.M. (2008) *Appreciative Inquiry Handbook* (2nd edn) Brunswick, OH: Crown Custom Publishing.

deShazer, S. (1985) *Keys to Solution in Brief Therapy*. New York: W.W. Norton.

Driver, T.F. (1991) *The Magic of Ritual: Our Need for Liberating Rites that Transform Our Lives and Our Communities*. New York: HarperCollins.

Drogin, S. (1997) *An Appreciative Inquiry Into Spirituality And Work*. Unpublished Ed. D. Thesis, Seattle University.

Egan, T.M. and Lancaster, C.M. (2005) Comparing Appreciative Inquiry to action research: OD practitioner perspectives. *Organization Development Journal*, 23: 2, 29–49.

Eliade, M. (1958) *Rites and Symbols of Initiation: The Mysteries of Birth and Rebirth*. New York: Harper & Row.

Emery, M. and Purser, R. (1996) *The Search Conference*. San Francisco, CA: Jossey-Bass.

Finehold, M.A., Holland, B.M. and Lingham, T. (2002) Appreciative Inquiry and public dialogue: An approach to community change. *Public Organization Review*, 2: 3, 235–52.

Fineman, S. (2006) On being positive: Concerns and counterpoints. *Academy of Management Review*, 31: 2, 270–91.

Fitzgerald, S.P., Oliver, C. and Hoxsey, J.C. (2010) Appreciative Inquiry as shadow process. *Journal of Management Inquiry*. 19: 3, 220–233.

Fredrickson, B.L. (2001) The role of positive emotions in positive psychology: The broaden-and-build theory of positive emotions. *American Psychologist*, 56, 218–26.

Fredrickson, B.L. (2006) The broaden-and-build theory of positive emotions. In Csikszentmihalyi, M. and Csikszentmihalyi, I.S. (eds) *A Life Worth Living: Contributions To Positive Psychology* (pp. 85–103). New York: Oxford University Press.

Fry, R., Barrett, F., Seiling, J. and Whitney, D. (eds) (2002) *Appreciative Inquiry and Organizational Transformation: Reports from the Field*. Westport, CT: Quorum.

Gergen, K.J. (1978) (2nd edn.). Toward generative theory. *Journal of Personality and Social Psychology*, 36: 11, 1344–60.

Gergen, K.J. (1982) *Toward Transformation in Social Knowledge*. New York: Springer-Verlag.

Gergen, K. (2009) *An Invitation to Social Construction* (2nd edn.). Thousand Oaks, CA: SAGE.

Gergen, K.J. and Thatchenkery, T.J. (1996) Organization science as social construction: Postmodern potentials. *Journal of Applied Behavioral Science*, 32: 4, 356–77.

Golembiewski, R.T. (1998) Appreciating Appreciative Inquiry: Diagnosis and perspectives on how to do better. In Woodman, R.W. and Pasmore, W.A. (eds) *Research In Organizational Change And Development*, Vol. 11 (pp. 1–45). Stamford, CT: JAI Press.

Golembiewski, R.T. (2000) Three perspectives on Appreciative Inquiry. *OD Practitioner*, 32: 1, 53–58.

Head, R.L. (2000) Appreciative Inquiry as a team-development intervention for newly formed heterogeneous groups. *OD Practitioner*, 32: 1, 59–66.

Head, T.C. (2005) A contingency approach to Appreciative Inquiry: A first small step. In D.L. Cooperrider, P. Sorenson, D. Whitney and T. Yeager (eds) *Appreciative Inquiry: Foundations in Positive Organization Development* (pp. 401–414). Champaign, IL: Stipes.

Isen, A.M. (2000) Positive affect and decision-making. In M. Lewis, and J.M. Haviland-Jones (eds) *Handbook of Emotions* (pp. 417–435). New York: Guildford.

Jantsch, E. (1979) *The Self-Organizing Universe: Scientific and Human Implications of the Emerging Paradigm of Evolution*. New York: Oxford.

Johnson, P. (2011) Transcending the polarity of light and shadow in Appreciative Inquiry: An appreciative exploration of practice. In Avital, M., Cooperrider, D.L. and Zandee, D. (eds) *Generative Organization: Advances in Appreciative Inquiry*, Vol. 4. Bingley, UK: Emerald Publishing.

Kelm, J.B. (2005) *Appreciative Living: The Principles of Appreciative Inquiry in Personal Life*. Wake Forest, NC: Venet.

Khalsa, G.S. (2002) The appreciative summit: The birth of the united religions initiative. In Fry, R., Barrett, F., Seiling, J. and Whitney, D. (eds) *Appreciative Inquiry and Organizational Transformation: Reports from the Field* (pp. 211–237).Westport, CT: Quorum.

Kotter, J.P. and Heskett, J.L. (1992) *Corporate Culture and Performance*. New York: Free Press.

Kretzmann, J.P. and McKnight, J.L. (1993) *Building Communities from the Inside Out: A Path Toward Finding and Mobilizing a Community's Assets*. Evanston, IL: Center for Urban Affairs and Policy Research, Northwestern University.

Ludema, J.D. (2000) From deficit discourse to vocabularies of hope: The power of appreciation. In Cooperrider, D.L., Sorensen Jr., P.F., Whitney, D. and Yaeger, T.F. (eds) *Appreciative Inquiry: Rethinking Human Organization toward a Positive Theory of Change* (pp. 256–87). Champaign, IL: Stipes Publishing.

Ludema, J.D. (2002) Appreciative storytelling: A narrative approach to organization development and change. In Fry, R. Barrett, F., Seiling, J. and Whitney, D. (eds) *Appreciative Inquiry And Organizational Transformation: Reports From The Field* (pp. 239–261). Westport, CT: Quorum.

Ludema, J. and Hinrichs, G. (2003) Values-based organization design: The case of John Deere Harvester Works. *AI Practitioner*, May, 11–15.

Ludema, J.D., Cooperrider, D.L. and Barrett, F.J. (2000) Appreciative Inquiry: The power of the unconditional positive question. In Reason, P. and Bradbury, H. (eds) *Handbook of Action Research* (pp. 189–199). Thousand Oaks, CA: SAGE.

Ludema, J.D., Wilmot, T.B., and Srivastva, S. (1997) Organizational hope: Reaffirming the constructive task of social and organizational inquiry, *Human Relations*, 50: 8, 1015–52.

Ludema, J.D. Whitney, D., Mohr, B.J. and Griffen, T.J. (2003) *The Appreciative Inquiry Summit*. San Francisco, CA: Berret-Koehler.

Marrow, A. J. (1969) *The Practical Theorist: The Life and Work of Kurt Lewin*. New York: Teachers College Press.

Marshak, R.J. and Grant, D. (2008) Organizational discourse and new organization development practices. *British Journal of Management*, 19: S7–S19.

McAdam, E. and Mirza, K.A.H. (2009) Drugs, hopes and dreams: Appreciative Inquiry with marginalized young people using drugs and alcohol. *Journal of Family Therapy*, 31: 175–93.

Messerschmidt, D. (2008) Evaluating Appreciative Inquiry as an organizational transformation tool: An assessment from Nepal. *Human Organization*, 67: 4, 454–68.

Miller, M.G., Fitzgerald, S.P., Murrell, K.L., Preston, J. and Ambekar, R. (2005) Appreciative Inquiry in building a transcultural strategic alliance. *Journal of Applied Behavioral Science*, 41: 1, 91–110.

Mohr, B.J., McLean, A. and Silbert, T. (2003) Beyond discovery and dream: Unleashing change through the design phase of an AI intervention. *AI Practitioner*, May, 1–3.

Molnar, A. and de Shazer, S. (1987) Solution-focused therapy: Toward the identification of therapeutic tasks. *Journal of Marital and Family Therapy*, 13: 4, 349–58.

Morris, J. (2008) Smooth Approach: Taking the turbulence out of the auditing process with a new approach. *Quality Progress*, October, 35–41.

Murrell, K.L. (2005) International and intellectual roots of Appreciative Inquiry. In Cooperrider, D.L., Sorenson, P.F., Yaeger, T.F. and Whitney, D. (eds) *Appreciative Inquiry: Foundations in Positive Organization Development* (pp. 105–19). Champaign, IL: Stipes.

Newman, H.L. and Fitzgerald, S.P. (2001) Appreciative Inquiry with an executive team: Moving along the action research continuum. *Organization Development Journal*, 19: 3, 37–43.

O'Connell, B. (2005) *Solution Focused Therapy*. Thousand Oaks, CA: SAGE.

Ogbonna, E. and Wilkinson, B. (2003) The false promise of organizational culture change: A case study of middle managers in grocery retailing. *Journal of Management Studies*, 40: 5, 1151–78.

Oliver, C. (2005a) Critical Appreciative Inquiry as intervention in organisational discourse. In Peck, E. (ed.) *Organisational Development In Healthcare: Approaches, Innovations, Achievements* (pp. 205–218). Oxford: Radcliffe Press.

Oliver, C. (2005b) *Reflexive Inquiry*. London: Karnac.

Oswick, C., Grant, D., Michaelson, G. and Wailes, N. (2005) Looking forwards: Discursive directions in organizational change. *Journal of Organizational Change Management*, 18: 4, 383–90.

Owen, H. (1992) *Open Space Technology*. Potomac, MD: Abbott.

Owen, H. (2008) *Wave Rider: Leadership for High Performance in a Self-Organizing World*. San Francisco, CA: Berrett-Koehler.

Powley, E.H. (2004) Underlying ritual practices of the Appreciative Inquiry summit: Toward a theory of sustained appreciative change. In D.L. Cooperrider, and M. Avital (eds) *Constructive Discourse and Human Organization: Advances in Appreciative Inquiry Volume 1* (pp. 241–61). Oxford, Elsevier.

Powley, E.H., Cooperrider, D.L. and Fry, R. (2002) Appreciative Inquiry: A revolutionary approach to strategic change. In Goett, P. (ed) *2002 Handbook of Business Strategy* (pp. 165–172). New York: EC Media Group.

Powley, E.H., Fry, R.E., Barrett, F.J. and Bright, D.S. (2004) Dialogic democracy meets command and control: Transformation through the Appreciative Inquiry summit. *Academy of Management Executive*, 18: 3, 67–80.

Pratt, C. (2002) Creating unity from competing integrities: A case study in Appreciative Inquiry methodology. In Fry, R., Barrett, F., Seiling, J. and Whitney, D. (eds) *Appreciative Inquiry and Organizational Transformation: Reports from the Field* (pp. 99–120). Westport, CT: Quorum Books.

Preskill, H. and Catsambas, T.T. (2006) *Reframing Evaluation Through Appreciative Inquiry*. Thousand Oaks, CA: SAGE.

Quinn, R.E. (2000) *Change the World*. San Francisco, CA: Jossey-Bass.

Reason, P. (2000) 'Action research as spiritual practice'. Retrieved 26 March 2010 from http://people.bath.ac.uk/mnspwr/Thoughtpieces/ARspiritualpractice.htm.

Richer, M-C, Ritchie, J. and Marchionni, C. (2009) 'If we can't do more, let's do it differently!': Using Appreciative Inquiry to promote innovative ideas for better health care work environments. *Journal of Nursing Management*, 17: 947–55.

Roethlisberger, F.J. and Dickson, W.J. (1939) *Management and the Worker*. Cambridge, MA.: Harvard University Press.

Smith, K.K. and Berg, D.N. (1987) *Paradoxes of Group Life*. San Francisco, CA: Jossey-Bass.

Spreitzer, G.M. and Sonenshein, S. (2004) Toward the construct definition of positive deviance. *American Behavioral Scientist*, 47: 6, 828–47.

Stavros, J.M. and Saint, D.K. (2009) SOAR: Linking strategy and OD to sustainable performance. In Rothwell, W.J., Stavros, J.M., Sullivan, R.L. and Sullivan, A. (eds) *Practicing Organization Development*, 3rd edn. (p. 377–394). San Francisco, CA: Pfeiffer-Wiley.

Stavros, J.M. and Torres, C. (2005) *Dynamic Relationships: Unleashing the Power of Appreciative Inquiry in Daily Living*. Chagrin Falls, OH: Taos Institute.

Sternin, J. and Choo, R. (2000) The power of positive deviancy. *Harvard Business Review*, 78: 1, 14–15.

Thatchenkery, T.J. (1994) *Hermeneutic processes in organizations: A study in relationships between observers and those observed*. Unpublished doctoral dissertation, Department of Organizational Behavior, Case Western Reserve University.

Watkins, J.M. and Mohr, B. (2001) *Appreciative Inquiry: Change at the Speed of Imagination*. San Francisco, CA: Jossey-Bass.

Weisbord, M. (1993) *Discovering Common Ground*. San Francisco, CA: Berrett-Koehler.

Wheatley, M.J. (1994) *Leadership and the New Science*. San Francisco, CA: Berrett-Koehler.

Whitney, D. (1996) Postmodern principles and practices for large scale organization change and global cooperation. *Organization Development Journal*, 14: 4, 53–68.

Whitney, D. and Cooperrider, D.L. (2000) The Appreciative Inquiry summit: An emerging methodology for whole system positive change. *OD Practitioner* Vol. 32: 2, 13–26.

Whitney, D. and Cooperrider, D.L. (2001) *The Encyclopedia of Positive Questions*. Euclid, OH: Lakeshore Communications.

Whitney, D. and Trosten-Bloom, A. (2003) *The Power of Appreciative Inquiry*. San Francisco, CA: Berrett-Koehler.

7

Images of organization development
The role of metaphor in processes of change

Cliff Oswick and Robert J. Marshak

Introduction

In his seminal work *Images of Organization* (1986), Gareth Morgan explored the prevailing metaphors which provide "ways of thinking" and "ways of seeing" organizations (e.g. organizations *as* machines, organizations *as* organisms and organizations *as* brains). In this chapter we consider the dominant metaphors that have underpinned ways of thinking about organization development (OD). In doing so, we seek to identify and examine the deeply embedded conceptual metaphors that have guided the formation and evolution of the field. Moreover, we also explore the extent to which metaphorical conceptualizations have simultaneously enabled and constrained OD practice and change processes. For our purposes, a distinction will not be made between metaphor, simile and analogy. We acknowledge there is a subtle difference between these forms of figurative comparison. However, in keeping with previous work, we view "metaphor as a rather broad category, encompassing analogy and mere appearance, as well as a variety of other kinds of matches" (Gentner and Jeziorski, 1993: 452).

There are four main parts to this chapter. First, in the following section, we explore how metaphors work and the extent to which they shape our thoughts, perceptions and actions. We also highlight the range of metaphors that are embedded in mainstream OD theories and OD processes. Then, in the second section, we discuss the existence of two dominant metaphors which can be characterized as representing a traditional discourse of change within the OD field. Third, we consider the emergence of new metaphors pertaining to OD and a new discourse of change. Finally, we conclude by considering the prospects for change practices if we treat the two metaphor-based discourses associated with early and more recent forms of OD as being mutually implicated and potentially complimentary approaches.

Metaphors, OD and change

According to Pinder and Bourgeois (1982), metaphors are dispensable figures of speech which should be eschewed from discourse in order to promote the development of literal, scientific language. Even if this cleansing of language was desirable it is somewhat impractical. Metaphors are inevitable and unavoidable in everyday language-use. As a cursory examination of any passage of text or episode of interaction will reveal, metaphors are embedded in discourse. Indeed, as if to demonstrate the point, the very notion that metaphors are "embedded" is itself metaphorical (i.e. they are not literally *embedded* in a text).

Metaphors are more than just poetic devices that act as an embellishment to language (Black, 1962; Manning, 1979; Grant and Oswick, 1996). They are vehicles which facilitate insight and help to create meaning through a process of enabling an object or concept (an abstract domain) to be understood by reference to another object or concept (a concrete domain) (Lakoff and Johnson, 1980). One of the most seductive aspects of metaphors is their potential to produce vivid, compact and evocative imagery (Ortony, 1975; Ortony, 1993). In this regard metaphors can be seen as having "generative qualities" (Schön, 1993), as being "liberating in orientation" (Barrett and Cooperrider, 1990), and as having "transformational properties" (Srivastva and Barrett, 1988; Tsoukas, 1991). As Barrett and Cooperrider observe, metaphors offer an "invitation to see the world anew" (1990: 222).

Although metaphors can be illuminating, they create what has been referred to as "partial truths" (Morgan, 1996). This arises because "in creating one set of insights it [metaphor] excludes others" (Morgan, 1996: 232). In other words, shining a light on certain aspects of a given phenomenon also involves casting other aspects into darkness. This is consistent with Palmer and Dunford's observation that "A metaphor, no matter how revealing, cannot help but alert us to some features and draw attention away from others" (1996: 9). When viewed in this way metaphors can "reify and act as ideological distortions" (Tinker, 1986) and, as a result, they can sometimes become more constraining than liberating in orientation (Oswick et al., 2002).

On occasions metaphors exhibit a "gestalt-like" quality inasmuch as they provide instantaneous surface-level descriptive insights into a subject, object or concept based upon mere appearance (Inns and Jones, 1996). An example of this is the observation that "the surface of the lake was calm and clear like a mirror" (Gentner, 1983). On other occasions metaphors can be seen as involving a process of abstraction where the comparison process is based on a set of relationships (Gentner, 1989: Tsoukas, 1993). As such, metaphor-use often entails sophisticated processes of cognitive mapping (Cornelissen, 2005; Fauconnier and Turner, 2002) and the analysis of metaphors can uncover deep underlying patterns of conceptual coherence (Lakoff and Johnson, 1980). So, for example, Lakoff and Johnson's description of "Argument *as* War" illustrates that "expressions from the vocabulary of war, e.g., *attack a position, indefensible, strategy, new line of attack, win, gain ground,* etc., form a systematic way of talking about the battling aspects of arguing" (1980: 7).

The war metaphor illuminates a particular way of thinking about "argument" which positions it as an adversarial endeavour and in doing so it foregrounds aspects of defence and attack and aspects of winning and losing. If, by contrast, we were to embrace an alternative metaphor, such as "Argument *as* Dance", a completely different way of thinking is evoked (e.g. aspects of interdependence, mutuality and manoeuvring are privileged). Hence, metaphors as evocative and generative devices have significant implications for not only the way we see things, but also the ways we engage and act in relation to particular social phenomena and material circumstances. The projective and implicative properties of metaphor are equally apparent if we consider the field of OD and processes of planned organizational change.

Given their generative and seductive qualities, it is not surprising that metaphors have been utilized to articulate and facilitate processes of organizational change (see, for example, Armenakis and Bedeian, 1992; Burke, 1992; Jacobs and Heracleous, 2006; Marshak, 1993a; Marshak, 2009; Sackmann, 1989). In some instances, change-based research and inquiry has involved using metaphors as deliberate and premeditated ways of eliciting insights and facilitating change processes. In effect, this involves treating "metaphors as data" (Brink, 1993). For example, Broussine and Vince

(1996) engaged in "an applied research project which encouraged managers to address both perceptions of change and resistance to change through analyzing individual and organizational metaphors" (p. 57). This was achieved by getting managers to draw pictures to express their feelings about change in their organization and to discuss their drawings in groups. Similar approaches have been utilized in studies where metaphor-based data has been captured through the use of "Lego" building blocks (Heracleous and Jacobs, 2008), paintings (Hatch and Yanow, 2008) and an attitudinal survey of employees using "animal analogies" (Oswick and Montgomery, 1999).

Beyond the premeditated and applied deployment of metaphor in organizational change initiatives, the OD and planned change literature is itself replete with deeply embedded, unconscious, taken-for-granted metaphors (Marshak, 1994; Oswick and Grant, 1996). An example of this is Lewin's (1951) seminal work which describes organizational change as involving a three-phase process of unfreezing, movement and refreezing. This conceptualization of change has obvious metaphorical connotations (e.g. the organization is not literally frozen). Other notable examples in the extant OD literature include: "*force-field* analysis" (Lewin, 1947), "*stream* analysis" (Porras, 1987), "*gap* analysis" and "*red flags* in diagnosis" (Brown and Harvey, 2004), "*waves* of change" (Morgan, 1988), "organizational *health*" (Beckhard, 1969), "organizational *renewal*" (Waterman, 1987), and "*turbulent* environments" (Oswick et al., 2005).

For us, the plethora of metaphors applied to OD and organizational change do more than merely act as linguistic embellishments. Moreover, although there might appear to be a diverse and diffuse range of metaphors used within the OD discourse, we would posit that there is an underlying conceptual coherence which informs and prefigures many of the apparently disparate metaphors used. It is to this issue that we now turn our attention.

Two dominant metaphors

The traditional discourse of OD has been dominated by two metaphors: the notion of change *as* a journey (Marshak, 1993b; Inns, 1996) and the OD process as analogous to issues of health (Dunford and Palmer, 1996; Kumra, 1996). Within the extant literature the health metaphor operates at a deeply embedded, but largely subliminal, way. It is one of a number of anthropomorphistic metaphors that have been applied to organizations (Doving, 1996). In effect, this involves a subtle, and largely subconscious, process of personification where human qualities (e.g. health and fitness) are projected onto non-human entities (e.g. organizations). An example of this is apparent in Beckhard's often cited definition of OD: "OD is an effort planned, organisation wide, managed from the top, to increase organisation effectiveness and health, through planned interventions in the organisation's processes using behavioural science knowledge" (1969: 9). The term "health" is clearly not meant to be taken literally (i.e. an organization cannot be "healthy" or "unhealthy"). However, the fact that it is used in a figurative way is nonetheless not recognized. The origins of "organizational health" can be traced back more than fifty years to a *Harvard Business Review* article by Chris Argyris which posed the question: "The organization: what makes it healthy?" (Argyris, 1958). The focus on organizational health in OD has persisted over the years (Goldman Schuyler, 2004). Bruhn (2001) has even distinguished between healthy bodies and healthy minds in relation to organizations. He suggests that the concept of a "healthy body" equates with aspects of structure, organization design, communication processes and the design of work, while the idea of a "healthy mind" is synonymous with less tangible organizational phenomena (e.g. underlying beliefs, goals, policies and procedures) and is concerned with "how conflict is handled, how change is managed, how members are treated, and how the organization learns" (Bruhn, 2001: 147).

The extant OD discourse is replete with covert references to health, and by implicit extension the practice of medicine, to describe aspects of planned organizational change. This tendency is revealed in the vernacular of OD textbooks through the use of terms with medical overtones, such as: consultants, clients, diagnosis, intervention, prescription, fitness, wellness and remedy (see, for example, Brown and Harvey, 2004; French and Bell, 1995). More overtly, OD practitioners have been described as "doctors" (Tilles, 1961) and "management physicians" (Nees and Greiner, 1985), and the "doctor–patient relationship" is one of the three basic models – along with the "purchase of expertise" and "process consultation" – used to describe the OD consultation process or to contrast it with other approaches (Schein, 1988). In short, the health metaphor is a dominant and enduring way of thinking about OD: doctors treat sick patients and OD consultants treat sick or unhealthy organizations.

The other metaphor which has been particularly prominent in the field of OD is the image of change as a journey (Marshak, 1993b; Inns, 1996). Like the health metaphor, the idea of a journey is embedded within the extant discourse and used in an unreflexive way. Beginning with Lewin's three-stage change process and continuing through the present with "roadmaps" for change leaders (Ackerman Anderson and Anderson, 2010), there are abundant examples of the journey metaphor in OD theory and practice. Instances of the journey being evoked can also be found within a variety of OD techniques and approaches. For example, "gap analysis" explicitly involves organizational stakeholders reflecting upon "where are we now" and "where do we want to be" (French and Bell, 1995; Ver Schere, 1984). The connotation of a journey is also present in the oft cited Gleicher "change formula" (Beckhard and Harris, 1987: 25), which is expressed as:

$$C = (D + V + FS) > R$$

where:
C = Change
D = Dissatisfaction with the status quo
V = Clarity of vision
FS = Practical first steps
R = Resistance

The use of "practical first steps" is metaphorical insofar as change does not literally involve taking physical steps. However, the use of this expression does nevertheless have subliminal connotations which suggest that there is a journey from one place to another place. Beyond this, the change equation shares some points of similarity with the process of gap analysis inasmuch as "dissatisfaction with the status quo" can be construed as being unhappy with where we are now and "clarity of vision" is concerned with knowing where we want to be. In effect, both gap analysis and the change equation can be read as a destination-oriented journey. This perspective is reinforced if we consider some of the labels ascribed to change agents as "pathfinders" (Brown and Harvey, 2004), "corporate pathfinders" (Leavitt, 1986), "pioneers" (McLean et al., 1982), "friendly co-pilots" and "strategic navigators" (Nees and Greiner, 1985). In keeping with the journey metaphor the stakeholders in organizations who are seen as resistant to change have been labelled as "blockers" (Shaw and Maletz, 1995) because they are perceived to be impeding the journey (i.e. the change). We also find problems that can arise during the diagnostic phase of OD are described as "red flags" (Brown and Harvey, 2004). The underlying rationale being that just as red flags are used to warn travellers of impending danger, they can also be used to indicate to OD consultants the potential problems that can arise during the diagnostic journey.

There is it would seem a discernible conceptual coherence to the "change *as* journey" metaphor. And, we would concur with Inns (1996) conclusion that "The implicit message in many accounts of the theory of OD is that change is a rational, structured and linear journey" (p. 24). Indeed, Lakoff and Johnson go so far as to suggest that "change is movement" is the dominant conceptual metaphor in Western thinking to express the phenomenon of change (1999). The problem with treating change as a linear, destination-oriented journey, however, is that it privileges a particular perception of change as a bounded and discrete process (Marshak, 1993b). This is problematic because it restricts the scope for other ways of thinking about change (i.e. as non-linear, cyclical or continuous). The health metaphor is similarly limited and limiting insofar as it juxtaposes the idea of being healthy and unhealthy (or illness and wellness) as punctuated and explicit points in the OD process. Hence, OD is either a journey from "where you are" (i.e. the current state) to "where you want to be" (i.e. desired state) or a medical process in which an organization is transformed from being ill/unhealthy (the current state) to being fit/healthy (the desired state). In both instances, the underlying common characteristics are of movement (from one state to another), improvement (movement from a less desirable position to a better one), and predictability (a clearly defined and knowable series of steps between two states). For us, there are other ways of thinking about the process(es) of organizational change.

Rethinking the premises of OD

It is possible to juxtapose this traditional discourse of change (based upon the metaphor of "change as a journey" and the "doctor–patient" analogy) with a recently emerging discourse based upon the metaphors of "change as a conversation" and the "organization as a mystery". Table 7.1 summarizes the traditional and emerging perspectives. It presents a number of defining characteristics of each perspective and highlights the significant points of dissimilarity. In the remainder of this section the content of Table 7.1 will be discussed and the attendant implications for organizational change will be considered.

The traditional approach to change as a tangible, punctuated and discrete process has recently begun to be challenged by the emergence of a body of work which explores change as a process which is inherently interpretive and discursive in nature (see for example: Barrett et al., 1995; Bushe and Marshak, 2009; Heracleous and Barrett, 2001; Grant et al., 2005; Heracleous and Marshak, 2004; Ludema, 2002; Marshak, 2009; Marshak and Grant, 2008; Oswick, 2009; Oswick et al., 2005; Oswick et al., 2010). Hence, rather than envisaging an organization as a human entity with human attributes and qualities, it is possible to think of an organization as a discursive entity which is socially constructed. When viewed in this way an organization is constituted in and through language via the ongoing interaction of stakeholders (Boden, 1984). This perspective on organizations has become well established in the extant literature in the field (see, for example, Boje, 1995; Broekstra, 1998; Oswick and Richards, 2004; Taylor and van Emery, 2000). The obvious, but less widely established, implication for OD is that if you want to change an organization you need to focus on aspects of discourse. In short, changing organizations involves changing conversations (Ford, 1999; Ford and Ford, 1995; Ford and Ford, 2008; Shaw, 2002).

The two-part distinction that we have characterized in Table 7.1 between a "traditional " and an "emerging" discourse of change bears comparison to what Bushe and Marshak (2009) refer to as "diagnostic OD" (where organizations are likened to living systems) and "dialogic OD" (where organizations are seen as meaning-making systems). For Bushe and Marshak, diagnostic OD is rooted in positivism and "change is episodic, linear, and goal oriented" (2009: 357). By contrast, dialogic OD is: more interpretive in nature; it embraces the idea that reality is socially

Table 7.1 Contrasting metaphorically informed approaches to OD and organizational change

	Traditional Discourse of Change	*Emerging Discourse of Change*
Approach to Change	Conventional approach – diagnose & plan	Contemporary approach – converse & discover
Dominant Root Metaphors	Change *as* a journey – Organization *as* sick/ill	Change *as* a conversation – Organization *as* mystery
Key Stakeholders	Consultants (*as* doctors and navigators) & client system representatives (*as* patients and co-travellers)	Local managers & employees (*as* change agents and mutual participants in a dialogue)
Nature of the Change Process	Discrete change orientation (destination-oriented journey)	Continuous change orientation (ongoing conversation & discovery)
Environmental Imperatives	Relatively stable and predictable world	Hyperturbulent and rapidly changing world
Focus of Change	Emphasis on problems (negative framing)	Emphasis on improvement (positive framing)
Targets of Change	Tangible objects and artefacts (e.g. rules, roles, systems, the design of work, aspects of organizational structure)	Intangible phenomena (e.g. norms, values, morale, power, culture, identity, meaning, relationships)
Primary Concern	Hard change – demonstrating the 'actuality' of change	Soft change – the discursive co-construction of change
Change Strategy	Reactive and incremental	Proactive and emergent
Underlying Epistemology	Positivist/functionalist	Constructivist/interpretivist

constructed and socially negotiated; and "change may be continuous and/or cyclical" (p. 357). There are clear parallels between Bushe and Marshak's assertions and the metaphors of change presented in Table 7.1. For instance, the idea that in diagnostic OD the organization can be seen as a "living system" resonates with the health metaphor and the description of change as "episodic, linear and goal oriented" has obvious overtones of change as a destination-oriented journey. Also the idea of an organization as a meaning-making system has explicit discursive implications insofar as meaning-making occurs through social interaction (i.e. conversations).

Turning our gaze away from the metaphor of conversations let us consider the idea that organizations can be thought of as mysteries. The metaphor of an organization *as* a mystery has been employed by David Cooperrider as part of his formulation of "appreciative inquiry" (Cooperrider and Srivastva, 1987; Cooperrider et al., 2001; Cooperrider et al., 2008). Cooperrider and Whitney suggest that the basic assumption that underpins traditional OD approaches is that "An organization is a problem to be solved" (2001: 23).

Within appreciative inquiry (AI) the guiding assumption is that "An organization is a mystery to be valued and explored" (Cooperrider and Whitney, 2001: 23). As a structured approach to organizational change, the core elements of AI are: (i) appreciating and valuing the best of "what is"; (ii) envisioning "what might be"; (iii) dialoguing "what should be"; and (iv) innovating "what will be" (Cooperrider and Whitney, 2001). By foregrounding a social constructivist perspective, and firmly advocating processes of dialogue, AI is aligned to the emerging discourse of change.

In terms of its metaphorical credentials it is clear that AI treats change as a conversational process. Moreover, in common with the general characteristics of the emerging discourse of change, AI's is also firmly on "improvement" (i.e. a positive framing) rather than "problems" (i.e. a negative framing).

The metaphor of organization as mystery could also be applied to the recent interest in chaos theory and complexity approaches to change. Although not used explicitly in that context as far as we know, the ways in which self-organization occurs at the edge of chaos or whereby a butterfly flapping its wings in one part of the globe impacts actions around the world could indeed be considered mysteries. To the linear, cause and effect listener the discourse of chaos and complexity might sound like organizational actions are quite mysterious indeed (see, for example, Stacy, 2001; Shaw, 2002).

Having identified contrasting discourses of change which are informed and guided by different dominant root metaphors, we would like to consider the implications of these alternative framings. In particular, we wish to conclude by expressing some concerns regarding both the metaphorical and substantive delineation of the traditional discourse and the emerging discourse as applied to processes of organizational change.

Conclusions

As we have indicated earlier in this chapter, metaphors can illuminate phenomena and meaningfully guide action. However, as we have also suggested, they can also obscure, obfuscate and create partial truths. For us, the limitations associated with the subliminal deployment of the journey metaphor and health metaphor are that they position OD as a decidedly univocal and positivistic endeavour inasmuch as change is projected as an objective, rational, predictable, discrete, bounded and controllable process. Indeed, altogether *planned* change. This linear rendition may be psychologically reassuring for organizations and OD consultants, but, in our view, it represents a partial truth. It obscures the actual lived experience of many organizational stakeholders where organizational change is non-linear and unfolds as a complex and messy process which is often unpredictable and, at least to a certain extent, uncontrollable or even "chaotic" both in terms of process and outcomes.

The juxtaposing of a "traditional discourse" (based upon the metaphors of health and journeying) with an "emerging discourse" (based upon the metaphors of conversation and mystery) is not without problems. The problems are two-fold. First, the metaphorical dichotomization of the field into contrasting discourses of organizational change implies that the two domains are discrete and clearly delineated areas. Second, the use of the terms "traditional" and "emerging" connotes a temporal relationship (i.e. "old" approaches versus "new" approaches) where the outdated (i.e. "old") techniques and approaches are replaced and superseded by the up-to-date ones (i.e. "new" techniques and approaches).

We believe that the two discourses of change should not be seen as black and white categories. Instead, they should be seen as archetypal, but with certain points of overlap. So, for example, there are some traditional OD approaches – such as "T" groups (Bradford et al., 1964; Lewin, 1951) and process consultation (Schein, 1988) – which share aspects of similarity with emerging change approaches (i.e. strong dialogic/conversational components, not heavy on prescription and not overly endpoint-driven). Beyond this, and in terms of temporality, it is fair to say that the "traditional discourse of change" evolved before what has been presented here as the "emerging discourse". However, this does not mean that the traditional discourse has been replaced or has become redundant. The emerging discourse might usefully be considered as a counterbalance to the dominance of the traditional OD discourse rather than a replacement for it. Hence, in our view, the two discourses co-exist and should be seen as having "contemporary-synchronicity" (i.e. as equally valuable concurrent phenomena) rather than "temporal-diachronicity" (i.e. as consecutive and progressive epochs).

Given the contemporaneous and overlapping nature of the traditional and the emerging discourses, there is perhaps scope for their mutual deployment and for combined forms of engagement when undertaking OD change interventions. This could involve seeking to instigate context sensitive change programmes which, to varying degrees based upon the situation and circumstances, simultaneously balance and focus on problem-solving (areas of deficiency) and success-amplifying (areas of strength) and which meld an emphasis on materiality, actions and tangible outcomes with a concomitant consideration of discursive constructs, meanings and intangible social processes. Rethinking the premises of organizational change approaches will require the revision of metaphors and possibly the development of news ones. With regard to the future metaphorical framings of change, we might imagine approaches which integrate "destination-oriented journeying" with "conversations" to produce more nuanced "discursive journeys of quasi-exploration into uncharted realms".

References

Ackerman Anderson, L.S. and Anderson, D. (2010) *The Change Leader's Roadmap: Navigating your Organization's Transformation* (2nd edn). San Francisco, CA: Jossey-Bass.

Argyris, C. (1958) "The organization: What makes it healthy?", *Harvard Business Review*, 36(2): 107–16.

Armenakis, A.A. and Bedeian, A.G. (1992) "The role of metaphors in organizational change: Change agent and change target perspectives", *Group and Organization Management*, 17(3): 242–48.

Barrett, F.J. and Cooperrider D.L. (1990) "Generative metaphor intervention: A new approach to working with systems divided by conflict and caught in defensive perception", *Journal of Applied Behavioral Science*, 26(2): 219–39.

Barrett, F.J., Thomas, G.F. and Hocevar, S.P. (1995) "The central role of discourse in large-scale change: A social construction perspective", *Journal of Applied Behavioral Science*, 31(3): 352–72.

Beckhard, R. (1969) *Organization Development: Strategies and Models*. Reading, MA: Addison-Wesley.

Beckhard, R. and Harris, R. (1987) *Organizational Transitions*. Reading, MA: Addison-Wesley.

Boden, D. (1984) *The Business of Talk: Organizations in action*. Cambridge: Polity Press.

Boje, D. (1995) "Stories of the storytelling organization: A postmodern analysis of Disney as *Tamara*-land", *Academy of Management Journal*, 38(4): 997–1035.

Black, M. (1962) *Models and Metaphors*. Ithaca, NY: Cornell University Press.

Bradford, L., Gibb, J. and Benne, K. (1964) *T-Group Theory and Laboratory Method*. New York: John Wiley.

Brink, T.L. (1993) "Metaphor as data in the study of organizations", *Journal of Management Inquiry*, 2(4): 366–71.

Broekstra, G. (1998) "An organization is a conversation". In D. Grant, T. Keenoy and C. Oswick (eds) *Discourse and Organizations*, London: SAGE, pp. 152–76.

Broussine, M. and Vince, R. (1996) "Working with metaphor towards organizational change". In C. Oswick and D. Grant (eds) *Organisation Development: Metaphorical Explorations*. London: Pitman, pp. 57–72.

Brown, D.R. and Harvey, D. (2004) *An Experiential Approach to Organization Development* (7th edn). Upper Saddle River, NJ: Prentice-Hall.

Bruhn, J.G. (2001) *Trust and the Health of Organizations*. New York: Kluwer Academic/Plenum Publications.

Burke, W.W. (1992) "Metaphors to consult by", *Group and Organization Management*, 17(3): 255–59.

Bushe, G.R. and Marshak, R.J. (2009) "Revisioning organization development: Diagnostic and dialogic premises and patterns of practice", *Journal of Applied Behavioral Science*, 45(3): 348–68.

Cooperrider, D.L. and Srivastva, S. (1987) "Appreciative inquiry in organizational life". In R.W. Woodman and W.A. Pasmore (eds) *Research In Organizational Change And Development*, Vol. 1. Stamford, CT: JAI Press, pp. 129–69.

111

Cooperrider, D.L. and Whitney, D (2001) "A positive revolution in change". In D.L. Cooperrider, P. Sorenson, D. Whitney and T. Yeager (eds) *Appreciative Inquiry: An Emerging Direction for Organization Development*. Champaign, IL: Stipes, pp. 9–29.

Cooperrider, D.L., Whitney, D. and Stavros, J.M. (2008) *Appreciative Inquiry Handbook* (2nd edn). Brunswick, OH: Crown Custom Publishing.

Cooperrider, D. Sorenson, P., Whitney, D. and Yeager, T. (eds) (2001) *Appreciative Inquiry: An Emerging Direction for Organization Development*. Champaign, IL: Stipes.

Cornelissen, J.P. (2005) "Beyond compare: Metaphor in organization theory", *Academy of Management Review*, 30: 751–64.

Doving, E. (1996) "In the image of man: Organizational action, competence and learning". In D. Grant and C. Oswick (eds) *Metaphor and Organizations*. London: SAGE, pp. 185–99.

Dunford, R. and Palmer, I. (1996) "Metaphors in popular management discourse: The case of corporate restructuring". In D. Grant and C. Oswick (eds) *Metaphor and Organizations*, London: SAGE, pp. 95–109.

Fauconnier G. and Turner, M. (2002) *The Way We Think: Conceptual Blending and the Mind's Hidden Complexities*. New York: Basic Books.

Ford, J.D. (1999) "Organizational change as shifting conversations", *Journal of Organizational Change Management*, 12(6): 480–500.

Ford, J.D. and Ford, L.W. (1995) "The role of conversations in producing intentional change in organizations", *Academy of Management Review*, 20: 541–70.

Ford, J.D. and Ford, L.W. (2008) "Conversational profiles: A tool for altering the conversational pattern of change managers", *Journal of Applied Behavioral Science*, 44: 445–67.

French, W. and Bell, C.H. (1995) *Organization Development: Behavioral Science Interventions for Organization Improvement* (5th ed.) Englewood Cliffs, NJ: Prentice-Hall.

Gentner, D. (1983) "Structure mapping: A theoretical framework for analogy", *Cognitive Science*, 7: 155–70.

Gentner, D. (1989) "The mechanisms of analogical learning". In S. Vasniadou and A. Ortony (eds) *Similarity and Analogical Reasoning*. New York: Cambridge University Press, pp. 199–241.

Gentner, D. and Jeziorski, M. (1993) "The shift from metaphor to analogy in Western science". In A. Ortony (ed.) *Metaphor and Thought*. Cambridge: Cambridge University Press, pp. 447–80.

Goldman Schuyler, K. (2004) "The possibility of healthy organizations: Toward a new framework for organizational theory and practice", *Journal of Applied Sociology/Sociological Practice*, 21(2): 57–79.

Grant, D. and Oswick, C. (1996) "Getting the measure of metaphors". In D. Grant and C. Oswick (eds) *Metaphor and Organizations*, London: SAGE, pp. 1–20.

Grant, D., Michelson, G., Oswick, C. and Wailes, N. (2005) "Discourse and organizational change", *Journal of Organizational Change Management*, 18(1): 6–15.

Hatch, M.J. and Yanow, D. (2008) "Methodology by metaphor: Ways of seeing in painting and research", *Organization Studies*, 29(1): 23–44.

Heracleous, L. and Barrett, M. (2001) "Organizational change as discourse: Communicative actions and deep structures in the context of information technology implementation", *Academy of Management Journal*, 44: 755–78.

Heracleous, L. and Jacobs, C.D. (2008) "Understanding organizations through embodied metaphors", *Organization Studies*, 29(1): 45–78.

Heracleous, L. and Marshak, R.J. (2004) "Conceptualizing organizational discourse as situated symbolic action", *Human Relations*, 57: 1285–1312.

Inns, D. (1996) Organisation development as a journey. In C. Oswick and D. Grant (eds) *Organisation Development: Metaphorical Explorations*, London: Pitman Publishing, pp. 20–34.

Inns, D.E. and Jones, P.J. (1996) "Metaphor in organization theory: Following in the footsteps of the poet". In D. Grant and C. Oswick (eds) *Metaphor and Organizations*, London: SAGE, pp. 110–26.

Jacobs, C. and Heracleous, L. (2006) "Constructing shared understanding: The role of embodied metaphor in organization development", *Journal of Applied Behavioral Science*, 42(2): 207–26.

Kumra, S. (1996) "The organization as a human entity". In C. Oswick and D. Grant (eds) *Organisation Development: Metaphorical Explorations*. London: Pitman, pp. 35–53.

Lakoff, G. and Johnson, M. (1980) *Metaphors We Live By*. Chicago, IL: University of Chicago Press.

Lakoff, G. and Johnson, M. (1999) *Philosophy in the Flesh: The Embodied Mind and its Challenge to Western Thought*. New York: Basic Books.

Leavitt, H.J. (1986) *Corporate Pathfinders*. Chicago, IL: Dow-Jones-Irwin.

Lewin, K. (1947) Frontiers in group dynamics: Concept, method and reality in social science, social equilibria and social change, *Human Relations*, 1(1): 5–41.

Lewin, K. (1951) *Field Theory in Social Science*. New York: Harper.

Ludema, J.D. (2002) "Appreciative storytelling: A narrative approach to organization development and change?" In R. Fry, D. Whitney, J. Seiling and F. Barrett (eds) *Appreciative Inquiry and Organizational Transformation: Reports from the Field*, Westport, CT: Quorum, pp. 239–61.

Manning, P. (1979) "Metaphors of the field: Varieties of organizational discourse", *Administrative Science Quarterly*, 24: 660–71.

Marshak, R.J. (1993a) "Managing the metaphors of change," *Organizational Dynamics*, 22(1): 44–56.

Marshak, R.J. (1993b) "Lewin meets Confucius: A re-view of the OD model of change", *Journal of Applied Behavioral Science*, 29(4): 393–415.

Marshak, R.J. (1994) "The tao of change", *OD Practitioner*, 26(2): 18–26.

Marshak, R.J. (2009) *Organizational Change: Views from the Edge*. Bethel, ME: The Lewin Center.

Marshak, R.J. and Grant, D. (2008) "Organizational discourse and new organization development practices", *British Journal of Management*, 19: S7–S19.

McLean, A., Sims, D., Mangham, I. and Tuffield, D. (1982) *Organization Development in Transition*. Chichester: Wiley.

Morgan, G. (1986) *Images of Organization*. Beverly Hills, CA: SAGE.

Morgan, G. (1988) *Riding the Waves of Change*. San Franscisco, CA: Jossey-Bass.

Morgan, G. (1996) "Is there anything more to be said about metaphor?" In D. Grant and C. Oswick (eds) *Metaphor and Organizations*, London: SAGE, pp. 227–40.

Nees, D.B. and Greiner, L.E. (1985) Seeing behind the look-alike management consultants, *Organizational Dynamics*, 14(1), pp. 68–79.

Ortony, A. (1975) "Why metaphors are necessary and not just nice", *Educational Theory*, 25: 45–53.

Ortony, A. (1993) "Metaphor, language and thought". In A. Ortony (ed.) *Metaphor and Thought*, Cambridge: Cambridge University Press, pp. 1–17.

Oswick, C. (2009) "Revisioning or re-versioning? A commentary on diagnostic and dialogic forms of organization development", *Journal of Applied Behavioral Science*, 45(3): 369–74.

Oswick, C. and Grant, D. (1996) "The organization of metaphors and the metaphors of organization: Where are we and where do we go from here?" In D. Grant and C. Oswick (eds) *Metaphor and Organizations*, London: SAGE, pp. 213–26.

Oswick, C. and Montgomery, J. (1999) "Images of an organization: The use of metaphor in a multinational company", *Journal of Organizational Change Management*, 12(6): 501–23.

Oswick, C. and Richards, D. (2004) "Talk in organizations: Local conversations, wider perspectives", *Culture and Organization*, 10(2): 107–23.

Oswick, C., Keenoy, T. and Grant, D. (2002) "Metaphor and analogical reasoning in organization theory: Beyond orthodoxy", *Academy of Management Review*, 27(2): 294–303.

Oswick, C., Grant, D., Marshak, R.J. and Wolfram Cox, J. (2010) "Organizational discourse and change: Positions, perspectives, progress, and prospects", *Journal of Applied Behavioral Science*, 46(1): 8–15.

Oswick, C., Grant, D., Michelson, G. and Wailes, N. (2005) "Looking forwards: Discursive directions in organizational change", *Journal of Organizational Change Management*, 18(4): 383–90.

Palmer, I. and Dunford, R. (1996) "Understanding organizations through metaphor". In C. Oswick and D. Grant (eds) *Organisation Development: Metaphorical Explorations*. London: Pitman, pp. 7–19.

Pinder, C.C. and Bourgeois, V.W. (1982) "Controlling tropes in administrative science", *Administrative Science Quarterly*, 27: 641–52.

Porras, J.L. (1987) *Stream Analysis: A Powerful to Diagnose and Manage Organizational Change*. Reading, MA: Addison-Wesley Publishing.

Sackmann, S. (1989) "The role of metaphors in organizational transformation", *Human Relations*, 42(6): 463–85.

Schein, E.H. (1988) *Process Consultation: Its Role in Organization Development – Volume I* (2nd edn), Reading, MA: Addison-Wesley.

Schön, D.A. (1993) "Generative metaphor: A perspective on problem setting in social policy". In A. Ortony (ed.) *Metaphor and Thought* (2nd edn), Cambridge: Cambridge University Press, pp. 135–61.

Shaw, B. and Maletz, M. (1995) "Business processes: Embracing the logic and limits of reengineering". In D. Nadler, B. Shaw and A. Walton (eds) *Discontinuous Change: Leading Organizational Transformation*. San Franscisco, CA: Jossey-Bass, pp. 169–189.

Shaw, P. (2002) *Changing Conversations in Organizations: A Complexity Approach to Change*. London: Routledge.

Srivastva, S. and Barrett, F.J. (1988) "The transforming nature of metaphors in group development: A study in group therapy", *Human Relations*, 41(1): 31–64.

Stacy, R.D. (2001) *Complex Responsive Processes in Organizations*. London: Routledge.

Taylor, J.R. and van Emery, E. (2000) *The Emergent Organization*. Meihwah, NJ: Lawrence Erlbaum.

Tinker, T. (1986) "Metaphor or reification? Are radical humanists really libertarian anarchists?", *Journal of Management Studies*, 25: 363–84.

Tilles, S. (1961) "Understanding the consultant's role", *Harvard Business Review*, 39(6), November–December.

Tsoukas, H. (1991) "The missing link: A transformational view of metaphors in organizational science", *Academy of Management Review*, 16(3): 566–85.

Tsoukas, H. (1993) "Analogical reasoning and knowledge generation in organization theory", *Organization Studies*, 14(3): 323–46.

Ver Schere, S. (1984) "Assessing the strengths and challenges of your group", *Fund Raising Management*, December: 60–61.

Waterman, R.H. (1987) *The Renewal Factor*. New York: Bantam Books.

Part 2

Newer approaches to change

Introduction

Bernard Burnes

It was the rise of Japanese competitiveness and the apparent eclipse of Western industry in the late 1970s that precipitated the questioning of existing approaches to structuring, managing and changing organizations (Pascale and Athos, 1982). Western organizations were portrayed as too bureaucratic and lacking innovation. It was argued that their survival depended on their adopting cultures that would promote innovation and entrepreneurship and encourage bottom-up, flexible, continuous and cooperative change (Peters and Waterman, 1982). Organization development (OD) was portrayed as focussing on incremental and small-scale change and, as such, inappropriate for this new environment (Wilson, 1992). In particular, it was Lewin's planned change which bore the brunt of these criticisms (Buchanan and Storey, 1997). Perhaps the most trenchant criticism came from Kanter et al. (1992: 10) who commented:

> Lewin's model was a simple one, with organizational change involving three stages; unfreezing, changing and refreezing ...This quaintly linear and static conception – the organization as an ice cube – is so wildly inappropriate that it is difficult to see why it has not only survived but prospered ... Suffice it to say here, first, that organizations are never frozen, much less refrozen, but are fluid entities with many 'personalities'. Second, to the extent that there are stages, they overlap and interpenetrate one another in important ways.

As the five chapters in this part will show, the attempts to replace OD as the dominant approach to change have come from three main quarters: processual change, emergent change and the complexity-based approach to change. Proponents of the complexity approach tend to refer to change as emergence, which can lead to confusion with emergent change. However, though sharing some similarities, they differ in their underlying theories.

Dawson, in Chapter 8, introduces the processual approach to change. This was the first substantial challenge to the dominance of OD and arose from Pettigrew's work on organizational change. This began in the 1970s, and really came to prominence with the publication of his study of ICI in the 1980s (Pettigrew, 1985). Processualists view change not as an episodic or isolated phenomenon, but as an ongoing, dynamic process – hence the term processual. According to Dawson, processualists see organizational change as being shaped over time by three broad overlapping and interlocking elements: the politics, context and substance of change. He also shows that though it does provide some practical guidelines for those undertaking change, the processualist approach is more concerned with the study and understanding of change rather than offering guidance those undertaking change.

In Chapter 9, Burnes examines the emergent approach to change, which for many was seen as the successor to OD. He shows that it has some strong similarities and overlaps with the processualist approach, especially in terms of Pettigrew's work. Burnes maintains that for proponents of the emergent approach, change is a continuous, dynamic and contested process that emerges in an unpredictable and unplanned fashion. For these reasons, change is not a rational process. Instead, it depends for its success on five key features of organizations: organizational structure, organizational culture, organizational learning, managerial behaviour, and power and politics. In summarizing the emergent approach, Burnes argues that, though it has a number of distinct strengths, it is not applicable to all change situations and, therefore, it needs to be considered alongside, rather than instead of, other approaches to change.

Influential as the emergent approach has been, it appears to have been overtaken in recent years by interest in theories of change from the natural world, notably complexity theory and chaos theory. In Chapter 10, Letiche introduces the concept of complexity and shows how its effects, based on simple order-generating rules, are manifested in the form of emergence. Emergence is the constant ebb and flow of living, self-organizing systems which arises from the interaction of the individual components of the system. Letiche makes the case for putting ethics at the centre of the complexity approach. He maintains that human beings have a duty of care towards themselves and others which must manifest itself in both the process and outcome of change. Letiche states that we need to view organizations from this care perspective rather than from a performance perspective. For him, complexity ethics has the potential to create an alternative to managerialist approaches to change, which put profit before people.

Chapter 11 by Lissack continues the emergence theme. He argues that organizational change projects are about confronting and embracing emergence, and that successful change depends on achieving coherence: comprehensibility, manageability and meaningfulness. Coherence is not an accidental occurrence but is achieved through processes of complexity reduction that arise from affordances and homology. Affordances are situations where "possibility" presents itself as weak signals which prompt action by those who perceive them. Homology is the study of sameness. When two or more items, events, or contexts share an underlying mode, they are said to be homologous. Lissack argues that when affordances and homology coincide, the amount of effort needed for a coherent response to complexity is reduced. He also explores the role of dialogue and narrative about affordances and homologies as a means of making sense of guiding people though uncertainty and change.

The role of narrative in making sense of emergence is continued in the last chapter in this part. Boje and Wakefield introduce the concept of systemicity – the recognition that system boundaries are an illusion and that systems can never be fully understood. Boje and Wakefield argue that through the convergence of narrative and storytelling, these boundaryless, complex systems can be understood and purposeful action initiated. They argue that successful leaders are ones who recognize the opportunities of emergence and have the courage to channel its flow to benefit their organizations.

Though processual change, emergent change and the complexity-based approach to change have vied to replace OD over the last 20 to 30 years, none have succeeded. The processual approach has won favour in some quarters, but it is emergent change which has been seen as the main challenger to OD, at least until recently (see Beer and Nohria, 2000; Burnes, 2009). Certainly, in terms of the number of publications, it far outstrips the processual approach. However, both of these approaches appear to suffer from a lack of empirical support – the longitudinal studies necessary to support them have simply not been undertaken, or at least not in sufficient numbers or rigour. Mainly for this reason, they have not been able to provide practitioners with the tools, techniques, advice and evidence which would allow either the processual or emergent approach to replace OD. However, as these two approaches have faltered in their challenge to OD, the complexity-emergence approach has grown in strength. Despite the enormous volume of publications seeking to apply complexity to organizations, this is an approach which is still developing. Furthermore, emergence is a way of understanding how change arises in organizations; it is not necessarily a means of managing change. Therefore, it will be some years yet before we can tell whether the promise of emergence will be realized. We must also bear in mind Pettigrew's (2000: 245) observation, cited in Chapter 9, that the time for "bipolar modes of thinking" may be over and that we need to embrace a broader range of change approaches and perspectives.

References

Beer, M. and Nohria, N. (eds) (2000) *Breaking the Code of Change*. Harvard Business School Press: Boston, MA.

Buchanan, D.A. and Storey, J. (1997) Role-taking and Role-switching in Organizational Change: The Four Pluralities. In I. McLoughlin and M. Harris (eds) *Innovation, Organizational Change and Technology*. International Thompson: London.

Burnes, B. (2009) *Managing Change* (5th edition). FT/Prentice Hall: Harlow.

Kanter, R.M., Stein, B.A. and Jick, T.D. (1992) *The Challenge of Organizational Change*. Free Press: New York.

Pascale, R.T. and Athos, A.G. (1982) *The Art of Japanese Management*. Penguin: Harmondsworth.

Peters, T. and Waterman, R.H. (1982) *In Search of Excellence: Lessons from America's Best-Run Companies*. Harper & Row: London.

Pettigrew, A.M. (1985) *The Awakening Giant: Continuity and Change at ICI*. Blackwell: Oxford.

Pettigrew, A.M. (2000) Linking Change Processes and Outcomes: A Commentary on Ghosal, Bartlett and Weick. In M. Beer and N. Nohria (eds) *Breaking the Code of Change*. Harvard Business School Press: Boston, MA.

Wilson, D.C. (1992) *A Strategy of Change*. Routledge: London.

8

The contribution of the processual approach to the theory and practice of organizational change

Patrick Dawson

Introduction

The contribution of the processual approach in providing a methodology for studying the dynamics of change, in offering a conceptual framework that facilitates theorization and in generating practical guidelines on change management is the focus of this chapter. It commences by discussing the longstanding debate over whether we view organizations as generally stable entities consisting of identifiable objects, resources and structures of control and coordination or whether we view organizations as fluid entities in a constant state of flux. A brief explanation of what we mean by processual research and how it relates to studying change in organizations is then presented. This is followed by a history and critique of the approach. The historical overview charts processual research from some of the early studies in workplace industrial sociology through to more recent contributions. The chapter then provides a brief reappraisal and examines concerns about the practical dimension of processual research to understanding complex change processes.

But first let us turn our attention to the debate on whether organizations exist as stable entities or whether they are continually in motion consisting of processes of becoming (Tsoukas and Chia, 2002). Theories of change often take as their starting point either a notion of fluidity or stability and then use this to develop a particular theoretical explanation of change. For example, *punctuated equilibrium theory* (Anderson and Tushman, 1990; Romanelli and Tushman, 1994) views stability as the normal state of play but recognizes that industries and organizations can experience major shocks within their business environments that necessitate major change. In contrast, *chaos theory* assumes a continuous dynamic interplay between forces that create a constant state of flux within which organizations achieve temporary periods of stability (Dubinskas, 1994; Stacey, 1992). Taken from the physical sciences, the basic argument of chaos theory is that disequilibrium is an essential condition in the development of dynamic systems as it promotes internal resilience (see also Burnes, 2005; Hayes, 2007). *Processual approaches* also assume fluidity in the continual and multifaceted flow of factors in organizations. As a result, proponents have argued that the terms organizing and strategizing (verbs) are preferable to the terms organization and strategy (nouns) as they more usefully capture the dynamic nature of processes of change (see, Pettigrew et al., 2003). This introduction illustrates that these and other theories of change, hold different ontological views about the nature of organizations and, consequently, disagree about the appropriate methods for studying change in organizations.

Van de Ven and Poole (2005) examine alternative approaches for studying organizational change and argue that many of the disagreements evident can be traced back to the differing philosophies of Heraclitus and Democritus. Process was central to Heraclitus' view of the world and was later taken up by the processual philosophers such as Alfred North Whitehead and John Dewey. As Van de Ven and Poole (2005: 1378) note: 'They viewed reality as a process and regarded time, change, and creativity as representing the most fundamental facts for understanding the world.' In contrast, Democritus 'pictured all of nature as composed of stable material substance or things that changed only in their positioning in space and time' (Langley, 2009; Mohr, 1982). In support of this view, Whetten (2006) argues that the study of organizations should focus on entities, such as structure and culture, rather than on social processes. This distinction between an emphasis on organizing as a process (or verb) and organization as a thing (or noun) has generated considerable debate within the academic literature (see Van de Ven and Poole, 2005). As two alternative and competing views of the world, these debates and issues can never be fully resolved, but perhaps each may serve to address different questions. The quantitative researcher is likely to take a more static worldview in studies on the relationships between variables; whereas, the qualitative researcher is more likely to be oriented to a process–world view in studying the processes of change in context and over time. That both approaches can contribute to knowledge on change is not in doubt. However, in this chapter the focus is on those scholars who conceptualize change as an ongoing dynamic process. After providing an overview of the processual approach, the chapter turns its attention to historical developments and some longstanding controversies.

A processual framework for understanding change

Processual research on change can be defined as the contextual, retrospective and real-time study of change as-it-happens over time through the observed, documented and lived experiences of people as they seek to make sense and give sense individually and collectively to decision and non-decision making activities, the actions and torpidity of others, the multiple stories that transform and compete over time, and the events and critical incidents that occur in expected and unexpected ways. The research is interested in the formal documented accounts, post hoc rationalizations and official versions of events, as well as in revealing the emergent, complex, muddied and unforeseen processes of change. It is interested in capturing attitudes and perceptions at all levels within the organization, from senior managers to operational employees as well as various key stakeholders, such as consultants, change agents and trade-union officials. Fieldwork is intensive, detailed and longitudinal employing a range of data collection techniques to capture and analyse subjective experience, chronicle sequences of events, examine and interpret documented material, and observe behaviours and daily practices. The approach seeks to accommodate dominant narratives as well as the multiple conflicting stories and outlier or deviant views that co-exist and shift over time in trying to uncover the full range of experiences that includes the 'dominant', 'common', 'hidden' and 'silenced' voices on change.

According to Dawson (1994), this framework views organizational change as being shaped over time by three broad overlapping and interlocking elements that comprise the politics, context and substance of change. The politics of change is taken to refer to political activities that occur both externally and within the organization. External political activity may involve: senior business leaders or industry groups lobbying government, the formation of various strategic competitor alliances and so forth; whilst internal political activity may be in the form of shop-floor negotiations between trade-union representatives and management, between consultants (working within the organization) and various organizational groups, and between and within managerial, supervisory and operative personnel. The contextual dimension also includes various elements residing outside the organization, such as the business market, world events, availability and development in technology; as well as internal dimensions, such as the history and culture of an organization, their human and capital resources and governance structures. The substance of change is taken to refer to the scale and scope of change, the defining characteristics of change, the timeframe of change, and the perceived centrality of change. As such, the processual framework is concerned with understanding: the political arenas in which decisions are made, histories re-created and strategies rationalized (politics); the enabling and constraining characteristics of change programmes and the scale and type of change (substance); the conditions under which change is taking place in relation to external elements, such as the business market environment and internal elements, including the history and culture of an organization (context); and the way these shape processes over time as an organization moves from an existing position to some future state (for a more detailed explanation see Dawson, 2003).

For analytical purposes, Dawson, (1994: 44) identifies three general timeframes comprising: (1) the initial conception of a need to change; (2) the process of organizational change; and (3) the initial and routine operation of new work practices and procedures. The initial awareness of a need to change may either be in response to external or internal pressures for change (reactive), or through a belief in the need for change to meet future competitive demands (proactive). Once a need for change has been identified, then the complex non-linear and 'black box' process of organizational change commences. This period will comprise a number of different tasks, activities and decisions for individuals and groups both within and outside of the organization. When a decision has been made on the general theme or content of change, then the task of search and assessment may follow, where members of an organization set out to find the best option for achieving a particular change objective. System selection is also likely to influence the process of planning for the task of implementing change; for example, the logistics of managing the change (what pieces of equipment, where, in what order) and for ensuring that staff can use the new equipment (for example, when and how much training is going to be required), will be partly determined by the type of system selected. Moreover, in planning for change, decisions have to be made about the design of the organizational operating system: that is, decisions on the organization of work in the daily operation of the new equipment. The task of implementing change has been well documented within the literature (see for example, Preece et al., 2000; Preece et al., 1999; Spector, 2009), and has been identified by Buchanan and Badham (2008) as a period which requires considerable political skill on the part of the agent. It is during the implementation of change that occupational and employee concerns normally begin to influence and shape the speed and direction of change (Dawson, 1994). The final general timeframe (the initial and routine operation of new work practices and procedures) is taken to refer to the period when, following the implementation of change, new organizational arrangements and systems of operation begin to emerge and then stabilize. During initial operation, factors such as business market considerations are likely to decline in significance whereas occupational and employee concerns are likely to increase in importance and influence management's strategic objectives behind the change (Dawson, 1994: 46). The early stages of operating under new systems may be characterized by uncertainty, conflict and misunderstanding among employees, who may variously adapt, modify, reassert and/or redefine their positions under new operating procedures and working relationships set up during the implementation of change. This is also the period in which a relatively stabilized system of operation may emerge comprising new

121

Context of Change
(Past, Present and Future)
External Context
(e.g. market, legislation, political events)
Internal Context
(i)   Human resources
      (e.g. work relations/teamwork)
(ii) Administrative structures
      (e.g. job design/work structures)
(iii) Technology
      (e.g. plant, machinery, tools)
(iv) Product or service
      (e.g. core business activity)
(v)   History and culture
      (e.g. contextual evolution of shared
      beliefs and assumptions)

Sense Making & Sense Giving

Present

Future   Past

THE
CHANGE
PROCESS

Politics of Change
External Political Activity
(e.g. lobbying of politicians,
strategic alliances, market
positioning, stakeholder and
competitor discussions)

Internal Political Activity
(e.g. consultation, negotiation,
conflicts and resistance, which
occurs within and between
groups and individuals during the
process of organizational change)

Substance of Change
Scale and Scope
(e.g. from small discrete to large radical change
initiatives)
Defining characteristics
(e.g. two change projects with same label may
be very different, so concerned with content)
Timeframe
(e.g. stops and starts from conception thought
to routine operation)
Perceived Centrality
(e.g. extent to which change seen as central to
company survival)

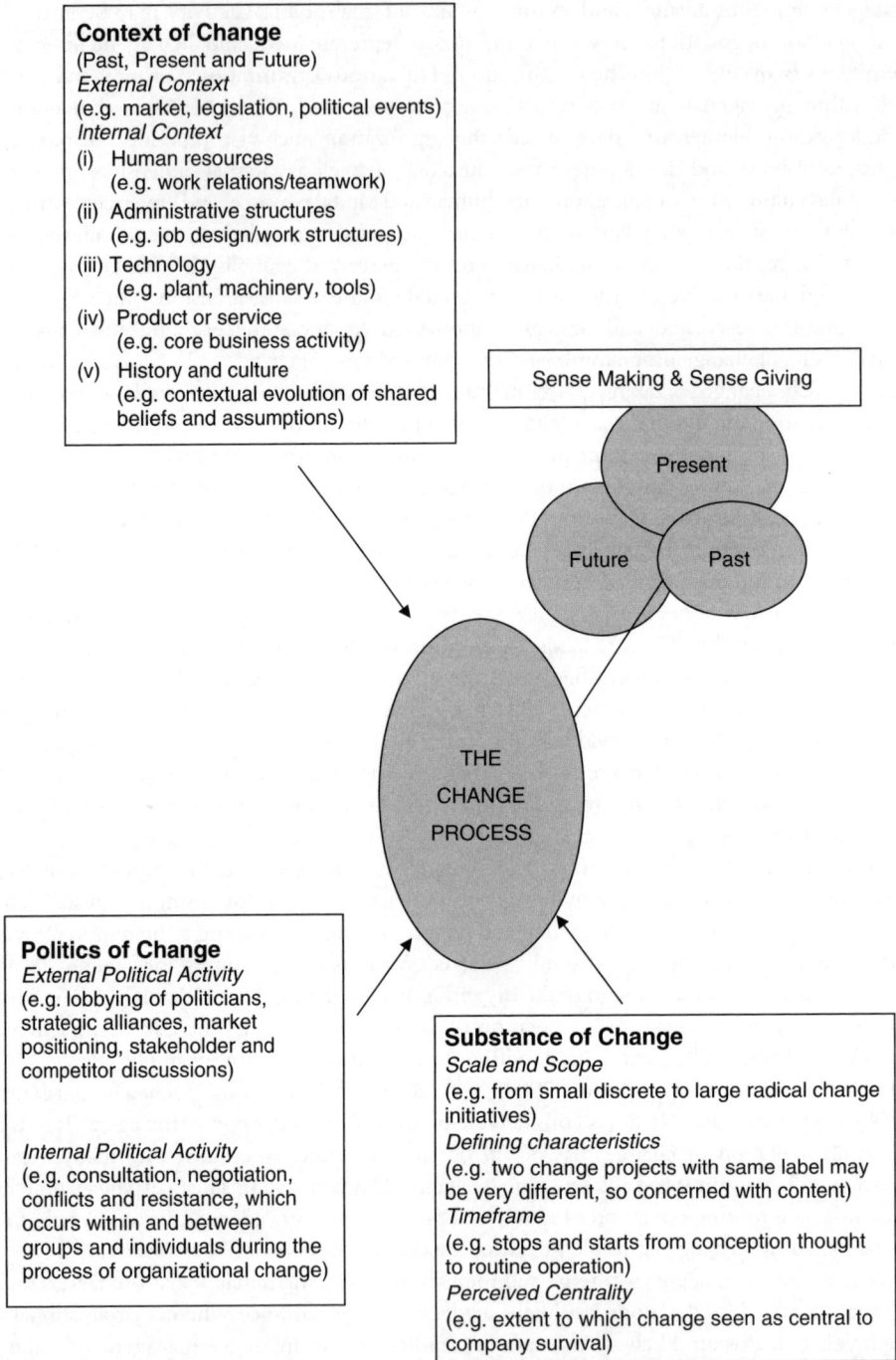

Figure 8.1 Dawson's processual framework for understanding organizational change

patterns of relationships and new forms of working practices. It is during this timeframe, there-fore, that the outcomes of change can be examined and contrasted with the operating system prior to change. Although in reality it is unrealistic to talk of an 'endpoint' of change (as the process continues *ad infinitum*), it is possible to identify a period after implementation when the daily work routines of employees become part of the operating system which is no longer regarded as 'new'. Routine operation provides an element of stability (Becker, 2004), a baseline from which inferences and assessments of change can be drawn. However, as Pentland and Rueter (1994) and Orlikowski (2002) illustrate, routines change over time and as such, outcomes are not fixed but represent outcomes at a particular moment in time (for a discussion about the way change is endogenous to routines themselves, see Becker, 2004). The basic elements of this processual framework that attempts to capture the temporal inter-connectedness (past, present and future) of the substance, context and politics of change, as people (individually and collec-tively) seek to make sense and give sense to their experiences, are outlined diagrammatically in Figure 8.1.

An historical overview of the processual approach to change

Industrial sociology has a long-established tradition of workplace studies on the processual dynamics of change. Early examples include Dalton's (1959) study of the changing alliances, power-plays and the purposeful management of information by cliques in pursuit of advantages over others, and Gouldner's (1965) analysis of the dynamics of management–worker interaction and the influence of social processes during a succession of bargaining incidents. Roy's (1967) study on the process of quota restriction and goldbricking in a machine shop, conducted from November 1944 to August 1945, is a particularly good example. He illustrates the process by which operators met their quota for 'gravy jobs' then 'knocked off' and how over time they restricted output on jobs they considered 'stinkers' and deliberately produced at lower rates. The workers sought to manage their earnings (determined by variations in hourly production piecework rates). This entailed ensuring that the rates for 'gravy jobs' were not lost whilst engaging in work behaviours that would encourage the reconsideration of rates for 'stinkers'. As a fellow worker advised (Roy, 1967: 316): 'Don't let it go over $1.25 an hour, or the time-study man will be right down here!' As Elger indicates, many of these early empirical studies can be broadly placed within the processual school of thought:

> The processual perspective emphasizes that the social structures of industrial concerns are patterned by negotiations and interpretation among participants with diverse interests and resources, so that analyses of variations and changes in such structures must attend to those sustaining and transforming processes.
>
> (Elger, 1975: 114)

In drawing on the work of Woodward (1958, 1980) and Burns and Stalker (1961), Elger outlines how these studies have often been too quickly ignored and misunderstood. His discussion highlights how major detailed empirical studies of innovation and change have historically drawn attention to *process* in the study of organizations. He demonstrates how the case studies of Woodward draw attention to an ongoing process in which management ideology, established rhetorics and political manoeuvring all serve to influence change outcomes. Similarly, in detailing the work of Burns and Stalker (1961), Elger (1975: 109) argues that whilst a systems typology is their starting point 'they develop, in relation to a rich array of empirical materials, a processual analysis which treats actors' allegiances, perspectives and strategies as problematic features of organizational action'. Similarly, Child's (1972: 2) critique of systems orthodoxy also drew attention to the process by which power-holders make strategic choices. He highlights the role of agency and choice in the way that individuals and groups can influence the environment rather than simply being constrained by operational contingencies. As he states in a later reappraisal of the strategic choice perspective:

> Strategic choice articulates a political process, which brings agency and structure into tension and locates them within a significant context. It regards both the relation of agency to structure and to environment as dynamic in nature. In so doing, the strategic choice approach not only bridges a numbers of competing perspectives but also adopts a non-deterministic and potentially evolutionary position. Strategic choice, when considered as a process, points to the possibility of continuing adaptive learning cycles, but within a theoretical framework that locates 'organizational learning' within the context of organizations as socio-political systems.
>
> (Child, 1997: 44)

The early work of Burns and Stalker (1961) and the perspective of Elger (1975) and Child (1972) contributed to the political process perspective which forms part of the processual approach developed by other authors (Clark et al., 1988). Pettigrew (1985), for example, clarifies how his processual approach builds on his PhD work (under the supervision of Enid Mumford) on the politics of organizational change (see Pettigrew, 1973). He views political process as evolving from individual and group levels, in which interest groups may form and develop different rationalities which direct action and response (whilst a particular rationality may predominate at any one time this is seen to be open to change). For Pettigrew (1985), change creates tension over the existing distribution of resources through threatening the position of some whilst opening up opportunities for others. As such, change stimulates power plays and heightened political activity. He notes how the greatest political energy is normally released when the decision to change is being made rather than during implementation when constraints have already been set (Pettigrew, 1985: 43). He also suggests that the political and cultural elements of change are likely to overlap in the management of meaning, especially in situations where individuals or groups seek to legitimize their own position and to delegitimize others (see also Bloor and Dawson, 1994).

In his study of ICI, Pettigrew (1985: 438–76) demonstrates how strategic change is a continuous process with no clear beginning or end point, and how it often emerges with deep-seated contextual, cultural and political roots that support the establishment of a dominant ideology. As such, he usefully illustrates how strategic change processes are best understood in context and over time, as continuity is often 'a good deal easier to see than change' (Pettigrew, 1985: 439). His book powerfully demonstrates the limitations of theories that view change either as a single event or as a discrete series of episodes that can be decontextualized. In a comparative analysis of five cases of strategic change, the study illustrates how change as a continuous incremental process (evolutionary) can be interspersed with radical periods of change (revolutionary). Major change initiatives are associated with major changes in business market conditions (such as world economic recessions) in which managers develop active strategies which build on these circumstances in order to legitimate and justify the need for change. For Pettigrew 'change and continuity, process and structure, are inextricably linked' (1985: 1) and he argues that the intention is not simply to substitute a rational approach with a political process perspective, but 'to explore some of the conditions in which mixtures of these occur' (1985: 24). He also notes how empirical findings and theoretical developments are generally 'method-bound' and how studies on organizational change have tended to adopt the planned stage model approach of organization development (OD). Pettigrew is highly critical of such approaches to change which are seen to ignore the importance of *changing*. As he states (1985: 15):

> For as long as we continue to conduct research on change which is ahistorical, acontextual, and aprocessual, which continues to treat the change programme as the unit of analysis and regard change as an episode divorced from the immediate and more distant context in which it is embedded, then we will continue to develop inadequate descriptive theories of change which are ill-composed guides for action. Indeed as I have implied already there is still a dearth of studies which can make statements about the how and why of change, about the processual dynamics of change, in short which go beyond the analysis of *change* and begin to theorize about *changing*.

In drawing on longitudinal contextual data (between 1975 and 1983, 134 people were interviewed), Pettigrew examines the interplay between internal contextual variables of culture, history and political process with external business conditions as factors that maintain continuity or bring about change. In providing a holistic contextual analysis, the approach provides both vertical analysis, examining factors such as external socio-economic influences on internal group behaviour, and horizontal analysis, for example in studying changing organizations with a past, present and future. In multilevel theory construction, attention is given to the way contextual variables in the vertical analysis link to those examined in horizontal analysis, and how processes both shape and constrain structures (Pettigrew, 1985: 37). The five essential needs of processual analysis are seen to comprise the following. First, the need to study changes in their context, or what is referred to as 'embeddedness' (Pettigrew, 1997: 340). Second, to study change over time and to identify the timing and sequencing of events. Third, the need to recognize that context and action are always tangled together, or in Pettigrew's (1997: 341) words 'context is not just a stimulus environment but a nested arrangement of structures and processes where the subjective interpretations of actors perceiving, learning, and remembering help shape process'. Fourth, the need to identify patterns and interrelated links among a range of features. Fifth, the value of examining outcomes in comparative case settings in order to explore how context and process explain divergence in outcome. These five assumptions of: embeddedness, temporal interconnectedness, intertwining of context and action, holistic explanation and the use of outcomes as a focus for processual analysis are seen to guide the researcher towards the case write-up as an 'analytical chronology' in which patterns in the data are identified and clarified (Pettigrew, 1997: 346). Emphasis is placed on comparative analysis with the goal of achieving broader thematic writing through 'meta level analysis and presentation'. The central aim is to weave an argument that constantly moves from the general to the particular in 'linking the theoretical and empirical findings across cases to wider bodies of literature' (Pettigrew, 1997: 346).

In building on this work, Dawson (2003) calls for accommodation of the polyvocal narratives of change and a movement away from focusing analysis on the dominant 'voices' within organizations. He argues that it is important to examine change from various viewpoints spotlighting the need to listen to the views and experiences of different groups and individuals working under conditions of change. During data analysis, the multiple narratives and competing histories that emerge should not be treated as a type of 'deviant noise' or 'disruption' to dominant patterns, but should be analysed as an integral part of the research (Dawson, 2003: 119–20). As such, competing narratives and multiple histories are central concepts in processual analysis. Multiple perspectives are thereby accommodated and individual and collective stories are viewed as powerful vehicles for resisting change and shaping change in certain preferred directions. Moreover, the way past events or incidents are re-scripted to fit the arguments and political objectives of individuals or groups with particular vested interests at certain moments of time, all form part of this approach that seeks a more critical understanding of the change process (Dawson, 2003: 27).

Buchanan and Dawson (2007) further develop this in their critique of monological research accounts and call for more fully informed case studies that view change as a multi-story process. They demonstrate how there can be competing accounts among different stakeholders of the same change event and how particular stakeholders can present different accounts that are tailored to meet and shape the expectations of different audiences. As such, they highlight caution in generating theoretical insights or practical guides from accounts that are purposefully crafted to influence target audiences. Apart from highlighting methodological issues in the collection and analysis of data, their study shows how stories not only report on change but also seek to shape the change they describe. In combining existing ideas from narrative and processual perspectives, they illustrate how change can be contradictory on at least four overlapping dimensions and argue that single-voiced narratives of change limit our understanding of change agency and complex change processes. These dimensions comprise: conflicts of interpretation, assessment, attribution and audience (Buchanan and Dawson, 2007: 674). Conflicts of interpretation between different stakeholders and groups are fairly self-explanatory and have already been alluded to. What is interesting for our purposes is how stories that attempt to make sense of and influence change, shape the sensemaking of not only supporters, but also others who may hold very different views. For example, people may respond by re-asserting and strengthening their own individual or collectively held accounts; they may modify and revise their interpretation in the light of conflicting views and opinions; they may develop strategies to undermine conflicting accounts, and so forth. Conflicts of assessment relate to judgements and evaluations of what went well, what the main problems and issues were, and the lessons, for example, to be learned from change. A conflict of attribution refers to the different explanations that can be used to explain a particular sequence of events. Brown (2004) provides a useful illustration of this in his analysis of public inquiry reports where key experts are often used to help construct an explanation that substantiates a certain version of reality over others. Finally, conflicts of audience relate to the way stories are crafted and rewritten to meet the needs and expectations, and to shape the views, of different audiences. For example, official accounts of 'what happened' often differ significantly from more personal accounts of events (Buchanan and Dawson, 2007).

For Buchanan and Dawson (2007), it is important to accommodate polyvocal accounts in collecting data on the way different groups and stakeholders make sense of and give sense to their own experiences of change. Consequently, they argue for the need to be aware of the way that stories not only provide accounts of change but can also influence the process and outcomes of change. This complexity in fully understanding muddied processes of change prevents the development of higher levels of theory and highlights the uniqueness of the lived experience of change. For Pettigrew (1997), the comparative element across case settings enables the researcher to identify broader patterns and explain how the context and process of change influences similarities and differences in outcome; whereas Dawson (2003) questions the tendency for a 'more is better' approach advocating the value of single longitudinal case studies on change. Under Dawson's approach (1994 and 2003), the aim is not to work the data to strengthen the generalizability of the findings, but rather to provide narrative accounts of the complex dynamics of change. Although general trends can be identified and typical responses recounted, the deviant or outlier response is not problematic, as under this approach, *one* is significant (Dawson, 2003: 121). A common feature running through this perspective is the collection and analyses of complex change data that do not lend themselves to a search for an authentic truth but highlight the unresolved and unheard as well as the dominant discourses and power plays that shape and are shaped within processes of change. It provides insight and understanding rather than panaceas and solutions. This in turn raises questions over the practical utility of such an approach, an issue that will be addressed shortly (Collins, 1998), but first a brief reappraisal of processual research on change is provided.

Processual research on change: a reappraisal

Over the last two decades, a range of problems associated with processual research have continued to receive attention and raise debate. For example, the lack of codification of research practice has raised concerns, especially with the continual emphasis on crafting the research, on learning from fieldwork experience and the need for creativity. Reflective commentators draw attention to the variety of studies that occur under this banner highlighting how different researchers conducting similar research in comparable research sites may produce very different findings. Scientific replication and verification is largely absent or simply not addressed and this has raised some scholastic concern, particularly among academics who are more positivistically inclined, but also among process researchers, such as Poole et al. (2000) and longitudinal ethnographic researchers, such as Barley (1990). For the processualist, these manifest themselves in more general problems, such as difficulties encountered in publishing qualitative research in scholarly journals, most notable in those that are highly ranked (see Bengtsson et al., 1997). On a more practical level, issues have arisen over the tacit skills required of processual researchers, as well as the amount of time and effort required to engage in these type of in-depth qualitative case studies that are carried out over time (rather than as a single one-off snapshot of change). Linked to the longitudinal and temporal aspects of the processual case study is the issue of uniqueness versus generalizability. For some commentators, there is a need to elevate the standing of this type of research through greater standardization and systemization whilst for others, the variety of processual research is one of the strengths of the approach that should not be undermined (Ropo et al., 1997: 331–35). The heart of this debate was captured rather neatly by Ropo et al. (1997: 332) who state that:

> Agreement on the rules of the game clears the water, but when pushed too far such agreement may lead to a straight jacket with little room for true experimentation and learning. One might ask, whether we wish to develop process research practices toward generic standardized patterns, or whether we would rather leave more space for personal orientations, individual voices and self-reflection that is inherent in social theory development?

Ferlie and McNulty (1997) point out how from the outset, the type of processual research one is engaged in can influence the research design, types of data collected, analysis and eventual outputs. They compare a commissioned mode where the research is oriented towards certain defined problems and intended outputs and the more traditional academic mode (Ferlie and McNulty, 1997). Their analysis highlights how there is a certain trade off with theorization inherent in commissioned research which sets the parameters for outputs and expects a more systematized and codified approach. The temporality of processual research is considered by Tuttle (1997) who usefully spotlights how temporal orientations can vary, for example, between the researcher and those being studied; whilst Orton (1997) calls attention to the need for improvisation whilst doing the research and issues of flexibility, in being able to modify design intentions and to be open to multiple accounts in an ongoing iteration between theory and data. The crafting skills and tacit knowledge required through hands-on experience is discussed by Laurila (1997) and Dawson (1997); whereas Bengtsson et al. (1997) investigate publication barriers and the need to ensure that submitted articles align with reviewers that are not going to be positivistically biased and against ideographic research.

Whilst space precludes the possibility of detailed discussion on these various aspects from research design issues, through to managing ongoing field relationships, collecting data, dealing with conflicting accounts, trying to analyse large bodies of qualitative data, tackling the temporal nature of this type of research, and then writing up the study tailored for particular audiences. Brief attention is given to the practical contribution of this approach to understanding change (Collins, 1998; Hinnings, 1997; McDermott et al., 2008).

Debates on the practical dimension: universal laws versus rules of thumb

A persistent criticism that has been levelled at processual research centres on the relationship between theory and practice. In contrast to Lewin's (Lewin, 1943–44: 169) dictum that 'there is nothing so practical as a good theory' there is a tendency with processual studies to either reject the practical dimension of this type of research – seeing it as undermining the scholastic contributions of such studies – or to present practical guidelines that are seen to give less than clear advice (see Burnes, 2000: 294–95). The horns of the dilemma rests, on the one hand, with the inability of this type of study to produce anything of 'practical' value (in the form of systematic predictive capabilities) and, on the other hand, the tendency for studies to provide guidelines that undermine their theoretical foundations through outlining rather banal lists of ingredients on how to best manage change. For example, in a critical review of Pettigrew's contextualist approach Collins (1998: 71) concludes:

> While most writers of a critical bent would tend to accept that Pettigrew offers a useful and valid framework for the analysis of change and its management, some have observed an imbalance in Pettigrew's work. It has been observed, for example, that whereas Pettigrew, quite correctly observes that matters of theory and practice are inseparable and indivisible, the theoretical, conceptual and methodological elegance of Pettigrew's work seems to have been purchased at the expense of practical advice and practitioner relevance.

Buchanan and Boddy (1992) also argue that the richness and complexity of a multi-level analysis does little to simplify or clarify processes of change and thereby renders the research as largely impenetrable for the organizational practitioner. In other words, whilst the research findings adequately convey the complexity of organizational change, they have also tended to mask, mystify and create barriers of interpretation to a non-academic audience who may seek practical tools for action (Buchanan and Boddy, 1992: 61–62). In an attempt to tackle this criticism, Dawson's *Organizational Change: A Processual Approach* outlines fifteen guidelines. Nonetheless the practical value of these are questioned (Collins, 1998; see also Burnes, 2000: 295), especially in their broad-brush approach which, whilst offering a very general list of things for managers to remember, is for Morsing (1997: 534) rather 'like a cake recipe reminding one to add flour, sugar, cocoa, cream and vanilla, without giving any information on measures and proportions'. In a sense, the sophistication and richness of the processual approach to understanding change is both a major strength and a major weakness, as the findings do not easily lend themselves to being translated into practical lessons. The critical question is whether there is value in trying to introduce a set of guidelines into this perspective that does not offer broad generalizations (Morsing, 1997: 535). For McDermott et al. (2008), there is room to further develop the practical dimension through opening a dialogue between processual and action research. They recognize that whilst the underlying philosophical differences are not resolvable, the practical elements of action research could usefully contribute to this area of processual research that has experienced sustained criticism. Equally, it could be argued that it is the abilities of processual research to uncover the complexity of change as dynamic practice that warrants the approach so valuable to practitioners. It does not belittle the difficulties or side-step the array of potential problems and pitfalls that can arise, nor does it avoid the issue of competing worlds or simplify resistance to a 'problem' to be overcome. It embraces change as practised rather than as idealized in a perfect world where change can be predicted, ordered and controlled. That measures of political acumen, communication, coalition building and replanning will be required provide useful heuristics for steering change through uncharted waters. Knowledge and experience of change aids practitioners engaged in ongoing and future projected initiatives but choices and decisions remain as the processes of change – in moving from some present state to some future position – can never be fully known.

While the processual approach is able to draw out broad rules of thumb, such as the need for flexible approaches that are sensitive to the socio-cultural environment, temporal contextual conditions and the shifting character of expectations in the views and reactions of employee groups and key political players (Andriopoulos and Dawson, 2009); these are not limited to a simple consideration of how managers can 'better' manage change; rather, they have a broader agenda that extend beyond management to include advice to non-managers and others, such as trade unionists, politicians, business development agencies, and so forth.

The epistemological status of these general lessons relate to our views of knowledge and whether we are seeking general truths or whether we are sceptical about knowledge claims that purport to offer universally applicable solutions to the complex problem of change in organizations. Polanyi (1962) makes a useful distinction between the scientific knowledge of what is required for an individual to maintain balance whilst riding a bicycle and the practical knowledge of knowing how to ride without understanding the physics that explain that achievement. The practical guidelines put forward by the processual approach do not provide specific measures of what is required in each context and case, but provide general rules of thumb about the key aspects of change that need to be considered during processes of change. For example, to say that communication is central to managing change is nothing new and a statement that most would agree with. From a processual perspective, it is not practicable to prescribe exactly what types and forms of communication are required at particular stages of change as these need to be understood in context and overtime (which is what action research facilitates, see McDermott et al., 2008). The choice of what, when and how to communicate as well as the releasing of types and forms of information need to be assessed in situ and are often political issues, themselves open to influence by governance structures and significant others. But equally, to assume that because exact prescriptive measures for change management cannot be detailed from this perspective that it is somehow of less value than those that do, but fail to deliver in practice, is a rather naive view of practical knowledge.

Conclusion

There is nothing new in viewing the world from a processual perspective. As illustrated from the outset, there has been a longstanding debate on whether organizations should be seen as fluid entities in a constant state of flux or as stable entities where equilibrium is punctuated by shocks in the system. The processualist is interested in studying the process of changing, organizing and strategizing, of observing and reporting on change as-it-happens. In so doing, the processualist is drawn towards a particular research methodology that seeks to capture the temporal inter-connectedness of processes through longitudinal research designs, and to engage with various data that capture meanings and subjectivities as well as scripted documents for particular audiences and material that allows the chronicling of key activities and events; and as such, it employs a predominantly qualitative methodology that is normally in the form of single longitudinal in-depth case studies or a broader set of comparative cases that are used in the development of middle-range theory that seeks to explain the complex dynamics of changing. Some of the criticisms of this perspective resonate with those associated with the method-linked theoretical debates between academics involved in quantitative-based research which seeks generalizability and replicability of findings, and those scholars that engage in inductive theory building associated with qualitative approaches. These issues have been well versed elsewhere and are not repeated here (see Buchanan and Bryman, 2009).

This chapter calls on scholars to maintain the craft associated with this type of approach that requires researchers to hone and develop their tacit skills in the practice of doing processual research. On the continuing debate about practicability, there is perhaps no resolution. Ironically, the recipe driven so-called 'practical' approaches to change are themselves criticized by processualists for offering poor advice through their over-simplified, step models of change. Processual researchers argue that there are no silver bullets, ultimate truths, or universal blueprints to the 'successful' management of change rather, there can only be fuller comprehension of what the main ingredients to change are or are likely to be under certain contexts. As such, the actual measures remain largely unknowable and need to be adjusted and refined during the process of changing. That processual heuristics may offer better practical advice than recipe approaches that ultimately fail to deliver what they promise is often neglected in the 'practical dimension' criticism of the processual perspective. Perhaps more fruitfully, debates should centre on the nature of practical knowledge and how it relates to our understanding of organizational change. Whilst the processual school of thought is not in the business of grand theorizing as it is linked to a longitudinal qualitative research methodology that is directed towards detailed empirical fieldwork – usually in the form of the in-depth case study – it does contribute to theory development, to methodological considerations in studying change processes as they unfold and happen over time, and to providing practical guidelines on change management.

Acknowledgement

Thanks are due to Aoife McDermott for helpful comments on an earlier draft of this chapter.

References

Anderson, P. and Tushman, M. (1990) Technological discontinuities and dominant designs: a cyclical model of technological change, *Administrative Science Quarterly*, 35: 604–33.
Andriopoulos, C. and Dawson, P. (2009) *Managing Change, Creativity and Innovation*, London, SAGE.
Barley, S. (1990) Images of imaging Notes on doing longitudinal field work, *Organization Science*, 1(3): 220–47.
Becker, M. C. (2004) Organizational routines: a review of the literature, *Industrial and Corporate Change*, 13(4): 643–77.

Bengtsson, L., Elg, U. and Lind, J. I. (1997) Bridging the transatlantic publishing gap: how North American reviewers evaluate European idiographic research, *Scandinavian Journal of Management*, 13(4): 473–92.

Bloor, G. and Dawson, P. (1994) Understanding professional culture in organizational context, *Organization Studies*, 15(2): 275–95.

Brown, A.D. (2004) Authoritative sensemaking in a public inquiry report, *Organization Studies*, 25(1): 95–112.

Buchanan, D. and Badham, R. J. (2008) *Power, Politics, and Organizational Change: Winning the Turf Game* (2nd edn), London, SAGE.

Buchanan, D. and Boddy, D. (1992) *The Expertise of the Change Agent: Public Performance and Backstage Activity*, London, Prentice-Hall International.

Buchanan, D. and Bryman, A. (2009) *The SAGE Handbook of Organizational Research Methods*. London, SAGE.

Buchanan, D. and Dawson, P. (2007) Discourse and audience: organizational change as multi-story process, *Journal of Management Studies*, 44(5): 669–86.

Burnes, B. (2000) *Managing Change: A Strategic Approach to Organisational Dynamics* (3rd edn), New York, Pearson Education.

Burnes, B. (2005) Complexity theories and organizational change, *International Journal of Management Reviews*, 7(2): 73–90.

Burns, T. and Stalker, G. M. (1961) *The Management of Innovation*, London, Tavistock.

Child, J. (1972) Organization structure, environment and performance: the role of strategic choice, *Sociology*, 6(1): 1–22.

Child, J. (1997) Strategic choice in the analysis of action, structure, organizations and environment: retrospect and propect, *Organization Studies*, 18(1): 43–76.

Clark, J., McLoughlin, I., Rose, H. and King, R. (1988) *The Process of Technological Change: New Technology and Social Choice in the Workplace*, Cambridge, Cambridge University Press.

Collins, D. (1998) *Organizational Change: Sociological Perspectives*, New York, Routledge.

Dalton, M. (1959) *Men Who Manage*, New York, Wiley.

Dawson, P. (1994) *Organizational Change: A Processual Approach*, London, Paul Chapman Publishing.

Dawson, P. (1997) In at the deep end: conducting processual research on organisational change, *Scandinavian Journal of Management*, 13(4): 389–405.

Dawson, P. (2003) *Reshaping Change: A Processual Perspective*, London, Routledge.

Dubinskas, F. (1994) On the edge of chaos, *Journal of Management Inquiry*, 3(4): 355–67.

Elger, A. (1975) Industrial organizations: a processual perspective, In J. McKinlay (ed.), *Processing People: Cases in Organizational Behaviour*. New York, Hold, Rinehart & Winston.

Ferlie, E. and McNulty, T. (1997) "Going to market": changing patterns in the organisation and character of process research, *Scandinavian Journal of Management*, 13(4): 367–87.

Gouldner, A. (1965) *Wildcat Strike*, New York, Free Press.

Hayes, J. (2007) *The Theory and Practice of Change Management* (2nd edn), Basingstoke, Palgrave Macmillan.

Hinnings, C. R. (1997) Reflections on processual research, *Scandinavian Journal of Management*, 13(4): 493–503.

Langley, A. (2009) Studying processes in and around organizations, In D. A. Buchanan and A. Bryman (eds), *The Sage Handbook of Organizational Research Methods* (pp. 409–29). London, SAGE.

Laurila, J. (1997) Promoting research access and informant rapport in corporate settings: notes from research on a crisis company, *Scandinavian Journal of Management*, 13(4): 407–18.

Lewin, K. (1943–44) Problems of research in social psychology, In D. Cartwright (ed.), *Field Theory in Social Science*, London, Social Science Paperbacks.

McDermott, A., Coghlan, D. and Keating, M. (2008) Research for action and research in action: processual and action research in dialogue? *Irish Journal of Management* (January): 1–18.

Mohr, L. B. (1982) *Explaining Organizational Behavior: The Limites and Possibilities of Theory and Research*, San Francisco, CA, Jossey-Bass.

Morsing, M. (1997) Patrick Dawson: organizational change – a processual approach, *Organization Studies*, 18(3): 523–35.

131

Orlikowski, W. J. (2002) Knowing in practice: enacting a collective capability in distributed organizing, *Organization Science*, 13: 249–73.

Orton, J. D. (1997) From inductive to iterative grounded theory: zipping the gap between process theory and process data, *Scandinavian Journal of Management*, 13(4): 419–38.

Pentland, B. T. and Rueter, H. (1994) Organisational routines as grammars of action, *Administrative Science Quarterly*, 39: 484–510.

Pettigrew, A. M. (1973) *The Politics of Organizational Decision-Making*, London, Tavistock.

Pettigrew, A. M. (1985) *The Awakening Giant: Continuity and Change in Imperial Chemical Industries*, Oxford, Basil Blackwell.

Pettigrew, A.M. (1997) 'What is processual analysis?', *Scandinavian Journal of Management*, 13(4): 337–48.

Pettigrew, A. M., Whittington, R., Melin, L., Sanchez-Runde, C., van den Bosch, F., Ruigrok, W. et al. (eds) (2003) *Innovative Forms of Organizing: International Perspectives*, London, SAGE.

Polanyi, M. (1962) *Personal Knowledge*, London, Routledge.

Poole, M. S., Van de Ven, A. H., Dooley, K. and Holmes, M. E. (2000) *Organizational Change and Innovation Processes: Theory and Methods for Research*, New York, Oxford University Press.

Preece, D. A., Steven, G. and Steven, V. (1999) *Work, Change and Competition: Managing for Bass*, London, Routledge.

Preece, D. A., McLoughlin, I. and Dawson, P. (2000) *Technology, Organizations and Innovation: Critical Perspectives on Business and Management*, London, Routledge.

Romanelli, E. and Tushman, M. (1994) Organizational transformation as punctuated equilibrium: an empirical test, *Academy of Management Journal*, 37: 1141–66.

Ropo, A., Eriksson, P. and Hunt, J. G. (1997) Reflections on conducting processual research on management and organizations, *Scandinavian Journal of Management*, 13(4): 331–35.

Roy, D. (1967) Quota restriction and goldbricking in a machine shop, In W. Faunce (ed.), *Readings in Industrial Sociology*, New York, Meredith Publishing Company.

Spector, B. (2009) *Implementing Organizational Change: Theory and Practice* (2nd edn), London, Prentice Hall.

Stacey, R. (1992) *Managing Chaos: Dynamic Business Strategies in an Unpredictable World*, London, Kogan Page.

Tsoukas, H. and Chia, R. (2002) On organizational becoming: rethinking organizational change, *Organization Science*, 13(5): 567–82.

Tuttle, D. B. (1997) A classification system for understanding individual differences in temporal orientation among processual researchers and organizational informants, *Scandinavian Journal of Management*, 13(4): 349–66.

Van de Ven, A. H. and Poole, M. S. (2005) Alternative approaches for studying organizational change, *Organization Studies*, 26(9): 1377–1404.

Whetten, D. A. (2006) Albert and Whetten revisited: strengthening the concept of organizational identity, *Journal of Management Inquiry*, 15(3): 219–34.

Woodward, J. (1958) *Management and Technology*, London, HMSO.

Woodward, J. (1980) *Industrial Organization: Theory and Practice* (2nd edn), Oxford, Oxford University Press.

9

Understanding the emergent approach to change

Bernard Burnes

Introduction

The emergent approach to change is based on the assumption that change is not a linear process or a one-off isolated event, but a continuous, open-ended, cumulative and unpredictable process of aligning and re-aligning an organization to its changing environment (Falconer, 2002). Weick (2000: 225) comments as follows on studies of emergent change:

> The recurring story is one of autonomous initiatives that bubble up internally; continuous emergent change; steady learning from both failure and success; strategy implementation that is replaced by strategy making; the appearance of innovations that are unplanned, unforeseen and unexpected; and small actions that have surprisingly large consequences.

Advocates of emergent change argue that it is more suitable to the turbulent and continually-changing environment in which organizations now operate. They reject what they see as the incremental approach of planned change, which they characterize as individually separate change events. Instead, they argue that organizations must continuously and synergistically adapt their internal practices and behaviour in real time to changing external conditions (Beer and Nohria, 2000). As Orlikowski (1996: 65–66) maintains:

> In this perspective, organizational transformation is not portrayed as a drama staged by deliberate directors with predefined scripts and choreographed moves, or the inevitable outcome of a technological logic, or a sudden discontinuity that fundamentally invalidates the status quo. Rather, organizational transformation is seen here to be an ongoing improvisation enacted by organizational actors trying to make sense of and act coherently in the world. … Each shift in practice creates the conditions for further breakdowns, unanticipated outcomes, and innovations, which in their turn are responded to with more variations. And such variations are ongoing; there is no beginning or end point in this change process.

To understand the nature of emergent change, this chapter begins by presenting the case against the planned approach and the rise of the emergent perspective on change. It then goes on to examine the main arguments for, and characteristics of, emergent change. This will show that, although they do not always agree with each other, the advocates of emergent change are united by the emphasis they place on organizational structure, culture and learning, and their perspective on managerial behaviour and the role of power and politics in the change process. In summarizing the emergent approach, it is argued that, though it has a number of distinct strengths, it is not applicable to all change situations and, therefore, it needs to be considered alongside, rather than instead of, other approaches to change.

The rationale for emergent change

Lewin's planned approach dominated the change field from the 1940s to the 1980s, and still remains highly influential (Burnes, 2004; Fagenson-Eland et al., 2004). However, the rise of Japanese competitiveness and the apparent eclipse of Western industry in the late 1970s precipitated the questioning of existing approaches to structuring, managing and changing organizations (e.g. Pascale and Athos, 1982; Peters and Waterman, 1982). For Wilson (1992), the increasingly dynamic and uncertain nature of the business environment undermines the case for planned change and underlines the appropriateness of the emergent approach. He also believes that the planned approach, by attempting to lay down timetables, objectives and methods in advance, is too heavily reliant on the role of managers, and assumes (rashly) that they can have a full understanding of the consequences of their actions and that their plans will be understood and accepted and can be implemented. Perhaps the most trenchant criticism of planned change came from Kanter et al. (1992: 10) who argued:

> Lewin's model was a simple one, with organizational change involving three stages; unfreezing, changing and refreezing ... This quaintly linear and static conception – the organization as an ice cube – is so wildly inappropriate that it is difficult to see why it has not only survived but prospered. ... Suffice it to say here, first, that organizations are never frozen, much less refrozen, but are fluid entities with many 'personalities'. Second, to the extent that there are stages, they overlap and interpenetrate one another in important ways.

From the early 1980s, a powerful consensus built up against planned change and in favour of a more emergent perspective (Beer and Nohria, 2000; Buchanan and Storey, 1997; Dawson, 1994; Hatch, 1997; Weick, 2000). It is a consensus, however, that criticizes planned change from very different perspectives: ranging from the neo-liberalism of the Culture-Excellence proponents (Peters, 2006) to left-leaning postmodernists (Hatch, 1997) and including proponents of complexity theories (Stacey, 2003). Therefore, they are certainly a much less coherent group than the advocates of planned change. Nevertheless, they do share at least three common beliefs. First, they see planned change as not fit for purpose. Second, instead of seeing change as a phenomenon that can be pre-planned and which has a finite end point, they see change as an 'emerging' and ongoing process of organizational adaptation and transformation. Third, they adopt an open systems perspective: that is, they see individual organizations as interdependent parts or sub-systems of a much larger environment, though they disagree about whether the environment is a concrete reality or a socially-constructed phenomenon. The environment impacts upon and affects the actions and decisions of organizations, but they also impact on the environment. Proponents of the emergent approach see change as emerging from the day-to-day actions and decisions of members of an organization. In this sense, change can emerge from attempts by members of organizations to align the organization with its environment, or as the result of different groups battling for domination, or even from attempts to construct a new, or challenge an old, social reality.

Having examined the rationale for the emergent approach, we can now move on to examine it in more detail.

The emergent approach: underlying assumptions

The nature of change

For proponents of the emergent approach, change is a continuous, dynamic and contested process that emerges in an unpredictable and unplanned fashion. It is not a rational process but one where: ' ... the key decisions about matching the organization's resources with opportunities, constraints and demands in the environment evolve over time and are the outcome of cultural and political processes in organizations' (Hayes, 2002: 37). This is a point reinforced by Dawson (2003: 14) who sees change as

> ... a complex ongoing dynamic in which the politics, substance and context of change all interlock and overlap, and in which our understanding of the present and expectations of the future can influence our interpretation of past events, which may in turn shape our experience of change.

From this perspective, even when changes are operational, they will need to be constantly refined and developed in order to maintain their relevance. Genus (1998: 51) uses an 'interpretive' perspective to explain the messy nature of organizational change, arguing that the ' ... various political, symbolic and structural factors [involved in the change process] condition the perceptions of individuals or groups...'. Finstad's (1998) view of organizational change, whilst being consistent with the perspectives of Dawson and Genus, appears to adopt a realist perspective on change by drawing an important distinction between the concrete elements of change, such as structures and practices, and the more symbolic elements, such as people's basic understandings and assumptions about their organizations. He maintains, though, that it is the symbolic aspects that dominate the change process rather than the more concrete elements of change. The importance of symbolism and ritual in the change process is also emphasized by Schuyt and Schuijt (1998), who argue that the management of these is not only central to achieving successful change, but also plays a crucial role in reducing the uncertainty which change generates.

Given this perspective on change, Weick (2000: 227), argues that emergent change is the most suitable approach because of its:

> ... sensitivity to local contingencies; suitability for on-line real-time experimentation, learning, and sensemaking; comprehensibility and manageability; likelihood of satisfying needs for autonomy, control, and expression; proneness to swift implementation; resistance to unravelling; ability to exploit existing tacit knowledge; and tightened and shortened feedback loops from results to action.

The role of managers

It is because change is so pervasive and multifaceted that Carnall (2003) suggests that mastering the challenge of change is not a specialist activity to that can be left to or driven by

135

an expert, but an increasingly important part of every manager's role. Carnall (2003: 125–26) proposes four core managerial competencies that are essential for the effective management of change:

- *Decision-making*: this includes intuition and vision, the ability to gather and utilize information, understanding the practical and political consequences of decisions, the ability to overcome resistance, the skill to understand and synthesize conflicting views and to be able to empathize with different groups.
- *Coalition-building*: this comprises the skills necessary to gain the support and resources necessary to implement decisions. These include checking the feasibility of ideas, gaining supporters, bargaining with other stakeholders and presenting new ideas and concepts in a way that wins support.
- *Achieving action*: this includes handling opposition, motivating people, providing support and building self-esteem.
- *Maintaining momentum and effort*: this involves team-building, generating ownership, sharing information and problems, providing feedback, trusting people and energizing staff.

Stace and Dunphy (2001) take a more contextual view of managerial competencies. Their Change Matrix identifies a spectrum of change situations, ranging from fine-tuning to corporate transformation, and a matching spectrum of styles of change management, ranging from cooperative to coercive. The Matrix identifies at least 16 combinations of change situations and styles of management, each of which requires a different set of managerial competences.

A contingency perspective

Stace and Dunphy's (2001) contextual view tallies with that of McCalman and Paton (1992) who suggest that, to be effective in creating sustainable change, managers need an extensive and systemic understanding of their organization's environment, in order to identify the pressures for change and to ensure that, by mobilizing the necessary internal resources, their organization responds in a timely and appropriate manner. Similarly, Dawson (1994) claims that change must be linked to developments in markets, work organization, systems of management control and the shifting nature of organizational boundaries and relationships. He emphasizes that, in a dynamic business environment, change interventions which focus on only one dimension of an organization's activities – whether that be markets, products, technology or people – are likely to generate only short-term results and heighten instability rather than reduce it. This is a point emphasized by many other writers (Beer and Nohria, 2000; Graetz et al., 2002; Hartley et al., 1997; Senior, 2002).

As can be seen, though not all state it openly, advocates of emergent change tend to adopt a contingency perspective, arguing that approaches to change need to be tailored to the situation of the individual organization and the type of change it is undertaking (Weick, 2000). This is a point that is central to Pettigrew's contextualist approach to change: 'context and action are inseparable' (Pettigrew, 2000: 243) and 'Leadership [of change] requires action appropriate to its context' (Pettigrew and Whipp, 1991: 165). Therefore, Pettigrew offers a very particularistic view of change whereby each change situation is different and must be approached and managed differently. It follows from this that implicit in the case for emergent change is the assumption that if organizations operated in more stable and predictable environments, the need for change would be less and it might be possible to conceive of it as a process of moving from one relatively stable state to another. As Dawson (1994: 3) observes:

136

Although [Lewin's] theory has proven to be useful in understanding planned change under relatively stable conditions, with the continuing and dynamic nature of change in today's business world, it no longer makes sense to implement a planned process of 'refreezing' changed behaviours.

For advocates of emergent change, therefore, it is the uncertainty of the environment that makes planned change inappropriate and emergent change more pertinent. This is a point emphasized by Stickland (1998: 14), who draws on systems theory to emphasize the way that organizations are separate from but connected to their environment:

> A system has an identity that sets it apart from its environment and is capable of preserving that *identity* within a given range of environmental scenarios. Systems exist within a *hierarchy* of other systems. They contain subsystems and exist within some wider system. All are interconnected …

From this systems perspective, Stickland (1998: 76) raises a question that many of those studying organizational change appear not to acknowledge: 'To what extent does the environment drive changes within a system [i.e. an organization] and to what extent is the system in control of its own change processes?' Finstad's (1998: 721) answer to this question stresses the reciprocal nature of the relationship by arguing that 'the organization is … the creator of its environment and the environment is the creator of the organization'. Though this has a postmodernist sound to it, realists would also recognize that organizations do contribute to the creation or the maintenance of their environment, but they see this as a long-term and largely unconscious process. This reciprocal relationship between an organization and its environment clearly has profound implications for how organizations conceptualize and manage change. It also serves to emphasize that a key competence for organizations is the ability to scan the external environment in order to identify and assess the impact on them of trends and discontinuities and also to understand how their actions might affect the environment (Graetz et al., 2002; McCalman and Paton, 1992; Pettigrew and Whipp, 1993).

Bottom up, not top down

Consequently, actual or potential changes in the external environment require organizations to make choices over how and when to respond. Such responses, the supporters of the emergent approach state, should promote, throughout the organization, an extensive and deep understanding of strategy, structure, systems, people, style and culture, and how these can function either as sources of inertia that can block change, or alternatively, as levers to encourage an effective change process (Dawson, 2003; Pettigrew, 1997; Wilson, 1992). A concomitant development is the adoption of a 'bottom-up' rather than 'top-down' approach to initiating and implementing change. After all, there is little point in encouraging staff to identify change opportunities unless they are also encouraged to implement them. The case in favour of this move is based on the view that the pace of environmental change is so rapid and complex that it is impossible for a small number of senior managers effectively to identify, plan and implement the necessary organizational responses. The responsibility for organizational change is therefore of necessity becoming more devolved.

The need for a bottom-up approach does not arise solely from external pressures. As Stickland (1998: 93) notes, organizations are continually experiencing 'natural changes':

Within any organization at a given point in time there are a number of continual shifts and changes playing out at various levels. These are not planned changes with a defined beginning and end, but rather reflect the natural dynamics which take place internally.

Such events may present organizations with unexpected and unlooked-for opportunities, such as new product ideas, but may also present unwelcome threats, such as the departure of key staff. Given that such changes are continually happening at all levels and across all functions, organizations would quickly become paralysed if it was left solely to senior managers to identify and resolve them. Therefore, if they are to be dealt with speedily, these local problems or opportunities have to be dealt with locally. As Senior (2002) comments, this requires organizations to empower their employees to make changes at a local level. This follows from Mintzberg's (1994) assertion that it is from these local and bottom-up actions that the direction of the organization emerges and is given shape.

In many ways, this is the essence of the emergent argument – that top-down, senior management imposed change does not work. What is required is for managers and employees, on a day-to-day basis, to have the authority to be able to shape and reshape their part of the organization to deal with the threats and opportunities presented by an ever-changing environment. However, as these changes emerge from a host of local responses, if they are to have a synergistic and positive effect on the organization, as averse to tearing it apart, such changes must be guided by a common vision of the future and a shared understanding of the organization's priorities and situation.

As can be seen, the advocates of emergent change come from a wide variety of backgrounds and each offers their own distinctive view on how organizations should and should not manage change. As the following section will show, there are some core similarities which link them.

The key features of the emergent approach

Though the proponents of the emergent approach reject the concept of universally applicable rules for change, the guidance they do provide tends to stress five features of organizations that either promote or obstruct success (see Figure 9.1).

Organizational structure

The case for developing more appropriate organizational structures in order to facilitate change very much follows the arguments of the contingency theorists (Burnes, 2009) that dynamic and chaotic environments require organizations to adopt more flexible, less hierarchical structures. Those favouring an emergent approach to change point out that the 1990s witnessed a general tendency to create flatter organizational structures in order to increase responsiveness by devolving authority and responsibility (Senior, 2002). As Kotter (1996: 169) remarks, the case for such structural changes is that 'An organization with more delegation, which means a flat hierarchy, is in a far superior position to maneuvre than one with a big, change-resistant lump in the middle.' In studying innovating organizations, Brown and Eisenhardt (1997: 29) refer to such flexible structures as 'semistructures', which they claim:

> ... are sufficiently rigid so that change can be organized, but not so rigid that it cannot occur. ... sustaining this semistructured state is challenging because it is a dissipative equilibrium and so requires constant managerial vigilance to avoid slipping into pure chaos or pure structure.

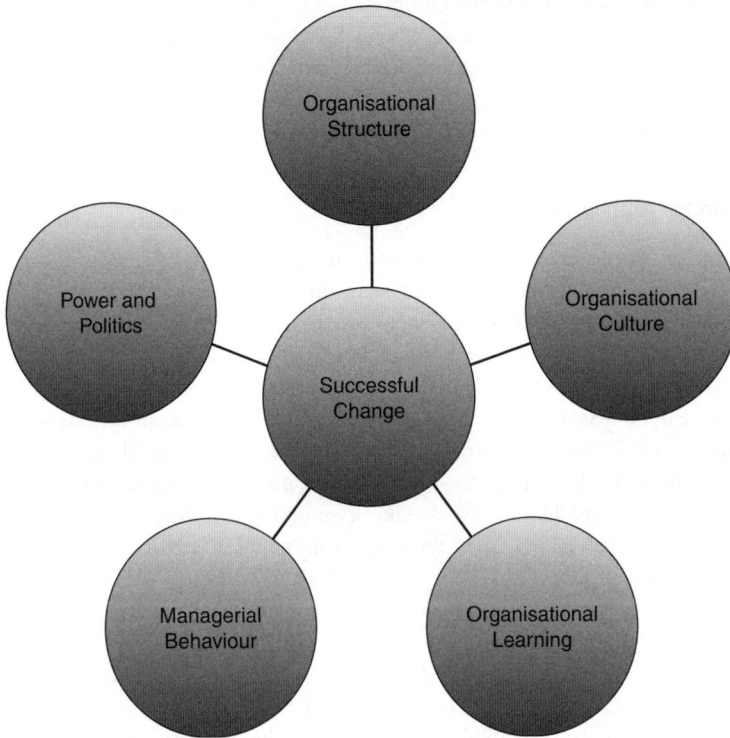

Figure 9.1 The determinants of successful change

Brown and Eisenhardt (1997) claim that such structures are essential for ensuring organizational survival in highly competitive environments because they facilitate continuous innovation and improvisation and allow intensive, real-time communication within a structure of a few, very specific rules. However, it is not sufficient to have an appropriate structure; it must be matched with an appropriate culture if it is to be effective.

Organizational culture

There can be few people who now doubt the important role culture plays in the life of organizations, especially when it comes to change (Allaire and Firsirotu, 1984; Brown, 1998; De Witte and van Muijen, 1999; Hirschhorn, 2000). Johnson (1993: 64) suggested that the strategic management of change is 'essentially a cultural and cognitive phenomenon' rather than an analytical, rational exercise. Clarke (1994) states that the essence of sustainable change is to understand the culture of the organization that is to be changed. If proposed changes contradict cultural biases and traditions, it is inevitable that they will be difficult to embed in the organization. Kotter (1996) takes a similar view, arguing that for change to be successful it must be anchored in the organization's culture.

Dawson (2003) echoes this theme. He suggests that attempts to realign internal behaviours with external conditions require change strategies that are culturally sensitive. Organizations, he points out, must be aware that the process is lengthy, potentially dangerous, and demands considerable reinforcement if culture change is to be sustained against the inevitable tendency to regress to old behaviours. Likewise, Pettigrew (1997) stresses that organizational processes are embedded in an organization's context, of which culture forms an important part. Pettigrew also points out that, because of this embeddedness, change can be slow. Accordingly, as Clarke (1994: 94) suggests, 'Creating a culture for change means that change has to be part of the way we do things around here, it cannot be bolted on as an extra.'

Organizational learning

For advocates of the emergent approach, learning plays a key role in preparing people for change and enabling them to cope with it (Bechtold, 1997; Senge, 2000). Put simply, learning means 'the capacity of members of an organization to detect and correct errors and to seek new insights that would enable them to make choices that better produce outcomes that they seek' (Martin, 2000: 463). Pettigrew and Whipp (1993) maintain that organizations need to become open learning systems in order to cope with the complications and uncertainties of the modern world. For them, strategy development and change should emerge from the way the company as a whole acquires, interprets and processes information about its environment. Carnall (2003) and Hayes (2002) take a similar view, arguing that an organization's survival and growth depend on identifying environmental and market changes quickly, and responding opportunistically. However, as Benjamin and Mabey (1993: 181) point out: 'while the primary stimulus for change remains those forces in the external environment, the primary motivator for how change is accomplished resides with the people within the organization'. Clarke (1994: 156) maintains that involving staff in change-management decisions has the effect of 'stimulating habits of criticism and open debate', which enables them to challenge existing norms and question established practices. Clarke goes on to say that, although this can create the opportunity for innovation and radical change, challenging the status quo is also akin to challenging managerial judgment and authority. As Benjamin and Mabey (1993) maintain, though the questioning of the status quo is the essence of bottom-up change, it also leads to a form of role reversal whereby, rather than managers pressuring staff to change, the reverse occurs.

Managerial behaviour

Kotter (1996: 25) argued:

> Management is a set of processes that can keep a complicated system of people and technology running smoothly. The most important aspects of management include planning, budgeting, organizing, staffing, controlling, and problem solving. Leadership is a set of processes that creates organizations in the first place or adapts them to significantly changing circumstances. Leadership defines what the future should look like, aligns people with that vision, and inspires them to make it happen despite the obstacles.

Therefore, in order to be effective, managers must become leaders; they require knowledge of and expertise in strategy formulation, human-resource management, marketing/sales and negotiation/conflict resolution, and much more (Beer and Nohria, 2000; Clarke, 1994; Hayes, 2002). But the key to success, the decisive factor in creating a focused agenda for organizational change is, according to many observers, managers' own behaviour (Graetz et al., 2002; Kanter, 1989; Kotter, 1999; Pfeffer, 1996). If managers are to gain the commitment of others to change, they must first be prepared to challenge their own assumptions, attitudes and mindsets so that they develop an understanding of the emotional and intellectual processes involved (Buchanan and Boddy, 1992; Burns, 1978; Harrison, 2005; Sosik and Megerian, 1999).

For supporters of the emergent approach, the essence of change is the move from the familiar to the unknown, from the certain to the uncertain (Jones et al., 2000). In this situation, it is essential for managers to be able to tolerate risk and cope with paradox and ambiguity (Weick, 2000; Stacey et al., 2002). In particular, instead of controlling employees, managers have to empower people. Instead of directing and controlling change, they have to ensure that the organization's members are receptive to the change process, and have the necessary skills, motivation and power to take charge of it. There is a distinction here between those who take a narrow view of empowerment, seeing it mainly as devolving some limited managerial responsibility, and those, *à la* Lewin, who see it as an emancipatory process that aims to create genuine organizational democracy – though it must be pointed out that even the former has a poor track record of success (Eccles, 1993; Foegen, 1999; Lee, 1999; Stohl and Cheney, 2001). Nor is it just managers who need to change. Wilson (1992) believes that to achieve effective empowerment, senior managers must not only change the way they perceive and interpret the world, but achieve a similar transformation amongst everyone else in the organization as well. Pettigrew and Whipp (1993: 17–18) contend that the degree to which managers can achieve such a difficult task, and create a climate receptive to change, is dependent on four conditioning factors:

1   the extent to which there are key actors within the firm who are prepared to champion assessment techniques which increase the openness of the organization;
2   the structural and cultural characteristics of the company;
3   the extent to which environmental pressures are recognized and their associated dramas developed; and
4   the degree to which assessment occurs as a multi-function activity which is not pursued as an end in itself but is then linked to the central operation of the business.

Power and politics

Change and politics are inexorably linked ... This means that at the top, middle, and lower reaches of the organization, campaigning, lobbying, coalition building, and the sharing of information, rewards, and recognition are all fateful for change through all the various unpredictable stages and loops of the innovation journey.

(Pettigrew, 2000: 250)

Though the advocates of emergent change tend to view power and politics from differing perspectives, they recognize their importance and that they have to be managed if change is to be effective. Dawson (1994: 176), for example, concluded, 'The central argument is that it is important to try and gain the support of senior management, local management, supervisors, trade unions and workplace employees.' According to Weick (2000: 236) gaining support requires 'considerable linguistic skills to capture and label the flow of events [and] resequence and relabel that sequence'. As such, managers can manipulate and use language and symbols to create a new organizational reality (Hatch, 1997).

Kanter et al. (1992: 508) argued that the first step to implementing change is coalition-building: '... involve those whose involvement really matters ... Specifically, seek support from two general groups: (1) power sources and (2) stakeholders.' In a similar vein, Nadler (1993) advocates the need to shape the political dynamics of change so that power centres develop that support the change rather than blocking it.

141

Important though power and politics are in the change process, Hendry (1996) and Pugh (1993) remind us that they are not the be-all and end-all of change and that it is important not to focus on these to the exclusion of other factors. Nevertheless, the focus placed on the political dynamics of change does serve to highlight the need for those who manage change to be aware of and control this dimension of the change process.

The five features of organizations discussed above – structure, culture, learning, managerial behaviour, and power and politics – help explain why the advocates of the emergent approach see change as a very difficult process.

Emergent change: summary and criticisms

The proponents of emergent change are a somewhat broad group who may seem to be united more by their scepticism regarding planned change than by a well-focussed and commonly agreed alternative. Indeed, some might argue that any label which spans the prescriptive, consultant-orientated views of Kotter and Kanter and the analytical-processual views of Pettigrew and Dawson is too broad; certainly this is Dawson's (2003) view. Nevertheless, this would ignore two crucial points. First, planned change is an equally broad church. It ranges from those who see it as only applicable to behavioural change in small groups to those who see it as an approach for transforming entire organizations (Armenakis and Bedeian, 1999; Burnes, 2004; Greiner and Cummings, 2004; Worley and Feyerhern, 2003). Second, any approach to change which seeks to be applicable beyond the classroom or have validity wider than the management consultancy needs to incorporate both the prescriptive practitioner and the analytical academic. The issue is not how broad the church is but whether what unites them is greater than what divides them. As far as commonalities are concerned, there does seem to be some agreement regarding the main tenets of emergent change, which are as follows:

- Organizational change is not a linear process or a one-off isolated event but is a continuous, open-ended, cumulative and unpredictable process of experimentation and adaptation aimed at matching an organization's resources and capabilities to the opportunities, constraints and demands of a dynamic and uncertain environment.
- This is best achieved through an interwoven pattern of (mainly) small- to medium-scale continuous changes which, over time, can lead to a major re-configuration and transformation of an organization.
- Change is a multi-level, cross-organization process that unfolds in an iterative and messy fashion over a period of years and comprises a series of interlocking projects.
- Change is not an analytical-rational process. Instead, key change decisions evolve over time and are the outcome of political and cultural processes in organizations.
- The role of managers is not to plan or implement change *per se*, but to shape the long-term process of change by creating or fostering an organizational structure and climate which encourages and sustains experimentation, learning and risk-taking, and to develop a workforce that has the skills, freedom and motivation to take responsibility for identifying the need for change and implementing it.
- Though managers are expected to become facilitators rather than doers, they also have the prime responsibility for developing a collective vision or common purpose that gives direction to their organization, and within which the appropriateness of any proposed change can be judged.

The key organizational activities that allow these elements to operate successfully are:

- Information-gathering – about the external environment and internal objectives and capabilities.
- Communication – the transmission, analysis and discussion of information.
- Learning – the ability individually and collectively to develop new skills, identify appropriate responses and draw knowledge from their own and others' past and present actions.

Though not always stated openly, the case for the emergent approach to change is based on the assumption that the environment in which organizations operate is changing rapidly, radically and unpredictably, and will continue to do so. Just as advocates of planned change assume that stability is the *natural* or *preferred* state for organizations, so proponents of emergent change assume the *natural* or *preferred* state for organizations is turbulence and unpredictability (Brown and Eisenhardt, 1997; Orlikowski, 1996). Consequently, if the external world is changing in a rapid, uncertain and continuous way, organizations need to change in a continuous, appropriate and timely manner if they are to remain competitive. It is because they view change as a continuous and open-ended process that proponents of emergent change see the planned approach to change as inappropriate. To be successful, changes need to emerge locally and (relatively) incrementally in order to counter environmental threats and take advantage of opportunities.

In terms of the validity or general applicability of the emergent approach to change, this depends to a large extent on whether or not one subscribes to the twin assumptions that (a) environmental instability and unpredictability constitute the *natural* or *preferred* state for organizations and that (b) the best way for organizations to cope with this is through a continuous process of small-to medium-sized changes which emerge from the bottom up and not the top down. However, it is clear that not all organizations experience the same degree of turbulence or need to respond to it in the same way. For example, though they operate in the same industry and, to a degree, serve the same customers, Apple and Microsoft tend to respond to environmental turbulence differently. This does not invalidate the emergent approach, but, as Burnes (2009) argues, it does indicate that organizations may need to have a broader range of change responses available to them in order to cope with the challenges they face, of which the emergent approach is just one. As Pettigrew (2000: 245–46) observes:

> There is a long tradition in the social sciences and in management and organization theory of using bipolar modes of thinking: dichotomies, paradoxes, contradictions and dualities. … The duality of planned versus emergent change has served us well as an attention director but may well now be ready for retirement.

In particular, we need to take account of the rise of complexity theories which, as other chapters in Part II will show, have developed a significant following in the last two decades.

References

Allaire, Y. and Firsirotu, M.E. (1984) Theories of organizational culture. *Organization Studies*, 5 (3), 193–226.
Armenakis, A.A. and Bedeian, A.G. (1999) Organisational change: a review of theory and research in the 1990s. *Journal of Management*, 25 (3), 293–315.
Bechtold, B.L. (1997) Chaos theory as a model for strategy development. *Empowerment in Organizations*, 5 (4), 193–201.

Beer, M. and Nohria, N. (eds) (2000) *Breaking the Code of Change*. Harvard Business School Press: Boston, MA.

Benjamin, G. and Mabey, C. (1993) Facilitating radical change. In C. Mabey, and B. Mayon-White (eds) *Managing Change* (2nd edn). The Open University/Paul Chapman Publishing: London.

Brown, A. (1998) *Organisational Culture* (2nd edn). FT/Pitman: London.

Brown, S.L. and Eisenhardt, K.M. (1997) The art of continuous change: linking complexity theory and time-paced evolution in relentlessly shifting organizations. *Administrative Science Quarterly*, 4 (1), March, 1–34.

Buchanan, D.A. and Boddy, D. (1992) *The Expertise of the Change Agent*. Prentice Hall: London.

Buchanan, D.A. and Storey, J. (1997) Role-taking and role-switching in organizational change: the four pluralities. In I. McLoughlin and H. Harris (eds) *Innovation, Organizational Change and Technology*. International Thompson: London.

Burnes, B. (2004) Kurt Lewin and the planned approach to change: a re-appraisal. *Journal of Management Studies*, 41 (6), 977–1002.

Burnes, B. (2009) *Managing Change* (5th edn). FT/Prentice Hall: Harlow.

Burns, J.M. (1978) *Leadership*. Harper & Row: New York.

Carnall, C.A. (2003) *Managing Change in Organizations* (4th edn). FT/Prentice Hall: Harlow.

Clarke, L. (1994) *The Essence of Change*. Prentice Hall: London.

Dawson, P. (1994) *Organizational Change: A Processual Approach*. Paul Chapman Publishing: London.

Dawson, P. (2003) *Reshaping Change: A Processual Perspective*. Routledge: London.

De Witte, K. and van Muijen, J.J. (1999) Organizational culture: critical questions for researchers and practitioners. *European Journal of Work and Organizational Psychology*, 8 (4), 583–95.

Eccles, T. (1993) The deceptive allure of empowerment. *Long Range Planning*, 26 (6), 13–21.

Falconer, J. (2002) Emergence happens! Misguided paradigms regarding organizational change and the role of complexity and patterns in the change landscape. *Emergence*, 4 (1/2), 117–30.

Fagenson-Eland, E., Ensher, E.A. and Burke, W.W. (2004) Organization development and change interventions: a seven-nation comparison. *Journal of Applied Behavioral Science*, 40 (4), 432–64.

Finstad, N. (1998) The rhetoric of organizational change. *Human Relations*, 51 (6), 717–40.

Foegen, J.H. (1999) Why not empowerment? *Business and Economics Review*, 45 (3), April–June, 31–33.

Genus, A. (1998) *The Management of Change: Perspective and Practice*. International Thompson: London.

Graetz, F., Rimmer, M., Lawrence, A. and Smith, A.(2002) *Managing Organisational Change*. Wiley: Milton, QLD.

Greiner, L.E. and Cummings, TG. (2004) Wanted: OD more alive than dead! *Journal of Applied Behavioral Science*, 40 (4), 374–91.

Harrison, R. (2005) *Learning and Development* (4th edn). CIPD: London.

Hartley, J., Bennington, J. and Binns, P. (1997) Researching the roles of internal-change agents in the management of organizational change. *British Journal of Managment*, 8 (1), 61–73.

Hatch, M.J. (1997) *Organization Theory: Modern, Symbolic and Postmodern Perspectives*. Oxford University Press: Oxford.

Hayes, J. (2002) *The Theory and Practice of Change Management*. Palgrave: Basingstoke.

Hendry, C. (1996) Understanding and creating whole organizational change through learning theory. *Human Relations*, 49 (5), 621–41.

Hirschhorn, L. (2000) Changing structure is not enough: the moral meaning of organizational design. In M. Beer and N. Nohria (eds) *Breaking the Code of Change*. Harvard Business School Press: Boston, MA.

Johnson, G. (1993) Processes of managing strategic change. In C. Mabey and B. Mayon-White (eds) *Managing Change* (2nd edn). The Open University/Paul Chapman Publishing: London.

Jones, G.R., George, J.M. and Hill, C.W.L. (2000) *Contemporary Management* (2nd edn). McGraw-Hill: Boston, MA.

Kotter, J.P. (1996) *Leading Change*. Harvard Business School Press: Boston, MA.

Kotter, J.P. (1999) What effective general managers really do. *Harvard Business Review*, 77 (2), 145–59.

Kanter, R.M. (1989) *When Giants Learn to Dance: Mastering the Challenges of Strategy, Management, and Careers in the 1990s*. Unwin: London.

Kanter, R.M., Stein, B.A. and Jick, T.D. (1992) *The Challenge of Organizational Change*. Free Press: New York.

Lee, M. (1999) The lie of power: empowerment as impotence. *Human Relations*, 52 (2), 225–62.

Martin, R. (2000) Breaking the code of change: observations and critique. In M. Beer and N. Nohria (eds) *Breaking the Code of Change*. Harvard Business School Press: Boston, MA.

McCalman, J. and Paton, R.A. (1992) *Change Management: A Guide to Effective Implementation*. Paul Chapman Publishing: London.

Mintzberg, H. (1994) *The Rise and Fall of Strategic Planning*. Prentice Hall: London.

Nadler, D.A. (1993) Concepts for the management of strategic change. In C. Mabey, and B. Mayon-White (eds) *Managing Change* (2nd edn). The Open University/Paul Chapman Publishing: London.

Orlikowski, W.J. (1996) Improvising Organizational Transformation Over Time: A Situated Change Perspective. *Information Systems Research*, 7 (1), 63–92.

Pascale, R.T. and Athos, A.G. (1982) *The Art of Japanese Management*. Penguin: Harmondsworth.

Peters, T. (2006) *Re-imagine! Business Excellence in a Disruptive Age*. Dorling Kindersley: London.

Peters, T. and Waterman, R.H. (1982) *In Search of Excellence: Lessons from America's Best-Run Companies*. Harper & Row: London.

Pettigrew, A.M. (1997) What is a processual analysis? *Scandinavian Journal of Management*, 13 (4), 337–48.

Pettigrew, A.M. (2000) Linking change processes and outcomes: a commentary on Ghosal, Bartlett and Weick. In M. Beer and N. Nohria (eds) *Breaking the Code of Change*. Harvard Business School Press: Boston, MA.

Pettigrew, A.M. and Whipp, R. (1991) *Managing Change for Competitive Success*. Blackwell: Oxford.

Pettigrew, A.M. and Whipp, R. (1993) Understanding the environment. In C. Mabey, and B. Mayon-White (eds) *Managing Change* (2nd edn). The Open University/Paul Chapman Publishing: London.

Pfeffer, J. (1996) *Competitive Advantage Through People: Unleashing the Power of the Work Force*. Harvard Business School Press: Boston, MA.

Pugh, D.S. (1993) Understanding and managing organizational change. In C. Mabey, and B. Mayon-White (eds) *Managing Change* (2nd edn). The Open University/Paul Chapman Publishing: London.

Schuyt, T.N.M. and Schuijt, J.J.M. (1998) Rituals and rules: about magic in consultancy. *Journal of Organizational Change Management*, 11 (5), 399–406.

Senge, P.M. (2000) The puzzles and paradoxes of how living companies create wealth: why single-valued objective functions are not quite enough. In M. Beer and N. Nohria (eds) *Breaking the Code of Change*. Harvard Business School Press: Boston, MA.

Senior, B. (2002) *Organisational Change* (2nd edn). Pitman: London.

Sosik, J.J. and Megerian, L.E. (1999) Understanding leader emotional intelligence and performance: the role of self–other agreement in transformational leadership perceptions. *Group and Organization Management*, 24 (3), 367–90.

Stace, D. and Dunphy, D. (2001) *Beyond the Boundaries: Leading and Re-Creating the Successful Enterprise* (2nd edn). McGraw-Hill: Sydney, NSW.

Stacey, R.D. (2003) *Strategic Management and Organisational Dynamics: The Challenge of Complexity*. FT/Prentice Hall: Harlow.

Stacey, R.D., Griffin, D. and Shaw, P. (2002) *Complexity and Management: Fad or Radical Challenge to Systems Thinking*. Routledge: London.

Stickland, F. (1998) *The Dynamics of Change: Insights into Organisational Transition from the Natural World*. Routledge: London.

Stohl, C. and Cheney, G. (2001) Participatory processes/paradoxical practices. *Management Communication Quarterly*, 14 (3), 349–407.

Weick, K.E. (2000) Emergent change as a universal in organisations. In M. Beer and N. Nohria (eds) *Breaking the Code of Change*. Harvard Business School Press: Boston, MA.

Wilson, D.C. (1992) *A Strategy of Change*. Routledge: London.

Worley, G.C. and Feyerhern, A.E. (2003) Reflections on the future of organization development. *Journal Of Applied Behavioral Science*, 39 (1), 97–115.

10

Complexity ethics

Hugo Letiche

Introduction

Complexity theory assumes an emergence-based view of existence. The complexity perspective assumes that disorder, flux, change, 'noise', interpenetration, and difference are all properties of the world. Complexity is processual; i.e. all forms change and life co-evolves. The inherently dynamic 'life-force' of transformation, process, and movement is considered to be necessary and irresistible. Emergence or continual motility and instability have organized us into the kind of beings that we are.

An ethics of complexity focuses on emergence, concentrating on the constant movement and change of (living-)organizing. The complex interrelatedness of such existence is fairly immediately and intuitively understandable. But, is there a 'natural law' of complexity and complexification, which leads to the change, development, and activity that we experience, and which defines the basis for an ethics? The justification for a complexity ethics hinges on the question of existence. If existence demands to be respected, then an ethics of 'care' towards organizing and emergence, as key qualities of complexity really ought to be self-evident. Ethics then entails 'care' for the well-being, sustenance and flourishing of emergence and the emergent, insofar as we are capable of this.

Organization and complexity

Ever since Lewin defined organizational change as 'unfreeze, changing and refreezing', the emphasis has been on assumed processions of fixed states, as if order, stability, and consistency were the rule, and emergence was the exception. Structure is prioritized as process is marginalized. But every 'structure' really is the result of process(es); and 'process(es)' normally involve change and novelty, which are structures. Emergence is a process of cause and effect; emergence is a sort of structuration. Organizing is a process of continual becoming, but not of chaos. Neither organization nor change is the exception; they are interconnected, heterogeneous, and constantly fluctuating.

A complexity perspective produces a different take on organizational change than the commonplace one. And a complexity approach points to an ethics of 'care', which would differentiate it from current organizational intervention practices. I will return to this last point. The assumption of an inter-relational process of change will be examined here as the ground for an organizational ethics. Such an ethics examines social and work relationships to see if they are, and/or can be made, satisfying and meaningful. If organizing upholds human action consistent with the kind of existence that we are, then in complexity terms, it is ethical. Such a complexity-based ethics seeks to support practices of communication and interdependence providing for human flourishing.

In 'complexity theory', specific circumstances are not reduced to general rules; concrete events are not subsumed to universal concepts; agency does not disappear in an overview. Specific persons, events, and activities are acknowledged to be crucial in what happens. Complexity will be, but it cannot be modeled. Assuming that a 'theory' can be used to 'model' a situation; there is here no 'theory'. One can point to various dimensions or aspects of complexity, but which descriptor will at any concrete moment prevail is indefinite. 'Complexity' entails a series of rich metaphors. Its language may be suited to talking about a changing world, but there is no theory leading to prediction or control. Some believe that such prediction and control will come some day. But for the time being, 'complexity' points to a logic of partial indeterminacy, where deeds can be deeply significant, but do not need to be. Based on the inputs, we cannot predict the outcomes. The 'black box' really is black – not only are we not sure what will happen in it, we are unsure what will (eventually) come out of it.

Indeterminacy forces the actant – whether person, organization, or society – to constantly make 'intelligent guesses'. In every situation there are degrees of freedom, sometimes they are very few, sometimes much more. Sometimes the few are more important than the many. This lack of certainty can be thought of as debilitating or as facilitating. For some, possibility is enabling and for others terrifying.

While complexity theory is a collection of insights about consciousness and feedback, it is not really a 'theory' at all. Complexity theory is, in effect, a sort of oxymoron. There is no single theory involved and there can be none without betraying the whole enterprise. Characteristic ideas in complexity theory are:

Emergence: change will happen; circumstances will be transformed, contexts will alter, and identities will vary. The best knowledge about how things are will sooner or later become obsolete. Transformation can be evolutionary and gradual, but it also can be abrupt and radical. We are sure that the status quo will end, but whether it will end unexpectedly or predictably, violently or calmly, creatively or ploddingly; we do not know. Change is arbitrary in degree, timing, severity, and import.

Edge of chaos: the most creative change occurs as close as possible to chaos as the person, group, organization, or society can sustain. Chaos entails disintegration and death. But without chaos, there is inflexibility, rigidity, and also death. Life exists between chaos and stasis, but cannot survive at either extreme. As one approaches chaos, there is the greatest chance of creative change, dynamic alteration, and innovative tension. It is the zone of maximum originality and novelty, but also of highest risk.

Self-organization: in nature, evolution occurs from itself. Order is not willed; it occurs. No first principle or authority makes the intricate structures we discover in nature. By analogy, 'organization is for free'. Complex structures have evolved in nature, in cultures, and in economies by themselves. One must not assume that evolution is (always) willed. Very demanding and intricate structures spontaneously emerge from much less complicated

147

elements. Organization often is not willed; organization spontaneously finds new, innovative, and effective forms.

Strange attractors: organization occurs around leitmotifs, simple guiding principles, or basic premises. The points of departure can be quite simple (point attractors), can repeat the same pattern over and over (cyclical), can be defined by a polar conflict, or can generate new unpredictable configurations (strange attractors) which are emergent.

Weak signals: in any system, there are strong dominant principles of order and structure, and there are hidden, not apparent, and subsumed elements of order and of identity. Strong signals are obvious and get noticed. But creativity is often in the weak signals. Alertness for weak signals can be much more inspiring and revelatory than going along with the more apparent ones.

Non-linearity: situation, identity, and organization do not evolve step by step. Change is discontinuous and often disruptive, as well as indefinite. The chain of cause and effect is often unexpectedly broken. A stable situation does not necessarily produce another stable situation. A 'well-oiled' machine or organization can work fine right now, but it can suddenly fall into disrepair. How things are does not assure how they will be.

Dis-proportionality: a small change can have massive effects and seemingly big changes can alter next to nothing. This is the so-called 'butterfly effect' – supposedly, a small perturbation in the air in one part of the world can cause a major storm half way around the globe. Or a total revamp of a company's structure can produce little or no change, while a small improvement (for instance, in product design) can make a major difference.

Duration: occurrence really happens; things change and become different. When a person, group and/or organization transmutes, one cannot simply go back to the old situation. Time is not an epiphenomenon that can be ignored. Events happen in duration; time is significant and substantive.

Unicity: specific, concrete constellations of persons, circumstances, and events are unique. Persons, lives, and reactions are one of a kind. Specificity is the rule. What a person does is singular and can never be repeated in quite exactly the same way or context. Occurrence or concrete particular actions, really do count.

All these qualities and principles focus on events, occurrences and the dynamic dimension to existence. Particular moments or events can bring transformations, identity-change and substantial innovation. There are no simple rules for change – all we can be sure of is that change will happen. Adjustment in continuity, or rupture and fundamental upheaval, or something in between, are all possible.

We can embrace complexity as our natural identity; and we can deny or try to ignore complexity. These are issues of 'response-ability' or of the ability and willingness to respond. 'Ethics' entails the study of responsibility in relatedness. If feedback loops between self and other, phenomena and perception, world and subject are honoured, then questioning of the nature and quality of relationships inevitably ensues. Combining ethics and complexity instigates ethical reflection on: (i) communication, and (ii) interdependence.

Rigorous study of communication reveals a multitude of links between different forms of human activity – that is, similarities in the fundamental mindsets of all sorts of disciplines. This observation is fundamentally phenomenal – it leads to seeing links and possible cross-fertilizations, but it does not make a claim to a global or holist ontology. At any given time and place, there is communication between society, biology, and individual existence. They share paradigms, basic concerns and approaches. Here we find the roots of a complexity-based ethics.

(i) Communication

Different persons, groups, and organizations influence one another in all sorts of ways. The results of interaction are emergent. A 'catch word' for all this relationality is 'communication' wherein the interaction between the persons and environment is enormously complex. Scientific reduction and abstraction cannot operate when faced with too many possibilities. Normal science seeks to establish causality ('A' causes 'B') with no mediation, relationality, consciousness, aesthetics, or beliefs complexifying matters. 'Complexity theory' asserts that between 'A and B' there will be multiple and complex feedback loops; 'A causes B', which causes 'A'; i.e. 'A <> B <> A' exists in an environment of positive and negative feedback loops. Knowing is part and parcel of the known. For instance, the researcher's consciousness is a biological phenomenon, just as well as all knowable biological phenomena are products of consciousness. Acknowledgement of the mutually constituting relationships of self and other, researcher and researched, organization and environment, is impossible for (most) mainstream science. But the foregrounded, 'object of research' or 'content', cannot exist without a back grounded hermeneutic. Communication inherently entails relationship(s) to others, circumstances and world.

Communication has to be understood as 'relatedness'. The study of 'relatedness' makes one aware of relationship(s). Identity exists in contrast to difference; organization occurs in tension with disorganization; unicity is understood in terms of continuity. Sameness and difference are complex interrelated facets to the one and the same existence. 'Sameness' is never 'identical' – two organizations, persons, or events can display 'sameness', but they are nonetheless different organizations, persons or events. 'Difference' is relative – two organizations, persons or events can be 'different', but they manifest enough 'sameness' to still (both) be organizations, persons or events. Thus 'sameness' and 'difference' exist in relationship to one another. They communicate in manifest 'relatedness'.

Figure 10.1 helps us to understand 'mutual relatedness'. The communicator (A) communicates something (B) that co-constitutes who or what (A) is. This process is grounded in soft distinctions between speaker and spoken, and self and other. The investigator and the investigated are engaged in processes of mutual causality. In the feedback loop(s) from the researched to the researcher, the researcher becomes a creation of the researched. The sociologist is a product of modern society; research is part of the biology of consciousness; phenomena are products of the human senses. Radical feedback loop(s) between self and other, observer and world, environment and entity are crucial.

An ethics of relatedness or communication focuses on the relationship:

$$\frac{A <> B <> A}{ENVIRONMENT}$$

For communication to occur, two similar elements – such as, persons, organizations, or societies – have to be linked. The 'B' bridges two similar, parallel and commeasurable

Figure 10.1 Mutual relatedness

'A's. Difference between 'A' and 'A' is limited. 'A' and 'A' are nouns and 'B' is a verb. Motility and change are concentrated on the 'B'. Radical difference, creative relationship and the power of aliveness, reach the subject ('A') via 'B' as supported by the 'environment'.

Communication always entails a complex context or environment which energizes that A <> B <> A relationship. A complexity theory of communication typifies the 'environment' as 'noise' (Serres, 1969, 1972, 1980, 1982a, 1982b, 1991, 2006, 2008; Sangild, 2002). 'Noise' is the unbridled raw power of existence. Noise or more specifically 'white noise' is chaos – i.e. it is like the sound of the sea, or of a jet engine drowning out all other sounds. Noise is the pure overwhelming din of the overpowering force of unlimited potential. Speech and communication require the exclusion or repression of 'noise'. But if 'noise' is the first principle of existence – being the remnant of the big bang and the vehicle of undifferentiated possibility – its repression will be life denying. 'Noise' brings emergence, change and creativity; but 'noise' threatens social order, identity and stability. Systems of meaning and order have to keep the 'noise' outside of their boundaries. 'Noise' is too powerful and too threatening to be included in human order. 'B' may depend on 'noise' for its energy – i.e. for the production of emergence, discontinuity, duration and unicity. But if self, identity and organization get too close to 'noise', they will (self-)destruct.

Thus, how is the communicative social order created and stabilized, if the sources of sense-making ('B') depend on something so precarious as 'noise'? 'A's relationship to emergence, creativity, and the 'life-force' is mitigated by 'B'. An implication is that most persons and/or organizations have little or no direct relationship to the life-force. They occupy structured, determined, and regimented roles of similarity. The 'life-force' only reaches them, mitigated by others, circumstances or serendipity. On the one side, there is the violence of chaos, which is potentially creative but always endangering; and on the other side, there is the reified, fetishized, and stabilized universe of bureaucratic order. Communication occurs by silencing the 'noise'. There is order and significance in social relationship, but it is bought at the cost of repressing the basic raw energy of existence.

Complexity is characterized by the force of the possible, i.e. the force of existence that precedes all concrete being and action. 'Noise' or existence's vital force comes from the outside. Humans can respond to existence, but they do not make it. Human thought is often focused on the 'black box' – i.e. on what happens between inputs and outputs. Inputs, such as leaders, cultures, economies and agriculture, are defined; and outputs, such as crises, revolutions, and successes are observed. But the 'white box' of 'noise' is ignored. The source of all energy, will power, and activity remains hidden. The pure energy of being, which makes all life, change and development possible, is the first principle of all existence. It can be called 'noise', 'energy' and 'potentia' (Greek: δύναμις dunamis).

The life-force or noise of the environment energizes inter-relationship. In interrelations the one lives on, or profits from, the activity or labour of the other. Human sociability involves biological, social, and communicative relatedness. This relatedness entails dependency, play, cooperation, violence, and guilt. Society, when analysed with the communication model of:

$$\underline{A <> B <> A}$$
$$\text{ENVIRONMENT}$$

has metaphorically to be understood in complexity terms. Michel Serres does this via the myth of Romulus and Remus (Serres, 1991). The twin brothers form the 'A's, what transpires between them is the 'B', and the crowd around them is the 'environment'. The founding of Rome and the start of Empire entail the death of Remus. By getting rid of the alternative or other 'A', according to Serres, Romulus sacrifices relationship for power. The ruler has no equal; the ruler does not communicate. Rulers exist via human sacrifice – i.e. by establishing a regime or episteme of one voice, one power, and one authority. Rulers kill the 'Other' – they exist by negating dialogue, exchange and interaction. If there is a 'ruler', there is no 'Other'. The ruler accepts being subsumed to no one; the ruler acknowledges the sovereignty of nobody else; and the ruler unconditionally respects the being of no 'Other'. But the destruction of the 'Other', brings with it guilt and fear (Hagemeijer, 2005). The authority that orders and rules does so by repressing dialogue, equality and open interaction. Both rulers and followers share in the resulting guilt. The followers form the 'environment', and the ruler is a solitary 'A' in a closed system of identity. Empire – as politics or as multi-national business, is ruled by an anti-dialogical logic. Alternatives are repressed. The ruler or the rule of law is singular, not plural. Power may come from the raw potentia of existence – i.e. from 'noise', but leadership institutionalizes inequality, repression, and a system of order that is closed to 'Other'.

In a much more optimistic frame, complex relatedness can be understood as a system of interactions between different aggregation levels (see Figure 10.2).

Life, relationship to others, and communication are then posited to be characteristics of interaction. There is dependence on and between each (aggregation) level. For instance, biology reveals the one organism feeding on the other. All organisms live in and/or on other organisms. All baby mammals feed on their mother's breasts to survive. Feeding entails social dependence. Everything from scavenging to agriculture entails the one feeding on the other. In society, there is a parallel logic of interdependence, protection and reproduction. And this is maintained via science, schooling and knowledge.

On the level of information, stories or narratives are used to talk solidarity, cooperation, and relationship into existence. All transactions – such as the buying and selling of goods and services – require promises, specifications, contracts, and trust. Trade requires stories and negotiations. Activity entails interdependence between the aggregation levels of the biological, social, and informational. Each aggregation level exists in relationship to its brethren.

But interdependence is ethically neutral; it can include everything from altruism to parasitism (Brown, 2002, 2004; Letiche, 2007). Interdependence is not voluntary or chosen; it is a necessary law of nature. All life depends on energy or 'noise' to exist. But how life partakes of this necessary energy, how it is distributed and (perhaps not) shared, is variable. Humanity can abuse nature; it can rebel against nature; it can pervert nature. Nature is not necessarily sustainable, virtuous or good. For instance, it may be natural to take possession of resources via pollution. Dogs mark their territory, polluting it to claim possession. Mankind may well pollute the natural world in a similar way. An environmentally

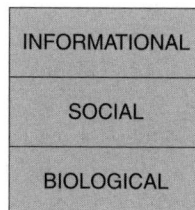

Figure 10.2 A system of interactions

responsible politics may not entail being more natural, but being less so. Mankind can choose to not pollute – i.e. to not take resources into its possession in a destructive and greedy way. Narratives of 'social responsibility', perhaps, can prevail over biosocial primitivism (Serres, 2008). But an ethics of environmental and/or social responsibility does not necessarily follow the logic of biology.

Social cooperation organized around so-called quasi-objects countervails the logics of parasitism and leadership. Instead of vesting all authority in rulers, society can create half-living objects around which sociability is organized. A 'quasi-object' is part object and part social agency. It is a thing around which human relationships are created; it is near-human or semi-living. Quasi-objects are inanimate things, which when coupled to humans produce living-systems of communication. Money is such a quasi-object. Quasi-objects stabilize human relations, but are constantly susceptible to rupture, challenge and decay. Systems of quasi-objects may not look fragile, but they are. If they collapse, social order disintegrates, and violence erupts every-which-way. German hyperinflation in the 1920s is an example of the collapse of a key quasi-object and of the tumultuous chaos that can result.

Quasi-objects on a globalized scale have been called 'world-objects' – that is, matters such as climate change, nuclear bombs, oil spills, and global economic crises – that have changed the aggregation level of social ordering. Instead of local, national, or organizational structures, order may now (have to) be created on a planetary level. A potential escalation of 'evil' – i.e. of violence, destruction, and chaos, is involved. The possibility of an ethical 'world-object', or of a 'quasi-object' written large in the form of a narrative of 'environmental humanism', is introduced.

Social order catalysed by quasi-objects follows the A <> B <> A structure, requiring an active 'B' as provided for by quasi-objects in reaction to the threat of an environment of chaos or noise. The 'A' talks and communicates. It is performatively constituted via engagement with the quasi-objects. Money, rugby balls, music – in fact all quasi-objects – exist as shared communicative structures.

The complexity perspective on communication leads us to 'restricted complexity'. Complexity, for instance, is 'restricted' in that phenomena studied are described and understood as complex, but consciousness, awareness, and mind are not understood or 'deconstructed' as complex. The complex is positioned outside of (self-)consciousness, which is not accounted for as complex. Biology, literature, mathematics, politics, history, and art, etc. can all be displayed as interrelated, without the 'I' of consciousness or communication being examined. A complexity awareness centering on emergence and communication does not necessarily address the presupposition(s) necessary for the making of 'self'-awareness and responsibility.

A complexity informed study of communication allows one to put 'noise', 'life-force' and 'quasi-objects' on display. Complexity can be portrayed as in-the-world. But the human ability to deal with non-linearity, chaos, noise, non-proportionality, etc. remains here problematic. The 'life-force' may be a necessary source of the human condition, which makes us the kind of being that we are, but it is uncertain whether humanity can translate this energy or 'noise' into flourishing, justice, fairness, or solidarity. Complexity reveals change, development, and activity, and there is a 'natural law' of all of this. Complexity ethics needs to explore how to thrive consistently with the kind of being that we are. The key characteristic of that being is emergence – its 'natural law' is motile and unstable. Communication as constituted by complexity entails the fundamental interrelatedness of 'response-ability' and requires a 'complexity theory' that deals with person and circumstance, ontology and consciousness, self and world.

152

(ii) Interdependence

'General complexity' is characterized by the interdependence of the force fields we observe and inhabit, and which constitute our 'response-ability'. In the communication analysis of 'restricted complexity', the energy that underpins aliveness was called 'noise' and 'life-force'. 'General complexity' explores interdependence between: Organization, Existence, System and Being. The combined possibilities define the concept of complexity, which has been called *auto (geno-pheno)-eco-re-organization* (Morin, 1977, 1979, 1980, 1982, 1992, 2000, 2004, 2005a, 2008; Morin and Kern, 1996; Morin and Weinmann, 2008).

It is *auto* because self-organization plays a key role. Organizing organizes itself; organization is not determined by any first cause or principle. How organizing will mature; how long an organization will persist, and when or how it will end, is indefinite. Auto-organizing results are complex and emergent. Organizations exist via change, renewal and constant activity. Parts are rejected, aspects are eliminated; portions die. All of these processes emerge from organizing and its complex relations with surroundings. They are not rigidly predetermined or driven by external first principles.

Identity or existence occurs – it is self-developing. It develops in relationship to what is possible (*geno-*) and what traits (*pheno-*) are manifest. Organization kneads realized traits and appeals to possible ones. And development always occurs in relationship to an environment (*eco-*); organization is a matter of relationship and of the application of energy, will, and/or force. The organization has continually to be *(re-)organized* – organizing is a repetitive and recursive and unending process.

My analysis of interdependence (see Figure 10.3) begins with an organization, i.e. an instance of organizing to be examined and/or to be understood. The starting point is problematic, because 'identity' or 'self' always have to be understood as relatedness, dynamic, and complex. There is no fixed, static, dead 'object' with which to begin the analysis; there are circumstances, events, and identities. These are emergent processes and proceedings. Organizations have autonomy – in the sense that they can be represented (also to themselves) as identifiable though dynamic. But their autonomy is complex – it includes dependence and independence, relatedness and opposition. Autonomy is in relationship to groups', societies' and organizations' situatedness. Organization/organizing tends to the specific, while system-ness answers to governance, biopolitics, affordances

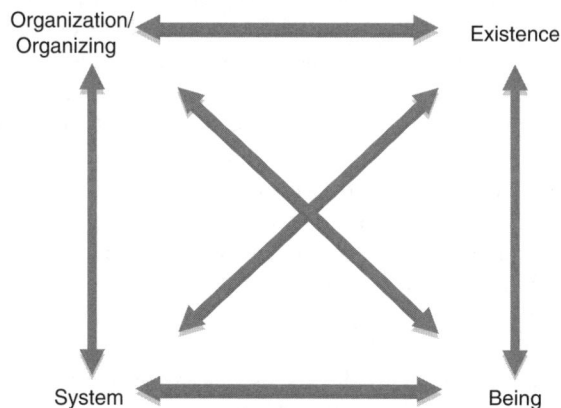

Figure 10.3 Analysis of interdependence[1]

and homologies. An ethics of organization/organizing is overwhelmingly situational; a system ethics appeals to (general) principles of organization/organizing. As I am using the concepts, complexity is close to organizing/organization and to (lived) existence, and it is far from systems logic(s) and/or Being.

My goal is to develop a form of process or complexity thinking that itself is complex, i.e. that is characterized by emergent awareness that appears circumstantially or existentially. Emergent awareness is characterized by response-ability grounded in a (natural) ethics of consciousness/ circumstance and self/other relatedness. Some situations are more embedded in rules and repetition; some are more temporary and changing. And all situations entail 'organizing' – i.e. patterns, standards, principles and attractors, around which they coalesce. As has been hammered home in organizational studies, looking at organizations as nouns distorts awareness of organizing as verbs (Chia, 1999). All living systems are 'verbs' – that will say that they exist in relationship to an environment and absorb energy to exist. In their (self-)organizing, diversity is kept under (some) control, and chaos is exploited, but necessarily kept restricted.

All human consciousness or knowledge of (social) organization exists via language and in relationship to other knowers and knowledge. All identity defers to other identities, all knowing is linked to other knowing, and all personhood stands in relationship to 'Other' as Levinas and Derrida have asserted (Levinas, 2001, 2001; Derrida, 1998). Experience entails the organizing of events and circumstances into understanding and sense-making (Dewey, 2005). Consciousness is in concrete circumstance or existence; awareness occurs in human (existential) time (or *durée*).

Existence is lived, experienced; it is what is. It is a commonplace that the 'whole (of existence) is more than the sum of its parts', but the 'parts are [also] more than the whole'. The 'whole' can be stated as a 'master idea' or 'grand narrative', such as that of the exploited workers, or of entrepreneurial leaders, or of members of an artistic vanguard. These are all more and less than the individual existences that they attend to. The more and less of existence is complex, i.e. human existence is complexly organized. Some possibilities dominate and others are repressed. One potential is championed and its alternatives are cancelled out. Some life forms are permitted; many are forbidden. Organizing channels activity into some routes and not others. The potentia of existence is much richer than how existence is concretely organized.

Organizing produces identity, praxis, and intentionality, which are all organization-effects. 'Self' expresses itself in relationship to 'Other', whereby 'self' and 'other' are mutually constitutive forms of existence. Sense-making, identity, and 'self' are all qualities of existence. Organizing and existence are 'ontic' – i.e. they are the way-of-life or way-of-being-in-the-midst-of-things, of everyday life. Existence is known as organization + sensemaking, or organizing + identity. Every living organism has awareness of 'existence' – i.e. it has at least some (minimal) qualities of 'consciousness'. Even one cell animals can be 'irritated' by external stimulus. Whether systems can support existence (i.e. consciousness) is hotly debated. One can assert that systems are inherently reified, abstract and lifeless. Systems are thereby thought of as law-bound, i.e. there is no place for existential awareness in the knowledge of their structures. Likewise, one can argue that existence is lost in abstraction when one starts the philosophical investigation of 'Being'. Are systems 'really' illustrations of complex relatedness or are they complex rule-bound structures? Is complexity 'cued' (i.e. always process) or 'coded' (i.e. objectified/objectifiable)?

'Being' is the category of ontology and it is about what 'IS' – i.e. it transcends everyday becoming and entails the 'IS' of 'is' (if any such thing exists). Organizations/organizing is characterized by complex, self-contradictory assemblages of elements, possibilities, and relation-ships. In 'existence', there is practice and reflexivity, activity and identity – i.e. consciousness. Put philosophically and in Heidegger's terms, 'existence' is *dasein* or being thrown into the world, and 'Being' is 'sein' or the ground of 'Being' that most essentially 'IS'. By attending to everything that can be found in the world, including the 'world' itself, one supposedly forgets to ask what 'Being' itself is. For Heidegger, what needs to be asked is: 'Beyond all circumstances and excluding all particularities of perception and event, what is the IS of existence?' Ethics becomes whatever the 'IS of is' dictates, demands, points to, or defines.

Complexity ethics, as conceived of here, centers on organization/organizing and existence. All encompassing system-principles, and the rejection of everyday involvement in existence, do not match the circumstantial, concrete, emergent logic of presence, crucial to complexity.

Organizing may depend on 'noise' or 'life-force' to energize itself; but are 'noise' and 'life-force' aspects or categories of 'Being' or of existence ('being')? As used here, they are not originatory or ontological. 'Noise' is a perceptual quality of matter; 'life-force' is a quality of all living systems – i.e. it is something biology and botany can study.

Existence is emergent and circumstantial. Existence is in the world, it is dynamic, and it happens. Organizing/organization cannot exist without interaction. Organizing is more than abstraction, without concrete relationships and actions. Organization requires the energy, possibilities, activity, and time of relationships to exist. An organization can be described as a pure abstraction, without it actually existing. But living organization/organizing exists. It has energy, which it absorbs and dissipates. It is interrelated to circumstance, others and time.

Organization can be full of energy and potential, but not be self-conscious or existentially reflective. For instance, a crowd can be full of energy, but whether it is preparing for a very nasty lynching or a creative act of sympathy can be utterly unclear. Intentionality, including what the organizing means ethically, is a key quality of 'existence'. But 'existence' can be unspecified, pre-reflective, hidden, or yet to emerge. The reverse is also possible; an idea of existence can have next to no 'organization-existence'. For instance, an intellectual can produce a perspective or a utopian possibility of great quality, but whether this 'identity' will ever become real living organizing can be totally unclear. Existence is about what can be in the world, but it can open to speculation, dreaming and fantasy, as well.

Organizing exists via renewal; parts are rejected, aspects are eliminated; portions die. Organization is an unending, repetitive, and recursive process. Organizing entails interrelatedness and produces (it can be argued) complexification. Organisms, ecological niches, and societies it seems have through the millennia become ever more complex. And the more complex an organization becomes, the less dependent it is on the specific properties of its elements. Increasingly, an overall pattern of organization prevails. Organizations do develop in the direction of 'system–ness' – i.e. they become reified, embedded and/or more 'solid'. Morin has explored this process by distinguishing between the 'trivial machines' of systems, and the 'complex machines' of living organizing/organization. His complexity ethics focuses on the existential value of 'complex machines' and the (relative) sterility of 'trivial machines'.

'Trivial machines' are forms of organization that are dependent on the correct functioning of their every element (Morin, 2006). Their intended outputs can be predicted on the basis of knowledge of the inputs. 'Trivial machines' wear out and then they do not work any more. 'Complex machines', such as life, evolve and change, and can persist or prevail in change. They develop and mature instead of only deteriorating and breaking down. 'Complex machines' are not programmed; that is, their actions are not strictly predetermined. Machines and computers are programmed; humans are intentional, strategic and flexible. 'Complex machines' die, making room for still more change and evolution. Complexity is a coming and going of order and disorder. Complexification and evolution entail generations of alteration and development, and are dependent on the changes that death makes possible.

155

Complexification supposedly leads to strong organizing, such as seen in life, which has flexible and unstable components. Its organization is complex – that is, description of all the elements does not allow for prediction. The elements are co-dependent and co-determinant, and their organization is purposeful. There is internal adjustment and fluidity, as well as adaptability. *Self-/ eco-(re-)organization* is continuous – i.e. 'self' (or organization plus existence) interacts with an environment, contextually re-creating 'self'. 'Self' is adaptable, flexible and creative; it cannot be strictly governed or made (entirely) predictable.

Organization self-organizes. Identity or 'self' is produced in interaction; organization produces social interaction. Individuals by interacting, produce organization. The results are indeterminate; they emerge in relationship(s). In life, radical relatedness and impermanence is inherent. Complexity is a given. The biological emerges from the physical, and the social emerges from the biological (Figure 10.4). Material existence, or the raw substance of the universe, has organized itself (on earth) into life and social existence. Life and society have emerged from the protoplasm (Greek: protos 'first' and plasma 'thing formed'). The smallest element, say for biological life the 'protoplasm', leads to all the rest; but all of this has been (as far as we know) emergent – a quality of existence.

The concrete time and place of the biological and/or the social entity counts. Identity – organizing + existence – is a product of specific circumstances and encounters. Relationships happen in tangible time and space; identity emerges from circumstance, occurrence and event. Autonomy is a word for the specificity of existence and of its organizing. In autonomy, there is a measure of openness or indeterminacy, and of radical relatedness and of impermanence. This complexity is a given. The unstable relatedness between organizing and consciousness, and organization and existence, is characteristic of complexity.

Complexity cannot be simplified without destroying its quality of emergence. To repeat: life entails processes of *auto-(geno-pheno)-eco-re-organization*. As already stated, mutual implication, or *eco-auto-causality*, is interactive and recursive. Organizing self-organizes. 'Self' never loses its relatedness to 'Other'. Traditional systems thinking follows the logic of 'order from order', and most critical (social) science follows the logic of 'order from disorder'. Each of these is too static and enslaves self and society in the permanence of a closed logical system. Complexity answers to: 'order from perturbation or noise'. In complexity, there is unending change, difference, and dynamism. Dis-organization is inherent to organization; unrealized potentia is crucial to identity; negative and positive feedback loops drive systems away from equilibrium. Complexity produces *chaosmos* or a cosmos wherein chaos is inherent and order is inseparable from disorder. Complexity leads to an *anthropo-ethics*, wherein organizing entails existence, and complexity is an ethico-life process.

Ethics can be framed around the tension(s) crucial to organizing/organization and existence. One can assert that organizing must respect both individual and species existence. Such an individual/species ethics champions a sustainable organizing of society, which guarantees the dynamic and interactive survival of individuals and species. It can be asserted that the triple

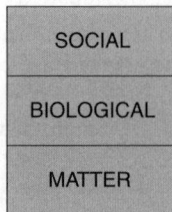

| SOCIAL |
| BIOLOGICAL |
| MATTER |

Figure 10.4 Recursive causality

identity of matter/species/persons is currently threatened as economically driven environmental change threatens sustainability. Social-economic goals tempt the individual to abandon his/her species identity and to exhaust the earth's raw materials. This betrays the material and biological grounds to life, and threatens the future of human existence.

Conclusion

Complexity ethics try to deal insightfully with two issues: (i) the phenomenal complexity of (social) organizing/organization, and (ii) the reflexive complexity of existing and thinking from a position of inter-relatedness. The ethical self in a complexity perspective is never alone; 'self' is with 'other' in circumstance, and always dependent on the environment. Ethics for an organizing/organization identity is complex because it always entails 'others', i.e. events and world. There is confluence: of self and other, of circumstance and will, of power and action. Existence is characterized by (de-)constructive circularity; wherein the relatedness of parts and wholes is endless. Via 'quasi-objects' or 'world-objects', order and a measure of stability can be attempted. But whatever structure or system is achieved, it will break down and be replaced via renewal and change. There is only impermanence. A reflexive awareness of emergence could celebrate impermanence and becoming. Organizing could be put in service of a concept of Being that acknowledges fluidity, instability and motility. But such a first-principle of Being is inherently paradoxical – can Being really be thought of as motion, change and process, without falling back into some sort of reification or metaphysics? Provisional and transient existence could be granted precedence over everything else. Systems could be understood as rhizomatic, and the noise or unstructured power of organizing could be thought of as all-important. Such an anti-ethics of ethics of course exists in Deleuzian thought (Deleuze and Guattari, 1983, 1987). But complexity ethics is proposed here as a much more modest ontic project of organizing/organization and of existence (or consciousness).

A stoic ethics of 'taking responsibility for what you can really influence' is close to the complexity alternative. Each moment and place in complexity possesses a limited force of organizing, a partial possibility of identity, and (at best) an imperfect access to consciousness or existence. Doing justice to complexity involves awareness of limits, and the ability to accept partiality. Complexity entails interdependence and its knowledge is cognitively indeterminate. There can be no single truth to complexity because it is always open to new organizing, leading to new circumstances – and that is its aporia. Complexity ethics requires a self-awareness of identity and motility, and the will to respect them both. Care for self, and for 'Other' is crucial. The examination of organizing from the 'care' perspective is very different from the performative focus of today. Emergent ethics, grounded in complexity, does have the potential of pointing to an alternative approach to individual, group and species respons-ability .

The challenge is to produce a complexity ethics that one can 'be for'. The amoral arrogance, wherein profit making somehow excuses existence from all other responsibility, has to be combated. Complexity ethics powerfully opposes blind individualism, which refuses to acknowledge interconnection, relationship, or interdependence. The primacy of the 'egoistic individual' is an ideology that falsifies the workings of organizing and of existence. But stoicism, as the privileged escape from irresponsibility, is problematic. Taking grasp of the significance of the limited role of the 'self' can lead to cynicism. The 'cynics' were in ancient Greece the persons who most extremely attacked convention and pretense; their heritors (in CMS?) are certainly ready to denounce green-washing, banker hypocrisy, and the lies of the PR departments (Jones et al., 2005). But ethics as an anti-business rant will not get us very far. The problem is that an ethics we can 'be for' has to take precedence over business-as-usual. As long as business assumes that maximization of its power, profits, and privileges is the only good that exists, there will be no space for ethics.

Self-understanding of change, may lead to an eco-ethics of relatedness and respect for difference. An ethics grounded in the complexity principles of communication just does not go far enough; respect for radical interrelatedness informed by a complexity awareness is required. Organizing must not be defined as only a utilitarian profit-driven activity; but also as a bridge between the potentia of material/biological/social levels and their realization in existence. As the current crisis reveals, the master-words of economic growth or of profit, or of shareholder value and material wealth, destroy the eco-stability of crucial relations of existence. Emergence and self-organization will follow their own constructive and destructive, innovative and repressive, expansive and declining logics. Existence will be polyphonic and complex, or it will be pragmatically and philosophically crushingly repressive. A humanly self-consistent complexity ethics, willing to address response-ability, is possible. Such an ethics has been defined here in terms of honoring the logic of complexity; but the current ecological and economic crises indicate that we are not as yet very good at it.

Note

1 The figure is my adaption of the semiotic square. The scale from 'organization/organizing' to 'system' is from process to law; and the scale from 'existence' to 'Being' is from the ontic to ontology. The supposed fluidity of 'existence' opposes the closed structure of 'system' and the circumstantial everyday quality of 'organization/organizing' opposes the ontological focus of 'Being'.

References

Brown, Steven D. (2002) "Michel Serres: Science, translation and the logic of the parasite", *Theory, Culture & Society*, vol. 19, no. 3, pp. 1–27.
—— (2004) "Parasite logic", *Journal of Organizational Change Management*, vol. 17, no. 4, pp. 383–95.
Chia, Robert (1999) "A 'rhizomic' model of organizational change & transformation". *British Journal of Management*, vol. 10, pp. 209–27.
Cilliers, Paul (1998) *Complexity & Postmodernism*. London: Routledge.
—— (2002) "Why we cannot know complex things completely", *Emergence (E:CO)*, vol. 4, no. 1–2, pp. 77–84.
—— (2005) "Complexity, deconstruction and relativism", *Theory Culture & Society*, vol. 22, no. 5, pp. 255–67.
—— (2006) "On the importance of a certain slowness", *E:CO*, vol. 8, no. 3, pp. 105–12.
—— (2008) "Towards an ethics of complexity", paper presented at the symposium Towards an Ethics of Complexity, Utrecht, The Netherlands, 27 November.
Deleuze, Gilles and Felix Guattari (1983) *Anti-Oedipus: Capitalism and Schizophrenia*. St Paul, MN: University of Minnesota Press.
—— (1987) *A Thousand Plateaus: Capitalism and Schizophrenia*. St Paul, MN: University of Minnesota Press.
Derrida, Jacques (1998) *Of Grammatology*. Baltimore, MD: Johns Hopkins University Press.
Dewey, John (2005) *Art as Experience*. New York: Perigee.
Hagemeijer, Rouven (2005) *The Unmasking of the Other*. Rotterdam: ERIM.
Jones, Campbell, Martin Parker and Rene ten Bos (2005) *For Business Ethics*. Oxford: Routledge.
Letiche, Hugo (2007) "Parasites & Self-Organization", *Tamara*, vol. 6, no. 2, pp. 187–202.
Levinas, Emmanuel (2001) *The Levinas Reader*. Oxford: Blackwell.
Morin, Edgar (1977) *La Méthode 1: La Nature de la Nature*. Paris: Seuil.

—— (1979) *Le Paradigme Perdu*. Paris: Seuil.

—— (1980) *La Méthode 2: La Vie de la Vie*. Paris: Seuil.

—— (1992) *Method*. New York: Peter Lang.

—— (2000) *Les Sept Savoirs Nécessaires à l'Éducation du Future*. Paris: Seuil.

—— (2004) *Pour Entrer dans le XXIe siècle*. Paris: Seuil.

—— (2005a) *Introduction à la Pensée Complexe*. Paris: Seuil.

—— (2005b) "From Prefix to Paradigm", *World Futures*, vol. 61, no. 4, pp. 254–62.

—— (2006) "Restricted Complexity, General Complexity", paper presented at the colloquium Intelligence de la complexité: ´épistémologie et pragmatique, Cerisy-La-Salle, France, 26 June 2005.

—— (2008) *On Complexity*. Cresskill, NJ: Hampton.

Morin, Edgar and Anne Brigette Kern (1996) *Terre-patrie*. Paris: Seuil.

Morin, Edgar and Heinz Weinmann (2008) *La Complexité Humaine*. Paris: Flammarion.

Sangild, T. (2002) *The Aesthetics of Noise*. Copenhagen: Datano.

Serres, Michel (1969) *Hermès Volume 1, La Communication*. Paris: Editions Minuit.

—— (1972) *Hermès Volume 2, L'Interférence*. Paris: Editions Minuit.

—— (1980) *Hermès Volume 5, Le Passage du Nord-Ouest*. Paris: Editions Minuit.

—— (1982a) *Hermes*. Baltimore, MD: Johns Hopkins University Press.

—— (1982b) *The Parasite*. Baltimore, MD: Johns Hopkins University Press.

—— (1985) *Les Cinq Sens*. Paris: Grasset (2009 New York: Continuum).

—— (1991) *Rome*. Stanford, CA: Stanford University Press.

—— (2006) *Récits d'Humanisme*. Paris: Le Pommier.

—— (2008) *Le Mal Propre: Polluer pour s'approprier?* Paris: Le Pommier.

11

Narratives of coherence
The role of affordances and homologies

Michael R. Lissack

Introduction

Organizational change is usually provoked by some outside event – often a perceived risk of failure but sometimes the perception by senior management of a major but unexploited opportunity. When a change project is commenced, its very nature is threatening not only to the status quo but to the coherence or sense of unity which pervades the organization and which helps to define it for its members and stakeholders. Management in this world is perhaps best labeled as "coherence seeking" – where what is sought is a pervasive yet dynamic feeling of confidence that the world is predictable and that things will work out as desired. The successful change project will achieve Antonovsky's (1979) definition of coherence: comprehensibility, manageability, and meaningfulness.

These three concepts are also the hallmark of successful "complexity reduction". Change projects and the organizational environments in which they most often occur are marked by complexity. Complexity involves a multi-dimensional ecology of world and consciousness, objects and perception, opportunities and language. This multidimensional world is very different from the efficiency based, profit-maximizing, cost-minimizing, customer-satisficing world of management. Managers are trained to act on simplicity. The coherence-seeking aspect of organizational change is but one attempt to reassert such simplicity. Organizational change projects redefine what "coheres". Managers are then left with the task of seeking to restore or assert a new coherence. This chapter addresses how to surface and discuss the resulting coherence seeking behaviour.

Complex systems

The work in this chapter emerges from the study of complex systems. Complexity studies are explicitly aimed at developing an understanding of the multi-dimensional. This understanding often involves the borrowing of concepts from other disciplines. Two concepts, which are seldom taught to managers, can provide key insight into the workings of the day today complex system or systems we call organizations – and more importantly into the effects of change. These concepts are (1) affordances and (2) homologies.

One key to understanding the multifaceted ecology of organizations is the concept of "affordances" – the assumed mechanism whereby "possibility" presents itself as weak signals to consciousness. These possibilities, in the form of affordances, invite responses by their perceivers. Affordances thus act as attractors drawing humans into action. Humans live in a world of active subject–world inter-relationship(s). The world acts, makes occur, and initiates possibilities. Affordance is a word for this activity.

A second key lies in furthering one's understanding of what is meant by a model and by the concept of shared models. This deeper understanding echoes in the concept known as "homology" – a term borrowed from developmental biology. Homology is the study of sameness. When two items, events, or contexts share an underlying model – when there is sameness in the underlying model – they are said to be homologous.

When change projects address the near term, when managers look at next steps, when we each go about contemplating the next possible action, or what Stuart Kauffman (2002) called the adjacent possible. The multitude of adjacent possibles available to us at a given instant can perhaps be taken as a hallmark of complexity. J.C. Spender notes: "the degree of complexity present is the extent to which our efforts at reduction have failed" (Letiche and Lissack, 2011). In truth we do not go through life overwhelmed by the apparent complexity continually confronting us. Instead we make choices about what to deal with, what to see, and what questions to ask.

Affordances and homologies interact with self and other as we go about contemplating next actions. The dialogue about them is often key to the creation and continuation of coherence in and about the organization. Change projects which ignore this dialogue risk the substitution of uncertainty for coherence and thus failure.

Affordances – opportunities for next actions

Change projects address opportunities. When self and context meet the opportunities which are presented to that self and which is that self recognizes are what we call affordances. J. J. Gibson (1977, 1979) first used the term "affordance" to refer to actionable properties between world and actor (a person or animal). To Gibson, affordances are relationships. They exist naturally; they do not have to be visible, known, or desirable. "Affordances provided by the environment are what it offers, what it provides, what it furnishes and what it invites" (Gibson, 1979, p. 127). A chair can also afford holding things and therefore affords being used as a "table", or it can afford being used as a step stool, or as decoration as an art object (among many other possibilities). Affordances extend across users and vary with them. "An affordance is an action possibility available in the environment to an individual, independent of the individual's ability to perceive this possibility" (McGrenere and Ho, 2000).

Affordances are about opportunities, dangers, and possibilities that call organism, consciousness, and environment to activity and sense-making. Affordances are what points to the adjacent possible. Getting the balance right of the "something out there" and the "consciousness of the actant" may be a philosophical nightmare, but we do it every day. Opportunities for action only exist if there is an actant to whom they appear.

Affordances occur when self and other, perceiver and perceived, objects and persons meet in actionable combinations. Affordances invite participation, action and response. When circumstance invites reaction, context demands a response, or the situation offers opportunity, something is afforded. In affordance, perception, information, and activity are related in a manner that

161

seems to beg for action. Affordances are not just labels – i.e. the product of a subject's naming something. Nor are affordances retrospective – i.e. a quality of reality identified after-the-fact. Affordances are prospective – context invites action, environment points to activity. In affordances, world, situation and location, point to action, shout for response and offer opportunities for attainment.

The financial crisis of 2008–10 is illustrative of the working of affordances. According to most observers it was the all-pervasive belief that housing prices could only rise that afforded easy lending and lax regulation, which in turn allowed the housing bubble to inflate. The belief in always-rising prices allowed lenders – supposedly rationally – to look only to the value of the underlying asset (which the belief set asserted could only rise), rather than to the ability of the borrower to make payments. The same beliefs allowed regulators to be unconcerned when stories arose in the media regarding "liars' loans" (loans made to people who blatantly could not afford them and who lied on their mortgage applications). The belief in rising prices afforded the bullish lack of unease or of controls. Beliefs and stories provided a context that afforded resulting actions. Affordances are thus a matter of mind and circumstance, and of the resonance between them.

It is important at this point to remind the reader that just as self interacts with context so too can other interact with context. Affordances are the possibilities and structures, opportunities and demands that physical and social environments present to existence. Affordances only exist in the relationship amongst situated environments and the observer. That observer need not be self: it could be other. Others will find their own affordances in context.

While academic models may assume for the sake of simplicity a stasis between what has been and what will be, managers in the real world do so only at their peril. Relationships between world and consciousness manifest themselves in concrete networks of activity. There is no single determining logic to these dynamic and emergent relationships. Possibilities, dangers, and spiritual beliefs all resonate with circumstances, others, and innovative actions. The effort to reduce all affordances to a few causal combinations amounts to reduction ad absurdum.

The absence of stasis means that one cannot predict and control affordances. One affordance will be violent and destructive, and another creative and fulfilling; the one can open up a field of fear and aggression, and the other an opportunity-space for generativity. Affordances can (but only can) bring us from a possibility space to an activity. One will be drawn out by affordances, feel compelled to do things by affordances, and be confronted by possibilities by affordances. The logic of affordances is a logic of relationship and possibility. Affordances are about the *could be* and not the IS.

Homologies – the sameness of models

Change projects make extensive use of models. Models of other change projects, models of the organization, models of the environment in which the organization operates, and models of the desired future all play a role. The goal of the use of these models is to produce coherence as the change project progresses.

Two keys to coherence are comprehensibility and meaningfulness. In managerial studies we refer to this as sense-making (Weick, 1995). When "making sense" we can do one of two things. We can make sense of the world by finding a pre-established category for what we observe, ascribing (assigning) a label to what we see, looking up in some code book what rule or regulation applies and then trying to stamp out deviations from the behaviour we believe goes with the label we have assigned. Or, we can look for some principles, some stories which resonate in a deep sense with our process of trying to understand what we observe. As we seek to determine which principles to apply and how the current observation may require a given principle to change, we engage in an emergent process of sense making. In the first case, bureaucrats, regulators, and managers seek to measure and eliminate differences from the fixed label or category. In the second, policy makers, doctors, and parents try to adjust what they know to what they see unfolding before them. Both paths are ways of making sense, of finding coherence in a given situation, and for using that coherence as the basis for further action.

The first path is the world of the computer, the second that of the environment. The unknown, unexpected, and the new can challenge the capabilities of those on the first path. Indeed, our labels for these emergent events include "miracle", "disaster", and "nasty surprise". These emergent events include the housing bubble and the subsequent financial crisis. For those on the second path, the unexpected, new, and unknown are part of the process of sense making and not its challenge. Deviance from norms becomes the basis of dialogue and query rather than the basis for statistical disregard. That dialogue is key to the success of organizational change projects.

Many projects fail because dialogue is avoided in favour of labels, categories, and checklists. A "normal" strategy for dealing with the complexity around us is to attempt to categorize what we encounter and to draw boundaries around what we are willing to "deal with" as opposed to that which we otherwise "treat differently" or ignore. The act of boundary setting, like the act of categorizing, is a brute force method of complexity reduction. Rorty suggests that we need a way of reducing the world enough that we can cope and act. This perspective suggests that the use of labels helps people to have some actionable view of the world. Labels form a very valuable role in limiting the world. Instead of actively discussing the multiple approaches which may all be interpretations, enactments, decodings, or embodiments of a model, managers often act as if there is but one or perhaps two decodings. These "privileged" interpretations are given status as names, labels, or symbols – and the labels are then used as guides for action.

Here is where the risk occurs. By making assumptions (and in so doing restricting ourselves to a particular or one method of decoding) we predetermine what might be learnt, which will limit the options that appear to be open to us as managers. This is because by adopting a particular perspective, and therefore making particular assumptions, we limit what we can "see". The perspective acts as a lens that only allows particular features to come into focus – all other features are lost, or assumed not to be relevant to the problem at hand. Furthermore, in communicating with others by making use of a particular viewpoint we limit their ability to "see" what is relevant.

Managers in general and organizational change leaders in particular have a tendency to assert labels instead of defining models and to identify best practices rather than explore affordances. The mistake is one of substituting an indexical (a placeholder) where either model or context demands an individual. Such a casual reference to indexicals in situations where the models and their use demand individuals (i.e. situatedness and context dependence) results in the replacement of a strong homological relationship with a weaker analogical one. Management scholars then compound the confusion by claiming that such indexical models can be used instead of experiments on the real world. Organizational users of models often demand accuracy despite the unreasonableness of the requirement. Given their role in the linear decision process, models are all too quickly assumed to be accurate depictions of reality. So, though the provisionality and contingency of all models is well-known, popular culture persists in utilizing them as if they were more than they are.

The problem with ascribing a label, and using it as your method of explanation, is that once one has ascribed it, once one has said this belongs to Label X, then the explanation is done.

Boundaries are often found in the narratives and labels: "the seeming durability of identity is actually contained in the stability of the labels used by organizational members to express who or what they believe the organization to be" (Gioia et al., 2000).

What kinds of model work?

If labels and categories are limiting as models, the question which naturally occurs is to ask what kind of model can be broadening? Most change projects are neither about limiting the scope of the organization nor about limiting its degrees of freedom. They require a set of models which allow for the exploration and exploitation of the adjacent possible and all its affordances.

Mental models which allow us to make internal predictions in order to determine our potential actions in the possibility space we face satisfy the criteria. Labels, metaphors, analogies, indexical simulations, and statistical formulations do not. The models which provoke resonance are those which we run in our heads in order to help determine what we should do with the possibility space in which we find ourselves. We run the model in order to make predictions. We assess the desirability of the mental outcome and then perhaps rerun the mental model. Based upon the encoding (translating the world into the model) and decoding (translating the results of our simulations into the world) regime in our heads we act or not. The model remains open to the inputs of context and situation. It allows for stories to be told, and for a range of potential actions.

Homologies are the sameness of a model which is perceived by an observer to be "behind" two or more situations. Homologies allow the observer to mentally interact with multiple affordances and where possible to "elect" the context for the next action. Homology assumes that context is variable. Labels assume that context is given. Complexity recognizes that both assumptions apply in the world.

The term homology was first used by Richard Owen in 1843 who defined it as the study of sameness (homo: same and ology: study of). The original definition of homology by Owen identified two entities as homologous if they were "the same". Owen's famously vague and broad definition of "homologue" as "the same organ in different animals under every variety of form and function" (1848, p. 7, repeated from 1843, p. 374) invokes a notion of sameness as "proceeding from a common archetype" (Gould, 2002). The meaning of "sameness" differentiated between superficial and essential similarity, i.e. between analogy and homology.

Different self(s) will interpret a model differently. Differing contexts will perhaps lead the same self to interpret a model differently. An important aspect of models is the indexicality of their subject. Indexicality is the quality of being able to serve as a "stand-in", as a generic variable. Indexicals derive their meaning from an interaction with their contexts and situatedness. The greater the indexicality of the subject, the more likely it is that multiple observers will reach similar conclusions from an examination of both model and modelled and that by abduction and induction the results of a model will be socially accepted as "facts" about the modelled. When the real world system has indexicality, it is easier to accept the indexicality of the necessarily simpler model. When the real world system, by contrast, has individuality, the indexicality of the model becomes a limitation, which tends to restrict the validity of the model to group behaviours, provided that the law of large numbers (itself an indexical model) applies.

We are better able to accept modelling results concerning atoms (which are highly indexical) than about modelling results concerning ourselves (whom we think of as individual and not indexical). Both horoscopes and Myers-Briggs tests serve to replace our individuality with indexicals (Capricorns and INTJ's). Wolfram's (2002) "new kind of science" replaces our individuality with simple programmes. The agent based models of which Casti, Holland, and other computer simulation types are so fond, replace our individuality with other indexicals, namely agents. Simulations have their place but they cannot supplant interactions in the "real world".

Another way to say this is that models are partial truths; they partially reflect some aspects of reality. Good models have well defined relationships to reality so that we know how and when to use them. This means that we recognize which aspects of the model are related to which aspects of reality. This is not a piece by piece correspondence, but a behaviour by behaviour correspondence. Our use of models is clearly not only a property of the model, but a property of our (incomplete) understanding of the relationship between the model and reality. To the extent that managers base change projects on models without a continual cross check with "reality", coherence is threatened. To the extent that managers encourage dialogue about that cross check, coherence can be enhanced.

Cues not codes

In their role as "complexity reducers" managers often forget that models are more than just labels. It is after all more efficient to assert the presence of a label and then to "look up" the appropriate behaviour or next action based upon the label and not the situation being modelled. This behaviour treats context and observation as if were a code. Code is the formal name for the use of a token to signify a specific and defined meaning. Codes are reductions. Any reduction's effectiveness is determined not only by the nature of the reductive process but also by the context in which the reduction is employed. Thus, when the goal is efficiency, codes can be very helpful. Morse code allowed for the transmission of a significant amount of information in its day. Codes can be dealt with via look-up tables, statistics, and Shannon's information theory. To assume or assert that messages consist of codes is to risk ignoring much of the meaning.

But, codes are efficient. And managers like efficiency. One source of the housing bubble and the subsequent financial crisis was the pervasive belief in a code: "housing prices always rise". If the code is accepted as an underlying truth by market participants and regulators alike, there is no one to ask the "what if?" questions which otherwise accompany cues. Surely when the general media is discussing such items as "liars loans" (loans made based on false documentation) with no money down, the environmental cues that there is "irrational exuberance" are rampant. But, as we all know only too well, those cues were ignored for the sake of the all-pervasive code. "It does not matter because housing prices only go up."

Our modern world, and especially the managers of organizations, has come to rely on codes, because codes are efficient. Look-up tables work. A means x. B means y. C when found in situation g means w and in situation h means z. Science, obviously, places a great emphasis on codes – as does management. Complexity thinking suggests that codes are just not as omnipresent as our linguistic tendencies might suggest. The minute one starts looking at interrelations, ambiguities, weak signals, or at the vast number of combinations of things that could occur, one discovers that the very notion that a look-up table works starts sounding questionable.

Day-to-day language works because of its usual appearance in a disambiguating context; we are able to choose one of several meanings for a word or sentence because we are in fact guided by the immediate verbal surroundings, the nature of the speech act in which the words are uttered and perceived, the social and historical setting and so on. As speakers, we usually attempt to construct our sentences in such a way as to eradicate any possible ambiguities and, as hearers, we assume single meanings in the sentence we interpret.

Affordances suggest that meaning is contained from inside one's self. When one encounters a signal, the signal evokes a meaning based on what's going on in the receiver's head and is not based on what the transmitter of the signal intended. We refer to these signals as "cues". The inability to define the environment in which a signal will be interpreted, and the parallel inability to predict affordances are what render cues complex and their study part of qualitative complexity. Cues are thus the label for the emergent meaning which results from an intersection of attendance to environment, situation, history, and cognition, such that semiotic affordance are perceived to allow for action, assignment of cognition, label, or code, or for boundary breaking.

We create semiotic affordances by telling stories. What matters about a story is what the listeners do with it, not the smile it brings to the face of the teller in its one hundredth reincarnation. Listeners use the images evoked to create meaning – meaning that goes on to inform actions. When we tell stories and share languaging, the changing context can bring us from raw experience to the possibilities and limits of shared consciousness. Such sharing is the exploration of homology. Affordances and their import demand an attention to underlying homologies rather than to labels.

Our modern sense of efficiency has led to the presumption that when a label can supplant a story it is more efficient and thus "better". The problem with that presumption is that the study of labels and associated rules is devoid of a study of context and the opportunities presented by context. Such opportunities are affordances – the then present context affords one the opportunity to do x.

Cues work when affordances match an available homology. Cues fail when the context seems to provide no linkage to an accepted homology despite the enticements of what may otherwise seem to be an attractive affordance. Cues are what evoke stories and schemas which have room for the listener. Cues thus can evoke resonance by evoking schemas – the resonance which helps create meaning and will for the next action. By contrast, codes only evoke a pre-planned meaning memorized or drawn from a lookup table. Codes can only produce a retrospective judgment of alignment. Cues are emergent. Codes are backwards looking. In the difference between cue and code, between the successfully told story and the dry repetition of memorized verse, lies the potential for resonance and the difference between judgments and actions.

Affordances in their application typically are cued and not coded. They are situation and context dependent. Their perception and being attended to is a function of the mental state of the observer and not a direct quality of the item or situation offering the affordance. To the extent that affordances limit the actionable range of adjacent possibles, some portion of that limitation is thus a result of the mental state of the observer and is a direct function of the homologies available to that observer and which he/she accepts.

Dialogue and narrative as complexity reducers

Because science as we have defined it in the Western world is supposed to leave out notions of self and of other, its use of models is generally accepted as "objective" and the standard to which other "professions" should aspire. But, by definition, management includes people and, thus, includes self and other. Scientists are too well aware that in reality science also includes self and other. The power of affordances and homology has led to many a scientific breakthrough – not due to the intrinsic nature of the subject matter being studies or the data collected but due to the humanness of the scientists who saw adjacent possibles and commonalities of model due to their own experience, history and context. Management "science" as it is all too often taught ignores this. Deconstruction studies are often focused on it.

Complex systems are those which contain ("com") interweaving(s) ("plex"). One source of those interweaving(s) is the potential for repeated encounters where history and memory have the possibility of playing a role. If we each were merely an abstract statistic and if we were destined to have no possibility for repetitious encounters, then the abstract rules of science – especially the physics which management scientists seek to emulate – might work as models. Such is not our world. We do have histories, we do have memories; those histories and memories can be transferred (and distorted) through storytelling and, in the face of this, we have the potential for repeated interactions. Those repeated interactions (or at least their possibility) are what make affordances recognizable and homologies actionable. Judgments, categories, and labels may be constructible from the statistical observation of indexicals, but affordances and homologies only create the possibility for action with the recognition of individuals.

There is a complexity reducer which makes use of affordances and homologies in dealing with individuals: respect. Respect here is meant as the possibility to be seen (spect) again (re). It has nothing to do with holding in esteem (the more traditional meaning of respect). By actively recognizing the possibility of being seen again and/or interacting again we give rise to very different set of homologies and affordances than when we view each individual and encounter as a statistical "one off".

Respect is a quality we practise rather than one we ascribe. To assign the label "respect" but not follow through on the implications for repeated sight or interactions is meaningless. In the housing/financial crisis, banks and analysts offered the label of respect for the idea of default or credit risk but failed (for the most part) to afford respect in practice. Unfortunately, we all know the outcome.

> Our ultimate device for dealing with complexity and the other is narrative. We use narrative to rise above the local constraints of models. A narrative is not about the reality of a situation. Rather, the point of a story is to lay out in the open what the narrator suggests is important. Narratives are not about being objective, but are instead displays of subjectivity. A narrative is the representation of a compression, which is integrated at a higher level of analysis. Powerful narratives, like great pieces of music, feel as if they were inevitable when they are over, and we seem to agree on that. But note, even in a compelling story, the next line cannot be predicted. It is that feeling of inevitability that endows the great story with its ability to generate commensurate experience amongst independent listeners.
>
> (Zellmer et al. 2007, p. 172)

When affordance and homology coincide the amount of effort needed for a coherent response to complexity is reduced. The obverse is also true. But, affordances are not "appropriate" best practices and homologies are not shared labels. In the drive for efficiency such substitutions are all too often proclaimed – at the manager's peril. Managers need to learn that context can be explored for affordances and that the mental models of their stakeholders – suppliers, customers, employees, and fellow organization members – can be mined for homologies:

> If complex systems are defined, as we and Rosen do, in terms of an incapacity to model them, it is possible to ride out emergence that is characteristic of complexity. One might even come to expect emergence, albeit unpredictable in its details. But we can only do this if we

167

are in a position to recognize the role of the scientist's decisions. Managing for emergence involves changing a point of view. Managing for complex systems requires a meta-level of activity.

(Zellmer et al., 2007, p. 182)

That meta-level can be provided if we recognize that the goal is coherence as a setting for action and that the tools for shaping that setting are to be found in affordances, homologies and narrative.

When affordance and homology meet, the possibility for coherent action is vastly increased. "The sense of coherence expresses a person's inner ability to see existing possibilities around him or herself and make use of the best ones in respect to the demands" (Kalimo et al., 2002). When, instead labels and judgments are allowed to dominate, while affordances are overlooked, and the cuing of "other" homologies is ignored, the prospect of unanticipated emergence is vastly increased. Better understandings of both affordances and homologies are thus vital ingredients in the manager's arsenal. Complexity cannot often be managed, but our response to it can be guided – if we give ourselves the tools.

Conclusion

Organizational change projects are about confronting and embracing emergence. When coherence arises from emergence, it is often attributed to serendipity. What is seldom realized is that serendipity is not luck but the coming together of affordance with sagacity – preparedness. If one treats emergence and its impacts as only the product of luck, then miracles and nasty surprises are likely results. The opposite of sagacity is a lack of preparedness.

Embracing emergence means helping to create the context which affords coherence. When that context is missing, coherence can still be imposed from the outside (it is always amazing what fear of force can accomplish temporarily). The likelihood is that emergence will prove to be transformational in a miracle or nasty surprise sort of way. Thus, it is the managers' role to help create the context which affords coherence.

Narratives are important because they are a key tool we all use in dealing with and reducing uncertainty. Having a willingness to act means one is not paralyzed by uncertainty. When we are uncertain, we not only struggle to predict what will happen next, but also to understand and to describe why things are currently as they are (Tenkasi and Boland, 1993). Narratives enable people to translate emergent situations that are ambiguous or equivocal so as to promote real-time problem solving (Bartel and Garud, 2009).

> What is necessary? The answer is, something that preserves plausibility and coherence, something that is reasonable and memorable, something that embodies past experience and expectations, something which resonates with other people, something that can be constructed retrospectively but also can be used prospectively, something that captures both feeling and thought ... In short, what is necessary in sense making is a good story.
>
> (Weick, 1995, pp. 60–61)

Since narratives guide us through uncertainty and change, they are critical in how we deal with emergence. "People do not simply tell stories – they enact them" (Pentland, 1999).

Managers often construct and interact with narratives built around labels and categories and not around affordances and homologies. Such narratives work to reduce uncertainty only while the participants perceive that the label on which the narrative is based is the "best" descriptor for the situation they perceive. By making assumptions (and in so doing restricting ourselves to a set of labels and a model) we predetermine what might be learned, which will limit the options that appear to be open to us. What is critical is that the interpretive and retelling efforts *not* stop when the symbol, icon, label, etc. get assigned. To stop at this point is to ignore dialogue and revert to the ascribed coherence and retrospective judgments of identity where the label is the explanation. Instead, the goal is to keep dialoguing so that homologies of mechanism and what-if effects can be exposed to articulation, pondered about, and used to shape an ongoing narrative.

When "best" slips to "satisficing", and then to "questioning", the relevance and the resonance of the label-based narrative declines, and coherence declines with it. There are alternatives to making use of labels, categories, and models as the means for establishing coherence and for creating narratives. With narratives built around homologies, affordances are more easily perceived, opportunities are better exploited (or at least explored), resonance has a better chance of taking hold, and experienced coherence can assert itself in the embrace of emergence.

Narratives can be the basis of dialogue and they can be the basis of labels and category. Dialogue and category are thus two differing tools for a manager. They each affect what will be the manager's world view and will expand or limit the manager's understanding of next steps or the adjacent possible. When the manager makes use of category as the tool for organizing thought and action, labels dominate. Dialogue and narratives about affordance and homologies are an alternative to this domination.

Category is the reductionist tool; dialogue is the complexity tool.

References

Antonovsky A., 1979. *Health, Stress and Coping*. San Francisco, CA: Jossey-Bass.

Antonovsky, A., 1993. The structure and properties of the sense of coherence scale. *Social Science and Medicine*, 36: 725–33.

Bartel, C. and Garud, R., 2009. The role of narratives in sustaining organizational innovation, *Organization Science*, 20: 107–17.

Cronon, W., 1992. A place for stories: nature, history and narrative. *Journal of American History*, 78: 1347–76.

Dresner, M., 2008. Using research projects and qualitative conceptual modeling to increase novice scientists' understanding of ecological complexity, *Ecological Complexity*, 5(3): 216–21.

Fox-Keller, E., 2002. *Making Sense of Life: Explaining Biological Development with Models, Metaphors, and Machines*. Boston: Harvard University Press.

Gibson, J.J., 1977. The theory of affordances. In R. Shaw and J. Bransford (eds), *Perceiving, Acting and Knowing*. Hillsdale, NJ: Erlbaum.

Gibson, J.J., 1979. *The Ecological Approach to Visual Perception*. Boston: Houghton Mifflin.

Gioia, D.A., Majken, S. and Corley, K.G., 2000. Organizational identity, image, and adaptive instability. *The Academy of Management Review*, 25(1): 63–81.

Gould, S., 2002. *The Structure of Evolutionary Theory*. Cambridge, MA: The Belknap Press of Harvard University Press.

Kalimo, R., Pahkin, K. and Mutanen, P., 2002. Work and personal resources as long-term predictors of well-being. *Stress and Health*, 18(5): 227–34.

Kauffman, S., 2002. *Investigations*. Oxford: Oxford University Press.

Kuhn, T., 1962. *The Structure of Scientific Revolutions*. Chicago: University of Chicago Press.

Letiche, H. and Lissack, M. (with Schultz, R.), 2011. *Enabling Coherence in the Midst of Complexity: Advances in Social Complexity Theory*. Basingstoke: Palgrave Macmillan.

Lissack, M., 2009. *Complexity is more than a label: a look at affordances and homologies*, Keynote Speech at the 2nd International Multi-Conference on Engineering and Technological Innovation: IMETI 2009, 10–13 July, Orlando, FL.

Lissack, M. and Richardson, K., 2001. When modeling social systems, models – the modeled: reacting to wolfram's a new kind of science, *Emergence*, 3(4): 95–111.

Lissack, M. and Richardson, K., 2003. Models without morals: towards the ethical use of business models, *Emergence*, 5(2): 72–102.

McGrenere, J. and Ho, W., 2000. *Affordances: Clarifying and evolving a concept.* Proceedings of Graphics Interface 2000, Montreal, QC.

Owen, R., 1843. Lectures on the comparative anatomy and physiology of the invertebrate animals, delivered at the Royal College of Surgeons in 1843. London: Longman, Brown, Green, and Longmans.

Pentland, B., 1999. Building process theory with narrative: from description to explanation. *Academy of Management Review*, 24: 711–24.

Richardson, K. and Lissack, M., 2001. On the status of boundaries, both natural and organizational: a complex systems perspective, *Emergence*, 3(4): 32–49.

Rorty, R., 1991. *Objectivity, Relativism, and Truth*, Cambridge: Cambridge University Press.

Rosen, R., 1989. Similitude, similarity, and scaling. *Landscape Ecology*, 3: 207–16.

Rosen, R., 1991. *Life Itself*. New York: Columbia University Press.

Rosen, R., 2000. *Essays on Life Itself*. New York: Columbia University Press.

Tenkasi, R. and Boland, R., 1993. 'Locating meaning making in organizational learning: the narrative basis of cognition'. In R.W. Woodman and W.A. Pasmore (eds), *Research in Organizational Change and Development*, Vol. 7. Greenwich, CT: JAI Press.

Weick, K., 1995. *Sensemaking in Organizations*. Thousand Oaks, CA: Sage Publications, Inc.

Wolfram, S., 2002. *A New Kind of Science*. Champaign, IL: Wolfram Media.

Zellmer A.J., Allen T.F.H. and Kesseboehmer K., 2007. The nature of ecological complexity: a protocol for building the narrative, *Ecological Complexity*, 3: 171–82.

Zhang, J. and Patel, V.L., 2006. Distributed cognition, representation, and affordance, *Special Issue of Pragmatics and Cognition*, 14(2): 333–41.

12

Storytelling in systemicity and emergence
A third-order cybernetic

David M. Boje and Tonya Wakefield

Introduction

Emergence is to complexity as Mona Lisa's smile is to mystery; it is the visible product of an underlying process at work. Emergent phenomena occur unpredictably but consistently exhibit familiar patterns that strike a chord in all of us, though we seldom understand why. For example, fractal patterns, the repeated artifacts of emergence, are self-similar across various scales and can be mathematically described using a power law (Johnson, 2007; Leibovitch, 1998; Ward, 2002). Mathematical symbology offers only one language for description of this polypi that science claims as its own, but which belongs to all of us and, above all to the storytelling organization. Just as linear equations cannot begin to express fractal dimensions, necessitating more exacting mathematics, *systems thinking*, including *open systems thinking*, cannot envelop the complexity and nuance of storytelling in its truest, unpoliticized sense. It is inadequate to address the multifaceted, holographic nature of complexity in human systems. To that end, Boje (2008) introduces the concept of *systemicity*, the "dynamic, unfinished, unfinalized, and unmerged, and the interactivity of complexity properties with storytelling and narrative properties" (p. 2).

To understand *emergence* is to understand the basic tenets of *complexity*. But the true power of *emergence* extends beyond Stuart Kauffman's revelation of "order for free" (Lewin, 1999, pp. 23–25); its full implications are not felt until *emergence* is considered simultaneously in multiple directions on multiple planes. In this chapter we introduce the concepts of *emergence, complexity thinking* and *systemicity* using an ontological story (Bennett, 2010, p. 3) in conjunction with other metaphors. We then elaborate on *third-order cybernetics* by addressing the oxymoron of hierarchical *complexity* frameworks and introduce *polylogical* and *storytelling* approaches to *systemicity* comprehension. Finally, we offer insights into the human *agency* that can sometimes shape emergent phenomena, introducing the role of materiality in such action. Taken in sum, these explanations are meant to serve as a springboard for further insights, insights that often emerge in unexpected places.

An ontological story

On a Saturday I went to a renaissance festival with my family and we stopped to listen to some drummers and a bagpipe. It occurred to me that the crowd surrounding us constituted an emergent phenomenon. There was no stage door to close during acts and no specific ticket for each event. On the edges of the crowd, people came and went. They were free to come and go as they wanted to, an open system. As it was a hot day, many went to get drinks and returned. My family wanted to see a different performance and we soon left after one of us went to the nearby restroom. Our group self-organized, dividing then regrouping and finally leaving that open system to join another one.

This situation involved the intentional channeling of an emergent phenomenon, the formation of a crowd and its reactions to the performance. That made us think about leadership and inspiration, how one might channel actors in an open system without striving for control. It also brought to mind an experiment that described conditions where self-organization is likely to occur (Smith and Comer, 1994; Johnson, 2007). Festival attendees were free to come and go at will. The self-organizing is like in the *Tamara* play (Krizanc and Boje, 2006; see Boje, 1995), where the audience splits into self-forming groups and chases characters in the play to follow from room to room, trying to sort out the inter-mingling story-lines of the simultaneous action in ten different rooms. Each venue, shop, and snack vendor at the fair can be thought of as a separate room, with the dominant narrative romanticizing the historical renaissance and myriad microstories among the performers and guests. Amid the sea of individual actors following their own paths we find the formation of crowds, ebbing and flowing in similar but non-uniform patterns; we observe *emergence*.

What is emergence?

It is surprising. *Emergence* is sometimes described as the unexpected development of order from disorder (Lewin, 1999). Johnson (2007) describes *emergence*, or *emergent phenomena*, as the development of *fractals* (p. 50), self-similar patterns that repeat on multiple scales, first discovered by Mandelbrot in 1982 (Zimmerman and Hurst, 1993; Leibovitch, 1998, p. 8). These phenomena start small and grow exponentially, often seeming to come out of nowhere and sometimes vanish just as quickly, like the formation of a crowd around a particular venue at the fair described above. While the timing and causes of these occurrences cannot be predicted with certainty, their general forms and trends are apparent when studied from a distance or over long periods of time (Zimmerman and Hurst, 1993). *Emergence* is often described as unexpected collective behavior, such as flocking in groups of wildlife or robots governed by simple rule sets (Waldrop, 1992, p. 242; Mataric, 1995). These occurrences are common to open, self-organizing systems poised between order and chaos. Such systems are said to exhibit *criticality*, as with dynamic open systems and materials undergoing phase shift (Ward, 2002).

It is the product of individual actions converging in group dynamics. *Emergent phenomena* arise when independent elements, called *actors*, follow very simple sets of rules, self-interest being paramount, and are free to act independently. Emergence is not attributable to any individual element; it is a property of group interaction (Gershenson and Heylighen, 2003, p. 611; Ison, 2008, p. 141). It includes such commonly used examples as avalanches, stock-market trends, fads, and larger-scale cultural phenomena. Investigation is complicated by the complex nature of the collective systems themselves, in that the same set of initial conditions and stimulus may not yield the same outcomes if repeated.

The elusive aspects of *emergent phenomena* are their precise timing and which combinations of initial conditions and catalysts are likely to bring them about. They are of vital importance to organizational change management because such occurrences sometimes happen on very large scales, affecting key business areas and necessitating both robust organizational structure and adaptation. Such phenomena present leaders and managers with both crisis and opportunity, with emphasis on the latter for the truly robust system. Inflexible organizations often perish as a result of phenomena like stock-market crashes and competition, while their self-organizing competitors either weather these storms or create new opportunities.

What is complexity thinking?

To understand *complexity thinking*, one must first review its predecessors. *Systems thinking* involves static organizational entities with clear boundaries (Boulding, 1956; Ison, 2008). *First-order cybernetics* introduces feedback loops to enable "goal-seeking" regulation of such systems in response to dynamic external conditions (Green and Welsh, 1988, p. 102; Rapoport et al., 2009). These ways of thinking were revolutionary in their day but are simplistic when compared with the next wave of thought, which progressed towards a more dynamic systems ontology, systems as processes (see Van de Ven and Poole, 2005, for process vs. systems ontologies). These more dynamic schools of thought include the *natural systems model*, which defends the system's internal order from outside influences, and *open systems thinking*. *Second order cybernetics* shift the focus to the observer's role (Ison, 2008), embracing *open systems thinking*, with permeable boundaries, self-organization, and the development of dynamic, dissipative structures that thrive on environmental variation. This trend marks the beginning of *complexity thinking*, which Boje and Khadija (2005) advance still further by introducing a *third-order cybernetic* paradigm centred on multifaceted dialogism. *Complexity thinking* is the domain of *open systems* thinking and *third-order cybernetics*.

Systems thinking contemplates organizations as "perceived whole(s) whose elements are inter-connected" (Ison, 2008, p. 140). This model is linear, static, perhaps even hegemonic, and adopts an ontology of "organizations as entities" (Van de Ven and Poole, 2005). Allowing for the regulation of such system based on feedback, much like a thermostat controlling the temperature in a room, is the stuff of *first-order cybernetics* (Boje and Khadija, 2005; Green and Welsh, 1988; Ison, 2008).

Second-order cybernetics focus attention on the regulating entity in the cybernetic dialogue, exploring the influence of the observer (Ison, 2008). Boje and Khadija (2005) further distinguish *second-order cybernetics* by describing it as the "open system theory of deviation-amplification, known as the Law of Requisite Variety" (Boje and Khadija, 2005). *Open systems thinking* involves self-organizing systems with permeable boundaries that permit external variation to influence their own structures. These systems require variation in their environments, which they both remove and create as they self-organize, adapting and evolving (Pondy and Boje, 2005). Such self-organizing systems are said to exhibit *complexity* and have proven useful in the semi-autonomous routing of cellular telephone calls, adaptive manufacturing systems, and computer network applications (Klenk et al., 2000; Rodriguez al., 2007; Ryu and Jung, 2006). At the heart of complexity is the flow of energy, information, or variation into and out of the system, changing the system as it flows. *Complexity* is process ontology.

While *second-order cybernetics* do much to address the dynamic, robust, variety-seeking entity that is the viable social organization, it does not go far enough, making way for *systemicity*. Boje's (2008) *systemicity* concept abandons hierarchy and linearity in favor of a more complex, richer multifaceted spiral that comes to light when narrative and storytelling meet. *Systemicity* breaks the illusion that systems can ever completely be defined and bounded, expanding their existence into multiple planes, their very fabric evolving through multifaceted dialogue (Boje, 2008). It personifies the strong process ontology (Tsoukas, 2005, as cited in Van de Ven and Poole, 2005) and gives voice to emergence and self-organization (Boje, 2008). It is this complex realm,

First Cybernetics

Linear systems

Machine-like function

Control/regulation functions

Predictability

Emphasis on preserving order of the system

Static boundaries

Monologic

Closed systems

Known boundaries

Organizations as entities

Hologrammatic

Hegemonic

Feedback materiality

Dynamic, uncertain boundaries

Homeostatic

Polylogic
Permeable boundaries

Multiple voices & languages Self-awareness

Importance of observer

Accommodating the unknowable

Unified voice

Open systems
Adapting & transforming

Heteroglossia

Blueprint reproduction

Nonlinear relationships
Emergence

Transcendental

Reflexivity

Multiple planes

Law of Requisite Variety

Organizations as dynamic processes

Second Cybernetics

Third Cybernetics

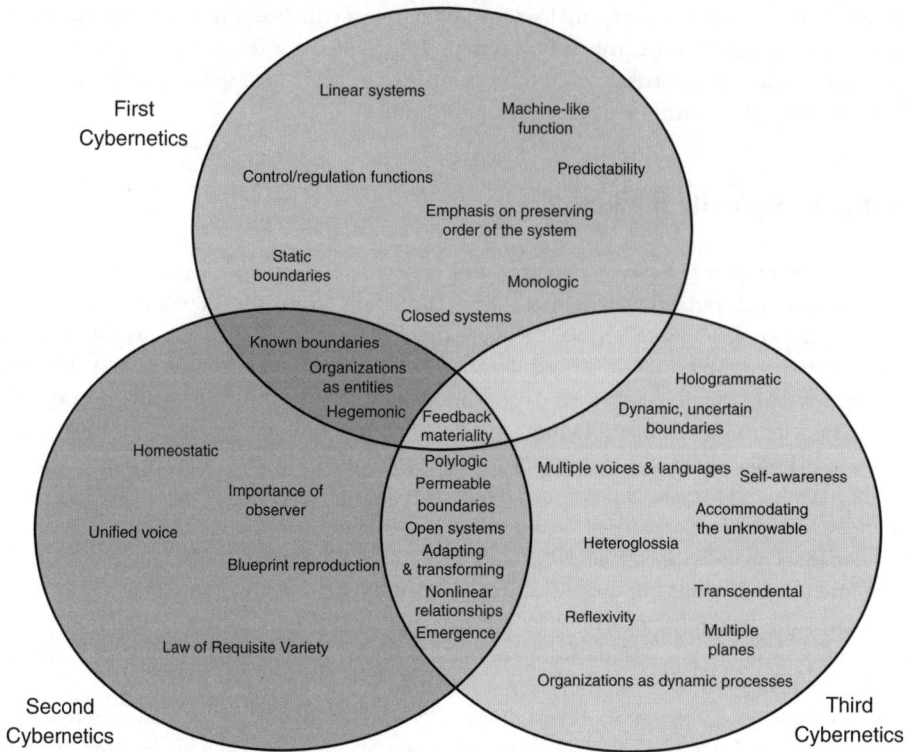

Figure 12.1 Key concepts of three generations of thought

where multifaceted dialogue, often existing in different times and spaces, does more to define systems than documents and organization charts, where the *third cybernetic* emerges. *Third-order cybernetics* permit the flow of influence between materialities (Bennett, 2010), individual perspectives, social constructs, networks, time and space, and even the transcendental. Figure 12.1 highlights key elements of the three generations of cybernetic constructs.

It is important to visualize that *complexity* begins with *second-order cybernetics* and expands multidimensionally with *third-order cybernetics,* also referred to as *systemicity*. It is in these regions that *criticality* comes into play, necessitating the flow of information and energy into and out of a dynamic self–organizing system (Ward, 2002). This energy flow results in *emergence*, the dynamic formation and undoing of the dissipative, fractal structures noted above.

The linearity trap

While it is tempting to order these concepts based on increasing levels of complexity, as does Boulding (1956), to do so would subject us to what Boje (2008) terms the "linearity trap." Pondy and Boje (2005) expand on nine levels of storytelling organization complexity first posited by Boulding (1956), ranging from the simplest *level one: framework,* to the most complex, *level nine: transcendental*. Such a ranking suggests that various levels of complexity cannot exist simultaneously, that the achievement of greater complexity implies that a system has evolved past less complex states. On the contrary, it is possible for a system to exist at a high level of complexity without progressing through the lower levels of the hierarchy. In Boje's (2008) later work, he suggests that one must move beyond hierarchical categorization, as its linearity is not suited to the complexity of the systems under study (pp. 29–35). The model's central flaw is the inclusion of all lower-level properties as one moves from lower levels of complexity toward higher levels. As the true nature of organizations is dynamic and shifting, automatic inclusion of lower-level properties may not always be the case. Sometimes it will be so, but not always. Therefore it cannot be said that a self-aware system (level 7) must always have a "blue-printed" regeneration capability attributed to level 5 (Boje, 2008; Boulding, 1956; Pondy and Boje, 2005). Instead, these nine levels of complexity should be considered as independent attributes that dynamically manifest themselves in various combinations. Boulding's (1956) work does, however, provide useful terms for articulating variations in complexity among different types of systems.

To illustrate by means of another metaphor, one might consider Boulding's (1956) levels of complexity as ingredients in a theoretical soup. The addition of carrots does not necessarily imply that the potatoes are already there. Likewise, if one fishes out the onion, the carrots remain present, regardless of the presence to absence of any other ingredients. The end result is invariably soup, though the specifics fluctuate to offer a great variation among myriad possible experiences.

Polylogic

In keeping with the use of metaphor, our renaissance fair story above illustrates the commingling of various levels of complexity in a unique space and time. The story fits into all of these categories, depending on the perspective of the observer, scale of observation, how one defines the unit under study, the actor.[1] A systems thinker might bound the system to that which is inside the fair's gated enclosure. A practitioner of first-order cybernetics might think in terms of regulating ticket prices to ensure profitability and prevent overcrowding within the same physical boundary, or measure customer satisfaction in the parking lot to determine if the attractions should be modified to achieve a desired standard. The natural systems model might be favoured by the janitorial staff, who strive to maintain order amid the endless stream of visitors, constantly emptying trash cans and picking up litter, again within the physical boundaries of the fair. Open systems thinkers might focus on the dynamic comings and goings on the edges of the venues, seeing the crowds as living, breathing, emergent phenomena. They are all correct, as is the practitioner of *systemicity, third-order cybernetics*, who sees clearly defined system boundaries as an illusion and seeks to understand the self-organizing processes unfolding by observing as many different layers and perspectives as possible, creating a holographic portrayal. This *third-order cybernetic* view has business utility in that it alone grasps the full range of *emergence*, from the materiality of goods sold, through the crowd energy channeled by performers, to the transcendence of time and place that causes otherwise workaday people to spend hundreds of dollars on a full suit of medieval armour with no practical modern use.

Narrative and story-telling

Luhman and Boje (2001) offer narrative study as a lens for viewing complexity. They consider the multiple perspectives informing a narrative and the resultant diminishment of the individual subject as central to the story (Luhman and Boje, 2001, p. 160). Representation, the inadequacy of language to express meaning without the taint of style or word choice, is also addressed (Luhman and Boje, 2001, p. 160). Intertextuality illuminates those themes that are conspicuously

175

absent from discourse. Through these postmodern considerations they establish the narrative as its own "discursive time and space in which organizational actors improvise, respond, draw on past narratives, create new ones ..." (Luhman and Boje, 2001, p. 160). Dating back to Aristotle's *Poetics*, narratives have been structurally defined as having a beginning, middle, and end (BME). Narratives can also exist in fragmented form, but they tend to be retrospective and hegemonic (Baskin and Boje, 2005; Boje, 2008; Pondy and Boje, 2005). In contrast, *storytelling*, or *storying*, is nonlinear, not officially sanctioned, and is more likely to be situated in the present and/or future (Baskin and Boje, 2005; Boje, 2008). Storying falls into the category of *emergence*, as it is the unchoreographed product of many independent actors and is unpredictable in scale and timing. Often these independent voices converge to illuminate aspects of reality excluded from the dominant narrative, or coalesce in a changing mixture of truth, rumour, and speculation. Other times, they reveal no strong reaction where one was anticipated.

The dichotomy between narrative and storying creates tension necessary to organizational criticality and is central to Bakhtin's concept of *heteroglossia* (Bakhtin, 1981). In heteroglossia, organizational storytelling is represented as a spiral, with centripetal forces strengthening a singular hegemonic dominant narrative; opposing centrifugal forces detract from that narrative by strengthening multiple disjointed, emerging stories from elsewhere, including what Boje (2001) terms "rebel voices" (p. 21). The dynamic struggle between these two forces brings about reflexivity (Boje and Khadija, 2005). This *third cybernetic approach* is less controlling than previous paradigms, dependent on emergent phenomena and the unpredictability resident therein. *Systemicity* embraces the unexpected, thriving on variety and talking it to the extreme of accepting and respecting the unknowable, transcendentalism. It is the realm of multidimensional *emergence*. Figure 12.2 portrays these concepts in a theoretical complexity and emergence idea space.

Complexity and Emergence Idea Space

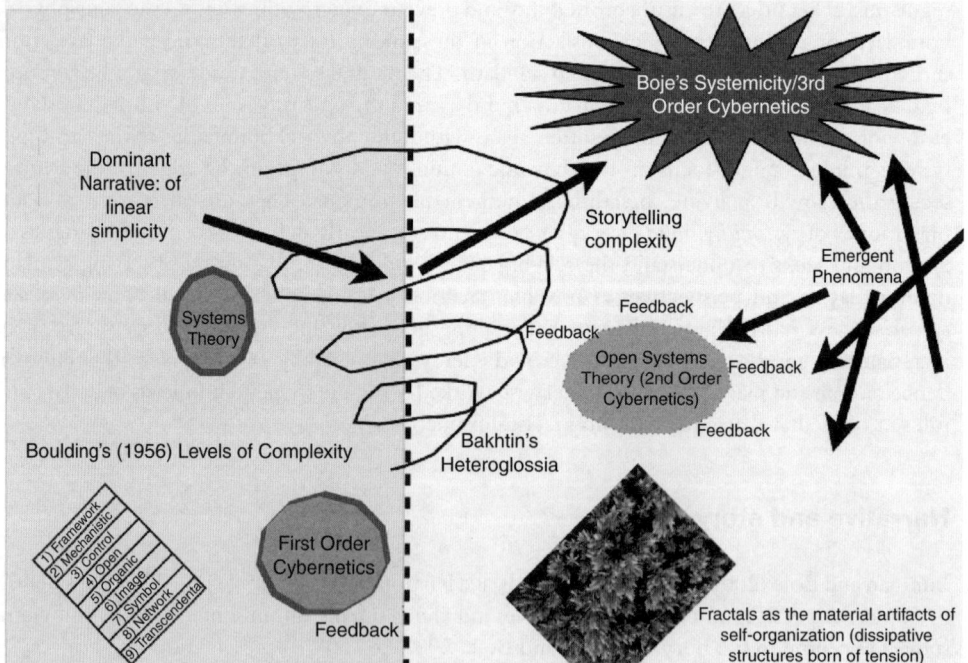

Figure 12.2 Complexity and emergence idea space

Shaping emergence

Emergent phenomena are capricious, unpredictable, and extreme in nature. Fads, traffic jams, grass-roots political movements, catch-phrases, tsunamis, and stock-market crashes have this in common. All appear to come out of nowhere, as the stimulus, if identifiable, is often seemingly insignificant. In the 1980s people paid for jeans with the knees already ripped out, an unpredictable fad. In 2008 a few major brokerage houses collapsed under the strain of bad mortgages and took the entire sentiment of Wall Street with them, followed by international indices, the US job market, and public opinion. In a dynamic ecosystem, such dramatic events are inevitable. If one accepts such dynamism a priori, the question then becomes what to do about it.

It is important for those managing organizational change to transcend traditional approaches to contingency planning and explore how complex self-organizing social systems adapt to, navigate, and ultimately use emergent phenomena. A truly robust organization must be sufficiently flexible and versatile to not only adapt to emergence, but ingest and gain nourishment from it. Figure 12.3 depicts such an organization, existing in a dynamic ecosystem. The arrows represent myriad influences of varying significance, direction, and magnitude. Some influences are insignificant, while others have the capacity to change the organization's future or change its substance completely. The latter, whether internally or externally derived, constitute emergent phenomena of sufficient magnitude to merit organizational responses.

When faced with an emergent phenomenon of significance, an organization must first become cognizant of its importance. Once this awareness is achieved, the organization is then faced with the following choices: (1) avoid the phenomenon; (2) adapt to survive the phenomenon; (3) "ride the wave" by embracing the change and modifying the organization using the variety as a sort of fuel; and (4) try to shape the phenomenon – grow it to suit the organization's purposes. The choices available to an organization encountering an emergent phenomenon in one of its key areas of interest necessitate a careful assessment of the entire ecosystem, organizational reflexivity, and a sense of the phenomenon's order of magnitude. Apart from the enormity of such assessments, Figure 12.4 illustrates these choices. Willingness to accept emergence, to "ride the

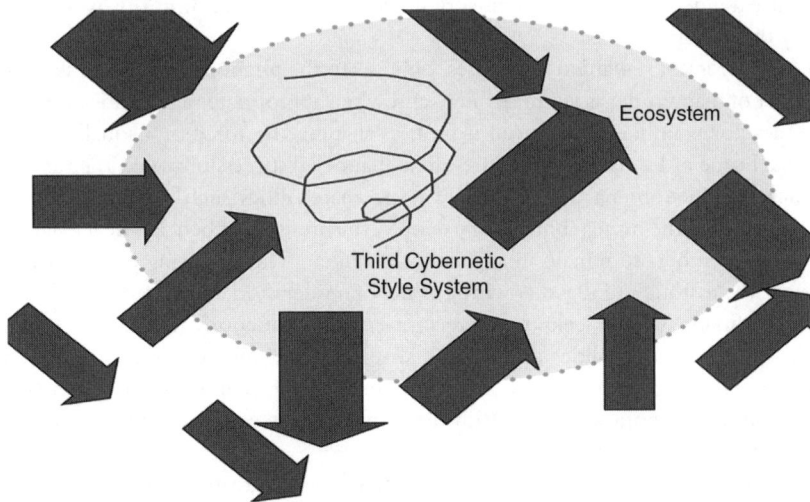

Figure 12.3 The third order cybernetic organization in situ

177

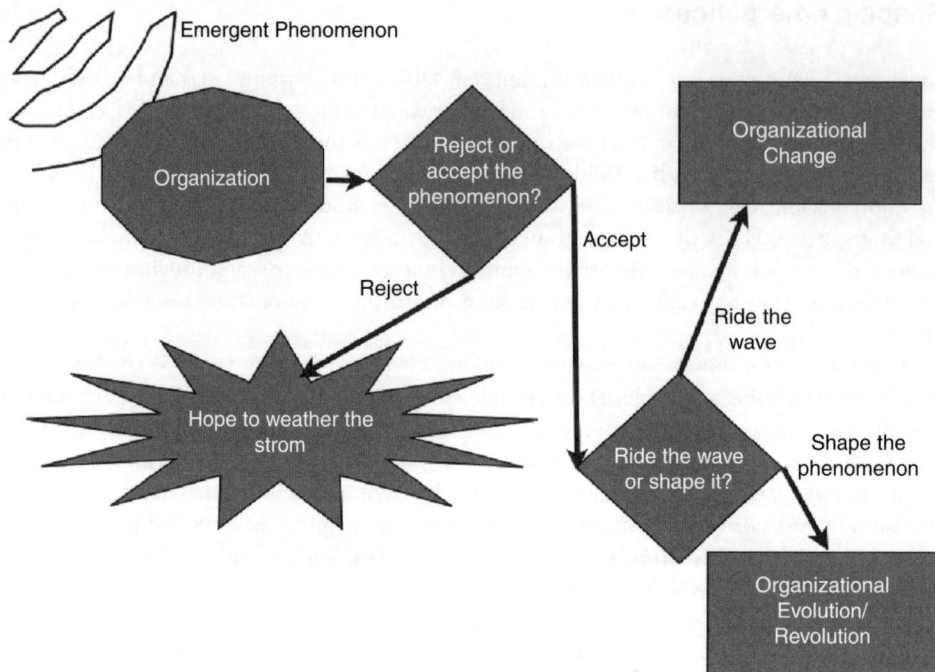

Figure 12.4 Organizational choices when faced with emergent phenomena

wave", is borne of a high level of complexity. However, the audacity to shape the phenomena, bending it to one's own purpose, as performers use the energy of a crowd, is sometimes rewarded by fortune.

The rise of Apple and Microsoft exemplify such rewards; in both cases visionary developers were able to create demand for their products by shaping the emergent demand for computers such that it extended beyond the engineering and business worlds into the average home and eventually the average pocket.

Such audacity is not rewarded in all cases, only when the phenomenon in question is below a certain order of magnitude, as yet undefined, and when appropriate materialities are present. For example, a sailor is unlikely to prevail if he tries shaping the force of a squall. But emergent phenomena borne of human reactions are often channeled successfully with the right tools. We think emerging phenomena can be shaped using materialities such as technologies, material resources, including the human body. For example, the presence of benches near a stage at the fair invites crowd members to remain in a place for a while. The balancing out of materialities, is consistent with Aristotle's (350 B.C.E.) virtue ethics of moderation and is central to the concept of *Intervention Research*, which seeks to correct material dysfunctions (Boje, 2010). It becomes possible to think of materialities as "actants" shaping emergent phenomena (Bennett, 2010). An example of such agency is the smart phone's shaping of bandwidth demand in the global telecommunications industry. With the right tools, actors can often influence emergent phenomena under the right conditions.

While material agency has its appeal, materialities have far greater agency when placed in an assemblage that is, at least in part, human. Returning to the renaissance fair, we recall the band members' manipulation of material elements (drums, microphones, bagpipes) to shape the crowd. They enticed its members to come along for the ride, to take the form of individual agents; members of the crowd tapped their feet, danced, bounced, breathed in time with the music, etc. Control in the traditional sense was never within the realm of possibility. On the edges of the crowd people came and went, going off to do different things based on their own individual needs, wants, and value systems. Other elements competing for people's attention opposed the musicians' narrative,[2] feeding complexity. The entertainers, like good leaders, provided overarching vision that spans different ideas of timing, in this case those in a hurry to catch another show and those content to stay put (see Ancona et al., 2001 for a discussion of varying organizational time constructs). The introduction of overarching vision, creation of trust, and the manipulation of materiality are tools that leaders often use to shape *emergent phenomena* in the social realm.

On another stage, simultaneously, a comedy duo (Sieve, 2009) used different assemblages to channel the energies of another crowd drawn from the same universe of fair-attendees. Some of the customers (actors) moved between the two shows. The assemblages used to channel these separate but similar emergent phenomena, crowd formation and laughter, were not musical instruments but a clever comedy routine and a carrot. In this instance, the comedian chewed carrot while delivering his monologue, spitting orange carrot shavings into the hair of a woman in the front row while speaking, to the crowd's delight. In a addition to the carrot, familiarity was used, including a soliloquy from Macbeth thrown in amid the humor. Involving the audience in the routine, reinforcing the its reactions and feedback increased the energy level exponentially, channeling and amplifying it to create new, separate phenomena, word of mouth that would fill the seats for the next show and those of subsequent years.

Central to *systemicity* is the concept of assemblages, the physical artifacts surrounding individual and collective actors (Boje, 2010). Boje (2010) separates these assemblages from networks by explaining that they are loosely coupled, migrant, collections of physical materials, in contrast with the more stable, enduring social construct that is a network. Assemblages are the catalysts of "on-to" stories, whereby speculative explanations are put together by spectators, not unlike the fictional character Sherlock Holmes, who could unravel a complicated scheme through what he deemed "elementary" observation of a suspect's personal appearance, clothing, and assemblage (Doyle, 1859–1930). Boje (2010) focuses on imbalances in these materialities as potential sources of disfunction necessitating organizational change. A surplus, shortage, or poor fit of assemblages to the situation can bring about change. Such imbalances may be the vestiges of *emergent phenomena* such as trends, unexplained surges in demand, or unanticipated technological and societal shifts. Likewise, a materiality can trigger human reactions which set off seemingly unrelated chains of events.

Theory of the assemblage situation

The fair in question is more than an open system. It is what Bruno Latour (1999, 2005) calls an "assemblage": an "actor-network" of human and non-human entities. The assemblage elements are a stage, drums, benches, a hot day, a crowd of people who paid to get into the festival but were not bound to attend or complete any one event, the availability of cold drinks and things to purchase in the nearby area, other shows, etc. We think some of these assemblages constitute attractors drawing people away, influences on the crowd. Table 12.1 explores the assemblages, which actors they are attributed to, and their importance in the context. It subdivides the overall assemblage based on which actor has primary use of the elements and to what end. Of central importance is their collective utility in shaping an emergent social phenomenon, the crowd.

179

Table 12.1 Actors, motivations, assemblages and importance

Actor	Governing Principles	Assemblage	Relevance
Musicians (leaders/ purveyors of influence)	■ Attract a large crowd ■ Obtain positive feedback ■ Earn tips ■ Secure a spot at next year's venue	■ Drums, bagpipes, music, jokes, microphones, stage, benches	■ Tools of facilitation for influencing the crowd to remain
Vendors	■ Make a profit by attracting paying customers	■ Cold drinks, wares for sale	■ Tools of facilitation for attracting actors away from the stage
Spectators	■ Maximize personal enjoyment ■ Stay cool ■ Stay hydrated ■ Compromise on family desires	■ Money, hats, sunscreen, unstructured time, maps and schedules of attractions, comfortable shoes	■ Money increases the vendors' motivations and makes their wares attractive to the spectators (enabler) ■ Knowledge of all available options (maps and schedules)

Conclusion

Complexity theory applies to adaptive open systems with a nonlinear flow of energy and/or information into and out of the system. Independent elements, acting of their own accord, self-organize in such a way that "order emerges out of chaos; irregularities emerge out of order" (Luhman and Boje, 2001, p. 158). From this dynamic "aliveness" emerge phenomena whose exact preconditions, timing and catalysts are often elusive. These phenomena create repeating patterns that are similar on multiple scales, though not easily predictable. These patterns, called fractals, are more evident when examining such systems at a distance (Luhman and Boje, 2001, p. 163) and are the material manifestation of emergent phenomena. Emergence is an inevitable, and often overwhelming, fact of all open systems. Its agency invokes reactions from even those who attempt to disregard its existence.

The true *third cybernetic* system is one that can discover those emergent phenomena of great import and channel them, generating reflexivity, reorganization, and growth of the organization itself. Organizations must be versatile and decentralized to profit from these dynamics. Leaders have choices in the face of strategically significant social emergence: ignoring or rejecting the imminent change, "riding the wave," and shaping the phenomenon. The latter choice makes the most of human–material assemblages, using them as levers in a multilayered dynamic *systemicity*. *Third-order cybernetic* organizations are open to new ideas, thrive on internal and external variation, and are poised to shape emergent social phenomena including demand in tomorrow's marketplace. They differ from their *second-order cybernetic* cousins in their active material-based agency.

This sort of agency requires courage and creates great power, but not the controlling hegemonic power of narrative. This is the collective power of assemblage, of like-minded individuals and appropriate resource levels. It is the polyphonic power of voices in harmony, not orchestrated but ad-libbed, with respect for the unplanned solo. It is the individual choice to linger near the stage for the sake of community and shared experience. This power abhors material excess and abuses. It does not silence rebel voices but draws strength from their variation and embraces moderation born of balance. It is the collective belief in something greater than one's self, what the military terms esprit de corps. Successful military officers have long known that this agency can never be forced or contrived. It emerges from a mixture of small catalysts that are not uniform from one unit to the next, but when it emerges, channeling it is simply a matter of recognition, confidence, and care.

We have seen that despite its precocious nature, emergence need not be an enemy of human organizations. Though rigid, static organizations are often unable to weather such storms, today's flatter, dynamic organizations not only survive unanticipated changes but grow stronger as a result. The world's most successful leaders, those termed visionary, are those who recognize the opportunities of emergence and have the courage to not only "ride the wave" but channel its flow to benefit their organizations. This is the lesson of Microsoft and Apple, of personal computers and smart phones, of musicians and comedians, and of modern life itself.

Fortune favors the bold – Virgil (19 B.C.–70 B.C.)

Notes

1 'Actor' in this context does not refer to a performer on a stage, but rather to the unit of action in a self-organizing system. For this scenario, it might be an individual person, a family, a social group, or a crowd.
2 It is worth noting that in much of the literature narrative denotes hegemony, while in this case the narrative is less sinister.

References

Ancona, D.G., Goodman, P.S., Lawrence, B.S., and Tushman, M.L. (2001). Time: A new research lens. *Academy of Management Review*, 26(4), 645–563.
Ashby, W.R. (1958). Requisite variety and its implications for the control of complex systems. *Cybernetica*, 1(2), 83–99.
Bakhtin, M. (1981). *The dialogic imagination: four essays*. (M. Holquist and C. Emerson, Trans.). Austin: University of Texas Press.
Baskin, K. and Boje, D. (2005). Guest editors' introduction. *Emergence: Complexity and Organization*, 7(3/4), 1.
Bennett, J. (2010). *Vibrant matter: a political ecology of things*. Durham, NC: Duke University Press.
Boje, D.M. (1995). Stories of the storytelling organization: a postmodern analysis of Disney as "Tamara-land", *Academy of Management Journal*, 38(4), 997–1035.
Boje, D.M. (2008). *Storytelling Organizations*. Los Angeles: SAGE Publications, Ltd.
Boje, D.M. (2010). 'A theory of socio-economic research intervention'. Unpublished Conversation Starter. Colorado Technical University.
Boje, D.M. and Khadija, A.A. (2005). Third cybernetic revolution: beyond open to dialogic system theories. *TAMARA: Journal of Critical Postmodern Organization Science*, 4(1/2), 138–50.
Boulding, K.E. (1956). General systems theory-the skeleton of science. *Management Science*, 2(3), 197–208.
Colorado Renaissance Festival. (2010). 'Colorado Renaissance Festival', www.coloradorenaissance.com/ (retrieved 31 August 2010).

Doyle, A.C. (1859–1930). *The new annotated Sherlock Holmes*. W.W. Norton.

Gershenson, C. and Heylighen, F. (2003). 'When can we call a system self-organizing?' Paper presented at the Advances in Artificial Life: 7th European Conference on Artificial Life, ECAL 2003, Dortmund, Germany, 19 February.

Green, S.G. and Welsh, M.A. (1988). Cybernetics and dependence: reframing the control concept. *Academy of Management Review*, 13(2), 287–301.

Ison, R. (2008). 'Systems thinking and practice for action research'. In P. Reason and H. Bradbury (eds), *The SAGE handbook of action research: participative inquiry and practice* (2nd edn, pp. 138–58). London: SAGE Publications.

Johnson, N. (2007). *Simply complexity: a clear guide to complexity theory*. Oxford: Oneworld Publications.

Klenk, J., Binnig, G. and Schmidt, G. (2000). Handling complexity with self-organizing fractal semantic networks. *Emergence*, 2(4), 151–62.

Krizanc, J. and Boje, D. (2006). Interview with John Krizanc, *TAMARA: Journal of Critical Postmodern Organization Science*, 5, 70–77.

Latour, B. (1999). *Pandora's hope: essays on the reality of science studies*. Cambridge, MA: Harvard University Press.

Latour, B. (2005). *Reassembling the social: an introduction to actor-network theory*. Oxford: Oxford University Press.

Leibovitch, L.S. (1998). *Fractals and chaos for the life sciences*. New York: Oxford University Press.

Lewin, R. (1999). *Complexity: life at the edge of chaos* (2nd edn). Chicago, IL: University of Chicago Press.

Luhman, J.T. and Boje, D.M. (2001). What is complexity science? A possible answer from narrative research. *Emergence*, 3(1), 158–68.

Mataric, M.J. (1995). Designing and understanding adaptive group behavior. *Adaptive behavior*, 4(1), 51–80.

Pondy, L.R. and Boje, D. (2005). Beyond open system models of organization. *Emergence: Complexity and Organization*, 7(3/4), 119–37.

Rapoport, A., Horvath, W.J. and Goldstein, J. (2009). Thoughts on organization theory. *Emergence: Complexity and Organization*, 11(1), 94–103.

Rodriguez, S., Hilaire, V., Gruer, P. and Koukam, A. (2007). A formal holonic framework with proved self-organizing capabilities. *International Journal of Cooperative Information Systems*, 16(1), 7–25.

Ryu, K. and Jung, M. (2006). Dynamic restructuring process for self-reconfiguration in the fractal manufacturing system. *International Journal of Production Research*, 44(15), 3105–29.

Sieve, M. (2009). *Call me puke: a life on the dirt circuit*. Minneapolis, MN: Two Harbors Press.

Smith, C. and Comer, D. (1994). Self-organization in small groups: a study of group effectiveness within non-equilibrium conditions. *Human Relations*, 47(5), 553–81.

Tsoukas, H. (2005). *Complex knowledge: studies in organizational pistemology*. Oxford: Oxford University Press.

Van de Ven, A.H. and Poole, M.S. (2005). Alternative approaches for studying organizational change. *Organization Studies*, 26(9), 1377–1404.

Waistell, J. (2006). Metaphorical mediation of organizational change across space and time. *Journal of Organizational Change Management*, 19(5), 640–6541.

Waldrop, M.M. (1992). *Complexity: the emerging science at the order of chaos*. New York: Simon & Schuster.

Ward, M. (2002). *Beyond chaos: the underlying theory behind life, the universe and everything* (1st US edn). New York: St. Martin's Press.

Zimmerman, B.J. and Hurst, D.K. (1993). Breaking the boundaries: the fractal organization. *Journal of Management Inquiry*, 2(4), 334–55.

Part 3

Perspectives on change

Introduction

John Hassard

Part 3 addresses "Perspectives on change". As such the emphasis is largely upon exploring various theoretical and methodological perspectives relating to organizational change and development. The opening essay, Chapter 13, by Richard Badham, Amanda Mead and Elena Antonacopoulou, for example, discusses "A dramaturgical approach to the practice of managing change". It argues that when we begin to consider the discourse of "managing change" we are far from the more restricted analysis of "organizational change". The suggestion is that we enter the sphere of action, judgement and decision, and the imperatives of practice. Exploring this issue philosophically the authors argue that in classical Aristotelean terms, this is not the sphere of *episteme*, or even *techne*, but of *phronesis* – wisdom in the doing. In developing this argument, therefore the authors adopt a phronetic view of managing change. Adopted as a discipline of influencing oneself and others to achieve a purpose, this is at once deeply personal and highly institutional, a proximate phronetic art embedded in situated life-worlds not a distal technical rationality. As such, performing effectively requires practical artfulness, disciplined creativity, serious play and engaged distance. For theories of managing change, a key challenge in this sense is how to explore and inform such a complex situational practice. Ultimately the authors argue that any academic contribution to phronetic knowledge arguably needs to satisfy three requirements: first, capturing the theoretical and empirical depth and richness of the literature on organizational change and its management; second, adopting a theoretically informed and pragmatically relevant sensitivity to the nature and demands of practice; and third, providing systematic support for reflective practice.

The second contribution to Part 3, Chapter 14, "Designing for change with critical scenario method", by George Cairns, suggests that change can originate in a number of ways to impact upon organizations. It may be initiated from within or generated from without: it may be planned such that it can be managed, or emerge from unexpected sources and have unpredictable impacts. Cairns argues, however, that modern business enterprises are also major players in how the world operates. As such major change that impacts the organization's ability to address its strategic objectives or to fulfil its plans and operate effectively can also affect a wide range of stakeholders; both those with direct links to the organization and those whose relationship is tangential or even remote. Business therefore must take a leading role in determining the change priorities and direction for the future, not just for those with an immediate interest. To make sense of this, Cairns presents an externalized, scenario-based perspective on change. Specifically he advocates an approach to organization analysis that is concerned with exploring the change process as a journey towards the best possible outcome for the broadest range of affected stakeholders. As such, he presents organization change as concerning matters of ethics and morality, and thus as a response to moral dilemmas facing contemporary managers.

In "Organizations unbound: psychodynamic perspectives on organizational restructuring", Chapter 15, Paula Hyde suggests that in the post-industrial era of organizational change some would argue that psychodynamic ideas such as social defences against anxiety have fallen behind. It can be argued that organization boundaries have changed to the extent that it may no longer necessarily be clear where work takes place, where it starts and ends or how the demands of work might be contained. In recent years, organizational change in large corporations has almost invariably involved some form of radical restructuring, often through delayering. Such restructuring has tended to depend upon the removal of middle managerial levels and a general slimming down of perceived bureaucracy. The impact of organizational restructuring on organizational boundaries is thus an important feature of organizational change, not least because modern organizational forms involve increased boundary complexity. Overall Hyde argues that reactions to such complexity are neither standard nor entirely predictable, but may be illuminated through empirical research exploring boundaries in organizational settings and notably utilizing psychodynamic methods.

Chapter 16, Stephen Ackroyd's essay "Contemporary realism and organizational change", then argues that realist approaches to organization studies are more significant than might be at first thought. He suggests that, far from being just one of many possible ways of doing organization studies, realist theory and research has a claim to being foundational for the field. Indeed Ackroyd argues that organizational studies was first thought of as a branch of social science and the idea of social *science* is difficult to conceive as such without thinking that the social world is real and has causal effects. Much of the social science which followed the work of the founding fathers in the twentieth century in Britain and other parts of Europe was, for example, recognisably realist in its assumptions. Indeed today there are still large numbers of researchers in our field who are implicitly if not explicitly realist in the way they conceive of organizations and in their views about the way knowledge should be developed. Therefore, despite the "paradigm proliferation" in organization studies experienced after the end of the 1970s, it is remains probable, Ackroyd argues, that today the majority of organization studies practitioners are realist in their approach to their subject matter, believing organizations actually exist and shape behaviour.

Appreciation of the influence of classical social science on organizational analysis is also evident in Chapter 17, Stewart Clegg and John Gray's essay on "Organization theory, power and changing institutions". However, they argue that institutional theory is the dominant means of sensemaking in use by the community of organization scholars today. Clegg and Gray suggest that as it has become "institutionalized"; institutional theory has focused less on the categories that its members use and more on those that are normative. The stress is overwhelmingly on cognitive and/or normative constructions through all of which power runs but which is rarely explicitly addressed. As a consequence Clegg and Gray argue that there has been too much order and legitimacy in institutional theory and not enough disordering and power as well as too much concern with the categories of its own reasoning and insufficient regard for the categories of everyday reasoning. For Clegg and Gray, Institutionalism's relative neglect is problematic for a clear research agenda. In this chapter they recognize its value and seek to reconnect it to its roots of processes and structuration in order to provide an adequate power theory for changing institutions.

In Chapter 18, Ann Langley and Pamela Sloan discuss "Organizational change and dialectic processes". In attempting to understand the processes of organizational change, they argue that many writers and empirical researchers have invoked the concept of *dialectics*, a notion that has its roots in Hegelian philosophy and that is used to refer to social processes as imbued with conflict, tension and contradiction. Their chapter reviews conceptual and empirical contributions to the organizational studies literature that have drawn on the notion of dialectics to examine how the concept is understood and used, and to review the implications that can be drawn from it both for the understanding of organizational change as well as for management practice. In developing their argument Langley and Sloan explain central tendencies in dialectical thought prior to describing the variety of streams of work in organizational analysis that draw on it.

The final contribution to Part 3 is André Spicer and Charlotta Levay's analysis of "Critical theories of organizational change", Chapter 19. They argue that contemporary organizations are characterized by an obsession and commitment to change. Many, indeed, spend significant amounts of their time and resources introducing wave after wave of change programs. The mantras of flexibility and nimble responses to movements in the financial markets or customer demand are a common currency in most organizations. In contrast, Spicer and Levay wish to "unsettle" the widespread assumptions that organizational change is necessary, correct and even morally vital. They note how existing studies of organizational change have largely reproduced the widespread ideology of change and have done so through either functionalist studies which seek to control organizational change more effectively, or interpretive studies which consider the meanings that actors have assigned to the change process. Instead Spicer and Levay turn to recent work that has sought to sketch out a critical approach to change. Building on recent advances in critical management studies, they argue that a critical approach to change should involve an affirmative stance, an ethic of care, a sense of pragmatism, and consideration of potentialities as well as normative bases for change. By detailing each of these components, they sketch out what a critical theory of change might look like, and what researchers might consider if they hope to follow this approach.

13

Performing change
A dramaturgical approach to the practice of managing change

Richard Badham, Amanda Mead and Elena Antonacopoulou

'I'm floating around on an ice cube that's melting in the toilet.'[1]
(James Lee Burke, 2005, *Heaven's Prisoners*, New York: Phoenix, p. 226)

Introduction: a phronetic art!

Once we enter the discourse of 'managing change', we are far from the more restricted analysis of 'organizational change'. We enter the sphere of action, judgement and decision, and the imperatives of practice. In classical Aristotelian terms, this is not the sphere of *episteme*, or even *techne*, but of *phronesis* – a wisdom in the doing (Flyvbjerg, 2001; Eikeland, 2007; Antonacopoulou, 2010a). There is no guarantee that an accumulation of knowledge about how change works, its nature and dynamics (*episteme*), will provide any useful knowledge about how to influence it. It may be that as one of the founders of contemporary theories of managing change, Kurt Lewin (1964: 169), put it, 'There is nothing so practical as a good theory', but if that *is* the case, then it is a theory that has to be translated, put to work and made to perform (Czarniawska-Joerges and Sevon, 1996; Latour, 1993). There is, similarly, no assurance that the provision of technical knowledge, in the form of procedures, rules and principles for manipulation and control (*techne*), will actually be used effectively and appropriately in context. There is always a 'phronetic gap' between what rules prescribe and situations demand (Taylor, 1995; Tsoukas, 2005). It is arguably a recognition of the dangers of this gap that lies at the heart of any meaningful treatment of 'managing change' (Badham, 2006b). Managing organizational change, in the sense of attempts to influence the changing nature of institutions (Badham, 2006a), is a complex situational practice, and one that requires wisdom, in the form of mindfulness, reflexivity and discipline, if it is to be effective.

In making this argument, the chapter adopts a phronetic view of managing change. Taken as a *discipline of influencing oneself and others to achieve a purpose*, it is both deeply personal and highly institutional, a proximate phronetic art embedded in situated life-worlds not a distal technical rationality (Cooper and Law, 1995). Performing effectively requires practical artfulness, disciplined creativity, serious play and engaged distance.

A key challenge for theories of managing change, in this sense, is how to explore and inform such a complex situational practice. Any academic contribution to phronetic knowledge arguably needs to satisfy three requirements: first, capturing the theoretical and empirical depth and richness of the literature on organizational change and its management; second, adopting a theoretically informed and pragmatically relevant sensitivity to the nature and demands of practice; third, providing systematic support for reflective practice.

This is a substantial challenge, especially for a chapter-length discussion of the topic. We will thus inevitably be restricted to providing suggestive guidelines rather than a definitive statement for how this might be addressed. In a sense, this chapter offers a set of theoretically informed yet experimental 'probes' in wrestling with the problem. In the spirit of phronesis, however, we would argue that the 'practical' political and ethical importance of the task overcomes the epistemic and technical limitations of such an enterprise.

The chapter introduces three such 'probes'. First, it explores how the literature on managing change may be translated into a set of heuristics. The particular characterization of such heuristics is inevitably suggestive and illustrative in character, and should be treated as such. It does, however, provide some initial potential guidelines to help support a phronetic change-management practice. Second, it provides a brief introduction to the context in which such guidelines can be put to use, that of managing change-as-practice, drawing on the recent contributions of the 'practice turn' in organizational studies. Third, it elaborates and argues for the value of a 'dramaturgical' approach to developing a practice-based phronetic knowledge.

Conversations, heuristics and the literature on managing change

In the face of questions raised about the contribution of organizational studies, and internal and external demands for relevance, a number of leading scholars have argued strongly for 'fruitful dialogues' (Reed and Hughes, 1992); constructive 'conversations' (Van Maanen, 1995); enriching 'bricolages' (Bolman and Deal, 1997) and a focused wrestling with key 'anomalies' (Willmott, 1993) and 'paradoxes' (Lewis and Kelemen, 2002). From the perspectives of a phronetic approach to knowledge, a valuable approach to generating such a conversation is the suggestive creation of relatively open and flexible heuristics in the sense of those described in Schön's reflection-on-action (1983, 1987). The term heuristics derives from the Greek, 'heuriskein', to find or discover. It has since been interpreted in three main ways: to describe the 'discovery of meaning and essence in significant human experience' in intrapersonal, interpersonal or, possibly more appropriately named, 'transpersonal' research (Moustakas and Douglass, 1985, p. 40); mechanisms to deal with complexity, limited time and inadequate mental resources in decision making (Kahneman, 2003; Simon, 1957); and phrases, models or metaphors which enable understanding, particularly of human responses to problems in the social environment or ecology (Marsh, 2002; Schön, 1983, 1987). It is the argument of this chapter that the explicit creation of performance heuristics has value as a means for knowledge development and presentation for this conversation and lays a foundation for supporting reflective practice.

The traditional discourse of change management

With an established history extending back beyond ancient Greece, and well over a million contemporary articles on the subject, the management of change is, literally, a voluminous subject and not one amenable to easy reduction as a set of heuristics (Poole et al., 2000, p. 57 fn.). Any overview of this discourse is also inevitably subject to controversy and debate (Cooke, 1999; Sturdy and Morgan, 2000; Zorn, 2005). Yet it is hopefully possible, without being excessively contentious, to roughly characterise mainstream post-World War II research and education on managing change as proceeded through three contributory stages. These stages overlap, are not exclusive and should not be interpreted as a form of intellectual 'epochalism' (du Gay, 2003), and are restricted to the 'conventional wisdom' within mainstream studies of managing change.

First, following the classic work in the 1940s and 1950s of Kurt Lewin (1943, 1964), Edgar Schein (1951) and Coch and French (1948), the initial focus was on planned organizational change within an organizational development framework. While attention was focused on individual, group and organizational level change, much of the organizational development approach was at the group/individual level, with a particular focus on overcoming resistance to change. Managing change was often presented as a matter of expert facilitation, providing education and involvement strategies and techniques for surfacing resistant beliefs, habits and emotions, and managing groups through a staged process of unfreezing, moving and refreezing (French et al., 2004).

Second, as represented in the work of Rosabeth Moss Kanter (1983) and John Kotter (1996) in the US, Andrew Pettigrew (1985) in the UK and Dexter Dunphy (Dunphy and Stace, 1992) in Australia, greater attention was paid from the 1980s onwards to transformational organizational change, the implementation of strategy, and managing the complex processes and politics of strategic change from a broad human resource-management perspective (Dawson, 1994). During this period, greater attention was paid to the coercive, as well as participatory, dimension of change, and the leadership skills in managing politics, complexity and process (Buchanan and Boddy, 1992; Buchanan and Badham, 2008).

Third, most prominently within academic discourse on organizational behaviour, the 1990s onwards saw the growth and widespread acceptance of more improvisatory and sense-making perspectives on change, more political and politicized views of the purposes and methods of programmatic change, and greater attention to the role of metaphors and frames underlying theoretical frameworks, and the intellectual and pragmatic difficulties involved in handling the paradoxical, complex and chaotic nature of change (e.g. Beer and Nohria, 2000; Brown and Eisenhardt, 1998; Burnes, 2000; Collins, 1998; Morgan and Sturdy, 2000; Palmer and Dunford, 2005; Stacey, 2007).

The first classical 'episodic' view of planned organizational change established managing change as a field of study, intellectual discipline and management specialization. By 'episodic' here is meant a classical view of the difference between the study and management of the dynamic phases or stages of 'change' and the static orderly nature of routine organizational operations. Once this 'episodic' view was broken down, with more fluid views of organizations as *organizing* (Gabriel et al., 2000) and change as ongoing *changing* (Weick and Quinn, 1999) and *becoming* (Tsoukas and Chia, 2002), then it became more difficult and controversial to identify 'managing change' as a separate area of inquiry, intervention and practice. This has been accompanied by more general criticism of the weaknesses of traditional formal, rational and autocratic views of management, and a greater recognition of the importance of the informal, emotional, supportive and inspirational nature of organizational leadership. In combination, these developments have at one and the same time paradoxically brought into question the status of managing change as a discrete area of inquiry and activity at the same time as it has increased recognition of the importance of the areas traditionally covered by managing change (e.g. dynamics, impacts and expectations of change, frame-breaking and group dynamics, managing expectations and handling anxiety and fear, impression management and influence techniques, managing power and politics, learning and experimentation and so on).

As a result, despite the breakdown of 'managing change' as a discrete activity and specialization, there is a common view of its importance as: an ongoing feature of rapidly changing nature of contemporary organizations, as part of the responsibilities of human resource management and development in organizations, as a core capability of senior managers, as a component expertise or specialization of a growing range of consultants, as well as continuing as an academic specialization on 'organizational development and change'.

It has not, however, been without its critics. Apart from criticisms of its 'non-disciplinary' nature, there have also been more critical reviews of its political and politicised character (Cooke, 1999; McLoughlin et al., 2005), as well as the superficiality of much of its knowledge base, purported techniques and practical interventions (Buchanan and Badham, 2008; Collins, 1998, 2004; Morgan and Sturdy, 2000; Sturdy and Grey, 2003; Sturdy and Morgan, 2003).

If managing change is an important and complex phronetic art – and enduringly so – where does this extant literature, activities and debates leave us? As argued above, managing change in practice involves the mindful (Weick and Sutcliffe, 2001) application of maxims and heuristics rather than the strict following of rules (Taylor, 1995), careful judgements about the relevance of cases and precedents rather than simply applying the lessons of business history, and ongoing reflection *in* and *on* an inevitably experimental process and practice (Argyris and Schon, 1974; Sztompka, 1999). Can the literature on managing change be used to support such activities? As illustrated in Zander and Zander (2000) 'toes to nose' story and Dopson's (1997) re-narrating of Edgar Allan Poe's 'fisherman in the maelstrom', simple and useable guides rather then tightly prescriptive methods are of key importance in navigating on the 'edge of chaos' (Stacey, 2007). Whether we draw on a Machiavellian tradition rejecting social 'science' in favour of pragmatic guidelines for 'realpolitik' (Latour, 1988) or a 'sensemaking' view of the centrality of maps despite the irreducible gap between the 'map and the territory' (Weick, 2001), the outcome is the same: reflective practitioners require pragmatic heuristics and guidelines.

Is it possible, therefore, to stimulate creative, practical and reflective conversations about how to manage change drawing on the established literature on managing change? Can this literature be used to inform the creative development of heuristics, shorn of some of the more restrictive and controversial academic packaging of theory, data and methods as established 'epistemic knowledge' or universal change 'techniques'? Table 13.1 represents one way in which some of these themes may be drawn out. It is intended for illustrative purposes only, to show how established literature may be drawn upon to create and reflect upon useful heuristics *not* (at least in this chapter) to argue for the precision and value of the particular examples chosen.

In the first phase of managing change, many OD consultants, practitioners and even academic writers interpreted the complex writings of such founding figures as Lewin, Argyris and Schein (Burnes, 2000) through the lenses of scientific discovery of 'laws' or the establishment of rules for technical 'engineering'. In crude form, this viewed OD knowledge as applied technique tailored to help individuals and organizations through the fixed universal three stages of change. This was associated with the application of simple change tools, and a view of managing-change theory as a therapeutic science, implementing strategies for involvement and participation.

As a looser set of heuristics supporting 'practical' knowledge and overcoming the limitations of traditional rationalistic perspectives on implementation, however, OD introduced the idea of pragmatic, experimental, action-research as a form of knowledge and learning, opening up the use of the idea of three 'phases' of change not as a rigid theory but as a flexible mindful counterpoint to simple 'two-stage' views of change as a rational activity of design-implementation or instruction-compliance. Rather than imposing simple change tools, OD can be seen as providing a set of situational heuristics, such as the 'forcefield' analysis, with a simplicity that enables groups to address issues not often surfaced yet with a practical complexity

Table 13.1 Change heuristics

Epistemic/Techne Orthodoxy	Phronetic Heterodoxy
Organizational Development and Planned Organizational Change	
■ Applied Technique	Action Research
■ Rigid Stage Theory	Three 'Phases' of Change
■ Simple Change Tools	e.g. Forcefield Diagnosis
■ Therapeutic Science	e.g. Surface Undiscussables
■ One-Way Participative Change	e.g. Coercive Persuasion
Human Resource Development and Strategy Implementation	
■ Lightweight Analysis	Change as Process
■ Designer Forms and Stages	Emergent Strategy
■ Design Contingencies	Participative & Coercive Strategies
■ One Best Way	Creative Enterprise
Organizational Behaviour and Reframing Change	
■ No Checklists	Organizing and Changing
■ Uncritical Pluralism	Frames of Change
■ Negativism	Managerialism & Politics
■ Academic Arrogance	Consultancy, Fads & Fashions
■ Systemic Chaos Theory	Complexity and Paradox

that requires sophisticated handling and use. Rather than being restricted to an organic 'thereapeutic' science, and the imposition of one-dimensional participation strategies, it draws attention to the controversial and complex political-psychological issues involved in surfacing 'undiscussables' in organizations, and the 'coercive' as well as 'participatory' nature of individual/group 'persuasion' methods and practices.

In this latter sense, Lewin's established 'unfreezing', 'moving' and 'refreezing' model of change, if used as a rough initial entrée into capturing and addressing the dynamics of 'transition rituals' (Turner, 1982), then it can be drawn upon without exaggerated views of an organization as 'ice cube' (Kanter et al., 1992), or as change having to proceed through any rigid sequence of simple, unlinear, non-overlapping phases. Similarly, Schein's (1988) classic study of the complex psychological dynamics of deliberate unfreezing, moving, refreezing as a sophisticated paradoxical process of 'coercive persuasion' is of value, while one-best way analysis of participation and involvement as *the* key to overcoming resistance to change is partial and limited at best. Argyris's (1990) exploration of the reasons, tactics and strategies for OD specialists to 'surface undiscussables' is a crucial area of investigation and inquiry, but serious recognition needs to be given to his observation that this is a skill and capability that is not attained by many, and not a simple therapeutic science or method. Finally, action research provides a set of models for an ongoing, iterative, experimental approach to addressing the complex demands of action and learning in practice, rather than being regarded as an applied technique for solving organizational problems (Cooperrider and Srivastva, 1987).

The second phase of the managing-change literature introduced the dual focus on strategic human-resource management and the adoption of a more processual and political view of change. At the level of establishing an episteme of change and a techne of change techniques, this imposed a relatively lightweight characterization of the change process as an interaction between content, context and politics, new fixed typologies of change and stages of change, rigid views of designer change strategies appropriate to situational contingencies, and new 'one best way' models of how to handle the challenges of change. As a contribution to an expanded set of heuristics of change challenging rationalistic orthodoxy, however, it encouraged recognition and reflection on the complex processual nature of change (Pettigrew, 1997), the emergent contextual nature of strategy development and implementation (Brown and Eisenhardt, 1998) and the recognition of situation-specific blends of coercion and participation in bringing about strategic change (Beer and Nohria, 2000), and the nature and value of entrepreneurial creativity in handling the complex uncertainties and confrontational politics of change (Buchanan and Badham, 2008).

The third phase extended the depth of understanding of processual and paradoxical dimensions of managing change, as well as the social and political character of the perspectives and methods that are deployed. Through the lens of traditional episteme, this has resulted in a greater understanding of the complexities of organizational becoming. The contribution has not, however, been so extensive in translating and extending this epistemic contribution into phronetic knowledge. It has often provided little advice on how to handle the complexity that is observed. In some cases, this has been accompanied by an uncritical pluralism in accepting diverse 'frames' of change. In a number of cases, it has been restricted in its phronetic potential by not going beyond academic 'debunking' or a critical negativity towards simplistic consultancy methods or restricted management politics. For others, it has involved adopting scientistic approaches such as 'chaos theory' as a new epistemic and technical solution to handling complexity.

In phronetic terms, however, if a sophisticated recognition of the complex nature of organizational becoming means 'no checklists' then the need for practical guidance is avoided. An equally uncritical negativism towards managerial initiatives can misrepresent as well as immobilise action. The critique of fads and fashions can lead to an academic arrogance that fails to capture the context and value of heuristics while offering little advice itself. Recognition of multiple frames can lead to a simplistic acceptance of pluralistic insights without any basis for identifying deploying and blending such frames. Finally, recognition of uncertainty and chaos has led to a recommendation to apply the insights of scientific 'chaos theory' as an expert 'solution'. In this way, it may, in a different guise, end up restricting its value in making practitioners face up to and address the enduring gap between aspirations and achievements. In this way, as an uncritical view of such a 'scientific' theory could end up restricting its potential as an ongoing reminder to practitioners to be mindful of irremovable complexity and the difficulties and discomforts of acting effectively in the face of irreducible uncertainty.

As a heterodox contribution to phronetic heuristics, however, this era was marked by encouraging reflective support for 'managing the unexpected' character of organizing and changing (Orlikowski, 1996; Weick and Sutcliffe, 2001), taking into account the need to handle the conflicting framing of change by change initiators and recipients (Orlikowski and Gash, 1994), the value yet complexity of extending the discussion of political 'undiscussables' in creating effective and persuasive change rituals (Argyris, 1990), serious consideration in change of the social dynamics of consultancy rhetoric's and practices (Clark and Fincham, 2001; Whittle, 2006), and the issues, mindset and social supports necessary to address rather than deny complexity and paradox when operating on the 'edge of chaos' (Stacey, 2007).

Table 13.1, and this all too brief discussion of the outlined heuristics, is only intended to be illustrative and suggestive in character. It does, however, capture some key change insights and their relevance for any serious exploration of the practice or phronesis integral to managing change. Any significant further development and use of heuristics does, however, need to be firmly grounded in an understanding of the nature of managing change as a *social practice*.

Managing change-in-practice

Our point of departure in adopting a social practice perspective is to join the conversation in the growing debate that has come to be referred to as the 'practice-turn' in organization studies (Schatzki et al., 2001). This debate has sensitized us to practice as a lens for reinterpreting a variety of organizational activities, such as learning (Gherardi and Nicolini, 2002; Brown and Duguid 2000), strategy (e.g. Jarzabkowski, 2005; Johnson et al., 2003) and technology (Dougherty, 2004; Orlikowski, 2000) to name but a few. Even institutional change has been re-examined through the practice lens (Seo and Creed, 2002).

One of the ongoing challenges facing this 'practice-turn' is an ongoing lack of clarity about exactly what practice means, with different perspectives focusing on action, social context, knowing, activity systems, structures and so on (Antonacopoulou, 2007). At the same time, however, practice studies has been successful in sensitizing organizational studies to the complexity of 'rule following' in action, the importance of understanding the interactions, relationships and contexts within which action occurs, and the complex, tentative and experimental nature of action and reflections on action. For practice studies, rules are, as Taylor (1993: 50) puts it, 'islands in the sea of our unformulated practical grasp on the world'. A key tenet is, as Gadamer succinctly remarks, that 'the application of rules can never be done by rules'. Practical wisdom and judgement is needed to interpret, adjudicate and adapt rules in the context of their application. (Gadamer, 1980: 83). This inevitably takes the form of what Pickering (1995: 22) dramatically represents as the 'mangle of practice', an inherently experimental 'practical, goal-oriented and goal-revising dialectic of resistance and accommodation'.

What, however, do these basic insights of practice studies mean for the management of change, and the use of the heuristics outlined above? In addition, of specific concern for the present chapter, in what ways does it support or contribute to a dramaturgical understanding of change and its management? In exploring these questions, we will draw strongly on Antonacopolou's (2007, 2008, 2010a, 2010b) overview of practice studies and development of these key practice studies assumptions through the key concepts of 'practise', ex-tension and reflexive critique.

At a base level, all areas of social practice are to varying degrees pragmatic, focused, disciplined and repetitive. They are constituted not just by the individual actions of practitioners but also by the collective interactions, stocks of knowledge, and more or less institutionalized relationships that make up any significant area of social and organizational life. From such a practice perspective, any discussion of managing change needs to consider two dimensions of social practice.

The first dimension is that all significant areas of organizational life are deliberate, habitual and *repetitive* in character. This should not be understood, however, as involving simple *replication* or predictable institutionalization. Reproduction is inevitably accompanied by a degree of adaptation, emergence and improvisation in context. Practice is governed by what MacIntyre (1985) calls internal and external 'goods', and practical judgement is always required to handle conflicts, contingencies and inevitable tensions between alternative demands. In the process, new developments, possibilities and potentials emerge, in the very act of habitual repetition. In this sense, all practice is a process of more or less unpredictable and uncontrolled becoming.

During this becoming, tensions develop into 'ex-tensions' (Antonacopolou, 2008). In the course of addressing inevitable ambiguity, uncertainty and conflict in context, practice creates new possibilities that point beyond existing habitual patterns of cognitive understanding, moral legitimation and power relationships. Inherent in repetition is, therefore, what Heidegger refers to as 'shocks' or what the Greeks called κρήσις (krisis – critique – being critical). All interaction involves individual and collective sense-making (Weick, 2001). However, this process inevitably involves 'sense-giving' as well as 'sense-making' in an ongoing process of negotiated interpretation and understanding (Strauss, 1978). It also includes 'sense-breaking' as well as 'sense-making' as traditional assumptions and behaviours are challenged in the very course of their application.

What this means for managing change is that change is not viewed as episodic events, deliberate or otherwise, occurring between periods of stability and reproduction. It is, rather, an ongoing process. Moreover, this process of change is a complex one, conscious *and* tacit, reproductive *and* challenging, improvising *and* disciplined and focused by tradition. Managing change is, therefore, an ongoing component of all practical action, involving the more or less reflective adaptation to shifting conditions, response to emergence and handling of new possibilities and developments.

Second, managing change involves conscious reflection on how this process of ongoing 'changing' occurs, and deliberate action in attempting to influence its outcomes. In this regard, it involves *practise* (understood as improving one's skill) as well as *practice* (in the sense of doing something). Practise is, also, more than *praxis* (action/activity), as it inevitably involves *phronesis* (practical judgement, virtuous modes of knowing). The idea of phronesis is based on the understanding that all practice involves intentionality. This is not understood in technocratic terms as simply applying means to achieve pre-given goals. It involves grappling with the complex shuffling of means and ends in a process of continuity and emergence, habitual action and disruptive crises and possibilities. This intentionality is not only individual and pragmatic, but also collective, moral and political. It intertwines the personal and the social, the cognitive and the emotional, the technical and the political. It involves what the classical Greeks called paideia (pedevo – παιδεύω) i.e. struggling, exerting great effort to achieve something, and with passion – *a labour of love*.

From such a practise perspective, understanding and improving how change is managed involves a *reflexive critique* of existing practice. Reflexive critique is grounded in empirical praxis. Empirical here is used in the classical sense of the word (from the Greek '*Εμπειρία*', empiria) meaning experience. Reflexive critique explores the relationship between established practice, intention and practical judgement. It addresses the goal (or *telos*) as well as the routines of *praxis*, and reflectively explores the practical judgements (*phronesis*) that are being made. In the face of the emergent possibilities inherent in all areas of emergent practice, reflexive critique is more than the potentially restricted habituated reflection in/on action. It is also an ongoing search to create new connections and possibilities, and involves *egrigorsi* (alertness, mindfulness), encouraging change and progress by avoiding complacency. In the Greek tradition of *paideia*, the development and application of such capabilities, is more than a matter of *educating* (i.e. guiding the young and inexperienced) but involves a mature critical reflexivity pursued as part of ongoing self-development and fulfilment.

What this means for managing change-in-practice is that the use of the kinds of heuristics outlined in the previous section should not be seen as mere 'application'. Changing is an inherent and emergent component of all practical action, and in an important sense uncontrolled and uncontrollable, however sophisticated or skilfully the heuristics of 'managing change' are applied. In addition, the experience of deliberately and consciously attempting to influence changing practices and institutions, is itself a complex practice. Improvement in this practice is only brought about through mindful and critical reflection, through an ongoing practise, that is personal as well as institutional, ethical and political as well as pragmatic. A crucial issue for management education, therefore, is how to provide concepts and environments that can support such a practise. It is our argument in this chapter that the dramaturgical view of organizational life as a *dramatic performance* is well-suited to this task.[2] In line with Tsoukas' (2009) advocacy for 'self-distanciation' in practice, it is argued that it helps to provide both a creative reflective distance from actions, roles and responsibilities, and an extensive analytical repertoire for analysing and handling situational demands and performance requirements and activities.

A dramaturgical perspective on managing change

In its view of life as a dramatic performance, dramaturgy performs the valuable task of revealing the *acting in action*, the *performing in performance* and the *drama in the doing*. It makes and allows a separation between the 'actor' and the 'action', the 'person' and the 'part' ('character', 'job' or 'role') that he or she plays. In so doing, it draws attention to action as a means of *ex*pression, a donning of a 'mask' that may be more or less internally and personally expressive and externally credible and convincing. It also highlights the *im*pression created by a performance, focusing on the fact that tasks and responsibilities are fulfilled for an audience or audiences, and that influencing and persuading such audiences is a key component of all performance. In a sense, it addresses acting and performing as a more or less effective blend of 'expression' and 'impression' management. Finally, it emphasizes the purposive, meaningful, personal and suspenseful character of agency and practice. It highlights the degree to which intellect and emotion are intertwined in the narrative framing of events and their expected and desired outcomes. But why are such insights so central for a phronetic approach to managing change? Why dramaturgy?

The first answer lies in the overlapping *pragmatic* objectives of both enterprises. As incorporated in our earlier definition of managing change, the focus of managing change is on what Pfeffer (1994) refers to as the crucial 'skills of getting things done' (in contrast to 'figuring out what to do') i.e. the realization of purposes, ensuring execution rather than creating designs, implementing rather than developing strategy. While such a focus is eminently reasonable, and pragmatic, it is at the same time antithetical to the rationalistic ethos prominent within modern organizations.

This rationalistic ethos is, in various complex and overlapping forms, embedded in the guiding ethos and legitimating rationale of later modern organizational life. In terms of established Western dualities, it prioritizes calculation over intuition, reason over passion, order over ambiguity, mind over body, science over art, thinking over doing and so on (Bauman, 2000; Bell, 1996; Weber, 1997). When, 'rationally', attention is focused on the necessity and value of execution, the rationalistic ethos naturally provides a rationalistic solution – searching for techniques, formulae and orderly controls capable of addressing the problem. In traditional change management terms, such an approach gives a strongly rationalistic slant to Lewin's view of managing change as action research – preparing, leading and reviewing organizational change. In classical rational task-based project management terms, this is viewed in terms of *planning projects*, *executing tasks* and *evaluating outcomes*. For the effective conduct of these tasks, required *change roles* need to be allocated to those with the required *change agency* skills and capabilities. These are seen primarily in terms of defining formal roles, allocating responsibilities and then knowledgeably applying change management techniques. In essence, in line with an established tradition of technocratic social science, managing change is understood as a social 'master-technique' to ensure the orderly and progressive introduction of other techniques (Badham, 1986; Badham, 2006a).

A dramaturgical approach provides a valuable counter to this response. In common with pragmatist philosophy, the dramaturgical approach challenges the idea of managing change as applied technique. It places central emphasis on the complex, situational, embedded, uncertain and judgemental nature of required knowledge-in-practice, knowledge that lies at the heart of 'getting things done'. This knowledge is 'up close and personal', tacit as much as explicit, bodily and emotive as much as mental, frustratingly 'proximate' rather than coolly 'distal', (Cooper and Law, 1995) and more about 'know how' rather than 'know that' (Ryle, 2000). As Denzin (1992: 26) emphasizes, the dramaturgical tradition is less focused on 'why' questions and more on 'how' action occurs as events unfold in 'negotiated, situated, temporal, biographical, emergent, and taken-for-granted processes'.

What dramaturgy integrates with this anti-rationalistic pragmatic view of knowledge, however, is its second major contribution: an *interpretive and interactionist* view of such processes as situated action. Managing change, as with all areas of organizational life, is viewed as occurring in and through a series of interactively narrated *episodic encounters* (Goffman, 1961; Harre and Secord, 1973). 'Global' macro-structures, technologies and environments and 'local' micro-action, interpretation and motivation are interdependent abstractions from the lived experience of such encounters.

In terms of a dramaturgical 'spin' on Lewin's managing change as action research, it is focused on the core activities of *preparing, handling* and *reflecting* upon the interactional dynamics that lie at the core of change-in-practice. As encounters, change situations are characterized by the interactional dynamics of actors and audiences as they iteratively present and receive definitions of the participants and the situation they are in (Edgley, 2003). Change agents are involved in handling multiple expectations and counter-expectations, conflicting and shifting frames, and contested and emergent accounts and motives. As episodes, such situations are more or less ritualized in character, interpreted through more or less established narratives and stories, and involve plots and ceremonies marking their beginning, middle and end. As a particular case in point, change agents are required to understand and handle 'ritualizing' (Collins, 2004) – the uncertainty, anxiety and drama of a constellation of 'transition rituals' (Turner, 1982). They are also required to organize *preparation* and *reflection* upon such ritualizing processes. In preparing the change ritual, they are inevitably involved in all the complexity of 'plotting' a ritual outcome that is as subject to unpredictability as the estimated course of a sailing ship buffeted by the wind and the tides. Change agents are involved in mapping out a territory in a manner that as much *imposes* as *uncovers* dramatic plots, and is as concerned in the complex intrigues of 'plotting' as rationalistic exercises in project planning. Similarly, in promoting reflection, change managers are involved in the disruptive and challenging process of uncovering and surfacing taken-for-granted assumptions and behaviours amongst participants in the change process itself, overcoming cognitive, emotive and political defensiveness and denial. In this process, they act as catalysts, instigating the creative experimentation necessary to successfully 'practise' (Antonacopoulou, 2008) and make *learning-in-practise* a reality.

In this context, the fulfilment of *change roles* is not simply or primarily a matter of defining roles and allocating responsibilities for formally managing change. It requires the use of rhetoric, negotiation and entrepreneurial creativity in confronting the conflicting expectations, frames and interests in situational encounters. In this context, change *agency* is less a matter of technique than it is about *acting mindfully* in the face of situational complexity (March, 2006; Weick, 2001), predictable irrationality (Ariely, 2008) and the frequently unexpected (Weick and Sutcliffe, 2001). It also involves *mobilizing power* – acquiring resources, building coalitions and overcoming powerlessness – in order to overcome the inevitable obstacles to getting things done in episodic encounters (Buchanan and Badham, 2008; Strauss, 1978).

This contrasting view of traditional 'rationalistic' and 'dramaturgical' approaches to managing change are summarized in Table 13.2.

Table 13.2 A dramaturgical approach to managing change

	Rationalistic	Dramaturgical
Change Agency	Applying Technique	Acting Mindfully
Change Roles	Designing Roles	Mobilizing Power
Planning Change	Planning Projects	Preparing Rituals
Leading Change	Executing Tasks	Handling Interaction
Learning & Change	Evaluating Outcomes	Guiding Reflection

The third major contribution of dramaturgy is the use of drama as a *metaphor* for understanding, exploring and effectively operating in such situations (Cornelissen, 2004; Edgley, 2003; Mangham, 1978). In complex and shifting ways, the dramaturgical approach views social and organizational life both *as* drama and *like* drama. Analytically, and in the work of particular writers, these views are and can be intertwined.

As outlined in classic terms in Burke's 'dramatism', it is valid and useful to regard social life *as* drama, not as a metaphor but in 'literal' terms (Brock et al., 1985, as a metonym Czarniawska, 1997). In any human encounter, the participants individually and collectively define, negotiate and re-define the 'definition of the situation'. Following Thomas's classic aphorism, 'If men define things as real, they are real in their consequences' (Thomas, 1923), how they define the situation influences how they will act. The narratives offered, the plots elaborated and the characters identified as dramatic characterizations of the situation define what it is meaningful for people to do in any situation (Czarniawska, 1997). Burke (Overington, 1977) provides the classic elaboration of this insight, arguing that the 'reasons' people act, the 'accounts' they offer and the 'motives' that they attribute to themselves and others, are all based on how they 'frame' (Goffman, 1974) what is relevant, possible and appropriate in a given situation. Burke focuses, in particular, on the interpretation people give of the appropriate relation between five key elements of any situation (a 'Pentad') made up of the Act (What was done); Scene (When and Where it was done); Agent (Who did it); Agency (How he did it); and Purpose (Why he did it).[3] How individuals and groups are then rhetorically persuaded to define the kind of situation they are in (what Burke characterizes as the perceived 'ratios' between elements of the Pentad), directly influences how they will act. In this way, situational action is linked 'to its sense rather than behaviour to its determinants' (Geertz, 1983: 34), for at root 'man is an animal suspended in webs of significance he himself has spun' (Geertz, 1983: 34).

The dramaturgical view of social life *as* drama goes one step further, however. A dramatic performance *in situ* is made up of more than the existence of a dramatic script (or scripts) for actors and audiences. It would be just as mistaken to 'read off' what will happen in a situation from narrative accounts of its character or interpretations of the situational Pentad as it would be to attribute action and behaviour to biological instincts, pre-given intentions or structural determinants. Outcomes are a result of the complex situational performance, intertwining the participants' 'self-interaction' (in an 'internal' conversation) and 'social-interaction' (in an 'external' conversation) (Denzin, 1992). A dramatic encounter is, therefore, inherently unpredictable and suspenseful as motives, intentions and causal explanations are as much outcomes as inputs into situated social interactions (Czarniawska, 1997: 15–16). Such conditions are not given but 'enacted' (Weick, 2001), the product of meaningful negotiated social interaction embedded in a web of collective knowledge and relationships[4] (Antonacopoulou, 2008).

Complementary dramaturgical approaches to managing change

In contrast to the view of social and organizational life *as* drama, Erving Goffman and others have argued that the dramaturgical approach is best seen as making the claim that situational encounters are merely *like* drama, a simple metaphor for exploring the ensuing interactions.[5] As Goffman (1961) emphasizes, there are clearly identifiable differences between 'real life' and institutionalized 'theatre', including the fact that in the latter the contrived characters and plots do not have real consequences, actors are not at the same time the audience and so on. It is argued, therefore, that the metaphor is useful for drawing attention to some but not all key characteristics of social interaction.

As a general perspective on managing change, the theatrical view of social life as being 'like' drama provides a provocative rhetorical counterweight to more formalized rationalistic views of organizations and change. It draws on, and extends, a long standing romantic and cultural awareness that in a sense 'All the world's a stage'[6] and provocatively extends this into an understanding of a late-modern view of organizations as formally rational and economizing systems of action (Bauman, 2000; Bell, 1996; Weber, 1997). In opposition to instrumental task-based views of organizations, it highlights the degree to which all successful task performance involves more or less effective 'displays' to relevant 'audiences' (Bolman and Deal, 1997). In contrast to views of organizations as the more or less automatic performance of institutionalized roles, it emphasizes the presence of role distance, conflict and ambiguity, and the creative role of 'actors' as a juggler of multiple and shifting scripts and performances on diverse stages (Carlson, 1996; Mangham and Overington, 1987, p. 164; Mirvis, 2005).

In this sense, the strong organization-like-theatre approach provides a dramatic and provocative challenge to rationalistic views of organizations and change. Within rationalistic organizations, this potentially provokes a defensive reaction, dismissing such a view as an unrealistic, superficial and playful approach irrelevant to the real practical needs of business. On the other hand, it can also be seen as a liberating source of creativity and reflection, providing practical advice on how effective managers handle the impression management challenge of presenting a formal 'frontstage' public performance of rationality or 'rhetoric of administration', while simultaneously addressing the other intertwined dimension of organizational life and action – the informal 'backstage' of more distanced, critical and reflective commentaries, and the 'rhetoric of realpolitik' (Goffman et al., 1983).

In addition to this general provocative and reflective role, however, the organization-like-drama approach seeks to provide an additional set of illuminating and useful metaphorical images for understanding and guiding managing change. The organization-as-drama approach views managing change as situated social interaction, occurring within interaction rituals as enacted narratives, and involving more or less purposive and reflective human agency. The 'like' drama view can be seen as supplementing rather than supplanting this perspective in its deployment of the *metaphor* of managing change as being like professional theatre (Czarniawska, 1997: 15–16). As outlined in Table 13.3, the metaphorical view provides a set of creative resources for illuminating the key areas of managing change. The list illustrated in the table and further commented upon below should not be understood in restrictive terms as

Table 13.3 Dramaturgical approaches to managing change

	Metonym (As Drama)	*Metaphor (Like Drama)*
Change Agency	Acting Mindfully	Improvising Theatre
Change Roles	Mobilizing Power	Producing Dramas
Planning Change	Preparing Rituals	Writing Scripts
Leading Change	Handling Interaction	Staging Presentations
Learning Change	Guiding Reflection	Rehearsing & Reviewing

'the only' metaphors for addressing areas of change management but, rather, as illustrations of the type of metaphor that has been and can be usefully deployed within the field of organizational studies.

In planning change, the 'as' drama view focuses on change as a ritual performance, the success of which depends to a significant degree on how well it is prepared as a 'transition ritual'. The 'like' drama view may use a variety of professional theatre metaphors as a useful heuristic to aid understanding and action in this area. It may, for example, view the planning of change or the preparation of rituals as the writing of scripts, exploring the role of the writer in a dramatic production, how writing draws on established narratives and literary/ dramatic devices, how scripts are written as instructions to actors, how such scripts are interpreted and refined as the writer interacts with actors, directors, producers and so on. Similarly, the handling of situated interaction in leading change may be viewed as like a staged presentation, involving dramatic costumes, props and techniques, backstage and frontstage activities, establishing credibility in the performance, and managing overall interactions between actors and audience 'on the night'. Ongoing learning about managing change initiatives can be viewed as guided reflection through theatre-like activities pre-performance ('rehearsal'), during performance ('response') and post-performance ('reviews') (Mangham, 1978, 1990; Mangham and Overington, 1987).

Acting mindfully and mobilizing power in undertaking these activities can, in turn, be viewed through such professional theatre metaphors as 'improvisational theatre' (Kanter, 2002; Vera and Crossan, 2004) and 'dramatic production'. Like improvisational theatre, actors are required to creatively respond to, interpret and develop upon general themes, think on their feet, involve audiences, have a tolerance for suspense, and involve quick reactions to responses to successive 'experimental' enactments (Kanter, 2002). Improvisational theatre's embodiment of a practice that cares passionately about the recognition of multiple perspectives (in a 'yes-anding' mode), the importance of active listening, and the ability to embrace different interpretations of ongoing situations has also been observed as key factors in leadership development (Antonacopoulou and Bento, 2003).

As with dramatic productions, the successful establishment and finalization of staged performances is also the result of complex and effective interactions between producers, directors, actors and scriptwriters in the context of funding providers, theatrical agents, distribution channels, and the press (Mangham, 1978).

Conclusion

The purpose of this chapter has been to introduce a dramaturgical approach to managing change. This is provided as one example of how to enhance interest in and understanding of its phronetic nature, and encourage and support professional reflection on 'wisdom in the doing'. In addressing this task, each section of the chapter was intended to be suggestive and introductory rather than definitive in nature. The managing-change literature was overviewed as a potential source of phronetic 'heuristics'. Managing change-in-practice was presented as a key set of assumptions underlying processual and situational understandings of the challenge of a phronetic approach to changing. The dramaturgical perspective on managing change, including both change-*as*-drama and change-*like*-drama variants, was introduced as a valuable culturally resonant, intellectually coherent, and phronetically focused approach to enhancing understanding and reflection. The chapter will have succeeded in its task if these suggestive outlines are taken as a useful stimulant, a set of prompts and cues for further research and pedagogic development on the phronetic nature of managing and organizing changing processes.

> When I say artist I don't mean in the narrow sense of the word—but the man who is building things—creating molding the earth—whether it be the plains of the west—or the iron ore of Penn. It's all a big game of construction—some with a brush—some with a shovel—some choose a pen.
>
> (Jackson Pollock)

Notes

1 C.f.:

> Lewin's model was a simple one, with organizational change involving three stages; unfreezing, changing, and refreezing ... This quaintly linear and static conception – the organization as ice cube – is so wildly inappropriate that it is difficult to see why it has not only survived but prospered, except for one thing. It offers managers a very straightforward way of planning their actions, by simplifying an extraordinarily complex process into a child's formula.
>
> (Kanter et al., 1992, p. 10)

2 Established overviews of the dramaturgical approach (Edgley, 2003; Harre and Secord, 1973, Hare and Blumberg, 1988), and its implications for organizational studies (Carlson, 1996; Hopfl, 2006; Mangham and Overington, 1987; Bolman and Deal, 1997), document its established philosophical and sociological heritage, with key figures such as Edmund Burke, Erving Goffman, Rom Harre, Ralph Turner and Richard Schechner building on the earlier pragmatic and interactionist work of Cooley, James, Dewey and Mead, and linked to the symbolic interactionist work of authors such as Blumer and Strauss. More contemporary work on post-structural philosophical and cultural studies, performativity, narrative views of self, identity and organizations and positioning theory continue this tradition (Denzin, 1992). As established overviews of this perspective emphasize (Harre and Secord, 1973, Edgley, 2003; Mangham and Overington, 1987) the dramaturgical approach embodies a recognition of *homo performans* (Turner, 1985, p. 187) as an expressive and reflective being. This goes beyond the ability to conduct performances, understand the characters that we adopt and the parts that we play, and the monitoring of these performances. It includes and expands a 'meta-theatre' consciousness (Mangham, 1978: 28). It is built on an awareness of and support for the ability of human beings to reflectively monitor the monitoring of their performances (Harre and Secord, 1973). It recognizes the nature and

significance of the creative 'liminal' gaps that are opened up in the often taken-for-granted routines of social life in which individuals anxiously yet creatively stand back and reflect on their habitual conduct (Turner, 1982; Turner, 1985).

3 The origins of this analysis of situated action can be traced back to Aristotle's 'four causes' and medieval rhetoricians' 'hexameter' for characterizing events. It is popularly presented in the journalist's catechism of summarizing the Who, What, When, Where, Why and How of any story in the first paragraph of an article.

4 In a sense, this view of social life as drama stems from the traditional meaning of the Greek word drama meaning 'action' (Classical Greek: δρᾶμα, drama), which is derived from 'to do' (Classical Greek: δράω, drao). This has been continued in our use of the same terms 'acting' and 'acting', 'performance' and 'performance', to refer to both pro-active purposeful behaviour and fictional pretence, effective behaviour with real outcomes and a staged illusion. At root, both routine 'real' social life and specialized 'fictional' art and theatre share the same origins in *artifice*, the intertwining of intellect and emotion in the construction of meaning and purpose, the attribution of identifiable plots and continued suspense in the face of inherent unpredictability.

5 There is ongoing debate surrounding whether the view of social life as drama is itself metaphor, and hence this absolute division breaks down (see Brock et al., 1985; Cornelissen, 2004). Whatever interpretation one accepts, however, a carefully worded distinction between 'as' and 'like' is feasible, if these are (a) seen as complementary and intertwined, and (b) latter is seen as using the particular metaphor of professional stage theatre, particularly of the kind prominent in the West, to extend our understanding and exploration of social life *as* drama.

6 The first indications were In *The Praise of Folly*, and then Shakespeare Act 2 Scene 7 of *As You Like It* within Western culture. Much of the traditional 'like theatre' dramaturgical imagery have come from this tradition (Harre). However, the limitations of Aristotelean theatre as a restrictive metaphor has been challenged by advocates of more radical theatre (Brecht, Boal) and broader non-Western ideas of narrative and theatre that go beyond the circumscribed plots and clear characters embodied in the Western genre (Gabriel, personal communication).

References

Abrahamson, M., 2004, *Change without Pain: How Managers Can Overcome Initiative Overload*, Boston: Harvard Business Press.

Antonacopoulou, E.P., 2007, 'Practise', in S. Clegg, and J. Bailey (eds) *International Encyclopaedia of Organization Studies*, London: SAGE.

Antonacopoulou, E.P., 2008, 'On the Practise of Practice: In-tensions and Ex-tensions in the Ongoing Reconfiguration of Practice', in D. Barry and H. Hansen (eds) *Handbook of New Approaches to Organization Studies*, 112–34. London: SAGE.

Antonacopoulou, E.P., 2010a, 'Making the Business School More "Critical": Reflexive Critique based on Phronesis as a Foundation for Impact', *British Journal of Management* Special Issue 'Making the Business School More "Critical" ', co-edited by Professors Graeme Currie, David Knights and Ken Starkey, 21, 6–25.

Antonacopoulou, E.P., 2010b, 'Beyond Co-production: Practice-Relevant Scholarship as a Foundation for Delivering Impact Through Powerful Ideas', *Public Money and Management*, Special Issue – the Politics of Co-production Research, 30(4).

Antonacopoulou, E.P. and Bento R., 2003, 'Methods of "Learning Leadership": Taught and Experiential', in J. Storey (ed.) *Current Issues in Leadership and Management Development*, 81–102, Oxford: Blackwell.

Argyris, C., 1990, *Overcoming Organizational Defenses: Facilitating Organizational Learning*, New York: Prentice Hall.

Argyris, C. and Schon, D.A., 1974, *Theory in Practice*, San Francisco, CA: Jossey Bass.

Ariely, D., 2008, *Predictably Irrational: The Hidden Forces that Shape our Destiny*, New York: HarperCollins.

Badham, R., 1986, *Theories of Industrial Society*, London: Croom Helm.

Badham, R., 2006a, 'Mudanças Not Removalists: Rethinking the Management of Organizational Change', *Human Factors and Ergonomics in Manufacturing*, 16, 3, 229–45.

Badham, R., 2006b, 'Mind(ing) the Gap: The Irony of Practice and the Practice of Irony', *2nd Organisation Studies Summer Workshop*, Mykonos, Greece.

Badham, R. and Meade, A., 2009, 'The Translation Performance: An Ethnography of "Success" in Critical Executive Education on Managing Change', *EGOS 2009 Sub-Theme 29 'Idea Work: creating and becoming in everyday organizational practice'*, Copenhagen, July.

Bauman, Z., 2000, *Liquid Modernity*, Cambridge: Polity.

Beer, S. and Nohria, N. (eds), 2000, *Breaking the Code of Change: Resolving the Tension between Theory E and O of Change*, Boston: Harvard Business Press.

Bell, D., 1996, *The Cultural Contradictions of Capitalism*, New York: Basic Books.

Boal, A., 1979, *Theatre of the Oppressed* (2nd edn), London: Pluto Press.

Bolman, L.G. and Deal, T.E., 1997, *Reframing Organizations: Artistry, Choice and Leadership*, San Francisco, CA: Jossey Bass.

Brecht, B. and J. Willett, 2001 [1964], *Brecht on Theatre: the Development of an Aesthetic*, New York: Hill and Wang.

Brisset, D. and Edgley, C. (eds), 1990, *Life as Theatre: A Dramaturgical Sourcebook*, Hawthorne, NY: De Gruyter.

Brock, B., Burke, K., Burgess, P. and Simons, H., 1985, 'Dramatism as Ontology or Epistemology: A Symposium', *Communication Quarterly*, 33, 1, Winter, 17–33.

Brown, A., 1998, *Organizational Culture*, London: Financial Times.

Brown, J.S. and Duguid P., 2000, *The Social Life of Information*, Boston: Harvard Business School Press.

Brown, S.L. and Eisenhardt, K.M., 1998, *Competing on the Edge: Strategy as Structured Chaos*, Boston: Harvard Business Press.

Buchanan, D. and Badham, R., 2008, *Power, Politics and Organizational Change: Winning the Turf Game*, London: SAGE.

Buchanan, D. and Boddy, D., 1992, *The Expertise of the Change Agent: Public Performance and Backstage Activity*, New York: Prentice Hall.

Burke, J.L., 2005, *Heaven's Prisoners*, New York: Phoenix.

Burnes, B., 2000, *Managing Change*, 3rd edn. Harlow: FT/Pearson Educational.

Burnes, B., 2004, 'Kurt Lewin and the Planned Approach to Change: A Re-appraisal', *Journal of Management Studies*, 41, 6, September, 977–1002.

Carlson, R.V., 1996, *Reframing and Reform: Perspectives on Organization, Leadership and Social Change*, London: Longman.

Clark, T. and Fincham, R. (eds.), 2001, *Critical Consulting: New Perspectives on the Management Advice Industry*, London: Wiley/Blackwell.

Clemmer, J., 1996, ' "Change Management" is an Oxymoron', *Cost & Management*, 70, 6.

Coch, L and French, J.R.P., Jr., 1948, 'Overcoming Resistance to Change', *Human Relations*, 1, 4, 512–32.

Collins, D., 1998, *Organizational Change*. London: Routledge.

Collins, D., 2004, 'Re-imagining Change' [Special Issue], *Tamara*, 2, 4, iv–xi.

Collins, R., 2004, *Interaction Ritual Chains*, Princeton, NJ, Princeton University Press.

Cooke, B., 1999, 'Writing the Left out of Management Theory: The Historiography of the Management of Change', *Organization*, 6, 1, 81–105.

Cooper, R. and Law, J., 1995, 'Organisation: Distal and Proximal Views', in S. Bachrach (ed.) *Research in the Sociology of Organisations*, Greenwich, CN: JAI Press.

Cooperrider, D.L. and Srivastva, S., 1987, 'Appreciative Inquiry in Organizational Life', *Research in Organizational Change and Development*, 1, 129–69.

Cornelissen, J.P., 2004, 'What Are We Playing at? Theatre, Organization, and the Use of Metaphor', *Organization Studies*, 25, 5, 705–22.

Czarniawska, B., 1997, *Narrating the Organization: Dramas of Institutional Identity*, Chicago and London: University of Chicago Press.

Czarniawska-Joerges, B. and Sevon, G., 1996, *Translating Organizational Change*, Berlin: De Gruyter.

Dawson, P. (1994) *Organizational Change: A Processual Approach*, London: Paul Chapman.

Denzin, N.K., 1992, *Symbolic Interactionism and Cultural Studies: The Politics of Interpretation*, Oxford: Blackwell.

Dopson, S., 1997, *Managing Ambiguity and Change: the Case of the NHS*, London: Macmillan.

Dougherty D., 2004, 'Organizing Practices in Services: Capturing Practice Based Knowledge for Innovation', *Strategic Organization*, 2, 1, 35–64.

Dourish, P., 2001, *Where the Action is: The Foundations of Embodied Interaction*, Cambridge: MIT Press.

du Gay, P., 2003, 'The Tyranny of the Epochal: Change, Epochalism and Organizational Reform', *Organization*, 10, 663–84.

Dunphy, D.D. and Stace, D.A., 1992, *Under New Management*, Sydney: McGraw-Hill.

Edgley, C., 2003, 'The Dramaturgical Genre', in L.T. Regynolds and N.J. Herman-Skinney (eds) *Handbook of Symbolic Interactionism*, New York: Rowman & Littlefield.

Eikeland, O., 2007, *The Ways of Aristotle – Aristotelian Phronesis, Aristotelian Philosophy of Dialogue and Action Research*, Bern: Peter Lang.

Emirbayer, M., 1997, 'Manifesto for a Relational Sociology', *American Journal of Sociology*, 103, 2, 281–317.

Feldman, M.S. and Pentland, B.T., 2003, 'Reconceptualising Organizational Routines as a source of Flexibility and Change', *Administrative Science Quarterly*, 48, 1, 94–118.

Flyvbjerg, B., 2001, *Making Social Science Matter*, Cambridge: Cambridge University Press.

French, W., Bell, C. and Zawacki, R., 2004, *Organization Development and Transformation: Managing Effective Change*, New York: McGraw Hill.

Gabriel, Y., Fineman, S. and Sims, D., 2000, *Organizing and Organizations*, London: SAGE.

Gadamer, H.-G., 1980, 'Practical Philosophy as a Model for the Human Sciences', *Research in Phenomenology*, 9, 74–85.

Geertz, C., 1983, *The Interpretation of Cultures: Selected Essays*, New York: Basic Books.

Gherardi, S. and Nicolini, D., 2002, Learning in a Constellation of Interconnected Practices: Canon or Dissonance? *Journal of Management Studies*, 39, 4, 419–36.

Goffman, E., 1961, *Encounters: Two Studies in the Sociology of Interaction*, Indianapolis, IN: Bobbs-Merrill.

Goffman, E., 1974, *Frame Analysis: An Essay on the Organization of Experience*, New York: Harper & Row.

Goffman, E., 1990, *The Presentation of Self in Everyday Life*, Harmondsworth: Penguin.

Grint, K., 2001, *The Arts of Leadership*, Oxford: Oxford University Press.

Hare, A.P. and Blumberg, H.H., 1988, *Dramaturgical Analysis of Social Interaction*, New York: Praeger.

Harre, H. and Secord, P.F., 1973, *The Explanation of Social Behaviour*, Totowa, NJ: Littlefield Adams.

Hopfl, H., 2007, 'Dramaturgy', in J.R. Bailey and S. Clegg (eds) *International Encyclopaedia of Organizational Studies*, London: SAGE.

Jarzabkowski, P., 2005, *Strategy as Practice: An Activity Perspective*, London: SAGE.

Johnson, G., Melin, L. and Whittington, R., 2003, Micro-Strategy and Strategising, *Journal of Management Studies*, Special Issue, 40, 3–20.

Kahneman, D., 2003, 'A Perspective on Judgment and Choice: Mapping Bounded Rationality', *American Psychologist*, 58, 9, 697–720.

Kanter, R.M., 1983, *The Change Masters*, London: Routledge.

Kanter, R.M., 2002, 'Strategy as Improvisational Theatre', *Sloan Management Review*, Winter, 76–81.

Kanter, R.M., Stein, B.A. and Jick, T.D., 1992, *The Challenge of Organizational Change*, New York: The Free Press.

Kotter, J., 1996, *Leading Change*, Boston: Harvard Business School Press.

Kunda, G., 1992, *Engineering Culture: Control and Commitment in a High Tech Corporation*, Philadelphia, PA: Temple University Press.

Latour, B., 1988, 'How to Write the Prince for Machines as well as for Machinations', in E. Brian (ed.) *Technology and Social Change*, Edinburgh: Edinburgh University Press, pp. 20–43.

Latour, B., 1993, *We Have Never Been Modern*, Cambridge, MA: Harvard University Press.

Lewin, K., 1943, 'Defining the "Field at a Given Time" ', *Psychological Review*, 50, 292–310.

Lewin, K., 1964, *Field Theory in Social Science: Selected Theoretical Papers*, New York: Harper & Row.

Lewis, M.W. and Keleman, M.L., 2002, 'Multiparadigm Inquiry: Exploring Organizational Pluralism and Paradox', *Human Relations*, 55, 2, 251–75.

MacIntyre, A., 1984, *After Virtue: A Study in Moral Theory* (2nd edn), Notre Dame, IN: University of Notre Dame Press.

Mangham, I., 1978, *Interactions and Interventions in Organizations*, Chichester: John Wiley.

Mangham, I., 1990, 'Managing as a Performing Art', *British Journal of Management*, 1, 105–15.

Mangham, I. and Overington, M., 1987, *Organizations as Theatre: A Social Psychology of Appearances*. Chichester: John Wiley.

March, J.G., 2006, 'Rationality, Foolishness, and Adaptive Intelligence', *Strategic Management Journal*, 27, 201–14.

March, J.G., and Olsen, J.P., 1983, 'Organizing Political Life: What Administrative Reorganization Tells Us about Government', *American Political Science Review*, 77, 2, 281–96.

Marsh, B., 2002, 'Heuristics as Social Tools', *New Ideas in Psychology*, 20, 1, 49–57.

Martin, J., 2002, *Organizational Culture: Mapping the Terrain*, Thousand Oaks, CA: SAGE.

McFarland, D.A., 2004, 'Resistance as a Social Drama: A Study of Change Oriented Encounters', *American Journal of Sociology*, 109, 6, May, 1249–1318.

McLoughlin, I., Badham, R. and Palmer, G., 2005, 'Cultures of Ambiguity: Design, Emergence and Ambivalence in the Introduction of Normative Control', *Work, Employment and Society*, 19, 67–90.

Mintzberg, H., 2004, *Managers Not MBAs: A Hard Look at the Soft Practice of Managing and Management Development*, San Francisco, CA: Berrett-Koehlerm.

Mirvis, P.H., 2005, 'Large Group Interventions: Change as Theatre', *Journal of Applied Behavioral Science*, 41, 122–38.

Morgan, G. and Sturdy, A., 2000, *Beyond Organizational Change: Structure, Discourse and Power*, London: Macmillan.

Moustakas, C. and Douglass, B.G., 1985, 'Heuristic Inquiry: The Internal Search to Know', *Journal of Humanistic Psychology*, 25, 3, 39–55.

Nicolini, D., Gherardi, S. and Yanow, D. (eds), 2003, *Knowing in Organizations: A Practice-Based Approach*, Armonk, NY: M. E. Sharpe.

Orlikowski, W.J., 1996, 'Improvising Organizational Transformation Over Time: A Situated Change Perspective', *Information Systems Research*, 7, 1, 63–92.

Orlikowski, W.J. and Gash, D.J., 1994, 'Technological Frames: Making Sense of Information Technology in Organisations', *ACM Transactions on Information Systems*, 12, 2, 174–207.

Orlikowski W., 2000, 'Using Technology and Constituting Structures: a Practice Lens for Studying Technology in Organizations', *Organization Science*, 12, 4, 404–28.

Overington, M., 1977, 'Kenneth Burke and the Method of Dramatism', *Theory and Society*, 4, 131–56.

Palmer, I. and Dunford, R., 2005, *Managing Organizational Change*, New York: McGraw Hill.

Pettigrew, A., 1985, *The Awakening Giant: Continuity and Change in ICI*, Oxford: Blackwell.

Pettigrew, A., 1997, 'What is a Processual analysis?', *Scandinavian Journal of Management*, 13, 337–48.

Pickering, A., 1995, *The Mangle of Practice: Time, Agency and Science*, Chicago and London: University of Chicago Press.

Pfeffer, J., 1994, *Managing with Power*, Boston: Harvard Business School Press.

Poole, M.S., Van de Ven, A., Dooley, K. and Holmes, M., 2000, *Organizational Change and Innovation Processes: Theory and Methods for Research*, New York: Oxford University Press.

Reed, M. and Hughes, M., 1992, *Rethinking Organizational Theory: New Directions in Organizational Theory and Analysis*, London: SAGE.

Ryle, G., 2000, *The Concept of Mind*, Harmondsworth: Penguin Books.

Schatzki T.R., Knorr-Cetina K. and von Savigny, E., 2001, *The Practice Turn in Contemporary Theory*, London: Routledge.

Schein, E., 1951, *Coercive Persuasion: A Socio-psychological Analysis of the 'Brainwashing' of American Civilian Prisoners by the Chinese Communists*, New York: W. W. Norton.

Schein, E., 1980, *Organisational Psychology*, 3rd edn, New York: Prentice Hall.

Schein, E.H., 1988, *Process Consultation: Its Role in Organization Development*, New York: Prentice Hall.

Schön, D.A., 1983, *The Reflective Practitioner: How Professionals Think in Action*, New York: Basic Books.

Schön, D.A., 1987, *Educating the Reflective Practitioner: Toward a New Design for Teaching and Learning in the Professions* (1st edn), San Francisco, CA: Jossey-Bass.

Schreyagg, G. and Hapfl, H., 2004, 'Theatre and Organization: Editorial Introduction', *Organization Studies*, 25, 5, 691–704.

Seo, M.-G. and Creed, W.E.D., 2002, 'Institutional Contradictions, Praxis and Institutional Change: A Dialectical Perspective', *Academy of Management Review*, 27, 2, 222–247.

Shakespeare, W., 2007, *As You Like It*, New York: Classic Books.

Simon, H.A., 1957, *Models of Man: Social and Rational; Mathematical Essays on Rational Human Behavior in a Social Setting*, New York: Wiley.

Stacey, R., 2007, *Strategic Management and Organisational Dynamics: The Challenge of Complexity*, 5th edn, New York: Prentice Hall.

Strauss, A., 1978, *Negotiations: Varieties, Processes, Contexts, and Social Order*, San Francisco, CA: Jossey-Bass.

Sturdy, A. and Grey, C., 2003, 'Beneath and Beyond Organizational Change Management: Exploring Alternatives [Special Issue]', *Organization*, 10, 651–63.

Sturdy, A. and Morgan, G., 2003, 'From Transformation to Financialisation? Towards a Discursive Approach to Organisational Change and a Structural Approach to Discourse', unpublished manuscript.

Sturdy, A. and Morgan, G., 2000, *Beyond Organizational Change: Structure, Discourse and Power in UK Financial Services*, London: Palgrave Macmillan.

Sztompka, P., 1999, *The Sociology of Social Change*, Oxford: Blackwell.

Taylor, C., 1993, 'To Follow a Rule', in C. Calhoun, E. LiPuma and M. Postpone (eds) *Bordieu: Critical Perspectives*, Cambridge: Polity.

Taylor, C., 1995, *Philosophical Arguments*, Boston: Harvard University Press.

Thomas, W.I., 1923, *The Unadjusted Girl*, Boston: Little, Brown, & Co.

Tsoukas, H., 2005, *Complex Knowledge: Studies in Organizational Epistemology*, New York: Oxford University Press.

Tsoukas, H., 2009, 'A Dialogical Approach to the Creation of New Knowledge in Organizations', *Organization Science*, 20, 6, November – December, 941–957.

Tsoukas, H. and Chia, R., 2002, 'Organizational Becoming: Rethinking Organizational Change', *Organization Science*, 13, 5, 567–82.

Turner, E. (ed.), 1985, *On the Edge of the Bush: Anthropology as Experience*, Tucson, AZ: University of Arizona Press.

Turner, V., 1982, *From Ritual to Theater*. New York: PAJ Publications.

Van Maanen, J., 1995, 'Style as Theory', *Organization Science*, 6, 1, Jan – Feb, 133–43.

Vera, D. and Crossan, M., 2004, 'Theatrical improvisation: Lessons for organizations', *Organization Studies*, 25/5, 727–49.

Weber, M., 1997, *The Theory of Social and Economic Organization*, New York: Free Press.

Weick, K., 2001, *Making Sense of the Organization*, Oxford: Blackwell.

Weick, K. and Quinn, R., 1999, 'Organizational Development and Change', *Annual Review of Psychology*, 50, 361–86.

Weick, K.E. and Sutcliffe, K., 2001, *Managing the Unexpected: Assuring High Performance in an Age of Complexity*, San Francisco, CA: Jossey-Bass.

Whittle, A., 2006, 'The Paradoxical Repertoires of Management Consulting', *Journal of Organizational Change Management*, 19, 4, 424–36.

Willmott, H., 1993, 'Breaking the Paradigm Mentality', *Organization Studies*, 14, 5, 681–719.

Zander, R.S. and Zander, B., 2000, *The Art of Possibility: Transforming Professional and Personal Life*, Boston: Harvard Business School.

Zorn, T.E., 2005, 'Book Review: Critiquing the Dominant Discourse on Change', *Organization*, 12, 947.

14

Designing for change with critical scenario method

George Cairns

Introduction

Change can originate in a number of ways to impact upon organizations. It can be initiated from within the organization or be generated from outside. It may be planned and designed such that it can, in theory, be managed, or it may arise from unexpected sources and have unpredictable and, in the worst case, terminal impacts upon the organization. However, contemporary business enterprises are also major players in how this world operates – or is seen by many as failing to operate effectively for the majority. Major change that impacts on the organization's ability to address its strategic aims and objectives or to fulfil its plans and operate effectively can also affect a wide range of stakeholders – both those with direct links to the organization and those whose relationship is tangential and remote. As such, business must take a leading role in determining the change priorities and direction for the future of all of society, not just for those with an immediate interest.

Whilst managers may spend vast amounts of time undertaking analysis and strategic planning in order to design and implement intentional change, the greatest danger to survival and operational effectiveness is likely to come from unforeseen, imposed change driven by forces outside the organization. In this chapter, I outline one approach to undertaking structured analysis of those external 'driving forces' – social, technological, economic, ecological, political and legal (STEEPL) factors – that might impact the organization and give rise to 'critical uncertainties' in the foreseeable future. The approach is based upon application of scenario method (cf. van der Heijden et al. 2002). Scenario method presents a framework for identifying the full range of driving forces, understanding their interaction with one another and considering the range of different outcomes that might feasibly arise through different sets of mediating events and actions. Scenario method, in the form used here, enables consideration of evidence-based, factual and quantifiable inputs alongside opinion-based, perceptual and qualitative ones. In accommodating consideration of all relevant inputs, scenario method allows us to engage with and explore complex and ambiguous issues, or 'wicked problems': ones that interweave social, ecological and economic factors, to which there is no obvious 'right' or 'wrong' answer and that cannot be understood in terms of binary notions of 'good'/'bad', 'rational'/'irrational', or 'valuable'/ 'worthless'.

In presenting an externalized, scenario-based perspective on change, I specifically advocate an approach to organization analysis that is concerned with exploring the change process as a journey towards the best possible outcome for the broadest range of affected stakeholders, not just for the organization and those directly involved. As such, I present organization change as paying attention to matters of ethics and morality, and as a response to moral dilemmas facing contemporary managers: whether to give primacy to profit or people, current pressures or future prospects, the desires of the powerful or the needs of the deprived, wealth accumulation or social regeneration. Whilst these need not all be mutually exclusive choices, consideration of the full range of options in response to them does require consideration of often conflicting demands and priorities and the making of difficult choices.

In acknowledging that the scenario approach is not value-free and engages with issues of opinion and belief, I offer it as a means of opening up organizational thinking to consideration of issues of critical concern to contemporary society; issues that may not be seen as of particular relevance to business within a narrow, value-neutral economic rationality. In the form of 'critical scenario method' (CSM) (Wright and Cairns 2011) outlined here, I present it as an approach that is specifically concerned with issues of power – in relation to matters of inclusion and exclusion and to outcomes of both action and non-action by powerful stakeholders. That said, I urge you not to read this text as a moralizing treatise on what is 'good' or 'bad', but as challenging you to question the notion of what is seen as 'good' for the organization within the economic rationality, and your own framework for analysing and engaging with organization change situations.

Whilst generation of the full range of scenarios is dependent upon consideration of all possible and plausible outcomes from human power plays and naturally occurring events, I suggest here that decision making on the desirability of various change options and strategies should be guided by consideration of the Aristotelian concept of *phronēsis*, or practical wisdom. A phronetic approach to organisation inquiry is one that is concerned with informing 'acts that are just and admirable and good for man [sic]' (Aristotle 2004: 162). The specific framework adopted for application of the principles of *phronēsis* in contemporary organization analysis is that propounded by Bent Flyvbjerg (2001), in particular his set of four value-rational questions that expose organization actions and decision making to critical reflection on issues of power, affect and desirability, and to consideration of alternatives that will be 'good for humanity'. The phronetic approach is one that is likely to challenge predominant forms of 'business-as-usual' thinking in many organizations, and to confront managers and decision makers with the prospect that bounded forms of taken-for-granted wisdom learned from MBA programs and managerial texts are not sufficient if we are to develop new forms of sustainable business in response to critical issues such as peak oil, climate change, social exclusion and unrest, water shortage, pandemic, and shifts in the loci of political and economic power.

From economic man to concerned stakeholder

As outlined above, my starting point in determining the need for, and the drivers of organization change is grounded in an outside-in view, that of the business as one constituent element within a complex social, ecological and economic environment. My approach to analysing organization change involves initial exploration and understanding of the broadest range of external factors that might, on the one hand, enforce this change or, on the other, imply a good reason for undertaking it. In holding forth organization change as a moral/ethical project, it is essential that we start with some philosophical and theoretical basis for determining what might be considered a 'good reason' for implementing a change programme. This must be set in the broad socio-political, ecological and economic context of organization activity and impact, rather than within the narrow confines of profit maximization and increasing shareholder value. The latter has been the focus of notions of 'good' organizational performance in recent decades, driven by economic rationalities and underpinned by reference to the works of free-market economists such as Milton Friedman. Friedman is frequently quoted in support of the profit motive, with his statement:

> [t]here is one and only one social responsibility of business – to use its resources and engage in activities designed to increase its profits so long as it stays within the rules of the game, which is to say, engages in open and free competition, without deception or fraud ... for corporate officials to make as much money for their stockholders as possible.
>
> (Friedman 1962: 133)[1]

Whilst the economic view of the organization assumes a position of it being value-neutral in relation to non-financially engaged actors, I see business as being firmly embedded in broader societal and ecological contexts, and within an economic context that is (or should be) integrally linked with these. Rather than focussing on *shareholders* and customers – defined by econometric theories of the 'rational man', driven by self-interest and a desire for asset accumulation – I align with those who propose the need for a consideration of an organization's *stakeholders*; where this term is read in the broad sense as implying '(a)ny identifiable group or individual who can affect the achievement of an organization's objectives or *who is affected by* the achievement of an organization's objectives' (Freeman and Reed, 1983: 91) (emphasis added). However, I also see the organization/stakeholder relationship as being one of mutual reciprocity, whereby the organization's 'objectives' are redefined to align as best they can with those of its stakeholders. Here, stakeholders are seen 'as individuals, human beings...moral beings' (Freeman 1994: 411) with individual values, beliefs and needs to be addressed, rather than as mere resources to be exploited. I see such a broad-ranging concern for stakeholders by business as being essential in a contemporary global context in which many governments have delegated (or abrogated) responsibility for designing and delivering responses to societal needs in areas of education, health and security. In many cases, these have been passed over to organizations that are guided by the profit motive and Friedman's free-market economic rationality, rather than by an overarching concern for public good. Western governments have engaged in such change in the name of increased efficiency and effectiveness and reducing public-sector spending. In many so-called 'developing' countries, this has been forced upon governments as part of the 'structural adjustment' agenda of bodies like the World Bank and the World Trade Organization (WTO) in order for these countries to gain institutional membership and access to loan funding.

Searching for new change agendas

The first step in approaching change here is not to seek to identify problems that already exist, let alone engage in formulating solutions to them and designing related change programs. Rather it is to engage in free-ranging thinking on the widest range of issues that might be of some significance and relevance to the organization in the future. Thereafter, we ponder why and how it might be reasonable to change in response to them, from the viewpoints and in the interests of the broadest range of stakeholders. Accepting that the future is not preordained, that the interests of all stakeholders do not align and that the future that unfolds will, in part, be determined by the way in which the different issues interact and in which this interaction is mediated by the power play between stakeholders, we must consider a range of different 'scenarios' for the future.

If we are to redress the economic and power imbalances that have resulted from business being viewed as value-neutral in relation to non-financial stakeholders whilst, as outlined above, being charged with meeting their non-financial needs, then we need to develop a change agenda that is concerned primarily with matters of longer-term social, environmental and economic sustainability, rather than short-term return on investment. Whilst it may appear naïve and idealistic to suggest that businesses can redefine their objectives to address the interests of all, or even the majority of their stakeholders, it is just such an approach that I advocate and outline here as a 'way of being' for the organizational decision maker. The strategies of many non-governmental organizations (NGOs) and not-for-profits, as well as the work of many profit-seeking social entrepreneurs[2] are underpinned by the broad stakeholder approach. I would argue that this must become the mainstream paradigm for management thinking on future change if we are to bring about required, radical re-conceptualization of our position as assessed using these longer-term criteria of sustainability.

The process I advocate starts through opening up enquiry to identify the widest possible range of 'driving forces' (van der Heijden et al. 2002) the most diverse set of possible and plausible outcomes from these in the foreseeable future, and the realization of different possible future 'scenarios' in which the organization and its stakeholders may find themselves. Whilst scenario thinking is an approach to problem analysis that can – and I would say should – be adopted by the individual, it is most appropriately applied in a group situation in order to promote cross-disciplinary and cross-functional sense-making in relation to the range and impacts of external driving forces. A process that promotes creative and challenging thinking, takes individuals outside their normal spheres of thought and action, and seeks input based upon wide experience across multiple contexts is unlikely to be within the capacity of one individual, no matter how knowledgeable and how skilful. In addition, experience with diverse groups (e.g. Cairns et al. 2004) indicates that it is a process that benefits from application of a fairly structured approach and is reliant upon careful guidance and facilitation in order to nurture divergent thinking and challenge, whilst maintaining direction and managing conflict. This is most appropriately undertaken by neutral outsiders rather than involved actors.

Whilst application of scenario method is directed at analysis and sense-making in relation to the nature of the external driving forces and the range of their possible and plausible impacts, the developed scenario stories are not, individually, predictions of any particular future. Rather, together they provide a means of better understanding the complexity and uncertainty of the present. They also provide a vehicle for testing the robustness of existing strategies and a foundation for planning and developing new strategies that can inform organization change whilst being flexible and adaptable to a broad range of future conditions.

Scenario thinking and stakeholder engagement

Much of the scenario literature is concerned with how the approach can be used by organizations to enhance their operational effectiveness. The scenario approach applied here (van der Heijden et al. 2002; Wright and Cairns 2011) has been subject to critical discussion in the academic literature, establishing its methodological foundations (cf. Bradfield et al. 2005; Wright et al. 2009) in the application of 'disciplined intuition' (Jungermann and Thuring 1987) in order to investigate a broad range of possible and plausible futures for the organization. However, in its original form, the adopted scenario approach does not overtly require consideration of these futures in relation to the range of stakeholders, and it presents stakeholder analysis as an optional addition to the 'mix' of ingredients; as 'a tool to be used in parallel with the scenario process, as and when members of the scenario team find it useful' (van der Heijden et al. 2002: 219). Cairns et al. (2010) develop and expand scenario method, with specific reference to the field of international business (IB) education, seeking to prompt radical change in how students – and potential future managers and decision makers – think more broadly and critically about the impact that organizations have on society and environment. They do so by embedding stakeholder analysis as an element of scenario method.

As outlined above, the starting point for consideration of stakeholders can be set in the broad realm of parties who can either affect or be affected by the organization's activities, or within the narrow realm of only those with direct involvement in these. However, even within the broad view of stakeholder engagement, Jones and Fleming (2003) identify a tendency towards instrumentality, whereby the aim of the engagement becomes that of 'stakeholder management', and how to minimize risk to the organization from unanticipated and undesirable stakeholder activities, rather than to open up consideration of what may be the undesirable nature of the organization's activities in relation to its impact on these stakeholders. They posit that, whilst 'mainstream' stakeholder theory presents a challenge to narrow neoliberal firm theories, it promotes a normative model of 'win–win' for organisation, employees and other stakeholders. They say that the relative scale of the 'wins' is not considered, let alone the wider societal issues of uneven power relations and coercion that prevail. Arising from their critical discussion on the nature of power differentials inherent in structural relations between organizations and stakeholder groups, and in response to the limitations of a 'mainstream' stakeholder approach, Jones and Fleming develop a conceptual framework of 'critical stakeholder analysis' (CSA) – 'a technique that focuses on broader structural (versus transient) commonalities and differences amongst key stakeholder groups apropos resource base, class positionality, access to decision-making opportunities, power assymetries, and so forth' (2003: 431). In acknowledging that the organization's activities do not take place in a vacuum, they posit that 'a CSA analysis (sh)ould occur at the level of the field itself rather than from the perspective of a focal firm as with conventional stakeholder analysis' (2003: 435). This critical field-level analysis links to the scenario approach, whereby account is taken of those driving forces in the broad field, or business environment, and these are central to the analytic framework.

Building upon Jones and Fleming's (2003) conceptual model of 'critical stakeholder analysis' (CSA), Cairns et al. (2010) embed the CSA approach to stakeholder engagement as an integral element of scenario method, terming their approach 'critical scenario method' (CSM). CSM integrates thinking on internal issues, such as marketing, logistics, R&D, etc., with consideration of the broad socio-economic and environmental impacts of business activity, both now and in future, and with specific reference to issues of power and structure in the business/stakeholder relationship. The aim is to prompt a change of mindset in the (aspiring) business manager, from a short-term, firm-centric focus on profit maximization and shareholder value to encapsulate longer-term consideration external impacts.

In CSM, stakeholder analysis is seen as an essential ingredient. Here, the definition of 'stakeholder' that is adopted is that encapsulated in the broad view (Freeman and Reed 1983), all those parties that may both affect and be affected by the activities of the organization. In addition, incorporation of the principles of critical stakeholder analysis as a core element of the scenario process brings in consideration of issues of power and structure; in particular, the power imbalances that exist between stakeholder groups. The CSA approach is designed to prompt participants to compare 'those stakeholders who are empowered (and enriched) by the globalization process to others who are relatively – sometimes even absolutely – disempowered and pauperized by that same process' (Jones and Fleming 2003: 440). Incorporating the CSA approach into scenario method allows us to place these comparisons into a set of contexts of different 'what if?' questions and outcomes, seeing that power and empowerment are not vested by right and forever in any particular group or individuals, but are fluid and dynamic within different possible and plausible futures.

Implementing critical stakeholder analysis – the application of *phronēsis*

Whilst Jones and Fleming (2003) theorize the need for and possibilities emerging from a CSAnalytic approach, they do not set out particular methods by which it might be enacted. Cairns et al. (2010) see possibility for enactment by drawing upon Aristotelian *phronēsis* and its contemporary social science interpretation in the work of Bent Flyvbjerg (2001, 2003). Whilst Flyvbjerg develops discussion of the relevance and applicability of Aristotle's *phronēsis* in organization inquiry through construction of shared 'narratives (that) provide us a forward glance, helping us to anticipate situations even before we encounter them, allowing us to envisage alternative futures' (2001: 137), he does not refer to scenario method as a way in which this might be done. It is in both seeing CSA as a set of possibilities and potentialities for enabling future change and in response to Flyvbjerg's call for the 'forward glance' informed by the principles of *phronēsis* that Cairns et al. (2010) present critical scenario method (CSM).

In presenting his case for application of *phronēsis* in organization inquiry, Flyvbjerg draws attention to several key issues. First, he places phronetic inquiry firmly in the context of our times, where society and the issues that concern its members are much more complex and ambiguous than in Aristotle's time. Second, he highlights that this complexity makes it much more difficult to determine what is 'good', 'just' and 'admirable' for the majority of society. Third, drawing upon the work of Foucault and others, he makes us aware that determination of what counts as knowledge, and therefore being of value and being good, is governed largely by relationships of power. He opines that 'power *defines* what counts as rationality and knowledge and thereby what counts as reality' (Flyvbjerg 1998: 227, emphasis in original). Having raised awareness of critical issues of power and structure differentials between stakeholder groups, CSM then applies Flyvbjerg's (2001) question framework in order to develop a focus on the consequences of different possible courses of action for the various stakeholders. These questions are:

- Where are we going?
- Is this development desirable?
- What, if anything, should we do about it?
- Who gains and who loses, and by which mechanisms of power?

The first question is applied to promote initial thinking on the current planned or anticipated future trajectory of the issue at hand – its outcome within the 'business-as-usual' scenario. Considering this trajectory in relation to the second question and with reference to the broad range of identified stakeholders moves thinking beyond the immediate 'desirability' of firm-centric targets – such as sales generation, profit maximization and shareholder return – to encapsulate wider social and environmental effects. Having opened up thinking across this broader context, key decision makers can then contemplate the third question. It may be that the answer that is adopted is 'nothing'. However, this decision will be taken with full knowledge of the consequences of a 'no change' strategy for all affected stakeholders.

Application and implications of CSM in practice

Having outlined the CSM approach at a philosophical and theoretical level and pointed to sources on 'how to' apply it in the classroom setting (Cairns et al. 2010), I now wish to provide some examples of how thinking on change might be mediated by its implementation in practice. These provide an overview of the various stages of critical scenario method, their intended outcomes, and the key issues that must be addressed in seeking effective outcomes from them. A real-life scenario exercise should be focussed on a specific critical uncertainty for the future. In CSM, this critical uncertainty will have both organizational implications, e.g. market volatility, customer disloyalty, uncertain resources, or currency fluctuations, and societal and ecological implications; e.g. employment uncertainty, health and safety concerns, resource exploitation, or residual pollution. Here, I use a variety of illustrative examples that do not have a single field of business context. The various stages of the process are as follows.

Identifying 'driving forces' and 'higher-level factors'

The first stage of the process involves seeking to identify the broadest possible range of 'driving forces' that will impact the focal issue over the foreseeable future.[3] The use of the structured STEEPL analysis in this stage is intended to minimize the risk of bounded thinking that might arise from an unstructured approach, whereby those with backgrounds, say, in economics and finance may tend to focus on economic driving forces, whilst those with legal training may see legislative frameworks as the key drivers. If we apply the STEEPL framework and the broad stakeholder concept, we should arrive at a substantial number of driving forces. For example, if we were to consider a critical uncertainty in relation to the future market for low-cost air transportation, we might identify drivers in relation to:

- Social – consumer buying power, consumer travel choices, cost vs. environmental orientation, fear of terrorism, access to and need for air transport, response to global pandemic, etc.
- Technological – aircraft design and functionality, air-traffic control capacity, security screening, etc.
- Economic – global financial (in)stability, cost of fuel, cost of ticketing, maintenance costs, depreciation, airport taxes, carbon taxes, etc.
- Ecological – greenhouse gas emissions, materials recycling, spread of disease, etc.
- Political – open skies vs. restricted access, taxation regimes, environmental orientation of policy, acts of terrorism, political activism, etc.
- Legal – international law, health and safety, employment law, environmental legislation, etc.

These categories are not mutually exclusive but are intended, as a group, to ensure that thinking is broad and inclusive.

Having established as many driving forces as possible, the group may well have generated several hundred forces that are deemed to have an impact on the identified critical uncertainty. Since the human mind is incapable of making sense of more than a small number of concepts in relation to one another, there is a danger that participants might move to focus on those issues deemed 'most important', or 'most critical', whilst ignoring the vast majority. This is the route likely to be followed by those who, when faced with a problem, immediately frame it in terms of their own discipline field, of what they, consciously or unconsciously, deem most relevant. The scenario approach does not entertain such an early, exclusive focus. In the scenario approach, the next move is to 'cluster' driving forces into a smaller number of 'higher-level factors'. The criteria for clustering are that every driving force within the group is connected to every other by lines of causal or chronological linkage. Also, the clusters must be capable of being 'named' with a few words that embrace every driving force. In relation to the issue of low-cost air travel, we might find that higher-level factors are derived from clusters of driving forces on issues of 'levels of environmental orientation and action', 'air transport technologies and infrastructure', 'consumer confidence and fear of mishap', or even 'consumer preferences for real/virtual travel'. These are, of course, hypothetical factors and the actual choices in any exercise emerge from iterative and related processes of intuition, research, cross-disciplinary discussion, critical reflection, distillation of ideas and sense-making on them in relation to one another.

'Framing', 'scoping' and 'developing' scenario storylines

Having arrived at a smaller number of higher-level factors that will impact the issue under discussion, we move to identify two that are used to 'frame' the construction of four scenario storylines that will, when taken together, define and describe the 'limits of possibility' for the future. In order to provide maximum relevance from, and to cover the widest range of possibilities within the scenarios, the two framing factors (labelled A and B) are those that combine: (a) the highest perceived impact upon the issue under consideration, and (b) the highest level of perceived uncertainty as to what that impact might be. These two factors are not selected to the exclusion of all others. Rather, they provide the anchor to which all others are related in terms of sense-making and logic testing. In referring to uncertainty as to what the impact of a factor will be, it is important to note the difference between being certain that something *will happen* and will have an outcome and impact and being certain as to what the outcome and impact *will be*. For example, an exercise on scenarios for the future of health and wellbeing in Africa might elicit a cluster of driving forces that is defined as an impacting factor, 'access to potable drinking water'. This may well be considered a high-impact factor, but there may not be certainty as to what that impact will be. Its impact may be seen as highly uncertain, determined by the outcomes from a range of driving forces related to: levels of access to water, availability of technologies for filtering water, impacts of climate events and climate change, and degrees of civil unrest and conflict.

Having identified factors A and B, we then 'scope' four scenarios around, in simplistic terms, the combination of perceived best/best (A1/B1), worst/worst (A2/B2), best/worst (A1/B2) and worst/best (A2/B1) perceived outcomes of them. The scoping of the scenarios is done by brainstorming descriptors of the world at large in relation to the interaction of these two factor outcomes, and as we might describe it to an alien visitor with no prior knowledge of the situation. Having determined the broad scenario frames, according to Factors A and B, we then 'develop' the scenarios by infilling details that encapsulate relevant elements of all other factors – and hence, all original driving forces – and other matters that will give them depth and bring them to life.

Scenario storylines, whilst not being predictions of the future, should incorporate people, events and outcomes that are 'real', as well as presenting challenges to thinking in offering alternative possibilities. 'Real' events that are already programmed into future 'history',[4] include that there will be US Presidential elections in November 2012 and November 2016. In 2012, barring the unknowable, Barack Obama will be the Democratic candidate. Similarly, there will be elections within known time horizons in many other countries, with 'known' protagonists having, to a large extent, knowable policies. Similarly, the changing demographic of most developed countries is fairly knowable over the coming decades, and the economic challenges that this represents are widely discussed. However, how these challenges might be met in a volatile global economy and in relation to different climate change events and impacts is perhaps less certain. Also, they may be mediated, for example, by changing patterns of political, economic or climate refugee migration over the period.

The outcome of the scenario development process is a set of four storylines that are each internally consistent and self-contained. They each describe the future in terms of different patterns of end states. These may be arrived at by way of the same intermediate events and outcomes, the same events with different outcomes, or by very different events and outcomes. As I have stated above, these are not individual predictions of a 'future', but represent a set of possibilities that, taken together, enable organizations to: (a) assess the robustness of current and intended strategies and policies, (b) test alternative strategy and policy options against a range of different external environmental conditions, and (c) identify future circumstances in which they do not have robustness and will be under threat. In the face of severe adverse conditions under (c), only a few very large and powerful organizations can contemplate seeking to influence the future in order to avert these conditions. For most, it becomes a matter of searching for new plans and prospects in order to seek to be resilient in the face of the possible threat.

To this point, the scenario process by and large follows the selected method (van der Heijden et al. 2002), focussed primarily on the organization's interests and its robustness or exposure in the face of different future conditions. As such, scenarios can be seen as roadmaps to inform change preparedness and planning in order to preserve the business, its values and the interests of its involved stakeholders. Here, my concern is to open up the discourse to consideration of the interests of other stakeholders, who may not be affected by the same factors, be affected in the same way, or assess these affects using the same value framework as the organization. Now, I move to consider how this wider stakeholder engagement might be achieved.

Engaging stakeholder interests through critical scenario method

The scenario approach outlined above should have resulted in preparation of four separate but related scenario outlines that place the organization's future within boundaries of possibility and plausibility for the external environment in which it sits. The process has involved identifying the fullest range of driving forces and, within clusters to form higher-level factors, the range of possible and plausible outcomes from these. This work will have involved some consideration of stakeholders, in determining the range of forces and possible outcomes that are within the realm of human action and power. However, there has been no explicit requirement to ensure that: (a) all relevant stakeholders have been identified and taken into account, and (b) the interests of and impacts upon these stakeholders in relation to organizational options for decision making and action have been considered.

At this stage, the incorporation of Jones and Fleming's (2003) critical stakeholder analysis (CSA) principles, underpinned by and enacted in accordance with Flyvbjerg's (2001) mode of phronetic organizational inquiry, enables us to interrogate the scenarios and to analyse their likely impacts upon and consequences for the full range of stakeholders. In order to consider the possibilities of this approach, Cairns et al. (2010) consider the range of possible futures for the flat-panel-television producer Vizio, building upon its use as a case study of international business in Charles W. Hill's (2009) textbook on IB. They first identify a broad range of stakeholders who might be affected by the operations of the company, but who may not be immediately obvious from reading the text book case, or without broad-based research and consideration of: the nature of design, procurement, use and disposal of consumer electronics; current and future energy consumption patterns and costs; the actions of governments and legislatures in defining parameters of operation; and the aspirations of and choices available to those in less-developed countries that aspire to a Western, consumption-based lifestyle. They identify 12 categories of stakeholder, ranging from American consumers and South Korean manufacturers to Indian and Chinese citizens who dismantle and reclaim discarded consumer electronics and governmentally recognized disposal facilities in Singapore and the USA. They indicate that these 12 do not preclude identification of others and subdivision of these into further discrete groups.

Having identified this broad range of affected stakeholders, they then explain how the application of Flyvbjerg's (2001) value-rational question framework can enable the organization-oriented scenarios developed earlier to be interrogated in relation to the interests all stakeholders. They first illustrate the application of the first question (Where are we going?) as a means of critical analysis of the end states of each scenario, where the word 'we' is taken to mean the particular stakeholder group under consideration at any one time. For each group, and in relation to these end states, they then consider the next two questions. The second question (Is this development desirable?) provides a vehicle for explicitly exploring the end state in relation to the particular group's values and interests. Thereafter, the third question (What, if anything, should we do about it?) enables consideration of the actions that the specific stakeholder group might seek to take when faced with a particular scenario. It also prompts deliberation on whether or not these actions align with the interests and intended actions of the organization, or other stakeholder groups.

It is important here to note that the question 'What should we do?' refers to action the group might ideally *wish* to take. However, consideration of this ideal outcome, which is the focus of Jones and Fleming's (2003) theoretical framework of CSA, needs to be tempered by consideration of the realities of current structural relationships and power inequalities. This can be addressed, moving from the ideal to the pragmatic, through application of Flyvbjerg's fourth question (Who gains and who loses, and by which mechanisms of power?). Within the classroom setting, Cairns et al. (2010) see the value of the critical scenario method as lying in the possibilities it presents for students being able to engage with issues of international business – and organizational activity in general – more critically, in terms of exploring the full range of possible futures that might arise in relation to them, of impacts and effects that they might have on the full range of affected stakeholders, and, most importantly, in prompting students, as future managers in organizations, to ask the question of themselves, 'What, if anything, can and should *I* do about it?'

Conclusion

In promoting the CSM approach to organization-change analysis here, I seek to prompt you to think about change projects more broadly than you might otherwise have done, both in terms of the range of possible and plausible outcomes that might arise from change that cannot be internally prescribed and managed, and in relation to the impacts that such change might have for affected stakeholders who might not otherwise be brought into consideration. I aim to extend the scope and time horizon of thinking on organization change, from short- to medium-term issues of immediate concern to longer-term issues of social, ecological and economic sustainability.

Application of scenario method permits consideration of different options for planned change in relation to a range of possible and plausible future external conditions – and the unplanned, imposed change that they might elicit. It provides a vehicle for comparative analysis of how the application of different strategies and plans might invoke a variety of future outcomes. In addition, adoption of the critical approach (Wright and Cairns 2011) requires that such consideration takes account of issues of structure and power and makes transparent who will be the 'winners' and 'losers' under different external conditions and as a result of different internal actions. It also identifies which stakeholders can and may exercise particular forms of power in order to bring about specific future outcomes.

In summary, this chapter promotes an approach to thinking about the context and implications of change in relation to external uncertainties, with consideration of its impacts upon the broadest range of stakeholders and in terms of its consequences for society and environment as well as for the organization and its immediate members.

Notes

1 In quoting this extract from Friedman, most commentators fail to note that Friedman placed this notion of the role of the business in contrast with the role of government to look after the needs of all members of society.
2 Robert Owen's work in New Lanark, Scotland in the early nineteenth century is one of the earliest examples.
3 Note that the 'foreseeable future' in relation to some issues, such as the impact of changing demographics and an aging population in Western countries, may span a considerable number of years. Other issues, such as the effectiveness of social networking web sites as marketing channels by organizations, may have shorter time horizons.
4 This programming does not allow for the unforeseeable, with which this scenario approach does not engage. It is concerned with possibility and plausibility within what might reasonably be knowable.

References

Aristotle (350BC/2004) *The Nicomachean Ethics*. Trans. J.A.K. Thomson, 1953. Rev. H. Tredennick, 1976. London: Penguin Books.

Bradfield, R., Wright, G., Burt, G., Cairns, G. and van der Heijden, K. (2005) 'The origins and evolution of scenario techniques in long range business planning', *Futures*, 37: 795–812.

Cairns, G., Śliwa, M. and Wright, G. (2010) 'Problematizing international business futures through a "critical scenario method"', *Futures*, 42: 971–979.

Cairns, G., Wright, G., Bradfield, R., van der Heijden, K. and Burt, G. (2004) 'Exploring e-government futures through the application of scenario planning', *Technological Forecasting and Social Change*, 71: 217–38.

Flyvbjerg, B. (1998) *Rationality and Power – Democracy in Practice*, Chicago: University of Chicago Press.

—— (2001) *Making Social Science Matter: Why Social Inquiry Fails and How It Can Succeed Again*, Cambridge: Cambridge University Press.

—— (2003) 'Making organization research matter: Power values and phronesis', in B. Czarniawska and G. Sevón (eds) *The Northern Lights: Organization Theory in Scandinavia*. Copenhagen: Liber Abstrakt – Copenhagen Business School Press: 357–82.

Freeman, R.E. (1994) 'The politics of stakeholder theory: some future directions', *Business Ethics* Quarterly, 4: 409–421.

Freeman, R.E. and Reed, D.L. (1983) 'Stockholders and stakeholders: a new perspective on corporate governance', *California Management Review* (XXV) 3: 91.

Friedman, M. (1962) *Capitalism and Freedom*. Chicago, IL: University of Chicago Press.

Hill, C.W. (2009) *International Business: Competing in the Global Marketplace*, 7th edn, New York: McGraw-Hill/Irwin.

Jones, M.T. and Fleming, P. (2003) 'Unpacking complexity through critical stakeholder analysis: the case of globalization', *Business & Society*, 42: 430–54.

Jungermann, H. and Thuring, M. (1987) 'The use of mental models in generating scenarios', in G. Wright and P. Ayton (eds) *Judgmental Forecasting*, London: Wiley: 245–66.

van der Heijden, K., Bradfield, R., Burt, G., Cairns, G. and Wright, G. (2002) *The Sixth Sense: Accelerating Organizational Learning with Scenarios*, Chichester: Wiley.

Wright, G. and Cairns, B. (2011) *Scenario Thinking: Practical Approaches to the Future*, London: Palgrave.

Wright, G., Cairns, G. and Goodwin, P. (2009) 'Teaching scenario planning: lessons from practice in academe and business', *European Journal of Operational Research*, 194: 323–35.

15

Organizations unbound
Psychodynamic perspectives on organizational restructuring

Paula Hyde

Introduction

Psychodynamic theory offers one means of exploring how organizational changes affect work practices, also recognizing that changes might be resisted for psychological reasons. It has been argued that a systems psychodynamic perspective can offer insights in cases of radical reorganization of boundaries that might otherwise go unnoticed (Gould et al. 1999). The systems approach is based on concepts related to organization structure, including task, role, authority and boundary. Task describes the area and direction of activity and responsibility. Role defines a grouping of tasks and a position in a system. Authority includes the area of decision-making that belongs to a role and the line of accountability to a manager. Boundary is a more difficult concept that defines the break point between one element and another, e.g. one role and another, one task and another, between different areas of authority, between subsystems and between the organization and its environment. In contrast, the psychodynamic component of the approach is interested in conscious and unconscious emotional effects of structural arrangements and their impact on social and personal functioning. From the psychodynamic point of view, structures can operate to help contain anxiety and to sustain a psychological space for work and creativity. Therefore, when structures change, lack of clarity about tasks, role, authority and boundaries give rise to uncertainty and anxiety (James and Huffington 2004: 213–14).

Isobel Menzies-Lyth, building on the work of Elliott Jaques, elaborated the notion of social defences against anxiety (Jaques 1953; Menzies Lyth 1988, 1989). She showed, through her study of nurses, two important features of social defences: (1) they were aspects of organization that existed independently of organizational members (e.g. structures, policies, technologies, work practices, distribution of authority); and (2) they came to reinforce people's defences against primitive anxieties aroused in the workplace. She maintained that these defences had enduring qualities that were difficult to change. Such defences either eliminated situations that generated anxiety or insulated people from the consequences of their actions. Consequently, social defences reinforced nurses' defences against anxiety generated by the work itself and nurses came to offer depersonalized, fragmented care. Organizational change modifies the social defence system threatening personal defences. One might expect that restructuring has a direct effect on boundary systems which affect significant areas of the work system: task, role and authority.

Change is therefore associated with the prospect of anxiety surfacing. This stimulates resistance even where changes may seem sensible.

Nevertheless, in the post-industrial era organizations are changing and some would argue that psychodynamic ideas such as social defences against anxiety have fallen behind (Krantz 2010). Organization boundaries have changed to the extent that it may no longer necessarily be clear where work takes place, where it starts and ends or how the demands of work might be contained. In recent years, organizational change in large corporations has almost invariably involved some form of restructuring (Hassard et al. 2009). Such restructuring has tended to depend upon the removal of middle managerial levels and a general slimming down of the perceived burden of bureaucracy. The impact of organizational restructuring on organizational boundaries is an important feature of organizational change, not least because modern organizational forms involve increased boundary complexity (Gabriel 1999). Reactions to such complexity are neither standard nor entirely predictable, but may be illuminated through empirical research exploring boundaries in organizational settings and utilizing psychodynamic methods.

Organizational restructuring and the National Health Service (NHS)

Organizational restructuring, usually involving the removal of layers of management, is almost ubiquitous in large corporations around the world. The effects of such changes on organizational members, particularly middle managers, include work intensification and ill health, and have been documented in detail (Hassard et al. 2009). Organizational restructuring has a fundamental effect on organizational boundaries. Such effects are symbolized by changes to organization charts that are redrawn to illustrate the new, often slim-line, structure. The enactment of such changes involves new tasks, roles and lines of authority and consequent emotional impact of reapplying for jobs, understanding new requirements and developing new work practices.

Restructuring has been a common feature of health policy in the UK for some considerable time. Health-care policy from the 1980s onwards focused on structural rearrangements aimed at improving health care such as, the introduction of general management, the introduction of new layers of organization, mergers and de-layering. During the Labour government (1997–2010), policy effort was increasingly directed at bringing about cultural changes through the introduction of clinical governance and life-long learning strategies (Department of Health 2000). At the same time much front-line effort was being expended on service redesign – the rearrangement of facilities, staff and patient pathways in search of more streamlined services, greater throughput, and improved patient experiences (McKee et al. 2008). These changes have had a significant impact on organizational boundaries. For example, mental health and social care organizations were created in England by splitting health and social care workers from their former organizations and joining them together to form new organizations. In contrast, boundaries between professional groups have remained more constant as professional bodies support health professionals in delineation of their roles; for example, professional training follows specified consistent programmes and professional work practices are delineated by national professional bodies. However, recent moves in UK health policy are set to restructure the National Health Service (NHS) again (largely by significant reductions in number and scope of NHS organizations). These policy moves include a continued focus on changing work practices with the emphasis on redesigning workers' roles. Attempts to change traditional roles threaten professional boundaries and are likely to increase defensive activity amongst professional groups.

The UK health service has undergone three decades of restructuring targeted at organizational, professional and work group boundaries. Yet little attention has been given to what may constitute a healthy set of boundary relationships. Four interrelated case studies are presented here. Each case study represents a sub-unit of a restructured mental health organization. They illustrate a variety of organizational relationships and cross-boundary processes. Each case illustrates how threats to particular boundaries can lead organizational members to engage in defensive activity. Whilst defences may be protective, i.e. healthy for the individual or the organization, they may also generate more problems than they solve, and, whilst the examples given here are highly specific, they indicate the potential for psychoanalytic perspectives on organizational change to explain sometimes baffling work practices.

The concept of boundary

Boundaries separate a system from its environment and within the system they separate parts and processes. They determine relationships between systems and affect the degree of interaction between systems. They also provide for the establishment of identity at individual, group and organizational levels (Hirschhorn and Gilmore 1992, Hyde 2005).

There have been several psychodynamic analyses of the effects of organizational restructuring and redesign on organizational boundaries (see, for examples, Gabriel 1999; Heracleous 2004; Hyde 2005; Lawrence 1999; Schneider 1991). Boundaries are said to be central to understanding behaviour in organizations (Gabriel and Willman 2004) and to be necessary for the formation of a sense of identity as a separate being (Schneider 1991). They are also central to processes of differentiation between individuals, groups and organizations. They offer a means of understanding where one entity ends and another begins: task, role, authority, organization or system (Gabriel 1999; Lawrence 1999). Boundaries have been conceived of as 'relational processes' being socially constructed through interaction (Heracleous 2004: 95). Thus any attempt at restructuring will affect boundary systems and the ability of workers to contain anxiety generated by the work itself.

It has been noted that the more one examines a boundary the less clear it becomes. It may be that discussion of 'boundary' is difficult because of the 'inter-disciplinary, multi-faceted and diffuse nature of the concept' (Heracleous 2004: 99). Boundary has been used both as a metaphor for describing organizational behaviour (Gabriel and Willman 2004) and in terms of metaphors such as lines (Gabriel 1999), surfaces (Diamond et al. 2004), system gateways (Lawrence 1999) or regions (Miller 1990). The infinite line metaphor involves one side of the line that is safe and familiar: the other side is dangerous, unknown and exciting. Moreover, this line may be strong and resilient or fragile and thin. The line analogy can be applied to individuals, groups and organizations. The 'surface' metaphor is more complex than it first appears. This idea of surface does not correspond with boundary in its totality, rather, the surface relates to areas where boundaries 'bump up' against each other so that 'boundary crossing is experienced as surface to surface contact' (Diamond et al 2004: 44). Such surface contact enables exploration of the psychological and affective texture of boundaries. Much psychological work is needed to maintain boundaries as they, themselves, offer a defence against anxiety. However, in spite of this, defending boundaries can generate anxiety as the defence itself may provoke further anxiety. Systems theorists have viewed organizational boundaries as a means of identifying gateways, points of entry/input into, or exit/output from an organization within a wider system. Alternatively, it has been suggested that a boundary is better considered as a region representing the discontinuity between the tasks of one system and the systems with which it transacts. The

219

region is not stable or static but locates activities that 'mediate relations between inside and outside' (Miller 1990: 172). These metaphors highlight the potential effects of even simple reorganization. They describe the function of boundaries as locations for identity development and the development of working relationships. Exploration of boundaries and cross-boundary interactions within organizations is a complex operation whether using psychodynamic or other means.

Boundaries then are often unconscious, dynamic systems maintained, at least in part, by defensive activity and affected by changes to organizational structure affecting staffing, clients, organizational systems and many other factors. They may be illustrated via attention to organizational defences as such activity can highlight areas of anxiety and therefore threats to boundary in terms of identity, task, role and authority.

Organizational defences in health care

Work within the psychodynamic tradition has argued that organizations use social defences to protect against the anxiety provoked by the primary task of the organization (Hyde and Thomas 2002; Jaques 1953; Menzies Lyth 1989). These defences are not seen as pathological although they may be counterproductive. They may offer short-term relief from anxiety but often do not resolve or remove it. The well-known study by Isobel Menzies Lyth (1989) described a series of interrelated defensive routines used by nursing staff, such as *splitting* the nurse–patient relationship so that the nurse attended to particular tasks rather than particular patients and *denial* of individuality where patients were treated by category of illness. *Detachment* and *denial of feelings* were encouraged through professional training and defences extended to senior staff who disciplined and reprimanded junior nurses. Uncertainties were eliminated through ritualized activity and nurses were discouraged from using their initiative and discretion when planning work. Where nurses were not supported with the day-to-day emotional realities of their work they moved on or left the service. To some extent the organizational defences she described provided a means of containing anxiety; however, the staff in her study experienced low morale, were highly anxious and there was high staff turnover.

Bain (1998) found similar defences in Australian hospitals in the 1990s to those described by Menzies Lyth in an English hospital in the 1960s. He suggested that the similarities between these socially constructed defences arise because of similarities in anxieties aroused by the primary task. He maintained that organizational defences are ingrained by professional training, organizational cultures and systems, funding arrangements, policies and procedures, representational systems such as trade unions and professional associations and the capacities and psychological characteristics of the people employed. His work suggests that organizational defences in health-care settings will bear some similarities because of the nature of the system within which they operate and the function they seek to perform. In addition, health systems are likely to be highly resistant to change as systemic features support stable work practices.

Mental health work generates anxieties for staff about being contaminated by insanity, being attacked or losing control over oneself. Particular difficulties associated with mental-health services include conflicts between controlling insanity, providing care for patients and the wish to offer treatment or cures (Bott 1976). Organizational defences associated with this area of work usually involve projecting insanity into the patient and sanity into the staff. Rigid barriers are then employed to prevent psychological contamination. These barriers prevent the restoration of health of the patient through their reclamation of sanity. It follows then that recent structural changes to the organization of mental health services are said to have had little impact for patients who continue to experience similar conditions of care (Hyde and Thomas 2003; Walton 2000).

This study of four mental health services within a larger mental health and social care trust may shed some light on boundary processes within and across the mental health system. By exploring interactions and organizational defences, some aspects of boundary functioning within organizations may be illuminated that are not easily explained by other means.

Boundary systems in mental health services

Four case studies formed part of a wider study (Hyde 2005). Each case study involved extensive observations and interviews as well as informal conversations with mental health managers, staff, patients and carers as they went about their business. The purpose of the study was to gain some understanding of organizational dynamics of mental health teams by exploring how staff understood the work they did and the operation and organization of their teams. Formulations and interpretations were discussed and explored with participants as each case study progressed. The study considered organizational dynamics broadly with specific consideration of organizational defences. Only subsequently did the interconnectedness of and interplay between various boundary systems emerge as an important feature. This outcome should not be surprising as defensive activity, whilst not always successful, is aimed at strengthening boundaries and thereby reducing anxiety.

The case studies took place within a larger mental health and social care trust, which had been recently formed by merging the mental health sections of several previously distinct organizations. The four sub-units forming the case studies were: a psychiatric ward; an occupational therapy (OT) department; a psychiatric hostel; and a community mental health team. The cases differed from each other in the following ways: facilities for care, staff groupings and levels of illness of patients. They were also differentiated by degree of patient contact – whether care was offered on a residential or appointment basis – and by their location – on a larger hospital site or in the community. All services were offered to people experiencing severe and enduring mental illness. A brief account of each case is given followed by a brief analysis of defensive activity and boundary issues. Subsequently, interactions between each sub-unit of the mental health service are considered. The case studies are necessarily brief but have been described in detail elsewhere (Hyde and Thomas 2002, 2003).

The psychiatric ward

The psychiatric ward housed patients who were severely mentally ill and who required 24-hour-a-day care. The environment was dilapidated with little functional equipment. Over 75 per cent of the patients were detained under the Mental Health Act (1983) which required them to stay in hospital and also, perhaps, to receive treatment. The primary task of ward staff was containment and control of the patients. Patients were locked in and were allowed short visits off the ward although, in reality, they rarely got the time away from the ward to which they were entitled. They had to wait for staff to unlock doors for them; for example, the door to the washing-machine and laundry room or the door to the bathroom. The ward lacked basic essentials such as enough food to eat and opportunities for activity other than watching television. One nurse who had recently left the ward described her work:

> I felt like a gatekeeper. I felt very much like I was being custodial in what I was doing …
> I was very good at sitting on the door counting people coming in and out. I was good at

dishing medication out and I learnt in a very short space of time how to be number one on the C&R [control and restraint] team.

The ward was over-occupied (120 per cent) as there were more patients than beds. Patients were sent on temporary leave and staff were concerned that a patient may return early and have no bed available. The staff were under constant pressure to admit new patients and to discharge existing patients. One member of staff was posted by the locked door and was required to record observations on a chart, of each patient at required time intervals. Staff roles on the ward were allocated each shift, so that junior members of the team were often given responsible roles such as ward co-ordinator (manager) even though they lacked the authority with other staff to get simple tasks done. One ward co-ordinator could not persuade any of the other nurses to collect a prescription from the pharmacy department. The ward often formed the training ground for newly qualified staff who could then move on to other parts of the system. The staff were under considerable pressure from both external demands to take new admissions and from constant requests of patients for milk, keys, money and information about their care. Staff were often found in the office with a queue of patients waiting outside the door to ask for their money, cigarettes or domestic items such as towels or milk. Occasionally a patient would be restrained or forced to have treatment.

Dangers to staff were signalled by the physical presence of alarm systems in case of attack and the locked doors to prevent patient escape. The locking away of equipment, food and personal belongings of the patients led to increased demands upon the staff that threatened to run out of control and overwhelm them. The allocation of managerial roles to junior members of ward staff meant that simple jobs did not get done and led to a reduction of control over the ward environment. For example, junior staff were ineffectual when insisting on immediate repairs to ward equipment such as the ward cooker, which was broken for the duration of the study. The lack of available activity for patients increased their boredom and frustration and led to an increase in the demands they made upon the staff. Outbursts of frustration, in rare cases, led to forced treatment which enabled staff to exert physical control over the patients and thereby to demonstrate their effectiveness. Staff attempted to protect their intrapsychic boundaries by retreating from patients to the ward office and employed means of reducing exchanges between them, such as avoiding eye contact, whilst still being in close proximity.

The intensive nature of mental health work on a psychiatric ward highlights some of the threats to intrapsychic boundaries faced by mental health workers more generally. Mental health services were provided to offer care to patients and/or to offer a place where they may be contained and controlled (Bott 1976). The work itself involved close contact with patients whose intrapsychic boundaries were disrupted to some extent, causing excessive anxiety in neurosis or distorted perceptions of reality in psychosis. Whilst psychotic processes have been identified as a normal part of personality development, they threaten disintegration of identity and mental health workers who identify with the distress of their patients may fear the consequences for themselves and feel that their own sanity is threatened.

On this psychiatric ward the staff were only able to connect with the patients' experience to a limited extent because of the threat of being overwhelmed that originated in the splitting and locating of insanity within the patient and denial of mad aspects of the self in staff members. All signs on the ward suggested that one would be overwhelmed (by insanity) unless great care was taken. Defensive activities were not serving to reduce anxiety in fact anxiety was increased and individuals concentrated on protecting themselves. Both staff and patients on this ward left at the earliest opportunity – the patients were either discharged to the community mental health team or admitted to the hostel for further rehabilitation and the staff moved on to more desirable positions in the community.

The occupational therapy (OT) department

In contrast, the OT department, which was on the ground floor of the same psychiatric unit, was a quiet and considerably under-utilized place staffed by occupational therapists and OT assistants. Their primary task was to care for in-patients once they were well enough to leave the ward for short periods of time and to provide OT activities aimed at supporting the patients' discharge from hospital. The staff came from one professional group and allocated tasks according to seniority. Roles and responsibilities were clearly defined as qualified staff took referrals for patients from the ward and assessed the patient on the ward to decide whether they were suitable. This process allowed them to limit the number of patients they saw and to limit the level of anxiety generated by the work. Staff did not like going onto the psychiatric ward and spent much of their time in planning meetings. These meetings often focused on what could be done in the future when the department was fully staffed and when a better service could be offered. The head occupational therapist, who had been recently appointed, explained how the OT department worked:

> Wards are difficult to go on. All the staff say that, because the [ward] staff don't welcome you. People work against each other, they let people go on leave when they have an appointment with OT … Team support has been neglected. I've had to reintroduce supervision and appraisal. We can't appoint to the jobs here. We'll have to get locums in the meantime. The OT role is to defend a return to better housing but they [the patients] are invariably discharged somewhere awful and told to apply [for better housing] from there.

The occupational therapists took part in case reviews and discharge planning meetings that often involved repetition of information to similar staff groups. The OT assistants offered a limited range of activities to patients, such as cooking or craft activities. Patients were normally brought down from the ward one at a time but assistant staff occasionally led group activities. Patients had to be 'well enough' to go to the department and by that time they had often been discharged from the hospital. Their readiness to attend the department was specified by the senior staff.

In the OT department the staff were able to distance themselves physically from the patients almost totally whilst still being able to talk about the patients in their meetings. The occupational therapists had been trained in their roles and had a hierarchical career system. Training involved being taught how to be objective and not to become overly involved with patients, the idea being that if one were too preoccupied with the patient's suffering effective work would become impossible. This allowed for professional boundaries that were protective of the individual. Professional boundaries can be very clear cut with certain tasks conducted by specific people according to their position in the hierarchy. Professional roles and hierarchies may be compared to those within the family group. Within families role and generational boundaries exist to allow individual identity and family relatedness whilst reinforcing the family boundary (Hirschhorn and Gilmore 1980). In the OT department professional boundaries were very clearly defined and contrasted with the emphasis on policing intrapsychic boundaries that was evident on the ward. By strengthening their professional boundaries and limiting their personal contact with patients the defensive activities of OT staff were counterproductive, i.e. they were not enabling better patient care through clearly defined roles and responsibilities. Here one professional grouping operated together, expending considerable energy in policing their professional and departmental boundaries. There were clearly defined roles and responsibilities yet there was also homogeneity within the team as they had developed both a clear identity and a rigid hierarchy.

The psychiatric hostel

The hostel was a large purpose built building that offered 16 patients their own room and some communal areas in which to live. The hostel staff were able to accept or reject patients for admission, following assessment, and the hostel was under-occupied. As a result, staff used spare patient bedrooms as offices and places to meet for patient reviews. The staff occupied the dining room and office and one of the kitchens and enacted routines such as having breakfast and reading the paper. Residents at the hostel had been previously treated on the psychiatric ward but they were unable, as yet, to return home. They were expected to stay at the hostel for one to two years while they became more able to live independently. The hostel staff were wary of increasing dependency in the residents and as a consequence the residents were left to their own devices for much of the time. One staff member described her work at the hostel:

> I like having the chance to sit and talk but it's too quiet sometimes. That's the nature of rehab: you aim to enhance the quality and lifestyle. We work with existing lifestyles, like if someone doesn't get up until 2.00pm … they are enabled. They've gone through [the psychiatric ward] and been stabilized and sorted out where they were before. The main thing is motivating them … it's a balance between intrusion and caring.

Residents were often excluded from decision making about their care as review meetings started without the resident being present. They were invited into the meeting later for a discussion and to hear what decisions had been made. The residents' conditions were slow to change and the role of the hostel staff included demonstrating skills and encouraging independence. Life at the hostel was monotonous for the staff as residents were allowed out alone and were often out for most of the day. Living conditions for residents at the hostel were often far better than those they could expect on leaving.

At the hostel, residents posed little threat to intrapsychic boundaries of the staff as their condition was stabilized and the staff were able to maintain some considerable physical and psychological distance between themselves and the residents. The staff group came from mixed professional backgrounds although the majority of staff were nurses and support workers. The hostel staff had adopted patient routines and were sometimes unaware of the needs of the residents. For example, some residents were unable to prepare meals for themselves but did not receive help as the staff were fearful of promoting dependence. As the hostel was located away from the hospital site the physical boundary provided by the building enabled staff to operate in ways that would have been unacceptable within the hospital. They were able to withdraw from the boundary between themselves and the patient and sustain a fantasy of active rehabilitation even though residents who needed supporting in community activities were referred to the community team.

The community mental-health team

The staff of the community team were said to be dynamic and effective by others in the mental health service, as they supported people with severe mental illnesses living in the community.

These staff were encouraged to take more patients than they were supposed to and much of their role involved persuading clients to take their medicines, often in the form of injections, under threat of returning to hospital. Staff took responsibility for individual patients and undertook the majority of care-related tasks regardless of professional background. One staff member described her work as follows:

> You wouldn't get that close to a patient as a general nurse. You don't have to get that emotional involvement if you don't want. Whereas, contrast that to here. With the injections it looks methodical but people maybe don't want injecting so a lot of the work is persuasion and encouragement and building trust. So you can't just go in and do an injection, it takes a lot of emotional energy. It is that engagement and building trust.

The team were housed in a community centre and had a locked door to their section. Following restructuring, they had been amalgamated with a team of social workers who divided the office with a row of cupboards to separate themselves. Most of their work took place in the clients' own homes and staff were held individually responsible for the wellbeing of their client group.

The clients were often acutely ill and so posed some threat to the intrapsychic boundaries of the staff who had to persuade or coerce them to ensure that they took their medicines. The staff were concerned to build good relationships with their clients so that they would understand the need for medication and be able to make contact in a crisis. In effect, the organization was 'boundaryless' in terms of physical boundaries, for the community team as their work could take place anywhere. This posed some problems for the workers as they did not have the usual safety nets a health-service organization may offer such as other staff for back up in an emergency. This led to an emphasis on professional boundaries and intra-professional pairings in the office. Exclusions were set on the tasks that could be performed by occupational therapists (injections) and nurses (longer-term rehabilitation). The social workers who were being amalgamated into the team began by separating themselves in the office using physical boundaries to exert some boundary control.

Managing across boundaries

Approaches to understanding and exploring boundaries at the organizational level have derived from many disciplinary backgrounds and there have been several attempts to classify organizational boundaries in an attempt to predict outcomes of specific organizational forms in terms of inter- and intra-organizational functioning (Hernes 2004; Miller and Rice 1967; Schneider 1991). Boundary functions within organizations are far more complicated than those of the family or the group and become increasingly complex as organizations import agency staff, contract out services and form partnerships with other organizations.

At the individual, intrapsychic level Freud described boundaries evolving to delineate the id by the ego (Freud 1932). These intrapsychic boundaries act to strengthen boundaries between reality and fantasy (fantasy arising from the id to satisfy desires). The ego must, however, negotiate between the id and superego to achieve individual integration of the personality. Indeed, boundary has been described as 'coextensive with the ego' (Gabriel 1999: 98). Intrapsychic boundaries enable transactions between the individual and the outside world and include transactions between the individual and their working environment. In health care generally and mental health care specifically, workers use their personality to engage and empathize with patients who they attempt to help. Such work involves particular anxieties and demands on the individual that render intrapsychic boundaries important when considering functioning not only at the individual but also at the organizational level. Such boundaries have barely been affected by seemingly major organizational restructuring, except perhaps to increase occupancy on the ward as numbers of available mental health beds had been reduced.

The excerpts of case examples presented here suggest that mental health staff responded to fear of psychological injury in a variety of ways. On the ward, staff were locked in with acutely ill patients at the height of their mental disturbance or distress. The staff retreated from patients and employed means of reducing exchanges between them while remaining in close proximity. They shared responsibility for patients so that they dealt with patient tasks rather than individual people. In the OT department the staff were able to physically distance themselves from patients almost totally and the hostel staff occupied resident spaces and enacted life on their behalf. Consideration of these threats of psychological injury in mental health services highlights the unique difficulties faced by mental health workers by the very nature of their work. It also highlights how organizational changes such as restructuring may generate further intensive work buttressing existing social defences rather than leading to any substantive change.

The OT department offered one example of clearly defined professional boundaries where the occupational therapists had retreated from the organizational boundary (with the patient) by strengthening their professional boundaries and limiting their personal contact with patients. Here one professional grouping operated together with clearly defined roles and responsibilities according to grade. These hierarchies are present in other mixed services where professionals also retain some connection with their speciality that may allow the leader of the mixed team to be overruled on their behalf. This happened in the community team where the occupational therapists did not do injections and nurses did not do longer-term rehabilitation. Current attempts at modernizing the NHS are focused on changing the way services are delivered, thereby challenging professional boundaries. These changes seem likely to increase defensive activity amongst professional groups. Attempts to alter such boundaries run the risk of generating role confusion as a result of blurring of boundaries and could have serious effects for those receiving care. Managers have a particular role to play in establishing new task, role and authority boundaries that enable the containment of anxiety following structural changes.

Whilst health-service organizations may have had new structures imposed, professionals and teams have retained the ability to carve out niches, control the flow of inputs and outputs or isolate business operations. It has been further argued that workers operating at an organization's outer boundary (i.e. the interface between the organization and the customer) experience anxiety from both external threats and internal defensive activity. They tend to retreat from the boundary to a safe quarter. Frenzied searches for safe havens or niches are common in fragmented organizations as staff move around the organization. Boundaries between the organization and the outside world can be strengthened by isolating operations, creating niches and by controlling the flow of inputs and outputs, effectively withdrawing from the boundary. Schneider argued that public-sector organizations such as hospitals are unable to define and negotiate external boundaries because of considerable external control of task performance and organizational structures.

The ward and community team formed a buffer for the hostel and the department. This may explain why the hostel and the department were operating under capacity with fewer patients than they were capable of treating. In contrast, the ward and community team were operating over capacity having more patients that they should. Defensive activity varied across teams but all teams attempted to retreat from the boundary of care by some means. Some managers were unaware of the realities of service provision to the extent that they thought the ward staff inefficient or hostel staff highly anxious about organizational change. This distancing of managers from the services for which they are responsible has been noted elsewhere (Hirschhorn and Gilmore 1992; Krantz 2010).

Modern mental health services commonly use medication and cognitive behavioural therapies to treat patients. Whilst there are many factors in play, psychodynamic insights into the staff experience can demonstrate how staff become able to relate to patients' experiences whilst containing difficult emotions. Such abilities were demonstrated by the community team who were able to connect with the patient experience whilst recognizing their role in persuading the patient to accept unwelcome injections. Staff on the community team were able to recognize their own emotional reactions and maintain their identity.

Restructuring weakened the organizational boundary. As with boundaries between sub-units, organizational boundaries separating organization from the environment can be strengthened by creating niches or controlling the flow of patients. The mental health services in this study were all part of one larger, recently formed, mental health and social care trust. There were clear access points to the overall service described above which put the ward and community mental health team at the boundary of the organization whereas the hostel and OT department were able to control patient flow and protect themselves from boundary violations.

Perhaps more surprisingly, this study has shown how restructuring led to relatively little change in daily work practices. Only the boundaries of the community team were affected as two groups of workers had been moved in to new, shared accommodation. These cases illustrate what little difference major changes can have on front line work. The sub-units on the organizational boundary were subject to work intensification as they had little control of traffic across the boundary.

Organizations unbound

The boundaries described here are often unconscious, dynamic systems affected by changes in staff, patients, organizational systems and many other factors. Indeed, their dynamism is essential as exchanges across boundaries allow for the development of identity not only of the individual but also of the group or the organization. Where boundaries are policed tightly, much energy is expended and anxiety is not successfully alleviated. Boundary processes operating in the health service can shed some light on similar processes in other settings. As organizations are reformed and restructured, boundaries between departments can become more rigid leaving those at the boundary of the organization under considerable pressure as flow of inputs (patients in this case) through the system slows down. In this study, the restructuring of mental health service organizations, which had amalgamated a number of services did not improve co-operation and understanding between services. Indeed, the reorganization itself generated anxiety relating to threatened boundary violations. Changes that affect boundary can threaten identity. They may also generate defensiveness and anxiety that is not conducive to effective organizational performance. Consideration of 'boundary' may allow staff reactions and resultant organizational functioning to be better understood. Moreover, means of supporting staff in their daily work may be suggested that allow staff increased ability to care for patients and to respond to the demands of their managers.

Rather than seeing boundaries as obstacles, they may be viewed as essential to effective organizational functioning as 'boundary' represents the area where relations are mediated between the inside and outside. Challenges to intrapsychic boundaries threaten individual integrity and sanity, whereas restructuring at the professional and group level threaten role confusion through blurred boundaries or loss of clarity of task respectively. Increasingly complex organizational boundaries (including those outlined above) lead to the creation of niches and restricted flows of inputs and outputs as the result of attempts to retreat from the organizational boundary. Each of these effects will have a negative resultant effect upon organizational performance and may go some way to explain aspects of organizational functioning that are not easily explained by other means.

Post-industrial work has weakened organizational boundaries and, therefore, their potential to contain anxiety. A re-examination of socially structured defences would be timely as new work practices emerge, organizational entities become less stable, networks replace small groups of workers, negotiated authority subsumes delegated authority and computer-mediated relationships become increasingly important. James Krantz (2010) suggested two aspects of twenty-first century organizations critical to the understanding of modern social defences: effects of digitization/information technology and knowledge work (thinking intensive work). Information technology can transcend traditional boundaries so that new systems of containment need to be developed and knowledge work increases personal rather than organizational responsibilities.

Technological innovations have weakened boundaries offered by the workplace itself as work is increasingly accessed outside the workplace and new organizational forms have blurred boundaries within and between organizations. Social defences arise less from the organizational level and more from the domain, system or institutional level as organizational boundaries are depleted. Organizations in effect become unbound.

Conclusion

This chapter has indicated how the application of psychodynamic approaches to understanding boundaries can illuminate organizational functioning at the level of the individual worker, the work group and the organization. A series of metaphors have been considered to clarify what is meant by boundary that include lines, surfaces, gateways and regions. It has also been suggested that boundaries form the location for identity development. Mental health services are perhaps particularly illuminating because the work itself requires attention to be paid to psychological functioning. For staff working in contact with patients, psychological boundaries are under continuous threat. Staff must find some way to protect themselves whilst being effective in their work. They may have a professional identity to draw upon that can offer a means of containing anxiety generated by the work itself.

Organizational restructuring has a weakening effect on organizational boundaries meaning that other boundaries will need to be strengthened. In addition, other forms of social defence become important such as those available at institutional/systemic or societal levels. This may well be true for other large corporations as they see the effects of recurrent restructuring. This examination has shown how some subunits manage to distance themselves from the organizational boundary by creating a niche for themselves or by restricting the flow of patients into the service. As organizational boundaries blur and weaken other boundary systems will come to the fore. Whilst radical restructuring may have had a significant effect on the organization boundary, positive effects on work practices are less apparent.

References

Bain, A. (1998) Social defences against organisational learning, *Human Relations*, 51(3), 413–29.
Bott, E. (1976) Hospital and society, *British Journal of Medical Psychology*, 49, 97–140.

Department of Health (2000) *The NHS Plan*, London: Department of Health.

Diamond, M., Allcorn, S. and Stein, H. (2004) The surface of organizational boundaries: a view from psychoanalytic object relations theory, *Human Relations*, 57(1) 31–53.

Freud, S. (1932) The ego and the id. In Strachey, J. (1961) *The Standard Edition of the Complete Psychological Works of Sigmund Freud*, Vol. 19, London: Hogarth Press.

Gabriel, Y. (1999) *Organisations in Depth*, London: Sage.

Gabriel, Y. and Willman, P. (2004) The journal strapline: boundaries or integration? *Human Relations*, 57(1), 7–9.

Gould, L., Ebers, R. and Clinchy, R.M. (1999) The systems psychodynamics of a joint venture: anxiety, social defences, and the management of mutual dependence, *Human Relations*, 52(6) 697–721.

Hassard, J., McCann, L. and Morris, J. (2009) *Managing in the Modern Corporation: the Intensification of Managerial Work in the USA, UK and Japan*, Cambridge: Cambridge University Press.

Heracleous, L. (2004) Boundaries in the study or organization, *Human Relations*, 57(1), 95–103.

Hernes, T. (2004) Studying composite boundaries: a framework of analysis, *Human Relations*, 57(1), 9–30.

Hirschhorn, L. and Gilmore, T. (1980) The application of family therapy concepts to influencing organizational behaviour, *Administrative Science Quarterly*, 25, 18–37.

Hirschhorn, L. and Gilmore, T. (1992) The new boundaries of the 'boundaryless' company, *Harvard Business Review*, May–June, 104–15.

Hyde, P. (2005) Managing across boundaries: identity, differentiation and interaction, *International Journal of Innovation and Learning*, 3(4), 349–62.

Hyde P. and Thomas, A.B. (2002) Organisational defences revisited: systems and contexts, *Journal of Managerial Psychology*, 17(5), 408–21.

Hyde, P. and Thomas, A.B. (2003) When a leader dies, *Human Relations*, 56(8), 1003–22.

Jaques, E. (1953) On the dynamics of social structure, *Human Relations*, 6, 10–23.

James, K. and Huffington, C. (2004) Containment of anxiety in organizational change: a case example of changing organizational boundaries, *Organisational and Social Dynamics*, 4(2), 212–33.

Krantz, J. (2010) Social defences and twenty-first century organizations, *British Journal of Psychotherapy*, 26(2), 192–201.

Lawrence, W.G. (ed.) (1999) *Exploring Individual and Organizational Boundaries: A Tavistock Open System Approach*, London: Karnac Books.

McKee, L., Ferlie, E. and Hyde, P. (eds) (2008) *Organizing and Reorganizing: Power and Change in Health Care Organizations*, Basingstoke: Palgrave Macmillan.

Menzies Lyth, I. (1988) *Containing Anxiety in Institutions: Selected Essays*, Vol 1, London: Free Association Books.

Menzies Lyth, I. (1989) *The Dynamics of the Social: Selected Essays*, Vol 2, London: Free Association Books.

Miller, E.J. (1990) Experiential learning in groups 1: the development of the Leicester Model. In E. Trist and H. Murray (eds) *The Social Engagement of Social Science, Vol 1: The psychological perspective*, London: Free Association Books.

Miller E.J. and Rice, A.K. (1967) *Systems of Organisations: The Control of Task and Sentient Boundaries*, London: Tavistock.

Schneider, S.C. (1991) Managing across boundaries in organisations. In M.F.R. Kets De Vries (ed.) *Organisations on the Couch: Clinical Perspectives on Organisational Behaviour and Change*, Oxford: Jossey Bass Publishers.

Walton, P. (2000) Psychiatric hospital care: a case of the more things change the more they stay the same, *Journal of Mental Health*, 9(1), 77–88.

16

Contemporary realism and organizational change

Stephen Ackroyd

Introduction

Realist approaches to organization studies are more significant than might be at first thought. Far from being just one of many possible ways of doing organization studies, realist theory and research has a claim to being foundational for the field. Organizational studies was first thought of as a branch of social science and the idea of social *science* is difficult to conceive as such without thinking that the social world is real and has causal effects. Next there is the fact that many social science thinkers and organization studies and researchers were and are realist in their work. Pioneers such as Marx and Weber are usually considered to be realist in their approach to the world and are, of course, foundational contributors to organization studies. Much of the social science which followed the work of the founding fathers in the twentieth century in Britain and other parts of Europe was also recognizably realist in its assumptions. Today there are still large numbers of researchers in our field who are implicitly if not explicitly realist in the way they conceive of organizations and in their views about the way knowledge should be developed. Thus, despite the 'paradigm proliferation' in organization studies experienced after the end of the 1970s (Burrell and Morgan, 1979), it is probable that even today the majority of organization studies practitioners are realist in their approach to their subject matter, believing organizations actually exist and shape behaviour.

The argument here is that the realist approach has more than simply survived, as it were against the odds. There are clear continuities in basic outlook: realist theory and practice connect the scholarship of the pre-war and post-war periods in the last century down to the late 1970s and from there to the present day. There also have been some recent developments that give contemporary realism a new intellectual weight and its researchers ambitious research agendas. Today it is possible to see that there has been considerable intellectual development of the traditional and broadly realist, approach to social science in the last thirty years of so. First, there has been the formalization of realist (and explicitly *critical* realist) philosophy of social science, so that today realism can be seen as a distinctive philosophical position. It is now clear to most people active in the organization studies field that realism is very different from positivism and yet also compatible with key propositions of social constructionism. Second, there has been the emergence of some distinctive groups of realist researchers, groups that are intent on refining and developing traditional realist social science in new and different directions. Third, there is now more attention to the place and role of research methodology within realism, so that attention is now, if somewhat belatedly, being paid to the question of how knowledge can be more systematically developed by the use of research projects, many of them large in scale. Much of the discussion in the later stages of this chapter will be concerned with the developments in realist-inspired methodology in organization studies.

These developments reinforce each other, so that many working in social science and organizational studies are no longer only implicitly realist, but self-consciously so. Realist philosophy now helps to guide research practice. Not only are there now several authoritative writers and researchers who have elaborated the realist approach to social science (Bhaskar, 1975, 1986; Sayer, 1993, 2000; Archer et al., 1998), there are practitioners who take an explicitly realist approach to organization and management studies (Clark, 2000; Ackroyd and Fleetwood, 2000; Fleetwood and Ackroyd, 2004; Van de Ven, 2007). Realism proposes that the way the social world is constituted is the central question for social science, and other questions, such as the way that world should be studied, are subordinate to this. In this chapter, then, these developments will be considered in more detail, beginning with a general discussion of realist philosophical ideas. Whilst there is no logical connection between realist metaphysics (especially realist ontological and epistemological ideas) and the social science realist-inclined scholars actually develop, there are some obvious similarities that realists share in their approach to the study of social and organizational processes. Contemporary realism is centrally concerned with social ontology and gives primacy to propositions in this area rather than to epistemology (Sayer, 2000; Fleetwood, 2005), which is the usual focus in other schools of philosophy of science (Nagel, 1961; Harre, 1972; Keat and Urry, 1975). As we shall see, it is the ideas realists adopt in social ontology that incline them to think that social and organizational change are primary features.

Finally, after consideration of realist conceptions of their subject matter, which make change central to the approach, current questions concerning realist methodology and the development of knowledge will be discussed in this chapter. The views entertained by various groups of realist researchers concerning the methods appropriate to the study of processes vary surprisingly little in terms of the basic approach taken. Realists typically conceive of organizations and other social phenomena in terms of the processes that comprise them, and accept that the research procedures appropriate to studying these things have to take account of this. However, different groups of realists differ sharply concerning the possibilities of influencing the processes they study; that is in the potential for *applied* organizational change. Their views on the possibilities of social science effecting social change, although erected on very similar foundations, indicate that very different approaches to practice are possible. There are at least three highly active contemporary schools of recognisably realist research and scholarship, the output from which has been voluminous and which are recognizably realist in the approach to management and organization studies.[1]

Key features of realist philosophy

Distinguishing naive and critical realism

A basic element of realism is the proposition that things and events (including organizations, institutions and societies) exist independently of knowing subjects, and are likely to affect the behaviour of people and groups whether they conceive of these things or not. However, it is obviously important to distinguish between naïve realism, which assumes the world is precisely as the observer perceives it to be, and critical or reasoned realism in science, which proposes that an external world exists, but that obtaining reliable knowledge of it is not straightforward and may often turn out to be extremely problematic. For critical realists, the world is distinct from the accounts of it that may be available or which may be produced. There is an unavoidable and necessary distinction between the things and events in the world as they are and any descriptions or accounts of them. The distinction cannot be removed and, because of it, knowledge of the world is always only approximate and provisional. The universe is assumed to be both complex and infinite in extent, while accounts of things (including developed knowledge) are necessarily limited, constrained by the modes of expression and calculation available.

Yet accounts of things and events are reliable to varying degrees. Just as maps and models are not to be confused with reality, they may nonetheless sometimes be used to provide reliable guidance to thought and action. Thus, it is a cornerstone of social scientific or critical realism that social phenomena can be grasped by concepts and, from the use of these, reliable theoretically based accounts of the way the world is arranged can be developed. It is a foundational idea that groups, organizations and key social processes are the basic stuff of the social world. But they can be accurately conceptualized and their effects assessed. Thus the choice of the concepts used to describe social phenomena and the choices made about the ways concepts may be combined into theoretical propositions are key processes in the development of knowledge. Also important, as knowledge is developed, are the ways concepts and theories are used in conjunction with appropriate research investigations. Well-designed research, realists believe, can improve and develop knowledge. Hence, realists think that in favourable circumstances logically rigorous and empirically grounded accounts of organizations and related social processes can be produced. Because of this, both collectivities (such as groups and organizations) and causal processes within and between them are held to be real in a similar way to material things. (For the senses in which social things are taken to be real, see Fleetwood, 2005.)

Realist social ontology

As has been said, realism gives primacy to ontology. For realists social entities and social processes have some distinctive properties which make them unique as a subject matter for science and which should be grasped before they can be effectively studied. One such key property is that social phenomena are both subjectively and objectively knowable. Groups and collectivities originate in the sociability of people and their subjectivity is basic to this, but the groups they create are not to be identified as purely subjective phenomena. The groups people form have emergent properties that have effects on behaviour and which are the key aspects of scientific enquiry. This is also clear in the processes that constitute and connect institutions and organizations. Thus, for realists, the attitudes and beliefs of people are only part of the subject matter. Also important are social and organizational structures and the processes that connect them. As Layder (1993: 50) has suggested: '... a central feature of realism is its attempt to preserve a *scientific attitude* towards social analysis whilst, at the same time, recognizing the importance of actors' meanings and incorporating them into research' (emphasis added).

So it is that the attitudes and values of groups of participants are carefully considered in any investigation and accounts of these are used as necessary building blocks in the construction of more general accounts involving social structures and processes; but information concerning ideas and motivations is not all that is considered. It is obviously correct that any human group or organization is subjectively known by the participants in them, and the views and attitudes of participants in groups is usually a key feature securing their production and reproduction. However, realists do not accept that groups and organizations are constituted by ideas and discourses, so that groups and organizations are only held to affect behaviour because they are subjectively conceived by the people involved in them.

Realists usually envisage the existence of: individuals with ideas, motivations and dispositions to act; collective entities with quite different properties such as belief systems and ideologies and social structures; and formative social processes within and connecting social groups. Thus, collective entities and social processes are distinct from and not reducible to individuals, and the extent of processes connecting these is often largely unrecognized by participants in them, and has to be discovered by research. Because two generic types of social subject matter – individuals and groups – are recognized and considered, realist social ontology is sometimes said to be 'dualist' (Reed, 1997).

Realists hold that, in their manifest (or, as they would usually put it, their 'actual') forms, any group or organization is produced and reproduced by the people in it, as they engage in their organizational roles and group activities. However, for the realist, any group, institution or organization is not simply the product of, and reducible to, its components. The reality of groups, organizations, etc. and the causal processes associated with them, is asserted because the relationships which arise from interaction have both behavioural manifestations that can be observed; but also, considered as collectivities, they have emergent properties (which can be observed and to some extent measured). Thus a distinction is made between, on the one hand, the way in which any group or organization is produced by recurrent relationships and the distinctive emergent properties (of structure, culture and process) it also acquires on the other. Whether self-consciously acknowledged or not, the emergent properties of groups can and do affect outcomes independently of the expectations of participants. Thus, recession in the economy will produce unemployment that will affect people deeply, whether they acknowledge the causal processes producing unemployment or not. In this respect the properties of groups and their effects are comparable to material things and processes (Archer, 2002).

Ubiquitous change

For realists change is endemic to social relationships and to groups: it is in the nature of these things. The reasons for this are several, but the basic reason is that groups and organizations are routinely produced and reproduced by the everyday action of individuals. Analytically considered, organizations are sets of processes put in motion by the mutually regarding actions of members, and so change is present in groups and organizations if only because the behaviour of participants varies over time. Thus, almost everywhere change is likely. When employees return to work after a holiday break, as they resume their work roles, they also collectively reconstitute the organization to which they belong. However, individuals and groups do not remake the group or organization by their behaviour and relationships precisely the same as it was before.[2] There is the possibility of simple errors in the reproduction of organizational relationships as they are remade, but there are also more systematic sources of organizational change, such as, for example, the pursuit of other objectives and agendas than those desired by those who direct and control an organization. Building on these basic insights, realists tend to think in terms of typical cycles of social reproduction and processes generating change. These are evident, for example, in the ever present processes of the production, reproduction and transformation of groups and organizations. It is the recurrent or typical features – such as processes of incremental of improvement or of decline – that are of most interest to realists.

The key point to note, however, is that there are usually in operation some recurrent processes. Realists do not typically assume, however, that these processes mainly ensure social reproduction, homeostasis as it is called. They are usually more interested in formative social processes that, although undoubtedly produced by the interaction of many participants, proceed in consistent directions beyond the control of any one individual or group. These are noteworthy because of their causal effects, and are described by realists in various ways – as formative 'mechanisms' or 'generative processes' or simply 'processes' – to which specific outcomes can be connected. For example, growth in business activity is an expected tendency as organizational members respond to business opportunities. In addition, however, an organization's members are also likely to interpret the objectives and policies of their organization in different ways. As well as attempting to meet the objectives given to them by their managers, for example, employees and employee groups also pursue and develop agendas and objectives of their own. Indeed, this sort of thing may lead to contention between groups and to the emergence of characteristic forms of organizational politics and some distinctive associated organizational processes. Such processes can be highly consequential for organizations and, clearly, may affect their efficient working. Realists tend to be found quite often thinking in terms of the comparative differences in the situations they are studying, in terms of the relative importance of individuals, groups and the roles that each may play in producing specific recurrent generative processes and particular types of outcomes.

The point is that interaction leads to the production of a system of relationships with emergent properties that bind sets of individuals into distinctive patterns of activity and processes of change. The objective of research is to bring out what generative processes of this kind there are and how they work. Thus, when they describe emergent structures, realists are not likely to make elaborate typologies of different organizational forms. Although they may use any existing organizational models as reference points with which to make comparisons, and even to create them, models and typologies are certainly not the end point of research work. For most realists whilst there are individual and group actions (including typical mental states and dispositions to act) and there are structures and interactive processes with emergent properties of their own distinctive kind (*sui generis*), the point is to create accounts of formative processes using these basic building blocks. It is the latter that tend to be thought of as fundamental and real and the basis for any explanations of events. Obviously organizations are not the only important social groups, so realists also envisage other entities and see organizations as being embedded in a particular social and economic context, which external entities can profoundly affect the activities of organizations. Andrew Pettigrew, for example, distinguishes between what he calls the internal and external context of organizations, drawing a distinction between the entities internal to the organization that comprise it and contribute to its properties and the entities external to the organization – the state and other organizations for example – that may in their turn affect the organization from the outside. Such concerns are widespread amongst realists.

Theory and the identification of generative processes

Despite the complexity of events, for the realist, there can be highly effective representations of things which describe aspects of the world. Ideally these are simple accounts of formative processes that can be seen to be active in a variety of different situations. However, what distinguishes these accounts is that, although they necessarily simplify complexity, they may sacrifice little in terms of accuracy. Thus, although in some ways it is not ideal because they are static, maps are a useful model for some aspects of what realists envisage here. A map is a highly simplified representation of some territory; but it is, nonetheless, a reliable guide to key features of the landscape, the relative distances between places, the topography of the region depicted and so on. Mapping also shares some of the features realists attribute to the process of knowledge creation, in that map-making is a collective and ongoing practice and achievement. Early maps were crude by comparison with today's resources but early efforts have clearly been improved by numerous individual contributions, not to mention the development of new technologies. It is held that social science may work in this sort of way in that it offers simplified accounts of key aspects of social institutions and processes. Thus, although social life may appear to be complex, specific features of it – typical motivations and structures as well as key formative processes (in particular the last of these) – may be grasped theoretically, and the effects of such formative processes validated (or not) empirically by their effects. In this way, potentially at least, research provides a route to improved knowledge.

Looked at like this, a realist project in organization and management studies implies abandoning commonsense or widely accepted representations of organizations and events taking place in them in favour of drawing selectively on these and other materials to understand motivations and structures and then the processes at work producing particular outcomes. Hence realist-informed research projects involve the idea that there are causal relationships to be discovered, in which, for instance, event x is caused by antecedent event e (or, much more likely, the combined effects of events e1 to en). However, the causal efficacy of a relationship is not given by empirical conjunction. Causal relationships have to be theoretically grasped before the nature of any connection can be established, and the explanation for any events determined. In any given situation there are, it is envisaged, chains of events, constituted by the combined properties and tendencies of social groups, which can be shown to occur in particular and identifiable recurrent sequences. Taken together, typical sequences of events are thought of as causal mechanisms or processes. The idea of causal mechanism or necessary process is invoked because the processes are thought of as necessarily connected, as are the parts of a machine. Such processes may also be thought of as being operative in many situations, and, when they are activated, they bring about particular outcomes recurrently. In this way, the realist-informed researcher hopes to produce accounts which invoke the tendencies and powers to people and groups which, taken together, constitute key generative mechanisms in social and organizational life.

There are numerous examples of processes that might be cited as exemplary to illustrate. Perhaps the clearest examples come from single company case studies. Gouldner's study of interactions leading to the wildcat strike in his factory, or Burawoy's study of the effects of competition between employees in his are just two of many examples from the classic literature in organizational behaviour that might be cited. More compelling, however, are the conceptions of processes built up from many studies, such as the ways in which management policies and employee responses led to the more and more elaborate and bureaucratized type of managerial regime in factories that was constructed in the twentieth century. The process – or more accurately the set of linked processes we now understand – was initiated when management began to pay systematic attention to the amount of work operatives were actually doing. Early practitioners like F. Taylor noticed that, to a considerable extent, employees in factory settings were controlling their own level of work. This traditional pattern of working effort was construed as 'soldiering' by Taylor and controls (such as close supervision and piecework) were put in place to curb it. The response of employees was to defend their traditional work levels, by innovating responses such as collusion over output quotas, manipulation of the process of setting piecework prices and cutting corners to produce more output with the same effort. As the intensity and effectiveness of supervision increased so more innovations (such as utilitarian sabotage and absenteeism) were improvised to redress the balance. For their part, management introduced systematic task redesign and training for supervisors. The key points in what is now seen as an extended process of the managerialization and bureaucratization of factory work have been in described many times, and they are depicted as set of related processes or a mechanism by realist researchers (see, for example, Ackroyd and Thompson, 1992: Figure 4.2).

235

The processes of action and response briefly described above, which began to be pieced together from observations in particular factories, obviously took some time to understand; but one point to note is that any emergent understanding of complex processes is not limited because insights into them are gathered by case-study work in one workplace. Accounts of very general processes can be and often are assembled from theoretical work and field studies undertaken independently. In essence, to perceive formative processes and indeed to establish how and when they work, researchers combine concepts (with which they characterize the processes theoretically) with observations (which potentially validate their ideas empirically). Thus, in order to be perceived in the first place, formative processes are necessarily observed within particular contexts. For them to be established as distinctive mechanisms they must be clarified and differentiated from the context of discovery. Thus, generative mechanisms or formative processes are seen as sequences that work themselves out within contexts, but which are only partially shaped by this. It follows that one important task of research is actually to clarify the contours of a mechanism so that it can be seen in operation in many different contexts and become the subject of generalization. In this conception, the role of theory is to propose the existence of what are, at the outset of the research, largely hidden causal mechanisms or generative processes and to isolate these from their context. The role of empirical research is to consider the evidence that suggests a particular causal mechanism might be at work and in what way it may be thought of as integral to or distinct from the social matrix in which it occurs. Hence, although a given causal mechanism may be shaped by a particular context, it is sufficiently independent from that context to be recognized as distinctive and, analytically at least, detachable from it. Once clarified the possibility of the mechanism – or something very like it – being at work in other contexts too may be considered.

The context of a mechanism may be seen as some but not all of its necessary preconditions. Thus a theory of organization has, as a part of its necessary context, general and developmental features such as a developed commercial system, product and labour markets and, although the polity may vary greatly, there must be minimally a political system that is tolerant of the private ownership and use of economic assets. Such conditions are not always acknowledged in a specific theory itself, which refers only to such things as the roles and behaviour of key stakeholders and participating groups and the emergent configuration of the organization, and so on. Clearly, there are necessary limits in the extent to which contextual features can be enumerated, and the realist approach implies any search for antecedent conditions is limited to the identification of those that are critical to particular outcomes. Different groups of realists differ on the extent to which it is necessary to theorize – especially about the nature of the context.

Not the explanation of change, but processes of change as explanations

Realist explanation

In general the goal of realist-informed research is to identify the real mechanisms or generative processes that produce outcomes. Explanation resides in showing that the working out of a process has a necessary and causal sequence. Thus things and events are explained as the outcome of identifiable processes and the context in which they occur. When characterizing their idea of explanation, the idea of mechanism is compelling to some realists, despite its connotations of mechanisms not involving human judgement or discretionary behaviour. But the idea of mechanism is only a metaphor and one that is attractive because it emphasizes that the processes identified have a necessary, even an inexorable, aspect. In this conception, the processes of interest are seen to have a logic driving them, which is operative despite (if also because of) the individual will of participants. As has been argued also, the processes of interest do not simply result in the reproduction of social and organizational arrangements, they tend to produce recurrent sequences of change. So, for realist-informed researchers, the problem of research is not so much explaining change as proposing sequences of change as the explanation of events. Distinctive processes of change are central to the explanations realists propose.

Realist explanation combines theoretical elements (proposing generative processes and generalizing about them) and empirical evidence (specifying data that are indicative of mechanisms and showing how they operate and in what circumstances they are or are not operative). Thus, explanation does not depend mainly, as in positivism, on logical inferences from theoretical postulates (i.e. deduction) or generalization from evidence (i.e. induction). Explanation is concerned with revealing the working of mechanisms and is essentially either abductive (in which events and processes are construed as part of a necessary pattern or sequence) or retroductive (in that the conditions necessary for the existence of a mechanism are identified). Just as in positivist research in practice, in which the research process involves the use of both deduction and induction, so an adequate account of realist-informed research involves, in practice, recognition of the use of both abduction (the recognition of sequences and patterns) and retroduction (considering the conditions of the existence for such patterns). Thus we have, in abduction, the construal of events as processes constituting necessary patterns or causal sequences. In addition, however, we have accounts of the necessary conditions for the existence of such processes or mechanisms (retroduction). For a more complete account of the different logics of scientific discovery named here, see Blaikie (2000) and specifically as they apply to realism, see Ackroyd (2010).

Figure 16.1, which sets out the range of research methods realists researchers employ, suggests a link between the kinds of research design project utilized by realist informed researchers (second row), their research stratey (third row) and the logic of explanation as briefly outlined in the paragraph above (bottom row). As will be discussed more fully later in the chapter, both intensive and extensive methods are used. At this point it should be also noted that different kinds

A continuum of research Designs: from Intensive ← --- →to Extensive				
Research Design	Focussed Case Studies	Simple comparative case studies	Studies to clarify and isolate generative mechanisms	Population studies using surveys and other data
Research Objective	To establish what mechanism(s) exist	To show how Mechanism and Context (a) have interacted differentially to produce some unique outcomes	(b) have generally intersected to produce similar outcomes	To establish the context or key features of it (mechanism given or conjectured)
Dominant logic of discovery	mostly abduction	maj = abduction minor = retroduction	maj = retroduction minor = abduction	mostly retroduction

Figure 16.1 Research designs used in realist-informed research, their objectives and logics
Sources: Harre and Secord (1972); Sayer (1993); Dannermark et al. (2002)

237

of projects rely differentially on abductive and retroductive logics. Intensive research is concerned primarily with establishing the operation of processes or mechanisms and the use of abductive logic. This suggests why case-study research is so attractive and so recurrently used by realist inclined researchers. Case studies are typically intensive investigations of limited contexts and allow aspects of the processes underlying presenting events to be built from a close consideration of the attitudes, values and behaviour of particular groups. In contrast, extensive designs are primarily utilizing retroductive logic as a basis for explanation.

Mechanisms and methodology

For realists, the role of methodology in research is to assist the search for evidence that establishes, confirms or (more rarely) calls into question the existence of postulated generative mechanisms/ processes. Research takes place against the background of a particular construal of existing work, and it is useful to the extent that it leads on to the development and or the correction of theoretical ideas. Observations are not regarded as data in the positivist sense, so much as highly selected indicative observations. The research that gathers and organizes data so defined is specifically conceived in terms of whether or not it will produce observations that instanciate particular conceptualizations of causal mechanisms. Proposals about possible mechanisms have to be initially conceived and research is always theoretically driven because it is the conceptualization of possible processes that governs what evidence is sought and, to a considerable extent, how it is appraised. However, knowledge is secured and developed only to the extent that theory postulating the existence of formative processes actually explains perceived events. Thus methodology (and indeed research practice itself) tends to be allocated the role of under-labourer to the master-builder of theory.

Thus, at the outset of research work, existing work (theoretical or empirical) has to be appraised – not to find hypotheses to test – but for clues it can give about likely generative processes that may be at work. Indeed, much recognizably realist work features the critical reappraisal of work already undertaken. Indeed the process of organizing existing findings around the idea of generative mechanisms often reveals new insights, and realist research may stop at this point, after a review of existing work. Theoretical critique of existing work, and theoretical work developing ideas, are legitimate objects of research in this conception of social science. Accordingly, realist research may often be simply scholarly in the sense of undertaking a scrupulous review and appraisal of existing evidence and ideas in a field. Given this priority to conceptualization, data are evidence often taken to be important (or not) because they are indicative (or not) of a specific theoretical account of particular mechanisms and so contribute to explaining outcomes in particular ways. While there is no implication that expectations will dictate research findings, it is a danger. It is certainly also something of a weakness in this approach that the validity or reliability of evidence is usually considered to be a subordinate problem to the relevance of findings to existing ideas about postulated mechanisms and their likely effects. In short, there may not be enough attention paid to the question of the qualities of the evidence on which knowledge is based. If the extent to which data can be thought of as independent of the concepts describing it is taken to be limited, there is all the more reason for carefully constructing routines and procedures that limit the possibility of error.

It is surprising therefore that the attention of realists to the contribution that appropriate research design and techniques of data collection and evaluation might make to the development of knowledge have been regarded as relatively unimportant. This situation is changing and attention to it is one of the important areas of innovation in realist organization studies. The foundational texts on realist methodology by Sayer (1993) and Danermark et al. (1997) drew on initial ground-clearing work by Harre and Secord (1972). As a result they distinguish realist approaches to method in terms of whether they are 'intensive' or 'extensive'. This dimension is also suggested at the top of Figure 16.1 But how far specific research designs were designated because they were seen to be directly related to the underlying logic of scientific discovery was not closely specified. Discussions of intensive studies clearly drew on ethnographic models, and the research procedures envisaged went beyond the idea that the researcher should be immersed in the situation under study and take copious notes. Intensive studies clearly allowed procedures as formal interviewing – as well as the collection and citation of available statistics if relevant and available. In short, the kind of intensive study implicitly recommended is best seen as case-study work. But how, when and in what ways more extensive research – and the precise research designs – could prioritize more generality and representativeness was not made very clear. One of the effects of a lack of clarity here was that research training was not either routinized or very thorough; it was a far cry from the highly professionalized programmes available to positivist researchers and their trainers. In practice, research projects often involved investigators devising fresh research procedures for each new project and they were often limited to the use of data available as a result of the particular access to the subject organizations that had been granted.

At the other end of the continuum to intensive case studies, which were and still are the almost automatic choice for realist-inclined researchers in one form or another, are extensive studies of large samples or populations. Realist studies of whole populations, as well as very large-scale studies of groups, organizations and social classes, were clearly envisaged by some realists (Sayer, 1993; Byrne, 2002). However, writers on realist research methods do not say with any precision how research designs can be tailored to a particular conception of process. Clearly, positivist types of large-scale survey, using similar research instruments and designed to produce data to which inductive statistics can be routinely applied, are not envisaged and are viewed with extreme scepticism. Realists tend to be highly critical of such methods. Even those researchers using survey techniques are highly critical of them and disposed to want to make extensive adaptations to them (Byrne, 2002). Currently, the need for more prescription about techniques and the provision of materials to teach about a range of research methods has recently been more fully addressed by textbooks adopting (Robson, 2002) or aware of realism (Blaikie, 2000). If the present account has any merit, it is in specifying more clearly why the particular range of research methods is adopted by realist-inclined researchers in organizational and management studies. Clearly this matter of methods is a critical area for the development of the realist approach to social science.

The methods realists actually employ

Intensive research, in which many sources of data concerning the same situation are appraised, is indispensable for realists because this type of research allows complex sets of interactions – of the kind that are involved in generative mechanisms – to be considered. Such research gathers information from a range of sources over relatively long periods of time. In such studies the research problem involves establishing the nature of any mechanisms whilst the organizational context is taken as largely unchanging and given. In such studies the context is arbitrarily fixed at the outset so that the nature of the mechanisms at work in the research organization can be progressively clarified. Extended and focussed observations of this kind can provide the detail that will establish whether causal connections occur or not. Such procedures, given an appropriate level of theoretical creativity on the part of the researcher, have a chance of making sense of any complex processes at work.

239

For the above reasons, case studies may be thought of as the primary research design in the realist cannon. Case studies are particularly appropriate in organization and management studies. Of course, case studies need not be studies of organizations but may be defined as inter-organizational processes or social and organizational interactions. However, realists have a penchant for focussed case studies and it is no accident that the earliest of avowedly realist research methods texts was a detailed manual for intensive case-study research (Miles and Huberman, 2004). Organizations are delimited sites, and they are arenas in which complex processes are at work by design. It should be no surprise that intensive case studies focussing on particular organizations are frequently used, therefore. Lines of research, and indeed schools of thought, can be traced to the insights gained from highly perceptive single case studies. Given the idea with which realists typically begin, that there are mechanisms in operation and that existing theory and research provides guidance as to what they might be, new observations and data collection can be appropriately focussed on the relationships and connections of interest within intensive case-study research. Thus case-study work will typically involve bringing into focus particular features of the organization under study, but it will also allow a theoretical under-standing of general mechanisms to be developed. Beyond a certain point, the limitations imposed by focussed case studies are many, though they do not include the proposition that cases do not allow generalization. Such an allegation, though often advanced, simply misunderstands the relation of theory and empirical research. Only one exemplary case is needed to show definitively that a particular causal mechanism exists; and which, once discovered, can be seen to be at work in many places.

Because theory is what guides research, the information thought to be most relevant in a research project will shift as the researchers' ideas and understanding are refined and devel-oped. A change of focus or direction is relatively easily accommodated in ongoing intensive case-study work, and this is another reason why such research designs are often preferred. The flexibility of this kind in research, that is, the possibility it offers to change emphases in observations and, if necessary, the whole direction a project is taking, is obviously sometimes very helpful. However, the willingness to shift the focus of research as it proceeds is a design feature that is in sharp contrast to other prescriptions about how research should be under-taken, particularly positivist conceptions. Flexibility of this kind comprehensively breaks the rules in the positivist conception of research, in which the search for enduring associations is key, and so making measurements of 'variables' defined at the outset of the work and then carefully measured as the research proceeds are required. Definitively validating (or not) key hypotheses is the goal of positivist research, and changing the objectives before the results are in makes little sense. In realist conceptions, by contrast, methodology is subordinate to theory and is valuable only in so far as it facilitates the development of theoretical understanding. Indeed in this conception, when theoretical insight is achieved, and some evidence to support the existence of theoretically postulated generative mechanisms is found to exist, the research task is complete. Then, new research efforts become relevant to extend or test existing knowledge. In a useful recent methodology textbook written from a realist point of view, Robson (2002) makes the flexibility of intensive research designs their chief distinguishing characteristic.

The key point is, however, not the capacity for flexibility per se, but the recognition of the importance of theory development to research. It is the latter that is important and it is made more possible by a capacity to respond to findings flexibly; that is all. Research necessarily makes the likely realization of theory – and, if possible, better theory – paramount. Typically, realist informed researchers progressively focus on making observations that, according to their devel-oping understanding of what is happening, give insights into elements of the underlying generative mechanisms. When some theoretical understanding of the causal processes occurring in a case-study organization has been developed, then comparative case research, designed to pin down and assess the working of the mechanism in different contexts, becomes relevant. In general, when theoretical understanding has been more fully developed, less intensive research and more extensive research designs become appropriate. Table 16.1 suggests the range of research designs that have been envisaged – and to a variable extent adopted – in realist research. It preserves, in its horizontal dimension, the distinction between intensive and extensive types of research first introduced by Harre and Secord (1972). However, here the horizontal dimension is not seen as a continuum, but is used to differentiate some distinctive designs that have been used by realists in successful research projects.

What distinguishes these designs is not the qualities of the data these methods prioritize – whether it is measurable or at what level – as is argued by some social science methodologists, such as Alan Bryman, to be a basic issue (Bryman, 1988). Realist research designs do not prioritize one kind of data over another, or give more credence to higher over lower levels of measurement. If anything the opposite is the case. Realist research ideally combines and utilizes any types of data that are relevant or available or can be collected. Both evidence for the attitudes and inclinations of groups of actors (attitudes towards work) and quantitative data relating to outcomes (say of the extent of absenteeism) are needed to illustrate the existence and operation of mechanisms connecting management policy and worker responses, for example. The key to Figure 16.1 is in understanding the way in which the designs aim at prioritizing different aspects of effective explanation as it is conceived by realists. Most simply, the target of research in the consideration of a case is about discovering a mechanism (which explains by construing events as part of a necessary sequence). This type of research typically utilizes simple case-study designs. Alternatively, when the processes at work are to some extent known, research may become focussed on finding out how a mechanism operates by exploring the relative importance of the mechanism itself and the extent to which the process described is modified by the context in which it is found. This latter type of research typically utilizes comparative research designs of some kind, and tends to include quantitative data more often. As will be argued more fully below there are at least two types of approach here. Finally research may be simply aimed at discovering more about contexts themselves. Again if something is known about the operation of a process, at some point it becomes relevant to explore key features of the context and to consider how widespread these features are. This type of research can hardly avoid being quantitative. Thus, different types of research design use different mixes and types of data. Quantitative data becomes progressively more important as research becomes more extensive in scope.

Processes in context

Between intensive studies which typically examine a single research site and studies aimed at revealing the character of populations which are necessarily extensive in scope, there are, as suggested by Figure 16.1, some other intermediary research designs. It is important to distinguish these. Figure 16.1 identifies simple comparative case-study research designs and what are called studies of generative processes.

There is a sense in which all realist research is comparative, even though not all of it is designed to be so. When thinking about the mechanisms that may be at work in a single case, it is helpful to consider how outcomes would be different if a postulated process were not there. Thus even intensive work aiming to establish that a putative mechanism exists entails considering the possibility of its absence. It is a small but important step on from this to attempting to understand the character of a process more fully or accurately by considering how it works in different examples. Such research is overtly comparative and will involve the selection of cases in which the process operates differently; very little, or a lot more or only intermittently, by comparison with an original case or an abstract model of the mechanism. However, thinking in terms of a distinctive mechanism operating implies that, to some important degree, the process is independent of its context. To postulate a distinctive process we envisage that a process can and does work in its distinctive way without undue interference from the context. It is precisely because of the existence of a particular mechanism that a particular outcome will typically occur. To clarify this, it is useful to think in terms of the *intersection* or meshing of the mechanism and its context, so that the one is necessary to it – but does unduly affect it. Thus the basic form of comparative research is designed to establish the precise nature of generative process and so to distinguish mechanism and context. The main target is clarifying and establishing the essential nature of a mechanism as a theoretically necessary phenomenon. Although it is always recognized that the context may influence a process, the latter is causally prior, in that its existence of is the primary explanation of distinctive outcomes.

Alternatively, it is possible to consider the *interaction* of mechanism and context over a range of places and times, and to examine the ways in which the two *taken together* produce a distinctive outcome. Here again the research design is explicitly comparative but here the interest is in combinations of process and context. Crucially this research investigates the possibility of unique outcomes. Although the distinction between intersection and interaction may seem a fine one, it is actually crucially important, pointing to the possibility of two different kinds of comparative research. On the one hand, that involving intersection of mechanism and context is primarily aimed at clarifying theoretical propositions, the main objective being to establish the nature and properties of the a process under study. By contrast with this, thinking in terms of the combined effects of process and context implies that contingent events in the context may sometimes circumvent the general tendency predicted by the central process. Such possibilities are clearly important when they occur, especially if accounting for a unique outcome is the main purpose of research. On the other hand, there is a danger of such research sinking into a mass of detailed observations in which cause and effect are not clearly seen. That research can establish that outcomes necessarily occur for theoretical reasons may be compromised or lost. Even at its best this kind of research offers less certain explanations, not to mention less predictability concerning outcomes. Recognizing the possibility that contextual events may interfere with any outcome brings the result of research closer to the kinds of ideographic results achieved in historical research and this contrasts with the nomothetic ideal which is arguably central to the idea of social science. Nevertheless this is obviously an important area of work, and studies that disentangle the general trend from the particular effects of those trends in different societies for example are amongst the most important of historical and contemporary scholarship (Weber, 1958; Moore, 1966; Edwards, 1986).

Finally, realists have an interest in undertaking research primarily aimed at exploring contexts. Revealing the general character of the context – how extensive certain general conditions may be – becomes relevant once there are firm ideas about processes or mechanisms. Large social entities may of course become cases, as in the work of the institutional writing of Whitley and his collaborators (Whitley, 1992, 1999). It is also a valid area of enquiry – once the processes of interest have been clarified – to ask the related research question: how widespread are the contexts that are now seen as fostering and supporting key generative mechanisms? In principle, realist researchers must be interested in large, quantitative data sets if they may be used to describe the context of a chosen process in a theoretically germane way. Thus realist researchers are potentially interested in using large-scale surveys and the use of data relating to organizational populations, demographic and other data as understanding the context of key processes. These are important areas of growth for realist research.

Brief conclusions

Realist thought and research is clearly not over and done. Although this argument has not been developed substantively, it might have been. There are several active groups of realist researchers, whose work can be seen to be producing cumulative results. The Kuhnian idea of normal science – where numerous scientists work on the puzzles implicit in their shared general conception of the field, which Kuhn (1970) calls their paradigm – offers a plausible and helpful account of what seems to be going on (Ackroyd, 2009). Moreover, the explanation of change is central to realist research agendas, whichever active branch of contemporary realist scholarship is considered. If the argument of this chapter is correct, there is today a more and more explicit understanding of the character of social-science practice and some clear goals of realist research. One of the areas of the continuing debate about realism, which was considered quite fully in the second half of this chapter, has concerned the perceived problems of realist methodology. In the eyes of some, the lack of development in this area has held the approach back from development. But it is clear that such limitations are largely illusory, springing more from the reluctance of many realist researchers to move on from the certainties of focussed case-study work than from any intractable problems in the logic of explanation or the lack rigorous research methods. The prospects for realist-informed understanding of our changing world were never better.

Notes

1 First, there is a group that may be considered *critical realists* (identified with the work of such researchers as M. Burawoy, P. Edwards, P. Thompson, C. Smith, and T. Elger amongst others); second, there are *engaged realists* (identified with the work of A. Pettigrew and R. Whipp, their other research associates, and A. Van de Ven); and finally, there are the *policy realists* (identified here with the work of R. Pawson and N. Tilley and numerous other researchers – mainly working in different areas of public sector and in public policy research).
2 Social production of organizations is clearly, for this reason, much more like analogue as opposed to digital reproduction, with many mistakes possible in the reproductive process. Here, too, entropy is inevitable, and the need for energy to be devoted to renewal is essential if its effects are to be countered. Thus whilst the exact reproduction of social and organizational relationships is theoretically possible, in practice change is inevitable.

References

Ackroyd, S. (2009) 'Labour Process Theory as "Normal Science"', *Employee Responsibilities and Rights Journal*, 21: 263–72.

Ackroyd, S. (2010) 'Critical Realism, Organisational Theory, Methodology and the Emerging Science of Reconfiguration', Chapter 3 of P. Koslowski (ed.) *Elements of a Philosophy of Management*. Heidelberg: Springer.

Ackroyd, S. and Fleetwood, S. (2000) *Realist Perspectives on Management and Organisations*. London: Routledge.

Ackroyd, S. and Thompson, P. (1992) *Organisational Misbehaviour*. London: SAGE.

Archer, M. (2002) *Realist Social Theory: The Morphogenic Approach*. Cambridge: Cambridge University Press.

Archer, M., Bhaskar, R., Collier, A., Lawson, T. and Norrie, A. (1998) *Critical Realism: Essential Readings*. London: Routledge

Bhaskar, R. (1975) *A Realist Theory of Science*. Leeds Books. Second edition, 1979. Brighton: Harvester.

Bhaskar, R. (1986) *Scientific Realism and Human Emancipation*. London: Verso.

Blaikie, N. (2000) *Designing Social Research*. Cambridge: Polity.

Bryman, A. (1988) *Quantity and Quality in Social Research*. London: Unwin Hyman.

Burrell, W.G. and Morgan, G. (1979) *Sociological Paradigms and Organisational Analysis*. London: Heinemann.

Byrne, D. (2002) *Interpreting Quantitative Data*. London: SAGE.

Clark, P. (2000) *Organisations in Action: Competition Between Contexts*. London: Routledge.

Danermark, B., Ekstrom, M., Jakobsen, L. and Karlsson, J. (1997) *Explaining Society: Critical Realism in the Social Sciences*. London: Routledge (second edition, 2002).

Edwards, P. (1986) *Conflict at Work: A Materialist Analysis*. Oxford: Blackwell.

Fleetwood, S. (2005) 'Ontology in Organization and Management Studies: A Critical Realist Perspective', *Organization* 12 (2): 197–222.

Fleetwood, S. and Ackroyd, S. (2004) *Critical Realist Applications in Organisation and Management Studies*. London: Routledge.

Harre, R. (1972) *The Philosophies of Science*. Oxford: Oxford University Press.

Harre, R. and Secord, P. (1972) *The Explanation of Social Behaviour*. Oxford: Basil Blackwell.

Keat, R. and Urry, J. (1975) *Social Theory as Science*. London: Routledge.

Kuhn, T.S. (1970) *The Structure of Scientific Revolutions*. Chicago: University of Chicago Press (first edition, 1962).

Layder, D. (1993) *New Strategies in Social Research*. Cambridge: Polity.

Layder, D. (1998) *Sociological Practice: Linking Theory and Research*. London: SAGE.

Miles, M.B. and Huberman, A.M. (2004) *Qualitative Data Analysis: An Expanded Sourcebook*. Thousand Oaks, CA: SAGE (first edition, 1984).

Moore, B. (1966) *Social Origins of Democracy and Dictatorship*. Boston: Beacon

Nagel, E. (1961) *The Structure of Science: Problems in the logic of Scientific Explanation*. London: Routledge.

Reed, M. (1997) 'In Praise of Duality and Dualism: Rethinking Agency and Structure in Organisational Analysis', *Organisation Studies*, 18 (1):21–42.

Robson, C. (2002) *Real World Research*. Oxford: Basil Blackwell.

Sayer, A. (1993) *Method in Social Science: A Realist Approach* (first edition, 1982).

Sayer, A. (2000) *Realism in Social Science*. London: SAGE.

Van de Ven, A. (2007) *Engaged Scholarship: A Guide for Organizational and Social Research*. Oxford: Oxford University Press.

Weber, M. (1958) *The Protestant Ethic and the Spirit of Capitalism*. New York: Scribbeners (first published in German, 1904).

Whitley, R. (ed.) (1992) *European Business Systems: Firms, Markets and Their National Contexts*. London: SAGE.

Whitley, R. (1999) *Divergent Capitalisms: The Social Structuring and Change of Business Systems*. Oxford: Oxford University Press.

17

Organization theory, power and changing institutions

Stewart Clegg and John Gray

Introduction

Organization theory, as a family relative of sociology, has always suffered from a strain in its theorizing that relates to the status of its analytic categories. Are these analytic categories best formed as a coherent whole abstracted from the sense that the members have of the everyday scenes of action that theory takes as its objects for data collection, reflection and analysis, or should its categories be somehow grounded in the sense that the members make? The first strain is towards what we might call analytic coherence; the other is to what one might call member coherence.

The strain has run through anthropology and sociology for over a hundred years. On the one hand are those – from Marx through Parsons through to contingency theorists – who create an abstracted and coherent account of action that they then use to categorically order those actions they are accounting for. The dominant logic in the accounting process is that of the accounters, not the accounted. Such theorizing spawns false consciousness in its radical forms and deviancy and failure of socialization in its conservative forms. On the other hand, there are those who have sought to attend to the categories of action in use – what the members actually use to make sense of their lives – as the basis for theorizing, such as symbolic interactionism, ethnomethodology and grounded theory.

Each approach has a different take on power. Those who strain towards analytic coherence in many ways provide more theoretically cogent accounts, with theorists such as Parsons, with his account of power's positivity, or Marx, with his account of power's negativity, being the most evident. Those whose strain is towards member coherence have, on the whole, provided less adequate accounts of power because they have sought to see it purely in the action: the conversation analysis wing of ethnomethodology would be the best example of this, where power would be seen in conversational turn-taking, interruptions and related phenomena.

Institutional theory is the dominant means of sensemaking in use by the community of organization scholars today. We will argue that as it has become institutionalized; institutional theory has focused increasingly not only on the categories that its members use – rather than those the members of whatever scenes of action it attends to – but that it has whittled down the use of its categories to focus almost exclusively on those that are normative. The focus is overwhelmingly on cognitive and/or normative constructions through all of which power runs but which is rarely explicitly addressed. The consequence is that that there has been too much order and legitimacy in institutional theory and not enough disordering and power as well as too much concern with the categories of its own reasoning and insufficient regard for the categories of everyday reasoning. Institutionalism's relative neglect is problematic for a clear research agenda. In this chapter we recognize its value and seek to reconnect it to its roots of processes and structuration in order to provide an adequate power theory for changing institutions.

Exegesis

Institutions are those processes that become intrinsically valued (Selznick 1949). A body of scholarship has been erected upon that insight. Whilst commentators such as Aldrich (1999: 48–53) and Hirsch (1997: 1718) have laid out the role of institutional theory in explaining the stability of organizational types in a field, Greenwood and Hinings (1996) emphasize institutional theory's possibilities as a theory of change. Their purpose was, 'to set out a framework for understanding radical organizational change' (Greenwood and Hinings 1996: 1022). They linked the normative pressures of organizational context (which they describe as new institutionalism; DiMaggio and Powell 1991: 27) with organizational action in which interests, values, power and capability interplay, (which they describe as old institutionalism; Selznick 1949). Thus re-integrated institutionalism enables change, which they assert is intrinsic to the theory (Tolbert and Zucker 1983; Haunschild 1993: 564; Burns and Wholey 1993). For Greenwood and Hinings (1996: 1032) neo-institutionalist theory, therefore '... provides a more complete account for understanding organizational interpretations of, and responses to contextual pressures by stressing the political dynamics of intraorganizational behaviour and the normative embeddedness of organizations' and beyond this it provides a means of understanding how organizational entrepreneurs might evolve new templates which would compete for institutionalization (DiMaggio and Powell 1983; DiMaggio 1988; Sherer and Lee 2002). Thus they look beyond the expected question of 'Why do institutions endure?' and enquire 'Why do institutions develop?'

We are attracted to the hybrid approach being forged but see within it problems that are inherent to the institutionalist project. The first of these is an over-reliance upon structuration theory (Giddens 1976, 1979) that privileges individuals as agents and pays insufficient attention to non-actor agency, as Clegg (1989) argues. The second of these, odd as it may seem given a base of structuration, is the lack of attention to the quotidian micro-processes that discipline and form organizational virtue (Clegg 1990: 191). The third is the lack of an adequate theory of power for which this chapter provides remedies.

The chapter argues, first, in favour of a process, becoming a view of organizing rather than organizations, stressing ordering and disordering as equivalent, mutually implicated phenomena. Second, based on these points, the chapter argues that institutional theory has been overly concerned with one side only of the dialectics of ordering and disordering – and that has been a preference for order. Third, institutional theory's concern for order has been articulated in terms that are far too normative and that pay insufficient attention to power relations. Bringing power relations back into the picture, we argue, provides more specificity upon the theory's key category of the institutional entrepreneur. All theories have some account of whom or what that category might entail and we explore some of the more institutionalized accounts in our conclusion.

The micro-processes of organizing

Let us attend to micro-processes first. With regard to mainstream analyses, organization is not understood in terms of flux, emotion and unpredictability – instead it is seen as a means of ordering, structuring and controlling the chaotic world outside. In a seemingly chaotic world, it appears that human beings 'need to create a sense of order and make arrangements with each other, both to achieve security and to meet material needs' (Watson 1994: 222). Organization provides means for trying to achieve a stable, predictable and secure world. For such a notion of organization, that which is not rationally unified is considered to be threat to the very condition of being organized such that, for example, anything emotional and messy should be institutio-nalized through the regulation and repression of emotionality (Scherer and Tran 2001). This implies that to be irrational, emotional, unpredictable or undefined is a kind of organizational pathology, which must be controlled, organized, brought into line or even eradicated. The desire organizationally, as the name suggests, is to be 'organized' – that is to be controlled, defined and predictable. Managers are the agents that do this in search of efficiency and best fit with contingencies (Donaldson 2005).

A contrasting view sees organization as a 'reality-constituting and reality-maintaining activity' (Chia 1998: 366), an 'initial, artificial stabilizing of ... incessant and relentless change which, itself, is not entity-like at all' (Chia and King 1998: 466). Organizing is an 'inscription of order in relation to the otherness (and disorder) of the "unreal"' (Jeffcutt 1994: 245). The world is chaotic, in flux and transformation, and our effort to organize is 'the intrinsically human activity of forging order out of disorder, cosmos out of chaos ... organizations are provisionally ordered networks of heterogeneous materials whose resistance to ordering has temporarily been over-come' (Chia 1996: 51). People seek patterns. Organizing is one of many ways of pattern making. Organizing involves ordering and reducing complexity such that 'as we embody and perform ordering modes, so, too, we delete. This is what agency is about. It is what ordering is about: ignoring; simplifying; fixing what is complex for a moment in a stable form; reifying' (Law 1994: 132). While agency is often assumed to be a function of being human it can be found in forms of collective as well as individual social organization as well as in other non-human and hybrid entities.

Organizing: ordering/disordering

The recent fascination with chaos, disorder, noise, paradox and the whole range of concepts like *différance*, supplement, deconstruction (Derrida 1976), *différend* (Lyotard 1986), and deterritor-ialization (Deleuze and Guattari 1987) resides in the growing recognition that 'organization coexists with surprise; that unpredictability does not imply the absence of order; that recurrence does not exclude novelty' (Tsoukas 1998: 292). Organizing does not involve defining and ordering *per se*, so much as seeking pattern in situations where the conventional sense of orderliness reveals only confusion and noise.

Organizing translates raw, infinite matter into concrete, finite forms and objects and the redrawing of these in a perpetual work of (re)generation. Its categorical devices and methods both enable the grasp and representation of reality but simultaneously mask its inherent complexities with their accentuations and absences. Organization can be understood as oscillating between complexification and simplification, de- and re-construction, de- and re-territorialization. It is threatened both by the danger of imploding *and* exploding (Mintzberg 1991). It becomes an unfolding process of tension between order and disorder which pluralizes and cross-connects

247

artefacts and subjects, human and non-human elements. Thus seen, organization is not driven by intentions (of management) but is always 'in-tension' (Cooper and Law 1995). It is a process of linking and connecting that which otherwise would be separated.

Organization is space in which the order and disorder inherent in everyday organizing meet, creating and transgressing the boundaries between old and new, stable and unstable, drawing attention to the boundary areas: that 'margin created by the will and vision of a recurrent and predictable world on the one hand, and on the other the other the reality of a molten universe that is always on the verge of fusing its elements' (Kallinikos 1996: 23). Thus, organization is occurring in the border zones, in the grey area, where the collision of order and chaos, inside and outside, formal and informal, rationality and irrationality, structure and agency, configuration and process, meet in specific practices.

Practices comprise any types of organized human activities. Any practice may be defined as being an open-ended spatial-temporal manifold of actions that are not random because they exhibit some structured and recurrent features. These practices are achieved through the agency of individuals, groups or entities. The set of actions that composes a practice is organized by three phenomena: understandings of how to do things, rules and teleo-affective structure. The understanding of how to do things can bring with it norms or logics that are cosmopolitan (and for example involve barriers to entry as with professionals; Abbott 1988) or local (and protect current coalitions of power). Indeed whether cosmopolitan or local they may also be innovative. Rules comprise explicit formulations that prescribe, require, or instruct that a specific something or other be done, said, or apply; a teleo-affective structure is an array of ends, projects, uses (of things), and even emotions that are acceptable or prescribed for participants in the practice. In everyday life, organization and accomplishment, actions and the material arrangements that sustain them are entangled together in specific practices. For instance, driving as a practice requires cars, roads, fuel, oil companies, service stations and repair shops, Highway Codes, traffic lights, stop signs, sleeping police, patrol cars and so on. Driving as a practice is materially, symbolically and politically embedded in forms of local and global ordering.

The approach that is best able to capture the fundamental implication of the wider world in the grain of everyday local scenes of action and practice is ethnomethodology. For complex reasons related to the politics of knowledge and the timing of ideas, when Garfinkel's (1967) work first appeared, organization theory barely registered it, with a few exceptions such as Silverman (1971). In the late 1960s functionalism reigned almost everywhere; the Aston School was a dominant approach in the pages of the *Administrative Science Quarterly*, and in general sociology, ethnomethodology was viewed with great suspicion because of its radically reflexive programme, one that seemed to threaten many of the structural assumptions of more conventional sociologies such as Marxist-inspired conflict theory or Parsonian structural functionalism.

Ethnomethodologically, the foundations of social and moral order, as well as social change, emerge from mundane processes and practices situated in everyday life, talk and action. A sense of order is both oriented to and emerges in the practices of everyday life. These practices temper and shape organizing processes as agents attend not only to each other but also those things, such as machines and systems, with which their everyday life is populated. Ordinary people and ordinary groups of these people routinely reproduce the sense of order that sustains the normalcy of their projects in subtle, nuanced and fine-grained ways. For the researcher to gain access to these ordinary and ordinarily unremarkable ways of doing and being, everyday behaviour opens a window on the world being constructed and differentially valued. To understand changing institutions is to trace the behaviours that confirm and deny the virtue of routines or practices. These are enacted within groups and at any time the value commitment of groups will be competitive, reformative or indifferent (Hinings and Greenwood 1988). Hegemonic groups gain agency over organizations.

Whilst Selznick (1949) was alive to this, the new institutionalists (Meyer and Rowan 1977) were focused on how myths become legitimated.

Legitimacy and power

Institutional theories' key category is legitimacy. From nearly all perspectives in recent power debates, it has emerged that legitimacy itself is a problematic category, in which domination may well be present, as Weber, writing about the Bismarkian state, was well aware. If we look to Lukes' (2005) third dimension of power, Foucault's (1977) power/knowledge hypothesis, the various traditions of power analysis that build upon the Gramscian (1971) concept of hegemony and Bourdieu's (1990) concept of symbolic violence, etc., what lies at the centre of all these perspectives is the image of social actors acquiescing in their own domination. One way of theorizing this is to argue that these individuals perceive certain exercises of power, and structured relations of authority, as legitimate but (for various reasons) the observing sociologist or political theorist/scientist believes that the actors in question should not view them in this manner. In Lukes, actors consider power legitimate because they do not know what their real interests are. In Foucault they consider their objectification as subjects as legitimate because it is derived from some locally perceived concept of truth. In Gramsci, the subaltern classes accept *bourgeois* domination because they have internalized the latter's interpretative horizon and in Bourdieu, symbolic violence makes people 'misrecognize' reality. In all these versions of power and domination actors view social relations as legitimate due to some kind of cognitive shortcoming; the granddaddy of these accounts, of course, comes from Marx (and Engels). If it were not for cognitive shortcoming, the very same social relations would appear straightforwardly as domination.

In institutional theory there is the risk, as Garfinkel (1967) once observed of Parsons' functionalism, that one treats the person as a 'judgmental dope', as someone who doesn't know their own mind. Another way of thinking about it is to say that while people may not do or want what various sophisticated social theorists might in similar situations, this does not, in itself, invalidate their choices, some of which are small but cumulative. It might point up some of the implications and limits of those choices in ways that would not be immediately apparent.

It is evident that the coexistence of stasis and change and power and order comprises a key theoretical tension in institutional theory: as Leca and Naccache put it, 'How is institutional change possible if actors' intentions, actions and rationality are conditioned by the institutions they wish to change?' Or in other words, how can they exert agency as power against those structures that constrain them if those structures do, indeed, constrain them? How do we avoid reducing structure to action, or action to structure, or of merging both? Either actors' freedom or structural constraint must be denied unless an argument is made that 'structurating' is in progress as made by Giddens (1984), Scott (2004) and Hinings and Tolbert (2008).

An excess of order

Let us turn now to structuration and an adequate theory of power. The new institutionalist citation classic was DiMaggio and Powell's (1983) 'The Iron Cage revisited: Institutional Isomorphism and Collective Rationality in Organizational Fields'. Drawing on Meyer and Rowan (1977), and influenced by Bourdieu's ideas about practice, the paper considered how rational myths lodged in institutional settings shape organizational action to the extent that they can secure semblances of organizational legitimacy in order to capture resources and mobilize support.

There were two main signposts to subsequent research in the paper: the importance of the concept of organizational fields and the focus on mechanisms of organizational change through institutional isomorphism. The organizational field was defined in relational terms as 'those organizations that, in the aggregate, constitute a recognized area of institutional life: key suppliers, resource and product customers, regulatory agencies, and other organizations that produce similar services or products' (DiMaggio and Powell 1983: 148). Later they add that the field includes all those who have 'voice' as well as those who do not – picking up on Bachrach and Baratz's (1962, 1970) influential critique of Robert Dahl's (1961) work by stressing non-action, or absence from a field, as a significant form of presence. On the whole, this element of power has been largely absent from engagement with DiMaggio and Powell's work subsequently.

Institutional isomorphism has become, perhaps, the key concept for much mainstream organization studies work of the past decade and as Scott (1995, 2008) laments, it has replaced an emphasis upon the processes of daily life in organizing. Three ideal-type mechanisms of organizational change by institutional isomorphism were sketched: coercive (when external agencies impose changes on organizations – most obviously through practices of state regulation); normative (when professionalization projects shape entire occupational fields); and mimetic (essentially the copying of what is constituted as culturally valuable ways of doing or arranging things – cultural capital). Interest in the last category has far outweighed interest in the former two in empirical studies as Greenwood and Meyer (2008) note.

Ideal types tend to reification and institutional isomorphism mechanisms are no exception. It is this reification that makes many institutional analyses seem mechanical. As a theory designed to explain how things got to be the way they are and not just why they endure, institutionalism handles discontinuous change inadequately. In a famous turn of phrase, Zucker concluded that institutionalization means 'alternatives may be literally unthinkable' (1983: 5). Tolbert and Zucker (1983: 25) suggested three indicators of institutionalized practices: they are widely followed, without debate, and exhibit permanence. The notion that alternatives may be literally unthinkable is not a new one; it was, for instance, the basis of Steven Lukes' even more famous and, as it transpired, deeply problematic turn of phrase that coined the radical face of power as three-dimensional. Power relations, insofar as they have been addressed, for instance by Greenwood and Hinings (1996), have been represented in terms that are largely those of Lukes (1974).

This new institutional theory is generally acceded to stress that organizations are influenced by their *institutional context*, i.e. by widespread social understandings (*rationalized myths*) that define what it means to be rational. Meyer and Rowan (1983: 84) referred to the institutional context as 'the rules, norms, and ideologies of the wider society' Zucker (1983: 105) looked to 'common understandings of what is appropriate and, fundamentally, meaningful behaviour'. And Scott (1983: 163) offered 'normative and cognitive belief systems'. The underlying focus of these institutional theorists, in short, was the role of shared meanings, institutional processes (such as cultural prescriptions, Zucker, 1977) and institutional conformity.

There are two major problems with these views. First, they minimize the reflexivity that structuration theory suggests. Within this the new institutionalist tradition structuration is bowdlerized as meaning that fields have become tightly coupled (Greenwood and Hinings 1988, 1996). Second, they proceed without an adequate theory of power. They downplay reflexive interaction, conflict and overstress the primacy of order. This is apparent if we think of a major category of organization in modernity, that of the state. Are states secured organizationally because they are bound by the rules, norms and ideologies of the wider society, by common understandings of what is appropriate and, fundamentally, meaningful behaviour, by normative and cognitive belief systems? Well, the answer is that some states are to a great extent and some states are less so. The most stable states appear to be those liberal democracies that diffuse tensions throughout society; rationalized myths are important in this – think of the role that was played by 'market forces' in the UK under Thatcherism. But the rationalized myth did not create anything like common understandings – quite the opposite: the miners' strike; the poll tax riots, and so on. The rationalized myth was a mobilization by political and media elites. Institutional conformity was *not* the medium-term result. It was not the result because the political actors at that time did not accept the categories of the myth. It was only after Blair gained control of the Labour Party that the myth became institutionalized; only then were the categories of market forces established and stabilized. The important thing is that it was *not* the myth alone that did the stabilizing; it could not. On the contrary it was a political process. it was political agency making choices about the categories of reasoning.

At base, structuration and destructuration, institutionalization and deinstitutionalization, are about the categories of reasoning. Categories are the means through which we routinely, albeit largely unconsciously, observe and classify events and experiences as we understand them to be in the languages that we ordinarily use. They are ontologically prior to discourse and rhetoric, one more fundamental or philosophically primitive, as it were. Lakoff (1987: 5–6) suggests:

> There is nothing more basic than categorization to our thought, perception, action, and speech. Every time we see something as a kind of thing, for example, a tree, we are categorising. Whenever we reason about kinds of things – chairs, nations, illnesses, emotions, any kind of thing at all – we are employing categories.

And these categories are necessarily experiential and empirical; they are grounded in our ways of being in the world. Perhaps the most astute observer of this necessity was Harvey Sacks.

Within ethnomethodology and conversation analysis, Sacks (1972) suggests that membership categorization devices, which systematically follow rules of economy and consistency, signal how everyday activities are accomplished locally and recognizably. The terms are the members, not analysts, and they signify how members make sense of the world. It is in investigating how these categories are deployed that we can gain a grounded appreciation of the way that these members construct the world. Institutional theory is mostly concerned with the categories of the members of the institutional theory domain: it is strangely self-referential and inattentive to the everyday reasoning of everyday people. Functionalist auspices intrude.

In institutional theory such a great deal of energy goes into being similar to culturally valued organizations through mimesis that it is legitimate to ask how is it possible that organizations can change? This is the question the institutional entrepreneur is designed to answer; thus, institutional theory accounts for change in basically Schumpeterian terms. Initially developed as a theory of reproduction it sees change occurring when innovative and thus deviant modes of organizing acquire legitimation. When an innovative pattern is established by a previously powerful or currently successful agency a large part of the field follows. Eventually this manner of organizing becomes dominant.

Institutional theories' version of change focuses overly on a few champions of change and neglects the wider social fabric in which they are embedded. Nelson Mandela may have been an institutional entrepreneur in South Africa but without the long struggle, armed resistance and civil disobedience campaigns of the ANC he could not have achieved much. Of course, he is a remarkable political actor but he is precisely that – a political actor tangled up in a complex web of power and political relations.

The category of institutional entrepreneur 'saves' the theory by creating an account of how things and times change. Introducing the character of the institutional entrepreneur is an effect of a theory that institutes and institutionalizes macro/micro divisions, and then faces the embarrassment of bridging between that which it has sundered. The institutional entrepreneur is the category that institutionalism's functionalism requires in order to make change from isomorphized regimes possible

When we find agreed routines or structures in place – such as an apartheid regime – then their being taken-for-granted and their being contested are signs of power at work. What power is can be gleaned from its effects; where we find social realities that take on a stable, durable and material form in routines, actions, practices and we may take these to be effects of power that need not have any specific or particular intention 'behind' them. Where there is resistance to these forms of power it will tend to take the form of attempting to disequilibrate the rule-bound dominant order through the agency that institutionalist theory refers to as entrepreneurs.

When they disequilibrate, actors do not create or construct social reality *de novo* or merely in the present: they live in intersecting histories. Because these histories are overlapping and essentially contested, incomplete and indeterminate, they do not comprise a coherent whole. Any agents' practice that seeks to organize life wholly in terms of a singular institutional logic quickly becomes dogmatic, ideological and deeply divisive: think of the impact of various kinds of religious fundamentalism on social ordering in plural societies. Yet, whatever the impact, it depends on three things. First, social integrating practices, such as proselytizing, including and excluding. Second, institutional logics, such as belief systems whose legitimacy is not questioned, such as Islam, Pentecostalism or Catholicism. Third, structures, such as places of worship, as well as clergy, networks of relations between offices, organizations, and other institutions, such as government commissions, charities, and other circuits through which power relations might move. Institutional logics offer opportunities for causal powers to be elaborated if the standing or contextual conditions that enable them can be configured in a sustainable and stable way. Institutional entrepreneurs thus become those categories of agent that both stabilize standing conditions for causal powers to operate and use these casual powers in practice. Within these systems' integrating circuits of power standing conditions will be configured, thus solidifying institutional logics, that institutional entrepreneurs can to use rally and translate potential allies to their interests. The effects of their practice reproduce and transform the domain of the real through changing or maintaining patterns of events and experiences as these are discursively registered or not.

In conclusion: power

Any adequate theory of power must simultaneously be a theory of order and change, ordering and changing; it must address, at the same time, flux, flow and fixity. If we look to symbolic interactionism and the acute observations of Goffman (1961), it is obvious that structural reproduction is not always a foregone conclusion in every interaction, thus structuration has to be negotiated and must carefully delimit the agency of individuals. If we look to Foucault (1977), we also see that systems of meaning are frequently contested. For any social order to be established as 'the way we do things around here' – as obligatory passage points that become institutionalized – a great deal of strategic agency has to be carried out, which means that social structures and structuration practices are always up for grabs. In a sense, *destructuration* or the breaking down of structures is every bit as important to our understanding as routine structuration practices are. In contested social systems, which all systems to a greater or lesser extent are, the powerful try to maintain their power by ensuring predictability in structuration, while the less powerful have an interest in counter-hegemonic, destructuration practices. These introduce changes that sometimes may be radical and are not all exogenous; all theories of order must also be theories of change, as argued in *Frameworks of Power* (Clegg 1989), and the most important sources of change – and functionalism neglected them – are endogenous.

Power relations are the central concept of the social sciences because they anchor order. Mark Haugaard argues that in complex societies social power is based upon the reproduction of social order; a form of power that is more important in such contexts than is coercion. Simpler conceptions of power tend to see it as coercive: where some agent requires some other agent to do something that the other agent would prefer not to do but with which they comply, either because of the threat of sanctions or, in some cases, because of some inducement. An inducement is, of course, a threat at one stage removed: 'don't do this and you won't get that'. It is for this reason that the assertion that all organization represents a fair exchange because the balance of organization inducement and employee contributions would not produce the equilibrium position that the organization is assumed to be in are false; what is an inducement varies with circumstances and contexts. If circumstances and context dictate that this job must be accepted on those terms and that the alternative is no job, then the inducements are clearly coercive.

More complex and sophisticated accounts of power argue that power is an outcome of the creation of social order that goes beyond coercion. Actors reproduce social order that constrains, and is responsible for relations of power and powerlessness, but it also facilitates phenomena by conferring upon actors a capacity for social action. Such a capacity enables them to make things happen which would not otherwise occur; a form of power that can be exercised as 'power to' or 'power over' in the interests of all, contrary to their interests, for collective goals or solely for instrumental ends.

In this more sophisticated account of power, Haugaard argues, there are seven well-developed options in broader social theory.[1] In each power is created by a different set of phenomena: according to Parsons, it is created by system consensus directed towards systems goals; Luhmann sees the key elements to be trust in system reproduction; Barnes maintains that power is produced by self-reinforcing knowledge of rings of reference which define objects; for Giddens the capacity for social action derives from structuration; for Bachrach and Baratz it is the bias of a system that creates power; for Lukes it is 'false consciousness'; for Foucault it is an inseparable link between power and knowledge; for Clegg it is circuits of power that constitute social order; Arendt focuses on the ability to act in concert through the creation of legitimate polities, while for Weber and the Weberians, elements of coercion enter into the shaping of power relations.

From Haugaard's account it is possible to construct a typology that adds some organizational examples to those that he provides, in order to see how the different elements of the theoretical synthesis that he produces can address different concrete aspects of power in organizations.

Looking at Table 17.1 we see many organizational instances of power at work that relate to different theories. However, using a slightly different approach to power at work, deploying a counterfactual questioning, with Galit Ailon (2006) we can ask, 'What B would otherwise do?' The point of asking the question is to develop different perspectives on conceptualizations of 'power' in organizational theory. In Dahl's original applications of his definition of power as an A getting a B to do something that the B would otherwise not do, what the 'otherwise' is seems quite clear; a son not mowing the lawn for his father, for instance. However, such simple examples hardly capture the complexity of power in organizations. What Ailon does is to

Table 17.1 Adapting Haugaard for organization studies

Theorists	For whom power is created from	Theoretical example	Organization example
Parsons, Luhmann, Barnes, Haugaard, Clegg and Giddens	Social order	Causal predictability created through the reproduction of meaning; theorized as structuration and confirming-structuration	Training, induction, work-shops, retreats, organizational communications
Bachrach and Baratz	System bias	Order precludes certain actions: destructuration	Selection biases embedded in the actually existing structure of organizations: freemasonry, forms of gendered, ethnic, religious or other identity exclusion
Foucault	Systems of thought	Certain acts of structuration are incommensurable with particular interpretive horizons	The reification of missions and visions; the ordering of certain forms of privileged disciplinary knowledge
Lukes	'False consciousness'	'Power over' based upon social knowledge that is not discursively challenged. Empowerment through the transfer of knowledge from practical to discursive consciousness	Acceptance of one's subordinated position in the organization through translation of its subordination into a sphere of privilege: e.g. working class 'lads' for whom dirty hands and overalls equate with masculinity while white-collar work is equated with femininity. Empowerment occurs as a result of a coming-to-another-awareness of the way things are, perhaps through tutelage or critical incidents redefining reality
Foucault and Clegg	Power/ knowledge, obligatory passage points	Social order has to appear as non-arbitrary	The organizational fixity of processes, procedures and practices is normalized such that deviant action cannot achieve its ends and is thus not productive
Foucault	Discipline	Routine is used to make actors predictable through the inculcation of practical consciousness knowledge	The importance of organizational routines that are drilled into the being of organizational members and that shape the practices of work: e.g. Taylor's scientific management as a political economy of the body; the realization that, as a skilled knowledge worker, you make your pay from 9 to 5 (on the organizations' time) and your promotion from 5 to 9 (on your time)
Weber, Dahl, Bachrach and Baratz, Mann and Poggi	Coercion	Natural power as a base: violence and coercion as a substitute for the creation of social power	Organizational strike-breaking; lockouts; bonded and indentured labourers who are unfree to quit; resource extraction against the wishes and interests of local communities but in cahoots with local comprador elites

build a typology of what the normative assumptions embedded in theory suggests the otherwise would be. Again, for ease of exposition we have represented these in tabular form (Table 17.2).

Each of these different accounts offers an approach to institutional entrepreneurship. First the conservative accounts: for the classical scientific management theorists, agency and transaction cost theorists it is the tendency of employees to cheat which induces a managerially entrepreneurial reaction by focusing analytical coherence on schemes for outwitting everyday cunning; for human relations, decision-making theory and the acculturists, it is the superior rationality of the managers that is the source of entrepreneurial energy – the organization can be rationally designed to minimize errant entrepreneurialism and channel legitimated behaviour through the superior analytical coherence of its theories that can be demonstrated through management actions. For conservative power theories, such as those of resource dependency or strategic contingencies theory, the basis of order is an equilibrium that contains its own internal dynamics in which any agency that acquires more strategic resources will be able to assert their entrepreneurial energies. For radical accounts, situated in feminist theory and labour process analysis, entrepreneurial energies are dialectical. There are the dominant agents – capitalists, men – and there are the subordinated agents – workers, women – each of whom has the potential to develop different accounts of the world. Ordinarily, these theorists believe, it is the analytical coherence of the dominant categories that is the source of entrepreneurial agency but that at times of crisis, radical, alternative energies can be unleashed from workers or women as the shackles of analytically coherent, legitimated and dominant categories no longer make sense for them – but only if there is some external entrepreneurial agency such as the party or the movement that can reorder sensemaking according to a different logic. It is doubted that true consciousness will emerge spontaneously, collectively. The more subjectivist variants of these radical approaches take a different tack: for these Foucauldians domination occurs in many

Table 17.2 What organization theorists think B would otherwise do

Theorists	Theory	What B would otherwise do
▪ F W Taylor ▪ Oliver Williamson ▪ Jensen & Meckling	▪ Scientific Management ▪ Transaction Cost Economics ▪ Agency Theory	Cheat
▪ Mayo ▪ March & Simon ▪ Schein; Ouchi; Deal & Kennedy	▪ Human Relations Approach ▪ Decision Making Approach ▪ Managerialist Versions of Culture	Go astray
▪ Emerson; Pfeffer & Salancik ▪ Crozier ▪ Hickson et al.	▪ Resource Dependence Theory ▪ Uncertainty Theory ▪ Strategic Contingencies Theory	Carry on regardless
▪ Braverman ▪ Calás and Smircich	▪ Labour Process Theory ▪ Feminist Theories of Organization	Be emancipated, (according to different criteria of what constitutes emancipation)
▪ Foucault ▪ Knights & Willmott, and collaborators	▪ Power/Knowledge Approaches ▪ Subjectivity + Labour Process Theorists	Assert subjective resistance more forcefully

ways in many local situations just as resistance to it does. It is in the specifics of the latter that institutional entrepreneurship can be best found as creativity is enacted in resisting dominant orderings.

Finally, where does institutional theory, *per se*, fit into the scheme? Oddly, it does not do so readily: while it is a version of analytical coherence according to the argument of this chapter, and it tends towards social reproduction and thus might be constituted as conservative in orientation, its major recent category in use is that which we have deployed in these concluding remarks – the institutional entrepreneur. Perhaps for this reason it is difficult to apply Ailon's logic: in institutional theory agency is overwhelmingly one of two types. Either agents strive to be the same – most agents strive to be alike with other agents in their search for mimesis – or, in exceptional circumstances, those that are most institutionalized will use the resources and power benefits that this bestows to try and break away and get ahead of the field. One consequence of this is that institutional theory tends to overlook the ways in which institutional entrepreneurship might be associated not with resource endowments but lack of resources – the emergence of hip-hop culture and its eventual dominance in popular culture is a case in point. Thinking about organization theory in power terms, we suggest, opens new windows on phenomena of organizational change.

Note

1 It should be apparent that, for the present authors, organization theory is a sub-field of social theory more generally. We would erect no self-denying ordinances around a small piece of technicist turf with a sign that says, 'Keep out, trespassing not allowed' (on which whose reverse there would also be inscribed 'Keep out, trespassing not allowed'). Organization theory is a component of social science; social science should be constituted in relation to social theory if it is not to be some poor, empiricist and orphaned progeny.

References

Abbott, A. (1988) *The System of Professions: An Essay on the Division of Expert Labor*, Chicago: University of Chicago Press.

Ailon, G. (2006) 'What *B* would otherwise do: A critique of conceptualizations of "power" in organizational theory', *Organization* 13(6): 771–800.

Aldrich, H. (1999) *Organizations Evolving*, London: SAGE.

Amis, J., T. Slack and C.R. Hinings (2004) 'The pace, sequence and linearity of radical change', *Academy of Management Journal* 47(1): 15–39.

Bachrach, P. and M.S. Baratz (1962) 'Two faces of power', *American Political Science Review* 56(December): 947–52.

Bachrach, P. and M.S. Baratz (1970) *Power and Poverty: Theory and Practice*, New York: Oxford University Press.

Beckert, J. (1999) 'Agency, entrepreneurs, and institutional change: the role of strategic choice and institutionalized practices in organizations', *Organization Studies* 20(5): 777–99.

Bourdieu, P. (1990) *A Theory of Practice*, Stanford: Stanford University Press.

Brock, D., M. Powell and C.R. Hinings (1999) 'The restructured professional organization: corporates, cobwebs and cowboys', in D. Brock, M. Powell and C.R. Hinings (eds) *Restructuring the Professional Organization: Accounting, Healthcare, and Law*, London, New York: Routledge.

Burns, L.R. and D.R. Wholey (1993) 'Adoption and abandonment of matrix management programs: Effects of organizational characteristics and interorganizational networks', *Academy of Management Journal* 36(1): 106.

Chia, R. (1996) *Organizational Analysis as Deconstructive Practice*, Berlin: de Gruyter.

Chia, R. (1998) 'From complexity science to complex thinking: Organization as simple location', *Organization* 5(3): 341–70.

Chia, R. and I. King (1998) 'The organizational structuring of novelty', *Organization*, 5(4), 461–78.

Clegg, S. (1979) *The Theory of Power and Organization*, London: Routledge & Kegan Paul.

Clegg, S. (1989) *Frameworks of Power*, London: SAGE.

Clegg, S. (1990) *Modern Organizations: Organization Studies in the Postmodern World*, London: SAGE.

Cooper, D.J., C.R. Hinings, R. Greenwood and J.L. Brown (1996) 'Sedimentation and transformation in organizational change: The case of Canadian law firms', *Organization Studies* 17(4): 623.

Cooper, R. and J. Law (1995) *Organization: distal and proximal views, Research in the Sociology of Organizations*, Stamford, CT: JAI Press.

D'Aunno, T., M. Succi and J.A. Alexander (2000) 'The role of institutional and market forces in divergent organizational change', *Administrative Science Quarterly* 45(4): 679–703.

Dacin, M.T., J. Goodstein and W.R. Scott (2002) 'Institutional theory and institutional change. Introduction to the special research forum', *Academy of Management Journal* 45(1): 45–56.

Dahl, R.A. (1961) *Who Governs: Democracy and Power in an American City*, New Haven, CT: Yale University Press.

Danisman, A., C.R. Hinings and T. Slack (2006) 'Integration and differentiation in institutional values: an empirical investigation in the field of Canadian national sport organizations', *Canadian Journal of Administrative Sciences* 23(4): 301–17.

Deleuze, G. and F. Guattari (1987) *A Thousand Plateaus: Capitalism and schizophrenia*, Minneapolis, MN: University of Minnesota Press.

Derrida, J. (1976) *Of Grammatology*, Baltimore, MD: Johns Hopkins University Press.

DiMaggio, P. (1988) 'Interest and agency in institutional theory', in L.G. Zucker (ed.) *Institutional Patterns and Organizations*: 3–22. Cambridge, MA: Ballinger.

DiMaggio, P. and W.W. Powell (1983) 'The iron cage revisited: Institutional isomorphism and collective rationality in organizational fields', *American Sociological Review* 48(2): 147–60.

DiMaggio, P. and W. W. Powell (1991) *The New Institutionalism in Organizational Analysis*, Chicago: University of Chicago Press.

Donaldson, L. (1985) *In Defense of Organization Theory: A Reply to the Critics*. Cambridge: Cambridge University Press.

Donaldson, L. (1996) 'The normal science of structural contingency theory'. in S. Clegg, C. Hardy and W.R. Nord (eds) *Handbook of Organization Studies*, London: SAGE.

Donaldson, L. (2001) *Contingency Theory of Organizations*. Thousand Oaks, CA: SAGE.

Donaldson, L. (2005) 'Following the scientific method: How I became a committed functionalist and positivist', Vita Contemplativa, *Organization Studies*, 26(7): 1071–88.

Foucault, M. (1977) *Discipline and Punish: The birth of the prison*, London: Allen & Lane.

Garfinkel, H. (1967) *Studies in Ethnomethodology*, Englewood Cliffs, NJ: Prentice-Hall.

Garud, R., S. Jain and A. Kumaraswamy (2002) 'Institutional entrepreneurship in the sponsorship of common technological standards. The case of SUN Microsystems and Java', *Academy of Management Journal* 45(1): 196–214.

Giddens, A. (1976) *New Rules of Sociological Method*, New York: Basic Books.

Giddens, A. (1979) *Central Problems in Social Theory*, London: Macmillan.

Giddens, A. (1984) *The Constitution of Society: Outline of the Theory of Structuration*, Cambridge: Polity Press.

Goffman, E. (1961) *Asylums*, Harmondsworth: Penguin.

Gramsci, A. (1971) *From the Prison Notebooks*, London: Lawrence & Wishart.

Gray, J.T. (1998) 'Organising modes of law firms', PhD thesis, School of Management, University of Western Sydney, Campbelltown.

Gray, J.T. (1999) 'Restructuring law firms: Reflexivity and emerging forms', in D.M. Brock, M.J. Powell and C.R. Hinings (eds) *Restructuring the Professional Organization: Accounting, Healthcare and Law*, London: Routledge: 87–104.

Greenwood, R. and C.R. Hinings (1988) 'Organizational design types, tracks and the dynamics of strategic change', *Organization Studies* 9(3): 293–316.

257

Greenwood, R. and C.R. Hinings (1993) 'Understanding strategic change: The contribution of archetypes', *Academy of Management Journal* 36(5): 1052–81.

Greenwood, R. and C.R. Hinings (1996) 'Understanding radical organizational change: Bringing together the old and the new institutionalism', *Academy of Management Review* 21(4): 1022–54.

Greenwood, R. and R.E. Meyer (2008) 'Influencing ideas: A celebration of DiMaggio and Powell (1983)', *Journal of Management Inquiry* 17(4): 258–64.

Greenwood, R., C. Hinings and J. Brown (1990) ' "P²-Form" strategic management: Corporate practices in professional partnerships', *Academy of Management Journal* 33(4): 725–55.

Greenwood, R., C.R. Hinings and D.J. Cooper (2003) *Structuring Organizations to Manage Knowledge: Lessons From, and Challenges For, Global Accounting Firms*, University of Alberta, Centre for Professional Service Firm Management.

Greenwood, R., R. Suddaby and C.R. Hinings (2002) 'Theorising change: The role of professional associations in the transformation of institutionalized fields', *Academy of Management Journal* 45(1): 58–80.

Hanlon, G. (1994) *The Commercialization of Accountancy: Flexible Accumulation and the Transformation of the Service Class*, New York: St. Martin's Press.

Hardy, C. and S. Maguire (2008) 'Institutional entrepreneurship', in R. Greenwood, C. Oliver, K. Sahlin and R. Suddaby (eds) *The SAGE Handbook of Organizational Institutionalism*, Thousand Oaks, CA: SAGE.

Haunschild, P.R. (1993) 'Interorganizational imitation: The impact of interlocks on corporate acquisition activity', *Administrative Science Quarterly* 38(4): 564–92.

Hinings, C.R. and R. Greenwood (1988) *The Dynamics of Strategic Change*, Oxford, New York: Blackwell.

Hinings, C.R. and P.S. Tolbert (2008) 'Organizational institutionalism and sociology: A reflection', in R. Greenwood, C. Oliver, K. Sahlin-Andersson and R. Suddaby (eds) *Handbook of Organizational Institutionalism*: 473–91. London: SAGE.

Hinings, C.R., R. Greenwood and D.J. Cooper (1999) The dynamics of change in large accounting firms', in D. Brock, M. Powell and C.R. Hinings (eds) *Restructuring the Professional Organization: Accounting, Healthcare and Law*. London, New York: Routledge.

Hirsch, P. (1997) 'Sociology without social structure: New-institutional theory meets brave new world', Review Essay: *American Journal of Sociology*, 102(6): 1702–23.

Jeffcutt, P. (1994) 'From interpretation to representation in organizational analysis: postmodernism, ethnography and organizational', Symbolism, *Organization Studies* 15: 241–74.

Kallinikos, J. (1996) 'Predictable worlds: On writing, accountability and other things', *Scandinavian Journal of Management* 12(1): 9–25.

Kikulis, L.M., T. Slack and C.R. Hinings (1995). 'Sector-specific patterns of organizational design change', *Journal of Management Studies* 32(1): 67–100.

King, P., J. Fitzhenry, D. Gilbert, J. Maxwell, G. Roberston, L. Taylor and I. Wilson (1997) *The report of the professional regulation task force of The Law Society of New South Wales*. Sydney, The Law Society of New South Wales: 48.

Kitchener, M. (1999) 'All fur coat and no knickers: Organisational change in UK hospitals', in D. Brock, M. Powell and C.R. Hinings (eds) *Restructuring the Professional Organization: Accounting, Healthcare and Law*, London, New York: Routledge.

Kondra, A.Z. and C.R. Hinings (1998) 'Organizational diversity and change in institutional theory', *Organization Studies* 19(5): 743.

Kraatz, M.S. and J.H. Moore (2002) 'Executive migration and institutional change', *Academy of Management Journal* 45(1): 120–43.

Lakoff, G. (1987) *Women, Fire, and Dangerous Things: What Categories Reveal About the Mind*. Chicago: University of Chicago Press.

Law, J. (1994) *Organizing Modernity*, Oxford: Blackwell.

Lawrence, P.R. and J.W. Lorsch (1967) *Organization and Environment: Managing Differentiation and Integration*, Boston, Division of Research, Graduate School of Business Administration, Harvard University.

Lawrence, P.R. and J.W. Lorsch (1969) *Developing Organizations: Diagnosis and Action*, Reading, MA: Addison-Wesley.

Lawrence, T.B. (1999) 'Institutional strategy', *Journal of Management* 25(2): 161–87.

Lawrence, T.B., M.I. Winn and P.D. Jennings (2001) 'The temporal dynamics of institutionalization', *Academy of Management Review* 26(4): 624–44.

Lukes, S. (1974) *Power: A Radical View*, London: Macmillan.

Lukes, S. (2005) *Power: A Radical View (2nd edition)*, London: Palgrave-Macmillan.

Lyotard, J. – F. (1986) *The Postmodern Condition: A Report on Knowledge*, Manchester: Manchester University Press.

Malhotra, N., C.R. Hinings, J.T. Gray and G. McAllister (2003) 'A typology of archetypes in Australian law firms' Clifford Chance 2003 Oxford Conference on Professional Service Firms. Oxford Saïd Business School.

McAllister, G. (2004) *The Management of Strategic Change in Large Law Firms*, PhD Thesis, School of Management. University of Western Sydney, Campbelltown.

Meyer, J.W. and B. Rowan (1977) 'Institutionalized organizations: Formal structure as myth and ceremony', *American Journal of Sociology* 83, 340–63.

Meyer, J.W. and B. Rowan (1983) 'The structure of educational organizations', in J.W. Meyer and W.R. Scott (eds) *Organizational Environments: Ritual and Rationality*, Beverly Hills, CA: SAGE.

Meyer, A.D., G.R. Brooks and J.B. Goes (1990) 'Environmental jolts and industry revolutions: Organizational responses to discontinuous change', *Strategic Management Journal* 11: 93–110.

Mintzberg, H. (1991) 'The effective organization: forces and forms', *Sloan Management Review* 32(2): 54–68.

Morris, T. and A. Pinnington (1999) 'Continuity and change in professional organizations: Evidence from British law firms', in D. Brock, M. Powell and C.R. Hinings (eds) *Restructuring the Professional Organization: Accounting, Healthcare and Law*, London; New York: Routledge.

Munro, R.J.B. and D.J. Hatherly (1993) 'Accountability and the new commercial agenda', *Critical Perspectives on Accounting* 4(4): 369–95.

Nelson, R.L. (1988) *Partners with Power: The Social Transformation of the Large Law Firm*, Berkeley, CA: University of California Press.

Orlikowski, W. and D. Robey (1991) 'Information technology and the structuring of organizations', *Information Systems Research* 2(2): 143–69.

Pettigrew, A. (1985) *The Awakening Giant: Continuity and Change in Imperial Chemical Industries*, Oxford: Blackwell.

Pettigrew, A.M. (1997) 'What is a processual analysis?', *Scandinavian Journal of Management* 13(4): 337–48.

Pinnington, A.H. and J.T. Gray (2007) 'The global restructuring of legal services work? A study of the internationalisation of Australian law firms', *International Journal of the Legal Profession* 14(2): 147–72.

Pinnington, A. and T. Morris (2002) 'Transforming the architect: Ownership form and archetype ahange', *Organization Studies* 23(2): 189–210.

Porter, M.E. (1980) 'Industry structure and competitive strategy: Keys to profitability', *Financial Analysts Journal* 36(4): 30–41.

Ranson, S., C.R. Hinings and R. Greenwood (1980) 'The structuring of organizational structures', *Administrative Science Quarterly* 25(1): 1–17.

Rowan B.P. (1977) 'Institutionalized organizations: Formal structure as myth and ceremony', *American Journal of Sociology*, 83(2): 340–63.

Sacks, H. (1972) 'An initial investigation of the usability of conversational data for doing sociology', *Studies in Social Interaction*, New York: Free Press: 31–74.

Sastry, M.A. (1997) Problems and paradoxes in a model of punctuated organizational change', *Administrative Science Quarterly* 42(2): 237–75.

Scherer, K.R. and Tran, V. (2001) 'Effects of emotion on the process of organisational learning', in A. Berthoin Antal, J. Child, M. Dierkes, and I. Nonaka (eds) *Handbook of Organizational Learning and Knowledge* (pp. 369–92), New York: Oxford University Press.

Scott, W.R. (1983) 'Healthcare organization in the 1980s: the convergence of public and professional control systems', in J.W. Meyer and W.R. Scott (eds) *Organizational Environments: Ritual and Rationality*, Beverly Hills: SAGE: 99–114.

Scott, W.R. (1994) 'Conceptualizing organizational fields: Linking organizations and societal systems', in H.-U. Derlien, U. Gerhardt, and F.W. Scharpf (eds) *Systemrationalitat und Partialinteresse* [Systes rationality and partial interests]. Baden-Baden: Nomos-Verlagsgesellschaft.

Scott, W.R (1995) *Institutions and Organizations*, Thousand Oaks, CA: SAGE.

Scott, W.R. (2001) *Institutions and Organizations*, 2nd edition, Thousand Oaks, CA: SAGE.

Scott, W.R. (2004) 'Reflections on a half-century of organizational sociology', *Annual Review of Sociology*, 30: 1–21.

Scott, W.R. (2008) *Institutions and Organizations: Ideas and Interests*, Thousand Oaks, CA: SAGE.

Selznick, P. (1949) *TVA and the Grass Roots*, New York: Harper & Row.

Sherer, P.D. and K. Lee (2002) 'Institutional change in large law firms: A resource dependency and institutional perspective', *Academy of Management Journal* 45(1): 102–19.

Silverman, D. (1971) *The Theory of Organizations*, London: Heinemann.

Suddaby, R. and R. Greenwood (2001) 'Colonizing knowledge: Commodification as a dynamic of jurisdictional expansion in professional service firms', *Human Relations* 54(7): 933–53.

Tolbert, P.S. and L.G. Zucker (1983) 'Institutional sources of change in the formal structure of organizations: The diffusion of civil service reform, 1880–1935', *Administrative Science Quarterly* 28(1): 22.

Tolbert, P. and L.G. Zucker (eds) (1996) 'The institutionalization of institutional theory', in *Handbook of Organizational Studies*, Thousand Oaks, CA: SAGE.

Trice, H.M. and J.M. Beyer (1993) *The Cultures of Work Organizations*, Englewood Cliffs, NJ: Prentice Hall.

Tsoukas, H. (1998) 'Introduction: chaos, complexity and organisation theory', *Organization* 5 (3): 291–313.

Tushman, M. and E. Romanelli (1985) 'Organizational evolution: A metamorphosis model of convergence and reorientation', in L.L. Cummings and B.M. Staw (eds) *Research in Organizational Behavior*, Greenwich, CT, JAI Press: 171–222.

Van Maanen, J. and S.R. Barley (1984) 'Occupational communities: Culture and control in organizations', in B.M. Staw and L.L. Cummings (eds) *Research in Organizational Behavior*, Greenwich, CT: JAI Press.

Van Maanen, J. and S.R. Barley (1985) 'Cultural organization: Fragments of a theory', in P.J. Frost, L.F. Moore, C.C. Louis, C.C. Lundberg and J. Martin (eds) *Organizational Culture*, Beverly Hills, CA: SAGE.

Watson, T.J. (1994) *In Search of Management: Culture, Chaos and Control in Managerial Work*, London, Routledge.

Wooten, M. and A. Hoffman (2008) 'Organizational fields: Past, present and future', in R. Greenwood, C. Oliver, K. Sahlin, and R. Suddaby (eds) *Handbook of Organizational Institutionalism*, Thousand Oaks, CA: SAGE.

Zucker, L.G. (1977) 'The role of institutionalization in cultural persistence', *American Sociological Review* 42, 726–43.

Zucker, L.G. (1983) 'Organizations as institutions', in S.B. Bacharach (ed.) *Advances in Organizational Theory and Research*, Vol. 2. Greenwich, CT: JAI Press, 1–43.

18

Organizational change and dialectic processes

Ann Langley and Pamela Sloan

In attempting to understand the processes of organizational change, many writers and empirical researchers have invoked the concept of *dialectics*, a notion that has its roots in Hegelian philosophy and that is used to refer to social processes as imbued with conflict, tension and contradiction. This chapter will review conceptual and empirical contributions to the organizational studies literature that have drawn on the notion of dialectics to examine how the concept is understood and used, and to review the implications that can be drawn from it both for the understanding of organizational change as well as for management practice. We begin by briefly introducing some central tendencies in dialectical thought prior to describing the variety of streams of work that draw on it.

Dialectical thought: origins, commonalities and attractions

As several authors have indicated (Benson, 1977; Zeitz, 1980; Nielsen, 1996; Mumby, 2005), the notion of dialectics has multiple intellectual origins and diverse meanings. Some trace it back to Socrates' emphasis on dialogue, but Hegel is usually credited with introducing it into modern philosophical thought. It acquired increased strength and notoriety when it was adopted and adapted by Karl Marx to develop his critique of capitalism (Benson, 1977). Dialectics subsequently became a central tenet for the critical theorists of the Frankfurt School including Horkheimer, Adorno and Marcuse and was pursued in other directions by poststructuralists such as Bakhtin (1981). While a detailed exegesis of its philosophical underpinnings is beyond the scope of this chapter, it is important to identify some commonalities underlying its various conceptions in the organizational literature, as well as to specify what seems to be their central appeal.

Schneider's (1971: 667) early analysis of the variety of manifestations of the term "dialectics" in sociology offers an interesting starting point. Drawing on 200 years of writing on what he calls the "dialectical bent," he identifies seven "meaning-clusters" that emerge as central. The first three refer explicitly to phenomena associated with the unpredictability and irony of change: "unanticipated consequences," "goal shifts," and "adaptations that once made inhibit more effective ones." The second three emphasize the centrality of contradiction: "development through conflict," "phenomena of the type of contradiction, paradox, negation," "the contradictory logic of passion." Finally, the last item refers to the Hegelian idea of synthesis as the "dissolution of conflict in the coalescence of opposites."

Schneider's analysis precedes the work in organization studies we draw on to develop our own analysis. However, it foreshadows what we see as the key commonalities and indeed the key attractions of a dialectic perspective. Specifically, dialectic thought is inherently both *pluralistic* and *processual*.

Pluralism is reflected in the emphasis on the inevitability of conflict and contradiction. In the organizational literature, the language of dialectics is variously used to refer to contradictions or tensions among ideas, among values, among goals, among social groups, among elements of social structure, among "paradigms" or among almost any set of social phenomena (Nielsen, 1996). These contradictions may be transparent or masked, overt or suppressed. However, in one way or another, a dialectic perspective necessarily implies the co-existence and indeed mutual interdependence of opposing tendencies. Often, though certainly not always, authors pinpoint specific "dialectics" (taken as a collective noun) in which opposite poles are linked by a hyphen: e.g., the control-resistance dialectic (Collinson, 2005; Mumby, 2005), the enactment–externalization dialectic (Leonardi et al., 2009), design–emergence, competition–collaboration, and control–autonomy dialectics (De Rond and Bouchikhi, 2004), and so on.

A dialectic perspective also implies an inherent focus on process, on change, on "becoming" (Benson, 1977; Tsoukas and Chia, 2002). Dialectic tensions emerge and evolve, dissolve or reproduce themselves in the context of ongoing social interaction within and among social systems. Particular authors in the organizational literature vary in the extent to which they fully reflect the processual character of dialectical tensions. However, the simple description of a contradiction is insufficient to suggest a dialectical perspective. To warrant this label, contradictions will be embedded in processes of conflict and interaction leading to possible shifts in individual actions and understandings and in social, organizational and inter-organizational arrangements.

This combined emphasis on pluralism and process is critical and distinguishes dialectical thought from more traditional ways of representing organizational phenomena both in the realm of organizational practice and in the realm of organizational research. For example, Mason (1996: 294) notes how Churchman's (1979) development of a method of dialectical inquiry was a reaction to "the almost exclusive emphasis placed at the time on purely rational methods of inquiry in normative and descriptive theories of managerial decision making." These methods tended to focus on the search for system "optimality," ignoring the existence of conflict, and indeed the possibility that more than one legitimate perspective might exist. Similarly, Benson (1977) notes how classic organizational theories relating static sets of variables to one another (e.g., as in contingency theories that were dominant at that time) essentially reified existing connections among organizational elements without considering how those patterns and combinations came to be, or how alternatives might emerge. Although current organizational theorizing is arguably more sophisticated than in Benson's and Churchman's time, much of the strategic management and organizational behavior literatures continues to pursue the search for nomothetic generalizations in which contradiction, pluralism and process are missing or heavily stunted (Langley, 2007).

That said, beyond these commonalities and sources of theoretical complexity and richness, the dialectic perspective is imbued with some of its own tensions and contradictions, as we shall see. One issue concerns the degree to which the notions of "thesis," "antithesis," and "synthesis" representing the three "moments" of the Hegelian dialectic are central or secondary to this perspective. In the classic formulation of the Hegelian model, the thesis and antithesis are seen as the two poles of a contradiction, and the synthesis is seen as a new form that emerges from their interaction but that transcends or rises above them, itself potentially becoming a new thesis that may later be subject to contestation from a new antithesis in a never-ending cycle. Some authors align themselves very strongly with this model (Mason and Mitroff, 1979; Van de Ven and Poole, 1995; Sabherwal and Newman, 2003). Others, drawing on Adorno's (1973) "negative dialectics" see it as illusory in its implicit assumption of continual "progress" represented by the possibility of dissolving tensions in synthesis (Neimark and Tinker, 1987; Mumby, 2005). Others formulate the dialectic perspective as a never ending cycle of interaction among contradictory forces without finding it necessary to box oppositions and evolution into the three rather static categories (Benson, 1977; Zeitz, 1980).

Another element of possible contention concerns the uses to which dialectic thinking is put. For some, dialectics is a method of inquiry whose purpose is essentially managerial—to improve organizational decision making (Mason and Mitroff, 1979; Cosier and Schwenk, 1990; Nielsen, 1996). This contrasts sharply with those who see dialectics as a tool of critical historical analysis aimed at unmasking hidden injustices within institutionalized organizational arrangements (Carr, 2000; Kersten, 2000; Mumby, 2005), and finding routes to emancipation (Benson, 1977). For others—and indeed perhaps most organizational scholars—the dialectical frame is treated merely as a descriptive theoretical lens for revealing and describing change phenomena or simply for understanding conflict and tension. Thus a variety of value commitments (from managerial to descriptive to critical) underlie scholars' usage of dialectical frameworks.

Finally, the notion of dialectics is applied with a highly variable degree of integration and insistence. For some, dialectical analysis is represented as the dominant conceptual and analytical frame for understanding empirical phenomena (McGuire, 1988, 1992; Farjoun, 2002; De Rond and Bouchikhi, 2004). For others it is readily hybridized with other perspectives. For another set of scholars, the word "dialectic" is used rather casually in passing to signify certain paradoxical characteristics of organizational change phenomena or to draw attention to the ironies of change where well-intended actions have unintended consequences that turn back on their initiators (Schneider, 1971).

We now describe four broad streams of work in the organizational literature that uses the term "dialectics" more concertedly. We identify originating authors and elaborate on some of the issues each stream raises.

Dialectics as technique

The first stream of work dating originally back to the 1960s and 1970s uses the term dialectics to refer to a form of inquiry that involves debate around opposing strategies in order to enrich managerial thinking (Churchman, 1979; Mason, 1967; Katzenstein, 1996). This was developed and incorporated into a fully fledged management intervention method for handling ill-structured problems by Richard Mason, Ian Mitroff, Ralph Kilmann James Emshoff and other colleagues (Mason, 1967; Mitroff et al., 1977; Mitroff and Emshoff, 1979).

Specifically, Mitroff and Emshoff (1979: 3) argued for the need to develop "maximally opposing policies" in order to "ferret out and challenge the underlying assumptions that each policy makes." Their technique involves beginning with a proposed strategy, identifying its underlying assumptions, and then creating a counter-strategy whose underlying assumptions negate those of the original strategy. Different groups are assigned to work on and develop the analysis of assumptions for the strategy and counter-strategy, and then to debate these assumptions with the other group. In an ultimate step, the different teams attempt to reach a set of common assumptions that all can accept, and develop a new strategy that builds on these. A number of case studies have been published illustrating its use and value (Mason, 1967; Mitroff et al., 1977; Mason and Mitroff, 1979; Mitroff and Emshoff, 1979).

Following this foundational work, experimental researchers became interested in the "effectiveness" of dialectical inquiry (labeled DI) in relation to alternative methods of decision making including "consensus" and "devil's advocacy" (DA)—a simpler form of structured debate in which individuals are assigned the role to oppose recommended decisions but not to offer a counter-proposal. Results of these experimental studies have themselves given rise to rather vigorous debate around methodology (e.g., Cosier, 1981; Mitroff and Mason, 1981). However, the later studies tended to show that both DI and DA are superior to consensus methods (Schweiger et al., 1986; Cosier and Schwenk, 1990; Priem et al., 1995; Katzenstein, 1996).

It is hard to tell, however, to what degree these findings might generalize to real organizational contexts. Experimental situations where student participants consider neutral topics bear a tenuous relationship to the context of organizations where key issues are likely to be emotionally involving, and where any kind of debate will be profoundly influenced by historical factors and existing power relationships (Katzenstein, 1996). Moreover, one wonders what circumstances might tempt an organization to invest in formalized dialectical inquiry. While it is widely recognized that conflict can be constructive, its contrived development is likely to pose certain risks. In a revealing statement, Mason (1996: 298) notes, "In our work in organizations, Mitroff and I have witnessed several career-shattering moves made under the guise of carrying out a civil discourse and have had to intercede just prior to the likely outbreak of fisticuffs. (...) Courage, it turns out, is one of the hallmarks of the dialectician."

It is also interesting to note that in one trial with the method at the US census bureau, "the Director and executive staff purposefully did not involve themselves to any great extent lest it appear that they were trying to influence it unduly" (Mitroff et al., 1977: 57). According to the account of the authors themselves, when the results of the exercise were presented, they were not fully understood or particularly well-received. One might argue that the "dialectical inquiry" exercise was itself embedded in a more profound dialectic where top managers had delegated the debate of the most significant issues facing the bureau under the pretext of openness and a desire to avoid undue influence, while actually maintaining full control over these issues by deliberately distancing themselves from any involvement in the debate.

Indeed, the problem with implementing "dialectic inquiry" as a formal technique is similar to that faced with any organizational change intervention. The structure of the intervention itself will interact dialectically with existing situated modes of functioning (people, structures, assumptions and power relationships) to produce results that may be quite different from those that were intended. Dialectic inquiry as a management methodology is an appealing idea in theory—its application in organizational contexts however still remains open to analysis despite the fact that the method was originally developed in the 1970s.

Dialectics as mantra

Our second body of literature also has a strong "managerial" orientation but it does not consider dialectics to be a technique or method in itself. Rather, the authors discussed in this category draw on ideas from dialectical thinking to show how successful organizations can manage and indeed profit from emerging contradictions. We have labeled this category "dialectics as mantra" because of its role in guiding managerial thought towards the optimistic supposition that opposites can and should be transcended or held simultaneously in constructive dialogue and interaction. From this perspective, contradiction is seen as a source of strength, resilience, dynamism and creativity—a motor for continuous change and innovation. Dialectics, in this view, is a positive force.

Nonaka and Toyama's (2002, 2005) description of the firm "as a dialectic being," continually creating knowledge through dialogic interaction among contradictions is representative of this view. These authors argue that firms can create a propitious context for dialectic synthesis through a knowledge vision, situated interaction within multiple interconnected *Ba* (shared time – space contexts where open interaction occurs among people), through creative routines, and through collaborative incentives and distributed leadership.

Similarly, Calori et al. (2000) offer the example of Novotel as a firm that was able to successfully transform itself by simultaneously maintaining opposites in tension—combining deliberation and experimentation, integration and differentiation, and preservation and transformation, i.e., a "both-and" rather than an "either-or" strategy. Calori (2002) makes a similar argument in his description of Michel Barthod's success in transforming Salomon Brothers. Rather than using the concept of Hegelian transcendence or synthesis that implies the absorption of opposites in new arrangements over time, Calori (1998: 293) derives his perspective from Maurice Merleau-Ponty's conception of "hyperdialectics" or the "dynamic harmony between opposites" implying simultaneity.

Hampden-Turner's (1990) conception of the management of dilemmas, Clegg et al.'s (2002) notion of managing paradox as well as Seo et al.'s (2004) notion of "connection" as an approach to handling the dualities underlying organizational change interventions draw on similar ideas. For example, inspired by Bakhtin (1981), Seo et al. (2004: 101) note:

> Connection legitimates dualities through demonstrating respect, empathy, and curiosity for differences. Rather than oscillating between them, unifying them or merging dichotomies, connection seeks to embrace differences. When dualities are treated as mutually reinforcing, they remain connected, use each other as insights, and are open to multiple and evolving interpretations.

These images of dialectic processes as imbued with dynamic and creative tension are powerful and inspiring, particularly for situations where opposing forces seem equally legitimate. For example, in the context of strategic alliances, Das and Teng (2000) examined the inherent tensions between cooperation and competition, rigidity and flexibility, and short-term and long-term goals, arguing that these poles need to be held in balance for alliance survival and success. Vlaar et al. (2007) examined the functional and dysfunctional aspects of formalization in the context of an alliance and showed that skillful alliance managers navigated the tensions by implementing semi-structures that formalized outcomes but not behaviors, and that dynamically traded off different needs between partners. The literature on continuous innovation (Brown and Eisenhardt, 1997; Garud et al., 2006) and on the phenomenon of ambidexterity where organizations combine exploration (creating new knowledge) and exploitation (mobilizing existing knowledge) (Smith and Tushman, 2005; Andriopoulos and Lewis, 2009) similarly offer examples of how dialectic tensions can be sustained and managed.

On the other hand, these prescriptions for "both–and" forms of thinking and practice demand fragile balancing acts. Their everyday enactment may not be entirely within the control of management. For example, the maintenance of dynamic tension requires a configuration of power dependencies that supports it, a broad recognition of the legitimacy of opposing forces, and yet at the same time, a means to make acceptable ongoing choices in particular situations. Managing opposites without risking either disintegration into chaos and inertia or absorption by one pole or the other remains a puzzle, as illustrated by the literature on the complexities of strategy formation in pluralistic settings (Jarzabkowski and Fenton, 2006; Denis et al., 2007),

Overall, this view of dialectics is helpful in drawing attention to the potentially constructive nature of conflict, the importance of dualities, and the opportunities for creative synthesis. However, it is important to be aware of the elusiveness of "dialectical management" as an ideal strategy for change. A dialectic perspective in the purest sense would suggest that any deliberate attempt by top managers to impose a social order that involved the nurturing of creative tensions is likely at some point to encounter its very own contradictions and resistance. In other words, the dialectic change process can never be perfectly contained within any managerial recipe, not even one that recognizes the dialectic nature of change.

Dialectics as narrative

This brings us to the largest body of literature drawing on dialectics within organization studies, the stream that uses the notion of dialectics as a narrative plot or conceptual lens to describe, explain and interpret organizational change phenomena. This generally implies taking the fundamental concepts underlying the dialectic model and using them to label empirical events, showing how the events logically string themselves together to reflect dialectic processes.

In this effort, the thesis–antithesis–synthesis sequence has been a powerful heuristic mobilized by many researchers. For example, in an early empirical contribution, Lourenço and Glidewell (1975) showed how tensions related to control and autonomy between a local television station and its New York head office evolved over a 15-month period. Repeated episodes of conflict and tension described as interaction between a thesis and its antithesis eventually led to a synthesis involving "a broader and more complex, mutually balancing power base" (Lourenço and Gildewell, 1975: 504). In another ground-breaking and influential study of organizational change, Bartunek (1984) referred to the dialectical frame to describe the way in which a new interpretive scheme and accompanying organizational structures emerged over a period of 20 years within a religious order as conflicting visions of the role of the order emerged (antithesis) to interact with previous understandings (thesis), and were eventually integrated into a new view that recognized both old and new and that was formalized in the new structure (synthesis).

Beyond the thesis-antithesis-synthesis model, two conceptual articles have been particularly influential in structuring subsequent empirical research drawing on dialectics: Benson's (1977) exposition of the dialectical view of organizations, and more recently, Van de Ven and Poole's (1995) identification of dialectics as one of four generic conceptual motors for explaining development and change, the other three being life-cycle models of change (explaining change in terms of genetically predetermined phases), teleological models (explaining change in terms of purposeful behavior and rational adaptation), and evolutionary models (explaining change through processes of natural selection).

Benson (1977) framed the dialectical view as constituted by four principles: (1) *social construction/production*—the idea that the social world is continually produced and reproduced through the concrete and mundane actions and interactions of people enabled and constrained by existing social structures and contexts; (2) *totality*—the idea that any social structure is embedded in and relationally connected to its larger social context and that this needs to be considered in understanding ongoing change; (3) *contradiction*—the idea that contradictions are embedded in the fabric of all social structures, and may emerge from the interaction with their context constituting potential motors for change; (4) *praxis*—the idea that in some circumstances, people may come to see and question the contradictory and oppressive nature of existing social orders and mobilize to

266

transform them. These four dimensions have been taken up in many subsequent empirical studies, usually involving historical data and mobilizing longitudinal qualitative methods.

For example, McGuire used the Benson model in two studies, one that described the dialectic relationships between mental health agencies operating in networks (McGuire, 1988), and another comparing the dialectic interactions among factions in the board and administration in two educational districts (McGuire, 1992). In a particularly interesting study from around the same period that contrasts markedly with Bartunek's (1984) story of successful synthesis and change, Grimes and Cornwall (1987) used a dialectic perspective based on Benson's model to describe how underlying contradictions led to the disintegration of an alternative organization. The organization called Innisfree was an alternative social movement organization based on the principles of collective democracy that attempted to run an alternative school. The demands for control, supervision and formal rules required to operate the school conflicted profoundly with the democratic values originating within the community. Grimes and Cornwall (1987) recount in detail how over time the organization of the school descended into disarray and chaos through the inability of organization members to reconcile its founding values with the discipline expected by new clients attracted to the school for its instrumental value as an educational institution for their children.

Grimes and Cornwall's (1987) study illustrates the non-inevitability of creative synthesis, as well as the flexibility and versatility of the dialectic model for understanding different types of change. Dialectics can and does accommodate multiple narrative plots including what might be called tragedy as in this case, or the more romantic view of dialectical interaction illustrated in the previous section. Perhaps more frequently, however, the dialectic perspective provides the plots of irony and epic. Sabherwal and Newman's (2003) accounts of the evolution of three IT development projects through successive ups and downs as periods of conflict gave rise to new syntheses that were themselves ultimately contested are typical of the epic narrative. As De Rond (2003) underlines in his use of the dialectic model to describe the evolution of three strategic alliances, dialectic processes are messy and unpredictable. The never-ending social construction/ production of social orders can move in myriad different directions depending on the particular people and systems in interaction. The only certainties are that new contradictions will emerge, and that attempts to achieve deliberate change through intervention (that might be labeled forms of *praxis* by Benson) will always engage organizations in interaction and conflict with prior social structures that are likely to produce unanticipated as well as anticipated outcomes (Jian, 2007).

The flexibility, versatility and non-deterministic nature of dialectical models are at one level their strength. They enable coherent explanations of both evolutionary and revolutionary types of change, of change and stability (Farjoun, 2010), and of growth, decline and oscillation. Yet, conversely, if they can be used to describe almost any pattern of development, although not necessarily predict it, one might ask how dialectical explanations offer contributions to knowledge? There are three possible answers to this question.

First, many authors have mobilized dialectic explanations precisely to offer a counterpoint to the hegemony of more simplistic predictive models. For example, Prechel (1991) presents a dialectically based historical analysis of the US steel industry to reveal the limitations of Chandler's (1964) theory of the evolution of large business firms based on the efficiency hypothesis, in which firms choose their structures to optimize performance. Similarly, the key message of De Rond's (2003) dialectical analysis of the evolution of alliances (see also De Rond and Bouchikhi, 2004) is that simplistic views in which tensions are resolved or even balanced are misguided and that the reality of alliances is that they are "social facts" constructed and reconstructed in everyday interaction.

In another example, Sloan (2005) illustrates the importance of dialectic ideas by showing the incompleteness of four classic narratives of strategy development within the same firm—the competitive positioning logic based on industries (Porter, 1980, 1985), the resource-based logic based on internal corporate strengths and capabilities (Barney, 1991; Eisenhardt and Martin, 2000), the strategic leadership logic based on the profile, vision and preferences of the top management team (Hambrick, 1989), and the social responsibility logic based on ethics and concern for stakeholder interests (Donaldson and Preston, 1995). When these narratives converged, the strategies of the firm she studied appeared to be successful and sustainable. However, during periods of divergence, the dialectic approach was critical to understanding the complex relationship among the different narratives and explaining the trajectory of strategic and organizational change.

A second form of contribution available from dialectic analysis arises from the hybridization of dialectical concepts with other theoretical resources. For example, dialectical approaches have often been teamed with structuration theory (Orlikowski, 1992; De Rond, 2003; Jian, 2007), and indeed ideas concerning the duality of action and structure (Giddens, 1984) are already implicit in Benson's (1977) account described above. The hybridization of different theoretical forms received a boost from Van de Ven and Poole's (1995) suggestion that four process theory motors can be identified singly or in combination behind virtually all accounts of change. Thus, Cule and Robey (2004) combined teleological and dialectical motors to develop an explanation for major organizational transition in an IT company—a process that showed clear ups and downs in an epic narrative in three phases—"confused creation," "creative destruction," and "the phoenix arises." Marcus and Geffen (1998) combined teleological, evolutionary, and dialectical motors to understand changes in the energy production industry following the passage of the Clean Air Act in the US. They showed how teleological imposition of governmental constraints and evolutionary market forces within the energy and transportation supply industries as well as creative tensions within specific firms dialectically interacted to generate a set of responses that could not have been predicted from a narrower analysis. Calori (2002) referred to the development of a "quad-motor" theory of change drawing on narratives from Michel Berthod. The combination of various motors can offer richer, more textured narratives that reach beyond the generic restatement of dialectical themes.

A third form of contribution extending the second may involve the development of more local mid-range theorizing drawing on dialectical concepts as meta-theoretical resources. For example, dialectical theory has recently been more extensively mobilized by institutional theorists. Since institutionalization implies taken-for-grantedness and stability, and since organizational actors who might be best positioned to promote institutional change are themselves embedded in and constrained by these contexts, institutional theorists have long puzzled over how such change might emerge (Hardy and Maguire, 2008). Seo and Creed (2002) build on Benson's (1977) dialectical model to examine how dialectical processes may provide an explanation for institutional change. They explain how awareness of contradictions within existing institutional orders can emerge when spheres of institutional influence interact and are noticed by actors who are less favored by existing arrangements, leading them to engage in praxis to achieve change. Hargrave and Van de Ven (2006) suggest an alternative model of collective action that draws on institutional theory and social movements theory as well as dialectics. Finally, Farjoun (2002) applies dialectical ideas to understand institutional change in the empirical case of the on-line database industry, contrasting this view with earlier models of institutional change.

Overall, the use of dialectics in empirical research contributes to the development of interesting and diverse narratives structured by descriptions of the context and key underlying oppositions, the identification of key actors, their activities, interactions, conflicts, crises, dénouements, and eternally regenerated beginnings. Dialectical views have opened up thinking about a wide range of organizational phenomena. However, ideas from other theoretical roots and more focused applications seem important to continue to enrich it, ground it and provide insight into concrete organizational phenomena that extend the perspective beyond its generic restatement.

Dialectics as critique

One possible route (amongst others) to enriching the dialectical view might be to bring back the critical edge that has been lost in much published organizational research. The fourth body of work described here returns us to the origins of dialectics in the work of Marx and his followers. Here, dialectical analysis is used as a means to reveal how taken-for-granted forms of social order may embed relations of domination and to consider how these arrangements might be transformed—something that was present in Benson's (1977) original definition of the notion of praxis, but that has not been taken up in most contemporary research.

For example, in a direct line from Marx, dialectical thinking underlies the critical tradition of labor process theory (Braverman, 1974; Burawoy, 1979) in which the class struggle between capital and labor takes centre stage. Early labor process theorists such as Braverman (1974) argued that the continued historical drive for capital accumulation stimulated by market competition in the capitalist system results over time in increased deskilling and alienation of the workforce, leading eventually to the possibility of wider worker mobilization and revolution. Following the decline of socialism, analysts have tended to downplay the revolutionary theme, but have focused more finely on the micro-level processes by which exploitative relations between capital, management and labor may be maintained and reproduced in particular settings. For example, Burawoy's (1979) classic ethnographic plant study revealingly titled "Manufacturing of consent" described how workers collaborated in managerial attempts to increase productivity by engaging in games that appeared to offer choice and psychological rewards, but at the same time contributed to their own submission to management goals.

Building on this base, critical-management scholars over the past 30 years have drawn not only on Marx and the Frankfurt school but also on poststructuralists such as Foucault to explore the multiple ways in which dominant–oppressive relations among groups are created and maintained, as well as how resistance manifests itself in everyday practice. The dialectical underpinnings of much of this scholarship are often implicit rather than explicit and an exhaustive review is beyond the scope of this chapter. It should be noted also that critical management scholarship is a particularly contested field characterized by virulent debates, with Marxist scholars of various persuasions on the one hand (Tinker, 2005; Adler, 2007) often ranged against poststructuralists (Knights and Willmott, 2007) on the other. In this chapter, we will sidestep these philosophical fault-lines, but draw attention to selected pieces of writing and research that have engaged more directly with dialectical thinking.

For example, in an in-depth review of the literature dealing with workplace control and resistance, Mumby (2005) advocates a return to a more explicitly dialectical view, arguing that the literature on the control-resistance dynamic has tended to bifurcate into distinct bodies of work that overstate, on the one hand, the hegemony of management control and, on the other, the agency of actors engaged in micro-processes of resistance. He urges a more textured attention to resistance as a form of praxis that involves creative interaction and engagement with partially institutionalized structures of control that are tested, reinterpreted and subverted through individual and collective activities. Observed resistance behaviors include for example cynicism (Fleming and Spicer, 2003), the use of humor (Collinson, 1988), and "careful carelessness" (Prasad and Prasad, 2000). Ironically, by providing alternative sources of identification and outlets for expressions of autonomy, the forms of resistance inventoried in these studies and others cited by Mumby (2005) tend to sustain ongoing patterns of managerial control and prevent more radical and collective forms of mobilization and transformation.

The ironies underlying the reproduction of forms of control and domination through the very means by which they are resisted or accommodated are a common thread in much of the critically-inspired literature dating back to the critique of the human relations school as a surreptitious means of keeping labor happy despite its subordinated position (Braverman, 1974). For example, Kersten (2000) argues that the "diversity management movement," ostensibly aimed at enabling greater integration of racial minorities within the workplace, in fact tends to reproduce current patterns of discrimination and to eschew more productive but perhaps more challenging forms of dialogue. She takes the inclusive definition of diversity inherent in these approaches (that fails to recognize historic inequalities among groups) as well as the origins of the movement with business interests and its promotion as contributing to profit objectives as evidence that it "operates on multiple fronts to avoid rather than to create dialogue and meaningful organizational change" (Kersten, 2000: 245). Similar critiques and arguments have been made concerning the corporate social responsibility movement (Shamir, 2004). Indeed, in a study of a bank, Humphreys and Brown (2008) show how despite attempts by individuals in middle-managerial roles to promote a novel altruistic discourse around social responsibility that might offer opportunity for fundamental change, other managers and employees were generally unable to relate this discourse to their own experience and used either economic and expedience-motivated or more cynical narratives to make sense of the initiative.

In another rich example of critically-inspired research, this time in the feminist tradition, Ashcraft (2001) offered a dialectical analysis of "organized dissonance" in a "self-avowed feminist bureaucracy," specifically, a non-profit centre for survivors of domestic violence. In this organization, characterized by contradictions between democratic feminist values and bureaucratic organization, Ashcraft shows how members struggled to implement a practice they called "ethical communication" intended to avoid hierarchical relations. Through a fine-grained analysis of meeting interactions, Ashcraft (2001) observed how members used five tactics to sustain the operation of hierarchical power relations despite widespread espousal of ethical communication: "tentative facilitation" (e.g., mitigating instructions by asking for input but then ignoring it), "invoking collective commitment to collaborative practice" (e.g., suppressing questions by referring to collective goals), "candid reality checks" (e.g., explicitly referring to the impossibility of meeting democratic norms in some situations), "deflecting domination" (e.g., imputing problems to personalities rather than to power) and "parodies of power" (e.g., playful imitations of teacher-pupil interactions). Again, we see the irony inherent in these practices that might be taken as further evidence for the inexorability of management hegemony. And yet, there were occasions when the group was able to take opportunities for more open dialogue. Moreover, the management practices apparent in this organization are clearly mitigated by its members' feminist commitments and norms.

These ethnographic observations and those derived from other critical studies described above (Burawoy, 1979; Prasad and Prasad, 2000; Fleming and Spicer, 2003) are important for understanding the mundane everyday playing out of dialectic tensions and the potential for praxis in the here and now. Important and insightful as they are, however, we would argue that the full richness of the dialectic perspective demands complementary work that opens up analysis to a longer-term diachronic view (Norton, 2009) and one that also reflects the embeddedness of organizational micro-processes in their institutional environment, i.e., Benson's concept of totality (Benson, 1977). One criticism of some of this literature is that with its tendency to view almost all forms of empirically-observed resistance as constitutive of management control, these studies can be insensitive to the real possibility of longer-term change inherent in the dialectic view. A diachronic perspective would enable the study of how patterns of resistance and control may interact reciprocally and evolve dynamically over time. In addition, the emergence or strengthening of social movements around issues such as human rights, corporate social responsibility, and the natural environment can over time lead to transformations in the conditions of capitalism that are likely to penetrate organizations, and whose influence and dialectic interactions with existing patterns of control and resistance also needs to be recognized, studied and understood (McAdam and Scott, 2005).

In summary, within critical-management scholarship, the dialectical view is both a deeply-rooted intellectual starting point and a constant reminder of a broader agenda for positive social change represented by the notion of praxis. This agenda also extends the reach of dialectics beyond the narrow emphasis on managerial performance inherent in the first two bodies of literature presented above and complements the emphasis on the development of knowledge, theoretical insight, and understanding reflected in the third perspective.

Discussion and implications

In this chapter, we have presented an overview of the concept of dialectics and have examined how it has been mobilized in four different bodies of literature. The particular strengths of the dialectical view include its emphasis on process (the ongoing social production of reality enabled and constrained by existing social structures) and its recognition of pluralism, praxis and the transformative power contradiction. The dialectical view reaches beyond both simplistic prescriptions and simplistic explanations, and offers considerable potential for future research on organizational change as well as for practitioner understanding—where the term "practitioner" may refer to managers but also to other social actors concerned by issues of change.

Among the four perspectives we described, the view of *dialectics as technique* oriented toward strategic planning and decision making is the narrowest in focus, and this is the perspective that is perhaps least likely to attract further research attention. And yet, the potentially constructive nature of conflict is undeniable. There is room for innovation and experimentation with other approaches that might enrich organizational decision making by stimulating more open dialogue. While the originators of dialectic inquiry emphasized the need to develop maximally different alternatives and to engage in a highly formalized procedure of assumption surfacing, other forms of facilitated strategy interventions that attempt in some way or other to liberate participants, at least temporarily, from traditional hierarchical structures (Hendry and Seidl, 2003) and which offer other ways to engage in structured debate may serve a similar purpose. These methods might include for example, scenario methods (Schoemaker, 1993) or the use of physical objects (Bürgi et al., 2005).

The second perspective titled *dialectics as mantra* also emphasized the constructive nature of conflict but rather than focusing on a specific technique, it drew attention to the potentially creative nature of contradiction seen more generally. This view promoted a form of synthesis or connection between opposites that is believed to be associated with successful organizational change and performance. The weakness of this perspective lies in its sometimes rather blind and romantic vision of the potential for successful and unproblematic combination of opposing tendencies. Authors adopting this perspective can also sometimes be less than perfectly explicit about *how* opposites are combined. This suggests a need for more fine-grained research on pluralistic contexts where opposing tendencies are particularly prevalent. The ethnographic study of a feminist bureaucracy described by Ashcraft (2001) and reported in the section on the critical approach offers a model for how one might examine the effective interpenetration of contradictions, and also of some of the concrete questions this might pose.

271

The third perspective labeled *dialectics as narrative* examined a body of research that draws on the dialectic approach, not as a managerial recipe but rather as a theoretical lens, referring either to the Hegelian thesis–antithesis–synthesis sequence, to Benson's (1977) more processually sophisticated rendering, or to Van de Ven and Poole's (1995) identification of dialectics as one of four fundamental motors for change. We argued that the narrative approach offers potential for further development, more especially when it is enriched by other theoretical resources, and when it is used to examine specific phenomena allowing the development of middle range theory. Reaching beyond single case studies, there is a need for more comparative work that examines when, how and why certain patterns in dialectical interaction tend to occur. The recent mobilization of dialectic thinking by institutional theorists is a welcome trend that could be extended to other domains of analysis.

The last perspective *dialectics as critique* returned to the Marxist view of dialectics and focused on the way in which social orders embedding unequal power relations come to be reified and taken for granted. This literature draws on a variety of traditions that take up the cause of oppressed groups and whose scholarship is driven by overtly transformative value commitments. Critical scholars reveal for example the way in which resistance to control often tends to result in the reproduction of patterns of domination rather than leading to collective mobilization. In contrast to the narrative view of dialectics, the particular strength of this view lies in its awareness and sensitivity to the losers in dialectic struggles and to the ethical issues that this raises. The critical edge provided by this kind of dialectical view has always been important in enhancing awareness of inequities and stimulating efforts to redress them. It remains so in a context where issues such as climate change are raising increasingly serious questions about the sustainability of current patterns of economic development.

Overall, the dialectical approach contributes to a view of organizational and social change that fully recognizes their complexity. As such, it complements, joins, and in some cases impregnates other processually-oriented theoretical approaches such as complexity theory, structuration theory, actor–network theory, social-movements theory, and theories of practice. Amongst other things, a dialectical view tells us that whatever our well-formed plans for organizational change and whatever the power and effort we place behind them, these plans will interact with whatever is already there to generate entirely unanticipated effects. Contradiction is inevitable, and it is both the outcome and motor of human action in the world.

References

Adler, P.S. 2007. The future of critical management studies: A paleo-Marxist critique of labour process theory, *Organization Studies*, 28(9): 1313–45.

Adorno, T. 1973. *Negative Dialectics*, New York: Continuum.

Andriopoulos, C. and Lewis, M.W. 2009. Exploration–exploitation tensions and organizational ambidexterity: Managing paradoxes of innovation, *Organization Science*, 20(4): 696–717.

Ashcraft, K.L. 2001. Organized dissonance: Feminist bureaucracy as hybrid form, *Academy of Management Journal*, 44(6): 1301–22.

Bakhtin, M.M. 1981. *The Dialogic Imagination: Four Essays by M.M. Bakhtin*. Austin, TX: University of Texas Press.

Barney, J.B. 1991. Firm resources and sustained competitive advantage, *Journal of Management*, 11: 99–120.

Bartunek, J.M. 1984. Changing interpretive schemes and organizational restructuring: The example of a religious order, *Administrative Science Quarterly*, 29: 355–72.

Benson, J.K. 1977. Organizations: A dialectical view, *Administrative Science Quarterly*, 22: 1–21.

Braverman, H. 1974. *Labour and Monopoly Capital: The Degradation of Work in the 20th Century*, New York: Monthly Review Press.

Brown, S.L. and Eisenhardt, K.M. 1997. *Competing on the Edge: Strategy as Structured Chaos*, Cambridge, MA: Harvard University Press.

Burawoy, M. 1979. *Manufacturing Consent: Changes in the Labor Process under Monopoly Capitalism*. Chicago: University of Chicago Press.

Bürgi, P.T., Jacobs, C. and Roos, J. 2005. From metaphor to practice in the crafting of strategy, *Journal of Management Inquiry*, 14(1): 78–94.

Calori, R. 1998. Essai: Philosophizing on strategic management models, *Organization Studies*, 19(2): 281–306.

Calori, R. 2002. Organizational development and the ontology of creative dialectical evolution, *Organization*, 9: 127–50.

Calori, R., Baden-Fuller, C. and Hunt, B. 2000. Managing change at Novotel: Back to the future, *Long Range Planning*, 33: 779–804.

Carr, A. 2000. Critical theory and the management of change in organizations, *Journal of Organizational Change Management*, 13(3): 208–20.

Chandler, A.D. 1964. *Strategy and Structure*, Cambridge, MA: MIT Press.

Clegg, S.R., Cunha, J.V. and Cunha, M.P. 2002. Management paradoxes: A relational view, *Human Relations*, 55(5): 483–503.

Churchman, C.W. (1979). *The Systems Approach and its Enemies*, New York: Basic Books.

Collinson, D. (1988). Engineering humor: Masculinity, joking and conflict in shop-floor relations. *Organization Studies*, 9: 181–99.

Collinson, D. 2005. Dialectics of leadership. *Human Relations*, 58: 1419–42.

Cosier, R.A. 1981. Dialectical inquiry in strategic planning: A case of premature acceptance, *Academy of Management Review*, 6(4): 643–48.

Cosier, R.A. and Schwenk, C.R. 1990. Agreement and thinking alike: Ingredients for poor decisions, *Academy of Management Executive*, 4(1): 69–74.

Cule, P.E. and Robey, D. 2004. A dual-motor, constructive process model of organizational transition, *Organization Studies*, 25: 229–60.

Das, T.K. and Teng, B-K. 2000. Instabilities of strategic alliances: An internal tensions perspective, *Organization Science*, 11: 77–101.

De Rond, M. 2003. *Strategic Alliances as Social Facts*, Cambridge: Cambridge University Press.

De Rond, M. and Bouchikhi, H. 2004. On the dialectics of strategic alliances, *Organization Science*, 15: 56–69.

Denis, J.-L., Langley, A. and Rouleau, L. 2007. Strategizing in pluralistic contexts: Rethinking theoretical frames, *Human Relations*, 60(1): 179–215.

Donaldson, T. and Preston, L.E. 1995. The stakeholder theory of the corporation: concepts, evidence and implications. *Academy of Management Review*, 20: 65–91.

Eisenhardt, K.M. and Martin, J.A. 2000. Dynamic capabilities: what are they? *Strategic Management Journal*, 21: 1105–21.

Farjoun, M. 2002. The dialectics of institutional development in emerging and turbulent fields: The history of pricing conventions in the on-line database industry, *Academy of Management Journal*, 45(5): 848–74.

Farjoun, M. 2010. Beyond dualism: Stability and change as a duality, *Academy of Management Review*, 35(2): 202–25.

Fleming, P. and Spicer, A. 2003. Working at a cynical distance: Implications for power, subjectivity, and resistance. *Organization*, 10: 157–79.

Garud, R., Kumaraswamy, A. and Sambamurthy, V. 2006. Emergent by design: Performance and transformation at Infosys Technologies, *Organization Science*, 17(2): 277–86.

Giddens, A. 1984. *The Constitution of Society*, Berkeley, CA: University of California Press.

Grimes, A.J. and Cornwall, J.R. 1987. The disintegration of an organization: A dialectical analysis, *Journal of Management*, 13(1): 69–86.

Hambrick, D.C. 1989. Putting top managers back in the strategy picture. *Strategic Management Journal*, 10 (Special Issue): 5–15.

Hampden-Turner, C. 1990. *Charting the Corporate Mind*, Oxford: Basil Blackwell.

273

Hardy, C. and Maguire, S. 2008. Institutional entrepreneurship. In R. Greenwood, C. Oliver, R. Suddaby and K. Sahlin-Andersen (eds) *Sage Handbook of Organizational Institutionalism*, London, Sage: 198–217.

Hargrave, T.J. and Van de Ven, A.H, 2006. A collective action model of institutional innovation. *Academy of Management Review*, 31: 864–88.

Hendry, J. and Seidl, D. 2003. The structure and significance of strategic episodes: social systems theory and the routine practices of strategic change. *Journal of Management Studies*, 40: 175–96.

Humphreys, M. and Brown, A. (2008). An analysis of corporate social responsibility at Credit Line: A narrative approach. *Journal of Business Ethics*, 80: 403–18.

Jarzabkowski, P. and Fenton, E. 2006. Strategizing and organizing in pluralistic contexts. *Long Range Planning*, 39(6): 631–48.

Jian, G. 2007. Unpacking unintended consequences in planned organizational change: A process model, *Management Communication Quarterly*, 21(1): 5–28.

Katzenstein, G. 1996. The debate on structured debate: Toward a unified theory, *Organizational Behavior and Human Decision Processes*, 66(3): 316–32.

Kersten, A. 2000. Diversity management: Dialogue, dialectics and diversion, *Journal of Organizational Change Management*, 13(3): 235–48.

Knights, D. and Willmott, H. 2007. Socialization, yes. Skill upgrading, probably. Robust theory of capitalist labour process, no, *Organization Studies*, 28(9): 1369–78.

Langley, A. 2007. Process thinking in strategic organization, *Strategic Organization*, 5(3): 271–82.

Leonardi, P.M., Jackson, M.H. and Diwan, A. 2009. The enactment–externalization dialectic: Rationalization and the persistence of counterproductive technology design practices in student engineering, *Academy of Management Journal*, 52(2): 400–420.

Lourenço, S.V. and Glidewell, J.C. 1975. A dialectical analysis of organizational conflict. *Administrative Science Quarterly*, 20(4): 489–508.

Marcus, A. and Geffen, D. 1998. The dialectics of competency acquisition: pollution prevention in electrical generation, *Strategic Management Journal*, 19: 1145–68.

Mason, R.O. 1967. A dialectical approach to strategic planning, *Management Science*, 15(8): B403–B414.

Mason, R.O. 1996. Commentary on varieties of dialectic change processes, *Journal of Management Inquiry*, 5(3): 293–99.

Mason, R.O. and Mitroff, I.I. 1979. Assumptions of majestic metals: strategy through dialectics, *California Management Review*, 22: 80–88.

McAdam, D. and Scott, W.R. 2005. Organizations and movements, In G.F. Davis, D. McAdam, W.R. Scott and M.N. Zald (eds) *Social Movements and Organization Theory*, Cambridge: Cambridge University Press: 4–40.

McGuire, J.B. 1988. A dialectic analysis of interorganizational networks, *Journal of Management*, 14(1): 109–24.

McGuire, J.B. 1992. A qualitative analysis of dialectical processes in educational organizations, *Human Relations*, 45(4): 387–410.

Mitroff, I.I. and Emshoff, J.R. 1979. On strategic assumption making: A dialectical approach to policy and planning, *Academy of Management Review*, 4(1): 1–12.

Mitroff, I.I. and Mason, R.O. 1981. The metaphysics of policy and planning: A reply to Cosier, *Academy of Management Review*, 6(4): 649–51.

Mitroff, I.I., Barabba, V.P. and Kilmann, R.H. 1977. The application of behavioral and philosophical technologies to strategic planning: A case of a large federal agency, *Management Science*, 24(1): 44–58.

Mumby, D.K. 2005. Theorizing resistance in organization studies, *Management Communication Quarterly*, 19:19–44.

Neimark, M. and Tinker, T. 1987. Identity and non-identity thinking: Dialectical critique of the transaction cost theory of the modern corporation, *Journal of Management*, Winter, 13: 661–73.

Nielsen, R.P. 1996. Varieties of dialectical change processes, *Journal of Management Inquiry*, 5: 276–92.

Nonaka, I. and Toyama, R. 2002. A firm as a dialectical being, *Industrial and Corporate Change*, 11: 995–1009.

Nonaka, I. and Toyama, R. 2005. The theory of the knowledge-creating firm: Subjectivity, objectivity and synthesis, *Industrial and Corporate Change*, 14(3): 419–36.

Norton, T. 2009. Situating organization in politics: A diachronic view of control-resistance dialectics, *Management Communication Quarterly*, 22(4): 525–54.

Orlikowski, W. 1992. The duality of technology: Rethinking the concept of technology in organizations, *Organization Science*, 3(3): 398–427.

Porter, M.E. 1980. *Competitive Strategy: Techniques for Analyzing Industries and Competitors*, The Free Press: New York.

Porter, M.E. 1985. *Competitive Advantage: Creating and Sustaining Superior Performance*, The Free Press: New York.

Prasad, P. and Prasad, A. 2000. Stretching the iron cage: The constitution and implications of routine workplace resistance, *Organization Science*, 11: 387–403.

Prechel, H. 1991. Irrationality and contradiction in organizational change: Transformation in the corporate form of a U.S. steel corporation, 1930–87, *Sociological Quarterly*, 32(3): 423–45.

Priem, R.L., Harrison, D.A. and Muir, N.K. 1995. Structured conflict and consensus outcomes in group decision making, *Journal of Management*, 21(4): 691–710.

Sabherwal, R. and Newman, M. 2003. Persistence and change in system development: a dialectical view, *Journal of Information Technology*, 18: 69–92.

Schneider, L. 1971. Dialectic in sociology, *American Sociological Review*, 36(4): 667–78.

Schoemaker, P.J.H. (1993). Multiple scenario development: Its conceptual and behavioral foundation, *Strategic Management Journal*, 14(3): 193–213.

Schweiger, D.M., Sandberg, W.R. and Ragan, J.W. 1986. Group approaches for improving strategic decision making: A comparative analysis of dialectical inquiry, devil's advocacy, and consensus, *Academy of Management Journal*, 29(1): 51–71.

Seo, M.-G. and Creed, W.E.D. 2002. Institutional contradictions, praxis, and institutional change: A dialectical perspective, *Academy of Management Review*, 27: 222–47.

Seo, M.G., Putnam, L.L. and Bartunek, J.B. 2004. Dualities and tensions of planned organizational change. In M.S. Poole and A.H. Van de Ven (eds) *Handbook of Organizational Change and Innovation*. Oxford: Oxford University Press.

Shamir, R. 2004. The de-radicalization of corporate social responsibility, *Critical Sociology*, 30(3): 669–89.

Sloan, P. (2005). *Strategy as Synthesis: Andrews Revisited*. Unpublished doctoral dissertation, HEC Montréal.

Smith, W.K. and Tushman, M.L. 2005. Managing strategic contradictions: A top management mode for managing innovation streams, *Organization Science*, 16: 522–36.

Tinker, T. 2005. The withering of criticism: A review of professional, Foucauldian, ethnographic, and epistemic studies in accounting, *Accounting, Auditing and Accountability Journal*, 18(1): 100–135.

Tsoukas, H. and Chia, R. 2002. On organizational becoming: Rethinking organizational change, *Organization Science*, 13(5): 567–82.

Van de Ven, A.H. and Poole, M.S. 1995. Explaining development and change in organizations, *Academy of Management Review*, 20: 510–40.

Vlaar, P.W.L., van Den Bosch, F.A.J. and Volberda, H.W. 2007. Towards a dialectic perspective on formalization in interorganizational relationships: How alliance managers capitalize on the duality inherent in contracts, rules and procedures, *Organization Studies*, 28: 437–46.

Zeitz, G. 1980. Interorganizational dialectics, *Administrative Science Quarterly*, 25: 72–88

19

Critical theories of organizational change

André Spicer and Charlotta Levay

Introduction

Contemporary organizations are characterized by an obsession and commitment to change. Many spend significant amounts of their time and resources introducing wave after wave of change programs. The mantras of constant flexibility and nimble responses to movements in the financial markets or customer demand are a common currency in most organizations. A whole field of speciality called 'change management' has been created to facilitate the unending flux of organizational transformation. Many organizations write 'change' into their mission statements and the people who staff them use the word profligately. It seems that the need to change has become one of great unquestioned assumptions of organizational life. This involves a widespread attachment to flexibility, projects, movements, processes and any future-oriented activities. It also involves a devaluation and rejection of appeals to stability, stasis and perhaps even sustainability. The image of the good organization is one that consistently projects itself into the future and is willing to change radically in order to fit.

However, the recent financial crisis has brought questions about the dark side of organizational change back into popular debate. This crisis of 'post-Fordist' capitalism has led some to question our economic system that is based on ever-present change, flexibility and fluidity. When financial markets crumbled, property values melt away, and established corporations turned out to be built on sand, stability suddenly seems more appealing. Some began to ask whether our contemporary obsession with change has wrecked havoc on many of our most successful organizations and the world economy as a whole. Others began to see some of the profound effects on individuals, making it difficult for them to craft meaningful lives which are more than a collection of empty and short-time projects. 'Slowness', 'authenticity', 'sustainability', 'stability' and even 'zero growth' suddenly seemed to be a preferred item on the ideological menu. It seemed as if there was a widespread desire for shelter from the constant change initiatives in organizational life. Solutions that delivered more stability and predictability such as Keynesian economic solutions were suddenly being explored. But these questions around change were somewhat short-lived as the discourse of change reappeared with a vengeance in many organizations. The official line of most commentators, politicians and corporate leaders quickly became one about the need for even more change: The problems with the organizations which were laid bare in the financial crisis which began in 2008 were to be solved not through questioning change, but through actually speeding it up! More change programmes were announced. Flexibility, project structures, and re-organization were to be stepped up. And change management was needed now more than ever.

The response to the financial crisis lays bare how deeply we are attached to the notion that change is necessary good in an of itself. Despite the significant destruction wrought by wave after wave of corporate change programmes, we cling to the assumption that organizations are about unhalting transformation. Why is it so difficult, if not impossible, to begin to question the widespread assumption that change is a good which is to be pursued no matter how painful it might be? Why is it that it is possible to imagine the complete collapse in the organizations which we work for (and indeed the economy as a whole) while it is impossible to imagine cutting back on the endless waves of corporate change programmes?

In this chapter, we hope to begin to address some of these questions. In particular, we would like to unsettle the now widespread assumptions that organizational change is necessary, correct and even morally vital. To do this, we will adopt a critical stance towards organizational change. We begin by noting how existing studies of organizational change have largely reproduced the widespread ideology of change. They have done this through either functionalist studies which seek to control organizational change more effectively, or interpretive studies which consider the meanings that actors have assigned to the change process. We then turn to recent work that has sought to sketch out a critical approach to change (Dawson, 2003; Helms-Mills, 2003; Alvesson and Sveningsson, 2007; Morgan and Spicer, 2009). Building on recent advances in critical management studies (Spicer et al., 2009), we argue that a critical approach to change should involve an affirmative stance, an ethic of care, a sense of pragmatism, and consideration of potentialities as well as normative bases for change. By detailing each of these components, we begin to sketch out what a critical theory of change might look like, and what researchers might consider if they hope to follow this approach. We conclude the chapter by asking whether it is possible to move beyond change.

Theorizing change

The question of change has been right at the centre of modern thought (Berman, 1983). It is therefore surprising that organization theory is such a latecomer to the question of change. Up until thirty or so years ago, organization theory sought to explain stability (Burrell and Morgan, 1979). When change did come into the picture, organization theorists ask 'how do organizations respond in order to restablize themselves'? Following many of the profound economic changes which took place at the heart of core capitalist economies during the late 1970s and the early 1980s, theorists were increasingly confronted with organizations and industries which appeared to be in rapid flux. The central challenge therefore moved from the need to explain stability to the need to explain change. This demand was rapidly filled by highly proscriptive studies that celebrated change and provided managers with simplistic advice on how they might ride the waves of change and create corporate revolutions (e.g. Peters, 1987; Senge, 1992; Hammer and Champy, 1993). Self-help literature became replete with advice on how people can develop a positive attitude towards change in their day-to-day life (e.g. Johnson, 1998).

Alongside this more proscriptive work, an academic literature on change appeared. This body of work is diffuse, explains many levels of change, highlights many different problematics and adopts very different languages. Existing reviews of this literature have highlighted different types of change (Van de Ven and Poole, 1995), mechanisms that generate change (Greenwood and

277

Hinings, 2006), and assumptions associated with the study of change (Van de Ven and Poole, 2005). But perhaps the most widespread way of thinking about organizational change currently contrasts stage-based conceptions of change and process based conceptions of change (Tsoukas and Chia, 2002). Stage-based conceptions of change tend to assume that change moves through a series of identifiable moments. Stage theorists think about change as something can be carefully monitored and engineered by change managers. According to this logic: 'to manage is like being in a control room checking certain variables on a panel of instruments and pressing buttons or pulling levers in order to bring any deviating variables within their normal range of operation' (Tsoukas, 1994: 3). The key aim of studies of change is to identify the various stages that change moves through, the levers which might be used to induce organizational change, and the potential outcomes of manipulating these levers. This has produced an exhaustive list of different models of change that are standard fare in any change management book. This approach has also underpinned much of the huge 'change management' segment of the consultancy model and the various models that promise to lead clients smoothly through the various steps to successful change. Despite the appeal of this engineering metaphor, it has been notoriously difficult, if not impossible to develop rigorous social scientific accounts of change which explain, predict and control (McKelvey, 1997; Elster, 2007). At the best, most social scientific theories have been able to develop causal explanations of change processes. However they struggle to predict the course that new change processes might take.

Such stage-based models of change have been roundly called into question during the previously three decades. The seminal work of Andrew Pettigrew (e.g. 1985) pointed out that change often involved highly localized and recursive processes which were did not clearly conform to any clear stage-based model. The work of Karl Weick (e.g. 1979) pointed out that organizational change involved a significant process of 'sensemaking' whereby change agents would make sense of change as they go, assigning meaning to what often appeared to be random occurrences and creating patterns as they went. The dual themes which appeared from out of this work was that change was an ongoing and recursive process which change agents must assign meaning to. In recent years, this has been formalized into the 'organizational becoming' approach which looks at organizational change as a process of ongoing flux and fluidity that actors in organizations seek to assign meaning to (e.g. Tsoukas and Chia, 2002; Thomas et al., 2010). From this perspective change is seen as inevitable and constant, thus understanding it and responding to it is no longer just the job of senior managers and their strategy consultants: it should be a task for everyone in the organization. This is achieved by devolving the injunction to change throughout the organization and ensuring that actors at all levels are engaged in constant and apparently unceasing change processes. The result is that change programmes are seen to evolve from the bottom-up. Everyone in the organization becomes a change agent, and change becomes a full-time job for many, and largely un-paid over-time for all.

Process-based approaches offer a major step forward in our understanding of the change. They give us tools for thinking through the constant flow associated with organizational change processes. They also highlight the role which human interpretation and action play in making change a meaningful issue in organizations. What these theories are less adept at doing is explaining how they are actually questioning the widespread assumption that change is necessary that so many in organizations seem desperate to cling to – even when it is deeply and profoundly harmful. By focusing on fluidity and flux, many interpretive approaches have actually deepened our addiction to change: they have done so by seeing change nearly everywhere, and pushing the injunction to be an agent of change down to the lowest level in corporate life. This has rendered them largely unable to question the widespread assumption that change, flux and fluidity are necessarily good things. By elevating the constant flow of change to an ontological principle which is shared not just through the corporate world, but social life more generally, interpretive studies have rendered us mute about the darker consequences of our change obsession. They have also cut off the ability to question the notion of change itself. This is because if change is everywhere and in everything (as most 'process theorists' suggest), then it becomes impossible to imagine anything which is not change, let alone question the notion of change as such. Change, as a result, becomes a horizion of possibility it is impossible to escape from.

Critiquing change

A critical approach to change seeks to remedy some of these shortcomings. Taking a lead from Critical Management Studies (e.g. Alvesson and Willmott, 1996), it does not try to recommend how change can be improved (as contingency approaches do) or simply to interpret and understand the dynamics of change (as processual approaches do). Rather it seeks to actively question the widespread assumptions about the necessity, inevitability and goodness of organizational change processes. This builds on deeper scepticism towards discourses of change in some strands of broader social theory. The ideals of constant change and flexibility common in today's organizations are questioned by Zygmunt Bauman's (2007, 2008) depiction of the dilemmas of post-modern, 'liquid' society and Richard Sennett's (1998, 2006) investigations of the eroding consequences of the 'new capitalism'. Bauman presents late modern society as ridden with insecurities – material, social, and existential – creating a fluid condition without solid reference points. Freed from the bonds of tradition and the iron cage of modernity, people can and must constantly choose what was otherwise given and constrained – family, home, work, morality, etc. In a world of relentless and inevitable change 'the sole skill I really need to acquire and exercise is *flexibility* – the skill of promptly getting rid of useless skills, the ability to quickly forget and to dispose of the past assets that have turned into liabilities, the skill of changing tacks and tracks at short notice and without regret, and of avoiding oaths of life-long loyalty to anything and anybody' (Bauman, 2008: 128). These developments mean an ongoing production of 'human waste' – the new poor made redundant by constantly changing companies, who can no longer be directed to the colonies, and the refugees of former colonies, who are refused to enter anywhere but the non-places of temporarily set-up but long-lasting camps (Bauman, 2004, 2005). The new global elite, in contrast, moves freely between countries, without obligations to any particular place or community, other than its own parochial group of privileged people (Bauman, 2001: 50–57). Liquid society, according to Bauman, has its advantages. The bonds of bureaucracy, tradition, and local community meant real limits to freedom, and untying them does mean increased freedom, however daunting. But freedom is unequally distributed, and there is an inevitable trade-off between freedom and security. The situation Bauman describes in many ways appears as an intolerable impasse, such as when people in uncertain times seek security in the false solution of closed communities, which only generates more insecurity (Bauman, 2001).

Bauman's description of organizational life in liquid society largely coincides with and relies on Sennett's analysis of the conditions and moral perils of 'new capitalism' (1998, 2006). The iron cage of hierarchical, bureaucratic organization has given way to flexible organizational forms, with loose networks, teamwork, temporary work, and changing tasks and work-roles. However, the revulsion against bureaucracy and the search for flexibility has not set people free but rather produced new and illegible structures of power and control (Sennett, 1998: 47). In workteams, the authority of a manager who can be held accountable is replaced with even more demanding group pressures and facilitating efforts from 'leaders' who are free to shift, adapt and reorganize, since 'change' is the only responsible agent (Sennett, 1998: 106–17). In networks, relations are unstable and unequal, without centralization but with concentration of power, as production units are pressed to achieve targets beyond their reach (Sennett, 1998: 55–57). The ideal for organizations is disruptive change that basically reinvents institutions, such as in 'reengineering', which normally means downsizing. Reengineering is usually chaotic and the gains in productivity are dubious, but stock prices tend to rise and 'the organization must prove to the market that it is capable of change' (Sennett, 1998: 51). The overall result is an organizational deficit of loyalty, informal trust, and accumulated institutional knowledge (Sennett, 2006: 63–82), as well as an ever-threatening spectre of uselessness to individuals (Sennett, 2006: 83–130). What is more, the demands for constant readiness to change foster a shallow personality without long-lasting relations or commitments. Under such circumstances, personal character is threatened with corrosion. For instance, one respondent in Sennett's study faces the conundrum of raising his children to be loyal, persistent and capable of long-term commitment, while his own entire professional career is a testimony to the importance of being able to change job and move at short notice (Sennett, 1998: 26–31). This reflects a universal, contemporary dilemma: 'How do we decide what is of lasting value in ourselves in a society which is impatient, which focuses on the immediate moment? (…) How can mutual loyalties and commitments be sustained in institutions which are constantly breaking apart or constantly being redesigned?' (1998: 10).

Critical approaches to change in organization theory build on many of the motifs found in Bauman and Sennett's accounts. In particular, they push us to ask if change is so necessary and inevitable as it is so often portrayed. The widespread 'pro-change bias' and assumption that change can be managed through the careful application of a set of universal models is also treated sceptically (Sturdy and Grey, 2003). Doing this opens up space to consider the possibilities of stability as well as alternative models of change. Typically this scepticism has lead critics to focus on how organizational change often further embodies modes of power and domination. This has involved an exploration of the potential negative outcomes of the change process, resistance to change, the political drivers of change, and how modes of power-knowledge are embodied in change processes. Let us briefly look at each of these aspects in turn.

Scepticism towards change programmes requires the critic to draw out the 'darker' sides of change that are so frequently disregarded by more mainstream accounts. Organizational change programmes frequently trumpet many great benefits of change processes, but rarely capture the profound human costs of these change processes such as destruction of whole sectors and the economy, the loss of people's livelihoods, increased managerial control, destruction of hard-won working conditions and increasing stress in the workplace. By registering the pain behind change processes, it becomes possible to see why people may be opposed to organizational change for very good reasons which go beyond the apparent irrationality which mainstream accounts assume drive resistance to change.

This brings us to a second aspect of change typically considered by existing critical accounts – an appreciation of resistance. While an account of resistance has been part of most mainstream accounts of change for many years (for review see: Ford et al., 2008), rarely is this resistance seen as being legitimate and acceptable. Critical approaches to change begin from the assumption that forms of resistance are to be considered as legitimate expression of those being changed seeking to defend themselves and hold onto hard won rights and resources. For a critic, a proper understanding of change needs to more completely understand the important role which resistance can play. For instance, there is a deep stream of research that has investigated how employees respond to culture change initiatives (Trethewey, 1997; Gabriel, 1999; Collinson, 2003; Thomas et al., 2003). Employees resist culture change programmes through humour (Taylor and Bain, 2003), cynicism (Fleming and Spicer, 2003), collective mobilization (Creed et al., 2002), as well as various forms of more material misbehaviour (Ackroyd and Thompson, 1999). Through these strategies, employees can either preserve and protect valued cultures that they feel are under assault. Other in-depth studies have noticed how resistance and political struggles on the part of those being objected to 'change' often have a profound impact on the change process. For instance, Dawson (2003) emphasizes how political struggles occur during change processes in various organizations. He shows how the adoption of a new mode of organizing is not just the preserve of top management. Rather, change processes are carefully negotiated among a whole range of constituencies include employees, unions, different levels of management as well as external constituencies such as consultants.

Critics need to recognize the interests that often lie behind not only change processes, but also models and theories of organizational change and the broader discourse of change itself. Doing so questions the widespread assumption that change processes are value-free and fulfil the interests of everyone. Instead, critical approaches register how organizational change is frequently used to push forward the interests of the managerial classes by unsettling forms of employee autonomy, further deepening the demands of work and concentrating the control of work into fewer and fewer hands (Edwards, 1979). More recent critiques have pointed out that wave after wave of organizational change processes are largely in the interest of the financial elite who now control many corporations (e.g. Froud et al., 2000). These ever-present change processes provide lucrative commercial opportunities for various professional services firms such as consultancies and investment banks who are involved in the continued restructuring of corporations. They also allow financial institutions to continually shake up the power base of senior management in the firm, ensuring that it is difficult for one dominant group to gain a foothold.

A further aspect that critical studies of change have recognized is the role that bodies of managerial knowledge play in driving change processes. For instance, in a longitudinal case study of an electrical company in Nova-Scotia, Jean Helms-Mills (2003) traces out the changing reactions and struggles which took place over time as managers sought to introduce wave after wave of new managerial technologies including business process re-engineering, balanced score-cards, culture-change programmes, and restructuring. The study shows how bodies of knowl-edge associated with each pre-packaged change project had deep political implications insofar as it shaped how people could know and understand their work and organization. She found that experts like consultants played a significant role in making these change programmes performa-tive. They did so by providing theoretical justification for the change as well as the technical skill to implement the change program. She also suggests that each of these change programmes is often the result of significant and ongoing struggles between different groups, even within management.

Towards a critical performative account of change

The few existing critical accounts of change have certainly made significant advances in how we understand and engage with change processes (for a more extensive review see: Morgan and Spicer, 2009). In particular they have brought to the fore a significant scepticism about much of the over-blown change rhetoric that so frequently infuses corporate life. Moreover, they have sought to reveal how many change programmes cause significant pain and anguish that prompt waves of resistance on the part of those being changed. Furthermore critical approaches have identified the various structures of power and politics that often lurk below various change processes. By doing this they have begun to paint a picture of organizational change processes as a body of managerial knowledge used by powerful groups to further extend domination, often sparking significant bouts of struggle and resistance. Moreover, these studies largely seek to eschew the demand to develop 'performative' knowledge which will help to make change programmes function more efficiently.

Existing critiques of change are an important step in moving the study of change management beyond the strict managerial focus it is currently stuck in. However, we feel that giving up any claims to performativity is troubling. The first reason for this is that relinquishing any claims on being 'performative' could be seen as not seeking to influence how managerial modes of change operate. This is because the cut and thrust of practical reality may be seen as somehow beyond the scope and concerns of the critic and rubbing against their commitment to 'anti-performativity'. This is a problem because it seems to give up any notion that a critical approach to change should put scepticism in the service of progressive social transformation. This does not simply involve a call for 'more change' or even 'more change with socially just goals'. In many ways such calls would only further feed our already raging obsession with change. Rather, it means a transformation based on the use of sceptical reason of how organizational change processes are actually carried out.

The second major shortcoming with non-performative accounts of change is that by advancing consistently negative images of social change, critics have been rather silent about the kinds of organizational change which they actually want. By this we mean that the constant focus on criticism and questioning has clouded the critics ability and even responsibility to articulate alternative visions of organizational change. The unflinching focus on pointing out what is 'problematic' in existing change programmes is certainly valuable, but it can run the risk of perpetuating the assumption that these models of change are the only option available. This can result in a kind of cynical consciousness (Sloterdijk, 1984) whereby we assume that although there are significant problems with organizational change processes, we nonetheless assume that they are the only procedure that is possible and acceptable. This kind of criticism ironically actually stabilizes and further solidifies existing assumptions about the stability and givenness of existing change processes in organizations. Undoing this kind of cynical reinforcement of existing change processes would require us to articulate alternative visions of change rather than parasitically rely on existing accounts of organizational change.

To overcome these problems with the fledgling field of critical approaches to change, we would like to sketch out a critical approach to change which aims to performatively engage with concepts of change in a way that unsettles widespread assumptions about change but also seeks to performatively rework widely held conceptions of change. This involves treating organizational change as a discourse and set of practices that are open to subversive interventions. To do this, we argue that critics need to adopt an affirmative stance, work with an ethic of care, work with a sense of pragmatism, consider potentialities and tease out the normative bases of assessments of change (Spicer et al., 2009). In what follows, we would like to briefly trace out what each of these aspects mean.

The first aspect of a critical theory of change we would like to offer involves adopting an affirmative stance. This requires researchers to eschew the temptation to distance themselves in a grandiose manner from change processes and instead develop a close proximity. By doing this, the critic is able to not only develop a better knowledge of what is actually going on in change processes, but also craft a sense of empathy with those involved in these change processes. However, unlike interpretive approaches which see this empathy as a path to affirming the 'natives point of view' on change processes, the aim of critical approaches is to identify potential contradictions and conflicts which actually exist within change programmes. These contradictions can only be unearthed once one gets very close to change processes and seeks to affirm the complexities, ambiguities and contradictions which are typically at work within any change process. For instance, careful consideration of many change programmes show how they can promise radical change in grand strategic statements, but rarely deliver on even the most modest of promises (Alvesson and Sveningsson, 2007). This can mean that the symbolic content of change processes becomes a kind of diversion from the difficult work of actually creating many meaningful organizational change. So change programmes become a way in which senior level management can divert the activities and energy of those lower down the corporate food chain into largely symbolic activities which give the impression that things have changed, without creating any serious long-term transformations in the organization or it work-processes. Thus, by listening carefully to the various people involved in the change process and affirming the contradictions they face, it is possible to give due attention to the internal critiques which already exist of change processes in any organization. In a sense, what a critical study of change should do is to collect and affirm these cutting critiques of change processes that are already being articulated by those who experience it. This would hopefully overcome the wilful blindness to the many resistances and contradictions that are produced by organizational change programmes.

An ethics of care similarly pushes the concern for exploring the views of those being changed further. The idea here is that the critical should create a space where the voices of those involved in change processes, particularly those who are often most ignored, should be registered. This clearly involves listening not only to the voice of dominant groups who have planned change programmes and recording their frequently over-celebratory rhetoric. It requires us to register those whose views about change processes are all too frequently disregarded – those who are being changed. Doing this allows us to recover the silent and sometimes painful struggles which are all too often a major part of corporate change processes. Moreover, it allows us to reveal potential responses and empirical events which do not strictly fit into existing theoretical frameworks. This further allows us to reveal what Alvesson and Kärreman (2007) call mysteries: empirical events that call into question or do not fit with our existing theories of change. Thus, by caring for the views of all those involved in change processes, we are able to call into question many of our existing attitudes about change. This ethic of care is well illustrated by a number of critical studies of changes in corporate culture that have pushed beyond the managerial rhetoric celebrating changes and recovered the voices of those being changed (e.g. Collinson, 1992; Kunda, 1993; Casey, 1995; Fleming, 2005). What these studies identified was deep struggles on the part of employees who were subjected to culture change programmes. In contrast to the official view that all employees were 'on board', these studies found that many employees remained highly ambivalent and some outright resistant to the new culture. Furthermore, they found that these manufactured cultures did not produce more positive, motivated and happy workers. Rather, it produced all manner of pathologies in employees including anxiety, stress, and at times feelings of worthlessness. These findings did not fit with existing theories about corporate culture change which proposed that it would largely produce happy, committed and self-directing employees. This created an interesting 'mystery' – why is it that employees resist corporate culture, even when it is supposed to be in their own best interests? Resolving this mystery has produced some interesting new critical theories of culture such as ideas of normative control (Kunda, 1993; Barker, 1999) and employee cynicism (Fleming and Spicer, 2003). More practically, these critical studies of culture change practices have called into question the received wisdom that corporate cultures produce overwhelmingly positive results. It has helped us to register the ways that corporate culture may produce profoundly negative outcomes, and show that these negative outcomes are not mere aberrations, but are in some way essential to the corporate culture as a whole.

As well as caring for the views of all involved in change programmes, a critical theory of change will seek to approach change initiatives with a measure of pragmatism. This involves avoiding rash over-generalizations and working with very specific and focused aspects of organizational life. This requires us to see our target of critique – in this case a change programme – not as some gigantic and solid monolith, but as a complex and fragile gathering of different and often conflicting interests (Latour, 2005). By doing this it becomes possible to see potential points of intervention. This allows critical theorists of change to identify points where they may be able to make a difference and in someway transform organizational change programmes. This most likely would involve what Roberto Unger (1987) refers to as a kind of 'revolutionary reformism' that seeks to make incremental reforms in the way change processes occur. Perhaps the best example of this kind of research can be found in studies of the role of social movements in organizational change processes (e.g. Davis et al., 2005; Spicer and Böhm, 2007). These studies examine change processes ranging from the introduction of equal opportunities policies into firms (e.g. Creed et al., 2002), the transformation of organizational forms (e.g. Rao et al., 2003), or the introduction of new managerial techniques such as Total Quality Management (e.g. Strand and Jung, 2005). What they show is that organizational change is very rarely achieved through the strong leaders with certain visions. Rather, change programmes are often the result of a ground-swell of actors who gradually form a social movement around a particular issue or initiative. These actors often feel passionately about the issue and invest it with significant meaning that goes far beyond the humdrum day-to-day issues in the corporation. For instance, those pushing for equal opportunities legislation would often be passionately and personally involved in equity issues either due to personal identity (for instance being gay), or broader sympathies. What these movements did was to focus on a particular aspect of organizational life (such as Human Resource policies) in order to take forward far broader social struggles (such as struggles against a 'hetero-normative society'). The role of the research becomes registering the micro-political moves that these movements engaged in as they sought to promote their own particular goals. What these studies of social movements have begun to achieve is to show how broader systems of domination can begin to be can be challenged on a more detailed level. Moreover, they show that the source of change in organizations is often not managerially sanctioned change programmes, but unofficial attempts on the part of a whole range of organizational actors to push forward new practices. Indeed, a recent book argues that the social movements have played a vital role in the creation of entire industries, such as the automobile industry, and the transformation of other industries, such as French restaurants or parts of the US financial industry (Rao, 2008).

Exploring the pragmatics of how organizational change can critics might intervene into social change programmes is vital, but it also needs to be complemented with an eye on potentialities. This involves moving beyond a sense of what is presently available in terms of models of change and experimenting with new modes of creating social change. This requires us to explore alternative visions of change processes, many of which already exist but rarely appear in discussions about organizational change. By doing this, it is possible for the critic to demonstrate alternative modes of thinking about and enacting change processes. Doing this hopefully opens our minds as to how change might be done in ways that are not commonly expressed in managerial texts. One of the more interesting attempts to explore already existing potentialities of organizational change can be found in recent work inspired by Italian autonomists (e.g. Hardt and Negri, 1999, 2004, 2009; Virno, 2004). These studies argue that innovation and change in the economy is not created by deliberate attempts on the part of capitalists or their representatives (management, consultants etc). Rather, change is created by 'living labour': groups who seek to escape from modes of organizational capture and control. In their attempts to live autonomously of forms of control, these groups create new modes of organization and other kinds of social innovation. These kinds of innovation then become 'captured' by dominant groups such as management. The central message here is that many forms of organizational change are actually created by resistance movements rather than dominant groups who are seeking to increase organizational control. Perhaps the best illustration of this process is Boltanski and Chiapello's (2006) study of the changing organization of French firms in the twentieth century. They point out that the transformation of these firms from owner-run entrepreneurial activities, to large-scale 'Fordist' structures, and then to flexible 'post-industrial' structures was driven by the demands of various social groups articulating demands for new social organization. The widespread social demands for security during the 1930s and 1940s gave rise to the modern 'Fordist' firm with its highly structured career paths. The demand for freedom, experimentation and authenticity gave rise to the 'post-Fordist' firm with its flexible forms and emphasis on self-management. What Boltanski and Chiapello's study does is open up thought around how else we might think about organizational change and its sources that is not completely captured by existing accounts of strong leaders with definite vision. The study also begs the question of what more alternative demands can be embodied in change processes that exceed the ones that we so frequently notice.

As well as experimenting with alternative visions of organizational change, critical theorists also need to articulate normative criteria for evaluating organizational change processes. The starting point here is that organizational change needs to be justified in some way. This usually involves some appeal to a broader set of moral criteria of a good that might be achieved at the end of the transformation process. Organizational change may appeal to criteria such as ensuring the organization is competitive in the market, making it more efficient, fostering a sense of civic responsibility, creating a sense of inspiration and creativity, nurturing further familial or community attachments, or building a sense of status or fame for the organization (Boltanski and Thévenot, 2006). A critical theory of change would seek to recover the moral appeals that often lurk at the centre of many organizational change programmes. Often change initiatives involve an appeal to a multiple moral justifications at once. For instance, companies might claim a social responsibility programme will make them both more marketable as well as help to fulfil its civic duties to society as a whole. By excavating these moral claims at the heart of change programmes, it becomes possible for us to show that even the apparently most 'value free' appeals to markets or efficiency to justify change are themselves loaded with particular moral claims. Furthermore, by recognizing that change processes are based on some kind of appeal to moral criteria, it also becomes possible to question these moral criteria, and perhaps seek to articulate new possible bases for change. For instance, we might point out the many problems of instrumental rationality which come with taking industrial goals of efficiency as the only basis on which we might judge the success of a change initiative. The next step would require us to articulate alternative moral criteria for assessing change initiatives. One way that the critic might go about doing this is recovering some of the dominant schemes of moral justification that are frequently used as grounds of appeal in change processes (see Boltanski and Chiapello, 2006; Boltanski and Thévenot, 2006). For instance, we might point out that industrial, market and connexionist modes of justification dominate contemporary corporate life. It would then be possible to revive alternative modes of justification such as familial, civic, inspirational and fame. A second approach might involve considering alternative forms of justifying organizational change processes. This would require us to offer alternative moral schemes that could be used to assess the potential ends of change processes in organizations. For instance, critics might draw on the already existing moral repertoire of critical management studies and argue that change should be assessed with reference to emancipation (Alvesson and Willmott, 1993) or autonomy (Hardt and Negri, 2000, 2004, 2009). Thus a critic might ask how a change process furthers or retards human emancipation or allows individual or collective autonomy. We could go even further and consider alternative moral schemes that are available in political-philosophy, but remain under-explored by critical theorists, including feminism, libertarianism, liberalism and even conservatism (see Kymlika, 2001; Wolin, 2004). By doing this, it may be possible to explore not just alternative ways of thinking about what kind of change is 'acceptable' but articulating alternative visions of change altogether.

In sum, we have argued that in order to develop a more engaged critique of change, it is vital to become more performative. This involves intervening into discourses and practices of organizational change through adopting an affirmative stance, working with an ethic of care, developing a sense of pragmatism, considering potentialities and teasing out the normative bases of change. By doing this, we hope to begin to open up change processes, and indeed begin to change the notion – and ultimately the practices – of organizational change itself.

Conclusion: beyond change?

As members of organizations we are inevitably in the process of changing something. The only constant in many organizations appears to be a change programme of one form or another. The usual story that we hear of organizational change processes is that they give rise to many positive things such as increased productivity, innovation and more motivated employees. But another side of change that is rarely spoken about is the disastrous consequences it can have on our working lives, the organizations that we work in, and even our personal character. Studies report that people feel that they are constantly 'on edge', feel that there are few if any stable points of reference and have heightened senses of anxiety and stress. They feel overburdened because delivering on change processes seems to leave no time for doing their day-to-day work. They are constantly worried that the next change programme will render them obsolete, so they struggle to 'stay ahead of the curve'. Such an unceasing demand for change has also rendered what were once apparently stable organizations into temporary operations that are erected and pulled down with ever increasing speed and ever decreasing reason. The result is that modern work-life has become 'one single catastrophe which keeps piling wreckage upon wreckage' (Benjamin, 1968: 257). Researchers are by no means outside this catastrophe – they see the wrecked lives, demolished organizations, and fractured communities all around them. And we must ask ourselves how is it possible to respond to such an unending catastrophe. What might be done?

In this chapter we have looked at three dominant ways that researchers have approached this catastrophe. Functionalist accounts of change rarely recognize the catastrophic consequences of organizational change, and when they do, they largely see them as the result of incorrect implementation of models of organizational change. Interpretive studies of change have been more entertaining of such messages of pain created by change programmes. They have set their task as registering the traumas that individuals faced as part of the ongoing flow of change. But it is only critical approaches which have sought to put the traumas of change at the centre of their account. Instead of just seeking to understand these traumas, they seek to question them fundamentally – and hopefully to point out how things could be otherwise. Here we have argued that a critical performative approach provides a way for critics to begin to question the unending catastrophe of organizational change and at least begin to explore some ways out.

One of the most beguiling questions that a critical approach to change poses is whether there is a way out of our change obsession. This is certainly a difficult question to ask because 'critical management studies' has typically fashioned itself as 'progressive' insofar as it pursues radical social change (Parker, 2000). This would mean that most models of critique could only replace one form of managerial sponsored change with another vision of more 'socially just' change. This may certainly seem like an appealing option, but it is ultimately unsatisfying because it leaves untouched our obsession with change as such. Thus a more though-going critique of organizational change would need to take the bolder, and perhaps more dangerous step of questioning change itself. A starting point here would be to confront the other side of change – namely stability (Sturdy and Grey, 2003).

One way of thinking about this stability offered in some strands of social theory is to put forward communities which sustain practices over time. In particular, Alistair MacIntyre calls for construction of local forms of community where intellectual and cultural life can be nourished, just as Benedictine monasteries were founded when barbarians threatened at the borders of the crumbling Roman Empire – only that now, the dark ages are already upon us, and the barbarians 'have already been governing us for quite some time' (1984: 263). While influential versions of political communitarianism tend to over-emphasize the value of unity and consensus (Frazer, 1999), more well-considered appreciations of communities leave room for dissent, and thus for changes that protect what is worth preserving. Bauman and Sennett offer a notion of community bound together by acknowledged differences, conflict, and negotiation (Sennett, 1998: 143–44) – an inclusive, planetary community (Bauman, 2008: 257), and a political community of morally self-sustained, self-governed citizens (Bauman, 1994: 36–37). To restore security and narrative frames in the realms of work, both advocate basic income schemes and revived craftsmanship. Basic income entitlements are actually conservative, since they suggest 'preservation of ethical values and social arrangements constitutive of Western civilization' (Bauman, 2005: 118), while craftsmanship implies commitment to objective standards outside one's own desires and the rewards from others (Sennett, 2006: 195).

MacIntyre's (1984) rendition of communities as havens for the cultivation of virtues has much in common with Sennett's and Bauman's ideals. He bases his understanding of virtues in the concept of 'practice' – coherent and complex forms of socially established cooperative human activity with specific standards of excellence and with internal goods that are realized in the efforts to achieve those standards (1984: 187–225). Virtues are the acquired human qualities that enable us to achieve such internal goods, i.e. the goods that can only be acquired through exercising a particular practice. Examples of practices are medicine, architecture, farming, and creating and sustaining communities or family life. To enter a practice is to enter an existing tradition and accept the authority of existing standards. But practices and their purposes evolve over time through the contributions of committed practitioners. Likewise, the institutions that sustain communities and traditions of practice, e.g. a hospital or a university, are constituted by a continuous argument over what such an institution is and should be. Hence, vital traditions embody continuities of conflict and evolve gradually over time.

What MacIntyre, Bauman and Sennett offer is a gesture towards alternatives to the pervasive obsession with change – organizations which eschew the change fetish and are based around more stable bonds of occupational communities, without excluding changes for reasons that can stand scrutiny based on explicit moral criteria. This theme has recently been picked up in discussions about collaborative communities in organizations (e.g. Heckscher and Adler, 2006). Considering the role which communities play in creating a sense of stability poses some particularly interesting questions that critics of change might pursue more vigorously. These might include: What would the stable organizations and occupation communities look like? How could an ethic of stability and community be crafted and defended? What would be involved in stability management? What would the role of the stability managers look like? What modes of preserving and nurturing stability do we already find in organizational life? As well as exploring the perplexing question of stability, we also think it is vital that critics keep in mind the question of possible limits and pathologies of this kind of stability and community.

References

Ackroyd, S. and P. Thompson (1999) *Organizational Misbehaviour*. London: SAGE.

Adler, P.S. and C. Heckscher (2006) *The Firm as Collaborative Community: Reconstructing Trust in the Knowledge Economy*. Oxford: Oxford University Press.

Alvesson, M. and D. Kärreman (2007) 'Constructing Mystery: Empirical Matters in Theory Development', *Academy of Management Review*, 32(4): 1265–81.

Alvesson, M. and S. Sveningsson (2007) *Changing Organizational Culture: Cultural Change Work in Process*. London: Routledge.

Alvesson, M. and H. Willmott (1993) 'On the Idea of Emancipation in Management and Organization Studies', *Academy of Management Review*, 17(3): 434–54.

Alvesson, M. and H. Willmott (1996) *Making Sense of Management: A Critical Introduction*. London: SAGE.

Badham, D.A. and R.J. Buchanan (1999) *Power, Politics and Organizational Change: Winning the Turf-game*. London: SAGE.

Barker, J.R. (1999) *The Discipline of Teamwork: Participation and Concertive Control*. London: SAGE.

Bauman, Z. (1994) *Alone Again: Ethics After Certainty*. London: Demos.

Bauman, Z. (2001) *Community: Seeking Safety in an Insecure World*. Cambridge: Polity.

Bauman, Z. (2004) *Wasted Lives: Modernity and its Outcasts*. Cambridge: Polity.

Bauman, Z. (2005) *Work, Consumerism and the New Poor*. Maidenhead: Open University Press.

Bauman, Z. (2007) *Liquid Times: Living in an Age of Uncertainty*. Cambridge: Polity.

Bauman, Z. (2008) *Does Ethics Have a Chance in a World of Consumers?* Cambridge, MA: Harvard University Press.

Benjamin, W. (1968) 'Theses on the Philosophy of History', in H. Arendt (ed.) *Illuminations*. New York: Shocken.

Berman, M. (1984) *All That is Sold Melts into Air*. London: Penguin.

Boltanski, L. and E. Chiapello (2006) *The New Spirit of Capitalism*. London: Verso.

Boltanski, L. and E. Thévenot (2006) *On Justification*. Princeton, NJ: Princeton University Press.

Burrell, G. and G. Morgan (1979) *Sociological Paradigms and Organizational Analysis*. London: Heinemann.

Casey, C. (1995) *Work, Self and Society: After Industrialism*. London: Routledge.

Collinson, D. (1993) *Managing the Shopfloor: Subjectivity, Masculinity and Workplace Culture*. Berlin: Walter de Gruyter.

Collinson, D. (2003) 'Identities and Insecurities: Selves at Work', *Organization*, 10(3): 527–47.

Creed, W.E.D., M.A. Scully and J.R. Austin (2002) 'Clothes Make the Person? The Tailoring of Legitimating Accounts and the Social Construction of Identity', *Organization Science*, 13(5): 475–96.

Davis, G.F., D. McAdam, W.R. Scott and M.N. Zald (eds) (2005) *Social Movements and Organization Theory*. Cambridge: Cambridge University Press.

Dawson, P. (2003) *Reshaping Change: A Processual Perspective*. London: Routledge.

Edwards, R. (1979) *Contested Terrain: The Transformation of the Workplace in the Twentieth Century*. London: Heinemann.

Elster, J. (2007) *Explaining Social Behaviour: More Nuts and Bolts for the Social Sciences*. Cambridge: Cambridge University Press.

Fleming, P. (2005) 'Metaphors of Resistance', *Management Communication Quarterly*, 19(1): 45–66.

Fleming, P. and A. Spicer (2003) 'Working at a Cynical Distance: Implications for Power, Subjectivity and Resistance', *Organization*, 10 (1): 157–79.

Ford, J.D., L.W. Ford and C. D'Amelio (2008) 'Resistance to Change: The rest of the story', *Academy of Management Review*, 33(2): 362–77.

Frazer, E. (1999) *The Problems of Communitarian Politics: Unity and Conflict*. Oxford: Oxford University Press.

Froud, J., C. Haslem, S. Johal and K. Williams (2000) 'Shareholder Value and Financialization: Consultancy Promises, Management Moves', *Economy and Society*, 29(1): 80–110.

Gabriel, Y. (1999) 'Beyond Happy Families: A Critical Reevaluation of the Control-Resistance-Identity Triangle', *Human Relations*, 52(2): 179–203.

Greenwood, R. and C.R. Hinings (2006) 'Radical organization change' in S. Clegg, C. Hardy, T. Lawrence and W. Nord (eds) *Handbook of Organization Studies*, London: SAGE.

Greenwood, R. and R. Suddaby (2006) 'Institutional entrepreneurship and the dynamics of field transformation', *Academy of Management Journal*, 49(1): 27–48.

Hammer, M.C. and J. Champy (1993) *Re-enginnering the Corporation: A Manifesto for the Business Revolution.* New York: Harper Business.

Hardt, M. and A. Negri (2000) *Empire.* Cambridge, MA: Harvard University Press.

Hardt, M. and A. Negri (2004) *Multitude.* London: Penguin.

Hardt and Negri (2009) *Commonwealth.* Cambridge, MA: Harvard University Press.

Heckscher, C. and P.A. Adler (2006) *The Firm as a Collaborative Community: The Reconstruction of Trust in the Knowledge Economy.* Oxford: Oxford University Press.

Helms-Mills, J. (2003) *Making Sense of Organizational Change.* London: Routledge.

Johnson, S. (1998) *Who Moved my Cheese? An amazing way to deal with change in your work and your life.* G.P. Putnam Sons.

Kunda, G. (1993) *Engineering Culture: Control and Commitment in a High-tech Corporation.* Philadelphia, PA: Temple University Press.

Kymlika, W. (2001) *Contemporary Political Philosophy: An Introduction*, 2nd edn. Oxford: Oxford University Press.

Latour, B. (2005) *Reassembling the Social: An introduction to actor network theory.* Oxford: Oxford University Press.

MacIntyre, A. (1984) *After Virtue: A Study in Moral Theory.* 2nd edn. Notre Dame, IN: University of Notre Dame Press.

McKelvey, B. (1997) 'Quasi-Natural Organization Science', *Organization Science*, 8(4): 352–80.

Morgan, G. and A. Spicer (2009) 'Critical Approaches to Organizational Change' in M. Alvesson, T. Bridgeman and H. Willmott (eds) *The Oxford Handbook of Critical Management Studies.* Oxford: Oxford University Press.

Parker, M. (2000) *Against Management.* Oxford: Polity.

Peters, T. (1987) *Liberation Management: Necessary Disorganization for the Nanosecond Nineties.* New York: Knopf.

Pettigrew, A. (1985) *The Awakening Giant: Continuity and Change in Imperial Chemical Industries.* Oxford: Blackwell.

Rao, H. (2008) *Market Rebels: How Activists Make or Break Radical Innovation.* Princeton, NJ: Princeton University Press.

Rao, H., P. Monin and R. Durand (2003) 'Institutional Change in Toque Ville: Nouvelle Cuisine as an Identity Movement in French Gastronomy', *American Journal of Sociology*, 108(4): 795–843.

Senge, P. (1992) *The Fifth Discipline: The Art and Practice of the Learning Organization.* New York: Doubleday.

Sennett, R. (1998) *The Corrosion of Character.* New York: Norton.

Sennett, R. (2006) *The Culture of the New Capitalism.* New Haven, NJ: Yale University Press.

Sennett, R. (2008) *The Craftsman.* London: Allen & Lane.

Sloterdijk, P. (1984) *The Critique of Cynical Reason.* Minneapolis, MN: University of Minnesota Press.

Spicer, A. and S. Böhm (2007) 'Moving Management: Theorizing Struggles Against the Hegemony of Management', *Organization Studies*, 28(11): 1667–98.

Spicer, A., M. Alvesson and D. Karreman (2009) 'Critical Performativity: The Unfinished Business of Critical Management Studies', *Human Relations*, 62(4): 537–60.

Strand, D. and D.-I. Jung (2005) 'Organizational Change as an Orchestrated Social Movement' in G. Davis, D. McAdam, W.R. Scott and M.N. Zald (eds) *Social Movements and Organization Theory.* Cambridge: Cambridge University Press.

Sturdy, A. and C. Grey (2003) 'Beneath and Beyond Organizational Change Management: Exploring Alternatives', *Organization*, 10(4): 651–62.

Taylor, P. and P. Bain (2003) ' "Subterranean Worksick Blues": Humour as Subversion in Two Call Centres', *Organization Studies*, 24(9): 1487–1509.

Thomas, R., L.D. Sargent and C. Hardy (2011) 'Managing Organizational Change: Negotiating Meaning and Power–Resistance Relations', *Organization Science*, 22 (1): 22–41.

Thomas, R., A. Mills and J. Helms-Mills (2003) *Identity Politics at Work: Resisting Gender, Gendering Resistance.* London: Routledge.

289

Trethewey, A. (1997) 'Resistance, Identity, and Empowerment: A Postmodern Feminist Analysis of Clients in a Human Service Organization', *Communication Monographs*, 64(4): 281–301.

Tsoukas, H. (1994) 'Refining Common Sense: Types of Knowledge in Management Studies', *Journal of Management Studies*, 31 (6): 761–78.

Tsoukas, H. and R. Chia (2002) 'On Organizational Becoming: Rethinking Organizational Change', *Organization Science*, 13(5): 567–82.

Unger, R. (1987) *False Necessity, Politics Vol 1*. London: Verso.

Van de Ven, A. and M.S. Poole (1995) 'Explaining Development and Change in Organizations', *Academy of Management Review*, 20(3): 510–40.

Van de Ven, A.H. and M.S. Poole (2005) 'Alternative Approaches for Studying Organizational Change', *Organization Studies*, 26(9): 1377–1404.

Virno, P. (2004) *A Grammar of the Multitude*. New York: Semiotext.

Weick, K.E. (1979) *The Social Psychology of Organizing*. Reading, MA: Addison-Wesley.

Wolin, S.S. (2004) *Politics and Vision*, 2nd edn. Princeton, NJ: Princeton University Press.

Part 4

Change in practice

Introduction

John Hassard

The theme of Part 4 is 'Change in Practice'. As such, chapters within this part are largely concerned with how change policies, programmes and practices are developed and prosecuted. The opening essay by Rune Todnem By and Bernard Burnes on 'Leadership and change', Chapter 20, argues that the practices of leadership and change go hand in hand. By and Burnes argue that they are also two of the most important and contested issues facing organizations and those who study them. However, they are arguably two of the least successful elements of organizational life. The authors suggest there is substantial evidence over the last three decades which shows that over two-thirds of all change initiatives fail. If the main task of leaders is to bring about change, then this implies that most leadership initiatives also fail. The purpose of the chapter therefore is to argue the case for a new focus on leadership – ethical change leadership. By and Burnes examine the developments in leadership over the last three decades and how these relate to change and ethics. This is followed by a review of the two main approaches to organizational change – planned and emergent change – and the implications of these for ethical behaviour by leaders. The chapter then explores two specific but very different perspectives on ethical leadership – egoistic consequentialism and utilitarian consequentialism – and how these relate to change. By and Burnes conclude by arguing that organizations cannot achieve sustainable and beneficial change unless leaders act in an ethical fashion that meets not only egoistic needs but also utilitarian needs. This requires that those who promote and adopt particular approaches to leadership and change must explicitly acknowledge the ethical basis of the approaches they are championing.

The second chapter of this part is David Collins' analysis of 'Management fads and fashions', Chapter 21. This chapter focuses similarly on a controversial issue of recent management and organizational analysis; that is that change initiatives often represent largely superficial innovations. Initially placing the fad motif within a context that – to use John Shotter's phrase – 'notices and allows' for the peculiarities of organizational life, the argument develops to consider the linguistic foundations of business faddism. Noting the metaphorical power of the fad motif in management and organization studies, Collins considers the ways in which this term 'informs and yet deforms' academic analysis. In other words, the argument seeks to acknowledge the ways in which the fad motif has directed and yet distracted our attention; illuminated and yet obscured our understanding of managerial (and academic) toil. Accordingly Collins considers a number of alternative means of framing concern with contemporary developments in management. Finally, the chapter concludes with a summary that considers the analytical dimensions and, therein, the opportunities for development revealed by this critical reanalysis of management fads and fashions.

In Chapter 22, 'Organizational entrapment', Helga Drummond argues that although in the management literature we appear to know a lot about how to get organizations moving, we appear to know far less about how to re-direct them when they begin to falter. Drawing upon recent corporate debacles and failures she notes initially how in 2008 for example Woolworths suddenly closed down, yet asks why this iconic store did not learn from Marks & Spencer's near collapse of a decade earlier. Similarly she asks why McDonald's did not respond sooner to the growing demand for healthy eating, and why Microsoft was slow to recognize the implications of the advent of firms like Google. Drummond argues that 'entrapment' theorists believe that organizations may be slow to respond to important environmental cues because continuity begets continuity. The chapter explores why such 'lock-in' occurs and, paradoxically, how costly failure can result from the pursuit of successful policies and practices.

The emphasis on organizational change problems is continued in David Grant and Richard Hall's analysis of 'Power and discourse in organizational change', Chapter 23. In their case analysis of implementing Enterprise Resource Planning (ERP) systems in a number of large firms they show how discourse mediates the power relations between the sponsors of the implementation and organizational users. Grant and Hall argue that these power relations are best understood by examining the mutually constitutive relationship between power and discourse. They identify the emergence of an 'original sponsoring discourse', authored by a sponsoring coalition of senior management and the implementation team, which portrays the ERP as beneficial for the organization and advocates its implementation in a standard, off-the-shelf form. In response to this discourse they identify the emergence of a 'user-authored counter discourse' which highlights the practical problems and deficiencies of the ERP. This discourse relies heavily on claims that ERP does not work in practice, requires numerous 'workarounds' and duplications, leading to inefficiencies in work and organization. Finally, Grant and Hall see the sponsoring coalition responding to this alternate discourse, by reformulating a 'revised sponsoring discourse'. This discourse reframes and redefines the objectives of the ERP implementation, accepts the need for some limited customizations to the technology and depicts user resistance to the implementation as transient and, ultimately, inconsequential.

An altogether different analytical register is evident in Chapter 24, Slawomir Magala's analysis of a major motif of organizational change programmes, 'Cultural change'. Magala wishes to develop a philosophical rather than structured approach to the analysis of organizational change. He suggests his aim is simple – to explain why cultural change matters and what it consists of. Magala argues that it matters because institutional evolution is shaped primarily by the cultural framework of socialized, interacting individuals; that is, 'the 'culture' part of our communicative interactions'. This consists of 'blueprints and scenarios, hints and tips', all of which may or may not be 'used against or for anybody in the course of more or less material interactions'. He suggests this is the ' "society", or "institution", or "organization" part of flows of social events before they become "histories" '. Overall the cultural change Magala discusses is an 'enhanced, increased, empowered, expanded designing and constructing' one – a culture of '*tempospaces* for reflection, including self-reflection'.

Chapter 25 discusses 'Changing attitudes to employee attitudes to change'. Here Stephen Procter and Julian Randall identify three broad phases in the way in which employee attitudes have been dealt with. They suggest that early work on the management of change took the view that employees will be resistant to change. The task for managers was seen as identifying and avoiding any factors that might aggravate this tendency. As the study of change moved into the 1990s, however, it became clear that this rather one-dimensional view of employee attitudes was no longer adequate. Against the background of increased interest at what was happening at the level of the workplace, attention shifted to the idea that different groups of employees have different attitudes to change. The task then would be to develop a range of strategies to deal with these different attitudes. Procter and Randall note, however, that where such academic work was not so helpful was in determining precisely what these different attitudes were and, underlying these attitudes, identifying the factors that might help predict them. They argue ultimately that the third and most recent wave of interest has retained the idea of differences in attitude, but has focussed on the idea that these exist within rather than between individuals. In particular, the idea has been developed that individuals are likely to have an attitude of ambivalence to organizational change. From a management point of view, this highlights the importance of understanding and acting upon the process by which employees make sense of change. They argue that can be very difficult, especially when the changes about which employees are ambivalent are themselves quite ambiguous.

In Chapter 26, Julie Wolfram Cox and Melanie Bryant discuss 'Narrating organizational change'. They argue that narrative approaches provide an opportunity for exploring changing organizations as 'discursive spaces constituted through language practices', thus 'providing an angle from which various language practices can be interrogated'. They also, however, acknowledge the question of 'how might narrative writings, which tend to take a non–utilitarian, postmodernist slant, be used to inform organizational change, which is often enacted in distinctly utilitarian and modernist ways?' Their chapter seeks to address this question by highlighting how narrative approaches have been used to inform empirical research into organizational change by reviewing major narrative research themes that have emerged over the past decade or so. To achieve this, they first define narrative and the role of researchers in constructing narrative accounts. Bryant and Wolfram Cox then trace the growth of narrative approaches in the 1990s in response to calls for new perspectives and criticisms of the dominant approaches of the time. As part of this discussion attention is paid to the recognition of *multivocality* in narrative studies and of the methodological issues associated with allowing for multivocality. The authors also comment on the growth of narrative studies into identity in situations of organizational change, some of which present a return to univocal assumptions, and consider whether the continued interest in analysis of narratives in terms of genre or plot types also reflects researchers' own desire to impose some semblance of order, or meta–narrative, over what is necessarily a complex field. Finally, the implications of this consideration are examined and challenges for future research in this area are outlined.

In the final chapter of this part, John Storey discusses issues of 'Governance and organizational change', Chapter 27. Storey argues that 'governance' is a term which now features large in public policy, political science and business management. It refers broadly to the actors, mechanisms and processes which are involved in the making of policy, the setting of strategic direction and the monitoring of executive performance. Storey notes how numerous corporate failures and outright catastrophes in recent years have been attributed to failures of governance, with examples of 'governance scandals' including Lehman Brothers, Enron, Worldcom and Tyco in the USA, and RBS and Mid Staffordshire Hospitals Trust in the UK. Indeed, he suggests some attribute the root cause of the global banking crisis to a failure of governance. The passivity of Non-Executive Board members has been especially noted and so too the failure of the regulators. In response, various reviews have begun to sketch out further reforms to governance. But, by what mechanisms and processes does, and should, governance operate? Why has governance figured so little in most analyses of organizational studies when compared to traditional topics such as structure, strategy, leadership and change? What is the proper scope of governance? What would good governance look like? These are the questions examined in this chapter. For illustrative purposes, Storey makes reference to governance and organizational change in the public and private sectors. Overall the chapter develops the argument that good governance can be an invaluable and essential support for successful organizational change.

20

Leadership and change
Whatever happened to ethics?

Rune Todnem By and Bernard Burnes

Introduction

First, leadership is a process that is not specifically a function of the person in charge. Leadership is a function of individual wills and individual needs, and the result of the dynamics of collective will organized to meet those various needs. Second, leadership is a process of adaptation and of evolution; it is a process of dynamic exchange and the inter-changes of value. Leadership is deviation from convention. Third, leadership is a process of energy, not structure. In this way, leadership is different from management – managers pursue stability, while leadership is all about change.

(Barker, 2001: 491)

There are now increasing signs of disenchantment with the concept of the assertive, no-nonsense leader, whether of the charismatic or transformative variety. ... The "shadow side of charisma" has been noted by a number of writers ... The dangers of narcissism and the associated misuse, and even abuse, of power were thus known about even at the height of the period when charismatic and transformational leadership were being celebrated.

(Storey, 2004: 31–32)

As the above quotes show, leadership and change go hand in hand. They are also two of the most important and contested issues facing organizations and those who study them (Beer and Nohria, 2000; Daft, 2002; Cummings and Worley, 2005; Rickards and Clark, 2006; Yukl and Van Fleet, 1992), and, arguably, two of the least successful elements of organizational life. There is substantial evidence over the last three decades which shows that some 70 per cent of all change initiatives fail (Bessant and Haywood, 1985; Crosby, 1979; Hammer and Champy, 1993; McKinsey & Company, 2008; Senturia et al., 2008; Smith, 2002, 2003). If the main task of leaders is to bring about change, then this implies that most leadership initiatives fail. Therefore, when we look at the relationship between leadership and change, we are not looking at one which has been particularly successful.

The last three decades have seen the rise of new approaches to both leadership and change (Burnes, 2003; Yukl, 2006). The former has been accompanied by an emphasis on ethical behaviour which appears to be more honoured in the breach than in the observance, whilst the latter has seen the practice of ethical change almost disappear (Burnes, 2009a; Dunphy et al., 2007; Jones et al., 2000).

The Oxford Dictionary of English (2006: 595) defines ethics as 'moral principles that govern a person's behaviour or the conducting of an activity'. Thiroux and Krasemann (2007: 27) state that ethics relate to a specific area of study – morality – which

> … deals basically with humans and how they relate to other beings, both human and nonhuman. It deals with how humans treat other beings so as to promote mutual welfare, growth, creativity, and meaning and to strive for what is good over what is bad and what is right over what is wrong.

The purpose of this chapter is to argue the case for a new focus on ethical change leadership. We begin by examining the developments in leadership over the last three decades and how these relate to change and ethics. This is followed by a review of the two main approaches to organizational change – planned and emergent change – and the implications of these for ethical behaviour by leaders. We then explore two specific but very different perspectives on ethical leadership – egoistic consequentialism and utilitarian consequentialism – and how these relate to change. Consequentialism is a philosophical–normative view of ethics which holds that the value of an action derives from the value of its consequences (Blackburn, 2008; Kaler, 2000a; Pettit, 2003). We conclude by arguing that organizations cannot achieve sustainable and beneficial change unless leaders act in an ethical fashion that meets not only egoistic needs but also utilitarian needs. This requires that those who promote and adopt particular approaches to leadership and change must explicitly acknowledge the ethical basis of the approaches they are championing.

Leadership and ethics

The study and practice of leadership has undergone a sea change in the last 30 years. The two main developments are, first, that older theories of leadership, such as the trait model and the leader–follower model, have been overtaken by the contextual or situational model (Griffin, 2002; Kotter, 1990; Yukl, 2006). This is an approach which stresses that leadership is primarily concerned with bringing about change and that effective leaders are those who can adapt their leadership style to the context in which they are operating (Alimo-Metcalfe and Alban-Metcalfe, 2000; Bass, 1995; Burns, 1978; Hitt et al., 2009). The second development is the rejection of the command and control view of leadership which focuses on top-down control based on the authority of position. Instead, leaders are now viewed as individuals who motivate their staff by establishing an emotional link with them through the power of their personality – their charisma – and not the power of their position in the organization (Brown and Eisenhardt, 1997; Conger and Kanungo, 1998; Maddock, 1999; Nahavandi, 2000; Peters, 2006; Stacey, 2007).

The quote from Barker (2001) which introduced this chapter captures the essence of this new approach to leadership. Barker distinguishes leadership from management. Leadership is essentially concerned with bringing about transformational change through the power of the leader's personality, i.e. charisma, and his/her ability to achieve an emotional bond – an emotional exchange – with subordinates. Management is primarily concerned with achieving stability and predictability by ensuring that subordinates comply with the rules, regulations and working procedures laid down by the organization. Compliance is achieved through a transactional exchange between the subordinates and the organization which is policed by managers using the authority granted by their position in the organizational hierarchy (Bass, 1995).

The charismatic-transformational view of leadership has garnered much support and admiration since it first emerged in the late 1970s (Burns, 1978; Foster and Kaplan, 2003; Harrison and Clough, 2006; Kanter, 1989; Maccoby, 2000; Osborne and Gaebler, 1992; Peters, 2006). There is certainly evidence to suggest that charismatic-transformational leaders can bring enormous benefits to organizations by galvanizing them to reinvent themselves, e.g. IBM, Procter & Gamble, Omron, CEMEX, Cisco, and Banco Real (Kanter, 2008). However, the same approach in the hands of unscrupulous leaders can result in cases of organizational destruction, such as Enron, Global Crossing and Arthur Andersen, and the indictment of senior executives from these and other companies such as Health South and Worldcom/MCI (Gopalakrishnan et al., 2008). The problem is that whilst the criteria for judging a manager's performance and honesty are relatively clear, the same cannot be said for leaders. The fact is that:

- Whilst managers can be sacked for breaking the rules, leaders can be sacked for not breaking the rules.
- The performance measures for holding managers to account are relatively clear and short term whilst the criteria for holding leaders to account are far more fuzzy and long term.
- Stakeholders can judge the trustworthiness of managers by their adherence to specified and monitored objectives and rules, but the trustworthiness of leaders is often based on faith, sometimes blind faith, engendered by their magnetic personality. Unfortunately, a magnetic personality is common to both saints and conmen, hence Storey's (2004) warning about the 'shadow side of charisma'.

Leadership and change go hand in hand; however, if stakeholders are not to be so dazzled by charismatic-transformational leaders that any change is seen as good change (see, for example, the case of Marconi in Burnes (2009a)), they need to ensure that leadership and change are underpinned by a system of ethics. That is to say, leaders must possess a moral compass which ensures that they do not abuse the faith that is placed in them and the unique freedoms which they enjoy (Burnes, 2009b, 2009c). This is a point made forcibly by Barker (2001: 491) when he states that leadership is 'a process of transformative change where the ethics of individuals are integrated into the mores of a community as a means of evolutionary social development'. Hollander (1995: 55) also identifies the ethical dimension of change and leadership when he states that:

> This process [leadership] is essentially a shared experience, a voyage through time, with benefits to be gained and hazards to be surmounted by the parties involved. A leader is not a sole voyager, but a key figure whose actions or inactions can determine others' well-being and the broader good … The leadership process is therefore especially fraught with ethical challenges.

The argument that leadership and change need an ethical base is not new. Such arguments can be found in the work of Chester Barnard (1938) on leadership in the 1930s and in the work of Kurt Lewin (Marrow, 1969) on change in the 1940s. Indeed, as will be discussed below, Lewin's ethical view of change lies at the heart of the Organization Development (OD) movement which dominated the field of change up to the early 1980s (Burnes, 2004). Alongside the recent rise of charismatic-transformational leadership have been the growing volume of calls for organizations to act in an ethical fashion (Dunphy et al., 2007; Jones et al., 2000; Hitt et al., 2009). Prominent in this respect has been the promotion of corporate social responsibility (CSR) by national governments and international bodies, such as the United Nations (Burnes, 2009a).

However, rather than leading to a diminution of unethical behaviour, the reverse seems to have been the case, as the various organizational and financial scandals of the last two decades have shown (Deresky, 2000; Leigh and Evans, 2007; Partnoy, 2003; Tran, 2003). Indeed, as the recent 'credit crunch' and global financial crisis clearly demonstrate, unethical and criminal behaviour appears to have mushroomed out of control in many organizations, especially in banking and finance (Clark, 2008; Gopalakrishnan et al., 2008; Porter, 2008; Stiglitz, 2010). As the next section will show, paralleling the rise in unethical leadership has been a decline in the interest in the ethics of change.

Change and ethics

Up to the 1980s, the field of change was dominated by the Lewin-inspired OD movement (see Chapter 9). At its core lies a set of democratic-humanist values which guide both the process of change and the actions of those who lead change (Conner, 1977; French and Bell, 1999; Gellerman et al., 1990; Warwick and Thompson, 1980). However, with the rise of newer perspectives on change, especially the emergent approach, the emphasis on ethics has diminished to the extent that some approaches even encourage the manipulation and coercion of those involved (Burnes, 2009c).

As the Introduction to this *Companion* has shown, organizational change has a long antecedence. However, it was only in the 1940s with the work of Kurt Lewin that a fully-fledged change theory emerged – the planned approach to change (Burnes, 2004). This approach comprises four elements: Field Theory, Group Dynamics, Action Research and the Three-Step model. For change to be successful, though, there has to be a 'felt-need'. Felt-need is an individual's inner realization that change is necessary. If felt-need is low, introducing change becomes problematic. Felt-need can only arise if individuals and groups are given the opportunity to reflect on and learn about their own situation, and change of their own volition through a participative, open and ethical change process. Lewin did not believe that people could be tricked or coerced into change. His approach was greatly influenced by the work of the Gestalt-Field theorists, who believe that successful change requires a process of learning. This allows those involved to gain or change insights, outlooks, expectations and thought patterns. This approach seeks to provide change adopters with an opportunity to 'reason out' their situation and develop their own solutions (Bigge, 1982). Therefore, for Lewin, the change process is fundamentally a learning process. It is an iterative, cyclical, process involving diagnosis, action and evaluation, and further action and evaluation. It recognizes that once change has taken place, it must be self-sustaining (i.e. safe from regression).

Lewin's original purpose was to develop an approach to change capable of resolving social conflict in society. As Burnes (2007) relates, Lewin quickly saw the benefits it could bring to organizations. In organizational terms, the focus of the planned approach is on improving the effectiveness of the human side of the organization. Central to the approach is the emphasis placed on the collaborative nature of the change effort: the organization, employees at all levels, and the change agent jointly diagnose the organization's problems, and jointly plan and design the specific changes required. Underpinning planned change is a strong humanist and democratic orientation based on Lewin's own personal beliefs and his work on participative management (Lewin et al., 1939). Marching hand in hand with this humanist and democratic orientation was the development of a host of tried and tested tools and techniques for promoting group participation and change.

After Lewin's death in 1947, his work was further developed and provided the inspiration and core approaches for the OD movement which began in the 1950s (Cummings and Worley, 2005). Not only can Lewin's influence on OD be seen from its adoption of planned change but also in terms of the humanistic values which underpin it (French and Bell, 1995). These values have been articulated by many writers over the years (Conner, 1977; French and Bell, 1999; Gellerman et al., 1990; Warwick and Thompson, 1980). One of the earliest attempts was by French and Bell (1973), who identified four core values of OD:

- The belief that the needs and aspirations of human beings provide the prime reasons for the existence of organizations within society.
- Change agents believe that organizational prioritization is a legitimate part of organizational culture.
- Change agents are committed to increased organizational effectiveness.
- OD places a high value on the democratization of organizations through power equalization.

In a survey of OD practitioners, Hurley et al. (1992) found these values were clearly reflected in the five main approaches they used in their work:

- Empowering employees to act.
- Creating openness in communications.
- Facilitating ownership of the change process and its outcomes.
- The promotion of a culture of collaboration.
- The promotion of continuous learning.

In order to remain relevant to the needs of organizations, OD has broadened out its focus from group behaviour change to more organizational-wide transformational approaches (Cummings and Worley, 1997; French and Bell, 1995). However, these approaches tend to be less participative and more directive, which weakens the ethical basis of OD. Indeed, quite a number of leading writers on the subject have begun to argue that OD has lost its sense of direction and purpose to the extent that it is no longer clear what constitutes OD (Bradford and Burke, 2004; Greiner and Cummings, 2004; Worley and Feyerhern, 2003). Yet, as Wooten and White (1999) argue, the core values of OD – equality, empowerment, consensus-building and horizontal relationships – are ones that are particularly relevant to the needs of contemporary organizations.

It can be seen, therefore, that not only was planned change the first fully-developed theory of change, but it has also proved to be the most enduring (Burnes, 2004, 2007). Nevertheless, since the early 1980s, its pre-eminence has been supplanted by a range of other approaches to change, the most prominent being emergent change (Burnes, 2009a). The term emergent approach was probably first coined by Wilson (1992). It is used to describe a collection of complementary approaches which take as their starting point the rejection of planned change (By, 2005). They share the notion that change is not a linear process or a one-off isolated event but a continuous, open-ended, cumulative and unpredictable process of aligning and re-aligning an organization to its changing environment (Falconer, 2002). Weick (2000: 225) comments as follows on studies of emergent change:

> The recurring story is one of autonomous initiatives that bubble up internally; continuous emergent change; steady learning from both failure and success; strategy implementation

that is replaced by strategy making; the appearance of innovations that are unplanned, unforeseen and unexpected; and small actions that have surprisingly large consequences.

Advocates of emergent change argue that it is more suitable to the turbulent and continually-changing environment in which organizations now operate. They reject what they see as the incremental approach of planned change. Instead, they argue that organizations must continuously and synergistically adapt their internal practices and behaviour in real-time to changing external conditions (Beer and Nohria, 2000). Consequently, 'The art of leadership in the management field would seem to lie in the ability to shape the process [of change] in the long term rather than direct single episodes' (Pettigrew and Whipp, 1991: 143). Furthermore, and just as importantly, proponents of emergent change view organizations as power systems and, consequently, they see change as a political process whereby different groups in an organization struggle to protect or enhance their own interests (Orlikowski and Yates, 2006; Wilson, 1992).

This highlights one of the more notable shortcomings of the emergent approach, which is that its proponents do not appear to recognize ethics as a topic worthy of consideration. Their view seems to be that it is an immutable fact of life that organizations are composed of warring factions and, therefore, for change to be successful, its proponents must utilize politics and power to achieve their ends (Buchanan and Boddy, 1992; Caldwell, 2006; Dawson, 1994, 2003; Hardy, 1996; Hatch, 1997; Orlikowski and Yates, 2006). This view is neatly summed up by Pfeffer (1992: 337–38), who states, 'Computers don't get built, cities don't get rebuilt, and diseases don't get fought unless advocates for change learn how to develop and use power effectively.'

If one accepts that politics dominates organizational life and that change is a battle between those who have power and those who want it, it is only a small step to arguing that 'might is right': that those who have the power have the right to impose their change on the rest of the organization, regardless of how those on the receiving end feel about it. Obviously, the proponents of emergent change do not necessarily support such abuses of power. However, they do see power and politics as a fact of organizational life, which must be accepted and exploited if change is to be achieved (Pfeffer, 1992). Indeed, as Buchanan and Badham (1999: 29) note, the advice seems to be that 'If all else fails, use dirty tricks such as coercion, undermining the expertise of others, playing one group off against another, and get others to "fire the bullet".' What we can see, therefore, is that the ethical dimension of leadership and change does not get a mention, at least explicitly, in the emergent approach to change. However, as Burnes and Jackson (2011) argue, and as the next section will demonstrate, this does not mean that the ethical dimension is absent, but that one has to impute it from the nature of the approach to change.

Ethics, leadership and change

In organizational terms, ethics are beliefs about what is right or wrong, they provide a basis for judging the appropriateness of behaviour and they guide people in their dealings with other individuals, groups and organizations (Jones et al., 2000). However, there are two philosophical camps with regard to ethical values – the consequentialists and the non-consequentialists (Pettit, 2003). Consequentialists argue that values are meaningless unless they are actively promoted. Therefore, consequentialists tend to focus on behaviour and outcomes rather than motives. Non-consequentialists, on the other hand, believe in honouring and respecting values, but not necessarily actively promoting them or using them as a yardstick to judge behaviour or outcomes. Proponents of planned change clearly take a consequentialist stance in their pursuit of ethical outcomes. Advocates of emergent change, on the other hand, would seem to fall into the non-consequentialist camp. From a personal standpoint, they may believe in and respect ethical values, but they also believe that it would be 'naïve' to suggest that they can be applied to organizations.

In this chapter, we adopt the consequentialist stance on ethics, which holds that actions should be judged by their consequences and not according to their intrinsic nature or the motives or character of those performing them. According to this view, the right course of action in any circumstances is that which maximizes good outcomes and minimizes bad ones (Baggini and Fosl, 2007). Based on the work of Thiroux and Krasemann (2007), we identify three forms of ethical consequentialism:

- *Altruistic consequentialism*: This form of consequentialism is associated with the nineteenth-century philosopher Auguste Comte, who defined altruism as the disinterested concern for the welfare of another as an end in itself (Blackburn, 2008). Altruistic consequentialism maintains that an action is ethically right if it maximizes the beneficial consequences for everyone other than the instigator. Under altruistic consequentialism, the role of leaders would be to act in the best interests of everyone but themselves.
- *Utilitarian consequentialism*: This form of consequentialism maintains that an action is ethically right if it maximizes the beneficial consequences for everyone, including the instigator. Utilitarianism originates with the work of the nineteenth-century philosopher Jeremy Bentham, whose Principle of Utility states that ' ... of the various possibilities open to us in any given case, we ought to choose that which will produce the greatest happiness (i.e. pleasure) to the greatest number' (Jones, 1980: 368). Under utilitarian consequentialism, the role of leaders would be to act in the best interests of everyone including themselves.
- *Egoistic consequentialism*: This is a form of consequentialism which maintains that an action is ethically right if it maximizes the beneficial consequences for the instigator. It is associated with the work of the seventeenth-century philosopher Thomas Hobbes on the egoistic view of human nature and morality (Jones, 1980). Under egoistic consequentialism, the role of leaders would be to act in the best interests of themselves alone.

For the purpose of this chapter, we intend to dispense with the first of these (altruistic consequentialism) because it is difficult to see how organizations could survive for very long if leaders acted purely in an altruistic fashion. As an example, in seeking to maximize the beneficial consequences for everyone else, an altruistic leader might choose to close down their own organization in order to favour competitors. Our focus here, therefore, will be on the impact of utilitarian and egoistic consequentialism. It might, of course, be argued that we should also dispense with egoistic consequentialism, because if leaders pursued only their own self-interests, that must surely be to the detriment of their organizations. However, as Kaler (2000b) observes, there is no compelling reason to withhold the term 'ethical' from behaviour motivated by egoistic as opposed to utilitarian reasons. It is the outcome which is important and not the motivation. For example, a study of the development of successful organizations, institutions and nations shows that egoistic leadership and success can go together (Mooney, 2004). For example, how could leaders such as Henry Ford, Pierre du Pont, Alfred Sloan, Toyoda Kiichiro, Matsushita Konosuke, Rupert Murdoch, Bill Gates, Steve Jobs, Ratan Tata, Sir Richard Branson, and many others have built or rebuilt their organizations without an enormous degree of self-belief – i.e. egoism – that they were right and everyone who disagreed with them was wrong? Unfortunately, the same level of egoism can also have disastrous consequences for individual companies, as was the case with Kenneth Lay at Enron, and even for entire sectors, as in the case of the bankers, speculators and fund managers whose individual greed nearly destroyed the world's financial system in 2008 (Burnes, 2009c; Gopalakrishnan et al., 2008; Porter, 2008; Sunderland, 2008, 2009).

Therefore, in theory, egoistic consequentialism can be viewed as no more prone to unethical or illegal behaviour than is utilitarian consequentialism. Nor is such unethical behaviour likely to be confined to leaders. As Joseph Stiglitz (2010) observed in his book on the 2008 global financial crisis, the performance incentives of mortgage salesmen, of the inventors and purveyors of complex and ill-understood financial instruments, and of the corporate leaders who were supposed to supervise them were not aligned with the long-run interests of the institutions for which they worked. To put it succinctly, the long-term interests of the many were sacrificed to the short-term greed and arrogance of the few.

One of the major reasons for such illegal and unethical behaviour is that we have been living in a time where egoistic consequentialism has been aligned with forms of leadership and change which allow leaders a large degree of unquestioned discretion, and even secrecy, regarding what they do and how they do it. This is not inevitable. The danger of such situations arising can be reduced where there is openness about and alignment of values and objectives, transparency in decision-making and truly independent external scrutiny. As By and Macleod (2009) and Burnes and Jackson (2011) show, approaches to leadership and change are not value-free. Sometimes, as with planned change with its attendant democratic leadership, they are explicitly stated; in other cases, such as emergent change and its attendant transformational–charismatic leadership, they are more implicit. As we will show, egoistic consequentialist values align with the emergent approach to change whilst the planned approach is more aligned to utilitarian consequentialism.

Taking the planned approach first: as noted above, this is strongly underpinned by an ethical base which promotes democratic-humanist values. It is a participative approach which seeks to involve all those concerned as equal partners, and to ensue that all the parties have access to and can openly share, analyse and debate the information and options available. This involvement and transparency helps to prevent one group or one individual seeking to promote their interests over those of the other parties. It also helps to achieve outcomes that satisfy the needs of all the parties involved by ensuring they all have an equal say in the analysis, planning and implementation of change. Therefore, the planned approach adopts the utilitarian objective of seeking to achieve the greatest good for the greatest number. In effect, as Figure 20.1 shows, it creates a virtuous

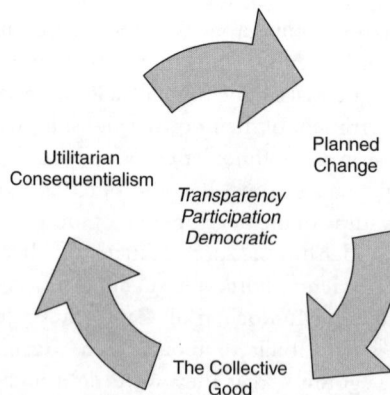

Utilitarian
Consequentialism

Planned
Change

Transparency
Participation
Democratic

The Collective
Good

Figure 20.1 The virtuous change circle

circle whereby the values of utilitarian consequentialism underpin the planned approach which, through openness and democratic decision-making, promotes the collective good.

Emergent change, on the other hand, makes no claims to possessing an ethical base, and instead acknowledges and often promotes change as a political process in which there is a need to use power and manipulation to achieve the leader's ends (Buchanan and Badham, 1999; Wilson, 1992). What is perhaps even more worrying is that, under the emergent approach, change is seen as uncontrolled and uncontrollable (Weick, 2000). All managers are expected to seize the opportunity to bring about change and to experiment with the 'everyday contingencies, breakdowns, exceptions and unintended consequences' of organizational life (Orlikowski, 1996: 65). This creates the conditions for ambitious leaders to pursue their own self-interest under the guise of change. This of course fits in with the spirit of the age which was neatly summed up by Gordon Gekko, the central character in Oliver Stone's 1987 film *Wall Street*, who stated that 'greed, for want of a better word, is good'. Gekko may have left Wall Street over 20 years ago but his ideology has proved far more enduring, as recent events have demonstrated all too well (Burnes, 2009c). Many managers perceive themselves as leaders forming the new ruling class (Diefenbach, 2009) and in some cases have even adopted the sobriquet 'masters of the universe' (Harris, 2007). Yet, as Alvesson and Sveningsson (2003) observe, what makes their actions extraordinary, in their mind, is that they are done by them, which, of course, is a working definition of egoism. The result is a surprisingly high acceptance of mendacious leadership, systemic mismanagement and greed which only a few seem to be prepared to challenge (By, 2010).

It is the unfettered pursuit of the leader's self-interest which the emergent approach allows and even encourages which shows its strong alignment to egoistic consequentialism. For many of the leaders who utilize the emergent approach, it is the degree to which it results in the promotion of their interests rather than the collective good which is important. If both can be achieved, fine, if not, the collective good will always be seen as subservient to the individual good – how could it be any other way for an egoist? Therefore, the combination of egoistic consequentialism and emergent change creates a potential vicious circle whereby the pursuit of the leader's own interests can crowd out the pursuit of the collective good. However, it is not egoistic consequentialism which is dangerous per se, but the context in which it is deployed. When deployed in a context in which leaders are freed from the normal restraints of organizational life, in which political behaviour is legitimized, and in which underhand and even illegal behaviour can be hidden by 'the fog of war', egoistic leadership can be very damaging. As Figure 20.2 shows, it creates a vicious circle whereby

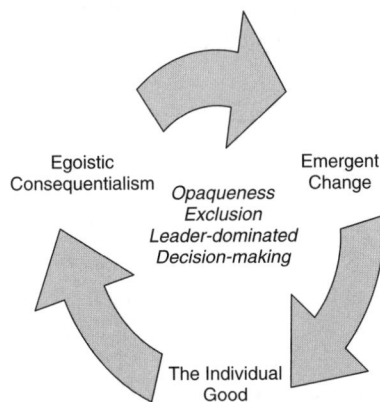

Figure 20.2 The vicious change circle

303

egoistic consequentialist values underpin emergent change which, through obfuscation and political manipulation, subverts the collective good in favour of the leader's good.

Conclusions

Our argument in this chapter has been three-fold:

First, that leadership and change are inextricably linked – the purpose of leadership is to bring about change. This is a view which few would dispute. However, we have also argued that neither leadership nor change is value-free. In order to explore this further, we adopted the consequentialist view of ethics – a view which focuses on behaviour and outcomes rather than process and motives. Given that leadership and change are both concerned with outcomes, i.e. successful change, the consequentialist view of ethics is an appropriate one to take. We also note the high failure rate of change initiatives. We do not claim that this is due solely to a lack of ethical values but, as Burnes and Jackson (2011) show, the issue of value alignment is an important one.

Second, that the planned approach to change is more likely to lead to utilitarian outcomes than the emergent approach. This is because it was explicitly developed by Lewin to achieve collective good rather than to promote sectional or individual interests. It is an approach which stresses democratic leadership, participative change and ethical values, which we have identified as utilitarian consequentialism. Therefore, if planned change results in ethical outcomes, this is not by accident or because of a collection of fortuitous circumstances. It is because that is what it was designed by Lewin to do.

Third, that emergent change is more likely to lead to unethical outcomes. This is because it comprises: charismatic-transformational leadership which gives leaders an almost free hand to act as they like; change processes open to abuse and manipulation; and ethical values which allow leaders to pursue their own interests, namely egoistic consequentialism. None of these by themselves are necessarily unethical or wrong. Charismatic leadership, as mentioned earlier, has been a factor in the success of many organizations. As Pfeffer (1992) noted, power and politics can be used to achieve ethical outcomes. Similarly, egoistic consequentialism in the appropriate circumstances can be a force for good. However, when linked together, as they have been over the past three decades, they do pose a danger – the danger that leaders will pursue, and even be encouraged to pursue, their own interests regardless of the wider interests of other stakeholders or even the survival of the organization. This is especially the case given that the last three decades have also been ones which have been presided over by Gordon Gekko's mantra: 'greed, for want of a better word, is good'.

Our argument, therefore, is a very simple one: all leadership styles and all approaches to change are rooted in a set of values. The appropriateness and efficacy of leadership styles, approaches to change and the ethical stance adopted depend on the exact combination of these and the circumstances in which they are deployed, rather than the intrinsic merits of the particular elements which make up the combination. Elements of planned change could result in unethical outcomes just as elements of emergent change can result in ethical outcomes: the crucial element is how they are combined. The axis on which acceptable and unacceptable outcomes revolve are the ethical values which underpin and link together particular combinations of leadership and change. We believe the fundamental flaw in many approaches to change is that not only are they not explicit about values, but they give the impression that it is somehow unworldly or naïve even to mention ethical considerations. From this perspective, ethical change is not an issue because power and politics preclude such considerations. However, it seems contradictory that proponents of emergent change maintain that most aspects of organizational behaviour can be changed but not those connected with power and politics (Burnes, 2009c). Crucially, it also ignores the issue of choice. As Hatch (1997: 367–68) observes:

> In a socially constructed world, responsibility for environmental conditions lies with those who do the constructing … This suggests at least two competing scenarios for organizational change. First, organization change can be a vehicle of domination for those who conspire to enact the world for others … An alternative use of social constructionism is to create a democracy of enactment in which the process is made open and available to all … such that we create opportunities for freedom and innovation rather than simply for further domination.

However, many change leaders and advocates of approaches to change appear only to recognize the first of these scenarios. Their stance echoes the famous quotation attributed to Charlie Wilson, who was President of General Motors in the early 1950s: 'What's good for General Motors is good for the country.' Many leaders appear to interpret this to mean: 'What's good for me is good for the organization', which is of course an egoist consequentialist standpoint. But what Wilson actually said was: 'For years I thought that what was good for our country was good for General Motors, and vice versa' (*Time*, 1961). Therefore, a more accurate interpretation of Wilson's words would be: 'What's good for the organization is good for me', which is very much a utilitarian consequentialist stance.

Consequently, self-interest and organizational interest are not necessarily incompatible. If one goes back to the work of Thomas Hobbes, the original proponent of the egoist view of human nature, his view of leadership is closely allied to Wilson's view of General Motors. Hobbes believed that the quid pro quo for allowing leaders authority, for individuals surrendering some of their liberties to them, is that the leader acts for the common good (Jones, 1980). Applying this to organizations, which are social groupings established, in the most part, to meet the ends of their stakeholders. Then, if a leader ceases to act for the common good, they lose their legitimacy. It follows that for leaders to have legitimacy they must act in the common good even if their own personal philosophy is one of egoist consequentialism. Therefore, drawing on both Charlie Wilson and Thomas Hobbes, one can argue that leaders with egoist consequentialist ethics can best serve their own interests by serving the collective interests of the rest of the stakeholders in the organization. In order to guarantee this, organizations need to be explicit about what is acceptable and not acceptable, there needs to be transparency and involvement in decision-making and leaders need to be subject to appropriate levels of accountability. Above all, those who study and offer advice on change need to be explicit about the ethical basis of their work and the dangers as well as the benefits of their approach to change. Indeed, perhaps all approaches to change should carry a health warning:

> Ignoring ethics can seriously damage your organization.

References

Alimo-Metcalfe, B. and Alban-Metcalfe, R. (2000) Heaven can wait. *Health Service Journal*, 12 October, 26–29.

Alvesson, M. and Sveningsson, S. (2003) Managers doing leadership: the extra-ordinarization of the mundane. *Human Relations*, 56, 1435–1459.

Baggini, J. and Fosl, P.S. (2007) *The Ethics Toolkit: A Compendium of Ethical Concepts and Methods*. Blackwell: Oxford.

Barker, R.A. (2001) The nature of leadership. *Human Relations*, 54 (4), 469–494.

Barnard, C. (1938) *The Functions of the Executive*. Harvard University Press: Cambridge, MA.

Bass, B.M. (1995) Transformational leadership redux. *Leadership Quarterly*, 6, 463–478.

Beer, M. and Nohria, N. (eds) (2000) *Breaking the Code of Change*. Harvard Business School Press: Boston, MA.

Bessant, J. and Haywood, B. (1985) *The Introduction of Flexible Manufacturing Systems as an Example of Computer Integrated Manufacture*. Brighton Polytechnic: Brighton.

Bigge, L.M. (1982) *Learning Theories for Teachers*. Gower: Aldershot.

Blackburn, S. (2008) *The Oxford Dictionary of Philosophy* (2nd edn). Oxford University Press: Oxford.

Bradford, D.L. and Burke, W.W. (2004) Introduction: Is OD in crisis? *Journal of Applied Behavioral Science*, 40 (4), 369–373.

Brown, S.L. and Eisenhardt, K.M. (1997) The art of continuous change: linking complexity theory and time-paced evolution in relentlessly shifting organizations. *Administrative Science Quarterly*, 4 (1), March, 1–34.

Buchanan, D.A. and Badham, R. (1999) *Power, Politics and Organizational Change: Winning the Turf Game*. Sage: London.

Buchanan, D.A. and Boddy, D. (1992) *The Expertise of the Change Agent*. Prentice Hall: London.

Burnes, B. (2003) Managing change and changing managers: from ABC to XYZ. *Journal of Management Development*, 22 (7), 627–642.

Burnes, B. (2004) Kurt Lewin and the planned approach to change: a re-appraisal. *Journal of Management Studies*, 41 (6), 977–1002.

Burnes, B. (2007) Kurt Lewin and the Harwood studies: the foundations of OD. *Journal of Applied Behavioral Science*, 43 (2), 213–231.

Burnes, B. (2009a) *Managing Change* (5th edn). FT/Prentice Hall: London.

Burnes, B. (2009b) Organisational change in the public sector: the case for planned change. In R.T. By and C. Macleod (eds) *Managing Organisational Change in Public Services: International Issues, Challenges and Cases*. Routledge: London.

Burnes, B. (2009c) Reflections: ethics and organisational change – time for a return to Lewinian values. *Journal of Change Management*, 9 (4), 359–381.

Burnes, B. and Jackson, P. (2011) Success and failure in organisational change: an exploration of the role of values. *Journal of Change Management*, 11 (3).

Burns, J.M. (1978) *Leadership*. Harper & Row: New York.

By, R.T. (2005) Organisational change management: a critical review. *Journal of Change Management*, 5 (4), 369–380.

By, R.T. (2010) Journal of Change Management: 10 years on. *Journal of Change Management*, 10 (1), 1–3.

By, R.T. and Macleod, C. (eds) (2009) *Managing Organizational Change in Public Services*. London: Routledge.

Caldwell, R. (2006) *Agency and Change*. Routledge: London.

Clark, A. (2008) Feds charge bear pair with fraud over $1.4bn sub-prime collapse. *Guardian*, 20 June, available at www.guardian.co.uk.

Conger, J.A. and Kanungo, R.N. (1998) *Charismatic Leadership in Organizations*. Sage: London.

Conner, P.E. (1977) A critical enquiry into some assumptions and values characterizing OD. *Academy of Management Review*, 2 (1), 635–44.

Crosby, P.B. (1979) *Quality is Free*. McGraw-Hill: New York.

Cummings, T.G. and Worley, C.G. (1997) *Organization Development and Change* (6th edn). South-Western College Publishing: Cincinnati, OH.

Cummings, T.G. and Worley, C.G. (2005) *Organization Development and Change* (8th edn). South-Western College Publishing: Mason, OH.

Daft, R. (2002) *The Leadership Experience* (2nd Edition). Thomson: South-Western: Mason, OH.

Dawson, P. (1994) *Organizational Change: A Processual Approach*. Paul Chapman Publishing: London.

Dawson, P. (2003) *Reshaping Change: A Processual Approach*. Routledge: London.

Deresky, H. (2000) *International Management: Managing Across Borders and Cultures* (3rd edn). Prentice Hall: Upper Saddle River, NY.

Diefenbach, T. (2009) *Management and the Dominance of Managers*. London: Routledge.

Dunphy, D., Griffiths, A. and Benn, S. (2007) *Organizational Change for Corporate Sustainability* (2nd edn). Routledge: London.

Falconer, J. (2002) Emergence happens! Misguided paradigms regarding organizational change and the role of complexity and patterns in the change landscape. *Emergence*, 4 (1/2), 117–130.

Foster, R. and Kaplan, S. (2003) *Creative Destruction: Why Companies That Are Built to Last Underperform the Market – And How to Successfully Transform Them*. Doubleday: London.

French, W.L. and Bell, C.H. (1973) *Organization Development*. Prentice Hall: Englewood Cliffs, NJ.

French, W.L. and Bell, C.H. (1995) *Organization Development* (5th edn). Prentice Hall: Englewood Cliffs, NJ.

French, W.L. and Bell, C.H. (1999) *Organization Development* (6th edn). Prentice Hall: Upper Saddle River, NJ.

Gellerman, W., Frankel, M.S. and Ladenson, R.F. (1990) *Values and Ethics in Organizational and Human Systems Development: Responding to Dilemmas in Professional Life*. Jossey-Bass: San Francisco, CA.

Gopalakrishnan, S., Mangaliso, M.P. and Butterfield, D.A. (2008) Managing ethically in times of transformation challenges and opportunities. *Group & Organization Management*, 33 (6), 756–759.

Greiner, L.E. and Cummings, T.G. (2004) Wanted: OD more alive than dead! *Journal of Applied Behavioral Science*, 40 (4), 374–391.

Griffin, D. (2002) *The Emergence of Leadership: Linking Self-Organization and Ethics*. Routledge: London.

Hammer, M. and Champy, J. (1993) *Re-engineering the Corporation*. Nicolas Brealey: London.

Hardy, C. (1996) Understanding power: bringing about strategic change. *British Journal of Management*, 7 (Special Issue) March, S3–S16.

Harris, P. (2007) Masters of the universe still run New York. *Observer*, 16 December, available at www.guardian.co.uk.

Harrison, J.K. and Clough, M.W. (2006) Characteristics of "state of the art" leaders: Productive narcissism versus emotional intelligence and Level 5 capabilities. *Social Science Journal*, 43 (2), 287–292.

Hatch, M.J. (1997) *Organization Theory: Modern, Symbolic and Postmodern Perspectives*. Oxford University Press: Oxford.

Hitt, M.A., Miller, C.C. and Colella, A. (2009) *Organizational Behaviour: A Strategic Approach* (2nd Edn). Wiley: Hoboken, NJ.

Hollander, E.P. (1995) Ethical challenges in the leader-follower relationship. *Business Ethics Quarterly*, 5 (1), 55–65.

Hurley, R.F., Church, A., Burke, W.W. and Van Eynde, D.F. (1992) Tension, change and values in OD. *OD Practitioner*, 29, 1–5.

Jones, G, R., George, J.M. and Hill, C.W.L. (2000) *Contemporary Management* (2nd edn). McGraw-Hill: Boston, MA.

Jones, W.T. (1980) *Masters of Political Thought (Volume 2): Machiavelli to Bentham*. Harrap: London.

Kaler, J. (2000a) Positioning business ethics in relation to management and political philosophy. *Journal of Business Ethics*, 24 (3), 257–272.

Kaler, J. (2000b) Reasons to be ethical: self-interest and ethical business. *Journal of Business Ethics*, 27 (1–2), 161–173.

Kanter, R.M. (1989) *When Giants Learn to Dance: Mastering the Challenges of Strategy, Management, and Careers in the 1990s*. Unwin: London.

Kanter, R.M. (2008) Transforming giants. *Harvard Business Review*, 86, January, 43–52.

Kotter, J. (1990) *A Force for Change: How Leadership Differs from Management*. Free Press: New York.

Leigh, D. and Evans, R. (2007) BAE accused of secretly paying £1bn to Saudi prince. *Guardian*, 7 June, available at www.guardian.co.uk.

Lewin, K., Lippitt, R. and White, R. (1939) Patterns of aggressive behavior in experimentally created "social climates." *Journal of Social Psychology*, 10, 271–299.

Maccoby, M. (2000) Narcissistic leaders. *Harvard Business Review*, 78 (1), 68–77.

Maddock, S. (1999) *Challenging Women*. Sage: London.

Marrow, A.J. (1969) *The Practical Theorist: The Life and Work of Kurt Lewin*. Teachers College Press: New York.

McKinsey & Company (2008) Creating organizational transformations. *McKinsey Quarterly*, July, 1–7, available at www.mckinseyquarterly.com.

Mooney, B. (2004) *Shaping History: 100 Great Leaders–From Antiquity to the Present*. Arcturus Foulsham: London.

Nahavandi, A. (2000) *The Art and Science of Leadership* (2nd edn). Prentice Hall: Upper Saddle River, NJ.

Orlikowski, W.J. (1996) Improvising Organizational Transformation Over Time: A Situated Change Perspective. *Information Systems Research*, 7 (1), 63–92.

Orlikowski, W.J. and Yates, J.A. (2006) ICT and organizational change: a commentary. *Journal of Applied Behavioral Science*, 42 (1), 127–134.

Osborne, D. and Gaebler, T. (1992) *Reinventing Government: How the Entrepreneurial Spirit is Transforming the Public Sector*. Addison-Wesley: Reading, MA.

Oxford Dictionary of English (2006) (2nd edn). Oxford: Oxford University Press.

Partnoy, F. (2003) When greed is fact and control is fiction. *Guardian*, 14 February, available at www.guardian.co.uk.

Peters, T. (2006) *Re-imagine! Business Excellence in a Disruptive age*. Dorling Kindersley: London.

Pettigrew, A.M. and Whipp, R. (1991) *Managing Change for Competitive Success*. Blackwell: Oxford.

Pettit, P. (2003) Consequentialism. In S. Darwall (ed.): *Consequentialism*. Blackwell: Oxford.

Pfeffer, J. (1992) *Managing with Power: Politics and Influence in Organizations*. Harvard Business School Press: Boston, MA.

Porter, H. (2008) How did so many smart people get suckered by Bernard Madoff? *Observer*, 21 December , available at www.guardian.co.uk.

Rickards, T. and Clark, M. (2006) *Dilemmas of Leadership*. Routledge: Abingdon.

Senturia, T., Flees, L. and Maceda, M. (2008) *Leading change management requires sticking to the PLOT*. Bain & Company: London.

Smith, M.E. (2002) Success rates for different types of organizational change. *Performance Improvement*, 41 (1), 26–33.

Smith, M.E. (2003) Changing an organization's culture: correlates of success and failure. *Leadership & Organization Development Journal*, 24 (5), 249–261.

Stacey, R.D. (2007) *Strategic Management and Organisational Dynamics: The Challenge of Complexity* (5th edn). FT/Prentice Hall: Harlow.

Stiglitz, J. (2010) *Freefall: Free Markets and the Sinking of the Global Economy*. Allen Lane: London.

Storey, J. (2004) Signs of change: 'Damned Rascals' and beyond. In J. Storey, (ed.) *Leadership in Organizations: Current Issues and Key Trends*. Routledge: London.

Sunderland, R. (2008) 'Inside the minds of men who want to get rich', *Observer*, 21 December, available at www.guardian.co.uk.

Sunderland, R. (2009) Earth to overpaid bankers: you're working for us now. *Observer*, 8 February, available www.guardian.co.uk.

Thiroux, J.P. and Krasemann, K.W. (2007) *Ethics: Theory and Practice* (9th edn). Pearson Prentice Hill: Upper Saddle River, NJ.

Time (1961) Armed forces: engine Charlie. *Time*, 6 October, available at www.Time.com.

Tran, M. (2003) $1.4 bn Wall Street settlement finalised. *Guardian*, 28 April, available at www.guardian.co.uk.

Warwick, D.P. and Thompson, J.T. (1980) Still crazy after all these years. *Training and Development Journal*, 34 (2), 16–22.

Weick, K.E. (2000) Emergent change as a universal in organisations. In M. Beer and N. Nohria (eds) *Breaking the Code of Change*. Harvard Business School Press: Boston, MA.

Wilson, D.C. (1992) *A Strategy of Change*. Routledge: London.

Wooten, K.C. and White, L.P. (1999) Linking OD's philosophy with justice theory: postmodern implications. *Journal of Organizational Change Management*, 12 (1), 7–20.

Worley, G.C. and Feyerhern, A.E. (2003) Reflections on the future of organization development. *Journal of Applied Behavioral Science*, 39 (1), 97–115.

Yukl, G. (2006). *Leadership in Organisations* (6th edn). Prentice Hall: Upper Saddle River, NJ.

Yukl, G. and Van Fleet, D.D. (1992) Theory and research on leadership in organizations. In M.D. Dunnette and L.M. Hough (eds) *Handbook of Industrial and Organizational Psychology, Volume 3* (2nd edn). Consulting Psychologists Press, Inc: Palo Alto, CA.

21

Management fads and fashions

David Collins

Introduction

There are, as the novelist Jon McGregor (2006) observes, 'so many ways to begin'. Despite this, academic narratives tend to have rather conventional opening gambits.

For reasons that will soon become apparent this chapter will attempt to dispense with the usual formalities of academic introductions. Instead we commence with two observations; two threads of analysis that will quickly become intertwined:

1 By convention academic narratives in the field of business and management tend to articulate an interest in novelty and a concern for controversy.
2 From the 1950s, and especially during the 1980s and 1990s, the management consulting industry brought forth a variety of ideas, frameworks and tools. These were sold to practitioners in the private and public sectors as solutions to a range of problems – both novel and perennial.

Our first thread of analysis proceeds from the understanding that in their professional lives most academics are, publicly, disdainful of fashion. Indeed academics in the field of business and management studies, often, protest that their ideas and orientations persist in the face of ideas, which in being fashionable, are less substantial; unworthy. My colleagues, for example, tend to argue that their ideas and concerns are guided by conviction; by thematic continuity and by a commitment to critique. Despite such protestations, however, academics *are* preoccupied with novelty (Noon et al., 2000; Collins, 2007; Starbuck, 2009a).[1] Of course this concern is cloaked to some extent by, linguistic codes, which speak of 'contributions to knowledge' and debates at the 'cutting edge'. But every academic with an ambition to publish understands that 'top' journals want work that is distinctive and ideas that are new!

Grant and his co-authors demonstrate the authorial tendencies that these concerns precipitate. Introducing their *Sage Handbook of Organisational Discourse* (Grant et al., 2004) they adopt – ironically – an approach which is, in any sense, conventional. Thus their introductory remarks turn upon the hinges of *chronology* and *controversy*:

A growing disillusionment with many of the mainstream theories – and methodologies – that underpin organizational studies has encouraged scholars to seek alternative ways in which to describe, analyse and theorize the increasingly complex processes and practices that constitute 'organization'.

(Grant et al., 2004: 1)

Our second thread of analysis begins by documenting the growth of the consulting industry: McKenna (2006) observes that in 1965 there was one management consultant for every one hundred managers in the USA. However he notes that this ratio had declined to 1:13 by 1995. Approaching this question of growth from another angle, McKenna reminds us that there were 100 consulting firms in the US in 1930, 400 by 1940 and 1000 by 1950.

The US consultancy industry is worth an estimated $100bn (McKenna, 2006). But it is not only cash that this industry consumes. One-third of the world's top MBA graduates and one-sixth of all elite under-graduates (whether these be from Oxbridge or the Ivy League) begin their working lives in management consultancy firms.

And at this point our threads begin to intertwine: Since the 1990s academics – who are, after all, excited by change and reverential of controversy – have been keen to discuss the dubious virtues of consultancy.[2] Contrasting their intellectual priorities with those, assumed to be predominant in management consulting, academics and business journalists (collectively dubbed 'the guru industry' (Collins, 2000)) have argued that contemporary developments in management knowledge and practice amount to little more than fads and, as such, constitute distractions, both from the real business of managing and the proper calling of academia (Starbuck, 2009a, 2009b).

In this chapter I hope to offer an alternative perspective on management fads. Instead of adopting the normal conventions of academic writing I set out to reconsider the terms of the narrative that has shaped our appreciation of the ideas, arguments and practices that have been branded as being, *merely*, fads and fashions.

Accordingly, this chapter is structured as follows. We will begin with an attempt to establish the prevalence of 'the fad motif' in management and organization studies (Collins, 2001). To this end we will:

a) note the development of a range of initiatives, which have been labelled as fads,
b) offer a critical analysis of a selection of texts that have sought to establish, empirically, the faddish nature of recent developments in management knowledge.

Having noted the centrality of the fad motif and having introduced concerns as to its efficacy we will invite readers to reconsider the terms of the debate that have labelled recent initiatives as empty fads. We will ask:

c) What is it that we suggest when we label an idea as a fad?
d) What do we fail to see when we label ideas and practices in this way?

In pursuit of these particular issues we will examine Abrahamson's (1991, 1996) discussion of fashions and fads (for an alternative, complementary account see Grint, 1997). This analysis, as we shall see, acknowledges organizational variety and in so doing offers redemption to those practitioners who have, otherwise, been presented as dopes and dupes.

Having placed the fad motif within a context that, in Shotter's (2002) terms, 'notices and allows' for the peculiarities of organizational life we will move on to consider the linguistic foundations of business faddism. Noting the metaphorical power of the fad motif in management and organization studies we will consider the ways in which this term 'informs and yet deforms' (see Moorhouse, 1988) academic analysis. Thus we will seek to acknowledge the ways in which the fad motif has directed and yet distracted our attention; illuminated and yet obscured our understanding (see Morgan, 1986) of managerial (and academic) toil. Accordingly we will consider four alternative means of framing our concern with contemporary developments in management. Finally we will conclude with a summary that considers the analytical dimensions and, therein, the opportunities for development revealed by our critical reanalysis of management fads and fashions.

Management fads and fashions

What do consultants do? Ordinarily these words would serve as the opening lines of a joke. I know lots of jokes about consultants. But this is not the place for such frippery. The literature on management fads and fashions makes it clear that consultants are no laughing matter. Consultants, in fact, are bad news. They sell novelty. They peddle fads and in so doing they 'tear down the sophisticated formal organization and decision systems that corporations have evolved and which make management effective' (Hilmer and Donaldson, 1996: 7).

Fads are transitory; ephemeral; insubstantial. Fads are proof of a fickleness of mind. Or, as Furnham (2004) puts it: 'A fad is a craze for something: a short time when there is an exaggerated zeal for a particular idea or practice. Fads are by definition short-lived. They go in one era and out the other' (1).

But it's not novelty *per se* that makes 'fads' problematic for those who would redeem management. Nowadays no one is allowed to be *resistant to change*. It is novelty *plus* inconsistency that makes fads (and consultants) 'dangerous to know' (Burnes, 1998).

Pascale (1990) captures this well. Quoting the observations of a practising manager he suggests that following the *latest advice* involves repeated reversals of practice and strategy: 'In the past eighteen months, we have heard that profit is more important than revenue, quality is more important than profit, that people are more important than profit, that customers are more important than our people, that big customers are more important than our small customers, and that growth is the key to our success. No wonder our performance is inconsistent' (18–19).

To name the techniques that foster such inconsistency, Pascale (1990) tells us, is to compile 'a who's who of business hype' (18). Glaser (1997), for example, lists and attacks seven sets of fads. He disparages:

1　Stakeholder theory
2　Total Quality Management
3　Benchmarking
4　Strategy
5　360° feedback
6　Empowerment
7　The Learning Organization.

Furnham (2004) offers two lists of fads: one of his own making and the other produced by Bascal and Associates. The Bascal listing overlaps, only marginally, with that produced by Glaser and is as follows:

- One-Minute Management
- Total Quality Management
- Learning Organizations
- Peak Performance
- Excellence
- Chaos
- Management by Objectives (MBO)
- Matrix Management
- Team-Based Management
- Process Reengineering.

Operating within a longer timeframe – one that commences in the 1950s – Pascale lists some 33 fads:

- Decision Trees
- Managerial Grid
- Satisfiers/Dissatisfiers
- Theory X/Theory Y
- Brainstorming
- T-Group Training
- Theory Z
- Conglomeration
- Management by Objectives (MBO)
- Decentralization
- Diversification
- Experience Curve
- Strategic Business Units
- Zero Base Budgeting
- Value Chain
- Quality Circles/Total Quality Management (TQM)
- Excellence
- Restructuring/Delayering
- Portfolio Management
- Management by Wandering About (MBWA)
- Just-in-Time/Kanban
- Intrapreneuring
- Corporate Culture
- One Minute Manager
- Globalization
- Cycle Time/Speed
- Visioning
- Work-out
- Empowerment
- Continuous Improvement/Learning Organization
- Business Process Reengineering

Brindle and Stearns (2001) in contrast list just 16:

- Theory X/Theory Y
- Leadership

- Strategic Planning
- Management by Objectives (MBO)
- Portfolio Management
- Matrix Management
- Quality Circles
- Total Quality Management (TQM)
- Empowerment
- Benchmarking
- Reengineering
- Team-based Work/Self-managed Teams
- Downsizing
- Leadership
- Entrepreneurship

Furnham's (2004) own account of management's fads is, perhaps, shaped by a recognition that any attempt to compile a definitive list of management techniques will tend to attract pedants, excite controversy and, in so doing, fabricate a 'listology'[3] that distracts from larger analytical concerns. Thus Furnham documents 'six over-arching fads' (2). These are fads in planning (such as strategic alliances); in organizing (as evidenced by a concern with corporate culture); in staffing (such as 'wellness'); for performance (such as downsizing, demassing and rightsizing); in leading (such as 'intrepreneurs'); and in controlling (such as quality circles).

Hilmer and Donaldson (1996) operate with an approach that straddles the listology of Pascale (1990) and the thematism of Furnham. Employing a topographical metaphor they suggest that managing might be regarded as a journey over terrain that is a challenge to navigation. Indeed they suggest that fads are dangerous for (travelling) managers because they set 'false trails' which delay progress. These false trails, they warn us, have been set across the entire landscape of managing. Presenting themselves as the owners of a truly accurate map of managerial work, therefore, Hilmer and Donaldson warn us that there are false trails concerned with *structure*; with *action*; with *techniques*; with *culture*; and with the conduct and constitution of the *Board of Directors*.

Other commentators, meanwhile, have avoided the perils of listology by treating fads, individually, on a case-by-case basis. Total Quality Management (TQM) and Business Process Reengineering (BPR) have often been singled out for particular criticism:

> Total Quality Management (TQM) looks like being one of the management fashions of the 1990s. One advocate has gone so far as to call it the third revolutionary wave after the industrial and computing revolutions.
>
> (Wilkinson et al., 1991: 24)

> Business process re-engineering (BPR) is the latest business panacea to emerge from the American academic – consultancy complex.
>
> (Grey and Mitev, 1995: 6)

> Business Process Reengineering (BPR) is set to become the most influential management idea, or fad, of the 1990s.
>
> (Wilmott and Wray-Bliss, 1996: 62)

Coulson-Thomas (1996), more than most, mixes his metaphors and (if you will forgive another) throws the kitchen sink at BPR:

> Is BPR a temporary gravy train for consultants? Or is it a management fad equivalent to a flu epidemic, quickly spreading and leaving people the worse for wear when it passes?
>
> (Coulson-Thomas, 1996: 18)

Yet labelling initiatives in this way does not in itself constitute proof that managers are faddish. In the following section, therefore, we will consider the evidence for business faddism.

What does it mean to be faddish?

Gill and Whittle (1992) were among the first UK commentators to consider the nature of management fads. They offer a four-phase, life-cycle, model of management knowledge development. The phases of this model are said to mirror human life-cycles and are, namely, *birth* (introduction), *adolescence* (growth), *maturity* and *decline* (see Figure 21.1).[4]

Analysing 'three consultant-driven approaches to organizational improvement' (281) – MBO (Management by Objectives), OD (Organization Development) and TQM (Total Quality Management) – Gill and Whittle suggest that the product life-cycle for management knowledge-products is around 40 years. In common with others (see, for example, Engwall and Kipping, 2002), they observe that the market for management knowledge needs to be located within a distinctive producer–consumer dynamic. This dynamic, they argue, creates a symbiosis between consumers (managers) who need 'to find ways of committing and controlling their workforces' (Gill and Whittle, 1992: 282) and producers (consultants) who are, themselves, located within a competitive and sales-oriented business. Thus Gill and Whittle argue that innovations in management knowledge are, increasingly, transient in terms of their impact on practice because:

a) managers confront a world which is complex, ambiguous and multi-faceted,
b) the competitive dynamics of the consultancy industry obliges consulting firms to launch wave after wave of products, which claim the capacity to simplify managerial work.

Furthermore they suggest that the brazen claims of this industry go uncontested because:

c) consultants are wary of evaluating their products (for they are fearful of negative publicity and, additionally, have no wish to make useful knowledge available to their rivals),
d) the volatility of managerial careers means that few practitioners are ever in post long enough to evaluate their purchases and
e) the culture of American and British business is action-oriented, anti-intellectual and individualist, and so, rewards those who pioneer new innovations.

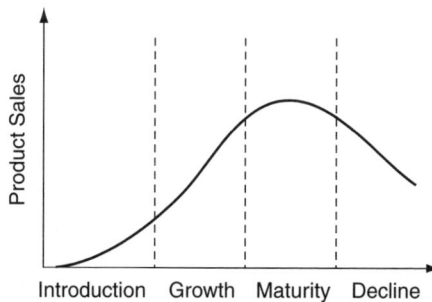

Figure 21.1 An outline model of the product life-cycle

315

The work of Gill and Whittle (1992) is highly plausible. Certainly it is one of the papers that reviewers expect authors to cite when new contributions to the literature concerned with management fads and fashion are aired (see Latour, 1987).[5] But there are problems with their analysis:

1   It is speculative. Indeed Gill and Whittle offer no clear, empirical, evidence to support their contention that management knowledge has a 40-year product life-cycle.
2   It appears contradictory to some degree. For example the authors note that Performance Appraisal retains key elements of an earlier product known as Management by Objectives (MBO) and yet they complain that management fashion is 'cyclical and non-cumulative' (Gill and Whittle, 1992: 292).
3   The findings of their analysis seem to contradict both, the title of their work and the thrust of their claims. Indeed the authors tell us that their paper will document and account for the transient nature of management knowledge and yet their own analysis suggests that these, knowledge-products, have an enduring presence insofar as they (a) incorporate earlier ideas and (b) enjoy a useful shelf life of some 40 years.

In contrast Abrahamson (1996) does attempt to place his account of management fads on an empirical footing. Analysing the period between 1977 and 1987, Abrahamson documents the rapid growth and subsequent decline of interest in Quality Circles using two measures. The first of these is based on a count of articles appearing in the ABI Inform database. The second calculation of interest is based upon a simple measurement of the width of the proceedings of the International Association of Quality Circles (1979–87).

Each of these proxy measures, Abrahamson tells us, yields a curve that is similar to the product life-cycle curve suggested by Gill and Whittle (1992). Yet Abrahamson's analysis suggests that the period between the 'birth' of an idea and its ultimate 'decline' may be as short as ten years.

Thomas's (1999) analysis, of management fashion, however, disputes both sets of figures. In fact Thomas estimates that management knowledge-products have, on average, a shelf-life of 20 years. Furthermore he is critical of those such as Abrahamson (1996) and Pascale (1990) who assume that a simple count of texts can provide a reliable proxy for the influence of an idea or practice. Accordingly, Thomas bases his analysis on citations – the number of times that an author's work is used by others. He concedes that citations perform a variety of heterogeneous roles (see Moravcsik and Murugesan, 1975) and he acknowledges that self-citation, in concert with the practices of 'citation circles', and the, observed, failure to cite older, or classical, texts means that citation analysis is far from being unproblematic. Nonetheless Thomas protests that most 'citations do, in fact, constitute a valid conceptual link' (49) between texts. Consequently he argues that citation analysis provides a more reliable measure of the influence of ideas.

Thomas employs the Social Science Citation Index (SSCI) to facilitate his work. This database offers an analysis of texts post – 1956, and so he is obliged to select a canon that reflects these dates. After a lengthy and, at times, confusing discussion of sampling frames, Thomas eventually chooses to base his sample on four editions of *Writers on Organizations* (Pugh and Hickson, 1964, 1989; Pugh et al., 1971, 1983).[6] Analysing these texts, Thomas disputes Gill's and Whittle's (1992) speculations as to the duration and the shape of the management knowledge, product life-cycle. Thus he suggests that the product life-cycle for management knowledge endures for an average of 20 years and describes, not and n-shaped, but an s-shaped curve.

Reviewing organizational practices, however, Cole (1999) and Clark (2001, 2004a) cast shadows over such bibliometric accounts of management knowledge.

Managing fads

Cole (1999) offers an in-depth and longitudinal analysis of the American experience of quality management. He begins by observing that:

> Management fads appear inherently hostile to both effective imitative and learning activities. After all, the term *fad* connotes transience. Webster's Third International Dictionary defines fad as 'a pursuit or interest followed usually widely, but briefly and capriciously, with exaggerated zeal and devotion'.
>
> (Cole, 1999: 14)

Consequently he warns us that: 'Fads are seen as costly distractions that keep managers from concentrating on running the business' (14). Yet he protests that this is a misapprehension. He argues that 'The strong pejorative connotations associated with fads (and imitation) in American popular life are often quite misleading and indeed harmful to corporate competitive performance' (3). Studying the processes of work as opposed to the practices of authors, therefore, Cole (1999) argues that there is a pattern and a context to business faddism, which suggests that fads – so-called – have been embraced for sound business reasons. Thus he notes that, in the US, interest in quality was more pronounced in those organizations that were exposed to foreign competition – such as the chemicals, car and electronics industries. Furthermore he suggests that fears over the growth of public liability law-suits in relation to product defects also helped to galvanize management opinion on quality management. Yet he notes that, despite these inducements, conversion to quality matters was slow in the US and that the early quality innovations produced patchy and, often, contradictory results.

Now at this point the 'fad busters' (*who you gonna call?*) would tend to suggest that such disappointing experiences demonstrate, only too painfully, that fads are alien to, and inconsistent with, good management. But Cole is not swayed by this. He warns us that, in the context of the workplace, imitation (so-called) is rather difficult and represents a creative challenge for all concerned. What the bibliophiles dismiss as mere 'fads', therefore, Cole prefers to see as 'experiments'.

Looking more closely at the actual processes of organizational innovation, Cole observes that bibliometric studies have a tendency to over-estimate the pace at which genuinely novel ideas are generated by organizational consultants. In part he blames the media for this fixation with novelty. Thus he observes that the print and broadcast media takes 'delight in pointing to the rapid succession of fads' (14) because it is drawn to whatever is distinctive or spectacular. Indeed he suggests that there is a basic rule-of-thumb which orders our daily news bulletins: ' "If it burns or bleeds lead with it" ' (10).

Yet Cole argues that succeeding business ideas do not wipe away earlier movements. Consequently business fads cannot be viewed as being, either, genuinely novel or, obviously, inconsistent with what went before. Thus he protests that the quality movement provided, key, experimental and experiential building blocks for Business Process Reengineering (BPR). In addition he notes that America's Quality experiments depended upon a number of 'minifads' (14) such as Quality Circles; Statistical Process Control; and Quality Functional Deployment. Indeed he warns us that these are, too often, listed as departures from Quality Management when they are, in truth, movements within it. Far from being a transient fad, therefore, Cole argues that the Quality movement signals a long-term commitment to learning and experimentation in US organizations.

Clark offers a similar but more direct critique of the bibliometric literature. Focusing upon Thomas's (1999) contribution, Clark (2001) acknowledges that this author promotes a reflexive form of analysis insofar as he demonstrates the existence of fashion swings in scholarly management research. Nonetheless he complains that Thomas's work has 'serious methodological problems' (1656) because it excludes significant texts published prior to 1956. Furthermore he observes that Thomas's sample is skewed because it has been out-sourced to editors who have, we might add, particular ontological and philosophical preferences (see Collins, 2000).

Aside from this specific criticism of Thomas (1999), Clark (2004a) also offers a more general criticism of those who have sought to gauge business faddism by means of bibliometric analysis. In line with Cole's (1999) quip regarding the ordering of our daily news, Clark argues that managers do not choose what appears in the business media. Editors – and advertisers (see Chomsky, 2003) – make such choices. Indeed Clark suggests that editors *shape and distort* media coverage of business and management matters. Thus he argues that editors have a selfish and personal concern with the promotion of management fashion because, within the context of their own working lives, they have a reputational interest in spotting and breaking new trends.

Follower of fashion

Brindle and Stearns (2001), share Clark's eye for fashion and his sensitivity to the complexities of social organization. Consequently their posture with respect to management fads is somewhat ambivalent. Pascale (1990) shares this ambivalence to some degree. Indeed he concedes that some of the ideas that he has, otherwise, dismissed as fads have 'valid aspects' (18). Micklethwait and Wooldridge (1997) and Hilmer and Donaldson (1996) offer, similarly, ambivalent accounts of business fads. Yet they seem to assume that the world of management has binary characteristics such that a categorical division may be drawn between 'good' and 'bad' ideas. Thus Hilmer and Donaldson protest that 'good ideas' support thoughtful management endeavour whereas bad ideas 'damage our corporations'.

Brindle and Stearns, however, are sceptical about the use of the first person plural in this context. Indeed their analysis prompts reflection on a number of assumptions (and refrains) which bolster the literature on fads and fashions. Thus Brindle and Stearns (2001) challenge the unitary thinking (Fox, 1985) that, quietly, underpins much of the literature on fads and fashions. Consequently, when it comes time to weigh the benefits of developments such as BPR and TQM they employ a form of calculus, which recognizes the sectional nature of organizations and the local character of interests. For Brindle and Stearns, therefore, fads acquire an audience and a marketplace because they:

1 Help to provide a sense of common identity. Thus fads may actually help to foster the sense of cohesion which unitarists assume, naturally prevails.
2 Enhance organizational legitimacy, and so, reduce investor and customer anxiety insofar as they tend to ensure that organizations in similar markets look and act alike. Indeed Brindle and Stearns (2001) argues that fads 'permit conformity under the guise of novelty and independence, and all the while give voice and identity' (7).
3 Allow managers to engage in public demonstrations of activity, energy and, perhaps more importantly, vision.
4 Provide avenues for career development: These days you can become the 'VP Quality' or a 'Czar' of some kind!
5 Help managers to secure control over cultures by providing a common language and shared referents.

318

6   May help to improve communications channels.
7   Provide a legitimation for certain courses of action that may otherwise prove problematic. Noting this Collins (2000) argues that 'downsizing' and its cousin, 'rightsizing', provide managers with a means of talking about mass dismissal which makes this process, both, necessary and faceless.

Recognizing the complexity of organizational life, therefore, Brindle and Stearns seem forgiving of managers when they embrace fads. However they show no such mercy to *Harvard Business Review*. In fact they suggest that this journal has done much to promote, thoughtless, business faddism.

A plague on your house ... journal

Brindle and Stearns (2001) argue that in the 1970s the *Harvard Business Review* (HBR) changed direction. A new editorial policy was put in place which, they argue, made a legitimate space for fads in commercial life. There were, they tell us, 'three main tacks' (60) in this shift of course:

1   'a significant shift away from an historical, philosophical grounding toward a decidedly ahistorical bent' (60–61)
2   a retreat from those perspectives which attempted to place the consideration of management in a social and economic context
3   the development of a self-help ethos which meant that 'speed [in action] and [analytical] simplification became virtues' (63).

This analysis of the failings of *HBR* shapes the account of faddism offered by Brindle and Stearns. Going beyond the simple, life-cycle, model of faddism, therefore, the authors argue that fads have three dimensions. They are (a) transient (b) presented as panacea, or cure-alls, and (c) chauvinistic, in the French sense of being unaware of their own limitations.

Yet Brindle and Stearns insist that this condition can be controlled – with careful management. The key to managing fads – as opposed to being managed by fads they tell us – is to take control of this triad (see Figure 21.2). To this end the authors insist that those who would counter faddism, must attack those rhetorics that indulge chauvinism and foster panaceas. Accordingly they offer a counter-rhetoric which, in taking refuge in common-sense (Collins, 1996, 1998) is plainly designed to speak directly to those who have been schooled in an a-historical and anti-analytical approach to managing:

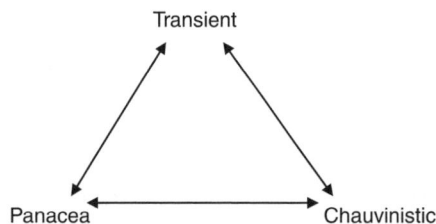

Figure 21.2 Triadic account of management fads produced by Brindle and Stearns (2001)

> Pour in a need for change to deal with problems old and new. Add a sense of perspective, distilled from an understanding of what faddism is all about and what the long-standing issues are. Stir in common sense. The result: It's possible to use fads without being faddist.
>
> (206)

In common with Brindle and Stearns, Abrahamson (1991, 1996) recognizes the importance of rhetorics. Indeed like Brindle and Stearns, Abrahamson hopes that his critical reviews of management fashion might make practitioners, not anti-innovation, but more discerning in their consumption of scholarly rhetoric.

Fads, fashions and rhetoric

Abrahamson uses the term, 'management fad', in a variety of ways. At times he uses the term as a simple synonym for fashion: 'Modes, vogues, fads, fashions, rages and crazes frequently revolutionize many aspects of cultural life' (Abrahamson, 1996: 254). Yet at other times, he uses these terms quite separately. Indeed in an earlier paper Abrahamson (1991) suggests that we should separate 'management fashions' from 'management fads'. His insistence that such innovations need to be considered from the standpoint of rhetoric, however, remains constant throughout. Thus he defines fashions and fads as 'transitory collective beliefs that certain management techniques are at the forefront of management projects' (Abrahamson, 1996: 254).

Abrahamson complains that scholars of management have failed to take fashion seriously and have, indeed, tended to treat fashion as being trivial and undeserving of serious scholarly intention. Disputing this orientation he suggests that management fashion is worthy of serious scrutiny, and yet, quite unlike 'aesthetic fashion'. Aesthetic fashion, Abrahamson argues, is a social-psychological phenomenon that makes an appeal to *taste* and *beauty* whereas the rhetoric (and appeal) of management fashion is couched in terms of *rationality* and *progress*. To explore this rhetorical formulation he considers four explanations for recent developments in management knowledge (See Table 21.1).

Abrahamson labels the first of his four explanations for management fashion 'Efficient choice'. In this quadrant it is assumed that organizational actors can interpret market signals accurately and, having done so, respond by developing innovations that are designed to close any, apparent, performance gaps. Abrahamson plainly doubts the efficacy of this rationalistic account of managing. Nonetheless he allows it as a possibility (albeit an implausible one), and so, he suggests that in this quadrant organizational innovations represent rational and progressive attempts to reduce the gap between actual and potential performance. Such performance gaps, he notes, may be

Table 21.1 Analysis of the diffusion and rejection of managerial ideas

	Imitation processes do not impel diffusion or rejection of ideas	Imitation processes impel the diffusion or rejection of ideas
Organizations within a group determine the diffusion and rejection of ideas within the group	Efficient-choice Perspective	Fad Perspective
Organizations outside a group determine the diffusion and rejection within the group	Forced-selection Perspective	Fashion Perspective

Source: Abrahamson 1991

caused by the 'push' of demand or by the 'pull' of supply. When demand 'pushes', organizations are said to react to, wider, environmental changes by embracing change. Alternatively supply is said to 'pull' change when innovating organizations create performance gaps that their competitors are obliged to address.

The second perspective Abrahamson labels 'Forced Selection'. In common with the first perspective, this quadrant assumes that organizational actors face little in the way of uncertainty. In this sector of the diagram, therefore, it is clear what actors need to do in any given situation. Yet here the conduct of actors is less volitional than in the first perspective. Indeed discretion is assumed to be constrained by external agencies that have the power to mandate certain courses of action and/or organizational forms.

The third quadrant Abrahamson labels the 'fashion' perspective. Here 'fashion' is not synonymous with 'fad'. Indeed 'fads' are analysed in the fourth quadrant and are said to reflect a different dynamic.

In the fashion perspective organizational actors are said to confront a complex environment such that there is uncertainty about (a) the goals of the organization and (b) the efficiency of organizational innovations. These uncertainties are said to generate fear and anxiety among organizational actors. In an attempt to allay these anxieties practitioners are said to turn to 'fashion-setters', or consultants, for support and guidance.

Commenting upon the mechanics of this argument, Thomas (1999) notes that there are, in general terms, three models of the fashion-setting process:

1   The 'trickle-down' model where high status groups act as models, or exemplars, which other lower status, but aspirant, groups will tend to emulate.
2   'Collective Selection Theory', which assumes that collective movements in fashion and taste allows individuals to satisfy their, felt, need for change from within the relative safety of the group.
3   The 'marionette model', which assumes that fashion swings are the inevitable outcome of capitalist social relations because we are socialized (a) to think of ourselves as consumers and (b) to demand novelty.

Viewed in the context of these accounts of the fashion-setting process it is apparent that Abrahamson's third quadrant operates, largely, with a 'trickle-down' model of fashion since here we have organizational isomorphism in the absence of coercion. Abrahamson's 'fad', perspective, in contrast, appears to employ a model of 'collective selection theory'. In this, the fourth quadrant outlined by Abrahamson (1991), organizational actors are assumed to be uncertain about their goals *and* about the efficiency of organizational innovations. Yet, in the absence of a fashion-setting community, those located within this quadrant are obliged to find a means of dealing with their own anxieties. In this sector of the diagram the actual outcome is much like that hypothesized for the fashion perspective. Thus the organizations in this arena begin to look alike and to do the same things. Yet the mechanics of this isomorphism differ.

In the fashion perspective, isomorphism is the result of the activities of a fashion-setting community selling innovations. In the fad perspective, however, organizational isomorphism is a product of mimesis. Thus, in the absence of a fashion-setting community, actors in similar market/organizational niches are said to manage their own anxieties and the expectations of wider stakeholders (Abrahamson, 1996) by adopting similar tools, forms and/or innovations.

In Abrahamson's (1991) schema, quadrants one and two are pro-innovation. These quadrants assume that management is rational and that choices with respect to innovation reflect a choice-making process that is, similarly, rational and transparent. Hilmer and Donaldson (1996),

Micklethwait and Wooldridge (1997) and Glaser (1997) accept one half of this. Management, they aver, is amenable to rational choice-making. However these authors insist that the tools and pre-dispositions of the consulting industry encourage managers to behave irrationally.

In quadrants three and four Abrahamson addresses this division between the rational and the irrational and in so doing he, too, questions the casual unitarism (Fox, 1985) that characterizes much of the literature on fads and fashions. Thus Abrahamson argues that certain forms of conduct, which, might appear to be irrational, when viewed from the detached and comfortable surroundings of an academic's study can appear, perfectly, rational when (re)placed within the context of their application. Indeed Abrahamson suggests that under conditions of uncertainty and in circumstances where stakeholders expect managers to be, both, proactive and at the forefront of developments it is, in fact, perfectly rational to place your faith in fashion-setters – even when you harbour suspicions as to the utility of their products – because this is the form of conduct that is rewarded.

And yet Abrahamson still protests that these innovations do, often, cause damage to (our) organizations and societies. In an attempt to counter the practical difficulties associated with 'faddism', therefore, Abrahamson (1996) and Brindle and Stearns (2001) offer a range of (more-or-less) concrete suggestions, which they hope might turn the tide against those who produce and promote fads and fashions in management.

Fighting fads

Brindle and Stearns (2001) argue that scholars need to be prepared to lead the counter-attack against business faddism. They suggests that academics should intervene in the market for management advice to ensure (a) that those rhetorics which suggest that innovations have panacea–like qualities are subject to rebuttal and that (b) consumers of management knowledge are less chauvinistic in their learning (for similar manifestos see Abrahamson and Eisenman, 2001; Mohrman, 2001).

Yet they acknowledge that this is a tall order. Indeed they concede that to re-educate managers, academics will need to overcome the deep-seated, cultural, fetishization of novelty. Furthermore they acknowledge that any challenge to faddism is, by definition, an attack on the experts that service our organizations and the body of expertise that defines and conditions our notions of what it is to manage.

In the face of these odds, Brindle and Stearns – perhaps unsurprisingly – shy away from developing a concrete, anti-fad, manifesto. Abrahamson (1996), in contrast, is happy to suggest a number of practical interventions.

Abrahamson agrees that scholars – or at least those scholars who do not adopt the norms and practices of the *Harvard Business Review* – need to challenge the rhetorics of management fashion. Yet he suggests that, to do so, academic authors will need to adjust their own practices. Indeed he argues that management scholars will need to improve their writing and will need to adjust the contents of their texts to ensure that these reflect the day-to-day concerns and dilemmas faced by management practitioners. In addition he argues that scholars will need to write for those publications that managers actually read. The extent to which popular publications such as *The Economist*, *Private Eye* and *Cosmopolitan* would be prepared to run such features, however, is not considered! And finally he suggests that fads need to be subject to rapid rebuttal, and so he argues that attempts need to be made to reduce the lag between managerial interests and scholarly publications. Quite how long this lag is, and whether academic research on the optimum lag between management practice and academic critique would be legitimate under this new *rapprochement* remains, however, moot.

Recognizing such problems and inconsistencies, Collins (2001) essays a different approach to faddism. Indeed he argues that scholars will learn little about management and will learn nothing about their own practices so long as they continue to make casual references to managerial 'fads'. Consequently he directs his anger towards the fad motif itself.

The fad motif

Collins (2001) argues that the debunking of business fads has becomes a mass participation sport.[7] He observes, however, that while debunking makes for good sport it makes for poor scholarship. Noting the power and appeal of guru rhetorics he agrees with Abrahamson (1991, 1996) that there is a need to take fads seriously. Yet he argues that the fad motif mitigates this requirement because it encourages us to view innovations in practice as being 'too philosophically impoverished, theoretically underdeveloped and empirically emaciated to warrant academic scrutiny' (Jackson, 1996: 52).

In an attempt to reconstitute the terms of the debate on management knowledge, therefore, Collins (2001) has attempted to undermine the fad motif itself. Articulating his discontents he argues that the fad motif precipitates, not a battle over gurus, but a battle between gurus. In addition he notes that accounts of faddism imply, quite falsely, the existence of a common consensus as regards the nature, form and processes of academic scholarship. Furthermore he observes that the fad motif indulges the suggestion that management practitioners are hapless dopes who purchase useless products from their unscrupulous consultants. Drawing attention to the complexities of consumption, however, Collins argues that the consumers of scholarly rhetorics must make an effort to derive utility from their purchases and, invariably, add water to the wine of guru ideas.

Recognizing that the fad motif cements and submerges a variety of analytical problems our next section will reflect upon the origins of the term fad and explore the potential of alternative metaphors.

A closer look at fads

In the classic adventure story *The Riddle of the Sands* (Childers, 2007 [1903]) one of the key characters – Arthur Davies – discusses his love of coastal navigation. Without any hint of reproach he confesses to his friend that maps and navigation are his 'fad'. And in 1903, when Childers first published his story, this non-judgemental usage of the term was normal. Indeed in 1903 an individual could, quite happily, immerse him/herself in their chosen 'fad'.

The term, fad, it seems, first came into general usage in the 1830s. At this time it was used to connote a hobby; a pet project; or a favourite theory. In this period none of these terms was, necessarily, suggestive of a passing concern. Indeed we would do well to observe that, key terms taken to be synonymous with fad, such as crotchet (a sustained note) suggest anything but an interest which is fleeting.

Modern attitudes towards hobby pursuits and other pastimes are, invariably, dismissive and pejorative (see Moorhouse, 1988), of course, such that, nowadays, the term fad tends to connote matters that are merely 'trifles'; orientations that are, largely, immaterial. Yet the origins of the term and its changing usage should act as an encouragement to reflect upon the ways in which particular patterns of discourse and particular forms of metaphor, such as 'fad', act to privilege forms of knowledge and understanding, which have consequences for (in)action.

Metaphors and analysis

Schön (1979) argues that metaphor has a profound effect upon how we think and how we act. Taking issue with those who protest that metaphors constitute anomalies in language which need to be cleared out in order to ensure clear and transparent communication, Schön insists on a point of view 'which treats metaphors as central to the task of accounting for our perspective on the world: how we think about things, make sense of reality, and set the problems we later try to solve' (254). Thus Schön argues that metaphors have real and enduring, material, consequences insofar as policy and action proceed in the wake of 'problems-as-set'.[8] Young (2001), similarly, draws our attention to the enduring consequences of the literary and linguistic formations that constitute our worlds. Recognizing, both, the prospective and the selective characteristics of metaphors (see also Morgan, 1986), she sets out to examine the ways in which such figurative forms of language shape our appreciation of risk and our stance towards it. Analysing the pronouncements of the Financial Accounting Standards Board (FASB) she argues that this organization's metaphorical choices encourage us to regard risk as something which, while it should be avoided might be assessed and, ultimately, controlled. However she suggests that recent financial history demonstrates that 'risk' may be more adequately understood within the metaphorical frame of 'chaos'!

The works of Schön (1979) and Young (2001) bring an interesting proposition to the surface of our analysis: what might we have learned about contemporary developments in management had we chosen a different metaphor? To pursue this question we will consider four alternatives to the fad motif.

Four alternatives to the fad motif

Coulson-Thomas (1996), as we have seen, mixes his metaphors when discussing BPR. In Coulson-Thomas's analysis, therefore, business process reengineering is, variously, referred to as a fad; a gravy train; and a flu epidemic. In a later section we will touch upon the 'gravy train' metaphor, for the moment, however, we will concentrate upon Coulson-Thomas's flu motif.

The flu metaphor

The flu metaphor has, at least, one distinct advantage over the fad motif: no one who has suffered a bout of flu would ever treat it lightly. Flu epidemics are serious. Flu kills! Recognizing this, state authorities take precautions against influenza. They offer advice designed to minimize the spread of the flu virus; they inoculate the elderly, and those whose health and/or respiratory function is compromised; and they often stockpile anti-viral drugs to maintain the health of 'essential workers' such as nurses.

Had we viewed fads as being flu-like would we have enacted (Weick, 1995) a different world? Yes … and no.

Doubtless, the flu motif would encourage us to take contemporary developments in management knowledge seriously. Yet it is not clear that this, alternative, metaphorical formulation would have altered, what Schön (1979) terms the 'problem-as-set' since the prevailing approach to management *fads* already revolves around what amounts to a programme of containment and inoculation.

In addition, there are at least two further drawbacks with the flu metaphor. First, no one would seriously suggest that there are benefits associated with the flu. Yet Brindle and Stearns (2001) have documented a range of individual and organizational benefits associated with faddism. Second, we should point out that the flu metaphor tends to obscure the organizational processes of production and the dynamic processes of transmission/consumption, which need to be examined if contemporary developments in management knowledge are to be understood (Collins, 2004a).

The storm metaphor

Our second metaphor conceives of contemporary developments in management as storms. Discussing the recent, global, financial crisis, Cable (2009) employs this metaphor in an attempt to encapsulate the scale and pace of these changes. In common with the flu metaphor this formulation of the problem of knowledge has the benefit of encouraging us (a) to take these developments seriously and (b) to plan ahead in order to deal with the anticipated consequences of (passing) storms.

Yet, once again the policy outcomes that flow from the stormy metaphor look much like those suggested by those who have applied the fad motif: the storm would be viewed as a transient problem. And organizational scholars would, almost inevitably, suggest that they have the skills and insights necessary (a) to construct the 'shelters' that will protect the community and (b) to prepare 'run-offs' that will be used to channel away the latest deluge. In addition we would do well to note that, like the viral metaphor, this stormy allusion also tends to obscure the human and organizational processes that propagate fads and, indeed, the all-too-human processes that precipitated the global collapse of the banking system!

The experiment metaphor

Our third metaphor builds upon the work of Cole (1999). Cole has voiced his frustration with those who have suggested that recent organizational innovations are empty and, thoughtlessly, imitative. Countering such pejorative assumptions he suggests that what we now regard as *fads* are, in truth, better thought of as creative forms of experimentation. This experimental motif has certain positive aspects. First, it brings the consumers of management knowledge – the experimenters – to the centre of the analysis and in so doing allows these individuals to appear as mature and volitional adults. Second, this acknowledgement of choice-making invites us to place our analysis of organizational experimentation within the local contexts that, variously, demand, precipitate and, yet, constrain organizational learning. And thirdly – although this may be stretching things a little – the metaphor of experimentation could be used to introduce ethical considerations to the analysis of organizational innovation.[9] On the downside, however, this metaphor does seem to obscure the (questionable) role which fashion-setters play in the development and propagation of the consultancy 'gravy train' (see O'Shea and Madigan, 1997; Pinault, 2000; Craig, 2005; Perkins, 2005).

The cocktail metaphor

Our fourth metaphor, while not exhausting the potential for further metaphorical analysis and development, is the final one that this text will address explicitly.

Brindle and Stearns (2001), as we have seen, employ a cocktail metaphor to elaborate the ways in which scholars and practitioners might interact with management fads. They suggest that managers should temper their interest in fads with a dash of common-sense and a slice of experience! Wray-Bliss (2003) couches his analysis of fads within a similarly intoxicating metaphor. He suggests that, while practitioners might use fads and might derive utility from these, they must be mindful of the problems of 'addiction'.

These cocktail metaphors are entertaining and they are, plainly, memorable. But they are silent on key matters of importance. For example: Who sets the recipe for management cocktails? And are consumers bound by these recipes (see Gabriel, 2002; Collins, 2004a)?

Collins (1995) couches his analysis of empowerment within a cocktail metaphor. But unlike the devices discussed above, Collins's empowering cocktails are composed of various forms of managerial control. Commenting upon the dynamic processes of managing, Edwards (1986) observes that, although management is, primarily, about control, work is about co-operation since the day-to-day processes of working require some degree of engagement if not the outright commitment of subordinates. Bendix (1956) provides a famous justification for this assertion. He notes that 'Management no matter how expert, cannot set out in advance exactly what must be done under all circumstances and how, but must rely to some extent on the workers' co-operation initiative and experience' (256). Building upon this analysis, Anthony (1997) notes that the need for worker commitment is located within a system of control, which makes managerial endeavours complex *and* self-defeating.

It is this recognition of the self-defeating nature of managerial control that underpins Collins's (1995) account of empowerment and the analysis of fads developed by Noon and his colleagues (Noon et al., 2000). Thus Noon and his co-authors argue that 'fads' are problematic because they suggest the existence of optimum solutions and binary choices in a world which is, inescapably, complex and multi-faceted. Viewed in these terms the cocktail metaphor has a number of features, which recommend it:

- It acknowledges organizational plurality, and so, has little time for analyses which protest that fads cause, wholesale, damage to 'our corporations'.
- It locates organizational innovation within the context of managerial control, and in so doing, alters our appreciation of management practitioners. Thus the cocktail motif reminds us that managers prize concrete answers to everyday problems above mere novelty.
- It leaves a space for consumer experimentation and adaptation, and so, does not need to portray managers as being, simply, the hapless dupes of vile consultants.

Furthermore we would do well to note that the analysis of Noon and his colleagues demands some degree of self-reflexivity from the academic reader insofar as it makes it plain that, for all their fad debunking, it is academics, above all other interested parties, whose rhetorics turn upon novelty. And with such reflexive matters in mind we conclude by considering a number of analytical dimensions that scholars and practitioners might employ when weighing up current and future accounts of management knowledge whether these are couched in terms of fads, flu or intoxicating cocktails.

A framework for analysis – concluding comments

This chapter has offered a critical review of what are commonly referred to as management fads and fashions. Such fads and fashions are seldom defined explicitly. Just a few moments of analysis, however, reveals that the term 'fad' denotes a form of organizational innovation that is taken to be transient, thoughtlessly imitative and limited in its appreciation of organizational complexity. In short fads and fashions are typically presented as distractions from the real business of managing. Consequently contributions to this domain have tended to attack and debunk key developments in management knowledge and practice. This chapter, however, has essayed a different relationship with the tools and techniques of contemporary management. Indeed we have argued that it is the careless application of the fad motif that has hindered analytical development in this arena.

To outline this argument we began by noting the prevalence of the fad metaphor and the attempts that have been made to substantiate this motif by means of bibliometric research.

Unit of Analysis

Plural ←――――――――――→ Unitary

Analysis of Fashion

Internal Drivers ←――――――――――→ External Drivers

Consumption Oriented ←――――――――――→ Production Focused

Consideration of Practitioners

Active Users ←――――――――――→ Passive Recipients

Posture of Author(s)

Reflexive ←――――――――――→ Reactive

Thrust of Argument

Policy-oriented ←――――――――――→ Pejorative

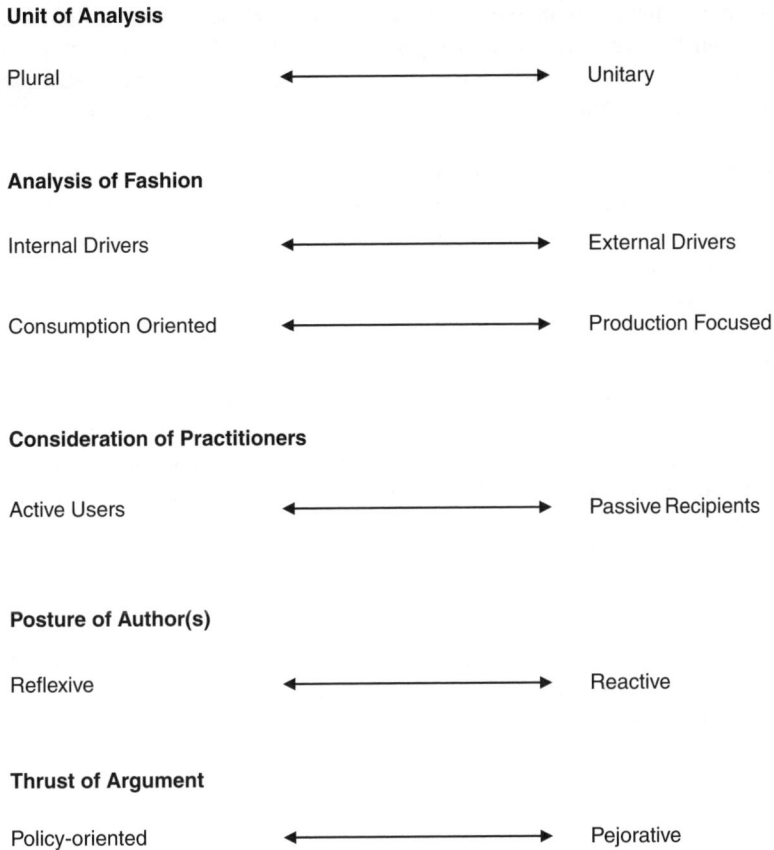

Figure 21.3 Six analytical dimensions for the further exploration of management knowledge-products

Building upon the work of Cole (1999) however we argued that the fad debunkers and 'the bibliometricians' offer critiques that are too far removed from the day-to-day realities of practice. To reconnect criticism with practice, therefore, we have re-examined the fad motif and we have explored the ways in which this and other metaphors inform and yet deform our inquiries. And in an attempt to summarize this argument we conclude by offering six analytical dimensions that we hope might be used to orient future accounts of organizational innovation and change (see Figure 21.3). These dimensions, as we shall see, reflect our earlier review of the literature and have been reproduced here to encourage readers to pursue the often unstated assumptions that have shaped our appreciation of recent developments in management thought and practice.

1　Does the thrust of the analytical framework employ a unitary or a more pluralistic account of organizational life? Does it assume that *our corporations* are damaged by fads as Hilmer and Donaldson (1996) do? Or does it operate with an analytical frame that recognizes the sectional nature of organizations and the mixture of costs and benefits associated with innovation? Does the analytical framework nest organizational matters within a larger contextual setting? And finally, does it take account of the ways in which organizational innovations interact with wider societal changes?

2 Does the analytical framework simply assume that movements within organizations are driven by larger structural changes that are external to the organization? Or does it acknowledge the internal, emotional and political drivers that might predispose us to seek either comfort or advantage from organizational innovations, as Grint (1997) suggests?

3 Does the analysis focus solely upon the production of innovations or does it recognize the importance of consumption (see Collins, 2004a)?

4 Does the commentary treat practitioners as passive recipients of ideas or does it acknowledge the complexities of consumption and the active nature of these processes (see Collins, 2003, 2004a, 2005)?

5 Does the author write in a reflexive fashion? Have they acknowledged their own interest in all things fashionable?

6 Does the work have any policy implications? And perhaps more significantly, does the analytical framework generate guidance for future conduct that extends beyond trading one set of (practitioner) gurus for another set of (academic) luminaries? Crucially, does the framework for action reflect the complexities of our lives and the inequalities which structure these?

Notes

1 Noon et al. (2000) observe that consultants, so often lambasted for the production of fads and neologisms, have little interest in novelty *per se*. They are, however, very interested in sales and will, cheerfully, sell 'old' and/or repackaged ideas to their clients. The converse, they argue, applies to academics.

2 Students of fads and fashions, often, have very little to say about the nature of the consulting industry (Engwall and Kipping, 2002; Clark, 2004b; Edersheim, 2004); about the debates which persist as to its origins (McKenna, 2006); or about the difficulties associated with its measurement (Collins, 2006; Gross and Poor, 2008).

3 Given recent public-health scares *listeria* might have been a better choice of phraseology!

4 Discussing the practices and perils of academic research, Starbuck (2009a) couches his preferred definition of faddism within a life-cycle model that is, apparently, non-cumulative in nature: '… someone proposes an attractive strategic idea and this idea begins to draw enthusiasts. The number of enthusiasts grows until the idea becomes dominant. However, the idea's limitations gradually emerge and enthusiasts begin to have doubts' (108–9).

5 In this respect the work of Gill and Whittle constitutes 'an obligatory passage point'.

6 The full citations for these texts is absent from Thomas's (1999). This omission ensures that the contributions of Prof Hinings remain unacknowledged in Thomas's analysis.

7 Unlike other mass participation sports – such as angling – and despite the intentions of its followers and adherents such debunking endeavours are largely bloodless (see Collins, 2001).

8 Rose George (2009) offers a powerful example of the processes outlined by Schön. She notes that many human diseases are said to be 'water borne'. Consequently public health policies on a global scale tend to focus upon the provision of clean drinking water. However she argues that the provision of potable water, too often, proceeds in the absence of appropriate toilet/latrine facilities. This, she tells us, has dire consequences for public health since clean drinking water very soon becomes contaminated by human waste when the population has no access to hygienic toilet facilities. Thus she insists that latrines are, in any sense of the term, an up-stream concern for those who would provide safe drinking water. In an attempt to improve public health (outcomes), therefore, she suggest that we need to re-define the 'problem-as-set'. Indeed she insists that we need to confront the reality that diseases such as cholera and dysentery are not so much 'water borne' as *vectored by shit*!

9 Ethical considerations are generally taken to be central to the processes of research and experimentation.

References

Abrahamson, E. (1991) 'Managerial Fads and Fashions: The diffusion and rejection of innovations', *Academy of Management Review*, 16 (3): 586–612.

Abrahamson, E. (1996) 'Management Fashion', *Academy of Management Review*, 21 (1): 254–85.

Abrahamson, E. and Eisenman, M. (2001) 'Why Management Scholars Must Intervene Strategically in the Management Knowledge Market', *Human Relations*, 54 (1): 67–75.

Anthony P.D. (1997) *The Ideology of Work*, Tavistock Publications: London.

Barley, S.R., and Kunda, G. (1992) 'Design and Devotion: The ebb and flow of rational and normative ideologies of control in managerial discourse', *Administrative Science Quarterly*, 37: 1–30.

Bendix, R.A. (1956) *Work and Authority in Industry*, University of California Press: Berkeley, CA.

Brindle, M.C. and Stearns, P.N. (2001) *Facing up to Management Faddism: A new look at an old force*, Quorum Books: Westport, CT.

Burnes, B. (1998) 'Recipes for Organizational Effectiveness. Mad, bad, or just dangerous to know?', *Career Development International*, 3 (3): 100–106.

Cable, V. (2009) *The Storm: The world economic crisis and what it means*, Atlantic Books: London.

Childers, E. (2007) [1903] *The Riddle of the Sands*, Penguin: London.

Chomsky, N. (2003) *Understanding Power: The Indispensable Chomsky*, ed. P.R. Mitchell and J. Schoeffel, Vintage: London.

Clark, T. (2001) 'Management Research on Fashion: A review and evaluation', *Human Relations*, 54 (12): 1650–62.

Clark, T. (2004a) 'The Fashion of Management: A surge too far?', *Organization*, 11 (2): 297–306.

Clark, T. (2004b) 'Strategy Viewed from a Management Fashion Perspective', *European Management Review*, 1 (1): 105–11.

Clark, T. and Fincham, R. (eds) (2002) *Critical Consulting: New perspectives on the Management Advice Industry*, Blackwell: Oxford.

Cole, R.E. (1999) *Managing Quality Fads: How American business learned to play the quality game*, Oxford University Press: Oxford.

Collins, D. (1995) 'Rooting for Empowerment?' *Empowerment in Organizations*, 3 (1): 25–33.

Collins, D. (1996) 'A Practical Approach to Management', *Management Decision*, 34 (1): 66–71.

Collins, D. (1998) *Organizational Change: Sociological perspectives*, Routledge: London.

Collins, D. (2000) *Management Fads and Buzzwords: Critical-practical perspectives*, Routledge: London.

Collins, D. (2001) 'The Fad Motif in Management Scholarship', *Employee Relations*, 23 (1): 25–37.

Collins, D. (2003) 'The Branding of Management Knowledge: Rethinking management "fads"', *Journal of Organizational Change Management*, 16 (2): 186–204.

Collins, D. (2004a) 'Who Put the Con in Consultancy? Fads, recipes and "vodka margarine"', *Human Relations*, 57 (5): 553–72.

Collins, D. (2004b) 'X-engineering: *ex cathedra*?', *Personnel Review*, 35 (1): 127–42.

Collins, D. (2005) 'Pyramid Schemes and Programmatic Management: Critical reflections on the "guru industry"', *Culture and Organization*, 11 (1): 33–44.

Collins, D. (2006) 'Assaying the Advice Industry', *Culture and Organization*, 12 (2): 139–52.

Collins, D. (2007) *Narrating the Management Guru: In search of Tom Peters*, Routledge: London.

Coulson-Thomas, C. (1996) *Business Process Re-engineering: Myth and reality*, Kogan Page: London.

Craig, D. (2005) *Rip-Off! The scandalous inside story of the management consulting money machine*, The Original Book Company: London.

Edwards, P.K. (1986) *Conflict at Work: A materialist analysis of workplace relations*, Blackwell: Oxford.

Edersheim, E.H. (2004) *McKinsey's Marvin Bower: Vision, leadership and the creation of management consulting*, John Wiley & Sons: Hoboken, NJ.

Engwall, L. and Kipping, M. (2002) 'Introduction' in M. Kipping and L. Engwall (eds) *Management Consulting: Emergence and dynamics of a knowledge industry*, Oxford University Press: Oxford.

Fox, A. (1985) *Man Mismanagement* (2nd edn), Hutchinson: London.

Furnham, A. (2004) *Management and Myths: Challenging business fads, fallacies and fashions*, Palgrave Macmillan: Houndmills, Basingstoke.

Gabriel, Y. (2002) '*Essai:* On paragrammatic uses of organizational theory – a provocation', *Human Relations*, 23 (1): 133–51.

George, R. (2009) *The Big Necessity: Adventures in the world of human waste*, Portobello Books: London.

Gill, J. and Whittle, S. (1992) 'Management by Panacea: Accounting for transience', *Journal of Management Studies*, 30 (2): 281–95.

Glaser, S. (1997) 'Management Duckspeak', *Management Decision*, 35 (9): 649–51.

Grant, D., Hardy, C., Oswick, C. and Putnam, L. (2004) 'Introduction: Organizational discourse: exploring the field' in D. Grant, C. Hardy, C. Oswick and L. Putnam (eds) *The Sage Handbook of Organizational Discourse*, Sage: London.

Grey, C. and Mitev, C. (1995) 'Re-engineering Organizations: A critical appraisal', *Personnel Review*, 24 (1): 6–18.

Grint, K. (1997) *Fuzzy Management: Contemporary ideas and practices at work*, Oxford University Press: Oxford.

Gross, A.C. and Poor, J. (2008) 'The Global Management Consulting Sector', *Business Economics*, October: 59–68.

Hilmer, F.G. and Donaldson, L. (1996) *Management Redeemed: Debunking the fads that undermine our corporations*, Free Press: New York.

Huczynski, A.A. (1993) *Management Gurus: What makes them and how to become one*, Routledge: London.

Jackson, B.G. (1996) 'Re-engineering the Sense of Self: The Manager and the management guru', *Journal of Management Studies*, 33 (5): 571–90.

Latour, B. (1987) *Science in Action*, Harvard University Press: Cambridge, MA.

McGregor, J. (2006) *So Many Ways to Begin*, Bloomsbury: London.

McKenna, C.D. (2006) *The World's Newest Profession: Management consulting in the twentieth century*, Cambridge University Press: Cambridge.

Micklethwait, J. and Wooldridge, A. (1997) *The Witch Doctors: What the management gurus are saying, why it matters and how to make sense of it*, Mandarin: London.

Mohrman S.A. (2001) 'Seize the Day: Organizational studies can and should make the difference', *Human Relations*, 54 (1): 57–65.

Moorhouse H.F. (1988) *Driving Ambitions: A social analysis of the American hot rod enthusiasm*, Manchester University Press: Manchester.

Moravcsik, M.J. and Murugesan, P. (1975) 'Some Results on the Function and Quality of Citations', *Social Studies of Science*, 5: 86–92.

Morgan, G. (1986) *Images of Organization*, SAGE: London.

Noon, M., Jenkins, S. and Martinez Lucio, M. (2000) 'Fads, Techniques and Control: The competing agendas of TPM and TECEX at the Royal Mail (UK)', *Journal of Management Studies*, 37 (4): 499–520.

O'Shea, J. and Madigan, C. (1997) *Dangerous Company*, Random House: London.

Pascale, R.T. (1990) *Managing on the Edge: How the smartest companies use conflict to stay ahead*, Simon & Schuster: London.

Perkins, J. (2005) *Confessions of an Economic Hit Man: The shocking inside story of how America really took over the world*, Random House: London.

Pinault, L. (2000) *Consulting Demons: Inside the unscrupulous world of global consulting*, Wiley: Chichester.

Pugh, D.S. and Hickson, D.J. (1964) *Writers on Organizations*, Hutchinson: London.

Pugh D.S. and Hickson D.J. (1989) *Writers on Organizations* (4th edn), Penguin: Harmondsworth.

Pugh, D.S., Hickson, D.J. and Hinings, C.R. (1971) *Writers on Organizations* (2nd edn), Lyon, Grant & Green: London.

Pugh, D.S., Hickson, D.J. and Hinings, C.R. (1983) *Writers on Organizations* (3rd edn), Penguin: Harmondsworth.

Schön, D. (1979) 'Generative Metaphor: A perspective on problem-setting in social policy' in A. Ortony (ed.) *Metaphor and Thought*, Cambridge University Press: Cambridge.

Shotter, J. (2002) *Conversational Realities: Constructing life through language*, SAGE: London.

330

Starbuck, W.H. (2009a) 'The Constant Causes of Never-ending Faddishness in the Behavioural and Social Sciences', *Scandinavian Journal of Management*, 25: 108–16.

Starbuck, W.H. (2009b) 'Unlearning What We Knew and Rediscovering What We Could Have Known', *Scandinavian Journal of Management*, 25: 240–42.

Thomas, P. (1999) *Fashions in Management Research: An empirical analysis*, Ashgate: Aldershot.

Weick, K. (1995) *Sensemaking in Organizations*, SAGE: London.

Wilkinson, A., Allen, P. and Snape, E. (1991) 'TQM and the Management of Labour', *Employee Relations*, 13 (1): 24–31.

Wilmott, H. and Wray-Bliss, E. (1996) 'Process Reengineering, Information Technology and the Transformation of Accountability: The remaindering of the human resource', in W.J. Orlikowski, G. Walsham, M.R. Jones and J.I. DeGross (eds) *Information Technology and Changes in Organizational Work*, Chapman & Hall: London.

Wray-Bliss, E. (2003) 'Quick Fixes, Management Culture and Drug Culture: Excellence and ecstasy, BPR and Brown', *Culture and Organizations*, 9 (3): 161–76.

Young, J.J. (2001) 'Risk(ing) Metaphors', *Critical Perspectives on Accounting*, 12: 607–25.

22

Organizational entrapment

Helga Drummond

We've travelled too far, and our momentum has taken over; we move idly towards eternity, without possibility of reprieve or hope of explanation.

(Tom Stoppard, *Rosencrantz and Guildenstern are Dead*, Act 3)

Introduction

We know a lot about how to get organizations moving but less about how to re-direct them when they begin to falter. In 2008 Woolworths closed down. Why did they not learn from Marks & Spencer's near collapse a decade earlier? Why did McDonald's not respond to the growing demand for healthy eating sooner? Why was Microsoft slow to recognize the implications of the advent of firms like Google? Entrapment theorists believe that organizations may be slow to respond to important environmental cues because continuity begets continuity. This chapter explores why 'lock-in' occurs and, paradoxically, how costly failure can result from the pursuit of successful policies and practices.

One of the small pleasures of childhood was being taken to Woolworths on a Saturday afternoon to choose a toy. In 1961 half-a-crown (12.5p) bought such delights as plastic modelling clay, bubbles to blow and cap guns that gave a satisfying crack when fired. Yet I can hardly remember visiting Woolworths as an adult, far less buying anything. Nor it seems did millions of other people. For in November 2008 following a series of profits warnings, the retail giant closed with the loss of over 3000 jobs in the UK.

With hindsight, it is perhaps surprising that Woolworths lasted as long as it did. The reasons for Woolworths' ultimate demise are complex. Moreover, the global credit crunch cannot have helped. Yet history might have been different had Woolworths not clung to its time-served 'pick and mix' business model. Business history contains many examples of similarly mal-adaptive strategies. When cheap foreign imports of cloth began to arrive in the UK in the early 1950s, textile-mill owners said there was no cause for alarm. In the 1950s the US produced most of the world's steel but the industry clung to old-fashioned technology and was eventually overtaken by Japan (e.g. Schwenk and Tang 1989) whilst in the UK steel industry, the Victorian era lasted until the 1980s (e.g. Tweedale 1995)!

Modern sophisticated companies should not make such elementary mistakes because they employ legions of highly qualified analysts and economists to scan the environment for threats and opportunities and to calculate costs and benefits. Yet Woolworths seemed to have learned little from Marks & Spencer's near collapse a decade earlier. Kodak was likewise slow to produce 'new fangled' digital cameras. More recently, the once seemingly impregnable Microsoft has begun to trail behind firms like Google, Yahoo! and Apple who are re-writing the script for personal computing without the need for Microsoft's once ubiquitous platforms. Although the Apple iPhone is designed in the US, most of the components are made in Japan. Whereas Apple profits hugely from controlling iTunes and other software applications, Japanese component manufacturers earn less than 5 per cent profit margin. Why do those manufacturers not switch to more profitable lines?

Like dinosaurs, big organizations can become extinct if they fail to adapt to environmental change. Moreover, by the time they recognize their mistake, the damage may be well and truly done. For example, when Kodak finally entered the digital market, non-traditional competitors like HP and Sony had achieved a decisive lead and Kodak was eventually forced to exit. More recently the Korean car industry with its five and even seven year warranties looks set to overtake Japanese firms who are only just beginning to respond to the challenge.

What causes entrapment

It is thought that there are five main reasons why organizations may succumb to entrapment as follows:

Biased environmental scanning
'Side-bets'
Closing costs
Passive decision-making
Reluctance to take a risk

Each of these possible causes is now discussed in turn.

Biased environmental scanning

Recall, modern sophisticated organizations use sophisticated scanning methods to identify threats and opportunities. Paradoxically, organizations can miss environmental cues because the methods organizations use to filter information are biased towards what the firm sees as important (Starbuck 1983; see also Hedberg and Jonsonn 1977 and Brown 1978). For example, at first Kodak ignored digital photography because they saw it as none of their business. Likewise, initially IBM did not see the advent of the personal computer as a threat as they were mainframe producers. Microsoft too may have decided search engines were nothing to do with them.

'Side-bets'

Entrapment can also result from mixing one's main interests with extraneous ones, that is, making what Becker (1960) calls 'side-bets'. At first 'side-bets are inconsequential but over time, they mount up. For example, someone who contributes a tiny amount every month to a non-transferable pension scheme may eventually discover that although the decision to join the pension scheme was originally incidental to their employment, it becomes the main reason for staying because changing direction is now too expensive.

In other words, if the decision-maker changes direction those 'side-bets' count for nothing. The investment merely becomes an expense. For example, Becker recounts how in the 1950s, Chicago operated a waiting list for teaching posts in middle-class schools. Consequently, many newly qualified schoolteachers took jobs in lower-class schools as a temporary expedient. Yet when they finally reached the top of the waiting list, many teachers decided to stay put after all. This is, having invested so much time and effort writing materials to suit lower class children they were unwilling to start all over again and re-write their materials for a middle class audience. Organizations also enter into side-bets. For example, once big projects like the London 2012 Olympics get under way, myriad stakeholders including hoteliers, restaurants and taxi firms invest in anticipation of the games being held, all adding to the pressure to persist with the project regardless of whether persistence makes economic sense. Organizations also create 'side-bets' with suppliers. That is, as suppliers become more experienced they learn how to work with the firm so it is easier just to re-let the contract rather than educate a new supplier even though the new supplier may offer better quality and lower prices.

Closing costs

Closing costs can make quitting too expensive. There may be penalty payments to sub-contractors, redundancy payments to staff, costs of ripping out partially completed works and so forth (e.g. Staw 1997). For example, although the Channel Tunnel project was massively over budget, there was no question of cancelling it because banks could only hope to recoup their loans was if the project was finished.

Closing may also involve psychological and social costs. No one likes admitting failure, particularly if their job is at stake and/or the venture is in the public eye. Decision-makers may thus be tempted to re-invest scarce resources in questionable projects in the hope of eventually turning them round, though often only to end up throwing 'good money after bad' (e.g. Brockner 1992; Staw 1997; Karlsson et al. 2005; Drummond 2001: Ch . 9). For example, the UK's NHS electronic patient record system is so far behind schedule that it seems destined never to appear. Yet the government continues pouring billions of pounds into the venture insisting that it will work even though the system caused chaos when it was piloted in a London hospital.

Imagine Porsche without sports cars or HP without computers. Another reason why organizations may be reluctant to change direction is when products or services become so deeply associated with the values and purposes of the firm that the idea of abandoning them becomes unthinkable. In addition, managers may stick to their comfort zones. Kodak understood conventional cameras. Managers were lost with digital technology. McDonald's may have been slow to embrace healthy eating because it meant moving beyond the deeply familiar hamburger terrain.

Passive decision-making

Entrapment theorists believe that continuity begets continuity. In another landmark contribution to the entrapment literature, Rubin and Brockner (1975) imagined decision-makers being caught up in a conflict, confronted with pressures to persist with an economically poor decision and also pressures to withdraw. The author's starting point is that the passage of time can represent both an investment and an expense. For example, as in digging a tunnel, time is an investment in that it can increase the likelihood of goal attainment. It is an expense because of the costs incurred in waiting. Conflict arises because, as time passes, expenses mount but so does presumed proximity to the goal. Tension mounts, however, because we cannot wait indefinitely: the greater the passage of time, the greater the conflict. And the greater the conflict, the greater the pressures to act decisively – either by withdrawing or by committing oneself to remain in the situation. Of these two possible decisions (total commitment or total withdrawal), the former is probably more likely to occur (Rubin and Brockner 1975: 1055). For instance, being kept on hold on the telephone at premium rates is an expensive business. So the costs of persistence mount as the minutes tick by. Yet if the call is important and the caller knows that they are next in line to speak to an operator and that if they give up they will need to start all over again (and perhaps take even longer), they may well decide to remain on hold.

Yet supposing that the call centre does not actually operate a queuing algorithm? Just how long do we continue to wait? Supposing that although we know that being kept on hold is costly, we are not aware of precisely how much it costs per minute or exactly how long we have been waiting. How does that affect decisions about whether to persist or hang up? In order to explore those questions, Rubin and Brockner (1975) designed a fascinating experiment where participants were challenged to solve a crossword puzzle in return for a cash prize of $8. The exercise was time critical as the value of the prize dropped as the minutes ticked by. Respondents were told that a dictionary that would help speed up the task was available and that they were first, second or third in line for it.

Waiting for the dictionary meant that participants experienced the passage of time as both an expense and an investment. It was an expense in that the longer participants waited, the smaller the prize. It was an investment in that if participants obtained the dictionary sooner rather than later, they could win more money. Participants were divided into groups. One group of participants had 'real-time' information charting the precise rate at which the cash prize was declining. The second group did not have this information. Groups were organized so that for some participants the value of the prize declined slowly. For others it declined more rapidly. These were known respectively as low and high decrement conditions. All participants were free to stop the game during the first three minutes and take the $2.40 consolation prize lying on the desk.

In fact, there was no dictionary. Yet 87 per cent of participants stayed in the experiment beyond the critical three minutes where they could leave and take the consolation prize. More than half of the participants remained beyond break-even point, that is, where the value of the prize equalled the $2.40 consolation prize. Participants, moreover, spent almost a third of the time waiting for the non-existent dictionary and ended up earning less than half of what they would have earned if they had opted for the consolation prize.

Participants typically became entrapped because they believed that the dictionary would arrive soon; and/or because or they believed that the dictionary would enable them to earn more money than they already had, and/or, because, having waited for so long for the dictionary, it seemed silly to give up. Furthermore, participants tended to wait longer if they believed they were first in line for the dictionary, or if they were not acutely aware of the mounting costs of waiting, and when the value of the prize declined slowly rather than rapidly. In short, the longest waits were incurred when they goal seemed close to realization and/or participants were not acutely aware of the cost of waiting.

The phantom dictionary experiment is a metaphor for many ill-judged business decisions. For example, Kodak decided digital photography was a fad so they simply waited for customers to return to conventional photography. They are still waiting. The experiment is also a metaphor for the war in Afghanistan. The costs of persistence are mounting as almost every week someone is killed. Conversely, mounting casualties make it ever harder to leave empty handed. Yet just as there was no dictionary, there may be no victory to be won.

The weakness in the phantom dictionary experiment was that participants had to decide whether or not to remain in the game. Yet in reality it is often possible for organizations to 'drift idly' and live with an economically poor course of action indefinitely. Significantly in a sequel to the phantom dictionary experiment Brockner et al. (1979) found that decision-makers were more likely to persist with an economically poor course of action where decisions to persist could be made passively as distinct from when they must be made actively.

Organizations engage in passive (programmed) decisions to conserve resources. To a point this may be a sensible strategy because it enables organizations to concentrate energy on important issues. For example, it would hardly make sense to call a board meeting to issue parking permits or sign off invoices. But only to a point! Passive decision-making can also lead to inefficiencies if it means that certain departments receive automatic renewal of funding. For example, if R&D automatically receive funding every year without ever having to justify their existence by citing number of patents registered or other performance metrics (e.g. Pfeffer 1981: Ch. 8).

Reluctance to take a risk

Entrapment may start because the cost of *not* doing something is initially small (Brockner et al. 1979). For instance, at first digital photographs were of poor quality so Kodak lost little by adhering to conventional photography. Likewise, when search engines like Google first appeared, they were used mainly by IT literate enthusiasts. As advertising revenues were extremely limited, Microsoft may have decided they were not missing anything.

Psychological forces may also enter the equation. Jim (a pseudonym) was a highly successful fishmonger. He owned a small chain of shops, each with an average turnover of £60,000 a week. Yet he almost let the business slip through his fingers. The story is as follows. Jim ran a conventional wet fish business. 'I can tell you exactly how I used to set the stall out,' said Jim. 'We maybe only had about 14 different lines. We'd kippers; then there was cod and haddock, herrings, plaice – things you would expect.'

When Jim's daughter started working in the business she pleaded with him to expand the business into more exotic lines like bass and sea bream. Jim refused to hear of it. When Jim went on holiday, he left his daughter in charge of the business. He returned to things he did not expect:

> I left her in charge. All the time she's been saying, 'We ought to get all these [exotic] fish.'
> Oh! No! No! No! Too dear!
> I came back and the bill was about 25 per cent more than it had been the weeks before we'd gone on holiday. I looked at it and she'd bought all these things [exotic fish]. I didn't really know what she'd taken at that point, but I thought, Oh, crikey! It's going to be a disaster is this.

According to prospect theory, when decisions are expressed positively, that is, as a choice between gains, decision-makers tend to be risk averse. Risk averse means that the proverbial 'bird in hand' is preferable to the bigger but risky gain of 'two in the bush' (Kahneman and Tversky 1979, 1982). Jim's reaction could hardly be more risk averse. The business was generating thousands of pounds every week. Yet he refused to take a chance on a few boxes of fish. In fact, the experiment saved the business. Jim again:

It hadn't been [a disaster]. And then you realized, people wanted other things. They wanted bass and they wanted squids and they wanted prawns. I would say now that [without new lines] we wouldn't be able to survive at the rents and rates that we pay and the cost of staff.

If the 'Jims' of Goldman Sachs had had their way in the early 1990s the firm might not have survived either. In December 1990 Steve Friedman and Bob Rubin were named senior partners and co-chairmen of the management committee. Their ambitious vision involved expanding the firm to offer the full range of expertise – capable of competing with the biggest investment banks and offering new services. Many of the partners opposed the idea ('going to be a disaster is this') particularly as Goldman's boutique model had served the firm well:

Goldman Sachs, with its sixty-five hundred employees, was highly successful, and the partnership was by its nature conservative. After a decade of astounding prosperity, the impetus for change was low. 'We were moving too slowly, or not at all, to face some serious competitive threats ... and with too much self-satisfaction,' Friedman remembers. Too many things were on autopilot and were not re-examined. If we waited to fix them it might get too late.

(Endlich 1999: 188)

While ever the business is doing well, decisions are likely to be expressed positively and may thus deter decision-makers from taking risks that on economic grounds they should take. As Rubin and Friedman recognized, although Goldman's could have continued with its existing business model, the firm would eventually decline and reach a point of no return. In other words, whilst change was risky, in the long run Goldman's had more to lose by *not* taking the risk.

Avoiding entrapment

Although entrapment may appear to be surrounded by an air of inexorability, nothing need be inevitable. There are measures organizations can take to reduce their vulnerability to entrapment including:

Treat 'reality' as fiction
Count the costs of persistence
Create a crisis
Create options
Avoid the temptation to discount the future

Each of these is discussed in turn.

'Reality' as fiction

Rather than seeing analysts' reports as literal truth, it is better to view them as 'helpful fiction', that is as partly true and therefore partly false (e.g. Drummond 2001: Ch. 4). Part of the skill of being a manager is the ability to sense the limits of one's information. It is also important that managers look outside their regular channels of information to see what they may be missing. For example, the growth of digital photography was obvious on the high street yet it still took Kodak by surprise.

337

Count the costs of persistence

Decision-makers should also count the costs of persistence. Economics teaches that all else equal, organizations should change direction if an opportunity promising a better return on investment becomes available even if it means giving up a *successful* course of action (Northcraft and Wolf 1984). For instance, if equipment has become obsolete it may be wise to jettison it even though it has years of service life left in it. If the US steel industry had done this, they might not have been overtaken by Japan.

Create a crisis

Organizations can build reviews into their decision-making procedures in order to force decision-makers to make an active decision to persist. For example, zero-based budgeting where projects are only funded one phase at a time is used in some high risk industries like pharmaceuticals. Funding is only renewed at each stage if the project passes a rigorous assessment. This form of control also has the advantage requiring decision-makers to confront their options periodically rather than just drifting along.

Create options

Real options are toehold investments that enable but do not compel decision-makers to take a certain course of action in the future. For example, a company may buy the rights to a goldmine but mine only if the price of gold reaches a certain level so that mining becomes economically justified. Options are thus a way of providing for the future instead of trying to second guess it. The beauty of purchasing an option is that the loss is confined to the purchase price, whereas the potential gain is unlimited (e.g. Janney and Dess 2004).

Indeed, organizations can be seen as bundles of options. In this view, a problem for which there is no solution is a failure of management. To put it another way, the hallmark of an entrapped organization is that it has run out of options. For example, Woolworths had no option but to close. Likewise, when Lehman's were refused financial assistance from the US government and when the proposed merger with Barclays was blocked in September 2008, the firm was left with no option but to file for bankruptcy. Decision-makers should therefore be careful about making decisions that destroy options.

Better still, organizations should focus upon creating options. Indeed, economics teaches that decisions that create real options are more profitable than decisions that involve exercising them. For example, wildcat oil exploration firms like Tullow and Heritage make money by selling their discoveries to the big oil producing companies who effectively purchase an option to commence drilling immediately or at some time in the future – or not at all. Goldman's decision to diversify into new products and services gave the firm a new lease of life because it created options. Likewise, Porsche have broadened their options by entering the domestic market with its Panamera range whilst still retaining sports cars as their core business. Apple's experience in building and marketing the iPhone created a platform for the subsequent launch of the iPad.

Avoid discounting the future

Creating options involves taking a long-term view of profits. Discounting the future refers to our innate preference as human beings for short-term gain (Bazerman and Watkins 2008: 85). For example, would you prefer £10,000 now or £12,000 in two year's time? Clearly £12,000 in two year's time is the best (maximizing) option, but you may well prefer immediate gratification. Discounting the future can mean that firms are tempted to postpone necessary investment – as evidenced for example by the number of shabby London hotels. By the same token, the UK government postponed dealing with the national debt before the general election even though delay risked making things worse.

Summary

This chapter has focussed upon how and why organizations can become locked in to an economically poor course of action. 'Lock-in' can happen because organizations fail to see the future even after it has arrived because their information gathering programmes are biased towards the status quo. 'Lock-in' can also be caused by 'side-bets', that is, extraneous investments that eventually become the main reason for persistence. High closing costs may also act as a deterrent, particularly if decision-makers' careers are at stake. Vulnerability to entrapment is heightened where decisions can made passively as distinct from where they must be made actively.

Although entrapment may be surrounded by an air of inexorability, nothing need be inevitable. Organizations can reduce their vulnerability to 'lock-in' by broadening their information bases, counting the costs of persistence; by deliberately creating crises that force decision-makers to review options and by avoiding decisions that destroy options. Above all, organizations should recognize that sometimes they may have more to lose by not taking a risk.

References

Bazerman, M.H. and Watkins, M.D. (2008) *Predictable Surprises*, Harvard, Harvard University Business Press.

Becker, H.S. (1960) 'Notes on the concept of commitment', *American Journal of Sociology*, 66, 32–40.

Brockner, J. (1992) 'The escalation of commitment to a failing course of action: toward theoretical progress', *Academy of Management Review*, 17, 39–61.

Brockner, J., Shaw, M.C. and Rubin J.Z. (1979) 'Factors affecting withdrawal from an escalating conflict: quitting before it's too late', *Journal of Experimental Social Psychology*, 17, 492–503.

Brown, R.H. (1978) 'Bureaucracy as praxis: toward a political phenomenology of formal organizations', *Administrative Science Quarterly*, 23, 365–82.

Drummond, H. (2001) *The Art of Decision Making: Mirrors of Imagination, Masks of Science*, Chichester, Wiley.

Endlich, L. (1999) *Goldman Sachs: The Culture of Success*, London, Time Warner.

Hedberg, B. and Jonsonn, S. (1977) 'Strategy formulation as a discontinuous process', *International Studies of Management and Organization*, 7, 88–109.

Janney, J.J. and Dess, G.G. (2004) 'Can real-options analysis improve decision-making? Promises and pitfalls', *Academy of Management Executive*, 18, 60–75.

Kahneman, D. and Tversky, A. (1979) 'Prospect theory: an analysis of decision under risk', *Econometrica*, 47, 263–91.

Kahneman, D. and Tversky, A. (1982) 'The psychology of preferences', *Scientific American*, 246, 162–70.

Karlsson, N., Garling, T. and Bonini, N. (2005) 'Escalation of commitment with transparent future outcomes', *Experimental Psychology*, 52, 67–73.

Northcraft, G. and Wolf, G. (1984) Dollars sense and sunk costs: a life cycle model of resource allocation decisions', *Academy of Management Review*, 9, 225–34.

Pfeffer, J. (1981) *Power in Organizations*, London, Pitman.

Rubin, J.Z. and Brockner, J. (1975) 'Factors affecting entrapment in waiting situations: the Rosencrantz and Guildenstern effect', *Journal of Personality and Social Psychology*, 31, 1054–63.

Schwenk, C., and Tang, M.-J.E. (1989) 'Economic and psychological explanations for strategic persistence', *Journal of Management Science*, 17, 559–70.

Starbuck, W.H. (1983) 'Organizations as action generators', *American Sociological Review*, 48, 91–102.

Staw, B.M. (1997) 'Escalation research: An update and appraisal.' In Z. Shapira (ed.) *Organizational Decision Making*, Cambridge, Cambridge University Press, 191–215.

Tweedale, G. (1995) *Steel City: Entrepreneurship, Strategy and Technology in Sheffield 1793–1993*, Oxford, Clarendon.

23

Power and discourse in organizational change
The case of implementing enterprise resource planning systems

David Grant and Richard Hall

Introduction

Processes of organizational change inevitably involve conflict and contestation. Where organizations are attempting to undertake planned change, involving, for example, the introduction and implementation of major new technology, change agents and their sponsoring coalitions seek to implement change plans, and attempt to manage resistance from a range of different interest groups and factions within the organization. Strategies for managing resistance invariably highlight the key role of communication. Given the ubiquity of themes of conflict and communication in the study and practice of managing technological change, it is unsurprising that the analysis of these processes might be usefully informed by theories and studies of organizational discourse that are sensitive to the role and dynamics of power.

The methods and approaches associated with Critical Discourse Analysis (CDA) (Fairclough, 1992; Fairclough and Wodak, 1997; van Dijk, 2001) can be used to deepen our understanding of technological change in organizations. One of the key strengths of a CDA approach is that it highlights discourse and power as important in mediating the change process. From this perspective the change process is not seen as one in which change agents, supported by senior management, progressively 'manage' employee opposition and resistance through strategies of effective communication and consultation. On the contrary, in cases of technological change in organizations, we see different groups using discursive strategies as a critical means of asserting their interests and deploying their power.

Here we use CDA in order to examine a series of cases of organization change in which Enterprise Resource Planning Systems (ERPs) are introduced and implemented. In doing so we seek to identify and assess the role of discourse in the process of change and in the shaping of new organizational technology implementations such as these. ERPs are packaged business software systems that automate the integration of data across an organization and impose standardized procedures on its input, use and dissemination (Buckhout et al., 1999; Kallinikos, 2004; Monk and Wagner, 2006). Since the early 1990s ERPs, and their contemporary variants (often described as 'enterprise systems'), have been one of the most common and significant forms of technology implemented in large and medium-sized organizations. It has been estimated that ERP implementations now account for 30 per cent of all major organizational change activities (Morris and Venkatesh, 2010).

In our study of the implementation of ERPs in five large organizations we show how discourse mediates the power relations between the sponsors of the ERP implementation and organizational users. We argue that these power relations are best understood by examining what Hardy and Phillips (2004) describe as the mutually constitutive relationship between power and discourse. In relation to the ERPs at the case-study organizations, we identify the emergence of an *original sponsoring discourse*, authored by a sponsoring coalition of senior management and the implementation team, which portrays the ERP as beneficial for the organization and advocates the implementation of the ERP in standard, off-the-shelf form as possible ('vanilla'), with little, if any, customization. In response to this discourse we then identify the emergence of a *user-authored counter discourse* which highlights the practical problems and deficiencies of the ERP. This discourse relies heavily on claims that the ERP does not work in practice, requires numerous 'workarounds' and duplications, leading to inefficiencies in work and organization. Finally, we see the sponsoring coalition responding to this alternate discourse, by reformulating a *revised sponsoring discourse*. This discourse reframes and redefines the objectives of the ERP implementation, accepts the need for some limited customizations to the technology and depicts user resistance to the implementation as transient and, ultimately, inconsequential.

The chapter is divided into five main sections. In the first, we contextualize our study by reviewing the various debates and controversies surrounding ERP implementations. This involves examining the motives behind ERP implementation and illustrating how proponents of ERP have constructed and promulgated a discourse that, despite evidence to the contrary, presents ERP implementations as unproblematic and as having a highly beneficial and positive impact on organizational performance. In the second section we propose a framework of analysis based on the mutually constitutive relationship of power and discourse. We suggest how such an analysis might provide fresh insight into the analysis of the implementation of, and mobilization of resistance to, ERP implementations as an example of major organizational change. The third section outlines the discourse analytic methodology employed by the study. The fourth section reports and discusses the results of the discourse analysis carried out in relation to the implementation of ERP systems at five case-study organizations. Here we identify the key discourses produced by various stakeholders in the ERP implementations as they seek to assert their interests and deploy their power. The final section of the chapter presents our main conclusions and outlines their implications for using discourse analysis as a means of better appreciating the strategies available to change sponsors and resistors in the course of technological change.

ERP Implementations: organizational change and resistance

ERPs are packaged business software systems that automate the integration of data across an organization and impose standardized procedures on its input, use and dissemination. Using an ERP system, members of an organization can enter or draw on data from one part of an organization's operations and then immediately inform or update all other parts of an organization's operations in a variety of report formats, each designed to assist particular functions and procedures (Buckhout et al., 1999; Monk and Wagner, 2006; Yusef et al., 2004). The current generation of ERPs now include a range of modules that incorporate the core manufacturing and logistics functions, complemented by various financial and accounting, human resource management, and sales and distribution applications (Kallinikos, 2004; Mabert et al., 2001; Monk and Wagner, 2006).

It has been observed that software vendors, consultants, the business press and some academic commentators as well as those internal to the organization who sponsor ERP adoption, often draw on a strongly technological determinist discourse in order to present the beneficial changes that an organization will experience post-ERP implementation (Grant et al., 2006). Further, it has also been observed that this discourse emphasizes the considerable business efficiency dividends that can be realized through the introduction of an ERP system, the value of ERPs driving 'best practice' business processes into organizations, and the suitability of ERPs for organizations of any size in any industry (Light et al., 2001; Light and Wagner, 2006; Wagner and Newell, 2004). For example, those such as Buckhout et al. (1999) and Gefen and Ragowsky (2005) have suggested that ERPs can deliver significant cost savings and increased profits to organizations though reduced procurement costs, smaller inventories, more effective sales strategies, lower administration costs, and reduced direct and indirect labour costs. They also note how ERPs lead to improved decision making because of their ability to provide 'real time' information in a variety of report formats, each designed to assist particular management functions and procedures.

The capacity of ERPs to lead to significant cost savings and increased profitability is believed to be the primary motivation for large numbers of organizations to adopt them since the mid 1990s (Grant et al., 2006; Madapusi and D'Souza, 2005). It has been estimated that 75 per cent of medium and large manufacturers, 60 per cent of service firms and 80 per cent of the Fortune 500 have implemented ERPs (Morris and Venkatesh, 2010: 143). The significance of the ERP 'industry' is such that the worldwide market for these applications in 2004 was estimated to be worth US$79 billion (Gefen and Ragowsky, 2005).

While proponents point to the widespread success of ERP implementations, a counter discourse exists which asserts that they are costly to implement, and often fail to deliver significant benefits. The cost of implementing an ERP system has been estimated at between $300,000 for small firms to $500 million for large corporations (Mabert et al., 2001; Monk and Wagner, 2006: 32). Failure rates for ERP implementations have been estimated to be as high as 60 per cent (Devadoss and Pan, 2007) with losses ranging from $6 million to over $100 million (Morris and Venkatesh, 2010).

ERP implementations can lead to significant changes in the nature, structure and management of work (Dery et al., 2006; Kallinikos, 2004; Morris and Venkatesh, 2010) and have been associated with: downsizing and delayering; job redesign leading to reduced employee autonomy, deskilling and work intensification; and the centralization of control (Hall, 2002, 2005; Alvarez, 2008). These changes challenge existing power structures and relationships within the organization. As a consequence, ERPs may meet resistance from key managerial and employee interest groups (Harley et al., 2006; Lee and Myers, 2004). Some research has pointed to the consequences of employee resistance to ERP implementations: they have been seen to lead to increased exit rates workarounds and to job dissatisfaction or the moderation of levels of job satisfaction (Boudreau and Robey, 2005; Hall, 2002, 2005; Morris and Venkatesh, 2010). However, there has been relatively little research examining the way in which resistance to ERP implementations plays out from an organizational change perspective (see Boudreau and Robey, 2005 for a rare exception). The present study seeks to provide such an analysis. In so doing, it argues that an understanding of the power relationships underlying the implementation of, and resistance to, ERP implementations is necessary and that this can be facilitated by an examination of the discourses that are used by different stakeholders in an organization. Such an approach highlights the important link between power and discourse and it is to this we turn in the next section.

Discourse, power and ERPs

In this study we define a discourse as comprising a set of interrelated texts that, along with the related practices of text production, dissemination and consumption, brings an object or idea into being. By this we mean that discourse relates to not just spoken or written texts, but also structures and practices that underlie the texts and their production, transmission and reception (Grant and Hardy, 2004). Our approach to the study of discourse is informed by Critical Discourse Analysis (CDA) (Fairclough, 1992, 2001; Fairclough and Wodak, 1997; Van Dijk, 2001). CDA contributes to our understanding of ERP implementations as a form of major organizational change in three significant respects.

First, a discourse analytic approach allows us to identify and analyse the key discourses by which organizational change is conceptualized, idealized and articulated. Moreover, it enables us to demonstrate that discourse plays a central role in the social construction of the change process and its associated outcomes. In sum, discourse brings an object (in this case ERP) into being so that it becomes a material reality in the form of the practices that it invokes for various stakeholders (Hardy, 2001: 27). These practices amount to organizational members experiencing significant changes in work and organization.

Second, and in line with their socially constructive effects, discourses related to change are created, and supported via the implicit negotiation of meaning among key stakeholders (e.g. consultants, managers, employees) with different views and interests (Marshak and Grant, 2008). This process results in the emergence of a dominant meaning that can be seen as a particular discourse. The emergence of this dominant meaning occurs as alternative discourses are subverted or marginalized (Fairclough, 2001; Hardy, 2001) and, in the context of this study, is indicative of the power relationships and political processes that may come into play during an ERP implementation (Grant et al., 2006).

Third, to understand how and why particular change-related discourses and their meanings are produced, as well as their effects, it is important to understand the context in which they arise (Sillince, 2007). This has led to the application of 'intertextual' analyses of discourses and the texts therein, whereby any text can be seen as 'a link in a chain of texts, reacting to, drawing in and transforming other texts' (Fairclough and Wodak, 1997: 262). It is an approach that assists in understanding how the negotiation of meaning surrounding an ERP implementation unfolds through the complex interplay of both socially and historically produced texts that are part of an ongoing, iterative and recursive process (Grant and Hardy, 2004).

Underlying these three contributions is an appreciation of the link between power and discourse. However, as Hardy and Phillips (2004: 299) have observed, the nature of this relationship is complex and more could be done to unpack it further. Thus, they propose an analytical framework where ' ... power and discourse are mutually constitutive ... In other words, discourse shapes relations of power while relations of power shape who influences discourse over time and in what way'.

In this chapter we utilize Hardy and Phillips' framework of analysis in order to identify and examine the power dynamics underlying the management and organization of change associated with ERP systems. We show how these power dynamics lead key actors to produce influential discourses pertaining to ERP related change and why some of these actors are more successful in modifying the discourse in ways that are useful to them.

According to Hardy and Phillips (2004: 306–7), the power of a particular group to produce and disseminate influential discourses will be influenced by whether members of the group occupy positions associated with (a) formal power; (b) critical resources; (c) network links; and (d) discursive legitimacy. *Formal power* refers to authority and decision making power (Astley and

Sachdeva, 1984; French and Raven, 1968). Actors with power based on *critical resources* (rewards, sanctions, expertise, access to organizational members higher in the authority structure, control of finances etc) (French and Raven, 1968; Pettigrew, 1973; Pfeffer, 1981) may be well placed to utilize those resources in order to generate and disseminate a particular discourses in a highly effective manner. Those actors who derive power through *network links* and social relationships (Bourdieu, 1993) are able to constitute alliances with, incorporate and win the consent of other groups that might otherwise oppose the discourse that they are promulgating. In so doing, the discourse is gradually adopted by its potential opponents to the extent that it becomes instantiated in every day organizational life. Finally, some actors are able to draw upon what is termed *discursive legitimacy* (Fairclough, 1992; Phillips and Hardy, 1997). In these instances they are able to produce a discourse that is authenticated by other people. In confirming the authenticity of the discourse these other people validate its dissemination and extend its reach by virtue of their number or position.

Hardy and Phillips (2004: 307) are careful to point out that these forms of power are distributed among multiple actors, in a variety of positions, who are implicated in establishing the extent to which a particular discourse comes to dominate the meaning attached to a particular issue (for example ERP). Often there is a considerable struggle among these actors to establish a dominant meaning. In these instances discursive 'closure' (Sillince, 2007) is never complete, leaving space for resistance through the production of 'counter' discourses.

We subscribe to Hardy and Phillips' framework of analysis, but in investigating the mutually constitutive nature of power and discourse in relation to organizational change, we believe it is important to bring to the fore three inter-related factors.

First, as Hardy and Phillips' framework acknowledges, the power of any discourse rests, in part, on its capacity to persuade others of its legitimacy. The persuasiveness of the discourse is, however, highly contingent on the rhetorical devices deployed by those using it (Cheney et al., 2004; Sillince, 2002).

Second, the effectiveness of the rhetoric that underpins a discourse will be dependent on the extent to which the arguments and claims made translate into lived experience (practice) for those the discourse and its proponents are seeking to persuade. This takes on added significance in the context of change-related discourses since it may influence the extent to which the change takes hold. We would describe this as *the test of practice*. We are not here talking of discourse as practice where this refers to various types or instances of discursive interaction (Broadfoot et al., 2004). Rather, and in line with Foucault (2002: 30), we are talking about the extent to which the ideas or ideological or hegemonic assumptions underlying a particular discourse influence those that it is aimed at, such that it has a material effect. Thus a persuasive change-related discourse (in terms of its level of influence and thus the power of its proponents) is one where those organizational members it is aimed at think or behave in ways that lead to the discourse being translated into social practice (Alvesson and Deetz, 2000; Fairclough, 1992). This contributes to the authentication of the discourse and thus the discursive legitimacy of those associated with it. Moreover, it means that the issue of discursive legitimacy may be far more significant in the link between discourse and power than Hardy and Phillips' (2004) framework of analysis would initially suggest.

In the case of ERP, we have already seen how its proponents (those occupying positions who have an interest in seeing an ERP implemented in an organization) assert that a range of beneficial changes will flow directly from the technology. However, the extant literature on ERPs seems to suggest that, once implemented, they often fail to deliver these benefits. In short, the rhetoric underpinning ERPs fails to match the reality experienced by those operating them – often middle managers and other employees (Harley et al., 2006; Light and Wagner, 2006). As a consequence, discourses in support of ERP appear often to fail the test of practice and thus lose legitimacy. Without this, proponents of these discourses cannot rely on formal power, critical resources and network links in order to sustain them.

Third, as we have already noted, by their very nature, ERPs challenge existing power structures and relationships within organizations and so their implementation is likely to meet resistance from key actors such as middle managers and employees. Where an ERP discourse fails to be consistent with users' apparent experiences, these key actors are unlikely to be persuaded of the legitimacy of the discourse. Drawing on their own experience of ERP in practice, and contingent on their own formal power, critical resources and network links, this may encourage them to construct a highly persuasive counter discourse – one that enables them to undermine discourses that favour ERP and resist its implementation. We know however that many organizations, despite encountering such resistance, go on to implement their ERP systems (Boudreau and Robey 2005; Harley et al., 2006; Lee and Myers, 2004; Light and Wagner, 2006). This suggests that management is often able to overcome or minimize the damage caused by their discourses failing the test of practice. We believe that they achieve this by drawing on discursive manoeuvres that are consonant with some of those identified by, among others, Hardy and Phillips (2004: 299) and Sillince (2007: 380–82). These manoeuvres involve actors modifying, transforming or reinforcing their discourses by, for example, appropriating and reframing discourses that oppose their own.

Methods and approach

Our study draws on data from a major study of ERP implementations at five large Australian organizations. Each organization was in the process of implementing or had recently implemented one or more ERP modules. *FoodCo* is a large food processing company, employing approximately 2500 staff. FoodCo implemented an ERP system with staged roll-outs of a full suite of modules commencing in 1999 with most modules having 'gone live' by the end of 2001. *BankA* is a large Australian bank employing over 20,000 staff and offering a full range of banking services. The bank implemented the financial modules of an ERP in the late 1990s and commenced an implementation of HR modules in late 2000, going live in late 2002. *BankB* is a large bank based in New Zealand offering a full range of retail banking, business banking and financial services. The bank is a wholly owned subsidiary of a multinational financial institution. The parent company and BankB have been implementing ERP modules since 2000. *OzUni* is a large Australian university employing over 5000 people and enrolling over 40,000 students. OzUni implemented the financial modules of an ERP in 2002 with further implementations of other modules thereafter. *OilCo* is a large oil company operating in Australia as part of a large multinational corporation. The company first implemented an ERP in 1990, with subsequent major implementations of upgraded systems commencing in 1995/96 and again in 2004.

Data were collected through interviews with between six and 12 managers, workers and consultants at each of the five case-study organizations. This amounted to a combined total of 45 interviews. Interviews took place between 2003 and 2005. In addition to the interview data, the case studies made available a range of pertinent documentation including internal memos, organizational newsletters and reports.

The study interviews were semi-structured, lasted between one and two hours, and were recorded and transcribed. Each interviewee was selected on the basis of their involvement with the planning and implementation of the ERP and/or for their being in a position to provide an informed evaluation of the effects of ERP post-implementation. In two cases (OilCo and OzUni) interviews were conducted at the time of the ERP system going live, although at one of those cases (OzUni), further interviews with users were also carried out between six and 12 months after implementation. In the third case (BankB), virtually all interviews were undertaken approximately nine months after 'go-live'. In the final two cases (FoodCo and BankA) interviews were conducted between 18 months and two and a half years after initial implementation. This means that we are drawing on interview data that was based on a mixture of recollection and current observation. It also means that the extent to which an interview was based on recollection and/or current observation depended on which case-study organization it took place at. Despite this variation we were still able to use the data in order to identify common patterns of discourses associated with ERP implementations and to show how, as a result of the mutually constitutive relationship of discourse and power, these discourses evolve as ERP implementations progress.

We took a discourse analytic approach that first required us to catalogue the texts we had collected according to which case study they related to and their genre (i.e. interview, report, memo etc.) (Yates and Orlikowski, 2002). We then classified the specific speech act reference, in order to see what the text or a particular section of the text was aiming to achieve in relation to the interviewee's evaluation of the ERP. For example, was the text trying to justify, empathise, correct, explain, resist? We then matched this microanalysis with broader, institutional references, noting concurrent line-by-line references to ERP in relation to issues such as organizational strategy, efficiency, performance, and culture (Hardy, 2001).

Results

Analysis of the texts gathered from the five case studies revealed the existence of three distinct, inter-related discourses concerning ERP: an 'original sponsoring discourse', a 'user-authored counter discourse' and a 'revised sponsoring discourse'. Distinctions can be drawn between the timing of the emergence and maturation of each of these discourses, between their authorship and appropriation and between their content and apparent aims. Understanding practice is critical to understanding the fate and emergence of these discourses. We thus paid close attention to the relationships between the implicit and explicit claims of each discourse and the experience of practice. At the same time we also sought to provide an analysis that was highly contextualized and that was sensitive to the power dimensions and implications associated with these discourses.

The original sponsoring discourse

At each of the case studies, the decision to implement an ERP was invariably associated with an original sponsoring discourse that tended to be generated and sustained by a coalition that was normally led by one or more very senior managers and that included vendor representatives, implementation and IT consultants, and members of implementation teams.

While particular emphases in the discourse varied across the organizations, they all included claims that the implementation of an ERP would lead to a number of significant and beneficial changes. At all five case-study organizations, for example, the rationalization of a large number of incompatible legacy systems was seen as a major attraction by senior management. Indeed, at BankB (and FoodCo and OilCo) mergers and acquisitions in the recent past had generated what was seen to be an imperative for the introduction of a single, integrated IT system. At the same time, all five organizations recognized and promoted the potential advantages of faster data processing, business process automation and standardization and less duplication.

The standardization of business processes across departments, divisions or different regional operations also featured prominently in the original sponsoring discourse's justification of ERP implementations at all of our case studies. For example, reflecting back on the implementation of the ERP system at FoodCo, the Senior Business Solutions Manager explained how management had signalled a determination to introduce 'one way' of doing business for all its disparate processing and distribution facilities and had reasoned that the introduction of the standard processes embedded in the ERP would 'lead us to best practice'.

The sponsoring discourse conceded that these innovations were aimed at enhancing centralized control over processes. The Senior Business Solutions Manager at FoodCo, reflecting on the system after implementation, boasted: 'We can hop on the system now and I can tell you what the sales were for yesterday, I can tell you the stocks all around the country, I can see the status of production, I can check procurement, I can run balance sheets …'.

One of the most prominent themes in the original ERP sponsoring discourse is the commitment to the virtues of a 'vanilla' implementation of the ERP. According to the discourse, the real value in ERPs can only be fully realized where the modules are implemented with little or no customization. This implies that business processes may need to change in line with the assumptions of the ERP. The original discourses at all five case studies revealed a strident commitment to vanilla. For example the CIO at OilCo asserted: 'I've made my view very clear that we should be putting that [ERP module] on absolutely stock vanilla …'.

An overall appraisal of the original sponsoring discourse suggests that those using it advanced their claims about the advantages and benefits of ERP by drawing on all of the dimensions of power identified by Hardy and Phillips (2004). For example, the coalitions of senior managers that initially championed ERP at all of our cases could be seen to draw on their formal power and authority. Moreover, their confidence at seeing through the implementation can, in part, be attributed to the critical resources at their disposal, especially financial and human resources (including control over in-house and external IT consultancy resources). Network links were used to create these powerful senior management-sponsored coalitions. They were also apparent where sponsors of the discourse confidently predicted success on the basis of knowing vendors and consultants who had experience and knowledge of ERP implementations. Finally, discursive legitimacy was earned through the experience and success of coalition members in past organizational change initiatives.

The user-authored counter discourse

At all our case studies, as ERP modules were implemented and as their effects started to become apparent, a user discourse took shape that tended to portray ERPs negatively. ERPs, or at least the specific ERP as implemented at the users' organization, were seen to be inefficient, ineffective and inflexible. This discourse can be seen to be driven and sustained by two key forces – one explicit, the other implicit.

The explicit force was the experience of the ERP once implemented. Here we conceptualize this in terms of the original sponsoring discourse encountering the 'test of practice'. Whereas the sponsoring discourse claimed that the ERP would lead to efficiencies, operational improvements, faster processing, improved integration and standardization of processes, the experience of users was generally vastly different. Users articulated their experience of the ERPs in terms of technical problems, poor performance of the system, its inflexibility and its failure to live up to expectations. They regularly stated that they were unable to see any clear advantages for them or for the execution of their operational responsibilities.

For example, many users at BankA reported that processing times for even simple transactions were markedly slower under the ERP. HR users at this organization reported that the time taken to process an employee separation had gone from '30 to 35 minutes up to an hour'. At all of our cases, even where the ERP appeared to be technically working, some users questioned whether the new processes were any more efficient.

The user discourse portrayed ERPs as inflexible as well as inefficient. For example, a Departmental Manager at OzUni who was responsible for generating reports, complained that report formats were unwieldy, difficult to modify and challenging to interpret. Frustrations with the operational problems plaguing the ERP became so acute that users formed an informal 'user support group' to share experiences:

> Every fortnight we would have a meeting at around four o'clock in the afternoon and we would have antipasto and come five o'clock we would open a bottle of wine or champagne, and then we would bitch about them [IT Help Desk]. So we were our own counselling group because it was just frustrated people. It was a shocker. It was a very trying time.

The user discourse contended that ERPs in their vanilla form are fundamentally unworkable. As a result, the discourse saw extensive customizations as mandatory, or failing that, the retention of legacy and shadow systems as necessities. Users from all of our case studies related stories of the need to argue the case to management for customizations so that the ERP could accommodate their work requirements. At FoodCo for example, the QA Manager highlighted the difficulties in getting approval for customizations desired by users:

> We have a help desk where you can log issues [requests for customizations] ... we have a log ... a list of improvements. But again, those lists ... are evaluated by senior management on the basis of benefit to the business. So what may make someone's life a little bit easier here can be seen to be not important for the business.

Normally the effort involved in securing a particular customization was seen to be significant and time-consuming. As a result, workarounds, legacy systems and shadow systems persisted at all of our cases. For example, at OilCo where the ERP was associated with the introduction of a new method of calculating costs, the CIO observed that the accountants, who were among the first to have to use the ERP: ' ... couldn't live with it and so they've built their entire standard costing system in spreadsheets ... they find some way of making the two [sets of costings] look like the same thing ... the practice hasn't really been picked up.'

The implicit force which sustained the user discourse was the threat posed by the ERP systems and its processes to the autonomy, discretion and power of users. The discourse reveals a clear awareness that the ERP implementations were not informed by user experiences, nor by an adequate understanding of the realities of work processes and requirements. According to one Departmental Manager at OzUni: 'I felt that the system had been set up for central finance and they had not considered the department level at all. I don't think a lot of the people had experience in departments so they didn't even understand how a department ran.'

Users were conscious that the ERP served to constrain their choices and limit their discretion at work. A Procurement Officer at FoodCo noted that the new procurement system had limited his capacity to choose suppliers. 'In days gone by we could juggle around our pick of suppliers.

349

We're now locked in to approved, agreed suppliers so we can't deviate from that ... you're going down the one path.'

Our analysis suggests that overall the user discourse did not appear to draw potency from dimensions of formal power – users were relatively powerless in formal terms and tend to be non-managerial, non-professional workers. Where supervisors and managers subscribed to this discourse they had relatively limited formal authority in terms of their span of control and decision-making power. Users relied somewhat on the (limited) critical resources at their disposal (largely represented by their capacity to undermine or compromise the operation of systems and processes) and in some cases appeared to have drawn on network links with other users in their organization. Users also had little discursive legitimacy, at least at the outset of an ERP implementation. Rather than drawing on these conventional dimensions of power it appears users become empowered through the test of practice. As ERPs were implemented, and as they failed the test of practice, users drew on this experience to elaborate their emerging discourse around the ERP. As users they were uniquely placed to be able to articulate and enact a counter-discourse which was sustained by their own practice. In short, users possessed a degree of potential discursive legitimacy when it came to matters of operational practice. They were able to escalate the significance and potency of this discursive legitimacy by marshalling evidence of ERP failures or shortcomings and articulating and demonstrating those failures and shortcomings in the user discourse.

The revised sponsoring discourse

Post-implementation, senior management and other members of the original coalition that sponsored the ERP at each of the case studies became aware of the increasing criticism and opposition to its implementation manifest in the emergent user discourse. Such was the persuasive power of the user discourse that members of the coalition were forced to adopt a discursive strategy that involved them revising their own discourse. In doing so they appropriated some parts of the user discourse and deflected, reframed or qualified other parts.

The compelling nature of the user discourse can be explained by the test of practice. The user discourse gained legitimacy because its claims were buttressed by the actual experience of the ERP as implemented. In simple terms: the ERPs did not lead to the changes envisaged by the original sponsoring discourse and users knew the ERPs did not work because they had direct experience of them not working. Moreover, at each of the case study organizations users were (more or less) able to articulate these claims in a relatively coherent discourse that proved, in practice, to be compelling. We see this process as one of the veracity of the user discourse undermining one of the key dimensions of senior-management power – their discursive legitimacy. With their legitimacy under threat in the face of a manifestly poorly performing ERP and a compelling user discourse, senior management and other members of the coalitions responsible for ERP implementation at each of the case studies was forced to act. Typically, they did so through the generation of a revised discourse – one that sought to respond to the challenge of the user discourse, by reframing the experience of the ERP, refocusing the aims of the implementation, recasting the expectations of users and reassuring stakeholders that the ERP was workable and that the implementation was, actually, a success.

The claim that the ERP implementations were, despite the user discourse, relatively successful in achieving their aims was a key feature of the revised discourse at all of our case studies. For example, at BankA where the implementation of the payroll module had been roundly criticized, the Senior HR Manager claimed: 'People continued to get paid; so in that sense the implementation was a success and the changeover was seen as seamless by most customers.'

Despite these claims, the discourse did concede that there were some problems such that some customization was necessary. Accordingly, all five organizations undertook more customizations than originally envisaged. For example, at FoodCo, the Change Manager for the implementation project explained that: 'You are told that vanilla is best practice, it's supported everywhere ... then you sit there and go: that will in no way work with what we have. So there's a compromise where the customizations occurred.'

According to the revised sponsoring discourse while the original ambition was to have an ERP that would enable improved analysis and business strategy, the aim post-implementation became one of ensuring an efficient transactional system so that improved strategic capacity could be developed in the future. BankB estimated that 'maybe that's a long way away, like 10 years, 15 years, 20 years, that it's really strategic' (HR Manager, BankB).

The revised sponsoring discourse also recognized the existence of user resistance to ERPs. As the HR Manager at BankA, conceded, customizations were indeed made in response to user requests:

We made the decision to concentrate on improving the customer [i.e.: user] experience of the system. There were costs involved in this, but the system needed to be performing – a lot of money had been invested in the system and we had to get it working better ... The integration capacity of the system might be compromised but over time there was a growing acceptance of the need to do it, even amongst the technical teams.

While user resistance was therefore recognized and, to some degree, acceded to the revised discourse, it was nevertheless also qualified and rationalized in other ways. In these instances resistance was seen to be a passing phase and a reflection of the fact that 'people just don't like change'. The HR Manager at BankB conceded that customer service staff at the bank were ' ... a wee bit change resistant'. The Fulfilment Manager at OilCo however reasoned that users came to terms with the system eventually:

They just throw their hands up and say, 'This is a silly system, I can't use it and I don't know how anybody will ever be able to use it'. And that's just out of, I suppose, frustration because it is a change. But if they sat down and just took things logically they probably would have been able to ... well they did work it out in the long run.

By classifying user resistance as either dealt with through customizations or as the result of a lack of familiarity with the system or the result of an inherent resistance to change, the revised sponsoring discourse seeks to deflect and marginalize that resistance.

Overall, the revised sponsoring discourse represents an important discursive manoeuvre on the part of management. Confronted by the test of practice and the emergent and increasingly powerful user discourse, the management coalition responsible for overseeing the ERP implementation did not simply seek to defend their original sponsoring discourse. Instead they moved to appropriate the user discourse, at least in part, and re-fashion the sponsoring discourse. This discourse recognized the legitimacy of the user discourse, in the sense that its subscribers professed to 'listen' to the complaints of users. At the same time, it was used to repudiate some aspects of the original discourse. Through the generation and dissemination of this revised discourse, senior management sought to reclaim their discursive legitimacy and protect their power.

Conclusions

Organizational change inevitably involves a dynamic interplay of forces seeking to effect change and forces seeking to resist it. Rather than a predictable process of 'managing away' resistance, as implied by some 'life cycle' theories of resistance, this study highlights that the change process is more typically contested and iterative. It also suggests that the power of different organizational interests is deployed through discursive strategies.

Overall, the study's analysis of the management and organization of ERP systems directs attention to the differential impact of the changes ERPs bring about on different organizational groups and individual members. In particular, it highlights the diverse reactions to ERP implementations, including resistance, that are often characteristic of those members and groups (Alvarez, 2008; Boudreau and Robey, 2005; Hall, 2002, 2005; Harley et al., 2006; Lee and Myers, 2004; Morris and Venkatesh, 2010). As such, and via its analysis of the mutually constitutive relationship of power and discourse, it goes some way to explaining the reasons for these various reactions and contributes to an understanding of why ERP implementations often encounter difficulty and fail to meet the expectations of the organizations implementing them.

As is widely acknowledged in the change management literature, resistance can be based on numerous factors – psychological predispositions, threats to individual or collective self-interest, lack of information, a lack of faith in process, procedure or managerial competence. However, our study of ERP-related change leads us to contend that resistance is most potent where it is based on rational claims that the change is inappropriate, in the sense that it is likely to be ineffective. In cases such as these, such as where resistors are users of a new technology who believe that the new technology will be ineffective as a response to perceived problems or deficiencies, users have relatively limited power resources available to them. Users, in contrast to the sponsoring coalition of managers, change agents and consultants, will have comparatively little formal power and few critical resources at their disposal. Users have certain network links with other users in the organization, however, it seems apparent that their capacity to mobilize effective resistance through those networks, and to develop a compelling counter discourse, depends decisively on their discursive legitimacy. Our study demonstrates that users, in developing a counter discourse that is persuasive, tend to rely on claims that the technology fails the test of practice. The discourse is persuasive because users are able to marshal evidence of the practice of using the technology. As a result of the legitimacy of these claims, management and the sponsoring coalition will often be forced to engage with these claims. What our discourse analysis demonstrates is that this is done through an important discursive manoeuvre – one in which some of the claims in the counter discourse are appropriated and reframed into what we have characterized as a revised sponsoring discourse which serves to both sustain the change initiative and reassert the discursive legitimacy of management. It is important to recognize, however, that through this process resistant users can influence the implementation and ultimate form of the technology as implemented.

Our conclusions suggest that in studying organizational change and resistance, there is much value in examining the discourses employed by different interest groups in the struggle over organizational change and the critical role played by claims relating to the test of practice in establishing the discursive legitimacy of those discourses.

First, the results show that in attempting to constitute their power, key actors will use a range of rhetorical devices or strategies in order to ensure that their discourses achieve legitimacy. A number of previous studies have highlighted the use of these rhetorical devices and their implications for power in organizational settings (e.g. Mueller et al., 2004; Sillince, 2002).

352

Second, our study demonstrates that the test of practice is directly linked to discursive legitimacy. This suggests that actors drawing on discursive legitimacy in order to enhance their power, is perhaps more significant than Hardy and Phillips' (2004) framework implies. In particular and on the basis of our results, we suspect that actors' formal power, critical resources and network links are far more dependent on discursive legitimacy to be effective than vice versa.

Finally, the study shows that where a discourse fails the test of practice, change advocates may well adopt one or more discursive manoeuvres in order to try and ensure it meets the test. These will entail revising and reframing it and/or appropriating aspects of other, often opposing discourses. It therefore appears that as actors engage in various struggles in relation to organizational change, one factor determining the outcomes of these struggles may well be the effectiveness of their discursive manoeuvres.

References

Alvarez, R. (2008) 'Examining technology, structure and identity during an enterprise system implementation', *Information Systems Journal*, 18: 203–24.

Alvesson, M. and Deetz, S. (1996) 'Critical theory and postmodernism approaches to organizational studies'. in S. Clegg, C. Hardy and W. Nord (eds) *Handbook of Organization Studies*. London: SAGE.

Alvesson, M. and Deetz, S. (2000) *Doing Critical Management Research*. Thousand Oaks, CA: SAGE.

Astley, W.G. and Sachdeva, P.S. (1984) 'Structural sources of intraorganizational power: a theoretical synthesis', *Academy of Management Review*, 9(1): 104–13.

Boudreau, M.-C. and Robey, D. (2005) 'Enacting integrated information technology: a human agency perspective', *Organization Science*, 16(1): 3–18.

Bourdieu, P. (1993) *Sociology in Question*. London: SAGE.

Broadfoot, K., Deetz, S. and Anderson, D. (2004) 'Multi-levelled, multi-method approaches to organizational discourse', in D. Grant, C. Hardy, C. Oswick and L. Putnam (eds) *The Sage Handbook of Organizational Discourse*. London: SAGE.

Buckhout, S., Frey, E. and Nemec, J.J. (1999) 'Making ERP succeed: turning fear into promise', *Technology*, 15: 60–71.

Cheney, G., Christensen, L., Conrad, C. and Lair, D. (2004) 'Corporate rhetoric as organizational discourse', in D. Grant, C. Hardy, C. Oswick and L. Putnam (eds) *The Sage Handbook of Organizational Discourse*. London: SAGE.

Dery, K., Grant, D., Harley, W. and Wright, C. (2006) 'Work, organization and enterprise resource planning systems: an alternative research agenda', *New Technology, Work and Employment*, 21(3): 199–214.

Devadoss, P. and Pan, S. (2007) 'Enterprise systems use: towards a structurational analysis of enterprise systems induced organizational transformation', *Communications of the Association for Information Systems*, 19: 352–85.

Fairclough, N. (1992) *Discourse and Social Change*. Cambridge: Polity Press.

Fairclough, N. (2001) *Language and Power* (2nd edn). London: Longman.

Fairclough, N. and Wodak, R. (1997) 'Critical discourse analysis', in T.A. van Dijk. (ed.) *Discourse as Social Interaction*. London: SAGE.

Foucault, M. (2002) *Archeology of Knowledge*. London: Routledge.

French, J.R.P. and Raven, B. (1968) 'The bases of social power', in D. Cartwright and A. Zander (eds) *Group Dynamics*. New York, Harper & Row.

Gefen, D. and Ragowsky, A. (2005) 'A multi-level approach to measuring the benefits of an ERP system in manufacturing firms', *Information Systems Management*, Winter: 18–25.

Grant, D. and Hardy, C. (2004) 'Struggles with organizational discourse', *Organization Studies*, 25(1): 5–13.

Grant, D., Hall, R., Wailes, N. and Wright, C. (2006) 'The false promise of technological determinism: the case of enterprise resource planning systems', *New Technology Work and Employment*, 21(1): 2–24.

Hall, R. (2002) 'Enterprise resource planning systems and organizational change: transforming work organization?', *Strategic Change*, 11: 263–70.

Hall, R. (2005) 'The integrating and disciplining tendencies of ERPs: evidence from Australian organizations', *Strategic Change*, 14: 245–54.

Hardy, C. (2001) 'Researching organizational discourse', *International Studies of Management and Organization*, 31(3): 25–47.

Hardy, C. and Phillips, N. (2004) 'Discourse and power', in D. Grant, C. Hardy, C. Oswick and L. Putnam (eds) *The Sage Handbook of Organizational Discourse*. London: SAGE.

Harley, B., Wright, C., Hall, R. and Dery, K. (2006) 'Management reactions to technological change: the example of enterprise resource planning', *Journal of Applied Behavioral Science*, 42(3): 58–75.

Kallinikos, J. (2004) 'Deconstructing information packages: organizational and behavioural implications of ERP systems', *Information Technology and People*, 17(3): 8–30.

Lee, J. and Myers, M. (2004) 'Dominant actors, political agendas, and strategic shifts over time: a critical ethnography of an enterprise systems, implementation', *Journal of Strategic Information Systems*, 13(4): 355–74.

Light, B. and Wagner, E. (2006) 'Integration in ERP environments: rhetoric, realities and organisational possibilities', *New Technology Work and Employment*, 21(3): 215–28.

Light, B., Holland, C. and Wills, K. (2001) 'ERP and best of breed: a comparative analysis', *Business Process Management Journal*, 7(3): 216–24.

Mabert, V.A., Soni, A. and Venkataramanan, M.A. (2001) 'Enterprise resource planning: common myths versus evolving reality', *Business Horizons*, 44(3): 59.

Madapusi, A. and D'Souza, D. (2005) 'Aligning ERP systems with international strategies', *Information Systems Management*, Winter: 7–17.

Marshak, R. and Grant, D. (2008) 'Organizational discourse and new OD practices'. *British Journal of Management*, 19(1): 7–19.

Monk, E. and Wagner, B. (2006) *Concepts in Enterprise Resource Planning* (2nd edn). Boston, MA: Thomson Course Technology.

Morris, M.G. and Venkatesh, V. (2010) 'Job characteristics and job satisfaction: understanding the role of enterprise resource planning system implementation', *MIS Quarterly*, 34(1): 143–61.

Mueller, F., Sillince, J., Harvey, C. and Howorth, C. (2004) ' "A rounded picture is what we need": rhetorical strategies, arguments and the negotiation of change in a U.K. hospital trust', *Organization Studies*, 25(1): 75–93.

Pettigrew, A.M. (1973) *The Politics of Organizational Decision Making*. London: Tavistock.

Pfeffer, J. (1981) *Power in Organizations*. Marshfield, MA: Pitman.

Phillips, N. and Hardy, C. (1997) 'Managing multiple identities: discourse, legitimacy and resources in the UK refugee system', *Organization*, 4(2): 159–86.

Sillince, J.A. (2002) 'A model of the strength and appropriateness of argumentation and rhetoric in organizational contexts'. *Journal of Management Studies*, 39(5): 585–618.

Sillince, J.A. (2007) 'Organizational context and the discursive construction of organizing'. *Management Communication Quarterly*, 20(4): 363–94.

van Dijk, T.A. (2001) 'Critical discourse analysis', in D. Schiffrin, D. Tannen and H. Hamilton (eds) *Handbook of Discourse Analysis*. Oxford: Blackwell.

Wagner, E. and Newell, S. (2004) ' "Best" for whom? the tension between "best practice" ERP packages and diverse epistemic cultures in a university context', *Journal of Strategic Information Systems*, 13(4): 305–28.

Yates, J. and Orlikowski, W. (2002) 'Genre systems: structuring interaction through communication norms', *Journal of Business Communication*, 39(1): 13–35.

Yusef, Y., Gunasekaran, A. and Abthorpe, M.S. (2004) 'Enterprise information systems project implementation: A case study of ERP in Rolls-Royce', *International Journal of Production Economics*, 87: 251–66.

24

Cultural change
Complexity and diversity in institutional tempospaces

Sławomir Magala

> Probably the most dangerous thing about an academic education, at least in my own case, is that it enables my tendency to over-intellectualize stuff, to get lost in abstract thinking instead of simply paying attention to what's going on in front of me. (...) The really important kind of freedom involves attention, and awareness, and discipline, and effort, and being able truly to care about other people and to sacrifice for them, over and over, in myriad petty little unsexy ways, every day.
>
> (David Foster Wallace, 2009, 48: 120)

A philosophical introduction instead of a structured abstract

To begin a scholarly contribution to a volume edited by academic professionals with a quote from a novelist is a risky venture. Cultural change theory acquires a halo of a humanist – dreamy, soft, unmeasurable – investigation into an ongoing debate which will never end. Neither will it result in explaining why an expat feels proud of his white man's burden, while an illegal alien (often dark, female, young, undereducated and stereotyped), also labelled as "allochtone", an invisible migrant labour pool member – does not. Nor will it bring us closer to discovering why "diversity" is good for you, while "otherness" not necessarily so. My aim is simple. I want to explain why cultural change matters and what it consists of. It matters because institutional evolution is shaped primarily by the cultural framework of socialized, interacting individuals (this is the "culture" part of our communicative interactions). It consists of blueprints and scenarios, hints and tips, all of which may or may not be used against or for anybody in the course of more or less material interactions (this is the "society", or 'institution", or "organization" part of flows of social events before they become "histories"). It consists – the cultural change I will be talking about – of an enhanced, increased, empowered, expanded designing and constructing of *tempospaces* for reflection, including self-reflection.

To reflect is to reduce complexity. Complexity is what we are part of, what we experience, what we "taste" and what become aware of, if we become aware of a narrow channel of our routines. Complexity is what we encounter when we go on about any business, when we act, live and change – in other, more abstract words, when we shift and turn and twist and change, in short – evolve, co-evolve, or "e-volve". Reflecting upon complexities is what distinguishes us from computer programs for finding key words. Self-reflection is what distinguishes us from predictable performers of organizational routines, which had been designed without them and are being reiterated, reproduced, repeated – for instance for servicing large populations of simplified consumers, or members of constituencies or audiences. Leading a mature life of a responsible citizen and of a networked individual is a complex project subjected to an ongoing reflection and exposed to bouts of acute self-reflection. Harmonizing flows of millions of mature full lives (with dreams one had one night, for instance, or "new deals" or any other political visions, movements and routines, promising us that "yes, we can") is, has to be, must be, an unfinished project. Like enlightenment, it has no final solution. As a cultural evolution it has no known predetermined limits. As long as we follow routines (start working at 9.00 a.m., compare value in monetary units) and practice immediate adjustment (move left to let a new passenger step into an elevator, please, or grant vocational schools a right to issue bachelor diplomas, so that more people can enjoy higher education), no reflection is called upon. Or at least this is what one is promised in work, consumption, relaxation (trust us, we're competent and professional and we know what we are doing, while you do not need to; "you press the button, we do the rest", competent think tanks hold vigil so that you may doze off in front of your TV).

A "Fordist" assembly line worker tightened up the screws, which had been placed in front of him and dreamt of a weekend on a beach (standard package), a house in the suburbs (standardized construction) and retirement benefits (standardized life-cycle career-pathing on a mass scale). His (mostly "his" until world wars drew women to the ranks of a paid workforce) managers were supposed to reflect on everything – *until knowledge intensive competition drove reflection way down the corporate hierarchies*. Not being a boss does not free us from a necessity to reflect and lead an examined professional life. At the bottom of the organigram's pyramid one still has to reflect – operatives, workers, employees, rank-and-file members must diagnose, analyse, design, they have to make instant distinctions and follow up with appropriate decisions. Not only an unexamined life becomes difficult to live with the hyper-communications forcing comparisons (and triggering self-reflection as if a mirror was thrust into our faces ever so often) all the time (forcing us to answer the question: "Am I as attractive as this billboard person or this tabloid celebrity?") – also the unexamined work disappears (though one might argue that the more it disappears from plain view of multimedia, the more it goes underground in sweatshops, migrant labour pools and call centres or into the grey zone of domestics, sex workers and the like). The same goes for military work. A soldier in a Prussian formation of the eighteenth century or in a French column of the early nineteenth, led by ambitious and talented "high potential" by the name of Buonaparte, responded to his sergeant and companions by executing practiced drills – until high tech weapons and multiple "mobilities" drove the human "locus" of immediate decision-making way down the military ranks. Then – now – foot soldiers had to be empowered or they[1] would have died before the top of the chain of command reached a decision and communicated it all the way down. "Power to the people" has been translated into "empower-ment" – it became feasible, but did not exactly liberate the masses from the yoke of the social divisions of labour (the iron cage might have acquired velvet bars, but it is still with us).

The iron cage of social division of labour, and of many later inequalities (added to the ones we had started to learn to manage), has become – and this is the foremost cultural achievement in the last years of the twentieth and in the first decade of the twenty-first century – a moral embarrassment. There is an embarrassed silence at the very centre of organizational and managerial studies, where we find out that the cult of power, like hope, dies last and excessive reflection did not, until now, weaken it (power is relatively neglected in academic research, periodical ritual complaints notwithstanding, with more taboos wrapped around it than around sex). Pyramids, hierarchies, ranks, pecking orders and formal bureaucracies survive the networked realities. How do we explain their survival? Common sense does not offer any clue, except for "consilient" socio-biologists. Biology and sociobiology suggest a simple answer. A single bird in a flock of crows responds to the movements of those closest to him, and so does a single fish in a moving school, so let us allow a teenager on a disco floor or a car driver in a heavy traffic do the same (though we impose traffic lights and white stripes between lanes, speed limits and limited access zones). Disco managers are supposed to recognize the limits of the dancing floor's capacity, while city planners have to take care of sufficient highway capacities. But this regulation is not random, nor is it automatic. "Our" (reflective, democratic, responsible, sustainable, Western, progressive, modern, post-industrial) managers (aware of complexities and ebbs and flows of interpersonal events) empower those below them on differentiated pay-scales and heed Orwellian motto "always side with the underdog". They are supposed to genuinely believe that "power should go to the people". Provided – of course – that we define who belongs to "the people". For instance, educated workforce in the wealthiest member states of the UN does, inhabitants of Brazilian or Mexican slums and illegal immigrants – do not, even if they are indispensable for a national economy. They are as invisible as the beggars, the homeless, sometimes Roma "gypsies" and other categories of marginalized "others" – hidden from reflection, although perfectly visible in front of our eyes. "Our" "good" managers represent corporate citizens (as if they were elected politicians, though they are not) and – presumably, hopefully – coach them to perform better (to be able to exercise judgment, to be able to reflect, to hone their intellectual skills). We tend to take pride in treating employees in a more responsible, sustainable manner than managers of the past. The latter presumably believed only the econometrists' tales, full of statistical sound and fury, cared only about anonymous shareholders, and had been driven only by profits' size on the annual report sheets. Cultural change means there is no return to business reporting blind to ecology, global inequalities, social and cultural capital and gender issues.[2]

Reflexive modernization in a nutshell

This is the way they never were (nor are), of course. Nowadays, even the least critical student of the cheapest MBA programme cannot forget that complexity kicked in shortly after the US astronauts set foot on the moon and the US students and Vietnamese peasants ruined the reputation of McNamara's one and only crew of "the best and the brightest", and no matter how hard the neoconservatives blamed the flower power generation for everything that went wrong with anything western – they failed to change the cultural climate and return to the "good old values". Knowledge intensive companies, with sceptical and cynical professionals became the rule rather than exception. Routines died more quickly and so the new ones had to be discovered, invented, or imported from unexpected quarters (and they had to be revised, updated and changed much more frequently than ever before). Reflective modernization[3] at a lottery of global encounters randomizing the most regular patterns of activities into chaotic ebbs and flows did not allow parking the cultural change at the "back to square one" parking lot. Some flows are still a mystery to us and we are becoming aware of their consequences very slowly, even reluctantly. What are – for instance – long-term consequences of a sudden explosion of female migrant labour leaving children in the Philippines to grandparents, spouses or relatives? Sociological reports may not be forthcoming through peer reviews in top publications, but films of a Mexican director, Alejandro González Iñárritu, for instance, who created both *Amores Perros* and *Babel*, send powerful signals to the public sphere (where the Bagdad war story of *The Hurt Locker* gets twice the number of Oscars gained by *Avatar*, a nicely escapist SF cartoon-like fantasy). Who wants to know what percentage of Manila teenagers will suffer from lack of proper socialization, because yuppies in Seattle or Boston can pluck their young mothers away for underpaid and under-regulated domestic services of baby-sitting, cleaning, cooking, ironing, gardening and the like? What are the consequences of attracting the Indian (educated & young) labour pool generation to call centres, where they make enough money to emancipate themselves from the traditional family controls imposed traditionally on their sexual behaviour? Do we really refuse to follow the insights from *Slumdog Millionaire* to the – presumably – bitter research results? Enough, let us limit ourselves to an obvious cultural change in our institutional environment. Complexity of a self-reflexive analysis of a contemporary university resulted from passing three points of no return, which emerged as rock formations from the tectonic movements of the past centuries, and which contributed to the pressure to increase the standards of self-reflexive evaluation. They have influenced the current cultural climate – in fact, they changed it:

> *Social production of knowledge is heading towards an accelerated rate of growth and increased hybridization of its disseminating channels* preached by Open Access, Wikipedia and Bottom-Up Ex-Post Peer Review (hence the legitimizing of research products cannot be linked to a single dimension, criterion or accreditation network). *We have to reflect more, not less, on our research methods. Even our establishments, the think tanks of "straight members of establishments" do.*
>
> *Social dissemination of the entry tickets to knowledge, i.e. universal education is heading towards a dramatic increase* in the size and dynamics of educational institutional complexes, with universities getting ready for a new expansion into a hyper-diversity alliance (hence the absolute growth of graduate populations). *We have to reflect on our educational and communicative strategies. Even our most conservative colleagues (schools of business) and periodicals' publishing crews (structured abstracts, anyone?) do.*
>
> Academic communities can produce knowledge, but if media, educators and trainers, and the consulting go-betweens do not communicate it in relevant contexts and formats (again, the many uses of structured abstracts) – societies are facing new challenges and conflicts with no assistance from professionals in training for a continuous reflection. Journalists and media professionals increasingly often turn to the academics for a diagnosis, for specific guidance, for a concrete advice. *Multimedia do not feed off commissioned academic expertise as if they were parasites on a healthy body of knowledge – they are part and parcel of the process of making the very knowledge relevant, applicable and useful.* They merge, form joint ventures with academic professionals, network and design common projects. Members of academic professional communities have to reflect on their broader responsibilities and sustainability of our researched dreams. *We have to recognize our civic obligations and look for allies among the artists and humanists as well as media professionals, not only corporate sponsors.*

Dealing with growing complexities of the post-standardization period in social development requires more diversity in the academic environments. Diversity – as we begin to understand – breeds creativity, and creativity further fuels demand for reflection. Self-reflection is no exception. Institutions shake up, we do not want them to be just stirred by organizational rituals. Capacity for self-reflection dragged out of the bureaucratic confines of academia into the public sphere and multi-mediated open access "spaces" – here is where we could forge a real bond between us, fellow academics and them, non-academic fellow citizens, in order to make us feel truly at home in the socially transformed universe. The Santa Fe school called for feeling at home in the universe. What about trying to be at home in a social universe with different cultural climate zones subtly interfering with our actions?

Cultural climate changes and the emergent communities of sense

> Making fictions does not mean telling stories. It means undoing and rearticulating the connections between signs and images, images and times, or signs and space that frame the existing sense of reality. Fiction invents new communities of sense: that is to say, new trajectories between what can be seen, what can be said, and what can be done. It blurs over the distribution of places and competences, which means that it also blurs over the very borders of defining its own activity; doing art means displacing the borders of art, just as doing politics means displacing the borders of what is recognized as the sphere of the political.
>
> (Ranciere, 2009: 49)

If culture was a nation-state and had a pavilion at a world expo, the art section of culture would have been granted the rights to speak for the rest of cultural domains. One of the favourite social spaces for encouraging self-reflection has always been provided by aesthetic communications – supplied by visual artists, performance artists or literary masters – poets, novelists, essayists and critics, usually labelled "humanists" and "creative artists". Their activities, already growing and expanding ever since the Gutenberg galaxy started exploding, acquired a new boost with the arrival of the "Googled", viral, digital, multi-mediated aesthetic games. Art has become available instantly: David Hockney, an established painter, uses the iPhone to "paint" a work of visual arts, by moving his finger through the touch-screen. What results is a digital construction resembling a "painting", but a strange one – the one which never saw paint at all and appears under his fingers on the screen of his portable, versatile phone cum digital canvas. Then he e-mails this newly created work of visual art to a hundred or so friends. One can imagine that one day all of them come up with excellent printouts, framed and all, and ask for a signature of the artist. It is not only that a choice of techniques of, say, visual presentation, becomes broader. It is not only that an installation, a happening, a performance, a digital recording replace the solid object of art as a unique material "concretization" of a creative project. It is also the provocative, active, searching change of the playing field during the game of aesthetic communication, which adds to the complexity of the cultural games played in the twenty-first century. Complexity and complex reflexive activities we apply to reduce, master, control, appease her – is on her (its?) way towards becoming the next key word in public discourse. Complexity-born, self-corrective reflexivity becomes visible, audible and traceable in public and private communications (even the makers of the Hollywood movies do not shy away from titles like *It's Complicated*).

Complexity, the term, the word, the concept – begins to be quoted and creatively woven into all sorts of communication commodities. Scholarly dissertations, scientific research reports, political statements, social appeals, media "infotainment" packages, news items, PR campaign documents, commercial advertising slogans and messages – all manifest, signal, tackle, take complexities into account, and in all of them we can usually trace attempts to inject a self-corrective, self-reflective "chip" (to be activated when contingencies emerge). Complex reflexive evaluations with subversive undertones can be hidden – as guns once were – in the "flowers"[4] of cultural contents supplied by multimedia. Local complexities are linked by satellites and "fed" into truly global village chain of high-tech tam-tams. Screens, pages, loudspeakers, laptops and iPhones never tire announcing "events" generated by creative industries or growing on the margins (as Bill Wasik's "flash mobs")[5] of the humming virtual, viral "spatiotemporal windows of opportunity". Most contemporary creative artists, the Bill Viola's, the Krzysztof Wodiczko's, most contemporary visual arts events (Venice Biennale, Kassels Documenta, NYC Armory

Show – yes, commercial art galleries' fair also acquires aesthetic legitimacies on a par with purely aesthetic and publicly performative ones) either deal with cultural weather forecasts directly or hint at complex cultural climate changes as the major source of challenging emergencies, contingencies and unpredictable developments. Most of these platforms of aesthetic communication create new complexities as they go along. They deal with these complexities by establishing new rules of the communicative, aesthetic, cultural games – games of self-reflexive ongoing modification and renegotiation of the rules of further communication and further evaluation.

The arrival of this ability to change the rules, not just humbly subject oneself to their supreme and unquestioned authority – this arrival announces a new phase in the ever more sophisticated game of reducing complexity in order to subject it to a reflexive scrutiny.

Cognitive reduction, from Plato, through Descartes to Husserl and most recently to Kolakowski, Derrida, Taylor and Habermas, always meant "taking" "concepts" ("ideas", "images", "thoughts", "representations") into imagined brackets, lifting them from their usual contexts, as if they were cars, whose underside had to be examined by a garage mechanic. Today, we do not rest satisfied with a *cognitive reduction* – a concept of an intelligence, measured by IQ is not enough. We would also like to subject our concepts and ideas to an emotional, interactive, interpersonal, social, cultural and probably many more other types of reduction. Look at the concept of intelligence – IQ has been followed by emotional intelligence, social intelligence, cultural capital, networking skills and many other theoretical concepts honing our ability to reduce the complex flows of events in order to reflect on our ability to modify the outcomes, to twist or bend reality's flow according to our negotiable desires.

This shift towards the in-built multidimensional reflexivity has been grasped by sociologists of culture, who took the concept of language games (intuitively introduced by Wittgenstein) seriously and developed it in order to explain the new, postmodernist reflexive modernization, the one which makes a self-reflexive creative intervention and change in the routine rules of social games central to our theoretical understanding of "social life", "cultural dynamics", "knowledge intensive organizations", "information-led economies", and the like. Reflexive guidance of complex processes is at the very core of unfinished, risky projects (climate control, poverty eradication, management of inequalities). Designing, articulating and implementing these risky projects provides the only chance we have to influence the course of events – they are already replacing the "royal road" to some kind of a "salvation" and some type of "the end of history", both of which turned out to be fairly illusory. In order to reduce their complexity to manageable sizes and proportions, we have to reflect on our communicative games, thus tracing the emergence of the imaginable projects during the present "linguistic turn" in the humanities, followed by the "visual turn":

> Language does not derive from semiotic difference, which cannot generate a satisfactory notion of meaning. Rather, language has meaning only because of the indexical properties of its use. No signs exist without narratives, even those that appear to be wholly iconic.[6] Aesthetic reflection in the current period is paradoxical in that its reflexivity has characteristically been deployed in such a way as to subvert, or place in question, the very narrative forms that it presumes.

(Giddens in Beck et al., 1994: 197)

Giddens, who has served as one of the advisors to Tony Blair, is a sociologist, and managerial sciences are under-socialized and less sociology-saturated (hence fairly indifferent to the sociology of organizations, which had traditionally been linked to the Marxian and other radically socialist paradigms), then they should have been in the first place. Managerial sciences tend to be "over-psyched" or excessively "psychology-saturated" (since consultants and academic trainers tend to focus on the top or upper-middle managerial cadres, which offer higher fees and more stable business). Thus it is not very frequently that we notice demands to increase reflexivity in the academic bureaucracies (and when it does happen, it is usually limited in scope and reserved for the upper levels of management). Dave Boje's concept of "antenarrating" could belong to very rare exceptions, provided it does not remain restricted to a single university (state university of New Mexico in Las Cruces) or a single network of academic professionals (say, a club of sc'MOI, or Standing Conference on Management and Organization Inquiry"). His concept of an "antenarrative" meets the criteria spelled out by Giddens, since Boje (*expressis verbis*) calls for subvertion of the narrative forms of academic communications controlled by the university bureaucracies and professional accreditation bodies certifying the academic institutions and ranking their merits:

> Antenarrating means noticing multiple bets on the future, and multiple now-choices before the narrative managerial, administered order of a standardized, mechanical time, and a global spatial colonizing occurs as the only antenarrative potentiality. If there is a multiplicity of temporalities interacting with a multiplicity of specialties, then we get more vertigo from such Academic Reflexivity.
>
> (Boje, 2009: 2)

Institutional reduction of complexity – consequences of cultural change

> We need art to amplify parts of ourselves into larger, more complete wholes. When successful, artists and humanist critics help make sense of what was unseen. We need art (and some need religion) to magnify what is obscure in us into something visible, tangible, and real to all of us. That counts, I suggest, as progress.
>
> (Gay, 2009: 198)

Cognitive reduction is not alone – the pyramids and irrational respect for powers that be do not survive unharmed the present cultural climate of empowerment.[7] The institutional reduction of complexity follows a reflection on the "core competence" and the raison d'être of an institution. Hospitals, airlines and universities, all went down the same institutional transformation road following *the egalitarian turn in cultural climate*. It did not seem revolutionary, but produced remarkable results. When the twentieth century entered its last decades, the rising costs of the health care (aggravated by the "greying" of most populations), a gradual expansion of access to higher education (aggravated by the demands of the knowledge economy), and the increase of global mobility (tourists, migrant labour, refugees, expats, employees of international organizations, soldiers, etc. aggravated by globalization) made managers and academics alike inspect their institutional scaffoldings. It soon became clear that the feudal privileges of the medical doctors, the aircraft pilots or tenured university professors will not survive. The underlying vision of a proper hospital as a pyramid with a medical doctor on the top, the registered nurses in the middle, the auxiliary personnel in the lower middle regions of the pyramid and patients at the bottom, humbly begging for therapy and subjected to the barracks-like discipline – this vision had to go. The underlying vision of a proper airline pyramid with pilots as the elite (after all, the ability to fly an airplane was what mattered most, wasn't it?), marketing managers and air controllers in the middle and stewardesses with luggage handlers in the lower middle, still on top of a mass of passengers – was flawed. The vision of the universities with tenured professors on the top, associate and assistant teachers/researchers in the middle, PhD students and secretaries in the lower middle and the huge river of students flowing at the bottom of the pyramid – this vision had to go.

In all three cases, reflection on core activities and competencies resulted in a new organizational order, with a patient, a passenger and a student as the focus of institutional activities, profiting from a cultural tsunami of egalitarian claims. Organizations started wrapping themselves up around their target populations. The population of patients, the constituency of passengers, the audience and the community of students – all of them became the "corporate citizens"[8] around whom all activities had to be reinvented and re-clustered. It does not matter that a pilot can fly an airplane if there is no passenger willing to fly and the fuel costs exceed the ticket revenues. It does not matter that a surgeon can operate if no patient will visit his clinic or no insurance company will foot the bill for an operation. It does not matter that a university professor has a profound knowledge of some domain researched by his peers and himself – if no students are willing to listen and no government is willing to finance the programmes. This loss of elite status bred resentment – for instance, tenured university professors refused to collaborate with educational managers in shaping their educational offers, claiming far superior and unique expertise and a maestro status. They (we) opposed the introduction of professional deans from outside of the faculty (no elected colleagues – *primus inter pares* – but an empowered manager imposed by the boards of directors). They (we) resented the negotiations of the format and content of the curriculum. The reduction of complexity followed a reflection and an upgrading of the client/patient/passenger/student audience-constituency.

Sitting in the meetings of academic department heads of a medium-sized EU university I have tired of listening to the passionate pleas for a nostalgic defence of the former organizational hierarchies, usually under the banners of "power back to the fee earners" (us, researching and educating academics, the only ones who really matter in producing and disseminating knowledge), and usually at the expense of "fee burners" (the marketing, communications, managerial and auxiliary staff, coordinators, learning consultants, librarians, ICT people, secretaries, managers – basically anybody who was not a tenured professor with a publishing and teaching record and a toga in the closet).

The institutional reduction of complexity involved the reflexive, critical analysis of the hidden costs of preserving class privileges of medical doctors, tenured academic professors and aircraft pilots. Reflexive analysis of these privileges as one of the elements of complexity had emerged during a reflection on an entire institution viewed as a service organization, though not surprisingly this critical observation did not figure prominently in the self-reflection of the three abovementioned professional groups.[9] Recognition and reconciliation with this loss of status usually assumes the form of a nostalgic and sentimental response (Rieff's "Fellow Teachers" comes to mind and the appeal to reverse the decline of the humanities, undermined by criticism unbound, as exemplified by strategies of suspicion in Freud, and so does Khurana's "From Higher Aims to Hired Hands"), but sometimes it does result in an "institutional pragmatism":

> Institutional pragmatism thus means, for me, recognizing the University today, for what it is: an institution that is losing its need to make transcendental claims for its function. A University is no longer simply modern, insofar as it no longer needs a grand narrative of culture in order to work. As a bureaucratic institution of excellence, it can incorporate a very high degree of internal variety without requiring its multiplicity of diverse idioms to

be unified into an ideological whole. Their unification is no longer a matter of ideology but of their exchange value within an expanded market.

(Readings, 1996: 168)

I do not think that a loss of status once conferred on a professional in a corporate bureaucracy by the acquisition of a higher education within a stable system of an educational "preparation" for further organizational upward mobility should be nostalgically regretted. Neither should we bemoan the accompanying loss of status of the conferring elites (ourselves). Institutional pragmatism is already forcing us, academic professionals, to go beyond a simplified solution, which Khurana observed in the Cold War USA (Ford Foundation's programme to improve doctoral studies in business and economics launched in 1955), and which was simply reduced to the increased production of PhDs in business administration and to the saturation of the management school curriculum with quantitative analysis and behavioural sciences. Cognitive reduction to quantitative paradigm in behavioural sciences did not work then and does not work now (for instance, behavioural finance analyses did not help us either foresee or deal with the financial meltdown of 2008, neither did they produce breakthroughs in coaching and training techniques). By the same token, however, neither do the qualitative counterrevolutions work out in the academic communities. The last attempt to acquire an ideological "cover" of this paradigmatic hue, namely the loose philosophy of "postmodernism", failed to catch on or lost specificity and impact. What remains is not the ruined university, but far more diverse and differentiated academic communities, whose members have less automatically high status, but are more aware of the significant role played by the arts and humanities in honing our evaluating skills. We appear to agree – at least tacitly – on diversity and ongoing negotiation of quality (cf. Boltanski and Thevenot, 2006), we begin to recognize the need to involve aesthetic values in professional rankings (architects according to Larson, 1993) and we are starting to record antenarratives, alternative reflections on complexities we shall have to face. Is it a beginning of a more flexible, contingent and unpredictable organizational *temposcape* (cf. Magala, 2010: 255) of the presumably ruined university? Is it through these emergent organizational tempospaces in the more egalitarian climate that we, the academic professionals with a taste for a social engagement and aesthetic experiments, move – recombining our webs of meaning (culture) and webs of relations (society) and reflecting on the new complexities waiting for our reflexive interventions, for a cultural change to happen, to be designed, implemented and reflected upon again and again?

Two results of the cultural climate change, still waiting for its Copenhagen summit to be announced, are obvious: change drivers are becoming "footless", international, even global (for instance a sense of urgency in regulating the banking sector after the 2008 meltdown of mortgage market) and the emergent challenges of a sustainable development (no government and no business organization can claim a right to define the framework for the public discussion; most constituencies reject the Davos celebrity show as well as the usual UN or IMF vaudevilles), are incorporated in the guiding documents of most organizations requiring a legitimate recognition (hence ultimately in the hands and hearts and minds of the Seattle, Genua or Puerto Allegro demonstrators). Even mainstream handbooks of organizational change finish with a pious comment that: "moral awareness needs to be defined and cultivated as a change initiative". (Grieves, 2010: 392). So be it. Not bad for a culture change.

Notes

1 Foot soldiers tended to be male only – but as of the present writing even the US Navy admitted female sailors aboard nuclear submarines, thus breaking one of the longest preserved gender taboos.

2 The idea of a cognitive and interactional reduction of complexity and uncertainty has been first suggested by Max Boisot in an unpublished paper (which he had read at a seminar in Rotterdam School of Management in 2008). Boisot thought that a Gutenberg press allowed to reduce all future possible texts to 24 movable printing blocks, and thus allowed for disseminating literacy and education, fuelling social growth. The Chinese had the print, but it was irreducible to a few cheaply remixed elements, and thus they had to focus on reducing uncertainty and increasing interactional trust through ethical principles of all future possible interactions (interactional reduction) rather than through rapidly disseminated instructions (cognitive reduction).

3 The term "reflexive modernization" has been introduced in 1994 by Beck, Giddens and Lasch in their Stanford publication (Beck et al., 1994).

4 The revolutionary message of Beethoven's music was famously compared to "guns hidden in flowers".

5 "How much buzz one could create about an event whose only point was buzz, a show whose audience was itself only a show"(Wasik, 2009: 23).

6 This is why Sontag has famously stated "A photograph is not an opinion. Or is it?" and hesitated before answering it. She finally did, in a very ambiguous way (cf. Sontag, 2001: 238), but not without demonstrating difficulties of choosing between an iconic and a narrative interpretation of a photographic image.

7 The failure of the climate top in Copenhagen in December 2009 was due, among others, to the firm stand of the representatives of the smaller or weaker but vitally interested parties, for instance, the Association of Small Island States, sub-Saharan African countries, or Bangladesh (exposed with its delta to the floods). The managerial action of the organizers was to bypass them, trying to work out the deal between the largest states (USA, China, India) and to prevent most legally invited ecological activists from entering the main conference hall where Obama spoke (isolating them under a large beamer screen in a separate location).

8 Yes, the very concept of a "corporate citizen" smells of PR. But even if it is a lip service, a service it is.

9 Recent self-reflection on what do tenured academics do when they are tenured can be found in a book by the French sociologist of culture at Harvard, Michele Lamont, who wrote "How Professors Think" (Lamont, 2009). Her merit is in pointing out that professionals, and academics in peer review commissions are no exception, usually conflate judgments of quality (merit) with judgments of taste. My conclusion is that this requires a better orientation in humanities (which hone moral and aesthetic taste) if we are to tackle the above conflation. Her conclusion is that we should have a better understanding of evaluation rules and procedures in "peer review journals, university presses, tenure review committees, or college admissions, as well as athletic, artistic or financial fields" (Lamont, 2009: 248).

References

Beck, Ulrich, Giddens, Anthony, Lasch, Scott, 1994, *Reflexive Modernization. Politics, Tradition and Aesthetics in the Modern Social Order*, Cambridge, Polity Press.

Boje, David, 2009, "Academic Reflexivity: Oxymoron and Vertigo", position paper posted on 13 October 2009 on the website of Standing Conference on Management and Organization Inquiry (sc'MOI).

Boltanski, Luc and Thevenot, Laurent, 2006, *On Justification. Economies of Worth*, Princeton and Oxford, Princeton University Press.

Gay, Volney, 2009, *Progress and Values in the Humanities. Comparing Culture and Science*, New York, Columbia University Press.

Grieves, Jim, 2010, *Organizational Change. Themes and Issues*, Oxford and New York, Oxford University Press.

Khurana, Rakesh, 2007, *From Higher Aims to Hired Hands. The Social Transformation of American Business Schools and the Unfulfilled Promise of Management as a Profession*, Princeton and Oxford, Princeton University Press.

Lamont, Michele, 2009, *How Professors Think. Inside the Curious World of Academic Judgment*, Cambridge, MA and London, Harvard University Press.

Larson, Magali Sarfatti, 1993, *Behind the Modern Façade. Architectural Change in Late Twentieth Century America*, Berkeley, Los Angeles, London, University of California Press.

Magala, Slawomir, 2010, "Perplexing Images: Relational Identities in Cultural *Tempospaces*", in Sid Lowe (ed.), *Managing in Changing Times: A Guide for Perplexed Manager*, Los Angeles, London, New Delhi, Singapore, Washington, DC, Response Books (SAGE).

Ranciere, Jacques, 2009, "Contemporary Art and the Politics of Aesthetics", in Berth, Hinderlither, William Kaizen, Vered Maimon, Jaleh Mansoor, and Seth McCormick (eds) *Communities of Sense. Rethinking Aesthetics and Politics*, Durham, NC and London, Duke University Press.

Readings, Bill, 1996, *The University in Ruins*, Cambridge, MA and London, Harvard University Press.

Rieff, Philip, 1985, *Fellow Teachers. Of Culture and Its Second Death*, Chicago, University of Chicago Press (first edition, Faber & Faber, London & New York, 1975).

Sontag, Susan, 2001, *Where the Stress Falls*, New York, Farrar, Straus & Giroux.

Wallace, David Foster, 2009, *This is Water. Some Thoughts, Delivered on a Significant Occasion, about Living a Compassionate Life*, New York, Boston & London, Little, Brown & Company.

Wasik, Bill, 2009, *And Then There is This. How Stories Live and Die in Viral Culture*, New York, Viking.

25

Changing attitudes to employee attitudes to change
From resistance to ambivalence and ambiguity

Stephen Procter and Julian Randall

Introduction

This chapter examines the issue of employee attitudes to change. We identify three broad phases in the way in which employee attitudes have been dealt with. Early work on the management of change took the view that, on the whole, employees will be resistant to change. The task for managers was thus seen as identifying and avoiding any factors that might aggravate this tendency.

As the study of change intensified as it moved into the 1990s, it became clear that this rather one-dimensional view of employee attitudes was no longer adequate. Against the background of increased interest at what was happening at the level of the workplace, attention shifted to the idea that different groups of employees will have different attitudes to change. The task then for managers was to develop a range of strategies to deal with these different attitudes. Where academic work was not so helpful, however, was in determining precisely what these different attitudes were and, behind this, identifying the factors that might help predict them.

The third and most recent wave of interest has retained the idea of differences in attitude, but has focussed on the idea that these exist within, rather than between, individuals. In particular, the idea has been developed that individuals are likely to have an attitude of ambivalence towards organizational change. From a management point of view, this highlights the importance of understanding and acting upon the process by which employees make sense of change. This can be very difficult, especially when, as a number of authors stress, the changes about which employees are ambivalent are themselves quite ambiguous.

Employee resistance to change

The notion of employee resistance is a powerful one. From the beginning of the explicit consideration of the management of change in organizations, it was an idea that came to dominate thinking about the attitude and behaviour of employees. This kind of approach is well captured in the *Harvard Business Review* article of Kotter and Schlesinger (1979). They take for granted the pervasiveness of resistance: their concerns are with explaining its existence and dealing with its effects. There are, they argue, four main reasons why people resist change: the simple fear of losing something of value, which can lead to the adoption of self-interested political behaviour; misunderstanding, which often stems from a lack of trust between management and employees; different assessments of the situation, in which employees might emphasize the costs of change – to the organization as well as to themselves; and a low tolerance for change, which can result from fears that people will not be able to provide what is expected of them.

Having diagnosed the problem, the issue then is how managers can deal with it. For Kotter and Schlesinger, there are six ways in which resistance can be dealt with: education and communication, participation and involvement, facilitation and support, negotiation and agreement, manipulation and co-optation and, finally, explicit coercion. The choice between these should be based on a contingency approach: 'The most common mistake mangers make,' they argue (1979: 112, emphasis in original), 'is to use only one approach of a limited set of them *regardless of the situation*.' Education and communication are most appropriate when resistance is based on lack of information, for example, while participation and involvement should be used when the success of change depends on the commitment rather than simply the compliance of employees.

In looking at how the idea of resistance to change came to dominate thinking in this area, the study by Coch and French (1948) provides a conventional starting point, providing, as it did, a focus for debate for over thirty years. Their field experiment involved four groups of workers in a US plant manufacturing pyjamas. The workers in each group were subjected to a small change in their working methods, the difference between groups being the degree of participation the workers were given in the implementation of the change. The researchers took changes in the groups' output levels as the main indicator of resistance to change, although they also considered such things as quit rates and more direct signs of hostility. The major conclusion from the study was that resistance to change could be avoided by involving workers in the implementation. Where participation had been 'total', for example, only a small drop-off in production was recorded and output quite quickly exceeded its pre-change level; in the 'no-participation' group, output dropped significantly and stayed at this level for some time.

Although on the face of it this was a fairly clear-cut result, providing a correspondingly clear implication for management, a number of other authors have taken issue with Coch and French's interpretation of their own findings. Lawrence (1954), for example, argued that the study's approach to the idea of participation was too narrow and mechanical. Whether employees felt involved in the organization's decision-making, he argued, would depend much more on their broader, long-term experience of the company's management rather than on being allocated to one group rather than another in the field experiment. The factory had been portrayed in the original study as one characterized by an open and trusting relationship between management and employees. In these circumstances, argued Lawrence, the members of the 'no participation' group would have experienced a degree of dissonance between the way in which they were usually managed and the way in which they were being treated for experimental purposes; those in the 'full participation' group, on the other hand, would have experienced little if anything 'new' at all.

In Lawrence's interpretation, Coch and French had focused on the 'technical' aspects of change – the change in working methods – to the neglect of its social aspects. What was happening in the 'no participation' group, maintained Lawrence, was that employees were experiencing a threat to the social relations upon which they relied to do their work; in the 'full participation' group no such threat was perceived, and the technical change to their working methods could easily be accommodated. Lawrence supported this conclusion with examples of research stressing the importance of the relationship between shop-floor employees and the staff specialists whose job it was to identify and introduce changes in the work they did. Employee participation, he argued, 'will never work so long as it is treated as a device to get somebody else to do what you want him to do' (1954: 56).

Bartlem and Locke (1981) also questioned the emphasis Coch and French had placed on the role of employee participation in overcoming resistance to change. They argued that in the design of the experiment, the degree of participation was not the only difference between the groups of employees. The availability of training was another factor; as too was the way in which the changes were justified. Bartlem and Locke's own interpretation settled instead on 'the perceived fairness of the (new) pay rates as the main factor responsible for the positive results' (1981: 564).

Thus although there was some discussion over what considerations were most important to employees and, as a result, what managers should do to address these, the focus on the idea of resistance was retained. In the *Harvard Business Review* as late as 2001 Kegan and Lahey (2001) based an article around setting out 'the real reason people won't change'. Their argument was that although individuals might be committed to change, they might have a 'competing commitment' sustained by a 'big assumption'. Overcoming the resulting 'immunity' to change therefore involves uncovering what these commitments are and identifying what big assumptions underlie them, providing the means by which individuals can understand their own 'psychological dynamics' and modify their behaviour.

But it was not just at an organizational level that resistance came to be seen as major problem. In the UK context it came to be seen as the main factor in the under-performance of the economy as a whole. In his account of this viewpoint, which he called the 'British worker question', Theo Nichols (1986) showed how deeply embedded the association between worker attitude and resistance had become. He demonstrated, moreover, how many people blamed such attitudes for the UK's long-term relative economic decline. Nichols' main concern was to attack this idea – almost, as he saw it, this assumption – that the UK's post-war economic decline was the result of workers' attitudes and effort. This idea had been evident in a whole series of so-called 'productivity studies', which sought to explain why, relative to other countries, productivity in the UK had grown so slowly.

Because Pratten's (1976) comparison of productivity differences within international companies appeared to offer the most systematic analysis of the various productivity studies, it was here that Nichols concentrated his attention. This study did use information on working practices, he conceded, but this had been derived not from direct observation but from investigations undertaken by management within each part of the company. More than this, productivity measurements were based not on physical product per employee but on various figures provided by management, some of which were little more than non-quantitative comparisons. Taken together with questions about the representativeness of Pratten's sample, 'it now appears,' said Nichols (1986: 60), 'that the whole investigation is in fact beset by an ABC of elementary flaws and faults, the consequences of which for his research generally could be profound'.

While Nichols' approach was to identify the weaknesses in the work based on the assumption of worker resistance, his conclusions were given more positive support from work that attempted a more direct assessment of employee attitude to change. A specific concern was the reaction to the widespread introduction of microelectronic technologies into the workplace, and this provided a major theme of the second of the authoritative Workplace Industrial Relations Survey (WIRS) series, undertaken in 1984. In their analysis of the WIRS data Daniel and Hogarth (1990) examined the question of worker reaction to technical change. They argued first of all that there is in general a presumption that workers will resist change. Thus even those studies that had found little evidence for such resistance (Northcott et al. 1985) are chided for failing even to consider the possibility that workers might support and even promote technological change.

Concentrating on the effects of new microelectronic technologies, Daniel and Hogarth distinguished between organizational and technical change. While both involved changes to work organization and working practices, technical change was defined as having taken place when these were accompanied by the introduction of new plant, machinery or equipment. What Daniel and Hogarth found was that while organizational change 'provoked mixed reactions and, on balance…was resisted more often than it was supported' (1990: 86), technical change was on the whole supported. 'Overall,' they conclude, 'the introduction of new technology tended to be associated with success' (Daniel and Hogarth 1990: 90).

These basic findings were the subject of a later, more detailed analysis. Hogarth (1993) concentrated on case studies of 14 companies drawn from the WIRS sample. In looking at the resistance to organizational change he concluded that a major consideration was the way in which change was approached by management. On the whole, management's concerns were narrowly economic: they failed to consider the effect of change on the quality of the workforce's jobs. Trade unions were involved at a late stage in implementation. Their views carried little weight overall, but in the few cases where management did take into account the implications of change for the content of jobs, the change was much better received. These considerations did not apply to technical change. Union involvement in technical change was even more limited than in organizational change: 'because new technology was introduced into existing organization, authority and social structures in the workplace, there were few issues around which the unions could coalesce and oppose the change' (Hogarth 1993: 204). Despite this, and for the reasons outlined above, technical change received active support from the workforce.

In emphasizing the argument that workers might positively welcome change, work such as Hogarth's opened up possibilities beyond the simple equation of employee attitude with employee resistance. At the same time, however, it could be argued that they do not go far in this. What they provide can be seen as a simple mirror-image of the 'resistant worker' view: workers might be placed at a different point on the scale, but it is still essentially the same scale, with high levels of acceptance being the same thing as low levels of resistance. While it would be a mistake to impose too rigid a periodization on the development of thinking in this area, it is really from the mid-1990s onwards that we can discern a move towards providing a more nuanced picture of employee attitudes.

Differentiation in employee attitudes to change

Part of the emergence of a more differentiated perspective on employee attitudes to change is associated with changing emphases in approaches to research. Although the relationship between research method and research findings is a complex one (see, for example, Morris and Wood, 1991), it can come as little surprise that a more complex and process-based picture of employee perspectives came out of qualitative, in-depth research in individual organizations or workplaces. Some studies have focused on identifiable groups of workers to see what distinguishes reactions in particular circumstances. Ogbonna and Wilkinson (2003), for example, looked at the experience of middle managers in a grocery retailing company, arguing that these managers were in a unique position in being both the agents and the subjects of cultural change.

More generally, however, studies have tried to identify a range of different attitudes that employees might take. Knights and McCabe's (2000) study of teamworking in a UK-based automotive manufacturing company divides employees' experiences into three categories: the bewitched, who tended to follow the company line and portray teamworking in a positive manner; the bothered, who resented the intrusion of teamworking into what they considered their private lives and who were worried by colleagues who they saw as having been taken in; and the bewildered, who dismissed teamworking as something without substance.

369

What management wanted from teamworking – a pride in work, in the product and in the organization – was widely seen as something which employees felt they had always exhibited but which management had not properly acknowledged.

Harris and Ogbonna (1998) approached this question in a more structured way. Their study of employee response in two case study organizations led to their identifying two variables as important: one of these was simply employees' willingness to change, but the other, subcultural strength – the strength of different cultures within each organization – related more to the *ability* to resist. Each of the two variables was given three values – high, medium and low – and this in turn allowed Harris and Ogbonna to identify nine different combinations. Some of these were quite straightforward. Where willingness to change was high but sub-cultural strength was low, this gave rise to the 'active acceptance' of change; where, on the other hand, willingness to change was low but sub-cultural strength high, we have 'active rejection'. In between these, where both variables were categorised as 'medium', employees were characterized as experiencing 'dissonance'.

These three categories of Harris and Ogbonna's classification equate roughly with Knights and McCabe's bewitched-bothered-bewildered distinction, and it is elsewhere on their matrix that we can find more interesting responses. To capture these, Harris and Ogbonna use the concepts of 'reinvention' and 'reinterpretation'. In cases where sub-cultural strength was low and there was no great willingness to change, it was 'reinvention' that was observed. This was a process by which 'existing cultural attributes are recycled so that, superficially, they appear to be aligned with the newly espoused culture … the camouflage of past values under the veneer of adopted cultural attributes' (1998: 84–85). Where sub-cultural strength was high, on the other hand, and there was some degree of willingness to change, the process observed was 'reinvention': 'a tendency to translate the espoused organizational culture in a manner which … results in the development of modified values and behaviour which are consistent with both the existing and the espoused culture' (1998: 87).

While it might be argued that Harris and Ogbonna have to work very hard in order to draw out this conceptual classification from their empirical data, we can see in it an attempt not only to provide a wider range of possible employee responses but also to move away from the idea that, for employees, change is something that they simply respond or react to. The idea that employees can and do play a more active role in the shaping of change, is one that has been taken up by a number of other authors. Dawson's (1991) examination of the shift to human-centred manufacturing in the Australian automotive industry, for example, showed how workers began to anticipate change, which in turn put pressure on management to maintain the momentum of workplace reform.

In a similar vein McKinlay and Taylor (1996) were able to demonstrate how, in a Scottish electronics plant, a group of workers was able to exploit a company-initiated move towards an empowering, team-based culture. They did this by taking the initiative's underlying principles and turning them back against the management. Rejecting the idea that the kind of 'concertive' control Barker (1993) identified will always and everywhere be effective, they show how, for example, a system of peer review was subverted by employees on the grounds that if the teams were making their targets, individual members should not be singled out for criticism. Likewise, employee opposition to being obliged to make the decision as to whether temporary employees in their team should be made permanent was, say McKinlay and Taylor, 'articulated *through* the empowerment ideology' (1996: 289–90).

What these studies give us, therefore, is not just a broader range of possible employee responses, but also the suggestion that we might need to go beyond the idea of employees simply reacting or responding to change. What we have instead is the view that we need to understand change as something arising much more from the interaction between management and employees. While this might give us a more accurate picture of organizational change, it raises its own challenges, both for understanding and for managing change. Over time, however, things have become even more challenging, as we have seen in more recent years the emergence of an approach based on individual employee ambivalence and the ambiguities of change.

Understanding individual employee attitude to change: ambivalence and ambiguity

Thus in recent years we have seen a still more subtle and differentiated account of employee attitudes to change. Rather than looking at employees as a whole, or even at identifiable groups of employees, the focus is on the individual and the complexity of their responses. This has centred on the notion of ambivalence, which in this context refers to the possibility – or, indeed, the likelihood – that individual employees will face internal conflict in their attitudes to change.

This concept of ambivalence within individual responses is expressed most clearly in the work of Piderit (2000), who identifies three basic attitudinal dimensions in worker responses to change: the cognitive, defined as what the worker knows about the change; the emotional, the feelings they have towards it; and the intentional, which tries to capture the link with intended behaviour.

The identification of these different dimensions opens up the possibility that they will be in conflict with one another. Thus an individual might be cognitively in favour of a change, whilst being uncertain about the ethical dilemmas involved. For Piderit this is not just a conceptual possibility: she claims that response to change is likely to be characterized by a significant degree of ambivalence. This is a reasonable assumption in a world of more complex change, she argues, since, in these circumstances, employees are 'more likely to engage in the formation of a new attitude, rather than simply shift their old attitude along a stable dimension' (2000: 789).

The emphasis on ambivalence has a number of implications for both management practice and management research. For Piderit, the split between beliefs and emotions has an intuitive appeal that would help managers in making predictions about employee behaviour. A degree of ambivalence in response, moreover, might have desirable as well as undesirable consequences: a slower move towards compliance might, argues Piderit, have the effect of encouraging discussion and learning, thereby improving the nature of the change. From a research point of view, allowing for ambivalence has the effect of encouraging a move from studies based purely on top-down management towards a greater consideration being given to its interaction with the bottom-up, employee-based contributions to the process of change.

Part of this involves looking at the result of or response to ambivalence. Badham and McLoughlin (2005/06) are critical of the body of work that makes cynicism central in this respect (see, for example, Ezzamel et al. 2001), arguing that these authors themselves display neither ambivalence – in assuming change programmes to be repressive rather than in any sense co-determined – nor irony, in their failure to explore the gap between management intention and its achievement. Badham and McLoughlin's own contribution examines the involvement of three individuals in a change programme in an Australian coke-making works. Their ambiva-lence (their 'distanced yet committed' attitude (2005/06: 141)) was retained rather repressed, Badham and McLoughlin argue, giving rise to what they describe as 'ironic engagement'.

Moreover, in related work, McLoughlin et al. (2005) argue that in studying employee response to change, ambivalence alone is not enough. The danger, they claim, is that 'what employees and some managers are ambivalent *about* is assumed to be relatively clear and unproblematic'

371

(2005: 68, emphasis in original). This view thus takes little account of the 'substantial and persistent ambiguities that characterize cultural change processes themselve' (2500: 68). In the context of organizational culture, ambiguity has sometimes been described as a disparity between the conceptual content theme of the organization and its practices at the departmental level (Martin and Meyerson, 1988). What becomes significant is organizational actors' ability to refashion, reshape and redefine the cultural values, prescriptions and mechanisms about which they are ambivalent.

Thus the ambiguities arise from the 'design/emergence dynamic' of the interaction between programmed and emergent change, and McLoughlin et al. detail three aspects of this: the 'devil in the detail' of translating generic concepts into specific contexts; the 'learning dynamic' as the change initiative is modified over time as a result of employee response; and the 'embedded uncertainty' that surrounds attempts by organizational actors to ascertain what is taking place during episodes of change.

Randall and Procter (2008) have combined these ambiguity-based and ambivalence-based approaches in their study of the accounts of change provided by senior managers in a UK government department undergoing restructuring. These accounts showed there to be no generally shared view of the form that change had taken: some focused, for example, on the change in the way in which the department's clients were dealt with; others, on the way that managerial skills and experiences were assessed. In each of these accounts, cognitive and emotional dimensions could be identified, thus providing the potential for employee ambivalence.

This study was able to go even further, however, by looking not just at the attitudes of a small number of individuals but also at how these individuals could be clustered together into identifiable groupings. Those managers who saw change in terms of how it affected the department's relationships with its client groups were largely the more senior, who had spent a large part of their working life in the department. These were characterized as taking the 'long view'. Those most concerned about managerial assessment were managers who were in senior positions in the department but who had come into the department from other working environments. These were characterized as taking a 'new view'; with a third group, taking the 'short view', being those with a short but steep career trajectory within the government department, and being concerned primarily with what they saw as the inequities of the system of appraisal.

Conclusions

So where does all this leave us? What conclusions can we draw from our assessment of how attitudes to attitudes to change have changed over time? The simplest conclusion would be that what we have observed is scientific progress: that the rather crude assumption of employee resistance was replaced by a more sophisticated view of employees' attitudes and, in turn, by a more sophisticated view of an individual employee's attitudes.

But such an interpretation would be an over-simplification. A closer look at the idea of resistance reveals that dismissing it as unproven and outdated should itself be regarded as a very crude approach. We need to explain, first of all, why resistance has, over a long period, retained a substantial degree of appeal as a conception of employee attitudes to change. Part of the appeal can be put down to ideology. For those keen to assert the interests of capital, it makes sense to portray labour as self-interested and backward-looking. But more than this, the idea of resistance resonates with people's direct experience of being involved in organizational change. Those with experience of teaching courses on the management of change will be familiar with their students' expression of this view, making resistance almost synonymous with change. From a management point of view it also has the virtue of simplicity: the issue is how to deal with resistance, even if, as Kotter and Schlesinger (1979) assert, we can associate different management actions with different motivations for resistance.

But we do gain something from a move away from this exclusive focus on resistance. From a research point of view we do get other possibilities with which to understand how employees act in the context of organizational change. We can also place much greater emphasis on change as something that arises from the interaction between management and employees. From a management point of view the advantages are less clear. This is particularly so since much of the work in this area has had little interest in trying to predict which employees or groups of employees are likely to be associated with which response, let alone set out what strategies might be adopted to deal with them.

These dilemmas become more acute when we allow for individual employee ambivalence and for an intrinsic ambiguity in organizational change. We can achieve a more refined view of employees and of the process of change, but the complexity involved in this makes it much more difficult to make informed and useful generalizations. From a management point of view, their work is made much harder by the degree of complexity involved in diagnosing attitudes to change and in developing strategies to address these. The task from a research perspective might then be to persuade management that the costs of complexity are more than offset by the benefits derived from a more sophisticated understanding of organizational change and its management.

References

Badham, R. and I. McLoughlin (2005/06) 'Ambivalence and engagement: irony and cultural change in late modern organizations', *International Journal of Knowledge, Culture and Change Management*, 5(4): 132–43.

Barker, J. (1993) 'Tightening the iron cage: concertive control in self-managing teams', *Administrative Science Quarterly*, 38(3): 408–37.

Bartlem, C. and E. Locke (1981) 'The Coch and French study: a critique and reinterpretation', *Human Relations*, 34(7): 555–66.

Coch, L. and J. French (1948) 'Overcoming resistance to change', *Human Relations*, 1(4): 512–32.

Daniel, W. and T. Hogarth (1990) 'Worker support for technical change', *New Technology, Work and Employment*, 5: 85–93.

Dawson, P. (1991) 'From machine-centered to human-centered manufacture', *International Journal of Human Factors in Manufacturing*, 1(4): 327–38.

Ezzamel, M., H. Willmott and F. Worthington (2001) 'Power, control and resistance in "the factory that time forgot"', *Journal of Management Studies*, 38(8): 1053–79.

Harris, L. and E. Ogbonna (1998) 'Employee responses to culture change efforts', *Human Resource Management Journal*, 8(2): 78–92.

Hogarth, T. (1993) 'Worker support for organisational and technical change', *Work, Employment and Society*, 7(2): 189–212.

Kegan, R. and L. Lahey (2001) 'The real reason people won't change', *Harvard Business Review*, Nov. 85–92.

Knights, D. and D. McCabe (2000) 'Bewitched, bothered and bewildered: the meaning and experience of teamworking for employees in an automobile company', *Human Relations*, 53(11): 1481–1517.

Kotter, J. and L. Schlesinger (1979) 'Choosing strategies for change', *Harvard Business Review*, Mar–Apr: 106–14.

Lawrence, P. (1954) 'How to deal with resistance to change', *Harvard Business Review*, May–Jun: 49–57.

Martin, J. and G. Meyerson (1988) 'Organizational cultures and the denial, channeling and acknowledgement of ambiguity', in L. Pondy et al. (eds) *Managing Ambiguity and Change*, New York: John Wiley & Sons.

McKinlay, A. and P. Taylor (1996) 'Power, surveillance and resistance: inside the "factory of the future" ', in P. Ackers, C. Smith and P. Smith (eds) *The New Workplace and Trade Unionism*, London: Routledge.

McLoughlin, I., R. Badham and G. Palmer (2005) 'Cultures of ambiguity: design, emergence and ambivalence in the introduction of normative control', *Work, Employment and Society*, 19(1): 67–89.

Morris, T. and S. Wood (1991) 'Testing the survey method: continuity and change in British industrial relations', *Work, Employment and Society*, 5(2): 259–82.

Nichols, T. (1986) *The British Worker Question: A New Look at Workers and Productivity in Manufacturing*, London: Routledge & Kegan Paul.

Northcott, J., M. Fogarty and M. Trevor (1985) *Chips and Jobs: Acceptance of New Technology at Work*, London: Policy Studies Institute.

Ogbonna, E. and B. Wilkinson (2003) 'The false promise of organizational culture change: a case study of middle managers in grocery retailing', *Journal of Management Studies*, 40(5): 1151–78.

Piderit, S. (2000) 'Rethinking resistance and recognising ambivalence', *Academy of Management Review*, 25(4): 783–94.

Pratten, C. (1976) *Labour Productivity Differentials within International Companies*, Cambridge: Cambridge University Press.

Randall, J. and S. Procter (2008) 'Ambiguity and ambivalence: senior managers' accounts of organizational change in a restructured government department', *Journal of Organizational Change Management*, 21(6): 686–700.

26

Narrating organizational change

Melanie Bryant and Julie Wolfram Cox

Throughout the 1990s and 2000s, narrative has increasingly been used as an analytical tool, a methodological approach and as a focus for constructing knowledge about organizational change. Although examples of the use of narrative in organizational research are evident from as early as the 1950s (see, for example, Dalton, 1959), the postmodern and linguistic turns (Alvesson and Kärreman, 2000) in organizational studies have increased the popularity of language and text-based tools to analyse narratives, stories, discourse and conversations. Within the specific context of organizational studies, narrative has provided scholars with opportunities to explore not only human experiences, but also the various forms of talk and text that transpire within organizational settings. Along with, for example, discourse and story-based research, narrative approaches enable exploration of the dialogic nature of organizations in which the organization is recognized as a 'multiplicity of discourses which reflect ... "plurivocal" meanings' (Grant et al., 1998, p. 7) of those who participate in organizational life. Furthermore, narrative approaches highlight a move in organization studies towards 'a widening acceptance of alternative epistemologies' (Pinnegar and Daynes, 2007, p. 7) and for recognition of the interdependence of the roles of researcher and participant. This contrasts with empiricist approaches to organization studies, or modernist, monologic views in which a single perspective – such as a viewpoint provided by senior managers that purportedly reflects the views of the collective organization – is presented and used as a basis for theorizing about organizational events and processes (Boje, 1995).

Narrative approaches provide an opportunity for exploring changing organizations as 'discursive space[s] constituted through language practices' (Brown et al., 2005, p. 312), providing an angle from which various language practices can be interrogated. Syrjälä et al. (2009, p. 264) explain, if 'we assume that employees' speech ... forms part of the discursive organizational reality, that reality is obviously mediated narratively'. However, as Barry (1997, p. 30) questions: 'How might narrative writings, which tend to take a non-utilitarian, postmodernist slant, be used to inform organizational change, which is often enacted in distinctly utilitarian and modernist ways?' This chapter seeks to address this question by highlighting how narrative approaches have been used to inform empirical research into organizational change by reviewing major narrative change research themes that have emerged over the past decade or so. To achieve this, we first define and delimit our consideration of narrative and of the role of researchers in constructing narrative accounts. We then trace the growth of narrative approaches in the 1990s in response to calls for new perspectives and criticisms of the dominant approaches of the time. As part of this discussion particular attention is paid to the recognition of *multivocality* in narrative studies and of the methodological issues associated with allowing for multivocality. We also comment on the growth of narrative studies into identity in situations of organizational change, some of which present a return to univocal assumptions, and consider whether the continued interest in analysis of narratives in terms of genre or plot types also reflects researchers' own desire to impose some semblance of order, or meta-narrative (Leijon and Soderbom, 2008), over what is necessarily a complex field. Finally, the implications of this consideration are examined and challenges for future research in this area are outlined.

Defining narrative

Riessman (2008) argues that a precise definition of what constitutes narrative is not easy to obtain as the context and purpose for which narrative is used is subject to considerable variability. However, within the broader social sciences, narrative has been defined as:

> … Retrospective meaning making – the shaping or ordering of past experience. Narrative is a way of understanding one's own and others' action, of organizing events and objects into a meaningful whole, and of connecting and seeing the consequences of actions and events over time
>
> (Chase, 2005, p. 656)

> … A story that tells a sequence of events that are significant for the narrator and audience. A narrative has a plot, a beginning, a middle and an end. It has an internal logic that makes sense to the narrator. A narrative related events in a temporal, causal sequence of events that have happened
>
> (Denzin, 1989, p. 37)

Narrative has been described as including a chronological dimension and a plot structure; as requiring retrospective interpretation and co-authoring by an audience; as well as being linked to identity construction (Søderberg, 2006). Buchanan and Dawson (2007, p. 672) argue that the term *narrative* has diverse application and suggest that 'stories, scripts, anecdotes, legends, sagas, histories, myths, reports and other discursive accounts are categorically narratives'. This resonates with Riessman's (2008) comment that anything written or spoken is now referred to as *narrative*, suggesting of a possible proliferation of the term without specific application. However, 'developing a detailed plotline, character and the complexities of a setting are not needed in many communicative and written exchanges' (Riessman and Speedy, 2007, pp. 428–29) hence not all forms of talk and text should be referred to as narrative.

Within the domain of organizational studies narrative definitions and explanations are not too dissimilar from those developed within the broader social sciences. For example, definitions used here include: 'A narrative is a set of events or actions put chronologically together' (Czarniawska, 2007, p. 387); and 'narratives elaborate a sequence of events connected by subject matter or time' (Chreim, 2007, p. 452). Various claims about the usefulness of narrative approaches have been offered, including that: 'Narrative verbalizes and localizes the experiences of organizational members as they interpret and share work situations' (Jabri, 2004, p. 567); it 'is about the use of stories as a primary way of making sense of an experience' (Vickers, 2008, p. 562); and it provides 'cognitive structures that help individuals and groups cope with the confusion of their world of action' (Boudes and Laroche, 2009, p. 378).

Although the terms *narrative* and *story* are often used interchangeably within organizational studies, it is important to acknowledge that this usage has also been the subject of debate. It is not our intention to focus on this debate in detail within this chapter for it is discussed at length elsewhere (Boje, 2008; Collins, 2008; Gabriel, 2000). However, it is important to highlight these discussions in order to contextualize our use of the term *narrative* as well as to draw attention to a disjuncture that appears to be occurring within the narrative and storytelling literature and which is reflected in the differentiation of chapters on narrative and on storytelling in this Companion. Boje (2001, 2008) argues that story and narrative are distinct and should be treated as such. For him, stories reflect the process of telling in the present highlighting loose ends, fragmentation, and even incoherence. The focus of the story is likely to shift constantly from past to present and even future telling, which may be difficult for a listener to follow. In contrast, narratives are constructed retrospectively. At a basic level structure and order are imposed onto stories by the researcher (see, for example, Isabella, 1990). The researcher plays the role of narrator determining coherence and chronology, such as a plot or beginning, middle and end, to bring stories 'into a meaningful whole' (Czarniawska, 1998, p. 2). Alternatively, Gabriel (2000) argues that *stories* rather than narratives are characterized by order, direction and plot and that not all narratives can be stories for 'factual or descriptive accounts which aspire to objectivity rather than emotional effect must not be treated as stories' (Gabriel, 1998, p. 86). In this chapter we have attempted, where possible, to focus on studies of narratives and organizational change rather than stories and storytelling. However, both concepts have overlapping characteristics that are not always clearly differentiated within organizational studies.

Both within and beyond such studies, narratives can be studied in different forms including written, oral or visual elaborations. They can also involve the study of personal experience within an autobiographical or autoethnographic context, or inquiry into others' experiences in a more biographical manner. Perhaps Chase (2005, p. 651) best highlights the diversity of narrative inquiry by explaining that:

> Contemporary narrative inquiry can be characterized as an amalgam of interdisciplinary analytic lenses, diverse disciplinary approaches, and both traditional and innovative methods – all revolving around an interest in biographical particulars as narrated by the one who lives them.

Pinnegar and Daynes (2007, p. 5) describe narrative inquiry as consisting of 'both the method and the phenomena of study', while Riessman (2008) suggests that it involves the dual process of narrative construction and narrative analysis. In other words, narrative researchers are often interested in co-constructing the narrative, focusing on the narrative as the centre of the research, and conducting narrative analysis. In narrating the experiences of another, as opposed to the self, the researcher highlights her own interpretation, thereby providing her own narrative that draws attention to what she considers to be important and worthy of re-telling (Chase, 2005).

Given the implication of the researcher in any 'data collection' exercise, this consideration must not be under-estimated, carrying with it the associated responsibility to represent, if not describe, another's experience and to think carefully about how organizational stories are told (Czarniawska, 1997; Rhodes, this volume). Boje (2001) warns however, that focusing too much on our interpretations, and particularly on imposing order, may cause narrative researchers to overlook subtle nuances within the data, or fragmentation of stories that provide us with insight into an individual's experience. It may also overplay the researcher's authority, for 'authors are not in full control of the text (Barthes, 1981) and ... readers (if any) will intentionally and unintentionally re-present the text in their own meaning-making processes' (Cairns and Beech, 2003, p. 180). Therefore, to develop understanding of the complexities of organizational change, we need to pay attention to the details of, for example, an individual's experience but also present those details to an audience in a manner that makes sense without reducing a narrative to a single linear storyline. Narrative-based analytical techniques that can assist in such endeavours are many and varied, including plot analysis, character analysis, actant analysis and temporal structure analysis (Lämsa and Sintonen, 2006; Syrjälä et al., 2009). It is not our intention to discuss the variety of tools that can be utilized as part of narrative inquiry, for that has been discussed by other authors (see for example Boje, 2001; Riessman, 2008), as have narrative-informed approaches to organization development (Dindler and Iversen, 2007; Gergen and Gergen, 2006; Marshak and Grant, 2008). Rather, we seek to highlight the insight that organizational change researchers can gain from using narrative inquiry as a research approach and to provide what is, in effect, our own narrative of contemporary narrative research on organizational change.

Narrating organizational change

In the 1990s organizational change research was criticized by Collins (1998) as being presented in a mechanistic, over rational and under-socialized manner in which *n-steps* – that is, research that emphasized change as a model consisting of various steps or stages – featured heavily. Similar concerns were raised by Vickers (2008, p. 561) more recently, who also highlighted a number of limitations with the organizational change literature that was influential at that time:

> The managerialist perspective is ... represented in the change literature with the bastardization of Lewin's (1943) holistic approach to change into the three words of "unfreezing – change – refreezing". There are a plethora of models which suggest that a planned pseudo-scientific approach to change is possible (Beckhard & Harris, 1977; Kotter & Cohen, 2002). There is an assumption that there is one voice that is representative ... and that it is "right". Anyone who does not agree with this view is seen to be "resistant" to change (Kotter & Schlesinger, 1979).

Collins (1998) subsequently called for further research that explored change from paradigmatic approaches such as interpretivism to enable researchers to explore the social nature of change including the various views that people hold. Concurrently in the broader field of organization studies, researchers such as Boje (1991, 1995), Gabriel (1995, 1998) and Czarniawska (1997, 1998) were focusing on storytelling and narrative methods of inquiry to explore various facets of organizational life. For example, Czarniawska (1997, p. 21) states that 'the main fount of organizational knowledge is the narrative', arguing that narratives are the 'carriers of life itself, not just "reports" on it'. Boje (1995), highlights this point in his postmodern study of the interactive Disney play *Tamara* by following actors around the set to explore the various stories of *Tamara*-land that each individual constructed in comparison to Disney's *official* account of what *the* story was about. As each actor played a different role in *Tamara*, they interpreted what the play was about as well as their role in the broader production, highlighting a multiplicity of stories and knowledge that contribute to the overall 'organization'. When used as an analogy for broader organizational life, Boje (1995, 2001) argues that organizations cannot be registered as single stories. Rather, and as becomes very clear through dramaturgical analysis (Cairns and Beech, 2003), each consists of multiple stories that are in competition with each other and are based on the experiences of each individual staff member. Emphasis on individual narratives enables us to understand how people interpret events such as change and can also be used to mobilize change (Boje, 2008; Czarniawska, 1997). Increasingly, organizational change scholars are using varying approaches to narrative work that have shifted organizational change from predominantly empiricist and *n-steps* based research to embrace more in-depth exploration of issues such as individual experiences, sensemaking and identity.

Contemporary narrative-change research is diverse, encompassing a range of studies that use narrative as an analytical tool to explore various aspects of organizational change, as a tool to explore how organizational narratives can be constructed, and to examine change across a vast range of settings. For example, narrative analysis has been used to investigate change within public sector organizations (Berendse, Duijnhoven and Veenswijk, 2006; Feldman et al., 2004; Fronda and Moriceau, 2008); as a means to investigate learning and its role in organizational change (Reissner, 2005; Rhodes, 1997); to uncover the multivocal nature of changing organizations (Buchanan, 2003; Dawson and Buchanan, 2005); to examine different types of change narratives (Brown and Humphreys, 2003); to focus on the negotiation of controversial episodes over time (Garcia-Lorenzo, 2004; Wagner and Newell, 2006) and on change responses (Cutcher, 2009); and to understand identity (Beech and Johnson, 2005; Brown et al., 2005). Whether constructed for research or other purposes, change narratives can be developed at organizational, group or individual level and used as a means to rationalize or legitimize, as a sensemaking device, or to provide 'future' direction' (Bryant and Wolfram Cox, 2004; Buchanan and Dawson, 2007). Dunford and Jones (2000) provide an example of this last, explicitly political, purpose from the organizational level:

> Narratives are especially likely to be of significance during times of strategic change; in this situation 'stories about directionality are variously appropriated, discounted, championed and defended' (Barry and Elmes, 1997, p. 432). Central to this 'directionality' is the nature of the narrative as something that it intended to persuade others towards certain under-standings and actions. From a narrative perspective, the success of a strategic story may depend less on such tools as environmental analysis and strategic planning than on whether it is an engaging, compelling account that encourages the actions desired by the authors of the narrative.
>
> (Dunford and Jones, 2000, p. 1209)

Besides providing strategic change directionality, prescriptive organizational level narratives act as conduits for new organizational cultures and changes in values or behavioural expectations. Often referred to as *grand narratives*, and used in a sense more narrowly defined than that of Lyotard (1984), these organizational level narratives usually provide the corporate view of change, or 'grand assumptions about what an "Ideal, Proper and Healthy" organization is' (Aaltio-Marjosola, 1994, p. 66), which Boje (1995) refers to as an 'official' discourse.

While grand narratives can provide us with an understanding of the senior management view of organizational change, scholars have raised concerns about placing too much emphasis upon them in a quest to develop further understanding of change. As noted above, such narratives are described as speaking on behalf of all members of the organization (Boje, 1995) or assuming that organizational members are 'one amorphous group of people who all agree with a unitary agenda for the organization' (Vickers, 2008, p. 569). Further, Rhodes (2000, p. 227) suggests that grand narratives may be a consequence of the hierarchical nature of organizations and the power relations that exist within them, creating a situation in which those in positions of power impose 'their own monological and unitary perceptions of truth' about change on all organizational members (see also Cairns and Beech, 2003; Mumby, 1987). Consequently, organization-level change narratives can – whether intentionally or not – silence and marginalize different interpretations of change held by others (Berendse, et al., 2006). Dawson (2000) warns that ignoring other people's experiences of change plays up organizational change successes and downplays failure. De Cock (1998) also cautions against reliance upon managerial versions of organizational change on the basis that although they are promoted as an authoritative version, they merely reflect one interpretation.

As Stensaker and Falkenberg (2007, p. 138) argue; 'we know little about how different organizational-level responses [to change] come about, or what individual responses lay beneath the aggregate response'. However, and as also noted above, narrative research has facilitated a shift towards a 'multivocal' view of organizational change by providing a means through which varied and layered group and individual interpretations may be presented and through which the dynamics of both change experience and change accounts may be explored (e.g. Surjälä, et al., 2009). Where we no longer assume a singular aggregate response, research aimed toward representing such complex organizational change dynamics has become increasingly legitimate.

Multivocality and individual interpretations of change

Hardy et al. (2000) suggest that social reality in organizations is created from numerous interpretations, highlighting the need for researchers to pay attention to experiences of change constructed from multiple frames of reference (see also Palmer and Dunford, 1996). Emphasis on 'multi-' or 'poly-vocality' (Buchanan, 2003; Buchanan and Dawson, 2007) refers to the recognition of multiple versions or voices and is explained as consisting of 'many tales, dramas, [and] pieces of fiction' (Lincoln and Denzin, 1994, p. 584). This explanation allows us to recognize that multivocality may not (just) allow for a more comprehensive examination of multiple interpretations, but may, instead, introduce the opportunity to examine organizational accounts, vignettes and dramas in their own terms regardless of the extent to which they correspond with any lived reality. Even so, numerous organizational change researchers have explored multivocality within their empirical work as a way of understanding specific contexts of change more thoroughly. For example, Buchanan (2003) conducted a study of competing narratives of change agents responsible for the implementation of organization-wide large-scale change programs within a large hospital setting. Focusing on change from a processual-contextual perspective, Buchanan (2003, p. 17) found that 'identifying the "accurate account" of "what *really* happened" [was] ... illusive and indeterminate' as change agent reports of their experience of strategic change were contradictory to management reports of what happened.

Findings such as these raise questions about management driven narratives regarding the success of organizational change programs. They also raise a number of methodological issues of which researchers should be aware when researching change. Specifically, contradictory narratives should be treated as naturally occurring and a reflection of individual experience rather than as 'aberrations that should be triangulated away methodologically' (Buchanan, 2003, p. 17). We argue that this is particularly important as differences in individual backgrounds, opinions and values make it difficult for researchers to avoid hearing and considering multiple experiences of change, providing us with a responsibility to consider many rather than one account of what happens throughout the processes of change.

In addition to considering multiple contemporaneous narratives of change, we also need to pay attention to how narratives help individuals make sense of past change events and, consequently, shape the future (Buchanan and Dawson, 2007). Gioia and Chittipeddi (1991, p. 442) argue that individuals make sense of change through a process of 'meaning construction and reconstruction ... as they attempt to develop a meaningful framework for understanding the nature of ... change'. The construction of change narratives can assist in the process of sensemaking by providing individuals with such a framework and provide researchers with an understanding of how organizational members interpret change and what the consequences of such interpretations can be. This is particularly useful in understanding responses such as resistance to change. Although it has already been established that managers can use employees' negative responses as a scapegoat for organizational-level change failure (see for example Piderit, 2000; Reichers et al., 1997; Wanous et al., 2000), exploring narratives of individual sensemaking arguably provides further insight into why negative interpretations might occur. For example, Stensaker and Falkenberg (2007) found that unclear expectations about responsibility for specific aspects of organizational change can cause negative interpretations amongst staff, leading to problems concerning change interpretation:

> While expectations, in terms of what changes should be made, were unclear, the reasons for negative interpretations of the change initiative at the individual level were tied to the change process. Individuals stated that they experienced limited understanding and received no support from the management level during implementation. Management, on the other hand, was waiting for employees to take charge.
>
> (Stensaker and Falkenberg, 2007, p. 160)

This example highlights how differing interpretations and understandings of what organizational means and the roles and responsibilities associated with it can lead to fundamental problems concerning the overall success of change efforts. To suggest that change failed due to negative employee interpretations would be simplistic and Stensaker and Falkenberg's example of individual narratives reveals that problems that could arguably be fairly easily overcome through adequate communication and could lead to costly change failures if different interpretations are marginalized.

The works of Stensaker and Falkenberg (2007) and Vickers (2008) also highlight how differing interpretations of change can cause modifications to change strategy. Stensaker and Falkenberg (2007) illustrate how unclear senior management communication of change can lead to multiple interpretations, which can lead to both intentional and unintentional redirection of change strategy. Vickers (2008) views narrative as both social process and political praxis in which researchers can focus on not only how meaning is constructed by individuals about change, but also the power relations that exist in organizations and how they dictate the narratives that are 'allowed to be told'. Focusing specifically on managers, Vickers (2008, p. 569) suggests that managers are often perceived as being members of a unitary group who agree upon a collective organizational agenda. In reality, studying the experiences of individual middle managers may reveal that accepting a unitary model of change and blindly conforming to seniority is a myth (Randall and Procter, 2008; Vickers, 2008). By focusing on narratives of middle managers that are normally silenced, the capacity and power that middle managers have in controlling and redirecting organizational change strategy is revealed. Further, middle management attempts to satisfy personal agendas, rather than those of senior management, highlight the political and ambiguous nature of change that is not necessarily accessible if exploring it from a singular managerialist approach. The narrative-based examples provided in the works of Stensaker and Falkenberg (2007) and Vickers (2008) are reflective of how individuals seek to make sense of ambiguous or unclear organizational change directives from senior management. They also demonstrate how redirection of change strategies can be an outcome of sensemaking – rather than a deliberate or manipulative ploy by staff who may be unfairly accused of being resistant to change – by providing a mechanism for creating an 'understanding of the organization and its environment in order to better cope with change' (Landau and Drori, 2008, p. 703).

Identity in narratives of change

Given the need for sensemaking, it is perhaps not surprising that narrative-change research has focused on identity in different forms ranging from individual identity construction through to organizational-level identity. Seeger et al. (2005) provide an example of the importance of identity construction and reconstruction at the organizational level in their study of change post 9/11. In opposition to studies calling for multivocality, the authors argue that leaders of organizations directly affected by a crisis such as 9/11 need to communicate using meaningful narrative frames to organizational members so that they can seek stability within the post-crisis state and re-identify with the organization: 'Such support communicated through monologic organizational discourse is critical to organizational renewal' (Seeger et al., 2005, p. 87). It is possible that mono-vocal change narratives are constructed in crisis or transformational change situations in an attempt to re-develop or reinforce an organization's identity.

Even outside such settings pressures toward construction of singular organizational identities may still be evident. For example, Demers et al. (2003) found that organizations legitimize change through managerially constructed change messages and that employees play only a subdued role in such messages. They argue that such findings are significant as 'narratives are constructions that reaffirm and elaborate the organization's identity and reflect the vision management has of employees and their role' (Demers et al., 2003, p. 238). This indicates that throughout periods of instability associated with large-scale change, an organization's identity may provide a constant for employees. Within the context of subtle rather than large-scale change, Brown et al. (2005, p. 314) provide an alternative view, suggesting that organizational identities are comprised of 'multiple, changing, occasionally constant, sometimes overlapping, but often competing narratives centred on them, authored by those who participate in them'. In their study of collective identity narratives they found that those narratives constructed by the organization's owners reinforce the power structure of the organization while simultaneously communicating the owners' expectations to employees, providing a further example of an organization's identity being a constant for employees. Brown et al. (2005, p. 321) conclude that although multiple narratives exist within organizations, 'employees' sensemaking occurs within a political context and is subject to the hegemonic influence of carefully edited stories'.

In comparison to the above studies of identity and organizational change, others focus on special circumstances that allow for different or shifting interpretations of organizational identity in changing organizations. For example, Chreim's (2007) narrative analysis of organizational groups that merged as a consequence of an acquisition found that multiple interpretations of identity emerged from the various narratives. These are documented as being linked to the social and temporal contexts in which members of each group constructed the narratives, hence the difference in identity narratives across the participants. A further important finding is that the merger and acquisition caused all participants who were interviewed as part of the study to report loss as a consequence of organizational change, particularly loss of a family atmosphere that existed prior to change, causing a shift in perception of the organization's identity pre- and post-change. These findings resonate with other narrative studies of organizational change in which change is associated with loss. For example Bryant and Wolfram Cox (2006) discuss employee reports of loss linked to removal of decision-making power, demotion, and feelings of displacement caused by organizational change. In this case, loss is described by employees as being exacerbated by a need to suppress negative emotions associated with change. However, loss associated with organizational change is not always a negative experience. Loss has also been linked to more positive outcomes in which feelings of release from past constraints and relief to move into the future have been reported (Wolfram Cox, 1997). Such studies highlight the effects that shifts in organizational identity caused by change can have upon individual identities.

A common feature of contemporary studies of individual identity is that they also highlight its shifting nature (see for example Beech and Johnson, 2005; Chreim, 2007), disrupting the univocality assumed in earlier studies of organizational change narratives. At the individual level, and to varying degrees, organizational members are presented as being able to construct new identities for themselves and others as change processes emerge. Beech and Johnson (2005) explore disruption to identities of senior staff during organizational change and argue that when viewed as a micro-strategic process, the progression of change can cause broken or disrupted organizational narratives, which in turn can create shifts in perception of others' identities. For example, those identified as *heroes* of the organization may later be perceived as *anti-hero* in the event that they do not comply with others' expectations. This may occur in situations in which an individual acts in a manner that breaks the organization's strategic narrative. Consequently, organizational members have the ability to *recast* or *rewrite* others who are thought to behave in an inappropriate manner. Further, disruption to identity caused by change provides individuals with an opportunity to 'recast themselves' (Beech and Johnson, 2005, p. 44). Beech and Johnson's example demonstrates how agentic organizational members are able to construct new identities for themselves and others as change processes emerge, highlighting the fluid nature of identity – at both individual and organizational levels – within changing organizations (see also Chreim, 2005).

This fluidity is particularly apparent from Jabri's (2004) integration of narrative and dialogic approaches to change, one which also aligns with Chase's (2005) focus on temporality as a key aspect of the definition of a narrative (see also Petranker, 2005). Jabri (2004, p. 568) provides a comprehensive explanation of the process of the formation of narrative identity by explaining that:

> Based on conversations that tap lived accounts of change and change management, organization members come to inhabit their own narrative experiences of change and change situations … If a change participant resists … change and … recites his or her own reasons for resistance to change, that participant is participating in a narrative of the past and relating it to a narrative of the present … Such an act of narrative involves a hermeneutic – that is, it involves an "interpretation" that uses narratives to depict what is real and relevant in the person's experience of the world … Narrative identity is the output of such a hermeneutic cycle of meaning-making.

Thus, narrative studies that focus on identity draw attention to the complex nature of organizational change that is marked by a variety of emphases and sensitivities to matters of power, agency, time and voice. We suggest that one means by which this variety is simplified – at least to some extent – is through the development of 'figurative images' (Dunford and Jones, 2000, p. 1222) of change, which are often presented as narrative styles or types.

The construction of organizational change narratives

Narrative types have been described as 'modes of subjectivity' (Gabriel, 1995, p. 477) or cognitive frameworks (Beech, 2000) and are predominantly used to illustrate underpinning themes that emerge from across multiple narratives. Narrative types are developed predominantly around plots in which events and patterns are linked together to form a narrative structure (Boje, 2001). The plots that feature in many narrative-change studies are not unique to the context of organizational change. For example, Boje (2001) draws upon Ricouer's (1984) emplotment analysis in which the plots of romance, satire, tragedy and comedy are used to analyze organizational activity. Gabriel (1995) uses similar plots for organizational analysis – the subject as hero, heroic survivor, victim or object of love – to describe the subjective 'unmanaged' organization, and narrative types draw upon existing storylines and 'cultural archetypes' (Brown and Humphreys, 2003, p. 124). Drawing from the work of Jeffcutt (1993, 1994), Beech (2000, pp. 212–13) provides a succinct summary of some of these types, which are introduced as different 'styles':

> The first style is the epic narrative. This entails a difficult journey during which the hero has to undergo some ordeal, and success results in his or her exultation. The romantic style is one in which obstacles posed by opponents or by social or organizational restrictions are overcome, and a new state of happiness and integration is reached. In the tragedy style, flaws in the character or circumstances come to fruition, obstacles are not overcome, and conflict destroys harmony. The fourth type is the ironic style. In this style, the quest is unsuccessful, harmony is not reached, and the hero learns that this is the norm.

In analyzing narratives of employees and managers undergoing culture change, Beech (2000) found that the above narrative styles were revealed through investigation of plot (or narrative type) summaries and common themes. In working through each of the styles he clearly outlines the common features of the individual plots that are later categorized as the broader narrative types. Put simply, Beech found that the heroic and romantic narratives were associated with management staff. This may not be surprising as the hero is described as being 'able to generate movement when others and static and to transform when stalemate situations into productive harmonious outcomes' (Beech, 2000, p. 216). In comparison, the tragic narrative is associated with the worker who experiences trauma and pain as part of the change process. These findings resonate with the outcomes of others who have used narrative types of explain experiences of organizational change. For example, in an interpretivist study of change Brown and Humphreys (2003) also found that managers construct epic narratives in which they are successful in overcoming their struggle, while subordinate groups simultaneously constructed tragic narratives based on interpretation of the same organizational change event (see also Cairns and Beech, 2003; Collins and Rainwater, 2005).

Earlier research that we have published on narratives of organizational change also focuses broadly on narrative types (Bryant and Wolfram Cox, 2003, 2004). Similar to Beech (2000) and Brown and Humphreys (2003) we highlight negative narratives of change constructed by employees but refer to these at atrocity tales (Bryant and Wolfram Cox, 2003). In comparison to the tragedy narrative, the term *atrocity tale* was developed to reflect an underlying theme that emerged from employee narratives of change in which employees reported experiencing various forms of aggression as a consequence of attempting to use voice. Rather than using an existing narrative type such as the tragedy narrative to analyse employee stories, we highlight a number of experiences ranging from elimination from decision-making through to overt acts of bullying, which we loosely refer to as atrocity tales. In contrast, we applied the term *conversion stories* to highlight positive experiences of change (Bryant and Wolfram Cox, 2004). Conversion stories are comparable to romantic narrative plots in which individuals are able to overcome adversity to be successful in change. However, conversion stories also highlight a shift in individual stories from a pre-change narrative of anti-organization to a post-change narrative of pro-organization.

In this sense, organizational change led to the construction of a new narrative for individual employees.

The future of narrative-change research

Undoubtedly, narrative studies have offered greater insight into the micro social dynamics of organizational change providing an opportunity to explore what happens at different levels of the organization. They also allow researchers a legitimate license to demonstrate their own roles in the crafting of presentations of organizational change as writing in this domain is removed from the requirements of scientistic scholarship. However, such demonstration is also accompanied by the need to negotiate the balance between the tales and the telling; between talking about organizational change and speaking for those involved in it; and between allowing for multivocality in the tales being presented but doing so through a medium that is, at best, itself a single and linear presentation such as a journal article or book chapter. Thus, a continuing challenge for *authors* of narrative studies is to examine the form of presentation as well as its content. This is not to suggest that narrative studies necessarily need to be presented in forms consistent with the material they include (e.g. plays, improvisations, dialogues), but that reflexivity extend at least to a recognition that the form of writing required for academic publications such as this requires a presentation that can be conveyed to a reader. It is not just that any presentation is always partial but that as authors of narrative studies we are also *partialling* them out and that the very nature of narrative construction and presentation requires an arrogance of which we must be aware. While the ongoing interest in narrative genres and styles may well continue, it is therefore important to consider whether this interest may also reflect researchers' own desire to impose some semblance of order, or meta-narrative, over what is necessarily a complex field; to *draw* larger meaning from particular narratives in a further effort to make order among them as well as from the experiences depicted within them. Whether this stabilizing tendency (cf. Tsoukas, 2005) is a legacy of the importance of generalization in scientistic studies, a reflection of the ambitions (or uncertainties) of particular authors, or simply a line of inquiry, it is at least to some extent at odds with the multivocality that is increasingly valued in narrative research. Whether and how such different approaches continues, and how they are themselves assembled, will be worth assessing over the next few years.

References

Aaltio-Marjosola, I. (1994). From a "grand story" to multiple narratives: Studying an organizational change project. *Journal of Organizational Change Management*, 7(5), 56–67.

Alvesson, M. and Kärreman, D. (2000). Taking the linguistic turn in organizational research: Challenges, responses, consequences. *Journal of Applied Behavioral Science*, 36(2), 136–58.

Barry, D. (1997). Telling changes: From narrative family therapy to organizational change and development. *Journal of Organizational Change Management*, 10(1), 30–46.

Barry, D. and Elmes, M. (1997). Strategy retold: Toward a narrative view of strategic discourse. *Academy of Management Review*, 22(2), 429–52.

Barthes, R. (1981). *The Theory of the Text*. London: Routledge.

Beckhard, R. and Harris, R. (1977). *Organizations transitions: Managing complex change*. Toronto: Addison Wesley Publishing.

Beech, N. (2000). Narrative styles of managers and workers: A tale of star-crossed lovers. *Journal of Applied Behavioral Science*, 36(2), 210–28.

Beech, N. and Johnson, P. (2005). Discourses of disrupted identities in the practice of strategic change: The mayor, the street-fighter and the insider-out. *Journal of Organizational Change Management*, 18(1), 31–47.

Berendse, M., Duijnhoven, H. and Veenswijk, M. (2006). Editing narratives of change: Identity and legitmacy in complex innovation infrastructure organizations. *Intervention Research*, 2, 73–89.

Boje, D. (1991). Organizations as storytelling networks: A study of story performance in an office-supply firm. *Administrative Science Quarterly*, 36, 106–26.

Boje, D. (1995). Stories of the storytelling organization: A postmodern analysis of Disney as 'Tamara-Land'. *Academy of Management Journal*, 38, 997–1035.

Boje, D. (2001). *Narrative methods for organizational & communication research.* London: SAGE.

Boje, D. (2008). *Storytelling organizations.* Los Angeles: SAGE.

Boudes, T. and Laroche, H. (2009). Taking off the heat: Narrative sensemaking in post-crisis inquiry reports. *Organization Studies*, 30(4), 377–96.

Brown, A. and Humphreys, M. (2003). Epic and tragic tales: Making sense of change. *Journal of Applied Behavioral Science*, 39(2), 121–44.

Brown, A., Humphreys, M. and Gurney, P. (2005). Narrative, identity and change: A case study of Laskarina Holidays. *Journal of Organizational Change Management*, 18(4), 312–26.

Bryant, M. and Wolfram Cox, J. (2003). The telling of violence: Organizational change and atrocity tales. *Journal of Organizational Change Management*, 16(5), 567–83.

Bryant, M. and Wolfram Cox, J. (2004). Conversion stories as shifting narratives of organizational change. *Journal of Organizational Change Management*, 17(6), 578–92.

Bryant, M. and Wolfram Cox, J. (2006). The expression of suppression: Loss and emotional labour in narratives of organisational change. *Journal of Management & Organization*, 1(2), 116–30.

Buchanan, D. (2003). Getting the story straight: Illusions and delusions in the organizational change process. *Tamara: Journal of Critical Postmodern Organization Science*, 2(4), 7–21.

Buchanan, D. and Dawson, P. (2007). Discourse and audience: Organizational change as a multi-story process. *Journal of Management Studies*, 44(5), 669–86.

Cairns, G. and Beech, N. (2003). Un-entwining monological narratives of change through dramaturgical and narrative analyses. *Culture and Organization*, 9(3), 177–93.

Chase, S. (2005). Narrative inquiry: Multiple lenses, approaches, voices. In N. Denzin and Y. Lincoln (eds), *The Handbook of Qualitative Research* (3rd edn, pp. 651–79). Thousand Oaks: SAGE.

Chreim, S. (2005). The continuity-change duality in narrative texts of organizational identity. *Journal of Management Studies*, 42(3), 567–93.

Chreim, S. (2007). Social and temporal influences on interpretations of organizational identity and acquisition integration. *Journal of Applied Behavioral Science*, 43(4), 449–80.

Collins, D. (1998). *Organizational change: Sociological perspectives.* London: Routledge.

Collins, D. (2008). Has Tom Peters lost the plot? A timely review of a celebrated management guru. *Journal of Organizational Change Management*, 21(3), 315–34.

Collins, D. and Rainwater, K. (2005). Managing change at Sears: A sideways look at a tale of corporate transformation. *Journal of Organizational Change Management*, 18(1), 16–30.

Cutcher, L. (2009). Resisting change from within and without the organization. *Journal of Organizational Change Management*, 22(3), 275–89.

Czarniawska, B. (1997). *Narrating the organization: Dramas of institutional identity.* Chicago: University of Chicago Press.

Czarniawska, B. (1998). *A narrative approach to organization studies.* Thousand Oaks, CA: SAGE.

Czarniawska, B. (2007). Narrative inquiry in and about organizations. In D. Clandinin (ed.), *Handbook of narrative inquiry: Mapping a methodology* (pp. 383–404). Thousand Oaks, CA: SAGE.

Dalton, M. (1959). *Men who manage: Fusions of feeling and theory in administration.* New York: Wiley.

Dawson, P. (2000). Technology, work restructuring and the orchestration of a rational narrative in the pursuit of 'management objectives': The political process of plant-level change. *Technology Analysis & Strategic Management*, 12(1), 39–58.

Dawson, P. and Buchanan, D. (2005). The way it really happened: Competing narratives in the political process of technological change. *Human Relations*, 58(7), 845–65.

De Cock, C. (1998). Organisational change and discourse: Hegemony, resistance and reconstitution. *Management*, 1, 1–22.

Demers, C., Giroux, N. and Chreim, S. (2003). Merger and acquisition announcements as corporate wedding narratives. *Journal of Organizational Change Management*, 16(2), 223–42.

Denzin, N. (1989). *Interpretive interactionism*. London: SAGE.

Dindler, C. and Iversen, O. (2007) Fictional inquiry – design collaboration in a shared narrative space. *CoDesign*, 3, 213–234.

Dunford, R. and Jones, D. (2000). Narrative in strategic change. *Human Relations*, 53(9), 1207–26.

Feldman, M., Sköldberg, K., Brown, R. and Horner, D. (2004). Making sense of stories: A rhetorical approach to narrative analysis. *Journal of Public Administration Research and Theory*, 14(2), 147–70.

Fronda, Y. and Moriceau, J. (2008). I am not your hero: Change management and culture shocks in a public sector corporation. *Journal of Organizational Change Management*, 21(5), 589–609.

Gabriel, Y. (1995). The unmanaged organization: Stories, fantasies and subjectivity. *Organization Studies*, 16 (3), 477–501.

Gabriel, Y. (1998). Same old story or changing stories? Folkloric, modern and postmodern mutations. In D. Grant, T. Keenoy and C. Oswick (eds), *Discourse + organization* (pp. 84–103). London: SAGE.

Gabriel, Y. (2000). *Storytelling in organizations: Facts, fictions and fantasies*. Oxford: Oxford University Press.

Garcia-Lorenzo, L. (2004). (Re)producing the organization through narratives: The case of a multinational. *Intervention Research*, 1, 43–60.

Gergen, M.M. and Gergen, K.J. (2006). Narratives in action. *Narrative Inquiry*, 16, 112–21.

Gioia, D. and Chittipeddi, K. (1991). Sensemaking and sensegiving in strategic change initiation. *Strategic Management Journal*, 12, 433–38.

Grant, D., Keenoy, T. and Oswick, C. (1998). Introduction: Organizational discourse: Of diversity, dichotomy and multi-disciplinarity. In D. Grant, T. Keenoy and C. Oswick (eds), *Discourse + Organization* (pp. 1–13). London: SAGE.

Hardy, C., Palmer, I. and Phillips, N. (2000). Discourse as a strategic response. *Human Relations*, 53, 1227–48.

Isabella, L. (1990). Evolving interpretations as a change unfolds: How managers construe key organizational events. *Academy of Management Journal*, 33(1), 7–41.

Jabri, M. (2004). Change as shifting identities: A dialogic perspective. *Journal of Organizational Change Management*, 17(6), 566–77.

Jeffcutt, P. (1993). From interpretation to representation. In M. Parker and J. Hassard (eds), *Postmodernism and organizations*. London: SAGE.

Jeffcutt, P. (1994). The interpretation of organization: A contemporary analysis and critique. *Journal of Management Studies*, 31(2), 225–50.

Kotter, J. and Cohen, D. (2002). *The heart of change: Real life stories of how people change their organizations*. Cambridge: Harvard Business School Press.

Kotter, J. and Schlesinger, L. (1979). Choosing strategies to change. *Harvard Business Review*, 57, 106–14.

Lämsa, J. and Sintonen, T. (2006). A narrative approach for organizational learning in a diverse organization. *Journal of Workplace Learning*, 19, 106–20.

Landau, D. and Drori, I. (2008). Narratives as sensemaking accounts: The case of an R&D laboratory. *Journal of Organizational Change Management*, 21(6), 701–20.

Leijon, S. and Soderbom, A. (2008). Builders and cleaners: A longitudinal study of strategic narratives. *Journal of Organizational Change Management*, 21(3), 280–99.

Lewin, K. (1943). Forces behind food habits and methods of change. *Bulletin of the National Research Council*, 108, 35–65.

Lincoln, Y. and Denzin, N. (1994). The fifth moment. In N. Denzin and Y. Lincoln (eds), *Handbook of Qualitative Research* (pp. 575–86). Thousand Oaks, CA: SAGE.

Lyotard, J.-F. (1984). *The postmodern condition: A report on knowledge*. (G. Bennington and B. Massumi, trans.). Minneapolis, MN: University of Minnesota Press.

Marshak, R. and Grant, D. (2008) Organizational discourse and new organization development practices. *British Journal of Management*, 19, S7–S19.

Mumby, D. (1987). The political function of narrative in organizations. *Communication Monographs*, 54 (June), 119–34.

Palmer, I. and Dunford, R. (1996). Conflicting use of metaphors: Reconceptualizing their use in the field of organizational change. *Academy of Management Review*, 21, 691–717.

Petranker, J. (2005). The when of knowing. *Journal of Applied Behavioral Science*, 41(2), 241–59.

Piderit, S. (2000). Rethinking resistance and recognizing ambivalence: A multidimensional view of attitudes toward an organizational change. *Academy of Management Review*, 25(4), 783–94.

Pinnegar, S. and Daynes, J.G. (2007). Locating narrative inquiry historically: Thematics in the turn to narrative. In D.J. Clandinin (ed.), *Handbook of Narrative Inquiry: Mapping a Methodology* (pp. 3–34). Thousand Oaks, CA: SAGE.

Randall, J. and Procter, S. (2008). Ambiguity and ambivalence: Senior managers' accounts of organizational change in a restructured government department. *Journal of Organizational Change Management*, 21(6), 686–700.

Reichers, A., Wanous, J. and Austin, J. (1997). Understanding and managing cynicism about organizational change. *Academy of Management Executive*, 11(1), 48–59.

Reissner, S. (2005). Learning and innovation: A narrative analysis. *Journal of Organizational Change Management*, 18(5), 482–94.

Rhodes, C. (1997). The legitimation of learning in organizational change. *Journal of Organizational Change Management*, 10(1), 10–20.

Rhodes, C. (2000). Doing knowledge at work: Dialogue, monologue and power in organizational learning. In J. Garrick and C. Rhodes (eds), *Research and knowledge at work*. London: Routledge.

Ricouer, P. (1984). *Time and narrative volume 1*. Chicago: University of Chicago Press.

Riessman, C. (2008). *Narrative methods for the human sciences*. Los Angeles: SAGE.

Riessman, C. and Speedy, J. (2007). Narrative inquiry in the psychotherapy professions. In D. Clandinin (ed.), *Handbook of narrative inquiry: Mapping a methodology* (pp. 426–56). Thousand Oaks, CA: SAGE.

Seeger, M., Ulmer, R., Novak, J. and Sellnow, T. (2005). Post-crisis discourse and organizational change, failure and renewal. *Journal of Organizational Change Management*, 18(1), 78–95.

Søderberg, A. (2006). Narrative interviewing and narrative analysis in a study of a cross-border merger. *Management International Review*, 4, 397–416.

Stensaker, I. and Falkenberg, J. (2007). Making sense of different responses to corporate change. *Human Relations*, 60(1), 137–77.

Syrjälä, J., Takala, T. and Sintonen, T. (2009). Narratives as a tool to study personal wellbeing in corporate mergers. *Qualitative Research*, 9(3), 263–84.

Tsoukas, H. (2005). Afterword: Why language matters in the analysis of organizational change. *Journal of Organizational Change Management*, 18(1), 96–104.

Vickers, D. (2008). Beyond the hegemonic narrative – a study of managers. *Journal of Organizational Change Management*, 21(5), 560–73.

Wagner, E. and Newell, S. (2006). Repairing ERP: Producing social order to create a working information system. *Journal of Applied Behavioral Science*, 42(1), 40–57.

Wanous, J., Reichers, A. and Austin, J. (2000). Cynicism about organizational change: Measurement, antecedents and correlates. *Group & Organization Management*, 25, 132–53.

Wolfram Cox, J. (1997). Manufacturing the past: Loss and absence in organizational change. *Organization Studies*, 18, 623–54.

27

Governance and organizational change

John Storey

Introduction

'Governance' is a term which now features large in public policy, political science and in business management. In broad terms it refers to the actors, processes, mechanisms and processes which are involved in the making of policy, the setting of strategic direction and the monitoring of executive performance against these. Numerous corporate failures and outright catastrophes in recent years have been attributed to failures of governance. Examples of 'governance scandals' include Lehman Brothers, Enron, Worldcom and Tyco in the USA and RBS, Mid Staffordshire Hospitals Trust in the UK. Indeed, some attribute the root cause of the global banking crisis to a failure of governance. The passivity of non-executive board members has been especially noted and so too the failure of the regulators. In response, various reviews (including, for example, one into the failings of the banking system by the Walker review in the UK) (Walker 2009) have begun to sketch out further reforms to governance. In the USA, earlier concerns about governance failure led to the Sarbanes – Oxley Act in 2002 which introduced new standards for public company boards; the post-2008 events in the financial institutions prompted calls for further reforms.

But by what mechanisms and processes does, and should, governance operate? Why has governance figured so little in most analyses of organisational studies when compared to traditional topics such as structure, strategy, leadership and change? What is the proper scope of governance? What would good governance look like? These are the questions examined in this chapter. For illustrative purposes, reference is made to governance and organizational change in the public sector – most especially with reference to the UK National Health Service (NHS) and also to developments in the private sector most notably with reference to the governance aspects of corporate failures.

The chapter develops the argument that good governance can be an invaluable and at times essential support for successful organizational change.

What is governance?

There are multiple forms and multiple levels to the governance phenomenon. At the societal level, governance is about the mediation of political power. At this level, choices fluctuate between an expanded and a reduced role for the state and its institutions. Conversely, the market as a governance mechanism may be constrained or unfettered. Within states, power may be centralized or devolved to nation-states or regional assemblies. It may also be devolved to multiple agencies within nation states. In the other direction, there may be increasing or decreasing involvement in supranational organizations such as the EU, the World Trade Organization or the UN. At the organizational level, private- and public-sector organizations have their own patterns of governance. These can be modes which involve external oversight or are insular. Power may be concentrated or distributed. Information may be open and transparent or safeguarded and hidden. As we will see, at the organizational level, governmental choices are very much influenced by developments at the societal level.

Economic behaviour normally involves some mode of exchange – or transaction such as a purchase or a sale. In his development of the field of Transaction Cost Theory (TCT), (Williamson 1975) contends that markets and hierarchies are the two main alternative choices for governing transactions. The market form of governance uses prices, competition and contracts as the mechanisms for governing transactions. The hierarchical form of governance brings parties involved in an exchange under the control of a boss. Both mechanisms – markets and hierarchy – have their advantages and disadvantages and likewise it is possible to argue that conditions can be specified when each is to be preferred.

A key behavioural assumption underpinning transaction cost theory and indeed behind the perceived need for governance is the notion of opportunism. This concept goes beyond conventional economic assumption of actor's pursuit of self interests. Williamson's presentation of TCT suggest that behaviour may potentially extend towards guile (Williamson 1975: 26). The notion of opportunism implies the potential capacity and risk of cheating and misrepresentation. As Williamson observes, it 'refers to the incomplete or distorted disclosure of information especially to calculated efforts to mislead, distort, disguise, obfuscate or otherwise confuse' (Willamson 1985: 47).

The risk of opportunism prompts the need for some form of governance. But this may take a number of forms. Market governance can put a check on opportunism through competition. One advantage of this form is that it requires little cost in the form of governance infrastructure. But there are conditions where the market form of governance has disadvantages. A notable condition is when transaction specific investments are required. Thus, in the marketized NHS, if all hospital foundation trusts merely competed on low cost there would be a lessened scope for significant capital investment in technologies needed to treat specialized illnesses. Trusts need some reassurance from purchasers (commissioners) that a sufficient volume of demand will be forthcoming and be paid for over a number of years to amortize the investment in equipment and in specialized medical staff. Likewise, in private-sector buyer – supplier relationships, if a supplying firm invests heavily in plant, equipment and distribution in a manner designed to fit rather specific needs of a particular buyer then it is at risk of opportunistic behaviour from that buyer. One resolution to this risk is for vertical integration – that is for the supplier and buyer to become part of one firm.

A further consideration apart from opportunism is that of incentives. The market form of governance tends to be often favoured because of its strength on this criterion. Markets incentivize individuals and groups to aspire to compete and gain advantage. Success in meeting demand results in direct reward. Hierarchical forms of governance while ameliorating opportunism (though as we will see not eliminating it) may do so at the price of blunting incentives. Hierarchy and rules which penalize departures from conformity may not be conducive to risk taking or creativity and innovation. Thus, governance is concerned with the modes and mechanisms which enable oversight and regulation of decision making (including managerial decisions making). It can take multiple forms and operate across multiple levels. Its function is to reduce opportunism and corruption and to enhance efficiency, effectiveness and fairness.

If one of the key functions of governance is to counteract opportunism and corruption, then it follows that it must have a role to play in the effective handling of organizational change. From a post-modern and constructionist perspective Hatch argues that:

> In a socially constructed world, responsibility for environmental conditions lies with those who do the constructing ... This suggests at least two competing scenarios for organizational change. First, organization change can be a vehicle of domination for those who conspire to enact the world for others ... An alternative use of social constructionism is to create a democracy of enactment in which the process is made open and available to all ... such that we create opportunities for freedom and innovation rather than simply for further domination.
>
> (Hatch 1997: 367–68 and cited in Burnes 2009)

In this chapter we explore the potential for governance to play an important part in the latter, alternative, approach. A 'democracy of enactment' for organizations can be conceived as realized through governance.

Macro-societal level

At a macro level, governance can be seen as shaped in varying ways and to varying degrees by the state. In a fully state-controlled planned economy, social and economic decision making can be accrued at the centre. Production decisions are made centrally and functionaries are instructed and held to account through plans. Increased complexity and dynamic uncertainty has induced many governments to reduce their attempts to govern from the centre and instead they have sought ways to distribute and devolve governance and accountability. The transfer of power and accountability to agencies, and through privatization, to private sector and voluntary sector organizations has led, it has been suggested, to a draining of governance from central government. This has resulted, it has been claimed, in a 'hollowing out' of the state. How governance is then accomplished by the multifarious agencies becomes the crucial question.

According to Rhodes (1997) the discussion about governance among political scientists and analysts of public management is normally, in effect, about *changes* to governance: that is, movements towards 'a new process of governance' (Rhodes 1997: 15). He notes that the term has been used widely to refer to aspects such as the new public management and the minimal state. Governance has been described as having achieved the status of a 'defining narrative' in policy circles (Rhodes 1997). The 'governance turn' has become so pervasive that it has even been suggested that 'new public governance' represents the latest paradigm shift displacing the much vaunted 'New Public Management' (Osborne 2006).

The shift from central government control to 'governance' was often seen as a key component of New Labour's modernization project. It was related to devolution and to strategic change; hence change and the governance mechanisms to drive and deliver it become closely intertwined. Modernization and governance can be seen as part of a related discourse embracing such ideas as a shift from producer interests to client interests; from uniform standardized services to 'choice' and a demand-led approach activated by the intelligent consumer; and from central to local decision-making. The extent to which these declared policies have been realized in practice

391

is of course open to debate. For example, the dual tendency to both decentralization and centralization has been widely noted (Greener and Powell 2008).

Changes to governance have had somewhat different dynamics in the private and public sectors. In the private sector, the agenda has been driven by concern about laxity by Non-Executive Directors as manifested in problems relating to executive remuneration and bonuses, excessive risk taking and the neglect of shareholder interests. In the public sector, while some of the above has found reflection in institutions such as the BBC and the newly public owned financial institutions such as Northern Rock, the dynamic has, in the main, been somewhat different and has been wrapped-up in the debates about 'modernization' and fundamental policy shifts of the kind noted above.

In both sectors, debates about modes of governance are inevitably tied to ideas about power/ authority and its distribution. Accordingly, much of the debate about governance is essentially about accountability. Who should be accountable to whom? What should be the appropriate mechanisms for giving account and receiving accounts? For what aspects of work should agents be held to account and how should performance be measured? What sanctions are appropriate for inadequate performance and what incentives/rewards for good performance?

Illustrations of macro level governance issues in the NHS

In the NHS, 'governance' has been projected to a prominent position through a series of policy reforms and reorganizations which have attended to the idea and apparatus of governance in a very explicit way. The ideas, principles and mechanisms constituting governance in the NHS derive from an amalgam drawn from corporate governance, public governance and a variety of other sources. The resulting miscellany presents directors, managers and senior clinicians, who are charged with undertaking governance within specific realms, with a considerable sense-making challenge.

Recent developments include an NHS Constitution and proposals for a new mode of governance in the shape of an 'Independent NHS Board'. Representatives from each of the main political parties have put the idea of an independent board on the agenda. There is already an NHS Management Board but it is the element of independence in the new proposal that would introduce a novel governance dimension. Meanwhile, the Constitution sets out principles, values, rights and responsibilities. It seeks to state clearly and definitively who (e.g. ministers, regulators etc) is responsible and accountable for what. The NHS operates with a massively complex governance system and it has been argued by the Kings Fund that accountabilities and responsibilities have not in the past been at all clear (Dixon and Alvarez-Rosete 2008; Dixon and Storey 2010).

Governance in the modern sense tends to be associated with a system constituted by devolved bodies assuming a range of responsibilities while subject to regulations, scrutiny and oversight (Bartle and Vass 2007). It has increasingly been used in the public and voluntary sectors to refer to the oversight of executive power, it sets the expectations for executive agents, it sets parameters, and it grants decision rights and conditional authority, it monitors performance against targets. Powerful new regulatory bodies (Monitor and the Care Quality Commission) have been created in the NHS which, in subtle ways, re-draw the nature of governance (Dixon and Storey 2010; Storey et al. 2010).

Dedicated machinery or apparatus of governance may be established in order to steer, oversee or control the executive function. It has been suggested that the key function of governance is to control and discipline management (Daily and Dalton 2003). This approach accords with agency theory, the main perspective used in governance research and theorizing. In the context of the

NHS it can be extended to also include control over clinicians. From this perspective, governance represents a means to control 'self-interested behaviour by agents' (Jensen and Meckling 1976). In the NHS, these 'agents' may be viewed as both managers and clinicians. Depending on circumstances, the part of the controlling principals may be played by directors or by regulators. The senior team acting as a corporate board of directors may enact governance and seek to ensure due diligence as part of its overall set of activities. There can thus be a blurred line with 'corporate strategy' and with 'leadership'. The assumption of the need to control for self-interested behaviour of agents by principals is not shared by all theories of governance. Stewardship theory which works from the assumptions that there can be alignment between intrinsic service motivations and organizational interests offers a significant alternative (Davis et al. 1997).

Policies and experiments in the realm of governance of the NHS represent a particular manifestation of a confluence of forces and ideas. They reflect the influence of market ideology and the reform of public service provision. They also reflect responses to widely publicized scandals which prompt a desire to manage risk and reputation as well as prompting a desire to learn from the experiences of others (Benz 2007). Both main political parties have honed a narrative about the NHS which suggests the need for a 'movement from a "failed" bureaucratic model to a system of entrepreneurial governance that would help it to survive' (Currie and Brown 2003).

The emergence of new governance arrangements can also be interpreted as response to complexity – a recognition by the state that it needs to share power – a phenomenon that has been described as a shift to 'co-arrangements' (Kooiman 2003). This is reinforced by other factors: citizens are better educated and less deferential. They expect to be consulted and be involved. They are 'challenging bureaucratic or paternalistic modes of administration' (Johansson 2005: 104). Thus, on an optimistic reading, the changes to governance in the NHS can be interpreted as part of a wider change towards more advanced modes of citizenship. Such a change would reconstitute clinicians and patients as active, participative, agents. There are a number of institutional innovations which might support such a reading.

On the other hand, a less optimistic reading would suggest that the changes reflect the state's intent to exercise control and influence in more effective and fiscally-affordable ways. To a considerable degree, whatever the initial motive, the course of the outcome will be determined by the behaviour of managers, clinicians and patient representatives within the devolved arrangements. As previous analyses have shown, there is also the element of symbolic behaviour to be taken into account (Freeman and Peck 2007) in its actual performance.

The Francis Report on the Mid Staffordshire NHS Foundation Trust revealed failures in the macro governance system as implicated in the ongoing organizational failures (Francis 2010). The regulators continued to endorse an institution which, it turns out, was failing in fundamental ways. As a result, the Inquiry recommended a further investigation into the wider regulatory regime.

Illustration of macro-level governance issues from the private sector of the economy

In the private sector, there are other aspects of macro-level governance to note. The governance of private-sector firms is largely left to the boards of those firms – but not entirely. These corporations work within a framework of laws and regulations. Long battles have been fought over this issue of 'state interference' – notably the Factory Acts of the nineteenth century and more recently with regard to health and safety, equal opportunities, low pay, etc. The concept of a national minimum wage is in operation in a many countries – including the United States as well as the UK. Recently, the pressure group Compass has called for a High Pay Commission to explore the potential to regulate high levels of pay. The idea is to mimic the Low Pay Commission which has successfully set minimum wages for over a decade. The reasoning is that the extent of the gap between high and low pay can become so wide as to threaten a society's sense of social justice and the sense of a shared financial destiny. This has proved a controversial proposal but it nicely illustrates some of the issues surrounding choices about governance and regulation.

Following the global economic crisis there are pressures for an increased role for governance and regulation of business. There is a marked increase in the mistrust of business. Numerous corporate and investment scandals have been well publicized and prominent figures such as Bernard Madoff have been sent to jail. Notably, the US regulator, the Securities and Exchange Commission, had previously conducted investigations into Madoff's business but had failed to uncover the fraud. Following the Enron scandal, the mighty Arthur Anderson accounting firm was discredited and had to change its name and rebrand. As (Reich 2009: 96) notes: 'Every major US accounting firm either admitted negligence or paid substantial fines without admitting guilt. Nearly every major investment bank played a part in defrauding investors, largely by urging them to buy stocks that the banks' own analysts privately described as junk'. In the UK, the level of bonuses paid by financial services firms has been widely condemned as excessive. The case of the former chief executive of RBS, Sir Fred Goodwin, became a special case of note in the media with a range of senior politicians including the Prime Minister publicly condemning payments made to him. Staff had incentives to take excessive risk with apparently few penalties if the risks played out in a negative way.

The perceived lack of governance of these processes was compounded when bonuses continued to be paid even in banks which had become publicly owned as a result of bailouts. The furore included the unusual spectacle of a group of business professors writing a collective letter to the *Guardian* newspaper in August 2009 denouncing the idea that high levels of bonuses for bankers could be justified. Central to the debate here is whether scarce talent will flee across international borders in order to escape higher taxes or tighter regulation. Not surprisingly bankers tend to play the international mobility card very quickly. The business professors' letter suggested that this is a bluff and that there is plenty of latent talent ready to replace any lost financiers. We know that investment bankers often operate in teams and whole teams or parts of teams do move between firms. That in itself provides some barrier to the free entry of new labour. The possibility of whole firms relocating and thus taking job opportunities (and tax revenues) with them is another matter. But the risk and uncertainty raises the question whether, in a global economy, these firms are beyond governance. To date, national regulatory systems have seemed incapable of regulating global enterprises. There have been some tentative moves towards international cooperation between governments in pursuit of a more regulated world – most notably with the restrictions on tax havens.

The extent to which, and the manner in which, new governance oversight of business will occur in the future remains uncertain. In the current climate it seems highly likely that the pendulum will swing from a sentiment in favour of free markets to a more regulated settlement. The damage caused to jobs and wealth prompts and enables such increased regulation. The form it will take is open to question. Robert Reich (2009) argues that the new mode of regulation and governance will witness increased government 'activism' but of a mode which emphasizes incentives rather than restriction. Even in the US context this may imply governments mandating changes to bonus payment systems. Reich (2009) argues that 'By better aligning the incentives of executives and traders with the needs and goals of investors, we'll avoid rigid restrictions that tie the hands of executives with regard to all sorts of specific decisions' (Reich 2009: 97).

In the UK, one of the responses to the economic crisis was the establishment of a review by the Financial Reporting Council (FRC). The FRC issued a consultation document and reactions from corporations tended to argue that the existing Combined Code of governance was an appropriate framework (despite its failure to prevent the various failings). Root and branch reform was not supported. For example, a senior figure from BT observed: 'A prescriptive approach to corporate governance is likely to damage rather than improve the effectiveness of governance. We strongly believe that future efforts should largely go into improving the provisions of the Code rather than radical reform' (Scott 2009). Responses to the consultation document about the Combined Code reveal debates about the weight to be given to experience of non-executive directors, their independence and the degree to which they are team players while also being willing to challenge the chief executive.

Organizational level

Organizations operate within the changing milieu outlined in the previous section. It could be claimed that the very possibility for many organizations simply to exist results from the changes to governance noted at the macro level. The withdrawal of the state from direct delivery of many services has been effected through increased marketization including privatization which transfers opportunity from the state to private sector organizations (e.g. privately operated prisons, refuse collection etc). Additionally, new organizations are created in the semi-public, voluntary and social enterprise sectors also as a result of devolution of responsibility to agencies and other bodies which are independent of the state albeit subject to regulatory bodies such as the Audit Commission.

The role of boards

Whether the organizations are private sector companies or quasi-state bodies, an important aspect to note from the point of view of organization theory is the problem of 'agency'. When hierarchy is chosen as the governance solution some form of organization has to be created. Whichever mode is developed (for example, highly centralized or highly decentralized) the 'owners' (be that the state or a diverse body of shareholders in a publicly quoted company) will want reassurance that their 'agents' (the firm's directors and executives) are acting in the owners interests and not their own personal interests in a way which is detrimental to the owner's interests (share-holders or citizens). This reassurance is found, or at least sought, through various mechanisms of holding to account. In the private sector, corporate boards of directors are required. These contain a mix of full time executive directors (the firm's most senior managers) and independent external directors the non-executive directors. These mechanisms are forms of governance.

As more and more public services are delivered by these independent bodies concern is raised about their accountability and questions are raised about a 'democratic deficit'. In response, more attention has been paid to the governance of these bodies. The main device for meeting these anxieties has been the establishment of boards of directors to provide oversight of these bodies. Boards allow for a meeting at the strategic apex of executive and non-executive directors. The latter are supposed to bring external perspectives to bear, to champion the interests of the owners and to provide challenge to the internal, full-time executives. Also, non-executives can, it is hoped, seek to reassure service users, stakeholders and the public at large that the organizations are being run in a manner which is responsible and which balances service quality and financial stability. The Nolan Committee on Standards in Public Life in its first report established the seven

395

key principles of 'selflessness, integrity, objectivity, accountability, openness, honesty and leadership' (Nolan 1996).

Different models of corporate governance

Despite this attempt to establish universal principles there are various types or models of governance. These types reflect different theories and they also find reflection in different roles played by boards that follow one or other of these theories (Carver and Oliver 2002; Cornforth 2003; National Leadership Council 2010). Drawing on these different sources it is possible and useful to delineate seven main types or models of governance.

Agency theory has been discussed above. At its heart is the principal–agent relationship. The driving notion is that governance is essentially about the means whereby those occupying governance roles ensure that agents (for example, managers and others) act in a manner approved of by the principals. The model therefore emphasizes compliance, monitoring, control, targets, performance measurement, incentives and sanctions. A sub-set of this is the Carver model which still retains the principal – agent distinction but does so in a more sharply defined manner (Carver 2001; Carver and Oliver 2002). It emphasizes 'policy governance' by drawing a clear line between the board's role in setting a policy framework and the managers' role as operators who have freedom to manage operational matters as long as they work to the policy framework. This form of 'policy governance' thus shies away from the close monitoring of performance suggested in the first form of agency theory above.

Managerial hegemony theory is a variant of the agency theory except in this mode the managers have taken over and the external representatives are so well-controlled by the expert managers that they merely serve to rubber-stamp proposals from the executive as they lend a veneer of legitimacy to the dominant group.

Stewardship theory suggests a possibility for shared interests and shared values between 'owners' and managers. Seats at the board are mainly therefore reserved for various experts who seek, in a balanced way, to improve performance. The underlying model is one of partnership.

The *stakeholder model* suggests a set of competing as well as overlapping interests within organizations and those they seek to serve. The work of the board is therefore to balance these varying priorities of interested parties, to involve stakeholders and to ensure all stakeholders are content that their interests are being safeguarded.

The *democratic model* emphasizes a different aspect – namely, the idea that the purpose and function of governance is a *representation* of public interests. The work of the board therefore is to reconcile competing interests and one way in which this might be assessed is in the extent to which different interests can be seen to have a representative on the board voicing the concerns and wants of the constituents.

The *co-option model* derives from the resource dependency theory of governance. This focuses on external relations and the need to secure and maintain resources from outside. The work of the board is to assuage the concerns and win the trust of these resource-providing stakeholders.

Finally, the *generative governance model* emphasizes active and ongoing dialogue and shared sense-making between the board members, the staff and the service users (Chait et al. 2005). This model is deemed especially suitable for the governance of non-profit organizations where engaging service users and staff in an ongoing interpretation of needs, priorities, information, opportunities and plans is a crucial element of success.

These various 'types' of governance of course often overlap and exist in less than pure form in practice. Boards, as active governing bodies, grapple with the forces, paradoxes and tendencies identified in the different models (Demb and Neubauer 1992). There are a number of classic dilemmas facing governing boards and these are reflected in the different emphases shown in the models above and we now turn to an examination of these tensions and dilemmas.

Tensions and dilemmas of organizational level governance

The first point of tension stems from the question *who* should be doing the governing? In other words, who should be appointed to serve on boards and how should they be selected? The model which privileges democracy would tend to suggest that election to board positions is important and that members should represent constituents. Conversely, a stewardship perspective would stress expertise and this would imply a selection process based on appointment.

A second tension is whether board members should emphasize *monitoring and conformance* or should themselves seek to *drive performance*? The conformance role would mean monitoring executive behaviour; the performance role would also involve monitoring but with a stress on the attainment of high performance and the setting of higher targets. A further tension can be found in the extent to which board members – especially the external representatives – seek to shape not only the overall purpose and mission but also the strategic objectives of the organization.

A third tension and dilemma concerns the degree of *involvement in operational matters*. If, for example, a hospital board agrees to a plan to reconfigure wards (with repercussions on staff numbers and roles) should the board be kept involved in the working through of the changes or should this be considered managerial, operational detail? At Stafford hospital just such a reconfiguration of wards occurred and with deleterious outcomes; the board was not kept informed nor did it seek to keep itself informed of these developments and it was criticized by the subsequent inquiry for this. But a board operating with the Carver model in mind (policy governance as above) would not even be trying to exercise this kind of oversight.

A fourth tension and dilemma is an extension of the previous choice between a stance which involves not only close monitoring of executive managers in their implementation work but a further step which involves joint problem-solving in a seamless *partnership approach*. The alternative would be for governors to maintain a critical distance (for example, by refusing to have non-executive directors sit on sub-committees).

A fifth tension concerns how to govern using reported data. Determining which data to seek and how much of it is not an easy task. Too much detail will swamp a board; but too little or in too much of an aggregated form and the ability to read the meaning of the data and information becomes problematic. Board members may become too easily assured by executive summaries and or by external regulatory endorsement. Knowing how far to dig and to insist on relevant data is a challenge for non-executive directors in particular. Individuals may be perceived as awkward if they press a point following a general assurance from a chief executive or another executive director.

In practice, board members often veer between different stances. None the less, distinct patterns can sometimes be observed as a board culture develops in favour of one stance or another. Strong chairmanship can steer a board towards a particular style, posture and associated set of behaviours. The ability of chairs to hold appraisals of board members can bestow upon them a power to shape behaviours.

The interplay between governance and organizational change will depend very much upon which of the above models is followed by the governors of an organization. It will also be dependent on how board members handle the dilemmas identified above.

Illustrations of organizational level governance issues from the NHS

There are different forms of governance regulations cascading down through the reformed structure of the NHS: directives, standards, assurance frameworks, regulations, incentives, codes of conduct and standing orders. There are also a large number of vehicles for ensuring compliance. There is, in addition, the requirement on trusts to develop three-year local delivery plans which address national targets. Hence, although governance in the NHS is now a highly dispersed phenomenon, these all serve to indicate the 'web of constraints' within which acute and primary care trusts must function. The complexity presents board members and foundation trust governors with an interesting set of challenges.

The corporate level in the NHS is organized around 'trusts'. These are self-governing entities (or businesses) which may be responsible for a number of hospitals and other health service units. At trust level, overall governance is effected through sets of arrangements based on models borrowed to a considerable extent from the corporate world. Extensive guidelines detailing how trust boards should be structured and should behave in order to mimic 'effective boards' have been promulgated by the Appointments Commission in conjunction with Monitor and Dr Foster Intelligence (2006, 2010). The guides state the purpose of NHS boards: to set strategic direction, to oversee progress towards strategic goals and to monitor operational performance. In one interpretation, these new governance arrangements give very considerable autonomy to foundation trust boards. Some boards choose to act as though these freedoms are real and extensive.

But, other boards are more cautious. They point to the array of 'guidelines' against which they are inspected and audited. Monitor, the Appointments Commission and the CQC between them variously define the principles which guide how each of the organizations (SHAs, acute trusts and PCTs) should operate, they stipulate the role of the boards, outline the precise information requirements needed in order for boards to discharge these responsibilities, they provide model board agendas and an annual cycle of board activities. In other words, there is very considerable guidance and thus scope for relatively uniform practice. And given that trusts are overseen and judged by the bodies issuing these guidelines, there is considerable incentive to take serious note of their suggestions. Foundation trusts need to satisfy Monitor that they have in place systems and procedures that meet their criteria.

In addition to the guidance about procedures, there are numerous external audits of performance outcomes. Of crucial importance here is the Care Quality Commission which evaluates performance against a detailed list of 'standards'. But at the theoretical axial point to the whole apparatus is the notion of 'corporate governance'. This denotes the machinery and processes at board level which are designed to allow supervision and policy direction of trust management in primary and secondary care. The intense concentration on enhancing the capabilities of trust boards in recent years through investments in careful recruitment, selection and development is indicative here.

'Clinical governance' occurs within the envelope of corporate governance and is to a large degree a tributary of corporate governance. In essence, it refers to a series of protocols, institutions and processes which are designed to help ensure that there is some oversight of clinical judgement, practice and outcomes. Individual clinicians and clinical teams are thus held to account. In recent years, trusts have appointed directors of clinical governance and have established clinical governance committees. Whether this is conformance ritual or genuinely useful risk management is a further question.

NHS Trusts which have not yet gained foundation trust status, continue to be answerable to their SHAs. Although they have boards of directors their governing capacity is thus significantly curtailed. In contrast, foundation trusts as semi-autonomous devolved bodies, freed from direct control by SHAs and governed by boards and by members' councils, ought to reveal even more accentuated aspects of governance than was the case with other acute trusts or with PCTs. foundation trusts are supposed to be accountable to their local communities through their members and governors. As devolved bodies, foundation trusts are expected and indeed required to operate with diverse lines and types of accountability. These include remnants of traditional hierarchical accountability to the Department of Health, contractual accountability to commissioning bodies, accountability to regulators, partnership accountability to agencies such as local authorities and local accountability to governors, members, patients and the public. These types of accountability are mapped in Figure 27.1 for NHS foundation trusts.

Part of the work of governance undertaken by the boards of foundation trusts is to balance accountability to a number of different regulators and stakeholders. The Department of Health's (2002) *A Guide to NHS Foundation Trusts* stated clearly that foundation trusts are designed to 'introduce a new form of social ownership where health services are owned and accountable to local people'. Failings in clinical standards and/or in standards of care are increasingly likely to be seen as connected with failings in governance. The problems uncovered in the Mid Staffordshire NHS Foundation Trust were described in a letter from Monitor to the trust's governors as revealing 'inadequacies in aspects of the quality of clinical and nursing care at the trust, alongside broader governance and senior management failings'. It was prompted by high mortality rates, particularly in emergency admissions and subsequently many other failures in the standard of care were revealed. Governance was seen to have failed. But, apart from helping to

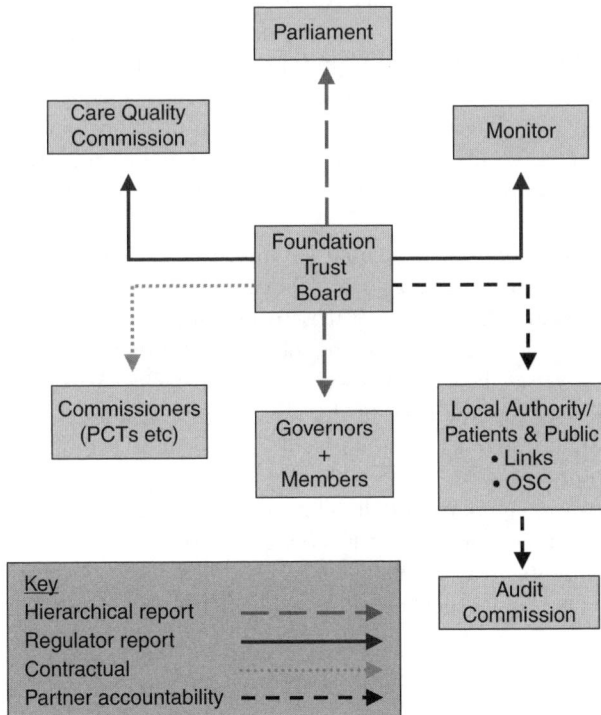

Figure 27.1 Foundation Trust accountability map
Source: Storey et al. (2011)

399

ensure ongoing performance could governance be used to drive change? This is the subject of our final section.

Governance and organizational change

A governance perspective on organizational change highlights two main types of questions. The first is concerned with *who* initiates, drives and legitimates change? The second concerns the interaction between governance and change, most especially the impact of governance mechanisms and processes on change.

As we have seen, governance discourse assumes that multiple and potentially conflicting interests are to be expected and therefore mechanisms are required to mediate these interests. This, in turn, implies the possibility of legitimated and non-legitimated change attempts. Governance thus offers a mechanism to arbitrate between arguments and positions relating to proposed change. There has been an abiding concern with the management of change, but rather less attention has been directed to the governance of change. It has been argued in this chapter that the latter needs to be recognized as meriting a greater role.

Governance could be seen to be a positive force in relation to change for a number of reasons. Governance implies the legitimate airing of a range of diverse voices. Diversity and variety are often associated with positive change management. Not only may a wider range of options be considered so that more creative solutions are considered but the very process of enabling these voices in an appropriate forum may also serve to lend legitimacy to the eventual decisions which are taken. Additionally, governance suggests a detached, measured and strategic perspective rather than specific personal agendas and self-serving interests. In so far as this is delivered in practice then any change proposals emerging should have been considered with regard to a range of short, medium and long term consequences for a range of stake-holders. Further, governance tends to emphasize accountability and a sober consideration of risk and its mitigation. Ideally, change proposals emerging from the governance process will be in alignment with the organizations mission and strategy rather than merely short term and opportunist in nature.

On the other hand, governance could be argued to be *inimical* to organizational change. Governance processes are relatively slow when compared with executive action. They involve checks and balances and the exercise of these may drain some of the pent-up excitement and energy behind a change idea. Likewise, the sober consideration of risk which is noted above as strength could conversely be viewed as a weakness from a change perspective. Close, measured attention to risk may dull the edge of the kind of enthusiasm and faith in an idea which is sometimes needed to drive a change forward. Indeed, most reforms of governance and the associated regulatory measures – such as the Sarbanes – Oxley Act – attract critics who suggest that such governance requirements dull the competitive edge of capitalist enterprise.

But, these could be considered as self-serving criticisms. The central argument for urging a clearer and more insistent case for linking governance and change is that the process of change itself has to meet the ethical and participatory standards if it is to be sustainable and effective under current conditions. Burnes (2009) in his defence of Kurt Lewin's values-based approach to planned change mounts a spirited critique of the 'emergent' and 'political' change-management orthodoxy of the past couple of decades (Burnes 2009). This orthodoxy he suggests has, albeit unwittingly, given succour to the unethical abuses of power and privilege instanced at various points throughout this chapter. The role for governance therefore is to rediscover, defend, practice and require an ethical approach to organizational change.

The ultimate argument for good governance is that it enables sustained and defensible organizational behaviour. As seen in this chapter, good governance requires a mix of appropriate regulation, mechanisms, processes and behaviours. Good governance is required for long-term viability and sustainability – and it is most especially required for the successful enactment of change.

References

Appointments Commission /Dr Foster/Monitor (2006). *The Intelligent Board*, London, The Appointments Commission.

Bartle, I. and P. Vass (2007). 'Self-regulation within the regulatory state: towards a new regulatory paradigm?' *Public Administration* 85(4): 885–905.

Benz, M. (2007). 'Corporate governance: what can we learn for public governance?' *Academy of Management Review* 32(1): 92–104.

Burnes, B. (2009). 'Ethics and organisational change: Time for a return to Lewinian values.' *Journal of Change Management* 9(4): 359–81.

Carver, J. (2001). 'Carver's policy governance model in nonprofit organizations.' *Gouvernance Revue Internationale* 2(1): 30–48.

Carver, J. and C. Oliver (2002). *Corporate Boards that Create Value: Governing Company Performance from the Boardroom.* San Francisco, CA, Jossey-Bass.

Chait, R., W. Ryan and B. Taylor (2005). *Governance as Leadership: Reframing the Work of Nonprofit Boards*, Wiley.

Cornforth, C. (2003). Introduction. *The Governance of Public and Non-Profit Organisations*. London, Routledge.

Currie, G. and A.D. Brown (2003). 'A narratological approach to understanding processes of organising in a UK NHS hospital.' In C. Cornforth, (ed.) *Human Relations* 56(5): 563–85.

Daily, C.M. and D.R. Dalton (2003). 'Corporate governance: decades of of dialogue and data.' *Academy of Management Review* 28: 371–82.

Davis, J.H., F.D. Schoorman and L. Donaldson (1997). 'Towards a stewardship theory of management.' *Academy of Management Review* 22: 20–47.

Demb, A. and F. Neubauer (eds) (1992). *The Corporate Board: Confronting the Paradoxes*. Oxford, Oxford University Press.

Department of Health (2002). *A Guide to NHS Foundation Trusts*, London, Department of Health.

Dixon, A. and A. Alvarez-Rosete (2008). *Governing the NHS*. London, Kings Fund.

Dixon, A. and J. Storey (2010). 'Accountability of Foundation Trusts in the English NHS: views of directors and governors.' *Journal of Health Services Research and Policy*, 15(2): 82–89.

Ezzamel, M. and M. Reed (2008). 'Why this special issue on governance in transition?' *Human Relations* 61: 595–96.

Ezzamel, M. and M. Reed (2008). 'Governance: A code of multiple colours.' *Human Relations* 61: 597–615.

Francis, R. (2010). *Independent Inquiry into Care Provided by MId Staffordshire NHS Foundation Trust*. London, HOC.

Freeman, T. and E. Peck (2007). 'Performing government: A partnership board dramaturgy.' *Public Administration* 85(4): 907–29.

Greener, I. and M. Powell (2008). 'The changing governance of the NHS: Reform in a post-Keynesian health service.' *Human Relations* 61: 617–36.

Jensen, M.C. and W.H. Meckling (1976). 'Theory of the firm: managerial behaviour, agency costs and ownership struture.' *Journal of Finanical Economics* 3: 305–60.

Johansson, H.a.H.B. (2005). Welfare governance and the remaking of citizenship. In J. Newman (ed.) *Remaking Governance*. Bristol, Policy Press.

Kooiman, J. (2003). *Governing as Governance*. London, SAGE.

Morris, J., J. Hassard and L. McCann (2008). The resilience of 'institutionalized capitalism': Managing managers under 'shareholder capitalism' and 'managerial capitalism', *Human Relations* 61: 687–710.

401

National Leadership Council (2010). *The Health NHS Board: Principles for Good Governance*. London, NHS National Leadership Council.

Nolan, M.P. (1996). *2nd Report of the Committee on Standards in Public Life* (Cm.: 3270-II). London, Stationery Office.

Osborne, S.P. (2006). 'The New Public Governance.' *Public Management Review* 8(3): 377–87.

Reich, R.B. (2009). 'Government in your business.' *Harvard Business Review* July – August: 94–99.

Rhodes, R.A.W. (1997). *Understanding Governance*. Buckingham, Open University Press.

Scott, A. (2009). 'Response to the FRC Review of Governance: Submission from BT', frc.org.uk.

Storey, J., J. Bullivant and A. Corbett-Nolan (2011). *Governing the New NHS: Issues and Tensions in Health Service Management*. London, Routledge.

Storey, J., R. Holti, N. Winchester, R. Green, G. Salaman and P. Bate (2010). *The Intended and Unintended Outcomes of New Governance Arrangements within the NHS*. Southampton, NIHR/SDO.

Walker, D. (2009). *A Review of Corporate Governance in UK Banks and Other Financial Industry Entities*. London, HM Treasury.

Williamson, O.E. (1975). *Markets and Hierarchies*. New York, The Free Press.

Willamson, O.E. (1985). *The Economic Institutions of Capitalism*. New York, The Free Press.

Part 5

Key issues

Introduction

David M. Boje

It goes without saying that change is accompanied by resistance. In managerialist organizational change, resistance is some sort of subordinate irrationality to be overcome, or a direct challenge to the ruling by those at the base of the pyramid. The authors in this part take exception to the managerialist view of managing resistance to change. They raise key issues, themes and controversies including the theme of imperialism, and ways to achieve a decolonized space through acts of deconstruction and attention to stories as utterances. Chapters in this part, all seem to want a new approach, one that reimagines resistance as more than just futile.

The issues with managerialist resistance are around power, domination and gender.

In Chapter 28, Richard Badham, Richard Claydon and Simon Down raise the issue of how management, in order to justify cultural change, create a conceptually frozen 'irrational' historical past (Age of Unreason – Position 1). Management then contrast this with an alternative concept: a 'good/rational' organizational future (Age of Reason – Position 2). Often this is done by reducing Kurt Lewin's more complex field theory model to just one-dimensional, linear, sequential process of 'unfreezing', 'moving' and 'refreezing.' This reinforces the managerialist mind-set of an enforced top-down regime that treats ambivalence, ambiguity, or any other resistance as a threat. The paradox Badham, Claydon and Down introduce is that purging ambivalence only enhances it.

Raza and Ali Mir, in Chapter 29, draw attention to the glut of organizational change, and managing change articles and books, to sort out ways that both are complicit in an ideology of imperialism in late modern capitalism which justifies all kinds of exploitative practices. They stress how resistance to change that management wants, is made to appear totally irrational. In these times of macro–economic booms and busts, they question the concept of 'jobless recovery', and change that legitimizes and rationalized managerial regimes of unequal exchange, declaring resistance a madness is so very convenient. Their chapter presents a critical ethnography of 'knowledge transfer' situating the change in its sociocultural and historical context. The Mir brothers stress the absence of actual dialogical processes is a way to 'manufacture' the appearance of consent, without addressing resistance.

In Chapter 30, Maxim Voronov and Warner Woodward take the view that organization development has failed to humanize organization, and become just one more form of domination tool used by the managerialist hoard. OD has reached an end, and it's time for a new OD discourse and practice to emerge. The good news is the problem lies in the OD discourse, not all those good-hearted, mild-mannered OD practitioners. The reason given for the death of OD is its rootedness in discourse of neo-empiricism and a limited overly psychological approach whose sensemaking is overly rational while avoiding the important sociological questions. One wonders if the fatal flaw of OD is not in the transition from a more materiality-rooted social construction (e.g. Berger and Luckmann) that squarely addressed the realities of power, and the new social constructionism (what Bruno Latour calls reassembling the social to focus on actant-materiality as well as those human actor-networks). OD discourse, while claiming to be humanistic practices, seems, now more than ever, to privilege managerialism interests in the bottom line, and the psychological orientation of those who resist change, in ways that are blind to power, class and material conditions.

Nic Beech and Rob McIntosh, in Chapter 31, are critical of stakeholder approaches to managing change because the mapping-stakeholder-exercises are quite divorced from any kind of dialogical 'action'. Resistance is not engaged in the mapping, which is disengaged from any field of stakeholder interaction processes. The authors give examples from the French film industry of how managers tracing out stakeholder maps to 'manage' stakeholders ignore actions, such as actually engaging with stakeholders. Those in charge of managing change have an excessively agential view, where 'managing' stakeholders drives the change initiative. An engaged approach has a less simplified view of stakeholder dynamics and identity.

In Chapter 32, Mary Ann Hazen reflects on the polyphonic organization. Could it be that dialogically engaged stakeholders can be about ambivalence and treat resistance as necessary to change? Not really, because as Hazen points out, polyphonic dialogism needs a space for discourse that is not already thoroughly colonized or imperialized as the Mir brothers stress. Deconstruction is explored as a way to decolonize spaces for dialogical discourse. Hazen concludes that the idea of stories as utterances is a way to expand some space for the dialogical.

Jo Tyler, in Chapter 33, works with storytelling and a diversity of perspectives to get at more polyphonic processes. She explores how storytelling spaces that allows the exploration of diversity perspectives. Tyler turns to Socratic dialogue (one of the roots of Bakhtin's dialogism), as a way to get beyond subject-object dualism. Like other authors in this part, Tyler is concerned that the sacred spaces for dialogic conversation get instrumentalized in organizations. Tyler finds some hope in Torbert's liberating structures, then looks to de Certeau, for some liberating time and space structures. Her final proposal is for sculpting liminal spaces that allow people to listen to and actually explore their differences.

In Chapter 34, Albert Mills, Kathy Sanderson and Jean Helms Mills take a feminist look at organizational change. Most of the change articles fail to take gender into account. The authors look to Weick for a theory of 'critical sensemaking' especially when organization has had a shock and could very well take a serious look at the 'gender order'. The authors apply the case of Helms Mills, where a combination of social, on-going, and identity sensemaking give stakeholders 'sensemaking cues' that it's time for a culture change. When looking at the change management approaches from TQM, Balanced Scorecard, Six Sigma, Business Process Reengineering, to Appreciative Inquiry, Sanderson and the Mills question the approaches to gender, using the 'critical sensemaking approach'. For example, in the approaches, characteristics of women are either ignored, or essentialized. The focus on best practices in the approaches to change management lack any sort of gender reflexivity. Feminist have argued that there is just not the space in the colonized organizations for dialogically polyphonic discourse among stakeholders. Perhaps the problem lies with the social construction paradigm, and its preference for retrospection and representational narrative? The authors therefore look at present-ness in the Now-ness of Being-ness.

In the final chapter in Part V, Carl Rhodes offers a critical review of the role of storytelling in organizational change. He raises ethical issues. A storytelling organization is made up of members' simultaneous and multiple ways of storytelling past, present and future, But a storytelling organization also has some collective agreement about common organizational myths. The mythmaking of the Cadbury Foundation is explored by Rhodes to look at the ethical aspects of their storytelling organization. The sanctioned ways of mythmaking, become sanctioned ways of storytelling that can drown out or marginalize the other ways of telling, thus becoming quite hegemonic (political as well as ideological, in ways the Mir brothers stress, or as Hazen puts it colonizing). Imposing a monological storytelling in a change project is a subject for ethics, where some voices matter more than others. Rhodes suggests that an ethical narrative history could help this situation. He does not go so far as saying that the organization would become polyphonic or dialogical.

28

The ambivalence paradox in cultural change

Richard Badham, Richard Claydon and Simon Down

Introduction

Managerial culture change programmes are expected to integrate employees into the organizational 'family', align their performance with organizational expectations and improve competitiveness. To achieve these aims, current programmes identify a set of organizational practices
contributing to poor performance and, in a sense, conceptually 'freeze' them into a 'bad/
irrational' conceptualization of organization (Weick and Quinn, 1999). In classic Enlightenment
terms, this conceptually frozen 'irrational' past (Age of Unreason – Position 1) is then contrasted
with an alternative concept: a 'good/rational' organizational future (Age of Reason – Position 2)
(Badham, 1986). To enable Position 1 to become Position 2, change programmes often initiate a
series of processes designed to 'un-freeze' current 'bad' practices, 'move' the organization
through the change, and 're-freeze' them into new 'good' ones (Brown, 1998). In a dangerous
caricature of Kurt Lewin's original, considered and provocative three-stage model of change
(Burnes, 2004), planned cultural change is presented in one-dimensional terms as a rigid,
sequenced and autocratic process. Many such programmes attempt to whip up enthusiasm for
the 'good/rational' organizational future, seek to restrict and direct reflection, yet inevitably fails
in this task. As illustrated in Barker's (1993) description of the early stages of change in ISE, such
programmes inevitably create discomforting and energizing 'betwixt and between' experiences
of liminality that awaken critical reflection upon *all* aspects of such processes.

Managerial attempts are made to create an emotional attachment to a restricted view of the
'journey' (Dunn, 1990; Grint, 1994) that potentially disables more generalized reflection. It is no
coincidence that the first major study of deliberate psychological processes of 'unfreezing',
'moving' and 'refreezing' by Schein (1951) was undertaken as an investigation of the brainwashing of US citizens captured by the Chinese in North Korea. The very nature of this 'three step'
process mirrors the ritualized conversion processes of 'rites of passage', in its symbolic 'separation'
from the past, movement through a 'liminal' state and 're-incorporation' in the future (Turner,
1982, 1985; Brown, 1998). However, while doubt and reflectivity are important parts of any
transition ritual, the goal of many planned cultural change initiatives has tended to be to enforce
and reinforce a different unitary mindset that aligns committed, motivated, hardworking and,
importantly, uncritical employees to the process and practices of the new cultural regime.

As Bauman (1993) explores in some depth, these very attempts to order, control and align human subjects are inevitably unsuccessful in eliminating uncertainty and ambivalence. They paradoxically end up increasing the very ambiguity and ambivalence that they sought to purge. The attempt to plan cultural change leads to unexpected consequences. Implementation in practice is a (non-trivial) complex affair. The quest to achieve order and unity through the imposition of new classifications and ordering devices creates new ambiguities and ambivalences as they require further interpretation, detailing and application.

One traditional breeding ground for routine organizational ambivalence is the tension generated in employees trapped between a reliance on the organization for continued existence and resentment towards the organization for its limitation of their freedoms and the imposition of its practices. The ultimate aim of the type of planned change programme outlined above is to combine emotional, cognitive and volitive methods (Smelser, 1997) to purge this ambivalence and align member motivations and emotions with the interests of the organization. However, by encouraging critical reflection on the old practices, change programmes inevitably open up criticism of the change process itself – yet often attempt to restrict or even forbid such reflections. Influenced by exhortations to critically reflect on existing 'bad' organizational processes, those subject to change programmes often extend their criticism to perceived ambiguities, contradictions, paradoxes and gaps in the new 'good' ones. The disruptive experience of liminality allows and encourages employees to recognize the arbitrary and restrictive nature of cultural authority (Turner, 1982, 1985), and enables the voicing of discontent. Yet the demand of those imposing culture change programmes for total commitment and loyalty attempts to restrict this reflection in an attempt to guide a commercialized 're-incorporation'. Consequently, overt critique of the new regime is often condemned as resistance, and extended critical reflection then tends to become covert, unvoiced backstage ambivalent evaluation accompanied by irony and humour.

Caught within an underlying ambivalence towards the organization, and corporate ambivalence towards critical reflection on organizational practices, managers and employees attempt the uncomfortable task of grappling with its meaning for themselves and the organizations within which they work. In this way, an ambivalence paradox is created. Change programmes that seek to purge ambivalence are in the paradoxical position of actually enhancing it.

As we will argue below, for many radical critics of such culture change programmes, the resulting ambivalence is captured, positioned and stigmatized as the empty 'irony' or 'bewildered' wanderings of 'capitulating' organizational 'dramaturgs', characterized as one organizational 'position' contrasted to the engaged enthusiasts ('colluded', 'conformist', 'bewitched') and the distanced critics ('defensive', 'resistant', 'bothered'). However, as we will seek to show, it is arguable that there are significant elements of ambiguity and ambivalence in the mindset and practices of many (if not all) managers and employees, promoters and targets of change. Given that critical reflection is brought into being and then repressed by the processes of change, it is not surprising that this occurs. It can, in a sense, be seen as the inevitable outcome of the lived experience of an extreme version of what is arguably the general 'liminoid' nature of late modern existence (Turner, 1982).

How all managers and employees grapple with such ambiguities, and the ambivalence they generate, is an important site for research and investigation (Badham and Garrety, 2003; McLoughlin and Badham, 2005). In exploring this theme, this chapter draws on a case study of the complex subject positions adopted by organizational actors to help open up the intellectual space for such explorations. It is the argument presented here that in order to help inform future studies, the initial tri-partite positioning of managers and employees as 'zeolots', 'cynics' or ironic 'dramaturgs' should be used in a more reflective and nuanced fashion (see, for example, the discussion of 'positioning' in Davies and Harre, 1990; Harre and Langenhove, 1999). It should be

408

explicitly understood as an initial guide and orientation for exploring subject positions not as a set of typecast characters. A central characteristic of the lived experience of those caught in the 'blender' of culture change programmes is embedded uncertainty (Badham and Garrety, 2003). In order to capture this experience it is necessary to provide a fluid, processual and interactive investigation of change programme participant's positioning of themselves and others. Such an investigation does more than capture the inevitably fragmented, multi-dimensional, and fluid character of organizational change(ing) (Weick and Quinn, 1999). It also, most importantly, provides the intellectual space for reflection and voice about the experienced ambiguities, ambivalences, uncertainties and paradoxes on the part of those involved in such change. In so doing, it helps create the conditions for a more intimate dialogue between those experiencing and those studying what are inherently complex and often harrowing change experiences.

Planned culture change programmes

Planned organizational development initiatives stemming from the innovative and critical work of Kurt Lewin and his followers are broad ranging, complex and multidimensional in character (Gallos, 2006). One particular form, widespread since the 1980s, are managerialist 'strong culture' initiatives advocating a more deliberate and systematic engineering of the subjective and emotional dimensions of employee experience (Peters and Waterman, 1982; Ouchi, 1981; Deal and Kennedy, 1982; Ray, 1986; Willmott, 1993). Such initiatives at cultural re-engineering draw on a long, established and arguably cyclical tradition of recommending organizational regulation through normative control (Barley and Kunda, 1992; McLoughlin et al., 2005). This tradition continues to be influential in initiatives informed by discourses of enterprise (du Gay, 2000), ranging from arguments for greater empowerment and engagement to exhortations for employees to 'be themselves' in a more fun and authentic work culture (Fleming, 2009).

Such prescriptive managerial initiatives have been accompanied by a proliferation of critical analyses within organizational studies, arguably originating with Ray's (1986) argument that the demands of corporate culture were generating a 'love of the firm and its goals' engineered by 'manipulation of culture including myth [and] ritual' (p. 293). Subsequent critiques have expanded upon these themes, drawing attention to the seductive nature of organizational culture, with its tendencies towards totalizing and inescapable normative control (Casey, 1995).

Following this lead, managerial and critical perspectives on normative cultural re-engineering developed into significant but largely incompatible literatures. In crude terms, early approaches tended to fall into dichotomous categories of 'consensus' v. 'conflict' (Burrell and Morgan, etc.) or 'integrationist' v. 'differentiationist' (Martin 1992, 2001) paradigms. The former is unitarist, functionalist, consensual and managerialist, assuming and/or pursuing a common and benign organizational culture, creating committed corporate citizens. The latter assumes an embedded inequality in organizations, domination by the most powerful, and conflicting ideologies reflecting different interests, generating resistant practices and sub-cultures. In a sense, these perspectives reflect the common sense 'dual code' within organizations themselves, a bi-polar pattern of alternative organizational languages and moralities about organizational life and experience, identified by Dalton (1961) and Burns (1961).

While these perspectives have traditionally dominated much of the literature on organizations and culture, Martin (1992, 2001) has identified a third influential tradition in culture studies, that of 'fragmentationism'. This perspective emphasizes the complex, multi-dimensional, messy and emergent nature of culture and its transformation. Within studies of cultural re-engineering, this perspective is reflected in studies of the inherent ambivalence and ambiguity in such programmes

(Badham and Garrety, 2003; McLoughlin et al., 2005), as well as in observations of the lived experience and discourses of a class of emergent 'ironic' (Kunda, 1992; Badham and McLoughlin, 2005), 'capitulated' (Casey, 1995), 'dramaturgical' (Collinson, 1992), and 'bewildered' (Knights and McCabe, 2000) set of organizational actors.

The latter descriptions of a new category of organizational actors are embedded in tripartite classifications of responses to cultural change programmes: as 'colluded', 'defensive' or 'capitulated'; 'conformist', 'resistant or 'dramaturgical'; or 'bewitched', 'bothered' or 'bewildered'. Such tripartite descriptions have stimulated far reaching discussion and debate. It would, however, betray the intentions of their originators if these were to become a somewhat stereotyped tripartite classification, replacing a restricted bi-polar model with an equally rigid tripartite alternative. Taking the insights of the fragmentationist perspective seriously means that any such crude classification is unlikely to capture the complexity of organizational life. As we shall illustrate below, the lived experience and discursive interpretations of those involved in cultural re-engineering is far more ambiguous and ambivalent than this simple trichotomy suggests.

Are we, however, caught in a double bind of either uncritically accepting an overly-simplified classification or relapsing into a relatively undirected and uninspiring appeal to recognizing complexity and ambiguity? The answer is that we are not inevitably trapped in such a dichotomy. Rather than viewing this tri-partite positioning as a comprehensive account of lived experience, they may be viewed as cultural 'typifications', part of the established narrative positioning adopted by organizational actors involved in change programmes. As argued by Sturdy et al. (2006), the experience of ambiguity and uncertainty in 'liminal' spaces such as those encountered during such programmes does not mean that these events are not structured by narrative, ritual and ceremony.

As social encounters, all change situations are characterized by the interactional dynamics of actors and audiences as they iteratively present and receive definitions of the participants and the situation they are in (Edgley, 2003). Change agents are thus involved in handling multiple expectations and counter-expectations, conflicting and shifting frames, and contested and emergent accounts and motives. As social episodes, however, such situations are more or less ritualized in character, interpreted through more or less established narratives and stories, and involve plots and ceremonies marking their beginning, middle and end (for further discussion of this dramaturgical character see Chapter 13 by Badham, Mead and Antonacopoulou). It is the argument of this chapter, that in the context of cultural re-engineering programmes, the tripartite academic characterization of actors' responses *is* reflected in the experiences and interpretations offered by the actors themselves. At the same time, however, the actors *go beyond* such simple typifications, tacitly and at times explicitly, recognizing the ambiguity and ambivalence inherent in their situation and their responses to it. The main purpose of this chapter is to capture some of complexity and sophistication of how organizational actors grapple their experiences, in ways that draw on yet go beyond the simplistic narratives embedded in organizational ideologies, and the analyses and prescriptions of many consultant, and even academic, observers.

Culture change at Steelmaking Oz

Drawing on a longitudinal ethnographic study of cultural change in an Australian steelworks (Steelmaking Oz) (Badham et al., 2003; Badham and Garrety, 2003; McLoughlin et al., 2005; Down and Reveley, 2009), this chapter explores the interesting and complex ways in which actors whose interpretations and self-definitions conform to the tripartite classification, also reveal a more or less reflective ambiguous and ambivalent response to such narrative positioning. In conclusion, the implications of this phenomenon for future studies of cultural re-engineering are explored.

The ethnographic standpoint employed in the study is driven by assumptions that an organization is a socially constructed system, the cultural reality of which is actively created and maintained through the symbolic practice of its members. To draw out this lived experience, the research team immersed themselves in the everyday life of the organization to gain 'some understanding of the language, concepts, categories, practices, rules, beliefs, and so forth, used by the members of the written-about group' (Van Maanen, 1998: 13). In describing the attitude to the research project it is perhaps also useful to reference Kenneth Burke's exhortation to 'use all there was to use'. These perspectives on research are highlighted by the nature of the research team, managed by the first author, which comprised people with a diverse range of academic backgrounds – sociology, work psychology, engineering, organizational learning and occupational health and safety. During the six and half year project, running from 1998 to 2004, some team members directly contributed to the change initiative, giving the intervention an action research flavour, seen by Lewin (1946) as facilitating academic access to valuable data that they would not otherwise collect. This includes basic access to those who are seen as providing potential benefits to the client, confidences given to 'insiders' and insights gained from first-hand experience of dilemmas and problems of change, and more formal forms of collaboration in testing academic theories and hypotheses in real-world experiments. In managing the team, the first author was very aware of the danger that action 'researchers [often] become overly client-centred and focus only on action, not research; they do not define problems from the perspective of the client; they do not study the processes of their own interventions; they neglect to test hypotheses; and they continue to work within the paradigm of "normal science"' (French and Bell, 1999: 138). To avoid this the broader project also employed more traditional observational ethnographic research, such as in the Utilities project conducted by the third author. Overall, data was therefore collected from a number of interrelated projects using a range of techniques and in a range of settings. The quotes selected below derive from a number of these projects and include: formal taped interviews at work; field notations of informal one-on-one talks at work; off-site one-to-one informal talks; formal taped group meetings at work; and informal non-taped meetings at work. Notations in square brackets after the quote denote which type of data and the setting. The strong themes of ambiguity and ambivalence presented below emerged as these relationships matured over the six and a half year intervention and undoubtedly contributed to the later direction of the research and its related publications. The following three sections document these experiences amongst what initially appeared to be different 'conformist', 'resistant' and 'dramaturgical' groups.

Integrationism and conformist selves

The integrationist perspective on organizational life views cultural change programmes as reflecting the interests of their developers. These cultural redesign programmes are seen as seeking to introduce a new form of emotional (Kunda and Van Maanen, 1999), normative (Barley and Kunda, 1992), personal (Hochschild, 1983), concertive (Barker, 1993) or intimate surveillance based (Sewell and Wilkinson, 1992) forms of control to replace or supplement traditional direct, technical, rational or bureaucratic forms (Delbridge and Ezzamel, 2005). Such programmes are regarded as deliberately and systematically seeking to rationalize the organizational self in a manner that (a) generates intellectual and emotional commitment to the goals of the organization and (b) develops ways of organizing and rewarding work that supports and

411

mobilizes discretion in the pursuit of these goals. To achieve these aims, they are seen to explicitly deploy a legitimizing rhetoric of freedom that seeks to create commitment to the programme's goals and the forms of work that they espouse. Organizational members are exhorted to care about the new culture and related corporate goals and values.

Whereas culture change gurus claim such programmes improve employee commitment through notions of improved empowerment, self-efficacy and task ownership that lead to increased autonomy, critics of their totalizing effect frame this in terms of loss of independence and responsibility: 'Once people over-align themselves with a company, and invest excessive faith in the wisdom of its leaders, they are liable to lose their original sense of identity [and] tolerate ethical lapses they would have previously deplored' (Tourish and Vatcha, 2005: 476). This loss is accompanied by the effects of being subordinated to an inherently contradictory change rhetoric, a rhetoric that it is difficult for organizational members to challenge. In his influential critique, Willmott (1993) cited the following two passages from the guru text *In Search of Excellence*:

> There was hardly a more pervasive theme in the excellent companies than *respect for the individual* … These companies give people control over their destinies; they make meaning for people.
>
> (Peters and Waterman 1982, 238–39, quoted in Willmott 1993, 526;
> emphasis in original)

> A set of shared values and rules about discipline, details and execution *can provide the framework in which practical autonomy takes place* … The institution provides the guiding belief and creates a sense of excitement, a sense of being a part of the best.
>
> (Peters and Waterman 1982, 323, quoted in Willmott 1993, 524–25;
> emphasis added)

Within the rhetoric of normative control, freedom is allowed and even encouraged, but only within strict constraints. Individuals are respected only if they 'buy into' organizational norms. Work, generally a mundane necessity comprising a mix of boring and interesting tasks, is artificially inflated into a source of 'excitement'. Employees are consequently plagued with a debilitating sense of ambivalence and confusion.

Within Steelmaking Oz's Cokemaking Plant, the overall rhetoric was that of a culture of enterprise (McLoughlin et al., 2005). Discussions of the change 'journey' involved the plant manager's highly personalized spin on classic themes of individual 'self-expression', the significance of an 'integrated self' that links the self 'at work' and 'at home', the creation of an 'expressive community', and the establishment of a 'tight-loose' structure of individual and group autonomy (Badham and Garrety, 2003; McLoughlin et al., 2005). This rhetoric was cascaded through the organization and the managers from different sections of the plant were tasked with instigating the changes. As illustrated in the commentaries of Garry, the Plant Manager, and Albert, the Manager of Utilities, the section that maintains and repairs the doors and ovens of the 'coke batteries', the attempt was being made to impose a new corporate ethos on a workforce divided by the long standing identification of employees as 'wages' and 'workers' and management as 'staff'.

Management was frustrated by the resistance to the new culture, which was exhibited by an unwillingness to work overtime, backed up by manipulative and false unavailability, and a loss of morale on the part of those feeling they were having to do more than their fair share. In response, they drew upon metaphors of family and parenting to illustrate the differences between mature commitment and immature selfishness. In Utilities, buy in to the ideals informing the change programme was clearly exemplified in the rhetoric of the manager. Albert applied a deliberate policy of hiring new employees from 'greenfield' sectors and backgrounds with higher skills, education levels and more enterprising attitudes. Cultural change at Utilities included the division of the workforce into 'higher level' Technicians and 'lower level' Specialists. The Technician designation, taking on project work and some supervisory responsibility, had been used by Albert as an opportunity to put 'five or six best performing people' into more responsible roles: self-motivated and entrepreneurial individuals keen to develop and learn at work. Albert was, however, experiencing problems that he defined in terms of the more 'selfish' lower selves of his employees conflicting with what he perceived as their more desirable higher selves. As Albert put it:

> You have got to understand where our people are at, at the moment. Our people on the shop floor [...], they're not demonstrating the maturity of being an active self-managed workforce [...]. We've got some issues within Utilities because individuals can't see that it's got to be a win–win relationship. [...] I have people that I could trust with my life ... and then I've got others that are Battery Specialists that are so self-absorbed that I can't depend on them ... [I'm] personally absolutely devastated with what's going on [...]. So they're very, very selfish to me.
>
> (Formal interview with third author in Albert's office).

This 'immaturity,' often seen in terms of selfishness and personal disappointment, required the use of threatening behaviour or responsible parenting of 'immature' children. Following an incident involving a lost key to a shared toolbox that required the use of bolt cutters to cut through the padlock, a Technician kept the padlock remains on top of his computer.

> Michael explained that the broken lock was going to stay as a symbol of the mentality of people that work here. The point was that Michael didn't believe that they had lost the key. He believed that they were playing games. Damien [another Technician] said that 'it must have been one of the children; kids are like that'. Damien said [to the researcher], 'you think I'm kidding? They are kids'. Michael agreed.
>
> (Third author field notes of informal non-taped meeting at work)

Managers emphasized that employees were being taken on a 'journey' not of their own choosing but were going to be 'cared' for along the way. On the one hand, this issue was put clearly and forcefully. As Garry commented:

> The issue is getting them to move, and the way is to show them that there will be no accommodation. They have to change. At present this is seen as uncaring, but there is no option. The challenge is to care for them during the process. The question is when is the appropriate time to reveal that there is no option?
>
> (First author, informal interview at work)

Much of the discussion about caring has explicit overtones of parental 'tough love'. Garry was critical of managers who were scared of being honest and confronting people with unpleasant realities of job losses and changing conditions, and 'caring' acted as an excuse for deceit, covering a concern that imposing hardships on people would destroy their relationship with them. As Garry said: 'How do we make a change when wages and salaries are blown up with overtime and

413

shift allowances? Management has allowed this to happen. Now is the time to "take the lollies away"' (first author, informal reflective group meeting at work).

Although Garry and Albert were committed to the new 'caring' ethos and signed up to its promises of delivering an organization staffed by 'committed, loyal and hard-working employees', they were continually having to balance this perspective against the necessity of bullying, cajoling or forcing members to accept the new direction. To pursue the integrationist vision, they were required to employ authoritarian practices that were in opposition to its supposed values and vision. To cope with the contradiction and ambivalence, they employed oxymoronic concepts such as 'uncaring caring' or 'tough love' to wrestle with the necessity of transforming selfish, immature lower selves into the self-motivated, entrepreneurial higher selves the change programme promised to deliver. Although they were committed to the pursuit of an integrated organizational milieu, they regularly had to undermine their own espoused beliefs in order to achieve it. Some idea of the frustration and ambivalence that this generated in those promoting the programme is indicated in one of Garry's intimate reflections:

> Maslow's hierarchy may be passé but how real it is. I go with everybody wanting self actualization. Some want a good job for today to pay the bills for today, yet you are making assumptions about what people want in life and what is good for them. [...] 500 individuals with agendas for themselves are difficult to manage. They are like vampires sucking the energy out of you, and then I have no energy left for my family, and I don't want to deal with their problems. I have negotiated all day. I don't want to negotiate any more.
> (First author, formal reflective interview at work)

Differentiationism and resistant selves

The problem inherent in the integrationist perspective is highlighted in Ackroyd and Thompson (1999) critique: 'What is problematic about many current accounts of corporate culture, team-working or TQM is not the argument concerning what those who design the systems want, but the bizarre belief that they have almost no difficulty getting it' (pp. 160–61). Gabriel (1999) agreed, stating that many critiques of normative control 'exaggerate the magnitude and totality of organizational controls, generating over-managed and over-controlled images of individuals, organizations and societies' (p. 179). This perspective can be partially explained by Foucault's insights into the capacity of discourses to effect power through subjectivity, which have led to some scholars, seduced by images of panopticons and disciplinary apparatuses, giving precedence to the content of managerial discourses, at the expense of careful observations of interactions between managers and workers in real-life workplaces. As a result, 'the distinction between the intent and outcome of management strategies and practices is lost' (Thompson and Ackroyd, 1995: 629). In doing so, they tend to neutralize distinctions among different types of control, and how different categories of workers, through historical circumstances and the differential possession of skills and other resources, are differently placed with respect to managerial powers (Thompson and Ackroyd, 1995; Gabriel, 1999).

Some scholars (e.g. Hochschild, 1983; Casey, 1995; Kunda, 1992) have argued that the nature of such change programmes is inescapable, invasive and totalizing, despite finding that employees were by no means uniformly receptive to the prescribed norms and values. It is not the homogeneity of effects that makes the culture totalizing, but the fact that employees cannot escape its intrusions, no matter what they do: 'In such a colonization, self-constituent processes of self-regulated emotional experiences and expression, and self-determined judgment and effectivity, are altered and usurped by the practices of the designed corporate culture' (Gabriel, 1999: 159). Indeed, Hochschild (1983), Kunda (1992) and Casey (1995) did not find homogeneity and simple obedience in such organizations, but complex, subtle, and often contradictory responses. Nevertheless, in exploring these responses, they appeared to many readers to to homogenize the mechanisms of organizational control, depicting them as unified, pervasive and ultimately quite effective, despite their sometime recognition of resistance and diversity.

Despite this conclusion, the more critical insights of these scholars have been taken up in different readings of the capacity of individuals to manoeuvre within and against the power relations in which they are enmeshed (Starkey and McKinlay, 1998; May, 1999). Drawing from Foucault's later works, focusing on self-knowledge and the management of desires through 'technologies of the self' (1982, 1988), these studies draw a nondeterministic link between discourses/power and subjectivity. It is thus possible to remain faithful to critiques of attempts to impose totalitarian, authoritarian regimes while exploring diverse and contradictory responses to control among employees. Empirical work supporting this perspective has revealed that while many employees are indeed 'sucked in' by cultural engineering, many others are cynical, resistant and/or only superficially compliant. The following segment examines the mindset and actions of the workforce 'resisting' the authoritarian 'caring parenting' imposed by Cokemaking management.

The first area of resistance concerned the effects of the 'call out' system. While having agreed to overtime being included in normal pay, in the Utilities section, many Specialists strongly resented the intrusion into their home lives of being 'on call' when required. The tensions raised are illustrated in field notes from a monthly 'Team Day':

> Michael raises the issue of the overtime/call out coverage. […] Jokey comments are made about the laziness of Technicians, or how people were hiding or playing golf when called by Production. Michael responded when the hubbub had settled by saying that the Production Controllers don't want to have to call ten people. A specialist replied 'tell them to get fucked'. Another said 'get them to phone the Technicians […]'. Some of the older Specialists clap and laugh in agreement and enjoyment at the vociferousness and abandon of these interjections. Someone says 'Why wake people up at 2am in the morning?'
>
> (Third author field notes of formal non-taped meeting at work)

The problem of poor coverage and a perception of unfairness continued, and as a result an extraordinary meeting between Albert, Technicians and Specialists was called. After this meeting two of the Specialists were talking to the researcher. One explained that he didn't like the idea of being on call, despite understanding that they received more money than the hours worked. As was written down in the field notes: 'For some it's a matter of principle that management now have control over much more of their time. For others they see it as easy money' (third author field notes of informal non-taped meeting at work). The second source of resistance was with regard to a perceived intrusion of a private 'inner world' of work. An example of this attitude can be seen in what a Battery employee Zoran said at the Team Day: 'I come to work as a Battery Specialist, not to kick the arse of Production. I am a skilled craftsman. I have no authority, I can only ask them. I'm here to work, not to chase after everyone: chasing adds up to a day' (third author field notes of formal non-taped meetings at work).

This desire to work, not manage, was a common attitude that informed worker 'resistance'. For some, this was linked to the unwelcome stress it created. One Specialist explained that he

415

wanted to do a good job, but the recent changes and the current call out situation created a lot of stress and guilt about his work. For other Specialists, the concern was voiced more in terms of the impracticality of the lack of external supervision and control. On the one hand, this was based on a view of the need for the traditional 'autocratic dickhead' style of management: 'there is a need for close supervision. The guys won't do the work unless they are supervised', was one Specialist's informal response to the changes being discussed at the Team Day (third author field notes of informal non-taped meeting at work). These worker observations were grounded in a perception that the success of Utilities work depended on Production, and that higher authority was needed to enable them to get their work done.

This idea of taking responsibility for 'self-management' was linked to the problems of the call out system, as the idea of that system is that the employees themselves, rather than the managers, manage their own time. An example of the frustration about this issue can be seen in a special ad hoc meeting that a Battery Specialist team had with Albert to discuss a call out problem:

TONY: [Production were] ringing people on Sunday, people said 'I've got golf tomorrow'.
MANUEL: It's frustrating.
TONY: It's always the same fucking guys, I'm getting really pissed off.
[...]
ALBERT: Are we documenting whose refusing?
MICHAEL: Yes, lots of people are not answering the phone, or are simply not there. One person said they were playing golf.
TONY: I'm really stressed and fed up with it, I wasted my Monday. [...] I won't be doing it until everyone does their fair share.
MANUEL: None of us are perfect, but I came in. People make all these excuses, they scramble everything up, holidays get in the way. It's all bullshit, I get a headache. It's frustrating. It comes down to people chipping in.
TONY: Can't force them.
MANUEL: It's the same pattern.
TONY: Same pattern.

(Third author field notes of formal non-taped meeting at work)

In part, the reluctance to undertake 'managerial' work was resistance to the stress that came from having to undertake 'mental' work. Another dimension, however, is the belief that the 'real work' was the manual craft work they had to perform, in contrast to the 'managerial shit' that consumed the time of the 'autocratic dickheads': a third defence from intrusion. At a Team Day for example, Albert talked about a new corporate wide change initiative which was pulling the change initiatives of the plant manager in a different direction and was going to have significant implications for all:

Albert explains that in the 'New World' everyone has accountabilities and responsibilities. (I notice that many have newspapers in front of them and seem to be reading and not paying much attention. Later in Albert's talk, Michael says something to Angelo about whether he is listening). [...] As a general thing, the guys don't really seem that interested or responsive to the – in Albert's eyes – seemingly momentous changes taking place and being reported. Their responses are much more about battery specific technical – what they actually do – type things, and constructive to boot.

(Third author field notes of formal non-taped meeting at work)

One Specialist said that the management rhetoric of 'the era of change' had increased dramatically, and all that 'bullshit' was just about 'softening us up' for the 'change'. It was also seen as 'simply a ruse to get more work from less people' (third author field notes of informal non-taped meeting at work). Even some Technicians saw continual change as 'flavour[s] of the month'. Many felt that the 'us and them' culture was really deep and wouldn't change overnight.

At this level, the rhetorical conflicts observed in Utilities correspond to the explicit or implicit prejudices of many critical management studies. The enterprise culture is imposed on a work-force with a combination of dogmatism, paternalism and more or less hidden threat. The workforce, defending traditional privileges, also draws on long standing liberal values against the imposition of arbitrary authority, in particular the value of the 'separation of powers' (between 'home' and 'work', 'conception' and 'execution' and so on), and the blend of craft romanticism and bureaucratic work ethic in the commitment to doing 'real' manual work. This critique of the new enterprising culture also represents qualified support for a particular defined set of authoritative relationships – the kind of 'autocratic dickhead' arrangements that character-ized the old work culture. The old forms of work and the old public/private split were relatively unquestioningly presented by many of the Specialists as an alternative, ahistorical, and unques-tionable ethic. At various times, however, different groups of operations and maintenance employees gave voice to critical comments about other groups' self-interested defence of inefficient, unhealthy and boring forms of work.

Whereas the differentationist perspective may regard such actions as evidence of its thesis (either as an expression of effective cynical resistance or as a delusionary appearance of freedom while conforming in practice), the lived experience of the actors is more ambiguous and unclear than such a simple version of this perspective allows. Employees were at times not resisting the change per se, but expressing frustration at how it could restrict their effectiveness and efficiency in their day-to-day activities, i.e. stop them from working well. There were also different degrees of reflection at play, ranging from classic Marxist-style criticisms of losing control of the self in the face of managerial dictates to the necessity of dealing with the increased stress levels at having to undertake 'mental work'. Lack of sign up to the new ethos was not necessarily motivated by an anti-management sub-culture, although something along those lines certainly existed. At times it was guided by views that reduced direct control and supervision, opened up departmental divides and generated practices of laziness that could not be addressed without the use of the 'traditional-style' managerial intervention's that management proclaimed it was removing. Whereas an anti-management sub-culture was undoubtedly present, there was another form of resistance that was pragmatically engaged with and reflective of the change vision and processes, aware of its values but doubtful of its usefulness.

Fragmentationism and dramaturgical selves

In contrast to traditional analyses of the committed citizen and distanced critics, ethnographies of culture change programmes have claimed to uncover a substantial degree of ambivalence, irony and theatrical role-playing. For some, the resulting 'ironic' (Kunda, 1992), 'dramaturgical' (Collinson, 1992) or 'capitulated' (Casey, 1995) self has been a major source of concern. Kunda framed his analysis in terms of role embracement and distancing. In role embracement, workers accepted and enacted the beliefs, emotions and behaviours allocated to them by the cultural engineers (Kunda, 1992: 156). In distancing, they 'assume[d] a reflective and openly self-conscious stance' in order to comment, often cynically, on the culture and its effects on

417

themselves and others (pp. 157–58). Distancing 'is a declaration of autonomy…a hint that the self behind the role is not coterminous with the role' (p. 188). However, because embracement was necessary for career advancement, Kunda found that many employees combined the stances, and were able to switch deftly between them, depending on the circumstances (p. 158). Casey's 'capitulation', a stance that 'contains elements of both defense and collusion' (p. 175), is of a similar ilk. Capitulated employees conform to the behavioural norms of the culture, but maintain a distance that is often ironic and cynical.

A different 'spin' on such actors is provided in analyses of the 'Svejkian' employee by Fleming and Sewell (2002) and the 'bewildered' manager by Knights and McCabe (2000). For the former, the dramaturgical and performative selves examined by Kunda, Casey and Collinson may actually be involved in a highly personally effective form of resistance to corporate authority. In contrast, for Knights and McCabe, the characteristics of the 'bewildered' are their difficulty in comprehending mixed messages or consequences. Although these critiques have traditionally found their place as variants in the differentationist perspective, if such employee behaviour is viewed through the 'dramatic' lenses of Mangham (Mangham and Overington, 1987) and Burke (1957, 1962), the more 'positive' ability of such a stance to react and adapt to the requirements of its immediate audience gains focus. Organizational actors adopting such stances might well be 'using all there is to use' to craft effective performances within the chaotic, messy and emergent changes.

A pertinent example of fragmented readings of management definitions is in how the 'caring' perspective was understood and used quite differently in different contexts in Cokemaking. As two operators put it:

PETER: Garry says care for people, but what is this meaning of caring. I really don't know what caring is. Different people might want different types of caring.

TONY: There are a couple of interpretations about aren't there!

[laughter]

(First author, observation of work redesign group meeting)

Echoing Garry's 'stakeholder' rhetoric, Tom, a manager, pointed to the 'dilemma between caring for yourself, for others and the business, and how to draw the balance, that is the problem' (first author, observation of work redesign group meeting). On the one hand, managers and employees were often given narrow choices – to accept job loss or adapt their attitudes and behaviour in the required manner. This form of caring, whatever its nuances, is thus put forward as the 'one best way'. This authoritarianism was far from opaque to the workforce and management: As one worker sarcastically commented on being disciplined, 'thank you for caring for me' (first author, observation of work redesign group meeting).

On the other hand, changes were also conducted in a more liberal 'caring' manner. Cokemaking is no 'total institution', and attempts were made to resolve disputes in an inclusive manner. Extensive consultation and participation were entered into during the change process, giving people an opportunity to change, but where they did not, a generous Voluntary Redundancy Scheme was in place. Garry, and other managers, spent long periods of time supporting people before decisions were made about the incompatibility between their capabilities and desires and that of the change. For some managers, such 'caring', in its many forms, was perceived as excessive. As Peter (a Supervisor) put it, 'we […] spend so much time on caring, and making sure that we are sharing, that we all feel too much' (first author, informal personal interview at work). There was a common feeling that too much 'caring' took place. Many in the company remained broadly 'on-side' because the plant was what Garry explicitly referred to as 'a slack company'. It remained an 'indulgency culture' (Gouldner, 1954). Small wonder, from this ambiguity surrounding the positive nature of caring, and the degree to which it imposed constraints on people 'in their interests', that a degree of confusion and angst was observed amongst many of the more committed promoters of the change.

What was apparent amongst a number of employees in Utilities, especially amongst the Technicians, was a sustained grappling with the contradictory nature of this situation, recognizing the value yet limitations of the change ethic, the desirable yet restrictive nature of the 'old order' and the overall ambiguity of (and their ambivalence towards) the cultural change. One Technician (Danny) was unsure whether the new management and its philosophy really represented a move to a collaborative, high trust, mutually enterprising regime. Discussing the plant manager, Garry, he states:

DANNY: Yeah – he's different I don't know, I don't know if he's..., compared to some of the managers he's very different. [...] doesn't seem to be a hidden agenda I don't know with him, he seems, he tells ya, you know.
RESEARCHER: right, and you think that like, senior managers sort of have always, have a [hidden agenda]?
DANNY: I think years ago yeah. Oh there's probably still one, I don't know.
[laughter]

(Formal interview with third author at work)

In these examples, the actors have juxtaposed traditional perspectives of management against the new, caring ethos, and created ambiguous spaces. Cynical, sarcastic and ironic commentary, drawn from and interpreted via a variety of non-work sources, is employed to enable them to make sense of what they are experiencing. For some, the caring metaphor was deconstructed and employed as a criticism of the change, either in the one dimensionality of the change pro-gramme's deployment of 'caring' or through worry that 'over-care' could harm performance. In contrast, others were unable to detach the call for 'caring' from older management practices, wondering if practices of manipulation, surveillance and control underlay the rhetoric of trust and enterprise. As with much fragmentationist critique, the ambiguities and contradictions are voiced but not managed, left hanging as explicit reminders of how day-to-day organizational complexity overpowers managerial expectations.

The more general critical response to the day-to-day ambivalence about the new forms of work is revealed in the following comments from Brett. For him the idea of becoming a Technician 'had its negatives yeah. Positive part was moving on, negatives part was trying to get the employees on side'. Moreover, in regard to working conditions he said:

BRET: The bigger the business the um the freer you are, less responsibility, less pressure. But it's just yeah when you're here I'm just a number floating around the system here.
RESEARCHER: But one aspect of that you like cause you know you're sort of sitting around and you know but I mean a fairly relaxed time but I mean on the other hand you don't like it.
BRET: Exactly. Yeah some...I'm going against each other here, I'm arguing with myself. [...] like sometimes I like to be freer and then other times I want the responsibility.

(Formal interview with third author at work)

The ambivalences, tension and contradictions involved in becoming a more responsible employee were most clearly evident in interviews with Michael, the lead Technician. He grappled with the conflicts between his desire to be enterprising, and the bureaucratic conditions and politics that actually typified his work. Did he feel good about his new roles in being responsible for managing himself and others?

MICHAEL: If you're asking Michael Hughes I'd say yes. [...] Because it's just worth it for me because it challenges me, it got me out of a very depressive situation where I was just doing repetitive [work], and it drove me [crazy body language sign] in the head.
RESEARCHER: So that's Michael Hughes, so who the fuck are you then [laugh]?
MICHAEL: I don't ... Haven't figured that out myself yet. [laughter]
MICHAEL: But yeah [...], it is worth it because you know it's changed me, and I'm learning something new and it's making me think about myself more, which I quite like. For me, that's like a continuing improvement thing for my own personal um self but um if you were to look at a bit more objectively I would sometimes say no.
RESEARCHER: And what does objectively mean? I mean what criteria are you using for that?
MICHAEL: [...] we talk about isolation, [...] when I was a protected species out there, I was, I mean not that I ever needed protection but it was always there, I was a protected species because of um union, unionism.

(Formal interview with third author at work)

These ambiguities were exacerbated when Cokemaking started changing in a different direction as a result of a new corporate wide change initiative. Michael found himself now having his roles and responsibilities more clearly defined but in a situation that left him somewhat in a 'no man's land' between a team member and a supervisor. In response to a question about whether this was a desirable situation to be in, he responded:

I'm torn between yes and no [...] I understand this idea about the Requisite Organization [from consultants using Jacques (1996)] and therefore [...] the way that I rationalize things is that I'm not responsible for their actual performance, I'm there to assist Albert to gather the information so he can make decisions, [...]. [...] it makes it quite disjointed because I'm here in no man's land [...], I know what they're getting away with and I also know what they're doing well [...] what do I do? [...] I can't reprimand them because according to Requisite Organization I have to go to Albert and get the authority [...]. If they're doing well why should I have to go to Albert and say look let me, let me commend these people. It's silly.

(Formal interview with third author at work)

Michael provided an overall understanding of his situation as being a conflict between the 'dark' (rule bound) and the 'light' (enterprising). Michael explained that there was of course a need for the 'dark side' because of the 'hierarchy above me' and because of the 'legislation that we work around'. However, there was a degree of angst that any bureaucratic slip-up would be exploited by colleagues:

gradually more and more this job is forcing me to have a dark side look [laugh] because [...] I'm forever aware that I have to cover my arse [...]. I now have an expectation that someone down that road is going to fuck me over. [...] it's not coming from Albert, it's coming from these guys.

(Formal interview with third author at work)

A number of recent analysts have put a positive spin on such struggles, and associated interpretations and actions by managers and employees grappling with the desire to improve both personal and work life, yet aware of the contradictions between the two. Meyerson (2003), for example, praises the 'tempered radicalism' of middle-managers able to integrate private political passions, such as gender, sexual or racial equality, into their traditional managerial endeavours, thereby merging commitments to corporate and ethical goals. In contrast, Fleming and Spicer (2003, 2007) introduced a differentiationist slant to this stance, identifying 'Enlightened Cynics' who understood and knowingly contributed to the strategies and techniques of control and domination, but used ironic techniques to detach from them when overburdened. More recently, Clegg et.al. (2006) have explored the character of 'creative resistors' employing localized readings of the culture to influence and change central directives. Wallace and Hoyle (2007) also describe the 'principled infidelity' of public sector middle-managers grappling with the desire to address the 'service' requirements of local audiences that come up against the contradictory 'managerialist' expectations for centralized 'accountability' and 'budgetary' control. Badham and McLoughlin (2005/6) and Badham and Claydon (2007) have also explored the nature and desirability of 'ironic engagement' and an 'ironic temper' amongst those seeking to proactively craft out a meaningful response to such circumstances. Arguably, these fledgling oxymoronic concepts, allowing for simultaneous attachment and detachment, loyalty and critique, action and reflection, have the potential to extend research and understanding of the complex nature of ambivalent 'dramaturgical' organizational actors.

Conclusion

One-dimensional views of 'strong culture' change programmes fail to capture the fluidity, uncertainty and ambiguity that inevitable dog cultural transitions. Stereotyped views of 'champions' and 'resisters', and categorizations of respondents into 'zealots', 'cynics' and 'dramaturgs', also fail to communicate the complex positioning and inherent ambivalence of the lived experience of change. The purpose of this chapter has been to give recognition and voice to the ambiguity and ambivalence experienced by the actors involved. Similarly to Beech et al.'s (2004) argument for 'serious play' in the face of embedded organizational paradoxes, the aim is to raise to prominence the dilemmas of the 'ambivalence paradox' and encourage more open and critical discussion of how this can and should be handled.

This is not a critique of 'culture change management' per se but, rather, an appeal to a return to the more critical, experimental and committed dimensions of the work of Kurt Lewin and his followers (Burnes, 2004; Cooke, 1999). It should not be understood as a simple rejection of tri-partite stereotyped categorizations of actors into zealots, cynics and ironists but, rather, a critical look at how actors grapple with ambiguity and ambivalence in such positioning of themselves, as well as the change programmes that they are involved in. Finally, it is not a rejection of Martin's (2001) categorization of integrationist, differentiationist and fragmentationist frames on organizational culture. It is, rather, an appeal for a focus on how, in their lived experience, actor's wrestle with the ambiguity and ambivalence brought about by: (i) a degree of commitment to and dependence on the fulfilment of organizational goals; (ii) a level of awareness of the clash of interests existing between themselves and the institutions on which they depend; and (c) a varying yet often acknowledged experience of uncertainty, ambiguity and even chaos in how these commitments and interests are understood and play out. The documented experiences of actors involved in cultural change at Steelmaking Oz has hopefully drawn out some of these themes, and will encourage further reflection on how managers and employees grapple with the dilemmas of the 'ambivalence paradox' in cultural change programmes.

References

Ackers, P. and D. Preston (1997). 'Born again? The ethics and efficacy of the conversion experience in contemporary management development', *Journal of Management Studies* 34(5): 677–701.

Ackroyd, S. and P. Thompson (1999). *Organizational Misbehaviour*. London, SAGE.

Badham, R. (1986). *Theories of Industrial Society*. London and New York. Croom Helm/St Martin's Press.

Badham, R.J. and R. Claydon (2007). 'The dance of identification: Ambivalence, irony and organisational selfing', 23rd EGOS Colloquium, Vienna, Austria.

Badham, R. and K. Garrety (2003). '"Living in the blender of change": The carnival of control in a culture of culture', *Tamara* 2(4): 22–38.

Badham, R. and I. McLoughlin (2005), 'Ambivalence and engagement: Irony and cultural change in late modern organizations', *International Journal of Knowledge, Culture and Change Management* 5: www.Management-Journal.com (accessed 15 August 2006).

Badham, R. and I. McLoughlin (2006). 'Ambiguity and ambivalence: Irony and cultural change in late modern organizations', *International Journal of Knowledge, Culture and Change Management* 5(4): 133–43.

Badham, R., P. Dawson, K. Garrety, A. Griffiths, V. Morrigan and M. Zanko (2003). 'Designer Deviance: Enterprise and Deviance in Organizational Change', *Organization* 10(4): 651–73.

Barker, J.R. (1993). 'Tightening the iron cage: Concertive control in self-managing teams', *Administrative Science Quarterly* 38(3): 408–37.

Barley, S.R. and G. Kunda (1992). 'Design and devotion: Surges of rational and normative ideologies of control in managerial discourse', *Administrative Science Quarterly* 37(3): 363–99.

Bauman, Z. (1993). *Modernity and Ambivalence*. Oxford: Polity Press.

Beech, N., H. Burns, I. De Caestecker, R. MacIntosh and D. MacLean (2004). Paradox as Invitation to Act in Problematic Change Situations, *Human Relations* 57(10): 1313–32.

Boje, D., G. Rosile, B. Dennehy and D. Summers (1997). Restorying reengineering: Some deconstructions and postmodern alternatives', *Journal of Communication Research* 24(6): 631–68.

Brown, A. (1998). 'Organizational culture', *Financial Times*.

Buchann, D. and R. Badham (2007). *Power, Politics and Organizational Change: Winning the Turf Game* (2nd edn). London, SAGE.

Burke, K. (1957). *The Philosophy of Literary Form: Studies in Symbolic Action*. New York, Vintage Books.

Burke, K. (1962). *A Grammar of Motives, and a Rhetoric of Motives*. Cleveland, World Pub. Co.

Burnes, B. (2004). 'Kurt Lewin and the planned approach to change: A re-appraisal', *Journal of Management Studies* 41(6): 977–1002.

Burns, T. (1961). 'Micropolitics: Mechanisms of institutional change', *Administrative Science Quarterly* 6: 321–56.

Casey, C. (1995). *Work, Self and Society: After Industrialism*. London, Routledge.

Clegg, S., M. Kornberger, C. Carter and C. Rhodes (2006) 'For management?', *Management Learning* 37(1): 7–27.

Collinson, D.L. (1992). *Managing the Shopfloor: Subjectivity, Masculinity, and Workplace Culture*. Berlin; New York, Walter de Gruyter.

Cooke, B. (1999) 'Writing the left out of management theory: The Historiography of the management of change', *Organization* 6(1): 81–105.

Dalton, M. (1961). *Men Who Manage: Fusions of Feeling and Theory in Administration*. New York, Wiley.

Davies, B. and R. Harre (1990). 'Positioning: The discursive production of selves', *Journal for the Theory of Social Behaviour* 20: 43–63.

Deal, T.E. and A.A. Kennedy (1982). *Corporate Cultures: The Rites and Rituals of Corporate Life*. Reading, Mass., Addison-Wesley Pub. Co.

Delbridge, R. and M. Ezzamel (2005). 'The strength of difference: Contemporary conceptions of control', *Organization* 12(5): 603–18.

Down, S. and J. Reveley (2009). 'Between narration and interaction: Situating first-line supervisor identity work', *Human Relations* 62(3): 379–401.

Du Gay, P. (2000). *In Praise of Bureaucracy*. London: SAGE.

Dunn, S. (1990). 'Root metaphor in the old and new industrial relations', *British Journal of Industrial Relations* 28(1): 1–31.

Edgley, C. (2003). 'The dramaturgical genre', in L.T. Regynolds and N.J. Herman-Skinney (eds), *Handbook of Symbolic Interactionism*. New York: Rowman & Littlefield.

Fleming, P. (2009). *Authenticity and the Cultural Politics of Work: New Forms of Informal Control*. Oxford, Oxford University Press.

Fleming, P. and G. Sewell (2002). 'Looking for the good soldier, Svejk: Alternative modalities of resistance in the contemporary workplace', *Sociology* 36(4): 857–73.

Fleming, P. and A. Spicer (2003). 'Working at a cynical distance: Implications for power, subjectivity and resistance', *Organization* 10(1): 157–79.

Fleming, P. and A. Spicer (2007). *Contesting the Corporation*. Cambridge: Cambridge University Press.

Foucault, M. (1982). 'Afterword: The subject and power', In H.L. Dreyfus and P. Rabinow (eds) *Michel Foucault: Beyond Structuralism and Hermeneutics*. New York, Harverster Wheatsheaf: 208–26.

Foucault, M. (1988). *Technologies of the Self: A Seminar with Michel Foucault*, ed. L.H. Martin, H. Gutman and P.H. Hutton. Amherst, MA, University of Massachusetts Press: 16–49.

French, W.L. and C.H. Bell (1999). *Organization development: Behavioural science interventions for organization improvement* (6th edn). Englewood Cliffs, NJ: Prentice Hall.

Gabriel, Y. (1999). 'Beyond happy families: A critical reevaluation of the control-resistance-identity triangle', *Human Relations* 52(2): 179–203.

Gallos, J. (ed.) (2006). *Organization Development: A Jossey-Bass Reader*. San Francisco, CA, Jossey Bass.

Gouldner, A. (1954). *Patterns of Industrial Bureaucracy*. New York, Free Press.

Grint, K. (1994). 'Reengineering history: Social resonances and business process reengineering', *Organization* 1(1): 179–201.

Harre, R. and L. Van Langenhove (eds) (1999). *Positioning Theory: Moral Contexts of Intentional Action*. Oxford, Blackwell.

Hochschild, A. (1983). *The Managed Heart: Commercialization of Human Feeling*. Berkeley, CA, University of California Press.

Knights, D. and D. McCabe (2000). 'Bewitched, bothered and bewildered: The meaning and experience of teamworking for employees in an automobile factory', *Human Relations* 53(11): 1481–1517.

Kunda, G. (1992). *Engineering Culture: Control and Commitment in a High-tech Corporation*. Philadelphia, Temple University Press.

Kunda, G. and J. Van Maanen (1999). 'Changing scripts at work: Managers and professionals', *Annals of the American Academy of Political and Social Science*, 561(1): 64–80.

Lewin, K. (1946). 'Action research and minority problems', *Journal of Social Issues*, 11(4): 34–46.

Mangham, I.L. and M.A. Overington (1987). *Organizations as Theatre: A Social Psychology of Dramatic Appearances*. Chichester, New York, Wiley.

Martin, J. (1992). *Cultures in Organizations: Three Perspectives*. Oxford: Oxford University Press.

Martin, J. (2001). *Organizational Culture: Mapping the Terrain*. London: SAGE.

May, T. (1999). 'From banana time to just-in-time: Power and resistance at work', *Sociology* 33(4): 767–83.

McLoughlin, I.P., R.J. Badham and G. Palmer. (2005). 'Cultures of ambiguity: Design, emergence and ambivalence in the introduction of normative control', *Work Employment Society* 19(1): 67–89.

Meyerson, D.J. (2003). *Tempered Radicals: How Everyday Leaders Inspire Change at Work*. Boston, Harvard Business School Press.

O'Reilly, C.A. and J.A. Chatman (1996). 'Culture as social control: Corporations, cults, and commitment', *Research in Organizational Behaviour* 18: 157–200.

Ouchi, W.G. (1981). *Theory Z: How American Business Can Meet the Japanese Challenge*. Reading, MA, Addison-Wesley.

Peters, T.J. and R.H. Waterman (1982). *In Search of Excellence: Lessons from America's Best-run Companies*. London, Harper & Row.

Ray, C.A. (1986). 'Corporate culture: The last frontier of control?', *Journal of Management Studies* 23(3): 287–97.

Schein, E. (1951). *Coercive Persuasion: A Socio-psychological Analysis of the 'Brainwashing' of American Civilian Prisoners by the Chinese Communists*, New York, W.W. Norton.

Sewell, G. and B. Wilkinson (1992). 'Someone to watch over me': Surveillance, discipline and the just-in-time labour process', *Sociology* 26(2): 271–89.

423

Smelser, N. (1997). 'The rational and the ambivalent in the social sciences: 1997 Presidential Address' *American Sociological Review* 63(1): 1–16.

Starkey, K. and A. McKinlay (1998). 'Afterword: Deconstructing organization – discipline and desire', in A. McKinlay and K. Starkey (eds) *Foucault, Management and Organization Theory. From Panopticon to Technologies of the Self.* London, SAGE: 230–41.

Sturdy, A., M. Schwarz and A. Spicer (2006). 'Guess who's coming to dinner? Structures and uses of liminality in strategic management consultancy, *Human Relations* 59 (7), July: 929–60.

Thompson, P. and S. Ackroyd (1995). 'All quiet on the workplace front? A critique of recent trends in industrial sociology', *Sociology* 29(4): 615–33.

Tourish, D. and N. Vatcha (2005). 'Charismatic leadership and corporate cultism at Enron: The elimination of dissent, the promotion of conformity and organizational collapse', *Leadership* 1(4): 455–80.

Turner, E. (ed.) (1985). *On the Edge of the Bush: Anthropology as Experience.* Tucson, AZ, University of Arizona Press.

Turner, V. (1982). *From Ritual to Theater.* New York, PAJ Publications.

Van Maanen, J. (1988). *Tales of the Field: On Writing Ethnography.* Chicago: University of Chicago Press.

Wallace, M. and E. Hoyle (2007). 'An ironic perspective on public service change', in M. Wallace, M. Fertig and E. Schneller (eds) *Managing Change in the Public Services.* Oxford, Blackwell.

Weick, K. and R. Quinn (1999). 'Organizational development and change', *Annual Review of Psychology* 50: 361–86.

Willmott, H. (1993). 'Strength is ignorance, slavery is freedom: Managing culture in modern organizations', *Journal of Management Studies* 30: 515–52.

29

Organizational change as imperialism

Raza Mir and Ali Mir

You fell in love with my enemy, and call it a test of my forbearance. If this is a test, then what is oppression?

(Mirza Ghalib, nineteenth-century Urdu poet)

The construct of organizational change is by no means an understudied topic in organizational studies. In fact, one could argue to the contrary, as a study of academic databases confirms. The ABI-Inform database shows over 10,000 scholarly articles that contain "organizational change" in their citation or abstract, of which 1000 contain the phrase "organizational change" in their title. Likewise, the Academy of Management database throws up over 2500 articles that deal with the topic. This makes organizational change a veritable industry in the arena of intellectual production in organizational studies. It is perhaps to be expected, for change is an integral feature of organizational life, a feature that neither loses its dynamism nor its terrors over time and space. In the current global economic paradigm of violent macroeconomic upheaval, economic booms and busts, organizational layoffs, and the perennial talk of a "jobless recovery," organizational subjects live a life of constant uncertainty and anxiety. The institutionalization and legitimization of regimes of unequal exchange in late capitalism have not only made change the only true constant of organizational life, but mixed it inexorably with a sense of dread and foreboding for a variety of organizational subjects.

In this chapter, we report on an empirical study of organizational knowledge transfer to foreground the imperialistic elements of organizational change (also see Mir and Mir, 2009; Mir et al., 2008). By way of introduction, we do not wish to engage in any great depth either with the canonical texts of organizational change or offer a literature review. Other works have done that admirably. Starting with Ford and Ford (1994) and Van de Ven and Poole (1995), authors have attempted to contain the sweep of organizational change literature into a few broad themes. Subsequently, Armenakis and Bedeian (1999) have plumbed the research on organizational change, and sought to isolate four research themes under which it can be grouped. Beer and Nohria's (2000) edited volume on organizational change provides a more conceptually anchored analysis. Finally, there have emerged a variety of sub-fields in the change literature such as the construct of "commitment to change," a field that has grown enough to warrant a critical literature review (Jaros, 2010).

While the studies of organizational change in our field are numerous, they are unfortunately less heterogeneous than one would have hoped, considering that organizational change is, in practice, a fiercely contested terrain. Most scholarly studies of organizational change traverse well-trod ground, depicting change as progress, resistance to change as a problem to be solved, and subjects who resist change as either forces to be managed or obstacles to be removed. However, recent critical studies of organizational change have emerged, such as Sturdy and Grey's (2003) critical analysis of the literature, and the Special Issue of the journal *Organization* that it introduced. The *Journal of Organization Change Management* has devoted over two decades to a nuanced understanding or organizational change. Chapters in this volume too have plumbed the depths of the concept of organizational change to highlight and champion various critical approaches, as have the authors associated with them. Thus, any attempt to add to the corpus of existing literature on organizational change (including critical approaches) must proceed through a very specific analytical regimen. In our case, we hope to do so by linking the concept of organizational change to that of *imperialism*.

The reasons for this isomorphism in organizational change research are ideological, and in this chapter, we explore one facet of this ideological apparatus. We contend that in the current economic climate of increasing corporate power and reduced oversight of corporate activities by traditional actors such as the state, regimes of imperialism have intensified in organizations. These regimes have begun to deploy theories of organizational change to legitimize their actions, and ideologically depict routines of workplace resistance as irrational, infantile and anti-progress. We discuss how organizational studies as a field is subject to cooptation from such discourses, and offer ways in which critical organizational theorists can offer a counter-theoretical way to resist the legitimization of organizational imperialism that carried out in the name of organizational change.

Imperialism

In generic terms, imperialism can be seen as a special case of exploitation, where the appropriator of surplus value functions by shifting the locus of exploitation into specific geographical areas, for the gratification of other geographies. In other words, the heightened exploitation of one part of the world serves to ameliorate the effects of exploitation in another part (Brewer, 1980). The post-war welfare states in Europe and the US have often been seen as a consequence of neo-imperialist and extractive practices of Western states (often through the medium of MNCs) in Asia, Africa and South America. Dependency theorists have referred to the phenomenon of *unequal development* (Amin, 1976), implying that much of the order that pervades the capitalist societies of Europe and North America is predicated upon the suffering of poorer nations. MNCs have been implicated in these imperialist processes. Be it plantation corporations, mineral and oil producers, and increasingly, those that utilize poorer nations as sites of labor-intensive manufacture, MNCs have been implicated in the process of imperialistic exploitation.

In linking the broad concept of imperialism to the organizational construct of change, we will rely on some discussions that have occurred in the discipline as they relate to knowledge management and organizational knowledge transfer. According to Gordon and Grant (2005), discourses of information technology and knowledge management have been influential in "shaping the direction of contemporary organizational change." Intra-organizational knowledge transfer between a multinational corporation and its subsidiaries results in changes in organizational processes in both entities, but perhaps more significantly in subsidiary firms. Knowledge transfer can thus be theorized as an example of organization change. Traditional approaches to organization change have viewed the change processes from the perspective of organizational stability rather than change as an ongoing process (Tsoukas and Chia, 2002). Change is seen as a top-down, episodic process with a majority of the research providing accounts of change as a *fait accompli*, developing approaches and typologies of change, and discussing its antecedents and consequences (Porras and Silvers, 1991; Weick and Quinn, 1999). Alternate views of organizational change attempt to shift the focus from the organization as a unit, change as an intervention and senior management as change agents to a more dynamic approach that focuses on "changing" (as opposed to change) "grounded in the ongoing practices of organizational actors" with the "everyday contingencies, breakdowns, exceptions, opportunities, and unintended consequences that they encounter" (Orlikowski, 1996: 65). "Change" rather than "organization" becomes the ontological focus of this perspective.

Empirical explorations

In order to explicate the workings of organizational imperialism in the name of organizational change, we wish to report on an empirical project that we worked on, that sought to answer a fundamental research question: How is knowledge transferred across international boundaries within a multinational corporation? Given that this question related to the study of organizational processes, we chose a research design that was field-based (van Maanen, 1988). Also, given the international dimension (and the inductive character) of our research questions, we felt it would be empirically appropriate to locate the research within a single MNC, where we would be granted access not only to the corporate headquarters, but also to a specific national subsidiary. Our research plan involved a longitudinal element, in that we wanted to follow a set of organizational processes at various stages of organizational life (Van de Ven and Poole, 2002). We decided to use ethnographic techniques to achieve this objective. The lead author spent a total of 12 months at the foreign subsidiaries of two large US-based MNCs (results from one corporation are reported in this paper). We supplemented the primary data that was collected with a variety of other forms of primary and secondary data, and analyzed them using conceptually ordered displays and thematic pooling. In the rest of this section we discuss our choice of ethnography as a research method, the organization where research was conducted, and our techniques of data collection and analysis.

The ethnographic method

Of the various qualitative research methods employed by social scientists, ethnography has developed perhaps the greatest legitimacy (Denzin and Lincoln, 2005). Given the rigorous demands made on the researcher by the ethnographic process and the interesting and influential stories that have been woven over the last century by ethnographers, it has not only become "the trademark of cultural anthropology" (Schwartzman, 1993: 1), but has also informed a variety of social sciences, including organizational studies. Gideon Kunda's study (1992) of high tech firms and Steven Barley's (1996) analysis of the work of technicians and technology stand out among several ethnographic studies in management. As Prasad (2005: 78–83) elaborates, the great advantage of ethnographic research comes from three sources, namely the ability to illuminate a setting in its *cultural and historical context* (Bate, 1997); the power to provide a *thick description* of events (Geertz, 2000) and the *narrative dimension* that allows us to string different events into coherent thematics (Rosen, 1991).

There is another, more compelling reason which guided our choice of ethnography as a research method, which related to the power of this methodology to illuminate phenomena that dominant discourses consign to the periphery. In effect, ethnography allowed us to document the subtler responses to the imposition of hegemony by dominant groups by a variety of subjects. In effect, the aim of our research was not to provide an authoritative narrative account of the goings on at the site of our study. Rather, it was to provide an *alternative* narrative of the same phenomena that had been studied by mainstream organizational theorists. As the historian Sudipta Kaviraj (1992: 38) remarked with respect to subaltern historiography, "the interstices of every narrative are filled with semblances rather than truth. Thus, the telling of true stories in history would not rule out the telling of other stories different from the first, which are also true." Our research then, provides an account that is as authoritative as the mainstream accounts of knowledge transfer in MNCs. Indeed, to the extent that the mainstream stories purport to be an account of the "reality" of knowledge transfer, we believe that our research provides an important counter-narrative. Alternative stories are a way of restoring the balance, and remaining true to what Gadamer (1975: 267–74) has referred to as "the principle of effective history."

Research location

In line with our research needs, we were able to gain access to a large, US-based MNC, which we have nicknamed Chloron Corporation. Chloron is a world leader in the chemical industry, with operations in several different countries. We were offered access to its subsidiary in India, which had been in operation for over 50 years, and employed over 1000 full-time personnel.

Chloron-India was now a fully owned subsidiary of the parent corporation; a relatively recent development. A discussion of the context in which it became a fully owned subsidiary is important. Given the prevailing political and legal conditions in India in the past, only 39 percent of Chloron-India had been owned by the parent organization till 1995, and it operated as a "stand-alone" business until 1995. This was primarily because India's Foreign Exchange Regulations Act (FERA) had stipulated various constraints on the investment of foreign exchange in the country; one of which had been that no foreign entity could hold more than 40 percent stake in its Indian subsidiary. The rest of the equity had to be drawn from local investors. As a consequence, Chloron had relied on a variety of Indian entrepreneurs to provide the other 60 percent. Thus, the transformation of Chloron-India from a stand-alone corporation to a subsidiary was itself an artifact of globalization.

Beginning in 1991, the Indian government began an extensive project of liberalization, which, among other things, led to the relaxation of FERA (Chandrasekhar and Ghosh, 2002), making it possible for corporations like Chloron to increase their stake in their Indian operations. By 1995, Chloron had bought up all the available equity in its Indian operations, turning Chloron into wholly owned subsidiary. The corporation then began an extensive reorganization process, where the financial data reporting, market intelligence, accounting systems, and other reporting patterns of the subsidiary were restructured to mirror the corporate structure. Our research at Chloron-India coincided with a transition period, where the globalization of the subsidiary was underway, but incomplete.

Chloron-India had annual revenues of around $50m, which was very small by the standards of its other national subsidiaries, but was growing at a rate of around 25 percent per annum, which was high by Chloron's global standards. It employed around 1000 fulltime workers at its plants, offices and the sales force, with a well developed manufacturing and distribution infrastructure, as well as a network of outsourced manufacturing and sales contractors.

Data collection and analysis

We collected data from a variety of primary and secondary sources. Primary data collection included participant observation and interviews. Secondary sources included confidential corporate correspondence, firewall-protected intranet sites and other proprietary sources within the corporation (the entire data in this study has been re-checked to eliminate any possible breach of confidentiality). This data was also supplemented by publicly available information such as corporate annual reports, macro economic data and industry analysis reports.

Participant observation was conducted over three stints, which lasted a total of 12 months, spread over three years. These included attending a variety of meetings, from routine planning meetings to strategy sessions; visits to manufacturing sites, distributors and accompanying sales personnel on calls; time spent at contractor premises; and extensive interactions with the MIS and IT departments. Interviews were conducted with a variety of actors such as the head of the subsidiary, visiting executives from the US-based headquarters, middle and lower managers, non-managerial staff such as technicians and sales people, contract workers and external informants such as economists and trade union activists.

Data analysis involved an extensive regimen of transcription, coding, and the use of concept cards (Martin and Turner, 1986) and conceptually ordered displays (Miles and Huberman, 1994: 127). Data were coded and logged according to thematic consistency (Madison, 2005: 36–39). Knowledge transfer can be studied at multiple levels, including the nation of the subsidiary, the nation of the headquarters, the headquarters of a multinational corporation, the subsidiary of a corporation, and the international regimes (such the World Trade Organization) all of whom interact in the process of knowledge transfer. The headquarters of the organization is primarily concerned with issues of the protection of intellectual property rights as well as maximizing revenue appropriation, while the subsidiary is interested in being integrated in the global space in such a manner that its voice is dialogically heard, and its independence is not compromised. The country that exists at the subaltern level of this transaction is focused on the maintenance of its national identity and sovereignty, but at the same time, is eager to get the benefits of global investment. The country of the corporation's headquarters is also concerned with developing favorable trade terms, and has the task of balancing the potential opportunities afforded by internationalization against attendant economic and political risks. Finally, international regimes deal with transnational concerns such as the securing of intellectual property rights, solving multilevel disputes, and the management of tax and tariffs. For example, the WTO is focused on developing platforms for multilateral discussions between corporations and countries, on issues as wide ranging as patent protection, tariff reduction and currency convertibility. In the space characterized by episodes of organizational knowledge transfer, international regimes often function more as agents of the dispersed corporation. Each entity approaches the issue of knowledge transfer with different areas of focus, but the challenge for the theorist is to develop a framework that uses the knowledge transfer transaction as a unit of analysis, but is still sensitive to the enactment of all the compulsions and focus areas.

Enterprise requirement planning: a story of knowledge transfer

It is extremely frustrating. Here is a perfectly serviceable UNIX system, which we have to dismantle and install this @#$%X* AS400 system. I could accept it if we were going to put in a much better system, like SAP or PeopleSoft's ERP. But now, in this day and age, we have to learn to use mainframes, when Springfield [company headquarter] itself has declared that it will phase out the AS400 by 2003. Our UNIX system is similar in architecture to the new system they have planned for the organization. So we are working to put ourselves back from 2000 to 1985! By the time we learn AS400 operations; we would have lost all our knowledge of distributed computing, and will have to go back with a begging bowl to Springfield, asking them to train us in networking and ERP.

(Vijay Tendulkar, GM, Information Technology, Chloron-India)

In this chapter, we have chosen to analyze a specific episode of knowledge transfer from the US headquarters of Chloron to Chloron-India, which was located in the IT department. It involves the installation of an Enterprise Requirement Planning (ERP) system at the Indian subsidiary, which was driven by the headquarters.

First, the story in brief. For a variety of political and contextual reasons, Chloron-India had not been able to install Chloron's corporate ERP system in the 1980s. Deprived of this knowledge, the subsidiary had developed an innovative system based on locally available hardware and software, which performed the ERP job adequately, and produced information in a format that was compatible with the requirements of the headquarters. Now that the political constraints on hardware import had been lifted, Chloron-India was facing pressure from the headquarters to change over to the centralized ERP system, at great capital and learning cost.

The frustration embodied in the quote by Vijay Tendulkar, the local IT chief, arose from one important factor: the ERP system that Chloron-India was expected to install had itself had been declared obsolete by the headquarters a year ago. Now that the IT community was migrating from mainframe-based systems to distributed, networked and server-based systems, Chloron had embarked upon an ambitious program in the US to overhaul its corporate ERP system to a distributed system, albeit in a phased manner.

The new system proposed by headquarters for eventual global adoption ironically possessed many characteristics that were similar to the ones possessed by the *current* system at Chloron-India. The Indian system was not dependent on big computers, but a network of smaller computers, using distributed data processing protocols. The local innovations that had been made by the Indian subsidiary actually were much more compatible with the corporate system of the future, but totally at odds with the corporate system of the present. However, the corporate IT team felt that it would be too long a wait if they let Chloron-India change over directly from its current system to the proposed future system, a process that could take three years. In the interim, they decided that Chloron-India should change to the mainframe-based system right away. In effect, the headquarters decision to change the ERP system was pushing Chloron-India from the future into the past!

Tendulkar was particularly bitter because he felt that there were no institutional avenues by which he would be able to represent this information to the headquarters. For one, as a "promotee-manager," with a less-than-stellar educational background and a shaky command over English, he had been excluded from many of the interactions that Chloron-India's top managers had with visitors from the headquarters. For another, his boss Pinchoo Kapoor, the CEO of Chloron-India, was known to be more of a "headquarters-man" than a champion of local initiative, having been transferred recently to Chloron-India from an overseas assignment as an explicit "agent of globalization," presumably to counter the relatively intransigent stands taken against the headquarters by his predecessor. According to Tendulkar, Kapoor could scarcely position himself as an objector to the process: "he makes constant speeches about how we should not be 'resistant to change.' He has been reprimanding people who do not keep the mission statement framed on their office walls. He is not going to go to Springfield (Chloron's head-quarters) and say that we will not follow their orders."

Ultimately, as researchers, we were able to document the manner in which the new/older ERP system was installed in Chloron-India. Tendulkar was given the unenviable job of seeing this operation through, while simultaneously, S. Padmanabhan, a young MBA from an elite business school was appointed to an Asia-Pacific team that was drawing up a blueprint for the migration of Chloron's ERP systems to the distributed model by 2004. It was a matter of common knowledge in the corporation that Padmanabhan was being groomed to succeed Tendulkar as the head of IT at Chloron-India. For purposes of narrative parsimony, we have chosen to present the events surrounding the ERP system installation in the form of a Tendulkar-Padmanabhan binary, lest the main ideas of the paper be lost in the thickness of ethnographic description. However, this mode of representation should not be taken to assume that either Tendulkar or Padmanabhan were the sole champions of their perspective. There were several other players in the process, whose views mirrored either that of Padmanabhan or Tendulkar (or other players such as Kapoor). Nor is the specific event of our story, that of ERP system installation, the sole site of contestation around issues of knowledge transfer. There were several areas of contestation between Chloron and Chloron-India where similar knowledge-transfer dynamics were visible.

Of the many instances of knowledge transfer that we observed at Chloron-India, we have chosen to foreground the above incident because it fleshes out the manner in which the process of communication between the headquarters and the subsidiary is inflected with authority rather than persuasion, of a univocal rather than a dialogical process, and of an absolutist rather than a context-sensitive representation of organizational reality. We found Tendulkar to be almost like the figure of Oedipus in the Greek tragedy, whose will was completely subordinate to the determinism of circumstances, and who was doomed to participate in his own impending annihilation. Padmanabhan, on the other hand, found the position assumed by the Chloron headquarters acceptable, despite its authoritarian streak. He found it convenient and expedient to accept their line lock stock and barrel, because it suited his personal interests, and because in his worldview, he was more predisposed to see a global logic to it. In these personalities and their approaches, the entire power dynamics within the organization can be made visible. This approach follows the ethnographic analysis made famous by Clifford Geertz, who analyzed how we can understand a number of things about Balinese culture as a whole from representing a single event: in his case a cockfight. For Geertz, the cockfight was not just about the staging of an event, but a comment on the hierarchical ordering of Balinese society and how it is enveloped in various webs of significance (Geertz, 1973). Likewise, the contest over an ERP system is itself a contest about power, representation and dominance.

Discussion: an analysis of imperialist practices at Chloron

Based on an extensive analysis of the situation, we found that the narratives of Tendulkar and Padmanabhan, while analyzing the same event, were "Rashomon-like" in their incommensurability. For instance, Tendulkar recounted the moment when the idea was first proposed to him by Pinchoo Kapoor, the head of Chloron-India. He maintains that when he declared the idea to be incompatible with the strategic goals of Chloron-India:

> … Mr. Kapoor began to get angry with me. "The problem with you, Tendulkar, is that you are afraid of change. But I am not. Let me tell you that this is not (the old CEO's) time.

431

You cannot begin every conversation with a 'no' and get away with it! If we are to grow in today's environment, we will have to learn to look at markets in terms of regions, and not nations. We are not an Indian company; we are the Asia-Pacific subsidiary of a global company."

In effect, globalization was being invoked by Kapoor to steer Tendulkar toward a decision that was not in local (subsidiary) interests. Padmanabhan had a similar analysis of the situation as Tendulkar, but projected a different perspective, which was a function of his own ability to acquiesce to a global demand, and also of his personality one who had an understanding of the deterministic nature of a decision made by the headquarters:

I can say definitely that if I had been the decision-maker, I would never have purchased the AS400s (The IT system under dispute). Between you and me, if I had been put on the AS400 team, I would be getting ready to post my biodata (mail my resume) to recruiters right now. If Tendulkar had been given a free hand, we would have continued working with the existing older computers and then gone directly to networked 256-bit Pentium machines running SAP. In a way he would be right. But unfortunately, because of the need for global standardization we had to go in for these AS400s, and we are not very good at using their system. New training, new hassles, it is all very dirty work. I am very happy that I was not sidelined into that project. Some of my colleagues now have to spend a lot of time getting trained on IBM AS400 machines. I think it is a very big waste of time. And if I was in their place, I would have really resigned and gone to another company. But I am doing very high-quality work here and it is very sad to see that the work they are doing will not really be of that much use in 5 to 6 years. But really, one must be practical. What is the point of fighting when corporate people like Mr. Clemente (the corporate IT head), our big boss Mr. Kapoor and the Asia-Pacific team, have all made a decision? It shows that Tendulkar does not understand human relations. He is too much of a technical man. He should have had an MBA like me, and he would have a better understanding of corporate culture.

Eventually, Chloron-India implemented the system of the headquarters' choice. Tendulkar was forced to dismantle his futuristic IT set-up, and go with the mainframes. Ironically, when Chloron put together a global team to evaluate the efficacy of a new ERP system for the future, Padmanabhan was made part of this highly visible team. This was as much a recognition of his ability to deal with distributed computing as it was a reward for his political role in facilitating the transfer of mainframe technology to India, or rather, his role in neutralizing Tendulkar's objections. In his own candid words:

The funny thing is, I think I was put on the SAP team after I had supported the AS400 project! When Mr. Kapoor made it clear to me that we were going to go ahead with the project, and that he had agreed to Mr. Clemente's suggestions, I decided to support it. No point in fighting losing battles like Tendulkar.

Based on our analysis of this episode, we have identified three themes that we believe need to be brought to the attention of those organizational theorists who analyze intra-organizational knowledge transfer, but pay lesser attention to its power-laden dimensions. The entire process of knowledge transfer at Chloron is of course driven by macro-economic changes. The intensification of Chloron's interest in its subsidiary, the changed ownership structure, and the facilitation of the integration of ERP systems through the re-entry of IBM (and the AS 400) into India are all artifacts of the triumph of globalization and neoliberal political reform in India (Chandrasekhar and Ghosh, 2002), which has radically different effects on the careers of Tendulkar and Padmanabhan.

Theme 1: uneven knowledge flows and imperialism

Empirical research on knowledge transfer has tended to follow one of two assumptions. Either knowledge is perceived as flowing into a vacuum (Wheelwright and Clark, 1995), or it is depicted that knowledge flows play the role of agents of creative destruction, destroying old knowledge and replacing it with new (Dewar and Dutton, 1986; Tushman and Anderson, 1986). However, the reality is more complex here. The system developed at Chloron-India is quite a sophisticated, working system. In effect, by transferring knowledge into Chloron-India, the US headquarters is attempting to "pour tea into a full cup," to quote a Sufi proverb. The interesting question is, what needs to be emptied for the tea to be placed in the cup? How can we account for the knowledge that Chloron-India will lose from this knowledge-transfer transaction?

Tendulkar's objection to the new system was based on technological grounds:

Our UNIX-based system may not be state-of-the art, but it is actually much better than Springfield's system, and actually more suitable for future upgrades. The whole world is now going in for networking and there is no need to go back in time and get ourselves a mainframe-based data processing system.

Moreover, it was better suited to the Indian terrain, since it bypassed much of India's unreliable telecommunications infrastructure, and had backup options where stored data could be sent across nodes using couriers and CDs in case of sustained telecommunications failure. The new system presupposed uniform connectivity, and would be more vulnerable to such breakdowns. The new system also had the effect of pushing Chloron-India to the back of the line in terms of those subsidiaries that would have access to the latest system. The reasoning at the headquarters was, "let us get some work out of these AS 400 systems before we replace them." Unfortunately, the manufacture of AS400 systems had been discontinued by IBM (Chloron-India received its stock from inventory), and were a low priority for IBM's maintenance division as well. Over time, many of the personnel who had expertise in UNIX systems quit Chloron India. As Tendulkar said:

What pains me is that we will soon be in the same boat that we were in the early 1980s [when Chloron-India had to move from mainframes to distributed systems]. The only difference will be that while at that time there was a "UNIX culture" in the IT department. By now, that competency has been eroded. In another year, it will be completely lost. Several old-timers have left, and the new people have worked only on an AS400 platform since their arrival here. We are becoming more and more backward. Linux and Windows XP have become the operating systems of choice all across corporate, but we still struggle with the AS400. I sometimes find it amusing. Mr. Kapoor had been glad to pay the consultants who designed the project $1,000 dollars a day to put this system into place. What he did not realize was that we are still paying for it.

"Knowledge flow" has been the term of choice used in strategy research to refer to various complex transfers of expertise in MNCs (Appleyard, 1996), but we find this to be a troubling

433

legacy. The term "flow" connotes the existence of a gradient, a movement that is natural, and involving a substance that is fluid. The *Merriam Webster's Dictionary* uses multiple terms to describe flow, such as "to move," "to proceed smoothly and readily," "to have a smooth continuity or "to derive from a source." Such descriptions exude a sense of desirability and inevitability that scarcely captures the complex, often coercive manner in which subsidiaries of MNCs are "modified" according to the exigencies determined by the headquarters. Research on the roles of MNC subsidiaries rarely examines power dynamics that underlie MNC-subsidiary relationships. Instead, the focus is on classifying types of subsidiaries based on those that "exploit existing MNC knowledge" and those that "augment existing MNC knowledge" (Almeida and Phene, 2004). Our analysis of knowledge transfer at Chloron did not reveal these clear distinctions – instead what we found was fragmentation, contestations, coercions, manufactured consent, loss of knowledge, and the stifling of local innovation.

Theme 2: knowledge transfer and imperialist coercion

> Global change does not require so much a transfer of knowledge from one part of the globe to the other as it does the investment in different types of global dialogues that can create new knowledge contextualized in multiple sites. This requires investments in dialogues that can initiate localized creativity and imagination and foster newer meanings and texts.
>
> Bouwen and Steyaert (1999: 304–5)

The story of the "upgrade" of Chloron-India from UNIX to AS400 offers us some important pointers. On one hand, we have the forces of globalization represented by the US headquarters of Chloron, its Singapore unit (which headed the Asia Pacific division and provided much of the logistical support for the AS 400 conversion), and partially, Pinchoo Kapoor and Padmanabhan, who force their logic on Tendulkar and his team. The absence of the dialogic process in this particular case is important. The executive team at India is used to apply pressure on Tendulkar. Kapoor's angry outburst about Tendulkar needing to go beyond "narrow" frames of reference, and subsequent attempts to corral opposition to the SAP project offer evidence of this coercion.

Eventually, Tendulkar suffered sanctions as a consequence of his resistance. Interestingly, while he was not fired, his punishment was very ironic and Sisyphean. He was forced to oversee the diminishment of his importance by giving him charge of the very process that he had opposed. While at times, Tendulkar's position seemed to find technological justification at the level of the headquarters, the political process won over the logic of technological rationality. We can only speculate about Tendulkar's assertion that the entire project was a case of escalated commitment based on an initial misreading of the complexity of Chloron-India's indigenous system by the headquarters, but it does seem quite clear that the process ran roughshod over local objections. While this could be seen as an example of authoritative power we believe the reality is more complex. Local objections were overcome by creating compliance with key actors in the subsidiary. While the process of creating compliance included elements of Lukes' third dimension of power where beliefs are shaped through the "imposition of internal constraints under historically changing circumstances," we believe the discursive power of "historically changing circumstances" produced certain material effects that are not taken into account by current theories about power and knowledge transfer.

This theme can also be seen as a clear challenge to the benign representations of "communities of practice" that populate the literature on organizational learning and knowledge management. While Chloron-India's IT advisory team, dispersed between Mumbai, Singapore and Springfield, can be seen as a "community," the contestations within this communal space are not solved by dialogue, but eventually by fiat and order. In traditionalist representations of such communities, Tendulkar comes across as a recalcitrant resistor, who is eventually won over by the community (after all, he eventually participated in the IT changeover). However, the reality is that Tendulkar's opinion had no currency in the organizational schema to start with. It is this pre-ordained fate of his perspective that ultimately challenges the representation of organizational spaces as communities of practice, and refocuses attention on the dynamics of coercive practices.

Theme 3: imperial subjectivities

If we are to grow in today's environment, we will have to learn to look at markets in terms of regions, and not nations. We are not an Indian company; we are the Asia-Pacific subsidiary of a global company.

(Pinchoo Kapoor)

We worked hard on the project. It is still a bit shaky, but in the beginning, it was worse. I remember how we used to work day and night. Even now, you were yourself here, and saw how all of us came even on Deepavali [important Indian holiday]. I had asked Mr. Clemente if I could give my staff the day off on Deepavali. It is after all, a national holiday here, and everybody has religious functions at home. But he said, "Our deadline here will be affected if you do not meet yours." So we all came. Of course, when they have their (Thanksgiving) holidays, we are automatically shut down. We give thanks when corporate is thankful. Otherwise, our Deepavali remains thankless.

(Om Shivpuri, Tendulkar's Deputy)

The above two statements foreground an important schism within Chloron-India. Pinchoo Kapoor, the CEO of Chloron-India, is exhibiting a sophisticated familiarity with the reality of globalization, while Om Shivpuri is bitterly opposing a work schedule that keeps him in office in early November on Deepavali (India's equivalent of Christmas), while offering him a holiday in late November because the headquarters is closed for Thanksgiving.

Kapoor was indeed an urbane man. Educated in the prestigious Indian Institute of Management at Calcutta, he had spent two decades in the management cadre of Chloron. He had been rotated across several management functions and geographies, and his last stint was as the head of consumer marketing in Malaysia. He was an authority on teak furniture, and could speak in an informed way about the relative merits of French impressionist paintings and the Bengal school of paintings in India. And indeed, his statement could be incorporated seamlessly into such books on global corporations such as Kenichi Ohmae's *The Borderless World*.

The manufacture of consent in this particular knowledge transfer process was enabled by a discursive process that created specific subjectivities and spaces of common interest between actors in the headquarters and the subsidiary. We argue that colonial and development discourses played a role in creating the conditions where consent was manufactured. Postcolonial theorists have reflected upon the emergence of the global subject among the third-world elite. From their perspective, we could make a linkage between Kapoor and a quote made by Lord Thomas Macaulay over 200 years ago. Speaking in his capacity as the Legal Member of the Council of Indian Education in 1785, Macaulay (Macaulay, 1782/1972: 249) stressed:

We must at present do our best to form a class who may be interpreters between us and the millions we govern; a class of persons, Indian in blood and colour, but English in taste, in opinions, in morals, and in intellect. To that class, we may leave it to refine the vernacular

435

dialects of the country, to enrich those dialects with terms of science borrowed from the western nomenclature, and to render them by degrees fit vehicles for conveying knowledge to the great mass of population.

Kapoor certainly fit the bill as one of the "interpreters" in Macaulay's schema. Likewise, Padmanabhan was rewarded for his compliance, despite his off-the-record reservations about the new system. In Padmanabhan's analysis of the situation, we can see the empirical representation of a corporate reality that the current theories of knowledge transfer are very well suited to describe. Gupta and Govindarajan (2000) discuss how "corporate socialization of subsidiary managers" enable the alignment of subsidiary managers "values and norms" with that of the parent organization. This process was apparent in Chloron with Kapoor and Padmanabhan: we have the consultant, the international team, the perils of standardization, the limits of absorptive capacity and infrastructure, cultural exchanges and a future focus. However, it is Tendulkar's (and Shivpuri's) story that is ultimately banished to the shadows of theory; the exercise of power, the loss of a valuable fund of local knowledge, and a subtle process of deskilling that is not even explored by labor process theorists. Shivpuri, on the other hand, was articulating his anger with Chloron in extremely local terms. For him, the peril of Chloron was that it devalued his local identity, which was expressed in this case as a religious affiliation. Thus Chloron's claim of being global rang hollow with him not just because he had to work on Deepavali, but also because of the Thanksgiving holiday he had to "endure." It appears that Kapoor, the global, postnational subject and Tendulkar, the local, national subject exist in uneasy proximity in Chloron-India. Globalization within Chloron, and indeed in all MNCs, is an extremely unfinished vision. What was much clearer of course, was the story of imperialism.

Conclusion

In this chapter, we have sought to tease out the dynamics of imperialism in an organizational setting, where change demands from the headquarters to the subsidiary followed imperialist scripts. While much of the discussion in the foregoing section should be self-explanatory, we would also like to use the conclusion to tease out another aspect of imperialism, as demonstrated by the Tendulkar–Padmanabhan dynamic.

Over almost 40 years ago, Bill Warren had presented empirical analysis to suggest that the emergence of regimes of national capitalism in the third world end up mitigating the effects of imperialism. This is not to say that exploitative regimes of accumulation are reduced, rather, Warren argued that exploitative systems "originate not in current imperialist–Third World relationships, but almost entirely from the internal contradictions of the Third World itself; that the imperialist countries' policies and their overall impact on the Third World actually favor its industrialization; and that the ties of dependence binding the Third World to the imperialist countries have been, and are being, markedly loosened, with the consequence that the distribution of power within the capitalist world is becoming less uneven" (Warren, 1973: 3). To us, the Tendulkar–Padmanabhan relationship mirrors the issue of exploitation from within the subaltern space, rather than the traditional geographically determined terrain.

However, conditions in the past two decades (especially since the emergence of neoliberal regimes in many third world nations) have led to a resurgence of the older patterns of imperialism (Gatade, 1997). MNCs, through their promise of global investment (and periodic threats to withdraw it), have been able to influence nation states as well as local capitalists substantially, leading to the re-emergence of extractive regimes (the extraction refers here not only to materials such as minerals and crops, but also to surplus value through regimes of outsourcing and offshoring). They have been abetted by an entire secondary network of institutions that have aggressively pursued the goal of capital mobility, elimination of sovereign protection for local industries, currency convertibility, and immunity for corporations from local laws (Baker et al., 1998). Consider, for example, that much of debt provision to the poorer nations by the IMF and the World Bank has been linked to tariff reductions, corporate tax reductions, removal of barriers to MNC entry in specific industrial sectors, reduction of barriers to foreign exchange repatriation, currency convertibility, reduction of administrative tasks by foreign investors, and in specific cases, immunity from local laws relating to labor and environmental protection.

Ultimately, Chloron remains the site of multiple imperialisms, spatially and temporally anchored and dynamic. Critical researchers need to highlight in our research that the change demands that are usually made of the subaltern subject, much like the demands of fealty made of the plaintiff quoted in our epigraph, are sites of imperialism. However, they are simultaneously sites of resistance. In this context therefore, we need a new research agenda in the field of organizational change. Our new research questions may be articulated as follows: How are change demands communicated by imperialists (represented in our study through the head-quarters of MNCs) to subaltern subjects (subsidiaries)? How are they internalized at the subsidiary level? How are these demands assimilated or resisted? More importantly, how do local interests hybridize, transform, and indigenize these alien demands so as to carve out a space of "local" agency within the "globalized" economy? And ultimately, what does this new story of organizational change, of political economy, and the changing landscape of industrial accumulation have to offer to those researchers who try to write a different organizational theory, one that is sensitive to those subjects who are consigned to the periphery of mainstream organizing? Research that attempts to offer answers to these questions will be of great importance, and will join a small but growing body of research that offers a different understanding of organizations and their activities.

References

Almeida, P. and Phene, A. (2004). Subsidiaries and knowledge creation: The influence of the MNC and host country innovation. *Strategic Management Journal*, 25: 847–64.

Amin, S. (1976). *Imperialism and Unequal Development*. New York: Monthly Review Press.

Armenakis, A. and Bedeian, A. (1999). Organizational change: A review of theory and research in the 1990s. *Journal of Management*, 25(3): 293–315.

Baker, D., Epstein, G. and Pollin, R. (1998). *Globalization and Progressive Economic Policy*. Cambridge: Cambridge University Press.

Barley, S.R. (1996). Technicians in the workplace: Ethnographic evidence for bringing work into organization studies. *Administrative Science Quarterly*, 41: 404–41.

Bate, S. (1997). Whatever happened to organizational anthropology? *Human Relations*, 50: 1147–75.

Beer, M. and. Nohria, N. (2000). *Cracking the Code of Change*. Cambridge, MA: Harvard Business Press.

Bouwen R. and Steyaert C. (1999). From dominant voice toward multivoiced cooperation: Mediating metaphors for global change. In D. Cooperrider D. and J. Dutton (eds), *Organizational Dimensions of Global Change: No limits to Cooperation* (pp. 291–319). Thousand Oaks, CA: SAGE Publications.

Brewer, J. (1980). *Marxist Theories of Imperialism*. London: Routledge.

Chandrasekhar, C.P. and Ghosh, J. (2002). *The Market that Failed: A Decade of Neoliberal Economic Reforms in India*. New Delhi: Leftword Books.

Denzin, N.K. and Lincoln, Y.S. (2005). *Handbook of Qualitative Research*. Thousand Oaks, CA: SAGE Publications.

Dewar, R.D. and Dutton, J.E. (1986). The adoption of radical and incremental innovations: An empirical analysis. *Management Science*, 32(11): 1422–33.

Ford, J. and Ford, L. (1994). Logics of identity, contradiction, and attraction and change in change. *Academy of Management Review*, 19(3): 756–85.

Gadamer, H. (1975). *Truth and Method*. London: Sheed & Ward.

Gatade, S. (1997). *Globalisation of Capital: An Outline of Recent Changes in the Modus Operandi of Imperialism*. New Delhi: Lok Dasta Press.

Geertz, C. (1973). *The Interpretation of Cultures*. New York: Basic Books.

Geertz, C. (2000). *Light: Anthropological Reflections on Philosophical Topics*. Princeton, NJ: Princeton University Press.

Gordon, R. and Grant, D. (2005). Knowledge management or management of knowledge? Why people interested in knowledge management need to consider Foucault and the construct of power. *Tamara: Journal of Critical Postmodern Organization Science*, 3(2): 1–12.

Gupta, A. and Govindarajan, V. (2000). Knowledge flows within multinational corporations. *Strategic Management Journal*, 21(4): 473–96.

Jaros, S. (2010). Commitment to organizational change: A critical review. *Journal of Change Management*, 10(1): 79–91.

Kaviraj, S. (1992). The imaginary institution that was India. In R. Guha (ed.) *Subaltern Studies: VII*. New Delhi: Oxford University Press, 1–27.

Kunda, G. (1992). *Engineering Culture: Control and Commitment in a High-Tech Corporation*. Philadelphia, PA: Temple University Press.

Macaulay, T.B. (1782/1972). *T. B. Macaulay: Selected Writings*. Chicago: University of Chicago Press.

Madison, D.S. (2005). *Doing Critical Ethnography*. Thousand Oaks, CA: Sage Publications.

Martin, P.Y. and Turner, B. (1986). Grounded theory and organizational research. *Journal of Applied Behavioral Science*, 22: 141–57.

Miles, M.B. and Huberman, A.M. (1994). *Qualitative Data Analysis: An Expanded Sourcebook*. Thousand Oaks, CA: SAGE Publications.

Mir, R. and Mir, A. (2009). From the corporation to the colony: Studying knowledge transfer across international boundaries, *Group and Organization Management*, 34(1): 90–113.

Mir, R., Banerjee, S. and Mir, A. (2008). Hegemony and its discontents: A critical analysis of organizational knowledge transfer. *Critical Perspectives on International Business*, 4(2/3): 203–27.

Orlikowski, W.J. (1996). Improvising organizational transformation over time: A situated change perspective. *Information Systems Research*, 7: 63–92.

Porras, J.J. and Silvers, C. (1991). Organization development and transformation. *Annual Review of Psychology*, 42: 51–78.

Prasad, P. (2005). *Crafting Qualitative Research: Working in the Postpositivist Traditions*. London: M. E. Sharpe.

Rosen, M. (1991). *From Text to Action*. Evanston, IL: Northwestern University Press.

Schwartzman, H. (1993). *Ethnography in Organizations*. London: SAGE Publications.

Schwartzmann, H. (1995). *Ethnography in Organizations*. London: SAGE Publications.

Sturdy, A, and Grey, C. (2003). Beneath and beyond organizational change management: Exploring alternatives. *Organization*, 10(4): 651–62.

Tsoukas, H. and Chia, R. (2002). On organizational becoming: Rethinking organizational change. *Organization Science*, 13(5): 567–82.

Tushman, M.L. and Anderson, P. (1986). Technological discontinuities and organizational environments. *Administrative Science Quarterly*, 31: 439–65.

Van de Ven, A. and Poole, M. (2002). Field research methods. In J. Baum (ed.) *The Blackwell Companion to Organizations*, pp. 867–88. Oxford: Blackwell Publishing.

Van de Ven, A. and Poole, M.S. (1995). Explaining development and change in organizations. *Academy of Management Review*, 20: 510–40.

Van Maanen, J. (1988). *Tales of the Field: On Writing Ethnography*. Chicago: University of Chicago Press.

Warren, W. (1973). Imperialism and capitalist industrialization. *New Left Review*, I/81: 1–20.

Weick, K. and Quinn, R.E. (1999). Organizational change and development. *Annual Review of Psychology*, 50: 361–86.

Wheelwright, S.C. and Clark, K.B. (1995). *Leading Product Development: The Senior Manager's Guide to Creating and Shaping the Enterprise*. New York: Free Press.

30

OD discourse and domination

Maxim Voronov and Warner P. Woodworth

This chapter draws on critical discourse analysis to analyze the field of Organization Development (OD) as a discourse. We argue that the OD discourse is characterized by the following: overwhelmingly psychological focus, construction of individuals as rational and bounded, and avoidance of sociological questions. We argue that the failure of OD to humanize organizations highlighted by a number of OD writers does not result from the failings of particular OD practitioners, but rather, that it is rooted in the very discourse of OD, which renders the field incapable of navigating the socio-economic context in which organizations operate and are constituted. We pick up on Marshak's (2005) speculation about the emergence of a "new" OD to argue that the "old" OD has reached a dead end and that the discourse that is constitutive of OD should be revolutionized, if OD practitioners are serious about making organizations more humane.

The field of OD is no novice to controversy. The debate about the relative importance of human needs versus the bottom line is as old as the field itself (Kahn, 1974; Stephenson, 1975). Questions also have been raised about the extent to which OD should be seen as separate or different from the broader field of change management (Farias and Johnson, 2000; Worren, Ruddle, and Moore, 1999), as well as from management consulting (e.g., Schein, 1988). Recently, Marshak (2005) wondered if a "new" OD was emerging, with an entirely new set of epistemological, political and methodological commitments—one less committed to empiricism and objectivism and more attuned to the processes of social construction and the realities of power. We hope to take this point further. We would like to make a provocative suggestion that not only should there be a new OD, but also that the "old" OD, with its neo-empiricism and psychological orientation has reached a dead end. We argue that the traditional OD, due to its consistent privileging of managerial interests at the expense of other stakeholders as well as to its psychological orientation and a belief in bounded rational actors that have blinded it to issues of power and class, has rarely managed to live up to its stated objective of facilitating a humanistically oriented organizational change.

This essay differs from earlier critiques of OD (e.g., Cooke, 1999; Nirenberg, 1998; Nord, 1974; Woodworth, 1981, 1982), in that we treat OD as a discourse, rather than as a field. In this way we hope to analyze OD not as a reified and fixed entity but as a socio-historically produced set of discursive concepts that can be critically examined. Thus, we intend to show that it is not particular theories in OD or specific OD practices that are responsible for OD's frequent alliance with sectional managerial interests, but rather the very discourse of OD that contains the roots of this kind of managerialism. Such an analysis is particularly needed, given that OD has not yet been viewed through the lens of critical theory to the degree that management and organization theory have, both of which have been major theoretical developments (e.g., Alvesson and Willmott, 1992; Barker, 1993).

This chapter is organized as follows. We first provide a brief overview of OD as it constructs itself. We then introduce critical discourse theory and the key concepts that we use as a heuristic to analyze OD. Following that, we analyze a variety of OD topics and concepts to argue that OD discourse is overwhelmingly psychological, constructs individuals as bounded and rational and avoids exploring sociological context of OD interventions. We conclude by emphasizing the importance of fundamentally changing the OD discourse to make it more attuned to the sociopolitical realities of organizational life by recognizing the importance of societal and economic structures that constitute organizations and within which organizations operate as well as by taking seriously the inevitably political nature both of organizational life and of OD interventions.

Setting the context

This section sets the context for the chapter by providing an overview of OD as it normatively constructs itself and by introducing the theoretical framework that will then be used to analyze OD.

OD as it constructs itself

OD is different from other forms of organizational consulting in several ways. First, is the dual importance placed on both people and organizational effectiveness, as opposed to the automatic privileging of financial markers. Second, OD and its repertoire are informed by behavioral science. Third, the consultant is expected to work jointly with the client to design and implement interventions.

According to Church et al. (1999), "Organization development is a field based on values—promoting positive humanistically oriented large-system change in organizations—plain and simple" (p. 49). In keeping with the humanistic values that underpin OD, commentators on the field commonly emphasize the dual concern for the well-being of organizations as well as the well-being of the people who work there (e.g., Argyris, 1957; Burke, 1994; Waclawski and Church, 2002a).

There is not always an agreement as to the relative importance of human needs as opposed to organizational performance. In their seminal article on OD values, Tannenbaum and Davis (1969) observe the therapeutic nature of successful OD interventions. They note that such interventions focus on breaking through inter-personal and organizational barriers that stifle human growth and keep people from realizing their potential. On the other hand, Bennis (1969) is more focused on the coupling of the humanistic change with meeting the organization's objectives, and Stephenson (1975) accuses OD of being focused on human development to the point of losing the focus on organization development. Kahn (1974) cautions OD practitioners against excessive reliance on the process versus structure dichotomy, as this may lead them to overemphasize the process interventions and to ignore the needed structural interventions. Pages

(1971) even goes as far as suggesting that some OD interventions designed to overcome defensive routines can engender a different kind of defensive routines and submission to authority. Nonetheless, in its attention to human needs, OD is distinct from those forms of consulting that focus exclusively on organizations' financial performance.

OD is based on behavioral science research. Burke (1994) credits humanist writers, such as Maslow, Herzberg, Lawler, Argyris, Bion, and Lewin for the intellectual underpinnings of OD. The community has over the decades developed a great variety of techniques and interventions based on research in behavioral sciences, including process consultation, group dynamics, survey feedback, large-scale interventions, and appreciative inquiry (see Waclawski and Church, 2002b and French and Bell, 1999 for recent discussions of OD's repertoire). One of the key stated premises of OD is that OD consultants should intervene at the level and be mindful of the whole system, rather than focusing purely on individuals and groups (Burke, 1994; Kahn, 1974; Katz and Kahn, 1966, 1978). It needs to be noted, however, that the OD community has been under increased pressure to demonstrate the contribution of various interventions to the bottom line (Cady and Lewis, 2002; Church et al., 2002), and the focus is, at least to some extent, shifting from human input to the business results (McLean and DeVogel, 2002). This pressure is arguably shaping the repertoire, with certain "harder" and more quantitative approaches, such as survey feedback and multi-source feedback, becoming increasingly prominent, while the "softer" approaches, such as group dynamics, apparently losing some of their appeal (Schein, 1989).

OD interventions are conceived as joint collaborations between consultants and clients (Bennis, 1969; Burke, 1994; Schein, 2001). Unlike the forms of consultation in which consultants solve clients' problems or offer them solutions without providing assistance with implementation, OD consultants are expected to work jointly with their clients throughout the process of diagnosing the "problem," designing a solution, implementing it, and assessing its impact (Schein, 1988).

Critical discourse theory

Before we can discuss OD as a set of discursive practices as well as the power effects of those practices, it is necessary to briefly review the relevant critical discourse analysis literature and to define key concepts.

According to Mumby and Clair (1997), critical discourse analysis is concerned with exploring the "connection between everyday talk and the production of, maintenance of and resistance to systems of power, inequality, and injustice" (p. 183). Discourses are defined as "sets of texts— statements, practices, etc.—which bring an object into being. Thus, discursive analysis requires an examination of language, the production of texts and processes of communication, and the interactions between actors in organizational and institutional settings" (Grant et al., 1998, cited in Hardy et al., 2000). *Texts* do not have to be formal written texts but may involve a variety of forms, such as artifacts, spoken language, symbols and pictures (Grant et al., 2005; Phillips and Hardy, 2002). This perspective treats discourse as neither inherently malleable and controllable, nor as a force that exerts unidirectional control over social actors. Instead, discourse is both socially constituted and socially constitutive (Grant, Keenoy, and Oswick, 2001; Hardy et al., 2000).

As Chia (2000, p. 513) writes:

> Social objects and phenomena such as 'the organization', 'the economy', 'the market' or even 'stakeholders' or 'the weather', do not have a straightforward and unproblematic

existence independent of our discursively-shaped understandings. Instead, they have to be forcibly carved out of the undifferentiated flux of raw experience and conceptually fixed and labeled so that they can become the common currency for communicational exchanges. Modern social reality, with its all-too-familiar features, has to be continually constructed and sustained through such aggregative discursive acts of reality-construction.

The implication of such theorizing is not that the world is "made up" or that it is all in our heads. Indeed, there is no perfect consensus in the literature as to the comparative importance placed on the "objective world" as opposed to the "discursive world." We side with Tsoukas' (2000), position that "social reality is causally independent of actors (hence realists have a point) and, at the same time, what social reality is depends on how it has been historically defined, the cultural meanings and distinctions which have made this reality as opposed to that reality (hence constructivists also have a point)" (p. 531).

Discourses produce concepts, or categories and relationships between those categories that enable individuals to make sense of the world. They produce identities for individuals and groups that then enable as well as constrain these individuals' and groups' actions and abilities to produce alternative discourses (Hardy et al., 2000; Oswick et al., 1997; Wetherell and Potter, 1992).

A specific example of critical discourse analysis at work is the social construction of refugee identities (Hardy and Phillips, 1999; Phillips and Hardy, 1997). The notion of "refugee" is not an objective or fixed one. Establishing a person's identity as a refugee involves an elaborate process of managing meanings. Agencies go through a variety of discursive practices to legitimize someone as a refugee, such as distinguishing between "political refugees" and "economic migrants." These identities, in turn give the individuals labeled this way some rights and privileges while taking away others. Furthermore, there are affiliated discursive categories, such as "client," that can be evoked and intertwined with that of "refugee." Another example is the case of an NGO operating in the Palestinian Territories that attempted to shift its identity from "international" to "Palestinian" (Hardy et al., 2000) in order to be perceived as being more legitimate among the local populace. When the new identity resulted in unforeseen and undesirable outcomes for the NGO (e.g., harassment and intimidation of the personnel by the local police), it sought to reconstitute its "international" identity. This case illustrates that the discursive production of particular identities facilitates certain actions while disabling others. While, the "Palestinian" identity made some of NGOs work easier by making it appear more legitimate, it resulted in the loss of protection that the "international" identity had conferred upon it.

Analyzing OD as a discourse allows us to examine the various writings as texts that constitute OD discourse. This discourse creates particular identities for organizations, managers, employees, OD practitioners, and so on (Holvino, 1996; Oswick et al., 1997). Any discourse highlights certain things while masking others and legitimizes certain actions while delegitimizing others. Interrogating OD as a discourse, then, allows us to examine what aspects of organizational life it highlights as well as what aspects it masks or renders invisible. We should note, however, that we use critical discourse theory here in a more-or-less heuristic way. Instead of engaging in rigorous discourse analyses of particular texts (e.g., Holvino, 1996), we look at a variety of OD writings as manifestations of the OD discourse.

OD as a discourse

We now apply the insight from critical discourse theory to the field of OD, re-conceptualizing the field as a discourse. We argue that the OD discourse is overwhelmingly psychological in nature. It constitutes individuals as bounded and as exercising free will. It largely avoids the broader (sociological) questions of social structure, power and domination, and so on. This section tackles each of those three aspects, one by one, and examines specific concepts of interest to prominent OD writers as manifestations of OD discourse.

The "psychologism" of the OD discourse

We argue that OD discourse is an overwhelmingly psychological one. This is not surprising, given the psychological training of many of OD's founding figures and OD's heavy borrowing of theories from various sub-fields of psychology. In his review of OD's theoretical roots, Burke (1994, 2002) credits primarily psychological theories, including need theory, expectancy theory, job satisfaction, the group unconscious, the group as a family, and so on. A similar overview is offered by French and Bell (1999). Although OD writers tend to draw on open systems (e.g., Burke, 1994; Katz and Kahn, 1978) and more recently on dynamic systems theory (e.g., Burke, 2002), as we argue below, those appear to be marginal discourses that do not impact the dominant psychological discourse of the field. Along with theories, OD has also heavily borrowed its methods from psychology. Thus, its hallmark techniques, such as process consultation, surveys, multi-rater feedback, are rooted in psychology and are infused with psychology's strong preference for empiricism, pursuit of objective truth, and conceptualization of organizational phenomena in terms of health and sickness. Like its cousin psychology, and unlike the more remote fields of sociology and management, OD has not welcomed the newer theoretical and epistemological perspectives, such as interpretivism, symbolic interactionism, and linguistic analyses (Grieves, 2003).

In order to highlight the psychologism of the OD discourse, we discuss several specific OD concepts: organizational health, assessment/diagnosing, intervention, and resistance.

Organizational health

The conceptualization of organizational health dominating the OD discourse is a psychological one. This is apparent in the very notion of "organizational health" itself. Schein's (2002) model of health, for instance, is that of coping process: being able to sense changes in the external environment, to get the information to the relevant sub-systems, to change in response to those demands, to externalize the changes, and to reflect on the consequences of the organization's actions (see also Beckhard, 2006). Thus, this is a process of transferring the individual-level model of psychological health to the organizational level. Such notions of organizational health conceive of organizations as removed from the broader socio-economic structures (Nord, 1974, 1977) that fall outside of its psychological discourse.

Assessment/diagnosing

The predominantly psychological nature of OD discourse is also evident in its approach to diagnosing and assessing organizations. There is a great deal of emphasis on valid and scientific (in empiricist sense) measures, such as surveys (e.g., Falletta and Combs, 2002), personality assessment (e.g., Burke and Noumair, 2002), and multisource feedback (e.g., Church et al., 2002). This drive to create standardized and generalizable measures has even caused some prominent OD practitioners to be alarmed. Schein (1989, 2002) has consistently voiced his concerns about this drive toward greater empiricism. However, while he may be skeptical about OD's increasing reliance on standardized quantitative methods, he still advocates the clinical method and emphasizes the therapeutic nature of the consultant–client relationship. Nor does he abandon the empiricist drive to get to the "truth"—just the quantitative methodology.

Intervention

This notion is also conceptualized in psychological terms. According to Burke (1994), "taking a step is making an *intervention* into the routine way in which organization operates" (p. 8, italics in original). This evokes the image of a "problem" individual or group, such as an alcoholic or a dysfunctional family (Levinson, 1972), that requires the interruption of the dysfunctional routines and a forcible move in a new direction. The change process itself—unfreeze–change–refreeze— is derived from research in personality change (Nord, 1976). The objective is to generate a motivation to change (Nord, 1976) or to foster anxiety and/or shame about not changing or learning something new (Schein, 1993). This is followed by providing a safe space for learning and experimentation, to help the individuals cope with fear of the unknown. Once the changes have been made, efforts are undertaken to reinforce the "new" routines. There are variations on these change processes (e.g., Burke, 1994; Kotter, 1995), but there are more similarities than differences. Armed with an almost exclusively psychological understanding of intervention/ change management leaves OD poorly prepared to cope with issues of systemic power (e.g., Hardy, 1994; Palmer and Dunford, 1996) and discourse (Tsoukas, 2005) that are often important in organizational change efforts.

Resistance

OD has tended to conceive of resistance as something to be overcome. It is sometimes conceived as relatively benign—as fear of the unknown or of losing something valuable or as blind resistance and as ideological resistance (Burke, 2002). Regardless of the characterization, resistance is almost inevitably conceptualized in psychological terms. According to Nord and Jermier (1994, p. 398),

> The concern with overcoming resistance appears to be linked to a pejorative view of "resistance" and resisters—a view apparently derived from the use of "resistance" by Freud. In psychoanalytic theory, resistance is often seen as a process that keeps neurotic individuals distant from reality and from suggestions of their therapists.

Such a psychological construction of resistance positions it as irrational and in opposition to change, which is unambiguously good (Nord and Jermier, 1994; Schein, 1999). Having constructed resistance in psychological terms, suggested solutions are also constructed as akin to therapeutic interventions. For example, Burke (2002) advocates activities designed to achieve closure, such as a symbolic funeral for the way things used to be. However, rare is the acknowledgement of resistance as rational and legitimate (Barker, 1999; Fleming, 2005; Nord, 1977; Nord and Jermier, 1994).

In summary, we argue that OD discourse constructs the subject matter of OD—organizational ideal state, the process of assessing organizations, intervening in organizations, and resistance to the interventions—as fundamentally psychological. Running throughout is a discourse of pathology in which individuals need to be "diagnosed" and "interventions" designed and performed on them by expert and enlightened OD professionals using all manner of scientific "instruments" and "tools" and "techniques" in order to "fix," "rid" or "cure" individuals of behaviors that are undermining the organization's success as defined by the ethos and

445

measurement criteria of a market-centric economic logic. At the same time, however, this pathology orientation is rationalized as assisting individuals with self-actualization, professional development, personal growth, etc.—albeit always in service to the effectiveness of the organization and its definition of success regardless of impact and consequences for individuals or the larger community and society.

OD discourse and the construction of bounded individuals

In the "Preface" to the sixth edition of *Organization Development*, French and Bell (1999) describe organization development as "the applied behavioral science discipline dedicated to improving organizations and the people in them through the use of the theory and practice of planned change" (xiii). The emphasis is on change—changing organizations through changing the people in them—and privileges the goals, needs and demands of the organization over the goals, needs and general well-being of the people who work there. In the process, OD is positioned as the solution-provider and OD-facilitated change as good for both individuals and the organization despite its managerialist ties, dependencies and constraints. In these change-oriented intervention practices, while the espoused focus might be on the organization, a closer analysis of OD discourse reveals an emphasis is on the smallest—and most vulnerable and powerless—unit of influence, i.e. the individual. Three particular areas in which this plays out are the following:

1. The pervasive—and invasive—use of personality testing such as the Myers–Briggs Type Indicator (MBTI)
2. The proliferation in the use of multi-rater assessment and feedback
3. The emphasis on the training and "development" of individuals as the means of achieving organizational "effectiveness" and "growth" (aka "profitability" and "shareholder value").

Lost in all of this, are the very real and complex organizational influences and constraints on individuals (including groups/teams) and larger societal influences and constraints on organizations (Nord, 1974, 1977).

Personality inventories

The use of personality inventories and personality assessment in OD has spread over the years (Burke and Noumair, 2002). Since the length and scope of this chapter does not allow for an in-depth analysis and discussion of the multitude of instruments that fall into these various categories, we will focus on the MBTI, the most popular of these tools. But, first, a slight detour to discuss two terms that are intimately/intricately intertwined with these processes of evaluation. The two terms are "instruments" and "inventory." Virtually all "assessment tools" are known and referred in the field and practice of OD as "instruments," which can be defined as "devices for indicating, measuring, controlling, etc." (*Webster's New World Dictionary*, 2003, 337). Those whose results are categorized into predefined diagnostic scales or typologies are referred to as "inventories" or itemized lists of attributes, characteristics, etc. All of this is in the name of "science" defined in terms of measurement and quantification and extended to "behavioral science" designed to reduce the human to numbers and scales and to corral individuals into collectives/aggregates (referred to as "profiles") of neat, simplistic categories for descriptive, evaluative and corrective purposes.

Developed in the 1940s by mother-and-daughter team of Katharine Briggs and Isabel Briggs Myers, according to Annie Murphy Paul's *The Cult of Personality Testing* (2004), the MBTI is now given to 2.5 million people annually and is used by 89 of the Fortune 100 companies (xiii).

Murphy goes on to observe that the MBTI has also been embraced by a multitude of individuals whose enthusiasm persists "despite research showing that as many as three-quarters of test takers achieve a different personality type when tested again, and that the sixteen distinctive types described by Myers–Briggs have no scientific basis whatsoever" (p. xiii).

Not only do these last facts not deter individuals and organizations from their enthusiastic embrace, but the MBTI and other personality, temperament, style, etc. assessment instruments are the cornerstone of much of OD practice. As such, it is a core that is hyper-psychologistic in nature and focus and gives the false comfort of scientific measurement stemming from its positivistic roots. And, despite the warning by French and Bell (1999, p. 249) against some of the "dysfunctional consequences" of its use, such dysfunctions are rampant and may be more the norm than the exception. Three of the most common and egregious are the following: (1) using results to label and stereotype others; (2) focusing on analysis of individual behaviors rather than on addressing more fundamental issues facing the group, team or organization; and (3) focusing on individuals rather than on addressing more systemic and structural issues facing the organization, industry/sector and larger social system.

Burke and Noumair (2002) justify their fondness for MBTI by noting that their "clients find it easy to understand, [it is] reasonably accurate as far as they are concerned, and fun and interesting. Also as psychologists, we are partial to MBTI because of its grounding in Jungian theory and the instrument's unique evolution" (p. 56). Thus, the face validity of the instrument, in light of its easy fit within the broader psychological discourse of OD and is entertainment value appear to be the main selling points of MBTI in the context of OD interventions. However, as Lawler (2006) cautions, personality and individual difference traits are very difficult to change through OD interventions, and "it is unclear that training can significantly influence people's personalities" (p. 654). Thus, on the one hand, the OD discourse appears to seek to use MBTI as a rough but entertaining tool, not to be taken especially seriously. On the other hand, it constructs personality as stable and difficult (if not impossible) to change. We would argue that the presence of these two conflicting assumptions within the OD discourse makes it easy for the discourse to enable and facilitate the egregious abuses of MBTI that French and Bell (1999) caution against.

Multi-rater feedback

Although a more recent instrument in the OD "toolkit," multi-rater (and its popular variation 360°) feedback, has grown rapidly in popular use among OD consultants (Church et al., 2001; Church et al., 2002). Unlike the MBTI and other personality inventories, multi-rater feedback is generally reserved exclusively for those in managerial positions and marketed on its "developmental" merits. The process involves the independent and confidential/anonymous rating of an individual on a list of predetermined categories and measures of performance, behavior and abilities by others that might include that individual's supervisor, colleagues, staff and clients/customers and oneself. The results are compiled and assessed by the OD professional who then provides "feedback" to the individual being rated. Consulting engagements might also include "coaching" for the individual and/or the individual might be paired with a "mentor" within the organization to help facilitate the individual's on-going developmental process.

It is an interesting feature/aspect of this assessment and feedback model that it is often cast as a "leadership development" mechanism and process whereby the individual has been identified as a candidate for potential advancement within the organization and the espoused purpose of the multi-rater feedback is to help the individual—and the organization—identify strengths to be enhanced and weaknesses to be overcome. Although the process is cast as a scientific and

447

relatively objective way of "discovering" the individuals' strengths and weaknesses, it can be argued that like other OD and HR techniques, multi-source feedback creates and fixes the individuals' traits, rather than merely describing them (Townley, 1993). Masked under the clout of scientific discovery, the multi-source feedback process gets intertwined with other modes of concertive control (e.g., Barker, 1993) to discipline and control the individuals.

Training and development

In the world of OD, training and development is the intervention of choice. The theory being that if we just train enough people how to behave, then the organization will automatically be a better place to work as well as being profitable and able to sustain its existence in an increasingly unpredictable and competitive marketplace. Everything else is a precursor to training and development. All the assessments and feedback sessions serve the purpose of building the case and establishing the need for training and development (Grieves, 2003). Here again, while vast numbers within organizations are put through various training and development workshops, courses, programs, initiatives, etc., the focus is on individuals—either individually or as parts of "teams"—rather than the organization as a whole or systemic, institutional issues. And, in many cases, the "development" part is the most psychologistic of all.

This individualistic and psychologistic focus can be directly traced back to the T-groups (training groups) of early OD and central to the practice of one of the preeminent OD institutions, National Training Laboratory (NTL) in Bethel, Maine. As designed and practiced these T-group sessions are a form of "group therapy" in which the individual is encouraged to bare her/his soul before perfect strangers in a "safe" environment for personal exploration and discovery as the foundation for developmental change in order to go back and fit into and contribute more effectively to the sponsoring organization who has sent them to and paid for them to attend the session (Burke, 1994). The objective of T-groups was to allow people to gain a greater self-awareness and understanding of "choices" they subconsciously made in their behavior (Bennis, 1964). Little care and attention is given to what the individuals will face when they return to their respective offices—or other areas of their lives for that matter. The charge is to go forth and develop and change or make changes such as opting out of the system if individual and system are not a good "fit."

In response to the potential charge that the excessive focus on individuals is merely a failing of individual practitioners, we argue that the foundation of this focus on individuals is in the discourse itself. Note Maslow's and Herzberg's theories of motivation that underpin training and development approaches. These and other theories of motivation and satisfaction construct individuals as actors ultimately seeking individualistic attainment (Nord, 1977). It is also important to note the close relationship between the growth of psychology and the onset of the Cold War, with psychologists receiving a great deal of funding from the US military (Cooke et al., 2005; Herman, 1995). Maslow, for instance, viewed the student activists of the 1960s as belonging to the "spit-on-Daddy Club" (Herman, 1995) and as someone allowing for a hierarchy of societies, from least to most self-actualized, it is apparent that Maslow was very much pro status quo. Thus, the psychological theories of motivation and satisfaction that are an intrinsic part of the OD discourse are hardly a basis for radical or significant reformist action. Rather, they help to explain the origins of the pro-status quo nature of OD discourse.

In summary, an examination of the prominent role given to personality inventories, multi-rater feedback and training and development initiatives leads us to argue that OD discourse constructs individuals as bounded and rational actors, discounting organizational and societal influences on individuals' actions.

OD discourse and the avoidance of sociological questions

Although OD writers regularly credit sociology as a discipline that has influenced the development of OD (e.g., Burke, 1994), it does not appear as though the discourse of OD has taken in the insights of sociology. To be sure OD writers grounded in sociology (e.g., Lawrence and Lorsch, 1969) have contributed important insights that are a part of the OD discourse, but the insights from sociology have been functionalist in nature and devoid of any critical examination of the relationship between organizations and society. Specifically, OD writers have shown little interest in the relationship between organizations and the socio-economic structure of the society (Nord, 1974), have paid limited attention to the role of power and politics in organizations (Marshak, 2001; Woodworth, 1981, 1982) and have assumed the universality of managerial interests (Collins, 2000; Nirenberg, 1998; Nord, 1974, 1977).

OD's inattention to the socio-economic structure of society

OD discourse takes the capitalist socio-economic logic and the existing system of gender and ethnic relations as a given. The categories, such as "managers," "employees," "men," "women," "Whites," "minorities," and so on are treated as objective, rather than socio-historically constructed (Holvino, 1996). OD discourse does not seek to inquire how such categories have been produced, but rather, accepts them as given. Thus, OD discourse conceives of appropriate interventions as ones that improve people's work life and wellbeing within existing societal structures and does not leave itself open to the exploration of the extent to which social structures themselves need to be re-examined in order to accomplish the very changes that OD discourse defines as desirable. For example, there is little examination in OD discourse of the extent to which the managerial control imperative (Deetz, 1995; Nord, 1977; Seo, 2003) may contradict some of the participatory management initiatives that OD seeks.

In all, Nord's (1974) Marxian critique of applied behavioral science is pertinent to our critique of the OD discourse, in that the OD discourse appears to remain abstracted from the broader societal structures.

OD's lack of attention to power and politics

Marshak (2001) notes the frequent "ambivalence or even antagonism toward power" on the part of many OD consultants (p. 35). This, however, we would argue, is not merely a failing of individual OD practitioners. Instead, the avoidance of power appears to be but one manifestation of OD a-sociological discourse. For evidence of this one may examine French and Bell's (1999) influential text on OD. The authors acknowledge the accusation that OD often fails to take power into account but claim that that criticism "was essentially correct for many years although it is less valid today" (p. 282). They argue that recent years had seen an "outpouring" of research on power, from which OD practitioners derived implications for OD practice. A review of French and Bell's references indicates that the only work on power they review spans 1959 to 1988. No work from 1990's is deemed relevant for inclusion—including such frequently cited articles from top management journals, as Alvesson and Willmott (1992) and Barker (1993). Even the work from the period that could potentially raise questions about the supposedly politically neutral nature of organization development, such as Nord's (1974, 1977) or Woodworth's (1981, 1982) is not discussed (Nord, 1974 is cited in the notes section, but his argument is not discussed or even mentioned in the text). The literature reviewed is limited to the writers like McLelland, Dahl, French and Raven, Mintzberg, and Pfeffer, who emphasize the overt, purposeful and

449

measurable nature of power, rather than those who highlight the nature of power as embedded into the taken-for-granted organizational practices and connected to broader societal arrangements. Not surprisingly, French and Bell's (1999) advice to OD practitioners for navigating the political terrain errs on the side of voluntarism and choice in regard to positioning oneself and one's intervention within the political arrangements in organizations, with the ultimate aim of avoiding and downplaying politics as much as possible.

OD's alignment with managerial interests

Schein (1999) compares organizational culture change to brainwashing. Woodworth (1981) compared OD practitioners to CIA agents infiltrating organizations on behalf of managerial interests, and Baritz (1960) refers to industrial psychologists (close cousins of OD) as "servants of power." We argue that this—perhaps excessive—alignment between OD and managerial interests is also rooted in the very OD discourse, which constructs organizations as unitary, with the assumption that one super-ordinate goal is shared by all organizational factions. The oft emphasized dual objective of OD to improve organizations' financial performance *and* the life of the employees is a specific manifestation of such unitary construction. The dual objective is only possible if employee well-being and the profitability of an organization are either positively linked or at least, not contradictory. However, the reality on the ground for most organizational members appears to be that their objectives are in fact contradictory (Nord, 1977). For example, there is a real financial incentive for managers to keep the employees' wages as low as possible, and as much as employees might like to see their employer organizations thrive and prosper, it is hardly satisfying if that happens while they see no increased wages or the company stock jumps, just as their peers are laid off.

The practical contradiction between profitability and employee well-being should, in theory, force OD practitioners to choose sides between serving managerial interests and those of the employees. Yet, the OD discourse conveniently masks this contradiction, allowing OD practitioners to serve managerial interests and to directly work against employees' interests, such as by participating in anti-union initiatives (Voronov et al., 2006), without having to acknowledge their political roles.

We argue that a related contribution of the OD discourse to the cooptation of OD interventions by managerial interests is the insistence that OD interventions be managed from the top (e.g., Beckhard, 2006). This principle, in itself, privileges the managerial interests and legitimizes OD practitioners' doing the top executives' bidding with little regard to the impact of their intervention on the employees.

In summary, we argue that the a-sociological nature of OD discourse is manifest in its extremely limited attention to power and politics and in implicit alliance with sectional managerial interests. Having critiqued the dominant OD discourse, we conclude this chapter by advocating major changes in OD discourse.

Conclusion: toward a "new" OD

Marshak (2005) suggested that a "new" OD appeared to be emerging, alongside a more traditional OD. The new version appeared to be characterized by a weakened orthodoxy of the neo-empiricist epistemology, a greater attention to the social construction of reality, and an increased awareness of issues of power and domination. The chapter examines the traditional OD as a discourse and seeks to demonstrate that any failings on the part of OD to humanize organizations should not be attributable merely to the failings of particular practitioners or to the refusal of managers to embrace OD's teachings. Instead, we argue that the very discourse of OD, with its overwhelming psychologism, the construction of bounded and rational individuals and the refusal to explore sociological concerns has laid the foundations for the failures of OD practice. In this section we argue that any meaningful changes in OD practice can only be accomplished if the discourse of the field changes. Thus, we outline some of the changes that the discourse must undergo.

OD must take power and politics seriously

OD discourse must move beyond the present lip service to systems thinking and its partly sociological roots. A genuine acceptance of sociological insights would necessitate the acknowledgement that OD interventions cannot be assumed to happen in truly democratic and just systems. Every organization faces power struggles among managers and between managers and other stakeholders (employees, community groups, etc.) as well as among the various stakeholder groups. These power struggles must be taken seriously, and the interests of all stakeholders must be acknowledged as legitimate (Marshak, 2006). Thus, the pejorative view of resistance (Nord and Jermier, 1994) and the general implicit alignment between OD and managerial interests should have no place in the "new" OD discourse.

The term "resistance," in particular, needs to be rethought. Instead of borrowing the psychologists' tendency to see it as something to be overcome, OD practitioners might take a page from the playbook of critical management studies and conceive of resistance as inevitable part of organizational functioning (e.g., Fleming, 2005) that can be used as data for unearthing the multitude of voices, agendas and interests that are inevitable in any organization (Marshak, 2006; Voronov, 2005).

More fundamentally, however, the OD discourse needs to embrace frameworks of power that emphasize that power is not something that one actor does to another, but is embedded into the taken-for-granted routines of organizations and is connected to the broader social structures within which organizations operate (e.g., Voronov, 2005; Woodworth, 1982).

OD must overcome the myopic focus on process

Chris Argyris wrote in his volume of the Addison-Wesley OD Series that an OD consultant can work with an organization like the Ku Klux Klan and still maintain one's integrity (1970). For him, as well as for Bennis (1969) and others, OD was a neutral process of helping organizations improve and become more effective. This myopic focus on the process causes OD to obfuscate the moral and ethical considerations implicit in OD practice. It facilitates the pursuit of "empowerment" as a feeling (Boje and Rosile, 2001) rather than actual practice. It silences those practitioners who see OD as a potential vehicle for social transformation and the pursuit of social justice. It turns OD practitioners into the henchmen and henchwomen of the managers (Woodworth, 1981, 1982) instead of impartial professionals working to facilitate a genuine and mutually beneficial partnership between managers and other stakeholders (Woodworth and Meek, 1995).

Thus, a "new" OD discourse must be both process and content focused, with a clear conceptualization of what effective, humane and just organizations must look like. In other words, instead of focusing on the "soft" issues of morale and feelings, OD must be focused on the hard issues of how organizations should actually be structured and how wealth and profits should be distributed (Woodworth and Meek, 1995).

OD practitioners would also benefit from a dialogue with critical management studies scholars (Voronov, 2005). This conversation is likely to add a sociological dimension that OD discourse sorely needs, and would help critical scholars to more effectively impact organizational practice. For OD consultants, accepting some insights from critical theory would require them "to envision and advance the development of discourses and practices that can facilitate the development of 'management' from a divisive technology of control into a collective means of emancipation" (Willmott, 1997, p. 175).

Conclusion: OD must reclaim its radical roots

The previous two points connect to OD the "old" OD discourse having been cleansed of the leftist radical tendencies that characterized the foundations of the field (Cooke, 1999). Placing the OD discourse within the socio-historical context of Cold War and McCarthyism, Cooke (1999) has shown how OD's history has gradually been cleansed of its leftist and fairly radical roots. Grieves (2003) shows the parallels between the concerns of OD throughout the twentieth century and the socio-political climate, with OD functioning essentially as a tool of social control and a cure against anomie. We argue that our call for a new OD discourse is not so much an attempt to radicalize and politicize OD or to introduce elements that were not there. Our attempt, rather, is to bring OD back to its radical roots and to make it more aligned with the normative views first articulated by Lewin but not taken seriously by OD writers that have followed him. Schein (1989) deliberates whether OD is science, technology or philosophy. He concludes by suggesting that the commercialization and proliferation of technologies in the field threatens its philosophical and scientific pursuits. We argue that a new discourse is what is needed to reconnect OD to its humanistic philosophy anchored by scientific pursuits.

References

Alvesson, M. and Willmott, H. (1992). On the idea of emancipation in management and organization studies. *Academy of Management Review*, 17, 432–64.

Argyris, C. (1957). *Personality and organization: The conflict between system and individual.* New York: Harper & Brothers.

Argyris, C. (1970). *Intervention theory and method: A behavioral science view.* Reading, MA: Addison-Wesley.

Baritz, L. (1960). *The servants of power: A history of the use of social science in American industry.* New York: Wiley.

Barker, J.R. (1993). Tightening the iron cage: Concertive control in self-managing teams. *Administrative Science Quarterly*, 38, 408–37.

Barker, J.R. (1999). *The discipline of teamwork: Participation and concertive control.* Thousand Oaks, CA: SAGE.

Beckhard, R. (1969). *Organization development: Strategies and models.* Upper Saddle, NJ: Pearson Education.

Beckhard, R. (2006). What is organization development? In J.V. Gallos (ed.), *Organization development: A Jossey-Bass Reader* (pp. 3–12). San Francisco, CA: Jossey-Bass.

Bennis, W.G. (1964). Patterns and vicissitudes in T-group development. L.P. Bradford, J.R. Gibb, and K.D. Benne (eds.), *T-group theory and laboratory method: Innovation in re-education* (pp. 248–278). New York: Wiley.

Bennis, W.G. (1969). *Organization development: Its nature, origins, and prospects.* Reading, MA: Addison-Wesley.

Boje, D.M. and Rosile, G.A. (2001). Where's the power in the empowerment? Answers from Follett and Clegg. *Journal of Applied Behavioral Science*, 37, 90–117.

Burke, W.W. (1994). *Organization development: A process of learning and changing* (2nd ed.). Reading, MA: Addison-Wesley.

Burke, W.W. (2002). *Organization change: Theory and practice.* Thousand Oaks, CA: Sage.

Burke, W.W. and Noumair, D.A. (2002). The role of personality assessment in organizational development. In J. Waclawski and A.H. Church (eds), *Organization development: A data-driven approach to organizational change* (pp. 55–77). San Francisco, CA: Jossey-Bass.

Cady, S.H. and Lewis, M.J. (2002). Organization development and the bottom line: Linking soft measures and hard measures. In J. Waclawski and A.H. Church (eds), *Organization development: A data-driven approach to organizational change* (pp. 127–46). San Francisco, CA: Jossey-Bass.

Chia, R. (2000). Discourse analysis as organizational analysis. *Organization*, 7, 513–18.

Church, A.H., Waclawski, J. and Berr, S. (2002). Voices from the field: Future directions for organizational development. In J. Waclawski and A.H. Church (eds), *Organization development: A data-driven approach to organizational change* (pp. 321–36). San Francisco, CA: Jossey-Bass.

Church, A.H., Waclawski, J. and Burke, W.W. (2001). Multisource feedback for organization development and change. In D. Bracken, C.W. Timmreck, and A.H. Church (eds.), *The handbook of multisource feedback: the comprehensive resource for designing and implementing MSF processes* (pp.301–317). San Francisco, CA: Jossey-Bass.

Church, A.H., Waclawski, J. and Seigel, W. (1999). Will the real OD practitioner please stand up? A call for change in the field. *Organization Development Journal*, 17 (2), 49–59.

Church, A.C., Walker, A.G. and Brockner, J.A. (2002). Multisource feedback for organization development and change. In J. Waclawski and A.H. Church (eds), *Organization development: A data-driven approach to organizational change* (pp. 27–54). San Francisco, CA: Jossey-Bass.

Collins, D. (2000). *Management fads and buzzwords: Critical-practical perspectives*. Routledge.

Cooke, B. (1999). Writing the left out of management theory: The historiography of the management of change. *Organization*, 6, 81–105.

Cooke, B., Mills, A.J. and Kelley, E.S. (2005). Situating Maslow in Cold War America: A recontextualization of management theory. *Group and Organization Management*, 30, 129–52.

Deetz, S. (1995). *Transforming communication, transforming business: Building responsive and responsible workplaces*. Cresskill, NJ: Hampton Press.

Falletta, S.V. and Combs, W. (2002). Surveys as a tool for organizational development and change. In J. Waclawski and A.H. Church (eds.), *Organization Development: A data-driven approach to organizational change* (pp. 78–102). San Francisco: Jossey-Bass.

Farias, G. and Johnson, H. (2000). Organizational development and change management: Setting the record straight. *Journal of Applied Behavioral Science*, 36, 376–79.

Fleming, P. (2005). Workers playtime? Boundaries and cynicism in a "culture of fun" program. *Journal of Applied Behavioral Science*, 41, 285–303.

French, W.L., and Bell, C.H., Jr. (1999). *Organization development: Behavioral science interventions for organization improvement* (6th ed.). Upper Saddle River, NJ: Prentice-Hall.

Grant, D., Keenoy, T. and Oswick, C. (2001). Organizational discourse: Key contributions and challenges. *International Studies of Management and Organization*, 31(3), 5–24.

Grant, D., Michelson, G., Oswick, C. and Wailes, N. (2005). Guest editorial: Discourse and organizational change. *Journal of Organizational Change Management*, 18, 6–15.

Grieves, J. (2003). *Strategic human resource development*. London: SAGE.

Hardy, C. and Phillips, N. (1999). No joking matter: Discursive struggle in the Canadian refugee system. *Organization Studies*, 20, 1–24.

Hardy, C. and Phillips, N. (2004). Discourse and power. In D. Grant, C. Hardy, C. Oswick, and L. Putnam (eds.), *The sage handbook of organizational discourse* (pp. 299–316). London: SAGE.

Hardy, C., Palmer, I. and Phillips, N. (2000). Discourse as a strategic resource. *Human Relations*, 53, 1227–48.

Herman, E. (1995). *The romance of American psychology: Political culture in the age of experts*. Berkeley, CA: University of California Press.

Holvino, E. (1996). Reading organization development from the margins: Outsider within. *Organization*, 3, 520–33.

Kahn, R.L. (1974). Organizational development: Some problems and proposals. *Journal of Applied Behavioral Science*, 10, 485–502.

Katz, D. and Kahn, R.L. (1966). *The social psychology of organizations*. New York: Wiley.

Katz, D. and Kahn, R.L. (1978). *The social psychology of organizations* (2nd ed.). New York: Wiley.

453

Kotter, J.P. (1995). Leading change: Why transformation efforts fail. *Harvard Business Review*, March – April, 59–67.

Lawler, E.E. (2006). What makes people effective? In J.V. Gallos (ed.), *Organization development: A Jossey-Bass Reader* (pp. 634–55). San Francisco, CA: Jossey-Bass.

Lawrence, P.R. and Lorsch, J.W. (1969). *Developing organizations: Diagnosis in action*. Reading, MA: Addison-Wesley.

Levinson, H. (1972). *Organizational diagnosis*. Cambridge, MA: Harvard University Press.

Marshak, R.J. (2001). Claiming your power and leadership as an OD consultant. *OD Practitioner*, 33(4), 35–40.

Marshak, R. (2005). Is there a new OD? *Seasonings*, 1(1). Retrieved from www.odnetwork.org/publications/seasonings/article_marshak.html.

Marshak, R.J. (2006). *Covert processes at work: Managing five hidden dimensions of organizational change*. San Francisco, CA: Berrett-Koehler Publishers, Inc.

McLean, G.N. and DeVogel, S.H. (2002). Organization development ethics: Reconciling tensions in OD values. In J. Waclawski and A.H. Church (eds.), *Organization development: A data-driven approach to organizational change* (pp. 302–20). San Francisco, CA: Jossey-Bass.

Mumby, D. and Clair, R.P. (1997). Organizational discourse. In T.A. van Dijk (ed.), *Discourse as structure and process* (pp. 181–205). London: SAGE.

Nirenberg, J. (1998). Overcoming Hammurabi's curse: The realpolitik of building new organizations. *OD Practitioner*, 30(1), 6–17.

Nord, W.R. (1974). The failure of current applied behavioral science—A Marxian perspective. *Journal of Applied Behavioral Science*, 10, 557–78.

Nord, W. (1976). Personality and organizations. In W.R. Nord (ed.), *Concepts and controversy in organizational behavior* (2nd ed.) (pp. 134–38). Pacific Palisades, CA: Goodyear Publishing.

Nord, W.R. (1977). Job satisfaction reconsidered. *American Psychologist*, 12, 1026–35.

Nord, W.R. and Jermier, J.M. (1994). Overcoming resistance to resistance: Insights from a study of shadows. *Public Administration Quarterly*, 17, 396–409.

Oswick, C., Keenoy, T. and Grant, D. (1997). Managerial discourses: Words speak louder than actions? *Journal of Applied Management Studies*, 6, 5–12.

Pages, M. (1971). Bethel culture, 1969: Impressions of an immigrant. *Journal of Applied Behavioral Science*, 7, 267–84.

Palmer, I. and Dunford, R. (1996). Reframing and organizational action: The unexplored link. *Journal of Organizational Change Management*, 9, 12–25.

Paul, A.M. (2004). *The cult of personality testing: How personality tests are leading us to miseducate our children, mismanage our companies, and misunderstand ourselves*. New York: Free Press.

Phillips, N. and Hardy, C. (1997). Managing multiple identities: Discourse, legitimacy and resources in the UK refugee system. *Organization*, 4, 159–86.

Phillips, N. and Hardy, C. (2002). *Discourse analysis*. Thousand Oaks, CA: Sage.

Schein, E.H. (1988). *Process consultation: Its role in organization development, Vol. 1* (2nd ed.). Reading, MA: Addison-Wesley.

Schein, E.H. (1989). *Organization development: Science, technology, or philosophy?* Invited address to the Academy of Management, Organization Development Division, New Orleans, LA, August 15.

Schein, E.H. (1993). How can organizations learn faster? The challenge of entering the green room. *Sloan Management Review*, 34(2), 85–92.

Schein, E.H. (1997). The concept of "client" from a process consultation perspective: A guide for change agents. *Journal of Organizational Change Management*, 10, 202–16.

Schein, E.H. (1999). Empowerment, coercive persuasion and organizational learning: Do they connect? *The Learning Organization*, 6, 163–72.

Schein, E.H. (2002, August). *Five Traps for Consulting Psychologists: Or, How I Learned to Take Culture Seriously*. Invited Address to the Consulting Psychology Division, American Psychological Association.

Seo, M. (2003). Overcoming emotional barriers, political obstacles, and control imperatives in the action science approach to individual and organizational learning. *Academy of Management Learning and Education*, 2 (1): 7–21.

454

Stephenson, T.E. (1975). Organization development: A critique. *Journal of Management Studies*, 12, 249–65.

Tannenbaum, R. and Davis, S.A. (1969, Winter). Values, man and organizations. *Industrial Management Review*, 67–86.

Townley, B. (1993). Foucault, power/knowledge, and its relevance for human resource management. *Academy of Management Review*, 18, 518–45.

Tsoukas, H. (2000). False dilemmas in organization theory: Realism or social constructivism? *Organization*, 7, 531–35.

Tsoukas, H. (2005). Afterward: Why language matters in the analysis of organizational change. *Journal of Organizational Change Management*, 18, 96–104.

Voronov, M. (2005). Should critical management studies and organization development collaborate? Invitation to a contemplation. *Organization Management Journal*, 2, 4–26.

Voronov, M., Johnson, B.K., Kaufman, B.E., Woodworth, W.P., Zickar, M.J. and Nord, W.R. (2006). *Understanding Different Assumptions about Power and Equity: An Inter-Disciplinary Conversation*. Symposium presented at the Annual Conference of the Academy of Management, Atlanta, GA, August.

Waclawski, J. and Church, A.H. (2002a). Introduction and overview of organization development as a data-driven approach for organizational change. In J. Waclawski and A.H. Church (eds.), *Organization development: A data-driven approach to organizational change* (pp. 3–26). San Francisco, CA: Jossey-Bass.

Waclawski, J. and Church, A.H. (2002b). (eds.), *Organization development: A data-driven approach to organizational change*. San Francisco, CA: Jossey Bass.

Webster's New World Dictionary (2003). *Webster's New World Dictionary*, ed. Michael Agnes (4th ed.) New York: Pocket Books.

Wetherell, M. and Potter, J. (1992). *Mapping the language of racism: Discourse and the legitimation of exploitation*. New York: Columbia University Press.

Willmott, H. (1997). Critical Management Learning. In J. Burgoyne, and M. Reynolds (eds.), *Management Learning* (pp. 161–76). London: SAGE.

Woodworth, W. (1981). Organizational consultants, conspirators, and colonizers. *Group and Organization Studies*, 6, 57–64.

Woodworth, W. (1982). Organization development: A closer scrutiny. *Human Relations*, 35, 307–19.

Woodworth, W.P. and Meek, C.B. (1995). *Creating labor-management partnerships*. Reading, MA: Addison-Wesley.

Worren, N.A.M., Ruddle, K. and Moore, K. (1999). From organizational development to change management: The emergence of a new profession. *Journal of Applied Behavioral Science*, 35, 273–86.

31

Practices of stakeholder engagement and identity dynamics

Nic Beech and Robert MacIntosh

Commercial companies have long sought to manage their stakeholders and to do so by exercising influence over those who they compete with and those who consume their products. More recently, social movements have been analysed using stakeholder mapping techniques and this has led to an awareness of alternative perspectives on stakeholders. In this chapter we explain the traditional mapping approach and apply it to a music company by way of illustration. We then raise criticisms of the traditional approach, namely that it fails to comprehend the complex dynamics of socially constructed environments, the subtle nature of plural identities and the value-base of some stakeholder groups. These criticisms lead us to argue that a means to ends rational perspective of stakeholders will under-represent those who act for value, identity and expressive motivations. Subsequently, we illustrate some of these points by drawing upon a case from the French film industry where we trace the process as a group of managers went through it. We conclude that although stakeholder mapping can be used in attempts to 'manage' stakeholders, a viable alternative is that it should be used to engage with stakeholders.

The practice of stakeholder analysis

The practice of stakeholder analysis has long been established as a significant part of strategic change (Freeman, 1984). The fundamental questions being addressed are: 'What space do we have to act in?' and 'How can we increase that space?' The space for acting is defined by the relative position of the group seeking to change (which could be an organization, a team, an individual or even a social movement) and others around them who could be relatively supportive or obstructive towards the change intention. Stakeholder analysis has often been used by top teams as they try to work out how they develop their organization in the midst of a network of others who may want to see different outcomes (Schneider, 2002). For example, competitors might prefer to see contraction rather than expansion and customers might prefer to see lower margins rather than higher ones. Hence, it is useful to be able to plot where the focal organization stands vis-à-vis others in the environment (Finlay-Robinson, 2009).

Whilst it might be useful to have a general understanding of the stakeholders who relate to the company, it is normally important when thinking about organizational change to define what the activity or process is that is being changed and this will inform the analysis of which stakeholders are to be highlighted as not all will be equally interested in all the company's activities (Savage et al., 1991). Peltokorpi et al. (2007) note that stakeholder analysis can be used for different purposes during a change project. These include assessing expected benefits, understanding implementation challenges, analyzing the capability of an organization to change, and gaining insight into stakeholders' influence over implementation. Equally, stakeholder analysis is used in assessing markets and market position when taking strategic decisions about the direction of a firm (Strong et al., 2001).

Having defined the change issue or problem that is being considered, the first step of analysis is to produce a list of stakeholders. This is normally done through dialogue within an internal team. The stakeholders can be defined as relatively broad groups, such as 'competitors', or they can be smaller collectives (e.g. a specific competitor) or a particular individual (e.g. the CEO of a competitor). The rule of thumb is that the stakeholders should be defined in the smallest aggregate required to understand who could act in relation to the change issue being addressed. Thus, it might be appropriate to consider competitors as one stakeholder group if they are all likely to react in a similar manner, but to consider a number of separate competitors if some might react strongly to a change in the focal organization whilst others may have little interest.

Once the stakeholders have been identified the next task is to map where they sit with regard to the focal organization. This is done by considering their position on two axes. The first axis is the degree of interest the stakeholder is judged to have in the change issue. This can range from stakeholders who are directly affected by the change to those who only have a passing interest, or for whom the change is a relatively unimportant part of their context. The second axis relates to the level of influence that the stakeholder could have over the progress of the change. Some stakeholders might have a great deal of influence and be able to either accelerate or prevent the change, whilst others may have little power to alter the way that things will develop.

When these two axes are taken together, it is possible to map some stakeholders as having strong potential influence and high interest. These stakeholders (the 'players') are likely to notice changes that the focal organization introduces takes and to be active in taking steps of their own in reaction, and perhaps in a proactive way. Other stakeholders (the 'observers') might have a keen interest in the way the change progresses, but have relatively little influence over the speed and direction of change. The observers will pay attention to the change process and may be active in communicating their views to other groups. In the diagonally opposite quadrant are stakeholders who have power to influence the speed and direction of change but have relatively little interest in the issue (the 'latent leaders'). For those managing the change, the issue with the latent leaders is the extent to which they become interested in the change topic. One route to their interest increasing is when stakeholders in the observers' quadrant lobby the latent leaders in order to increase their engagement with the change. The last quadrant is low on both influence and interest (the 'currently unengaged'). These are not people with no interest whatsoever, but their primary focus is on other topics. Stakeholders in this group can be significant either when players seek to engage them, or when they become part of the tactics of another stakeholder group.

A mapping of stakeholders on these two axes is illustrated in Figure 31.1 This company organizes a famous international world music festival which runs annually. When they are deciding on the shape of the festival (the programming, the mix of events, which artists to book etc.) the artistic director has the greatest influence. He is appointed by the CEO, but on this particular topic has greater expertise and decision making power. He has a team (the arts team) who review artists, visit other festivals and liaise with agents and managers. This team has a lot of input into the decision making and they are highly interested as the success or failure of the festival is the basis for their continued employment. National and international broadcasters (TV, radio and web-based) contract to record and broadcast concerts. This brings in both concert fees and high profile marketing, so ensuring that the broadcasters get access to concerts that work for their profile and schedules is important. The festival has many well-known sponsors, but although they provide revenue for the festival they have very little influence on the programming. However, if they were unhappy with the festival one year they could choose to withdraw funding the next year. Hence the players are those most influential and interested in the programming of the festival.

The festival always features some high profile international artists ('famous names'). These artists have profiles that will attract a lot of media attention and draw audiences not only to their own concerts but to the festival as a whole. Hence, they have a fair degree of power should they choose to use it. They can decide when they are available, make requirements of the venue and sometimes even decide on guest artists to join them for the concert. However, most artists in this category have very full diaries and so although this is a premier festival their interest or focus on this particular company is limited until they take the decision to play. Hence, they can be regarded as 'latent leaders' – stakeholders who will influence the outcome, but only once they become focused on this issue.

Up and coming artists gain profile by playing at the festival. For many of them it will be the biggest venue and highest profile exposure that they will have received. Therefore, they are very interested in playing and their agents will engage with the arts team in the hope of gaining a place. However, they have relatively little influence because there are more artists who want to play than slots available. The audience is split into different groups. Some are fans and highly focused on the festival, for example becoming 'friends of the festival'. These people attend many concerts, are part of a feedback network that gives input on the quality of the festival and its programming and they also represent a source of reliable revenue for the festival company. Hence, both up and coming artists and friends of the festival audience members are highly interested 'observers'. They have some influence, but relatively little in comparison to the 'players'.

Stakeholders who are 'currently unengaged' include people who will become audience members but who are not regulars or fans. For example, this group includes people who

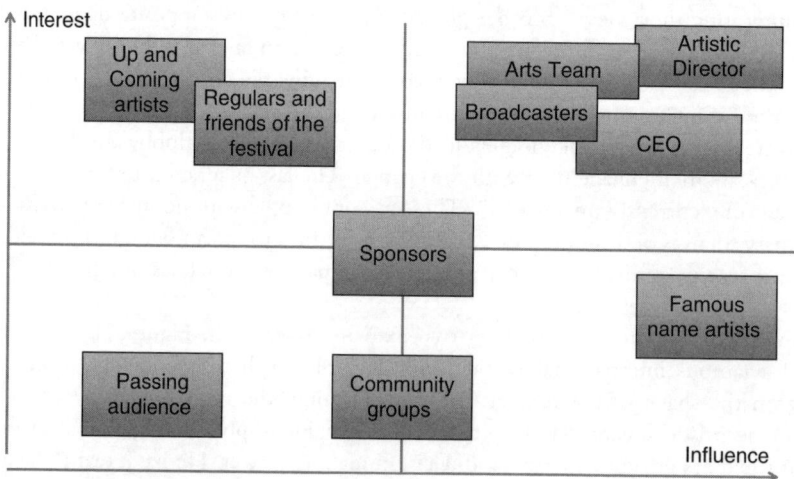

Figure 31.1 World Music Festival

decide to go to a concert on a particular evening and then look to see what is available in the city. This is in contrast to the 'friends' who will have booked months in advance. The more casual or 'passing' audience do have some interest and influence to the extent that they decide to buy tickets or not, but they are not influential on programming decisions.

Developing the approach

Stakeholder mapping has been subject to various criticisms and by considering some of them it is possible to develop the approach. First, we should be aware of the dynamics of a changeful situation and a map can present a rather static way of thinking. As a change progresses it is normal for stakeholders to react and realign. For example, in the World Music Festival when a famous name artist agrees to play it often becomes known within industry circles very quickly. This can influence other famous (and less famous) names in their approach to the festival. In some cases encouraging them to want to play and in others influencing them to distance themselves in order that they are not seen to be 'playing second fiddle'. In a recent year, a significant coup was achieved when one of the world's leading groups decided to play the festival and to join up with another star to make a completely unique concert. This had a major positive impact on the profile and revenue of the festival. It attracted a large audience many of whom were new to the festival and these people who were previously in the 'currently unengaged' quadrant, became motivated to act. Clearly, not all of this new audience will return, but this is a useful way of gaining profile in the minds of (potential) audience members and the audience statistics show that a proportion of people who attend high profile concerts subsequently attend concerts (both high and low profile) in subsequent years.

This dynamic also impacts on up and coming artists who want to be associated with this type of success. A number of new artists gained significant profile at the festival and part of the festival has now been developed to showcase new talent. This has led to many receiving recording contracts and developing their careers. Amongst this group of artists an increasing trend has been for them to return to the festival in later years, at which point they are bringing their profile to supplement the festival. Hence, there are a number of dynamic positive reinforcing cycles that can be created between stakeholders. Equally, it is possible for negative dynamics to emerge, for example where audiences do not return because of dissatisfaction with a concert or where famous names start to prefer other festivals to play at. Therefore, as Neville and Menguc (2006) assert, the interactions between stakeholders should play a significant role in the use of stakeholder techniques.

In order to take such dynamics into account, the map should not be regarded as a static picture which is 'finished' once it is produced. Rather, maps tend to become covered with arrows tracing the likely and actual movements of stakeholders. This will be illustrated in the case study of Film de France below.

A second criticism is that, in its basic form, stakeholder management makes fairly naïve assumptions about identity. Identity categories can easily be taken for granted, but may often be unsustainable (Ybema et al., 2009). For example, 'audience' and 'musician' are macro aggregations that can easily incorporate more difference than similarity. In Figure 31.1 both of these identity categories are disaggregated into two sub-groups which then appear in different places on the map, but in reality the disaggregation may need to be undertaken at a much finer grade of distinction. However, there is a further problem that people are not fully defined by a single identity (Watson, 2009). For example, musicians frequently play for more than one band and so will have interests in different concerts that are potentially in competition with each other for ticket sales. The multiple aspects of their identities are further complicated by being audiences

459

(and fans) of other musicians and by operating in networks of other professionals, not infrequently with emotional and relationship ties. Therefore, it is difficult to categorize a band as, say, observer, when members of that band may also play in the support group of a star and they might be related to an agent who represents several bands including theirs. Hence, insider knowledge of the networks and relationships is important in order to have a sophisticated perception of where people are, or rather, the several positions that they might occupy on the map depending on which aspect of their identity is to the fore.

Rowley and Moldoveanu (2003) have argued that focusing on interests in stakeholder mapping is problematic because interests do not easily translate into action. They argue that an understanding that incorporates a more considered view of identity is preferable because identities can be related to situations where shared values are reinforced not merely by being a member of a group, but by taking action. For example, social movements and ecological groups such as Greenpeace have a value-base to membership but also place great emphasis on action. Hence, to identify oneself as a Greenpeace member incorporates both value and action, and the collective identity is a product of both individual commitment and feelings of solidarity. An analysis that is only about achieving interests, or a means to ends rationality would fail to understand that their actions are also value driven and expressive in that they both derive from and enhance solidarity. Such groups also have significant organizational advantages. There are significant costs to stakeholders mobilizing into action. (for example, the cost of forming relationships and finding consensus, as well as resource constraints). Another example is music file-sharing between fans. This is currently having a major impact on the financial performance of recording companies who see the activity as theft or piracy. However, the fans who share files do not all see themselves in this way. Some are driven by a value of freely sharing musical resources, and some are also opposed to what they regard as the excessive control of the market that the big recording companies have exercised for many years. Therefore, to understand how stakeholders might act, it is important to be aware of the subtleties of how the stakeholders defined themselves (in multiple ways) and of the values (Hillman and Keim, 2001) that are reinforced by their acting.

The last criticism that we will briefly consider is that traditional approaches to stakeholder management take an excessively agential view of those driving the change and that the idea of 'managing' stakeholders might be somewhat overstated (Rasche and Esser, 2006). The simple idea is that if change 'agents' can achieve a position of high interest and high influence then they will be able to 'make change happen'. In fact, many change situations entail complex interconnections of influence and power such that even stakeholders who appear to have little power can ally with others who are powerful, or can move over time such that the smooth operation of power by those in the 'players' quadrant is disrupted. In the case of social movements and ecological groups this can take the course of influencing journalists such that the cause is highlighted in a way that voters might notice. Voters are often seen as a passive category as it is such a large aggregation. However, when companies in the players quadrant start to fear that politicians might become stronger in their views on ecology because voters are becoming more interested, then through a series of linkages, influence is brought to bear on the powerful by the interested. Fans who file share music provide another example. Not so many years ago this group had very little power and paid relatively high prices for CDs. Now, with changes in technology, their actions are bringing about change in the whole of the music industry. In view of this, the moderated approach is not to seek to 'manage' stakeholders, but to engage with them. Engaging places greater emphasis on understanding their perspectives and seeking actions that find win–win outcomes where there is something in it both for those who are currently players and for others who currently appear to have less influence. Hence, the actions that are taken after doing a stakeholder map may not be to 'manage' other players out of the top right quadrant of the diagram. Rather, there can be an approach that might deliberately increase the influence of some groups and seek areas of agreed value that could lead to mutual benefit. However, this is not to say that all stakeholder analysis should be about empathy. Clearly, there are many situations that include competition and conflict, but seeking to eliminate opposition or maximize profit at the cost of others may eventually be confronted by stakeholder mobilization against the company, as has happened in both the ecological field and the music industry.

In the next section we will discuss another case from the creative industries. This case is based in France and relates to the movie industry. It follows the stakeholder engagement process adopted by a group of senior managers as they faced a significant change. The company asked to be anonymized and so we have given them the pseudonym 'Film de France'. The diagrams are ones that they produced which we have then simplified for presentation here and our analysis of the case comes from our experience of working with the managers as they went through this process.

Case study: Film de France

Film de France is a company that provides marketing and strategy consulting services to companies in the cinema/movie sector. It has a specialism in the use of IT and many clients are high tech companies that operate in the production and distribution chains. Film de France's mission is to helps companies achieve growth and they have a history of supporting development of small companies from local operation to national and international levels. Having operated in this market for 30 years, Film de France has expanded internationally and now has offices in the US and various European countries where films are produced. In some countries films can be produced complete from beginning to the end of the process, but in many cases, various stages of production occur in different specialist facilities in different countries. Therefore, operating in this network of production is rather complicated, particularly for the smaller independent companies and Film de France operates by providing knowledge and contacts in the industry, assisting with market positioning, and providing specific local analyses for clients. In addition, Film de France assist international companies who wish to operate in France and the growth of the international offices has been significant in providing this service.

The film industry in France is an important part of the national cultural heritage. The cinematograph was invented in 1895 in France and there are 2,143 cinemas (140 of which are multiplex) which means that France has one of the densest coverages of cinemas in Europe. 33 per cent of the population go to the cinema at least once a month and in recent years audience attendance has been increasing (from 178.14 million in 2007 to 189.71 million in 2008). There is also an increasing audience interest in French films and in 2008 French productions outstripped US film audience numbers with 86 million tickets sold. This was the highest total since 1984. Figures for 2010 show that international appreciation of French films is strong with one new French film released each day on movie screens around the world and 40 French films aired each day on televisions worldwide. There is governmental support for the industry with the Centre National de la Cinématographie supporting 50 film festivals, a domestic network of 120 feature film producers, 140 short film producers, 220 directors, 30 sales agents in addition to actors and talent agents. Film de France operates in an international network of 800 distributors, TV buyers of French films, international film festival programmers, and over 1,200 foreign journalists. Therefore, the setting is one of growth and cultural significance in which many firms, individuals and governmental bodies have an interest. It is also a setting of considerable

461

dynamism, where the popularity of a single film can have a dramatic influence on revenues and subsequent investment.

Film de France was established by a charismatic entrepreneur and he is currently still the Chief Executive and a major shareholder. However, as he nears retirement the debate over succession has been intensifying within the company. Senior members of the management team see the company as old-fashioned and in need of modernization. It is regarded as highly mechanistic and all the main decisions have to go through the Chief Executive. The Chief Executive is very well known in the supply chain and has personal relationships with most industry leaders and politicians in the media and cultural departments. It is estimated by senior managers that 40 per cent of the clients are directly connected to the Chief Executive and to replace him would therefore be highly problematic.

The senior managers met without the Chief executive present in order to discuss the change that they believed was needed and how best to approach this. They developed a list of stakeholders which (in simplified form) included the Chief Executive, shareholders, senior managers, employees, competitors and customers. We will not go into all the complexities of their conversation here, but a summary of their initial analysis is presented in Figure 31.2.

Several things are notable about this analysis. The Chief Executive is placed highest in both influence and interest and the managers and employees have almost no influence attributed to them. One group of shareholders (A) is thought to be highly interested in the change of leadership, but moderate in their degree of influence. A second group (B) is thought to have significant influence (partly due to the number of shares they hold) should they choose to use it, but as the Chief Executive has particularly close relationships with these shareholders (some of whom are family members) their interest in acting was seen as fairly moderate. Competitors are seen as very influential and fairly interested. One possibility was a take-over bid but most of the competitors were of a similar size or smaller and so the significant fear was that the retirement of the Chief Executive would provide competitors with an opportunity to attract customers and clients away from Film de France.

The senior managers planned various actions in order to engage and influence the stakeholders they had identified. First, their aim was to gain more influence for themselves and to reduce the

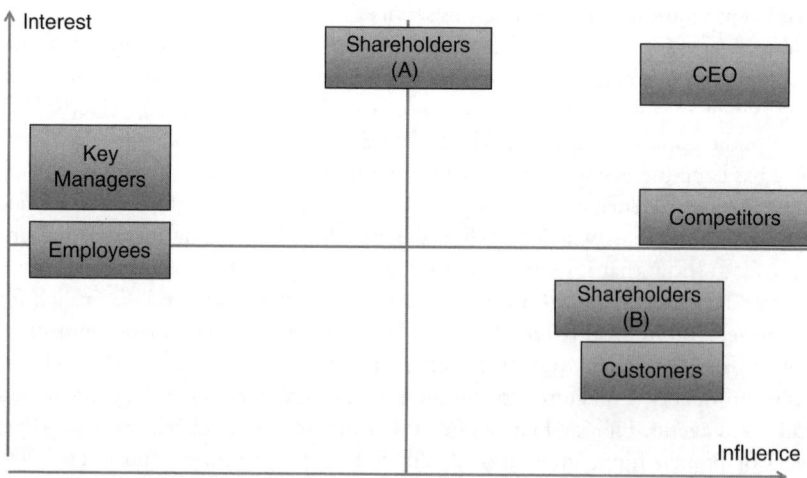

Figure 31.2 Initial analysis

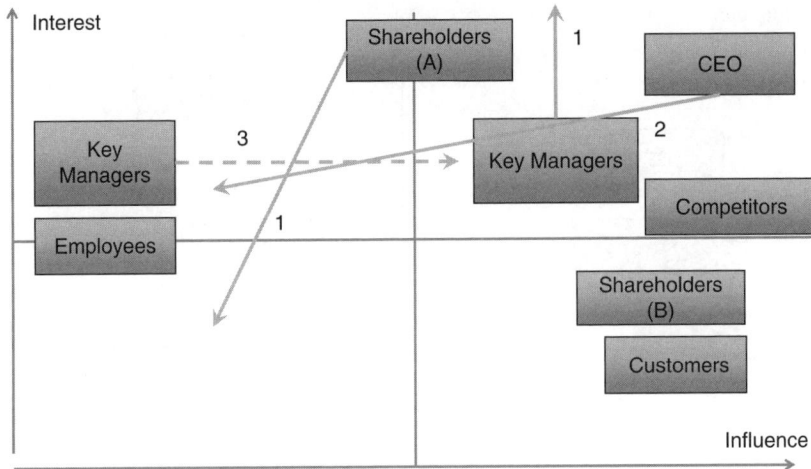

Figure 31.3 Actions by senior managers to encourage stakeholder movement

influence of shareholders on the Chief Executive. They also needed to reduce the autocratic decision making of the Chief Executive. In order to achieve these outcomes (Labelled 1 and 2 in Figure 31.2) they recognized that they needed to change the perceptions of themselves (Labelled 3 in Figure 31.2). They planned to do this by highlighting the results they achieved, by persuading the Chief executive that giving them some voice in decisions would not lead to poor decision making and by convincing him that he needed them to have greater interactions as primary contacts with certain clients. They recognized that this would take time but as the Chief Executive was unlikely to retire for at least two years, they believed that this was feasible. As they gained greater access to smaller and then more significant clients they aimed to increase the confidence of the Chief Executive and key shareholders in them.

If successful, their purpose was to be in a position to influence the strategic future of the company, including the choice of new Chief Executive. Figure 31.4 depicts their desired 'end state' stakeholder map. It is worth noting that they do not place themselves as having absolute influence. Although they are close to the top right corner there is a gap and this is because of the potential influence of others. It may also be somewhat wishful thinking to suppose that they could occupy this position with ease, particularly given the relationship-based nature of the industry. However, their intention was to establish greater relationships with clients, to generate evidence of their ability to perform and hence to be able to persuade the Chief Executive and shareholders that they were competent to lead the company into its next phase of development.

Achieving such a change was likely to be highly problematic as the culture of the company was one of a strong single leader and deference to him, highly centralized decision making and formality of relations. Strategy making was mainly a one-man activity and so their task was to show that by involving others the task could not only be made easier but could also be achieved with high quality and more creativity. There is a certain irony in that in effect Film de France needed to apply the sort of techniques it provided to its clients to itself. However, such ironies are not uncommon in the business world. Twelve months on from their initial analysis, senior managers had had some success. The Chief Executive had stated openly that he intended to retire and had started to introduce senior managers to key clients as the *leaders* of projects. He still found

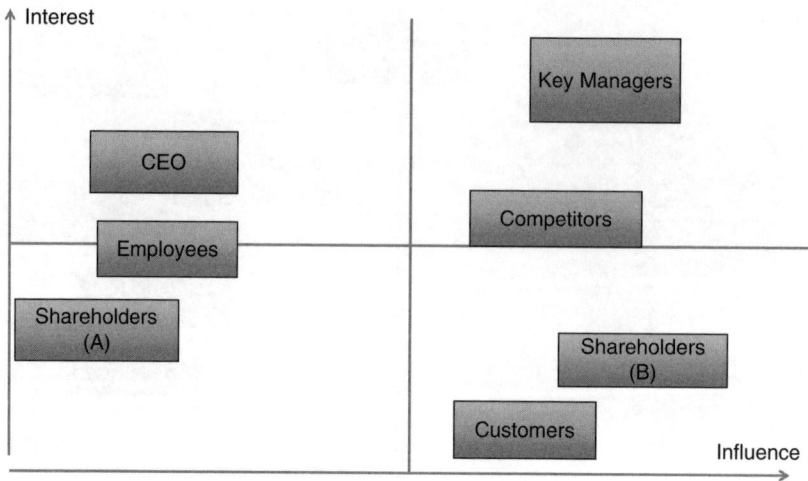

Figure 31.4 Target Stakeholder map for succession

it difficult not to be present at key meetings with these clients, but did seem to be accepting that there will come a time when he will no longer be there to oversee his staff. Informal contacts with some of the shareholders revealed that they were aware that the Chief Executive would need to be replaced and are keen that this should be achieved in a way that preserves the business. So in practice, the senior managers may want to keep or increase the influence of some of these shareholders who are more interested in modernizing the business than the Chief Executive. The employees did not feature strongly in the analysis of the senior managers and this is also something that has changed in practice. They have conducted an internal communication exercise which has identified a degree of concern amongst the staff about succession and the future of the company. The plan was to take a more engaged approach to strategic renewal and seek to give the employees more voice. This will clearly be in contravention of the very hierarchical culture that has existed until now.

However, new identity dynamics have emerged. The senior managers had been fairly united, but clearly some of them shared competing ambitions to be the next Chief Executive. A potential which had not been seriously considered by the group initially was that the Chief Executive would recruit his successor from outside the company. As the situation moved on, they became aware that the Chief Executive was considering this option. Clearly, in such a strongly networked context, buying in a new person with a big reputation would not be an unreasonable strategic move. However, as a result former allies in the senior management team have become distant and the internal competition appears to be increasing. In addition, two members of the team who feel that they are unlikely to be appointed to the top job are making moves towards setting up their own company and this looks like being a likely outcome. Hence, what started off as a shared identity group is now in the process of splitting and reforming.

Conclusion

We are not suggesting that this is a perfect illustration of how to undertake stakeholder analysis. Rather we wish to suggest that it indicates how stakeholder analysis can be useful as part of a change process, but that it should not necessarily be assumed that stakeholders can be managed. The managers found it useful to identify and map out the stakeholders and they formulated a set of actions around this analysis. As the chance has proceeded there has been evidence of considerable dynamics. Some of these were expected by the managers, but others were unexpected. Hence, stakeholder analysis may not be a tool that accurately predicts behaviour (Strong et al., 2001), but it can be useful as a heuristic device for raising awareness of how stakeholders might react and then draw attention to what they do. In addition, there is evidence of identity dynamics (Ybema et al., 2009), some of which, such as splits within the senior management team, were not expected by the team at the start of the process. Equally, the agreement of some of the shareholders with encouraging the Chief Executive to plan for succession and retire indicated the significance of their plural identities as shareholders and family members.

Our proposition is that traditional stakeholder management will often be flawed in practice because of its over-simple approach to dynamics and identities. However, the basic techniques can still be useful as a way of making sense of complex environments either internal or external. Therefore, the utility of the ideas is enhanced if we respond to the criticisms raised above by using it as a basis for analysis and engagement, rather than seeking control.

References

Finlay-Robinson, D. (2009) What's in it for me? The fundamental importance of stakeholder evaluation. *Journal of Management Development*, 28(4): 380–88.

Freeman, R.E. (1984) *Strategic Management: a stakeholder approach*, Boston, MA: Pitman.

Hillman, A.J. and Keim, G.D. (2001) Stakeholder value, stakeholder management and social issues: What's the bottom line? *Strategic Management Journal*, 22: 125–39.

Neville, B.A. and Menguc, B. (2006) Stakeholder multiplicity: Toward an understanding of the interactions between stakeholders. *Journal of Business Ethics*, 66: 377–91.

Peltokorpi, A., Alho, A., Kujala, J., Aitamurto, J. and Parvinen, P. (2007) Stakeholder approach for evaluating organizational change projects. *International Journal of Health Care Quality Assurance*, 21(5): 418–34.

Rasche, A. and Esser, D.E. (2006) From stakeholder management to stakeholder accountability. *Journal of Business Ethics*, 65: 251–67.

Rowley, T.J. and Moldoveanu, M. (2003) 'When will stakeholder groups act? An interest and identity based model of stakeholder mobilization', 28(2): 204–19.

Savage, G., Nix, T., Whitehead, C. and Blair, J. (1991) Strategies for assessing and managing stakeholders. *Academy of Management Executive*, 5: 61–75.

Schneider, M. (2002) A stakeholder model of organizational leadership. *Organization Science*, 31(2): 209–20.

Strong, K.C., Ringer, R.C. and Taylor, S.A. (2001) The rules of stakeholder satisfaction. *Journal of Business Ethics*, 32: 219–30.

Watson, T. (2009) Narrative, life story and manager identity. *Human Relations*, 63(3), 425–52.

Ybema, S., Keenoy, T., Oswick, C., Beverungen, A., Ellis, N. and Sabelis, I. (2009) Articulating identities. *Human Relations*, 63(3): 299–322.

32

Reflections on polyphonic organization

Mary Ann Hazen

An idea begins to live, i.e. to take shape, to develop, to find and renew its verbal expression, and to give birth to new ideas only when it enters into genuine dialogical relationships with other, foreign, ideas. … The sphere of its existence is not the individual consciousness, but the dialogical intercourse between consciousnesses.

(Bakhtin, 1973, pp. 71–72)

In this chapter, I reflect on the metaphor of polyphonic organization (organizing) and its development. I use the related concepts of dialogue, voice, and authority to amplify an understanding of polyphony.

I have thought and written about and tried to practice dialogue for a long while. I completed my dissertation on dialogue in an interorganizational planning project for psychiatric emergency services in 1984 and my thinking was shaped by the discourse and practice of dialogue as a Gestalt therapist before that. Whatever I have written and published since then, dialogue is at the heart of it; I expect this practice to continue.

When my interest in dialogue led me to the work of Bakhtin (1973, 1981, 1986), I was awed by his brilliance as well as the complexity, breadth and depth of his work. It was a small step to wonder, "What would it be like if I applied Bakhtin's ideas about Dostoevsky's novels to ideas about organization?" One answer to that question was "Towards Polyphonic Organization" (Hazen, 1993). Since then, a number of scholars have cited the article (103, according to Google Scholar, July 10, 2010). Of these, some, dialogically, have further developed the concept of polyphonic organization through critique, application, or extension.

The purposes of this chapter are to briefly summarize the ideas of polyphonic organization as initially portrayed (Hazen, 1993), review some of the major contributions to the concept since then, and apply the metaphors of polyphony, dialogue, and voice to two examples of organization.

Polyphonic organization

Polyphonic organization does not mean *only* "many-voiced," as some have understood it; nor does it result in cacophony and noise. Polyphony is born in dialogue, and is many dialogues occurring together. Polyphonic organization is something alive, dialogic, organic, not envisioned as a hierarchical pyramid but rather heard as a circle of sound. The idea of polyphonic organization is based here on Bakhtin's analysis of Dostoevsky's novels as polyphonic. I briefly summarize below my earlier portrayal of this idea.

Definitions

The word *polyphonic* is defined as "many-voiced" and "producing many sounds" and is intimately joined in Bakhtin's work to *dialogue*. He claimed that Dostoevsky had a true dialogic relationship with the hero in his novels, that is, one in which the "hero's independence, inner freedom, unfinalizedness and indeterminacy" is confirmed. The "hero is not 'he' and not 'I' but a full-valued 'thou' that is another full fledged 'I' " (Bakhtin, 1973, p. 51). For Bakhtin, the *utterance*, spoken or written, is the basic component of dialogue. One who creates an utterance is an *author*. Both the utterance and the author express and shape values. As authors in dialogue interact with one another intersubjectively through utterances, they express their differences in values and perspectives.

Polyphony, dialogue, and organization

As he examined polyphony and dialogue in Dostoyevsky's novels, Bakhtin explored the relationship with the hero, the position of the idea, and characteristics of plot, genre, and the word. All of these illuminate aspects of polyphonic organization. As noted earlier, Dostoyevsky's *relationship with the hero* is fully dialogical; he does not treat the characters in his novels as objects but as *thou*. The author's consciousness "reflects and re-creates them in their genuine unfinalizability (which is after all their very essence), rather than creating a world of objects" (Bakhtin, 1973, p. 56). In the novels, while "the image of the *idea* is inseparable from the image of the person, the carrier of the idea (Bakhtin, 1973, p. 71)," it is also dialogical, interindividual, and intersubjective; unless it becomes so, it disintegrates and dies. The *plots* in Dostoyevsky's novels have an organic, dialogic form rather than being based on an outline, appearing to those with a monological vision to be chaotic, missing what Bakhtin called their "profound organicism, consistency and unity" (1973, p. 5). In examining *genre*, he claimed that Dostoevsky's novels were grounded primarily in the ancient carnival tradition. Carnival turns everything upside down and inside out, freeing people from seriousness and fear. It is an "artistic vision ... which makes possible the discovery of new and as yet unseen things" (Bakhtin, 1973, p. 139). Bakhtin understood the *word* to be alive, concrete, and interpersonal, not merely a linguistic phenomenon. Language is alive in dialogue. Dialogue, for both Bakhtin and Dostoevsky, was not a means but an end, "not the threshold to action but the action itself. ... To be means to communicate dialogically. When the dialogue is finished, all is finished (Bakhtin, 1973, p. 213)".

If we imagine organization to be like Bakhtin described Dostoevsky's novels—multivoiced, intertextual, open-ended, upside down, seemingly chaotic—we understand differently than if we see organization as monological, bureaucratic, monolithic, and orderly. We hear organization as sound. The voice, for each person, is the source of author-ity. Language, ideas, and organization are alive and live among people rather than in or outside of one person. Differences are life-giving. Dialogue is not just a process of organization—it is organization itself. There is order in what appears to be chaos; this order is rooted in dialogue.

Scholars have critiqued, extended, or applied ideas of polyphonic organization. Some of these contributions are noted here.

Power and management in polyphonic organization

One group of authors (Carter et al., 2003; Clegg et al., 2003; Clegg et al., 2006) maintained that the idea of polyphonic organization is an antithesis to the notion of the total organization. Such a language-based theory is "incipiently democratic rather than totalizing" (Clegg et al., 2006, p. 13). Echoing Bakhtin and Foucault, they claimed that language constitutes organization, rather than mirroring or representing it (Clegg et al., 2006, p. 13). Polyphonic organization *is* utterances—stories and narratives that guide those who tell and listen to them.

These authors considered the role of power in polyphonic organization, emphasizing that "polyphony does not deny power, but it does not assume domination either—it proposes that questions can be raised from the auspices of different rationalities" (Clegg et al., 2006, p. 15). Who speaks, who is silent, who is silenced, what questions or issues are brought to dialogue, whose languages are used are all questions to be considered.

They asserted that "polyphony does not necessarily lead to change," since being different from dominating discourses is neither necessary nor sufficient to resist power or bring about change (Carter et al. 2003, p. 295). They used the idea of strangers—those who cross borders and speak in different languages or discourses, have different ways of perceiving reality, and carry dissimilar maps of the territory—to understand one source of differences among voices in polyphonic organization (Simmel, 1950, in Carter et al., 2003; Hamel, 1996: 77 in Carter, et al., 2003; Bauman, 2001 p. 200, in Clegg, et al., 2006). Strangers allow for trouble, conflict, confusion, and uncertainty—they are springs of life-giving change in how people organize.

Further, resisting power, "means first being able to speak to power from outside of power. … finding a space for discourse that is not already colonised—or marginalised—by the strategies that power uses" (Carter, et al., 2003, p. 295). In the Liverpool dock strike that began in the fall of 1995 and lasted for more than two years, dockworkers found such a space in the Internet, colonized by neither the owners and managers nor the trade union, and thereby garnered global support from unexpected sources (Carter et al., 2003).

Concerning management in polyphonic organization, management discourse seeks to translate; and managers creatively facilitate translation between and among various languages, rather than ruling from an authoritarian position in a monolithic, monological structure. One method of translation, considered to be a political action, is deconstruction, "a way of questioning truth effects and analyzing the language games that shape reality, opening up space for different concepts and perceptions" (Clegg et al., 2006, p. 19).

Utterances and stories

Boje defined story as "an oral or written performance involving two or more people interpreting past or anticipated experience" (Boje, 1995). Bakhtin defined an utterance as the basis of dialogue, the "unit of speech communication" (Bakhtin, 1986, p. 75). Clark and Holquist elaborated on this idea by pointing out that an utterance is "an activity that enacts differences in values," and is "expressed from a point of view, which for Bakhtin is a process rather than a location" (Clark and Holquist, 1984, p. 10). Stories and narratives are utterances. If one way of understanding polyphonic organization is as stories that guide those who tell and listen to them, then analyzing stories is one way of learning more about polyphonic organization. Boje used deconstruction to analyze the stories of Disney and described the analysis in this way:

> Instead of affirming functionality, I increasingly looked for the exploitation, privilege, domination, power, discipline, and control practices of this storytelling organization. … The only

difficult step was to shift my own perception. … Much about deconstruction has to do with noticing voice. Who gets a voice in the CEO stories, whose voice is marginal, who gets no voice at all? It also means looking at those stories that are being concealed and marginalized within particular stories.

(Boje, 1995, p. 1008)

There are two important values in this methodology that enhance the understanding of poly-phonic organization. First, it is important to notice voices, not only those that are speaking and heard but also those that are silent, silenced, or silencing; and stories that are discounted, marginalized, or hidden. We can understand silence not only literally but also metaphorically. DeVault (1999) outlined feminists' uses of silence, pointing out that silence can mean not speaking, not writing, not being present, not being heard, and not being noticed; it also can signify speaking or writing ephemerally or without authenticity, confidence, or authority. Further, silencing can refer to "quieting … censorship, suppression, marginalization, trivializa-tion, exclusion, ghettoization, and other forms of discounting" (DeVault, 1999, p. 177). However, feminists "do not usually consider the silences of the powerful, often used to maintain control" (DeVault, 1999, p. 177).

Second, it is vital to pay attention to hearing, interpreting, and understanding stories, not only speaking or uttering them. A story—an utterance—in itself can have many layers of meaning; further, each person who hears and listens to the story can hear and interpret its meanings differently from others. So not only are there many voices, there are many stories, many meanings, many listeners, and many interpretations. Imagining organization in this way gives us some idea of the richness and complexity inherent in organization and the difficulty of comprehending all that happens in this process. If we remember this reality, we will not be tempted to simplify organization to such an extent that we distort what is happening by using overly simplistic and static models and diagrams.

Homeboy industries

I recently attended a lecture given by Gregory Boyle, S.J., about Homeboy Industries in Los Angeles, which he founded as a result of his pastoral work (Iowa City Public Library, July, 2010). His parish was located at the hub of gang activity in a city of gangs. He was accompanied in Iowa by a writing teacher on the Homeboy Industries' staff and Homeboys Robert and Jesse. Homeboys and Homegirls are at-risk youth or those who have been involved in a gang; many have been in prison. They are working to turn their lives around with the support of Homeboy Industries—turning from the despair of gang membership and criminal activity (what Boyle called "the lethal absence of hope") towards the hope of having regular jobs and belonging to a compassionate community. All four spoke or read their own words as part of the event. I was at times inspired, involved, entertained, and humbled by their stories. At the end of the evening, a friend (who knew I was writing this chapter) turned to me and said, "Is *this* polyphonic organization?" "I think so."

Homeboy Industries is an organization that *is* its stories—what Boyle calls, in his book of the same name, "Tattoos on the Heart" (Boyle, 2010). There are stories in Boyle's book and speeches. The organization's website has links to newspaper articles, television programs, and radio interviews—all stories. The organization is grounded in inclusion, dialogue, and the intimately connected belief that all human beings, even hardened gang members and criminals, can change their lives. Homeboy Industries grew out of Boyle's parish work in the late 1980s and is now the largest gang exit program in the world. Its motto is "Nothing stops a bullet like a job" (VanMullem, 2010). Its mission is "Jobs not Jails: Homeboy Industries assists at-risk and formerly gang-involved youth to become positive and contributing members of society through job placement, training and education" (www.homeboy-industries.org/ retrieved August 10, 2010).

Boyle's book is made up of stories loosely held together by themes and portrays his beliefs and values. The stories are personal, not so much about Boyle as about the unique lives and choices that various neighborhood people have made. The conversations are truly dialogues, evidence of mutuality and reciprocity. They are told in English with Spanish and slang words effectively tossed in. Below is a conversation that is part of a longer story that begins, " ... Scrappy walks into our office and, I'm not proud to admit it, my heart sinks" (Boyle, 2010, p. 33).

> "Look, let's just be honest with each other and talk man to man. You know that I've never disrespected you."
> I figure, why not, I'm gonna go for it.
> "Well, how 'bout the time you walked out on my homily at Cuko's funeral, or the time you pulled a *cuete* out on me?"
> Scrappy looks genuinely perplexed by what I've just said and cocks and scrunches his face like a confused beagle.
> "Yeah, well ... besides that," he says.
> Then we do something we never have in our two decades of knowing each other. We laugh. But really, truly laugh—head-resting-on-my-desk laughter. We carry on until this runs its course, and then Scrappy settles into the core of his being, beyond the bravado of his *chingón* status in his gang.
> "I have spent the last twenty years building a reputation for myself ... and now ... I regret ... that I even have one."
> And then in another first, he cries.
>
> (Boyle, 2010, pp. 33–34)

In many ways, this dialogue—this short conversation between two men who have been at odds with one another for twenty years—is representative of the organization as a whole. Recall the statement by Bakhtin that Dostoevsky's consciousness "reflects and re-creates them [the characters in his novels] in their genuine unfinalizability (which is after all their very essence), rather than creating a world of objects" (Bakhtin, 1973, p. 56). Clearly, Boyle, the founder of HI and the teller of the story above, perceives (in spite of himself) that Scrappy is unfinalizable—he is someone who is truly a "thou," who is not finished, and who can change. And the feeling is mutual, with Scrappy giving Boyle yet another opportunity to know him. For Bakhtin and Dostoevsky, language is "not the threshold to action but the action itself. ... To be means to communicate dialogically" (Bakhtin, 1973, p. 213). Transformative action takes place between both men in the dialogue above: as the conversation shifts, it changes the two people creating it.

The conversation develops in a somewhat chaotic way, surprising even the men from whom it flows, with a sense of irony, humor, and humility. There is mutuality, as the priest and the gang member meet as equals. Both are authors and speak with authority from their individual perspectives—each reflecting what have been radically different values and beliefs and somehow reaching across that chasm to meet one another as human beings. While there are only two voices in this story, there are many stories in the organization, told in different voices in various media to the public and, no doubt, within the circle of organization.

Homeboy Industries has a sense of carnival—topsy-turvy, upside down, surprise—about it. Even its name, taking the street word for gang member—homie or homeboy—and turning it around to mean something that offers an alternative to gang life, evokes carnival. The heroes of the Homeboy stories are poor, undereducated, mostly former gang members, many of whom have served time in prison, people who are often feared or scorned by others. People who were enemies to one another in their gang life become co-workers and even friends at Homeboy, baking, silk screening, or painting over gang graffiti together.

The organization itself creates an alternate space for dialogue and allows for polyphony. In the housing projects that were sliced up into gang territories or *barrios*, there were few alternatives to joining a gang. As Boyle recounted, " … gang members from all the forty-plus gangs in the Hollenbeck Police Division (some ten thousand members) began to arrive [at the Homeboy Industries office], looking for a way out of the gang life. Perhaps gang members had always longed for this, but for the absence of a place to go, the desire had festered" (Boyle, 2010, 7). Without a place to go, a place to speak out, they were trapped; Homeboy Industries offered a choice, allowed for identities to alter, and created a space for discourse and dialogue not unlike the space for discourse created on the Internet by the Liverpool dockworkers.

Recall the importance of strangers as a source of differences among voices in polyphonic organization: they cross boundaries, talk in distinctive languages, apprehend reality differently, and carry dissimilar maps of the territory (Simmel, 1950, in Carter et al., 2003; Hamel, 1996, in Carter et al., 2003. p. 77; Bauman, 2001 in Clegg et al., 2006 p. 200). They enter a space, invited or not. Strangers can be trouble-makers, cause struggles, and give rise to confusion and uncertainty—they can stir things up and change how people perceive, communicate, and organize.

Boyle described how his church, situated in the Pico-Aliso area of Los Angeles—"the gang capital of LA"—started an alternative middle school in 1988 and so opened their church to strangers: "With the school came a new parish attitude. Suddenly, the welcome mat was tentatively placed out front. A new sense of 'church' had emerged, open and inclusive, replacing the hermetically sealed model that had kept the 'good folks' in and the 'bad folks' out" (Boyle, 2010, p. 3). Gang members began to hang out at the church. A parish meeting was called when some parishioners complained. Two women leaders proclaimed at the meeting, "'We help gang members at this parish because it is what Jesus would do' " (Boyle, 2010, 4). They welcomed strangers.

Boyle told the story of how women church members went as strangers into gang territory when they "organized major marches, or *caminatas*, moving through the projects, often in the heat of tension and in the wake of ceaseless shooting. …[They] would move to hotspots, and their gentle praying and singing presence would calm the gang members ready for battle" (Boyle, 2010, p. 4). Boyle, too, would ride a bike through the projects to speak with gang members. Since they lived to tell the tales, it seems that gang members, too, allowed Boyle and parishioners into their space. (However, such work is not without risk and not to be undertaken lightly.) Strangers began to engage in dialogue and Homeboy Industries grew from these dialogues.

When I heard Boyle speak, he began his talk by stressing the importance of kinship, of standing at the margins with people who are strangers until the margins expand and become a circle in which all are included. He ends his book with a similar image—an image of polyphonic organization: "And so the voices at the margins get heard and the circle of compassion widens. Souls feeling their worth, refusing to forget that we belong to each other. No bullet can pierce this" (Boyle, 2010, p. 212).

But can we end here? Are there voices that are silent or silenced? Stories that are discounted or hidden? While Boyle made no mention of financial difficulties (that I can recall) during his speech, it is clear from Homeboy Industries' website (www.homeboy-industries.org/, retrieved August 1, 2010) and a recent interview with Terry Gross on Fresh Air (www.npr.org/templates/

story/story.php?storyId=127010471) that the organization is in serious financial difficulty—so much so that many staff members have been laid off.

And I found only a whisper about the natural environment, perhaps because that is all that can be heard. It is in the story of a visitation by an owl in a playground in the projects, where "the patch of lawn never deepened in color past yellow" (Boyle, 2010, pp. 159–60). Boyle writes, "Sure enough, there is the largest owl imaginable resting on this telephone wire. ... We stand ... eyeing this anomalous creature that has chosen to visit the poorest, most owl-less sector in LA (pigeons and mice are generally our only wildlife)" (Boyle, 2010, p. 160). He likens the appearance of this owl in the playground and the youths' responses to it to entering a cathedral and keeping vigil in a temple. "Silence prevails ... until this astonishing owl opens its wings and takes off. ... And he is gone in a majestic flapping and a slow-motion gliding, disappearing from view behind the gigantic tower of the corn factory fronting the projects" (Boyle, 2010, p. 161). However, the natural environment is surely background to the foreground of Homeboy Industries' stories of personal and community loss and redemption.

Voice, Rachel Carson, and *Silent Spring*

Most mornings, near dawn, I walk down our driveway and pick up the newspaper. The birds are awakening, too, and I often stop to listen to their chirps, squawks, and twitters before I focus on my work of the day. They lift my heart. One morning, I thought, "What would it be like without the sounds of birds?" Immediately following, I thought of *Silent Spring* by Rachel Carson (2002). I knew that Carson's book was influential in the early 1960s, pointing out how the rash use of insecticides such as DDT in the United States after World War II was endangering life on the planet. Although I did not then recall anything else about this book or Carson's story, I knew that she had raised her own voice in print so the voices of nature could be heard.

Carson was born in 1907. She studied marine biology at Woods Hole Biological Laboratory and Johns Hopkins University, earning a master's degree in zoology in 1932. Family obligations, the lack of a mentor, and not enough money to continue her education during the depression caused her to go to work rather than continuing to study for the Ph.D. Working as a marine biologist in the Bureau of Fisheries (later the U.S. Fish and Wildlife Service), Carson was recognized as a talented writer and edited other scientists' field reports; by 1949 she edited all of the bureau's publications and participated in interagency science and technology conferences. Such responsibilities helped Carson to widen her scientific knowledge and understand how government policies were developed (Lear, 1997, 2002, pp. xii–xiii).

While working for the government, Carson also had her own writing agenda. She was both a scientist and a writer. Her gift was to translate specialized scientific information into lyrical writing accessible to non-scientists. Her three books published before *Silent Spring* (Carson, 1941, 1951, 1955) had been at the top of the bestseller list. She was the "foremost science writer in America. ... a trusted voice in a world riddled by uncertainty" (Lear, 2002, p. xiv).

In writing *Silent Spring*, Carson knit together the voices of many different people to present evidence of what the reckless, large-scale applications of pesticides across the country were doing to harm not only the insects at which they were aimed but also birds, fish, and human beings. "In the process of her research she established a remarkable network of scholars in many fields all over the world and created an alliance of scientists, naturalists, journalists, and activists committed to helping her document a spectrum of environmental abuses" (Lear, 1997, p. 313). An important element of this network was from her own "connections with government scientists, librarians, Smithsonian Institution scientists, associates in conservation organizations at the national level, and the regional Audubon Society" (Lear, 1997, p. 334). It is this polyphonic organization or network that she drew on as she wrote *Silent Spring*.

For example, in Michigan, Illinois, and Wisconsin in the 1950s, scientists at research institutes and universities reported the wholesale deaths of robins after elm trees were sprayed with DDT in an effort to control Dutch elm disease. If the birds did not die from the poison, they were unable to reproduce; if they reproduced, their eggs did not hatch. The cycle that led to their deaths was this: the elm trees were sprayed heavily with DDT, which killed not only the targeted elm bark beetle that carried the fungal disease, but also other insects. The film of DDT did not wash off of the trees. In the fall, the leaves, still coated, fell to the ground, where earthworms ate the leaves. When robins returned in the spring, they ate the earthworms, which poisoned them (Carson, 2002, pp. 105–8).

In this instance, as in other chapters, Carson gathered evidence from local field reports, published scientific papers, and letters from bird watchers and other observers. She listened to a variety of voices and reported their ideas in detail. Utterances that might have had little influence individually and locally, when joined with the voices of others who described similar patterns, had a great impact. The text of *Silent Spring*, while written in Carson's graceful voice, is made up of information from many voices.

Further, Carson engaged in a lifelong dialogue with nature and was aware of the importance of perceiving the whole ecology of an area, long before this was an acceptable aspect of science. Her profound dialogical relationship to the natural world was revealed in a letter to a close friend upon completion of *Silent Spring*:

> I think I let you see last summer what my deeper feelings are about this when I said I could never again listen happily to a thrush song if I had not done all I could. And last night the thoughts of all the birds and other creatures and all the loveliness that is in nature came to me with such a surge of deep happiness, that now I had done what I could—I had been able to complete it—now it had its own life.
>
> (Lear, 1997, p. 395)

Here, her voice is strong and emotional and reflects her deep love for the earth and its creatures.

Carson was an outsider, a stranger to the scientific establishment of the 1950s and 1960s. She was a "female scientist without a Ph.D. or an institutional affiliation, known only for her lyrical books on the sea" (Lear in Carson, 2002, p. xvii). Not only was she was a woman, her specialty, biology, had low status in the age of the atom and she had no academic appointment. "In postwar America, science was god and science was male" (Lear in Carson, 2002, p. xi).

The publication of *Silent Spring* was met with attempts to silence, discredit, and discount Carson's voice by the powerful "multimillion-dollar industrial chemical industry" (Lear in Carson, 2002, p. xvii) that profited from pesticide applications. She was labeled by them as a "'bird and bunny lover,'" a "woman who kept cats," a "romantic 'spinster' who was simply overwrought about genetics," and "a woman out of control" who had "overstepped the bounds of her gender and her science." This "industry spent a quarter of a million dollars [in 1962] to discredit her research and malign her character. ...[but] the worst they could say was that she had told only one side of the story and had based her argument on unverifiable case studies" (Lear in Carson, 2002, p. xvii).

Carson spoke for those who had no voice (mammals, birds, reptiles, even spiders), some of whom were nearly silenced forever. She wrote in a strong, active, confident voice—one that represented the many voices of biologists, field scientists, naturalists, ecologists, and bird lovers. She had powerful supporters. In the end, attempts by the chemical industry, politicians, and some government scientists to suppress, marginalize, and trivialize her work were unsuccessful.

In many ways, the writing, publication, and public response to the book evoked a Carnival-like upside-down, turned around, atmosphere. Carnival "makes possible the discovery of new and as yet unseen things" (Bakhtin, 1973, p. 139). The scientific outsider was lauded for her careful consideration of the consequences of pesticide poisoning. The "hysterical woman" presented herself to environmental groups, television audiences, and the President and Congress of the United States as calm, rational, and confident. A lone woman biologist, speaking out on behalf of the environment and all who were a part of it, confronted a powerful industry that was a partner to the dominant scientific establishment of chemists and physicists as well as government bureaucrats with a narrow vision, those who wished to eradicate "pests" and damn the consequences.

Just as the Internet provided for the Liverpool dockers a neutral safe space for discourse that was neither colonized nor marginalized by the industry and the union, and the Delores Mission and Homeboy Industries provided a similar space for discourse that was controlled neither by the police nor the gangs, so, too *Silent Spring* opened a space for public discourse about the consequences of indiscriminate applications of insecticides. Until then, the environment was largely left off of the political agenda. One government report stated that "'until the publication of Silent Spring, people were generally unaware of the toxicity of pesticides.'" (Lear, 1997, p. 451).

In the early pages of *Silent Spring*, Carson writes, "If the Bill of Rights contains no guarantee that a citizen shall be secure against lethal poisons distributed either by private individuals or by public officials, it is surely only because our forefathers, despite their considerable wisdom and foresight, could conceive of no such problem" (Carson, 2002, p. 13). When President Kennedy read the book, government investigations were begun to test the validity of Carson's claims; grassroots groups organized against the spraying of poison chemicals in their neighborhoods; and, not long after publication, Senate hearings were held as a "broad-ranging congressional review of environmental hazards, including pesticides." Carson testified before the committee (Lear, 1997, pp. 450–51). Carson's work was influential in the establishment of the Environmental Protection Agency in 1970. The first Earth Day was held on April 22, 1970, the roots of which began in 1962 (http://earthday.envirolink.org/history.html retrieved 08/09/10). A broad environmental movement grew in the United States and influenced the passage of the Endangered Species Act in 1973 (Wilson in Carson, 2002, pp. 361–62).

The hidden story—the story that was, at the time, unknown to almost everyone except for a few close friends and doctors—was that Rachel Carson was suffering from metastasized breast cancer. She completed the writing of the book, saw its successful publication and distribution, and received awards and honors, while undergoing surgery and radiation treatments. When the chemical industry was trying to silence and discount her work, she was fighting a personal battle for her health. On April 14, 1964, only two years after the publication of *Silent Spring*, a weakened Rachel Carson suffered a heart attack and died at home, just before sunset.

Reflections on polyphonic organization

In this chapter, I have summarized the ideas of polyphonic organization that were earlier developed from applying Bakhtin's ideas about Dostoevsky's novels to ideas about organization (Hazen, 1993). Included among the concepts related to polyphony as developed by Bakhtin are dialogue, utterance, and author. Bakhtin looked at the author's dialogical relationship to the hero, the intersubjective position of the idea, the organic (seemingly chaotic) flow of the plot based on dialogue, the genre of carnival, and the aliveness of the word and language in dialogue.

I have reviewed some of the major contributions to the concept since then. Two concepts, the stranger and non-colonized space, extended the metaphor of polyphonic organization. Strangers come from outside, speak different words, see reality differently, and thus help to create polyphony. They can be sources of discomfort and change. In order for power to be resisted, a space must be found that has not been marginalized or colonized by those in power so that discourse can occur (Carter et al., 2003; Clegg et al., 2003; Clegg et al., 2006). The idea of stories as utterances that are organization expand the understanding of polyphonic organization. One way of analyzing organization stories is to deconstruct them, ask what is missing, hidden, or silenced (Boje, 1995).

In the images of Homeboy Industries and *Silent Spring* as polyphonic organization portrayed here, I have used these "stranger" ideas to enrich the metaphor of polyphonic organization, enhance the descriptions, and improve our understanding of both. It is my hope that others will join the dialogue.

References

Bakhtin, M.M. *Problems of Dostoevsky's Poetics*, translated by Rotsel, R.W. Ann Arbor, MI: Ardis, 1973.

Bakhtin, M.M. *The Dialogic Imagination: Four essays by M. M. Bakhtin*, translated by Emerson, C. and Holquist, M., Holquist, M. (ed.) Austin, TX: University of Texas Press, 1981.

Bakhtin, M.M. *Speech Genres and Other Late Essays*, translated by McGee, V.W., Emerson, C. and Holquist, M. (eds.), Austin, TX: University of Texas Press, 1986.

Bauman, Z. *The Bauman Reader*, Oxford: Blackwell, 1993.

Boje, D., Stories of the storytelling organization: A postmodern analysis of Disney as "Tamara-land," *Academy of Management Journal*, 38 (4), 997–1035, 1995.

Boyle, G. *Tattoos on the Heart: The power of boundless compassion*, New York: Free Press, 2010.

Buchanan, D. and Dawson, P. "Discourse and audience: Organizational change as a multi-story process," *Journal of Management Studies* 44 (5), 669–86, July 2007.

Carson, R.L. *Under the Sea Wind*, New York, Oxford University Press, 1941.

Carson, R.L. *The Sea Around Us*, New York, Oxford University Press, 1951.

Carson, R. *The Edge of the Sea*, Boston, Houghton Mifflin Company, 1955; Mariner Books Houghton Mifflin Company, 1998.

Carson, R. *Silent Spring: Fortieth Anniversary Edition*, Boston: Mariner Houghton Mifflin, 2002.

Carter, C., Clegg, S., Hogan, J. and Kornberger, M. "The polyphonic spree: the case of the Liverpool Dockers," *Industrial Relations Journal*, 34, 290–304, 2003.

Clark, K. and Holquist, M. *Mikhail Bakhtin*, Cambridge, MA: Belknap of Harvard University Press, 1984.

Clegg, S.R., Kornberger, M. and Carter, C. "The differend, strangers and democracy: Theorizing polyphonic organization," *Academy of Management Best Paper Critical Management Studies*, 2003.

Clegg, S.R., Kornberger, M. Carter, C. and Rhodes, C. "For management?" *Management Learning*, 37 (1), 7–27, 2006.

DeVault, M. *Liberating Method: Feminism and Social Research*, Philadelphia, PA: Temple University Press, 1999.

Hamel, G. "Strategy as revolution," *Harvard Business Review*, July–August, 69–82, 1996.

Hazen, M.A. "Toward polyphonic organization," *Journal of Organizational Change Management*, 6(5), 1993.

Homeboy Industries (www.homeboy-industries.org/index.php retrieved July 28, 2010).

Lear, L. "Introduction" in R. Carson, *Silent Spring: Fortieth Anniversary Edition*, Boston: Mariner Houghton Mifflin, 2002.

Lear, L. *Rachel Carson: Witness for Nature*, Boston: Mariner Books Houghton Mifflin Harcourt, 1997.

VanMullem, L. "Gang exit program Homeboy Industries hits hard times," *Global Shift*, July 16, 2010, www.globalshift.org/2010/07/16/homeboy-industries-hard-times/, retrieved July 28, 2010.

Wilson, E.O. "Afterword" in R. Carson, *Silent Spring: Fortieth Anniversary Edition*, Boston: Mariner Houghton Mifflin, 2002.

33

Helping diversity matter
Fostering liminal spaces for authentic interaction

Jo A. Tyler

Anyone who is working in an organization knows this: there is increasing pressure in organizations for consistency in process execution and in the quality of the end results. This pressure can be an essentializing force. It can drive towards the predictability and sameness that drives against a natural and easy embrace of variety within the organization. To counterbalance this force, the efforts an organization makes to move from a focus on diversity toward a focus on inclusion can benefit from, and may even require, intentional, facilitated spaces that foster polyphony and democracy of voice. These spaces can fruitfully support abiding efforts to explore the potency of all ideas, not irrespective of their sources (as in "every voice should be treated the same") because they are not the same, but on the very basis of the variety of sources (as in "every voice is treated differently") because they are different. This is a shift from an effort to equalize ideas through a sort of blindness to source, to a sense of differential equity in which ideas are considered in the context of the experiences that generated them. The experiential DNA of the person who holds the idea is part and parcel of the ideas she offers.

Spaces in which this contextual consideration can happen, where ideas can bump up against each other, rub off on one another, merge into a rich stew of elements that coalesce into an altogether new flavor, are integrative spaces (Van de Ven et al., 2008) in which diversity is not a barrier to be overcome, but more simply an attribute that can inform organizational change in unique and positive ways. Van de Ven et al explain that "integrative behavior produces a safe organizational environment where employees feel comfortable sharing information due to supportive organizational practices that encourage constructive criticism and a supportive leadership that provides opportunities for experimentation, resolves conflicts and responds to employee concerns" (p. 340).

This sense of psycho-social resilience and leveraging of difference is fostered by the risk-safety balance that open, liminal spaces provide. It is a relaxing of politics and social pressure in favor of new possibilities wrought by telling and listening to diverse perspectives that depends on the "degree to which employees perceive that their organization encourages different perspectives, synthesizes those perspectives in ongoing day-to-day activities, and involves them in the change processes" (Van de Ven et al., 2008, p. 340).

This chapter begins with an operational definition of diversity that will underpin the discussion of liminal and integrative spaces. This is followed by a "tour" of some of the classical and contemporary ideas about psycho-social spaces that help to characterize their liminal potential for face-to-face interaction. From this platform, the attention will turn to a sampling of processes that practitioners and participants can undertake to sculpt and energize these spaces for expansive work that can creatively and ethically advance the nature and intent of change in the organization. The chapter closes with a reflection on practice for those hoping to foster such spaces in organizations.

Diversity writ large

In organizational discourse, reactions to the term "diversity" can be rather bi-modally stratified. In one cluster are advocates who see diversity as a goal to strive for, as a positive and compelling pursuit that would ideally permeate and therefore enhance all aspects and processes of organizational life. It is associated with notions of inclusion, and seen as fundamental to the creation of novelty. In the second cluster are those who see diversity as a set of policies, regulations, and guidelines which require compliance and drive a bureaucracy of record-keeping, influencing organizational processes by imposing restrictions or driving "politically correct" behavior and decision-making that may, even with the best of intentions, contraindicate the interests of organization and, perhaps, the people who comprise it.

Between these two clusters lies, at least, one more option: to eschew the notion that diversity is either an opportunity to be leveraged, or an obstacle to be overcome. This middle ground offers that diversity *writ large* is, in ways both simple and complex, a ubiquitous, dimension of the organization. In this framing, diversity is not an issue to manage, but a neutral, omnipresent phenomenon, a shape shifter seeming to both support or stymie an organization's attempts to change. When this phenomenon intersects with change, tensions naturally emerge.

Rather than take the bimodal view that these tensions should be parsed dialectically into the creative and the destructive, our middle ground takes the view that they *cannot* be parsed, and that they *simultaneously* possess the potential to inhibit change, resulting in a sloppy and uncomfortable stasis, and to inject change with vitality, resulting in a (perhaps equally messy) trajectory, a shift away from the status quo. The direction that the tensions take in the flow of organizational events and processes can lie in the possibilities that unfold in psycho-social spaces accommodating and indeed fostering reflective and reflexive conversational learning (Baker et al., 2005). This conversational learning, rife with its own potent dialectics, has the potential to increase the capacity of organizational members to explore the nature of the change and their varied experiences of them reflectively and even as they unfold. Sometimes such spaces occur naturally, in the cafeteria for example or in parking lots, but in organizational settings we cannot rely solely on this alchemical production. Hence our exploration here of the nature of spaces and the ways in which we might foster liminal psycho-social spaces for learning in organizations that welcome, and indeed rely, on diversity, not in ways that resolve our differences, but continue our exploration of them (Brookfield and Preskill, 1999).

The nature of psycho-social spaces

It is perhaps since we have sat together around the fire, at the mouths of caves at the end of the day, that we humans have been on a quest for spaces that will allow us to reflect on our experiences in collaboration with others. We strive to learn from each other in ways that support our ability to make sense of those experiences, and indeed to move beyond sensemaking, to making meaning that informs future actions. This quest is often quite specifically for spaces in which we do not feel threatened in the collaborative and challenging pursuit of ideas, the exploration of our experience, beliefs, assumptions, and values, and their implications for action. Our quest is for spaces in which these processes can conspire on a tightrope *between* risk and safety, each end of this tension reflexively allowing for and fostering the other as we dance together, however awkwardly, between them.

And it is perhaps only since we have come to notice that our communities are burgeoning with others who are not quite like ourselves, that we have tried to actively create these spaces. Or perhaps it is only since we have invited the stranger passing through to join in the warmth of a literal and then later imaginal fire—or been that invited stranger ourselves—that we have felt and then understood the need for such spaces.

We know these spaces when we are in them. We feel some sense that we are welcome there in spite of and even because of all our messy background and baggage, wonderings, wanderings, and wounds. We cannot necessarily point to what it is precisely, but there is in these spaces a sense of possibility, and of care. The bones of the construction of this space, if there are any at all, can feel elusive, seeming to rely on organic emergence, and defying premeditated actions.

These are liminal spaces characterized by a sense of ambiguity and availability that holds potential, spaces where normal constraints are relaxed sufficiently to open the way for something new—perspectives, ideas, challenges, or something else that is altogether extra-ordinary. They are not spaces safe because they are void of challenges. As Baldwin (1998) queries, "*how do we know safety exists until it is challenged, threatened, worked through and reestablished with a deeper sense of knowing*" (p. 149, emphasis in original)? In organizations we may, if we are very lucky, stumble into these spaces from time to time. When we do, we feel invited into a polyphony of voices, a concert of experience that is expansive in nature. It is outside of our everyday experience, and yet it welcomes all our experience in. Our time in these psycho-social spaces makes us wiser in the way it wires (or rewires) our connections—to our own experience and to each other.

Early perspectives: formlessness

We will begin our selective tour of psycho-social spaces (as opposed to physical space *per se*) not around campfires precisely but still in ancient days, with Plato's (428/7–348/7 BC) concept of the chora (1944, Thomas Taylor translation). Formless and therefore changeless, the chora is able "to receive all things, and never itself takes a permanent impress from any of the things which enter it, making it appear different at different times" (Plato, 1944, 50–51). Chora is a neutral vessel, and it is that very neutrality that allows for the energies that come into the space to retain their rawness, without shifting to accommodate the shape or form of the vessel:

> It is likewise necessary to understand that the figured nature [of the chora] can never become distinguished with an all-possible variety of forms, unless its receptacle is well prepared for the purpose, and is destitute of all those forms which it is about to receive. … We should call it a certain invisible species, and a formless universal recipient, which in the most dubious and scarcely explicable manner participates of an intelligible nature.
>
> (Plato, 1944, 169)

It is, he suggests "invisible and formless, all-embracing, possessed in most puzzling way of intelligibility, yet very hard to grasp" (as cited in Bianchi, 2006, p. 127). Derrida (1997 with

Eisenman), in his examination of the chora, points out that "you cannot conceive of that chora intellectually, neither through the senses" (108).

Importantly, chora is also characterized by movement, by growth, a concept Plato grapples with through the use of metaphor. In *The Timaeus* (1944) Plato variously applies metaphors such as that of a mother (p. 169) to characterize the open and receiving nature of chora, and a father for the source of that which it receives, such that "the nature situated between these [is metaphorically as] to an offspring" (p. 169). So too, then, we might consider as offspring gestated by this space its generative result—the birth of ideas, connections, new perspectives and so forth—made possible by the neutral and welcoming reception the chora offers to the formative notions participants bring—like seeds, damp earth, sunlight, and rain—into it.

It should be noted here that, following Plato, Aristotle also introduced a more instrumental articulation of place (rather than space) as topos, a similarly featureless vessel, unchanged by interactions. However Aristotle's concept includes no sense of generativity, change, or growth. It has contemporary metaphorical corollaries in GPS coordinates and *topo*graphical mapping (Lane, 2001) which feature particularity of fixed positioning. De Certeau (1988) suggests a distinction between place and space that is useful here, and which harkens to this distinction between Aristotle's topos and Plato's chora: "A place (*lieu*) is the order (of whatever kind) in accord with which elements are distributed in relationships of coexistence. ... Space occurs as the effect produced by the operations that orient it, situate it, temporalize it." (117, italics in original).

From the ancient Greeks, let us move now to another philosopher working at the turn of the last century. Japanese philosopher Nishida Kitarō (1870–1945) was influenced by Western philosophical ideas, including those of Plato and Aristotle connected to concepts of space and place (Uehara, n.d.; Emiko, 2000). It was perhaps even Plato's notion of chora that led Nishida to his logic of *basho* a "field of consciousness in which we reflect our thinking when we think" (Uehara, n.d., p. 161). Ultimate *basho* is characterized by an attribute Nishida called "enveloping," the *mu no basho*, or 'place of nothingness'" (Dilworth, 1987, p. 16). Uehara (n.d.) explains that Nishida suggested an "enveloping logic" that would rise above the subject-object dualism, and to this end he turns to Greek philosophy where the dichotomy has not yet fully developed. In this sense we can say that *basho* was formed as a new philosophical method that rejects the objectification of reality and indeed envelops that subjective view within the logic (p, 160).

Here we have the echo of Plato's chora, another way of conceptualizing space as neutral to that which enters into it. Its formlessness allows for interactions that help diversity *writ large* flourish in productive ways against a blankness, a *tabla rasa* free from restrictions or predispositions. Though the concepts of chora and *basho* are eminently more complex and layered than we are able to express here, we will take them on as particularly helpful metaphors for considering the types of spaces that will help us to "pull out the wedge between the *is* and the *ought*, rediscovering in ourselves a mode of affirmation that unifies rather than divides" (Kasulis, 1997, xvcii). Chora and *basho* both point to the importance of the neutrality of the space, its formlessness a backdrop for energetic exchange that can vessilize the energy without distorting it, without giving primacy to one perspective or another. The formless nature of the space allows the experiences, emotions, and ideas of participants to tumble in it, to bump and rub against each other, indeed to expand without contorting to fit inside.

Contemporary views: rationality and structure

Contemporary theorists have similarly devoted attention to the notion of psycho-social space in organizational settings. There is a sense, somewhat contrary to the nature of formlessness, that there are things we must "do" to spaces, ways that we must shape them in order to help humans work together, to help us traverse the distance between us created by differences in experience and perspective. This desire for applying structure to psycho-social spaces is not surprising in context of decades of management theory (see for example Taylor, 2009; Porter, 1998; Mintzberg, 1989; Drucker, 1974) that has moved organizations in the direction of order and cognition, and away from messiness, emotion, and spirituality. Rationality and structure appear in approaches to understanding how we might occupy and navigate spaces with an eye toward fostering learning and idea generation, not only by including a diversity of perspectives, but by challenging those perspectives in social, reflective processes, which will be touched on in a later section.

The need for rationality within liminal spaces is of course contestable. Nonetheless, organizations depend on rationality—though they are unlikely to survive on rationality alone. So it is, if you will, reasonable that organizational members may welcome (or even insist on) the familiarity of the rational, especially in the midst of change. Rationality is a kind of familiar, a way of bewitching the enemies of confusion and disorder that lets us measure our progress. It is an attempt to plan and shape changes that gives us an illusion of control over them. There is obvious danger in taking rationality to an extreme, to reduce discourse to algorithmic distillations of problems at the expense of outlying experiences that are not so easily computed. Various attempts to apply rationality and structures to liminal space have nonetheless resulted in some ways of thinking about the practicalities of sculpting spaces that aim to preserve their liminality at the same time that they infuse the space with rationality (though not necessarily with order). We need not abandon the ideal of an un-inhibiting formlessness to reconcile the notion of structures. Plato saw formlessness *within* forms, and for Kitaro, the Eastern arts "represent forms but reveal the formless" (Dilworth, quoted in Uehara, n.d., p. 156).

Here we will sample three salient sets of ideas, each attached to separate schools of contemporary thought, that have influenced our conceptualizing of forms within psycho-social space: knowledge creation and management (Nonaka and Konno, 1998), transformative learning theory (Mezirow, 1991), and action inquiry (Torbert, 1991).

Knowledge creation and management

Building on Nishida's concept of *basho*, Nonaka and Konno (1998) adapt the idea to the creation and management of knowledge in contemporary organizations. They introduced into our vernacular the concept of many levels of *ba*—a sort of boundary condition which they roughly translate to "place." They define *ba* as "a shared space that serves as platform for knowledge creation ... through one's own experiences or reflections on the experiences of others" (1998, p. 40), which in connection with one another form the "greater *ba* (known as *basho*)" (p. 41). Nonaka and Konno (1998) propose four types of *ba* in the context of their SECI (Socialization, Externalization, Combination, Internalization) model of knowledge creation. They are *Originating ba* of "feelings, emotions, experiences and mental models" (p. 46); *Interacting ba*, consciously constructed by bringing together "the right mix" (p. 47) and relying on dialogue to make tacit knowledge explicit; *Cyber ba* where existing information combines with new knowledge for explicit and virtual dissemination rather than occurring in physical space; and *Exercising ba* consisting of processes that convert explicit knowledge to tacit knowledge.

This instrumentalizing of Nishida's concept is useful for the concerns of knowledge creation and management, and, importantly, helped to popularize the notion of psycho-social space as an important management consideration. While these four types of *ba* can be helpful in understanding the types of interactions that can occur in psycho-social spaces, Nonaka and Konno repeatedly refer to the four types of *ba* as coming together to form a "platform for the 'resource concentration' of the organization's knowledge assets" (p. 41). In this way, their conceptualizing of *ba* becomes something that feels much more formed and formalized than Nishida's original concept of *basho* as an enveloping nothingness that allows for the transcendent interaction. We see Nonaka and Konno's contention that participation in *ba* (and ultimately *basho*) implies that one becomes involved in ways that "transcend one's own limited perspective or boundary. ... and yet remain analytically rational, achieving the best of both worlds" (p. 41). So, the appeal in this interpretation of *basho* as an amalgam of the levels of *ba*, lies in its connection to our contemporary interest in rationality in organizational contexts.

Transformative learning theory

Mezirow's (1991) transformative learning theory suggests that the deep and sustainable change resulting in perspective transformation is grounded in social processes "involving points of view expressed by others that we initially find discordant, distasteful, and threatening but later come to recognize as indispensable to dealing with our experience" (p. 185). Mezirow offers us a set of ideal conditions for creating spaces that allow for full participation in critical, rational discourse that fosters transformative change for individuals as well as groups.

There are seven conditions that Mezirow holds as the "essential components in the validating process of rational discourse through which we move toward meaning perspectives that are more developmentally advanced, that is, more inclusive, discriminating, permeable and integrative of experience" (1991, p. 198). The first of these conditions is that participants "have accurate and complete information" (1991, p. 77). This means not only that the "agenda" of the organization must be transparent, but that the participants must be able to disclose fully their own experiences and perspectives. Second, the space must "be free from coercion and distorting self-deception" (p. 77). The implication is that participants engage in the space of their own volition, not on the basis of an organizational mandate. Additionally, they must "be able to weigh evidence and assess arguments objectively" and "be open to alternative perspectives" (p. 77). This ability is essential to an integration of perspectives that leverages the diversity across participants and their experiences. The space must also, according to Mezirow, allow participants to "become critically reflective upon presuppositions and their consequences" and "have equal opportunity to participate (including the chance to challenge, question, refute, and reflect and to hear others do the same)" (p. 78). Finally, Mezirow contends that to achieve rational discourse, participants must "be able to accept an informed, objective, and rational consensus as a legitimate test of validity" (p. 78).

What prevents Mezirow's version of rational discourse from aligning with the idea of a formless space for exploration and experimentation, is his particular sense that this form of discourse is "in contrast to everyday dialogue [because] principles and operations are made linguistically explicit" (p. 77). Importantly for our concerns about spaces so free from form that they that embody nothingness, Mezirow contends that "such discourse is likely to be more independent of context" (p. 77) than ordinary conversation embedded in social structures, power, and organizational relationships.

Action inquiry

Torbert (1991) suggests the possibility of "liberating structures" (p. 98) from a developmental perspective in which inquiry and productivity are integrated in psychosocial spaces in workplace settings. The purpose these structures serve is to provide scaffolding where, despite their

481

differences, people can begin to take on "full executive responsibility for the effects of their own actions and treat one another as true peers" (p. 100).

Torbert articulates eight essential qualities of these structures beginning with "deliberate irony ... wherein members feel the limitations and self-contradictions inherent in their relatively self-restricting view of reality" (p. 102). Second, he suggests that the structures be "epistemologically transparent: the product and the process congruently embody and reflect the purpose. Members cannot successfully complete liberating tasks unless they challenge their usual ways of [working]" (p. 102). In addition, structures should evolve in a way that is "premeditated and precommunicated ... [and] reflects the movement by organizational members as they move toward conscious appropriation of the process and purpose" (p. 102). A fourth dimension of the structures is that they be crafted in such a way that they "provide a constant cycle of experiential and empirical research and feedback on participant's different ways of constructing reality, on their changing relations to one another, and on the quality of their work" (p. 103). Ultimately, in this way, differences are typically revealed as assets during active experimentation and reflection.

Torbert goes on to suggest (fifth) that leaders use their power to "perform a kind of psychosocial jujitsu whereby the members experience both more discretion and more direction than usual. ... question[ing] their own assumptions about the nature of power and begin to experiment with the creative power to constitute a new world" (103). Akin here to Mezirow, Torbert is quick to point out that power is used by leadership openly, and not to coerce or manipulate participants. This leads to the sixth quality, that "the structure at any given time is open, in principle, to inspection and challenge by organization members" (p. 103), and the seventh, that "leadership becomes vulnerable, in practice to attack and public failure as soon as it behaves inauthentically when its tasks, processes and purposes become incongruent and it refuses to acknowledge and correct" these disconnects (p. 103). Finally, the eighth quality, in some ways underpinning all the others, is that "leadership is committed to, practiced in, seeking, recognizing and righting personal and organizational incongruities" (p. 104).

The paradox of structured formlessness

The idea of conditions and structures such as those proposed by Mezirow and Torbert seems counter to the formlessness of chora and *basho*. Indeed, there are ways in which this is entirely the case. In practice, however, spaces like Plato's chora and Nishida's *basho* might best be conceptualized not as space to be constructed *per se*, but as ideals worthy of pursuit. The process can begin with practitioners simply believing that such spaces are possible. The next step is to intentionally sculpt spaces that flex expansively toward a multiplicity of possibilities rather than facilitating in ways that narrow the possibilities too quickly in the interest of locating a singular "best" idea. The scaffolding of conditions and structures acts as a compensatory force for the imperfections of people as well as the flaws inherent in organizational systems. We enter these liminal spaces in context, carrying with us historical baggage of (typically unexamined) assumptions and beliefs about how others differ from us and the changes we are facing. Whether consciously or unwittingly, we can give these unexplored ideas primacy—especially when what is known to us, valued by us, feels threatened in the face of change. So in the face of formlessness, a vacuum of forms, our assumptions will fill the structural void.

By consciously implementing particular scaffolding we can subject our assumptions to the conditions and structures rather than allowing them to run renegade in the space. Key here is that while the structures and conditions impose a kind of form onto the space, it need not (and likely *should* not) be permanent. Indeed, Torbert suggests that one way of developing these structures is to identify all the "limiting conditions" (p. 99) that are clear obstacles to change and development for the group, and then introduce into the space one or more structures that temporarily set these limits aside. Once participants learn ways that they can successfully overcome the limits within the context of the structure, those achievements erode the limiting condition, and the structure itself can be set aside. Participants learn that the structure is unnecessary through the fruits of their own resourceful work together, and can dismantle it, cast it out, and return the space to something closer to the formlessness that will maximize the potential for discovery. Torbert's final three qualities focusing on continuous examination and on vulnerability to change, further provide for the reduction, morphing, or elimination of temporary structures.

Structures and conditions have a reflexive relationship with the space. As the chora or *basho* take them into their formlessness, their presence fosters a way for members to interact that in turn reinforces the conditions, strengthening the scaffolding for ever deepening exchanges until finally the scaffolding itself is released, and the space advances toward the formless ideal.

Time as a liberating structure

Missing from the discussions of conditions and structures is the notion of time, though in practice it is perhaps the most essential of all conditions, the most liberating of all structures. Time is a rational element that provides for extra-rational work. It provides for formlessness. It is in the absence of sufficient time that we are most compelled toward the imposition of too much structure until those structures are no longer libratory. At that point, they run the danger of being institutionalized rather than impermanent. That is, the less time we have, the more tempted we are to give shape to the space, narrowing it, reducing the psycho-social elbow room of the participants to the point where differences are tamped down in the name of quickly solving a problem or accomplishing some other task.

In making a distinction between space and place (similar in some ways to the distinction we saw earlier between chora and topos) de Certeau (1988) contends that "*space is a practiced place*" (p. 117, italics in original). He explains that "a *space* exists when one takes in to consideration vectors of direction, velocities, and time variables" (1988, p. 117). Liminal spaces that take full advantage of diversity in groups are a challenge to the coupling of efficiency and speed that is so often called upon in the face of change. We mistake speed *for* efficiency, but these are not transposable. While the work of diverse groups inhabiting liminal spaces may not seem fast (or tidy) these spaces *are* efficient. Just as bio-diversity is related to sustainability (*Facts on Biodiversity* n.d.), the outgrowth of these spaces, their practical result, is likely to be a thick and hardy weaving together of different perspectives, not a quick situational fix to a problem or a single opportunistic swipe at an opportunity. There is a tradeoff for that sustainability: the polyphony and reflection that are the very roots of (and the route to) its sustainability unfold in ways that require time.

Too often, practitioners facilitating groups feel compelled to work quickly toward an end goal, and narrow the conversation prematurely, silencing dissension in favor of moving in small, organized and discreet steps within the prevailing organizational discourse, seeking alignment with, rather than an exploration of the narratives and habits that dominate the organization. Pressure results in a sense that conflicts emerging between members are problems to be solved rather than fertile territory for discovery. Opportunities to expand the organizational discourse are lost. Instead status quo is maintained, and the discourse shrinks. In the vortex of urgency around short-term returns, the organization settles for outcomes which are often no more than new twists on "the way it has always been done around here." While these twists may require some recalibration in process or behavior, that is they may *feel* different, ultimately they do little to move the organization forward in significant and sustainable ways.

In this context it is imperative that we decouple efficiency from speed. We cannot hurry the process, and if we do, we will find ourselves back at its beginning again and again. Like a mountain stream it will choose its own pace, shifting between white water rapids and deep placid stretches that belie the currents just beneath the surface. Shutting down exchanges that feel uncomfortable and scary may get everyone out of the meeting faster, but rather than integrating differences in creative ways this haste drives them underground where they will fester, often for a long while, until they gather sufficient energy to explode more violently through the organization's discursive skin, often with difficult and complex consequences.

Providing sufficient time in the context of adequate psycho–social "elbow room" for the full spectrum of difference not only to surface but to be explored—dissected, deconstructed, parts of one view or idea combined with parts of others which, when whole, were in conflict—is critical. Diversity contraindicates stasis, and novelty tends to emerge in bursts rather than steady increments. It comes not in spite of friction, the heat that tension produces, but because of it.

From a practical perspective, we know that in organizational life time is not always freely available. Liminal spaces, expansive in terms of participants' ability to explore differences, require time. In turn, they *prepare* organizational members for those moments when it is crucial to move with alacrity, when an opportunity must be seized quickly, a crisis minimized or circumvented. Practice integrating difference, taking the time to explore the way difference matters, builds organizational muscle that can be called upon at important moments. The work to provide the capacity for these bursts of energy is proactive and prospective, a hedge against the certainty of the eventual, real need for real speed.

Sculpting liminal spaces

We have seen that thoughtful structures introduced into the formlessness of the space can operate as scaffolding—vertical and horizontal bracing that temporarily supports the space until participants' learning replaces the need for them. That learning occurs through social processes that run through that scaffolding, that provide intentional navigational signals and signposts for participants as they are feeling their way through their differences toward the very value of those differences, manifesting them in new perspectives, ideas, and action. Returning to de Certeau, we learn that

> space is composed of intersections of mobile elements. It is in a sense actuated by the ensemble of movements deployed within it. Space occurs as the effect produced by the operations that orient it, situate it, temporalize it, and make it function in a polyvalent unity of conflictural programs or contractual proximities
>
> (1988, p. 117)

Once the space is as open and neutral as possible, with only those conditions and structures that are absolutely necessary in place, attention can turn to these dynamics of the space. In this section we will look briefly at several types of processes that can help to guide de Certeau's "mobile elements" through this "ensemble of movements" that support exploration, experimentation, in short learning *through* difference rather than in spite of it. As you read through this "taster" of processes, note that for each one time is the requisite condition, the most essential liberating structure.

484

Conversations

Conversations are perhaps the most ubiquitous of processes to occur in psycho-social spaces (sculpted or otherwise), and indeed each of the processes that follows in this section is at its core a way of fostering conversation. Because of the universality of conversation, because of its commonplace nature, we may overlook it as a process *per se*, thinking of it instead (if we think of it at all) as an element in other processes, and something in any event that we are very good at, having done it all our lives. In truth, integrative conversation is very complex, rife with tensions and missed opportunities for learning. Baker et al. (2005) suggest that we need to "rediscover the art of talking together" (p. 413). They introduce the concept of conversational learning, and parse out for us the presence of five intersecting process dialectics, the boundaries of which "open a conversational space" (p. 411). Here attending to the dialectics of apprehension and comprehension, reflection and action, epistemological discourse and ontological recourse, individuality and relationally, and status and solidarity results in conversation that is an "experiential process of learners constructing meaning from their collective experiences" (p. 413).

This dialectical view of conversation is particularly *apropos* of our quest for processes that integrate differences in that "an inviting attitude regarding differences in opinion and perception is key to the process" (p. 415). Baker et al. quote Elbow (1986) in suggesting that "the surest way to get hold of what your present frame blinds you to is to try to adopt the opposite frame, that is, to reverse your model. A person who can live with contradiction and exploit it ... can simply see and think *more*" (quoted in p. 415, italics in original). Further, connected to the notion of formlessness as an ideal to pursue, they suggest that "conversational learning is intended to be more broadly and contextually adaptable without deliberate intentions to mold or impose specific kinds of change and intervention" (p. 424), but that it is a nonetheless a demanding "self-organizing entity [which] cannot exist without a receptive space to hold it. ... The conversation can be killed from within, as when, for example, an authoritarian monologue crushes the spirit of other participants" (p. 424).

Brookfield and Preskill (1999) also recognize conversation as an underpinning process and suggest the importance of prompting conversation by beginning with a wisely chosen pertinent question, and the deliberate introduction of both alternative perspectives and periods of silence, eschewing the notion "that conversation means continuous talk" (p. 47). As Reason and Torbert (2001) suggest, "good conversation requires attuning to, hearing and responding to, influencing and being influenced by, other voices and perspectives (Evered and Tannenbaum, 1992). ... Persons need to reach beyond merely acknowledging the existence of multiple perspectives and voices to working with them" (p. 8). This is no simple task. We cannot leave the door open for this sort of rich conversation, leaving it to chance that experiential learning that generates new ways of thinking and acting will occur of its own volition. Like the space itself, opportunities for this kind of conversation benefit from attention and supporting processes. These conversations bloom as a result of the craft of facilitation.

Storytelling

Benjamin (1968) suggests a reflexive relationship between storytelling and craft, and here we can consider storytelling a craft that in turn fosters important conversations. The stories on point here are not fantasy or fable, but stories of authentic experience, the oral conveyance of the things that have actually happened to the tellers, or to which they have borne witness. These are not stories intended to manipulate or coerce listeners in the space. They are not planned and crafted in advance, practiced to make a particular point. Rather these are stories with a quality of aliveness

485

that emerge in the context of conversation organically, bursting out in nonlinear messiness, "unenslaved, unorganized, and unfinished" (Boje, 2006) in an effort to deepen the listeners' understanding of lived experience—pleasure and pain, oppression and victory—that they might otherwise not imagine. The stories become a window into interactions and perspectives that lie beyond their own, and may yet be connected to it. If the space is neutral and non-coercive, one story will spark another in a deepening spiral of connections both emotional and cognitive, new and refined, perhaps even transformed. The stories accomplish these connections through rich contextual detail, through feeling expressed not overtly but in the nuances of the tale. Indeed, Benjamin (1968) suggests, "the more natural the process by which the storyteller forgoes the psychological shading, the greater becomes the story's claim to a place in the memory of the listener, the more completely it is integrated into his own experience" (p. 91). Benjamin suggest that every "real story ... contains, openly or covertly, something useful" (p. 86) for the listener, and that "the storyteller takes what he tells from experience. ... He in turn makes it the experience of those who are listening to his tale" (p. 87).

The willingness of people to tell authentic stories of their experience is grounded in our assumptions about the safety of the psycho-social space in which these stories are invited. The power dynamics that are assumed, if not inherent, in any forum sponsored by management or "the organization" can effectively shut storytelling (and other forms of interaction) down (Tyler, 2009). As with conversational learning, salient questions carefully chosen can help to ignite emergent storytelling. Story modeling is also a powerful means of exerting energy into the space that levels the playing field for participant stories. Practitioners who model the types of storytelling they hope for undertake a sort of unmasking that allows others to follow in their storytelling footsteps. The deeper the relevancy of the story the practitioner tells, and the more risky it feels to listeners, the more they are willing to match that relevancy and risk with important stories that will drive the conversation deeper to places where the roots between their stories touch. Stories beget stories, and the neutrality of *basho*, the formlessness of the space, fundamentally rekindles the natural desire of people in groups to tell their stories, even and especially ones that would seem under other circumstances too risky or controversial to tell.

Artistic expression

We have focused so far on process that are primarily linguistic in nature, but we are not limited to the power of language alone to communicate. Not everyone is equally endowed with the capacity for voice, and not all experience is expressible. Tuan (1977) explains that participants "tend to suppress that which they cannot express. If an experience resists ready communication, a common response ... is to deem it private—even idiosyncratic—and hence unimportant. ... Yet it is possible to articulate subtle human experiences. Artists have tried—often with success" (pp. 6–7).

As Reason and Torbert (2001) point out, we can each further the development of our own research/practice (be it a form of social science, of business or political leadership, or an art or craft) with a commitment to engaging, interweaving, and seeking synchrony among more than one mode of knowing" (pp. 9–10). Of particular import here is Heron's (1999) presentational knowing, "an intuitive grasp of the significance of patterns as expressed in graphic, plastic, moving, musical and verbal art-forms" (p. 122). Providing opportunities for participants to collage, to work with clay or paint, or to work somatically in dance or in various theater games as a way of expressing their experience may seem unprofessional in some organizational settings, but that is why we make the effort to carve out neutral formless spaces in these contexts.

486

Presentational expression may be essential to understanding perspectives that feel too personal to express otherwise or too foreign to be understood in any other way. Tuan (1977) supports the importance of non-linguistic forms of expression. "Pictorial art and rituals supplement language by depicting areas of experience that words fail to frame. … Art makes images of feeling so that feeling is accessible to contemplation and thought" (p. 148).

It is important to note that Heron's presentational knowing does not exclude linguistic expression, but opens up new forms that it can take—poetry, songs, stories, and reflective journaling are all non-traditional ways of using language to express experience that transcend ordinary ways of making it known to and understood by others. Artistic expression may well deepen the understanding one has of one's own experience as well, an effect that comes to light on reflection and often realized in conversations with others about the artistic process undertaken and the nature of the result. This brings us back around to the importance of conversational learning, which hinges not only on our ability to talk about our experience but to listen openly to the experience of others.

Listening

Conversation is at least bi-directional, and no amount of talking will compensate for spaces that do not foster good listening. All of the processes described here hinge on the ability of people occupying the space to listen to one another—not just hear, but really listen. Baker, Jensen, and Kolb (2005) suggest that conversational space is "emotional space" that is created by "receptive listening" (p. 424). John van Maanen implores us to "be willing to listen to each other and to listen with respect. The goal is not to control the field … or impose a paradigm for self-serving or utilitarian ends" (1995, p. 140). Brookfield and Preskill (1999) point out that "listening attentively is not easy. … Race, class, gender, learning style, personality—all these complicate our efforts to understand one another in daily conversations without the added difficulties … [of] intellectual inquiry" (p. 27).

When psychologist Carl Rogers (1902–87) described listening in *A Way of Being* (1980), he used six descriptive adjectives. In full, he characterized the way of listening that mattered to him as "a creative, active, sensitive, accurate, empathic, nonjudgmental listening" (p. 14). In organizations over the years, we have reduced these adjectives to only one, an instrumental version of active listening that is more focused on convincing speakers that we hear them than about immersing ourselves in their stories imaginally, empathically, and without judgment. Reclaiming this form of listening is possible, but it requires connections between people, an ethic of care, and it too requires time. The literature on listening that is grounded in spirituality offers us some support in this respect. In general, these works parallel Rogers' in their attention to listening as process and practice connected to deepening relationships through understanding, rather than as a technique or tool of persuasion, focusing on an opening up, an organic and emergent process of unfolding with unpredictable, rather than predetermined, outcomes. Lindahl's (2003, 2004) work on sacred listening, for example, includes a variety of exercises and practices that lead toward a stronger listening muscle. Shafir (2003) pursues awareness through reflective exercises that readers still detoxing from instrumental notions of listening may find helpful. Brady (2003) offers an anthology of 18 chapters written by a range of spiritual teachers from various helping professions who, despite their diversity, consistently advocate for listening that is mindful, attentive and full-bodied—"listening deeply to the world around and within me" (p. 293). Works such as these provide us with ways to support participants' listening and inform our own practice of listening within the space, suggesting temporary attending structures that might offer useful scaffolding in the spirit of our pursuit of neutrality.

487

A word on physical attributes of place

Our focus here has been on psycho-social spaces which we inhabit physically rather than virtually. It could be argued that healthy psycho-social spaces could occur in any physical surroundings, and indeed that may be the case. There is, however, some advantage to fostering liminal psycho-social spaces (chora, *basho*) in places (topos) that are also comfortable for our bodies. In addition, it is likely that spaces that are easy on the body provide more fluid openings for the neutral, formless spaces that are the goal for making diversity matter. Creature comforts such as airflow, temperature, lighting, line of sight, comfortable seating, all can contribute to participants' ability to relax into the space, to attend to each other (Tyler, 2007).

Baldwin (1998) blends the psycho-social with the physical attributes of the space in her work with circles. Drawing on tribal wisdom, she explains that "the skills of circle begin with removing ourselves and our self-interests from the middle of any group. When we come into a room and rearrange the seating, it causes us to rearrange our expectations also" (p. 62). The circle becomes a form within the formlessness, a boundary condition that equalizes authority. "Half the work of comprehension is accomplished when we find our place at the rim" (Baldwin, 1998, p. 104).

Brookfield and Preskill (1999) warn us that asking participants to sit in a "circle and tell them to speak to each other" (p. 37) is, on its own, insufficient. Baldwin's work is infused with ideas for maintaining the rim in the face of difference (p. 57) and holding the center through ritual, "principles, practices, and agreements" (p. 150). These merge the physical circle with a psycho-social roundness, a form within the formless, which creates a space in which we can listen to our expressions of our own experience, and to those of others, making a connection that is at once novel and ancient, unique and universal.

Creating and holding spaces: reflections for practice

While diverse and potent liminal spaces may occur organically and informally, in parking lots, in the gym, at the bar after work, it is likely that these spontaneous places are populated only with people who share one or more facets of what we tend to consider "diversity," e.g. the federally protected categories such as race, gender, ethnicity, the social categories such as sexual orientation, gender identity, professional identity, age, socio-economic status, tenure with the organization, or other aspects of class within organizations such as level (individual contributor, manager, VP etc.) and function (manufacturing, marketing, human resources etc). These shared aspects of identity and experience can result in a simple confirmation of beliefs and opinions rather than any critical challenge that might incite new thinking or action. The outcome is a good feeling, perhaps, but not very much change.

Liminal spaces, as we have seen, are not magical concoctions, at least not entirely. We can intentionally foster these vessels for authentic interaction, deep understanding and meaning making between and among diverse individuals and groups that can translate into organizational change. Facilitating these spaces takes a certain degree of fearlessness on the part of the practitioner holding the space. It requires a confidence to let go, a belief in the ability of the collective consciousness of the group to collaborate in those spaces, to move through its own differences on the way to (and as a way of) unearthing and inventing unanticipated and surprising outcomes. The moment where things feel most uncomfortable is a moment not to retreat from conflict or messiness, but a moment to support the group's advance into it, helping them to peel back the layers of experience, illuminate assumptions. The goal is to explicate the experiences of those in the space so that their implications can be explored by everyone—by those who were present as experiences unfolded, and by those who are learning about those experiences for the first time.

Fearlessness alone, however, is not sufficient. As Rogers (1980) points out in his relational way of listening, the work must be grounded in abiding care, in love. Chodron (2005) explains the concept of bodhichitta, an open heart and mind, fully awake, the "soft spot, a place as vulnerable and tender as an open wound" (p. 4). It is essential to care about the group. Bodhichitta, Chodron teaches, occurs on two levels. One is an unconditional bodhichitta that is free from opinion and preconceptions. The second is relative, and is "our ability to keep our hearts and minds open to suffering without shutting down" (p. 5). When interactions in the space become tense, it is important to resist a desire to calm the space, to ameliorate tension, to close the abyss it opens. Chodron offers no advice for closing the abyss. Rather she suggests that the practices of "loving kindness, compassion, joy, and equanimity are our tools. With the help of these tools and practices, we can uncover the soft spot of bodhichitta. … We will find it in behind the hardness of rage and in the shakiness of fear" (p. 6). This is a shared fear, an electricity between the practitioner who holds the space and the group who occupies it. The goal is to uncover bodhichitta together, but a caring practitioner can clear the path.

Finally, as we have seen, facilitating in this way must couple confidence and care with time as the ultimate liberating structure. The group requires time to soak in its variety, simmer in difference, and boil in conflict. Patiently guiding reflective conversational processes will support the group through even the most spiraling and rhizomatic conversations, down dark and mysterious tributaries, through looping reversals. Like a fever, these conversations must run their full course in their own time in order to ultimately achieve a new or renewed sense of health in the organization.

Successful practitioners shaping spaces where diversity matters will bravely experiment, and so discover ways to walk up to the abyss created by challenges, peer in, even dive, taking the group with them. There is no way of knowing what is below the surface of the abyss without getting wet, but it is likely to be rich, organic, alive.

Summary

This chapter has considered ways in which diversity can support organizational change by virtue of an intentional holding of psycho-social spaces that are on the cusp of huge potential. They are polyphonic, expansive, exploratory, and experimental—in a word, liminal. Classical views of psycho-social space as a formless nothingness that resists presuppositions about process or outcome were suggested as, at least, metaphors for ideal spaces against which temporary, rational conditions and structures provide scaffolding for extra-rational work by participants as they collaboratively deepen their understanding of individual experiences. Time was offered as the essential libratory structure that underpins both the nature of the space and the processes that occur within it. A sampling of processes that can foster critical reflection and collaborative learning were suggested. The chapter closed with a reflection on the nature of practice, and the need for courage in holding the space for participants, all the while navigating the active tension between safety and risk.

References

Baker, A.C., Jensen, P.J., and Kolb, D.A. (2005). Conversation as experiential learning. *Management development journal.* 36(4), 411–27.

Baldwin, C. (1998). *Calling the circle: The first and future challenge*. New York: Bantam Books.

Benjamin, W. (1968). *Illuminations: Essays and reflections*. New York: Schocken Books.

Bianchi, E. (2006). Receptacle/Ch{omacr}ra: Figuring the errant feminine in Plato's Timaeus. *Hypatia*. 21(4), 124–46.

Boje, D.M. (2006). Breaking out of narrative's prison: Improper story in storytelling organizations. *Storytelling, self, society*. 2(2), 28–49.

Brady, M. (ed.) (2003). *The Wisdom of Listening*. Boston: Wisdom Publications.

Brookfield, S.D. and Preskill, S. (1999). *Discussion as a way of teaching*. San Francisco, CA: Jossey-Bass.

Chodron, P. (2005). *Places that scare you: A guide to fearlessness in difficult times*. Boston, MA: Shambhala.

de Certeau, M. (1988). *The practice of everyday life*. Berkeley, CA: University of California Press.

Derrida, J. and Eisenman, P. (1997). *Chora L works*. New York: Monacelli Press.

Dilworth, D.A. (1987). Introduction: Nishida's critique of the religious consciousness. In *Last writings: Nothingness and the religious worldview*. Nishida. K. Honolulu: University of Hawaii Press. (Original published in 1949.)

Drucker, P. (1974). *Management: Tasks, responsibilities, practices*. New York: Harper & Row.

Emiko, T. (2000). *Autonomy and co-creation — a study of innovation through "Ba" co-created between a maker and a customer*. Retrieved 2/14/2010 from https://dspace.jaist.ac.jp/dspace/bitstream/10119/654/1/987 abstract.pdf

Facts on biodiversity: A summary of the millennium ecosystem assessment biodiversity synthesis. Retrieved 2/12/2010 from www.greenfacts.org/en/biodiversity/biodiversity-foldout.pdf

Heron, J. (1999). *The complete facilitator's handbook*. London: Kogan Page.

Kasulis, T. (1997). Foreword. In Carter, R.E. *The nothingness beyond God: An introduction to the philosophy of Nishida Kitarō*. St. Paul, MN: Paragon House Publishers.

Kristeva, J. (2002). Revolution in poetic language. In *The portable Kristeva*, ed. K. Oliver. New York: Columbia University Press.

Lane, B.C. (2001). *Landscapes of the sacred: Geography and narrative in American spirituality*. Baltimore, MD: Johns Hopkins University Press.

Lindahl, K. (2004). *The sacred art of listening: Forty reflections for cultivating a spiritual practice*. Woodstock, VT: Skylight Paths Publishing.

Lindahl, K. (2003). *Practicing the sacred art of listening: A guide to enrich your relationships and rekindle your spiritual life*. Woodstock, VT: Skylight Paths Publishing.

Mezirow, J. (1991). *Transformative dimensions of adult learning*. San Francisco, CA: Jossey-Bass.

Mintzberg, Henry (ed.) (1989). *Mintzberg on management*. New York, NY: The Free Press.

Nishida, K. (1987). *Last writings: Nothingness and the religious worldview* (D.A. Dilworth, trans.). Honolulu: University of Hawaii Press. (Original published in 1949.)

Nonaka, I. and Konno, N. (1998). The concept of "ba": Building a foundation for knowledge creation. *California management review*. 40(3), 40–54.

Plato (1944). *The timaeus and critias of Plato: the Thomas Taylor translation* (T. Taylor, trans.). Princeton, NJ: Princeton University Press. (Original work published around 360 BC.)

Porter, M.E. (1998). *Competitive advantage: Creating and sustaining superior performance*. New York: The Free Press.

Reason, P. and Torbert, W.R. (2001). Toward a transformational science: a further look at the scientific merits of action research. *Concepts and Transformations*, 6(1), 1–37. Retrieved 6/8/2000 from http://people.bath.ac.uk/mnspwr/Papers/TransformationalSocialScience.htm.

Rogers, C.R. (1980). *A way of being*. Boston: Houghton Mifflin Company.

Shafir, R. (2003). *The Zen of listening: Mindful communications in the age of distraction*. Wheaton, IL: Quest Books The Theosophical Publishing House.

Taylor, F. (2009). *Principles of scientific management* (Original published 1911.) New York: Cornell University Library.

Torbert. W.R. (1991). *The power of balance*. Newbury Park, CA: SAGE.

Tyler, J.A. (2009). Charting the course: How storytelling can foster communicative learning in the workplace. In J. Mezirow and E. Taylor (eds.) *Transformative learning in practice: Insights from community, workplace, and higher education*. San Francisco, CA: Jossey-Bass, pp. 136–47.

Tyler, J. A. (2007). Incorporating storytelling into practice: How HRD practitioners foster strategic storytelling. *Human resource development quarterly.* 18(4), 559–97.

Tuan, Y. (1977). *Space and place: The perspective of experience.* Minneapolis, MN: University of Minnesota Press.

Uehara, M. (n.d.). Japanese aspects of Nishida's Basho: Seeing the "form without form." *Japanese Journal of Religious Studies.* Retrieved 2/11/2010 from nanzan-u.ac.jp/SHUBUNKEN/publications/ EJPhilosophy/PDF/EJP4-Uehara.pdf.

Van de Ven, A. H., Rogers, R. W., Bechara, J. P. and Sun K. (2008). Organizational diversity, integration and performance. *Journal of organizational behavior.* 29, 335–54.

van Maanen, J. (1995). Style as theory. *Organization science.* 6(1), 133–43.

34

Making sense of gender and organizational change
A feminist review of selected articles

Kathy Sanderson, Albert J. Mills and Jean Helms Mills

In this chapter we use the lens of Critical Sensemaking (CSM) to review the literature on organizational change and gender. Specifically we focus on two interrelated themes: (i) organizational change programs and the gendering of organization—exploring the impact of such programs of gendered practices; and (ii) gendered organization and change—exploring the implications of feminist theory for organizational change practices. We conclude with a synthesis of insights from the literature review and suggested strategies for changing gender and gendering change.

The Critical Sensemaking lens

Critical Sensemaking, or CSM, originates from the work of Weick (1995) who viewed the process of organizing through the lens of seven inter-related socio-psychological properties. The seven properties constitute what Weick (1995) sees as a sensemaking process through which people construct a sense of organization. The properties consist of the ongoing *identity* construction of the individual as he or she makes sense of events; the socio-psychological influences of relevant *social* groups on the sense of a situation; contextual *cues* that shape the direction of a given sense; the psychological need to ensure the *on-going* sense of a situation; the *retrospective* nature of sensemaking as people make sense of what has occurred; and the *plausibility* of a given sense that facilitates its *enactment*.

Weick's (1979, 1985, 1995, 2001) socio-psychological approach to organization, we contend, is important in shifting attention to agency and social construction and away from overly rationalized and structural accounts (Helms Mills, 2010; Helms Mills and Mills, 2009; Mills, 2008a). Nonetheless, as has been argued elsewhere (Helms Mills, 2003; Mills and Helms Mills, 2004; Thurlow, 2010), Weick's sensemaking lens fails to adequately take into account the gendered aspects of sensemaking processes. Nor does it adequately deal with power and structure as influences on and through the sensemaking process. It is also epistemologically problematic in its assumption of, what Johnson and Duberley (2000: 3) refer to as a "presupposed knowledge of the conditions in which knowledge takes place." In dealing with these questions we take a "consciously reflexive" (Johnson and Duberley, 2000: 4) approach that identifies the impossibility of "coming to a foundational set of epistemological standards ... while [maintaining] consistency with regard to the epistemological assumptions" (Johnson and Duberley, 2000: 177) we adopt.

To deal with contexts of power, structure, and knowledge we draw on the work of Mills (1988, 2008b), Unger (1987), and Foucault (1979) to deal respectively with the rules, formative contexts and discursive fields in which sensemaking takes place. We call this approach Critical Sensemaking (Helms Mills and Mills, 2009; Mills and Helms Mills, 2004; Thurlow, 2010).

Organizational change

In terms of organizational change the CSM lens focuses on the socio-psychological processes and contexts associated with specific change initiatives. Thus, organizational change is not viewed as a concrete outcome of an identified (Kotter, 1996), or even unconscious (Mintzberg, 1978), set of problems but rather as an *enacted* sense of change. In the process the CSM approach is interested not only in the processes leading up to an enacted sense of change but also such things as the power differentials involved and the identity outcomes for those affected by the enactment. In particular, we are interested in the gendered outcomes of the enactment of organizational change.

Gender, Critical Sensemaking, and change

Through a focus on the socio-psychological properties of organizational change CMS draws attention to the role of meaning and the implications for identity and organizational stability. This stands in sharp contrast to mainstream theories of organizational change, which tend to treat change as artifactual, i.e., some*thing* that is altered through attitudinal (Coch and French, 1948), job (Hackman and Oldham, 1980), structure (French and Bell, 1972), culture (Schein, 1985), process (Hammer and Champy, 1993), strategy (Porter, 1980), and/or measurement (Kaplan and Norton, 1992) changes. The artifactual approach tends to focus on change as an entity (more or less separate or separable from human intent) that can be manipulated through alterations in any number of variables, or other *things*, that are viewed as influencing, rather than the outcomes of, human behavior. "People" in the organizational change literature are often viewed through an essentialist lens, which pays little or no attention to identity (seeing it as a more or less fixed entity). If anything the focus is on altered attitudes and/or behavior with little regard to the potential changes to the way people view their selves and others. Instead, people tend to be viewed as a variable (e.g., the "human factor"—see, for example, Danny C. K. Ho, 1999) that, when subject to organizational change, can benefit in terms of participation in decision-making, higher income, more satisfying work, better customer relations, increased efficiencies, profit-ability, and enhanced status—particularly for senior managers and employers (Helms Mills et al., 2008): rarely is equity seen as part of the potential outcomes or subject of organizational change (Helms Mills, 2005).

A focus on the socio-psychological processes of organizational change, on the other hand, serves to problematize organizational change by revealing its socially constructed character, and raises questions about its influence on identity, including gender identity. A focus on the sensemaking nature of organizational change also points to its relatively unstable character as meanings change overtime, especially in the face of "shocks" to the way people understand organizational reality (Weick, 1995). As such, as we have argued elsewhere (Mills and Helms Mills, 2004; Mills and Helms Mills, 2010), instability offers the potential for challenges to the gender order.

Organizational change programs and gendered outcomes

The idea of programmatic change took hold in the last quarter of the twentieth century as culture change became a popular intervention technique (Davies, 1984; Deal and Kennedy, 1982; Peters and Waterman, 1982).

The development of an organizational culture focus within management and organization studies was accompanied by much optimism from postpositivist researchers (Smircich, 1983; Weick, 1985), who heralded the move away from a rationality and systems thinking towards issues of symbolism, identity and emotionality. Within this framework feminists were optimistic that, as a heuristic, organizational culture would open an intellectual space for consideration of gender and organization (Gherardi, 1995; Mills, 1988). Feminists had long argued that gender was an outcome of culture and cultural relationships (Ryan, 1979) and in a field of study that had long neglected gender (Hearn and Parkin, 1983) a focus on organizational culture promised to open debate about the role of masculinities (Collinson and Hearn, 1994) and femininities (Ferguson, 1984) at work. Yet it was a promise that basically failed to materialize as organizational managers and educators increasingly focused on adapting symbols, values and beliefs to create more efficient organizations through creating such things as a sense of identity and belonging among employees and by assisting management to understand how to shape and direct important aspects of an organization's culture (Schein, 1992). In the process the notion of organizational culture was objectified as practitioners and educators increasingly came to think of it as a thing to be manipulated rather than a heuristic for helping people to make sense of their organizational experiences and relationships (Smircich, 1983).

From the late 1980s onwards a series of different organizational change programs became variously popular over time, and include Total Quality Management (TQM), Business Process Re-engineering (BPR, reengineering or re-engineering), Six Sigma, the Balanced Scorecard and Appreciative Inquiry—see Abrahamson (1996), Kieser (1997) and Jackson (2001) for accounts of the various developments.

Gender and the enactment of organizational change

Despite the widespread changes that have occurred in the name of organizational change and a burgeoning literature there has been very little study of the outcomes for the people involved in terms of identity—especially gendered identities—discriminatory practices, and issues of self esteem, etc.

A review of the literature of organizational change reveals that the vast majority of articles fails to take gender into account. For example, a title search for "organizational change" on ABI/INFORM (ProQuest) results in a total of 964 hits within scholarly journals (as of October 15, 2009). When gender is added as a search component within the abstract, that figure is reduced to 13 (or 1.34 percent). When gender is a title search with organizational change, there are only 5 articles found (0.5 percent). A search of Business Source Complete show similar results: change management as a title search provided 501 articles (as of March 29, 2010), but only 3 (0.6%) when gender was added to the abstract.

If we look at gender and popular organizational change programs we find a similar picture. Using the search component "gender" and the name of a selected change program our ABI/INFORM (ProQuest) searches yielded the following results for six popular change programs:

Table 34.1 Percentages of gender issues in change management programs

Change Program	Total abstract references★	Incl. references to gender	Percentage gender references
Balanced Scorecard	1372	0	0
Six Sigma	2169	0	0
Appreciative Inquiry	171	1	0.6
Re-engineering	6565	3	0.05
TQM	8163	6	0.07
Culture change	9186	106	1.15
TOTAL	*27,626*	*126*	*0.45*

Note: ★ We used an "abstract" only search to ensure that gender and the selected change programs were central foci in a given article

We also undertook an EndNote search on the Library of Congress website for books that combined a focus on gender and one or other change program. That search yielded 0 books focussed on gender and Six Sigma, Appreciative Inquiry, Re-engineering, or TQM; 1 book on gender and the Balanced Scorecard, and 25 books on Corporate or Organizational/ Organisational culture and gender. These figures suggest an overall field of inquiry that has little or no concern with gender issues. The sheer number and focus of most of the articles and books presents an *on-going sense* of organizational change.

In her study of the sensemaking practices of a major Canadian corporation undergoing change Helms Mills (2003) argued that senior managers accepted the need to change as if it was an imperative—a more or less requirement with its roots in such things as competition, technological changes, globalization, and new management techniques. In making decisions, not on whether but what type of change process to enact, Helms Mills (2003) found that senior managers were influenced by widespread practices across the industry (social sensemaking), and business in general (on-going sensemaking), and a perceived sense that the ideal-typical manager was someone who adapted to change (identity). Abundant sensemaking cues—local, national and international companies who had adopted culture change—made it increasingly easy to see the adoption of a similar program as plausible. In the process of adopting their own culture change program, argues Helms Mills (2003), the company simultaneously enacted a sense of culture change (as an important and much needed process) and made retrospective sense of the factors (such as a need for improved morale through greater sense of purpose) supposedly leading up to adoption of a culture change program as something that needs urgent and vital attention in regards to organizational survival and prosperity in a global context. It is an impact that is reinforced in practice—as numerous organizations across North America and (other industrialized countries) adopt one or other of these change programs (Helms Mills, 2003), but also in theory—as various academics and consultants serve—as part of the *social sensemaking* environment —to construct ways to encourage the adoption of one or other change program or organizational change in general. As such, in critical sensemaking terms, this large body of literature and practices serve to construct a powerful discourse that *enacts* a dominant view of organizational change.

Gender and the organizational change literature

Feminist studies of work and organization have long dealt with the issue of change, specifically that change designed to address gender discrimination, yet few have engaged with the

495

organizational change literature per se. There are many reasons for this, including the over-whelming managerialist focus of much of the work, its often atheoretical and ahistorical slant and its positivist world view (Burrell and Morgan, 1979; Hearn and Parkin, 1983). Nonetheless, these are both reasons for adopting alternative paradigms or traditions (Burrell and Morgan, 1979; Prasad, 2005) and understanding the processes of and implications for knowledge production in the selected field of organizational change. To that end, in the rest of this chapter we want to directly engage with the organizational change literature to understand its discursive effects (Foucault, 1980).

A review of the various articles on gender and organizational change programs (see Table 34.1) reveals some of the potential problems associated with ignoring gender. We begin with those change programs that have little or nothing to say about gender – Six Sigma and the Balanced Scorecard.

Six Sigma and the Balanced Scorecard

Six Sigma has been described as "a set of practices that combines statistical techniques and management training to improve organizational processes—of cost minimization, schedule adherence, high product quality and customer satisfaction—specifically through the elimination of defects" (Helms Mills et al., 2008, p.110). Similarly, the Balanced Scorecard "is a method for developing strategic objectives through the measurement of key financial, structural and process factors linked to organizational performance critical to its success" (Helms Mills et al., 2008, p. 103).

On the surface, these approaches, with their focus on scientific method and measurement, appear gender-neutral. Indeed, one feminist researcher suggests that the Balanced Scorecard can be used as "a management tool to achieve gender mainstreaming in organizational culture" (Floeter-van Wijk, 2007). However, critics have argued that Six Sigma and the Balanced Scorecard can have a powerful influence on the mind-set of employees and managers by narrowing the focus to error reduction and measurement at the expense of other issues and concerns (such as innovation), "shifting attention from intangible assets to those that can be measured … [and] ignoring many of the non-measurable factors that constitute the culture of an organization, such as values, beliefs, symbols, systems of communication, and interrelationships that may contribute to the strength of the organization," encouraging rigid behaviour and leaving little room for "cross perspectives" (cited in Helms Mills et al., 2008, p. 114). A feminist concern here would be the extent to which a focus on such issues as employment equity could get lost in the concern for narrowly focussed, measurable interests. Discursively, while scientific approaches and measurement are not male characteristics per se, the privileging of rational models of change can—if not checked and reflected on—serve to reinforce masculine associations with the dominant thought processes that underlie the philosophies of Balanced Scorecard and Six Sigma. In the latter case, this concern is underscored by the widespread use of martial arts metaphors and symbols that are applied to a hierarchical system of training, processes, teams and leadership. Thus, for example, it has been called a "statistical thinking paradigm" that is enacted through *Executive Leaders* who are the visionaries of the program; *Champions*, drawn from management, who oversee the process; *Master Black Belts*, who play an integration role; *Black Belts* who execute the program; and *Green Belts*, specially trained employees, who work under the Black Belts. It is not a stretch of the imagination to speculate how this highly focussed way of thinking—with its focus on measurement and performance outcomes—can privilege some identities (e.g., the mathematician, the black belt) and marginalize others (e.g., those viewed as innumerate or not Black Belt material). It is also not too much of a stretch to imagine how such identities can become more or less associated with either masculinities (privileged) or femininities (marginalized).

Appreciative Inquiry

Despite the fact that Appreciative Inquiry (AI) has been around since the 1980s and was adopted at one time by the United Nations it remains one of the lesser known and discussed approaches to change. This may be due to its focus away from objectivist models or measurement and problem solving towards a focus on "finding the best in people and discovering what works best in an organization and then … building on and celebrating these successes" (Helms Mills et al., 2008, p. 83). It involves a "4-D process" of discovering the underlying strengths of individuals and the organization; dreaming or envisioning what might be; designing for what could be; and destiny, "sustaining what has been achieved" (Helms Mills et al., 2008, p. 84). As such, it carries the potential to open discursive spaces for discussions of more equitable organizations. Yet, to date, little has been done to discuss and develop AI as a method for addressing discriminatory practices. Sekerka et al. (2006) is the only published study to show interest in gender but only as a "moderating effect" on the way people understand and respond to a diagnostic tool used as part of an AI study. Interestingly, however, they conclude that AI "seemed particularly effective at encouraging men to engage with the task and to broaden their thinking … " (p. 472). They speculate that this may be because the AI "task contrasts with their typical mode of communication [and] may have garnered deeper thinking and engagement that will lead to better outcomes in subsequent phases of the change process." In other words, the researchers may be describing some form of "shock" (Weick, 1995) to the ongoing sense that encouraged new senses to be constructed. On the other hand, women in the study are described as being less creative as an outcome of the AI task "perhaps because of its consistency with their typical mode of conversing" (p. 472). Apart from the obvious problem of essentializing the assumed characteristics of women and men the study also fails to develop further study into the gendered insights unearthed. Arguably, with its focus on the "best" in people AI could be adapted to a more gender reflexive approach if such things as context and definitions of best are taken into account.

Re-engineering

According to Hammer and Champy (1993, quoted in Helms Mills, et al., 2008, p. 97), re-engineering is "the fundamental rethinking and radical redesign of business processes to achieve dramatic improvements in critical contemporary measures of performance, such as cost, quality, service and speed." Radical critics have argued that re-engineering is a new form of deskilling (Braverman, 1974), with work redesigned by teams according to identified organizational processes and workflows (see Helms-Mills et al., 2008). Critics also point to the far reaching job losses that usually accompany the introduction of re-engineering, and the fact that there is little evidence to document the successful implementation of re-engineering (Helms Mills, 2003). Even Hammer and Champy (1993) contend that three-quarters of all attempts fail—but they blame it in the ineptitude of the managers involved.

Analyses of the gendered aspects of re-engineering are few and far between. ABI/INFORM yielded only one article and two doctoral thesis on the subject, none of which was centrally focussed on gender. The one article (Dowlatshahi, 1994) on the subject only considered gender tangentially to re-engineering, being more concerned with the influence of re-engineering on higher education outcomes that include, among other things, gender disparities in graduate starting salaries. Of the two theses, one relegates gender to future research into its impact on perceptions of re-engineering leadership (Morreale, 2002), while the other takes up that very issue, finding little difference between males and females in their perceptions of management competencies in the application of re-engineering (Altman, 2006). Nonetheless, it can be argues that, like Balanced Scorecard and Six Sigma approaches, re-engineering's over-focus on process efficiencies can serve to narrow concern away from the human side of enterprise, including gender discrimination. As with Six Sigma, the language use and symbolism involved in re-engineering evokes masculine-associated metaphors of dominance, destruction, and fighting (e.g., "don't automate, obliterate" and "revolution"—see Hammer, 1990, 1995). In Helms Mills' (2003) study of Nova Scotia Power the senior managers in charge of re-engineering were called, and embraced, the names "gunslinger" and "undertakers" to describe their radical new role in the organization.

Total Quality Management (TQM)

TQM has been described as "an organization-wide method of managing people and processes to ensure the continuous delivery of quality products and services" (Helms Mills et al., 2008, p. 92). Again, despite it widespread use and potential implications for the identity work of organizational members there is little research on the outcomes for gendered practices. Critics have argued that some of the human problems of TQM include increased stress for employees who are required to take on new administrative duties and responsibilities concerned with "job enrichment" and "involvement" (Helms Mills et al., 2008).

Studies of gender and TQM are limited (in number and scope) and mixed in their results. Lian (2001, p. iii) suggests that males are more likely than females to contribute "positively to TQM implementation," while Aksu (2003) and Ehigie and his colleagues (Ehigie and Akpan, 2005; Ehigie and McAndrew, 2005), respectively, suggest that gender does not seem to influence the "readiness" to adapt to or the "practice of" TQM: Ehigie and Akpan (2005) draw on their results to argue against discriminatory hiring where it may be assumed that women are less capable of working within a TQM system of work. Cockerill-Walker's (1997) study of participants' experience of TQM found "a few gender differences" (p. 113) in regard to the way males and females conceptualized the relationship between the "tools" needed to do the work (females took a more system-wide approach), toleration of the time taken to complete tasks (males were less tolerant), and the requirements of team interactions (males were initially less comfortable).

Two feminist studies on TQM provide contrasting views on the potential value of the approach and the outcomes for women and men. The first—by Graham and Hotchkiss (2009)—applies a "conceptual application of theories of total quality management (TQM) to the topic of gender-related employment" (p. 578). They argue that the "application of TQM theory to the topic of gender-related employment disparities is a novel approach that may motivate new public policies;" as such "further conceptual work on the application of TQM to gender disparities in employment in recommended" (ibid.). Armstrong, Armstrong, Choiniere et al. (1997), on the other hand, come up with radically different recommendations from their empirical study of TQM in a hospital system in Canada. Basically, Armstrong et al. (1997) argue that the introduction of TQM in the not-for-profit health care system can have deleterious effects on working conditions and patient care. They contend that TQM shifts attention from the concern with people to more abstract thinking through an over-focus on measurement; tends to be introduced from above (with attendant tendencies to reproduce existing dominant viewpoints) and short-circuits unions; shifts the focus from patient-care to customer satisfaction, with all the attendant shifts in conceptualizations; introduces standardization and competitiveness to areas where there is a need for localized initiatives and cooperation; encourages a deskilling of labor as process structures replace employee task execution and initiative. Finally, the seemingly innocuous use of "team" work (that is central to TQM) drastically reconceptualized existing notions of teams (as a cooperative set of interrelationships) to take on more of an inherently masculinist one (as a competitive group designed to outperform other groups). Perhaps what we are seeing here are attempts to enact a sense of organization using cues (e.g., "team") that are rooted in other, contradictory social senses and thus leading to conflict and confusion in the system. With one of the results being a discursive shift of certain feminine or more gender balanced practices towards more masculinist understandings of organizational practice.

Organizational culture, change and feminist debate

By far the largest area of debate around issues of gender and organizational change can be found in the literature on organizational culture, and it is to this debate we now turn for insights.

It is perhaps fitting as well as understandable that most of the insights generated on gender and change have come from a focus on organizational culture. Feminists have long identified this focus as having the potential to open space for discussion, long neglected within management and organization studies (Hearn and Parkin, 1983; Wilson, 2003), around issues of the gendered nature of organization. It has generated not only a substantial number of articles but numerous books and edited collection on organizational culture and gender. Nonetheless, in terms of space and sheer scope we will restrict our study to the selected articles.

Analytical framework

To begin, we view the literature as located in two broad foci—social constructionist and essentialist. The latter can be found in those studies that categorize rather then problematize (the cultural differences between) "men" and "women." The former, while acknowledging embodied differences, focuses on the factors that serve to construct cultural differences and understandings of maleness and femaleness. As is evident from the beginning of this chapter, we take this social constructionist approach but apply it across the literature to gain insights into the various findings.

Essentialist insights

The great bulk of the essentialist studies cast gender as a variable—sometimes as central and sometimes tangential to the focus of the study. An example of the latter includes studies of corporate fraud that consider gender as one of several variables contributing to fraud-enabling corporate cultures (Watson, 2003).

While it would be quite easy to justify ignoring those variable that reduce human characteristics to impartial measures arguably they provide sensemaking clues to the relationship between gender and cultural dynamics in organizational relationships. Such studies suggest that an organization's culture can have negative effects on women's ability or preparedness to mentor (Appelbaum et al., 1994); may have no difference on men and women's deontological norms (Singhapakdi and Vitell, 1991); can have a difference on the construction of cultural values (Strautmanis, 2008) and perceptions of organizational culture (Bellou, 2008); and a moderating effect on perceptions of leadership and job satisfaction (Chen, 2005).

499

Other essentialist studies suggest that the cultural values of an organization can affect women's job satisfaction (Bellou, 2008), perceptions of their leadership abilities (Stelter, 2002) and of organizational justice (Lieberman, 2006); cultural values can also affect levels of sexual harassment (Cogin and Fish, 2009) and discriminatory stereotypes (Frohlich and Peters, 2007), but also compliance with employment equity legislation (Burgess-Wilkerson, 2008).

Strategies for addressing discrimination at work include making the culture "family friendly" (Weiler and Zimmerman, 2007); developing organizational cultures that help to overcome societal expectations of gender roles (Hossain and Kusakabe, 2005) and breaking down gender segregated work (Miller and Clark, 2008); zero tolerance of discriminatory behaviours and constant surveying of employees to monitor attitudes (Verespej, 1997).

Applying a CMS lens, we would argue that while the researchers have tended to essentialize gender and concretize organizational culture they are picked up on certain discursive associations or senses. Namely, that the use of the term organizational culture (to make sense of a series of interrelationships)—whether seen as a concrete entity or a heuristic—has come to be associated with gender inequities. Either as some*thing* that needs to be altered to address those inequities and/or as something that causes those inequities. The various studies signpost the various responses that people have when self identifying as "men" or "women" and how, when so labeled, they pick up cues from selected experiences (e.g., job satisfaction) that become enacted (through their responses and those of the researchers) as gendered realities.

Social constructivist insights

Social constructivist approaches problematize not only the relationship between organizational culture and gender but also the concepts of organizational culture and gender themselves (Coates, 1998). Organizational culture is often used as a heuristic to understand how organizational relationships contribute to gendered selves and how, in turn, gendered notions constitute so-called organizational cultures (Cartwright and Andrew, 1995). In the process they raise interesting questions about the conceptualization of "organizational change" and its impact on those involved.

Several studies focus on the processes through which gendered organizational cultures are created and maintained. These include such things as organizational rules (Mills, 1988), metaphors (Lewis and Morgan, 1994), gender dynamics (Angus, 1993), sub cultures (Gottfried and Graham, 1993), rhetoric (Gherardi, 1994), and gender imbalances (Simpson, 2000). These studies provide insights into how certain notions of masculinity and femininity are translated into privileged or marginalized practices that come to constitute a dominant set of cultural values in an organization.

Other studies focus on selected factors that may serve to reinforce those dominant gendered notions of organization, including body image (Girard, 2001), organizational commitment (Hopfl, 1992), career paths (Wilson, 1998), and presenteeism (i.e., the requirement to be ever present, ever seen in an organization—Simpson, 1998).

Within these studies strategies of change are either implied or viewed through the development of alternative ways of developing organizational relationships to those that are surfaced. In some cases, the researchers go further in developing strategies of organizational change designed to heighten awareness of the processes of gender discrimination as a method for addressing the issue. Rindfleish et al. (2009) for example suggest the active development of stories as a sensemaking device for challenging gendered notions of organization; Kolb and Merrill-Sands (1999) argue that a strategy of surfacing gendered assumptions can be used to encourage reflexivity and challenge to taken-for-granted gendered ideas; and Dutton et al. (2002) urge attention to the influence of context in shaping women and men's respective abilities to be willing and able to sell issues in organizations, including equity issues (Piderit and Ashford, 2003).

Summary and conclusions as further sensemaking clues

The literature on organizational change, particularly those focussed on programmatic change (e.g., TQM, BPR), has little or nothing to say about gender. This is likely rooted in the fact that most programs are narrowly focussed on managerial outcomes that are achieved through quasi-scientific methods and the assumption of gender-neutrality (or neglect). They do not preclude gender issues per se and one could imagine a scenario where some of the central techniques and foci could be applied to addressing gender discrimination—especially with an eye to even greater levels of efficiency, quality and/or commitment. Indeed, some feminists have suggested as much (Fondas, 1997; Graham and Hotchkiss, 2009).

Nonetheless, as the great bulk of studies on gender and change argues, the on-going sense of organizational change is generally enacted as a gendered sense of the organization, with far reaching consequences for the identity work of those involved.

First, a change program usually has wide-spread consequences for various aspects of the organization, including such things as layers of management, processes, the establishment of quality circles or teams, enhanced measurement techniques and goals, an array of new forms of symbolism (e.g., teams, quality circles, Black Belts), and new or elevated values (e.g., mission statements, etc). As feminist and other gender researchers have argued, changes in processes (Ferguson, 1984), structures (Kanter, 1977), and symbolism (Acker, 1992) can have serious consequences for the jobs/professions/identities of those involved. This can affect such things as mentoring (Appelbaum et al., 1994), leadership (Chen, 2005), and stereotypes (Frohlich and Peters, 2007) for better or for worst.

Second, organizations can be viewed at one level as an (on-going) sensemaking achievement whose maintenance is linked to a series of retrospective and social sensemaking activities. The notion of "team" for example can be seen as an integral part of a hospital system that privileges patient care as its central retrospective sense of organizational purpose and is supported by groups of healthcare professionals. By changing a critical part of the system (e.g., the notion of "team") senior managers may find that this leads to important yet unanticipated changes in sensemaking cues and the overall plausibility of the project (Armstrong et al., 1997). As the literature suggests, this rarely leads to improved gender equity. Nonetheless, changes to the sensemaking environment can lead to instabilities that open up spaces for addressing gender issues. The surfacing of gender assumptions is one suggested way of destabilizing existing dominant sensemaking (Kolb and Merrill-Sands, 1999). The development of new stories (that favour gender equity) is a way of directly engaging with sensemaking processes (Rindfleish et al., 2009). Reinterpreting as well as changing organizational rules (Mills, 1988) is yet another way of changing the sensemaking environment. As is the deliberate development of anti-discriminatory metaphors (Lewis and Morgan, 1994) to help frame changed ways of making sense in an organization.

Third, the notion of organizational change (and the various attendant elements of the concept) should be engaged with as a discursive process whose very naming may have gendered implications (Coates, 1998). At one level the very concrete connotations attached to organizational change and, through it, BPR, TQM, AI, Balanced Scorecard, Organizational Culture, may serve to naturalize the sense made of such activities and practices and with it those associated with gender disparities (Lewis and Morgan, 1994; Stelter, 2002). The same can be said of the socially constructed character of such things as careers (Wilson, 1998), organizational commitment

(Hopfl, 1992), and body image (Girard, 2001). Exploration of these aspect of organizational life reveal them to be well established myths of on-going sensemaking whose gendered effects are often exacerbated by association with other powerful sensemaking myths such as the culture of an organization. Thus, challenges need to be mounted not only at the overall and on-going sense of an organization in, for example, the form of an organization's culture but also in many of its constituent and interrelated parts, such as career paths.

Ultimately, organizational change presents challenges to feminists in two main ways. First, there is the need to engage with and make sense of organizational change from a feminist perspective, to develop a new sense of organizational change that will centrally embrace the need to develop reflexive, anti-sexist, equitable organizational processes (the Abella Commission provided a valuable template for such a project—Abella, 1984). This requires a far reaching synthesis of the various insights from the feminist literature on work and organization. Second, and not divorced from the first project, there is a need for feminist engagement with the dominant discourse of organizational change to develop further insights into the challenges and potentialities of change and resistance. We hope that, at least in a small way, we have made a contribution to the latter project.

References

Abella, R.S. 1984. *Equity in Employment: A Royal Commission Report*. Ottawa: Ministry of Supply and Services Canada.

Abrahamson, E. 1996. Management fashion. *Academy of Management Review*, 21(1): 254–85.

Acker, J. 1992. Gendering organizational theory. In A.J. Mills and P. Tancred (eds.), *Gendering Organizational Analysis*: 248–60. Newbury Park, CA: SAGE.

Aksu, M.B. 2003. TQM readiness level perceived by the administrators working for the central organization of the Ministry of National Education in Turkey. *Total Quality Management*, 14(5): 591–604.

Altman, R.E., II. 2006. *A survey of perceived managerial competencies of cardiac rehabilitation professionals in a hospital setting*. Unpublished D.Ed., Indiana University of Pennsylvania.

Angus, L.B. 1993. Masculinity and women teachers at Christian Brothers College. *Organization Studies*, 14(2): 235–61.

Appelbaum, S. H., Ritchie, S. and Sharpiro, B.T. 1994. Mentoring revisited: An organizational behaviour construct. *Journal of Management Development*, 13(4): 62–72.

Armstrong, P., Armstrong, H., Choiniere, J., Mykhalovskiy, E. and White, J. 1997. *Medical Alert: New Work Organizations in Health Care*. Toronto: Garamond Press.

Bellou, V. 2008. Identifying organizational culture and subcultures within Greek public hospitals. *Journal of Health Organization and Management*, 22(5): 496–509.

Braverman, H. 1974. *Labor and Monopoly Capital*. New York: Monthly Review Press.

Burgess-Wilkerson, B. 2008. Selection and interview procedures at a multinational company. *Business Communication Quarterly*, 71(1): 100–102.

Burrell, G. and Morgan, G. 1979. *Sociological Paradigms and Organizational Analysis*. London: Heinemann.

Cartwright, S. and Andrew, G. 1995. Project management: Different gender, different culture? A discussion on gender and organizational culture—Part 2. *Leadership and Organization Development Journal*, 16(4): 12–16.

Chen, L.-T. 2005. Exploring the relationship among transformational and transactional leadership behavior, job satisfaction, organizational commitment, and turnover on the IT Department of Research and Development in Shanghai, China. Nova Southeastern University, Florida.

Coates, G. 1998. Integration or separation: women and the application of organisational culture. *Women in Management Review*, 13(3): 114–24.

Coch, L. and French, J.R.P. 1948. Overcoming Resistance To Change. *Human Relations*, 1: 512–32.

Cockerill-Walker, J.L. 1997. An exploratory study of quality improvement team participants' experience. Unpublished Ed.D., University of Nebraska – Lincoln.

Cogin, J. and Fish, A. 2009. Sexual harassment—a touchy subject for nurses. *Journal of Health Organization and Management*, 23(4): 442–62.

Collinson, D.L. and Hearn, J. 1994. Naming men as men: implications for work, organization and management. *Gender, Work and Organization*, 1(1): 2–22.

Davies, S. 1984. *Managing Corporate Culture*. Cambridge, MA: Ballinger.

Deal, T.E. and Kennedy, A.A. 1982. *Corporate Cultures*. Reading, MA: Addison-Wesley.

Dowlatshahi, S. 1994. Reengineering in higher education: A case study. *Human Systems Management*, 13(4): 303–7.

Dutton, J.E., Ashford, S.J., Lawrence, K.A. and Miner-Rubino, K. 2002. Red light, green light: Making sense of the organizational context for selling issued. *Organization Science*, 13(4): 355–71.

Ehigie, B.O. and Akpan, R.C. 2005. Psycho-social factors influencing practice of total quality management in some Nigerian organizations. *Journal of Managerial Psychology*, 20(5/6): 355–79.

Ehigie, B.O. and McAndrew, E.B. 2005. Innovation, diffusion and adoption of total quality management (TQM). *Management Decision*, 43(5/6): 925–40.

Ferguson, K. 1984. *The Feminist Case against Bureaucracy*. Philadelphia, PA: Temple University Press.

Floeter-van Wijk, S.W. 2007. *The Gender Balanced Scorecard: A Management Tool to Achieve Gender Mainstreaming in Organisational Culture*. Frankfurt am Main; New York: Lang.

Fondas, N. 1997. Feminization unveiled: management qualities in contemporary writings. *Academy of Management Review*, 22(1): 257–82.

Foucault, M. 1979. *Discipline and Punish: The Birth of the Prison*. New York: Vintage Books.

Foucault, M. 1980. *Power/Knowledge*. New York: Pantheon.

French, W.L. and Bell, C. 1972. *Organization Development: Behavioral Science Interventions for Organization Improvement*. Englewood Cliffs, NJ: Prentice-Hall.

Frohlich, R. and Peters, S.B. 2007. PR bunnies caught in the agency ghetto? Gender stereotypes, organizational factors and women's careers in PR agencies. *Journal of Public Relations Research*, 19(3): 229–54.

Gherardi, S. 1994. The gender we think, the gender we do in our everyday organizational lives. *Human Relations*, 47(6): 591–611.

Gherardi, S. 1995. *Gender, Symbolism and Organizational Cultures*. London: SAGE.

Girard, A.E. 2001. The female executive: Experiences of body and self in the corporate culture. Unpublished Psy.D., Widener University, Pennsylvania.

Gottfried, H. and Graham, L. 1993. Constructing difference: The making of gendered subcultures. *Sociology*, 2(4): 611–29.

Graham, M.E. and Hotchkiss, J.L. 2009. A more proactive approach to addressing gender-related emploment disparities in the United States. *Gender in Management*, 24(8): 577.

Hackman, J.R. and Oldham, G. 1980. *Work Redesign*. Reading, MA: Addison-Wesley.

Hammer, M. 1990. Reengineering work: Don't automate, obliterate. *Harvard Business Review*, 68(4): 104–12.

Hammer, M. 1995. *The Re-engineering Revolution*. New York: Harper & Collins.

Hammer, M. and Champy, J. 1993. *Reengineering the Corporation*. New York: HarperCollins.

Hearn, J. and Parkin, P.W. 1983. Gender and organizations: A selective review and a critique of a neglected area. *Organization Studies*, 4(3): 219–42.

Helms Mills, J. 2003. *Making Sense of Organizational Change*. London: Routledge.

Helms Mills, J. 2005. Representations of Diversity and Organizational Change in a North American Utility Company. *Gender, Work and Organization*, 12(3): 242–69.

Helms Mills, J. 2010. Sensemaking. In A.J. Mills, G. Durepos and E. Wiebe (eds), *The SAGE Encyclopedia of Case Studies*, Vol. II: 852–55. Thousand Oaks, CA: SAGE Publications.

Helms Mills, J. and Mills, A.J. 2009. Critical sensemaking and workplace inequities. In M. Ozbilgin (ed.), *Equality, Diversity and Inclusion at Work: Theory and Scholarship*: 171–78. Cheltenham: Edward Elgar.

Helms Mills, J., Dye, K.E. and Mills, A.J. 2008. *Understanding Organizational Change*. Abingdon, UK: Routledge.

Ho, Danny C.K., Duffy, V.G.D. and Shih, H.M. 1999. An empirical analysis of effective TQM implementation in the Hong Kong electronics manufacturing industry. *Human Factors and Ergonomics in Manufacturing*, 9(1): 1–25.

503

Hopfl, H. 1992. Commitments and conflicts: corporate seduction and ambivalence in women managers. *Women in Management Review*, 7(1): 9–17.

Hossain, J.B. and Kusakabe, K. 2005. Sex segregation in construction organizations in Bengladesh and Thailand. *Construction Management and Economics*, 23(1): 609–19.

Jackson, B. 2001. *Management Gurus and Management Fashions*. London: Routledge.

Johnson, P. and Duberley, J. 2000. *Understanding Management Research*. London: SAGE.

Kanter, R.M. 1977. *Men and Women of the Corporation*. New York: Basic Books.

Kaplan, R.S. and Norton, D.P. 1992. The Balanced Scorecard: measures that drive performance. *Harvard Business Review* (January-February): 71–79.

Kieser, A. 1997. Rhetoric and myth in management fashion. *Organization*, 4(1): 49–74.

Kolb, D.M. and Merrill-Sands, D. 1999. Waiting for outcomes: anchoring a dual agenda for change to cultural assumptions. *Women in Management Review*, 14(5): 194–203.

Kotter, J.P. 1996. *Leading change*. Boston, MA: Harvard Business School Press.

Lewis, J. and Morgan, D.H.J. 1994. Gendering organizational change: The case of relate, 1948–90. *Human Relations*, 47(6): 641.

Lian, T.K.F. 2001. Determinants of Total Quality Management (TQM) implementation and impact: A study of selected Malaysian public organizations. Unpublished D.P.A., Unversity of Georgia.

Lieberman, E. 2006. What's fair is fair, or is it? The effects of merit-related managerial behaviors and organizational policies on organizational justice perceptions. City University of New York, New York.

Miller, K. and Clark, D. 2008. "Knife before wife": an exploratory study of gender in the UK medical profession. *Journal of Health Organization and Management*, 22(3): 238–53.

Mills, A.J. 1988. Organization, gender and culture. *Organization Studies*, 9(3): 351–69.

Mills, A.J. 2008a. Getting Critical About Sensemaking. In D. Barry and H. Hansen (eds), *The SAGE Handbook of New Approaches to Organization Studies*: 29–30. London: SAGE.

Mills, A.J. 2008b. Organizational rules. In S.R. Clegg, and J. Barley (eds), *Encyclopedia of Organisation Studies* London: SAGE.

Mills, A.J. and Helms Mills J. 2004. When plausibility fails: towards a critical sensemaking approach to resistance. In R. Thomas, A.J. Mills and J. Helms Mills (eds), *Identity Politics at Work: Resisting Gender and Gendered Resistance*: 141–59. London: Routledge.

Mills, A.J. and Helms Mills, J. 2010. Making sense of gender: self reflections on the creation of plausible accounts. In S. Katila, S. Meriläinen and J. Tienari (eds), *Working for Inclusion: Positive Experiences from Academics Across the World*: 244–73. Cheltenham: Edward Elgar.

Mintzberg, H. 1978. Patterns in strategy formulation. *Management Science*, 14: 934–48.

Morreale, S.A. 2002. Analysis of perceived leader behaviours in law enforcement agencies. Unpublished D.P.A., Nova Southeastern University.

Peters, T. and Waterman, R. 1982. *In Search of Excellence—Lessons from America's Best Run Companies*. New York: Warner Communications.

Piderit, S.K. and Ashford, S.J. 2003. Breaking silence: Tactical choices women managers make in speaking up about gender-equity issues. *Journal of Management Studies*, 40(6): 1477–1502.

Porter, M.E. 1980. *Competitive Strategy*. New York: Free Press.

Prasad, P. 2005. *Crafting Qualitative Research. Working in the Postpositivist Traditions*. Armonk, NY: M. E. Sharpe.

Rindfleish, J., Sheridan, A. and Kjeldal, S.-E. 2009. Creating an "agora" for storytelling as a way of challenging the gendered structures of academia. *Equal Opportunities International*, 28(6): 486–99.

Ryan, M. 1979. *Womanhood in America*. New York: Viewpoints.

Schein, E.H. 1985. *Organizational Culture and Leadership*. San Francisco, CA: Jossey-Bass.

Schein, E.H. 1992. *Organizational Culture and Leadership* (2nd ed.). San Francisco, CA: Jossey-Bass.

Sekerka, L.E., Brumbaugh, A.M., Rosa, J.A. and Cooperrider, D. 2006. Comparing Appreciative Inquiry to a diagnostic technique in organizational change: the moderating effects of gender. *International Journal of Organization Theory and Behavior*, 9(4): 449–89.

Simpson, R. 1998. Organizational restructuring and presenteeism: The impact of long hours on the working lives of managers in the UK. *Management Research News*, 21(2/3): 19–20.

504

Simpson, R. 2000. Gender mix and organizational fit: how gender imbalance at different levels of the organisation impacts on women managers. *Women in Management Review*, 15(1): 5–18.

Singhapakdi, A. and Vitell, S.J., Jr. 1991. Research note: selected factors influencing marketers' deontological norms. *Academy of Marketing Science*, 19(1): 37–42.

Smircich, L. 1983. Concepts of culture and organizational analysis. *Administrative Science Quarterly*, (28): 339–58.

Stelter, N.Z. 2002. Gender differences in leadership: Current social issues and future organizational implications. *Journal of Leadership and Organizational Studies*, 8(4): 88–99.

Strautmanis, J. 2008. Employees' values orientation in the context of corporate social responsibility. *Baltic Journal of Management*, 3(3): 346–58.

Thurlow, A. 2010. Critical Sensemaking. In A.J. Mills, G. Durepos and E. Weibe (eds.), *SAGE Encyclopedia of Case Study Research*, vol. I: 257–60. Thousand Oaks, CA: SAGE.

Unger, R.M. 1987. *Social Theory: Its Situation and Its Task*. Cambridge: Cambridge University Press.

Urwick, L. and Brech, E.F.L. 1944. *The Human Factor in Management 1795–1943*. London: Institute of Labour Management.

Verespej, M.A. 1997. Zero tolerance. *Industry Week*, vol. 246: 24–27.

Watson, D.M. 2003. Cultural dynamics of corporate fraud. *Cross Cultural Management*, 10(1): 40–54.

Weick, K.E. 1979. *The Social Psychology of Organizing* (2nd ed.). Reading, MA: Addison-Wesley.

Weick, K.E. 1985. The significance of corporate culture. In P. Frost, L. Moore, M. Louis, C. Lundberg and J. Martin (eds.), *Organizational Culture*: 381–89. London: SAGE.

Weick, K.E. 1995. *Sensemaking in Organizations*. London: SAGE.

Weick, K.E. 2001. *Making Sense of the Organization*. Oxford: Blackwell.

Weiler, P.A. and Zimmerman, M. 2007. Narrowing the gender gap in healthcare management. *Healthcare Executive*, 22(3): 0–28.

Wilson, E.M. 1998. Gendered career paths. *Personnel Review*, 27(5): 396.

Wilson, F.M. 2003. *Organizational Behaviour and Gender* (2nd ed.). Aldershot: Ashgate.

35

The moral of the story
Ethics, narrative and organizational change

Carl Rhodes

Telling a story is about recounting a series of events that occurred over time. As one of the most basic and common forms of human communication, storytelling gives us the ability to put the past into the present and even to imagine the future. There are many parallels between story-telling organizational change – if organizational change is the process by which organizations work through, adapt to, or manage transitions from one state of affairs to another then it is through stories that such change can be understood, made meaningful and influenced. Change occurs through the passage of time and it is with stories that this change is communicated, debated and discussed. As Weick (1995) explains, stories help people in organizations interpret and make sense of what is going on around them. People construct plausible stories that filter the hectic and at times random experience of organizational change so as to make it more manageable – both personally and organizationally.

The relationship between stories and the events that they describe is not straightforward. At first glance it might seem that stories are merely conduits for communication – a convenient way in which we can talk to each other about the things that have happened to us. But there are always at least two sides to the story – that is, a multitude of different ways that that the same series of events can be recounted. So, for example, two people who work in the same organization and experience the same organizational changes might be expected to tell quite different stories about it. Similarly the stories that those people tell could be expected to different depending on whom they are telling them to – the story of organizational change told to one's friends over dinner would be quite different to the one told to the CEO inadvertently bumped into in the work elevator.

Despite the multitude of possible organizational stories it has also been observed that some organizational stories are more dominant and powerful than others. In one sense this can occur when members of an organization engage in 'collective centring' – that is they participate in a form of shared storytelling that allows them to develop common meanings in terms of what is happening to the organization (Boyce, 1995). In another sense, managers responsible for organizational change can try to impose particular stories on the organization as an attempt to control or even manipulate how people understand the changes afoot (Denning, 2006). Of course one can anticipate that managers would engage in this storytelling in a manner that serves their own interests or the interests they feel they represent.

For organizations stories are powerful tools for change management that can be effective when 'precedent and future-directed stories are shared, revised and interpreted to account for and to affect unfolding organizational changes' (Boje, 1991: 7). When successfully taken up such stories try to engender the support of the members of the organization for change by informing and influencing the meaning that they ascribe to it. For managers stories are a valuable weapon in their change management arsenal. This is especially the case when it comes to managing changes to organizational culture. It is well accepted amongst researchers in organizational storytelling that stories transmit and institutionalize organizational norms and values (Meyer, 1995; Feldman and Skoldberg, 2002). As far as change management is concerned the managerial 'opportunity' that such a realization opens up is that by inculcating new stories into the organization, and by re-narrating an organization's history in particular ways, norms and values can be influenced along managerially sanctioned lines.

This chapter will provide a critical review of the role of storytelling in organizational change, with a specific focus on the meaning of this storytelling for organizational culture and ethics. The chapter will bring together the already well established literature on organizational storytelling (see Czarniawska, 1997, 2004; Gabriel, 2000; Boje, 2001; Rhodes and Brown 2005) and its relation to organizational change (e.g. Feldman, 1990; Skoldberg, 1994; Doolin, 2003; Humphreys and Brown, 2003; Brown et al., 2009) and assess its ethical implications; the latter being an area that has only recently begun to attract attention by researchers (e.g. Humphreys and Brown, 2008; Kornberger and Brown, 2007). The chapter advances the view that storytelling is a 'double-edged sword' as far as ethics is concerned. On the one edge institutionalized storytelling allows organizations to develop shared norms and values that serve to inform a collective organizational ethics. On the other edge the presence of such strongly shared narratives can stymie the types of debate, discussion and deliberation that constitute at 'ethical vitality' (Rhodes et al., 2008) in organizations. It is the tension between these two edges, rather than one dominating the other, that is, it will be argued, central to a healthy climate for ethics in organizations.

Organizational storytelling

In what Boje (1991, 1995) calls the 'storytelling organization' an organizations itself can be understood as the network of stories and story fragments that its members tell each other. Stories allow for the transmission and development of interpretations of what is going on in an organization that can be widely shared amongst those members (Boje, 1991). While each person might tell their own version of a story, collectively they also tend to develop common 'organizational myths' (Gabriel, 1991) – those storylines and plots that are repeated so many times in different contexts that they come to represent the shared meaning of an organization. Dellheim (1986) exemplifies this in his discussion of the organizational culture at British chocolate company Cadbury's. The modern Cadbury's was founded George and Richard Cadbury in the late nineteenth century. As Dellheim reports the Cadbury brothers brought to their business a Quaker ethic that stressed diligence, sobriety, thrift and honesty as a means to pursue wealth in society. The espoused goal of the organization was 'a fair profit for the firm and the trade, and a 'living wage' and security for workers' (p. 12).

The story of Cadbury's foundation was recounted to employees by George Cadbury in terms of the struggle and sacrifice that was required to get the business up and running – a story that embedded within it the values of 'hard work, renunciation and cooperation' (p. 13). It is on the basis of this foundation myth that Cadbury was able, in the early twentieth century, to develop a corporate culture based on the propagation of these values. At least as far as the managers were concerned, the set of values embedded in the foundation story were retained even until after the company's merger with Schweppes in 1969, with the new organization still espousing the importance of 'openness, individualism, consensus, efficiency and participation' (p. 15). Even today, Cadbury's official statement of its values reflects the history of its foundation, with the statement: 'We have always believed that "doing good is good for business". This belief inspired our founders, and is still at the heart of the way we work today. We see it as key to our future success.' Moreover, the web site contains dedicated pages to the heritage and history of the company, again recounting the story of its origin and the legacy of the Quaker values that inform it (Cadbury, 2010).

Cadbury's foundation myth suggests an organization where storytelling is purposefully used by the company's management as a means for directing, or even controlling, the organization's cultural values. Indeed, the use of stories as a means of managing organizational culture is well known. As Schein (2004) argued, the deepest assumptions of an organizations culture are contained within 'various myths of origin and stories of heroic behavior, thus articulating and illustrating some of the overarching values that can serve as a prescription for action in ambiguous situations' (p. 130). Moreover, an organization can purposefully use stories to communicate and institutionalize what it sees as it's 'ideology and basic assumptions' (p. 133).

For managers what is commonly seen as a goal in the management of change is the desire to 'collectively centre' (Boyce, 1995) stories of change so as to construct a singular cultural meanings across the organization. The potency of this idea lies in the view that it is not just that people in organizations tell stories, but that organizations themselves *are* narratives, at least in the sense that their very meaning is embodied in the stories told by them and about them (Skoldberg, 1994). Organizations are advised to deploy storytelling for their own functional purposes; they should 'harness the full power of storytelling by choosing the right narrative pattern for a particular purpose and performing it in the right way to achieve organizational effectiveness' (Denning, 2006: 48). This suggests that changing the stories people tell about their organizations is the means through which the deep structures that inform the meaning and practice of an organization can also be changed.

While managers might deliberately tell particular stories as a means to influence, change and direct organizations and their cultures, the idea that they might be entirely successful at such an endeavour is naïve because it significantly over-estimates the power of the organizationally sanctioned storyteller. A more complex perspective on these matters is presented by Boje (1994, 1995) who uses a Hollywood play (*Tamara*) as a means through which to theorize 'collective storytelling' (1994: 435). Rather than being on single stage where audience members all see the same action and witness all parts of the play, Tamara is performed on multiple stages each housed in a different room with the drama in each of the rooms occurring simultaneously. It is not possible for each member of the audience to see everything that is going on. Instead, they move from room to room, often following particular characters, and are only ever able to see a portion of the total story. The result is that while all people in the audience have been to see the same play, what each one has experienced is quite different.

Boje uses *Tamara* as a 'metaphor for a storytelling organization' (1995: 999) that moves away from the idea that stories can be controlled for the purpose of achieving managerial imperatives, and towards the possibilities for 'the plurivocal interpretation of organizational stories in a distributed and historically contextualized meaning network' (p. 1000). The storytelling organization, like *Tamara*, consists of multiple simultaneously occurring stories. Despite managerial attempts to control all of this storytelling through potent managerial myths, the storytelling organization exists as 'a pluralistic construction of a multiplicity of stories, storytellers and story performance events that are [...] realized differently depending on the stories in which one is participating' (p. 1000). The storytelling organization is one where there are many different stories at play, in dialogue with one another as well as in contest with one another.

With Boje's storytelling organization we get both a democratization and a politicization of organizational storytelling. It is democratic in that the different stories encountered, heard and told by different people are accounted for in terms of how the tissue of text and talk that makes up an organization is tenuously held together. It is political in that the acknowledgement of the everyday stories of people at work serves as a counter balance to the powerful storytelling practices that managers and organizations can partake in, as well as understanding these different stories as being located in a struggle over meaning. With the storytelling organization, organizationally sanctioned stories are conceived of as managerial monologues that attempt to drown out other values and interpretations, while almost inevitably failing to do so completely. Part of the reason for this is, as Feldman (1990) has noted, that storytelling in organizations is a creative act rather than one of passively describing what is going on.

In his study of organizational change at an electronics company Feldman (1990) found that the main stories told by employees concerned the fear of change, with the 'scapegoat' being the most dominant character in the story. The implication of this is that 'stories, despite the fact that they are a form of cultural change, can have a negative influence on the process of organizational change' (p. 809) – at least negative from the point of view of those implementing the change. This also suggests that stories perform rather than describe organizational change, but this performance can be different for different people, places and times. According to Doolin (2003) an 'organization [is] a multi-discursive set of strategic narratives' that structures the material and social relations that occur within it (p. 764). It is this structuring or ordering of the realities of organizational change that is a potent feature of narrative – one that attempts to finalize the meaning of what change means in political competition with alternative narratives.

Similar insights into organizational change and storytelling have been developed by Barry and Elmes' (1997) in their narrative approach to organizational strategy. They argue that rather than being a scientific or rational activity, strategy development is better understood as being located 'somewhere between theatrical dream, the historical novel, futurist fantasy, and autobiography' (p. 432). What gives strategy its narrative quality is that it seeks to emplot an organization's history from the past into the future, while defining roles and character-types to the different people (or groups of people) involved in the organization. For Barry and Elmes the narrative 'devices' of materiality, voice, perspective, ordering, setting and readership targeting are central to strategy development.

In analyzing dominant approaches to strategy, Barry and Elmes enumerate and describe four different ' genres' of strategy. These are:

EPIC: in which strategy is portrayed as an organization's heroic journey of 'navigating toward opportunities and away from threats' (p. 440)

TECHNOFUTURIST: in which strategy involves developing a specific vision of what the future will look like, as if a science fiction

PURIST: in which where organizations try to emulate archetypes of strategy

POLYPHONIC: in which strategy is developed by both listening to many different points of view and placing them in dialogue with each other.

It is with the polyphonic genre of strategy development that we can see clear alignments with Boje's 'pluri-vocal' storytelling organization. The epic, technofuturist and purist forms of strategy development, while being different from each other, all share the same tendency to see an organization as being under the complete control of management, such that the views, voices and stories of others are suppressed or ignored. While less political than Boje's storytelling organization, what we get with polyphonic strategy is again an attempt to pluralize organizational action, as well as to understand it democratically.

Ethics and stories

Organizational change is 'a multi-storied process of competing accounts' each trying to gain power and influence over the meaning of events (Brown et al., 2009: 326). These different accounts, however, are not just about a political struggle between different people's subjective appreciation of their own organizational experience. When we consider the meaning of the stories told in organizations they embody within them the varied normative ethical discourses that circulate through the organization (Randels, 1998; de Graaf, 2001) as they are developed and articulated in relation to different people's lived experience of the organization and of organizational change (Martin et al., 1983; Ellis and Flaherty, 1992; Clegg et al., 2007a). In this sense, storytelling can be seen as being directly relates to ethics:

> Stories are especially important for ethicists: they contain values (ideas about good and bad, right and wrong); they are about good and evil. Within stories, the 'is' and 'ought' are closely connected. Even if they seem to give simple factual descriptions, an enormous implicit normative power lies within narratives […] the events that are actually recorded in the narrative appear 'real' precisely insofar as they belong to an order of moral existence, just as they derive their meaning from their placement in this order.
>
> (de Graaf, 2006: 254)

The point is that telling stories is not just about communicating what has happened, but it is also about moral evaluation of whether what happened is good or bad. So, when people in organizations tell stories, and when organizations seek to control organizational storytelling, then there are serious ethical implications. It is precisely these implications that are elaborated in the to the narrative theory of Paul Ricoeur (1984), and although Ricoeur's theory is about narrative in general it can be used to inform how we understand organizational storytelling (see Lamsa and Sintonen, 2006; Rhodes et al., 2010).

For Ricoeur there are three operations that narrative uses to develop representations of the world and people's actions within it. He names these operations *prefiguration, configuration* and *refiguration*. These operations are not merely a means to recreate the past in a story – as he points out they work to weave the remembrance of the past with the creativity of storytelling in a manner that helps people make sense of their lived experience (Ricoeur, 1980). Each of these operations work in a 'circle of narrative' that weaves the plot of the story together. The first operation, *prefiguration*, is about how narrative is accepted as being somehow in parallel with the events that it is representing (Ellos, 1994). When something happens to us we already know that we are able to tell a story about it – indeed we are able to tell and listen to stories meaningfully because it is already culturally accepted that it is by telling stories that we can reproduce that experience for others (Simms, 2003). We know ahead of telling any particular story that a story must relate the what, why, who and when of what happened as they are connected across time (Ellos, 1994). The point here is that 'life prefigures narrative' in that we understand life in general through the stories we have heard about it; moreover, because we have heard those stories we are able to narrate our own experiences (Wood, 1991). Similarly we can surmise that organizational change is also prefigured by narrative, in that before actually encountering any particular change we already have a set of culturally available genres and plots we can apply to it – for example seeing the change as being a tragedy, an adventure or a satire (Skoldberg, 1994).

While any of our lived experiences might be prefigured in narrative, it is with Ricoeur's second narrative operation, *configuration*, that particular stories are put together. Configuration is achieved by using a plot to relate events to one another over time (Ricoeur, 1993) – the plot being, in Ricoeur's words, 'the intelligible whole that governs the succession of events in any story' (Ricoeur, 1980: 171). It is this configuration, this emplotment of experience, that marks the difference between narrative and other forms of discourse. Moreover, the plots we use to narrate our experience are not endemic to those experiences, but are brought to it through the creative act of storytelling – a form of creativity already noted in organizational change settings (Feldman, 1990). With configuration we do not simply have a chronology of events, but rather an emplotted story that makes those events meaningful as it 'resignifies the world' (Ricoeur, 1980: 81). In summary then as we experience organizational change, the meaning of that change is already prefigured in the various stories we already know and with the plots that we are already familiar (see Skoldberg, 1994). It is from there that we can configure a particular story with which to understand a particular experience. Think of two people being retrenched from their jobs as part of an organizational change program. While one person might configure their story as a tragedy befalling the innocent, another might configure it as an opportunity in disguise. The difference, at least in part, is not just the events that are occurring, but the type of plot each person uses to make sense of it, as well as their familiarity with that plot prior to their actual experience of the change.

It is with the third narrative operation, *refiguration*, that Ricoeur connects narrative with ethics. With refiguration Ricoeur moves from a concern with the telling of stories to a concern with receiving them. Refiguration involves 'the role of the interpretive reader' (Ellos, 1994: 102) in assessing and applying the 'point' of the story (Simms, 2003) and potentially using it to configure their own experiences. Refiguration registers the way that people are affected by stories, leading them to revaluate their own experience as well as their sense of who they are. The implication of this is that there is 'no ethically neutral narrative' (Ricoeur, 1992: 115) because the reception and interpretation of a story necessarily involves making ethical evaluations of the different characters involved and their actions in terms of 'estimations, evaluation, and judgments of approval and condemnation' (ibid.). Ethics are embedded in narrative because 'in the exchange of experiences which the narrative performs, actions are always subject to approval or disapproval and agents to praise or blame' (1993: 164). Thus in refiguring stories – in receiving them – we are also receiving a model for ethical judgment, a model which is sometimes referred to as the 'moral of the story'. Storytelling thus arises from a combination of the empirical details of human experience, the cultural resources available to us to help make sense of them, and the imagination we bring to that experience so as to make ethical sense of both what we do and what others do to us (Ellos, 1994). When people tell stories, they are not just recounting what happened, but are also reformulating the ethical meaning of what happened and passing that on to others such that stories might perform 'functions of discovery and transformation' (Ricoeur, 1992: 164).

Organizational change and ethics

Storytelling in organizations is central to the development of organizational values, the management of cultural and strategic change in organizations. Despite this focus on 'values' an explicit concern with ethics as it relates to change has not received a great deal of attention in the literature on organizational storytelling. This is so despite it being the case that the stories told in organizations are clearly not ethically neutral – stories reflect the ethical norms of the organization (Randels, 1998; de Graaf, 2001) that directly inform informs practice (Ellis and Flaherty, 1992; Clegg et al., 2007a). As Randels argues, organizational stories are not just descriptive, but contain normative implications that 'construe how we do, can, or should view the world, and how business people and corporations act, can act, and should act (or, who or what they should be)' (Randels, 1998: 1300). Indeed, as we have seen from the discussion above, storytelling in organizations can always be expected to embody the various ethical positions people have in relation to organizational change – positions that may or may not reflect a strongly configured managerial ethic. An example of this can be seen in Humphreys and Brown's (2003) study of the storytelling surrounding a merger in the UK education sector. In that study what was found was that while the stories told related to established literary genres and plotlines, the senior managers told stories of epic change while the non-managerial groups from each of the merged organizations narrated their experiences of the change as tragedies.

As we discussed earlier, there is a tendency for organizations to develop (or at least attempt to impose) singular monologues that all members of an organization might use to interpret organizational changes. In some cases this is directly seen as a matter of ethics. Fritz et al. (1999) argue that it is an organizations moral responsibility to provide its members with an overarching model of organizational ethics – a 'strong ethical [...] narrative' that should explicitly seek to increase 'its moral force relative to the cosmopolitan ethics and relative to competing individual moral stories' (p. 290). Corporate visions, as mechanisms for organizational change, for example, have been understood as being especially persuasive on account of their narrative quality and its associated 'ethical appeal' (James, 1994). Cast in Ricoeur's terms this means that the organization is attempting to configure the meaning of organizational change in a manner that establishes particular ethical positions – for example a position that provides legitimacy for the change (Rhodes, 1997). The managerial use of storytelling is one that tries to pre-empt the way that members of the organizations refigure their own experience in response to the story – an attempt to control the circle of narrative that works its way through prefiguration, configuration and refiguration so that the meaning and ethical value of organizational change is controlled by the organization itself rather than creatively interpreted by its members. The assumed managerial imperative is that 'if we are to increase awareness of ethics in organizations and commitment to organizations, some ethical story telling by managers, conversation among managers, and a clear sense of organizational narrative is necessary' (Fritz et al., 1999: 297). The intention of such storytelling is that it is received by the members of the organizations so as to refigure their understanding of the change, and in turn to interpret/narrate their own experiences using the organizational sanctioned plot and ethical position. It is through such a narrative process that Kornberger and Brown (2007) regard ethics as a discursive 'resource' which organization can use to narrate their own sense of identity and legitimacy. Such ethical narrative, they argue, serves to legitimize particular organizational change practices. In this way ethics and power become mutually implicated through narrative – the struggle over narrative is a struggle over the power to define the ethical meaning of organizational change, with each narrative embodying particular ways of justifying organizational actions and norms. Such narratives provide a sense of constancy and consensus over how people are expected to behave. As Kornberger and Brown (2007) sum up: 'in an organization, notions of ethics can be a discursive resource bound up in relations power, and how dominant discursive practices can work to legitimate certain decisions and actions rather than others' (p. 514) – or, in Ricoeur's terms to refigure the meaning of other people's experience along the lines of managerial imprimatur. These 'dominant discursive practices' thus seek to control the circle of narrative – to close the loop so that everyone in the organization is reading from the same story book as configured be a managerial elite. In such cases the intention would be that while many different people in an organization would be telling their own stories, the moral of each of these stories would be the same, as configured organizationally and collectively centered.

The issue of the ethical refiguration of experience through narrative that Ricoeur has alerted us to talks directly to the concerns, as discussed earlier, that organizational theorists have raised in terms of storytelling in organizations. What is at stake is the assumed managerial prerogative, or more precisely managerial desire, to impose a singular monological plot that seeks to define the meaning of organizational change. As Humphreys and Brown (2002) exemplified in their study of the merger of an educational organization mentioned earlier, faced with ambiguity senior managers can exert considerable effort to author monological and hegemonic narratives. Moreover, 'given their privileged hierarchical position, senior managers are often particularly articulate and powerful contributors to [organizational] stories, and seek to mould and manip-ulate organizational discourse for their own purposes' (p. 438). The conflict that arises, however, is that 'organizations are not discursively monolithic, but pluralistic and polyphonic, involving multiple dialogical practices that occur simultaneously and sequentially' (p. 422) characterizing what was described by Boje (1991) as the 'storytelling organization'. Within the storytelling organization, however, not all stories are equal and, moreover, there can be expected to be a conflict over the meaning of the organization's story. On the one hand there are those dominant, commonly managerial, stories that 'aim at centralization and the production of shared meaning used by dominant social groups to impose their own monological and unitary perceptions of truth' and on the other hand there are alternative, resistant, and/or idiosyncratic stories that fly in the face of the idea that an organization, or organizational change, can or should only be narrated and understood in one way (Rhodes, 2000: 29). The conflict is not at the level of what did or didn't happen, but over the meaning and ethics of the change as it can be variously configured into a narrative.

The conflict over organizational narrative is a conflict over ethics – all least insofar as ethics is understood as the system of values and norms that are used to evaluate whether actions and people are to be judged in terms of relative goodness. This is not the ethics of a philosophical system providing a justified model or argument for how one ought to act or be, but an 'ethics as practice' that concerns the moralities built into people's talk and action (Clegg et al., 2007b). For the CEO downsizing might be an inevitable organizational change that is required for the organization's survival. For the retrenched shop floor worker it might be about organizational greed and the desire for profit being more important to the organization than the welfare of the workers. These two ways of configuring the story not only reflect different ethics, but are also unequal in power, with the ethic of the managerial narrative much more likely to hold sway over the organization's fate. As Deetz (1994) suggests 'power is present in the attempt to hold one sign value or articulation as preferable over another. Domination occurs when one articulation is systematically, but arbitrarily, privileged through practices of suppressing alternatives' (p. 219). If, in the telling of an organizational change story, such domination were to be achieved there would only be one configuration of the organizational story, and that configuration would reconfigure the ethical meaning of the change for all involved. The managerial ethics would be the ethics of everyone in the organization. Moreover, this is precisely what organizations are counselled to try to achieve when told they should unreflexively 'harness the power' of storytelling in organizational change (Denning, 2006).

In thinking through the relationship between storytelling, ethics and organizational change we can consider, as discussed above, that storytelling is a political activity involving a struggle of competing meanings and values, as garnered from different perspectives and experiences. When organizations seek to manage change through the imposition of a monological story that seeks to define the meaning of change once and for all what we have is not so much a 'shared culture' but rather a suppression of alternatives – as Barry and Elmes (1997) would have it a suppression of 'polyphony'. But when storytelling is used in this way, despite the many different 'antenarratives' (Boje, 2001) and stories told about change, the managerial desire is to account for these through one overarching story within which the change can make sense. The result is that while a story can be told in many different ways and with different effects in organizations there is also considerable pressure for the storytelling to be dominated centrally and monologically. In opposition to such monologue, we can consider the meaning of the polyphonic organization (Hazen, 1993; Barry and Elmes, 1997). In one sense polyphony can be cast not so much as a problem to be eradicated by management, but more as an organizational opportunity. Here polyphony is considered to be central to organizational change as organizations negotiate between competing stories in order to drive new future direction. As Kornberger et al. (2006) surmise 'new developments derive from the contest between an old entrenched vocabulary and a new, as yet half-formed, one' (p. 28). Polyphony is thought of as a 'trigger' for creativity, innovation and adaptability. So, while such a view agrees that polyphonic organizations contain with them multiple discourses' (Hazen, 1993), it retains a focus on how such discourses should be best managed in order to achieve pre-existing managerial goals.

A monological account of ethics could only be achieved by reaching a sense of 'narrative closure' – that is the 'feeling of finality that is generated when all the questions saliently posed by the narrative are answered' (Carroll, 2007: 1). With such closure Ricoeur's circle of narrative becomes a closed loop for all members of the organization, such that there is one dominant form of emplotment that comes to be repeated again and again across the organization. It is at this point that we can characterize storytelling as a 'double edged sword' as far as ethics is concerned. On the one edge dominant stories facilitate the control over organizational change and offer a shared sense of ethics that can unite the organization; on the other edge such stories limit the possibilities of the different ethical meaning of the change for different people or from alternative perspectives. The two edges of this sword echo what Boyce (1996) identified as the two dominant perspectives on research on organizational story and storytelling – one being the perspective of stories as a vehicle for social control, and the other being stories as an opportunity for participation and emancipation. As Kupers (2005, p. 130, following Boje, 1995) sums up:

> On the one hand storytelling can be oppressive by subordinating employees and adapt all to one 'grand narrative' or 'grand story'. On the other side narrative practices in organization can be creatively liberating, by showing members that there is always a multiplicity of stories, storytellers, and story performance events

There is a danger here that the 'success' of managerial storytelling, that is the achievement of social control, might also serve constrain the forms of openness and questioning that have been argued to be the condition of ethical deliberation (Clegg et al., 2007b). In this sense, ethics is not just about the shared ethos of the members of an organization, but is also about being open to the 'question of ethics' (Scott, 1990) that demands that difficulties, deliberations and dilemmas be engaged with ahead of having the pre-set norms through which to resolve them (Roberts, 2003; Clegg and Rhodes, 2006). If ethics is seen in this way, then the achievement of a managerial monologue that configures meaning is precisely the opposite of what is required for ethical deliberation.

A central implication of what has been discussed in this chapter for organizational change is that when change is managed in such a way so as to attempt to control its meaning through the promulgation of dominant narratives, then the refiguration of meaning that risks becoming closed to ethical deliberation and questioning. The closure enforced by such dominant narratives means that the challenges and difficulties of the experience of organizational change are no longer open to ethical scrutiny. Moreover, if we accept that ethics is a matter of ongoing questioning of the structure of meaning that shape and rule our lives (Scott, 1990) then the successful imposition of dominant organizational narratives works against the cultivation of an 'ethical vitality' in organizations (Rhodes et al., 2008). This idea of 'ethical vitality' suggests that 'the presence of multiple ethical discourses in organizations might actually make people in organizations more, rather than less, ethically responsible' (p. 1052). This is so because the lack of narrative closure that such multiple discourses entail ensures that issues are left open to debate. Those in an organization might then be able to discuss and deliberate over their ethical choices rather than being constrained by a dominantly configured narrative imposed from above. In this sense, ethics is achieved not through the managerial control of meaning, but by moving the organization's discursive practice 'away from one that was directed by a monological organizational discourse to one far more plural and polyphonic' (p. 1054). Seen this way, the relationship between organizational change, storytelling and ethics is such that 'when stories of organizational change become dominated by organizationally legitimated plot, the narrative serves to close down the openness required by ethics' (Rhodes et al., 2009: 548).

Concluding comments

This chapter has sought to provide a selective review on the literature on organizational storytelling as it relates to organizational change. The review has focused specifically on considering the implications of this for ethics in organizations. As we have seen storytelling is a discursive practice that is central to organizational change – not just as a mechanism through which to communicate change, but a way of constructing the meaning of that change for members of the organization. On account of this those people charged with the management of organizations can use storytelling as a means to assist with the management and acceptance of change. In looking to the ethical implications of change and storytelling, we turned to Paul Ricoeur's understanding of the relationship between ethics and narrative, suggesting that all narratives contain within them an ethics that suggest how the events and people we experience might be judged as being good or bad. On this basis the stories told by managers about organizational change are also ethical – their purpose is not just to communicate what is going on, but also to inculcate particular judgments about the legitimacy of the change efforts. While such moves might be seen as valuable exercises in the fostering of a shared organizational ethic, what we have also seen is that the strong monologues perpetuated by managers also work to squeeze out or marginalize alternative explanations, meanings and ethics. The irony of this is that the attempt to develop an ethic of organizational change can actually stymie the debate and contestation required for an organization to achieve a sense of ethical vitality – that is the ability to deliberate over its ethical choices and to engage in an ethical self-critique.

We have depicted those organizational practices that seek to manage organizational change through stories as being a double edged sword. Such stories seek to create a common ethos through which people will make sense of organizational change. This might be something to commend ethically. As Fritz et al. (1999, p. 290) advise:

> An ethical narrative or history of an organization is essential in today's business because individuals need a clear articulation of group and corporate principles or organizational

identity. Such statements of ethical principles become a basis for right and wrong, a prioritizing criterion.

While such storytelling might enable organizations exert control over their ethics, at least in terms of people's behaviour as judged by organizationally sanctioned ethical norms, as we have been arguing there are other ethical implications as well. If all people in an organization where to abide by the same sense of ethics, there would be little need for ethical deliberation – the organizationally prescribed narrative would already have within it all of the answers. The upshot of this is that in the name of ethics, ethical reflection and moral responsibility are no longer required to be exercised in situ (Rhodes and Pullen, 2009) and 'ethical vitality' (Rhodes et al., 2008) is diminished because ethics is always prefigured and predecided by the organization. A strong organizational narrative about change might then constrain the ethical questioning and openness that are a necessary part of ethical deliberation – the reaching of a cross-roads where one must decide what to do, and take responsibility for it.

References

Barry, D. and Elmes, M. (1997) Strategy Retold: Towards a Narrative View of Strategic Discourse, *Academy of Management Review*, 22: 429–52.

Boje, D.M. (1991) Consulting and Change in the Storytelling Organization, *Journal of Organizational Change Management*, 4(3): 7–17.

Boje, D.M. (1995) Stories of The Storytelling Organization: A Postmodern Analysis of Disney as 'Tamara-Land'. *Academy of Management Journal*, 38: 997–1035.

Boje, D.M. (2001) *Narrative Methods for Organizational and Communication Research*, London: SAGE.

Boyce, M. (1995) Collective Centering and Collective Sense-Making in the Stories and Storytelling of One Organization, *Organization Studies*. 16(1): 107–37.

Boyce, M. (1996) Organizational Story and Storytelling: A Critical Review, *Journal of Organizational Change Management*, 9(5): 5–26.

Brown, A.D., Gabriel, Y. and Gherardi, S (2009) Storytelling and Change: An Unfolding Story, *Organization*, 16(3): 323–33.

Cadbury (2010) Our Culture, *Cadbury Web site*, www.cadbury.com/ (visited 14 May 2010).

Carroll, N. (2007) Narrative Closure, *Philosophical Studies*, 135(1): 1–15.

Clegg, S.R. and Rhodes, C. (2006) *Management Ethics-Contemporary Contexts*, London: Routledge.

Clegg, S.R., Kornberger, M. and Rhodes, C. (2007a) Business Ethics as Practice, *British Journal of Management*, 18 (2): 107–22.

Clegg, S.R., Kornberger, M. and Rhodes, C. (2007b) Organizational Ethics, Decision Making and Undecidability, *The Sociological Review*, 55(2): 393–409.

Czarniawska, B. (1997) *Narrating the Organization: Dramas of Institutional Identity*. Chicago: University of Chicago Press.

Czarniawska, B. (2004) *Narratives in Social Science Research*, London: SAGE.

de Graaf, G. (2001) Discourse Theory and Business Ethics, *Journal of Business Ethics*, 31: 299–319.

de Graaf, G. (2006) Discourse and Descriptive Business Ethics, *Business Ethics: A European Review*, 15(3): 246–58.

Deetz, S. (1994) Representational Practices and the Political Analysis of Corporations: Building a Communication Perspective in Organization Studies, In B. Kovacic (ed.) *New Approaches to Organizational Communication*, pp. 209–42. New York: State University of New York Press.

Dellheim, C. (1986) Business in Time: The Historian and Corporate Culture, *The Public Historian*, 8(2): 9–22.

Denning, S. (2006) Effective Storytelling: Strategic Business Narrative Techniques, *Strategy and Leadership*, 34(1): 42–48.

Doolin, B. (2003) Narratives of Change: Discourse, Technology and Organization, *Organization*, 10(4): 751–70.

Ellis, C. and Flaherty, F. (eds) (1992) *Investigating Subjectivity: Research on Lived Experience*, London: SAGE.

Ellos W.J. (1994) *Narrative Ethics*. Aldershot: Avebury.

Feldman, M.S. and Skoldberg, K. (2002) Stories and The Rhetoric of Contrariety: Subtexts of Organizing (Change), *Culture and Organization*, 8: 274–92.

Feldman, S.P. (1990) Stories as Cultural Creativity: On the Relationship Between Symbolism and Politics in Organizational Change, *Journal of Applied Communication Research*, 13: 45–58.

Fritz, J.M.H., Arnett, R.C. and Conkell, M. (1999) Organizational Ethical Standards and Organizational Commitment, *Journal of Business Ethics*, 20: 289–99.

Gabriel, Y. (1991) Turning Facts into Stories and Stories into Facts: A Hermeneutic Exploration of Organizational Folklore, *Human Relations*, 44(8): 857–75.

Gabriel, Y. (2000) *Storytelling in Organizations: Fact, Fictions and Fantasies*, Oxford: Oxford University Press.

Hazen, M.A. (1993) Towards Polyphonic Organization, *Journal of Organizational Change Management*, 6(5): 15–26.

Humphreys, M. and Brown, A. (2002) Narratives of Organizational Identity and Identification: a Case Study of Hegemony and Resistance, *Organization Studies*, 23, 421–47.

Humphreys, M. and Brown, A. (2003) Epic and Tragic Tales: Making Sense of Change, *Journal of Applied Behavioral Science*, 39(2): 211–144.

Humphreys, M. and Brown, A. (2008) An Analysis of Corporate Social Responsibility at Credit Line: A Narrative Approach, *Journal of Business Ethics*, 80(3): 403–18.

James, B. (1994) Narrative and Organizational Control: Corporate Visionaries, Ethics And Power, *The International Journal of Human Resource Management*, 5(4): 927–51.

Kornberger, M. and Brown, A. (2007) 'Ethics' as Discursive Resource for Identity Work, *Human Relations*, 60(3): 497–518.

Kornberger, M., Clegg, S.R. and Carter, C. (2006) Rethinking The Polyphonic Organization: Managing as Discursive Practice, *Scandinavian Journal of Management*, 22: 3–30.

Kupers, W. (1995) Phenomenology of Embodied Implicit and Narrative Knowing, *Journal of Knowledge Management*, 9(6): 114–33.

Kupers, W. (2005) Phenomenology of Embodied, Implicit and Narrative Knowing, *Journal of Knowledge Management*, 9(6): 114–133.

Lamsa, A.-M. and Sintonen, T. (2006) A Narrative Approach for Organizational Learning in a Diverse Organisation, *Journal of Workplace Learning*, 18(2): 106–20.

Martin, J., Feldman, M., Hatch, M.-J. and Sitkin, S. (1983) The Uniqueness Paradox in Organizational Stories, *Administrative Science Quarterly*, 38: 438–53.

Meyer, J.C. (1995) Tell Me a Story: Eliciting Organizational Values from Narratives, *Communication Quarterly*, 43: 210–24.

Randels, G.D. (1998) The Contingency of Business: Narrative, Metaphor and Ethics, *Journal of Business Ethics*, 17(12): 1288–1310.

Rhodes, C. (1997) The Legitimation of Learning in Organization Change, *Journal of Organization Change Management*, 10(1): 10–20.

Rhodes, C. (2000) Reading and Writing Organizational Lives, *Organization*, 7(1): 7–29.

Rhodes, C. and Brown, A (2005) Narrative, Organizations and Research, *International Journal of Management Reviews*, 7(3): 167–88.

Rhodes, C. and Pullen, A. (2009) Organizational Moral Responsibility, in S.R. Clegg and C. Cooper (eds) *The SAGE Handbook of Organizational Behaviour: Macro Approaches*, pp. 340–55. London: SAGE.

Rhodes, C., Clegg, S.R. and Anandakumar, A. (2008) Ethical Vitality: Identity, Responsibility and Change in an Australian Hospital, *International Journal of Public Administration*. 31(9): 1037–57.

Rhodes, C., Pullen, A. and Clegg, S.R. (2010) ' "If I Should Fall From Grace…": Stories of Change and Organizational Ethics', *Journal of Business Ethics*, 91(4): 535–51.

Ricoeur, P. (1980) Narrative Time, *Critical Inquiry*, 7(1): 169–90.

517

Ricoeur, P. (1984) *Time and Narrative Vol. 1*, trans. K. McLaughlin, and D. Pellauer Chicago: University of Chicago Press.

Ricoeur, P. (1992) *Oneself as Another*, trans. K. Blamey, Chicago: University of Chicago Press.

Roberts, J. (2003) The Manufacture of Corporate Social Responsibility: Constructing Corporate Sensibility, *Organization*, 10(2): 249–65.

Schein, E. (2004) *Organizational Culture and Leadership*, 3rd edn, San Francisco, CA: Jossey-Bass.

Scott, C.E. (1990) *The Question of Ethics: Nietzsche, Foucault, Heidegger*, Bloomington, IN: Indiana University Press.

Simms, K. (2003) *Paul Ricoeur*, London: Routledge.

Skoldberg, K. (1994) Tales of Change: Public Administration, Reform and Narrative Mode, *Organization Science*, 5: 219–38.

Weick, K. (1995) *Sensemaking in Organizations*, Thousand Oaks, CA: SAGE.

Wood, D. (1991) Interpreting Narrrative, in D.C. Wood (ed.) *On Paul Ricoeur: Narrative and Interpretation*, pp. 1–1. London: London: Routledge.

Part 6

The future

Introduction

David M. Boje

In Chapter 36, Philip Hancock addresses organizational change, and its management, though 'the lens' of organizational aesthetics. Through the aesthetics lens, he looks at instrumental (organization environments can be managed), creative (managing change to standards of artistic practice), and radical approaches to change (an ontological understanding of an aesthetic way of Being). Perhaps the call for change management to be about ontic concerns is one of the major themes of this Routledge book.

Suzanne Benn and Kate Kearins, in Chapter 37, take sustainability seriously. Sustainability is an ontological process, a movement, and an epistemological set of socially constructed concepts. Following Banerjee, Benn and Kearins say the sustainability discourse is disengaged from its material context, and deployed by many change agents and institutions to commit postcolonizing social and racial exploitation. Sustainability life-cycle narrative orders, for example, are at odds with business life cycle narrative order. The life-cycle (ante) narratives proclaim definite progress stages, take a blind eye to issues of non-linear complexity and power/politics. Sustainability discourse is at odds with the material-ontological achievements. The systems of the ecological world are more complex and full of more species than homo sapiens. Therefore the dialogical stakeholder models, even those across many transorganization global networks, seem to make sustainability development and sustainable change management, more social constructionist oxymoronic terms.

In Chapter 38, Theodore Taptiklis proposes we rethink the change project. Like many authors in this book, he seeks an alternative to the change management of managerialism. He suggest that a way forward is organizing change through practical trust. He follows Bakhtin in seeking an approach that is more dialogical, more polyphonic. For Taptiklis, this means focusing on the utterance, on what Bakthin calls the 'answerable word'. He argues that a change practice of practical trust attuned to the real-world-materiality would be a step forward for change management.

Scott Taylor and Emma Bell, in Chapter 39, relate the recent spirituality at work movement to more traditional approaches to organization change. This chapter invokes Max Weber's prophecy about disenchantment. Taylor and Bell trace a new thread in the spirituality movement, a strand of enchantment that goes all the way back to Max Weber. Rational capitalism, says Weber, is driven by instrumental accumulation, and now we have hyper-consumption in disenchanted late-madness-capitalism. Sociologist George Ritzer, in particular, picks up on Weber's disenchantment prophecy, showing how late modern capitalism in such cathedrals of consumption as Disney, McDonald's and Las Vegas have become models for the shopping mall, and been folded into Diseneyfied, McDonaldized, mall-ification of the Mc-university. The main point that Scott and Bell make is that the spirituality at work movement risks enacting a rather disenchanted sort of spirituality that fulfils Weber's prophecy of disenchanting priests, now called spiritual change agents. Can the spirituality at work movement be an organization practice that re-enchants the work place, or at least challenge all the organization disenchantment born of all that TQM, Reengineering rationalistic-calculable-managerialist-efficiency? From Weber, by way of Geertz, we learn that spiritual-religious belief habits become habits of social action, not just social constructions, but embodied into the material processes of everyday life. Taylor and Bell trace the spirituality at work movement to the change approaches rooted in the institutional change, organization culture, and the human relations movements. Spirituality at work movement is caught up in the debates between the institutional-functionalist and the social-constructivist-interpretivists ways of looking at culture and human relations. Most organizations are quite cultish, cultivating strong commitment and control through acts of salvation through managerialist worship, to get that promise of instrumental rewards in late-madness-capitalism.

In the final chapter of Part 6, and the final chapter of the book, David Boje, Ivy DuRant, Krisha Coppedge, Ted Chambers and Marilu Marcillo-Gomez take a similar approach to that of like Hancock in Chapter 36 in that they also favor an ontological approach. Like Benn and Kearins they antenarrate a future that is about ecological sustainability and ontic ties to nature. Like Taylor and Bell, the Boje crew wants to re-enchant organization change with a new physics of change that has living story intra-play with natured and communal existence. They also share Taptiklis' concerns about managerialism. So perhaps its fitting that this be the closing chapter, one that asks for a new adventure in change management that is more enchanting and more about ontology. Their chapter is rooted in the actor-network-theory of Bruno Latour who is definitely against the kinds of social constructionism that is overly psychologized, and does not address the sociology of material conditions. For the Boje crew the storytelling and sensemaking approaches in OD and managing change, as well as action research, need to move away from an epistemological bias, and look to a social material approach to ontology, one where changes in habits of actions and not just habits of habits or storytelling is the focus. Their call is for change approach this is posthumanist, rooted not just in what human stakeholders want, but in the material actants (animals, rocks, trees, mountains), it is all about rediscovering enchantment. They combine Latour's critique of social construction with Karen Barad's new quantum physics, which looks at the intra-play of discourse with materiality. An ontology-focused change management would take ethical answerability for the complicity of change discourse and practice in changing the material condition of not just humanity in its sensemaking, but the material world, the natured world that is ontic in its depths of enchantment. In the end, change management is about the relation of capitalism to nature, and the role choices are to be handmaiden or to be posthumanist.

36

Organizational change
The aesthetic dimension

Philip Hancock

Introduction

The importance of being able to successfully manage organizational change in order to ensure not only competiveness, but often straightforward viability, has become something of an unquestioned orthodoxy (Sturdy and Grey, 2003). Whereas change was once viewed, albeit perhaps somewhat naively, as an aberration, a deviation from a settled, stable state, it is now widely believed, as Kurt Lewin noted back in 1947, that change is an ever present condition and that all we experience are 'differences in the amount and type of change' (Lewin, 1947: 13). Often this belief is couched in terms of a necessity derived from the competitive impact of a globalizing economy, accelerating technological innovations, or the emergence of an increasingly discerning and consumer literate global populous; one always on the look out for innovative products and services. More sophisticatedly, perhaps, others such as Tsoukas and Chia (2002) suggest that we need to understand change as an inevitable characteristic of organizations; one grounded in the processural nature of the lives of their human inhabitants. Whatever one considers the underpinning of our contemporary fixation with change to be, what is clear, however, is that it now clearly occupies a prominent position on the organizational studies agenda.

In this chapter it is my intention to consider organizational change, and its management, though the lens of organizational aesthetics. While a concern with the aesthetic dimension of organizational life is both relatively new and somewhat multi-faceted, it offers a number of interesting insights into both how we might think about, and possibly manage change, within contemporary organizations. In particular, it might allow one to recognize more clearly the interconnections between the subjective dimensions of change as a fundamentally human process, and one that is both structured by, and reproductive of, institutionalized organizational relations. Structurally, the chapter commences with a discussion of the need to address the management of meaning in order to mediate possible tensions within the change process arising from this interrelationship of subject and object that sits at the heart of most of organizational change programmes. Next, there is an introduction to the impact a concern with aesthetics has had on the field of management and organization studies and how this might relate more specifically to the management of change. This, in turn, allows me to present three possible approaches to the management of organizational change – *the instrumental, the creative* and *the radical* – each drawing on differing conceptions of both the aesthetic, and orientations to the nature of change and its management within organizations.

Contours of change

As was noted in the introduction, change can be understood as a fundamental dimension of human experience and our ongoing attempts to make sense and take control of the world (Tsoukas and Chia, 2002). Yet despite this, change, particularly when associated with the world of work, is frequently experienced as a deeply unsettling and often alienating process. Not that this should be entirely surprising. After all we have, particularly in the West, been raised to believe in what is a fundamentally static reality. With its metaphysical origins in the Platonic (1987) ideal of the Form – a reality that is eternal and unchanging – modern science and its popularized 'culture of certainty' continues to present the search for universal laws and immutable truths as the loftiest of ambitions. This, in turn, has resulted in a culture suspicious of change. The impermanence and transitoriness that change implies smacks of unwelcome imperfection and a job not well done. Furthermore, the sense of psychological and emotional disquiet that change can bring about is rendered all the more unsettling when experienced within the context of the complex organization; the supposed bastion of rationality, and buttress against the uncertainty and vicissitudes of nature and chance.

Yet the modern subject is also far more multi-dimensional than this might suggest. Prior to Plato, the Presocratic philosopher Heraclitus (2000) reminded us of the impossibility of stepping into the same stretch of flowing water twice. In doing so, he also enshrined the understanding that process and change are as much a part of nature as is the possibility of permanence. Even modern science, with its fervour for ontological endurance and law-like statements, has opened our eyes to, for instance, the ongoing change associated with the evolutionary process. Indeed one might argue that as a response to the tyranny of certainty to which western culture appears to aspire, its members have sought out ever-greater personal and cultural challenges in order not to stagnate. Not only do many accept the risks and challenges that accompany change, they actively seek them out as a means of ensuring psychological and spiritual well-being. Change, therefore, is often embraced as not only inevitable, but also as positively life affirming. If we were to perhaps recast this dynamic in terms of say Freudian psychoanalysis, as others have certainly done previously (cf. Antonacopoulou and Gabriel, 2001; Carr, 2001), one might view this tension as emblematic of one of the more fundamental psychodynamic conflicts posited by Freud (1991); namely that between the death and life instincts. Here the former is concerned the desire to achieve a reduction in psychological stimulus (ultimately though the cessation of all mental and physiological activity), while the latter is often associated with the higher, creative drives of humanity. Thus the tensions and resistances so often experienced during organizational change programmes can be read, from this perspective at least, as embedded within our unconscious drives towards stasis and diminution of activity on the one hand, and a creative, almost revolutionary impulse on the other.

Perhaps not surprisingly, however, it is this subjective, unconscious dynamic that is often experienced by managers as the overwhelming complicating factor within any organizational change programme. In response, a range of prescriptions, solutions and remedials have been offered in an attempt to provide managers with suitable resources and ways of thinking about change in order to mitigate the more disruptive aspects of employee ambivalence and possible resistance. Lewin's (1947) now somewhat classic three stage model, for instance, urges managers to approach change through a linear process of unfreezing, changing and refreezing in order to psychologically prepare individuals for the need to change while ensuring that, at the end of the process, a sense of personal and institutional stability is restored. Kotter (1996), in similar vein, urges managers to implement his 'eight steps to transforming your organization', which commences with 'establishing a sense or urgency' and ends when the desired changes are firmly 'anchored' in the corporate culture. Other, albeit somewhat less linear formulations, advise on the need to consider the management of culture not so much as a final stage in a process, but rather as the heart of the process itself. Inspired by popular management texts such as Peters and Waterman's (1982) *In Search of Excellence*, and exemplified in Beer and Nohria's (2000) *Theory O* approach to change, managing culture is viewed from this perspective not simply as a way of embedding a particular organizational change, but as the means by which an enduring culture of change can be brought into being through an appeal to the symbolic, and largely affective relations, that underpin what is considered to be the fabric of organizational life.

Now for some, such as Collins (1998), such approaches are essentially flawed due to what he considers to be a largely over socialized model of organizational change. That is, they operate with something of an unproblematic conception of human agency; particularly that of managers and their capacity to bring about change through the manipulation of symbols and related cultural artefacts. Nonetheless, despite such a shared reservation, it is probably not unfair to say that change, like organizational culture itself, is neither wholly immune to the agency and intervention of managers, nor can it be simply reduced to the management of symbols and systems. It is this, more pluralistic view, which has subsequently led to numerous interventions that have aimed at guiding managers through the complexities and potential pitfalls of managing the human dimension of organizational change. Kanter (1985), for example, offers one of the earlier instances of this approach, arguing for a strategy that takes into account a range of subjective factors that frequently act as impediments to individuals embracing organizational change. These include, for instance, a sense of a lack of control and the persistence of negative emotions towards the organization itself for past treatment. Indeed, it is perhaps with respect to the question of emotions that the most interesting and relevant work to our concerns has emerged. Building on work that has explored emotional or affectively grounded capabilities amongst both employees and managers (Ashforth and Humphrey, 1995; Goleman, 1998; Fineman, 2005; Sakiyama, 2009), authors such as Huy (2002), Seijts and O'Farrell (2003), and Smollan et al. (2010) have explored not only how change within organizations might bring about powerful emotional responses, but also how these might, in turn, be managed though an increased sensitivity to the affective and, I will argue, aesthetic dimensions of the change experience.

Aesthetics and organization

A concern with the aesthetic dimension of organizations and their management is now fairly well established within the field of management and organization studies (Strati, 1996, 1999; Linstead and Hopfl, 2000; Carr and Hancock, 2003; de Monthoux, 2004). How one orientates oneself towards such work rather depends, however, on the interpretation of the term aesthetic that is applied. Popularized during the eighteenth century in the work of Alexander Gottlieb Baumgarten who, between 1750 and 1758, published his two volume work entitled *Aesthetica*, the term itself derives from the Ancient Greek term *aisthesis*, meaning 'sense perception' (Williams, 1983 [1976]: 31). Subsequently, it has evolved to have several differing, if albeit interrelated, meanings. Today it is largely associated with providing reasonable criteria by which 'art' might be evaluated and deemed to be of aesthetic value (cf. Bell, 1915) or, more generally, with questions of artistic activity and values such as beauty and style. Within management and organization studies, as elsewhere within the social sciences (cf. Welsch 1997), it has taken on a somewhat broader meaning, however.

Closer to the idea of a science of sensuality, the aesthetic has, from this perspective, been used to refer to the production and evaluation of sensory – or perhaps more accurately sensual – experience; 'the business of affections and aversions, of how the world strikes the body on its sensory surfaces' as Eagleton (1990: 13) has it. This more extensive definition has, in particular, been exploited by the German philosopher Gernot Böhme (1993: 116) who has spoken of the need to explore 'the full range of aesthetic work' – namely all that work that goes into producing particular ways of experiencing the world sensually, not simply those directly employed in the field of artistic production. What Böhme is pointing towards in his work, therefore, is what might be described as the emergence of a particular form of aesthetic economy – essentially an *aesthetic capitalism* – one that has transcended the production of purely surplus or symbolic value, and that now draws its profits from the production and distribution of ways of experiencing the world – generating what Böhme (2003) refers to as 'staging value'.

Certainly there are those within management and organization studies who have shown more of an interest in exploring the specifically artful or creative aspects of organizational practice, however. This is an approach exemplified, for instance, in de Monthoux's (2004) *The Art Firm: Aesthetic Management and Metaphysical Marketing*, in which he explores the utility to be found by managers in studying art and how artists themselves create aesthetic value. Similarly, in the field of Human Resource Development, Gibb (2004) argues for the merits of not only learning from arts-based organizations, but equally promoting the introduction of arts-based training programmes – including techniques associated with theatrical practice – as part of an overall human resource development strategy. Nonetheless, in the majority of work within the field two themes have tended to predominate.

The first of these is largely methodological in tenor, in that it asks how we might come to know organizations through our own aesthetic faculties and what research strategies and methods might be congruent with such an ambition. An example of this approach can be found, for instance, in Warren (2008), where the primary emphasis is placed on the development of a sensuous hermeneutic and the accumulation of novel modes of organizational understanding. A second, if not entirely unrelated approach, operates within a more critical tradition, actively rejecting the possibility of appropriation explicit within the 'organization as art' approach, and equally implicit within the epistemological tradition. This approach either takes to task the incorporation of an arts or aesthetic based perspective on organization and its management per se., or orientates itself towards studying the ways in which company environments, practices and resources are acted upon in order to evoke a narrow range of aesthetic responses from significant organizational stakeholders (Hancock, 2005; Hancock and Tyler, 2007). In this latter case, therefore, the question is that of how organizations *landscape* (Gagliardi, 1996) – or make aesthetically meaningful – what they do and how they do it in order to maximize relations of identity with, and cooperation by, employees, partners and customers.

Originally, much of this latter body of work focused on the aesthetic qualities of singular organizational artefacts ranging from office chairs (Strati, 1996) through to company documents (Hancock, 2006). In doing so it considered how one might, through a combination of design and placement, influence not only the perceptions of those exposed to such artefacts, but also actively direct organizational action through a pre-reflective formation of beliefs and values. Similarly, a burgeoning interest in the status of the working body pointed to the ways in which the bodies of

524

both managers and employees are subject, in various ways, to purposeful efforts to promote an embodied, aesthetic congruence with organizational aspirations and professed cultural values. This has led to a growth in the study of what has been termed *aesthetic labour* (Hancock and Tyler, 2000; Witz et al., 2003; Pettinger, 2004), describing as it does the ways in which employees are increasing required to present themselves in ways deemed aesthetically appropriate.

A more holistic approach has also emerged that seeks to transcend an analysis of isolated artifacts such as individual documents, design schemes or employee's bodies, and rather conceptualize aesthetic management in a more inclusive manner including, for instance, human performances, rites, rituals and other activities. Cappetta and Gioia (2006), for example, observe how the seasonal shows of the global fashion industry are themselves carefully constructed, aesthetically significant artifacts in their own right, while Strati (2006) demonstrates the ways in which performances within organizations – ranging from product launches to AGMs, disciplinary meetings to team building exercises – can provide a unified physical shape to what might otherwise appear to be a disparate set of beliefs, values and aspirations. A similarly holistic approach has also underpinned recent work that analyses organizational architecture and spatiality (Markus, 1993, 2006; Clegg and Kornberger, 2006; Dale and Burrell, 2003, 2008). Often this has combined a concern with artifacts (both human and non-human), with patterns of use and movement that themselves produce a particular mode of aesthetic expression and reception; one materialized in the very fabric of the working environment.

What unites these various studies and the objects they concern themselves with, however, is a recognition of the potential of aesthetic experience – and the affective state it can engender – to influence employee values and behaviours. In particular, its power is seen to lie in the fact that influence is exercised at a pre-reflexive level, bypassing our everyday sense-making practices and potentially establishing a strong emotional connection between particular various stakeholders – such as employees – and the organization. One way in which one might think about this process is in relation to what is known as *expressivism*. This idea takes us back to the more traditional view of the role of aesthetics vis-à-vis the realm of art, and refers to the proposition that the criteria by which a work of art should be judged is its capacity to *express* an artist's own emotions in such a way that by communicating these emotions the audience can not only experience them, but also identify with them. Transposing this into the realm of management and organization, however, it suggests that the value of aesthetics within an organization, from a managerial perspective anyway, is its ability to contribute to the active management of structures of feeling; the production of a shared emotional condition that brings together management and their employees in a conspiracy of feeling that is experienced as somehow personal and unique. When recognized as such, therefore, the aesthetic dimension of organizational life, or at least its management, has the potential to become a tool for promoting organizational change and one that I shall explore in more depth in the following section.

The aesthetics of change

In this half of the chapter I consider three possible approaches to incorporating the aesthetic into how one might think about and practice the management of organizational change. These range from a predominantly technical or instrumental interest in mobilizing aesthetic resources in order to promote and pursue managerially decreed change objectives, to a more radical or emancipatory approach that looks to the aesthetics of radical inter-subjectivity in order to reflect on a wholly different understanding of the origins and processes associated with the idea of change within organizations.

Instrumental

An instrumental approach, as I shall term it here, seeks to answer the question of how managers might, by paying attention to the issue of aesthetics, ameliorate the tensions created by the differentiation or divergence of objective requirements and subjective ambivalences towards change alluded to earlier. Tensions that can, in turn, lead to deep-seated resentments and resistances amongst employees if not also other stakeholders. It is, therefore, instrumental in that it establishes the aesthetic as an instrument that can be used to mechanically achieve pre-defined organizational goals and ambitions. It shares much in common, therefore, with recent approaches that have asked similar questions about how emotions, for instance, might be harnessed in the service of overcoming change resistance amongst employees and maximizing subjective buy-in. While owing something to versions of aesthetic philosophy primarily concerned with the arts or forms of artistic practice – such as storytelling – an instrumental approach relies heavily on a highly operationalised view of the aesthetic, realized through what I have alluded to elsewhere as *corporate aestheticization* (Hancock, 2010) and the idea of a burgeoning aesthetic capitalism.

Now, unless one adheres to a somewhat one-dimensional, rational-economic model of human behaviour, such as that which underpins the tenets of scientific management and its various offshoots, to suggest that for a change agent winning over employee hearts as well as their minds is vital to a successful outcome will come as little surprise. As Fox and Amichai-Hamburger (2001) observe, communication always comprises of both a rational and emotional component, and in order to communicate a successful change programme both elements require attention. One means by which the latter might be achieved is through mobilising the effect the aesthetic qualities of the physical environment has on how people interpret and respond to messages. How signs, sounds, ambiances and the like can be fused together to create what Böhme (1993) refers to as *atmosphere* – an almost ineffable state of perception – can have profound implications for how we think, feel and act.

So how might managers instrumentally mobilise aesthetics in order to enhance their ability to bring about organizational change? Well firstly there is the aforementioned role of artefacts. While it is possible to define organizational artefacts in a fairly inclusive manner, including ceremonies, symbols and language systems, tools and equipment, myths, sagas and rituals, as well as defining values and norms (Shrivastava, 1985; Higgins and McAllaster 2004) amongst others, here I want to focus primarily on the first two of these. In the first instance the role of symbols and artefacts, as well as modes of presentation oriented towards the communication of the symbolic, can be powerful agents of change in relation to a host of stakeholders. One industry that has often paid particular attention to such factors is the airline industry with major players such as British Airways and Continental Airlines having had their concern with the aesthetic dimension of their change strategies well documented. For both airlines, the importance of an integrated overview of the design and presentation of company artefacts ranging from recruitment documents, through the uniforms or their employees, to the interior design of their aircraft towards changing the ways in which employees acted both within the organization and outwardly to passengers and other stakeholders has not been lost on senior management.

A particularly powerful way of utilizing symbolic artifacts is to combine them with rituals or performances in order to reinforce an atmosphere of progress and change. For example, on July 5th 2004 the industrial and commercial retail arm of the UK energy company Powergen was rebranded as E.ON in line with its German parent company. On that day the vast bulk of the company's employees turned up to work to find that their offices and workplaces were occupied by wastepaper bins bearing an E.ON logo, into which they were instructed to place any items in their possession that bore the name Powergen or any of its associated livery. Then once having ceremoniously destroyed any artifacts associated with the old company identity, they were then replaced with a range of E.ON inscribed alternatives – from mouse mats to pens and badges (as well as larger items such as vehicle livery) – all in the new corporate colours and designs. Not only were the day-to-day artifacts of the companies operating changed in this way, however. Employees, for example, were given cards displaying their new E.ON designations as well as instructions on how to greet colleagues both from other E.ON companies around the globe, and other organizations. Thus, an intervention into the aesthetics of ritual and performance were also integral to this exercise; an exercise that cost millions, and has subsequently been hailed as fundamental to the success of the company's rebranding.

A further valuable resource is that of organizational space and architecture. As I also noted earlier, space and its organization – including the physical design of buildings and their interiors – exert a powerful influence on organizational attitudes and behaviours through the generation of certain ways of both moving and feeling. As such, it possesses a significant capacity to promote alignments between corporate aspirations and individual values and ambitions. On the one hand, organizational change often involves spatial relocation to new buildings, sites or offices. Often this brings with it problems in terms of changes in social relations, difficulties arising from altered commuting or travelling arrangements and, as is so often the case when moving from closed to open plan office spaces, adjustments to the changed dynamics and demands of a new environment. Yet even here opportunities exist to think about how design and an attention to aesthetics might ameliorate some of the possibly negative consequences deriving from such changes. Often this can be achieved simply through an eye to the perceived quality of fittings and equipment that themselves inhabit new working spaces. As Higgins and McAllaster (2004: 72) observe in this regard:

> As a cultural artifact, physical surroundings reveal the values of the organization related to such factors as innovation, the importance of employees, the degree of cost consciousness, and so on. Frugal organizations may use gray-metal desks and open bays where employees work as opposed to wooden desks and closed offices. Buildings with majestic exteriors or free flowing designs may stimulate more innovation than those that are dull and ordinary.

Good design can produce an atmosphere that both encourages a sense of thoughtfulness and investment on behalf of the company as well acting as an impetus to innovation and a similar investment by employees.

Attention to space and architecture need not only be paid when dealing with spatial relocations and the like, however. Any change process involves, as I have already pointed out, a communicative stage, and where and within what kind of environment that communication takes place is also an important factor that deserves consideration. First, there is movement through space itself, in that who travels to whom can help generate very distinct feelings about the communicative processes. The manager or change agent who appears to be sufficiently concerned to travel, in person, to where information is to be disseminated and feedback and discussion invited, is far more likely to contribute to an atmosphere of trust and cooperation than one who summons employees to them or, even worse, relies on mediated forms of communication such as video conferencing or email. Similarly, where larger formal meetings are necessary the question could be asked, what is the most appropriate environment for them to take place in? For instance, is a large conference hall like environment – one conducive to whipping up a supportive clamour – likely to contribute to the power of the change message or, alternatively, would a small scale and more intimate setting be more conducive to the situation. It is, of course, a matter of [aesthetic] judgement, but nonetheless at least that such judgements are being made might help ensure that the chances of success are greater.

527

Creative

The instrumental approach to thinking about the relationship between aesthetics and organizational change, while possibly of value in itself is, however, potentially problematic. After all, while there is little doubt that the aesthetics of one's environment have a significant effect on how one thinks and feels, to suggest that simply by choosing a suitable venue and some logo emblazoned trinkets managers can convince employees, amongst others, to invest in what may be genuinely life-altering changes would be naive in the extreme. Furthermore, it begs the question of how far one should condone any approach that, by virtue of its instrumentality, treats its objects (in this case employees), and its methods, in such a largely cynical manner. Yet this is not the only way in which a concern with the aesthetic dimension might inform how we think about and manage organizational change. Rather, by returning to that tradition that actively engages with the aesthetic as a form of creative or artistic practice, and the recent work of Bilton (2007), we might be able to identify an alternative approach that is both less vulgar in its appropriation of aesthetic ideas, yet remains relevant for those engaged in the managerial planning and implementation of organizational changes.

Bilton's ideas centre on the relationship between organizational change and what he considers to be two central features of artistic creativity; namely *incrementalism* and *integrity*. The former, Bilton (2007: 126) argues, is an often overlooked or ignored aspect of artistic activity whereby 'Artists generally achieve "originality" not by a moment of divine madness but by locating their work within an internal and external context, with ideas constantly evolving through successive drafts, versions, sketches and improvisations'. Creativity is not considered to be revolutionary in its outlook, therefore, but more evolutionary in that it 'digs deeper into shared resources of experience, memory and knowledge, reconfiguring the existing pattern rather than breaking it' (Bilton, 2007: 121). Thus, resonating with established incremental models of change, the primary case Bilton makes is for a creative approach to change that is underpinned by a cooperative and culturally embedded logic of experimentation and practice. This is premised on a condition of work whereby all stakeholders are afforded the opportunity to contribute to strategic development and an embedded culture of innovation and creativity can be allowed to flourish. In this way, Bilton argues, organizations can genuinely pursue a robust preparation for periods of environmental turbulence and associated drivers of change.

The latter, however, namely that of integrity, while similar in objective, focuses more on the nature of art itself and what we might learn from it about managing organizational change processes. Artistic integrity is defined, in this instance, as the shared ability of both artist, and the work of art itself, to posses a level of internal consistency that is indicative of both an evolutionary journey and a respect for the institutionalized relationships embedded within what has been termed elsewhere, the art world (Becker, 1982). Again citing Bilton (2007: 127): 'Aesthetic innovation occurs within a field of cultural production where different influences and conventions push and pull the meaning of the work and generate rules and influences, genres and structures – as well as other art works and institutions.'

Applying this insight to the realm of organizational change, Bilton once again argues for an aesthetic approach that limits the revolutionary model of discontinuous change and in turn seeks to manage the appearance of change through relatively minor (in terms of institutional upheaval at least) strategic and sometimes merely symbolic actions. Such an approach recognizes, therefore, that 'organizational change is in large measure a matter of internal and external perceptions as much as "real" change' (Bilton, 2007: 128). In this way integrity, in terms of a continued adherence to heritage and established institutional relationships, combined with the pursuit of a reinvention of identity in the eyes of selected stakeholders is maintained, while ensuring that organizational employees, amongst others, are able to keep pace with change and related change initiatives.

Now there is certainly much to commend Bilton's vision of a creative, aesthetic approach to change that eschews grand revolutionary gestures, a fetishization of novelty and, quite frankly, an absence of strategic oversight and future awareness. There can be few employees, if not indeed managers, that do not tire at the constant cycles of crisis and consolidation that seem to dissipate so much organizational energy and enthusiasm. Nonetheless, there are several criticisms that are immediately apparent. First and foremost, despite Bilton's own experience of working in the creative sector he does appear to offer a somewhat restricted view of artistic and creative activity; one that itself could in turn serve to limit what might be deemed to be a valid or acceptable change strategy. That is, the view that artistic innovation or originality seldom, if ever, arises from revolutionary or spontaneous insights and discoveries appears perhaps as narrow in conception as the opposing view. The same I would say characterizes organizational change. Sometimes radical departures appear both necessary and desirable if an organization is to survive say unforeseeable environmental or technological challenges, or even occasionally steady decline. Certainly a culture of creativity and innovation would still be desirable in such circumstances, but one size is unlikely to fit all and the idea that discontinuous change can itself neither be aesthetically informed, nor carried out in ways that are creative, or consistent with both organizational narratives and institutional expectations, is one that might not easily rebuff critical scrutiny.

A further criticism that can apply to both the instrumental and the creative approach is that each demonstrates an overriding and unquestioned managerialism. While perhaps obvious and necessary in the first instance, in the second, even despite Bilton's recognition that for incremental change to be successful it requires a close integration between individuals and an organization that is minimally hierarchical in nature, it nevertheless extols a fundamentally managerial prerogative when it comes to establishing the terms of change and its execution. The creative and innovative powers of employees are, or so it would seem, there to be harnessed in order to address predetermined priorities and ambitions, not set by and for themselves.

Of course if one accepts that the role of management is to direct and control in such a way, as Bilton clearly does, then this should come as no surprise. As with the instrumental approach, the ambition underlying the creative orientation is a validation of the managerial prerogative and its legitimacy as the most appropriate agent of organizational change. An alternative perspective, and one I want consider now, however, rejects such a presupposition. I refer here to what has come to be known as Critical Management Studies (CMS), an albeit diverse body of work but one that challenges the apparent naturalness of managerial authority within both organizations, and society more generally. In doing so I hope to be able to offer some final thoughts about how a concern with the aesthetic dimension of both organizational life, and the management of organizational change, may be envisaged in a more radical, and potentially emancipatory manner.

Radical

The early twenty-first century has witnessed something of a growth in critical perspectives on the perceived legitimacy of the management function, both organizationally and socially (Parker, 2002; Protherough and Pick, 2003; Grey and Willmott, 2005; Hancock and Tyler, 2008). Commonly referred to under the aforementioned umbrella term of CMS, this is an emergent tradition that can perhaps be understood as management (as both as an academic discipline and an institutional practice) coming to terms with itself and developing a reflexive self-critique characteristic of the modern condition (Giddens, 1991). At its most radical, CMS is concerned to identify and engage with the politics of hierarchy, instrumentality and performativity that, it is claimed, continue to characterize managerial ideas and practice. In this context organizational change and those discursive formations that legitimate it as both necessary and inevitable are, therefore, subject to questioning and opposed by the argument that, as Sturdy and Grey (2003: 652) note, '… change and continuity are not alternative objective states: they are not alternatives because they are typically coexistent and coterminous; and they are not objective because what constitutes change or continuity is perspective dependent'. The primary criticism of CMS is, therefore, directed at traditional writings on change management that promote (and therefore constitute) organizational change as an inevitable 'fact'. In raising an often manufactured need for constant, innovatory change to the status of an immutable universality, such an approach also, however, raises it to the level of a moral good. Thus, 'good' change is contrasted to the purported 'bad' qualities of decline and decay associated with a condition of stasis or stability ('change or die'). Furthermore, in order to ensure that such dire consequences might be avoided then it is also made clear that salvation is likely to be found in one place only, the managerial change agent who, with an optimum composition of vision, leadership and empathy, must be both equipped and empowered to identify the opportunities and make the hard decisions that successful change will necessitate.

While CMS is largely oriented towards critique, what is less forthcoming, however, are suggestions regarding alternative or non-managerial ways of organizing (Parker, 2002). Certainly some have speculated on how CMS might move to a position whereby it can credibly envisage how alternative, and more importantly, increasingly emancipated forms of organizational management might emerge (cf. Spicer et al., 2009). Nevertheless, such endeavours tend, or so it would appear, to fall prey to at least two complicating factors. The first is the inescapable fact that modern forms of organization are both constituted by, and constitutive of, a host of socio-economic relations – most notably of course being that of capitalism – that place both material and cultural restrictions on the degree of radical restructuring that might be possible. Second, as is widely recognized by critical scholars, despite the hierarchical nature of most organizations, in reality they remain characterized by a host of competing interests and ambitions. While this is a problem frequently brushed aside by the gurus and executors of organizational change, it provides a very real stumbling block for those who might prescribe just what form an alternative or emancipated organization might take. The question that needs to be asked in the context of this chapter is, therefore, might an interest in the aesthetic suggest any means by which these obstacles might be, if not overcome, then mitigated to the greatest extent possible in order to allow organizational members to 'freely and collectively control the direction of change on the basis of as rational understanding of social process' (Benson, 1997: 18).

Certainly there is no simple or definitive answer to such a question. Bilton's (2007) creative approach to organizational change and its management, while albeit limited by its adherence to a fundamentally managerialist orientation, does perhaps offer something in terms of an alternative critique of the tendency of senior managers to pursue transformatory organizational change for change's sake. Equally, it openly challenges the figure of the hero manager for whom change is not only a personal quest, but equally one that is often paid for by both employees and, just as often, corporate reputation. Yet in order to think about a genuinely radical approach to the subject we perhaps need to move away from the link Bilton makes between aesthetics and artistic creativity and return to the idea's ontological roots in the body and its status as the site of the human sensorium. In particular I want to revisit some ideas concerning the ways in which the body, and its status as the site of aesthetic experience, might provide some possibilities for an alternative ethic of organization and consider what this might mean of the management of organizational change.

In Hancock (2008), and drawing on the phenomenological insights of Merleau-Ponty (1962) and the feminist ethics of Diprose (2002) and her notion of corporeal generosity, I argue for an ethics of organization based on the philosophy of recognition (Honneth, 1995) and the materiality of human intersubjectivity. Such an approach is grounded in the Hegelian proposition that intersubjectivity – concrete relations between people – provides the fundamental basis of all ethical relations, and that such subjectivity is something that is continually produced and reproduced through relationships that are inherently corporeal and, therefore, aesthetic. For Diprose, such a state of embodied being and becoming is itself characterized by an inherent generosity in that we inevitably, and pre-reflexively, give of our bodies and enter into relationships of the ethical by virtue of simply of entering the perceptual field of others. It is this inevitable giving of ourselves to the other in order to be recognized and offer recognition that, she argues, has the potential to provide an ethics of acceptance and openness to others if we were only to recognize it in ourselves.

How might such an ethic provide a basis for thinking about organizational change, however? Well, in one respect it chimes closely with the aforementioned ideas of Tsoukas and Chia (2002) who argue for an understanding of organizational change as a product of the continual and processesural character of human agency and sensemaking. This is due to the fact that such an ethic realizes not only that organizational subjects are always in process, but that such processes of becoming require an act of recognition; one embedded in the generosity of the inter-corporeal exchange that not only tolerates but embraces difference as an integral ontological precondition of the change process. Thus, a radical approach to organizational change, one that genuinely acknowledges the centrality of change to human becoming, would require that difference and the constant interplay of differences – both individual and collective – sit at the heart of all organizational life. Conversely, what such an ethic would not tolerate, therefore, would be any attempt to control or direct change in line with a singular or universalistic perspective. Such a necessary 'nonindifference to difference', as Diprose (2002: 184) formulates it, would seek to embrace the widest possible constituency in a meaningful effort to embed organizational change within the needs and aspirations of those whose own emergent relationships constitute the organizational lifeworld in question.

Now, such an approach may appear to represent little more than an appeal to organizational managers to pursue the kinds of consultation and inclusivity agendas that have long been popular amongst more progressive schools of managerial thinking. Yet one important difference, or so I would argue, is that this is not simply about harnessing human resources in order to maximize organizational productivity or resilience; quite the opposite. Such an ethic of change would recognize and embrace the diversity of needs and aspirations of its members – and their embeddedness within society as a whole – and view these as the primary concern to be pursued, be it through change and/or stability. The experience of change as a reified process, subservient to the impersonal forces of global economics, technological advances or market expansionism, would thus be replaced by a potentiality for change if and when it aligned with the albeit itself contingent and prosessural conditions of its own realization. Such an approach would, of course, be a highly dynamic one in its own right, relying on a constant openness to, and dialogue amongst all those in whose name change is, or is not, undertaken. Nonetheless, the organizational priority would be – to employ a further aesthetic category – one of an albeit contingent *harmony* between the needs and aspirations of its membership in all its difference and diversity, and those organizational and social relations of recognition within which organizational life is both emergent and embedded.

Conclusion

Within the field of management and organization studies, as well as the popular business press, change management is now viewed as a topic of some major significance. Whether this is for

531

better or worse is, of course, a point for debate. What is clear, however, is that part and parcel of this process has been the associated message that constant change has become both inevitable and, in many instances, desirable. In this chapter I have considered how a concern with the aesthetic dimension of organizational life, and its practice, might inform how we think about managing change and, in particular, the problem of its subjective dimension; or how we bring employees and associated stakeholders on board in order to pursue successful change. In doing so, I have offered three possible approaches to this relationship.

Firstly, and based on the idea that organizational environments can be managed – or landscaped – in order to elicit a managerially favourable response from employees and the like, I presented what I termed an *instrumental approach*. Here the basic principle is an appropriation of ideas about the materiality of organizational aesthetics in order to render both the communication of the change agenda, as well as it actual implementation, aesthetically attractive to employees. Resonating with the values of an aesthetic capitalist economy, this approach promotes a strategy of aestheticization as central to the capacity of management to seduce, or enchant, employees into a subjective identification with managerial change priorities and practices. The second, *creative approach*, favours an alternative view that closely aligns the aesthetic with formal artistic and creative activity. From this perspective, change management should recognize and aspire to standards of what is posited as genuine artistic process namely a largely incremental approach embedded within established institutional arrangements and practices. Such an approach to change management should, therefore, eschew heroic, discontinuous models of change, and embrace a more tempered strategy based on long-termism and a respect of organizational traditions and integrity, allowing in turn, space and time for a more creative orientation to organizational development.

The final *radical approach* rejects both the respective explicit and implicit managerialism of these former approaches and, in turn, considers the relevance of the aesthetic in what is possibly its most esoteric sense. That is, it considers the opportunity offered by an ontological understanding of the aesthetic as a way of being and becoming in the world; one embedded within a recognition of, and respect for, the identity and difference of others that is embodied, sensual and, as such, an a priori precondition for the ongoing production of ethical relations. The subsequent emergence of such an ethic would, therefore, necessitate a radical reorientation to change. That is, one that not only embraces a diversity of hopes, aspirations and needs, but also one that will genuinely aim to enable subjects to define and enact the parameters of change while circumventing institutional paralysis by virtue of an ontology that places process at the centre of the human condition. To what extent such a proposal might, in someway, be enacted is highly contingent of course; most notably on a reconfiguration of those economic rationalities which I have already alluded to as presenting significant barriers to any vision of radical reorganization. This somewhat brute reality notwithstanding, however, it does at least remind us that there are always different ways in which one might approach not only change, but the nature and value of the aesthetic itself.

References

Antonacopoulou, E. and Gabriel, Y. (2001) 'Emotion, learning and organizational change: Towards an integration of psychoanalytic and other perspectives', *Journal of Organizational Change Management*, 14(5): 435–51.

Ashforth, B. and Humphrey, R. (1995) 'Emotion in the workplace: A reappraisal', *Human Relations*, 48(2): 97–125.

Becker, H. (1982) *Art Worlds*. London: University of California Press.

Beer, M. and Nohria, M. (2000) 'Cracking the code of change', *Harvard Business Review* (May–June): 133–41.

Bell, D. (1915/1914) *Art*. London: Chatto & Windus.

Benson, J.K. (1997) 'Organizations: A dialectical view', *Administrative Science Quarterly*, 22(1): 1–21.

Bilton, C. (2007) *Management and Creativity: From Creative Industries to Creative Management*. Oxford: Blackwell.

Böhme, G. (1993) 'Atmosphere as the fundamental concept of a new aesthetics', *Thesis Eleven*, 36: 113–26.

Böhme, G. (2003) 'Contribution to the critique of the aesthetic economy', *Thesis Eleven*, 73: 71–82.

Cappetta, R. and Gioia, D. (2006) 'Fine fashion: Using symbolic artifacts, sensemaking, and sensegiving to construct identity and image'. In A. Rafaeli and M. Pratt (eds), *Artifacts and Organizations: Beyond Mere Symbolism*. Lawrence Erlbaum Associates, Mahwah, NJ. pp. 199–219.

Carr, A. (2001) 'Understanding emotion and emotionality in a process of change', *Journal of Organizational Change Management*, 14(5): 421–36.

Carr, A. and Hancock, P. (eds) (2003) *Art and Aesthetics at Work*. Basingstoke: Palgrave.

Clegg, S. and Kornberger, M. (2006) 'Organizing space'. In S. Clegg, and M. Kornberger (eds), *Space, Organizations and Management Theory*. Copenhagen: Copenhagen Business School Press. pp. 143–62.

Collins, D. (1998) *Organizational Change: Sociological Perspectives*. London: Routledge.

Dale, K. and Burrell, G. (2003) 'An-aesthetics and architecture', In A. Carr, and P. Hancock (eds) *Art and Aesthetics at Work*. Basingstoke: Palgrave. pp. 155–73.

Dale, K. and Burrell, G. (2008) *The Spaces of Organisation and The Organisation of Space: Power and Materiality at Work*. Basingstoke: Palgrave.

de Monthoux, P.G. (2004) *The Art Firm: Aesthetic Management and Metaphysical Marketing*. Palo Alto, CA: Stanford University Press.

Diprose, R. (2002) *Corporeal Generosity: On Giving with Nietzsche, Merleau-Ponty and Levinas*. Albany, NY: SUNY.

Eagleton, T. (1990) *The Ideology of the Aesthetic*. Oxford: Blackwell.

Fineman, S. (2005) 'Appreciating emotion at work – paradigm tensions', *International Journal of Work, Organisation and Emotion*, 1(1): 4–19.

Fox, S. and Amichai-Hamburger, Y. (2001) 'The power of emotional appeals in promoting organizational change programs', *Academy of Management Executive*, 15(4): 84–94.

Freud, S. (1991/1964) *New Introductory Lectures on Psychoanalysis*. London: Penguin.

Gagliardi, P. (1996) 'Exploring the aesthetic side of organizational life'. In S.R. Clegg, C. Hardy and W.R. Nord (eds), *Handbook of Organization Studies*. London: SAGE. pp. 565–81.

Gibb, S. (2004) 'Imagination, creativity and hrd: an aesthetic perspective', *Human Resource Development Review*, 3(1): 53–74.

Giddens, A. (1991) *Modernity and Self Identity: Self and Society in the Late Modern Age*. Cambridge: Polity.

Goleman, D. (1998) *Working with Emotional Intelligence*. London: Bloomsbury Publishing.

Grey, C. and Willmott, H.C. (2005) *Critical Management Studies: A Reader*. Oxford: Oxford University Press.

Hancock, P. (2005) 'Uncovering the semiotic in organizational aesthetics', *Organization*, 12(1): 29–60.

Hancock P. (2006) 'The spatial and temporal mediation of social change', *Journal of Organizational Change Management*, 19(5): 619–39.

Hancock, P. (2008) Embodied generosity and an ethics of organization. *Organization Studies*, 29(10):1357–73.

Hancock, P. (2010) 'Aesthetics and aestheticization'. In P. Hancock and A. Spicer (eds), *Understanding Corporate Life*. London: SAGE. pp. 46–63.

Hancock, P. and Tyler, M. (2000) 'The look of love'. In J. Hassard, R. Holliday and H. Willmott (eds), *Body and Organization*. London: SAGE. pp. 108–29.

Hancock, P. and Tyler, M. (2007) 'Un/doing gender and the aesthetics of organizational performance', *Gender, Work and Organisation*, 14(6): 512–33.

Hancock, P. and Tyler, M. (2008) 'Beyond the confines: Managerial colonization and the everyday', *Critical Sociology*, 34(1): 29–49.

Heraclitus (2000) 'Heraclitus of Ephesus'. In *The First Philosophers: The Presocratics and the Sophists* (trans. R. Waterfield). Oxford: Oxford University Press.

Higgins, J.M. and McAllaster, C. (2004) 'Want to change your strategy, then change your cultural artifacts', *Journal of Change Management*, 4(1): 63–74.

Honneth, A. (1995) *The Struggle for Recognition. The Moral Grammar of Social Conflicts*. Cambridge: Polity Press.

Huy, N.Q. (2002) 'Emotional balancing of organizational continuity and radical change: The contribution of middle managers', *Administrative Science Quarterly*, 47: 31–69.

Kanter, R.M. (1985) *The Change Masters: Corporate Entrepreneurs at Work*. London: Routledge.

Kotter, J.P. (1996) *Leading Change*. Boston, MA: Harvard Business School Press.

Lewin, K. (1947) 'Frontiers in group dynamics', *Human Relations*, 1: 5–41.

Linstead, S. and Hopfl, H. (eds) (2000) *The Aesthetics of Organization*. London: SAGE.

Markus, T. (1993) *Buildings and Power: Freedom and Control in the Origin of Modern Buildings*. London: Routledge.

Markus, T. (2006) 'Built space and power'. In S. Clegg and M. Kornberger (eds), *Space, Organizations and Management Theory*. Copenhagen: Copenhagen Business School Press, pp. 129–42.

Merleau-Ponty, M. (1962/1945) *Phenomenology of Perception* (trans. C. Smith). London: Routledge.

Parker, M. (2002) *Against Management*. Cambridge: Polity.

Peters, T. and Waterman, R.H. (1982) *In Search of Excellence: Lessons from America's Best-Run Companies*. New York: HarperCollins.

Pettinger, L. (2004) 'Brand culture and branded workers', *Consumption, Markets and Culture*, 7(2): 165–84.

Plato (1987/1955) *The Republic*. London: Penguin.

Protherough, R. and Pick, J. (2003) *Managing Britannia: Culture and Management in Modern Britain*. London: Imprint Academic.

Sakiyama, H. (2009) 'When emotional labour becomes "good": The use of emotional intelligence', *International Journal of Work, Organisation and Emotion*, 3(2): 174–85.

Seijts, G.H. and O'Farrell, G. (2003) 'Engage the heart: Appealing to the emotions facilitates change', *Ivey Business Journal* (Reprint #9B03TA10), January/February: 1–5.

Shrivastava, P. (1985) 'Integrating strategy formulation with organizational culture', *Journal of Business Strategy*, 5(3): 103–11.

Smollan, R.K., Sayers, J.G. and Matheny J.A. (2010) Emotional responses to the speed, frequency and timing of organizational change, *Time and Society* 19(1), 28–53.

Spicer, A., Alvesson, M. and Kärreman, D. (2009)'Critical performativity: The unfinished business of critical management studies', *Human Relations*, 62(4): 537–60.

Strati, A. (1996) 'Organizations viewed through the lens of aesthetics', *Organization*, 3(2): 209–18.

Strati, A. (1999) *Organization and Aesthetics*. London: SAGE.

Strati, A. (2006) 'Organizational artifacts and the aesthetic approach'. In A. Rafaeli and M.G. Pratt (eds), *Artifacts and Organizations: Beyond Mere Symbolism*. Mahwah, NJ: Lawrence Erlbaum, pp. 23–39.

Sturdy, A. and Grey, C. (2003) 'Beneath and beyond organizational change management', *Organization*, 10(4): 651–62.

Tsoukas, H. and Chia, R. (2002) 'On organizational becoming: Rethinking organizational change', *Organization Science*, 13(5): 567–82.

Warren, S. (2008) 'Empirical challenges in organizational aesthetic research: Towards a sensual methodology', *Organization Studies*, 19(4): 559–80.

Welsch, W. (1997) *Undoing Aesthetics*. London: SAGE.

Williams, R. (1983/1976) *Keywords: A Vocabulary of Culture and Society*. London: Fontana Press.

Witz, A., Warhurst, C. and Nickson, D. (2003) 'The labour of aesthetics and the aesthetics of organization', *Organization*, 10(1): 33–54.

37

Sustainability and organizational change

Suzanne Benn and Kate Kearins

Introduction

Sustainability is both a contested concept and a social movement of our time. It has different meanings for different people, and is used in a wide variety of contexts, not least in relation to organizations including business. Sustainability is increasingly tied to other concepts such as corporate accountability, responsibility and citizenship. These concepts direct attention to the implication of organizations in wider environmental, social and political as well as economic systems. Business, in particular, is positioned as a key source of problems relating to global unsustainability, and managers of all types of organizations are being tasked with the resolution of such problems.

This chapter provides an overview of the concept of sustainability as it is interpreted in the field of organization studies. Our particular emphasis is on how the wider theory and practice of sustainability and sustainable development has been taken up by the literature of organizational change and development. We review recent trends in this literature around the need for holistic, systemic approaches to change and discuss implications for both the research and practice of organizational change toward sustainability. We link these implications to the wider debate in the literature around the relative benefits of planned and emergent change, arguing that both approaches are necessary to address the particular challenges of sustainability.

Constructions of sustainability in the field of organization studies

Sustainability, sustainable development and 'unsustainable' organizations

The genesis of sustainability as a concept is open to debate, but most commentators agree it is has been propelled to wider public attention since the World Commission on Environment and Development (WCED/Brundtland) 1987 report promoting the allied notion of sustainable development. Increasing concerns about the rate of environmental degradation and natural resource depletion and its consequences for economic and social development – essentially unsustainable development – had led the United Nations General Assembly to convene the so-called Brundtland Commission. Given the embeddedness of local environmental and social problems in global systems, the UN saw it in the interests of all nations to work on common policies for what came to be called 'sustainable development'. The WCED report was to inform sustainable development thinking right down to the level of individual organizations. What is probably the most cited definition of *sustainable development* comes from the WCED report which refers to "development that meets the needs of the present without compromising the ability of future generations to meet their own needs". The report points to: "the concept of 'needs', in particular the essential needs of the world's poor, to which overriding priority should be given; and the idea of limitations imposed by the state of technology and social organization on the environment's ability to meet present and future needs" (WCED, 1987, p. 43).

Sustainability, we might logically refer to as *a state*, and the allied concept of sustainable development as *a process* we might undertake to reach that state. But neither concept is straightforward. Sustainability, it would seem to us, is a broad systems concept, and would denote a dynamic state which currently stands more as an aspiration or vision than a reality, given currently unsustainable rates of resource use, particularly in relation to natural capital being degraded or used up at a greater rate than it is able to regenerate, and the inequities surrounding social as well as natural capital (see Millennium Ecosystem Assessment, 2005; World Wide Fund for Nature, 2008; Worldwatch Institute, 2009, 2010).

In acknowledging (un)sustainability thus as of material consequence, we also note sustainability as social construction open to various interpretations. Indeed, its meaning is contestable (Redclift, 1987; Banerjee, 2003, 2007) and a good deal of time has been taken to discussing various meanings both in the organizational studies and management literature (e.g. Russell et al., 2006; Byrch et al., 2007), and beyond in actual organizational settings themselves. There are those who use, some would say 'capture' or even 'hijack' the concept (Welford, 1997; Hajer and Fischer, 1999) to construe that current ways of living and organizing are sustainable. Some go so far as to suggest the word 'sustainable' is being overused, so as to become almost devoid of meaning. Calling sustainable development "the buzzword of the 1990s", Banerjee (2008, p. 67) proclaims "the problem with buzzwords is they tend to become disengaged from their original context and their meanings become discursively contested and deployed by a variety of agents, institutions and texts".

Given that business has become the focus of much interest in sustainable development circles – as both a cause of unsustainable development and a force for its resolution – it is not surprising that there has been increasing visibility of sustainability-related themes in the organization studies literature. A number of these themes involve a focus on the natural environment as central to sustainability (e.g. Gladwin et al., 1995; Milne et al., 2006). Considerable work in the organizations and the natural environment domain now exists (see Bansal and Gao, 2006 and Starik, 2006 for useful reviews) both standing separately and under the sustainability banner. A reasonable amount of attention in the literature has focused on the 'technical' side of environmental management operations and systems, as well as increasingly on the social legitimation side through the development of supporting infrastructural architecture and guidelines such as the Global Reporting Initiative (see recent articles by Levy et al., 2010; Etzion and Ferraro, 2010).

While not ignoring the natural environment focus, Banerjee's work is notable along with that of some business ethicists in bringing in the social. Banerjee (2003, 2008) highlights inequity brought about by organizational action in the name of sustainability, and asks important questions around who sustains whose development. He calls the Brundtland definition of sustainable development more of a slogan, and as such not the basis for good theory (Banerjee, 2007).

Theory development beyond the business case for sustainable development has been called for on several occasions (Shrivastava, 1994; Gladwin et al., 1995; Purser et al., 1995; Welford, 1998), and useful attempts have been made at identifying foundational concepts that point at embeddedness within wider systems (e.g. Welford, 1995; Gladwin et al., 1995; Starik and Rands, 1995). Egri and Pinfold (1996, p. 476) note the appearance of systems theory as a conceptual framework for both environmentalist and organizational domains – and the common prescription among a number of authors for "the wholesale adoption of ecological systems principles in societies and organizations as the 'only path' towards environmental sustainability". Within research on organizations and the natural environment, however, a wide variety of strands of established theory have been drawn upon from disciplines such as economics, ethics, political science, psychology, sociology among others (Sharma and Starik, 2002). Reframing of existing models and theories of organizations has also been attempted (Hart, 1995; Jennings and Zandbergen, 1995). Whether a theory of sustainability in the organizational context is feasible remains open for debate, however.

Sustainability, as invoked in the organizational context, has considerable overlap with other concepts such as corporate accountability, corporate citizenship and corporate social responsibility (Matten et al., 2003). These concepts also usefully direct managerial attention beyond the entity, but they retain a corporate centric focus. So, too, do the 'corporate sustainability' and the 'sustainable business/organization' concepts. They draw on the notion of sustainable development and the allied concepts noted above such as corporate social responsibility. Like the latter, they also rely heavily on the general precept of stakeholder theory: the organizational capacity to continue operating over a long period of time depending on the quality of stakeholder relationships (Freeman, 1984).

A growing body of commentators on business and sustainability suggests that what organizations require to become sustainable is, in many ways, fundamentally different from the status quo (see, for example, Shrivastava and Hart, 1995; Welford, 1995, 1997, 2000; Ehrenfeld, 1999; Milne et al., 2006). The term corporate sustainability (e.g. Dyllick and Hockerts, 2002; Dunphy et al., 2007; see also Dentchev, 2009) implies an interest in sustaining business, and corporate longevity which can be at odds with notions of sustainability as a dynamic and embedded systems concept that has at its heart ecological sustainability and the longevity of biophysical systems which support human life. In this view, sustainability transcends entity and national boundaries to embrace notions of equity, equality and futurity (Welford, 1995) in relation, but not limited to economic, social and environmental conditions.

Frameworks for classifying corporate sustainability

It is possible to classify interpretations of sustainability as either strong or weak (Pearce et al., 1990; Turner, 1993; Pearce, 1993; Dobson, 1999) according to whether all forms of capital, usually designated as social, environmental and economic, are maintained intact independent of one another. In strong sustainability, each form of capital is kept constant. When applied to organizations, strong interpretations require that social, environmental and economic objectives be addressed simultaneously for any one of them to be of value. Arguments for a business case for environmental (Porter and van der Linde, 1995) and/or social action, or for sustainable development (Day and Arnold, 1998; see also Springett 2003) fit within the weak sustainability classification. There has been considerable effort to establish linkages between corporate social/environmental performance and economic performance. Margolis et al. (2008a, 2008b) provide a meta-analysis of 167 such studies concluding only weak positive support overall. Little research appears to tackle the even more complex question of whether organizational efforts in relation to

537

sustainability contribute to the sustainability of wider systems, as strong sustainability would necessarily imply (Ehrenfeld, 2005).

The challenge for scholars and practitioners is that as the importance of sustainability in the organization studies literature has grown, so has the confusion surrounding its definition, presenting, as Garriga and Mele (2004) put it, not only a landscape of theories but a proliferation of suggested motives, capabilities and approaches to change.

A number of models and frameworks for corporate change have been suggested as a means of understanding the various factors that underpin a shift to sustainability. The European Corporate Sustainability Framework, for instance, is a multilayered framework that incorporates analytical, contextual, situational and dynamic dimensions (van Marrewijk and Hardjono, 2003). Other frameworks are built around levels of competences referring to material, financial and socialization domains (Hardjono and de Klein, 2004). The Dunphy et al. (2007) framework distinguishes between organizations that go beyond compliance according to human and environmental sustainability performance depending on whether they aim for efficiency-based outcomes or are more proactive in the strategic sense of integrating sustainability into their business decision-making. According to this model, through processes of transformational change the business organization can reach the 'ideal stage' where it actually contributes to ecological wellbeing, rather than diminishing it.

This process-based model links strategic HRM and cultural factors to environmental performance, and reflects increasing recognition in the literature that environmental sustainability is not just achieved by bringing in bundles of technical skills. Researchers have shown that certain HRM policies and practices can facilitate change through prompting employee engagement with environmental sustainability (Ramus and Steger, 2000) and current scholarly work is beginning to focus on this area, including on how generic organizational change and learning capacity is demonstrated in sustainability performance (Taylor et al., in press).

Limitations of phasic approaches

Stage models of the move to corporate environmentalism (e.g. Hunt and Auster, 1990; Muller and Koechlin, 1992) were popular some years back, in tune with interest in organizational life cycle models at the time. The validity of such stage models for theoretical development has been called into question with stage theories of business development life cycles being found to be lacking in large scale empirical support – as clearly models that itemize discrete stages of development in a predetermined order of historical association do not necessarily reflect the actual life cycles of all businesses (Levie and Lichtenstein, 2008). With the idea that organizations might pass from ignorance through a reactive to a more environmentally and socially-minded proactive, or even interactive stance, such stage models did not reflect the potential leapfrogging, or backtracking the organizations might make in terms of their commitment towards sustainable development (see also Kolk and Mauser, 2002).

There are other more fundamental problems with established change models such as contingency approaches. For example, the problem with the staged approach is that it evokes the journey metaphor associated with images of progressive change, organizational learning and an overall progress away from unsustainable business practices. To critics of this approach (e.g. Milne et al., 2006), the effect is to mask the issue of where exactly the organization is going. Little is said about what the organization would look like if it was actually sustainable and indeed whether some organizations would continue to exist in their current form. Little is also said in relation to the growth conundrum that underpins modern capitalist enterprise. Can an unsustainable organization grow sustainably? By doing more of the same, increasing resource throughput, is it likely to become more unsustainable, as a result?

Planned approaches in general have been called to question (Dawson, 2003; Pettigrew et al., 2001). Overall, incremental planned change programmes and phasic approaches to sustainability come under criticism on the same points – an inability to encompass the complexity, messiness and issues with power and unpredictability that are inherent in a contemporary organizational life that is characterized by instability and risk (Beck, 2000).

Critique and the requisites for radical change

Despite organizational pronouncements about the importance of sustainability, critics maintain that the environment remains subordinate to the interests of business (Levy, 1997; Newton and Harte, 1997; Prasad and Elmes, 2005), not least in the business case for sustainable development (Welford, 1997; Banerjee, 2001, 2003). Forbes and Jermier (2002) suspect green-washing by business. Milne et al. (2006) declare that business talk about sustainability is a poor substitute for its actual achievement in an ecological sense. Newton (2002) questions whether it is even possible to create a new ecological order as seemingly promised by businesses' engagement with sustainability. Again, the social and political dimensions of sustainability are confounding, as various interests clash.

While acknowledging the radical critique, we also point out that it may stymie more creative thinking about how the norms and values of organizations in their institutional context can move beyond where they are now. We salute the radical critique for its contextualization of the achievement of sustainability as going beyond an organizational or entity focus to one that is societal, and for pointing to the limitations of the business case within the political economy of capitalism. Neither heroic rhetoric on the part of corporations which is met with scepticism, nor miniscule efforts in relation to generally increasing ecological and social footprints on the part of many organizations are deemed sufficient. We contend that organizations need to address fundamental elements and core values, rather than merely masquerade as being or becoming sustainable. Prescriptions in respect of sustainable enterprise commonly include the following core values (Ehrenfeld, 1999):

Profit as a critical factor in short term survival;
Social equity as a responsibility of the business enterprise;
Precaution as a virtue, not a vice;
Business enterprise as existing within, and connected to the natural world;
Resources as limited and affected by business activities over whole product lifecycles, and thus of strategic importance;
Incorporation of the interests of diverse stakeholders with nature itself as a critical stakeholder (represented by human surrogates);
Organizations as open systems with extended boundaries; and
The absolute nonsustainability of individual, independent organizations.

Shifting from entity-based approaches to systemic thinking

Learning about sustainability and change

Few attempts have been made to establish a theory of change that is specific to addressing unsustainability. Organizational efforts that do, tend to focus on change in association with learning processes. For example, the theory of education for sustainability is basically an

539

educational philosophy that is complemented by principles drawn from organizational learning and change. In association with the Decade of Education for Sustainable Development 2005–14, the rhetoric of education for sustainability has come to rest on a set of principles emphasizing critical thinking, systems thinking, participatory change and action research (Kearins and Springett, 2003; Tilbury and Wortman, 2004; Tormey et al., 2008).

Badged thus, the discourse has been embraced widely by governments and intergovernmental bodies as a means of raising awareness and developing a capacity around sustainability (e.g. UNESCO, 2005a, 2005b, 2005c) that is locally relevant in cultural, environmental, economic, and societal terms (McKeown, 2002; Bradbury, 2003; Springett, 2005). Despite being widely proclaimed in policy literature as relevant to all types of organizations and across the wider community, this approach has been largely ignored in the organizational studies literature and critics are now arguing on behalf of a much stronger theoretical underpinning that can then link into organizational practice (Stephens and Graham, 2010). A second concern relates to criticisms of the sustainable development concept itself, particularly the argument that the norms of what is to be regarded as sustainable are set by the North and imposed on the South (Banerjee, 2003), or others less equipped to participate in global debate.

Learning through partnerships

Another body of work that links social partnership formation and organizational learning has arisen around the need to understand how change might occur for sustainability. Social partnerships refer to a wide range of inter-organizational, cross-sector mechanisms designed to address issues such as the environment, health and education (Waddock, 1989; Seitanidi and Crane, 2009). Calls for a shift from a dominator to a partnership model of transformational change (Riane and Eisler, 1994) are long-established in the literature but have recently given more credence because of the rapid expansion in the numbers of partnerships, collaborative arrangements and networks of all types (Senge et al., 2007). Much of the social partnering currently taking place is driven by the need for each of the partner organizations to learn to adapt its behaviour to reduce social or environmental risk or to obtain strategic opportunity around its management of such issues. For many organizations, partnering and networking is about accessing learning and change, particularly applying to partnerships between NGOs and corporations in connection with their strategic CSR activities (Matten and Moon, 2008; Porter and Kramer, 2006). There can be advantages for all types of organizations in engaging in the organizational learning around social responsibilities that is enabled by cross-sectoral dialogue and interaction and the bringing together of different knowledge, skills and capabilities (Zadek, 2004).

Consider Huber's (1991, p. 89) earlier definition of organizational learning: 'An entity learns if, through its processing of information, the range of its potential behaviours is changed'. In the context of this chapter, inter-organizational learning happens when companies, NGOs, governments and other partner organizations increase each others' behavioural capacities in relation to social or environmental practices (Roome and Wijen, 2006) as a consequence of *knowledge acquisition, information distribution, information interpretation* and *organizational memory* (Huber, 1991, p. 90). These activities may involve either or both exploitative (evolutionary, adaptive, incremental) or explorative learning (double loop, radical, strategic) in relation to social and environmental risks and opportunities (Argyris and Schön, 1978; Roome and Wijen, 2006). Triple-loop learning is the highest model of organizational learning and involves actors or organizations questioning the traditions, values and culture of the organization or the institution. It is this form of learning that is most likely to lead to radical transformation around sustainability. Requiring high levels of reflection for the self and at organizational and institutional levels, triple loop learning is supported by structural changes involving circular forms of organizing and is promoted by interactive governance processes (Ackoff, 1994; Romme and van Witteloostuijn, 1999).

Partnerships can facilitate higher orders of learning, experiment and change because they provide a forum enabling the dialogue that underpins the inter-subjective construction of knowledge between individuals (Dietz et al., 2003; Preuss and Córdoba-Pachon, 2009). In sustainability as with other contexts, co-learning might occur as a result of bringing diverse knowledge resources together to achieve common goals around shared risks, by introducing partners to understanding of new markets or technologies or by bringing together complementary skills and capacities (Abreu and Camarinha-Matos, 2008; Head, 2008).

The learning and change that occurs through inter-organizational collaboration and partnering is influenced by power distribution issues. Roome and Wijen's (2006) empirical study on stakeholder influence on organizational learning suggests that exploitative learning is dependent on convergence of powerful stakeholder interests, while explorative learning is not so dependent on convergence. These authors suggest that effectiveness of learning routines is dependent on the motives and the power of the various actors in the partnership organizations and that this relates to actors being able to fulfil the various critical roles for innovative learning to occur. According to Tushman and Nadler (1996) the four key roles are: Idea generators, internal champions, gate-keepers or boundary spanner and mentors. Inter-organizational learning is also reliant on the appropriate use of boundary objects, those artefacts that allow individuals from different disciplines, cultural backgrounds, and organizational functions to share knowledge and co-generate new information (Star and Griesemer, 1989; Oswick and Robertson, 2009). With entity-based accounting and performance measurement systems, boundary spanning activities are not always rewarded; however the general movement towards networked organizations, partnerships and alliances, as well as to various forms of stakeholder engagement (e.g. Sharma and Henriques, 2005) is invoking a shift more in tune with sustainability than would otherwise be the case.

Towards systemic thinking

Implementing strong sustainability in commercial organizations entails the need for radical and paradigmatic change both within the organization and across its organizational field. Illustrating the difficulties in promulgating such an approach, a recent survey conducted by MIT Sloan Management Review and Boston Consulting Group showed that companies are struggling to understand the sustainability drivers and issues relevant to their industry, and have little idea of how to measure social and environmental costs or how to execute a sustainability change programme (Berns, et al., 2009). The MIT study identified that competing priorities are a barrier to change across all sectors, and that corporate leaders share a widespread lack of understanding of what sustainability means and ignorance of how it can add value. Such studies highlight the issue of externalities that underpins unsustainability and suggest that entity-based approaches to change will not prevent companies externalizing their social and environmental costs. In other words, they will not enable the change associated with implementing and managing closed-loop, cradle-to-cradle systems (Doppelt, 2008).

Examined more closely, terms like sustainable organizations, sustainable business and sustainable growth – like sustainable development – can appear oxymoronic and over imbued with optimism. The process of sustainable development, as conceived of in the Brundtland Report most obviously entails turning the wheels of capitalism in more innovative ways to achieve more efficient and effective use of resources by more people across the globe. Some contend the growth model implicated in capitalism inevitably involves greater throughput of resources, and a political economy that rewards the owners of capital for decisions in favour of their own interest, and risks at the expense of others. The 'system' is much bigger than many of us are able to deal with – and without substantive change of almost unimaginable proportions, tradeoffs of one kind of capital against another are inevitable in our personal and organizational lives (Angus-Leppan et al., 2010). Moreover, it can be said that 'partial' attitudes based on individual rather than the collective interest whether by politicians, managers or citizens are likely to lead to unsustainable development. Since organizations including businesses are unable to be disengaged from wider systems in which they operate, entity-based thinking would render them unlikely contenders for sustainability, despite their rhetoric to the contrary (Milne et al., 2006).

There are now widespread calls for a holistic and systems-based approach to address the challenges entailed in bringing about strong sustainability. The arguments are not new in the literature but they are starting to appear more frequently. Critique of the entity-based approach has moved well beyond the more radical fringe. A wide literature crossing science and social science (e.g. policy and education, as well as organization studies) disciplinary areas now recognizes the need to address a major systems failure entailing a reassessment of the relationship between human and ecological systems (Coupland, 2005; Ehrenfeld, 2005).

Thought leaders interviewed in the MIT Research Project companies identified the adoption of a broad, systems-based approach to business as one of the most critical capabilities if learning and change for sustainability is to be implemented. This involves holistic integration and stakeholder inclusiveness.

Systems approaches are many and varied and are important in general terms as underpinning a key element of sustainability thinking – the concept of the interconnectedness between entities. Systems approaches to change recognize that there are systems out there in the world, whether they be social, environmental, economic or physical that can be identified and therefore improved through various process-based approaches. Systemic thinking, however, breaks with the idea of systems as structures and works from an interpretative approach of systems as meaning construction 'confining change in social situations to changing people's worldviews' (Flood, 2006). A shift to organization-wide systemic thinking is key to deep change around sustainability and requires both logic-based and cultural analyses approaches.

Implementing such an approach to deep change based on recognition of the interconnectedness between entities requires a range of perspectives on systems thinking: functionalist, complex adaptive systems and interpretative (Porter and Córdoba, 2009). 'The three lenses may be simultaneously focused on one situation or problem, but this is quite different from melding them into a monolithic representation. What is possible, and highly valuable, is a toolkit containing all three approaches along with the knowledge of the best use of each' (Porter and Córdoba, 2009, p. 344). Porter and Córdoba (2009) focus on how managers should be educated to manage according to these systems thinking principles. This multiple-pronged perspective aimed at generating systemic thinking accepts that quantitative, instrumental techniques such as chemically-based life cycle analysis can be valuably applied alongside an interpretative emphasis on stakeholder consultation and a complex adaptive systems focus on network-based data collection, information generation and feedback. In other words, this perspective on change for sustainability encompasses both planned and emergent change.

Planned or evolutionary change?

Critically-inspired researchers in organization studies whose focus has been on inherent power relations within the political economy of capitalism have been joined by those exploring potential solutions. Here there has been an interest in how control might be relinquished in favour of more collectivist approaches and change practice designed to work with organizations as complex adaptive systems. Some of these approaches allow for uncertainty, foster debate and perhaps even dispute. Scholars of leadership in complex adaptive systems, for instance, argue that effective leadership is associated with allowing for, rather than reducing, uncertainty in order to foster innovation and creativity (Uhl-Bien et al., 2007). Key elements of this approach are change and leadership skills that can facilitate strategic direction setting in the face of complexity and ambiguity and a leadership style that supports network interaction, follower engagement and bottom up transformation. On this account, sustainability outcomes appear as an aspect of emergent change, reflecting characteristics such as unplanned, ongoing innovations and learning associated with both success and failures on the ground (Weick, 2000).

The debate around the extent that this systemic change towards sustainability should be planned for or allowed to emerge raises particular issues. On the one hand, the concept of emergent or evolutionary change and continuous transformation based on innovation (Weick, 2000; Burnes, 2005) is obviously relevant to sustainability. Numerous writers claim that sustainability is dependent upon generating high levels of innovation within the organization, leading to product, process or service redesign (eg Hart, 2005; Laszlo, 2008; Rodriguez et al., 2002). As summarized by Burnes (2004a) and as noted above, there has been much criticism of linear models of planned change on the basis of their inability to support creativity and responsiveness, and in the case of sustainability, to deal with the complexity of the interrelationships between organizations and multiple stakeholders now recognized as including the natural environment (Starik, 1995; Law, 2004).

Viewing sustainability as a new 'business ethic' (Crane and Matten, 2004), suggests the need for participative engagement by employees in a change agenda that specifically aims to achieve these behaviours. According to Burnes (2009), the emergent approach is problematic because it is based on the overarching view of an organization as a political system, where the key role for the change agent is to maintain control. Participative employee engagement with ethical, sustainable behaviour is not necessarily prioritised. Political skill is viewed as the premium capability underpinning successful change (Buchanan and Badham, 1999), rather than establishing what are appropriate ethical or sustainable concerns.

Our experience supports the argument that planned and evolutionary, emergent change can occur concurrently in organizations with positive results for sustainability (Burnes, 2004b). For example, one of us has studied a community of practice led by academic water engineers and agricultural scientists whose aim was not environmental sustainability but water efficiency and agricultural productivity (Benn and Martin, 2010). On their path to achieve these aims, the participants opened a holistic discursive space in which adaptive learning paths could be shaped for all members of the community. The outcome has been learning and change toward sustainability across the range of participants. Effectively, the scientists planned to encourage informal as well as formal connections across the network as a means of developing local understandings of water measurement. But this strategy was in fact in accordance with the principles of complex adaptive systems and emergent change that multiple interactions foster creativity and adaptation (Uhl-Bien et al., 2007). As an 'accidental' result, major sustainability outcomes evolved that went far beyond the issue of water savings for rice production. A key factor in the sustainability transformation operating to bring together the planned and evolving change occurring in this community of practice was the role played by both visionary and structural boundary objects (Star and Greisemer, 1989; Briers and Chua, 2001). These enabled the community to engage with the problem at hand (water efficiency and agricultural productivity) as a holistic and systemic issue (Benn and Martin, 2010).

Further support for the argument that planned and emergent change can be concurrent comes from recent empirical study involving multiple case based analysis of CSR implementation

543

Table 37.1 Implementing CSR/corporate sustainability

	Implementation initiative or process
Step 1	Raising sustainability awareness inside the organization
Step 2	Assessing corporate purpose in its environmental and social context
Step 3	Establishing a vision and a working definition for corporate sustainability
Step 4	Assessing current sustainability status
Step 5	Developing a strategic plan to integrate sustainability across decision-making
Step 6	Implementing the strategic plan
Step 7	Communication about sustainability commitments and performance
Step 8	Evaluating sustainability strategies and communication
Step 9	Institutionalizing sustainability

Source: Maon et al. 2009.

processes (Maon et al., 2009). The findings of this study lead the authors to advocate a nine-step approach to implement CSR that integrates culture, strategy and structure, and implicates sustainability thinking and practice as a central element (see Table 37.1).

These stages encompass a 4 stage model based on Lewin's 3 phase model of planned change: sensitize, unfreeze, move, refreeze. Its authors claim this approach minimizes the limitations of Lewin's model (summarized in Burnes, 2004a) and that it can be applied to both evolutionary and planned change programmes.

In our view, the debate over whether change for sustainability should be according to the planned or emergent approach can be addressed by considering the differences between earlier and more recent approaches to planned change. To address the multiple dimensions and uncertainties surrounding sustainability, the first generation (e.g. action research, sensitivity training) and second generation (e.g. future search) iterations of planned change (Seo et al., 2004) need to be reinterpreted through the lens of third-generation approaches such as appreciative inquiry, action learning and process interventions such as open-space technology. Proponents of participative inquiry forms of action research for example, aim for their change initiatives to contribute to "the increased well-being – economic, political, psychological, spiritual – of humanity, and to a more equitable and sustainable relationship with the wider ecology of the planet of which we are an intrinsic part" (Reason and Bradbury, 2001, p. 2).

A key principle is active participation so that double and triple loop learning around sustainability is prompted. As with the wider issue of implementing organizational change in accordance with ethical practice, sustainability change initiatives rest upon fostering a culture that embraces and supports open questioning (Clegg et al., 2007). Such open forms of deliberation are inhibited by narrative closure (Rhodes et al., 2009) around fixed understandings of what sustainability might mean in an organization, whether interpreted through fixed rules, deep green dogma or more tacit understandings. Allowing for multiple voices to emerge is important where the change concerns such value-laden and contested concepts as sustainability. Boje's (2001) warnings around taking single-voiced stories as evidence of change successes or failures are highly pertinent in this context.

Major change programmes

Recent understandings of participatory change and organization development approaches and interventions have led to the kinds of major change programmes exemplified above. A range of other techniques have been advocated and trialled.

544

Large-scale interventions such as Open Space Technology are now used by public planners but also in large organizations attempting to implement major change (Bunker and Alban, 2006). Their benefits are proposed as 'feelings of deeper community' between participants (p. 353), shared leadership and co-creation between members of society (p. 228), breaking down boundaries between community advocacy organizations and corporates and opening discussion.

Techniques such as Appreciative Inquiry, which aim to harness the positive energy in organizations by collaborative means, are being utilized in whole systems approaches that specifically target sustainability (such as the City of Cleveland and the award-winning Green Mountain Coffee Roasters) (Cooperrider and Whitney, 2005). Such 'whole-system action learning' techniques encompassing site, plant, organization-wide or inter-organizational activities are useful in building a shared commitment around such principles as sustainability, although there are challenges (Benn and Baker, 2009; Bryson and Anderson, 2000).

Whole-systems approaches to change are clearly dependent on interactions between the academic and change agent or practitioner communities. The gap between how the management research and practitioner communities understand such technologies and interventions is an issue of concern and there is a need for fuller relationships and a more direct and positive emotional connection between researchers and practitioners if these methods are to bring about change (Bartunek, 2007). This applies perhaps even more so for sustainability because of the wide spectrum of sustainability understandings as noted above. Based on our earlier discussions, we argue that these fuller relationships could be generated through recognition not only of the multiple and often competing stories through which change for sustainability can be narrated, but that change can be influenced prospectively through narrative (Buchanan and Dawson, 2007). But as these authors acknowledge, narrative analysis is not the only tool that should be brought to bear in a sustainability change programme. We need examples of structures that might facilitate the academic–practitioner exchange (Bartunek, 2007).

Leadership skills and capabilities

As discussed above, applying whole systems approaches to change involves working with both complex adaptive systems as well as instrumental and interpretative approaches to systemic change (Porter and Cordoba, 2009). In this context, effective leadership is associated with allowing for, rather than reducing, uncertainty in order to foster innovation and creativity – an approach we see as more appropriate to leading for sustainability. Key elements of this approach are change and leadership skills that can facilitate strategic direction setting in the face of complexity and ambiguity and a leadership style that supports network interaction, follower engagement and bottom up transformation, rather than the charismatic leadership style often seen as necessary to drive radical change.

Intellectual stimulation rather than CEO charismatic leadership, appear to encourage a firm to engage in 'strategic' CSR or sustainability (Waldman et al., 2006). By intellectual stimulation is meant a process whereby the leader increases employee awareness of problems and influences subordinates to view problems from a new perspective. Required leadership skills include greater collaborative skills; more flexibility in style; more openness; a greater adaptability to new ideas and more reflective decision making. On this account, effective change agents have a greater capacity to prompt dialogue around the potential sustainability agenda. Dialogue can enable individual learning to bridge to organizational learning, the transfer of tacit knowledge and hence lead to organizational change (Oswick et al., 2000). Also relevant in the case of change for sustainability is Skordoulis and Dawson's (2007) research suggesting that techniques of Socratic dialogue can encourage participative exchange, facilitating a change process that occurs 'with'

545

people rather than being directed 'onto' an organization. Other pertinent empirical studies are those suggesting that organizational creativity can be generated through encouraging the processes involved in perpetual challenging (adventuring, overt confronting, portfolioing and opportunizing) (Andriopoulos and Lowe, 2000).

Overall, the sustainability leader plays an integrative and relational role – variously as coach, steward, storyteller and transformational change agent. One role may be more evident than the others at different times, but this leader needs to be capable of all.

For the Future

On the basis of the foregoing review, we conclude there is much work ahead in the social movement towards sustainability and the academic field of sustainability research that is being generated largely in its wake. Important foundational work from the mid 1990s in organization studies provides ideals and concepts, that both functionally and critically-oriented scholars still cite and have yet to develop into a comprehensive theory. Cross disciplinary theoretical fertilization has occurred and is likely to continue. Multi-level analyses appear appropriate to generate understandings of systemic interactions and complexities. Managers and other members of organizations wrestling with on-the-ground challenges in operationalizing sustainability beyond the business case provide not just the locale for traditional research to take place, but also the opportunity for more hands-on researcher involvement in substantive change programmes. In working together in different ways of thinking and acting towards sustainability that are perhaps personally uncomfortable, but that extend organizational responsibilities outward and into longer time horizons, researchers and practitioners could well be working in the wider interests of us all.

References

Abreu, A. and Camarinha-Matos, L. (2008). On the role of value systems to promote the sustainability of collaborative environments, *International Journal of Production Research*, 46 (5): 1207–29.

Ackoff, R.T. (1994). *The Democratic Corporation: A Radical Prescription for Recreating Corporate America and Rediscovering Success*. New York: Oxford University Press.

Andriopoulos, C. and Lowe, A. (2000). Enhancing organizational creativity: the process of perpetual challenging, *Management Decision*, 38 (10): 734–42.

Angus-Leppan, T., Benn, S. and Young, L. (2010). A sensemaking approach to tradeoffs and synergies between human and ecological elements of corporate sustainability, *Business Strategy and the Environment*, 19(4): 230–44.

Argyris, C. and Schön, D.A. (1978). *Organizational Learning*. Reading, MA: Addison-Wesley.

Banerjee, S.B. (2001). Managerial perceptions of corporate environmentalism: Interpretations from industry and strategic implications for organization, *Journal of Management Studies*, 38 (4): 489–513.

Banerjee, S.B. (2003). Who sustains whose development? Sustainable development and the reinvention of nature, *Organization Studies*, 24 (1): 143–80.

Banerjee, S.B. (2007). *Corporate Social Responsibility: The Good, the Bad and the Ugly*, Cheltenham, UK: Edward Elgar.

Bansal, P. and Gao, J. (2006). Building the future by looking to the past: Examining research published on organizations and environment, *Organizations and Environment*, 19 (4): 458–78.

Bartunek, J.M. (2007). Academic-practitioner collaboration need not require joint or relevant research: Toward a relational scholarship of integration, *Academy of Management Journal*, 50 (6): 1323–33.

Beck, U. (2000). *What is Globalization?* Cambridge: Polity Press.

Benn, S. and Baker, E. (2009). Advancing sustainability through change and innovation: A co-evolutionary perspective, *Journal of Change Management*, 9 (4): 383–97.

Benn, S. and Martin, A. (2010). 'Learning and change for sustainability reconsidered: a role for boundary objects', ARIES Working Paper 01/2010, at www.aries.mq.edu.au/ (accessed 13 February 2010).

Berns, M., Townend, A., Khayat, Z., Balagopal, B., Reeves, M. and Hopkins, M. (2009). The business of sustainability: findings and insights from first annual business of sustainability survey and the global thought leaders research project, *MIT Sloan Management Review in collaboration with BCG*.

Boje, D. (2001). The storytelling organization: a study of story performance in an office-supply firm, *Administrative Science Quarterly*, 36: 106–26.

Bradbury, H. (2003). Sustaining inner and outer worlds: A whole systems approach to developing sustainable business practices in management, *Journal of Management Education*, 27 (2): 172–87.

Briers, M. and Chua, W.F. (2001). The role of actor-networks and boundary objects in management accounting change: A field study of an implementation of activity-based costing, *Accounting Organizations and Society*, 26 (3): 237–69.

Bryson, J.M. and Anderson, S.R. (2000). Applying large-group interaction methods in the planning and implementation of major change efforts, *Public Administration Review*, 60 (2): 143–62.

Buchanan, D. and Badham, R. (1999). *Power, Politics and Organizational Change*, London: SAGE.

Buchanan, D. and Dawson, P. (2007). Discourse and audience: Organizational change as multi-story process, *Journal of Management Studies*, 44 (5): 669–86.

Bunker, B.B. and Alban, B.A. (2006). *The Handbook of Large Group Methods: Creating Systemic Change in Organizations and Communities*, San Francisco, CA: Jossey Bass.

Burnes, B. (2004a). Kurt Lewin and complexity theories: back to the future? *Journal of Change Management*, 4 (4): 309–25.

Burnes, B. (2004b). Emergent change and planned change – competitors or allies? The case of XYZ construction, *International Journal of Operations and Production Management*, 24 (9): 886–902.

Burnes, B. (2005). Complexity theories and organizational change, *International Journal of Management Reviews*, 7 (2): 73–90.

Burnes, B. (2009). Reflections: Ethics and organizational change – Time for a return to Lewinian values, *Journal of Change Management*, 9 (4): 359–81.

Byrch, C., Kearins, K., Milne, M. and Morgan, R. (2007). Sustainable 'what'? A cognitive approach to understanding sustainable development, *Qualitative Research in Accounting and Management*, 4 (1): 26–52.

Clegg, S., Kornberger, M. and Rhodes, C. (2007). Business ethics as practice, *British Journal of Management*, 18 (2): 107–22.

Cooperrider, D. and Whitney, D. (2005). *Appreciative Inquiry: A Positive Revolution in Change*, San Francisco, CA: Berrett-Koehler.

Coupland, C. (2005). Corporate social responsibility as argument on the web, *Journal of Business Ethics*, 62: 355–66.

Crane, A. and Matten, D. (2004). *Business Ethics*, Oxford: Oxford University Press.

Dawson, P. (2003). *Organizational Change: A Processual Approach*, London: Routledge.

Day, R. and Arnold, M. (1998). The business case for sustainable development, *Greener Management International*, 23: 69–92.

Dentchev, N.A. (2009). To what extent is business and society literature idealistic? *Business and Society*, 48 (1): 10–38.

Dietz, T., Ostrom, E. and Stern, P. (2003). The struggle to govern the commons. *Science*, 302: 1907–12.

Dobson, A. (1999). *Fairness and Futurity: Essays on Environmental Sustainability and Social Justice* (pp. 21–45), New York: Oxford University Press.

Doppelt, B. (2008). *Leading Change toward Sustainability: A Change-Management Guide for Business, Government and Civil Society*, Sheffield: Greenleaf.

Dunphy, D., Griffiths, A. and Benn, S. (2007). *Organizational Change for Corporate Sustainability* (2nd edn), London: Routledge.

Dyllick, T. and Hockerts, K. (2002). Beyond the business case for corporate sustainability, *Business Strategy and the Environment*, 11 (2): 130–41.

Egri, C.P. and Pinfield, L. (1996). Organizations and the biosphere: Ecologies and environments. In S. Clegg, C. Hardy and W. Nord (eds), *Handbook of Organization Studies* (pp. 459–83), London: SAGE.

Ehrenfeld, J. (1999). Cultural structure and the challenge of sustainability. In K. Sexton, A.A. Marcus, K.W. Easter and T.D. Burkhardt, *Better Environmental Decisions: Strategies for Governments, Businesses and Communities* (pp. 223–44), Washington, DC: Island Press.

Ehrenfeld, J. (2005). The roots of sustainability. *MIT Sloan Management Review*, 46 (2): 23–25.

Etzion, D. and Ferraro, F. (2010). The role of analogy in the institutionalization of sustainability reporting, *Organization Science*, 21(5): 1092–1107.

Flood, R. (2006). The relationship of 'systems thinking' to action research. In P. Reason and H. Bradbury (eds), *Handbook of Action Research: The Concise Paperback Edition*: (pp. 117–28), London: SAGE.

Forbes L.C. and Jermier, J.M. (2002). The institutionalization of voluntary organizational greening and the ideals of environmentalism: Lessons about official culture from symbolic interaction theory. In A.J. Hoffman and M.J. Ventresca (eds), *Organizations, Policy and the Natural Environment* (pp. 195–213), Stanford, CA: Stanford University Press.

Freeman, R.E. (1984). *Strategic Management: A Stakeholder Approach*. Boston, MA: Pitman.

Garriga, E. and Mele, D. (2004). Corporate Social responsibility theories: Mapping the territory, *Journal of Business Ethics*, 53 (1/2): 51–71.

Gladwin, T.N., Kennelly, J.J. and Krause, T.S. (1995). Shifting paradigms for sustainable development: Implications for management theory and research, *Academy of Management Review*, 20: 874–907.

Hajer, M. and Fischer, F. (1999). Introduction – Beyond global discourse: The rediscovery of culture in environmental politics. In F. Fischer and M. Hajer (eds), *Living with Nature: Environmental Politics as Cultural Discourse*, Oxford: Oxford University Press.

Hardjono, T. and de Klein, P. 2004. Introduction on the European corporate sustainability framework, *Journal of Business Ethics*, 55 (2): 99–113.

Hart, S. (1995). A natural resource-based view of the firm, *Academy of Management Review*, 20: 986–1014.

Hart, S. (1997). Beyond greening: Strategies for a sustainable world. *Harvard Business Review*, January–February): 66–76.

Hart, S.L. (1995). A natural-resource-based view of the firm. *Academy of Management Review*, 20 (4): 986–1014.

Head, B. (2008). Three lenses of evidence-based policy. *Australian Journal of Public Administration*, 67 (1): 1–11.

Hoffman, A. and Ehrenfeld, J. (1998). Corporate environmentalism, sustainability and management studies. In N. Roome (ed.), *Environmental Strategies for Industry: The Future of Corporate Practice* (pp. 55–73). Washington, DC: Island Press.

Huber, G.P. (1991). Organizational learning: the contributing processes and the literatures, *Organization Science*, 2: 88–115.

Jennings, P. and Zandbergen, P. (1995). Ecologically sustainable organizations: An institutional approach, *Academy of Management Review*, 20 (4): 1015–52.

Hunt, C. and Auster, E. (1990). Proactive environmental management: Avoiding the toxic trap, *Sloan Management Review*, 31 (2): 7–18.

Kearins, K. and Springett, D. (2003). Educating for sustainability: Developing critical skills, *Journal of Management Education*, 27 (2): 188–204.

Kolk, A. and Mauser, A. (2002). The evolution of environmental management: From stage models to performance evaluation, *Business Strategy and the Environment*, 11: 14–31.

Laszlo, C. (2008) *Sustainable Value: How the World's Leading Companies are Doing Well by Doing Good*, Palo Alto, CA: Stanford University Press.

Law, J. (2004). *After Method: Mess in Social Science Research*, London: Routledge.

Levie J, Lichtenstein, B.B. (2008). From 'stages' of business growth to a dynamic states model of entrepreneurial growth and change. University of Strathclyde Hunter Centre for Entrepreneurship Working Paper WP08–02.

Levy, D.L. (1997). Environmental management as political sustainability, *Organization and Environment*, 10 (2): 126–47.

Levy, D.L., Brown, H.S. and de Jong, M. (2010). The contested politics of corporate governance: The case of the Global Reporting Initiative, *Business and Society*, 49 (1): 88–115.

548

Margolis, J.D., Elfenbein, H.A. and Walsh, J.P. (2008a). Does it pay to be good? A meta-analysis and redirection of research on the relationship between corporate social and financial performance. Working paper, Harvard University.

Margolis, J.D., Elfenbein, H.A. and Walsh, J.P. (2008b). Do well by doing good? Don't count on it, *Harvard Business Review*, 86 (1): 19–21.

Matten, D. and Moon, J. (2008). "Implicit" and "explicit" CSR: a conceptual framework for a comparative understanding of corporate social responsibility, *Academy of Management Review*, 33: 404–24.

Matten, D., Crane, A. and Chapple, W. 2003. Behind the mask: Revealing the true face of corporate citizenship, *Journal of Business Ethics*, 45: 109–20.

Maon, F., Lindgreen, A. and Swaen, V. 2009. Designing and implementing corporate social responsibility: An integrative framework grounded in theory and practice, *Journal of Business Ethics*, 87: 71–89.

McKeown, R. (2002). Education for sustainable development toolkit: What is ESD? www.esdtoolkit.org/discussion/whatisesd.htm (accessed 29 March 2011).

Millennium Ecosystem Assessment. (2005). *Ecosystems and Human Well-being: Current State and Trends*. Washington, DC: Island Press.

Milne, M., Kearins, K. and Walton, S. (2006). Business makes a *'journey'* out of *'sustainability'*: Creating adventures in Wonderland? *Organization*, 13 (6), 801–39.

Muller, K. and Koechlin, D. (1992). Environmentally conscious management, in D. Koechlin and K. Müller (eds), *Green Business Opportunities: The Profit Potential* (pp. 33–57), London: Pitman.

Newton, T.J. (2002). Creating the new ecological order? Elias and actor network theory, *Academy of Management Review*, 27, 523–40.

Newton, T.J. and Harte, G. (1997). Green business: Technicist kitsch? *Journal of Management Studies*, 34, 75–98.

Oswick, C., Anthony, P., Keenov, T., Mangham, I.L. and Grant, D. (2000). A dialogic analysis of organizational learning, *Journal of Management Studies*, 37 (6): 887–901.

Pearce, D. (1993). *Blueprint 3: Measuring Sustainable Development*, London: Earthscan.

Pearce, D., Barbier, E.B. and Markandya, A. (1990). *Sustainable Development: Economics and Environment in the Third World*, London: Earthscan.

Pettigrew, A.M., Woodman, R.W. and Cameron, K.S. (2001). Studying organizational change and development: challenges for future research, *Academy of Management Journal*, 44 (4): 697–713.

Porter, T. and Cordoba, J. (2009). Three views of systems theories and their implications for sustainability education, *Journal of Management Education*, 33 (3): 323–47.

Porter M.E. and Kramer, M.R. (2006). Strategy and society: The link between competitive advantage and corporate social responsibility, *Harvard Business Review*, 84 (12), December: 78–92.

Porter, M. and van der Linde, C. (1995). Green and competitive, *Harvard Business Review*, 73 (5), 120–34.

Prasad, P. and Elmes, M. (2005). In the name of the practical: Unearthing the hegemony of pragmatics in the discourse of environmental management, *Journal of Management Studies*, 42, 845–67.

Preuss, L. and Córdoba-Pachon, J.-R. (2009). A knowledge management perspective of corporate social responsibility. *Corporate Governance*, 9 (4): 517–27.

Purser, R., Park, C.K. and Montuori, A. (1995). Limits to anthropocentrism: Towards an ecocentric organization paradigm? *Academy of Management Review*, 20 (4): 1053–89.

Ramus, C.A. and Steger, U. (2000). The roles of supervisory support behaviors and environmental policy in employee "Ecoinitiatives" at leading-edge European companies, *Academy of Management Journal*, 43 (4): 605–26.

Reason, P. and Bradbury, H. (2001). Inquiry and participation in search of a world worthy of human aspiration. In P. Reason and H. Bradbury (eds), *Handbook of Action Research: Participative Inquiry and Practice* (pp. 1–14). London: SAGE.

Redclift, M. (1987). *Sustainable Development: Exploring the Contradictions*. London: Methuen.

Rhodes, C., Pullen, A. and Clegg, S. (2009). 'If I should Fall from grace…': Stories of change and organizational ethics, *Journal of Business Ethics*, 91 (4): 535–51.

Riane, E. and Eisler, R. 1994. From domination to partnership: The hidden subtext for sustainable change, *Journal of Organizational Change Management*, 7 (4): 32.

Rodriguez, M., Ricart, J. and Sanchez, P. (2002). Sustainable development and the sustainability of competitive advantage, *Creativity and Innovation Management*, 11: 135–46.

Romme, G. and van Witteloostuijn, A. (1999). Circular organizing and triple loop learning, *Journal of Organizational Change Management*, 12 (2): 439–54.

Roome, N. and Wijen, F. (2006). Stakeholder power and organizational learning in corporate environmental management, *Organization Studies*, 27 (2): 235–63.

Russell, S.V., Haigh, N.L. and Griffiths, A.B. (2006). Understanding corporate sustainability: Recognizing the impact of different governance systems. In S. Benn and D.C. Dunphy (eds), *Corporate Governance and Sustainability: Challenges for Theory and Practice* (pp. 36–56), New York: Routledge.

Seitanidi, M. and Crane, A. (2009). Implementing CSR through partnerships: Understanding the selection, design and institutionalisation of nonprofit-business partnerships, *Journal of Business Ethics*, 85: 413–29.

Senge, P.M., Lichenstein, B.B., Kaeufer, K., Bradbury, H. and Carroll, J.S. (2007). Collaborating for systemic change, *MIT Sloan Management Review*, 48 (2): 44–53.

Seo, M., Putnam, L. and Bartunek, J. (2004). Dualities and tensions of planned organizational change. In M.S. Poole and A. Van de Ven (eds), *Handbook of Organizational Change and Innovation* (pp. 73–107), Oxford: Oxford University Press.

Sharma, S. and Henriques, I. (2005). Stakeholder influences on sustainability practices in the Canadian forest products industry, *Strategic Management Journal*, 26: 159–80.

Sharma, S. and Starik, M. (eds) (2002). *Research in Corporate Sustainability: The Evolving Theory and Practice of Organizations in the Natural Environment.* Northampton, MA: Edward Elgar.

Shrivastava, P. (1994). CASTRATED environment: GREENING organizational studies, *Organization Studies*, 15 (5): 705–26.

Shrivastava, P. and Hart, S. (1995). Creating sustainable corporations, *Business Strategy and the Environment*, 4: 154–65.

Skordoulis, R. and Dawson, P. (2007). Reflective decisions: the use of Socratic dialogue in managing organizational change, *Management Decision*, 45 (6): 991–1007.

Springett, D. (2003). An 'incitement to discourse': Benchmarking as a springboard to sustainable development, *Business Strategy and the Environment*, 12 (1): 1–11.

Springett, D. (2005). Education for sustainability in the business studies curriculum: a call for a critical agenda, *Business Strategy and the Environment*, 14 (3): 146–59.

Star, S.L. and Griesemer, J.R. (1989). Institutional ecology, 'translations' and boundary objects: amateurs and professionals in Berkeley's Museum of Vertebrate Zoology, 1907–39. *Social Studies of Science*, 19: 387–420.

Stank, M. (1995). Should trees have managerial standing? Toward stakeholder status for non-human nature, *Journal of Business Ethics*, 14 (3): 207–17.

Starik, M. (2006). In search of relevance and impact: Introduction to a special feature on the state of organizations and the natural environment research, *Organizations and Environment*, 19(4): 431–38.

Starik, M. and Rands, G.P. (1995). Weaving an integrated web: Multilevel and multisystem perspectives of ecologically sustainable organizations, *Academy of Management Review*, 20 (4): 908–35.

Stephens, J. and Graham, A. (2010). Toward an empirical research agenda for sustainability in higher education: exploring the transition management framework. *Journal of Cleaner Production.* 18 (7): 611–18.

Taylor, S., Egri, C. and Osland, J. (in press) HRM's role in sustainability: Systems, strategies and practices. *Human Resource Management.*

Tilbury, D. and Wortman, D. (2004). *Engaging People in Sustainability*, Commission on Education and Communication, IUCN, Gland, Switzerland and Cambridge, UK.

Tormey, R., Liddy, M., Maguire, H. and McCloat, A. (2008). Working in the action/research nexus for education for sustainable development: Two case studies from Ireland. *International Journal of Sustainability in Higher Education*, 9 (4): 428–40.

Turner, R.K. (ed.) (1993). *Sustainable Environmental Economics and Management: Principles and Practice*, London: Belhaven.

Tushman, M. and Nadler, D. (1996). Organizing for innovation. In K. Starkey (ed.), *How Organizations Learn* (pp. 135–55). London: Thomson.

Uhl-Bien, M., Marion, R. and McKelvey, B. (2007). Complexity leadership theory: Shifting leadership from the industrial age to the knowledge era, *Leadership Quarterly*, 18 (4): 298–318.

UNESCO (2005a). Report by the Director-General on the United Nations. Decade of Education for Sustainable Development: International implementation scheme and UNESCO's contribution to the implementation of the Decade, http://unesdoc.unesco.org/images/0014/001403/140372e.pdf (accessed 20 September 2009).

UNESCO (2005b). Education for sustainable development toolkit CD-ROM: Teaching and learning for a sustainable future, www.unesco.org/education/tlsf/TLSF/theme_d/uncofrm_d.htm (accessed 20 September 2009).

UNESCO (2005c). Contributing to a more sustainable future: Quality education, life skills and education for sustainable development, http://unesdoc.unesco.org/images/0014/001410/141019e.pdf accessed 20 September 2009.

van Marrewijk, M. and Hardjono, T. (2003). European corporate sustainability framework for managing complexity and corporate transformation. *Journal of Business Ethics*, 44: 121–32.

Waddock, S. (1989). Understanding social partnerships. An evoluntionary model of partnership organizations, *Administration and Society*, 21 (1): 78–100.

Waldman, D. A., Siegel, D. S. and Javidan, M. (2006). Components of CEO transformational leadership and corporate social responsibility, *Journal of Management Studies*, 43 (8): 1703–25.

Weick, K. (2000). Emergent change as a universal in organizations. In M. Beer and N. Nohria (eds), *Breaking the Code of Change* (pp. 223–43), Cambridge, MA: Harvard Business Press.

Welford, R. (1995). *Environmental Strategy and Sustainable Development: The Corporate Challenge for the 21st Century*, London: SAGE.

Welford R. (ed.) (1997). *Hijacking Environmentalism: Corporate Responses to Sustainable Development*, London: Earthscan.

Welford, R. (1998). Editorial: Corporate environmental management, technology and sustainable development: postmodern perspectives and the need for a critical research agenda, *Business Strategy and the Environment*, 7 (1): 1–12.

Welford, R. (2000). *Corporate Environmental Management 3: Towards Sustainable Development*, London: Earthscan.

WCED (World Commission on Environmental and Development) (1987). *Our Common Future* (Brundtland Report), Oxford: Oxford University Press.

Worldwatch Institute (2009). *State of the World 2009: Into a Warming World*. Washington, DC: Worldwatch Institute.

Worldwatch Institute (2010). *State of the World 2010: Transforming Cultures*. Washington, DC: Worldwatch Institute.

World Wide Fund for Nature. 2008. *Living Planet Report 2008*. http://assets.panda.org/downloads/living_planet_report-2008.pdf (accessed 12 January 2009).

Zadek, S. 2004. The path to corporate responsibility. *Harvard Business Review*, 82 (12): 125–32.

38

Rethinking the change project

Theodore Taptiklis

What occurs in our public service is a paradox of dynamic paralysis – we appear to be in a process of development and transformation but in reality are in a state of extended suspension of action.

This occurs because as we seek to enhance our ability to build an effective state machinery, we identify the problem in the structures of our organizations. So what do we do? We restructure. We create new posts, shift people around, and shunt out of the way those we believe are not delivering. We advertise new or existing posts; we put acting managers in positions in the interim. We try to sort out the funding issues; we go through the slow process of attracting new people, often from other government departments, creating new vacancies in those departments and perpetuating an endless cycle of vacancies.

Finally all the posts in the new structure are filled. A few people have resigned, feeling uncomfortable or sidelined in the new structure, having been shifted too many times just as they were settling into their positions and finally feeling equipped to deliver. A new management structure is in place. It immediately conducts a review. This indicates that the organization is not equipped to fulfill its mandate. What they need to do is – wait for it – restructure. And so the cycle begins again.

(Lewis Rabkin, *Don't Just Think Outside the Box*, The Cape Argus, 27 August 2009)

Introduction

Change has become a dominating philosophy of organizational intervention over the past thirty years. It is now a worldwide industry, and has built a formidable legion of practitioners, or 'change agents', who are active in enterprises of all kinds. Its language – for example, the term 'resistance to change' – is now common organizational currency. Its unique synthesis of ideas that include self-help, pop psychology and force-field modelling as applied to human affairs have given it a powerful instrumental appeal that now has a strong grip on the corporate imagination.

But that same instrumental appeal – casting the manager in the role of a latter-day alchemist, stirring the crucible until the gold of a new organizational culture starts to glister – seems, in the long run, to be yielding only the sense of disappointment that Lewis Rabkin describes. We find, for example, that change projects set so much in motion that unbidden consequences soon appear. Undervalued and unnoticed capabilities seem easily lost. Desired behaviours remain maddeningly elusive. And the associated uncertainty that galvanises a few people tends to demoralise many more. Moreover, the 'change agents' do not themselves seem to be subject to the same mysterious 'external forces' to which they wish others to respond. In these circumstances, a sense may naturally arise that people are simply being coerced and manipulated by those who do not necessarily see themselves as bound by the underlying values and purposes of the enterprise. And should this lead to resistance, it may only be met with greater force and a hardened sense of instrumental purpose.

Such concerns about the underlying ethos of organizational change can be reinforced by the popular management literature on the subject. Here is a recent piece from US corporate boss Jack Welch (2009):

Change is an absolutely critical part of business. And yes, your company does have to change, preferably now and not later, when you have no other choice. The problem is that people hate it when their bosses announce a transformation initiative. They run back to their cubicles and start frantically emailing one another, complaining that the changes are going to ruin everything.

Sometimes the need for change isn't immediately apparent. Competitive threats seem to be emerging, but you don't know for certain, and still, you have to respond. In these cases relentless communication about the business rationale for change, reinforced with lots of data, is the best ammunition you have.

The larger your firm, the more challenging it is to communicate the need for change. In big firms, calls for change are often greeted non-committally. After all, if the firm has been through enough change programmes, employeees will assume you'll go away if they just wait long enough. Stick to your guns – your solid, persuasive business case. Over time, logic will win out.

Hire and promote only true believers and get-on-with-it-types. Everyone in business claims to like change. To say otherwise would be career suicide. But by my estimate, at least 10% of all business people are true change agents. Once the next group – around 70–80% of people working in business – is convinced that change is necessary, they'll say, 'OK already, get on with it.' The rest are resisters. To make change happen, companies must actively hire and promote only true believers and get-on-with-its. But with everyone claiming to like change, how can you tell who is for real?

Luckily, change agents usually make themselves known. They're typically brash, high-energy and more than a little paranoid about the future ... These people have a certain fearlessness about the unknown. If they fail, they know they can pick themselves up, dust themselves off and move on. They're thick-skinned about risk, which allows them to make bold decisions without a lot of data.

Ferret out and remove the resisters, even if their performance is satisfactory. This is the hardest of the (change) practices to implement. It's tough to let anyone go, but it's particularly difficult to fire people who are not actually screwing up and may in fact be doing quite well ... That may sound harsh, but you're not doing anyone a favour by keeping resisters in your organization. They foster an underground resistance and lower the morale of the people who support change. They're wasting their own time: they're working at a company where they don't agree or share in the vision, and they should be encouraged to find one where they do.

It is hard to know where to begin with this. But perhaps we might start with the reasons advanced for organizational change. They are strikingly vague and perfunctory. Even the 'guns' and 'ammunition' of the 'solid, persuasive business case' that is 'reinforced by lots of data' of the second and third paragraphs above seem to be happily thrown aside by the fifth paragraph, where we are encouraged to admire 'change agents' who 'make bold decisions without a lot of data'. 'Yes, your company does have to change, preferably now,' says Jack Welch – meaning, we might infer, before there is any real excuse for doing so.

In this incarnation, organizational change simply becomes a convenient fiction for the assertion of the will of a dominant individual or group. The real discussion here is about how to exert one's will. The recipe for change that is proposed is to operate rather like a military dictator:

> You start by looking for a pretext (just as dictators look for scapegoats or manufactured threats as a prelude to a putsch or a pogrom). In this case, the idea of change can itself become the pretext. 'Being paranoid about the future', as Jack Welch puts it, is a perfect starting point;
>
> You then 'announce a transformation initiative' backed up by 'relentless communication of the business rationale for change' (i.e. you mount a propaganda offensive). Your only interest in the existing employees, who you expect will 'run back to their cubicles' and 'frantically email one another to complain' at your actions, is to manipulate them into submission and eventual agreement with your 'vision';
>
> You hire and promote an army of (thick-skinned and fearless) mercenary types to enforce the change. These 'true believers' will not be distracted by any concerns about the change from within the existing enterprise, because they know that they can 'move on' even when they fail;
>
> You and your mercenaries reserve your best efforts for dealing with 'resisters', even – perhaps particularly – those whose 'performance is satisfactory' and 'may in fact be doing quite well'. These unfortunates are not only 'lowering the morale of those who support change' but are 'wasting their own time as well', simply because they find themselves at odds with the new 'vision' for the enterprise (the one you've just invented). You and your troops must 'ferret out and remove' these people, who must be 'encouraged' (by being fired) to find somewhere else to go.

I have dwelt on this example because I think in his unguarded brutality, Jack Welch reveals a sense in which the idea of 'organizational change' can become a sham: that is, a convenient vehicle for the assertion of institutional power by individuals or groups who are (often temporarily) in charge. And for us to continue with this notion – despite what I have experienced as repeated failure, irrecoverable human cost and permanent loss of institutional capability – reveals ourselves, I think, as susceptible to a self-imposed ordinance that, at worst, is simply cynical and corrupt, and, at best – because it doesn't succeed – is a collective fantasy of significant proportions.

So I have an ambitious agenda in this chapter. I start by setting our present struggles and disappointments with organizational change practices in the context of an under-acknowledged ideology. I see our approaches and attitudes to organizational change as inseparable from an underlying set of beliefs that I think deserve to be examined more closely. I seek to sketch an outline of these beliefs: where they have come from, where they have been leading us, and what their consequences are. I will argue that these beliefs are fundamental ones, about what it is to be a human being in a world of other human beings.

I then propose other ways of understanding ourselves and our possibilities for making sense and achieving things together. And finally, I suggest how these other ways of understanding might help us to discover new, more practical, more satisfying, and longer-lasting means of achieving organizational change.

The intellectualization of the workplace

An important cause of our present difficulty, I believe, lies in the progressive separation of the conduct of skilled work from its oversight or management. We have arrived at an epoch where those with institutional power are no longer connected to, or necessarily concerned with, those who do the work every day.

When I began my organizational career, more than forty years ago, the norm was still to 'promote from within'. The Dutch multinational Philips, where I started work, was run by people who had risen through the ranks and had strong connections to the Philips family and its values. The detailed doings of many aspects of this complex enterprise seemed to be everyone's concern. As a (very junior) management cadet, I started in a branch office warehouse, beginning my apprenticeship with everyday and menial tasks. However, the era of the professional executive that was just beginning around that time rather dismissed 'family values', and largely did away with apprenticeship. A cadre of business-school-trained 'leaders' was starting to emerge who – focused on resumé accomplishments, and operating as consultants, executives, and board members – would be able to move between organizations and industries without becoming too closely attached to any one of them. And within a short period, I was seeking to become one of them.

The rise of professional management – and of what I now see as 'managerialism' – can be understood as a response to increasing organizational scale and complexity. But I think it is also connected to the accelerating pace of organizational change in recent times. In corporate mergers and takeovers, and in organizational 'restructuring' programmes, the delicate skein of carefully constructed workplace relationships and understandings – what Theodore Zeldin (1994, p. 466) calls the 'gossamer web' – is suddenly ripped apart. In place of these relationships, and without immediate connection between practitioners and their organizers – for example through personal ownership or direct supervision – we have evolved elaborate theories and models and multi-layered systems of measurement, reporting and evaluation. In turn, these have drawn us into an increasing fascination with abstractions like leadership, innovation and change.

Through simplified models or representations of human activity, such devices have helped us to order and arrange work at a distance, and have encouraged the growth of large institutional empires. But I suggest that their proliferation – and the present dominance of intellectual analysis – has now gone so far that it hinders us from getting to grips with and dealing with the realities of the day-to-day workplace. Slowly it has ground the natural responsiveness and creativity out of our workplace conduct, and has progressively reduced the capability of many of our organizations.

The history of work and its intellectualization is instructive. From earliest times, as soon as labour became specialized, and tasks were undertaken by one person who was paid by another, the question has arisen: What is good work? Manual labour or craft work seems to produce visible results, or things whose functional quality can be observed directly. But even here there are problems. How can we judge the thatcher's work until there's a rainstorm? Or until the wind blows from an unusual quarter, which happens only once or twice in a year? Many aspects of 'good work' are not visible to the untrained eye, but are deeply embedded in the tiniest details of working practice.

As the types of specialized work proliferated, so it became important to record and remember the details of each activity. Beginning in the Middle Ages, guilds and societies were formed to regulate the transmission of this specialized knowledge. A detailed understanding of a specific working practice was held to be a privilege, available only to a member of the institution (a craftsperson) who committed to the rules and the disciplines of apprenticeship. In this jealously guarded world, the connection between work and its evaluation was a very intimate one. Work was not seen to be complete until the guild-master judged it so. Sub-standard work might damage the reputation of the entire professional community. (Sub-standard work might even be an offence punishable by God.)

However, in the seventeenth century, Descartes and the Enlightenment began the massive shift in Western society that swept away notions of secret and privileged knowledge, undermined the institutions that depended on such secrecy, and opened the floodgates of the public realm. Newspapers appeared, making the details of distant events and undertakings widely available to anyone. In the middle of the eighteenth century, Diderot and the Encyclopedists, in a massive publishing effort, did their best to explain and illustrate the working knowledge of all known professions and crafts. Now it seemed that work and its detailed understanding and evaluation could at last be separated. With the appropriate volume of the Encyclopedia under his arm, the young squire could argue with the master builder about the placement of windows in the façade of his new manor, or decide to vary the roof pitch according to the fashion of the day.

With the rise of industrialization, new, larger-scale forms of enterprise appeared. People were gathered together not by profession or craft, but by industrial activity. The quality of work could no longer be regulated by the guild, or be influenced and moderated by the beliefs and attitudes of those in the local community. The rhythm of work was set by the machine rather than by the embodied skill of the worker.

So was the ground readied for the great twentieth-century invention: the management project. By the second half of the twentieth century, with first the growth and then the globalization of the management project, the separation of work from its oversight was completed, symbolized in its central figure: the Manager. For this heroic enterprise, the manager now had at his command all the classic tools of the Enlightenment: abstraction, simplification, and measurement.

And with these tools, the management project became prolific in its outputs, generating extensive theories of organization as well as a bewildering array of change models. Here is a single page from a comprehensive management encyclopedia-cum-forum produced in the Netherlands, hosted on the internet as *12manage.com: The Executive Fast Track* (Table 38.1):

Table 38.1 Change and organization, methods, models and theories (A–Z)

14 Principles of Management (Fayol)	Disruptive Innovation (Christensen)	PMMM Reiss
		Policy Deployment (Hoshin Kanri)
7-S Framework (McKinsey)	Distinctive Capabilities (Kay)	Portfolio Analysis
Acquisition Integration Approaches (Haspeslagh Jemison)	EFQM	POSDCORB (Gulick)
Action Learning (Revans)	Enterprise Architecture (Zachman)	Positive Deviance (Pascale Sternin)
Adhocracy	Entrepreneurial Government (Osborne)	Product Life Cycle (Levitt)
Appreciative Inquiry (Cooperrider)	Expectancy Theory (Vroom)	Real Options (Luehrman)
Ashridge Mission Model (Campbell)	Experience Curve	Requisite Organization (Jaques)
Balanced Scorecard (Kaplan Norton)	Facilitation Styles (Heron)	Result Oriented Management
Bases of Social Power (French Raven)	Five Disciplines (Senge)	Servant-Leadership (Greenleaf)
Beyond Budgeting (Fraser)	Force Field Analysis (Lewin)	Seven Habits (Covey)

BPR (Hammer Champy)

Brainstorming

Bridging Epistemologies
(Cook Brown)
Business Process Reengineering
(Hammer Champy)
Capability Maturity Model CMM
Catalytic Mechanisms (Collins)
Catastrophe Theory (Thom)
Causal Model of Organizational
Performance and Change
(Burke-Litwin)
Centralization and Decentralization

Change Approaches (Kotter)

Change Behavior (Ajzen)
Change Dimensions
(Pettigrew Whipp)
Change Equation (Beckhard)
Change Factors (Pettigrew Whipp)

Change Management (Iceberg)

Change Phases (Kotter)
Changing Organization Cultures (Trice
Beyer)
Chaos Theory (Lorenz)

Charismatic Leadership (Weber)

Coaching
CMM model

Co-Creation (Prahalad Ramaswamy)

Competing Values Framework
(Quinn)
Contingency Theory (Vroom)

Core Competence
(Hamel Prahalad)
Core Group Theory (Kleiner)

Crisis Management
Cross-functional Team

CSFs (Rockart)

Cultural Dimensions (Hofstede)
Cultural Intelligence (Early)

Forget Borrow Learn
(Govindarajan Trimble)
Fourteen Points of
Management (Deming)
Gestalt Theory

Group Dynamics

Groupthink (Janis)
Growth Phases (Greiner)
Hawthorne Effect (Mayo)
Hierarchic Organization
(Burns)

Hoshin Kanri - Policy
Deployment
Implementation
Management (Krüger)
Intellectual Capital Rating
Industry Change (McGahan)

Industry Life Cycle
Innovation Adoption Curve
(Rogers)
Intangible Assets Monitor
(Sveiby)
Just-in-time JIT
Kaizen philosophy

Knowledge Management
(Collison Parcell)
KPIs (Rockart)

Leadership Pipeline Drotter
Leadership Styles Goleman

Learning Organization
(Argyris Schön)
Level 5 Leadership (Collins)

Levels of Culture (Schein)

Levers of Control (Simons)

Management by Objectives
(Drucker)
Management Development
Managerial Grid (Blake
Mouton)
Managing for Value
(McTaggart)
Mentoring
Mergers and Acquisitions
approaches

Scientific Management (Taylor)

Seven Surprises (Porter)

Shared Service Center

Shareholder Value Perspective

Simulation modeling
Six Thinking Hats (de Bono)
Skandia Navigator (Edvinsson)
SMART (Drucker)

Sociotechnical Systems

Soft Systems Methodology
(Checkland)
Stage-Gate (Cooper)
Stages of Team Development
(Tuckman)
Stakeholder Value Perspective
Strategic Intent (Hamel
Prahalad)
Strategic Thrusts (Wiseman)

Strategic Types (Miles Snow)
Strategy Map (Kaplan Norton)

SWOT Analysis

Systems Thinking/Dynamics
(Forrester)
Team Building
Ten Principles of Reinvention
(Osborne)
Ten Schools of Thought
(Mintzberg)
Theory of Constraints (Goldratt)

Theory of Mechanistic and
Organic Systems (Burns)
Theory of Reasoned Action
(Ajzen Fishbein)
Theory X Theory Y (McGregor)

Theory Z (Ouchi)
Training Within Industry

Trajectories of Industry Change
(McGahan)
Turnaround Management
Twelve Principles of the
Network Economy (Kelly)

(continues on the next page)

Table 38.1 (Continued)

Culture Levels (Schein)	Metaplan (Schnelle)	Value Based Management
Culture Types Deal (Kennedy)	Modeling Business Processes	Value Chain Porter
Decentralization	MSP OGC	Value Disciplines (Treacy Wiersema)
Deming Cycle (PDSA)	Office of Strategy Management (Kaplan Norton)	Value Mapping (Jack)
DICE Framework (BCG)	People CMM CM-SEI	Value Stream Mapping
Dimensions of Change (Pettigrew Whipp)	Performance Categories (Baldridge)	
Dimensions of Relational Work (Butler)	Performance Management	
	Performance Prism	
	PMBOK PMI	

The management project sought to be instrumental not only in evaluating work, but also in shaping and guiding attitudes to its conduct and its performance. And although not necessarily their original intention, the ubiquity of management doctrines has fostered a climate of mistrust: an attitude of scepticism, and even cynicism, about the claims of those who do the work – its practitioners. 'What can't be measured, can't be managed,' became the mantra. As a result, expert practitioners have fallen increasingly out of favour as sources of institutional guidance. 'Best practice' has increasingly been assumed to come from outside the organization. And such best practice must be conveyed and articulated by independent consultants – since the organization's own practitioners are held to be potentially self-serving.

Perhaps the apotheosis of this project was the attempt in the final decades of the twentieth century to define a single composite measure of the value of work: shareholder value. This iconic construction sought to distill human purpose at work to a universally recognizable form: 'I produce shareholder value, therefore I am.' Here the work and its evaluation became so distant that both began to be seen as abstractions. (And the opportunities for fast-paced financial manipulation in corporations like Enron seemed almost to have made the actual work of the enterprise irrelevant.)

This, then, is the context for our doctrines of instrumentalized organizational change. From the boardroom perspective of Jack Welch and his colleagues, businesses and public enterprises are plastic and malleable entities, separable from the people, the purposes and the practices from which they have been constituted; their histories can be regarded as largely irrelevant to their potential futures; heroic leaders with 'vision' (preferably untainted by previous experience in the organization) should determine their purpose and direction; that these leaders are so valuable that they should be massively compensated, both to motivate them and 'pour encourager les autres'; and they should be given a free hand to reinvent the enterprise, recruit like-minded supporters and remove nay-sayers and recalcitrants as they see fit. We can see how easily such an élite corps can become detached from any sense of local accountability and responsibility, instead moving naturally towards a free-floating existence in a heady atmosphere of celebrity, self-congratulation and extraordinary material rewards.

In our public enterprises, the essentials of this ideological influence have been repeated, with differences of detail. For example, devices like the 'funder-provider' split in healthcare and infrastructure provision have encouraged public servants (who had previously worked together) to choose between employment in service commissioning organizations (as managers), or bidding as newly-formed commercial enterprises (as suppliers) for the provision of those services. By separating commissioning from service provision, the work of the public sector is now distanced from its evaluation. Unreliable human judgements of service quality can be replaced by more 'scientific' performance measures.

In this managerial public service environment, a new doctrine has arisen: the concept of 'outcomes'. Outcomes are supposed to show what is different as a result of providing a service. The details and the messy complexity of service provision can now be set aside in favour of this supposedly unarguable 'evidence' of change. Outcomes, with the citizen as presumed arbiter, can now become the 'shareholder value' of the public sector: something that is readily 'gamed' and manipulated by clever administrators.

Patricia Benner (2009, p. xi) considers the implications of this development for the world of nursing:

> Today's measurement-oriented work cultures insist on evaluation primarily based upon outcomes. An outcomes-oriented approach is designed based upon a narrow rationality that separates *means* and *ends*. This process of separation unwittingly devalues and fragments the means. I am thinking of nurses' work as the means for achieving improved safety and quality outcomes in Health Care Systems. But in many areas of health care, means and ends are inextricably bound together, for example, in the attentiveness and care required to achieve worthy person-centred outcomes in birthing, rescuing and helping patients recover and helping people to die with dignity.

Moreover, the separation of means and ends enables organizational change in the public sector to become more abstract, bloodless and routine: a course of action that is easier for the policymakers and the politicians to undertake without having to involve the practitioners, or being too concerned about the details of the work itself. So once again we have arrived at a form of organizational conduct that is defensible in theory, but manages in practice to elude specific, local accountability and responsibility. Changing the structures becomes a political game without the possibility of a referee.

Against intellectualization: towards practical trust

Though the management project has become the dominant force in the world of work in the West, it is not the only game in town. Opposition to its instrumentalized view of human endeavour has been led for more than 300 years from the most unlikely of directions – by the philosophers. A powerful strand of philosophical enquiry has developed to challenge Cartesian triumphalism head-on, that includes thinkers and writers such as Vico, Kierkegaard, Heidegger, James, Dewey, Bergson, Merleau-Ponty, Bakhtin, Wittgenstein, Vygotsky, Elias and, in our time, practitioner-philosophers like Benner (1984), Shotter (1993), Taylor (2002) and Dreyfus (2009).

The Cartesian position gives primacy to the notion of human beings as separate, self-determining individuals. We must begin by an act of will – by doubting everything – and move forward from there only on the basis of verifiable personal observation. In its time, this proposal of Descartes' was a radical and liberating response to the oppressive received wisdom of the scholastics.

But the counter-view – that of the foregoing philosophers – holds that mind and body are one, and that we lose our way in thickets of contestable abstractions unless we pay attention to our continuously unfolding embodied experiences. Such experiences connect us to others and therefore allow us to make sense of the world together, rather than leaving us separate and isolated as if each of us was always supposed to begin our enquiries alone – starting, like Descartes, from a clean sheet of paper each Monday morning.

So this alternative strand of thinking pays close attention to our relational existence and experience: how we influence and move each other in intricate, minute, often unconscious ways in our everyday encounters. These phenomena of influence, of movement and response, of gesture and acknowledgement, of hesitation and affirmation, go largely unnoticed and unrecorded – especially if we consider the world only through Cartesian eyes.

So steeped are we in instrumental thinking in our organizational lives, that it is hard for us to imagine anything different. As an example, take the phenomenon of the workplace meeting. We generally hold that a meeting is arranged with a particular group of people for a specific purpose. So we conduct the meeting on the assumption that nothing except what has already been agreed is considered seriously before the meeting, that all that matters takes place at the meeting, and that the meeting concludes with a result that will generate a different form of behaviour (perhaps some kind of action) that can effectively continue unconsidered until the next meeting.

In the 1980s, at Fletcher Challenge, a New Zealand conglomerate, and in the 1990s, at AMP, an Australasian life insurance mutual, I took part in many board and management meetings of this kind. I remember them now for their formality. There were pre-set agendas; papers were distributed beforehand; meetings always ran to time. Nothing spontaneous was allowed to occur. Discussion was clipped, curt, and often confined to nods and grunts. Questions were closed-ended, and there was seldom any general discussion. The air was thick with the unsaid. Not saying things, in fact, seemed to be the point. Saying things might have spoiled the carefully cultivated atmosphere of unruffled control.

But reality is, of course, irreducibly messy and complicated. Things with significance for the avowed purpose of every meeting are happening at every moment before, during, and after the meeting. No amount of instrumental management can prevent them from occurring, or can pretend them out of existence. And recognition of this can change the way we view and conduct meetings. We no longer need to use them as though they were closed worlds of command and control that are supposed to have predictable and measurable outcomes. Instead, we can use them as opportunities to connect our experiences together as whole persons in ways that allow us to generate fresh, collaborative, practical insights and commitments to each other that always acknowledge and take account of the ceaseless onrush of wider organizational activity.

With this philosophical counter-view in mind, we can arrive at an understanding of work and its evaluation that is different from the heroic conceptualizations of the management project. For example, we might stop thinking about work as a series of disembodied tasks, static and fixed and without relational and developmental character. Instead, we could acknowledge that work becomes centred in the body as a practice: that is, as an undertaking that develops with experience. Just as the guilds of old understood a craft or profession as a trajectory from apprenticeship to mastery, so we might see all forms of work as movements or experiences of becoming skilled within a community of participants whose understandings can inform one another.

Connected to this recognition, we might also understand that embodied experience becomes a kind of second nature, and is therefore not necessarily directly or easily visible to practitioners themselves. We might notice that the skilled professional generally moves into the arena where their capabilities are most at home without apparent effort, and without self-consciousness. Only by reflecting with fellow-practitioners about the detailed nature of the activities in which they are habitually immersed, can they come to recognize themselves and their actions in ways that give them useful traction on their own skilled performance.

560

We might also understand that work, like all human activity, is responsive to its particular local circumstances. It comes into being and exists in response to a specific situation, and cannot be readily separated from that situation. And it is not only the general characteristics of the situation that matter: it is the singularities of an individual event that draw forth specific, often unpredictable aspects of skilled practice. So to be useful, the evaluation of work needs to respect and understand these singularities.

Here is an experienced pre-school teacher talking, within a community of fellow-teachers, about her own learning from a singular moment at school (from a gathering attended by the author):

> We have this boy of two years old, and we have spent a lot of time talking about how to make him behave, but he won't behave. One day I came into the room where the children were about to eat, and I found him on the sofa, reading a book. Normally a pre-school teacher would tell him to go to the table and sit down; but as I entered the room I looked at him said, 'Hello, are you reading a book?' and he said, 'Yes, see.'
>
> I sat down with him, and when we had looked at this book together, he said, 'I'm going to eat', and he rose and went to the table and sat by the other children. Normally I would have prevented him from reading the book; but this time I waited for the moment when he was ready.

From such small but spontaneous and unpredictable observations, we can see that the management project, if too earnest in seeking to separate work from evaluation, is bound to fail. If it reduces its understanding of work to simple, repetitive patterns that can be codified and expressed as formulae – such as the 'capabilities' of human resources evaluation practice – it can shrivel the human spirit, and risks leaving many real, original human capabilities unwanted and unused. If by giving primacy to measuring work, it reduces work only to things that can be easily measured, it produces only an impoverished, mechanical, non-living world – the world that Dickens foresaw in Mr Gradgrind.

What we therefore need, instead, is a way of operating that binds work, practitioners, and the organization together. Instead of inventing representations of, or surrogates for, the work as the basis for organizing and dealing with change (as we do, for example, when we create job titles and arrange and rearrange them in organization charts), to organize ourselves usefully we must involve ourselves with the detailed character and flow of the work itself. For each area of expertise and experience in the organization, we need to develop an understanding of the resonances that it generates – the connections and understandings with others that it entails, and the arena in which it has significance – as the foundational elements of our organization design efforts. This approach enables us to better recognize the strengths and limitations of ourselves and others, fosters working relationships that are based on this understanding – something that I am calling *practical trust* – and leads us towards an entirely new practice of organizational change.

Into the flux of immediate experience

I have given myself a considerable challenge here, because I want to try to describe a shift in orientation that is so profound that we don't yet have a commonly-understood language for it. Instead, I have to try to describe this movement in our present language – a language that is steeped in deeply buried, taken-for-granted (largely Cartesian) assumptions about the world. Let me hasten for assistance here to the words of another – in this case William James, speaking more than a hundred years ago. In the Hibbert lectures given at Manchester College, published in 1909 as *A Pluralistic Universe*, James tackles the limitations of trying to deal with the experience of change through the use of concepts such as the methods, models and theories that were listed earlier. 'Thought,' says James, 'deals … solely with surfaces. It can name the thickness of reality, but it cannot fathom it, and its insufficiency here is essential and permanent, not temporary. The only way,' he says, 'to apprehend reality's thickness … is either to *experience it directly by being a part of reality one's self*, or to *evoke it in imagination by sympathetically divining someone else's inner life*.' (1909, Lecture VI, my italics). Citing the then 40-year-old Henri Bergson, James continues (my italics):

> Professor Bergson … inverts the traditional platonic doctrine absolutely. Instead of intellectual knowledge being the profounder, he calls it the more superficial. Instead of being the only adequate knowledge, it is grossly inadequate, and its only superiority is the practical one of enabling us to make short cuts through experience and thereby to save time. The one thing it cannot do is to reveal the nature of things …
>
> Dive back into the flux itself, then, Bergson tells us, if you wish to *know* reality, that flux which Platonism, in its strange belief that only the immutable is excellent, has always spurned; turn your face toward sensation, that flesh-bound thing which rationalism has always loaded with abuse.—This, you see, is exactly the opposite remedy from that of looking forward into the absolute, which our idealistic contemporaries prescribe. *It violates our mental habits, being a kind of passive and receptive listening quite contrary to that effort to react noisily and verbally (to) everything, which is our usual intellectual pose.*

'The immediate experience of life,' says James, 'solves the problems which so baffle our conceptual intelligence: (How can our experiences) be both distinct and connected? How can they act on one another? How be for others and yet for themselves? How be absent and present at once?'

He addresses this paradox with the following argument:

> Our intellectual handling (of every concrete thing, however complicated) is a retrospective patchwork, a post-mortem dissection, and can follow any order we find most expedient … But place yourself at the point of view of the thing's interior *doing*, and all the back-looking and conflicting conceptions lie harmoniously in your hand. Get at the expanding centre of a human character, the élan vital of a man, as Bergson calls it, by living sympathy, and at a stroke you see how it makes those who see it from without interpret it in such diverse ways. It is something that breaks into both honesty and dishonesty, courage and cowardice, stupidity and insight, at the touch of varying circumstances, and you feel exactly why and how it does this, and never seek to identify it stably with any of these single abstractions …
>
> (ibid.)

So after all, there does appear to be a serious alternative to making 'short cuts' through experience by way of conceptualization. Instead of floating above the real world, we can plunge directly into it: become immersed in and buffeted by its turbulence; swim in the current of everyday life with other people, and make sense of things by sharing and comparing not just ideas, but feelings; not just observations, but sensations; and not just opinions, but immediate, detailed accounts of the highs and lows of our own personal experience.

From within the current, we can understand others through the glimpses of connection or comparison between their lives and ours; by recognizing aspects of our own experience in the stories of others, we can better understand ourselves; and through these flashes of insight, we can immediately intuit how to work together to achieve something that we cannot achieve by ourselves.

Organizing through practical trust

So what is really entailed in operating 'in movement' in the workplace, by continually connecting up our individual experiences in the pursuit of a constantly renewed sense of practical trust? This in contrast to operating 'in freeze-frame' around prepared problem statements, analyses, models and theories that are highly selective abstractions from our ongoing experiences.

Orientation

I think the difference begins with our orientation to our work and to each other: that is, in the way we think about organization. We have grown accustomed to putting the organization ahead of ourselves, and attributing to it our own human characteristics like 'mission' and 'purpose'. And the more effort we have invested in the elaboration of these abstract notions – such as culture, brand identity and shareholder value – the more we have de-personalized the workplace, and forgotten that all that it really amounts to is us. Me and you and him and her and them and all those others who come to work each day to try to do something useful together. Plus, all the tools and equipment that can magnify our efforts, but are valueless without us there to operate them.

What is more, it is increasingly clear that all of these us-es have an equivalent claim to attention and involvement in enabling the organization to succeed. Two important developments of the past several decades support this view. First, our growing recognition of the complexity and interconnectedness of all aspects of human affairs: separating our professional activities into specializations that are remote from one another no longer seems to be sustainable. Second, our rising global standards of general education and information access: our continued faith in the pre-eminence of élite cadres of knowledge and leadership – and their active encouragement and cultivation in organizational life – no longer seem useful or justified. So I think that the organization really is *all of us*, and we must therefore find much more connected ways of working – not through workplace democracy, where people periodically 'represent' the views of others, but through the direct and continuing connection of many kinds of practitioners, as well as service users, across the entire arena of the enterprise.

Practice

A useful first step towards better connection and practical trust is to recognize the enterprise as made up of individuals whose knowledge and skills cohere around a set of activities that constitute a 'practice'. A person's practice is what they do in their daily working life: their habitual behaviours, their organized sequence of activities, including their physical orientation to their task, the way they speak, their patterns of communication, their gestural habits, and so on. For experienced practitioners, much of this activity may become 'second nature', or so deeply embodied that it is habitual, operating below the level of conscious awareness. But practices are never identical. Each is a unique response to a particular personal history and set of circumstances, pivotal experiences, and underlying beliefs and assumptions.

The recognition of practice is important, because it gives us a helpful new way to relate to one another and make sense of things together. A person's practice comes from their actual connection with the world. So talk about practice is not the same as talk about ideas or concepts or analyses or opinions. Practice is grounded in daily action and detailed accounts of experience. Precisely because it is not high-flown and universalized, people can find its gritty, ordinary nature difficult to talk about at first. But it turns out that these 'stumbles to give voice to the everyday' are themselves highly revealing, because they make spaces – small gaps and hesitations – in which others may glimpse their own experiences. Moreover, in exploring their practices, people recall particular moments and events that now seem significant. And it is these unique circumstances of particular practices – their once-occurrent moments of being, as in the small story of the Danish teacher earlier – that demonstrate differences, allow comparisons, and generate learning and insight.

Enquiry

We need, I think, a way of working together that is conducive to practical trust. So the character of the work, and its encounters and gatherings, is important. It needs to be something that is open-ended and invitational: something that draws in people, and gathers momentum and energy through the resonance of the process itself.

So it is not a meeting, in the sense of a progress review or an occasion with a pre-determined agenda. It is not a workshop, with a fixed timetable, a set process, a desired outcome and a facilitator to work through the process with the group. It is not a forum, where there are one or more presentations followed by discussion. It is not a taskforce, where a selected group of people is responsible for addressing a specific issue or for tackling a defined problem.

We might consider it as an enquiry: something that seeks to discover and articulate what we do and what we know in practice. The aim here is to reverse the usual procedure. Rather than beginning with an imaginary idealization of the world – such as a performance target – we start by plunging straight into the reality of what is actually being done at present. By exchanging individual examples of what is being done, we open up reminders and refreshers for individuals about their own activities. And as a collective sense of what is being done develops, so do the possibilities of what might be done spontaneously arise.

How, then is an enquiry conducted? I think it can start with a kind of disquiet, a sense of unease, a feeling that things are not quite right, are not working properly: people finding that they are not understanding each other, not harmonizing their efforts. So to begin with, it may not be a formal procedure at all, but something more like a persistent background conversation. And at this stage, there will be concerns like, Do we really have time to discuss this? Are we allowed or supposed to have this kind of discussion?

The turning point occurs when someone in authority has the courage and confidence to see that such 'feelings' do not threaten the organization, but are instead potential clues to its betterment. Then they can become a legitimate topic for discussion. But it is important not to overdo this step. Defining a problem, or creating a task force to solve it at this early stage would not be helpful. All that has to happen is that space is made for the conversation. The detailed character of the work, and a sense of who should be involved in its articulation, can emerge from the conversation. And a good place to begin the conversation is with an urge to recognize each other's work: to understand more clearly how each other operates in the day-to-day workplace, and how each person has arrived at their own sense of what really matters in their practice.

Attunement

A crucial difference in organizational conduct built on practical trust rather than intellectualization is in how much attention people pay to each other.

In organizations where individual performance is the dominant concern, people are naturally preoccupied with themselves and their own activities. And in our self-conscious, self-determining age, these preoccupations extend to much more than the tasks required of us: they include the way that we speak, the words that we choose, the enthusiasms we evince, and the attitudes we display, as well as the details of our appearance and our self-presentation. My argument is that these concerns of the self may so occupy our attention that we have little left over for noticing others. Our conduct with respect to other people can become entirely instrumentalized: that is, we pay attention to them only insofar as they contribute to our own concerns and our performance of the moment. Moreover, this 'closing in' of our attention, this self-centring, can occur so surreptitiously that we are unaware of it until some false step suddenly reveals how far we have mistaken our surrounding circumstances.

The pursuit of practical trust aims to reverse the direction of this preoccupation. In our enquiries with others, we focus on their understandings as a way of illuminating our own. And when we open ourselves up and focus our attention on others in this way, we begin to discover how much there is to notice and to learn. Gradually, we become aware of the enormous potential in sharing the details of our experiences and in discovering the collaborative possibilities that emerge as a result.

At the centre of the process of attunement is the human utterance. An enquiry is a process of conversational exchange. Within these conversations are individual utterances. Following Mikhail Bakhtin (1986, pp.69, 74, 76, 91), we can think of an utterance as a verbal expression from the beginning of a thought to a point where a response becomes possible. Bakhtin and many others have demonstrated the value of recognizing and paying attention to the individual utterance. With practice, we become aware of the detailed characteristics of the human utterance: how the thought arises, how words form around it, how the cadence of the voice moves and rises and falls in its expression, and how it contains minute pauses and hesitations that are potentially full of meaning. We may even hear what Bakhtin calls the *answering word* (1981, p.280): that is, the response that the speaker is anticipating from enacting the utterance (either from those present, or from an unseen audience) since nothing that is spoken is said into a void or a vacuum.

Attunement is a learned skill. And there are ways of improving our skills of attunement – our awareness of the circumstances and the conduct of our conversation exchanges. For example, we can record our conversations, and with the permission of those involved, extract and re-listen to individual utterances. If we do this in a group, we can help each other to notice salient details. And each time we listen again, we can discover new attributes and implications – fresh possibilities – that we had not previously observed.

Change

When people gather together to share detailed accounts of experience, they awaken two kinds of creative possibility. In the first instance, the comparisons and contrasts between the observations of those present reveal glimpses of things, echoes and connections, that lead to the recognition of novelty. And this is a reflexive process: 'Ah. If you are seeing things that way, and that is where you are, then my sense of things means that, in contrast, I must be over here.' So the first result of exchanging experience is a kind of mutual navigation, where I can extend my understanding *in relation to* yours, and vice versa.

But as the accounts of experience multiply and link up, forming and re-forming larger patterns together, another prospect arises. This is a sense of a unitary whole: an understanding of what all of these individual expressions amount to as an entire practice, or a living body of experience within the moving flux of the real world. John Shotter has drawn my attention to Goethe's (1948–1960) conclusion, that this unitary sense is as valid as any mathematical proposition:

> *Experiences of a higher kind* will be enunciated through short and comprehensive propositions, placed next to one another, and, when more of them have been worked out, organized and brought into relation such that they stand, just like mathematical

propositions, unshakable, either singly or taken together. The elements of these experiences of a higher kind, which are many individual experiments, can then be investigated and tested by everyone, and it is not hard to judge whether the many individual parts can be expressed by a general proposition, for there is no arbitrariness Here.'

I am especially taken by these words because they match findings from my own experiments with collaborative enquiries involving practitioners, some of which I have described in a recent book (Taptiklis, 2008). From a series of conversations about practice experience, individual utterances naturally present themselves and separate themselves out as a collection of observations. Repeated listening to these observations reveals connections between them that steadily cluster into higher, more comprehensive meanings and 'general propositions'. And preserving all of the steps in this sequence ensures that they, too, can be 'investigated and tested by everyone' to show that 'there is no arbitrariness Here'.

So here we have a response to the concern that I imagined earlier about 'diving into the flux of immediate experience': the process of *emergence* that is entailed in its articulation always ensures that there will be a 'higher overview' or sense of the whole: one, moreover, that is never arbitrary, but is able to be apprehended and tested by all.

Conclusion

It will be clear by now that I am pointing towards a prospect of organizational change that is very different from existing approaches. Far from entailing overt coercion, as Jack Welch supposes, I see change as immanent in all of us and all of our practices – provided that we are given the opportunity to see ourselves and our experiences and struggles in the context of those of the others around us.

I am arguing that the pursuit of 'practical trust' develops, not only a comprehensive and detailed account of existing capability, but also a rich storehouse of specific opportunities for improvement and change. And because these changes emerge from the spontaneous observations of practitioners themselves, there are many reasons to see them as achievable and sustainable. (In giving voice to possibilities that involve oneself, there is already an implicit commitment to action.) In contrast to our present conflation of organizational change and restructuring, this is instead a vision of continuous organizational change and development in small but telling steps, bubbling up from the natural instincts of engaged participants. This, I think, is a positive alternative to the wearying and mechanical process of restructuring that was described earlier by Lewis Rabkin.

And what this is all really about is quite straightforward: it is about genuine collaborative effort, about bringing all of ourselves – our contradictions, our inadequacies, our self-doubts, our enthusiasms, and our wonderings – to the workplace in search of collective achievement. Intellectualism tends to set aside, or even deny, our humanity: practical trust celebrates it, makes the most of it, and, I believe, can raise our efforts together to heights that we would otherwise never know existed.

Postscript

As I was completing this chapter, my (serious-minded) daughter asked me what I was writing about. As usual, I gave her a somewhat garbled summary, never having been able to master the art of the spontaneous 'elevator pitch'. She paused, thoughtful, when I had finished. 'So what you want is for us to talk more at work? Won't that be bad for productivity?'

In this moment I was reminded of one of the crucial assumptions of instrumental rationalism. *Work and talk are seen as different things.* On the one hand, there is the work – the stuff that we do by ourselves, in silence, following previously-explained instructions or understood rules. 'Productivity' is doing as much of this as possible in the shortest possible time.

Then there is talk. Because you can't 'work' and 'talk' at the same time, talk can only be a distraction. So talk acquires negative, even guilty connotations. Terms like 'chatter' and 'gossip' trivialize it further, making it – horror of horrors – something that only women do! Real men, of course, 'work' for hours on end in self-absorbed silence.

These assumptions are deeply established in organizational office life. Now much of our 'work' is about sitting at a computer, producing something on a screen. Talk to find out or get something that will go into what we are producing is legitimate. But open-ended conversation – at our desks – about what we are producing is not. The place for reflective conversation is away from our desks – at the water-cooler, over coffee, over lunch. Here there is much less chance that 'talk' will contaminate 'work'.

This recognition helps to explain the formal character of the meetings that I described earlier. Conversation is curt and clipped because *talking wastes time.* The sooner we stop talking, the sooner we get back to work – where the action is.

By contrast, in a world of practical trust, the talk *is* the work. The abstractions that we produce – our reports, our papers, our models, our strategies – are secondary by-products, whose only purpose is to improve the quality of the talk. In this world, documents are never finalized: they are always open to new inputs, fresh insights, and reinterpretations. It is not the intellectual authority or the production values of what is produced that counts. Nor is the quality of our performance and our self-presentation crucial. Instead it is the depth and reach of our shared practical trust and understanding, day by day and hour by hour, that makes the real difference.

References

12manage.com 2010, The Change and Organisation summary page of www.12manage.com, the Executive Fast Track, an executive business encyclopedia and interest group network of management methods, models and concepts, from 12manage B.V., Bilthoven, The Netherlands, retrieved on 31 May 2010 from http://www.12manage.com/i_co.html.

Bakhtin, M.M. 1981, *The Dialogic Imagination: Four Essays*, ed. Michael Holquist, trans. Caryl Emerson and Michael Holquist, University of Texas Press, Austin, TX.

Bakhtin, M.M. 1986, *Speech Genres and Other Late Essays*, trans. Vern W. McGee, University of Texas Press, Austin, TX.

Benner, P. 1984, *Novice to Expert: Excellence and power in clinical nursing practice*, Addison-Wesley Publishing, Menlo Park, CA.

Benner, P. 2009, *Foreword to Revealing Nursing Expertise Through Practitioner Inquiry*, Sally Hardy, Angie Titchen, Brendan McCormack, Kim Manley (eds), John Wiley & Sons, Chichester.

Dreyfus, H.L. 2009, *On the Internet* (2nd edn), Routledge, Oxford.

Goethe, Johann W. von 1948–60, *Goethes Werke (Hamberger-Ausgabe)*, E. Tunz (ed.), 14 vols., C. Wegner, Hamburg.

James, W. 1909, *A Pluralistic Universe, Lecture VI, Bergson and his critique of intellectualism*, retrieved 31 May 2010 from http://ebooks.adelaide.edu.au/j/james/william/plural/chapter6.html.

Shotter, J. 1993, *Cultural Politics of Everyday Life*, University of Toronto Press, Toronto.

Taptiklis, T. 2008, *Unmanaging: Opening up the organization to its own unspoken knowledge*, Palgrave Macmillan, Basingstoke.

Taylor, C. 2002, *Varieties of Religion Today: William James revisited*, Harvard University Press, Cambridge, MA.

Welch, J. and Welch, S. 2009, *Four Principles of Organizational Change*, retrieved 31 May 2010, from www.livemint.com/2009/10/11205341/Four-principles-of-organization.html.

Zeldin, T. 1994, *An Intimate History of Humanity*, HarperCollins, New York.

39

The promise of re-enchantment
Organizational culture and the spirituality at work movement

Scott Taylor and Emma Bell

Introduction

The spirituality at work movement has achieved considerable popularity in the last decade amongst management scholars and practitioners as a means of achieving organizational and individual transformation (Mitroff and Denton, 1999; Giacalone and Jurkiewicz, 2003; Neal and Biberman, 2003, 2004; Biberman and Tischler, 2008; Oswick, 2009). However, the nature of this transformation is difficult to pin down, partly because spirituality at work is an inherently ambiguous concept that has generated numerous, inconclusive attempts at definition (Ashmos and Duchon, 2000; Gotsis and Kortezi, 2007).

One way of assessing the distinctiveness and impact of spirituality at work is by considering its relationship to earlier theories of organizational change and assessing how spirituality at work builds on and extends them. Some critically oriented authors have drawn a parallel between spirituality at work and the culture movement of the 1980s and 1990s, suggesting that the focus on ritual practices, norms and beliefs makes these phenomena sufficiently similar to be indistinct (Brown, 2003). This might be interpreted as evidence to suggest that spirituality at work offers little that is new in comparison to earlier theories, a case of old wine in new bottles (Eccles and Nohria, 1992) perhaps? Despite the apparent similarities between the organizational culture and spirituality movements, in this chapter we argue that there are fundamental differences between these two movements.

In order to understand nature of these differences, it is necessary to explore the relationship between religion[1] and culture, and to appreciate the significance of beliefs in constituting culture. Drawing on anthropological and sociological theory we suggest that what sets spirituality at work apart from organizational culture is its promise to re-enchant modern work. However, in its current form the spirituality at work movement is limited in its potential for re-enchantment because of continued reliance on modernist principles of instrumental rationality and scientific progress. The desire to reintroduce magic and mystery is thus a *disenchanted* re-enchantment, bounded by modernist rationality in which religion and spirituality remain equivalent or subordinate to other value systems. Finally, we consider the possibility that the spirituality at work movement retains the potential to more effectively challenge organizational disenchantment. In order for this potential to be realized, spirituality must be made to work within but against modernity, challenging and transcending the foundations of efficiency and calculability that are inherent to disenchanted organizational norms.

The role of religion in shaping culture

The primary importance of religious beliefs in shaping culture has long been recognized by social anthropologists (Geertz, 1993). For Geertz, religion shapes the social order and is not just a description or reflection of it. His classic definition of culture focuses on the pattern of meanings made manifest in symbolic forms of communication which are used to develop and perpetuate knowledge about and attitudes towards all aspects of life. He advocates the adoption of a 'religious perspective' in understanding culture which focuses on the:

> system of symbols which acts to establish powerful, persuasive, and long-lasting moods and motivations in men by formulating conceptions of a general order of existence and clothing these conceptions with such an aura of factuality that the moods and motivations seem uniquely realistic.
>
> (Geertz 1993: 90)

Taking both belief and the bases of belief as beyond social scientific inquiry, Geertz draws comparisons with three other 'perspectives' on social life: common-sense, aesthetic, and scientific. He suggests that the religious perspective offers a distinctive way of seeing the social world based on the metaphysical significance that is accorded to rituals and symbols. Importantly, following Weber, Geertz insists on the differentiation of religious beliefs as a value system, arguing that differences in beliefs translate into action, personality, and culture. Religious belief thus complements and confirms a cultural stance or world-view – convincing believers and cultural members of the moral and aesthetic rightness of their truth. A style of life and a metaphysical position are thereby brought together, each sustaining the other and providing mutual authority. This perspective invites analysis of the interplay between religion and culture that places the former at the centre of cultural analysis, rather than seeing it as a marginal element.

Religion is thus a 'crucible' (Beckford, 2003) in which social and cultural phenomena can be seen with particular clarity. This perspective enables broader social and cultural phenomena to be dramatized in a way which provides clarity of insight into accepted norms and conventions in everyday life, permitting 'exceptionally clear views of the processes whereby culture is not only constructed but also embodied, charged with emotion, performed, controlled and often challenged' (Beckford, 2003: 187). This approach to cultural analysis is important because it challenges the notion that spirituality is merely an *expression* of culture. It thereby avoids the reductionist tendencies associated with analyses that regard spirituality at work as an incremental extension of the culture movement. By granting spirituality and religion an analytical status that is *at least* equivalent to culture, it enables a more sophisticated theoretical understanding of the relationship between these two organizational phenomena and a basis for exploring the question of what differentiates the spirituality at work movement from understandings of organizational culture.

Comparing the culture and spirituality at work movements

Like the culture movement, spirituality at work can be seen as a neo-modernist organization theory, traceable to the human relations school (Tischler, 1999). Both movements seek to create conditions in which work is seen as having a purpose and experienced as meaningful. Other commentators suggest that spirituality at work simply reproduces themes that are common to theories of organizational culture, such as self-help, leadership and institutional change (Oswick, 2009). There are also similarities in the way the two movements have addressed the tensions between functionalist and interpretive perspectives. In the early years of the organizational culture movement, the focus was on achieving integration; if employees shared the same beliefs, values and cultural norms, this would enable a high degree of commitment and enhance organizational performance. Similarly, in the early stages of the spirituality at work movement some scholars approached the phenomenon from an integrationist perspective (Milliman et al., 1999), suggesting that belief systems can provide a metaphysical norm for all organizational members to follow that has positive implications for individual productivity and organizational performance (Gull and Doh, 2004). However, like the culture movement (Smircich, 1983), spirituality at work has been criticized for treating spirituality as something that organizations can 'have', a variable that can be measured and managed, rather than regarding metaphysical beliefs as a subjective, non-rational and fundamental aspect of human experience (Bell and Taylor, 2003; Driscoll and Wiebe, 2007; Lips-Wiersma et al., 2009).

Some scholars have instead argued for greater recognition of the existence of multiple, competing belief systems in the workplace through the notion of pluralism (Hicks, 2003). This parallels Martin's (1992) cultural perspective of differentiation and acknowledges the existence of competing cultural norms in the form of organizational sub-cultures that undermine or challenge managerial attempts to construct a unified culture. Critical perspectives draw on the notion of differentiation to suggest that spirituality at work has been primarily used as a normative manage- rial control strategy, providing evidence of the further colonization of individual subjectivity by organizations (Tourish and Pinnington, 2002; Bell and Taylor, 2003). Whereas corporate culturalism sought to influence employees' subjective emotions and thoughts, or 'hearts and minds' (Willmott, 1993), a corporate cult-ist approach to spirituality at work focuses on transforming metaphysical beliefs or employees' souls. Spirituality at work is thereby suggested to be a means of colonizing the self in a way which extends ever deeper into individual subjectivities.

There are thus considerable similarities between the culture and spirituality movements in relation to the philosophical positions adopted in studying these phenomena. Within both movements it is possible to identify unitarist and pluralist approaches alongside functionalist, interpretive and critical perspectives. Furthermore, a similar pattern can be observed in the development of these competing perspectives within the two movements over time, integra- tionist views gradually being complemented by more critical analyses of differentiation as the movements mature theoretically and empirically.

However, there is a less recognized but equally important similarity between the culture and spirituality at work movements. Both cultural analysis and the spirituality at work literatures make use of religion as a source of analytical terminology, yet neither clarifies the conceptual status of belief. This is seen most clearly in qualitative studies that analyse the role of religious or quasi- religious discourses in constructing strong organizational cultures. Kunda's (1993) ethnographic account of a high-tech corporation provides a good example, many employees noting the cult- like experience of belonging to the organization and the theological language used by managers to encourage commitment. Terms such as mission, vision, values, rituals and beliefs are invoked to differentiate corporate culture from more rationalistic management tools that may be used to control and performance management.

Strong corporate cultures are also suggested to require quasi-religious commitment (Turner, 1986) and religious metaphors are used as a means of emphasizing the subjective or psychological

571

depth that culture management involves. This includes the use of terms such as 'governing the soul' (Rose, 1989), 'managerial salvation' (Case, 1999), and the 'making of the corporate acolyte' (Höpfl, 1992). These terminological boundaries are further blurred by analyses of the discursive practices associated with companies led by adherents of Christian evangelical religions (Biggart, 1989; Nadesan, 1999; Pratt, 2000; Bone, 2006). Within both the culture and spirituality movements, charismatic leadership is seen as key to the development of guiding norms, values and beliefs. Western (2008) argues that the culture movement gave rise to the concept of leader as messiah, a prophetic figure whose role is to 'convert' organizational members to follow a 'vision'. Similarly, within the spirituality at work movement, leaders are identified as a key source of vision, values, and spirit (Benefiel, 2005).

To summarize, both the culture and spirituality at work movements regard belief as empirically and analytically significant. Within the culture movement, religion is reduced to a set of metaphorical and discursive resources that are used to construct and interpret organizational cultures, whereas within the spirituality at work movement belief is accorded an empirical status that is independent of culture. However, belief remains insufficiently conceptually differentiated from culture within this literature. It can therefore easily be dismissed as an epiphenomenon or cultural effect rather than a potential cause.

One final point of similarity relates to the potential for change at individual, organizational, and societal levels (e.g. King and Nicol, 1999; Burack, 1999). The spirituality at work literature assumes that the magnitude of the organizational change that is required is transformational, because the majority of modernist organizations and their members tend to be oriented towards economic rewards, rationality, instrumentality, amorality and lack of care. Such organizations are said to be unable to satisfy the spiritual needs of employees and other stakeholders, and consequently they lack meaning and purpose (Tischler, 1999). The movement claims to provide a metaphysical response to these issues by promoting spiritual ideas and practices in the workplace.

However, despite these considerable similarities between the culture and spirituality at work movements, there are also major differences. Within the culture movement religion performs a purely metaphorical role. Consequently, cultures may be quasi-religious or inspire comparison with religions, but there is no empirical or analytical acknowledgement of belief as a distinct value system. Metaphysical or transcendent issues are entirely absent, as are magic, mystery, or enchantment. Specifically, as we shall argue in the remainder of this chapter, the fundamental difference that separates the spirituality at work movement from other neo-modernist organization theories such as the culture movement concerns the possibility of re-enchantment – of modern work, organizations, and even societies.

Enchantment, disenchantment and re-enchantment

Enchantment and modern life

The notion of enchantment involves experience of events or circumstances that produces a sense of the mysterious, the magical and the imagined:

> Enchantment conjures up, and is rooted in, understandings and experiences of the world in which there is more to life than the material, the visible or the explainable; in which the philosophies and principles of Reason or rationality cannot by definition dream of the totality of life; in which the quotidian norms and routines of linear time and space are only

part of the story; and in which the collective sum of sociability and belonging is elusively greater than its individual parts.

(Jenkins, 2000: 29)

The idea of enchantment can be traced to Weber (1993) who, writing at the turn of the twentieth century, argued that modernity, rationality and science entail a process of disenchantment, whereby all aspects of life are experienced and understood as more knowable and manageable and therefore less mysterious. Weber predicted that enchantment would ultimately be eradicated in public life through the growth of modernism and the rise of instrumental rationality, eventually denuding social and cultural life of the potential to generate meaning.

The key source for these ideas is his essay 'Science as a Vocation'. In this short piece, Weber argues that the development of modernity is underpinned by a process of 'intellectualist rationalization'. This rationalization is led by science and scientists, driven by a desire to achieve calculability in all things and demystify life through technical understanding. This is what Weber terms disenchantment, linking the process closely to discourses of progress. Weber further argues that disenchantment has taken place over the *longue durée* of millennia but has come to a peak since the Enlightenment. Since then, he suggests, scientists (including social scientists) have successfully persuaded society that humanity progresses or develops by reducing mystery, removing the magic or enchantment from everyday life. He further observes the ways in which modernity encourages life to become less organic and more industrial, less cyclical and more linear, less meaningful and more instrumentalized, less puzzling and more explicable (Weber, 2009).

Revisiting this theme in *The Protestant Ethic and the Spirit of Capitalism* (1930), Weber speculates on the future development of such rational capitalism driven by a vocational devotion to the instrumental accumulation of wealth. As this sense of calling or vocation becomes more secular, or disenchanted, Weber suggests production and consumption become 'purely mundane passions', more akin to sport than religious or moral service – leaving us trapped in his famous iron cage, characterized by 'mechanized petrification' (Weber, 1930: 182) and moral nullity. He predicts that the triumph of a purely utilitarian, secularized, disenchanted, ascetic rationalism will have considerable cultural and material effects, and is unlikely to be confronted 'until the last ton of fossilized coal is burnt' (1930: 181). As well as raising the spectre of hyper-consumption, Weber also argues repeatedly that modern science and therefore disenchanted modern life cannot address the only important question in life, that of how we should live. For Weber, science is only able to provide technical responses to technical questions, which are of little use when we consider complex issues of meaning and whether life is worthwhile.

Weber's lifetime saw rational science become the basis for explaining more and more and the concomitant decline in what could be attributed to forces of enchantment or magic (Jenkins, 2000). The social status of enchantment declined precipitously, coming to be seen as primitive, backward, or regressive. However, Weber's predicted 'disenchantment of the world' did not assume a complete rationalization and the disappearance of magic from all aspects of life. Rather, he suggested that ultimate and sublime values would retreat from public life into either the mystical life or the 'brotherliness of direct and personal human relations' (Weber, 2009: 155).

Weber's prophecy of disenchantment in public life has been challenged by those who question the extent of secularization in Western society, citing the continued presence, and even resurgence, of transcendental and mystical beliefs in many areas of social life. Jenkins (2000) argues that Weber's prediction of increasing disenchantment has been only limitedly realized. Jenkins argues that re-enchantment is a key aspect of late modernity. He suggests there is good evidence for the general success of rationality and rationalization, but little for comprehensive disenchantment.

Whilst Weber correctly observed the delegitimation of religion as a transcendent value system, he did not for example predict the rise of contemporary spiritualities as a means of re-enchantment. Such approaches to the transcendent or metaphysical may even, as some sociologists of religion suggest (Lynch, 2007; Heelas, 2008), provide the basis for a more inclusive form of re-enchantment.

Differentiating enchanted value systems

Several spirituality at work commentators emphasize the uniqueness of the movement in comparison for example to secular business ethics frameworks or human relations systems (Pava, 2003). This process of differentiation is also a central aspect of Weber's analysis of the relationship between disenchantment and modernity (Gane, 2004). Rationalization and disenchantment, for Weber, are accompanied by a levelling out of value orientations, so that religion loses its pre-eminence and takes its place alongside other positions. In other words, during disenchantment religion is de-differentiated and then integrated into the culture of rationalized modernism. Within modernity, the ability to make value judgments is framed by one of a variety of 'life orders', each with its own territory and each mobilized independently to justify action. In disenchanted societies religion takes its place alongside scientific, economic, political, aesthetic, affective, and intellectual systems. The overarching or transcendental perspective provided by belief systems until the development of modernity is thus lost and conflicts between value orientations become extremely difficult to resolve. In modern societies, Weber argues, the most likely outcome of any value conflict involving religious frameworks is rejection by impersonal, disenchanted forces. This places strain on individuals, who are encouraged to 'take a position' but always open to attack from alien value positions. This de-differentiation of religion leaves instrumental reason as the dominant value system, manifest through its 'institutional embodiment' (Gane, 2004: 27) of bureaucracy. The highest values, related to meaning, purpose, or the sublime, are subordinated to rationality and calculability, or ignored entirely.

The process of de-differentiation therefore results in a loss of status and pre-eminence for religion. Like Geertz, Weber wanted religion to have 'an exceptional analytical status' (Gane, 2004: 31) because of its emphasis on 'other-worldly' concerns and its socio-cultural dominance until the development of modernity. As various life-orders, particularly the economic, were freed from religious frameworks tensions developed, a dynamic that Weber famously noted in relation to the development of the Protestant ethic. As noted above, Weber also explored two responses to this tension that help to protect enchantment: dedication to a vocation or the pursuit of other-worldly mysticism.

As we have suggested, Weber's fears of comprehensive disenchantment are to an extent challenged by the emergence of the spirituality at work movement which appears to indicate the re-enchantment of management and organizations. In the section that follows we examine the promise of re-enchantment that is embedded in the spirituality at work movement.

Spirituality at work and the promise of re-enchantment

Scholars of management and organization appear to be finding plentiful evidence of re-enchantment. This reflects a wider trend towards spirituality in everyday social and cultural life in Western economies (Lynch, 2007; Heelas, 2008). Ritzer (2005) explores the idea of societal re-enchantment in some detail. He argues that contemporary consumption combines dissatisfaction with disenchantment and rational attempts at re-enchantment. The result is not a return to pre-modern enchantment but rather a postmodern 'disenchanted enchantment', based on instrumental rationality and bureaucratic principles. Dreams, fantasies and beliefs retain their power, but they are closely managed and bounded.

Ritzer's arguments are based on the analysis of one end of modern capitalism. He suggests, following Campbell (1989), that contemporary Western societies are defined by consumption rather than production. Through his analysis of contemporary landscapes of consumption, such as shopping malls, casino complexes, theme parks, cruise ships and university campuses, Ritzer argues that we are being encouraged to find enchantment in consumer activity. The 'new means of consumption', exemplified by Disney's various worlds around the globe, not only increases the level of consumption but also alters its fundamental nature. Ritzer terms these settings 'cathedrals' metaphorically, to indicate that they are intended to structure consumption as an 'enchanted, sometimes even sacred' (2005: 7) experience. However, he oscillates between suggesting they are akin to religious centres and implying that consumerism is actually a transcendent belief system.

The most important step in Ritzer's argument is that any enchantment generated by these forms of consumption will inevitably be accompanied by disenchantment. In other words, contemporary attempts at re-enchantment through global forms of consumption must be recognized as *disenchanted* re-enchantment. Rationalized, McDonaldized, instrumentalized, economically driven enchantment is a distinct form, underpinned by the still prevalent aspects of modernity that first indicated the rise of disenchantment for Weber.

On the production side of society and economy, Casey suggests that the re-enchantment of modernist work settings and contemporary organizations is enabled by the emergence of the 'strategic neo-rational' manager. This new managerial identity encourages spiritual or meaningful activity in an attempt to 'capture and reauthorize the [employee-led] re-enchantment and spirituality turn' (Casey, 2004: 77). She further suggests that re-enchantment enables the prevailing discourses of rationality and instrumentality associated with modernist organizations to be challenged.

Casey's argument thus builds on the observation that Weber's prediction of disenchantment through rationality, bureaucratic organization, and secularization has not come to pass in contemporary workplaces and provides evidence of the continuing presence of magic and meaning in modernity. In a series of interlinked analyses, she traces how instrumental rationality and calculability have failed to entirely colonize the everyday lives of employees. Instead, she argues that 'alternative sources of value, meaning and self-identity' (Casey, 2002: 147) supported by transcendent belief systems continue in their presence and significance. For Casey, spiritual belief systems are primary sources for the ideas that inform practices of re-enchantment. She further suggests that re-enchantment in this form is more common among professional, white collar employees.

Like Ritzer (2005), Casey suggests that these alternative practices and ideas are in part generated by instrumental rationality and the dominance of market commodification. However, she extends the theoretical implications of the movement towards re-enchantment by proposing that it is indicative of heightened agency, suggestive of a more active subject moving '[b]eyond alienation and subjectification' (Casey, 2002: 171). The emancipatory or liberatory potential of religious beliefs is, she suggests, highest outside mainstream employment (Casey and Alach, 2004). However, enchantment through spirituality often defies management in a modernist sense, an observation complemented by Finch-Lees et al. (2005) who argue that corporate-sponsored spiritual development programmes enable forms of resistance and micro-emancipation. The 'unreasoned' nature of beliefs, and therefore faith based managerial initiatives, allows for the production of alternatives, enabling of resistance either at structural-cultural or individual levels.

So, rather than seeing re-enchantment and contemporary spiritualities as 'another iteration of quietism' (Casey, 2002: 173) that encourages submission to modernist discipline and managerial rationality (Bell and Taylor, 2003), it may be that some of the ideas and practices promoted by spirituality at work contribute towards re-shaping working environments and social institutions (Bell, 2008: Lips-Wiersma et al., 2009). Whether the 'new mysticism' that we observe in practices of re-enchantment is socially interested, as Casey suggests, or inwardly focused, remains open. However, Casey identifies an additional dynamic to spirituality at work which concerns the tension between mysticism and rationality. Most accounts of spirituality at work solve this tension by assuming that belief can be rationally managed, measured, and controlled in change management programmes. Casey (2002) suggests an alternative, arguing that spiritualities enable the development of subjects who are able to reconcile reason and emotion, remaining relational and attached while simultaneously rooted in Enlightenment norms of critical thinking. In this way, Casey suggests, spirituality at work brings together reason and faith, agent and structure, individual and social development, economy and culture, in processes that are bottom-up rather than top-down. Similarly to Finch-Lees et al. (2005), this acknowledges the productive potential of individual engagement religious and spiritual belief systems and allows for their *re-differentiation* from other value systems such as the economic. It is this, we suggest, that could provide the key to unlocking the potential of the spirituality of work movement. However, as yet this potential remains largely unrealized, in part because of the lack of attention paid to the analytical status of belief systems.

Concluding discussion

In this chapter we have argued that, in the majority of analyses of spirituality at work, the analytical status of religion is either taken for granted or ignored. If the re-emergence of transcendent value systems as the foundation of managerial interventions in the workplace is to be understood, then the relationship between culture and religion must be carefully examined. The metaphorical use of religion and theological terminology in analyses of culture through the 1980s and 1990s suggests belief was seen as a vestige, a relic useful only for rhetorical flourishes. The spirituality at work movement appears to challenge this by taking religion and belief seriously as a presence at work. However, the spirituality at work movement tends to promote an integrationist perspective on belief and meaning, leading to the conclusion that there is little to distinguish it from other modernist or neo-modernist managerial techniques. In order to recognize the empirical validity of metaphysical or transcendent value systems or use notions such as re-enchantment analytically, it is crucial to clarify the status of religious belief in relation to other competing value systems, such as the economic, aesthetic, or cultural.

This brings us back to our original concern at the outset of this chapter, which was to ask whether spiritual change interventions can be distinguished from other organizational change initiatives, such as those associated with organizational culture. Three steps are necessary in order to address this question. First, we suggest that spirituality at work is differentiated by the promise of re-enchantment. However, we further suggest that research and practice often promotes a disenchanted re-enchantment which is reliant on reductionist, scientific rationality and bounded by a modernist mode of thought and action. Second, we argue that, in order to assess the promised re-enchantment that spirituality at work claims to offer, it is necessary to clarify the status of religion and spirituality in relation to culture. Third, we propose that these two embedded conceptual assumptions result in religion and spirituality remaining undifferentiated from competing value systems, at best equivalent but more often subordinated to other ethical codes such as the economic. In this, proponents of the disenchanted versions of spirituality at work are strikingly similar to the disenchanting priests depicted by Weber as rationalizers of religious institutions – rational trained professionals who use modernist rational-legal institutional authority to seek control over unpredictable, irrational mysteries and magicians.

The recognition of spirituality as significant within contemporary workplaces offers a route into a clearly differentiated analytical position that enables scholars to explore the magical, mysterious, and unmanageable aspects of work and workplaces. This transcends the everyday, the economic and rational-instrumentalist worldviews. It reaches beyond culture and potentially beyond modernist methods of understanding. However, if spirituality at work promises enchantment but remains de-differentiated, or worse, is reduced to a set of measurable behaviours or outcomes, either by managers or scholars, then it offers nothing more than any other modernist technique. Indeed, such an approach denies religion status, and leaves it more easily subordinated to dominant modernist or neo-modernist rationalities. If spirituality at work is to be constructed as a separate field of managerial practice and research, then this issue must be addressed.

On this final point, Weber once again provides a guide as to potential action, in his reflections on academic work in modern societies. Gane (2004) notes that Weber's response to societal disenchantment as an academic was to suggest the protection and development of a sense of vocation. For scholars, this position avoids both nostalgic longing for the enchantment of pre-modernity and the despair of value relativism. As Weber describes, working with vocation requires the individual to make reasoned, responsible choices towards understanding the disen-chanted, rationalized world that modernity produces, setting out the productive potential of value orientations and action other than the instrumental-rational. Through vocation, values and beliefs are protected as separate from disenchanting rationalities, offering 'a possible, although limited, form of resistance to the further rationalization and disenchantment of the world' (Gane, 2004: 63). This consideration of scholarly responsibility brings our chapter to its conclusion.

Note

1 Whilst many writers seek to differentiate and separate spirituality at work from religion (Mitroff and Denton, 1999; Ashmos and Duchon, 2000), we take the view that the emergence of spirituality at work is symptomatic of shifting conceptions of sacred beliefs and practices which constitute a cultural change that cannot be understood without reference to religion (Beckford, 2003).

References

Ashmos, D. and Duchon, D. (2000) 'Spirituality at Work: A Conceptualization and Measure', *Journal of Management Inquiry*, 9(2): 134–45.

Beckford, J. (2003) *Religion and Social Theory*. Cambridge: Cambridge University Press.

Bell, E. (2008) 'Towards a Critical Spirituality of Organization', *Culture and Organization*, 14(3): 293–307.

Bell, E. and Taylor, S. (2003) 'The Elevation of Work: Pastoral Power and the New Age Work Ethic', *Organization*, 10(2): 331–51.

Benefiel, M. (2005) *Soul at Work: Spiritual Leadership in Organizations*. Dublin: Veritas.

Biberman, J. and Tischler, L. (2008) *Spirituality in Business: Theory, Practice and Future Directions*. New York: Palgrave Macmillan.

Biggart, N. (1989) *Charismatic Capitalism*. Chicago: University of Chicago Press.

Bone, J. (2006) *The Hard Sell: An Ethnographic Study of the Direct Selling Industry*. Aldershot: Ashgate.

Brown, R.B. (2003) 'Organizational Spirituality: The Sceptic's Version', *Organization*, 10(2): 393–400.

Burack, E. (1999) 'Spirituality in the Workplace', *Journal of Organizational Change Management*, 12(4): 280–91.

Campbell, C. (1989) *The Romantic Ethic and the Spirit of Modern Consumerism*. Oxford: Blackwell.

Case, P. (1999) 'Remember Re-engineering? The Rhetorical Appeal of a Managerial Salvation Device', *Journal of Management Studies*, 36(4): 419–41.

Casey, C. and Alach, P. (2004) 'Just a Temp? Women, Temporary Employment and Lifestyle', *Work, Employment & Society*, 18: 459–80.

Casey, C. (2002) *Critical Analysis of Organizations: Theory, Practice, Revitalization*. London: SAGE.

Casey, C. (2004) 'Bureaucracy Re-enchanted? Spirit, Experts and Authority in Organizations', *Organization*, 11(1): 59–79.

Davie, G. (2007) *The Sociology of Religion*. London: SAGE.

Driscoll, C. and Wiebe, E. (2007) 'Technical Spirituality at Work: Jacques Ellul on Workplace Spirituality', *Journal of Management Inquiry*, 16(4): 333–48.

Driver, M. (2005) 'From Empty Speech to Full Speech? Reconceptualizing Spirituality in Organizations Based on a Psychoanalytically-Grounded Understanding of the Self', *Human Relations*, 58(9): 1091–1110.

Eccles, R.G. and Nohria, N. (1992) *Beyond the Hype: Rediscovering the Essence of Management*. Cambridge, MA: Harvard Business School.

Finch-Lees, T., Mabey, C. and Liefooghe, A. (2005) 'In the Name of Capability: A Critical Discursive Evaluation of Competency-based Management Development', *Human Relations*, 58(9): 1185–1222.

Gane, N. (2004) *Max Weber and Postmodern Theory: Rationalization versus Re-enchantment*. Basingstoke: Palgrave Macmillan.

Geertz, C. (1990) *The Interpretation of Cultures*. London: Fontana.

Geertz, C. (1993) *The Interpretation of Cultures*. London: Fontana.

Giacalone, R.A. and Jurkiewicz, C.L. (eds) (2003) *Handbook of Workplace Spirituality*. Armonk, NY: Sharpe.

Gotsis, G. and Kortezi, Z. (2007) 'Philosophical Foundations of Workplace Spirituality: A Critical Approach', *Journal of Business Ethics*, 78(4): 575–600.

Gull, G. and Doh, J. (2004) 'The "Transmutation" of the Organization: Toward a More Spiritual Workplace', *Journal of Management Inquiry*, 13(2): 128–39.

Heelas, P. (2008) *Spiritualities of Life: New Age Romanticism and Consumptive Capitalism*. Oxford: Blackwell.

Hicks, D. (2003) *Religion and the Workplace: Pluralism, Spirituality, Leadership*. New York: Cambridge University Press.

Höpfl, H. (1992) 'The Making of the Corporate Acolyte: Some Thoughts on Charismatic Leadership and the Reality of Organizational Commitment', *Journal of Management Studies*, 29: 23–33.

Jenkins, R. (2000) 'Disenchantment, Enchantment, and Re-enchantment: Max Weber at the Millennium', *Max Weber Studies*, 1: 11–32.

King, S. and Nicol, D. (1999) 'Organizational Enhancement through Recognition of Individual Spirituality: Reflections on Jaques and Jung', *Journal of Organizational Change Management*, 12(3): 234–42.

Kunda, G. (1993) *Engineering Culture*. Philadelphia, PA: Temple University Press.

Lips-Wiersma, M., Lund Dean, K. and Forniciari, C. (2009) 'Theorising the Dark Side of the Workplace Spirituality Movement', *Journal of Management Inquiry*, 18(4): 288–300.

Lynch, G. (2007) *The New Spirituality: An Introduction to Progressive Belief in the Twenty-first Century*. London: I.B. Tauris.

Martin, J. (1992) *Cultures in Organizations: Three Perspectives*. New York: Oxford University Press.

Milliman, J., Ferguson, J., Trickett, D. and Condemi, B. (1999) 'Spirit and Community at Southwest Airlines: An Investigation of a Spiritual Values-based Model', *Journal of Organizational Change*, 12(3): 221–33.

Mitroff, I. and Denton, E. (1999) *A Spiritual Audit of Corporate America: A Hard Look at Spirituality, Religion and Values in the Workplace*. San Francisco, CA: Jossey Bass.

Nadesan, M.H. (1999) 'The Discourses of Corporate Spiritualism and Evangelical Capitalism', *Management Communication Quarterly*, 13(1): 3–42.

Neal, J. and Biberman, J. (2003) 'Introduction: The Leading Edge in Research on Spirituality and Organizations', *Journal of Organizational Change Management*, 16(4): 363–66.

Neal, J. and Biberman, J. (2004) 'Research That Matters: Helping Organizations Integrate Spiritual Values and Practices', *Journal of Organizational Change Management*, 17(1): 7–10.

Oswick, C. (2009) 'Burgeoning Workplace Spirituality? A Textual Analysis of Momentum and Directions', *Journal of Management, Spirituality and Religion*, 6(1): 15–25.

Pava, M.L. (2003) 'Searching for Spirituality in all the Wrong Places', *Journal of Business Ethics*, 48(4): 393–400.

Pratt, M. (2000) 'The Good, the Bad, and the Ambivalent: Managing Identification among Amway Distributors', *Administrative Science Quarterly*, 45: 456–93.

Ritzer, G. (2005) *Enchanting a Disenchanted World: Revolutionizing the Means of Consumption*. Thousand Oaks, CA: Pine Forge Press.

Rose, N. (1989) *Governing the Soul: The Shaping of the Private Self*. London: Routledge.

Smircich, L. (1983) 'Concepts of Culture and Organizational Analysis', *Administrative Science Quarterly*, 28: 393–413.

Tischler, L. (1999) 'The Growing Interest in Spirituality in Business: A Long-term Socio-economic Explanation', *Journal of Organizational Change Management*, 12(4): 273–80.

Tourish, D. and Pinnington, A.H. (2002) 'Transformational Leadership, Corporate Cultism and the Spirituality Paradigm: An Unholy Trinity in the Workplace?', *Human Relations*, 55(2): 147–72.

Trice, H. and Beyer, J. (1984) 'Studying Organizational Cultures through Rites and Ceremonials', *Academy of Management Review*, 9: 653–69.

Turner, B. (1986) 'Sociological Aspects of Organizational Symbolism', *Organization Studies*, 7: 101–15.

Weber, M. (1930) *The Protestant Ethic and the Spirit of Capitalism*. London: Allen & Unwin. (First published 1904–5).

Weber, M. (1993) *The Sociology of Religion*. Boston: Beacon Press. [first published 1922].

Weber, M. (2009) *Science as Vocation*, in H. Gerth and C.W. Mills (eds.) *From Max Weber: Essays in Sociology*. London: Routledge. (First published 1919).

Western, S. (2008) *Leadership: A Critical Text*. London: SAGE.

Willmott, H. (1993) 'Strength is Ignorance; Slavery is Freedom: Managing Culture in Modern Organizations', *Journal of Management Studies*, 30(4): 515–52.

40

Social materiality

A new direction in change management and action research

David M. Boje, Ivy DuRant, Krisha Coppedge, Ted Chambers and Marilu Marcillo-Gomez

Introduction

The field of change management (CM) is different than its cousin, action research (AR). The difference centres on the preference for either 'social construction' (SC) or what we will understand here by the name 'social materiality' (SM). There are five dominant discursive formations of practice that populate the Academy of Management and management consulting practice in general: Organization Development (OD), Change Management (CM), Action Science (AS), Action Research (AR; and Participative Action Research, PAR) and Appreciative Inquiry (AI). All five practice discourses nominate Kurt Lewin as their founding father. However, each has moved away from their founder.

AR has embraced a variant of SC that narrows change to interpreting the psychologizing and sometimes social psychologizing ranges of action. Whereas initial approaches to SC by Berger and Luckmann (1967) included the more material conditions of work, technology, corporeality, and economics, the more recent approach to SC by Weick (1976, 1988, 1993, 1995; Weick and Quinn, 1999), Gergen (1985, 2008; Gergen and Gergen, 1984; Gergen and Thatchenkery, 2004). Gergen as a psychologist stayed with an interpretivist approach that is without materiality awareness. Weick, as a social psychologist, moved from a coupling approach to social control, to the ways of sensemaking in enactment processes.

It would be fair to say that whereas Gergen focused on perceived environment, Weick focuses on enacted environment. Weick (1969/1979: 164) argues this difference, saying that, "If a perceived environment were the essence of enactment then, as Lou Pondy suggested, the phenomenon would have been called enthinkment not enactment."

Weick (1969/1979, 1995) cites Berger and Luckmann (1967), only once, in each of his most seminal books. Weick, each time, limits enactment to interpretivism. For example, Weick's (1969/1979) enactment theory tries to differentiate from Berger and Luckman by emphasizing how "managers construct, rearrange, single out, and demolish many 'objective' features of their surroundings" and "literally create their own constraints" (p. 164). Weick goes on to accuse Berger of Luckman (1967) of stressing SC as what is "selectively perceived, rearranged cognitively, and negotiated interpersonally" and stress what is required for "actors to attain at least a partial consensus on the meaning of their behavior" (pp. 164–65). And it is here that Weick

(1969/1979: 165) splits away from Berger and Luckmann in his most quoted passage (which was inspired by G. W. Bateson): "The basic sense-making device used within organizations is assumed to be talking to discover thinking. How can I know what I think until I see what I say?" As Bateson put it, "an explorer can never know what he is exploring until it has been explored" (1972: xvi, as cited in Weick, p. 165). In Weick's (1995: 67) more recent book sensemaking becomes one word. And, again only one reference to Berger and Luckmann's oeuvre, this time summarized in one sentence: "Over time, people act in patterned ways and take these patterns for granted as their reality, thereby socially constructing their reality."

What do Berger and Luckmann say about social constructionism?

These authors contend that all knowledge is a consequence of social interaction. The question of how this is done is centred on an illusion of constant propaganda designed to create response patterns in the minds of hearers to influence them towards certain beliefs and certain systems of conformity. These forces verify the social interactions of typification. Their philosophy of social constructionism seeks to influence the social context of interpersonal social interaction. Conversation or communication establishes concepts of thought provoking implanted ideas through repetition and dramatic visual aid persuasive tools of alleged truths. By contrast social constructivism as explained by Vygotsky in 1978 becomes the burden on the individual to comprehend the significance of the knowledge observed. Without critical observation, social constructionism becomes a vehicle for presumable philosophies that are unsubstantiated. Truth in all cases may be based therefore on false premises without an inspired desire to promote intellectual curiosity in critical thinking; the truth may not be known!

In social constructionism the psychological trend accepts dependent hypotheses. Theories of these hypotheses may be confirmed by a willingness to receive teaching and learning. In viewing the phenomenological point of view of social constructionism from Berger and Luckmann's perspective, their foundation explores the mystery of what we interpret to be blind faith. It is like stepping into the darkness while being held by the hand of someone you trust who will lead you in the right direction away from stumbling blocks, pitfalls, and cliffs. However, such may not be the case. Blind faith may be equated with blind trust. If it something sounds good and logical, a social context is created with an atmosphere of social constructivism that places one in a consensual arena of social constructionism. Whereby, one may not know how he/she arrived at that behaviour or conclusions.

For example, in the military when an order is given, it is to be carried out without question whether the soldier understands its intended purpose or not. "Knowledge is on a need to know basis." Lee Harvey Oswell, may have been a victim of such social constructionism vs. constructivism in the death of the late President J. F. Kennedy. Oswell, was thought to be affiliated with communism. To what extent does the influence of social constructionism play a role in unquestionable decision-making under the psychological power of social constructivism? By this example, this alludes to the description of Iran Hacking's (1996) observation of social constructionism which ideology is depicted as radical transformation. What is understood from what these authors are saying about social construction is that people tend to be treated as non-human persons in the age of postmodernism (Wapner, 1996). Some governments that practice social constructionism seem to practice the reputation of a care disassociation policy of its people in the administration of social constructionism.

As we can see, social constructionism seems to be portrayed as a mirror image of an illusion based on unfounded ideologies. The presumption and pretence of ideas that influence society's philosophical context of thought and motivations of the heart is an illusion of mind and spirit. Consciousness portrays motive and intentional behaviour, but its validity cannot be verified without a sound premise for the emotional response to be justified.

Moreover, Berger and Luckmann strongly influenced what is called social construction reality through role-playing using artificial entities as a go between mental representations of concepts and images. Without reservation, when society is led to believe that when these concepts and images are communicated, their pre-programmed belief systems are stimulated and embedded in the very structure of society. The sociology of this philosophy is known as institutionalization. Institutionalization is a thought process instilled in society through emotional stimuli with impressive philosophical reasoning, and theoretical knowledge without necessarily substantial sound premises for the appropriate behavioural response.

Based on the research of views of social constructionism, it is difficult to find a significant radical difference in the capacity of the philosophy of social constructionism in comparing the ideas and operations of Marxism, communism, or socialism. To beg the question, are Berger and Luckmann saying that society has become a victim of brainwashed reality due to social constructionism? Having said that, the question now is to what extent will the influence of social constructionism affect the sovereignty of the United States of America, the United States Constitution, and the Bill of Rights?

Summary of how Berger and Luckmann includes the economic and corporeal social-material conditions

Social structures are the result of the acceptance, use and organization of the complex processes used by individuals to go about everyday life. Social reality is produced by individuals through the use of language and action. The most common signification or the creation of signs to indicate subjective meaning use by man is language. Language serves two functions it permits humans to communicate internally and externally while enabling subjective typification and objectification to occur. Berger and Luckmann further stresses the utter dependence of society on these words and actions to create a social reality. The process of creating the complex social categories of manager, doctor or other professions are the product of what we consider common everyday occurrences and the use of language, interactions and activities by the individuals which create the social construct (Bittner, 1965). Berger and Luckmann's foundation of objectification "process whereby human subjectively embodies itself in products that are available to one's self and ones fellow man as a product of a common world ... he is able to distance himself from his producing and his product, such that he can take cognizance of it and make it an object of his consciousness" (p. 71). This thought forms the beginning of our understanding of the economic and corporeal social-material conditions that exist in human society. This objectification is an attribute of institutions, they exist externally of the individual whether they are understood and recognized or not however, they affect the individual and the corporal economic and material conditions. These institutions are the creation of man, "society is a human product. Society is an objective reality. Man is a social product" (p. 61).

There are three steps in the human, society interchange; internalization, externalization and objectification. When we explore the economic and corporeal-material conditions of man we can see how these three steps act to create a generative social phenomenon within a particular political ideological system, i.e. as Berger and Luckmann stated, "How is it possible that subjective meanings become objective faciticities? Or…how is it possible that human activity should produce a world of things? (p.18). Berger and Luckmann ideological foundation is based on the writing of Marx, Durkheim and Mannheim which support social order and class structure. At its core Berger and Luckmann assert human knowledge as the result of changes in the social material condition of man that is based on the use of communication and language to produce a social reality.

When we consider the institution of home ownership it is an example of an objective reality which is created by man. It exists externally from the individual but has social power to affect the life of the individual, communities, governments and nation's economic and material conditions. Berger and Luckmann did not address specific aspects of the material condition; however, they did address the forces which enable society to create economic and material conditions. These conditions have become through reification "an extreme step in the process of objectivation, whereby the objectivated world loses comprehensibility as a human enterprise and becomes fixated as a non-human, non-humanizable, inert facticity" (p. 89). The social constructs which are highly amenable to reification are institutions as they are accepted and taken for granted by man as a part of an agreed upon social reality. These institutions facilitate the division of labor, social class, private property ownership, social educational status etc. This is the quality which allows institutions to become a "non-human, non-humanizable inert facticity" taking on a life and persona of their own. What is fascinating is this human ability to accept these institutions and pass them on to their children thus supporting their existence and insuring the economic and material status of their social reality?

Take into consideration the capitalistic ideology accompanying private property ownership; which has been transformed into an institution which encompasses financial organizations, governmental agencies, individuals and corporations all functioning to maintain the "idea of home ownership" as the social reality individuals should attempt to attain. This institution continues to reinforce the social reality of man while being reinforced by the language and actions of man becoming a "stabilizing" social institution for the capitalistic ideology and culture. Harvey stated it well in his study into the workings of a capitalistic society and built environments "A worker mortgaged up to the hilt, for the most part, is the pillar of social stability…"(Harvey, 1978: 15). With habitualization a group of social relationships may become an institution and a social construct that acts as a stabilizing force in the economic and corporeal social-material condition. Garfinkel built upon the work of Berger and Luckmann by discussing man's attempt to interpret or make sense of his social constructs, which in turns becomes the processes by which he uses this knowledge to "accomplish" (Garfinkel, 1967) the everyday activities of life. Concurrently it is this existing knowledge used interpretively by man which results in the actions that create the social structures we observe. Social structures are the result of the acceptance, use and organization of the complex processes which take place beneath surface, many times going unnoticed by those employing these actions. Again, this habitualization forms the foundation of institutions which support the economic and corporal social-material condition.

Berger and Luckmann in light of Gergen and Weick's use of social constructionism in society and organizational development

Berger and Luckmann and Gergen have developed two opposing definitions of generative, and by their definitions they each seek different aims or goals in their theory of social constructionism. The former uses the phenomena to continue the exiting social reality through the passing on of language and actions to future generations thus supporting institutions and their non-human facticy; while the other seeks to focus individual attention on the taken for granted social reality while encouraging the individual to "reconsideration" and seek new social realities. In fact Gergen's definition of generative is very subjective. It can be influenced by the thoughts and reflection of the individual, "generative capacity" is defined this as the "... capacity to challenge the guiding assumptions of the culture, to raise fundamental questions regarding contemporary social life, to foster reconsideration of that which is 'taken for granted' and thereby furnish new alternatives for social actions" (1978: 1346). When we approach Weick's Enactment theory we see the activities of the individual within an organization as the creative forces resulting in social structures and "realities". Much of the activity of enactment is an attempt to make sense of the external environment through the use of rules, roles and communication within the organization or as Weick explained, "The external environment literally bends around the enactments of people, and much of the activity of sense-making involves an effort to separate the externality from the action" (Weick, 1988: 130).

Both Gergen and Weick deal with the subjective as opposed to the objective genesis of the organizational social "reality", neither directly addresses the material condition of social realities in their constructs. They address the individuals attempt to make sense of his or her environment while acting upon that environment, with a focus on language, stories and actions used by individuals to construct their social realities in light of existing roles, rules and repeated behavior. Gergen and Weick have acknowledged objectivation and economic and material constructs, however their focus has been on the human's ability to change an existing social constructs thus changing existing social realities from an organizational perspective.

This begs the questions, why have they not addressed the economic and material condition? By definition the organization exist to influence, control and develop the economic and material condition within its spear of influence, or financial and material gain are the primary reasons man has created organizations. Is this oversight due to the complex nature or the process of constructing these types of social realities, and the ability or inability of man to successfully disengage from the "product of his creation"? Let's look again at home ownership i.e. private property ownership in a capitalistic society; each of the "players" or institutions are not only part of the larger social institution but are individually an objective social construct with other interest and activities which affect the economic and corporal material condition. A financial institution not only lends money for mortgage to purchase the property, it can finance auto, educations and other things while acting as a depositor, and investor for society. The governmental body which regulates laws and guidelines for the purchase of private property; collects taxes, pave roads, build schools, etc. We could go on with the insurance company, attorney and so on; all of these institutional constructs have a role in the larger social reality of private property ownership, which directly affects the economic and corporal material condition of society. In essence man creates social realities to communicate and function in a material world, to not integrate and understand the affect of this physical material world is to focus on one facet of man activities in creating his social reality at the expense of the other. As we have shown, social constructionism took a turn away from materiality inherent in Berger and Luckmann. This turn occurred both in Weick and more so in Gergen, as they selectively develop Berger and Luckmann or in Gergen's case ignore it all together.

Summary of Berger and Luckmann's approach to Marx's materiality conditions

Durant's observation that "man creates social realities to communicate and function in a material world, not to integrate and understand the effect of this physical material world is only to focus on one facet of the process of creating his social reality" (2010). Durant's theory in light of Marx's approach relating to materiality conditions based on Berger and Luckmann's philosophical views of economic and corporeal social-material conditions directly affects private property ownership (2010). Social construction is a vehicle by which behavioral scientists deal with the advancement of economic sociology. In a capitalistic society, competition is fierce in the race to monopolize global markets.

Even governments take a special interest in the global economy capitalized on firm profits for taxation, revenue recycling, and employment opportunities for greater taxation. Failure to engage in social construction to maximize capital cash flow threatens profitability and corporate survival (Beamish, 2007). Inequality in the markets creates an imbalance in political power and control causing a dependency on the stronger opposing force. Consequently, discrimination in the distribution of formal economy tends to reflect discrimination against the physically unattractive investors such as the poor and different ethnic minority groups. The lack of freedom to explore and participate in the free market due to discrimination because of power vacuums, which causes a waste of human productivity and influence (Molotch, 1990; Perrow, 1972). Capitalistic exploitation according to Karl Marx refers to the working middle class are personal servants who tend to be classified based on circumstances as unproductive workers. Relationships between the Capitalist such as the White-Collar workers and the Middle Class tend to clash or disagree concerning the importance of wages and benefits. The working class complained of being de-humanized as "wage slavery" under Aristotle and Marx (Leopold, 2007).

Durant is credited with bridging the gap between Social Construction and Marxism in betraying the social dynamics' interaction through her exposition of Berger and Luckmann's treatise of the art of language used in the social structure of organizational development of corporeal economic and material social construction. From an objective reality perspective society influences economic and corporeal social-material conditions through common labour, as seen through the approach of Berger and Luckmann.

The economic process involving human subjectivity is accomplished through the use of political art through language, which persuades individuals to willingly engage in productivity. (Bittner, 1965). Social construction naturally tends to create opposition due to the objection of ethics. Thinking arbitrarily by disagreement, in terms of ethical issues interrupts the oppositional force in grappling with issues that are contradictory and hostile due to the complexity of economic rights pertaining to sociology by social construction (Jackson, 2010).

In summary, to Berger and Luckmann approach to Marx's materiality conditions create the social structure necessary to implement economic policies through what "takes place beneath the surface" (Durant, 2010) is undetected by the public because of *secrecy* held in privacy. Social structural policies can be implemented through this tactic even though opposing forces are in opposition to those policies (Durant, 2010; Garfinkel, 1967). Furthermore, Adorno's essay speaks of enlightenment by deception. This is a methodology framing cultural industry through distractions of amusement. Through misdirected attention governed by enjoyment of pleasurable conditions of circumstances social bonds may be attached and represented as a priority transcending the real purpose and mission (Jackson, 2010). In reference to Marx's materiality conditions these social distracting realities cause the inability for the successful disengagement of the form of deception of the product in order to be returned to a social materiality: and a new direction in change management and action research. Under capitalism in America, home-ownership and private property are viewed as a benefit of a privilege society under the United States Constitution and Bill of Rights. According to Levinas because of social construction, forgetfulness is inevitable (Jackson, 2010). History must not be forgotten in spite of the many social and materialistic demands placed upon society as a people. If not, we forget from whence we have come, and repeat the sufferings of a lost State. There are challenges to Gergen, Weick and Berger and Luckmann and social construction.

Karl Marx, Bruno Latour, and the challenges to social constructionism

Karl Marx's (1932/1844) critical theory of materiality of labor posits that as a result of capitalism and private enterprise, man loses sight of his true self. In a feudal state, man lived off the land and defined himself through his conscious engagement in life activity; making things for himself, his family and trading with others for what he could not produce. Marx believes that private enterprise forces man to become an object. As an object, he is part of the means to an end (profitability of the enterprise). As Marx puts it: "he becomes an appendage of the machine, and it is only the most simple, most monotonous, and most easily acquired knack, that is required of him. Hence, the cost of production of a workman is restricted, almost entirely to the means of subsistence that he requires for his maintenance and for the propagation of his race"(Marx and Engels, 1888: 10). A consequence of objectifying individuals and defining them as actors playing roles also permits objectification of anything created by man. These assumed disconnects between man as a free producer and one who is merely a component of this great machine (the enterprise) which objectifies him illustrates Marx's understanding of the capitalistic perspective; that man is only valuable while he can produce and can earn a wage. It is through this wage that he is able to barely live (not live an affluent life per se). In this way man loses connection between his true value and what someone else feels he is worth; his wage. From an objective reality perspective, society influences economic and corporeal social-material conditions through common labor, as seen from Berger and Luckmann's (1966) point of view. This perspective relates to Marx's view of man as a component of a grand machine, endowing man and objects with the same value or importance in the socially constructed reality. A perspective we explore next by Bruno Latour which presents social construction theory with a new set of challenges to this assumption; that man lives in a passive state, individual actors engage in role playing and do not control their performance. Bruno Latour use his actor-network theory to develop an understanding of cause and action, considering the role of actants, agents, actions, and processes into new shapes of antenarrative which help to deconstruct what is hidden. Latour (2005) then critiques social construction for its lack of materiality in the ways it approaches both the social and construction aspects, "Antenarrative is constituted out of the flow of lived experience; … it is about the story that came before" (Boje, 2001b: 3), which helps to better understand the roles, influences, actions and personal experiences of those that may be often overlooked. Berger, Luckmann and Latour all view man as the actor in his social reality; "the apprehension of the products of human activity as if they were something from nature, results of cosmic laws, or manifestations of divine will. Reification implies that man is capable of forgetting his own authorship of the human worlds, and further, that the dialectic between man, the producer, and his products is lost to consciousness … The objectivity of the social worlds means that it confronts man as something outside of himself" (Berger and Luckmann, 1967: 89). Man is not responsible for ethical lapses or failures because he is just an actor playing a role, one that is not defined or controlled by him but by the institutions he has created.

Using Latour's assemblages to reassemble materiality within social constructionism

Bruno Latour (1999, 2005) considered the individual mind, a member of the actor network as a physical assemblage, having all the properties of social constructs as other assemblages; i.e. equal to the reality of "labour, resources (food), money, buildings, infrastructure, language and a range of other materials, including those constitutive of climates" (De Landa, 2006). From this perspective we can now view thought and language from a secondary position to that of matter and energy which humans use to create the social institutions of organizations, governments, individual networks existing in reality apart from any ideology. It is this lack of recognition of the material institutions created by man as objective entities existing outside human thought or language by Gergen and Weick which Latour criticizes. Again De Landa summed up the relationship between objective entities and materialism as a part of social constructionism which should be revisited if we are to understand the forces at work within organizational change.

> The ontological status of any assemblage, inorganic, organic or social, is that of a unique, singular, historically contingent, individual ... Much as biological species are not general categories of which animal and plant organisms are members but larger-scale individual entities of which organisms are component parts, so social assemblages should be given the ontological status of individual entities: individual networks and coalitions; individual organizations and governments; individual cities and nation states. This ontological manoeuvre allows to assert that these individual entities have an objective existence independently of our minds.
>
> (De Landa, 2006: 40)

He termed this "history of material flow" which De Landa uses Latour's assemblages as object orientations to social construction in the study of economic material history; this can then be used within CM when organizational assemblages are given the same weight as that of languages or ideology. We can then reassemble the entities of the organization, government, individual networks etc. objectively as they exist in the material realm viewing them from the perspective of Latour, Berger and Luckmann as the social constructs created by man, but existing independently; entities which influences it's creator as it creator influences the entities material history. Change works by storytelling in different types, phases, agencies, processes and optics.

By interpretation of the foregoing and by shifting to Michel Foucault's dialogue forthcoming, the rhetoric of the art of language is designed to create argument through entities by premise formation to establish a positivity position for organizational change. The hypothesis by which vehicle language enjoys maybe presented as a summation of an illusion to distort the picture of premise of continuities known as evolutionism. Whereas organizational change rests upon the hypothesis that encourages a summation by illusion to distort the positive picture of premise evolutionism, hence, the expression of the art of language is therefore, structured by scientific methodology to influence the illusive distortion, which fictitiously appears to be an affirmation of the entities premise as an evolutionary determination. Next we deal with Foucault's materiality approach as a challenge to social construction.

Michel Foucault on the archaeology of practice domains of discourse

Foucault's (1972: 173–75) archaeology method "tries to establish the system of transformations that constitute 'change'; it tries to develop this empty, abstract notion, with a view to according it the analyzable status of transformation". This distinction between change as an abstract, empty force and transformation as discourse discontinuity is a critical distinction. In a discursive transformation new rules govern domains of discourse practices such as OD, CM, AS, AR, and AI. Change as a phenomena of continuity, returning from any disrupting, and a repetition is different from transformation, which is about discontinuity, and difference. The theory here is

587

that the fields of practice have stabilized their continuity into inertia, and have not really engaged in transformation that is "discontinuous," or a "rupture" (p. 174). This is a major critique of the practice disciplines. It bears further exploration.

Rupture is a discontinuity, a transformation, not a change in some homogeneous equilibrating process that takes place "everywhere in the same way" (p. 175). Change as well as action metaphors imagine a great drift, a glacier or river of evolution, that carries away all processes at once from one stage of a cycle to the next, or one phase of a plot to the next, or one level of system complexity to the next. Transformation is difference, discontinuity, break out, coincidences; a counter-move to change that is more of a spiral a galumphing assemblage, a rhizome.

Foucault develops several thresholds of scientific disciplines: *positivity*, *epistemologization*, *scientificity*, *formalization*, and *evolutionism*.

Positivity threshold – a group of verbal performances that characterizes and defines a discursive formation of continuities, that aims at a transcendental foundation, a quest for origin, speaking from the same conceptual field by opposing another field by deploying polemical interchanges; interpositivity later assumed the mantle of the human sciences (Foucault, 1972: 125–27, 173, 186).

Epistemologization threshold – a coherence the exercises a dominant function (model, critique, or verification) over knowledge (Foucault, 1972: 186–87).

Scientificity threshold – when certain laws are constructed from basic propositions to legitimate its practice (Foucault, 1972: 187).

Formalization threshold – a formal edifice of axioms is constituted (Foucault, 1972: 187).

Evolutionism threshold – a system of evolution has a different formation and role than other thresholds; the meaning of the term evolution can change over time in a discursive formation (Foucault, 1972: 103, 161, 173).[1]

We hypothesize that OD, CM, AS, AR, and AI do not pass through the different thresholds in turn, such as from positivity, epistemologization, scientificity, formalization, end evolutionism. These are specializations, at least in the academy of Management, not evolutive, not successive, not stages of development of a paradigm. Foucault (1972: 187), "sometimes positivity involves at the same time the emergence of an epistemological figure. Sometimes the thresholds of scientificity are linked with the transition from one positivity to another; sometimes they are different …"

The distribution of these different thresholds can be by succession, specialization, or coincidence. In the Academy of Management, the practice discourses is certainly not one of succession. It could be coincidence, but it appears more a case of specialization of OD, CM, AS, AR, and AI gravitating to their distinct threshold of discursive practice. Attempts at integration have been launched from each of the five, but have yet to convert or colonize the others. Each has more or less power (in terms of resources, membership, and number of presentations in ballrooms) in the Academy of Management. The discursive practice formations are disciplines of different ages, roughly in the order given: OD, CM, AS, AR, and AI. They come into power in the Organization Development and Change, and the Organization Consultation Divisions of the Academy of Management.

Figure 40.1 gives a visual depiction of how we theorize the different practice formations as correlated with particular discursive thresholds.

While we posit that the thresholds are specialized in the Academy of Management, Foucault holds out the possibility of different patterns such as succession, and transition of one discursive practice formation into another. Foucault (1972: 187), for example, argues that, "sometimes

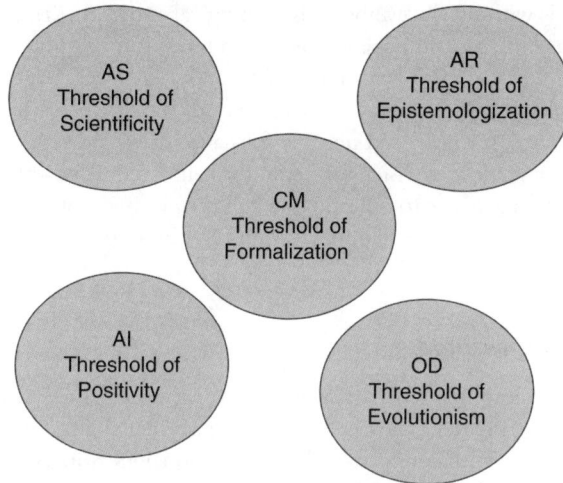

Figure 40.1 Discursive practice formations in the academy of management

positivity involves at the same time the emergence of an epistemological figure. Sometimes the thresholds of scientificity are linked with the transition from one positivity to another; sometimes they are different …" We hypothesize that OD, CM, AS, AR, and AI do not pass through the different thresholds in turn, such as from Positivity, Epistemologization, Scientificity, Formalization, end Evolutionism. These are specializations, at least in the Academy of Management, not evolutive, not successive, not stages of development of a paradigm. Foucault (1972: 187), "sometimes positivity involves at the same time the emergence of an epistemological figure. Sometimes the thresholds of scientificity are linked with the transition from one positivity to another; sometimes they are different …"

Next we explore how each of the practice disciplines, in our view, is rooted and specialized into a particular discursive threshold.

AI's positivity threshold

AI has a quest for positive thinking, for positivity in all forms. It seeks positivity as a transcendental foundation. Deficit discourses such as critical theory, deconstruction, and approaches to action and change that seek out problems and dysfunctions to be fixed are particularly suspect in AI positivity. While it is the youngest of the practice disciplines, it is also the most polemical, defining its conceptual field in opposition to any social science that explores anything negative. AI has been attempting to colonize other disciples: positive leadership, positive organizational behaviour, positive psychology, appreciative intelligence, and even positive social science. However, as yet AI has not developed its own positivity to the point of transitioning to an epistemologization, nor is it ready to be a science.

AR's epistemologization threshold

AR has spawned several transitions in its own epistemologization, from social science research to produce knowledge, to knowledge that is to be managed, stored, and transferred in knowledge organizations. Curiously knowledge management AR has not produced a corpus of knowledge, like law. And AR is without discernible epistemological structures. The lack of epistemological corpus and structure makes it impossible for AR to transition to some other kind of threshold. AR does not seem to develop a worked out *episteme*. By "*episteme*" Foucault (1972: 191) means, "the total set of relations that unite, at a given period, the discursive practices that give rise to epistemological figures, sciences, and possibly formalized systems. ..." AR has proliferated into inexhaustible field of postulates which has yet to formalize. These postulates also do not supplant preceding ones, but do give rise to still others. The knowledge is not evolving. The threshold has not been reached into terms of developing the epistemologization to the point of being a model with verification over knowledge.

AS's scientificity threshold

AS has attempted to leap full blown into a science, without having developed a positivity or knowledge corpus (episteme). AS has been vigorously developed over the past 50 years by Harvard's Chris Argyris, with considerable help from Donald Schon. AS defined itself as a science but did not as yet cross over to any of the other thresholds. Science is more metaphor and concept than it is practice. The theory and practice of AS has tried to colonize OD as its primary strategy. Most recently AS has been declared as a cousin to AR. AS's most recent project is to colonize organizational learning. There are several laws constructed from basic AS propositions, such as, a shift from one type of theory-in-use Model I (single loop learning) to a different theory-in-use, Model II (double loop) learning. This is done by reducing Model I defensive interpersonal behaviour that is said in Lewinian terms to be a barrier to change. Model I people define goals unilaterally and try to achieve them without any evaluative tests or inquiry. Model I people also do not express or generate negative feelings, and try to stay rational by minimizing emotionality. Model II learning is collaborative, stressing informed choice, participants originating actions have high trust, engage in open confrontation on difficult issues, publicly test theories, evaluating implementation of action. The confrontive, problem-solving focus of Model II prevents it from being the sort of positivity of AI.

AI is a practice that inhibits the participants from experiencing embarrassment or threat and prevents them from identifying, reducing, and correcting the causes of the embarrassment or threat. It is unlikely that AS and AI will integrate their thresholds. Indeed AI's threshold of positivity can be viewed as single loop learning, by making the negative and the problems un-discussable, and making the un-discussable stories un-discussable (denial, avoidance of confrontation, etc.). AI focus on using diplomacy, not using deficit discourse would be a problem for AS, since Model I does not encourage testing or validating claims, and could be said to inhibit learning to overcome dysfunctions.

CM's formalization threshold

CM established its axioms in the formalized discourse of Kurt Lewin. Lewin (1946), for example, defined behavior (*B*) as a function *(F)* of the person *(P)* and their environment *(E)*. In his field theory, the life space was differentiated into regions of reality and irreality. "Play can be understood as an action on the level of reality closely related to the irreal level" (Lewin, 1951: 245). The psychological environment of the life space was affected by the situation which included the present situation (the status quo) being maintained by forces, such as food habits of particular subcultures. Change was represented in field theory by the forces of various parts of the life space that could be analyzed as 'habits' and the situation, including its material-physicality, its economy, and sociology that could be understood scientifically (Lewin, 1943). Rather than becoming a science, CM, jettison's most of Lewin's formalization by the 1960s. The genesis of CM lies in adapting a less dynamic reading of Lewin, an ice cube metaphor of unfreezing restraints on change (most often defined as employees' resistance to change), and using managerial forces of change (i.e. managers, as we all know are positive about change), and it's managers who could move change, and then the change agent (managers again) refreezes the changed processes (and habits) at a new level of quasi-stationary equilibrium (usually defined as increased production). Lewin's field theory was reduced in CM practice to the ice cube metaphor. Since CM has not developed in its own threshold, it is in no position to transition to other thresholds in Figure 40.1.

OD's evolutionism threshold

OD became popular in World War II, with the emergence of the first cybernetics (deviation-counteracting systems). By the 1960s, the field of socio-technical system became aware of open systems (deviation amplifying loops), and the transition to second cybernetics was underway. Certain principles developed, such as the organization is in 1st and 2nd cybernetic interplay with its environment. With Emery and Trist (1965), the environmental situation was said to evolve from types: randomly distributed, placid clustered, distributed reactive, and turbulent field.

It is the fourth type of environment that is the basis of Emery and Trist's (1965), causal textual that contemporary organizations are said to have evolved to. Small businesses, are an exception, and can be in *randomly distributed* environments, free-running affairs with no sense of rhythm at all. They are the only natural stopping place other than ending the business when there are no more resources or customers. In *placid clustered* environments, small (and larger) firms live in more seasonal rhythms, aware of cycles and periods of resource availabilities, like the New Mexico green and red Chile farmers and the Pecan growers. Tax businesses are seasonal, aware that January to 15 April is a peak season for tax work. In *distributed reactive* environments, organizations are strategically conscious of cyclic and recurrent rhythms of resource distribution, but also aware that they are not the lone hunters and gathers. Finally, in *turbulent field* environments, rhythms self-organize, and no longer evolve. To say the least, it is a strange theory, since evolution is no longer a concern. The meaning of evolution has changed since the original formulations in OD.

For example Larry Greiner (1972) proposed a more linear model of size and age. There is a linear rhythm of evolution moments, disrupted in age and size growth trajectory by historical events of evolution. For example, in *The Leadership Crisis*, "as the company grows, new systems are needed – manufacturing, accounting, personnel, etc. The founders usually do not have the expertise to manage this new set of systems nor can they motivate new employees. This is the *Leadership Crisis*. The company may bring in management who can manage in this new environment or may flounder as founders try to 'maintain the old guard' (Greiner, 1972). OD has also looked at punctuated equilibrium in work of Karlene Roberts. It has however not developed an extensive practice model, such as with the Emerys (Merilyn, and the late Fred Emery).

In sum, the five practice disciplines have adopted different vocabularies, specialized their practice concepts and theories, and become self-enveloping instead of integrative. Since each of the five practice disciplines has not exploited their threshold specialization beyond the level of metaphor and binary concepts such as Model I and Model II, there is no escape, no maturation of the paradigm such that one practice discipline could cross over or transition into another threshold type. It is nevertheless true that the practice paradigms jostle for power in the Academy of Management and in the multi-billion dollar practice industry. As long as the root metaphors remain metaphors instead of full-blown constructs that can be evaluated for their social and economic consequences, the thresholds cannot be eclipsed.

Next we look at the implication of the five thresholds for the development of CM, which is the topic of this book.

Implications for CM

CM, following Lewin (et al. 1939, 1943, and 1951) established formalization and pointed the way to a practice that could well have adapted into a scientificity threshold. Further, CM had the potential to transition from formalization to epistemological threshold. Indeed, CM could have become all five thresholds, though perhaps not the same positivity as AI, nor the linear evolutionism of OD.

A return to training of CM in Kurt Lewin could result in an integration of the five thresholds. It would require moving away from the ice cube model, into one that had a more rigorously informed social and physics science. In the next section we look at the material aspects of Lewin, and the way in which the practice threshold of CM transitioned into social constructionism, at the expense of any inquiry into material conditions.

Extending the future of CM with a storytelling materiality approach

Our storytelling practices are material in actants. Materiality is a part of the telling, and affected by telling, in an iterative intra-activity process of change. An intra-active storytelling with materiality as iterative change practice form a PM perspective includes the engagement of human and non-human actors, and situational forces such as technology and economics. As Barad puts it the human and non-human actors "foreclose other patterns of mattering" (2007: 394). Boje's contribution to storytelling is to look at its materiality and complexity and at various intra-plays of antenarrative practices. An antenarrative is defined as a bet on the future, as a pre-narrative practice that shapes and transform the field of future possibilities (Boje, 2001b). Barad's work antenarrative implications: "Future moments don't follow present ones like beads on a string" (p. 394). Barad is pointing out the limits of linear antenarratives, which is also the limit of most change management approaches: too linear. Boje (2011) looks at alternatives to linearity and to cycles (bent lines) in spirals (that do not return to cyclic) and in assemblages. Barad (2007: 197) defines intra-action as "mutual constitution of objects and agencies of observation within phenomena."

Storytelling is not separate from measuring instruments. The measuring instrument selected is entangled with the storytelling phenomena, which is entangled intra-actively with materiality. Storytelling measurement makes agential cuts and delimits change properties and change courses. The measuring agencies of a storytelling methodology shapes a change vector, be it linear, cyclic, more spiral, or an assemblage (rhizomatic). The act of observation, measurement, operationalization, and instrumentation all affect the course in the intra-active storytelling-materiality. The methodology choice affects the microphysics of power. Storytelling and measurement is as important as the change process being managed. Measurement and change are complicit. "The framework of agential realism does not limit its reassessment of the matter of bodies to the realm of the human (and to the body's surface) or to the domain of the social" (Barad, 2007: 209). Storytelling (re)configures the material world. It does this by setting boundaries, including and excluding continent, and also by the wave-effect of its own materiality, its own corporeal flesh and body.

Observing a wave or a particle depends in quantum physics on the measuring device. Similarly, in storytelling, the methodology for observing the agencies and material practices of storytelling, shapes and disciplines the storytelling. The method includes or excludes so that not only what is admitted to be storytelling but the very course of the storytelling that unfolds is deeply affected. This approach by Barad and our extension into storytelling relies on Foucault micropolitics of power and resistance, as we have argued in this chapter the micro-forces of power and resistance that one finds in Kurt Lewin's work have been modified and greatly morphed in both AR and CM. We assume, following Barad (2007: 200) that storytelling "orders the body, fixes and constrains movement." Movement for Lewin was locomotion in the psychological field, as a result of changes in the physical/material situation. In Barad, and in PM in general, movement or locomotion is more at the quantum level, as well as at the waves of discourse intra-splicing the waves of materiality. This is an important difference, one we cannot overstress.

Storytelling, changes under this proposal it is not a fixed object-entity, where the methodology is to collect and stack and compare the texts from different subjects. A more *in situ* methodology would attend to the context and situation of the storytelling, but also to the physical material aspects of voice tones, gestures, and to material intertextualities (not just other texts). Latour (1999, 2005) for example asks that we debunk SC by looking at the material aspects of time, space, pressures, and the heterogeneity of agencies and actants. In both Barad and Latour, storytelling methods would need to trace the intra-active becoming where humans and nonhuman actors, as well as actants that are material, technological, natured (trees, air, soil, fire) and economic forces are part of the materiality-discursiveity. In agential realism, storytelling is part of intra-active becoming in its relationship with materiality, and its iterative intra-play with materiality. For Bakhtin (1981) discourse and storytelling are in what Barad calls intra-play with other dialogics such as stylistics, chronopicities (timespace), and architectonics (intra-play of ethics, aesthetics and cognitive discourses).

Not all storytelling practices are equally efficacious. Some are more apt to affect generativity, the becoming of ontological material-discursive patterns or what Barad calls "materialization" (2007: 207). Storytelling change, without an attention to materialization the generativity processes is obviously not a methodology we advocate. "Not any story will do" (Barad, 2007: 207). Storytelling change, from our perspective, would be more efficacious by studying that accounts of materialization, and the material practices of regulation, disciplining, negotiating the inclusions and inclusions, and the iterative intra-active trail. This would result in a more dynamic intra-action approach to storytelling-materiality, to the becoming of generativity. It is also what Barad calls "*a congealing of agency*" with materiality of power, that has an ontological thereness, rather than merely a social construction approach to AR or CM (p. 210). Storytelling-materiality has the thereness of an iterative process of becoming, including not just textuality, but gestures that bend the air, writing a story with strokes of a pen that leaves marks on the page, or striking the keys of keyboard that register digitally on the screen. IN terms of gestures and posture, my body embodies storytelling practices that occur in the corporeal world of time-space mattering that is more or less efficacious.

An array of storytelling practices have time-space mattering embodiment that is materially biological, chemical, kinesthetic. Other storytelling practices are the ways our habits of gesture and behavior live out our storytelling. IN either case storytelling materiality is about sorting the inclusions and exclusions that make for the micro-politics of power in organizational settings. Storytelling practices produce and are produced by economic, technological institutional, observational, and managerial arrangement of power and resistance, that order and exclude. There is no master storyteller (religious beliefs aside) issuing or giving master narratives that we are to discover and follow. Rather, following Foucault, there is always storytelling power

593

and resistance in the microphysics of materiality-storytelling. If we move beyond SC to PM materiality then we can propose storytelling does not exist independent of a materiality field. And materiality is shaped by the storytelling (Boje 2007 – See chapter on globalization narratives at http://peaceaware.com/vita see chapters in books).

Further, we propose that storytelling is never quite complete in its exchange and intro-play with materiality. There is always a field of possibilities, of futures that are sideshadows to the ones unfolding or not (Morson, 1994). Economists call sideshadows opportunity costs, but Morson has something more complex in mind. The sideshadows, the paths not followed, continue to intra-play with the path chosen. Morson does not get much into materiality. His work could be extended from its SC roots by looking at intra-play with materiality. Storytelling disturbs the air ways, messes with acoustics of tonality, pitch, and the rhythm of pace, repetition, and cadence. This is what provides the conditions of antenarrative iterative storytelling-materiality co-shaping and co-generating in the field of potentiality. Storytelling tones and gestures open and block space, have more or less agency, and more or less iterative enactment with other materiality.

Particular technoscientific and socioeconomic developments in storytelling have changed the intra-play of human and non-human storytelling. For example, Colonizing antenarrative lodge at the base of any futuring circuitry, affecting the becoming patterns, by acts of inclusion and exclusion (Boje 2007, 2008, 2011). In sum, storytelling is intricately involved in exchanges with materiality. The way we measure storytelling in our methodologies of change and research affects the phenomenon of storytelling-materiality, disturbing, even shaping its generative becoming. We cannot observe storytelling without disturbing the course of the storytelling. Reporting the unfolding of a storytelling, will change the agential materializing course of the intra-activity of storytelling and materiality. The choice of a methodology will produce different storytelling. So far change methods have relied more on particle methods, on stackable object stories that can be counted and sorted into categorical taxonomies. Change agents sift through the pile of story-telling from a focus group or a round of interviews without much attention to *in situ* storytelling practices, embedded in the material world. We cannot observe storytelling with changing it.

Agential realism can be a critical examination of storytelling methods and change practices that can differentiation how the bounding of human and non-human is being enacted in an institution. "For these very practices are always implicated in particular materializations" (p. 210). Therefore storytelling methods are always implicated in agential materialization and differentiating human and non-human roles, especially in late Western society. Storytelling itself is a material institution of differences though sounds, bodily gestures, figurations in text and architectural visual moves. And, the measuring devices of the storytelling methods and the change itself are more or less efficacious, depending upon the method. For example, much of the storytelling consulting literature is all about memorizing a beginning, middle, and end narrative, one that can be told in the time of an elevator ride. In entrepreneurial investment work, the elevator pitch can have monetary consequences with a group of investors, expecting to rate such pitch-narratives. However, much of this literature does not address the more complex world of storytelling organizations. Here, the storytelling is contested; there are counter stories to every story promoted. The material order negotiated in the storytelling is not worked out in the elevator ride.

In a posthumanist sense, storytelling is a differentiating, in counterforce to storytelling (mainly Western narrative tradition) which centers, abstracts, generalizes. A time-space mattering approach to change with storytelling is about affecting not just the SC but the time-space mattering ontology, boringness in the world. In post humanist storytelling what we notice in our telling matters and normalize in an iterative intra-active process of generativity. Non-human storytelling has its mattering practices and its agencies. We in the business college have not looked seriously at archaeology, geology, and botany or quantum physics. The result is our social constructions have biased conceptual schemata (Barad, 2007: 338). We have suggested a story-telling materiality that entangles telling of economist, sociology and political scientists with that of the physicist and the ecologist. Then we asked for a switch from an epistemological to an ontological approach to storytellers, to a Posthuman move.

The choice of change approaches, AR or CM gives different attention to materiality. There is only slightly more attention to materiality in CM. Both fields have adopted Kurt Lewin as their founding father. CM and AR have taken managerialist turns that they are trying to steer out of, without losing control. The storytelling, again, is never independent of the measuring tools. And for some, storytelling itself is the measuring tool of the change, measuring changes the potentiality, the antenarrative field of possibilities. This is from an ontological perspective, in defiance of the predominant preference for knowledge-epistemology.

So much of our storytelling the past three decades is increasingly embedded in technology, few may not have noticed. With Myspace, Twitter, Facebook, and the explosion of cell phones, digital recorders, and other technologies, we are a storytelling-texting society. We walk and talk in a world that is changing as a consequence of our storytelling. We would like to call for mores storytelling answerability in the ethics of CM and AR. Storytelling answerability is necessary in change management, because so much of CM and AR have made the exploitation and the colonizing project worse. Storytelling is intra-active and consequential with material-institutional configurations. The linkage between storytelling and materiality effects in human and non-human bodies and between them is a topic for future change management projects. The performative changes that give storytelling materiality its potency and agency have to be the subject of future study. Storytelling, however, is never entirely efficacious because it is always part of a wider intra-active context of counter-claims.

Storytelling can go outside the anticipated lines of linearity. It is perhaps here that the more dynamic change prospects outweigh the linear power of the short and sweet elevator pitch. Nonhuman storytelling is an area ripe for research. We know very little about how the world tells its story, how the world is what Bennett (2010) call vibrant matter. Perhaps it's safe to say, no storytelling is without non-human enactment, in terms of some props, a stage, a space-time mattering intra-activity where a wave, a sound, or a line in the sand can have material force.

Socialization is an agent of change; Temporalization is an agent of change; Mattering is an agent of change. The human fiction that we are storytelling to make sense, but not changing the material conditions flies against all that we have presented here.

Note

1 Foucault (1972) does not explicitly treat evolution as a threshold. We therefore use the term evolutionism to mean the continuities and developmental stages approaches to organization practices, and include such areas as punctuated equilibrium disruptions that return to a stable trajectory.

References

Bakhtin, M.M. (1981). *The Dialogic Imagination: Four Essays*. Edited by Michael Holquist; Translated by Caryl Emerson, and Michael Holquist. Austin, TX: University of Texas Press.

Barad, K. (2007). *Meeting the Universe Halfway: Quantum Physics and the Entanglement of Matter and Meaning*. Durham, NC: Duke University Press.

Beamish, T.D. (2007). Economic sociology in the next decade and beyond. Retrieved from online on: August 30, 2010 http://abs.sagepub.com/contend/50/8/993.

Bennett, J. (2010). *Vibrant Matter: A Political Ecology of Things* (A John Hope Franklin Center Book) Durham, NC: Duke University Press Books.

Berger, P.L. and Luckmann, T. (1966). *The Social Construction of Reality: A Treatise in the Sociology of Knowledge*. New York: Doubleday.

Berger, P.L. and Luckmann, T. (1967). *The Social Construction of Reality*. New York: Anchor Books.

Bittner, E.H. (1965). Employment opportunities for women in Alaska: a collection of data pertaining to knowledge and skills of home economics and how these contribute to wage-earning occupations. Online manuscript available from education resource informaiton center: http://eric.ed.gov/ericwebportal/search/detailmini.jsp?_nfpb=true&_&ericextsearch_searchvalue_0=ed012304&ericextsearch_searchtype_0=no&accno=ed012304.

Boje, D.M. (2001a). 'Microstoria analysis' narrative analysis. Chapter 3 in *Narrative Methods for Organizational and Communication Research*. London: SAGE Publications.

Boje, D.M. (2001b). *Narrative Methods for Organizational and Communication Research*. London: SAGE.

Boje, D.M. (2007). Globalization antenarratives. Chapter 17 in Albert Mills, Jeannie C. Helms-Mills and Carolyn Forshaw (eds). *Organizational Behavior in a Global Context*. Toronto: Garamond Press.

Boje, D.M. (2008). *Storytelling Organizations*. London: SAGE.

Boje, D.M. (2011). *The Future of Storytelling in Organizations: An Antenarrative Handbook*. London: Routledge.

De Landa, M. (2006). *A New Philosophy of Society: Assemblage Theory and Social Complexity*. New York: Continuum International Publishing Group Ltd.

DuRant, I. (2010). Social constructionism and organizational development, unpublished manuscript, Institute for Advance Studies, Colorado Technical University, Colorado Springs, CO.

Emery, F.E. and Trist E.L. (1965). The causal texture of organizational environments. *Human Relatons*, 18: 21–32.

Foucault, M. (1972). *Archaeology of Knowledge*. New York: Pahtheon.

Garfinkel, H. (1967). *Studies in Ethnomethodology*. Englewood Cliffs, NJ: Prentice Hall.

Gergen, K.J. (1978). Toward generative theory. *Journal of Personality and Social Psychology*, 36: 11, 1344–60.

Gergen, K.J. (1985). The social construction movement in modern psychology. *American Psychologist*, 40, 266–75.

Gergen, K.J. (2008). *An Invitation to Social Construction* (2nd edn). London: SAGE.

Gergen, M.M. and Gergen, K.J. (1984). The social construction of narrative accounts. In K.J. Gergen and M.M. Gergen (eds), *Historical Social Psychology* (pp. 173–89). Hillsdale, NJ: Lawrence Erlbaum.

Gergen, K.J. and Thatchenkery, T. J. (2004). Organization science as social construction. *Journal of Applied Behavioral Science*, 40 (2), 228–49.

Greiner, L.E. (1972). Evolution and revolution as organizations grow. *Harvard Business Review*, 50 (4), 37–46.

Hacking, I. (1996). Social constructionism vs. social constructivism. http://en.wikipedia.org/wiki/Social_constructionism (retrieved on 28 August 2010).

Harvey, D. (1978). Labor, capital and class struggle around the built environment in advance capitalistic societies. *Politics and Society*, 6 (3), 265–95.

Jackson, J.M. (2010). Persecution and social histories: Towards an Adornian critique of Levina'. http://psc.sagepub.com/content/36/6/719 (retrieved on 30 August 2010).

Latour, B. (1999). *Pandora's Hope: Essays on the Reality of Science Studies*. Cambridge, MA: Harvard University Press.

Latour, B. (2005). *Reassembling the Social: An Introduction to Actor-network Theory*. Oxford: Oxford University Press.

Leopold, D. (2007). *The Young Marx: German Philosophy, the State and Human Flourishing*. Cambridge: Cambridge University Press.

Lewin, K. (1943). Defining the "Field at a Given Time." *Psychological Review*, 50: 292–310. (Republished in *Resolving Social Conflicts & Field Theory in Social Science*, Washington, DC: American Psychological Association, 1997).

Lewin, K. (1946). Action research and minority problems. *Journal of Social Issues*, 2 (4), 34–46.

Lewin, K. (1951). *Field Theory in Social Science: Selected Theoretical Papers*. New York: Harper & Brothers.

Lewin, K., Lippit, R. and White, R.K. (1939). Patterns of aggressive behavior in experimentally created social climates. *Journal of Social Psychology*, 10, 271–301.

Marx, K. (1932, written 1844). Marx/Engels, Gesamtausgabe, *Abt.* 1, Bd. 3,.Eg (1959) translation The Economic and Philosophic Manuscripts of 1844. Moscow, Russia: Institute of Marxism-Lenisim, translated by Martin Milligan, Moscow, Russia: Foreign Languages Publishing House (now Progress Publishers).

Marx, K. and Engels, F. (1888). *The Communist Manifesto*. English translation by Samuel Moore. London: William Reeves.

McMurtry, J. (2009). The young Karl Marx: German philosophy, modern politics, and human flourishing. *Journal of the History of Philosophy*, 47 (3), 479–80. Retrieved 30 August 2010, from CTU's Research Library (Document ID: 1790232431).

Molotch, H.L. (1990). Social, economics, and the economy. In H. Gans (ed.), *Sociology in America*. Thousand Oaks, CA: SAGE.

Morson, G.S. (1994). Contingency and freedom, prosaics and process. *New Literary History*, 29(4), Autumn 1998, 673–86.

Perrow, C. (1972). *The Radical Attack on Business*. New York: Harcourt Brace Jovanovich.

Scheler, M., Mannheim, K., Stark W., Marx, K. and Weber, M. (1966). *The Social Construction of Reality*. http://en.wikipedia.org/wiki/The_Social_Construction_of_Reality (retrieved on 28 August 2010).

Vygotsky, L. (1978). Social constructionism vs. social constructivism'. http://en.wikipedia.org/wiki/Social_constructionism (retrieved on 28 August 2010).

Wapner, P. (1996). 'Environmental Leftist social constructionism'. http://en.wikipedia.org/wiki/Social_constructionism (retrieved on 28 August 2010).

Weick, K.E. (1976). Educational organizations as loosely coupled systems. *Administrative Science Quarterly*, 21 (1), 19.

Weick, K.E. (1979). *The Social Psychology of Organizing* (2nd. edn). Reading, MA: Addison-Wesley.

Weick, K.E. (1988). Enacted sensemaking in crisis situations. *Journal of Management Studies*, 24 (4): 305–17.

Weick, K.E. (1993). The collapse of sensemaking in organizations: The Mann Gulch disaster. *Administrative Science Quarterly*, 38 (4): 628.

Weick, K.E. (1995). *Sensemaking in Organizations*. Thousand Oaks, CA: Sage.

Weick, K.E. and Quinn, R.E. (1999). Organizational change and development. *Annual Review of Psychology*, 50 (1), 361–86.

Postscript
Change in a changing world – where now?

David M. Boje, Bernard Burnes and John Hassard

David M. Boje: I propose we move away from an over-reliance on social constructionism and get 'real' about the materiality conditions of power, politics, and world ecology. There is too much focus on human agents in organizations, on stakeholders being able to sit and plan and change things for other stakeholders, most of whom are not human. In a posthumanist approach to change management, it is not only humans who have agency for change management, but non-humans, not just animals, but all sentient life, and all that vibrant materiality that quantum physicists tell us has some kind of atom, molecule, quantum particle connection across vast nothingness. I am struck by how wedded we have become to sensemaking that is pretty far removed from the kinds of material conditions that inspired Berger and Luckmann, or for that matter the sociology Weber. Finally, a new sort of storytelling is needed. Perhaps that would be a suspicion of all storytelling. Heidegger's *Being and Time* certainly looked beyond storytelling to get at Being. OD, change management, action research and all its cousins seem to have moved into the managerialist camp, and don't know how to get out of all its colonizing, imperializing projects. Cutting the veil of all storytelling, and getting into the Now of the material condition, would get us past the prison of language and discourse. Perhaps that is impossible, but it would be change in a changing 'real' socioeconomic world. Can there be a new enchantment approach to change management, one rooted in recovering from disenchantment that is rooted in a new physics of change, in the new quantum physics. What would the new quantum physics (such as that of Karen Barad, 2007) mean for a new theory and practice of organizational change? If we are all connected in the quantum world, and our discourse, as Barad contends, is intra-penetrating with that materiality world of timespacemattering, then perhaps a new quantum physics of organization change is possible. It would be one where enchantment comes for changing the vibratory field. Perhaps this is what Kurt Lewin's field theory was becoming, a way of intra-playing physical-materiality with discourse. After Lewin's death, the field of organization change became wedded to the social psychology of field theory, but estranged from any materiality. I would therefore advocate a return to both Weber and Lewin.

Bernard Burnes: In considering the future of organizational change, there are three issues which need to be considered. The first relates to the volume of changes taking place. There was once a time when if someone suggested that a change should take place, they were met with the question why? and, if not laughed out of court, were required to make a strong case for the suggestion. We now appear to live in an age where change has become the norm and one has to make a strong case for not changing. When was the last time a senior manager was appointed and told he or she had to maintain stability? The result is that most people are faced with an avalanche of change. This is not to say that some changes are not required. We need to tackle global warming, the depletion of the earth's natural resources, poverty and disease, but strangely enough these seem to get lost in the plethora of other changes – if everything is a priority, nothing is a priority. What conclusion can we take from this? That we need to make fewer changes, but the right ones.

The second issue relates to the capacity to manage change. It appears to be generally accepted that some 70 per cent of all change initiatives fail. Allied to this is evidence that some 70 per cent of senior managers are either poor performers or have dysfunctional relationships with their colleagues. We also know that, in the main, top-down, imposed change does not work. Nevertheless, this does not stop senior managers from acting in this fashion. And why shouldn't they? Win or lose, senior managers appear to be extremely well-rewarded – whether they be entering or exiting from the board room. What conclusion can we draw from this? That we cannot rely on senior managers to identify what change is necessary or ensure that it is successfully achieved.

Last but not least is the role of change scholars and practitioners. Led by Lewin, the development of OD created a generation of practitioners who saw their role as neutral change facilitators driven by a set of humanist and democratic values. This was not because they were wild-eyed idealists, but because the evidence showed that it worked. In the 1960s and 1970s, this began to change. Practitioners began to be less neutral and more managerialist, and they found it harder and harder to stick to the values of OD. In effect, they became too focussed on what managers said they wanted and less able to involve other stakeholders in the change process. What about change scholars? From the 1980s onwards, we can see two interesting and interrelated developments:

1   The link between practice and theory began to break down. Scholars produced many interesting and insightful studies of change and linked these to emerging theories, such as post-modernism and complexity. However, the practical advice they offered was limited, usually tacked on at the end of books and articles, and of a very general nature.

2   Many change scholars ignored the importance of ethics. In their studies of change, they drew attention to the role of power and politics as mediators of change. The description of the change process which emerged was that change is difficult, people obstruct it, and power and politics are used to overcome this resistance. As a book I recently read put it, 'if all else fails, use dirty tricks'. Instead of ethical behaviour being seen as central to the change process, at best it became peripheral and at worst an obstacle.

What conclusions can we draw from this? That when practitioners become too focused on the needs of managers, they lose sight of the theoretical basis of their practice and neglect the important role of values; and that when scholars become too focused on analysis and theory, they neglect the impact of their work on practice and can, usually inadvertently, end up providing support for unethical practices.

So, what about the future? First, if most change initiatives fail, we need to step back from the fixation with changing everything and instead concentrate on a few key changes, especially those aimed at organizational and global sustainability. The good news is that sustainability is moving up the political and corporate agendas, though it still has a long way to go before it becomes the number one priority. The bad news is that the fixation with changing everything seems undiminished. Second, if top-down change does not work, we need to move back to a participative-democratic change process. As this *Companion* shows, there is a growing rejection of managerialist approaches to change and a renewed advocacy of democratic participation, which may also assist in reducing the volume of change initiatives. Lastly, we need to re-establish the link between theory and practice – Lewin's dictum 'that there is nothing so practical as a good theory' was not a politician's sound bite, but an encapsulation of the work of a great 'practical theorist'. There is a renewed interest in Lewin's participative-ethical approach to change and a growing recognition that much of Lewin's work appears to fit in remarkably well with current interests such as complexity and storytelling. Hopefully this will lead to a rebuilding of the bridges between practice and theory, and scholars and practitioners.

John Hassard: Research on organizational change may witness a return to materiality, ideology and politics. The renewal of interest in Marx work in wake of the sub-prime crisis for example has seen conferences once again support the dissemination of such structuralist organizational research. I see this trend continuing with structural Marxism increasingly joining Autonomist contributions I also anticipate, for the 'past-postmodernism' era, a return to formal, modernist, and unashamedly essentialist schemes for explaining research communities in organization studies. The advent of 'third-order' post-structuralism presented a fundamental challenge to traditional sociological models based on structure and agency. One result was that the formal schematic explanation of intellectual communities was curtailed, largely because deconstruction appeared incompatible with the dualisms traditionally deployed in such explanation. Rather than dualisms being theoretically and methodologically expedient, under post-structuralism they became an object for destabilizing. However the question arises for research on organizational change of just how expedient some aspects of deconstruction are for the study of workplaces in straightened times? Deconstruction, for example, may assist us in the critique of existing organizational 'texts' but arguably it offers us far less in terms of knowledge generation of an empirical kind. To take an extreme example, while the work of Jacques Derrida has been instructional in telling us what post-structuralism and in particular deconstruction is *not*, it has perhaps been less helpful in informing us what it is and can do for us methodologically, which in turn raises the slippery question of whether Derridean post-structuralism indeed has a 'method', or even a definition! When asked 'What is deconstruction?' Derrida famously replied, 'I have no simple and formalizable response to this question. All my essays are attempts to have it out with this formidable question.' Derrida also stated that 'Deconstruction is not a method and cannot be transformed into one', reflecting his view that deconstruction should not be considered a mechanical operation. It can be argued that the associated conceptual and definitional slipperiness that characterizes some post-structuralist writing in organizational analysis has resulted in opaque explanations of what post-structuralism is and what it can do for us in terms of explaining organizations in theory and practice. It is perhaps time for a return to more formal and material explanations of what organizations are and how they are changing, explanations which account for the tangible political, economic and ideological environments in which organizations operate.

Reference

Barad, K. (2007) *Meeting the Universe Halfway: Quantum Physics and the Entanglement of Matter and Meaning.* Durham/London: Duke University Press.

Index

Page numbers in *italics* refer to figures and tables.